THE
NEW BOOK
OF
KNOWLEDGE

THE
NEW BOOK
OF
KNOWLEDGE

Grolier Incorporated, Danbury, Connecticut

VOLUME 12

M

ISBN 0–7172–0519–3 (set)

The publishers wish to thank the following for permission to use copyrighted material:
E. P. Dutton & Co., Inc., for ''Missing'' from *When We Were Very Young* by A. A. Milne, copyright
1924 by E. P. Dutton, renewed 1952 by A. A. Milne.

Trademark
THE BOOK OF KNOWLEDGE
registered in U.S. Patent Office

M, the 13th letter in the English alphabet, was also the 13th letter in the ancient Hebrew and Phoenician alphabets and the twelfth letter in the classical Greek alphabet. The Hebrews and Phoenicians called it *mem*. The Greeks called it *mu*.

Many language scholars believe that the Phoenician word *mem* meant water and that the form of the letter was a simplified picture of waves. The letter *mem* looked like this: ⳋ.

The Greeks based their alphabet on that of the Phoenicians and borrowed the Phoenician letter M without changing its sound. The Greek *mu* looked like this: M.

Since the time of the Greeks, neither the consonant sound nor the shape of the letter has changed very much. The Romans learned the Greek alphabet from another ancient people, called the Etruscans. They wrote the letter as the Greeks had written it: M. It is this version that is used in the English alphabet today.

In English the sound of M, as in *mat*, is produced by pressing the lips together and making the sound while the air blocked by the lips passes through the nose. Unlike many other letters, the letter M is never silent except before N in a few words derived from the Greek language, such as *mnemonic*.

In Roman numerals, M is the symbol for 1,000. An M with a line above it ($\overline{\text{M}}$) denotes 1,000,000. M is also the abbreviation for Master in college degrees. A small m can stand for either mile or meter in measurements. It can also stand for married in genealogy. In Germany, M stands for mark, the basic unit of money.

M is found in many other abbreviations, among them mm, which stands for millimeter. In chemistry, Mg stands for the element magnesium. In French, M. stands for monsieur, just as Mr. denotes mister in English. In the U.S. Army, Maj. is the standard abbreviation for major, and MP stands for military police. In England, however, an M.P. is a member of Parliament.

Reviewed by MARIO PEI
Author, *The Story of Language*

See also ALPHABET.

See also ALPHABET.

SOME WAYS TO REPRESENT M:

Mm *M m*

The **manuscript** or printed forms of the letter (left) are highly readable. The **cursive** letters (right) are formed from slanted flowing strokes joining one letter to the next.

The **Manual Alphabet** (left) enables a deaf person to communicate by forming letters with the fingers of one hand. **Braille** (right) is a system by which a blind person can use fingertips to "read" raised dots that stand for letters.

The **International Code of Signals** is a special group of flags used to send and receive messages at sea. Each letter is represented by a different flag.

■■ ■■

International Morse Code is used to send messages by radio signals. Each letter is expressed as a combination of dots (•) and dashes (−−).

MAC ARTHUR, DOUGLAS (1880–1964)

General Douglas MacArthur was one of the most brilliant and controversial American military leaders. He was born on January 26, 1880, in Little Rock, Arkansas. His father, Arthur MacArthur, was a famous general. Young MacArthur graduated from the U.S. Military Academy at West Point in 1903 at the head of his class. Years of service in various parts of the world followed. During World War I, he commanded the 42nd (Rainbow) Division in France. He was wounded a number of times and cited for bravery seven times.

MacArthur returned to West Point as its superintendent in 1919. In 1930 he was appointed U.S. Army chief of staff—the youngest man ever to hold the post. In 1935, MacArthur became military adviser to the government of the Philippines. After the United States entered World War II in 1941, Japanese troops invaded the Philippines. MacArthur commanded the Filipino and American soldiers in a heroic but hopeless resistance. Ordered to Australia, he made his famous promise, "I shall return."

From Australia, MacArthur led the Allied campaign in the Southwest Pacific that brought him back victoriously to the Philippines and that helped defeat Japan. After the war ended in 1945, MacArthur was given command of the occupation forces in Japan. He introduced reforms, including a democratic constitution, that greatly changed Japanese society. It was a surprising development in a general often criticized for authoritarian tendencies.

When the Korean War broke out in 1950, MacArthur was named commander of the United Nations forces. His bold amphibious landing behind North Korean lines at Inchon seemed the decisive blow of the war. But the entry of Chinese troops into the war led to prolonged, bitter fighting. MacArthur wanted to strike at Chinese territory. Forbidden to do so, he publicly criticized U.S. Government policy. In 1951, President Harry S Truman angrily removed him from command. MacArthur returned to the United States, where many Americans greeted him as a hero.

MacArthur was mentioned as a possible Republican candidate for president in 1952 but failed to get the nomination. He died in Washington, D.C., on April 5, 1964.

Reviewed by Jules Archer
Author, *Front-Line General: Douglas MacArthur*

MACBETH

Shakespeare did not invent the plots of his plays. He found them in various books, and one of his favorite books was a history of England, Ireland, and Scotland, the *Chronicles* of Raphael Holinshed. It was here he found the story for his great tragedy *Macbeth*.

The story of King Macbeth is told in a very matter-of-fact way in the *Chronicles*. Macbeth was a nobleman of Scotland who killed the king in order to get the throne. Shakespeare turns this unpromising material into a tragedy of blood and darkness without making many changes in the story. Holinshed, for instance, describes three women in strange attire who greet Macbeth with the promise he will become king. It is Shakespeare who turns them into the three witches on the heath who set the atmosphere of gathering darkness.

Every line of *Macbeth* is heavy with a weight of evil and an implication of the power of supernatural forces. When Lady Macbeth first thinks of murder, she prays to the powers of darkness to give her strength, so that she will no longer feel the pity that would be natural to a woman.

> Make thick my blood,
> Stop up th' access and passage to remorse,
> That no compunctious visitings of nature
> Shake my fell purpose. Come, you spirits
> That tend on mortal thoughts, unsex me here,
> And fill me, from the crown to the toe, topfull
> Of direst cruelty!

When Macbeth finally nerves himself to commit the terrible act of murdering the king, he sees himself in league with darkness.

> Now o'er the one half-world
> Nature seems dead, and wicked dreams abuse
> The curtained sleep. Witchcraft celebrates
> Pale Hecate's off'rings; and withered Murther,
> Alarumed by his sentinel, the wolf,

Whose howl's his watch, thus with his stealthy
   pace,
With Tarquin's ravishing strides, towards his
   design
Moves like a ghost.

In Holinshed's account Macbeth rules for 10 years in Scotland after he kills the King, until he has to commit another murder to protect himself. But in Shakespeare's play Macbeth is immediately forced to clutch at safety with his bloody hands, and he commits murder after murder in a desperate attempt to feel secure. The atmosphere of darkness and terror in the play thickens as the spirits of evil close in around the man and woman who have invoked their power. They have lost all sense of peace, and Lady Macbeth is the first to find that she cannot endure the weight of what they have done.

Lady Macbeth had called upon the powers of evil to support her, and they gave her strength to commit the act of murder but not to endure the mental agony that followed. In the famous sleepwalking scene, in which she tries to wash imaginary blood from her hands, she shows the terror of the inward torment that she and her husband must now endure. When she dies and Macbeth receives the news, it is almost impossible for him to feel any emotion because life no longer has any meaning.

                              It is a tale
Told by an idiot, full of sound and fury,
Signifying nothing.

In Holinshed's story Macbeth is promised by a witch that he will be safe until Birnam Wood comes to his castle of Dunsinane. When he learns that the wood is moving because his foes have cut the boughs of trees to shield their advance, he knows that the witch has misled him and that he must die. But in Shakespeare's great play Macbeth is self-deceived and dead already when his foes surround him, for he has killed his own spirit.

MARCHETTE CHUTE
Author, *An Introduction to Shakespeare*

MACCABEES. See HANUKKAH.

MACDONALD, SIR JOHN A. (1815—1891)

Sir John A. Macdonald is rightly called the father of Canadian Confederation. It was his ability to persuade political opponents to co-operate and compromise that helped create the Dominion of Canada in 1867.

John Alexander Macdonald was born in Glasgow, Scotland, on January 11, 1815. He came as a boy to Kingston, Upper Canada, and grew up to become a successful lawyer. When the provinces of Upper and Lower Canada (now Ontario and Quebec) were united in 1841, Macdonald became active in politics. In 1844 he was elected to Parliament as a moderate Conservative. Two years later he became a cabinet member. Macdonald rose steadily in his party and laid the foundation for the alliance of English Conservatives and French Liberals that came to power in 1854. In 1857 he became leader of the Conservatives.

The union of the two Canadas gave each equal power in Parliament. Because of this and because of religious and language differences, no party could get enough support to stay in office more than a few years. By 1864 the Canadian Parliament was deadlocked, and Macdonald was ready to consider some basic change in the constitution. The leader of the Liberals, George Brown, was a personal enemy of Macdonald's. Nevertheless, Brown offered to join with him to break the deadlock.

Later in 1864 Macdonald, Brown, and other leading Canadians visited a conference of statesmen from the Maritime colonies held at Charlottetown, Prince Edward Island. They persuaded these men to consider a federation of all British North America. At a second conference, in Quebec city, terms were agreed on for a new federal constitution—the British North America Act. Macdonald led in these developments. So it was natural that he should become Canada's first prime minister when the Dominion was formed in 1867. He was knighted that same year.

Only the provinces of Nova Scotia, New Brunswick, Ontario, and Quebec joined the Confederation in 1867. But Macdonald worked to extend the new Dominion from the Atlantic to the Pacific. In 1869 the lands that are now the Prairie Provinces were bought from the Hudson's Bay Company. In 1870 British Columbia joined, and in 1873 Prince Edward Island was added. British Columbia entered because Macdonald had promised to build a transcontinental railroad. He won an election in 1872, but he was forced from office by his political enemies when it was learned that his party had accepted campaign funds from Hugh Allan, a shipowner who wanted the railroad contract. This incident is called the Pacific Scandal.

The Liberals held office from 1873 to 1878. But Macdonald easily won re-election in 1878 with promises to build the railroad and to help industry in eastern Canada by a "National Policy" of higher tariffs, or taxes, on foreign-made goods. With government help the Canadian Pacific Railway was completed in 1885. Macdonald's National Policy seemed so successful that it was carried on by later Liberal governments.

However, Macdonald faced problems that threatened to destroy his young country. Twice—in 1870 and 1885—Louis Riel led rebellions in the western territories against their inclusion in the Dominion. Riel's execution in 1885 for treason cost Macdonald the support of many French Canadians, who thought Riel was fighting for French Canadian rights. Macdonald was also opposed by some provinces who claimed that the federal government was too powerful. In 1891 Macdonald won his last election—a campaign to defend his National Policy. But the strain of the campaign led to a stroke and his death on June 6, 1891.

Throughout his life Macdonald suffered many family misfortunes, including the death of his first wife and one of their sons. Popular with everyone for his happy, carefree manner, John A., as he was called, was never a great orator. But his political strength came from his ability to talk with everyone and to win compromises even from his enemies.

JOHN S. MOIR
University of Toronto

MACDOWELL, EDWARD (1860–1908)

Edward MacDowell, one of the first American composers to receive international recognition, was born in New York City on December 18, 1860. Because of his exceptional talent, Edward's music teachers advised him to continue his musical education in Paris. Edward and his mother moved there in 1876.

For two years he studied piano at the Paris Conservatory. He then went to Germany to study piano and composition with some of the leading teachers of the time. The great Franz Liszt heard MacDowell, and in 1882 he arranged for him to play before an important international music society.

When MacDowell's formal studies were completed, he decided to stay in Germany. He earned a living teaching piano and giving concerts; he devoted his spare time to composition. One of his first piano pupils was an American, Marian Nevins, whom he married in 1884. Four years later they returned to the United States and settled in Boston.

MacDowell's reputation as a composer, concert pianist, and teacher grew steadily. In 1896, Columbia University appointed him its first professor of music, calling him "the greatest musical genius America has produced." Nine years later tragedy struck in the form of a severe mental illness that ended MacDowell's career. He died on January 23, 1908.

Although only 47 when he died, MacDowell had already achieved considerable fame. His two piano concertos and *Indian Suite* for orchestra are still played. Probably his best-known works are the short pieces for piano, *Woodland Sketches* (especially "To a Wild Rose"), *Fireside Tales,* and *New England Idyls.*

After his death, MacDowell's admirers established the MacDowell Colony as a memorial to him. The colony, located in Peterborough, New Hampshire, offers young American artists an inexpensive place to work in quiet and inspiring surroundings.

Reviewed by MARGERY MORGAN LOWENS
Peabody Conservatory of Music
The Johns Hopkins University

MACHINES. See WORK, POWER, AND MACHINES.
MACHINE TOOLS. See TOOLS.

MACKENZIE, SIR ALEXANDER (1764–1820)

The first white person to cross North America and reach the Pacific Ocean above Mexico was the explorer Alexander Mackenzie. Mackenzie was born in Scotland in 1764. When he was a child the family moved to New York. In 1778 young Mackenzie was sent to school in Montreal, but he soon left school to join a fur-trading company.

In 1784, Mackenzie's employers sent him to Fort Detroit on a trading and exploring expedition. But to his disappointment, he found that much of the area had already been explored, and he returned to Canada.

On June 3, 1789, Mackenzie started out on an expedition for the newly formed North West Company. With a small party of Canadians and Indians, he left Fort Chipewyan on the shores of Lake Athabasca in central Canada. For the next three weeks, the group sought an outlet from the frozen waters of Great Slave Lake to the Pacific Ocean. Finally they discovered a river—but it flowed northwest to the Arctic Ocean, instead of west to the Pacific. Mackenzie called it the Disappointment River, but the great stream now bears his name. In September the disgruntled party returned to the fort, traveling 4,800 kilometers (nearly 3,000 miles) by canoe.

In 1793, Mackenzie set out on a new attempt to reach the Pacific Ocean. Starting on the Peace River, he led his small party westward. On July 22, 1793, after a slow and dangerous journey, the group finally caught sight of the Pacific Ocean, at Dean Channel in what is now British Columbia.

After this victory, Mackenzie turned to fur trading and became rich. Later he went to England, where he published a book about his explorations. In 1802 he was knighted by King George III. Sir Alexander returned to Canada and served for several years in the Legislative Assembly of Lower Canada. In 1808 he settled in Scotland, where he remained until his death on March 11, 1820.

Reviewed by NOEL B. GERSON
Author, *The Magnificent Adventures of Alexander Mackenzie*

MACKENZIE, WILLIAM LYON (1795–1861)

William Lyon Mackenzie, known as the "little rebel," was born on March 12, 1795, near Dundee, Scotland. In 1820 he emigrated to Canada. He became a storekeeper. Then, in 1824, in Queenston, he started a newspaper, the *Colonial Advocate,* which he soon moved to York. In 1822 he had married Isabel Baxter.

Mackenzie became deeply involved in politics as a Reformer. His criticism of the Family Compact, the small group that ran the colony of Upper Canada, led to an attack on his printing shop. But this only served to make him a popular hero.

In 1828 Mackenzie was elected to the Legislative Assembly. A fiery speaker, he was expelled from the Assembly five times for criticizing it. But each time he was re-elected. In 1835, when York became Toronto, Mackenzie became its first mayor. The following year he wrote most of the famous *Seventh Report of the Committee on Grievances.*

Mackenzie had said many harsh things against the government. But he never suggested rebellion until the lieutenant-governor, Sir Francis Bond Head, interfered in the elections of 1836 to defeat the Reformers. In December, 1837, Mackenzie led a revolt in Toronto. It was poorly planned, and only a few hundred men joined him. The rebellion was easily put down, and Mackenzie escaped to Navy Island in the Niagara River. There he hoped Americans would help him make Upper Canada a republic. He received some support from American sympathizers, but the United States Government sent him to prison for violating the neutrality laws.

After his release from prison Mackenzie lived with his family in New York City until 1849, when he was allowed to return to Canada. From 1851 to 1858 he again sat in Parliament, but he had little influence. Mackenzie died on August 28, 1861, in the city of Toronto.

JOHN S. MOIR
University of Toronto

MACRAMÉ

Macramé, the art of decorative knotting, is a fascinating craft, and is not difficult to learn. Most macramé pieces are made by tying cord or yarn into just three different kinds of knots —the square knot, the double half hitch, and the overhand knot—and simple variations of these knots. If you can tie a shoelace, you can learn to make these knots.

You can use these knots to make many useful items—key chains, watch straps, necklaces, lamp shades, pillows, placemats, purses and book bags, and belts for every size and shape of person. You can also make purely decorative items such as wall hangings and holiday decorations. As your skill in macramé increases, more ideas will occur to you.

Macramé is a very old craft. In Spain and Italy during the 1400's, macramé lace was used to decorate items used in churches. Since that time, interest in macramé has faded and revived many times. In the mid-1800's, American and British sailors whiled away the hours during long voyages by knotting, and they became quite skilled. The most recent revival of interest in macramé began in the United States in the 1960's. Today most knotters use heavier cords than were used in the earlier days.

▶**GETTING STARTED**

To get started in macramé, you will need some tightly twisted cord or yarn; several long, sturdy pins (''T'' pins); a pair of scissors; and a ruler or tape measure. You will also need a board about 30 by 46 centimeters (12 by 18 inches) on which to do your work. It should be firm, but soft enough for pins to be pushed into it.

The supplies are easily found. Sturdy pins are available wherever sewing supplies are sold. Craft shops carry cord that is specifically made for macramé. It comes in an assortment of lovely colors and is available in a number of weights or textures. Hardware stores also have cord that is excellent for knotting. It is called seine twine, chalk line, or mason line. It is often white or yellow and is made of either cotton or nylon. Cotton cord is easier than synthetics for a beginner to work with because it is less slippery. Good sizes for knotting are numbers 18 and 24.

A piece of insulating board or wallboard makes a good knotting board. You can also use a plastic foam pillow form or even a stack of cardboard or corrugated cardboard pieces, glued together at the edges.

That is all the equipment you need, but there are other items that are fun or helpful to have on hand. You may want some beads or bells with large holes, a few small dowels or sticks, or a key ring for your projects. Other useful items are rubber bands, for holding loose ends of cord, and a small crochet hook, to help pull the cords through the beads.

▶**HINTS FOR MAKING PROJECTS**

Before starting on a project, you will want to practice your knotting technique. The best way to do this is to make a sampler. Complete instructions for a sampler follow on page 7a. The Knotting Chart on the opposite page will guide you in tying the basic knots from which your sampler and most other macramé pieces are formed.

When you are comfortable with the basic knots, you are ready to attempt your first projects. The simple project shown on page 7b will get you started. Here are some tips that will help you in making this and other macramé items:

• It is hard to know how long each cord should be cut. Tightly knotted work requires more cord than open work. As a general rule, measure each cord eight times longer than your finished work will be. You will fold each cord in half when you mount it, so each knotting cord will be four times longer than the finished work.

• If the cords are very long, they will be difficult to work with. Shorten each one by rolling it into a neat bundle and fastening it with a rubber band.

• Use pins freely to anchor your work and to pull against while knotting.

• Before you tighten each knot, make sure it is in the place where you want it to be.

• Firmly knotted pieces tend to look neat and handsome.

• Knots look crisp and clear when tightly twisted cords are used. Other cords and yarns may be used, but the effect will be different.

As you become more skilled at the art of macramé, you may want to try other variations of the basic knots. If you look at books devoted to macramé, you will find inspiring pictures and ideas, as well as shortcuts and other helpful hints.

KNOTTING CHART

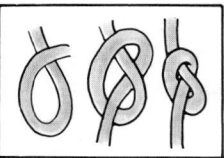

OVERHAND KNOT

Make a loop. Bring the end of the cord through the loop. Pull to tighten the knot.

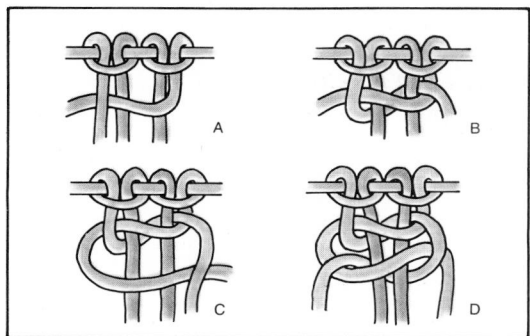

LARK'S HEAD KNOT

Fold the cord in half. Place the loop in front of the dowel or knotting cord (A). Pull the loop behind the dowel (B). Pull the 2 ends of the cord through the loop (C). Tighten.

HALF KNOT/SQUARE KNOT

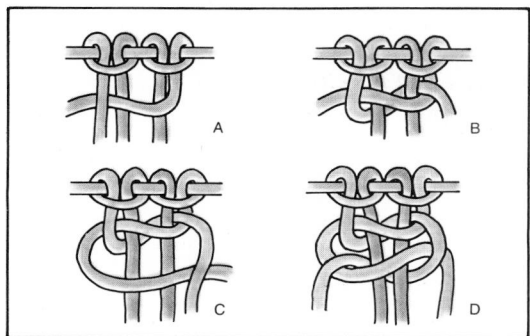

Put the right cord over the 2 center cords and under the left cord (A). Then pass the left cord under the 2 center cords and through the loop formed by the right cord (B). Steps A and B complete a half knot. To make a square knot, continue to diagram C, placing what is now the left cord over the 2 center cords and under the right cord. Then pass the right cord under the 2 center cords and through the loop formed by the left cord (D). Tighten.

HALF HITCH/DOUBLE HALF HITCH

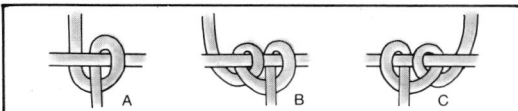

To make a half hitch, place the knotting cord behind the holding cord. Bring it under the holding cord, then up and over it, passing the end of the knotting cord through the loop (A). To form a double half hitch, continue by passing the knotting cord up and over the holding cord and pulling it through the loop (B). Tighten. Diagrams A and B show a half hitch worked from left to right across a holding cord. Diagram C shows the same knot worked from right to left.

HORIZONTAL DOUBLE HALF HITCH

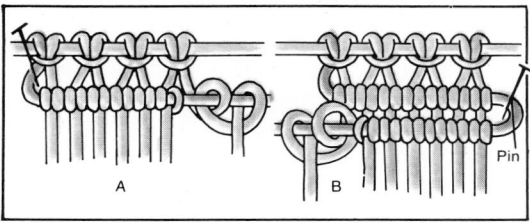

Place a pin as shown in diagram A to anchor your holding cord so you can keep it in a horizontal position across the other cords. Tie a double half hitch with the first cord at left. Repeat with each of the cords across the row (A). To reverse direction, move your pin to the right side and, using the same holding cord, position it in the opposite direction and tie a double half hitch with each cord, working from right to left (B).

ALTERNATING SQUARE KNOTS

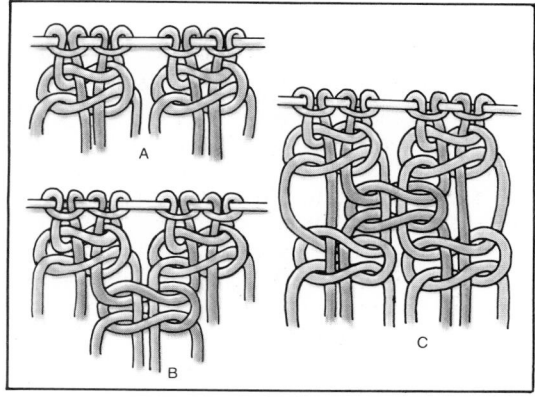

Begin by making a row of square knots with each group of 4 cords (A). Then for the next row, put the first 2 cords aside. Tie a square knot with 2 cords from the first knot of the previous row and 2 cords from the second knot of the previous row. Continue, using 2 cords from the second knot and 2 from the third, and so on. The last 2 cords will remain unused (B). The third row repeats the first row (C), the fourth row repeats the second row, and so on.

DIAGONAL DOUBLE HALF HITCHES

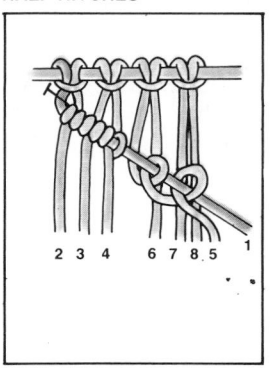
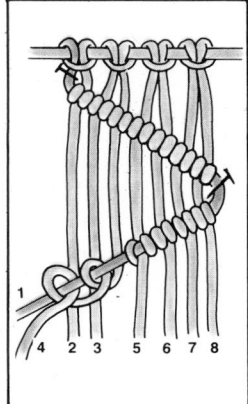

To make a line of diagonal double half hitches from upper left to lower right, place the pin between cords 1 and 2 and use the far left cord (1) as the knotting cord. Place it at the desired angle across the other cords and make a double half hitch with each cord (A). To reverse direction, place the pin to the right of cord 8. Position the holding cord at the desired angle across the other cords, and tie double half hitches, beginning with cord 8 as shown.

In order to clarify the knotting procedures, the holding cords appear slightly darker than the knotting cords in these diagrams.

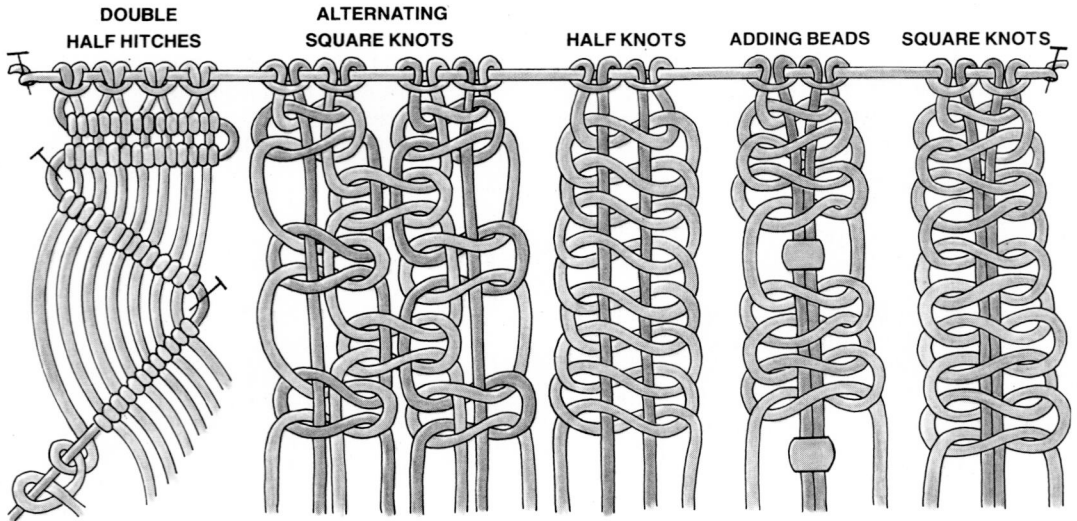

DOUBLE HALF HITCHES | ALTERNATING SQUARE KNOTS | HALF KNOTS | ADDING BEADS | SQUARE KNOTS

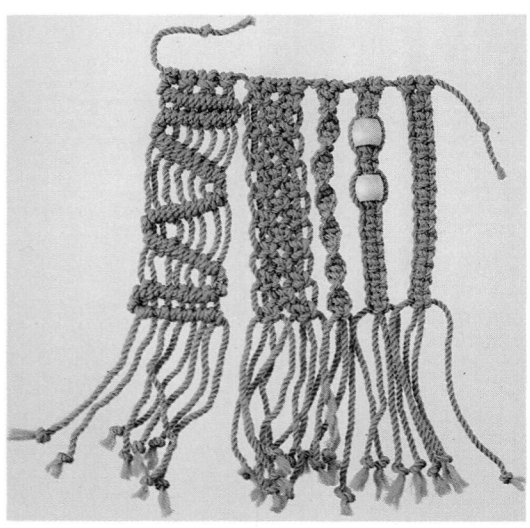

▶MAKING A SAMPLER

A good way to learn macramé is to make a sampler showing some basic kinds of knots. You will need about 15 meters (50 feet) of cord and a few beads of a size that will slide onto the cord. Begin by cutting 13 cords, each 115 centimeters (45 inches) long. (The sample in the photograph was made with 2- to 3-millimeter macramé cord, but any cord or twine will do.) Cut another cord 36 centimeters (14 inches) long. This short cord will be your mounting cord; the others will be your knotting cords.

Make an **overhand knot** near each end of the short cord (see the Knotting Chart). Spread

the cord on your knotting board. Push a strong pin through each knot and into the board to hold the mounting cord in place.

Now you are ready to attach your knotting cords to the mounting cord. Attach the first cord with a **lark's head knot** as shown in the Knotting Chart. Then take another cord and mount it to the left of the first one. You now have four cord ends with which to knot.

Square Knots. Your first piece of work will be a sennit, or row, of square knots. To make a square knot, follow the diagram in the Knotting Chart.

Continue making square knots until the sennit is about 10 centimeters (4 inches) long.

Adding Beads. Make another sennit that includes beads. Attach two more cords to the mounting cord and make two square knots. Then thread the core cords through the center of a bead. Push the bead up until it rests just below the last square knot. Make another square knot just below the bead, to hold it in place. Then continue making square knots, inserting beads wherever you please.

Half Knots. A spiral sennit will form if you make just the first half of the square knot and repeat that over and over again. Attach two more knotting cords and start making half square knots, one right under the other.

Alternating Square Knots. Alternating square knots form an interesting pattern. The procedure is shown in the Knotting Chart. Attach four knotting cords to your board so that you have eight free ends with which to knot.

Make a square knot using the first four cords and another square knot using the last four cords. Then take the first two cords and the last two cords and pin them out of the way. Make a square knot using the four center cords. Release the cords you have set aside. Make square knots again—one from the first four cords and one from the last four cords. Repeat the above steps alternating between rows of one and two square knots until your sennit reaches the desired length.

Double Half Hitches. Your last sennit will be made up of double half hitches. See the Knotting Chart for instructions on how to form the knots. Again, attach four cords so that you have eight free ends with which to knot. Think of them as being numbered 1 through 8, from left to right. Put a pin just below the mounting cord, between cords 1 and 2. Then place cord 1 on top of all the other cords, just below the mounting cord. This cord will be your **knot-bearing cord.**

Repeat these steps with cords 3, 4, 5, 6, 7, and 8 to make a row of horizontal double half hitches. Then reverse directions. Put a pin between your last cord and the knot-bearing cord, and bring the knot bearer all the way over to the left, just under your first row of knots. Hold the knot bearer with your left hand. With your right hand, make another row. Follow the same steps, but start from the right, using cords 8, 7, 6, 5, 4, 3, and 2.

Next, use double half hitches to make angles, as shown in the Knotting Chart. Begin from the left. Place a pin between your knot-bearing cord and cord 2, and bring your knot bearer over to the right. Hold it at about a 45-degree angle to your last row of knots. (If you want your angles to be perfect, you can draw a 45-degree angle on your knotting board and use it as a guide.) Make a row of double half hitches all along the knot bearer from left to right. Then change directions. Bring the knot bearer back to the left at another 45-degree angle, pin it in place, and knot from right to left along it.

Continue to practice double half hitches by angling to the right again. Finish with two rows of horizontal double half hitches.

Finishing the Sampler. You will notice that some of the cords of your sampler are much longer than the others. The cords in the center of the square-knot sennits are longest because they stayed in place while the other cords

made knots around them. To finish your sampler, trim the cords so that they are all the same length. Near the bottom of each cord, make an overhand knot. If your cords are slippery, make an overhand knot just below the last knot of your sampler, too.

Your sampler is now complete. If you would like to practice some more, just cut more cords and attach them to the mounting cord.

HELENE BRESS
Author, *The Macramé Book*

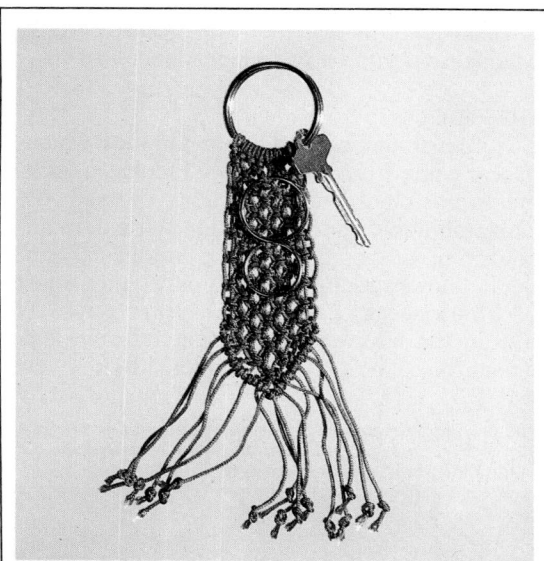

ALTERNATING-SQUARE-KNOT KEY HOLDER

Materials:
1 large round key ring
2 small round key rings
10 meters (33 feet) of 1-millimeter macramé cord or number 18 seine twine

How to Make the Key Holder:
(1) Cut eight cords, each 122 centimeters (48 inches) long.
(2) Fold the cords in half and mount them onto the key holder. Use the same lark's head knot that you used when you attached cords to the mounting cord of the sampler. You will have 16 free cords with which to knot.
(3) Make four square knots across the first row. Use the first four cords for the first knot, the second four cords for the second knot, and so on.
(4) Pin cords 1 and 2 and cords 15 and 16 to the side. Make a square knot using cords 3, 4, 5, and 6. Make another knot with cords 7, 8, 9, and 10, and a third knot with cords 11, 12, 13, and 14.
(5) Keep repeating steps three and four. Attach the small key rings by sliding them under the core cords of a square knot, just as you attached beads to your sampler.
(6) Outline the bottom of the key holder with double half hitches. The example is worked with angled double half hitches, with the area inside the angle filled in with extra alternating square knots.

MADAGASCAR

Madagascar is an island nation located in the Indian Ocean off the southeastern coast of Africa. It is the fourth largest island in the world, after Greenland, New Guinea, and Borneo. Its people, who are called Malagasy, have developed a unique mixture of Asian and African cultures. Formerly a French colony, Madagascar gained its independence in 1960.

▶ THE PEOPLE

Some of the earliest inhabitants of Madagascar came from what is now Indonesia. Others were black Africans who crossed the Mozambique Channel from the African mainland. The descendants of the Indonesian settlers, known as the Merina, once ruled most of Madagascar. Today the Merina generally live in the interior near the capital city, Antananarivo. They are outnumbered by the various groups of black African descent, who live mostly along the coast.

There have been conflicts between the Merina and the descendants of the black Africans. But the two groups of people have been intermarrying for generations. Over the centuries they have developed a common language and have come to share a common culture.

Language and Religion. Malagasy, a language much like Indonesian, is spoken throughout the country. Both Malagasy and French are official languages. More than half of the people follow traditional religious beliefs based on ancestor worship. About 40 percent are Christians, and another 5 percent are Muslims.

Way of Life. In the larger towns and cities, people live in stone, cement, or brick houses that usually have steep, pointed roofs. Houses in the countryside are made of wood or mud and often have two or three stories. Most rural families live in lofts above the areas where their animals are kept.

A traditional garment worn by both Malagasy men and women is the *lamba,* a large white shawl usually made of unbleached muslin. City dwellers sometimes wear the *lamba* over European-style clothing.

▶ THE LAND

Madagascar is an island of contrasts. Along the eastern and western coasts and in the north, the soil is fertile. Temperatures are warm. Annual rainfall is heaviest in the north and along the eastern coast. Less rain falls in the cooler, mountainous interior, and the south is hot and dry. The heart of the interior is the densely populated central plateau around Antananarivo. Many of the trees have been cut down, and the soil is badly eroded. The highest point in the country is Mount Maromokotro in the north, which rises to 9,436 feet (2,876 meters).

▶ THE ECONOMY

Madagascar's economy is based primarily on agriculture. Most of the people make their living as subsistence farmers, growing food for their own use on small plots, or as animal herders. Cattle raising is important in the sparsely populated south. Coffee, sugarcane, vanilla beans, tobacco, sisal (a fiber used in making cord and twine), cloves, and cotton, grown on large plantations, are the leading

The marketplace in Antananarivo, the capital and largest city of Madagascar. The Rova, the royal estate of the old Merina kingdom, overlooks the city.

commercial crops. Rice, the staple food, is the most important food crop, but supplies of rice must be imported to meet the country's needs.

What little industry exists is based largely on the processing of agricultural products. Textiles, soap, and cement are also manufactured, and a refinery at Toamasina processes imported oil. The country has known deposits of a variety of minerals. But only chromite, graphite, and mica are mined in any quantity. The economy is controlled at least partly by the government.

Madagascar spends much more for imports than it receives for its exports. This has caused serious economic problems in recent years.

▶ CITIES

Antananarivo is the capital and largest city of Madagascar. It was also the capital of the Merina kingdom. Relics of the monarchy can still be seen in the Rova, the former royal estate that overlooks the city from atop a huge rock. Toamasina, on the eastern coast, is the chief port of Madagascar. It is linked with Antananarivo by a railroad.

▶ HISTORY AND GOVERNMENT

The Malagasy had already developed their distinctive language by the time Arab traders began to visit the area in the 10th century. Europeans first sighted Madagascar in the

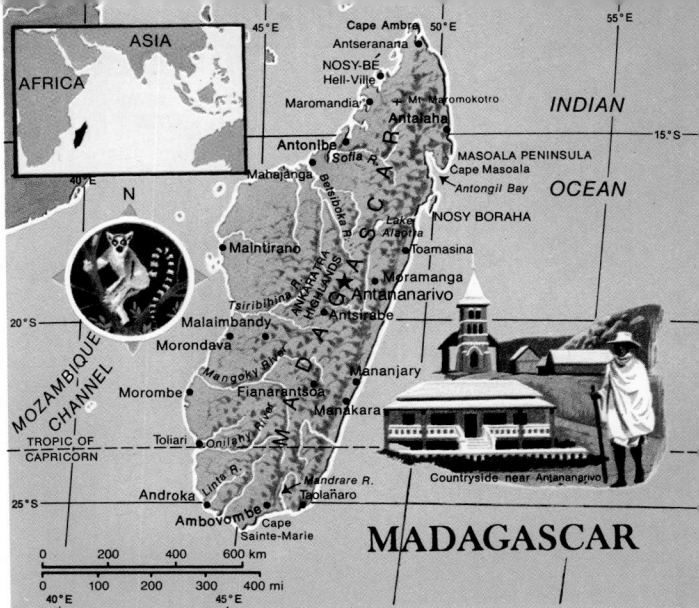

FACTS AND FIGURES

DEMOCRATIC REPUBLIC OF MADAGASCAR is the official name of the country. It is called Repoblika Demokratika Malagasy in Malagasy and République Démocratique de Madagascar in French.

THE PEOPLE are known as Malagasy.

LOCATION: Indian Ocean, southeast of Africa.

AREA: 226,657 sq mi (587,041 km²).

POPULATION: 9,500,000 (estimate).

CAPITAL AND LARGEST CITY: Antananarivo.

MAJOR LANGUAGES: Malagasy, French (both official).

MAJOR RELIGIONS: Traditional, Christian, Muslim.

GOVERNMENT: Head of state—president. **Head of government**—prime minister. **Legislature**—National People's Assembly.

CHIEF PRODUCTS: Agricultural—rice, coffee, sugarcane, vanilla beans, tobacco, sisal, cloves, cotton, livestock. **Manufactured**—processed food, textiles, cement, soap. **Mineral**—chromite, graphite, mica.

MONETARY UNIT: Malagasy franc (1 franc = 100 centimes).

NATIONAL ANTHEM: *Ry tanindrazanay malala ô* (''O, Our Beloved Fatherland'').

early 1500's. The French established a permanent settlement in the mid-1600's.

After the 1780's the powerful Merina kingdom was able to unify almost all of the island. During this period, Britain and France were competing for control of the Indian Ocean. King Radama I welcomed European missionaries and traders, but later Merina rulers often tried to drive them from the island. The European rivalry for influence in Madagascar ended in 1885, when Britain recognized a French protectorate over the island. In 1896, Madagascar was made a colony of France, and the Merina kingdom came to an end.

Recent Events. Madagascar won full independence in 1960 as the Malagasy Republic. Its first president, Philibert Tsiranana, served until 1972, when he was forced to resign after a period of political and social unrest. The government was then led by a series of military officers. A new constitution, approved in 1975, changed the name of the country to the Democratic Republic of Madagascar.

The president, who is elected for 7 years, is the head of state and chief executive and serves as chairman of the Supreme Revolutionary Council, the highest policy-making body. A prime minister, appointed by the president, handles the day-to-day management of the government. The legislature is the National People's Assembly. Admiral Didier Ratsirika was elected president in 1975 and re-elected in 1982.

EDWARD J. MILES
University of Vermont

JAMES MADISON (1751–1836)

4TH PRESIDENT OF THE UNITED STATES

MADISON, JAMES. James Madison is perhaps best known to Americans as the father of the Constitution. This title was given him because of the leading part he played in framing the charter of government under which the American people have lived since 1789. Madison was only 36 years old when that work was completed, but he had been in public life for 11 years and was unsurpassed as a student of government.

▶ **BACKGROUND AND EARLY YEARS**

Madison was born on March 16, 1751, at Port Conway, Virginia. His great-great-grandfather, a ship carpenter, had emigrated from England in 1653 and become a tobacco farmer in the Virginia tidelands. Later generations of Madisons pushed westward as the country opened. James Madison's grandfather and father built up a farm of about 6,000 acres in what is now Orange County, Virginia. This great farm, Montpellier (now spelled Montpelier), remained James Madison's home throughout his 85 years.

James was taught to read and write by his mother and grandmother. Soon after his 11th birthday he was sent to Donald Robertson's famous boarding school in King and Queen County, Virginia. After a year devoted to English, mathematics, French, and Spanish, James took up Latin at the age of 12. Within 2 years he was reading Vergil, Horace, Justinian's *Institutes,* Ovid, Phaedrus, Terence, and Sallust. The intellectual fare fed to the teenage boy also included Montesquieu's *Spirit of Laws,* John Locke's *Essay Concerning Human Understanding,* and Descartes' astronomy. Long afterward Madison said of schoolmaster Donald Robertson: "All I have been in life I owe largely to that man."

Two years of tutoring at home by the local Episcopal rector made the boy ready for college. James was sent to the College of New Jersey (now Princeton University). He completed the 4-year course in 2 years, sleeping only 5 hours a night and considerably damaging his health. Madison acquired his basic knowledge of government and international relations at college. Then, for 5 years after his graduation in 1771, he continued his extensive studies at home. These included a good part of a lawyer's training, though Madison had no intention of becoming a lawyer. At the same time he was teaching the younger children of the family.

During these years young Madison witnessed scenes that made him think religious persecution the worst of all evils. In a neighboring county half a dozen dissenting clergymen were in jail for preaching according to their own beliefs. All Madison's efforts to win their release were in vain.

The approaching Revolutionary War, however, turned Madison's thoughts in another direction. Three Madison brothers enlisted for military service in the Revolution. But James was forced to drop out, because of the physical strain, before his company was called to active duty. He turned at once to political service.

▶ **EARLY POLITICAL CAREER**

In 1776 the 25-year-old Madison was elected a delegate to the Virginia Revolutionary Convention. There he wrote the strong guarantee of religious freedom in the Virginia Declaration of Rights. He helped pass a resolution asking the Continental Congress to issue the Declaration of Independence. Madison then served a year in the Virginia legislature but was defeated for reelection because he refused to furnish whiskey to the voters. He was immediately appointed a member of the governor's council, which managed the state's war efforts. After 2 years of this work he was sent as a delegate to the Continental Congress. Though he was one of its youngest members, and was boyish in appearance, Madison quickly rose to leadership, especially in the conduct of American relations with France and Spain. Through his efforts, too, the vast vacant lands of the West came under national ownership.

With the coming of peace in 1783, Madison devoted his efforts to strengthening the weak national government set up under the Articles of Confederation. Elected again to the Virginia legislature, he persuaded his state to issue a call for a convention of the states. He went as a delegate to the Annapolis Convention of 1786 and then to the Constitutional Convention at Philadelphia in 1787. Madison's understanding of government made him a leader in the work of framing the Constitution. His devotion to democratic self-government made it the keystone of the American political system.

Madison's Ideas on Government

The essential problem facing the framers of the Constitution was to find some way to establish power and yet maintain liberty. This called for the republican form of government, in which the people are sovereign (supreme) but rule through elected representatives. Up to Madison's time most students of government had assumed that small republics were more virtuous than large ones. Madison observed that the opposite was true in America. Tyrannical majorities ruled the smallest states. In the larger ones, however, the greater diversity of interests prevented one faction, or interest group, from acquiring undue power.

So, Madison reasoned, let the United States have the republican form of government at all levels, with each state controlling its local affairs. Let a supreme federal government manage national affairs and interstate matters —those between the states. The larger such a federal republic became, the more liberty it could enjoy with safety, for the different interests of the various sections of the country would split the factions that might produce tyranny in a small republic.

Madison presented this idea to the delegates at Philadelphia. It overcame the fear many of them had of democracy, and the government of the United States was built on the basis of Madison's ideas. He then joined with Alexander Hamilton and John Jay in writing *The Federalist* papers, explaining the Constitution to the people in order to secure

---

IMPORTANT DATES IN THE LIFE OF JAMES MADISON

1751	Born at Port Conway, Virginia, March 16.
1771	Graduated from College of New Jersey (now Princeton University).
1776	Delegate to Virginia Revolutionary Convention.
1776–1777	Served in Virginia legislature.
1778–1779	Member of Virginia state council.
1780–1783	Delegate to Continental Congress.
1784–1786	Served in Virginia legislature.
1786	Delegate to Annapolis Convention.
1787	Delegate to Constitutional Convention at Philadelphia.
1788	Supported Constitution at Virginia ratifying convention.
1789–1797	Served in United States House of Representatives.
1801–1809	Secretary of state.
1809–1817	4th president of the United States.
1826	Succeeded Thomas Jefferson as rector of University of Virginia.
1836	Died at Montpellier, June 28.

Before the British burned the White House in 1814, Dolley Madison saved certain state papers and a portrait of George Washington.

its ratification. Madison led the supporters of the Constitution at the Virginia ratifying convention. He was then elected to the House of Representatives in the 1st Congress of the United States.

▶ THE NEW GOVERNMENT

In Congress he proposed and took a leading part in the passage of the first 10 amendments to the Constitution. Madison is thus known both as father of the Constitution and as principal author of the Bill of Rights.

Madison served in Congress from 1789 to 1797, rising to leadership of the entire House of Representatives. Then, as political parties began to form, he became leader of those men (later called Democratic-Republicans) who wished the government to give special thought to the welfare of the common people. Opposed to this was the Federalist Party, led by Alexander Hamilton, who wanted to strengthen the new government by linking it with the interests of persons of wealth and power. Hamilton's party won in Congress.

Early in this contest Thomas Jefferson arrived home from France, where he had been American minister, and took over leadership of the Republicans. Madison became his foremost supporter. When Jefferson was elected president in 1801, Madison was appointed secretary of state. In this capacity Madison helped promote the purchase of the Louisiana Territory from France.

Meanwhile, in Europe the Napoleonic Wars were raging. Great Britain was impressing (forcing into service) seamen from American ships to man its Navy against France. Both Great Britain and France were seizing American ships and cargoes. Secretary Madison strongly upheld the right of a neutral country to trade with warring nations through unblockaded seaports. But all his protests were ignored. President Jefferson attempted to preserve peace by the Embargo Act, forbidding American ships to leave port. But this only resulted in violations of the act.

▶ PRESIDENT

Thomas Jefferson's support helped Madison win election to the presidency in 1809. Madison's first action on becoming president was to inform Great Britain that if it would stop interfering with American commerce and France continued to seize American ships, he would ask Congress to declare war on France. At the same time a similar offer was made to France—to go to war against Great Britain if France would stop its seizures and Great Britain continued them. But both countries continued to seize American ships. In 1810 Congress authorized the President to cut off trade with either country if the other agreed to stop its oppressions. An agreement to do so by the French, though false, led to a commercial break with Great Britain in 1811 and to war in 1812.

The War of 1812

Congress, however, was more willing to declare war than to provide the means of fighting it. The War Department consisted of a secretary of war and eight clerks. The United States had virtually no army and only a small navy. While the little American Navy was winning brilliant triumphs at sea, the inexperienced soldiers met with defeat after defeat. Washington, D.C., itself was captured by the British. Part of the city, including the White House, was burned, and Madison was forced

Montpelier as it looks today. James and Dolley Madison are buried nearby.

to flee with other members of the government. Young army officers, however, were gaining experience, and so was the President. Newly disciplined American troops drove the Duke of Wellington's veterans from the field in successive battles. This change of fortune led to a satisfactory peace in the Treaty of Ghent in 1814.

All through the War of 1812 the Federalist Party of New England had opposed what they called "Mr. Madison's war." Nevertheless, Madison had refused to place any restraints on speech or the press. Amid the rejoicings over peace the Federalist Party broke down and soon vanished from existence.

When Madison left the presidency in 1817, the citizens of Washington held a mass meeting at which he was congratulated on "the untarnished glory" of his administration. During the war, they declared, Madison had held military authority within its proper limits, directed it with energy, and "won power and glory . . . without infringing a political, civil, or religious right."

▶ **LATER YEARS**

During the remaining 19 years of his life Madison engaged in scientific farming at Montpellier. He originated methods of agriculture that did not become common until a century later. With his wife, Dolley, famous as a White House hostess, he welcomed visitors from all over the United States and Europe. Equally welcome were the children of relatives, for Madison had no children of his own.

Although a slave-owner by inheritance, Madison hated slavery and did all he could to put an end to it. As an adult he never belonged to any church, but in his mature years he expressed a preference for the Unitarian faith. After Jefferson's death in 1826, Madison succeeded his old friend as rector (in effect, president) of the new University of Virginia.

Madison's last great service to the United States began in 1828. In that year South Carolina claimed the right to nullify (declare null and void) acts of Congress. For the next 6 years the aged statesman fought this doctrine of nullification. He wrote articles against it when he was so crippled with rheumatism that he could barely move his fingers.

Madison died at Montpellier on June 28, 1836. His earliest political thought had been for the liberty of America. His last thought and his final message to his countrymen concerned the way in which that liberty could be preserved: "The advice nearest to my heart and deepest in my convictions is that the Union of the States be cherished and perpetuated."

IRVING BRANT
Author, *James Madison*

See also BILL OF RIGHTS; WAR OF 1812.

MADONNA. See MARY, VIRGIN.

MADRAS

Madras is India's fourth largest city. It is the capital of the state of Tamil Nadu ("home of the Tamils"), formerly known as Madras state. The city proper has a population of over 3,000,000. An additional 1,000,000 people live in the metropolitan area. The city lies along the southeast coast, on the Bay of Bengal, and is a leading port. With its fine highways, railroads, rivers, and canals, Madras is an important transportation terminal. The city is serviced by an international airport situated nearby at Minambakkam.

Mount Road is the main thoroughfare of Madras. It passes through the city's central shopping and hotel areas before reaching the residential district in the south. An attractive city sight is the wide shore drive called the Marina. At one end of it is the Roman Catholic Cathedral of Saint Thomé, believed to be the burial place of the Apostle Thomas. Nearby is the early Portuguese settlement of Saint Thomé, established in 1504 and later incorporated into Madras. Between the cathedral and Madras' busy harbor are government buildings, residential houses, Madras University, and Fort Saint George, the original site of Madras.

George Town is the city's main commercial district. Near George Town are industrial areas where cotton textile and handloom industries flourish. The famous Madras cloth derives its name from the city where it is made. Other industries are engineering works, bicycle factories, iron foundries, and tanneries.

Madras was founded in 1639. At that time, an Indian rajah granted a strip of land to Francis Day, a British subject and chief agent of the East India Company. On this site, Fort Saint George was established. Between 1702 and 1801, the fort was captured in turn by the Moguls, Marathas (people of west and central India), and the French. It also was taken by the forces of Haidar Ali, Muslim ruler of Mysore. By 1801, most of the territory that presently makes up the state of Tamil Nadu had been ceded (given over) to the British by defeated Indian rulers. The city of Madras then became the capital of one of the largest administrative units of British India.

Today beautiful Hindu temples, the Horticultural Gardens, and the Central Museum highlight this city that has become the cultural center for India's Tamil-speaking population.

Reviewed by BALKRISHNA G. GOKHALE
Wake Forest University

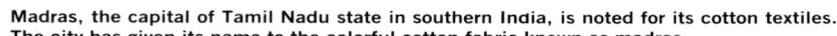

Madras, the capital of Tamil Nadu state in southern India, is noted for its cotton textiles. The city has given its name to the colorful cotton fabric known as madras.

MADRID

Madrid is located on a high, windswept plateau almost in the geographic center of Spain. With a population of more than 3,000,000, it is the largest city in Spain and one of the largest capital cities in Europe.

The Moors, a Muslim people who invaded Spain in the 8th century A.D., built a fortified village on the site of present-day Madrid. Conquered in 1083 by Alfonso VI, the king of Leon and Castile, it remained an unimportant place until 1561. In that year, King Philip II made Madrid the center of his vast empire. It has been the capital of Spain ever since, except for a brief period (1601–06) when the court was moved to Valladolid.

Much of the sprawling city was built during the 1600's and 1700's. This part, once surrounded by walls, is known as Old Madrid. Madrid has expanded rapidly in recent years by annexing nearby communities.

In the middle of Old Madrid is a plaza called the Puerta del Sol (Gate of the Sun). Streets fan out from the Puerta del Sol like the sun's rays. Those going west lead to the Opera House, the Plaza Mayor (Main Plaza), and the Royal Palace and Armory. The Plaza Mayor is another historic square. It was built in the 1600's as a kind of outdoor theater. From the balconies of the surrounding buildings, nobles and kings once watched festivals, bullfights, horse races, and ceremonies. The interiors of the huge stone Royal Palace are hung with fine silks and Flemish tapestries. The Royal Armory in the left wing of the Royal Palace houses one of the finest collections of weapons and armor in the world.

One of Madrid's best-known streets is the Paseo del Prado, a broad, parklike boulevard lined with museums, monuments, government buildings, and plazas. On the Paseo del Prado is the Prado, a world-famous art gallery housing paintings and sculptures collected by Spanish kings. Madrid has many other fine museums and libraries. Among the institutions of higher learning in the city is the University of Madrid, in University City.

The people of Madrid are called Madrileños. They are known for their love of night life. As in other parts of Spain, dinners and social gatherings start at about ten o'clock or even later. Movies, concerts, and plays often begin performances at the same hour.

Like all Spaniards, Madrileños love soccer, *pelota* (jai alai), and, of course, the bullfights at the Plaza de Toros. They often visit one of the largest of the city's many parks, the Retiro. It has playgrounds, gardens, bridle paths, lakes, a zoo, an outdoor theater, and café-restaurants where Madrileños enjoy eating and dancing. Restaurants in Madrid range from those serving typical Spanish dishes to those offering an international menu.

Madrid remains the political and cultural capital of Spain. It is also the center of Spanish printing, publishing, and moviemaking. And since the country developed a modern network of roads and railroads converging on the city, Madrid has become the leading manufacturing center of Spain.

> Reviewed by RAFAEL MILLÁN
> Former editor, *Aguilar* (Madrid)

See also PRADO.

The Avenida de José Antonio, or Gran Via, lies in the center of Madrid. It is one of the city's main avenues and is known for its fine shops and hotels.

There is a magazine for nearly every activity or interest. It is estimated that in North America alone, more than 65,000 different magazines are published.

MAGAZINES

The meaning of the word "magazine" is "storehouse" or "treasury"—and a magazine is truly a treasury of interesting material. Magazines give readers more specialized information than any other channel of mass communication, including newspapers, radio, and television. A magazine will tell you how to build a model plane or how to lose weight, which are the best jogging sneakers, or what your favorite celebrity eats for breakfast.

Magazines are sometimes called periodicals because they are published regularly at specific times. In the United States alone, there are 9,000 magazines that are published at least four times a year.

Magazines are divided into general- or special-interest magazines, sometimes called consumer magazines, and business magazines, sometimes called trade magazines. There are also scholarly journals, which report on research in various fields. A **business magazine** deals with the commercial and financial aspects of a particular business. **Special-interest** magazines, sometimes called hobby magazines, contain information on a specific subject—computers or horseback riding, for example. **General-interest** magazines are designed to appeal to a wide variety of readers. They include **newsweeklies,** which summarize

the news, and **digests,** which reprint material from other publications. Some carry articles of interest to certain reader groups—men, women, or children, for example. **Intellectual** and **opinion** magazines analyze current events. General- and special-interest magazines are sold on newsstands or by subscription.

▶ PRODUCING MAGAZINES

The production of a magazine involves many steps before the final product is distributed to the newsstand or mailed to a subscriber's home. Story ideas are the backbone of every issue.

Suppose a writer has an idea for an article and sends a letter describing the idea to an editor of a general-interest magazine. The editor may have the title of science editor or entertainment editor, depending on what the article is about. If the editor likes the proposal, it is then discussed with other editors—perhaps the articles editor, managing editor, and editor in chief. If they all agree that the article would be of interest to their readers, the writer is given the assignment. The editors send a contract that states what the fee will be and when the article is due.

The author sends in the article at the deadline time, and it is read sometimes by as many as five editors. The author may be asked to make revisions or to make the article shorter or longer. Then the editors decide where it will be placed in the magazine and whether it will be illustrated with photographs or drawings. They also decide on a working title.

The editor in charge of the article sends copies to the picture editor, who will either assign a photographer to take pictures or have a researcher find appropriate pictures. If artwork is to be used, an artist will be commissioned to do drawings or paintings.

The next step is the design of a **page layout** —a mock-up of what the finished pages will look like. This is done by the art director. Suppose the story will take four pages and have five photographs. The art director must measure the length of the story and decide how large the illustrations will be. The art director also decides how much space to allow for a title, a blurb (a brief statement that tells readers something about the article), a byline (the author's name), and picture captions.

The layout is given to the editor, who must cut and edit the manuscript to fit it. Then the article is sent to a copy editor, who makes sure that it fits the magazine's style (its normal usage in punctuation and grammar). Many magazines have a fact checker who must verify every important fact, date, and name.

After the managing editor and the editor approve the copy, it is ready to be set in type by computer. The set copy comes out in long sheets called **galleys.** Then the printer makes a **mechanical,** cutting the galleys and pasting them up to fit the page layout. The mechanical is photographed to produce a negative, which is then exposed onto an **offset** plate. You will find more about the offset process in the article PRINTING in Volume P.

The four pages of the article are printed as part of a **signature**—a large sheet that when folded will form a section of the magazine. After all the signatures are printed, other machines fold them, bind them together, cut the pages free, and address copies to subscribers.

▶AMERICAN CHILDREN'S MAGAZINES

Youth's Companion, founded in 1827, was the first magazine published especially for children. Its publishers, Nathaniel Willis and Asa Rand, wanted to encourage ''virtue and piety'' and ''to warn against the ways of transgression.'' In the 1850's *Youth's Companion* had the largest circulation of any American magazine.

Other magazines imitated *Youth's Companion. Student and Schoolmate,* begun in 1854, published travel articles, stories in serial form, sheet music, poems, and declamations. (Declamations were speeches or recitations with dramatic gestures.)

A similar magazine was *Our Young Folks,* popular from 1865 to 1873. Then came the magazine for children that was probably the most popular of all, *St. Nicholas.*

First issued in 1873 by Roswell Smith, *St. Nicholas* was edited for its first 32 years by Mary Mapes Dodge, author of *Hans Brinker, or, The Silver Skates.* Mrs. Dodge recruited well-known writers for her magazine. Mark Twain's *Tom Sawyer Abroad* first appeared in its pages. So did Frances Hodgson Burnett's *Little Lord Fauntleroy* and Rudyard Kipling's *Jungle Book* stories. Louisa May Alcott and Kate Douglas Wiggin were regular contributors.

Mrs. Dodge encouraged young readers to send in their own stories and poems. Budding writers whose work was published in *St. Nicholas* became members of the St. Nicholas League. Some of them later became famous. Edna St. Vincent Millay, Robert Benchley, Ring Lardner, William Faulkner, Rachel Field, and Stephen Vincent Benét all wrote for *St. Nicholas* when they were children.

St. Nicholas and *Youth's Companion* were the most popular youth magazines in the country when *American Boy* appeared in 1899. It had adventure and nature stories. Similar magazines followed—*Boy's Life* (1912), which is still published, and *Open Road* (1919), which published correspondence between young people in the United States and other countries.

After World War I the old favorites began to lose popularity. *Youth's Companion* survived until 1929, when it merged with *American Boy.* A year later *St. Nicholas* was sold to *Scholastic,* but it did not re-appear until 1935. *St. Nicholas* changed hands several times before it vanished finally in 1941. *American Boy* published its last issue in July, 1941.

Since that time many new children's magazines have come on the market to take the place of those that disappeared. Some of the most popular ones are listed on the following page.

SOME POPULAR MAGAZINES FOR CHILDREN

The following children's magazines are those with the highest home circulation in the United States and Canada. Included in the annotation are the year of first publication, the recommended age range for readership, the number of issues each year, and a brief description.

Boy's Life. 1911, 8–18, monthly. Fiction and nonfiction articles emphasize outdoor life, sports, and recreation.

Child Life. 1922, 7–9, 9 issues. Stories, articles, activities, and puzzles focus on teaching good health habits.

Children's Digest. 1950, 8–10, 9 issues. Fiction, nonfiction, and activities are intended to augment the well-being of children.

Cobblestone. 1979, 8–14, monthly. Each issue covers an aspect of American history, developed through both fiction and nonfiction.

Cricket. 1973, 6–12, monthly. A literary magazine that features stories and poems and some nonfiction—all nicely illustrated.

Ebony Jr! 1973, 6–12, 10 issues. "Mirrors the hopes, ideals, and accomplishments of Black children throughout the world."

The Electric Company Magazine. 1974, 6–10, 10 issues. Colorful education-oriented publication based on the popular television show.

Enter. 1983, 10 up, monthly. News, reviews, puzzles, technical articles, and games—all aimed at computer buffs.

Highlights for Children. 1946, 2–12, 11 issues. An emphasis on creativity combined with puzzles and games help children learn while having fun.

Humpty Dumpty's Magazine. 1952, 4–6, 9 issues. Puzzles, crafts, and humorous stories are geared toward teaching better health habits.

Jack and Jill. 1938, 6–8, 9 issues. Exciting and humorous stories emphasize health, safety, exercise, and nutrition.

National Geographic World. 1975, 8–13, monthly. A general-interest magazine with history, science, and human-interest articles.

Odyssey. 1978, 8–14, monthly. The scope is described by the subtitle, *The Young People's Magazine of Astronomy and Outer Space.*

OWL. 1976, 8–12, 10 issues. A Canadian magazine designed to teach children about their environment and their nation.

Penny Power. 1980, 8–14, 6 issues. Published by the publisher of *Consumer Reports;* emphasis is on consumerism and wise use of money.

Ranger Rick. 1967, 5–12, monthly. Teaches about natural history and the environment through stunning photos and lively text.

Sesame Street Magazine. 1971, 2–6, 10 issues. Games, puzzles, and picture stories further the educational goals of the television show.

3-2-1 Contact. 1979, 8–14, 10 issues. A science magazine characterized by lively writing and attractive graphics.

Turtle Magazine for Preschool Kids. 1979, 2–5, 9 issues. Stories, poems, and activities convey positive messages on health.

Wee Wisdom. 1893, 6–12, 10 issues. A Christian magazine with a stated purpose of "character-building," through fiction and features.

Young Miss. 1941, 12–17, 10 issues. Fashion and beauty tips combined with articles on problems likely to be faced by teenage girls.

Your Big Backyard. 1979, 3–5, monthly. Simple crafts and easy-to-read stories are enhanced by large color photographs of animals.

The first magazine was a weekly, *The Review*. It was started in 1704 in London by Daniel Defoe, who wrote *Robinson Crusoe*. Defoe had strong opinions about the British Government's policies, and he wanted to publish his ideas so that people could read them. He published his periodical by himself until 1713.

Other magazines followed *The Review*. The most popular was *The Tatler,* published by Richard Steele in 1709. It was the first magazine to sell space to advertisers. In 1710 a scholar named Joseph Addison joined the magazine, and the two men wrote essays. *The Tatler* became famous for humorous essays on all subjects, from national and foreign affairs to London society and the theater. In 1711, Addison and Steele started another magazine, *The Spectator*. Essays from both magazines are considered to be the first literature of merit to come from magazines, and they are collected in many anthologies.

The first periodical to use the word "magazine" in its title was *The Gentleman's Magazine* (1731). It was a collection of articles and poems copied from newspapers and journals by Edward Cave, a London bookseller, who used the name Sylvanus Urban.

Benjamin Franklin and Andrew Bradford, two rival printers in Philadelphia, published the first American magazines. Franklin (who later became a distinguished statesman, writer, and philosopher) was publishing a newspaper, *The Pennsylvania Gazette,* as well as *Poor Richard's Almanack.* But he wanted to start another publication that would be read throughout the British colonies. He called his monthly magazine *The General Magazine, and Historical Chronicle, for All the British Plantations in America.* The first issue was 70 pages long and was dated January, 1741, although it did not actually go on sale until February 16.

Meanwhile, Bradford had learned of Franklin's idea and rushed to print his magazine. It was called *The American Magazine, or a Monthly View of the Political State of the British Colonies.* His publication went on sale on February 13, three days before Franklin's.

After six months, Franklin stopped his magazine. Bradford's lasted for only two issues. But there were more magazines to take their place. The aim of these magazines was to spread the idea of revolt against England. History gives credit to one magazine for doing more than all the rest to bring about the Revolutionary War. This was the *Pennsylvania Magazine,* published by Thomas Paine. In 1775 it carried Paine's famous essay "On Liberty."

Magazines were so numerous after the revolution that in 1824 the *Cincinnati Literary Gazette* published this verse:

This is the age of Magazines—
Even Skeptics must confess it:
Where is the town of much renown
That has not one to bless it?

The special-interest magazine was born in the 1800's. There were religious magazines, farm magazines, literary magazines, and magazines for doctors, teachers, bankers, druggists, homemakers, and children. The first popular children's magazine, *Youth's Companion,* started in 1827. The first women's magazine, *Godey's Ladies Book,* started in 1830. *Godey's* crusaded for women's education at a time when more than half the women in the United States could not read. For 68 years it influenced the manners and tastes of American families. During the 1800's, three other women's magazines were started, and they are still published. They are *Harper's Bazaar* (1867), *McCall's* (1870), and *Ladies' Home Journal* (1883).

Many famous American writers had their stories first published in magazines. Washington Irving, James Fenimore Cooper, Nathaniel Hawthorne, John Greenleaf Whittier, Oliver Wendell Holmes, and Henry Wadsworth Longfellow contributed to *The Knickerbocker.*

LISTS OF MAGAZINES

Ulrich's International Periodicals Directory lists the magazines of all countries, classified according to subject. *Ayer Directory of Publications* lists newspapers and magazines in the United States and Canada. *The Standard Periodical Directory* is the largest of the directories for U.S. and Canadian publications. It has information on more than 60,000 publications. *Consumer Magazine and Farm Publication Rates and Data* lists U.S. and international consumer magazines. Other sources are *Literary Market Place* and the *Readers' Guide to Periodical Literature,* which lists magazine articles by topic and author. Most libraries have at least some of these directories.

This magazine was the first really popular monthly and was published in New York from 1833 to 1865. Rival magazines soon sprang up, including *Graham's Magazine, The Saturday Evening Post, Harper's Magazine,* and *The Atlantic Monthly.*

By the 1900's the United States had improved transportation and mail services. Brand-name products were being distributed over a wide area. And advertisers wanted to promote their products in the pages of magazines. When publishers discovered that advertising could cover their expenses, they cut the prices for copies of their magazines. *McClure's Magazine, Munsey's Magazine,* and *Cosmopolitan* were lively, entertaining 10-cent monthlies. *The Saturday Evening Post* and its chief rival, *Collier's,* were the leading 5-cent weeklies.

Gradually, magazines that did not get enough advertising went out of business. Drawing many readers was not enough to guarantee success. For example, *Collier's* folded in 1956 with 4,000,000 readers.

The single largest category of magazines is women's magazines. *Ladies Home Journal* has been published for more than a century.

But there were always new magazines coming along. *The New Yorker,* started in 1925, became known for its excellent fiction. And in the 1920's, two new types of magazines appeared. The first was *The Reader's Digest,* which condensed longer articles that had appeared in other magazines. It was an overnight success. By 1935 its circulation had reached 1,000,000. Then it tripled and continued to multiply. Today it is one of the most popular general-interest magazines. It is published in 41 different editions, which are written and edited in 17 different languages.

The second new type was *Time,* a weekly newsmagazine that summed up important events around the world. Two young graduates of Yale University, Henry R. Luce and Briton Hadden, introduced the magazine in 1923. Time Incorporated soon became a publishing giant. In 1930 the company launched *Fortune,* a monthly for business executives. In 1936 a weekly picture magazine, *Life,* was started. It continued until 1972 and was revived as a monthly in 1978. Other magazines published by Time Incorporated include *Sports Illustrated* (1954); *Money* (1972); *People* (1974), a magazine of gossip and articles on celebrities; and *Discover* (1980), a science magazine.

Meanwhile, *Time's* newsweekly format was so successful that it was copied. In 1933, *U.S. News & World Report* and *Newsweek* entered the market. All the newsweeklies have international editions. *National Geographic* and *Business Week* are two other important magazines that publish overseas editions.

Today magazines publish less fiction than they did in the early days. Special-interest magazines have become more and more popular. *TV Guide,* which carries television program listings, has one of the largest circulations of all magazines in the United States. Traditional women's magazines are still widely read, but the women's rights movement has given rise to such magazines as *Ms., Working Woman,* and *Savvy,* a magazine for women executives. *Ebony* and *Essence* were started for black readers. City and regional magazines have sprung up. *Sunset* reports on life in the West, and *Southern Living* on life in the South. And most major cities now have city magazines.

BARBARA BELFORD
Columbia Graduate School of Journalism

In 1520, Portuguese explorer Ferdinand Magellan found the narrow channel at the tip of South America that connects the Atlantic and Pacific oceans. Called the Strait of Magellan, it is 560 kilometers (about 350 miles) long.

MAGELLAN, FERDINAND (1480?–1521)

Ferdinand Magellan, the famous Portuguese navigator, was probably born in the former province of Entre-Douro-e-Minho, in northern Portugal, in 1480. Little is known of his early life, but when he was 25 he sailed to India, where the Portuguese were building an empire. In 1509 he traveled as far east as Malacca, near modern Singapore. The next year he helped conquer Goa in India. He became interested in the spice trade and learned that cloves, the costliest of all of the spices, grew mostly in the Molucca islands, east of Malacca. By this time an expert navigator, Magellan began to think about a possible route to reach the Moluccas from the west instead of by the usual route, around Africa and eastward across the Indian Ocean.

The Spaniards had found the New World. But they had not found the strait at the southern tip of South America, between the Atlantic and Pacific oceans. Magellan believed such a waterway existed. The best way to reach the Moluccas, he thought, would be to find this passage and sail west. Magellan and most other people thought that the Pacific would prove to be a small body of water.

By 1513, Magellan was back in Portugal from the East. He found that King Manuel had no interest in sending him to the Moluccas. In 1518 he decided to look to Spain for backing for his voyage. The Spanish king, Charles I, was interested at once. Magellan had little trouble in getting 5 ships and about 240 men. He did not intend to sail around the world but meant to find the Moluccas, load his ships with spices, and return by the same route.

The fleet left the Spanish port of Sanlúcar on September 20, 1519. Magellan sailed along the west coast of Africa and then crossed to Brazil and followed the South American coast to Patagonia, stopping for the winter in a desolate bay. There he crushed a mutiny led by Spanish officers who disliked sailing under a Portuguese. When warmer weather came, he pushed on. He found the strait now named for him and entered the Pacific Ocean. He called the ocean Pacific (peaceful) because it seemed very calm. He had only three ships left, for one had been wrecked near the strait and another had deserted.

What Magellan had thought would be a small ocean now proved enormous. He and his men ran out of food and fresh water. Many died of scurvy, a disease caused by a lack of vitamin C. They all might have died if they had not sighted the Ladrone Islands (now the Marianas). They took all the provisions they could find and sailed on to the Philippines. There, Magellan took sides in a war between two local chiefs, and he was killed in a battle on the island of Mactan on April 27, 1521. He had not sailed completely around the globe but had come very near to doing it.

After Magellan's death, his crews elected the Spaniard Juan Sebastian del Cano their leader. Cano found the Moluccas and loaded his one remaining ship, the *Victoria,* with spices and food. He decided to go home the shortest way—by completing the voyage around the world. There was again a shortage of food and much suffering. But Cano brought the *Victoria,* with 18 surviving crew members and a few East Indians aboard, back to Sanlúcar on September 6, 1522. The first voyage around the world had taken almost three years.

CHARLES E. NOWELL
Editor, *Magellan's Voyage Around the World*

Abracadabra! The woman seems to have been sawn in half. Only very experienced magicians can attempt this trick, here performed by Doug Henning.

MAGIC

Magic is the use of spells, charms, or tricks to produce certain effects. One who practices magic is a magician. In ancient days, magicians were believed to have extraordinary powers with which they could perform all sorts of marvelous acts. They supposedly could heal the sick, make rain fall, cast out evil spirits, and communicate with the dead. Naturally the ancient peoples held their magicians in awe.

Records going back more than 1,000 years show that magic was performed for entertainment in Egypt, China, and India. In Europe, magic flourished particularly during the Middle Ages. During that period (from about A.D. 500 to 1500), self-styled wizards traveled about, giving magic shows. They used the scientific discoveries of the day to perform their so-called magic, and they carefully guarded their secrets.

A trick they often did was called "Cups and Balls." It is one of the oldest tricks known, and magicians today still perform it. Three metal cups are set in a row, upside down. A small ball is placed underneath each cup. With a magic wand, the magician taps a cup and then raises it. The ball has disappeared. A second cup is tapped, then raised, and the magician finds two balls there. The balls seem to have jumped, invisibly, from cup to cup. Suddenly the magician tips over the cups, and there is now an orange, or some other large object, underneath each cup.

This trick is done by **sleight of hand,** which is the art of deceiving, or tricking, the eye by skillful movements of the hands. By the use of sleight of hand, small objects, such as balls, cards, or coins, can be made suddenly to appear or vanish or to "change" into something else.

▶MODERN MAGICIANS

Modern magic as a form of entertainment started around the middle of the 19th century. One of the greatest magicians of that day was a Frenchman, Robert Houdin (1805–71), who is known as the father of modern magic. Houdin created a sensation in Paris.

The French Government sent him to Algeria to match his skill against that of the rebellious Marabouts, a group of Arabs who controlled the people with their acts of magic. Houdin announced that he had the power to take away the strength of the Arab leaders. He then performed one of his great tricks, in which he used the principle of electromagnetism to make light objects seem heavy.

On a floor rested a small wooden box with a metal bottom. Houdin called on a man from the audience to lift the box, which he did with ease. Pretending to take away the man's strength, Houdin dared him to lift the box again. At this point, Houdin's hidden assistant turned on a strong electromagnet concealed beneath the stage. This held the metal-bottomed box fast to the floor, and the man struggled in vain, unable to lift the box. The Arabs viewed this demonstration with awe and soon concluded that French magicians were more powerful than their own.

After Robert Houdin other magicians became famous as entertainers. The name of each was usually identified with a particular type of magic or with some outstanding trick or illusion. (In the language of magicians, an illusion is an elaborate trick in which a human being or animal is used.)

Harry Kellar (1849–1922) was one of the great magicians of the 20th century. He held audiences spellbound by his illusion "The Princess of Karnac." By supposedly hypnotic influence, he caused a "hypnotized" girl to rise slowly from a couch into mid-air. He then passed a solid hoop around her as she floated in space, seeming to prove that her body had no means of support.

Howard Thurston (1869–1936) was another famous illusionist. One of his illusions was sawing a woman in half. He placed a woman in a coffin-like box, her head sticking out at one end, her feet at the other. Using a large saw, Thurston then sawed through the box and the lady. When the separated halves were brought together again, the woman sprang up from the box, whole and sound.

Harry Houdini (1874–1926) achieved worldwide fame as an escape artist. His specialty was escaping from handcuffs, leg irons, and shackles, and he took chances few others would. One of his feature tricks was the "Milk Can Escape." Handcuffed, Houdini stepped into an airtight metal can filled with water.

The can's cover was then locked on from the outside with padlocks. Houdini made his escape from this dangerous enclosure within minutes, while the audience watched breathlessly. He was a master showman.

Ching Ling Foo (1854–1922) amazed audiences by producing from empty shawls large bowls of water filled with goldfish.

Joseph Dunninger (1896–1975) gained his reputation and fame as a "mentalist." He mystified millions of people with his performances on stage and television. Dunninger, who apparently read the minds of members of his audience, was a fascinating performer.

Other famous modern magicians are Herrmann the Great (1843–96), Harry Blackstone (1885–1965), Horace Goldin (1873–1939), The Great Leon (1876–1951), Jarrow (1876–1960), Cardini (1895–1973), Doug Henning (1947–   ), and David Copperfield (1956–   ).

▶THE ART OF MAGIC

Magic appeals to everyone because people love to be mystified. The amateur magician who can entertain with a few clever tricks is always welcome in any social gathering.

Many of the most baffling tricks are extremely simple. Some are done by sleight of hand. Others are performed with the help of a cleverly constructed mechanical aid. A great many tricks require neither sleight of hand nor special equipment. They can be learned easily and can make one an effective magician.

Knowing how the tricks are done is one thing. Performing them so that they mystify and entertain is another. There are some important rules to follow, and one also has to know something of the psychology of deception, or trickery.

The Art of Misdirection. The old saying that "the hand is quicker than the eye" is supposed to sum up the art of the magician. This is false. The real secret of the magician's art lies in fooling the mind rather than the eye. The means by which this is done is called misdirection.

Misdirection is a form of mental suggestion. It is the art of transferring the attention of the audience to what the magician wants them to see and of drawing it away from all the secret actions so that they go unnoticed. For example, if you are the magician, you

"MYSTERY OF THE FOUR ACES"

1. Before beginning this trick, put the four aces facedown on top of the deck. Then place the deck facedown on the table and announce you will not touch the cards again until the trick is ended. Ask a helper to cut the deck in half, placing the upper half to the right of the lower half.

2. Ask your helper to cut the decks in half again, placing the upper halves below the lower halves to form a square (now the aces will be on top of Packet D).

3. Ask your helper to pick up Packet A, remove the top three cards, and place them facedown on the space that Packet A just occupied.

4. Now have your helper deal one card from Packet A to the top of each of the other packets, B, C, and D.

5. Finally, your helper must lay the balance of Packet A on top of the three cards that were first removed. Using Packets B, C, and D, your helper must repeat steps 3 to 5, placing the cards on the packets in clockwise order. When all four packets have been dealt, wave your hand over the packets and turn up the top cards to reveal four aces.

throw a small ball into the air with an upward motion of your hand. Every eye in the audience will follow the ball as it rises and falls. You also pointedly move your head and eyes to follow the course of the ball in flight. Repeating the action, this time you only pretend to throw the ball upward; actually you keep it in the palm of your hand. (This is known as palming.) Again you follow the imaginary flight of the ball with your head and eyes exactly as you did the first time, when the ball was in actual flight. Imitating you, the audience does the same thing. The magician's eyes peer upward for a moment. Then, with a look of surprise, they are turned to the audience, as if to ask, "What happened to the ball?" To the audience, it appears that the ball has vanished in mid-air.

Another method of controlling spectators' attention calls for entertaining talk by the performer. This diverting talk is called patter. It not only holds the audience's attention but it also makes the trick more enjoyable and helps hide the magician's secret moves from those watching.

Magicians' Rules. Here are some rules that good magicians carefully follow:

(1) Never tell the audience what trick you intend to perform; otherwise the element of surprise is lost, and the chance of detection is increased.

(2) Never perform the same trick twice on the same program. What the audience missed the first time it may discover upon seeing a trick the second time.

(3) Practice even the simplest tricks before attempting to perform them. Once you have gained some skill, you may broaden your knowledge. One way of doing this is to read good books on magic and get new ideas from them.

The following tricks will be a good start for you as a beginner magician. Although they are mystifying, they are easy to do.

▶ SPIRIT RING ON ROPE

In this baffling trick, your wrists are tied with a length of cord. You then take a solid ring, which has been examined, and turning your back for a few moments, you cause the ring to appear on the cord.

The secret is that, unknown to the audience, two rings are used. They may be plastic bracelets, alike in size and color, obtainable at any store selling novelty jewelry.

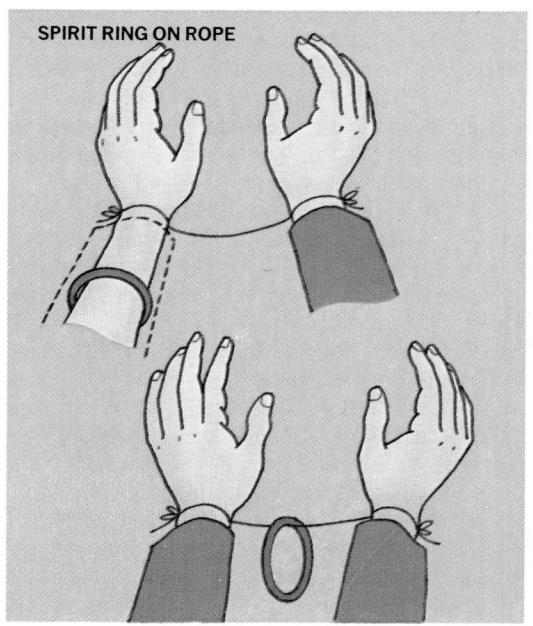

SPIRIT RING ON ROPE

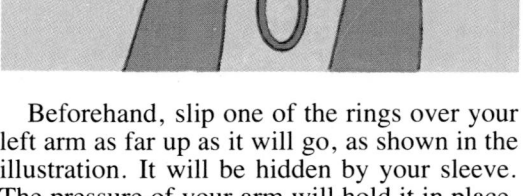

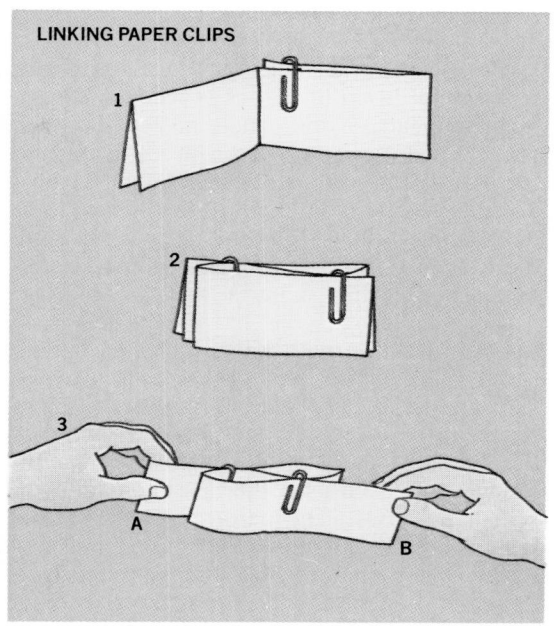

LINKING PAPER CLIPS

Beforehand, slip one of the rings over your left arm as far up as it will go, as shown in the illustration. It will be hidden by your sleeve. The pressure of your arm will hold it in place.

Have a friend tie a piece of cord fairly tight around your wrists, as shown. There should be about 30 centimeters (1 foot) of cord between the wrists. Hold your hands up while they are being tied, to prevent the ring on your arm from slipping down.

Next, hand out the duplicate ring for examination. When it is returned, turn your back and quickly put this ring into your shirt pocket or inside coat pocket, at the same time allowing the ring on your arm to slip down over the cord. Turn around and show the ring now hanging from the cord.

▶ LINKING PAPER CLIPS

To do this easy but puzzling trick, fold in half, lengthwise, a rectangle of paper about 20 centimeters (8 inches) long and 8 centimeters (3 inches) wide, keeping the folded edge on top. Now fold the paper into three parts, accordion style. Place a paper clip over the middle and back folds. (Illustration 1.)

Place another paper clip over the front and middle folds. (Illustration 2.)

Grasp ends A and B firmly and pull the paper straight. (Illustration 3.) The two paper clips will fly off, mysteriously linked together.

▶ THE DIGIT PROBLEM

Here is a mystifying mind-reading trick that you can perform for your friends at a party or some other gathering.

Ask two persons to assist you. Instruct them that when you turn your back and say "Ready," they must both hold up from one to five fingers and then call aloud the total of the two hands.

When this has been done, you immediately announce the number of fingers each of them is showing.

The secret is simple and ingenious. One of the two persons who participates is your secret assistant. The first time it is worked, your assistant must hold up two fingers. When the total is called, you simply subtract 2 and announce the number of fingers each of them has extended.

Contrary to the usual rule, you now offer to repeat the trick. This time your assistant must hold up the same number of fingers that the other person held up previously. Since you also know what that number is, you subtract it from the new total called and again announce the number of fingers each of them is showing. At each repetition it is your assistant's duty to hold up the same number of fingers as were last extended by the other person.

GEORGE G. KAPLAN
Author, *The Fine Art of Magic*

MAGNA CARTA

On June 15, 1215, King John of England met with a group of barons at Runnymede, a meadow near London. There he put his royal seal on a document, written in Latin, called the Magna Carta (Great Charter). The Magna Carta was the first attempt to limit the power of the king by law. John did not wish to sign the Magna Carta, but he had become so unpopular with his subjects that he had no choice.

Dissatisfaction with King John had begun many years before the signing of the Magna Carta. His subjects were angry with the King for his ruthlessness. He taxed them heavily so that he could carry on military campaigns in France. Often he used the taxes for his own selfish purposes. The barons had asked the King many times to agree to their demands for rights, but each time John refused. Stephen Langton, Archbishop of Canterbury, helped organize the barons' opposition to the King. In fact, it was Langton and the barons who drew up the Magna Carta. In the spring of 1215, the barons occupied London. King John finally realized that he had to give in to the barons' demands and agreed to the meeting at Runnymede.

The Magna Carta established the principle that certain customs and laws had more authority than the king and that if the king did not observe these laws, the people had the right to force him to do so. Many of the 63 articles in the Magna Carta dealt with specific problems of the times, such as payments of feudal dues and justice in the law courts. One of the articles guaranteed the freedom of the church. Other articles in the Magna Carta listed the barons' rights and privileges.

The most famous article, number 39, stated that "no freeman shall be arrested or imprisoned . . . except by the lawful judgment of his equals and according to the law of the land." It was later expanded to guarantee a jury trial for everyone. This was followed by article 40, which stated, "To no one will we sell, to no one will we refuse or delay right or justice." Another famous article was number 12, which stated that "no scutage [taxes] or aid shall be levied . . . unless by the common consent of our kingdom." During their fight for independence, American colonists extended this to mean "no taxation without representation."

At the time it was issued, the Magna Carta was not very effective. Civil war soon broke out between King John and the barons. It was still raging when John died on October 19, 1216. The charter was re-issued several times after his death. But only in the 1600's did the Magna Carta become a symbol of English liberty. Defenders of Parliament used the document to support their attempts to limit the power of King Charles I. By the end of the century, supreme authority rested in the hands of Parliament, as it does today.

In an attempt to simplify the laws of England, parts of the Magna Carta have been revised or repealed. But these changes have not destroyed or diminished the importance of this famous document. After more than 700 years, it remains a cornerstone of freedom in the Western world.

Reviewed by GOLDWIN SMITH
Author, *A History of England*

King John signed the Magna Carta reluctantly, since signing it was admitting that he was bound by the law.

MAGNESIUM

Magnesium is a silvery white metal that is very light in weight. It is the lightest of the engineering metals—the metals most often used in industry. Magnesium is also one of the easiest metals to shape with machine tools.

Like many other metals, magnesium is given added strength and durability when it is alloyed, or mixed, with other metals. The metals most commonly alloyed with magnesium are aluminum, manganese, and zinc.

Because they are light and strong, magnesium alloys are used in airplanes, missiles, rockets, and lightweight machine parts. They are also used in other products that need to be light, such as luggage, portable tools, hand trucks, and ladders.

Magnesium is one of several ingredients in chlorophyll, the green food-making substance in plants. Magnesium is also found in animals, where it is part of the chemical process in which sugar is broken down to provide energy. Beans, liver, nuts, and whole-grain cereals are foods that are rich in magnesium.

Magnesium compounds are used in several medicines. Epsom salts, for example, is actually magnesium sulfate. Milk of magnesia is a mixture of magnesium hydroxide and water.

When magnesium is powdered, or when it is shaped into thin ribbon or wire, it ignites easily and burns with an intense white flame. For this reason it is used in fireworks, signal flares, photographic flashbulbs, and incendiary bombs.

The printing industry uses large quantities of magnesium for making photoengraving plates because the metal can be etched very easily. Reproductions of drawings and photographs are etched on the plates, which are used for printing illustrations in books, magazines, and newspapers.

▶ SOURCES OF MAGNESIUM

More than 60 minerals contain magnesium. The most important mineral sources of magnesium are dolomite and magnesite. No magnesium metal is found uncombined in nature.

Magnesium compounds were known and used for many years before the pure metal was extracted from them. The compounds were confused with lime (a chemical containing calcium) until 1755. In that year, the Scottish chemist Joseph Black proved that lime and magnesium compounds were different substances. He did this by showing that they react differently when treated with the same acids.

In 1808 the English chemist Sir Humphry Davy extracted a small amount of magnesium metal from a compound of magnesium by heating it with potassium and mercury. He called the metal magnium but later changed the name to magnesium. The name comes from an area in ancient Greece called Magnesia, where deposits of magnesium compounds were found.

One of the largest supplies of magnesium is found dissolved in seawater. The element makes up about 0.13 percent of seawater. The supply of magnesium is almost unlimited because there are methods for extracting the metal from seawater.

In 1833, electricity was first used by the English scientist Michael Faraday to extract magnesium metal from magnesium chloride. In this kind of process, called electrolysis, an electric current is used to break down a chemical compound into its elements.

This is the method now used to extract large quantities of magnesium from seawater. In huge tanks, seawater is treated with several chemicals to obtain magnesium chloride. Then an electric current is passed through the magnesium chloride, which breaks down into magnesium metal and chlorine gas. More than 1 kilogram (2.2 pounds) of magnesium can be obtained from each metric ton of seawater with this method.

Reviewed by WILLIAM S. WISE
University of California—Santa Barbara
See also METALS AND METALLURGY.

FACTS ABOUT MAGNESIUM

CHEMICAL SYMBOL: Mg.

ATOMIC WEIGHT: 24.312.

SPECIFIC GRAVITY: 1.74 (nearly 1¾ times as heavy as water).

COLOR: Silvery white.

PROPERTIES: Lightest structural metal produced in quantity; is easy to machine and to etch; ignites easily in powdered form or when shaped into wire; burns with an intense white flame.

OCCURRENCE: Sixth most abundant element on earth; third most abundant engineering metal (after aluminum and iron); occurs as carbonate or silicate, never as a native metal.

CHIEF SOURCES: Dolomite; magnesite; magnesium chloride extracted from seawater.

MAGNETS AND MAGNETISM

If you have ever handled a small magnet, you know that it can pick up metal objects such as paper clips or nails. A magnet seems to have some kind of mysterious pulling power. Even if you lay a piece of paper over the nails, the magnet still pulls them. This pulling power is called **magnetism.**

People first noticed magnetism thousands of years ago. They discovered that pieces of a certain kind of black rock had a strange force, which came to be called magnetism. No one knows just how the name was chosen. There is a story that the force was named for a shepherd named Magnes, who discovered that the iron nails in his sandals were pulled strongly when he stood on a large black stone. Another story is that the name came from a place called Magnesia, in Asia Minor, where this kind of stone was first found. There are fanciful stories, too, from ancient times, about iron statues held in mid-air by magnets and about magnetic mountains that could pull the nails out of wooden ships that sailed too near.

After a while, people discovered some useful facts about the black rock, or magnet. They found that when a long, thin piece was hung by a thread, it would swing back and forth and finally stop in a north-south position. The same end of the piece always pointed toward the north. This meant that a magnet could be used as a compass.

Sailors began to use such compasses to guide their ships when the moon or stars could not be seen. The magnetic rock became known as **lodestone,** meaning ''leading stone.'' To make a compass, a sailor took a sliver of lodestone and laid it on a piece of wood floating in a tub of water. Afloat, the lodestone turned freely into the north-south position. You can make a compass of this kind by placing a small bar magnet on a plastic jar lid and floating it in a bowl of water. Try it.

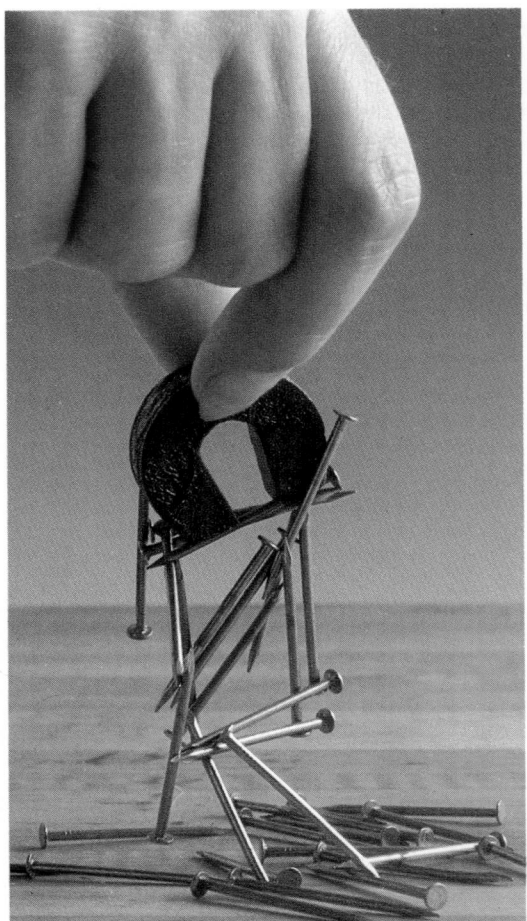

Magnetism can extend beyond the magnet itself. Common nails become slightly magnetic when they touch a magnet and can lift other nails from a table.

▶ EXPERIMENTING WITH MAGNETS

There are other important facts about magnetism that you can easily find out for yourself. Lay a bar magnet on a pile of tacks and then pick it up. The tacks will cling to the bar mainly near its two ends.

These two areas where the force is strong are called the **poles** of the magnet. When the bar is used as a compass, one end swings toward the north. The pole near this end of the bar is called a north pole, or simply N-pole. The other one is a south pole, or S-pole.

If you experiment with two bar magnets, you will find out something more. You will see that the two poles of an ordinary magnet are of opposite kinds. If you bring the N-pole of one bar near the S-pole of the other, the two will attract each other and even snap together. But if you put the N-poles of the two magnets near each other, you will find that they push apart. The same pushing apart happens when the two S-poles face each other.

The push-and-pull rule was discovered long ago, but scientists were not satisfied with just that. They wanted to find out more about these mysterious pushes and pulls of magnetism. They measured the strength of the forces and found that these become rapidly weaker if the poles are moved farther apart. If the distance between two poles is doubled, the force becomes only one fourth as strong as before. If the distance is tripled, the force becomes one ninth of what it was, and so on.

▶ LINES OF FORCE SHOW HOW A MAGNETIC FIELD LOOKS

How can one magnetic pole push or pull on another through empty space? In thinking about this, people found it helpful to imagine that the poles of a magnet are joined by invisible threads. They called the threads **magnetic lines of force.**

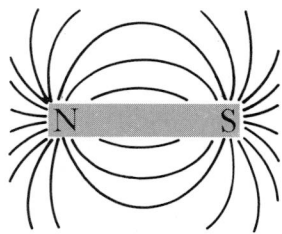

About 150 years ago the English scientist Michael Faraday went on to picture the push-and-pull rule for the forces between magnet poles. He imagined that the lines of force can stretch like rubber bands. Besides this he assumed that the lines push each other sideways. The drawings show the lines of force between two opposite poles and between two like poles.

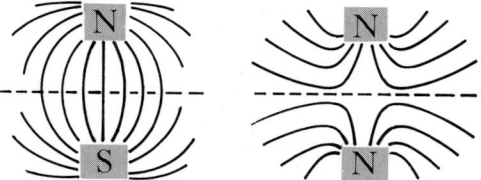

For opposite poles the lines stretch from one pole across to the other, as if trying to pull the two poles together. For the like poles, the lines from one turn away from the lines of the other, pushing sideways and forcing the two poles apart. The space around magnets where these forces are found is called a **magnetic field.** The lines of force help us to map out magnetic fields.

Lines of magnetic force are no more real than the latitude and longitude lines on a map. But they are very helpful in thinking about magnetic fields. You can make their shape visible by this experiment: Lay a magnet on the table and place a piece of stiff cardboard over it. Make some iron filings by rubbing a large nail with a file. Scatter the filings evenly over the cardboard and tap it a few times with a pencil. The filings will line up to give a picture of the lines of force.

In your experiment, notice that the iron filings seem to collect at the edges and corners of the magnet. That is because the lines of force bunch together at such places.

Magnetic lines of force become visible around a bar magnet when metal filings are scattered over the magnet. The area around the magnet is called a magnetic field.

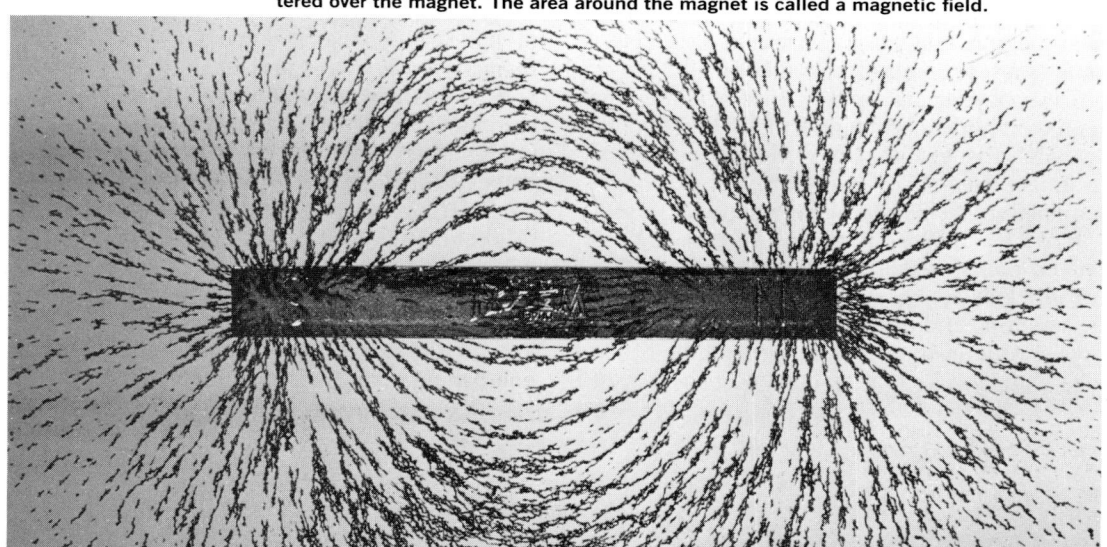

A compass is used by travelers to indicate direction. It is a reliable aid because the magnetized needle always points north.

▶ TEMPORARY AND PERMANENT MAGNETS

What makes a compass needle set itself in a north-south position? It does so because the earth itself has a magnetic field. This fact was discovered nearly 400 years ago by William Gilbert, an English scientist who was also the physician of Queen Elizabeth I. He cut a piece of lodestone in the shape of a ball and put bits of iron all over it. The magnetic field of the ball lined up the pieces of iron in the same way that compass needles line up at various places on the earth. This showed that the earth is like a magnetized ball.

The strength of any magnetic field can be measured in a unit called a **gauss** (rhymes with ''mouse''), named for a German scientist. The strength of the earth's field is only about one-half gauss. The strength of a strong horse-shoe magnet that might be found in a class-room is a few hundred gauss.

Some objects are very magnetic, while others have almost no magnetism at all. This observation made scientists wonder what makes an object magnetic. Two simple experiments demonstrate the answer they eventually found.

Make a magnet out of an ordinary unmagnetized piece of steel, such as a large sewing needle. This can be done by stroking the needle with one end of a bar magnet or even with a piece of lodestone. Start at the middle of the needle and stroke toward one end. The end of

the magnet must be moved along the needle in only one direction. On the return trip to the middle of the needle, keep the magnet some distance away. Do this about ten times. Then turn the needle around. Using the other pole of the magnet, stroke this half of the needle about ten times. The needle is now a magnet, too, and will be able to pick up tacks or paper clips.

Try another experiment: Lay a medium-sized bar magnet on the table with one pole sticking out over the edge. Hang several small nails from the pole by adding one after another, as in the picture.

Now take hold of the top nail and carefully pull it away from the magnet. The nails will cling together for a second or two and then drop off. They act like little magnets only when they are near the bar magnet. As soon as they are taken away, they are magnets no longer.

What made the steel sewing needle keep its magnetism and the iron nails lose theirs almost at once? These and many other facts can be explained by assuming that iron and similar materials are made up of a great many tiny magnets. An ordinary unmagnetized bar has its little magnetic units pointing in all possible directions. This bar does not act like a magnet at all.

But if it is stroked with a strong magnet, the tiny units will line up with one kind of pole facing one way and the other kind facing the opposite way.

In a steel bar, once these unit magnets have swung around into position, they stay in place. The bar becomes a permanent magnet with an N-pole near one end and an S-pole near the other. That is what happened with the sewing needle.

Something like this happened to the nails hanging from the pole of the magnet. The field of the strong magnet lined up the tiny unit magnets in the nails and made them all face one way. Each nail then became a small bar magnet. The attraction of the opposite poles of neighboring magnets made them cling together. But in the kind of iron used for nails, the tiny magnets swing around much more easily than in steel. As you took the nails out of the strong field of the bar, their unit magnets got out of line again. The nails were only temporary magnets. Even if you had stroked them as you did the needle, you could not have made them permanent magnets.

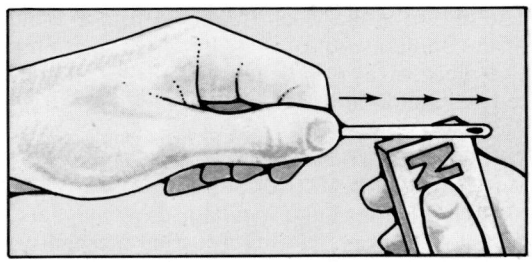
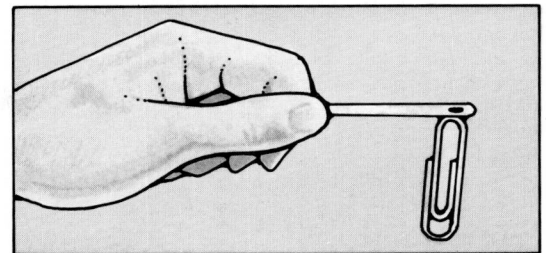

A steel sewing needle can be turned into a weak magnet if it is stroked with a magnet. The magnetism is not permanent, but it will last long enough to pick up a light object.

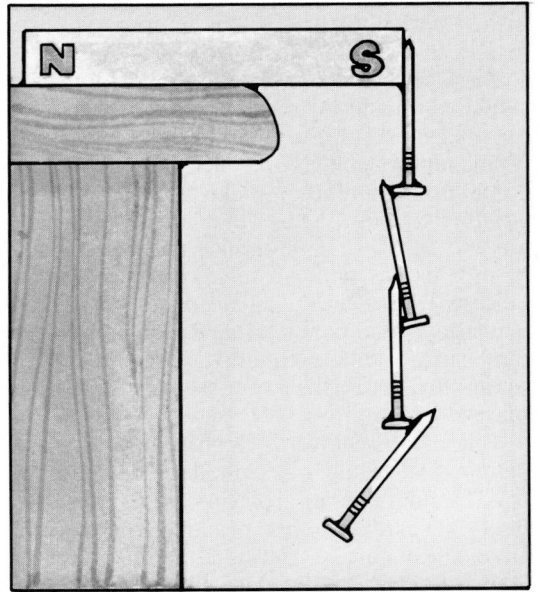
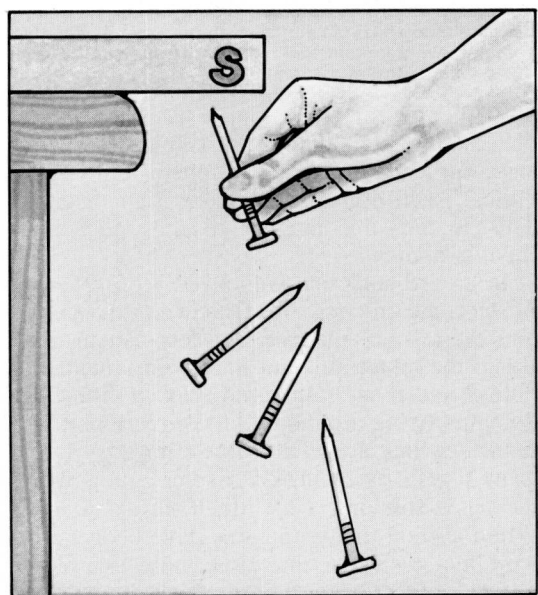

Iron nails can pick up other iron nails, but only when there is contact with a magnet. Unlike a steel sewing needle, iron nails do not remain magnetic and so immediately drop off.

▶WHERE MAGNETISM COMES FROM

One big question remains: What are the little unit magnets found in iron and steel and a few other materials? More than a century ago, the French scientist A. M. Ampère had the idea that these little magnets might be caused by tiny electric currents flowing inside the molecules of the material. Scientists already knew that magnetic fields could be produced by electric currents, and Ampère's idea proved to be right.

It is now known that the currents creating the unit magnets come from the movement of electrons inside the atoms of certain materials. Some of the magnetism comes from the circling of electrons around the center of the atom. But the main part is due to the spinning of an electron on its axis. Each electron has a spin much like that of a toy top.

In most atoms all these electron motions cancel out. As a result the material is non-magnetic. In atoms such as iron, cobalt, and nickel, the magnetic effects of the circling and spinning motions do not quite cancel out. The movement left over makes these materials magnetic.

An important point is that unit magnets are not single atoms or electrons but special groups of atoms. In a material such as iron, the atoms gather together in clusters. All the little atom magnets in the cluster line up in much the same direction. Such a cluster is

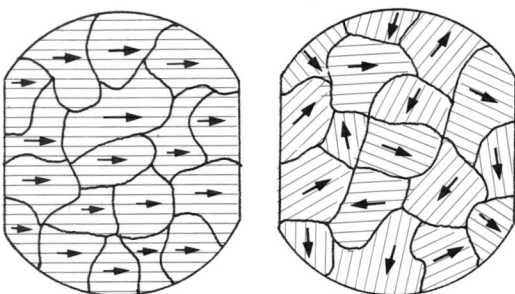

MAGNETIC DOMAINS IN MAGNETIZED METAL

MAGNETIC DOMAINS IN UNMAGNETIZED METAL

Tiny magnetic units, called magnetic domains, determine a metal's magnetism. A strong magnet makes the domains swing around and face in one direction. When this happens, the metal temporarily becomes magnetic.

called a **magnetic domain.** It is microscopic in size, but it may contain millions of billions of atoms. Each domain acts like a tiny magnet. This is the unit magnet that Ampère first thought about.

In an ordinary, unmagnetized piece of iron or steel, the tiny domains face in all directions, and their small magnetic effects cancel out. But if the material is put in a strong magnetic field, two things happen. Little by little the domains swing around into the direction of the field. As they come into line, they may also grow bigger by taking over some atoms from the other domains, which then shrink in size. When a great many domains have been fairly well lined up in one direction, the whole piece of iron or steel becomes a magnet.

Scientists know that bumping a steel magnet or heating it can make it lose its magnetism. The reason is that such treatment forces some of the domains out of their lined-up positions. If a piece of iron is heated until it glows dull red, it cannot be magnetized at all.

▶THE STRONGEST MAGNETS USE NEW MATERIALS AND METHODS

Certain alloys have special uses as magnets. An alloy of iron and nickel, called permalloy, can be easily magnetized, even in a very weak magnetic field. As soon as the field is taken away, the alloy loses its magnetism. This fact makes permalloy useful for temporary magnets in telephones, electric motors, and transformers. In these the magnetic field must be switched on and off many times a second.

Other kinds of alloys make especially good permanent magnets. One such alloy is alnico, containing aluminum, nickel, and cobalt, in addition to iron. Alloys that last even longer are the ferrites, ceramiclike materials made of iron oxides with nickel, cobalt, or certain other metals. Recently, scientists developed new alloys made of cobalt and elements called rare earths. One such alloy, of cobalt with samarium, makes the strongest, longest-lasting magnet known.

Television receivers, electric motors, computers, and many other modern devices depend for their operation on very strong magnetic fields. These fields are produced by passing an electric current through a coil of wire. Such a coil is called an **electromagnet.** Its mag-

A simple electromagnet is made with a battery (source of electricity), insulated wire, and an iron core. When electricity moves through the wire, the iron core becomes magnetic.

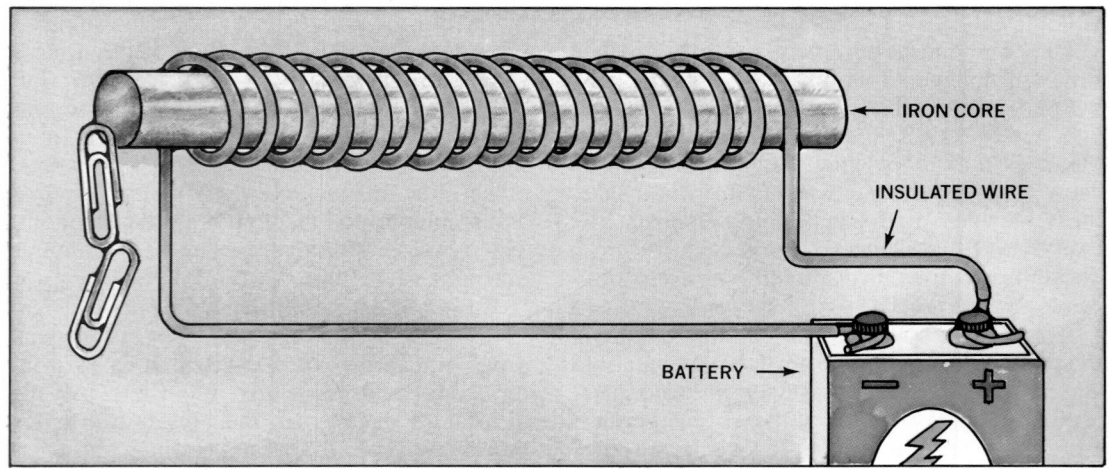

IRON CORE

INSULATED WIRE

BATTERY →

netic field can be made thousands of times stronger by placing a core of some magnetic material inside the coil.

The strongest fields that can be produced with permanent magnets reach a few thousand gauss. Huge atom-smashing machines, such as the synchroton, use electromagnets with fields of around 10,000 gauss. The magnets in many large atom smashers are in the form of huge rings, a thousand or more meters across. They contain many thousands of tons of iron.

There are many difficulties in building very strong magnets. Enormous amounts of heat are produced by the huge electric currents that are needed, and the magnets must be cooled by flowing water to keep them from melting. The strong fields also pull the metal of the magnet with a tremendous force that is almost enough to pull it apart and make it "explode."

The magnet with the strongest field ever made uses no magnetic core at all. It is a small coil of wire made of special alloys of metals such as niobium, rhenium, and zirconium. These alloys act in a very unusual way when they are cooled to extremely low temperatures—they become **superconductors.** This means that if an electric current is started in such a material, the current may keep flowing by itself forever. Through the use of superconductors, it may be possible to produce magnetic fields of 500,000 gauss or more.

To make a coil superconducting, it must be cooled to within a few degrees of absolute zero. This temperature is 273.16°C (459.69°F) below zero. This is difficult to do. It is also very expensive because it requires the use of liquid helium, which is costly.

Scientists are trying to make superconducting magnets that will operate at temperatures that are not so low. They hope to use these magnetic fields to learn many important facts about atoms. For example, the use of superconducting magnets should make it possible to build a synchrotron more powerful than any now in existence and to keep its size down to not more than a few meters across. Superconducting magnets should also make it possible to design and perform many new experiments dealing with the effects of strong magnetic fields on plants and animals.

Ira M. Freeman
Rutgers, The State University of New Jersey

See also Atoms; Electricity; Nuclear Energy.

A huge superconducting magnet (*above*) is used to study particles that make up atoms. An electromagnet (*below*) lifts heavy loads of scrap metal. The load is released when the electric current is turned off.

MAHLER, GUSTAV (1860–1911)

Gustav Mahler, the great Austrian composer and conductor, was born in July 7, 1860, in Kalischt, Bohemia (now Kaliste, Czechoslovakia). At the age of 15, he was enrolled at the Vienna Conservatory, where he studied piano and composition.

In 1880, Mahler began to conduct at small opera houses. Gradually he moved on to important positions at larger theaters in Prague, Budapest, and Hamburg. In 1897 he became artistic director of the Imperial Opera in Vienna. There he brought about needed reforms in the preparation and staging of operas. The Imperial Opera gained international prominence under his direction. During summers in Vienna, when the opera house was closed, Mahler worked on his own compositions. He wrote song cycles and symphonies. Gradually he was recognized as an important composer for the way he combined songs and symphonies and created new instrumental combinations. He was known especially for expanding the traditional form of the symphony and for using many performers. His Eighth Symphony has been described as a "symphony of a thousand." It requires a large chorus, many soloists, and a huge orchestra.

Mahler was a very demanding conductor, and his occasional fits of temper made him enemies. In 1907 he resigned from the Imperial Opera and accepted a position with the Metropolitan Opera in New York City, where he remained for three seasons (1908–10). His conducting of the operas of Mozart and Wagner account for some of the finest performances in the history of the Metropolitan. He also conducted the New York Philharmonic Orchestra.

Mahler's last three years were marred by ill health. He spent as much time as he could composing because he hoped to leave behind works of lasting importance. Some of his best-known works—the symphonic cycle *Song of the Earth,* the Ninth Symphony, and the unfinished Tenth Symphony—were composed during his last years. He died in Vienna on May 18, 1911. Mahler's fame grew after his death. Today he is regarded as one of the greatest composers of his generation.

WILLIAM ASHBROOK
Philadelphia College of the Performing Arts

MAIL ORDER

Mail-order shopping, a form of direct marketing, is a convenient and popular way to make purchases from home. In recent years a wide variety of goods have become available through this method of shopping, and more and more people are making use of it.

All forms of direct marketing use advertising to offer goods and services directly to people. Direct mail, using the postal system, is one type of advertising used in direct marketing. Mail order is a type of direct mail that allows people to order products from their homes or offices.

▶DIRECT MARKETING

The means of communication used in direct marketing may be catalogs or letters, magazine or newspaper advertisements, radio or television commercials, or the telephone. Whatever method is used, people are asked to respond directly by mail or phone.

Direct marketing is a very efficient way to sell and deliver goods—it does not necessarily require a store or in-person sales calls. For this reason it is used by many types of businesses—magazine and newspaper circulation departments, credit card companies, book and record companies, financial services, and insurance companies. Some businesses that use direct marketing, such as catalog and other mail-order firms, have no stores. Others use direct marketing along with other selling methods. Even retail stores sell merchandise through the mail or by telephone. Direct marketing is also used by colleges and universities and by most fund-raising groups.

▶HOW MAIL ORDER WORKS

Mail order is basically a simple process. A business selects a product or a group of products to offer to you and mails an advertisement or a catalog to your home. There is usually an order form for you to fill in and mail if you wish to buy something. Or there may be a telephone number, so that you can call and place your order personally. Payment is usually mailed with the order (or separately, if the order was placed by telephone.) Many mailers allow customers to charge purchases. Some allow payment on delivery.

After the company receives your order, it packs the product and ships it. Sometimes, in the United States, the merchandise is sent through the U.S. Postal Service. Sometimes other carriers, such as United Parcel Service, are used. Mail-order firms usually allow customers to exchange or return most items.

But mail order involves more than just assembling a list of products and sending out mail describing them. The products themselves must be selected wisely. The offer must be presented in a bright, original way, to show the customer its interest and value. And the seller must fill orders promptly.

Direct mail advertisements must reach the right people—people who are likely to be interested in the product being offered. Mailing lists help the seller reach these people. They are drawn up according to information on income, education, interests, home ownership, marital status, and other factors. Thus a firm that wanted to sell a lawn sprinkler through the mail, for example, would probably look for a list of homeowners.

▶ THE GROWTH OF MAIL ORDER

Mail-order shopping began to grow in the late 1800's, in the American Midwest. It filled the important role of providing goods to rural families who did not live near stores. These families had little means of getting the products they needed in their daily lives. In time such early mail-order companies as Montgomery Ward (which started in 1872) and Sears (1886) grew to become huge marketers of general merchandise, providing household, personal, and even automotive products to a vast number of shoppers.

Today mail order is a big business, generating $60,000,000,000 (billion) in sales a year and growing at a rate of 10 to 15 percent a year. There are several reasons why mail order has grown in recent years. One is the variety of merchandise available. You can purchase almost any kind of product through the mail, from teddy bears to telephones.

Another reason is the convenience of shopping at any hour of the day or night from the comfort of home. This is especially helpful to working people who have busy schedules.

A large mail-order operation looks more like an office than a store. The incoming orders are entered into a computer, which makes it possible to handle a large number of accounts efficiently and accurately.

These people have little time to shop in stores, but they must still feed and clothe themselves and their families and furnish their homes. Older people also use mail order because they find shopping at home safe and easy. Young professionals, college students, hobbyists, sports enthusiasts—there is hardly a group that has not begun to shop at home.

A new way of shopping at home is available in some parts of the United States. It is videotex, a two-way system that allows you to order merchandise by using a home computer or similar electronic device. Videotex transactions are recorded instantly, making shopping from home even simpler and faster. As more families acquire computers, it is likely that there will be more such systems.

Mail order and other methods of direct marketing are efficient and economical ways to do business. In recent years they have changed the way many people in the United States shop. It is likely that mail order will continue to grow because it fills the needs of so many different kinds of people.

ROBERT F. DeLAY
Direct Marketing Association

See also SALES AND MARKETING.

MAINE

Almost everyone knows the story of the first permanent English colony in America at Jamestown, Virginia, in 1607. The story of the Plymouth Colony, which was founded at Plymouth, Massachusetts, in 1620, is also well known. Not so well known is the story of the 100 or more colonists who came to Maine in 1607.

The Maine colonists were sent by Sir John Popham, chief justice of England. Their leader was George Popham, a relative of Sir John's. They landed at the mouth of the Kennebec River in August, 1607. Immediately they built a fort, houses, and a church. They also built a ship, the *Virginia*—the first ship built by the English in North America. Then troubles arose. The winter was unusually severe. Food supplies ran low, and the leader and many others died.

Supplies arrived the next year, but the remaining colonists felt that they could not survive another winter, and the colony was abandoned in 1608. The Fort Popham Memorial at present-day Popham Beach commemorates the settlement that was made in New England 13 years before the Pilgrims arrived.

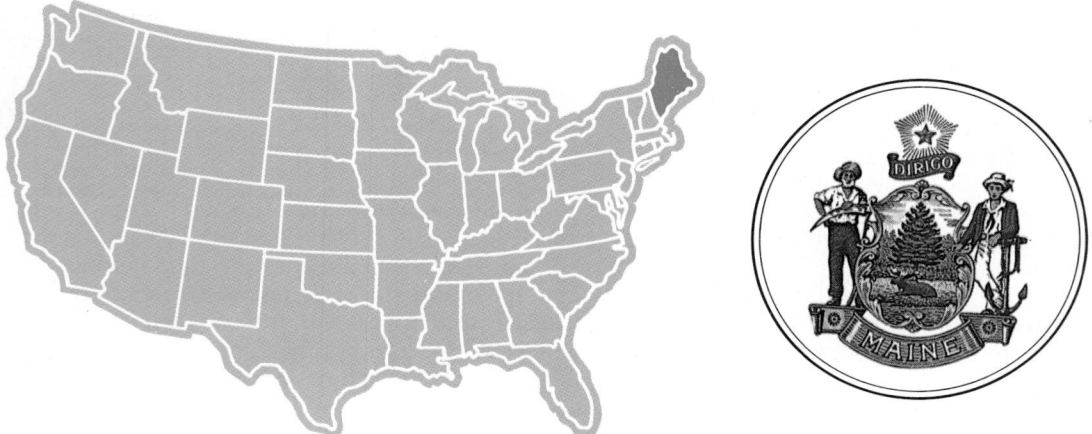

Maine is an interesting land of variety and change. It has long been known as the Pine Tree State. New Englanders call it Down East because ships sailing north from Boston sail downwind to get to Maine. The state might also be called Vacationland. Its lakes and mountains, great forests, and rugged coastline with many snug harbors make a delightful setting for year-round sports and recreation.

Maine is also a manufacturing, agricultural, and fishing state. The pulp and paper industry supplies the material for many of the books, newspapers, and magazines printed in the United States. Factories turn out a variety of wood products—from toothpicks to ships. Other factories produce shoes, textiles, and electronic equipment. The state's farms and fishing grounds contribute such famous Maine foods as potatoes, blueberries, and lobsters.

Maine is the easternmost of all the 50 states—the first to greet the morning sun. There is endless friendly argument about which one of several points receives the very first rays. Is it West Quoddy Head, the easternmost point in the state and the nation? Is it Mars Hill in eastern Aroostook County, or Cadillac Mountain on Mount Desert Island? Probably these points share the honor at different seasons.

Maine's location in the northeastern corner of the nation makes it a truly international state. It borders on only one other state—New Hampshire—but on two Canadian provinces —Quebec and New Brunswick. The people of Maine share common problems and holidays with their friends in Canada.

Maine did not become a state until 1820, but it has a long history. Viking explorers are said to have visited present-day Maine about the year 1000. Europeans fishing in Maine waters possibly also knew the area long before history recorded their visits. Colonists came to Maine several years before the Pilgrims landed at Plymouth, Massachusetts, in 1620. Blockhouses, monuments, and historic buildings are reminders of Maine's proud, eventful past. Its military and naval bases indicate that it plays an important part today in the defense of the United States.

▶ THE LAND

Maine is the most northeasterly as well as the largest of the New England states. It is almost as large as all the others combined.

The 45th parallel of latitude runs near the center of Maine. Several towns on this line of latitude can boast that they lie midway between the North Pole and the equator.

Landforms

The rugged surface of Maine is an ancient, worn-down land. The mountains of the present day are only the stumps of mountains that once were very high. During the Ice Age, all of present-day Maine was covered by moving ice. The great weight of the ice pushed the land down, submerging, or drowning, much of the coastal area. Today the land rises toward the northwest in a series of three steps. These steps divide the state into three natural

STATE FLAG.

STATE TREE: Eastern white pine.

STATE BIRD: Chickadee.

STATE FLOWER: Eastern white pine cone and tassel.

MAINE

CAPITAL: Augusta.

STATEHOOD: March 15, 1820; the 23rd state.

SIZE: 86,156 km² (33,265 sq mi); rank, 39th.

POPULATION: 1,125,027 (1980 census); rank, 38th.

ORIGIN OF NAME: Probably named by French explorers in the 1500's for Maine, a historical region of northwestern France; called Maine by early New Englanders to distinguish the main, or mainland, from the many islands along the coast.

ABBREVIATIONS: Me.; ME.

NICKNAME: Pine Tree State.

STATE SONG: "State of Maine Song," by Roger Vinton Snow.

STATE MOTTO: *Dirigo* (I direct, or guide).

STATE SEAL: A farmer resting on a scythe and a sailor resting on an anchor stand on either side of a shield. They represent agriculture and commerce. Both water and land are shown on the shield. On the land is a pine tree with a moose lying beneath it. Above the shield is the North Star with a streamer bearing the state motto. The name of the state appears on a streamer below the shield. All these figures make up the state coat of arms.

STATE FLAG: The state coat of arms appears on a blue field of the same shade as the blue field in the flag of the United States.

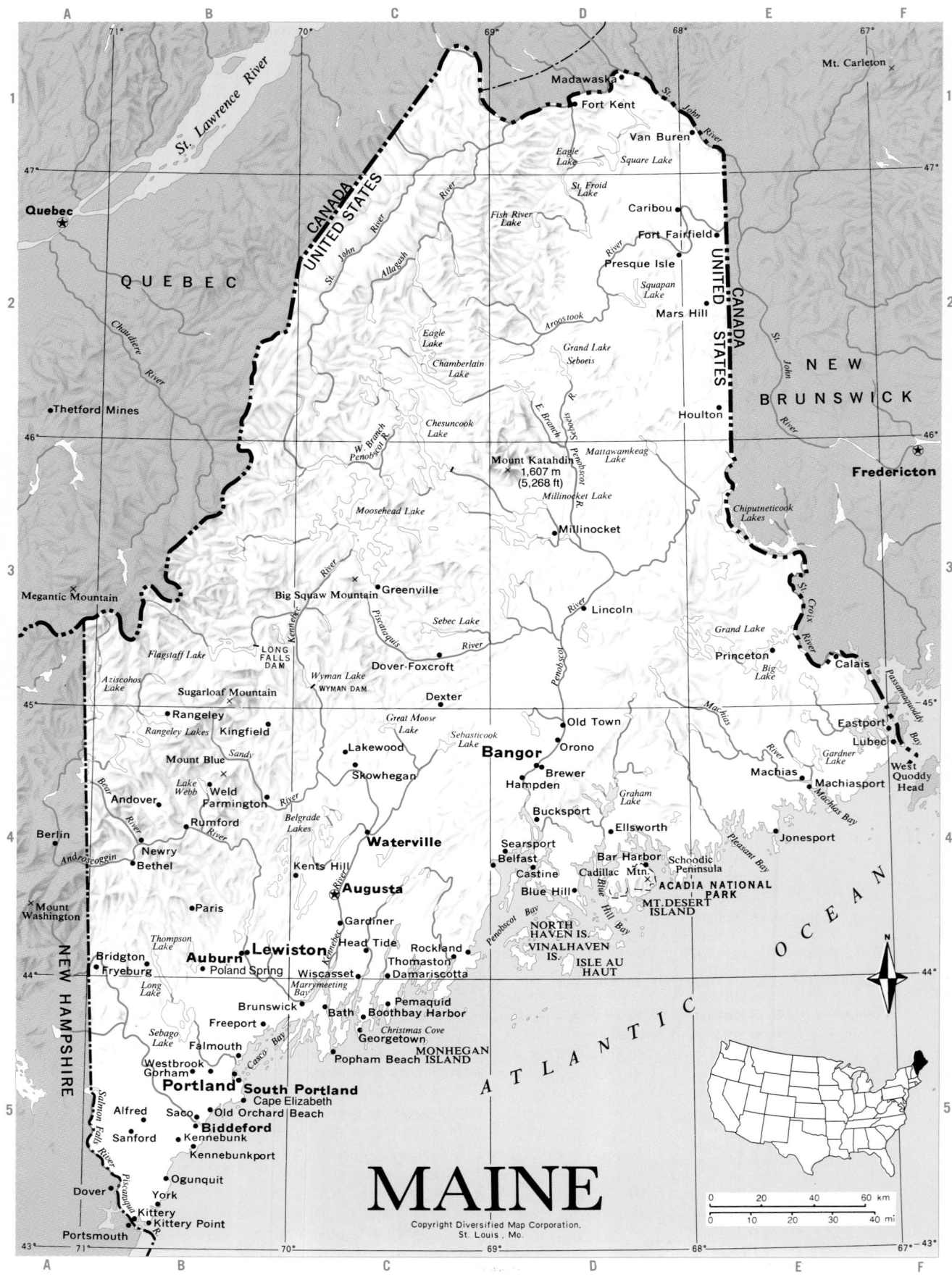

MAINE

Copyright Diversified Map Corporation,
St. Louis, Mo.

regions—the Seaboard Lowland, the New England Upland, and the White Mountains region.

The Seaboard Lowland is the name given to the sloping coastal border of New England. In Maine this region extends inland for distances ranging from about 30 to 95 kilometers (20 to 60 miles). In general it is lower than the adjoining upland. But the Seaboard Lowland is broken in places by hills.

Along the coast southwest of Casco Bay, there are numerous sandy beaches and tidal marshlands. Old Orchard Beach has one of the longest and finest sand beaches on the entire Atlantic coast. The rest of Maine's coastline is rugged and deeply indented—the true "rockbound coast of Maine." It was formed by the submergence of parallel rows of old, worn-down mountains and hills. The tops of these mountains extend into the sea—some as rocky peninsulas and others as islands. Mount Desert Island is the largest of the more than 1,000 islands. Cadillac Mountain on this island is the highest point—467 meters (1,532 feet) on the Atlantic coast of North America.

The New England Upland is a rolling area, averaging between 90 and 300 meters (300 and 1,000 feet) in elevation. Rivers have cut deeply into the land. Towns and cities are located in the river valleys. The upland slopes are forested. The central basin, which includes Augusta and Bangor, and the northern Aroostook basin are the state's chief agricultural areas.

The White Mountains region extends into Maine from New Hampshire. In Maine this region averages above 300 meters in elevation. It has a plateaulike surface with groups of mountains rising abruptly above the surrounding land. Maine's highest peak, Mount Katahdin, is in the White Mountains.

Rivers, Lakes, and Coastal Waters

The St. John River forms part of Maine's northern boundary with the Canadian province of New Brunswick. The St. John and its tributaries, the Aroostook and the Allagash, drain the northern part of the state. The chief rivers of southern Maine are the Androscoggin, Kennebec, Penobscot, and St. Croix rivers. The Androscoggin joins the Kennebec below Augusta to form Merrymeeting Bay. The Penobscot flows to Penobscot Bay. The St. Croix forms Maine's eastern boundary.

Maine has more than 2,000 lakes and ponds, connected by a wide network of brooks, streams, and rivers. Rock basins, scoured out by the glaciers, filled with water to create the largest lakes in the state. Moosehead Lake, southwest of Mount Katahdin, is one of the nation's largest freshwater lakes entirely within a state's borders. The Rangeley Lakes include six lakes, five in Maine and one on the border between Maine and New Hampshire. The Belgrade Lakes form another chain. Artificial lakes, such as Wyman and Flagstaff, help to control the rivers.

Maine's general coastline measures 367 kilometers (228 miles). But the total shoreline, counting all the inlets and bays, is 5,596 kilometers (3,478 miles) long.

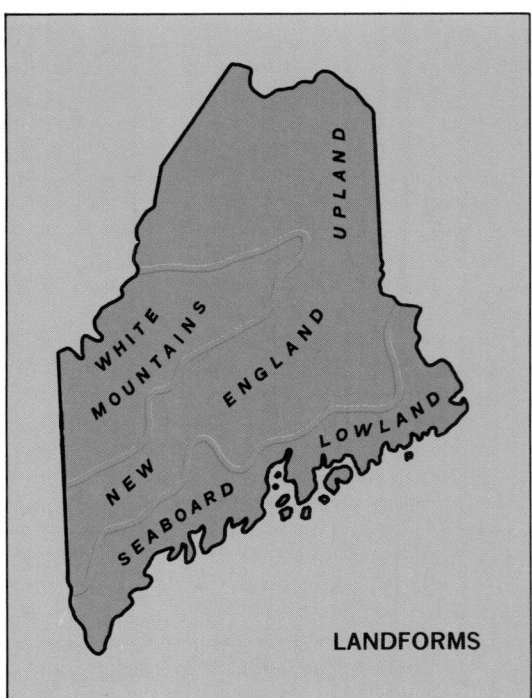

LANDFORMS

THE LAND

LOCATION: Latitude—42° 59' N to 47° 28' N. **Longitude**—66° 57' W to 71° 05' W.
The Canadian provinces of Quebec and New Brunswick to the northwest, north, and east; the Atlantic Ocean to the south; New Hampshire to the southwest.

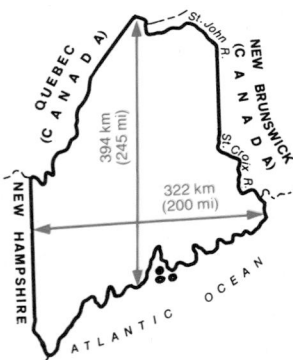

ELEVATION: Highest—Mount Katahdin, 1,607 m (5,268 ft). **Lowest**—Sea level, along the Atlantic coast.

LANDFORMS: Seaboard Lowland, New England Upland, White Mountains.

SURFACE WATERS: Major rivers—Androscoggin, Kennebec, Penobscot, St. John, St. Croix. **Major artificial lakes**—Wyman, Flagstaff. **Largest natural lakes**—Moosehead, Rangeley, Sebago, Chesuncook.

CLIMATE: Temperature—Caribou's January average, —13°C (9°F); July average, 18°C (64°F). Portland's January average, —6°C (21°F); July average, 20°C (68°F). **Precipitation**—Yearly average statewide, 1,000–1,170 mm (40–46 in). Snowfall, about 125–180 cm (50–70 in) along the coast; about 150–230 cm (60–90 in) elsewhere. **Growing season**—140–160 days along the coast; 120–140 days in the interior.

Climate

Maine's cool, moist climate is one of its great assets. Summer temperatures are usually not extremely high. Even the warmest summer days are followed by cool nights. January temperatures along the coast are well below freezing. In northern areas the January average is even more frigid.

Rainfall is fairly well distributed throughout the state. But it is the coastal areas that receive most of the snow. "Spells of weather" are common. Cool, clear, dry periods are followed by warm, moist, stormy days. The variety of weather produces a bracing climate.

Natural Resources

Forest and water resources are especially abundant in Maine. These resources support the major industries, including the growing resort and tourist industry.

Maine has strong environmental laws to conserve its resources and to control how land is developed and water resources are used. Only returnable bottles and cans may be sold in the state. Rivers and lakes cannot be used for dumping of untreated wastewater, and solid waste is deposited in sanitary landfills. The state's Land Use Regulation Commission is responsible for the use of wild forested lands; and the Department of Environmental Protection oversees the development of land

and the use of shorelines in the more populated parts of the state.

Forests. Maine's original forests have been cut down. But the cool, moist climate encourages the growth of trees, and more than half the state is covered with magnificent wild forests. The need to protect this valuable resource has made Maine a leader in conservation. The first continuously operated fire tower in the United States was built on Big Squaw Mountain in 1905. There are more than 400 tree farms, where trees receive the kind of care usually given only to grain or vegetable crops. Each year, millions of young trees are planted to ensure a supply of wood for the future.

Soils. The clay loams of central Maine and of Aroostook County are excellent for farming. Elsewhere the soils generally are thin and not very fertile.

Water. Waterfalls abound on the rough surface of Maine. The force of falling water was used to turn the waterwheels that powered the earliest factories—the sawmills and gristmills. Today waterpower is used to make electricity. Maine is New England's leading producer of hydroelectric power.

The thousands of lakes and streams within the state are important resources. They provide water for homes and industries and places for fishing and boating.

Wildlife. Fish and game are of special importance to the resort business. Salmon, trout, and bass are some of the inland species that lure many fishing enthusiasts to Maine. Tuna fishing is popular along the coast. Deer, bear, ruffed grouse, woodcock, and duck are found in Maine. The puffin, a rare seabird, has returned to Maine for the first time since the early 1900's. Restrictions on the hunting of moose have allowed these animals to increase in number to an estimated 20,000.

Minerals. Maine has a variety of metallic minerals. Aroostook County has millions of tons of low-grade manganese ore. The southern part of the state has deposits of nickel, copper, lead, and zinc. Gold is found in several of the rivers, and people enjoy panning for it. But there are not enough high-grade ores to make mining an important industry.

The chief minerals are nonmetallic—stone and sand and gravel. Stone includes granite, limestone, and slate. Maine also has semiprecious gemstones, such as tourmalines, rose quartz, agates, and mica.

▶THE PEOPLE AND THEIR WORK

The majority of early white settlers were English or Scotch-Irish. Some of them came to Maine from Europe. Others moved into the state from Massachusetts. Through the years

Potatoes have been Maine's leading crop since the late 1800's. Most of the state's crop comes from farms such as this one in Aroostook County.

Above: Maine's annual lobster catch is the largest of any state. Below: Forestry, like lobster fishing, was one of Maine's first industries. The state is a leading producer of pulp and paper.

various other national groups have come to Maine, including three different groups of French-speaking people. French Huguenots came directly from Europe in the 17th and 18th centuries. The Huguenots were Protestants who came to America in search of religious freedom. Those who came to Maine settled along the coast. Another group of French-speaking people, the Acadians, came to the St. John River valley in 1755. They were driven from their homes in Acadia (Nova Scotia) when they refused to swear allegiance to England. In more recent times large numbers of people have come to Maine from French-speaking Canada to work in the mills and the factories. Today many people in Maine speak both French and English.

Descendants of Maine's first people, the American Indians, still live in the state. In recent times, members of two tribes—the Passamaquoddy and the Penobscot—laid claim to a large area of northern Maine. This land, they said, had been taken from their ancestors illegally in the 1790's. The dispute was settled in 1980. Congress passed laws providing money for the tribes to use in buying land and setting up trust funds.

Where the People Live

Most of the people live in the southwestern part of the state. The northern and northwestern parts are sparsely populated. Maine's northernmost county, Aroostook, is larger than Connecticut and Rhode Island together, but only 8 percent of the state's people live there.

Population grew slowly during the first 120 years of statehood. White settlement of the interior was delayed by troubles with Indians and later by the lack of roads. Then, shortly after settlement began, people were attracted away from the state. They left at first to seek agricultural lands on the western frontier. Later the promise of jobs in industrial centers outside the state caused many farmers, especially hill farmers, to abandon their homes. Since the 1940's, opportunities for employment in Maine have improved steadily. The population experienced its greatest growth in the decade from 1970 to 1980.

Industries and Products

Maine might be called a natural resources state because its industries depend directly on those resources that nature has supplied.

Fishing. Maine's first industry, fishing, remains important to the extent that Maine ranks second to Massachusetts as a producer of fish in New England. Lobsters are by far the most valuable item in Maine's total catch. Ocean perch, clams, sardines, and flounder are also important.

Forest Industries. Forestry, like fishing, began in Maine before the time of white settlement. Europeans who visited the fishing banks near Maine came ashore and cut trees to repair their ships, to build drying sheds or platforms, and to smoke fish. Drying and smoking were early methods of preserving fish. Maine's tall white pine trees were eagerly sought for ship masts and lumber.

As the coastal forests were used up, the search for lumber spread throughout the state, especially along the rivers, which could be used to carry logs to mills and to the sea. By the middle of the 19th century, Bangor was an important lumber capital.

Forestry remains Maine's basic industry, although lumber is no longer the chief product. Instead the state has become a leading producer of pulp and paper. Large mills are located in Livermore Falls, Rumford, Millinocket, and Bucksport. Birch and other hardwoods supply the many factories that manufacture products from wood. White pine is important in the building industry.

Agriculture. The first farming was a combination of methods and products brought from Europe and borrowed from the Indians. Corn, an Indian crop, became the basis of mixed farming. Farmers produced small grains, vegetables, fruits, and a few animals. Hay became a leading crop, partly because it was needed as feed for the horses and oxen used in lumbering. The demand for hay dropped sharply as automobiles, trucks, and tractors came into use.

Potatoes became the leading agricultural crop in the late 1800's, after the construction of the Bangor and Aroostook Railroad provided an easy means of transporting potatoes to market. Today Maine is known as a leading producer of potatoes. Aroostook County supplies an important part of the nation's seed potatoes, table potatoes, and processed potato products, such as potato chips.

Maine's other leading agricultural products are livestock and fruit and vegetables, including strawberries, sweet corn, and apples. Blueberries are grown on the sparsely settled lands in the eastern part of the state.

Manufacturing. The first factories were in the homes of settlers. They spun and wove cloth and made farm implements. Later, gristmills and sawmills were built near waterfalls. The textile industry began in the early 1800's. It developed rapidly and soon became the main industry. Cotton mills were built at Lewiston, Biddeford, Saco, and Sanford. Woolen mills were located at Dexter, Lewiston, Guilford, and other places. Since the 1950's the importance of the textile industry has been sharply reduced by competition from textile industries outside the state.

Leathermaking and the boot and shoe industry were brought to Maine by the first white settlers, who had to make their own shoes. Later, shoes were made by traveling shoemakers. Leather came from the hides of animals slaughtered on the farms. It was tanned with tannin from the bark of hemlock trees. Maine ranked high in the tanning industry after the U.S. Civil War. Auburn became a famous shoe center. When cheaper tanning chemicals replaced hemlock, Maine was forced to import material for tanning hides. For a time, competition from growing shoe centers outside the state depressed the industry. Recovery began in the 1930's, and the manufacture of leather and footwear is again an important industry. Today its major competition comes from foreign imports.

Shipbuilding began when the Popham colonists of 1607 built the *Virginia*. During the 1800's, sailing ships built in Maine were a familiar sight in the great world ports. Kittery and Bath are the chief shipbuilding centers today. Many small shipyards along the coast build fishing boats and yachts with the skill that comes only from long experience.

Today manufacturing is increasing rapidly,

WHAT MAINE PRODUCES

MANUFACTURED GOODS: Paper and related products, footwear and other leather products, lumber and wood products, processed foods, textiles, nonelectrical machinery, electric and electronic equipment, boats and ships.

AGRICULTURAL PRODUCTS: Potatoes, milk, cattle and calves, eggs, broilers, apples, blueberries, greenhouse and nursery products.

FISH AND SHELLFISH: Lobsters, flounder, ocean perch, clams, sardines, herring, whiting.

MINERALS: Sand and gravel; stone, chiefly granite and limestone; cement; clays.

both in the number of plants and in the variety of products. Processed foods and electrical machinery are two of the newer products.

Mining. Granite from Maine has been used in the construction of many of the nation's important buildings and monuments. Throughout the state there are huge, gaping holes where busy quarries once existed. Today granite is not mined very much. Other minerals once mined in quantity are slate and limestone. The major mineral product today is sand and gravel, which is used in road construction, landscaping, and cement. Maine's gemstones are finding an increasing market with costume jewelers.

The Recreation Industry. Maine's long-established recreation and tourist industry brings an important part of the state's total income. People were first attracted to Maine by the beauty of the wilderness and the coastline or by hunting and fishing. Resort centers—such as Old Orchard Beach, Bar Harbor, Rangeley, Boothbay Harbor, and Sebago Lake—became famous after the Civil War. Their hotels were filled with summer guests. Bar Harbor was especially well known for its palatial summer homes. Millions of visitors now travel in the state each year, enjoying its fine hotels and motels, campgrounds, and natural attractions.

Transportation and Communication

Waterways were the first highways in Maine. Boats and canoes traveled up and down the rivers. Sailing ships brought passengers and freight from New York, Philadelphia, and Boston to Maine's coastal and river ports. Later, steamships offered the same service. Today ocean travel is limited to local motorship and ferry service. The harbor at Portland is one of the largest in the United States.

The first railroad in Maine was built between Bangor and Old Town in 1836. By the end of the 1800's, several small lines had been merged into two major railroads—the Maine Central Railroad and the Bangor and Aroostook Railroad. Portland is connected with Boston by the Boston and Maine Railroad. Automobiles, trucks, and buses speed over modern highways, carrying people and goods to all parts of the state.

Maine has about 45 commercial and municipal airports and half that many seaplane bases. Commercial air service links the principal cities to Boston and New York. The use of small planes allows the Forestry Department to keep close watch on the forests, the potato farmers to dust their crops, and travelers to reach even remote areas of the state.

Maine's first newspaper, the *Gazette*, appeared in 1785. It was published at Falmouth (now Portland). The first daily paper, the *Courier*, began in 1826, also in Portland. Today the state has about 10 dailies and many weeklies. The largest dailies are the *Bangor Daily News* and the *Portland Press Herald*. There are more than 70 radio and television stations.

▶**EDUCATION**

In general the early history of education in Maine is the same as that of Massachusetts. An education law passed in 1789 required all towns of 50 families to provide six months of schooling. Towns of 200 families were required to support a grammar school.

Schools and Colleges

A school code was adopted in 1820, the year in which Maine became a state. The code assured free education to all persons between the ages of 5 and 21. A state superintendent of schools was installed in 1854, and free public secondary schools were set up in 1873. Two schools for the training of public school teachers were established in the 1860's—one at Farmington and another at Castine.

Bowdoin College, at Brunswick, established in 1794, was the first college in Maine. Its long list of distinguished graduates includes Henry Wadsworth Longfellow and Nathaniel Hawthorne. Other well-known private colleges are Colby College, at Waterville, and Bates College, at Lewiston.

The University of Maine was established at Orono in 1865. Today, in addition to the Orono campus, the university has branches at Farmington, Fort Kent, Machias, and Presque Isle. The University of Southern Maine, at Portland, is also a part of the system. The state supports two-year vocational and technical institutes at Auburn, Bangor, Aroostook, and South Portland and the Maine Maritime Academy, at Castine. The academy trains officers in the merchant marine and the naval reserve.

Libraries, Museums, and the Arts

The first public library was organized at Falmouth (Portland) in the 1760's. It was burned during the British bombardment in

1775. But it was rebuilt, and it has become one of the best in the Northeast. Bangor also has an especially well equipped library. Other cities and towns have libraries that serve their areas. The State Library was organized at Augusta in 1836. It has a large collection of materials pertaining to Maine. The library also maintains bookmobiles.

The Maine State Museum, at Augusta, contains historical materials and displays of mounted native wildlife. The Penobscot Marine Museum, at Searsport, has interesting maritime exhibits. The Nylander Museum, at Caribou, contains an excellent collection of Maine minerals. Many kinds of foreign and domestic trolley cars may be seen at the Seashore Trolley Museum, at Kennebunkport. Important collections of fine arts are in the William A. Farnsworth Library and Art Museum, in Rockland; the Portland Museum of Art, in Portland; and the art museums at Bowdoin College, Colby College, and the University of Maine at Orono.

Portland and Bangor have symphony orchestras. Throughout the state there are summer music camps. Lakewood, near Skowhegan, is the oldest summer playhouse in the nation. Its success encouraged summer theaters to open at Boothbay Harbor, Kennebunkport, Ogunquit, and other places.

▶ **PLACES OF INTEREST**

Maine is a storehouse of historic sites and buildings. The beauty of the state is being preserved in a growing number of publicly owned parks.

National and State Areas

National areas include the Moosehorn National Wildlife Refuge in eastern Maine and a part of the White Mountain National Forest, shared with New Hampshire. The Appalachian National Scenic Trail, which extends 3,200 kilometers (2,000 miles) from Georgia, ends at Mount Katahdin in Maine.

State recreational areas number about 35. They are of two kinds—state parks and state memorials. Most of the state memorials are located on the sites of historic forts. The following are some of Maine's largest or best-known public recreation places.

Acadia National Park is located on parts of Mount Desert Island, Isle au Haut, and Schoodic Peninsula. A scenic drive leads to the top of Cadillac Mountain. There are numerous nature trails. A museum in the park contains relics of prehistoric Indians who once lived in the area.

St. Croix Island National Monument, across the St. Croix River from Canada, marks the site of an attempted French settlement in 1604.

Allagash Wilderness Waterway, along the

Maine's coastline is noted for spectacular scenery. Acadia National Park, on Mount Desert Island, was established in 1919 and is New England's only national park.

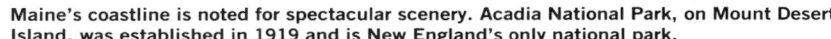

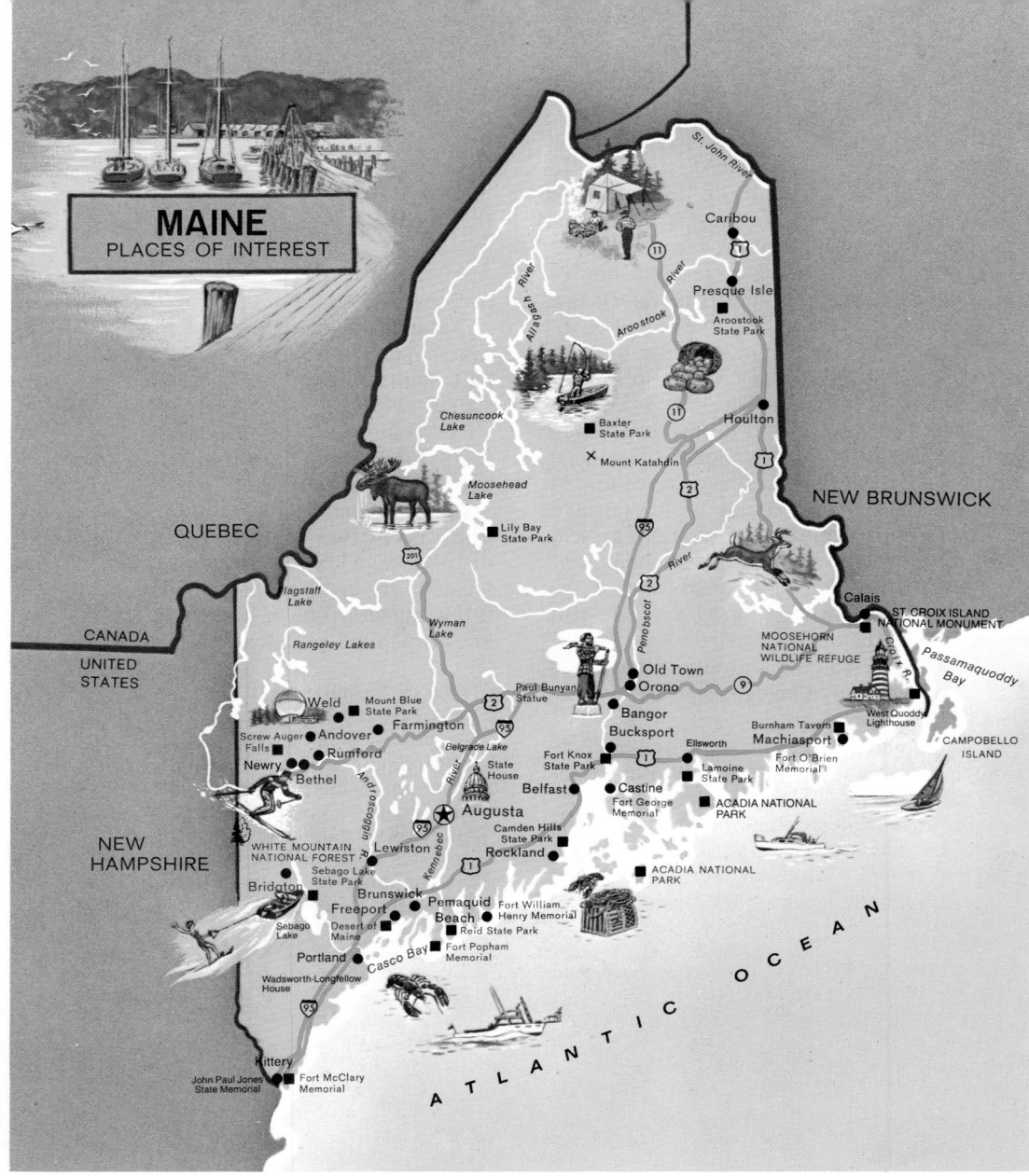

MAINE
PLACES OF INTEREST

Allagash River in northern Maine, preserves one of the nation's few remaining wilderness rivers. The area, which includes campsites, was established through federal-state co-operation.

Baxter State Park, the largest park in Maine, is located in the north central wilderness. It includes Mount Katahdin, the highest point in the state. The park is a sanctuary for wildlife, where moose, deer, bear, and beaver may be seen in their natural surroundings. It is named for Percival P. Baxter, governor of Maine from 1921 to 1925, who bought the land and gave it to the state.

Fort Knox State Park, near Bucksport, is on a site that was selected for fortification at the time of the dispute between Maine and New Brunswick over Maine's northeastern boundary. The dispute, sometimes called the Aroostook War, was settled in 1842. Construction of the fort was begun in 1846. It was used during the Civil War and World War I. It was named in honor of General Henry Knox, associate of George Washington and first United States secretary of war. After his retirement, General Knox lived in Maine.

Mount Blue State Park offers many different kinds of recreation—camping, mountain climbing, and swimming and fishing in Lake Webb.

The fire tower at the top of Mount Blue is a point of special interest.

Reid State Park, at Georgetown, features surf bathing, striped-bass fishing, and beautiful coastal scenery.

Sebago Lake State Park has beautiful sandy beaches on the shores of Sebago Lake. Swimming, fishing, and boating are the chief activities.

Fort George Memorial, in Castine, preserves the site of a fort built by the British in 1779. After the Revolutionary War, the fort passed into possession of the United States, but it was occupied again by the British during the War of 1812.

Fort McClary Memorial, at Kittery Point, is on the site of a fort authorized by the Massachusetts Bay Colony in 1715. It was later called Fort William in honor of Sir William Pepperell, a prominent citizen of Kittery. At the time of the Revolutionary War, the name of the fort was changed to Fort McClary, in memory of Major Andrew McClary, who was killed at Bunker Hill.

Fort O'Brien Memorial, at Machiasport, preserves a fort also known as Fort Machias. Near this fort the British ship *Margaretta* was captured in 1775 in one of the earliest naval battles of the Revolutionary War. Nearby in Machias is **Burnham Tavern,** where Jeremiah O'Brien and other patriots planned the capture of the *Margaretta*. The tavern is now a museum.

Fort William Henry Memorial, at Pemaquid Beach, is a replica of a part of Fort William Henry, built in 1692 and destroyed by the French in 1696. Earlier forts on the site include one built about 1630 for defense against pirates.

John Paul Jones State Memorial, at Kittery, is a memorial to the soldiers and sailors of Maine. It is near the site where the U.S.S. *Ranger* was built and launched in 1777. The *Ranger*'s first commander was John Paul Jones. On this ship he received the first salute to be given to the United States flag in international waters.

Other Places

The following are a few of the other interesting places, varying from an international park to lighthouses.

Campobello Island, in Passamaquoddy Bay, is a part of New Brunswick, Canada, but it is connected to Maine by a bridge at Lubec. On this island is the house that was the summer home of President Franklin D. Roosevelt. The area around the home is an international park shared by the United States and Canada.

The Desert of Maine, south of Freeport, is an unusual area of sand dunes. Sandstorms constantly raise and lower the area, creating deep gullies and high multi-colored dunes.

Screw Auger Falls, on the Bear River near Newry, are interesting for holes worn by swirling water in the solid rock of the riverbed. The holes vary in depth from about 0.3 to 6 meters (1 to 20 feet). They look as if they had been made with an auger—a tool for boring holes.

Wadsworth-Longfellow House, at Portland, home of the poet Henry Wadsworth Longfellow, is one of Maine's most famous places of interest. Part of the three-story brick house was built by Longfellow's grandfather, General Peleg Wadsworth, in 1785. The home contains possessions of the Wadsworth and the Longfellow families.

West Quoddy Lighthouse, on West Quoddy Head, provides splendid views from the easternmost point in the United States. Another famous lighthouse is the one at Portland, which was built in 1791. It is Maine's oldest lighthouse.

Annual Events

Winter carnivals are held during January, February, and March. Rangeley and Greenville are noted for their carnivals. National and international ski events are held at Sugarloaf Mountain near Kingfield. Yacht regattas, boat races, and water carnivals on coastal and inland waters fill the calendar from July to September. Agricultural fairs and festivals begin in July and run through October. Belfast holds a broiler festival during the summer, and Rockland has a lobster and seafood festival.

▶CITIES

Small cities are the rule in Maine. Only Portland has more than 60,000 people.

Augusta

Augusta, the capital, is on the Kennebec River about 70 kilometers (45 miles) from the Atlantic Ocean. In 1628 the Pilgrims of the Plymouth Colony had a prosperous fur-trading post on this site. The present city grew up around Fort Western, which was built in 1754 to protect settlers.

Augusta was incorporated as a town in 1797. It has been the capital since the seat of government was moved from Portland in 1832. The State House was designed by the famous architect Charles Bulfinch and was built of native granite. Another point of special interest is old Fort Western, which has been restored and opened as a museum. The main activities of the city are related to the work of the state government. Industries include the manufacture of paper products, textiles, and boots and shoes.

Portland, Maine's largest city, is also its chief seaport and a popular summer resort. It is located on a hook-shaped peninsula extending into Casco Bay.

Portland

Portland, Maine's largest city, was built on the site of Falmouth—a settlement that was started in the 1630's. It took the name of Portland in 1786. When Maine became a state in 1820, Portland was selected as the capital.

Portland is called the Forest City because of its thousands of shade trees. It is the chief seaport and the industrial and cultural center of the state. A few of its products are marine instruments and equipment, clothing and shoes, wood products, and processed foods.

Offshore in Casco Bay are the Calendar Islands, so called because there are about 365 of them—one for each day of the year.

Lewiston

Lewiston, the second largest city in Maine, is located on the Androscoggin River. Its twin town, Auburn, stands on the opposite bank of the river. Abundant waterpower from the river helped develop Lewiston's famous textile industry. Auburn is an important shoe center. Other products of the two cities are metal products, plastics, and bakery goods. Lewiston is the home of Bates College.

Bangor

Bangor is located at the head of navigation on the Penobscot River. It is the commercial center for eastern Maine and the gateway to northern and eastern parts of the state. Settlement of the present city began in 1769. It was known first as Kenduskeag Plantation and then as Sunbury. It acquired the name Bangor—from the old hymn tune known as "Bangor"—at the time of its incorporation as a town in 1791. During the middle 1800's, Bangor was a leading lumber market. A 9.4-meter (31-foot) statue of Paul Bunyan, legendary hero of the lumber camps, stands on Main Street.

Bangor produces pulp and paper, furniture and other products made of wood, machinery, shoes, and clothing. Orono, the original home of the University of Maine, is nearby.

COUNTIES

▶GOVERNMENT

Maine entered the Union in 1820. The state constitution adopted at that time has been in force ever since.

The executive branch of the state government is headed by the governor. In 1975 the voters approved a constitutional amendment abolishing the seven-member executive council. The council, which was elected by the legislature to advise the governor, had been in existence since 1820.

The legislative branch is made up of the Senate and the House of Representatives. The legislature held regular sessions in odd-numbered years until a constitutional amendment of 1975 authorized yearly sessions.

The Supreme Judicial Court is the highest court in the state. Other courts are the Superior Court and the regional courts.

▶FAMOUS PEOPLE

Maine has been called the Poets' Corner because it has produced a number of distinguished poets. The following are a few of the famous persons—poets and others—whose names are associated with Maine.

Sir Ferdinando Gorges (1566?–1647), an Englishman, is known as the founder of Maine because of his interest in promoting settlement in the early days. He helped to provide colonists and money for the Popham colony in 1607 and for many other settlements after that time. By 1639 the king of England had given him a charter to all the land between the Piscataqua and the Kennebec rivers. Gorges was never able to go to Maine, but he sent his son and his nephew to represent him.

Sir William Pepperell (1696–1759), wealthy colonial merchant and shipbuilder, was born at Kittery Point. In 1745 he took part in capturing the French fortress on Cape Breton Island, Nova Scotia, because the French were interfering with Maine's fishing and shipping. Later he was invited to England, where he was made a baronet. He was the first native of America to receive this honor.

Dorothea Lynde Dix (1802–87) was an educator, social worker, and author of children's books. She was born in Hampden. A biography of Dorothea Dix is included in Volume D.

Henry Wadsworth Longfellow (1807–82), born in Portland, was the first American poet to win wide recognition in other countries. A biography of Longfellow is included in Volume L.

Hannibal Hamlin (1809–91), vice president of the United States under Abraham Lincoln, was born in Paris Hill, a part of present-day Paris. After serving in the state legislature, he was elected to Congress in 1842. There he served for many years, chiefly as a senator. For a brief time in 1857, Hamlin was governor of Maine.

James Gillespie Blaine (1830–93), born in Pennsylvania, became a resident of Maine after his marriage to Harriet Stanwood of Augusta. In 1881 he became secretary of state in the cabinet of President Garfield. Earlier he had represented Maine in the United States House of Representatives (1873–76) and in the Senate (1876–81). The governor's mansion in Augusta was the home of the Blaine family.

Thomas Brackett Reed (1859–1902), from Portland, was a political leader of his state before being elected to the United States House of Representatives. There he served as Speaker for three terms. A fiery but respected debater, he was nicknamed Czar Reed.

Edna St. Vincent Millay (1892–1950), born in Rockland, became known when her poem ''Renascence'' was published in 1912. In 1923 she won the Pulitzer prize for *The Harp Weaver and Other Poems.*

Two other famous poets born in Maine are Edward Arlington Robinson (Head Tide) and Robert P. Tristram Coffin (Brunswick). Robinson won three Pulitzer prizes for poetry —in 1921, 1925, and 1927. Coffin, who was also a writer of prose, won the Pulitzer prize for poetry in 1935. Kenneth Lewis Roberts (Kennebunk) received a special Pulitzer award for his historical novels in 1957.

Other noted persons are sculptor Benjamin Paul Akers (Westbrook); singer Lillian Nordica (born Lillian Norton, Farmington); publisher Cyrus H. K. Curtis (Portland); essayist and novelist Mary Ellen Chase (Blue Hill); Margaret Chase Smith (Skowhegan), who served as U.S. senator from Maine for four terms; and Edmund S. Muskie (Rumford), U.S. senator and secretary of state.

The writer and editor E. B. White was born in New York state but moved to Maine in 1937. His biography appears in Volume W.

The painter Winslow Homer brought fame to Prouts Neck, a rocky promontory south of

Portland, where he lived and worked from 1884 until his death in 1910. A biography of Winslow Homer appears in Volume H.

▶HISTORY

It is believed that Indian peoples inhabited what is now Maine as long as 11,000 years ago. Later peoples are known as the Red Paint people because of the ocher found in their graves. Ocher is an earthy mineral—usually red or yellow—that can be used as coloring matter in paint. Graves containing ocher have been found along the coast.

At Damariscotta and many other places, there are great shell heaps. Scientists believe that these heaps are from 1,000 to 5,000 years old. It is thought that they were made by Indians who came to the coast in summer to feast on shellfish. Arrowheads and other implements found in the heaps are different from implements found in the Red Paint graves.

At the time of the European explorations in the 1500's and 1600's, the Indian tribes in Maine were of the Abnaki (or Wabanaki) Confederacy. They hunted and fished, and their birchbark canoes were wonders of boat construction. The confederacy broke up in the late 1800's, but members of two of the tribes, the Penobscot and the Passamaquoddy, still live in Maine.

Exploration and Settlement

No one knows who the first Europeans in Maine were. The Vikings may have been there around the year 1000. The age of exploration brought sailors from many nations. Voyages of John and Sebastian Cabot in the late 1490's gave the English their claim to the land. Verrazano's voyage in 1524 gave the French their claim. Reports from explorers spurred others to come to Maine for trading, fishing, and further exploration. Samuel de Champlain explored the coast westward from the St. Croix River and named Mount Desert Island in 1604. French missionaries established a mission on the Penobscot River in 1611 and another on Mount Desert Island in 1613. The Mount Desert mission was destroyed in the same year by the English under Captain Samuel Argall of Virginia.

George Weymouth of England visited Monhegan Island and explored the coast in 1605. He captured five Indians and took them back to England. Three of them he gave to Sir Ferdinando Gorges. They aroused Gorges' interest so much that he spent the rest of his life promoting the settlement of Maine. Captain John Smith explored the coast in 1614 and named Christmas Cove. Pemaquid had a fishing and trading post in the early 1600's. The colony established at present-day Popham Beach in 1607 did not succeed, but lasting settlements soon were made. A group of settlers representing Sir Ferdinando

---

IMPORTANT DATES

1000	Leif Ericson and other Vikings may have sailed along the coast of Maine.
1497	Voyages of John and Sebastian Cabot, 1497–99, gave England its claim to Maine.
1524	Giovanni da Verrazano, exploring for France, established the French claim.
1604	Samuel de Champlain explored the coast and named Mount Desert Island.
1605	George Weymouth explored the coast and kidnapped five Indians, whom he took to England.
1607	The Popham Colony, first English colony in New England, established at the mouth of the Sagadahoc (Kennebec) River; colony abandoned in 1608.
1614	Captain John Smith explored and mapped the coast.
1622	Sir Ferdinando Gorges and John Mason received lands between the Merrimack and the Kennebec rivers.
1629	Gorges and Mason divided their lands; Gorges received the area between the Piscataqua and the Kennebec.
1639	King Charles I granted a charter to Gorges, naming Gorges' lands the Province of Maine.
1652	Massachusetts took control of Maine.
1691	Maine officially became a part of Massachusetts.
1763	France gave up all claims in Maine at the end of the French and Indian War.
1775	First naval battle of the Revolutionary War fought at Machias; Falmouth (Portland) burned by the British.
1785	First newspaper in Maine, the *Gazette*, published at Falmouth.
1794	Bowdoin College, the first college in Maine, established at Brunswick.
1820	March 15, Maine admitted to the Union as the 23rd state.
1832	State capital moved from Portland to Augusta.
1836	First railroad in Maine built between Bangor and Old Town.
1842	Webster-Ashburton Treaty settled northeastern boundary dispute between Maine and New Brunswick.
1865	University of Maine established at Orono as an agricultural college.
1919	Congress created Lafayette National Park (renamed Acadia National Park in 1929).
1920	Maine celebrated its 100th year of statehood.
1933	Lands purchased and donated to the state by Percival P. Baxter named Baxter State Park.
1962	Radome at Andover used in the first transatlantic television broadcast.
1968	U.S. Senator Edmund S. Muskie was Maine's first vice-presidential candidate since 1896; he served later (1980–81) as U.S. secretary of state.
1975	James B. Longley took office as Maine's first independent governor in the 20th century.
1980	The Indian Land Claims dispute was settled, benefiting the Passamaquoddy and Penobscot tribes.

Gorges built cabins near present-day Biddeford in 1616.

In 1622, Gorges and John Mason, another Englishman, were granted all the land between the Merrimack and the Kennebec rivers. The Merrimack is in the northeastern part of present-day Massachusetts. In 1629, Gorges and Mason divided their claim. Gorges took the part between the Piscataqua and the Kennebec. The Piscataqua forms a small part of the present-day boundary between New Hampshire and Maine. In 1639, King Charles I issued a charter confirming Gorges' grant. In this charter the King stated very exactly that the land was to be called the County or Province of Maine. During the 1620's permanent settlements were made at Monhegan, Saco, and York. At present-day York—known at first as Agamenticus—Gorges planned a magnificent city to be called Gorgeana. The towns had local government, but there was no effective central government. After Gorges died in 1647, the Massachusetts Bay Colony claimed Maine. Massachusetts took control in 1652, but many overlapping grants of land led to confusion about actual ownership. The claims of the Gorges heirs were settled by payment in 1677. In 1691 the Province of Maine became officially a part of Massachusetts.

For many years, troubles with the Indians and the French kept Maine from growing. A series of wars began in the late 1600's and lasted, for Maine, until peace was made in 1760. The French did not finally give up all their claims until 1763, when the Treaty of Paris was signed, ending the French and Indian War.

The first naval skirmish of the Revolutionary War took place at Machias in 1775. Falmouth (now Portland) was bombarded and burned by the British.

Statehood and Later Times

The Revolutionary War was barely over before the people of Maine began to express their dissatisfaction with control by Massachusetts. They charged that Massachusetts took little interest in Maine, that the capital (Boston) was too far away, and that Maine was unfairly taxed.

Several votes were taken before it was clear that Maine wanted to be a separate state. Then Maine's entry into the Union was delayed because of the struggle in Congress to keep a balance between the free states and the slaveholding states. Finally, under the Missouri Compromise, Maine entered as a free state in 1820, and Missouri as a slave state in 1821.

The lack of a well-defined boundary on the northeast caused both Maine and New Brunswick to claim the forest wealth of northeastern Maine. Tempers flared on both sides, and preparations were made for war—the famous "Bloodless Aroostook War." But calm heads prevailed, and the boundary was settled without bloodshed by the Webster-Ashburton Treaty of 1842.

Between 1820 and the Civil War, Maine developed rapidly. Plenty of available land, the rise of industry, improved methods of farming, the development of transportation —all helped the state to grow. A sharp decline followed the Civil War. The principal reasons were war problems, increasing competition from industries outside the state, and loss of population.

The early 1900's brought another upswing in Maine's economy. Hydroelectric power plants were built. The pulp and paper industry developed, and there was an improved market for farm products. The loss of textile industries in the 1920's and the Depression of the 1930's dealt Maine a severe blow. But since 1945, growth has continued. Specialized farming has led to production of foods needed by the great population of the northeastern United States. State and local leaders have worked together to encourage a flow of new industries into the state. The tourist industry has increased greatly.

The Future

Maine's economic growth in the early 1980's was among the highest of the 50 states. Important gains have been won in the battle for conservation of Maine's forest and water resources. And a new pioneering spirit ensures that Maine will continue to draw on its variety of people and resources to meet the needs of changing times.

MYRON STARBIRD
University of Maine at Farmington

Reviewed by ALBERT R. MITCHELL
University of Maine at Farmington

MALAGASY REPUBLIC. See MADAGASCAR.

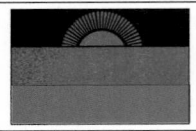

MALAWI

Malawi is a nation in southeast Africa, slightly larger in area than the state of Pennsylvania. It is bordered by the nations of Tanzania, Mozambique, and Zambia. Formerly called Nyasaland, Malawi was a British protectorate before gaining its independence in 1964. It was named Malawi, which means "broad water," after the huge lake along its eastern border.

▶ THE PEOPLE

Most of Malawi's people are Africans of Bantu origin. The chief groups are the Chewa, Lomwe, Nyanja, Yao, Ngoni, and Tumbuka. There are also a few Europeans and Asians and people of mixed origin. Most of the Europeans live in the larger towns and work for the government, the Christian missions, industries, and the tea plantations. The Asians also are town dwellers, who work in small shops. Some of the Asians were expelled from the country in 1976.

Most of Malawi's people are farmers. Their chief food crops are maize and cassava. Fish is also an important food. Because there are not many jobs where people can earn money, many people journey to nearby countries to work.

Fishermen prepare for a day's work on Lake Malawi.

They stay away for two or three years and then return to farm their land again.

Malawi needs many trained people to help build the country. Education is therefore very important. Nearly all children now go to school. Most elementary schools are run by the Christian missions. The government also runs some schools and helps run others. New schools are being built, often by the parents and children themselves. Adults, as well as children, are learning to read and write. English and Chichewa are the official languages of the country. Many of Malawi's people are Presbyterians. Others are Muslims or followers of tribal religions.

▶ THE LAND

About one fifth of Malawi's area is made up of lakes. The largest is Lake Malawi, one of the largest lakes in Africa. Lake Malawi lies within Africa's Great Rift Valley, which runs through the country from north to south. On either side of the lake are towering plateaus that rise to their greatest height in the Nyika Plateau. To the south of Lake Malawi is the Shire River valley. The Shire Highlands rise to the east of the river. The highest point in the country—3,000 meters (9,843 feet)—is in the Mlanje Mountains in the southeast. Low, marshy areas surround the lakes along the southeastern border.

Because Malawi is mountainous, it does not have an extremely warm climate. Only the Shire River valley is really hot. Generally, temperatures average from 18 to 30°C (65 to 85°F). Rainfall is heaviest in the mountains, where as much as 2,500 millimeters (100 inches) of rain may fall in a year.

▶ THE ECONOMY

Malawi's farms produce enough food for the people's own use, with some for export. Tobacco, sugarcane, and tea are the leading exports. Tea is grown on fertile, heavy red soil in the Shire Highlands and the Mlanje Mountains. Tobacco and coffee are grown in the northern highlands. Cotton is grown in the lowlands, much of it for export. Rice, peanuts, other food crops, and the oil-producing tung tree are also grown there. Since the future of the country depends on farming, the government has founded farm institutes to help improve crops. The government is also trying to expand the fishing industry, which is concentrated mainly in Lake Malawi.

Most of Malawi's industry involves the processing of agricultural products for export. Manufactures include cement, bricks, textiles, rope, and footwear. Malawi's extensive wildlife, its scenic beauty, and pleasant climate have made tourism an increasingly important part of the economy.

Malawi has few minerals in amounts large enough to be useful. Limestone, used as building stone, is the most important mineral. Since Malawi has no oil or coal, hydroelectric power projects are being developed.

▶CITIES

Blantyre, situated in the Shire Highlands of the south, is Malawi's largest city and its commercial and manufacturing center. Blantyre's twin city, Limbe, has factories and is the site of an auction where tobacco is bought and sold. Zomba, also located in the south, is the former capital of the country. The seat of government was transferred to Lilongwe, in the central region, in 1975. Lilongwe is a growing city, now the second largest in the nation.

▶HISTORY AND GOVERNMENT

Malawi was settled by Bantu peoples. The Portuguese were the first Europeans to enter the area, in the 17th century. David Livingstone, a Scottish medical missionary, made

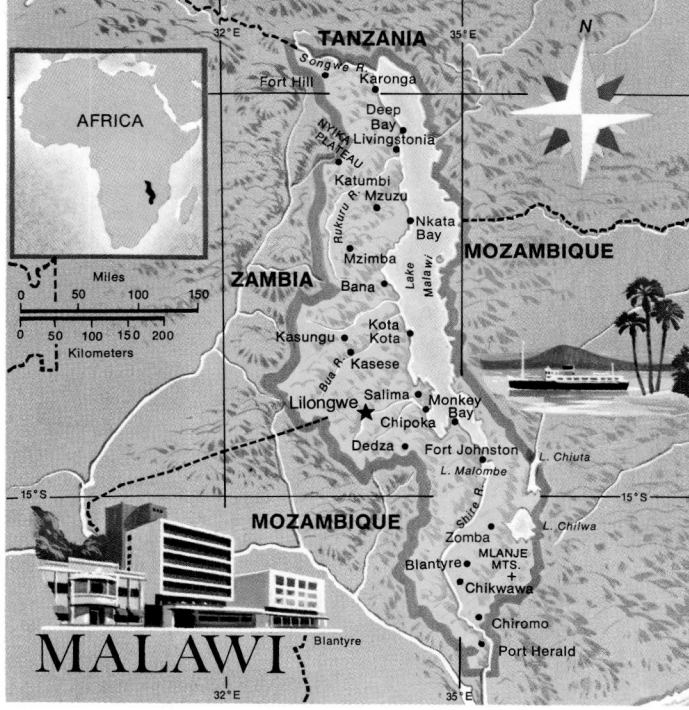

MALAWI

FACTS AND FIGURES

REPUBLIC OF MALAWI is the official name of the country.

THE PEOPLE are known as Malawians.

LOCATION: Southeastern Africa.

AREA: 45,747 sq mi (118,484 km²).

POPULATION: 7,000,000 (estimate).

CAPITAL: Lilongwe.

LARGEST CITY: Blantyre.

MAJOR LANGUAGES: English, Chichewa (both official).

MAJOR RELIGIONS: Christian (Protestant, Roman Catholic), Muslim, traditional African religions.

GOVERNMENT: Republic. **Head of state and government—** president. **Legislature**—National Assembly.

CHIEF PRODUCTS: Agricultural—tobacco, sugarcane, tea, cotton, coffee, maize (corn), potatoes, sorghum, cassava. **Manufactured**—processed agricultural products, cement, bricks, textiles, rope, footwear. **Mineral**—limestone.

MONETARY UNIT: Kwacha (1 kwacha = 100 tabala).

NATIONAL ANTHEM: "O God, Bless our Land of Malawi."

---

the first exploration of the region, discovering Lake Malawi, which he called Lake Nyasa, in 1859. Livingstone also helped to eradicate the widespread slave trade in the area. The city of Blantyre is named after his birthplace in Scotland. (For more information on Livingstone, see the article STANLEY, HENRY MORTON, AND DAVID LIVINGSTONE in Volume S.)

Nyasaland, as the region was then called, became a British protectorate in 1891. It was joined with the British dependencies of Northern and Southern Rhodesia (now the nations of Zambia and Zimbabwe) in the Federation of Rhodesia and Nyasaland in 1953. Nyasaland became self-governing in 1963 and won complete independence as Malawi in 1964.

Malawi is a republic under a president who serves both as head of state and government. The legislature, called the National Assembly, is elected for a 5-year term. All candidates must be members of the Malawi Congress Party. Hastings Kamuzu Banda, who led Malawi's independence movement, officially became president for life in 1971. The number of elected members in the National Assembly was raised from 87 to 101 in 1983. The president may also appoint additional members to the legislature.

HUGH C. BROOKS
Director, Center for African Studies
St. John's University (New York)

MALAYSIA

Malaysia is a nation of Southeast Asia. It is the only country of the region that is part of both the mainland of Asia and of the islands that form a part of Southeast Asia. A federation of states, Malaysia is divided into two sections, separated by about 400 miles (645 kilometers) of the South China Sea. One section occupies part of the Malay Peninsula. The other is located on the large island of Borneo.

The nation of Malaysia was created in two steps. The British-ruled states of Malaya won independence in 1957. With the addition of Sarawak, Sabah, and Singapore in 1963, Malaysia itself came into being. Singapore later withdrew from Malaysia to form its own nation.

FACTS AND FIGURES

MALAYSIA is the official name of the country. It is made up of Peninsular Malaysia and the states of Sabah and Sarawak (East Malaysia).

THE PEOPLE are known as Malaysians.

LOCATION: Southeast Asia.

AREA: 127,317 sq mi (329,749 km²).

POPULATION: 15,000,000 (estimate).

CAPITAL AND LARGEST CITY: Kuala Lumpur.

MAJOR LANGUAGES: Bahasa Malaysia (official), English, Chinese, Tamil, others.

MAJOR RELIGIONS: Muslim (official), Buddhist, Hindu, Christian.

GOVERNMENT: Constitutional monarchy. **Head of state—** *yang di-pertuan agong* (supreme head of state). **Head of government—**prime minister. **Legislature**—Senate and House of Representatives.

CHIEF PRODUCTS: Agricultural—rubber, oil palm, rice, coconuts, copra (dried coconut meat), sago, cassava, maize (corn), spices, hemp, tobacco, fruits, vegetables, livestock. **Manufactured**—palm oil, coconut oil, processed rubber, smelted tin, refined petroleum and petroleum products, forestry products, processed food, steel, tobacco products, textiles, television sets, motor vehicles, handicrafts. **Mineral**—tin, petroleum, natural gas, iron ore, bauxite (aluminum ore), gold.

MONETARY UNIT: Ringgit (1 ringgit = 100 sen).

NATIONAL ANTHEM: *Negaru-Ku* ("My Country").

▶THE PEOPLE

Malaysia's people are a fascinating mixture of races and cultures. The native Malays are the largest group, followed by the Chinese. There are also many people from India, Pakistan, Sri Lanka, and Bangladesh, as well as several aboriginal tribal groups. In recent years, refugees from Vietnam and Kampuchea (Cambodia) have settled in Malaysia.

Most government jobs are held by Malays. The Chinese dominate the commercial field. Many of the people from South Asia are professionals. The nation's ethnic diversity has sometimes created problems. The government has to be careful that each group feels it is a full partner in the nation's development.

Languages. Malay, officially called Bahasa Malaysia, is the national language of Malaysia. It is very similar to the national language of neighboring Indonesia. The two countries are working together to create a single language for use in both nations. English is used in business and government. Chinese and Tamil (a language of southern India and Sri Lanka) are also widely spoken.

Education. Children receive nine years of free, public education—six years of primary school and three years of lower secondary school. After nine years of basic education, Malaysian students who pass a series of examinations may go to upper secondary school for two years. Institutions of higher learning include teacher-training colleges, technical colleges, and several universities. The largest university is the University of Malaya, in Kuala Lumpur.

Religion. Islam (the religion of the Muslims) is the official religion of Malaysia. But the constitution gives freedom of worship to all, and various religions are practiced. Many ethnic Chinese are Buddhists. Most Indians are Hindus. Some of the tribal peoples of Sabah and Sarawak are Christians, while others follow traditional religions of their ancestors. The graceful minarets (towers) of a

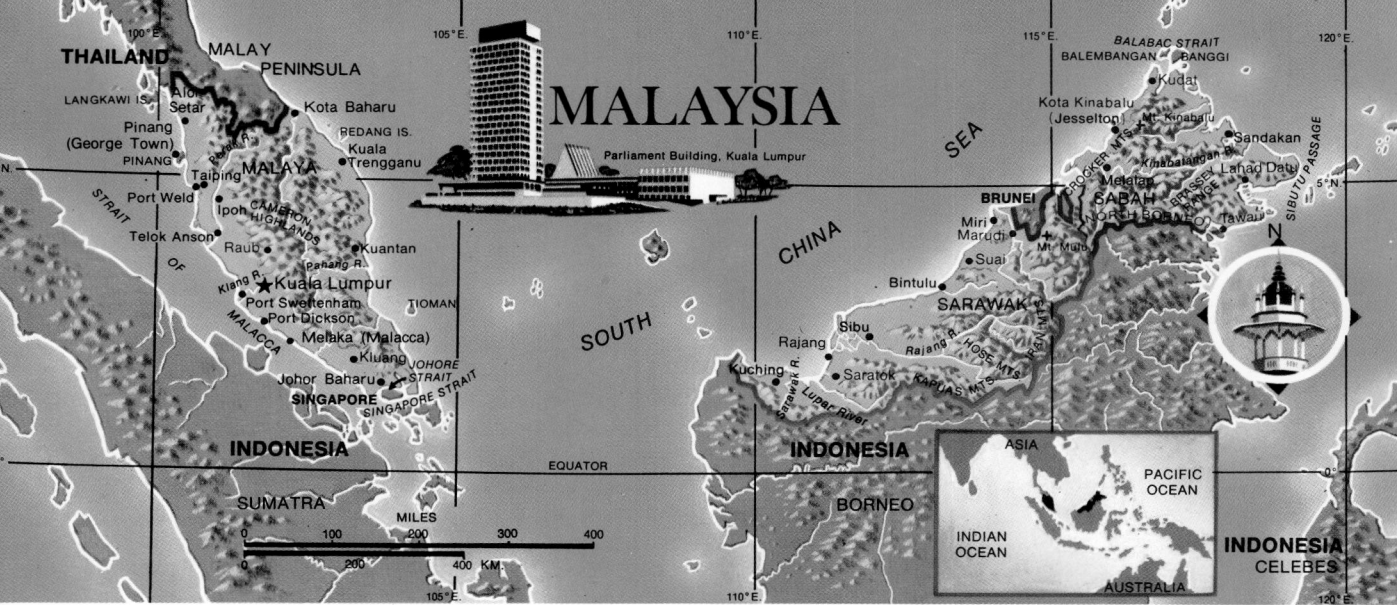

Muslim mosque often rise next to a Chinese-style Buddhist temple. Members of the various religious groups hold special festivals throughout the year.

Way of Life. In the Malay villages, wooden houses with thatch-palm roofs are often raised above the ground on pilings. In towns and cities, many of these traditional houses have been replaced by modern architecture. The Sea Dayaks (Ibans) and Land Dayaks of Sarawak often live in villages made up of longhouses, which contain multiple families.

Curry and spices flavor Malay dishes of rice, fish, vegetables, and meat. Alcoholic beverages are not drunk by Malays because their religion, Islam, forbids it. Instead, mineral water, tea, and coffee are consumed. Both Chinese and Indian people cook their own national dishes. Restaurants offer European, Chinese, Indian, and Malay foods.

The traditional national costume of Malay women is a sarong tied around the waist, a *baju*, which is a loose blouse, and a *selendang*, a scarf draped over one shoulder. Malay men wear loose shirts and trousers. A knee-length sarong skirt, tied at the waist, is often worn as informal attire. On their heads they wear a *songkok*—a black velvet cap with no brim. Indian women wear saris (long, loose robes). Chinese women wear the pajamalike *sam-foo* or the straight dress with side slits called *cheongsam*. Most Indian, Chinese, and Malay men wear Western-style clothes in towns and cities.

The country's most important holidays are the Hari Raya Puasa (an Islamic religious holiday), Deepavali (a Hindu religious holiday), Christmas, the Chinese New Year, and Freedom Day (August 31). On weekends and holidays, Malaysian families often picnic, fish or hunt, attend celebrations, or visit relatives. Adults and children enjoy riddles and the recitation of proverbs and stories, both national and foreign. Folktales are passed on from generation to generation.

Malaysians enjoy various kinds of entertainment. They like Malay operas, shadow plays, and the traditional Malay drama called the Menora. The shadow play is performed by puppets behind a screen. The audience watches the puppets' shadows, which appear on the screen. The Menora plays are presented on platforms or in huts lighted by lanterns, colored lights, or torches. Indian plays and dances and the telling of Hindu and Buddhist legends are also popular throughout the country. Audiences enjoy musical plays in which a wide variety of Chinese instruments are used. Chinese puppet shows and classical dramas are also performed. Traditional dancing, called *joget*, movies, and Western-style theater are other popular forms of entertainment. People watch and participate in sports such as soccer, badminton, rugby, cricket, swimming, field hockey, and tennis.

▶ **THE LAND**

Malaysia is divided into two distinct regions: Peninsular Malaysia and East Malaysia. Peninsular Malaysia is located in the south

An oil-drilling platform in the South China Sea off the coast of Malaysia.

ern part of the Malay Peninsula. East Malaysia is composed of the states of Sabah and Sarawak, which are located in the northern part of the island of Borneo.

A mountain chain rising at some points to over 7,000 feet (2,100 meters) runs down the middle of the Malay Peninsula. Between the hills and the sea are plains of low elevation. The plains, which extend to both the eastern and western seacoasts, have many large freshwater and saltwater swamps. The eastern coast has beaches but only two good harbors, Kota Baharu and Kuantan. The western coast, although covered by mangrove swamps, has good harbors at Pinang (George Town), Port Swettenham, Telok Anson, and Port Weld. Most of the towns, agricultural centers, and mining centers are located on the western coast. Except for the Pahang River valley, the land east of the mountains is underdeveloped and covered by dense forests.

Two high mountain peaks, the Gunong Tahan and the Gunong Korbu, are located in this region.

About three quarters of the eastern, or Borneo, region of Malaysia is sparsely populated jungle area. In Sabah, the low hills along the coast run into a central mountain range about 4,000 to 6,000 feet (1,200 to 1,800 meters) high. They reach a peak in Mount Kinabalu, the nation's highest mountain. The coastline of both Sabah and Sarawak consists of alluvial and swampy land. Farther inland in Sarawak, the country is rolling and intersected by mountain ranges. Mount Mulu, the highest peak in Sarawak, rises in a mountainous region in the interior. To the south, the Kapuas Mountains and Iran Mountains separate Malaysian Borneo from Indonesian Borneo.

Major Lakes and Rivers. The Pahang River, the longest on the Malay Peninsula, rises in the northeast. It flows south and east before emptying into the South China Sea. In the west, the Perak River rises on the border with Thailand and flows south to the Strait of Malacca. Both these rivers are flanked by cultivated land. There are many rivers in Sabah, the longest being the Kinabatangan, which waters Sabah's largest plain. In Sarawak, the Rajang and the Sarawak rivers have the longest navigable stretches.

Natural Resources. Malaysia abounds in palm, teak, camphor, sandalwood, and ebony trees. Elephants, rhinoceroses, crocodiles, lizards, wild pigs, and tigers roam through the country's forests, hills, and swamplands. Butterflies, other insects, and birds are plentiful.

The Malay Peninsula has a vast supply of rubber and palm oil and a large amount of timber. Tin, iron ore, bauxite, and gold deposits are also found on the peninsula. Considerable bauxite deposits are located in Sarawak. There are important petroleum and natural gas reserves in the South China Sea off the coast of Malaysia.

▶**THE ECONOMY**

Malaysia leads the world in the production of tin, palm oil, and natural rubber. The nation is rich in resources, and its economy is developing rapidly.

Agriculture. About 40 percent of the people in Malaysia are farmers. Many live on small farms, where they produce food for their own families and a small amount for sale. Rice, coconuts, fruit, and vegetables are grown on these farms. Rice, cassava, maize, and pepper are the main crops grown for domestic use in Sarawak. Rice is the country's second most important crop, after palm oil. But Malaysia must still import rice to feed its many people.

Rubber, palm oil, coconuts, and rice are the chief commercial crops of the Malay Peninsula. The chief cash crops of Sabah are rubber, copra, hemp, and tobacco. Poultry and other animals are raised there, and timber is exported in large quantities. Rubber, sago, coconuts, and spices are among Sarawak's exports.

Industries. Fishing, mining, commerce, finance, and manufacturing are Malaysia's chief industries. Most manufacturing is based on Malaysia's abundant resources. Oil is extracted from coconuts and oil-palm kernels, natural rubber is processed and packed for shipment, and tin is concentrated and smelted. Rice is milled, and fish, which are plentiful in local waters, are salted and cured. There are timber mills and oil refineries in Sarawak. One of the largest refineries is located at Port Dickson, on the west coast of the Malay Peninsula. A huge natural gas plant is planned at Bintulu, in Sarawak. Petroleum is used by many other industries in making such products as ammonia, solvents, plastics, automobile parts, and various consumer goods.

The handicraft industry is particularly important in Sarawak. Malaysian handicrafts include basketware, jewelry, silverware, and batik cloth. (Batik cloth designs are produced by coating the cloth with wax, cutting designs out of the wax, and dyeing the unwaxed areas.)

Transportation. The Singapore-Bangkok railroad runs from Singapore through the Malay Peninsula to Thailand. It has branches going to Port Weld, Telok Anson, Port Swettenham, and Port Dickson on the western coast and Kota Baharu on the eastern coast. There is also a very good all-weather road system on the peninsula. In Sabah a railroad joins Kota Kinabalu with the inland town of Melalap. Good highways serve the coastal area of the Borneo region of Malaysia. The country has several international airports.

A crowd at a bus stop in downtown Kuala Lumpur shows Malaysia's ethnic diversity.

▶ CITIES

For every Malaysian living in a city, there are three who live in the country, mostly in small villages. Malaysian cities are generally small in size and few in number. Kuala Lumpur, the national capital, is the financial, educational, medical, and transportation center of western Malaysia. Examples of beautiful Moorish architecture stand next to modern skyscrapers. The city is located in the center of a productive tin-mining and rubber-growing district on the Klang River. Port Swettenham is its seaport. Adjoining is Petaling Jaya, a flourishing model industrial center.

Kota Kinabalu, the capital and chief port of Sabah, is a trade and stock-raising center. Rubber is exported, and there are fisheries and rice mills.

Kuching, the capital of Sarawak, is a port on the Sarawak River. It is a center of local trade and industry.

▶ GOVERNMENT

Malaysia consists of 13 parts. There are the nine original Malay states—Johore, Kedah, Kelantan, Negri Sembilan, Pahang, Perak, Perlis, Selangor, and Trengganu. Together with Malacca (now Melaka) and Penang (now Pinang), they made up the former Federation of Malaya. The remaining two parts are Sabah and Sarawak, on the island of Borneo.

The head of state is the *yang di-pertuan agong* (supreme head of state), elected for a 5-year term by the rulers of the nine original Malay states, who choose one from their group. The legislature is made up of two houses, the Senate and the House of Representatives.

Actual executive power is exercised by the prime minister, who is appointed by the supreme head of state. The prime minister, however, must be a member of the House of Representatives and must have the support of that body to remain in power. The prime minister is assisted by a cabinet whose members are appointed by the supreme head of state on the advice of the prime minister.

▶ HISTORY

The modern history of Malaysia began around 1400, when a Malay ruler founded a settlement at Malacca. The city grew quickly. Arab missionaries and traders brought the religion of Islam to Malacca, and from there it spread to the rest of the Malay Peninsula and to the Indonesian islands. As the center of Islam as well as the center of trade, Malacca soon became the most powerful area in Southeast Asia.

The military power of Malacca, however, was no match for the Europeans. In 1511 the Portuguese captured Malacca. In 1641 the Dutch took the city from the Portuguese. The British got a foothold on the Malay Peninsula in 1786 by taking control of the island of Penang. In 1824 the Dutch ceded Malacca to Britain.

Meanwhile, Sir Thomas Stamford Raffles of the British East India Company founded a British settlement at Singapore in 1819. And in 1841 an Englishman named Sir James Brooke was installed as rajah of part of Sarawak. Both Sarawak and British North

Some people in Sarawak travel to market on a river ferry.

Kuala Lumpur, once a muddy tin-mining camp, is now a modern capital with many high-rise buildings.

Borneo (formerly controlled by the British North Borneo Company) came under the protection of Britain in 1888.

At this time, the Malay Peninsula was politically divided into nine states. Eventually all these states came under British protection. And by World War II the British were in control of all of Malaya. The Japanese occupation during World War II brought much hardship to the Malayan people. In 1945 the British re-occupied the peninsula, and in 1948 Britain established the nine Malay states as the Federation of Malaya.

Between 1948 and 1960, a state of emergency was declared by the Malayan Government as a result of a Communist revolt. In 1957 the Federation of Malaya became independent. At that time Britain gave up the settlements of Penang and Malacca, which became states in the Federation of Malaya.

In 1959 Singapore, a British crown colony, gained self-government within the Commonwealth of Nations. In 1961 the prime minister of Malaya, Tunku Abdul Rahman, conceived the idea of forming a Malaysian federation by joining the Malayan states with Singapore and the territories of British Borneo—Brunei, Sabah, and Sarawak.

Malaysia officially came into existence on September 16, 1963. But Brunei chose not to join, and Singapore withdrew from the federation in 1965 to become an independent country. Serious racial disturbances broke out between Chinese and Malays after the 1969 parliamentary elections. Parliament was suspended until 1971. In the late 1970's, Malaysia's racial stability was again threatened by the arrival of thousands of refugees from Indochina. In recent years the government has been working to bring the mineral-rich eastern states and the more industrialized Malay Peninsula closer together.

THOMAS FRANK BARTON
Indiana University

MALDIVES

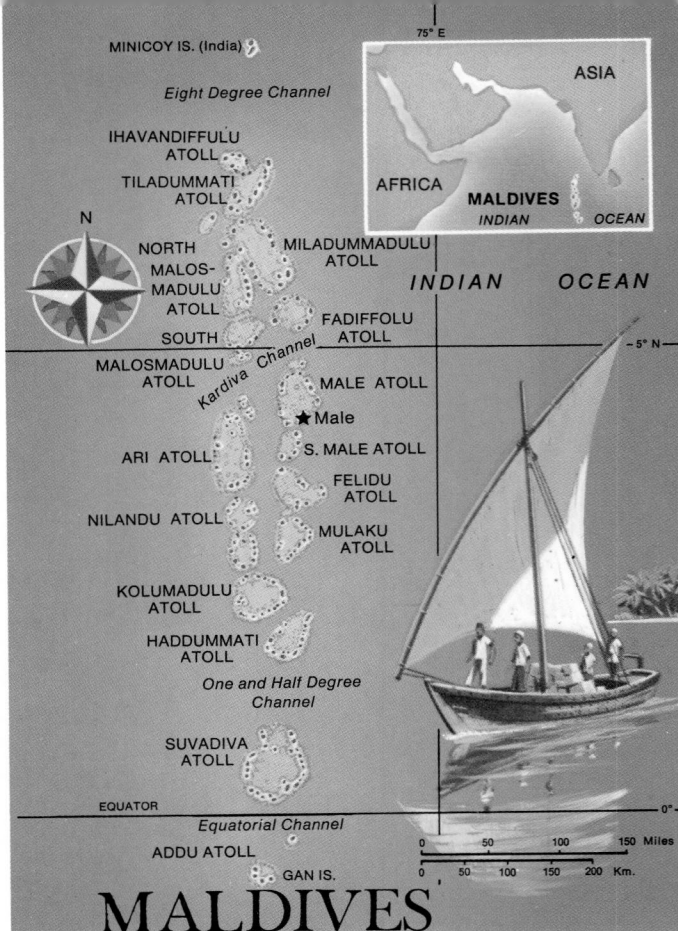

MALDIVES

Maldives is a small island nation in the Indian Ocean, lying southwest of India and the nation of Sri Lanka. The Maldives islands form an archipelago, or chain of islands, many of which are uninhabited.

The People. The Maldivians are believed to be descendants of people from India, Sri Lanka, and from Arab lands. Their language, Divehi, is related to the Sinhalese of Sri Lanka. English and Arabic also are spoken. Most of the people are Muslims.

The Land and Climate. The Maldives chain is made up of more than 1,000 small coral islands, or atolls. In fact, the word atoll, meaning a coral reef surrounding a lagoon, comes from the Maldivian language. Only about 200 of the atolls are inhabited. The capital and only large town is Male located on Male atoll. The climate of the islands is generally hot and humid with considerable rainfall.

The Economy. Maldives is considered one of the most underdeveloped nations of the world. Its economy is based largely on fishing and coconut products, including copra (dried coconut meat), coir (coconut fiber, used to make rope), and coconut palm mats. Seashells, tortoise shell, and lace are other important products. The chief export is dried fish, called Maldivian fish. The scenic beauty of the islands has led to the development of a growing tourist industry.

History and Government. According to Maldivian legend, the islands' first ruler was a Sinhalese prince whose ship was becalmed in Maldivian waters. Arab traders introduced the Muslim religion to the islands in the 12th century. Maldives later fell under Portuguese and Dutch control, then became a British dependency in 1887. The islands won independence in 1965.

The government is led by a president, who is elected for a 5-year term and serves as both head of state and government. The legislature is called the Majlis, or Citizens' Assembly. Most of its members are elected by the people. Eight are appointed by the president, who also appoints the cabinet of ministers. Maldives joined the Commonwealth of Nations in 1982.

Reviewed by ALEXANDER MELAMID
New York University

FACTS AND FIGURES

REPUBLIC OF MALDIVES (Divehi Jumhurija) is the official name of the country.

THE PEOPLE are known as Maldivians.

LOCATION: Indian Ocean, South Asia.

AREA: 115 sq mi (298 km²).

POPULATION: 170,000 (estimate).

CAPITAL AND LARGEST TOWN: Male.

MAJOR RELIGION: Muslim.

MAJOR LANGUAGE: Divehi.

GOVERNMENT: Republic. **Head of state and government**—president. **Legislature**—Majlis.

CHIEF PRODUCTS: Agricultural—coconuts, millet, fruits, vegetables. **Manufactured**—dried fish, coconut products (copra, coir, coconut palm mats), lace.

MONETARY UNIT: Rufiyaa, or Maldivian rupee (1 rufiyaa = 100 laris).

NATIONAL ANTHEM: Opening line (in English): "Together in national unity we salute you".

MALI

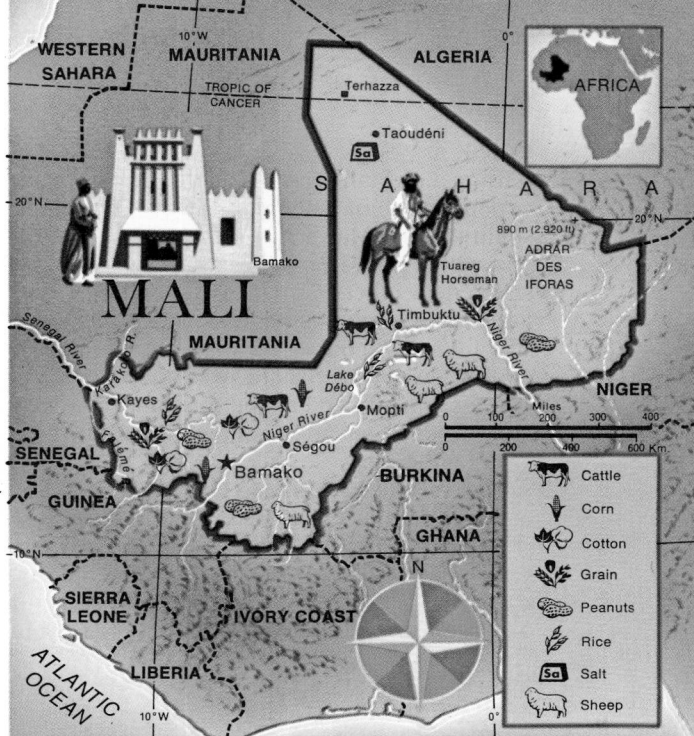

Mali is a large but thinly populated nation in West Africa. It was once one of the richest and most powerful of the ancient West African empires. In contrast, Mali today is one of Africa's poorest countries. Only about one quarter of its land can be used for farming. The rest is desert—part of the great Sahara desert —or semi-arid land suitable only for grazing livestock, such as cattle, goats, and sheep. A former French colony, Mali became an independent republic in 1960.

▶ THE PEOPLE

Mali lies at a crossroads of Africa, where people from the north meet those from tropical Africa. In the north live the Tuareg, desert nomads related to the Berbers of North Africa. The Fulani (Fulbe) are cattle raisers, who travel the semi-arid region below the Sahara seeking pasture for their herds.

The more fertile and heavily populated southern part of the country is the home of several black African peoples, most of whom are farmers. The most numerous are the Bambara. Others include the Songhai, Marka, Malinke, Senufo, and Dogon.

Language and Religion. French is the official language, but a variety of African languages also are spoken. The most commonly used language is Bambara. Most of the people are Muslims. Some Malians follow traditional African religions, and a few are Christians.

Education. Malian children are required to attend school for nine years, but presently only about 30 percent are able to do so because of a shortage of classrooms and teachers.

▶ THE LAND

Mali includes part of the Sahara in the north and parts of the savanna zone of western Africa in the south. It is a continental country, having no coastline at all. The south is the country's chief farming region because it receives a great deal of rain between July and October. It is hot all year, and in the northern desert areas it almost never rains. In the

northeast, near Algeria, is Mali's only mountain range, the Adrar des Iforas.

The Niger River sweeps across the middle of Mali in a great arc. Part of the Niger Valley, situated approximately in the center of the country between the cities of Ségou and Timbuktu, was once a large lake. Over the centuries it was filled in by mud washed down by the river and by sand blown in from the desert. This land can now be used for growing crops. Today Lake Débo is all that remains of the original lake.

▶ THE ECONOMY

Mali's economy is based chiefly on farming and livestock raising. The main food crops are millet, sorghum, corn, and rice. Peanuts and cotton are among the most important export crops. Cattle, goats, and sheep, once numbering in the millions, have been severely affected by drought in recent years.

Mali has some mineral resources, including iron and gold, but most have not been developed. Traditionally, the most important mineral has been salt. Salt mining is less important than it once was, but camel caravans still carry salt from the "salt city" of Taoudéni in the north to Timbuktu, where it is exchanged for food and other goods. The chief industries are the tanning of animal hides, food processing, and the manufacture of textiles.

▶ CITIES

Bamako, Mali's capital and largest city, has a population of about 500,000. Located in southwestern Mali, it is an important market city where goods from all over the country are shipped to other parts of West Africa. Other large towns include Ségou, Mopti, and Kayes. The fabled Timbuktu, situated in central Mali on the edge of the Sahara, was once an important trading city and a stop for camel caravans crossing the Sahara. It is now a small town.

▶ HISTORY AND GOVERNMENT

Several ancient empires once thrived in what is now Mali. The Empire of Mali, which was established in the 11th century, lasted until the 17th century. Its greatest emperor was Mansa Musa (ruled 1312–1337), who founded Timbuktu and made it a center of learning and culture. In 1591 the city was captured by invaders from the north, and it soon declined in importance. Today its once famous university is no longer in existence.

The French began to explore and conquer the region in the late 19th century. They called

FACTS AND FIGURES

REPUBLIC OF MALI (République du Mali) is the official name of the country.

THE PEOPLE are known as Malians.

LOCATION: West Africa.

AREA: 478,767 sq mi (1,240,000 km²).

POPULATION: 8,200,000 (estimate).

CAPITAL AND LARGEST CITY: Bamako.

MAJOR LANGUAGES: French (official), Bambara and other African languages.

MAJOR RELIGION: Muslim.

GOVERNMENT: Republic. **Head of state and government**—president. **Legislature**—National Assembly.

CHIEF PRODUCTS: Agricultural—millet, rice, corn, sugarcane, sorghum, peanuts, cotton, livestock. **Manufactured**—tanned animal hides, processed food, textiles. **Mineral**—salt, iron, gold.

MONETARY UNIT: African Financial Community (CFA) franc (1 CFA franc = 100 centimes).

NATIONAL ANTHEM: *A ton appel, Mali* ("At your call, Mali").

the territory French Sudan and made it part of French West Africa.

After World War II, France allowed its African territories some say in governing themselves. Mali, then called the Sudanese Republic, gained self-government in 1958. In 1959 it joined with Senegal to form the Mali Federation. In 1960 the federation was dissolved, and the Sudanese Republic declared its independence as the Republic of Mali.

Mali's first president, Modibo Keita, established a socialist government. Economic problems and discontent with Keita's rule led to his overthrow in 1968 by army officers, who formed a military government. A new constitution was approved in 1974, which called for a president to be elected for a 6-year term, and the legislature, the National Assembly, to be elected every three years. The sole political party is the Democratic Union of the Malian People (UDPM). The first elections under the new constitution were held in 1979.

Mali has had a long-standing border dispute with neighboring Burkina. The dispute led to a brief conflict between the two countries in 1985–86 before it was resolved in 1986.

H. R. JARRETT
University of Newcastle (Australia)
Author, *Physical Geography for West African Schools*

The Dogon, a people of southeastern Mali, live in distinctive villages often built on hillsides. They are believed to be among the earliest inhabitants of Mali.

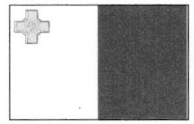

MALTA

The nation of Malta is composed of several small, rocky islands located in the Mediterranean Sea south of the Italian island of Sicily. Malta has few natural resources and owes its historical importance to its strategic location in the central Mediterranean. For most of its history Malta was occupied by a series of conquerors. The last foreign power to control the islands was Britain, for whom Malta served as an important naval base. The British governed the islands from the early 19th century until 1964, when Malta gained its independence.

▶ **THE PEOPLE**

The Maltese people today reflect their country's rich cultural heritage. Their earliest ancestors included the Phoenicians, an ancient seafaring people from the Middle East, and the Carthaginians, a related people who once ruled a great empire in North Africa and the Mediterranean.

Religion and Language. Most Maltese are Roman Catholics. They trace their Christian faith to Saint Paul, who is said to have been

MALTA

shipwrecked on Malta in the 1st century A.D. Maltese is a Semitic language. It has similarities to Arabic, for the Arabs occupied Malta from the 9th to the 11th century. But it also has been influenced by Italian. Both Maltese and English are official languages.

▶ **THE LAND**

Three main islands and two tiny uninhabited islets make up the nation of Malta. The main islands are Malta, the largest and most heavily populated; Gozo; and Comino, the smallest island. Most of the land is covered with low, rolling hills. There are no rivers or mountains. The climate is dry and hot in the summer, and mild, with periods of rainfall, in the winter. The capital, Valletta, and the largest city, Sliema, are located on Malta island. Valletta is built around an excellent natural harbor, which is one of the country's most important assets.

▶ **THE ECONOMY**

Malta's thin, rocky soil can be farmed only with great difficulty. Wheat, barley, potatoes, onions, and grapes are grown. Some potatoes and wine are exported, but Malta must import food to meet its needs. In the past many Maltese left the islands to seek their livelihoods in other countries.

Malta's economy was long dependent on military spending by the British. But even be-

FACTS AND FIGURES

REPUBLIC OF MALTA (Repubblika Ta' Malta) is the official name of the country.

THE PEOPLE are known as Maltese.

LOCATION: Mediterranean Sea, south of the Italian island of Sicily.

AREA: 122 sq mi (316 km²).

POPULATION: 375,000 (estimate).

CAPITAL: Valletta.

LARGEST CITY: Sliema.

MAJOR LANGUAGES: Maltese, English (both official).

MAJOR RELIGION: Roman Catholic.

GOVERNMENT: Republic. **Head of state**—president. **Head of government**—prime minister. **Legislature**—House of Representatives.

CHIEF PRODUCTS: Agricultural—wheat, barley, potatoes, onions, grapes, livestock. **Manufactured**—shipbuilding, textiles, clothing, processed food, wine.

MONETARY UNIT: Maltese pound (1 pound = 100 cents).

NATIONAL ANTHEM: *L'Innu Malti* ("The Maltese Hymn").

Malta's coastline is deeply indented, with many scenic bays like this one.

fore independence, the growth of manufacturing and tourism was encouraged. Fishing and the making of lace, buttons, pipes, gloves, beer, wine, and cigarettes are traditional industries. New factories produce cotton yarn, woolen goods, processed foods, chemicals, and clothing. An important source of income is the port of Valletta. Maltese work in the shipyards and on the docks. Others keep shops and restaurants to serve visitors.

▶ HISTORY AND GOVERNMENT

One group after another has conquered this small nation. The Phoenicians, Greeks, Carthaginians, and Romans all occupied Malta in turn. In 1530 the Holy Roman Emperor Charles V gave Malta to the Knights Hospitalers (or Knights of Malta). Under their rule Malta became a Christian fortress. They built beautiful churches, monasteries, and palaces, some of which still stand. After they defeated the Turks in 1565, their leader, Jean de la Valette, built the capital Valletta to commemorate the victory.

Napoleon conquered Malta in 1798. The Maltese rebelled against him, and Malta came under British control at its own request. It was formally annexed in 1814 and became an important British base on the route to India. During World War II, frightful bombings wrecked many old buildings and art treasures. For its bravery, the whole population was awarded the George Cross.

Malta was granted internal self-rule in 1947, but the islanders wanted either full independence or integration into the United Kingdom. Malta became an independent country within the Commonwealth of Nations in 1964. The constitution was amended in 1974, and the islands became a republic. A president replaced the governor-general (who represented the British monarch) as head of state. A prime minister is head of government.

Reviewed by E. Firman
Formerly, Secretary to His Excellency
the Governor-General of Malta

Modern Knights Hospitalers on Malta devote themselves to charity. Their order is the oldest combined military and religious order in the world.

MAMMALS

Mammals are the most advanced of all the different classes of animal life. They are also the animals that we know best. Our pet dogs and cats are mammals. So are the squirrels and rabbits that come into our yards. The bat that flutters above the treetops is a mammal. So is the mole that burrows through the soil.

Domestic animals, such as horses and cows, sheep, goats, and pigs, are mammals. So are elephants, gazelles, giraffes, sea lions, tigers, polar bears, baboons, mountain lions, and mice. For that matter, human beings are mammals, too.

▶ SIZES AND SHAPES

Mammals vary greatly in size. Largest is the blue whale, which sometimes measures 100 feet long and may weigh 130 tons—260,000 pounds. Smallest is a tiny shrew with a body little more than 2 inches long. It weighs less than many insects. Mammals also vary greatly in shape and appearance. Most of them walk about on four legs, but not all of them do. Bats have wings and fly through the air. Whales and dolphins have lost their hind limbs. They have fishlike shapes and spend their entire lives in the ocean.

Most mammals are covered with thick coats of hair, or fur. The whales, however, have hairless skin. Porcupines have quills, and armadillos wear suits of armor. Pangolins, strange mammals that live in Asia and Africa, are covered with overlapping scales. What makes all of these very different creatures mammals?

▶ WHAT IS A MAMMAL?

Mammals are vertebrates—animals with backbones. But so are fishes, amphibians, reptiles, and birds. All of these animals have bony skeletons inside their bodies. They are different from insects, worms, shellfish, and many other creatures that do not have bony internal skeletons. All mammals have lungs and breathe air. But so do birds, reptiles, and many amphibians. All mammals are "warm-blooded." That means that they are able to maintain fairly constant body temperatures regardless of the outside temperature. But birds are also warm-blooded animals.

Mammals and birds—both warm-blooded, both very active—have another important characteristic in common. Both are equipped with four-chambered hearts, which provide for quick and efficient circulation of the blood to all parts of the body.

All mammals, except two primitive types that lay eggs, give birth to living young. So do many fish, reptiles, insects, and other animals. But mammals are superior to all other animals in the care and protection they provide for their young, both before and after birth.

Mammals differ from all other animals in several ways. They are the only animals that possess true hair, or fur. They are the only animals that produce milk. The word "mammal" comes from the Latin word *mamma*, which means "breast." All female mammals nurse their young with milk that comes from glands, usually called breasts, on their bodies.

Those are two important characteristics that set mammals apart from all other animals.

Other Mammal Characteristics

Mammals have other characteristics that are not so obvious.

The mammal's lungs and heart are separated from its stomach and intestinal tract by a wall of muscle called the diaphragm.

The mammal's lower jaw consists of a single bone on each side. Most mammals have several different types of teeth—each type adapted for some particular use, such as cutting, tearing, grinding, or gnawing.

Most important of all, mammal brains are much more highly developed than the brains of any other animals. Man has the most highly developed brain of all and is the most intelligent of all mammals. Chimpanzees and gorillas are usually ranked next in intelligence, but some people consider that porpoises and dolphins should hold that place.

The Most Advanced Animals

Superior brains, warm blood, and improved methods of caring for their young give mammals great advantages in the struggle for survival. Mammals thrive from Arctic snowfields and polar seas to tropical jungles and rivers, from lofty mountaintops to blazing deserts. Mammals are the dominant, or ruling, animals of the world today.

THE ORDERS OF LIVING MAMMALS

MONOTREMATA
Mammals that lay eggs
Examples: Platypus, echidna (spiny anteater)

MARSUPIALIA
Young very immature at birth;
females usually have pouches
Examples: Kangaroo, opossum

INSECTIVORA
Small insect-eating mammals
Examples: Mole, shrew

DERMOPTERA
Gliding mammals
Example: "Flying lemur," or colugo

CHIROPTERA
Mammals with wings
Example: Bat

PRIMATES
Mammals with highly developed nervous
systems; most have opposable thumbs
Examples: Slender loris, monkey,
chimpanzee, gorilla, man

EDENTATA
Mammals that usually have simple, peglike
teeth
Examples: Anteater, sloth, armadillo

PHOLIDOTA
Mammals with coverings of overlapping scales
Example: Pangolin

LAGOMORPHA
Small- to medium-size mammals with clawed
toes; tails are either stubby or lacking
Examples: Rabbit, hare, pika

RODENTIA
Gnawing mammals
Examples: Rat, squirrel, beaver

CETACEA
Water-dwelling mammals with fishlike forms
Examples: Whale, porpoise

CARNIVORA
Flesh-eating mammals
Examples: Dog, cat, weasel, bear, seal, walrus

TUBULIDENTATA
Long-snouted, long-clawed, insect-eating
mammals
Example: Aardvark

PROBOSCIDEA
Huge mammals with trunks
Example: Elephant

HYRACOIDEA
Small, rodentlike mammals with hooves
Example: Hyrax

SIRENIA
Water-dwelling mammals with flippers, paddle-
shaped tails, and no hind legs
Examples: Manatee, dugong

PERISSODACTYLA
Hoofed mammals with odd numbers of toes
on each hind foot
Examples: Horse, tapir, rhinoceros

ARTIODACTYLA
Hoofed mammals with even numbers of toes
on each foot
Examples: Cow, goat, sheep, deer, antelope

RODENTIA

CETACEA

CARNIVORA

LAGOMORPHA

PHOLIDOTA

EDENTATA

TUBULIDENTATA

PRIMATES

PROBOSCIDEA

HYRACOIDEA

CHIROPTERA

SIRENIA

DERMOPTERA

PERISSODACTYLA

INSECTIVORA

ARTIODACTYLA

MARSUPIALIA

MONOTREMATA

THE RISE OF MAMMALS

Mammals arose from the reptiles, strange as that may seem. This probably began to happen at the beginning of the Mesozoic era, about 200,000,000 years ago. The Mesozoic was the Age of Reptiles, when cold-blooded, scaly creatures—especially the great dinosaurs—ruled the earth.

Very gradually one branch of reptiles began to change. They started to grow coats of hair instead of scales or armor. They became warm-blooded. Instead of laying eggs, as most reptiles did, some of them began to keep their eggs inside their bodies. Their young were protected and nourished inside the mother's body until they were born. In short, these animals became the first mammals.

The first mammals were tiny, timid creatures, about the size of rats and mice. They hid during the day and ventured out mostly at night to find food.

But conditions on earth gradually changed. The climate became cooler; the vast tropical swamplands began to disappear. The dinosaurs could not adapt to these new conditions. Their numbers grew smaller and smaller. They finally died out about 65,000,000 to 70,000,000 years ago. Now the more adaptable mammals had their chance.

Mammals Take Over the World

Mammals spread all over the world and branched out in many different directions. Some became grazers and developed hooves, on which they ran swiftly over the grasslands. Others developed hunting skills and became meat eaters. A few became adapted to a life in the sea. One branch developed wings and took to the air. There were all sorts of strange and wonderful mammals that flourished in the Miocene epoch, approximately 12,000,000 to 30,000,000 years ago.

About 3,000,000 years ago, vast ice sheets began to spread over great portions of the earth. This was the beginning of the Ice Age. Many of the mammals did not survive the frigid temperatures and other hardships of the Ice Age. Mastodons, saber-toothed cats, giant ground sloths, and many others became extinct. But a great number of other mammals adapted to the changing conditions and survived. They were the ancestors of mammals that inhabit the earth today.

Between 3,500 and 5,000 different species of mammals live in the world today. There are perhaps four or five times that many different varieties or subspecies. As you know, these modern mammals come in a bewildering variety of sizes and shapes. Scientists group them according to their body structures and relationships. All told, there are 18 different groups, or orders.

WALKING AND RUNNING

The mammals in each order have become adapted for some particular way of life. And it is often their limbs that give the best clue as to where and how each animal lives.

All of the land dwellers have four limbs, which they use in moving about. Man is the only one that stands erect and always walks and runs on two feet only. Man usually walks on the entire sole of his foot. So do bears and raccoons. Dogs, cats, and many other mammals walk on their toes, with their heels not touching the ground. (Our heels do not touch the ground either, when we are running.) Horses, deer, and antelopes move about on the very tips of their toes, which are encased in hard, protective hooves. Their limbs are adapted for swift, sustained movement.

The fastest speed a man can reach is about 20 miles an hour, and he can keep that up only for a few minutes. Race horses can move twice that fast, and so can many deer and antelopes. The pronghorn is probably the fastest mammal in North America. It has been clocked at speeds of 50 miles an hour, or more. Most scientists agree that the cheetah, a big cat of Asia and Africa, is the fastest of all mammals. It can speed along at close to 70 miles an hour for short distances.

Some mammals jump most of the time, instead of running. In jumping, the two hind legs move together. Kangaroos use only their powerful hind legs when they jump, holding their small front legs close to their chests.

LIFE IN THE TREES

Many mammals spend most of their lives in the trees. Most of them have sharp, curved claws that help them to hold on as they climb. Sloths, which spend large portions of their lives hanging upside down from branches, have enormous claws that act as hooks. Many tree dwellers also have tails that are adapted

MAMMAL HAIR

RHINOCEROS

MOLE

PORCUPINE

SHEEP

FOX

Mammals are the only animals that grow hair on their bodies. The hair appears in a variety of forms, ranging from the long, thick fur of the fox to the kinky wool of the sheep. The bristles on a mole's muzzle and the sharp, pointed quills of a porcupine are varieties of hair. So is the horn of a rhinoceros, which is made up of a mass of closely packed hair.

for grasping. When wrapped around a branch, the tail acts as a fifth hand. Mammals as different as New World monkeys, South American tree porcupines, and opossums have tails like that. Opossums and monkeys also have opposable, or grasping, thumbs like ours, and big toes to match. These aid them greatly in climbing.

GLIDING AND FLYING

A few mammals have become specialized for gliding. The flying squirrels are the best-known examples. They have developed thin membranes of fur-covered skin, which stretch between their legs on either side. Leaping from a high perch, the flying squirrel spreads its legs. The membranes, which act like sails or parachutes, allow the animals to glide for long distances from tree to tree.

Certain pouched mammals of Australia have developed similar gliding membranes. And so has the little-known colugo, or "flying" lemur of southeastern Asia and the Philippines.

The only mammals that can actually fly are the bats. Their forelimbs have become wings. Bats have very long and slender arms and fingers. These provide the framework for thin membranes of skin that stretch between them.

LIFE IN THE WATER

Practically all mammals, except possibly the great apes, can swim to some extent. Many spend a great deal of their time in the water and have special adaptations that make them expert swimmers. Otters and beavers, for example, have webbed hind feet. The beaver also has a broad, flat tail that can be used as either a rudder or an oar.

Seals, sea lions, and walruses spend most of their lives in the water and are even more specialized. Speedy, graceful, and streamlined in the water, they are awkward on land. Their four limbs have become shortened and flattened into flippers, which propel and steer them through the water.

The most specialized of all, however, are the sea cows and the whales. They live in the water from birth to death. Their short, flat forelimbs act as paddles for steering. Their hind limbs have disappeared, and their broad, flat tails move up and down, propelling them through the water.

▶ HAIR AND FUR

Only mammals grow hair. Hair insulates their bodies and helps to control their body temperatures. It also serves to protect their skin.

There are many different types of hair. Sheep have warm coats of kinky wool, and most horses have short, smooth coats of straight hair. Pigs have a thin covering of stiff bristles. Moles have coats of fine hair as soft as velvet. Foxes have thick coats of long, soft fur. The stiff whiskers that mammals have on their muzzles are special kinds of hairs. So are the manes and tails of horses.

The typical fur-bearing mammal really wears two coats in one. Next to his skin is a thick, warm undercoat. And over that is a topcoat of longer guard hairs. Most mammals shed their coats once or twice a year and grow new ones. Many of them grow a thick, warm winter coat each fall. They shed it in springtime for a shorter summer coat.

Coloration

These summer and winter coats may be different colors. The sleek summer coat of the white-tailed deer, for example, is a rich, reddish color. Its longer winter coat is a grayish brown. Weasels and snowshoe hares often have brown summer coats and white winter ones. The white coat helps to hide them against a snowy background.

The young of many mammals have fur coats that look quite different from their parents' coats. Fawns of white-tailed deer are spotted, in contrast to their plain-coated parents. Solid-colored big cats, such as African lions and American panthers, also have spotted young. Various seal pups are born with fluffy white coats, which are replaced after a few days by short, dark coats like those the parents have.

Some kinds of mammals have several different color phases. The American black bear, for example, comes in various shades—black, brown, and cinnamon. Silver, black, and cross foxes are all simply color varieties of the common red fox and may occur together in the same litter.

▶ DIFFERENT TEETH FOR DIFFERENT DIETS

Anything that can be eaten serves as food for some kind of mammal or another. Many are meat eaters. A great many other mammals

Mammals with sharp, pointed teeth are meat eaters. Their jaws open and close like a door hinge. Other mammals move their jaws from side to side, grinding with broad, flattened teeth. These are plant eaters. Mammals with both kinds of teeth and jaw movements can eat plant or animal food.

MAMMAL TEETH AND JAWS

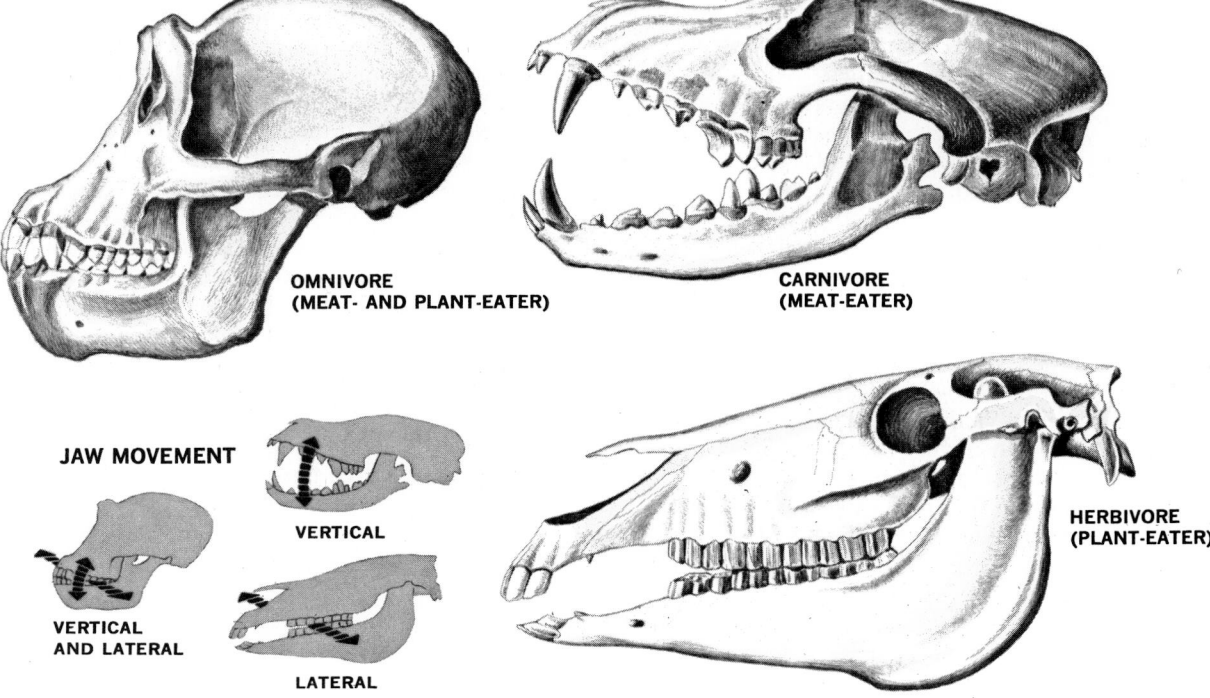

OMNIVORE
(MEAT- AND PLANT-EATER)

CARNIVORE
(MEAT-EATER)

JAW MOVEMENT

VERTICAL

VERTICAL
AND LATERAL

LATERAL

HERBIVORE
(PLANT-EATER)

are vegetarians. Still other mammals eat both plant and animal matter.

Each mammal has teeth that are adapted for dealing with the particular type of food it eats. Carnivores, or meat eaters, have long, sharp canine teeth for stabbing their victims. Their side teeth have sharp cutting edges for shearing the flesh into pieces. Insect eaters, such as bats and shrews, have many sharp, cutting teeth—ideal for chopping insects into pieces suitable for swallowing. Grazing mammals, such as horses and cows, have spadelike front teeth, suited for seizing grass and breaking it off. Their molars, or cheek teeth, prepare the plant material for swallowing. These have broad, grinding surfaces.

Rodents are vegetable eaters, too, but their teeth are adapted for gnawing. They have chisel-like front teeth—two in the upper jaw, and two in the lower—which shear against each other in cutting vegetable matter or gnawing through the hard shells of nuts. Rodent front teeth keep growing throughout the animal's life. They wear away against each other, however, and so remain a constant length.

Special Food Adaptations

Some mammals have very specialized diets. The giant panda of Asia eats bamboo shoots for the most part. The teddy-bear-like koala of Australia lives on a diet of eucalyptus leaves. **Anteaters**, as their name suggests, specialize in eating ants and other insects.

The anteater's front feet have huge, curved claws, ideal instruments for tearing open anthills and termite nests. The muzzle is long and slender, and the anteater has a sticky, wormlike tongue that can be extended several inches beyond the mouth. Thrusting this long tongue deep into the passageways of an ant colony, the anteater collects the ants and eats them. Such different mammals as the scaled pangolin, the echidna, and the African aardvark, or "earth pig," have similar equipment for gathering and eating ants and termites.

Most bats are insect eaters, but the vampire bat thrives on a diet of blood. Settling on a sleeping victim, it makes tiny punctures in the skin with its teeth and then laps up the blood that oozes out. A few bats are fish eaters and catch their prey with hooked claws while swooping low over a stream. Others feed only on nectar, which they collect by hovering over blossoms and extending very long, brush-tipped tongues into the cup.

Baleen, or whalebone, whales feed on tiny ocean animals called krill, which thrive near the surface. Rushing through the water with open mouth, the whale strains the water through plates of brushlike material—baleen—that hang from its upper jaws. The krill is collected on the baleen and swallowed.

Storing Food

Many mammals collect food and store it for future use. Even meat eaters will eat their fill and then hide the remainder of their kill for a meal some other day. Rodents, however, are probably the most famous storers of food. Many of them harvest food during the summer and fall and lay it away for winter eating.

Chipmunks, deer mice, and many other rodents collect seeds and nuts and pile them in their burrows. Pine squirrels are probably the champion hoarders. They often collect several bushels of food in a single storeroom, as insurance against winter hunger.

The little pika and the mountain beaver, or aplodontia, of western North America are both haymakers. They cut grass industriously during the summer, store it in stacks, and dry it for winter use.

▶ DEFENSE AGAINST DANGER

From birth onward, all mammals live with the threat of sudden death. But they have many different ways of protecting themselves. When danger threatens, most mammals try to avoid it. A rabbit may "freeze" in his tracks to avoid detection. If the enemy discovers him, he flees. Hoofed mammals—the usual prey of many large meat eaters—are unusually swift runners. They have keen senses that help them avoid danger.

Most mammals have dull-colored coats that blend with their surroundings. Even spots or stripes fade into the shifting lights and varied background of the jungle or woodland. A spotted fawn curled up at the base of a tree is practically invisible as long as it remains motionless.

Some mammals, however, depend chiefly on their armored bodies to protect them. The armadillo, for example, has bands of hard plates that cover its back and sides. When danger overtakes the armadillo, the animal curls up in a ball—protecting his soft undersides and presenting only the hard plates to his enemy. Pangolins do the same thing. But they are protected by tough, overlapping scales instead of plates.

Spines are the protective armor of the porcupine and hedgehog. Curling up when danger threatens, the hedgehog looks like a bristling pincushion. The porcupine, on the other hand, erects his sharp quills and sometimes even backs up toward the enemy. Each of his barb-tipped quills—there are about 30,000 in all—comes out at a touch and lodges in the enemy's skin. There it works its way deeper and deeper into the flesh.

▶ WEAPONS FOR ATTACK

Any mammal will fight if it has to, and many of them have deadly weapons. Cats attack with razor-sharp teeth and claws. Hoofed mammals slash about with their hooves. A big kangaroo can rip open an enemy with its clawed hind legs. Even a rabbit will kick out desperately if cornered. The elephant tramples its victim or tosses him with its tusks. The walrus stabs with a pair of downward-pointing tusks.

Skunks rely on a chemical attack. A skunk sprays the enemy with a choking, overpowering scent, squeezed from glands on either side of its tail. Hit in the face, the enemy is blinded for the moment and usually retreats.

The tiny, short-tailed shrew uses poison from its salivary glands. The shrew can quickly paralyze and kill a mouse with its bite. The male platypus uses poison spurs in his hind legs.

Horns and Antlers

Many hoofed mammals rely on horns or antlers as weapons of attack. Usually both males and females grow horns. These are formed of keratin, the same substance of which claws and hooves and fingernails are made. The horns of a rhinoceros are solid. Cattle and antelope have hollow horns, which grow over bony cores on the skull. Year after year the horns grow larger, until they have reached their full growth. The American pronghorn is the only horned mammal that sheds its weapons yearly, as deer shed their antlers.

Antlers differ from horns. They are solid bone and are usually shed and regrown each year. With the exception of the caribou and reindeer, only the male deer grows antlers. Starting as buds in the spring, the antlers grow and branch. By fall they have gained full growth. After using his weapons during the mating season, the buck drops the antlers during the winter. Then, the next spring, he starts to grow a new pair.

▶ MAMMAL HOMES

Most mammals have homes in which they sleep, take shelter, and raise their young. Many live in holes in trees or in burrows. Ground squirrels, woodchucks, and many others are skilled diggers. They dig out underground homes with several entrances and chambers. Many other mammals are skilled nest-builders. Some mice make woven nests of grass and other material. Squirrels often build bulky leaf nests high in the treetops. Wood rats, also, make huge nests of twigs and branches.

Muskrats make moundlike lodges of cattails and matted vegetation. Beavers, however, probably make the most elaborate mammal homes of all. Their roomy lodges are usually built in their ponds. Skillfully constructed of logs and branches, the lodge has an underwater entrance, a sleeping platform, and an opening in the top for ventilation. The thick walls are chinked with mud and vegetation, and the lodge is warm and snug throughout the winter.

▶ MIGRATIONS

Some mammals lead a wandering existence. Many of them make long journeys every year as they travel from summer feeding grounds to wintering areas, and then back. Such regular journeys are called migrations. Every spring herds of Barren Ground caribou of Canada and Alaska travel northward to tundra areas, where they graze on lichens during the summer. Along the way, their young are born.

As winter approaches, the caribou head southward toward the sheltering tree belt, where they spend the winter. Many species of deer carry out similar but shorter migrations. Elk, for example, often summer high in the mountains, then descend to sheltering valleys and lowlands as colder weather approaches.

A VARIETY OF LIVING MAMMALS

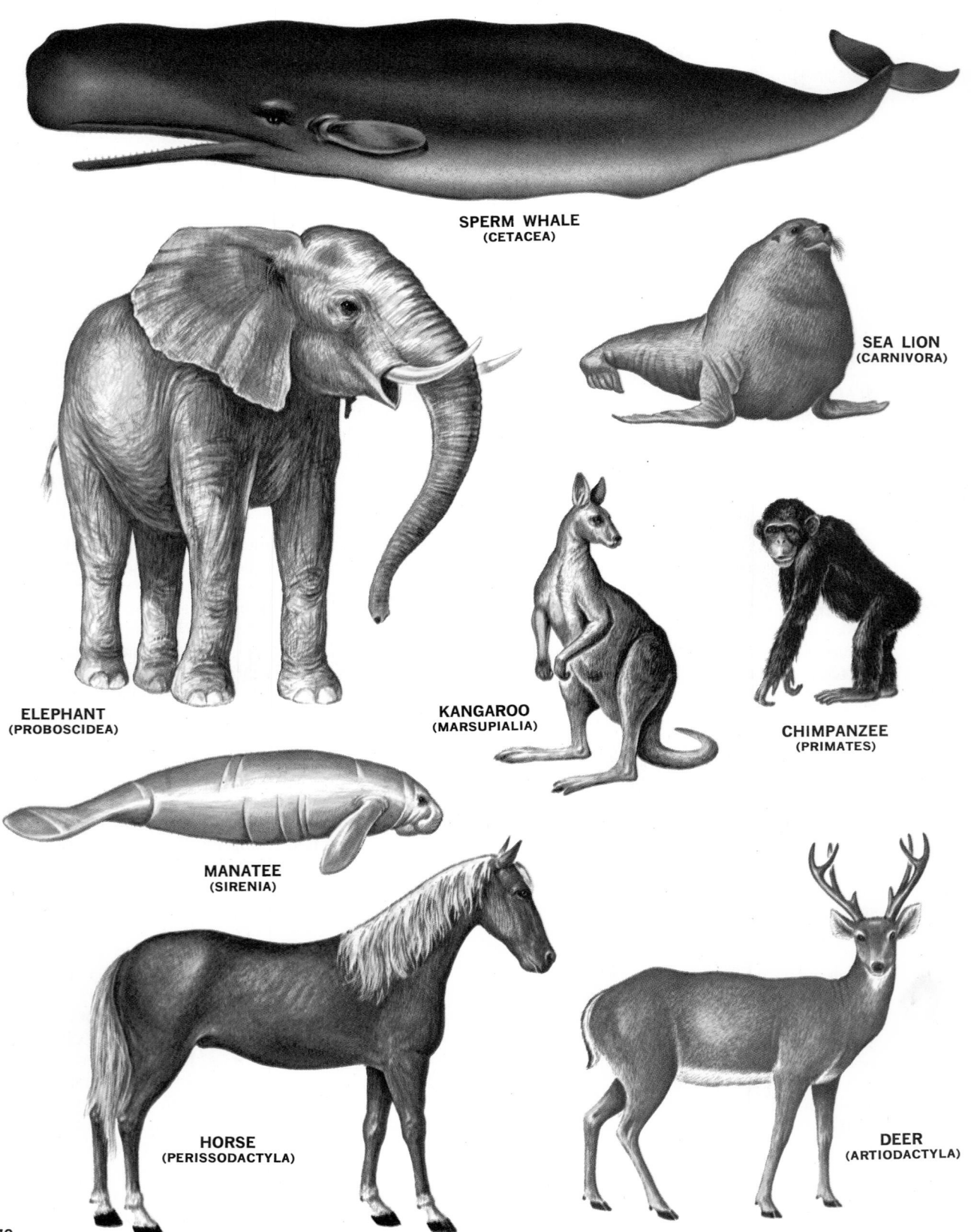

SPERM WHALE
(CETACEA)

SEA LION
(CARNIVORA)

ELEPHANT
(PROBOSCIDEA)

KANGAROO
(MARSUPIALIA)

CHIMPANZEE
(PRIMATES)

MANATEE
(SIRENIA)

HORSE
(PERISSODACTYLA)

DEER
(ARTIODACTYLA)

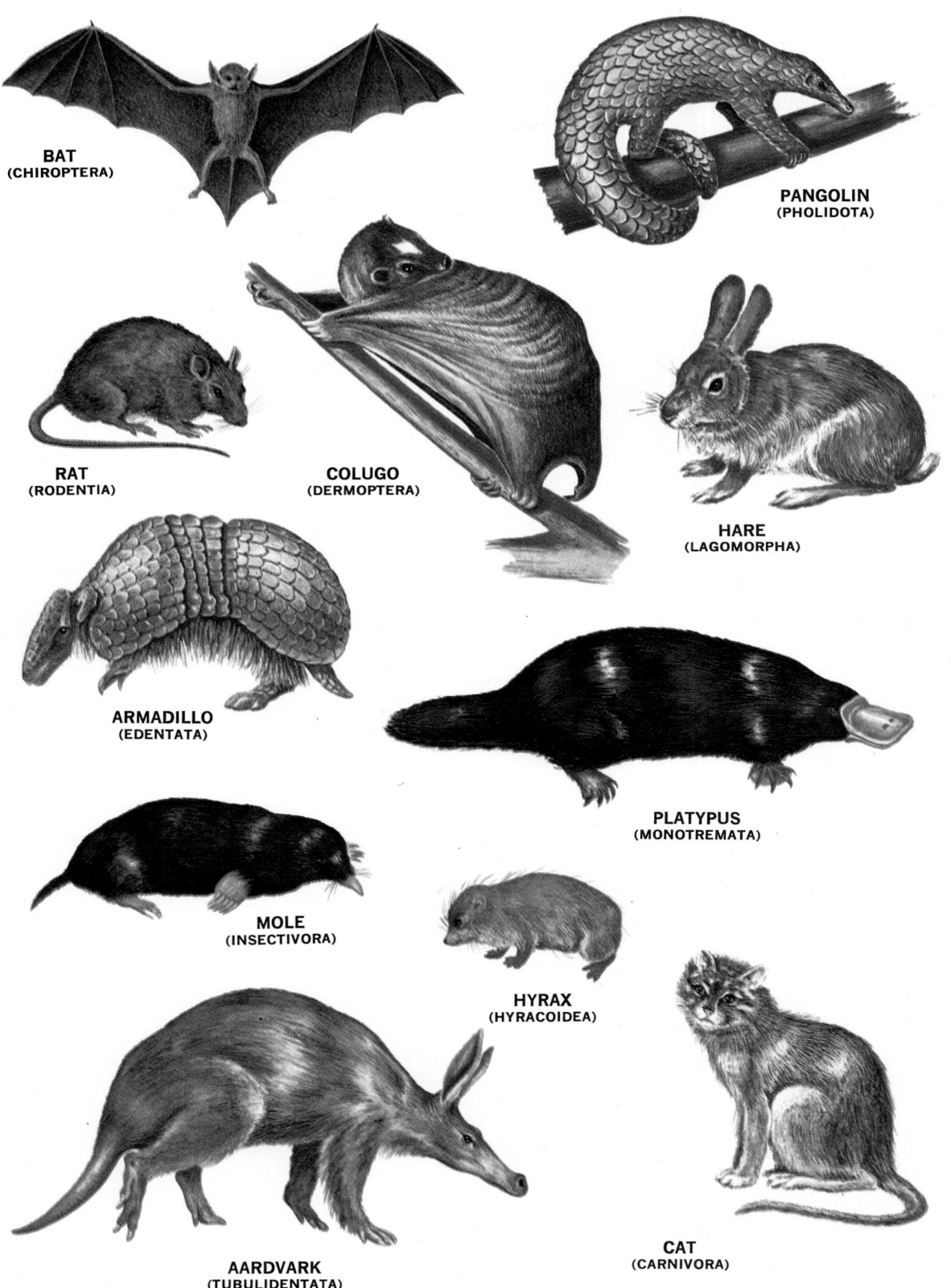

BAT
(CHIROPTERA)

PANGOLIN
(PHOLIDOTA)

RAT
(RODENTIA)

COLUGO
(DERMOPTERA)

HARE
(LAGOMORPHA)

ARMADILLO
(EDENTATA)

PLATYPUS
(MONOTREMATA)

MOLE
(INSECTIVORA)

HYRAX
(HYRACOIDEA)

AARDVARK
(TUBULIDENTATA)

CAT
(CARNIVORA)

Many ocean mammals perform long migrations to reach breeding grounds and seasonal feeding areas. For example, whales are almost constantly on the move as they head from one feeding ground to another. Gray whales usually winter in sheltered lagoons off the coast of Lower California. Here their young are born. But when springtime comes, they travel northward to feeding grounds in the cold waters of the North Pacific.

▶ MAMMALS IN WINTER

Many mammals remain in the same home territory throughout the year. They do not need to migrate, because they prepare for winter in other ways. Some of them store food. Others eat heavily during the autumn and build up stores of body fat that tides them through cold weather. Skunks, opossums, and many others retire into their burrows during extremely bad weather. Sometimes they do not come out for weeks. In northern areas many bears sleep the whole winter away in their dens.

A few mammals fall into a very deep winter sleep called hibernation. Groundhogs hibernate. So do ground squirrels, jumping mice, and many bats.

▶ MAMMAL SOCIETIES AND BREEDING BEHAVIOR

Many mammals live alone, except during the breeding season. But others are more sociable. Beavers usually live together in family groups throughout the year. So do wolves and lions. Monkeys and baboons often travel in troops, and many hoofed mammals travel in enormous herds. Prairie dogs live in colonies that sometimes include thousands of individuals. Some mammals, such as the fur seal, come together in huge gatherings only at breeding season.

A few mammals, such as the wolf and beaver, are thought to be faithful to one mate throughout life. Most mammals, however, are not so faithful. Many of them accept a number of different mates during each breeding season.

▶ REPRODUCTION

Among mammals there are three different methods of reproduction.

Two primitive mammals of the Australian region lay eggs, just as birds do. These mammals are the platypus and the echidna. All other mammals bear living young.

The marsupials, or pouched mammals, give birth to very tiny and immature young.

Some mammals, such as lions, live in devoted family groups.

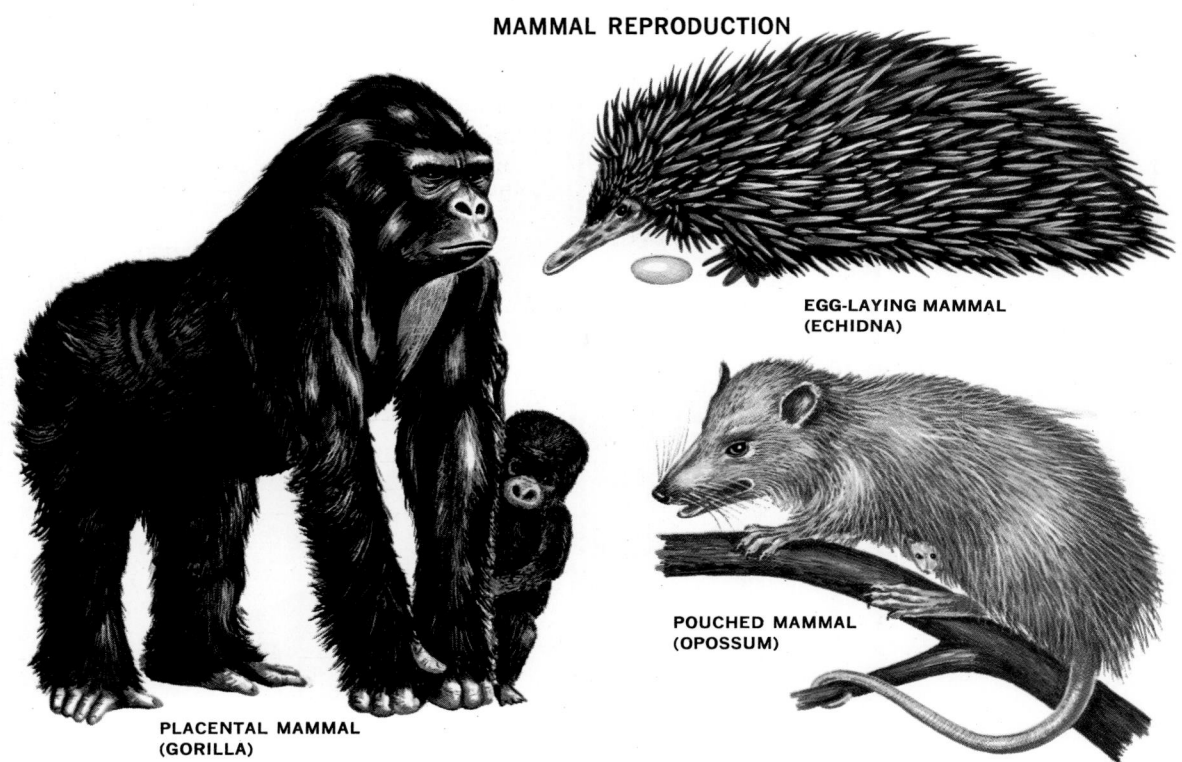

EGG-LAYING MAMMAL (ECHIDNA)

POUCHED MAMMAL (OPOSSUM)

PLACENTAL MAMMAL (GORILLA)

Two kinds of mammals—the platypus and the echidna—lay eggs, covered by an outer shell. The young develop inside the eggs. Pouched mammals give birth to tiny, undeveloped young. The young are nourished and protected in a pouch, or outer pocket, on the mother's body. In all other mammals the young develop inside the mother's body. At birth the young are well-developed, smaller versions of their parents.

Female marsupials usually have pouches on their undersides. Crawling into the pouch as soon as they are born, the tiny young hang onto nipples in the pouch. They grow and develop in this protective sack until they are mature enough to come out.

Most mammals, however, reproduce in the third way. With them, the developing young are nourished and protected inside the mother's body until they are ready to be born. These are called placental mammals. Their system of reproduction is much more advanced than the system used by the egg-laying platypus and echidna.

Egg-Laying Mammals

The platypus, or duckbill, is an extraordinary-looking mammal. About the size of a muskrat, it has sleek brown fur, a flattened tail, webbed feet, and a broad, leathery bill, with which it gathers its food. It lives in burrows in the banks of Australian streams and feeds by night on worms, insects, crustaceans, and other small animals that live in the stream.

When the female platypus is preparing for a family, she makes a nest of leaves in her streamside burrow. Plugging the burrow entrance, she retires to the nest and lays two round white eggs with wrinkled shells. Curling about them, she guards and incubates them for about 10 days until the young hatch. Milk oozes out of pores on her underside and trickles onto the fur, where the young get it.

Echidnas, or "spiny anteaters," also lay eggs. These are carried by the female in a pouch that forms on her belly during the breeding season. Echidnas have a covering of stiff spines, like hedgehogs. They have long tube-shaped snouts and huge claws.

Pregnancy and Birth

The platypus lays her eggs about 2 weeks after mating. The unborn young continue to develop inside the eggshell—but outside the mother's body—for another 10 days before they hatch. With marsupials and placental mammals, however, the young stay inside the mother's body until they are born. The time between mating and birth is called the period

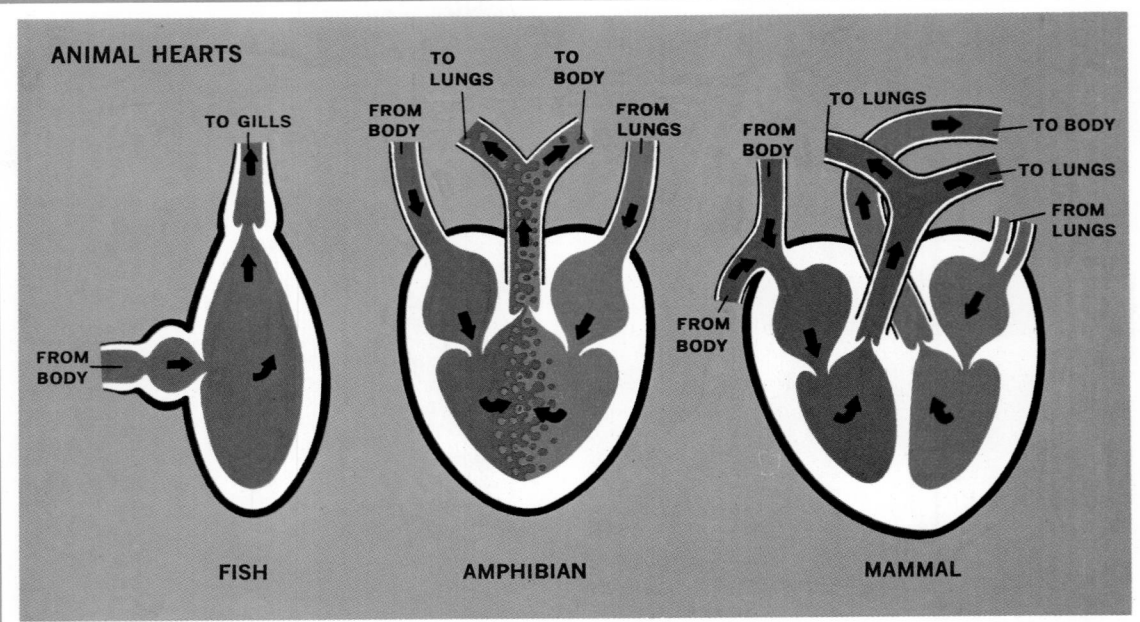

ANIMAL HEARTS

TO GILLS

FROM BODY

FISH

TO LUNGS
TO BODY
FROM BODY
FROM LUNGS

AMPHIBIAN

TO LUNGS
TO BODY
TO LUNGS
FROM BODY
FROM LUNGS
FROM BODY

MAMMAL

THE FOUR-CHAMBERED HEART

Both mammals and birds are equipped with four-chambered hearts. This means that they really have two hearts in one. Each side of the four-chambered heart provides for a distinct and separate circulation of the blood. The two chambers on the right side of the heart receive waste-carrying blood from the body. They pump it to the lungs and then back to the left side of the heart. While in the lungs the blood passes off waste gases and receives fresh oxygen. Returning to the left side of the heart, this fresh blood is pumped to the various parts of the body. Arteries carry blood away from the heart. Veins carry blood to the heart. The arteries that carry blood from the heart to the lungs are the only arteries with waste-carrying blood. The two separate pumps maintain the blood pressure at a high level and push the blood along quickly.

Mammals and birds need efficient double circulation. They are very active and must be able to function in all kinds of weather. Warm-blooded animals, they burn up much greater amounts of food and oxygen (in proportion to their body sizes) than the cold-blooded vertebrates do.

A fish has a two-chambered heart—a simple pump that sends blood to the gills, and from the gills to the rest of the body, all in one circuit. This is not a very efficient system. Much of the circulatory pressure is lost in the maze of gill capillaries (tiny blood vessels).

Amphibians and reptiles usually have three-chambered hearts—two upper chambers and one lower chamber. Such an arrangement partially provides for two circulations of the blood—one to the lungs and one to the rest of the body. It is not so efficient as the four-chambered heart, however. Waste blood from the body and fresh blood from the lungs are mixed in the single lower chamber.

of pregnancy, or the gestation period. This varies greatly with different mammals.

Mice are born about 3 weeks after the parents have mated. Domestic dogs and cats develop within the mother for about 2 months, and the young of big cats like lions and tigers for about 3 months. Human babies are carried for about 9 months, but many mammals have even longer periods of pregnancy. The fur seal carries its young for nearly a year, the giraffe for 14 months, and the rhinoceros for 17 or 18 months. The elephant carries its baby the longest time of all—20 to 22 months.

As might be expected, the condition of the young at birth varies, too. Baby mice are blind, naked, and helpless at birth. But the young of many hoofed mammals can stand up and follow their mothers within a few hours after they are born. Their eyes are open, and they have full coats of hair.

Care of the Young

With few exceptions, male mammals have very little to do with the care of the young. Several, such as the wolf and fox, are good fathers. They hunt and help to guard the young. Usually, however, the female has the entire responsibility. She takes good care of her young—nursing them and cleaning them and keeping them warm. If danger threatens, she fights to protect them or carries them to a new hiding place. When the youngsters are ready, she weans them from milk onto solid foods. Gradually they learn how to find food for themselves. They learn how to avoid danger and how to do all the things they need to know. Finally they launch out on their own.

ROBERT M. McCLUNG
Author, science books for children

See also AGING; ANIMALS; ANIMALS: COMMUNICATION AND SOCIAL ORGANIZATION; ANIMALS: INTELLIGENCE AND BEHAVIOR; ANIMALS: LOCOMOTION; EGGS AND EMBRYOS; EVOLUTION; FEET AND HANDS; FOSSILS; HIBERNATION; HOMING AND MIGRATION; KINGDOMS OF LIVING THINGS; LIFE, ADAPTATIONS IN THE WORLD OF; LIFE, DISTRIBUTION OF PLANT AND ANIMAL; REPRODUCTION; TAXONOMY; articles on individual animals.

MANAGEMENT. See LABOR AND MANAGEMENT.
MANCHURIA. See CHINA.

MANET, ÉDOUARD (1832–1883)

Édouard Manet was born on January 23, 1832, in Paris, the son of wealthy parents. As a child he was interested in art. Rather than study law, as his father wished, Édouard became an apprentice on a ship. When he returned home with his luggage full of drawings, his father finally allowed him to study art.

In 1850 Manet entered the studio of Thomas Couture (1815–79), an excellent teacher. After six years he left to work on his own—painting everyday life in Paris.

In 1861, Manet's painting *The Guitar Player* was accepted by the Paris Salon, the official exhibition of the French Academy of Fine Arts. *Olympia*, a painting of a reclining female nude, was accepted in 1865. It caused a great scandal. *Olympia* was considered improper, as were a painting of a drunken woman in a tavern and a nude seated on the grass of a public park. People could not understand why Manet bothered with such lowly or "vulgar" subjects. After that, most of his works were rejected by the Academy.

Manet was somewhat like the realist painters of his day in his choice of subjects and his manner of painting them. He was also often called the leader of the impressionists. But he never thought of himself as an impressionist painter. He remained firmly rooted in classical composition. And he longed for recognition by the Academy.

Manet died on April 20, 1883. By then his critics had become less harsh. *Olympia* was exhibited in the Louvre in Paris in 1907.

Reviewed by FRANK GETLEIN
Author, *The French Impressionists*

Woman with a Parrot (1866), by Manet.

MANGO AND OTHER TROPICAL FRUIT

Many different delicious fruits grow in the tropical regions of the world. Bananas and pineapples are so popular that they are the subjects of separate articles in this encyclopedia. Other important tropical fruits are described in this article.

The **mango** is native to tropical Asia but is now grown in nearly all tropical and subtropical countries. Most mangoes are kidney-shaped, but some may be nearly round or long and thin. Mangoes also vary in size. Some are the size of a plum. Others may weigh 2 kilograms (4½ pounds) or more. At the center of the fruit is a large, flat seed. Around the seed is the fleshy, fragrant, and juicy orange-yellow pulp. The mango is eaten as a fresh fruit. It is also used in chutneys and preserves.

One of the most common tropical fruits is the **papaya.** It is native to tropical America but now grows in other tropical areas. Papayas may be from 8 to 50 centimeters (3 to 20 inches) long and may sometimes weigh as much as 9 kilograms (20 pounds). The fruit may be round or oblong. The yellow or orange flesh has a sweet, somewhat musky flavor. It has a hollow center lined with many small seeds. Papaya may be served fresh in salads, or it may be boiled and served as a vegetable. It is also used in preserves, jellies, and sherberts. The meat tenderizer called papain, a digestive enzyme, comes from young papaya fruit. Papaya juice is used to help relieve some digestive disorders.

The **avocado** is native to tropical America, but it now grows in many tropical and subtropical areas. Avocados may be pear-shaped or round. They range in color from green to dark purple. The greenish yellow flesh has a buttery texture and a nutty taste. The avocado is often served fresh in salads. Mashed avocados are blended with other ingredients to make guacamole, a popular Latin-American dish.

The **plantain** is a type of banana widely used for cooking in tropical countries. It is starchy rather than sweet. It looks like a very large, yellowish green banana—about 30 centimeters (12 inches) long and 5 to 8 centimeters (2 to 3 inches) in diameter. It is picked when green and may be roasted, boiled, or baked. It is also dried and ground to be used in making breads, cakes, puddings, or soups.

The **breadfruit** is cooked as a vegetable. It is a sweet, starchy fruit that tastes like a sweet potato. The best types are seedless, usually round, twice the size of a grapefruit, and covered with a thick, greenish rind.

The fruit of the **guava** is known especially for the delicious, wine-red jelly that is made from it. The thin-skinned red or yellow fruit also has many other uses. It is eaten with the hand, sliced and served with cream, stewed, preserved, and cooked in pies.

One of the best fruits of the American tropics is the **sapodilla.** The sapodilla fruit may be round, oval, or even cone-shaped. It has a thin, brown skin. The flesh is yellowish brown, translucent, and sweet. It is eaten with the hand. The bark of the sapodilla tree is tapped for a milky substance that yields chicle, a gum used in making chewing gum.

The **tamarind** is a tropical fruit native to Africa. The acid, brownish pulp is contained in pods. Tamarind pulp is added to chutneys and curries and is used to pickle fish. The diluted syrup makes a beverage.

Reviewed by RODNEY W. DOW
State University of New York Agricultural
and Technical College at Farmingdale

See also FRUITGROWING.

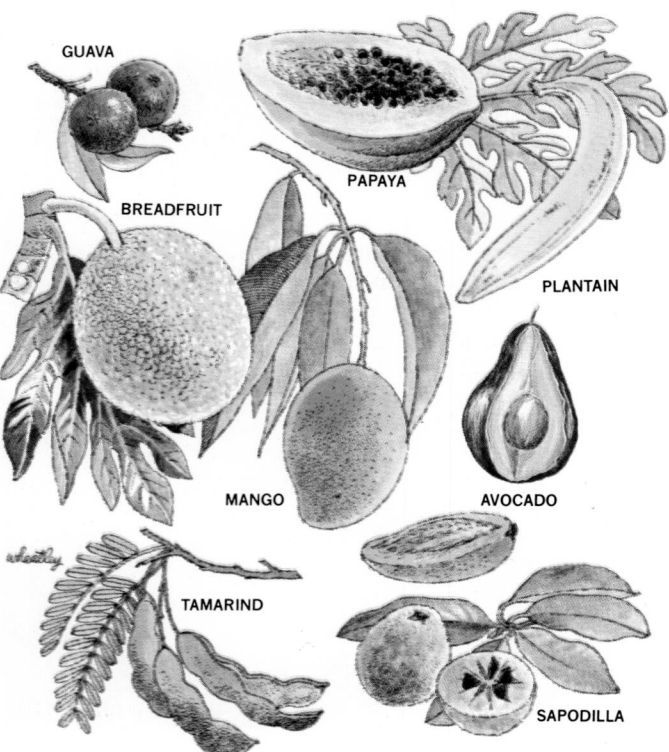

GUAVA

PAPAYA

BREADFRUIT

PLANTAIN

MANGO

AVOCADO

TAMARIND

SAPODILLA

MANILA

Manila is the capital and largest city of the Republic of the Philippines. It is a busy metropolis, an international port, and the center of the nation's cultural and commercial life. Early in its history it was known as Maynila, meaning "place of the nila flower," because of the flowering nila plants that once grew there. Manila is often called the Pearl of the Orient because of its natural beauty.

The city lies on a coastal plain in the southwest part of the island of Luzon. It is an ideal seaport because of its location on the eastern shore of Manila Bay at the mouth of the Pasig River. The climate is generally warm and humid. Temperatures average between 24 and 29°C (75 and 85°F).

Manila has a population of more than 1,600,000. In 1975 a larger community known as Metro Manila was created. It includes Manila, Quezon City, and many nearby cities and towns, with a total population of about 6,000,000.

OLD AND NEW

Manila is a city that combines the old and the new. In modern Manila, people work in tall office buildings and live in modern apartment houses. Automobiles speed along the wide boulevards and over the many bridges that span the Pasig River. Sugar, copra, lumber, and other goods are shipped all over the world from the busy docks on Manila Bay.

Near the port is the old Spanish city of Intramuros, which is surrounded by thick walls. Fort Santiago and the Church of St. Augustine, the oldest church in the Philippines, are located there. Many historic buildings and plazas are being restored.

Malacañang Palace, the official home of the president of the Philippines, is located in Manila on the banks of the Pasig River. There are many colleges and universities in Manila. The oldest is the University of Santo Tomás, founded by Spanish missionaries in 1611. One of Manila's leading attractions is the modern Cultural Center complex, built on land reclaimed from Manila Bay. The observatory of Manila, founded in 1865, is famous for its studies of weather conditions. The National Museum of the Philippines houses exhibits of anthropological and geological interest. The Lopez Memorial Museum and Library, in nearby Pasay, houses the works of many famous Filipino painters and writers.

HISTORY

The Portuguese explorer Ferdinand Magellan claimed the Philippines for Spain in 1521, and Manila became the headquarters of the Spanish government of the islands in 1571. In the 1700's Manila was attacked by both the British and the Dutch. British forces occupied Manila from 1762 until 1763, when it was returned to Spain. With this brief exception, Spain controlled Manila for over 300 years. The city was greatly influenced by Spanish customs and culture. Many Spanish missionaries came to Manila, where they became powerful in religion, education, and government.

During the Spanish-American War, United States warships under Commodore George Dewey defeated the Spanish fleet in Manila Bay in 1898. Manila was captured four months later with the aid of Filipino troops. The peace treaty that ended the war ceded the Philippines to the United States.

In World War II the Philippines were invaded by the Japanese. They occupied Manila in 1942 after first bombing the city. Manila was liberated by United States forces in 1945. But much of the city, including almost all of Intramuros, was destroyed in the fighting. After the war, it was completely rebuilt.

When the Philippines became independent in 1946, Manila became the nation's capital. Two years later Quezon City replaced Manila as the seat of government. But Manila again became the official capital in 1976. In recent years, the government has done much to provide housing, hospitals, roads, and schools for Manila's poor. It has also encouraged the building of hotels, a new airport, and a modern convention center to serve the important tourist industry.

CAROLINA S. MOULTON
Philippine Consultate (New York City)

MANITOBA

The name Manitoba comes from the Indian words *Manito waba,* meaning "great spirit's strait." These words probably refer to a narrow strait in Lake Manitoba where the waves dash against the rocks and produce great echoing sounds. Manitoba was the first of the Western Canadian provinces to be settled. Thomas Douglas, fifth Earl of Selkirk, established a colony for Scottish tenant farmers who had been forced off their land. The first of the Selkirk settlers arrived in 1812. They took up land along the lower Red River between Winnipeg and the present town of Selkirk.

▶ THE LAND

Manitoba lies within two major landform regions that extend across the interior of Canada. To the north and east is the Canadian Shield. Its rolling surface is dotted with many lakes and swamps and muskegs (peat bogs). Long ago the surface was scraped by a vast glacier. Only a thin layer of soil remains. While the Shield has very little land for cultivation, it is a storehouse of valuable minerals. Much of its surface is covered with forests suitable for pulpwood and lumber. Its principal rivers, the Churchill and the Nelson, are important sources of hydroelectric power.

FACTS AND FIGURES

LOCATION: Latitude—49° N to 60° N. **Longitude**—89° W to 102° W.

JOINED CANADIAN CONFEDERATION: July 15, 1870, as the 5th province.

POPULATION: 1,071,232 (1986 census). **Rank among provinces**—5th.

CAPITAL AND LARGEST CITY: Winnipeg, pop. (metropolitan area) 625,304 (1986 census).

PHYSICAL FEATURES: Area—650,090 km² (251,000 sq mi). **Rank among provinces**—6th. **Highest point**—Mt. Baldy, 832 m (2,729 ft). **Rivers**—Assiniboine, flowing east; Nelson, Churchill, and Red, flowing north; Winnipeg, flowing northwest. **Lakes**—Winnipeg, Winnipegosis, Manitoba, Southern Indian, Island, Cedar, Moose.

INDUSTRIES AND PRODUCTS: Manufacturing (especially oil refining and grain and meat processing), agriculture, mining, fishing, lumber, fur.

GOVERNMENT: Self-governing province. **Titular head of government**—lieutenant governor, appointed by governor-general of Canada. **Actual head of government**—premier, elected by the people. **Provincial representation in federal parliament**—6 appointed senators; 14 elected members of House of Commons. **Voting age**—18.

PROVINCIAL FLOWER: Prairie crocus.

South of the Shield is the Manitoba Lowland. This region contains three very large lakes—Winnipeg, Winnipegosis, and Manitoba. Three large rivers flow into these lakes—the Saskatchewan, the Assiniboine-Red, and the Winnipeg. During the Great Ice Age a huge continental glacier lay to the north of these lakes, cutting off their flow to Hudson Bay. This produced Lake Agassiz, an enormous ancient glacial lake that was bigger than Lake Superior. When the glacier melted, Lake Agassiz drained northward, leaving exposed the flat, fertile plain of the Red River Valley. Some of the finest agricultural land in western Canada is found in this valley.

In the southwestern part of Manitoba, the Manitoba Escarpment rises abruptly from the lowland. Unlike the flat lowland, the higher upland is rolling and covered with soil left by the retreating glacier. At places along the escarpment, the land rises steeply, giving the impression of low mountains. Such places as Duck Mountain, Riding Mountain, and Pembina Mountain are not actually mountains but are merely the steep edges of the escarpment. The highest point in Manitoba is Mt. Baldy, located on Duck Mountain. Hilly surfaces are well forested and provided with lakes. They make fine recreational areas. Elsewhere, the western upland is covered with fertile, black soil that provides good agricultural land.

Climate

Like the other Prairie Provinces, Manitoba has a continental climate. Winters are long and cold. Summers are short and occasionally quite warm. Snow comes in November and lasts until April. Farmers can count on a frost-free season varying from 120 days in the south to about 100 days at The Pas on the northern edge of the farming region. North of this, farming is not profitable. At the port of Churchill on Hudson Bay, the ground is permanently frozen.

Annual precipitation around Winnipeg is about 500 millimeters (20 inches). Farther west it drops to 400 millimeters (16 inches). About a fourth of the precipitation falls as snow. Most rain falls in the spring and early

Railroad yard at Winnipeg, transportation center of the prairie region.

summer, when newly planted grain needs it most. Usually the fall season is dry enough to allow the easy harvest of grain crops.

Natural Resources

Manitoba's chief natural resources are excellent soil, minerals, forests, waterpower, wildlife, and fish. Southern Manitoba has rich, black soils that are highly productive. Forests cover much of the Canadian Shield. The major minerals include nickel, zinc, copper, gypsum, clay, and limestone. The Canadian Shield is believed to contain untold resources, including gold, silver, and iron, waiting to be developed. There are oil deposits in southwest Manitoba. Among the creatures of the forests are fur-bearing animals such as fox, beaver, and muskrat. Many kinds of fish are found in the lakes.

▶ THE PEOPLE AND THEIR WORK

Most of the people live in the southern part of the province. One half of them live in the metropolitan Winnipeg area. But it was not always this way. When Manitoba became a province in 1870, nine out of ten people lived on farms or in rural areas. But farming areas have steadily lost people. With the development of modern machinery, small farms combine to make large farms that require fewer workers. Today only 6 percent of the people live on farms. The rural population of Manitoba is heaviest in the Red River Valley. Many people live in small towns, villages, pulpwood camps, and mining communities.

Manitoba's people come from different backgrounds. The largest group (over 40 percent) is of British origin. Ukrainians are next in number, followed by Germans, French Canadians, and Poles. Among the early settlers were Mennonites from the Ukraine. They are farmers who live mainly in the southern part of the Red River Valley. Another group is made up of Hutterites, who originated in Russia and went to Canada by way of the United States. They live in villages and own everything communally. As early as 1875, Icelanders settled along the shores of Lake Winnipeg and Lake Manitoba, where their descendants still carry on fishing and farming. Manitoba has the largest concentration of French Canadians in western Canada. They settled near the banks of the Red and Assiniboine rivers. Many live in small towns and continue to speak French.

Manitoba has some 30,000 Indians, many of whom live on reserves (reservations) scat-

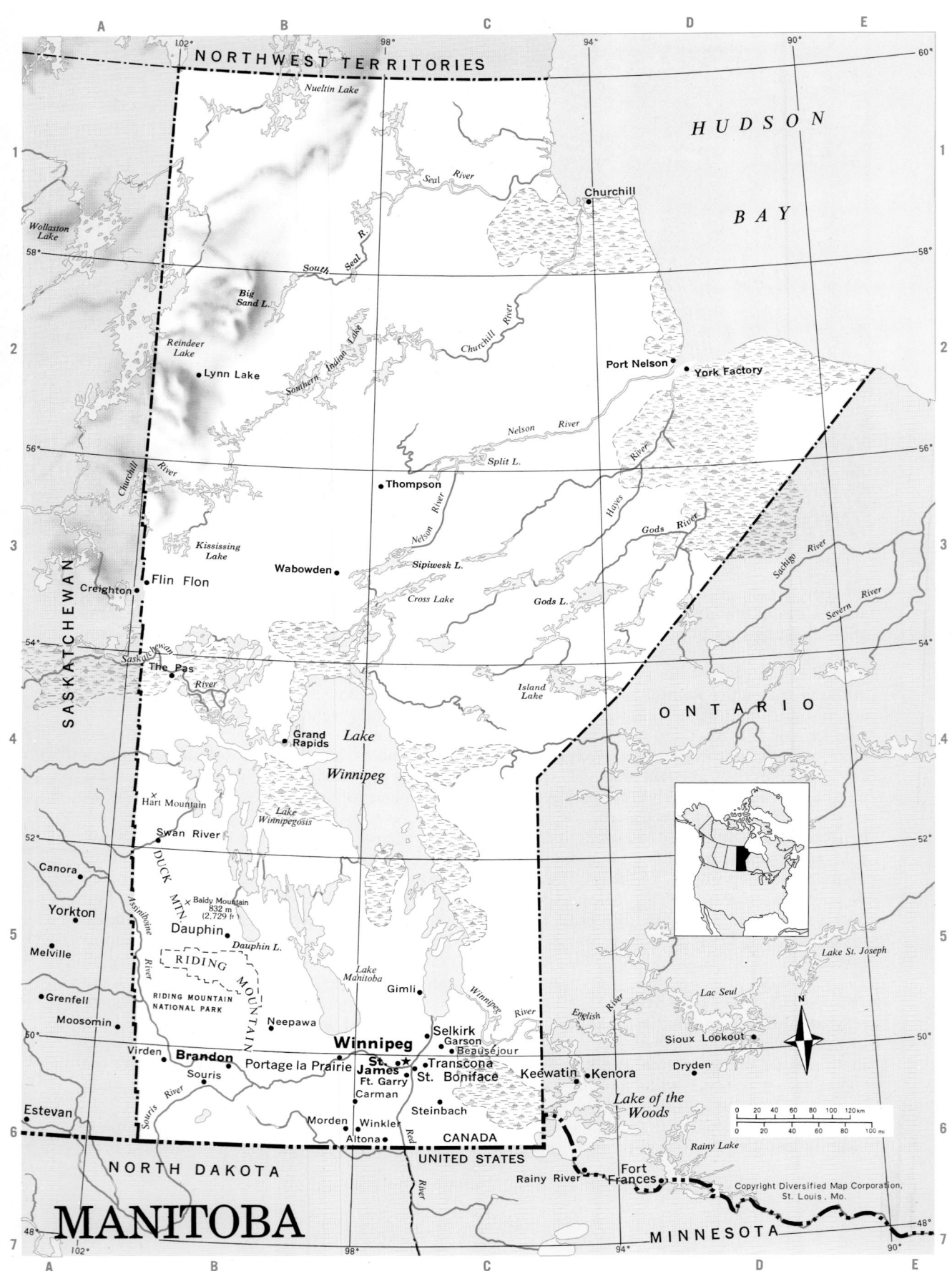

MANITOBA

NORTHWEST TERRITORIES

HUDSON

BAY

Nueltin Lake

Seal River

Churchill

South Seal R.

Big Sand L.

Reindeer Lake

Churchill River

Lynn Lake

Port Nelson • York Factory

Nelson River

Southern Indian Lake

SASKATCHEWAN

Churchill River

Split L.

Thompson

Nelson River

Kississing Lake

Hayes River

Gods River

Creighton • Flin Flon

Wabowden

Sipiwesk L.

Sachigo River

Severn River

Cross Lake

Gods L.

ONTARIO

Saskatchewan River

The Pas

Island Lake

Grand Rapids

Lake

×Hart Mountain

Winnipeg

Lake Winnipegosis

DUCK MTN

Swan River

Canora

×Baldy Mountain
832 m
(2,729 ft)

Yorkton

Dauphin

Dauphin L.

RIDING

Melville

RIDING MOUNTAIN
NATIONAL PARK

MOUNTAIN

Lake Manitoba

Gimli

Winnipeg River

Lake St. Joseph

Grenfell

Neepawa

English River

Lac Seul

N

Moosomin

Selkirk

Sioux Lookout

Virden

Brandon

Portage la Prairie

Winnipeg

Garson
Beauséjour

Dryden

Souris

St. James

Transcona

Estevan

Souris River

Ft. Garry

St. Boniface

Keewatin • Kenora

Carman

Morden

Winkler

Steinbach

Lake of the
Woods

0 20 40 60 80 100 120 km
0 20 40 60 80 100 mi

Altona

CANADA

Red River

UNITED STATES

Copyright Diversified Map Corporation,
St. Louis, Mo.

NORTH DAKOTA

Rainy Lake

UNITED STATES

Rainy River • Fort
Frances

MINNESOTA

Air view of Winnipeg. Legislative Building is in the foreground.

tered throughout the province. There are also about 30,000 métis—people mainly of mixed Indian and French background.

Industries and Products

Agriculture, manufacturing, mining and the processing of minerals, forest industries, fishing, hydroelectric power, and tourism—all add a share to the economy of the province.

Agriculture. Only 13 percent of the total area of the province is farmed. But this still amounts to much fertile farmland. Wheat, barley, and oats are the chief grain crops. Many farms produce cattle, hogs, and poultry.

Market gardening and dairy farming are important along the Red River north and south of Winnipeg. Many special crops such as sunflower seeds, sugar beets, corn, potatoes, and vegetables for canning are produced in the southern Red River Valley and near Portage la Prairie. Large grain farms are found on the western plains.

Manufacturing. The leading manufacturing industries—meat-packing and flour milling— are based on local agriculture. Winnipeg and Brandon are the main food processing centers. The iron and steel industry is located mainly in Selkirk and Winnipeg, where transportation equipment, farm implements, mining machinery, and structural steel are produced. Other manufactured products are aircraft engines, clothing, fur garments, and printed materials.

Mineral Industries. Nickel is the most important mineral in Manitoba. It comes chiefly from mines at Thompson and Lynn Lake. Zinc and copper are mined at Flin Flon. Petroleum is produced in southwest Manitoba near Virden. In parts of the Red River Plain, deposits of gypsum and clay are mined. Excellent hard limestone for buildings is quarried east of Winnipeg, at Garson and Tyndall. Ore smelters are located at Thompson and Flin Flon. Oil refineries using oil chiefly from Alberta are located in Winnipeg and Brandon.

Forest Industries. One third of Manitoba is covered with commercially productive forests. The most important forests lie in the southern part of the Canadian Shield. Spruce trees are in demand for pulp and paper. Other trees are made into plywood, mining timber, telephone poles, fence posts, and rough lumber for construction work.

Fur Trade. Indians and métis in the northern woods still make a living by fur trapping. But most of Manitoba's furbearing animals are raised on fur ranches. Mink and muskrat are the chief furs produced this way.

Commercial Fishing. Freshwater fishing is a small but important industry. Commercial fishing is based chiefly on Lakes Winnipeg, Manitoba, and Winnipegosis and in the larger lakes in northern Manitoba. Species include whitefish, pickerel, saugers, and northern pike.

Waterpower. Hydroelectric power is one of Manitoba's chief assets in attracting industry. The chief sources are the power plants on the Winnipeg, Saskatchewan, and Nelson rivers. The Nelson has many other potential sites.

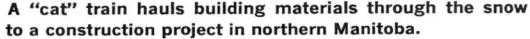

The International Nickel Co. mine at Thompson, one of the world's largest nickel-producing centers.

The Grand Rapids power plant on the Saskatchewan River produces much of Manitoba's hydroelectric power.

A "cat" train hauls building materials through the snow to a construction project in northern Manitoba.

Tourism. Manitoba's lakes and connecting waterways, forest areas, and parks attract about 2,000,000 tourists yearly. Fishing and hunting, canoeing, waterskiing, and sailing are popular summer activities.

Transportation and Communication

Winnipeg's role in transportation is similar to that of Chicago. Centrally located in Canada, Winnipeg is the focal point of all road, air, and rail lines. Both the Canadian National and Canadian Pacific railways pass through Winnipeg. An important branch line, the Hudson Bay Railway, extends north to Churchill. The Winnipeg International Airport is one of the largest airports in Canada.

Highways serve all parts of southern Manitoba and extend north to Grand Rapids, The Pas, Flin Flon, and Thompson. But more than half the province has no road or rail connections. Freight boats serve settlements along the shores of Lake Winnipeg. In the north, rivers and lakes provide landing places for small aircraft. Mining towns that were once isolated from the rest of the province can now be reached quickly by plane.

Manitoba has two daily newspapers and a number of foreign-language papers that serve its varied ethnic communities. There are several television and a number of radio stations.

▶ EDUCATION

The first schools in Manitoba were provided by the churches. In 1871 a public school system was established.

Children in outlying districts are transported to central schools by a school-bus system. School attendance is compulsory from 7 to 16 years of age. The Canadian Government provides schools for the Indians on the Indian reserves. Special schools are also provided for technical and vocational training.

The University of Manitoba, located in Winnipeg, is the largest university in the province. Other universities are the University of Winnipeg, formerly United College, and Brandon University, in Brandon. There are several community colleges.

Libraries and Museums. Public libraries are located in all cities and towns. Regional libraries serve the rural areas. Special libraries in Winnipeg include the Manitoba Legislative Library and the Public Archives of Manitoba.

The Manitoba Provincial Museum in Winnipeg specializes in natural history. Other museums are the Winnipeg Museum of Man and Nature and the St. Boniface Historical Museum. The Winnipeg Art Gallery is one of Canada's finest. The Manitoba Theatre Centre is in Winnipeg.

▶ PLACES OF INTEREST

The following are among the many scenic, historical, and recreational areas.

Assiniboine Park, in Winnipeg, contains one of the largest zoos in Canada.

Churchill, on Hudson Bay, serves as the terminus of the Hudson Bay Railway and gives Manitoba an outlet to the sea.

Delta Waterfowl Sanctuary, on Lake Winnipeg, is an important wildlife research center.

Grand Rapids Power Plant, on the Saskatchewan River, is the site of Manitoba's largest dam and hydroelectric power plant.

International Peace Garden, on the Manitoba-North Dakota boundary, is a monument to peaceful relations between Canada and the United States.

Lower Fort Garry, on the banks of the Red River north of Winnipeg, is a museum and the oldest standing stone fort in western Canada.

Ojibway Indians Mosaics, in Whiteshell Provincial Park, are large stone figures of birds, animals, and reptiles made by prehistoric Indians.

Riding Mountain National Park is a famous recreational area and a buffalo sanctuary.

St. Andrews Church, built by the Selkirk settlers, is the oldest church in western Canada.

▶ CITIES

A diagonal line—from the southeast corner of Manitoba northwest to The Pas—divides the almost uninhabited north and the well-settled south. Winnipeg, the capital, is the largest city and the chief industrial and transportation center of Manitoba. An article on Winnipeg appears in Volume W.

Brandon, Manitoba's second largest city, has a population of over 35,000. It is an industrial and marketing center and the home of a provincial university. Thompson and Portage la Prairie have populations of over 13,000. Selkirk has about 10,000 people, Dauphin about 9,000, and Flin Flon about 8,000. Thompson and Flin Flon are northern mining cities. Selkirk depends largely on steel mills. The others are mainly supply centers for farming districts.

GOVERNMENT

Manitoba is a self-governing province. Like the other provinces, it is headed by a premier, who is chosen from the controlling party in the provincial assembly. The lieutenant governor is appointed by the governor-general of Canada and is the titular head of the province. Manitoba is represented in the federal parliament by 6 appointed senators and 14 elected members of the House of Commons.

HISTORY

In 1612 a British explorer-trader, Sir Thomas Button, visited the western coast of Hudson Bay and claimed the entire area for England. He spent the first winter at the mouth of the Nelson River and traded with the Indians for furs. Other English explorers and fur traders followed, gradually pushing northward and westward as they explored the rivers that flowed into Hudson Bay.

In 1670 King Charles II of England granted a charter to the Hudson's Bay Company giving it the right to all lands draining into Hudson Bay. This huge area was named Rupert's Land after Prince Rupert, the first director of the company. It included Manitoba and most of the other Prairie Provinces.

From 1670 to 1870 the Hudson's Bay Company controlled the vast interior of British North America. York Factory on Hudson Bay and, later, Fort Garry served as the principal forts and trading posts in the fur trade. In 1811, Lord Selkirk, a Scottish philanthropist, bought 260,000 square kilometers (100,000 square miles) of land in the Red River Valley from the Hudson's Bay Company. He planned to establish a farming colony for poverty-stricken Scottish and Irish tenant farmers. This was the Red River colony in southern Rupert's Land. By the late 1860's the Selkirk colony had grown to about 12,000 settlers. Many of the new settlers came from Ontario. Many others were métis. From time to time conflicts arose between the settlers, who were farmers, and the métis, who saw the settlers as a threat to their fur trade.

When the Dominion of Canada was formed, in 1867, the Canadian Government wanted to acquire Rupert's Land. By 1870 Canada had bought the rights to the western land from the Hudson's Bay Company and made it part of the Northwest Territories.

The Red River colonists resented this. They wanted to join Confederation as a separate province—not part of a loosely organized territory. Negotiations resulted in the Manitoba Act of 1870, by which the new Province of Manitoba (the fifth province) was formed. The land was opened to settlers through free land grants called homesteads.

Gradually the lands of the Red River and Assiniboine valleys were settled. By 1891 there were 150,000 people living in Manitoba. In 1901 there were 250,000 and in 1921, 620,000. By the beginning of World War I no good free land was left.

In 1870, when Manitoba became a province, its area extended over only the south central part. Because of its small size, it was known as "the postage stamp province." In 1881 the borders were extended to the present east-west boundaries, and north to 53° north latitude. In 1912 the northern boundary was extended to its present limit of 60° north latitude.

THOMAS R. WEIR
University of Manitoba

IMPORTANT DATES

1612 Thomas Button explored the west coast of Hudson Bay and wintered at the mouth of the Nelson River.

1670 King Charles II of England granted a charter to the Hudson's Bay Company.

1690–1692 Henry Kelsey explored inland from Hudson Bay as far west as Saskatchewan.

1738–1739 The Sieur de la Vérendrye reached the present site of Winnipeg.

1812 Lord Selkirk established the first permanent agricultural settlement on the Red River.

1821 The North West Company merged with the Hudson's Bay Company.

1835 Upper Fort Garry erected by the Hudson's Bay Company at the forks of the Red and Assiniboine rivers.

1869 Louis Riel led a rebellion (Red River Rebellion) against the Canadian government; rebellion put down by Canadian troops.

1870 Manitoba became the fifth province of Canadian Confederation.

1876 First shipment of wheat exported from Manitoba.

1885 The North West Rebellion suppressed and Louis Riel executed.

1912 Present boundaries of Manitoba established.

1924 Manitoba Wheat Pool organized.

1932 International Peace Gardens opened on the international boundary between Manitoba and North Dakota.

1960 Atomic Energy of Canada development started on the Winnipeg River.

1964 Grand Rapids hydroelectric project began producing power.

1965 First reactor opened at the Whitehall Nuclear Research Establishment on the Winnipeg River.

1967 Pan-American Games held in Winnipeg.

1970 Manitoba celebrated its 100th anniversary as a province of Canada.

1979 Canada Winter Games held at Brandon.

MANN, HORACE (1796–1859)

The man who has been called the father of the American free public school was born on a farm in Franklin, Massachusetts, on May 4, 1796. Perhaps it was his own lack of proper schooling that led Horace Mann to struggle for the important reforms in education that he helped bring about.

When Horace Mann was still a boy, his father and brother died. The young Horace had to take over many of their chores. Like most of the children in his town, he was unable to go to school more than eight or ten weeks each year. Then, in 1816, a classics teacher named Samuel Barrett arrived in the town. He began teaching Latin to Horace. In addition, Reverend William Williams, a Baptist minister who lived near the Mann farm, taught him geometry. Both teachers helped Horace, an apt student, enter the sophomore class at Brown University. In 1819, Horace graduated with honors. He went on to study law in Connecticut, and in 1823, he became a member of the Massachusetts bar.

Mann was married twice. In 1830 he married Charlotte Messer, who died two years later. His second wife was Mary Tyler Peabody, whom he married in May, 1843. They had three children.

Mann entered politics and served in the Massachusetts legislature from 1827 to 1837. As president of the state Senate, he signed a historic education bill that became a law on April 20, 1837. This bill set up a state board of education. Mann was asked to be the board's first secretary. He willingly gave up a successful legal practice and political career because of his great desire to serve the cause of education.

During the twelve years that he was secretary of the board of education, Mann reorganized the public school system. Through his efforts the first state-supported normal school for the training of elementary-school teachers was established in 1839 at Lexington, Massachusetts. By 1840 there were three normal schools in Massachusetts.

Under Mann's leadership, a law was passed that increased the school year to a minimum of six months. Through his efforts more public money was made available for building schools, and the teachers received badly needed increases in their salaries. The twelve annual reports he submitted are still read by students of American education.

Mann was elected to the United States House of Representatives in 1848 to fill the vacancy caused by the death of John Quincy Adams. In 1852, Mann was offered the nomination for governor of Massachusetts. He declined in order to accept the presidency of Antioch College in Yellow Springs, Ohio. He continued as president of Antioch until his death there on August 2, 1859. In his last commencement address at Antioch, Mann said, ''Be ashamed to die until you have won some victory for humanity.''

Reviewed by Jonathan C. Messerli
Author, *Horace Mann, A Biography*

MANNERS. See Etiquette.

MANUFACTURING

The objects you use every day at home and at school were made from raw materials. Someone took these materials and turned them into pencils, books, shirts, or chairs. Making raw materials into useful products is called manufacturing.

Manufacturing is the shaping and changing of materials. This can be done by cutting away unwanted pieces, beating or stretching the material, or changing it by heating or chemical processing. When the materials are prepared and shaped, the final product can be made.

People in small, non-industrialized societies use the simplest manufacturing methods and tools. People in industrialized nations usually have developed more complex methods and tools with which to manufacture products.

The development of modern manufacturing was based on two things—sources of power and machines. For centuries the only sources of power were human and animal strength and waterwheels. Machines could not be used efficiently because there was no good way to power them. The invention of a practical steam engine in the 18th century provided the power that was needed. The rapid growth of industry at that time, known as the Industrial Revolution, was based on the power of the

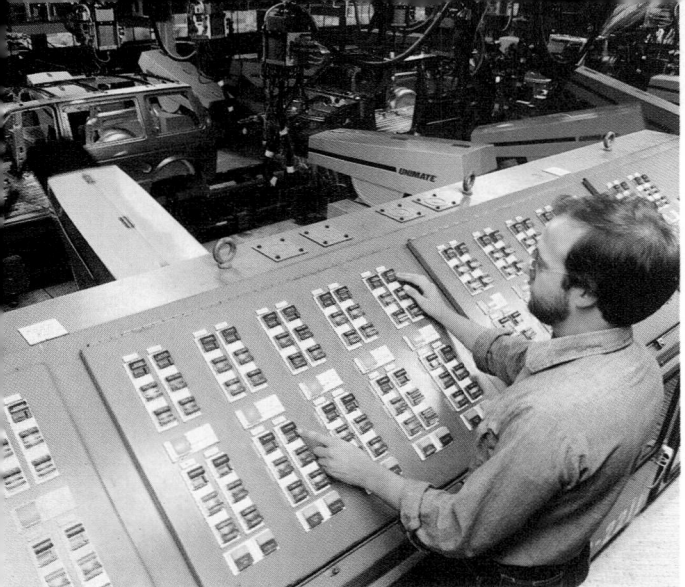

Computers are now important in many manufacturing processes. In this Canadian assembly plant, one worker at a control station directs many complex operations.

steam engine. Later other sources of power, such as electricity, were developed.

The discovery of a cheap way to produce steel was another important event. For many years, iron was the chief industrial metal. But steel is stronger and easier to work than iron. When Henry Bessemer introduced a cheap steelmaking process in 1856, steel began to replace iron for most uses. Besides being used to make tools and machines for factories, steel became valuable as a raw material for a great number of products.

As industries began using machinery to help increase production, another problem arose. To use the machines efficiently, manufacturing had to be planned and organized to get the most production. The machines had to work together to produce the final product.

New Ways of Organizing Manufacturing

Until the Industrial Revolution, manufacturing was organized in a casual way. Artisans did their work in small shops or in their own homes. In making textiles, for instance, spinners would spin the yarn in their homes. The yarn was then taken to the weavers' cottages, where it was woven into cloth.

The Industrial Revolution introduced many changes. The new machines could not be jammed into a worker's cottage. Factories were built to house the machinery. Conditions were harsh and unpleasant, especially in the early years of industrialization, but production was faster. Later changes helped make

manufacturing even more efficient. The most important of these changes were the standardization of parts, assembly-line production, and automation.

Standardized parts are important to mass production. Instead of making one part at a time, large quantities of a part are made. For example, a clock manufacturer will make all the mainsprings of the same type clock the same, all the minute hands the same, and so on. Since a particular part is identical to all its mates, the parts are interchangeable. A manufacturer wanting to put a clock together can use any one of the mainsprings made.

Speed of production is one of the advantages of this method. The separate parts can be put together rapidly to make many duplicates of a product. Another advantage is that it is cheaper for workers to make parts in large quantities than to make a few at a time.

The idea of standardized parts was developed early in the 1800's by two Americans— Simeon North and Eli Whitney, the inventor of the cotton gin. Both North and Whitney had their own workshops for manufacturing guns for the U.S. Government. Each man had the idea independently of the other to use standardized parts for the guns. After all the separate parts were made, a gun was assembled by passing it from one worker to another, with each worker adding a new part. Other manufacturers soon started using this method. Some of the first products, besides guns, to be made with standardized parts were clocks, watches, sewing machines, and farm machinery.

Rapid production was achieved by using both standardized parts and a moving assembly line. Henry Ford (1863–1947) was one of the first manufacturers to use this method in making automobiles. The bare frame of the famous Model T Ford started at one end of the assembly line. As the frame moved slowly along the conveyor, parts were added. Each worker was responsible for putting on a part —a fan belt or a door handle, for example.

With this method the time needed to assemble a car was eventually reduced from 12 hours and 23 minutes to only 93 minutes. Soon cars were being mass-produced by the thousands.

Automation

Production can be faster and easier if machines run and control themselves. This is called automation. The word is a short way of saying "automatic mechanization."

Advancement in automation has been rapid since World War II. At that time, research was focused on devices that could automatically guide airplanes, missiles, and rockets. Much of this research has been applied to making automatic controls for factory machinery.

In many factories today, at least part of the production is performed by automated machines. Some of these machines are robots, with "arms" and "hands" that perform tasks on the assembly line. There are some fully automated factories that use few workers but turn out large quantities of products. Bottles, cans, light bulbs, paper, and cigarettes are some of the things made by automated production. Many oil refineries are automated.

New Materials

Chemically made (synthetic) substances are among the most important new materials that are manufactured. One of the first such materials was the artificial textile fiber rayon. It is made of cellulose. Many other synthetic fibers, such as nylon, Dacron, and Orlon, were developed later. These fibers are replacing natural fibers such as wool and cotton for many purposes. To learn more about these new fibers, see the article NYLON AND OTHER SYNTHETIC FIBERS in Volume N.

Plastics, which are also chemically produced, have come into wide use in the past 25 years. Plastics are used for a great variety of products—everything from raincoats to ballpoint pens. Most of the new plastics are made from coal, natural gas, and petroleum. An article on PLASTICS appears in Volume P.

Manufacturing in the United States

Between 1800 and 1900, the United States changed from an agricultural to an industrial country. The greatest changes were made after the U.S. Civil War. In 1820 more than 70 percent of the people were engaged in farming. By 1900 this figure had dropped to about 40 percent, and by 1980 less than 4 percent of all workers were employed in farming. As industry grew, people left the farms and moved to jobs in factories. Automated farm machinery helped food production remain high even with the loss of farm workers.

In recent years another change has taken place. The number of production workers in

Electronic robots work on many automobile assembly lines. They can work almost nonstop, need little care, and, if programmed properly, do not make mistakes.

manufacturing has dropped, mostly because of automation. The number of office jobs has increased. More and more people have gone into professional jobs as lawyers, doctors, and teachers.

Manufacturing Around the World

Most of the nations of Europe are highly industrialized. In Asia, Japan is the leading industrial country. India and Communist China are in the early stages of industrial development.

In many nations of the world, industrialization is not yet well established. This is especially true in Africa, much of Asia, and South America. One of the first problems the underdeveloped countries must solve is the production of enough food to feed their people. When that problem is taken care of, the countries should be able to make rapid industrial progress. They will be able to use much of the knowledge already available in the industrialized nations.

PHILMORE B. WASS
University of Connecticut

See also AUTOMATION; INDUSTRIAL REVOLUTION; INDUSTRY; IRON AND STEEL; MASS PRODUCTION; ROBOTS.

MANUSCRIPTS, ILLUMINATED. See ILLUMINATED MANUSCRIPTS.

Mao Tse-tung's portrait heads a Peking parade.

MAO TSE-TUNG (1893-1976)

Mao Tse-tung, revolutionary leader and poet, was the founder of the People's Republic of China and its ruler for nearly 30 years. He was born on December 26, 1893, in Shao Shan, a village in Hunan province, South China. His father, a stern man, was a successful rice merchant and farmer.

Mao went to a nearby primary school. When he was thirteen, his father made him give up schooling for farm work. By that time the boy already had a great love for books—especially those filled with adventures and rebellions.

Mao worked on the farm for three years and then returned to school, where he was a brilliant but rebellious student. When the Chinese revolution against the Manchu dynasty broke out in 1911, he joined the revolutionary army. Mao stayed in the army for six months and then resumed his schooling. He was disappointed with the new Chinese Republic and thought the revolution had failed to win needed reforms. At school Mao headed a group of students who debated how to achieve those reforms.

In 1918 Mao went to Peking. He worked in the Peking University library as a fetcher of newspapers, but on the side he edited a monthly paper of his own. On May 4, 1919, the Peking students rebelled against the government. An associate of Mao's was the guiding spirit of this movement, which protested the transfer of former German lands, or "concessions," in China to Japan. Though most of these students were Socialists, a few called themselves Communists.

In July, 1921, Mao was one of the founding members of the Chinese Communist Party, which met in Shanghai. Within six years he had become one of the party's most important members.

The Communists joined forces with the Kuomintang, China's chief party of reform. But suddenly, in 1927, Chiang Kai-shek, leader of the Kuomintang, turned on the Communists and began to massacre them. Mao and his followers set up a base in the mountains of Kiangsi province and fought off five Kuomintang attacks. Then, with Chou En-lai and Chu Teh, the Commander-in-Chief of the Red Army, he led the Communist armies on the Long March. This 9,700-kilometer (6,000 mile) trek took them to the borders of Tibet and then north to the valley of Yenan, where, in 1936, they set up a power base.

In the following year the Japanese invaded China. For a time the Kuomintang and the Communists united against the common enemy—but this unity did not last long. Chiang Kai-shek's armies were forced to retreat while the Communist guerrilla armies fought on behind the Japanese lines. By the time the Japanese were defeated in 1945, it was clear that the Communists had more support among the Chinese people than did Chiang Kai-shek's forces. A civil war followed, ending in a Communist victory in 1949.

In Peking, on October 1, 1949, Mao proclaimed the People's Republic of China. The landlords were stripped of their holdings, the government took control of industry, and communes (communities where everything is owned in common) were set up. The entire country came under the control of the Communist Party. The control was so rigid that Mao feared the revolutionary spirit would die out. At various times, without much success, he tried to lessen the power of the Communist bureaucrats (government officials). The Great Proletarian Cultural Revolution in the late 1960's, led largely by Mao's wife, Chiang Ching, was an effort to cleanse the bureaucracy by giving power to young soldiers called Red Guards.

Mao's health began to fail in the late 1960's. He died in 1976 at the age of 82.

ROBERT PAYNE
Author, *Mao Tse-tung*

MAPLE SYRUP AND MAPLE SUGAR

Maple syrup and sugar are made from the sap of maple trees. The maple trees that are tapped, or opened, for maple sap, are all native to North America. Eighty percent of the maple syrup and sugar produced in North America comes from the Canadian province of Quebec. In the United States the leading producers of these products are New York and Vermont.

Long before Europeans appeared in North America, the Indians knew how to make maple syrup and sugar. In late winter or early spring, they made gashes in the trees with their tomahawks. They put in a reed or a piece of grooved bark for a spout and caught the sap in a trough or birchbark dish. The sap was reduced to a thick syrup by dropping hot stones into it. This syrup was dark in color. It had a smoky taste and contained impurities.

The Indians showed the European settlers how to make maple syrup and sugar. Often maple sugar was the only sugar the settlers could get. Sugar from sugarcane was scarce. Today, cane sugar is comparatively inexpensive and plentiful. Maple sugar is still used. But because of its high cost, it has become something of a delicacy. It is used to make candies and flavorings. Maple syrup is used on waffles, pancakes, French toast, ice-cream sundaes, and other foods. It can be used in baking, as a substitute for molasses.

▶ **THE SUGAR MAPLE TREE**

The sugar maple tree, sometimes called the hard or rock maple, is the best maple for sugar making. The sap from it is sweeter than the sap of black, silver, and other maple trees. The sugar maple lives a long time. It is easy to grow, but it grows slowly. The trees are not ready to be tapped until they are about 40 years old and about 30 centimeters (12 inches) in diameter.

During the winter the starch that the tree made during the previous summer and stored in its roots is turned to sugar. In early spring, sap begins to rise in the trees, gathering sugar with it.

Many factors determine the flow of the sap and the quality of the final product. The type of tree and its age, health, and size are all important. The quantity of leaves on the tree during the previous summer and the condition of the roots also affect the sap. The weather, both during the previous summer and during the sugaring season, can change the flow. Frosty nights and thawing days—days of 7 to 10°C (45 to 50°F)—provide ideal sapflowing weather.

▶ **PRODUCING SYRUP AND SUGAR**

At the beginning of the sugaring season, a small hole is bored in the tree trunk, about 90 centimeters (3 feet) above the ground. A spout is driven in, and a bucket is hung on it. Today, many farmers use plastic bags or plastic tubes connected to the spouts. From the tubes the sap flows into a pipeline system that takes it to storage tanks in the sugarhouse. Adding a vacuum pump to the pipeline can increase the flow of sap by as much as one half.

Immediately after the sap is collected, it is strained. Then it is boiled in huge evaporating pans. Steam from the boiling sap rolls out of an opening in the sugarhouse roof—sometimes until very late at night.

When the sap has been boiled to 104°C (219°F), it has become maple syrup. It must be boiled for a longer period of time for maple sugar.

Saps vary in sweetness. Some saps have 1 percent sugar. Others contain up to 6 percent sugar. It takes an average of 130 liters (35 gallons) of sap to make 4 liters (1 gallon) of syrup. A good tree gives as much as 150 liters (40 gallons) of sap in one season.

MAURICE TESSIER
Agriculture Canada

SUGAR-ON-SNOW PARTIES

When steam is pouring out of the sugarhouses and snow lies all about, sugar-on-snow parties are popular. Maple syrup is boiled for about 15 minutes and then poured over the snow. There it cools to a waxy taffy, which youngsters and grownups alike happily scoop up with forks. For those who do not want to stop eating, sour pickles are served. These cut the sweetness, so the eaters can go right back to enjoying more sugar-on-snow.

If you ever want to have a sugar-on-snow party in the summertime, use large cakes of ice or crushed ice instead of snow. Watch your syrup carefully so that it does not boil over the pan or get very thick. Serve unsugared doughnuts and deviled eggs as well as pickles. It's fun.

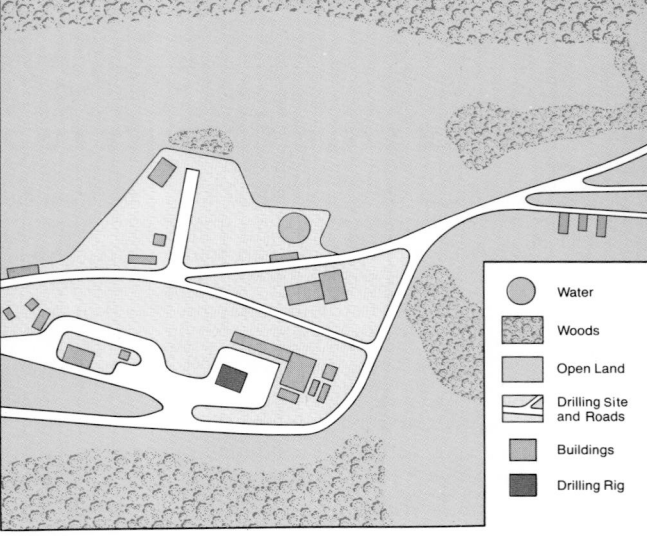

This photograph and map both show the same oil-drilling site. Unlike the photograph, the map uses symbols to represent things. Find the drilling rig in the photograph. Then use the map legend to find the drilling rig on the map.

Legend:
- Water
- Woods
- Open Land
- Drilling Site and Roads
- Buildings
- Drilling Rig

MAPS AND GLOBES

A map is a kind of picture of an area as seen from above. It will usually include symbols and other information to make it easier to understand. A map could show the street on which you live—or the entire world. Maps help people find their way from one place to another and record all kinds of information about people, places, and things.

Because our planet is round, a round globe gives the most accurate picture of the shapes and sizes of the land and water areas of the earth. But flat maps are cheaper and easier to handle, and they can show small areas in greater detail than a globe. For these reasons flat maps are more widely used than globes.

Maps have taken different forms through history. Long ago, Middle Easterners drew maps on clay tablets and directed travelers by arranging stones on the ground. Polynesians once sailed the Pacific using maps made of palm fiber and shells. Later, maps drawn on sheepskin told of trade and treasure routes. Maps once took a long time to make and were very rare and costly. It was not until the printing press and the process of copper engraving had been invented that maps could be produced cheaply and in large quantities. They then became part of everyday life.

The first maps were designed to help people move from place to place. Today maps come in many forms and are used for many purposes. Maps can show how land is used and who owns it. They can depict physical features such as mountains and lakes or record information about population or economic activities. There are even weather, undersea, and star maps. A person who makes maps is called a **cartographer.** The science of map making is known as **cartography.**

▶ MAP SKILLS

To be able to use maps, you must know how to read them. The language of maps is simple, and good maps include instructions to help you understand them. Once you become familiar with the language of maps, you can use them to find out about many things.

Finding Location

One basic use of maps is to locate specific places or features. All location is relative. You need a starting point. All else can then be described as being a certain distance and direction from this point. The earth has two natural starting points—the North and South poles. Because people needed a way to describe location between the two poles, the ancient Greeks invented a **geographic grid.** This grid is still in use today. It is made up of two sets of imaginary lines that cross each other at regular intervals. One set of lines is a series of circles running east and west around the earth parallel to the poles. The other set stretches north and south between the poles. The east-west lines are called **parallels of latitude.** The north-south lines are known as **meridians of**

SOME MAP AND GLOBE TERMS

Arctic Circle—a line of latitude around the north polar region at 66° 30′ N. The **Antarctic Circle** is a line of latitude around the south polar region at 66° 30′ S.

Atlas—a bound volume of maps.

Cartography—the science of map making. A **cartographer** is a person who makes maps.

Compass rose—a symbol used to show direction on a map.

Co-ordinates—a set of two numbers (usually latitude and longitude) used in specifying the location of a point.

Degree—a circle can be divided into 360 equal degrees. A degree, represented by the symbol °, is divided into 60 **minutes,** represented by the symbol ′. Latitude and longitude are shown in degrees.

Globe—a round representation of the earth.

Great circle—an imaginary circle on the earth's surface that divides the earth into two equal parts.

Grid—a network of evenly spaced horizontal and perpendicular lines. Lines of latitude and longitude form an imaginary **geographic grid** on the surface of the earth.

Hemisphere—half of a round object. The equator divides the earth into the **Northern and Southern hemispheres.** The prime meridian and the 180th meridian divide it into the **Eastern and Western hemispheres.**

International date line—an imaginary line at roughly 180° longitude, where a calendar day begins and ends.

Latitude—the distance in degrees north or south of the **equator** (° latitude). A **parallel of latitude** is an imaginary line circling the earth and connecting points on the earth's surface having the same latitude. Parallels of latitude never meet. They are numbered from 0° to 90° north and south of the equator.

    High latitudes are latitudes between 60° and the pole in the Northern and Southern hemispheres.

    Low latitudes are latitudes extending north and south of the equator to 30° latitude.

    Middle latitudes are latitudes between the high and low latitudes.

Longitude—the distance in degrees east or west of the **prime meridian** (0° longitude). A **meridian of longitude** is an imaginary line connecting points on the earth's surface having the same longitude. Meridians of longitude meet at the poles. They are numbered from 0° to 180° east and west of the prime meridian.

Map projection—the method by which the curved surface of the earth is represented on a flat map.

North Pole—the point farthest north on the earth's surface (90° N). The **South Pole** is the point farthest south on the earth's surface (90° S).

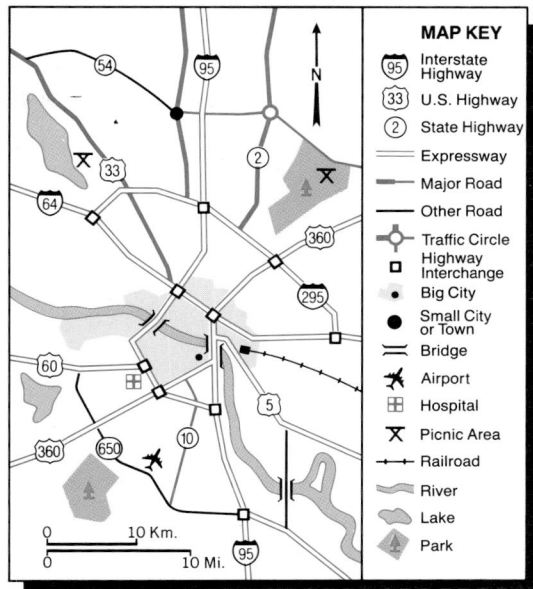

One of the most widely used kinds of maps is the road map. The symbols in the legend make the map easier to understand. On this map, north is at the top. If you were traveling from north to south, you might orient the map by turning it upside down, so that its directions would coincide with directions on the ground.

Orienting a map—making the map's directions coincide with directions on the ground.

Scale—the ratio between distance on a map and distance on the area being mapped.

Sea level—the level that the ocean would reach if it were as still as the water in a pond. Height, or **elevation,** is always measured from sea level, which is the same all over the world. **Contour lines** connect places of equal elevation on a map.

Symbol—something that represents something else. Letters, drawings, lines, and color are used as symbols on maps. The map **legend,** or **key,** is the place on the map where the symbols are explained.

Tropic of Cancer—a line of latitude lying 23° 30′ north of the equator. The **Tropic of Capricorn** is a line of latitude lying 23° 30′ south of the equator.

The globe on the left has been divided at the equator (0° latitude) into two equal halves—the Northern and Southern hemispheres. The globe on the right has been divided in half at the prime meridian (0° longitude) into the Eastern and Western hemispheres.

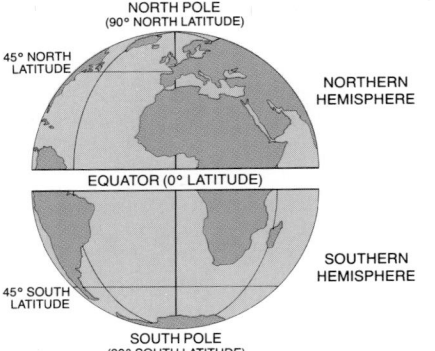

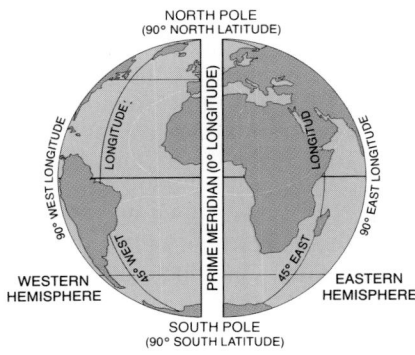

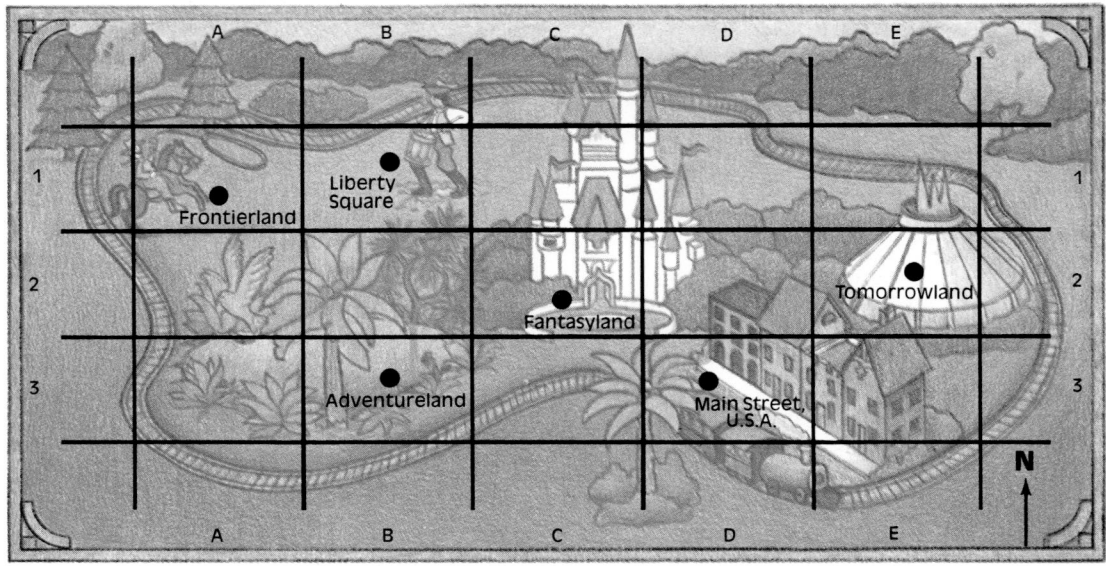

A map grid makes it easier for you to locate places on the map. To find Fantasyland on this map of the Magic Kingdom in Walt Disney World, follow section C to where it crosses section 2. Where on the map would you tell someone to look for Tomorrowland?

longitude. All latitude-longitude grid lines are circles or parts of circles and are shown in degrees (°).

Why do map makers need two sets of lines? Giving location only in latitude would be like telling people that you lived on Main Street instead of telling them that you lived at the corner of Main Street and Second Avenue. A place at 30 degrees north latitude (usually written 30° N) could be in Spain or China, in the middle of the Atlantic or Pacific oceans, or even near New Orleans, Louisiana. But any place on earth can be located exactly if you know both its latitude and its longitude.

There are other kinds of map grids that help you locate places. Many maps have a series of letters beginning with "A" running across the top and bottom of the map, and a series of numbers beginning with "1" running along the right and left margins. To find a place located at A-3 in the **map index** (the list of place names on the map), you just look in the box formed where sections A and 3 cross each other.

Finding Direction

Another thing maps tell us is direction. On most modern maps, north is at the top of the map. But "north" and "up" are not the same. "Up" is away from the surface of the earth. "North" is toward the North Pole. If you face north, east will be to your right, west will be to your left, and south will be behind you.

It is easy to find north on a globe—just look for the North Pole. On a flat map an arrow or

compass rose will tell you which way north is. If you are drawing a map of your town and want to add a compass rose, use a compass— holding it flat—to find north. Many places have features oriented to direction—for example, a city may have a North First Street or an East Meadow Drive.

A map can show direction and distance. If you look at the compass rose, you will be able to tell that the cabin is north of the picnic grounds. Use the map scale and a ruler to find out how far north of the picnic grounds the cabin is. Compare this map's scale to the scale on the map of Chad on the facing page. Which map shows a larger area on the ground?

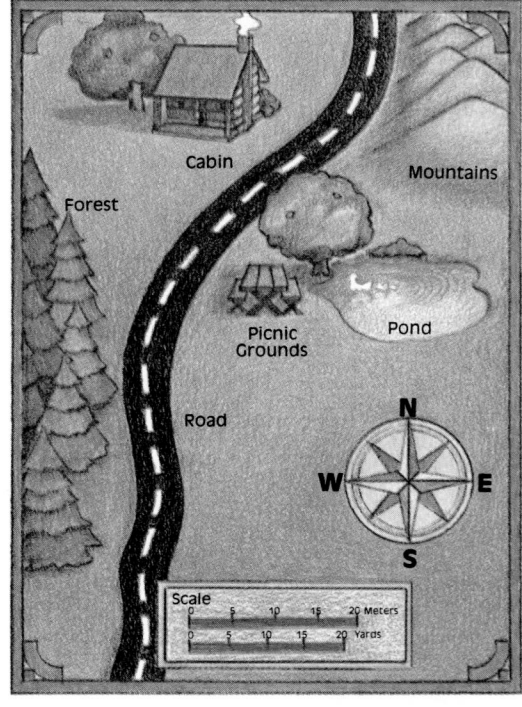

This is one of the many maps used throughout this encyclopedia. Why do you think the tiny map of Africa inserted in the corner is called a locator map? The symbols in the map legend represent the chief products of Chad. Most of these symbols are in southern Chad. Northern Chad, in the Sahara, receives very little rainfall. Where do you think most Chadians live? Why?

Finding Distance

Maps can do more than tell us where and which way. They can also tell us how far. Because areas being mapped are usually hundreds or thousands of times larger than the map itself, cartographers had to find a way to describe the relationship between the map and the area being mapped. So they let a small length on the map represent a large one on the ground. This relationship is called **scale.**

Expressions of scale can be written in several ways. The most common expression of scale on road maps and maps in textbooks or encyclopedias is the **graphic,** or bar, **scale.** This is a line that is subdivided to show distance on the area being mapped. To find the distance between two cities on a map with a graphic scale, mark the distance between the two places on the edge of a piece of paper or on a ruler. Place the paper or ruler along the graphic scale and read the distance. If you want to measure distances along waterways or other curved features, use a piece of string.

A **verbal scale** gives the relationship between the map and the ground in simple English. It might read, ''1 centimeter equals 100 kilometers'' (''1 inch equals 160 miles'').

Cartographers can show elevation on a flat piece of paper by using contour lines to link places of equal elevation. Contour maps are often used to show ocean depths as well as the height of land above sea level. This contour map includes a side view of the mountain being mapped so that you can see the relationship between the contour lines and the area being mapped.

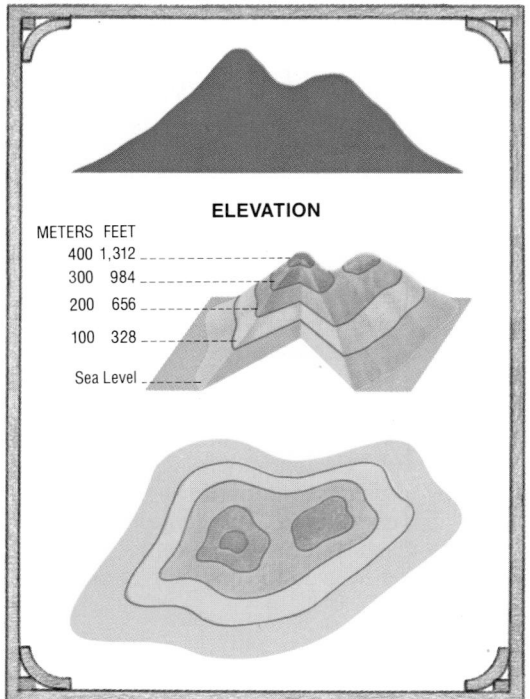

Another scale often used on flat maps is a **representative fraction (RF)** or ratio. This states the relationship between a unit of measurement on the map and the same unit of measurement on the area being mapped. Thus 1/10,000 or 1:10,000 means that 1 centimeter, inch, or other unit on the map represents 10,000 centimeters, inches, or other units on the area being mapped. With an RF scale it does not matter what system of measurement is being used. The larger the second number in the RF, the smaller the scale. The smaller the second number, the larger the scale will be. You can convert a graphic or verbal scale into an RF by multiplying the number of kilometers per centimeter by 100,000 (the number of centimeters in a kilometer) or the number of miles per inch by 63,360 (the number of inches in a mile).

There is another way to find approximate distances between points north and south of each other. Each degree of latitude equals about 111 kilometers (69 miles). If you find the difference in degrees of latitude between two north-south points and multiply it by 111 (or 69), you will get an approximate distance. This method will not work with east-west distances, because meridians of longitude are not the same distance apart along their entire length.

Distances over large areas are measured by **great circles** rather than straight lines. A great circle divides the globe into two equal halves.

The **equator** is a great circle. It divides the earth into the **Northern Hemisphere** and the **Southern Hemisphere.** Any meridian when joined with its opposite is also a great circle. The **prime meridian** (0° longitude) forms a great circle when linked with the 180th meridian. This great circle divides the globe into the **Eastern and Western hemispheres.**

Stretch a string between New York City and Moscow on a flat map and figure the distance between the two cities. Next, take a globe and turn it until both cities lie on the **horizon ring** (the ring going around the globe or from pole to pole). If you position one of the cities at the zero mark on the horizon ring, you can read the distance between the cities. Compare the distance you calculated on the flat map and the distance on the great circle route. Can you see why navigators use great circles to find the shortest distance between two points?

Using Maps to Find Time

Meridians of longitude can be used to tell time at any place in the world. The earth rotates from west to east at the rate of 15 degrees of longitude an hour (360 degrees in 24 hours). The time 15 degrees west of a point is 1 hour earlier; 15 degrees east it is 1 hour later. Thus, when it is 6 P.M. on the East Coast of the United States, it is only 3 P.M. on the West Coast. There has to be some place on the globe for an old calendar day to end and a new one to begin. This place is the international date line, a line roughly following the 180th meridian. If you cross the international date line heading west, "today" becomes "tomorrow." If you cross the line heading east, "today" becomes "yesterday."

Using Map Symbols

Relief or **physical maps** show natural features, such as mountains, oceans, rivers, and islands. **Cultural maps** include people-made features, such as political boundaries, highways, towns, oil wells, and dams. Cartographers often use **symbols** to stand for various features on a map. Map symbols often look like what they represent. The outline of an airplane, for example, may be used to locate airports. Colors, lettering, and lines are also used as symbols. Water, for example, is almost always blue.

Symbols and other information to help you understand the map are usually placed in a box called the **map legend,** or **key.** Since not all maps use the same symbols, it is important to refer to the map legend when using a map.

Physical relief features, such as mountains, hills, and valleys, are among the hardest things to show on a map. This is because they must be shown from above, rather than from ground level. Cartographers deal with this problem by using **contour lines** to show elevation above sea level. The contour lines link points with the same elevation. Color and shading are also used to show elevation.

MAP INDEX

Barranquilla	B-1
Bogotá	B-2
Caracas	C-1
Cartagena	B-1
Maracaibo	B-1
Medellín	B-2
Panama City	B-2
Puerto Rico	C-1

This is part of a physical-cultural map of South America. It shows both natural features of the land and cultural features such as political boundaries and cities. The map legend will help you identify different kinds of vegetation in the region. Use the grid and the map index to find Bogotá and Barranquilla. What direction would you travel to get from Bogotá to Barranquilla? How far would you travel?

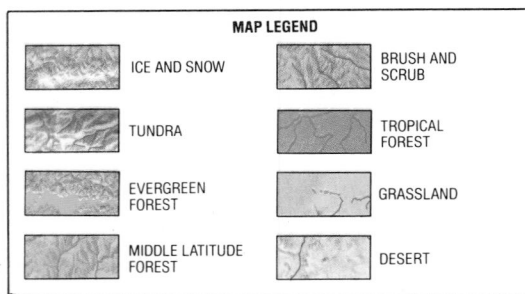

MAP LEGEND

ICE AND SNOW

TUNDRA

EVERGREEN FOREST

MIDDLE LATITUDE FOREST

BRUSH AND SCRUB

TROPICAL FOREST

GRASSLAND

DESERT

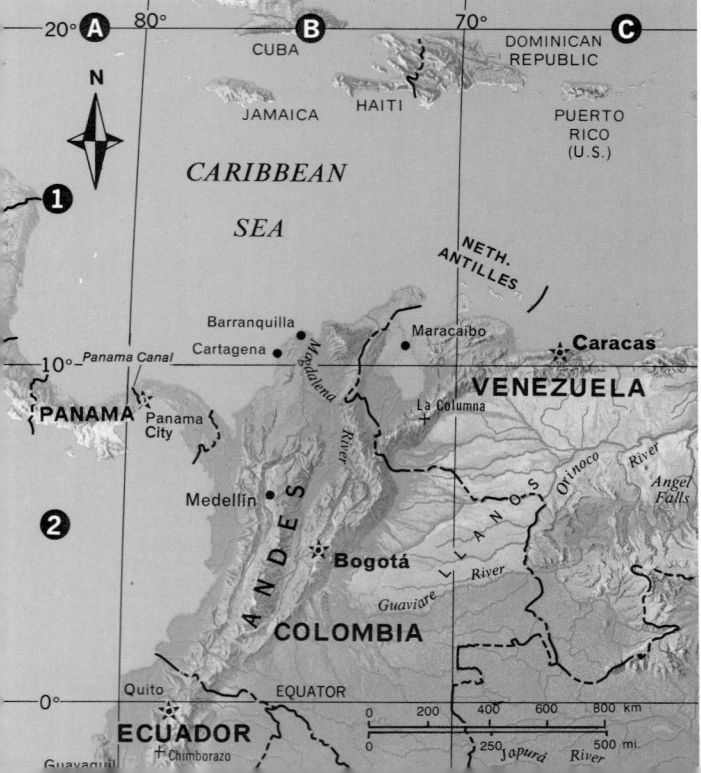

MAP PROJECTIONS

It is impossible to show the surface of the round earth accurately on a flat map. Some parts of the area being mapped will always be distorted (changed in size or shape) or broken apart as they are flattened. The smaller the area being mapped, the less distortion there will be. A city, for example, can be shown on a flat map with no apparent distortion. But distortion is a major problem on flat maps of large areas.

In map making, cartographers project the geographic grid of the round earth onto a flat piece of paper. They generally use mathematical formulas to determine the arrangement and spacing of the lines of latitude and longitude on which the flat map will be drawn. There are many kinds of map projections. Each was invented to keep relatively unchanged some particular property or properties of the round earth, such as distance, area, shape, or direction. The cartographer chooses a projection that will most accurately present the information needed by the people who will be using the map.

Cylindrical Projections. Imagine a cylinder of thin paper enclosing a transparent globe. A light source inside the globe projects the latitude-longitude grid and the continents onto the cylinder. This projection stretches the areas of the land masses toward the top and bottom of the map, although shapes remain true. Compare the sizes and shapes of Greenland and Africa on the Mercator projection below and on a globe. What does this tell you about distortion in a Mercator projection? The Mercator projection was invented by the great Flemish map maker Gerhard Mercator in 1569. It is still useful to navigators because it shows the true direction between any two points.

Conic Projections. Imagine a paper dunce cap (cone) placed over the Northern Hemisphere of a transparent globe. A light in the middle of the globe projects the grid and land features of the hemisphere onto the cone. At the point where the cone touches the globe, distance and direction and shape are true. This kind of projection works well for maps of countries. (A cartographer could make a fairly accurate map of the United States from the conic projection below.) But it is not appropriate for world maps because shapes and sizes away from the point where the cone touches the globe are badly distorted. **Polyconic projections** combine many conic projections, each touching the earth's surface at a different point.

Plane Projections. This time, imagine that a light is projected onto a piece of paper touching the globe at only one point. The point at which the globe and the paper touch is often the North or South pole, but it could be anywhere. Plane projections emphasizing the round shape of the earth are popular for mapping hemispheres. But shapes and sizes are greatly distorted away from the center. The azimuthal equidistant projection below is often used by pilots flying great circle routes over the North Pole. Every point is the correct distance and direction from the center.

Some Other Projections. Interrupted projections like the one below can show the whole world. Land areas are usually accurate, but water areas are broken apart. **Oval projections** like the mollweide projection below can show the whole world without interruption. Area and distance are true, but shape and direction are badly distorted toward the outer edges of the map.

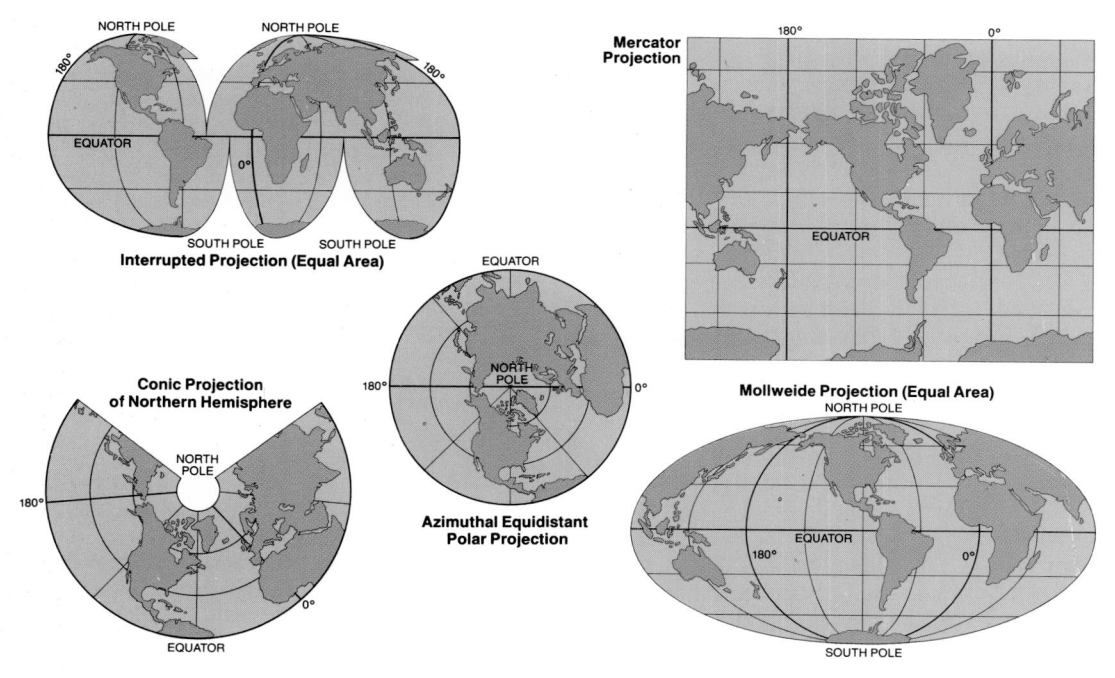

Interrupted Projection (Equal Area)

Conic Projection of Northern Hemisphere

Azimuthal Equidistant Polar Projection

Mercator Projection

Mollweide Projection (Equal Area)

The work of a French map maker of the mid-1500's, this map shows a portion of the northeast coast of Canada as described by explorer Jacques Cartier.

▶A HISTORY OF MAP MAKING

Civilizations throughout history have made and used maps. The oldest surviving maps date back to Babylonian times, more than 4,000 years ago. The ancient Greek geographers, including Herodotus, Pytheas, Eratosthenes, Hipparchus, and Strabo, are recognized as the founders of scientific cartography. Claudius Ptolemy, who lived in the second century A.D., is perhaps the most famous Greek geographer. He explained some of the basic principles of map making in his *Geography*. This work included a number of maps, directions for making a simple projection, and the latitude and longitude for many places in the world.

The Romans used maps to wage war, build roads and aqueducts, and administer their conquered provinces. They were not interested in mathematics, or in how maps were made. After the fall of the Roman Empire, European maps were made mostly in monasteries. Maps usually showed the Holy Land at the center of the world. Scientific cartography during this period was preserved and advanced chiefly by Islamic scholars. The Chinese also made many maps. The oldest printed Chinese map (1155) was made about 300 years before the first map was printed in Europe.

The Age of Exploration and Discovery (1470–1700) increased people's knowledge of the world and led to great advances in cartography. The oldest existing globe (1492) was the work of the German merchant and navigator Martin Behaim. The first map to use the name America was made 15 years later by another German, Martin Waldseemüller. In 1570 the Flemish publisher Abraham Ortelius reproduced many maps of the same size and bound them into the first modern atlas, *Theatrum Orbis Terrarum*. But the term **atlas** did not come to be used for a bound volume of maps until after Gerhard Mercator published his book of maps entitled *Atlas* in 1595.

European explorers and navigators made and used sailing charts. But little attention was given to mapping the inland areas of the continents until the 1700's, when all sorts of commercial and military activities created a great demand for accurate maps. Elaborately decorated atlases were published in Belgium and the Netherlands. France became the leading center of scientific cartography. A new tech-

---

BE YOUR OWN MAP MAKER

Let's explore the nature of contours by making and mapping a mountain. You will need a waterproof container, a large piece of modeling clay, and an old ballpoint pen. Set aside a small piece of the clay. Use the rest to form a make-believe mountain in the shape of an irregular cone. Place the mountain in the container. Put the small piece of clay on the bottom of the container and press the zero end of the ruler into it so that the ruler stands upright. Pour water into the container until it reaches the 2.5 centimeter (1 inch) mark on the ruler. With the pen, draw a line around the mountain where the water touches it. Continue to add water and draw contour lines at 2.5-centimeter (1-inch) intervals until the water covers the mountain. Remove the mountain from the container and look at it from above. The lines you have drawn mark off the contours.

To make a map of your mountain, use a fine wire or a piece of fishing line to cut apart the contour intervals. Cut through each contour line, beginning with the highest one, until all the contour intervals have been removed from the mountain.

Place the lowest contour interval on a heavy piece of paper and trace around its base. Remove the clay interval and set it aside. Place the next higher interval on the paper, positioning it correctly within the first interval's outline. After you have traced around it, place it on top of the clay base. Continue tracing around the clay intervals until you have rebuilt the mountain. When the mountain has been rebuilt, the contour map is complete. Compare the map and the mountain as viewed from above. Can you see why contour lines are a useful way to show relief on a flat map?

nique for measuring latitude and longitude enabled Jean Dominique Cassini (1625–1712) to construct a much more accurate map of the world. Jean's son, Jean Jacques Cassini, began a survey of France in 1733. This was the first of many national surveys undertaken by various European countries during the late 1700's and 1800's. Gradually, surveying and mapping became a government responsibility.

As the United States expanded westward, so many facts needed recording on official documents and verification on official maps that cartographic activity became primarily government sponsored. The U.S. Geological Survey, founded in 1879, began a national mapping program that continues to this day.

Ptolemy and Mercator would be amazed by our maps. We have so many of them. They are not very expensive, and they are colorful and accurate. Modern cartographers, assisted by computers, remote sensing devices, and satellite photographs, can even make maps of the moon, Mars, and the ocean depths.

MICHAEL L. HAWKINS
University of Georgia

See also EQUATOR, INTERNATIONAL DATE LINE; LATITUDE AND LONGITUDE; TIME; GEOGRAPHY; CLIMATE.

MARBLE. See QUARRYING; STONE.

MARBLES

Marbles is a game that is played all over the world. The history of the game goes back to the ancient civilizations of the Nile Valley and the Tigris and Euphrates valleys. Small balls of clay, flint, and bone have been found in the tombs of pharaohs and in caves in Europe dating to prehistoric times. Statues from the pre-Christian era show children playing at "knucklebones," which may have been an early marbles game. (Children in Iran still use sheep's knucklebones for marbles in a game called *ashog*.) The ancient Indian peoples of North America played marbles.

Marbles are mentioned in the writings of the Roman poet Ovid, and historians believe that Emperor Augustus played marbles. As long ago as the 16th century, marbles, or "Taws," was played in England. The game spread to America, and it is known that George Wash-

ington and Thomas Jefferson were marbles players. Abraham Lincoln was expert at a marbles game called "Old Bowler."

A Circle Game. Many marbles games are played in a circle. One of these, "Ringer," is perhaps the most famous. Thirteen marbles are placed in the shape of a cross in the center of a circle 3 meters (10 feet) in diameter. The surface should be hard and level so that shooters can aim accurately. The players try to knock marbles out of the circle by shooting at them—with a special shooting marble—from the edge of the circle. The winner is the first player to knock seven marbles out of the circle. To shoot, a player must "knuckle down," which means that the shooting hand must be turned so that four knuckles rest on the ground. The marble is held in the curved index finger and propelled by the thumb.

Pot, or Hole, Games. "Pot," or "Hole," games are somewhat like miniature golf. The object is to get your shooter into the hole and to knock your opponent's shooter out. If you knock a marble out, you win it. Games can either be played just for fun or for "keepsies." In "keepsies," all marbles won are kept by the winner.

FRED FERRETTI
Author, *The Great American Marble Book*

Marbles are smooth and perfectly round. They may be as small as peas or as large as golf balls. Glassies—glass marbles—may be clear or opaque. A purie is clear (pure) glass, such as the gold marble in the left corner. To the right of the gold purie is a blue aggie. Aggies are made of agate, marble, or limestone.

March

March was originally the first month of the year in the Roman calendar. The Romans named the month after Mars, the god of war. Later March became the third month.

Place in year: 3rd month.
Number of days: 31.
Flowers: Jonquil and daffodil.
Birthstone: Bloodstone or aquamarine.
Zodiac signs: Pisces, the Fishes (February 19–March 20), and Aries, the Ram (March 21–April 19).

1
- **Frédéric Chopin** born 1810
- U.S. Articles of Confederation ratified, 1781
- Ohio became the 17th state, 1803
- Nebraska became the 37th state, 1867

2
- **Samuel Houston** born 1793
- **Pope Leo XIII** born 1810
- **Pope Pius XII** born 1876
- **Dr. Seuss (Theodor Geisel)** born 1904
- **Mikhail Gorbachev** born 1931
- Texas declared its independence from Mexico, 1836
- First round-the-world nonstop airline flight successfully completed, 1949

3
- **Alexander Graham Bell** born 1847
- Missouri Compromise passed, 1820
- Massachusetts became first state to pass child labor laws regulating work hours, 1842
- Florida became the 27th state, 1845
- "The Star Spangled Banner" officially declared the national anthem of the U.S., 1931
- Feast of Dolls (Hina-Matsuri) in Japan
- Independence Day in Morocco

4
- William Penn received the charter to Pennsylvania, 1681
- U. S. Constitution went into effect, 1789
- Vermont became the 14th state, 1791
- Frances Perkins became first woman to be appointed to a U.S. presidential Cabinet, 1933

5
- Redcoats shot at a mob in the Boston Massacre, 1770
- Independence Day in Equatorial Guinea

6
- **Michelangelo** born 1475
- **Elizabeth Barrett Browning** born 1806
- Antonio Santa Anna, Mexican general, captured the Alamo, 1836
- Independence Day in Ghana

7
- **Luther Burbank** born 1849
- **Tomáš Masaryk** born 1850
- **Piet Mondrian** born 1872
- U.S. Congress ratified first treaty with a South American country, Republic of Colombia, 1825
- Alexander Graham Bell patented the telephone, 1876

8
- **Oliver Wendell Holmes, Jr.,** born 1841
- **Kenneth Grahame** born 1859

9
- The *Merrimack* fought the *Monitor* in the U.S. Civil War, 1862

10
- First paper money issued by the U.S., 1862

12
- **William Lyon Mackenzie** born 1795
- Juliette Low founded the organization that became the Girl Scouts of the U.S.A., Savannah, Georgia, 1912
- *National holiday* in Mauritius

13
- **Joseph Priestley** born 1733

14
- **Albert Einstein** born 1879
- Eli Whitney patented the cotton gin, 1794

15
- **Andrew Jackson** born 1767
- Julius Caesar assassinated, 44 B.C.
- Maine became the 23rd state, 1820

16
- **James Madison** born 1751
- U.S. Military Academy founded at West Point, New York, 1802
- U.S. Marines won major victory at Iwo Jima during World War II, 1945

17
- **Kate Greenaway** born 1846
- **Bobby Jones, Jr.,** born 1902
- *St. Patrick's Day* in Ireland and the U.S.

18
- **John C. Calhoun** born 1782
- **Grover Cleveland** born 1837
- Plans announced for formation of NATO, 1949

19
- **David Livingstone** born 1813
- **William Jennings Bryan** born 1860

20
- **Henrik Ibsen** born 1828
- **Martin Brian Mulroney** born 1939

21
- **Johann Sebastian Bach** born 1685
- **Benito Juárez** born 1806
- Vernal equinox, in which day and night are each just 12 hours long all over the world

22
- **Anthony van Dyck** born 1599
- Massacre of settlers in Jamestown, Virginia, 1622

23
- Patrick Henry delivered famous speech in which he declared "Give me liberty or give me death," 1775
- *National holiday* in Pakistan

25
- **Arturo Toscanini** born 1867
- **Béla Bartók** born 1881
- British Parliament abolished slave trade, 1807
- *Independence Day* in Greece

26
- **Benjamin Thompson** born 1753
- **Robert Frost** born 1874

27
- **Tennessee Williams** born 1911
- First savings bank of the U.S. chartered, in New York City, 1819
- *Independence Day* in Bangladesh

28
- Most serious accident in nuclear power industry's history, Three Mile Island, Pennsylvania, 1979

29
- **John Tyler** born 1790

30
- **Francisco Goya** born 1746
- **Vincent van Gogh** born 1853
- U.S. agreed to purchase Alaska from Russia for $7,200,000, 1867
- Fifteenth Amendment to U.S. Constitution, stating that a person cannot be denied the right to vote because of race or color, ratified, 1870

31
- **René Descartes** born 1596
- **Joseph Haydn** born 1732
- Commodore Matthew C. Perry signed treaty between the U.S. and Japan, 1854
- U.S. acquired the Virgin Islands from Denmark, 1917
- Daylight Saving Time introduced in the U.S., 1918
- Newfoundland became the 10th province of Canada, 1949
- *National holiday* in Malta

Holidays that may occur in either March or February: *Shrove Tuesday,* or *Mardi Gras; Ash Wednesday; Purim.* Holidays that may occur in either March or April: *Palm Sunday; Easter; Passover.*

The calendar listing identifies people who were born on the indicated day in boldface type, **like this.** You will find a biography of each of these birthday people in *The New Book of Knowledge.* In addition to citing some historical events and historical firsts, the calendar also lists the holidays and some of the festivals celebrated in the United States. These holidays are printed in italic type, *like this.* See the article HOLIDAYS for more information.

Many holidays and festivals of nations around the world are included in the calendar as well. When the term "national holiday" is used, it means that the nation celebrates an important patriotic event on that day—in most cases the winning of independence. Consult *The New Book of Knowledge* article on the individual nation for further information on its national holiday.

Marconi is shown at age 22 with his wireless receiver, now known as the radio. Several years later, Marconi sent the first radio message across the Atlantic Ocean.

MARCONI, GUGLIELMO (1874–1937)

Guglielmo Marconi, the inventor of wireless telegraphy, was born in Bologna, Italy, on April 25, 1874. He was the son of a successful Italian businessman. His mother was Irish. He was not a strong child and was also very shy, so his parents decided to have him educated at home by private teachers instead of sending him to school.

Guglielmo spent a great deal of his free time reading in the library of the Marconi home. The library had a good collection of science books. Almost as soon as Guglielmo could read, he began to read these books.

By the time he was 12 years old, Guglielmo was working with wires and batteries in an attic workshop he had set up. Then, when he was about 16 years old, he began to study electricity under the guidance of a physics professor. But he never became a regular student at any university.

In the summer of 1894, while on vacation, Marconi read a magazine article about the work of a German scientist, Heinrich Hertz, who had died earlier that year. Hertz had produced certain kinds of electric waves by means of electric sparks. They were called Hertzian waves. (They are now called radio waves.)

Marconi's imagination was fired by what he had read. He thought it might be possible to use these radio waves to send wireless dot-and-dash messages like those used in the telegraph. When he returned from his vacation, Marconi began to experiment in order to work out his ideas. His father encouraged him in this and set aside a part of the garden for these experiments. Within a year, Marconi was successfully sending weak dot-and-dash signals to a receiver across the garden. Before long he was able to send stronger signals that could be received by an assistant 13 kilometers (8 miles) away.

Marconi then recognized that he had a useful invention. He also thought that its greatest use would probably be in communicating with ships at sea. With his father's financial help, he went to England, one of the world's great shipping countries, to perfect his wireless. He felt his invention would be readily received there.

By 1899, Marconi was able to send messages across the English Channel to France, about 45 kilometers (28 miles) away. But his great dream was to set up wireless communication across the Atlantic Ocean. To do this he set sail for America and, on December 6, 1901, landed in Newfoundland. Assistants remained behind to operate a powerful transmitter on the coast of England.

On December 12, 1901, Marconi received a signal in dot-and-dash code sent from the station in England, 4,800 kilometers (3,000 miles) away. Wireless communication across the Atlantic was a success. And within a few years the usefulness of wireless communication from ships at sea was also proved.

Many countries now showered honors on Marconi. He became a wealthy man. In 1909 he won the Nobel prize in physics for his invention of the wireless.

Marconi remained a shy, serious-minded man even when he became famous. He was married twice and had four children.

Marconi continued improving his wireless, which had come to be called radio. During World War I, he became commander of the Italian Army's wireless service. By means of his own invention—wireless, or radio—the world learned of his death in Rome on July 20, 1937.

DAVID C. KNIGHT
Author, science books for children

MARCO POLO. See POLO, MARCO.
MARDI GRAS. See CARNIVALS.

MARIE ANTOINETTE (1755–1793)

Marie Antoinette was the beautiful and willful queen of France who was executed during the French Revolution. Born in Vienna on November 2, 1755, she was the daughter of Maria Theresa and Emperor Francis I of Austria. At 15 she married the dauphin, or crown prince, of France. When his father died in 1774, the Prince became King Louis XVI. Marie Antoinette became the Queen.

The Queen was a light-hearted woman who wastefully spent fortunes, not unusual for royalty of the day. But unemployment and hunger were widespread among the lower classes, and they blamed the Queen for their miseries. They could easily believe the rumor that when told that the people had no bread, she quipped, "Let them eat cake."

The French Revolution began. During the French Revolution, the people stormed the palace. The King and Queen were imprisoned in August 1792. On January 21, 1793, the King was beheaded.

The following October, Marie Antoinette was charged with treason and brought before a revolutionary tribunal. She was treated like a commoner. Throughout her trial the Queen remained serene and dignified. She calmly heard her sentence pronounced. On October 16, 1793, she went to her death on the guillotine.

OWEN CONNELLY
University of South Carolina

See also FRENCH REVOLUTION.

MARIJUANA. See DRUG ABUSE.

MARINES. See UNITED STATES MARINE CORPS.

MARION, FRANCIS (1732–1795)

One of the most successful officers of the Revolutionary War was a South Carolinian named Francis Marion. Although he had no military training, he became an elusive and skillful soldier, using the protection of rivers, hills, and swamps. An angry British officer once exclaimed, "But as for this damned old fox, the Devil himself could not catch him!" The nickname stuck—Marion became known as the Swamp Fox.

Francis Marion was born in 1732 in Berkeley County in the Low Country of South Carolina. Before the war began he fought with the state militia against the Indians. He also served one term in the South Carolina Provincial Congress.

When the Revolutionary War began, he was made lieutenant-colonel in the Continental Army. His leadership qualities were recognized quickly. In time he was made a general. He and his followers, called Marion's Brigade, gained fame by using guerrilla tactics of surprise attack and rapid movement. They were known as hard fighters.

As fighting slowed between 1782 and 1783, General Marion worked to heal the wounds of war. After the war he was twice elected to the state legislature. He was also a delegate to the state's Constitutional Convention in 1790.

On April 20, 1786, at the age of 53, Marion married his cousin, Mary Esther Videau. They lived happily at their plantation at Pond Bluff, near Charleston, South Carolina.

Francis Marion died in 1795. He was buried at Belle Isle, a short distance from Pond Bluff.

JOSEPH T. STUKES
Francis Marion College

MARIONETTES. See PUPPETS AND MARIONETTES.

MARK, SAINT. See EVANGELISTS, THE.

MARKETING. See SALES AND MARKETING.

MARQUETTE, JACQUES. See JOLLIET, LOUIS, AND JACQUES MARQUETTE.

MARRIAGE CUSTOMS. See WEDDING CUSTOMS AROUND THE WORLD.

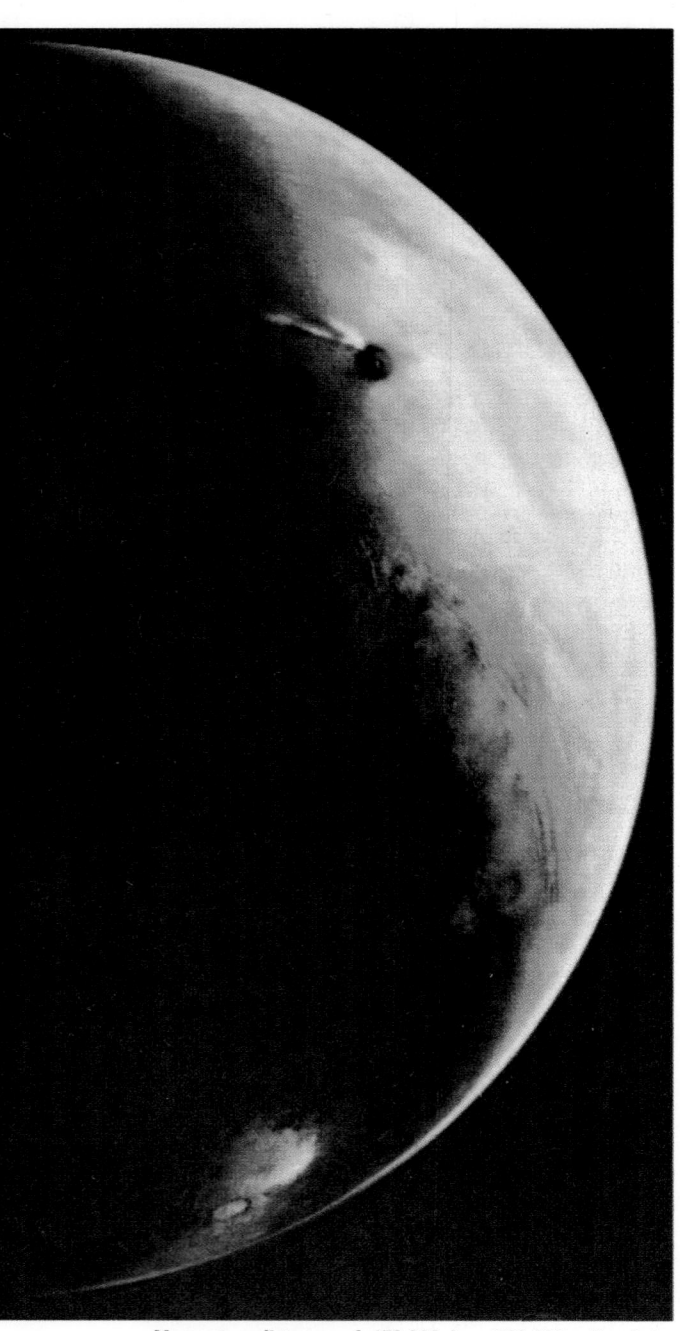

MARS

The earth is one of nine planets in the solar system. For centuries people have wondered what the other planets were like and whether life existed on any of them. Of all the planets, Mars always aroused the greatest curiosity, because conditions there seemed to be the best for the support of living things. This interest in Mars was greatly increased by the work of two astronomers, one Italian and one American.

The Italian was Giovanni Schiaparelli (1835–1910), director of the Brera Observatory in Milan. His special interest was the solar system. In 1877, like many other astronomers, Schiaparelli turned his attention to Mars, because it was especially close to the earth that year. Schiaparelli observed straight dark lines on the planet's surface and drew maps showing these lines. Most astronomers, then and later, were unable to see the lines. Schiaparelli called the lines *canali*, the Italian word for "channels." But the word was wrongly translated into English as "canals."

Mars at a distance of 450,000 km (280,000 mi), photographed by Viking 2 spacecraft. The dark, buttonlike object toward the top of the picture is a huge volcano named Ascraeus Mons. The two white plumes stretching away from Ascraeus are clouds; each is about 1,000 km (600 mi) long. The parallel lines near the center of the picture are part of Valles Marineris, a system of canyons over 4,000 km (2,500 mi) in length. At the bottom (south) is the Argyre Basin. The basin is covered with frost, which extends northward across part of the planet.

When at opposition, Mars is lined up directly with the earth and sun. Oppositions occur about every 780 days—slightly under 2 years, 2 months.

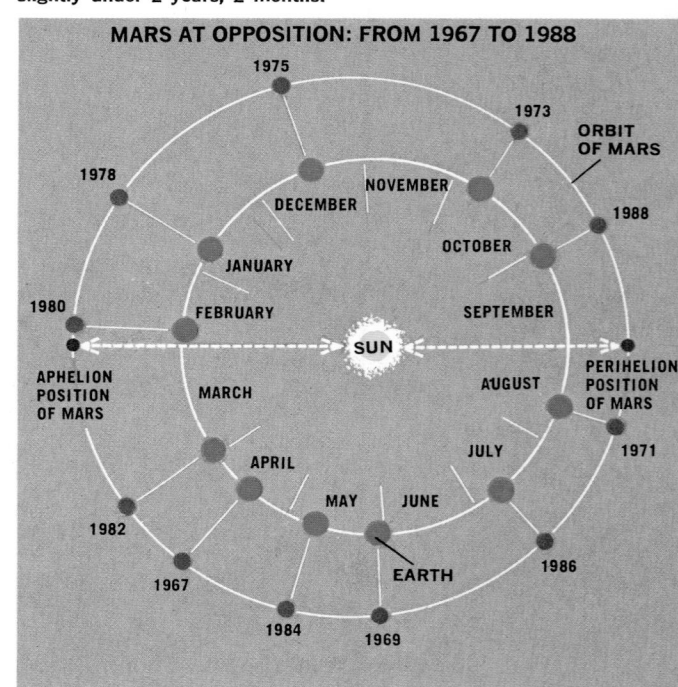

MARS AT OPPOSITION: FROM 1967 TO 1988

The straightness of the lines and the use of the word "canals" caused many people to jump to the conclusion that Schiaparelli had seen structures made by intelligent beings.

Schiaparelli thought the lines were long ditches of some kind, but he did not insist that they had to be the work of intelligent creatures. However, many people, including some astronomers, were convinced that the channels were artificial. One such astronomer was the American Percival Lowell (1855–1916). He drew maps of the planet, showing the canals in great detail. He insisted that the canals were there and that they had to be the work of intelligent beings.

Arguments over the existence of the canals went on for a long time, helped along by the exciting idea that there could be intelligent life on another planet. Popular interest in Mars rose to a new peak in 1965, when an American space probe, Mariner 4, flew within 10,000 kilometers (6,000 miles) of Mars. The probe transmitted 22 television pictures of the planet's surface. In 1969 Mariners 6 and 7 flew by Mars, sending back more pictures. Then, in 1971, Mariner 9 was put into orbit around Mars, 1,395 kilometers (865 miles) above the planet. The probe operated for nearly a year. It sent over 7,000 clear pictures of the surface, clouds, and satellites of Mars.

In July, 1976, another American probe, Viking 1, went into orbit around Mars. Part of the probe detached itself from the orbiter and landed on the planet. Both the lander and the orbiter sent many pictures of the surface, as did a later probe, Viking 2.

The pictures made by the probes show some straight channels, but not where Schiaparelli and Lowell had mapped the canals. What had these men seen, then? There are many small, dark-colored areas on some parts of the Martian surface. Scientists of the various Mars projects think that these areas were the cause of an optical illusion, in which lines seemed to connect the dark spots. These lines were the "canals."

▶ THE RED PLANET

Like all planets, Mars has no light of its own. We can see it glowing brightly in the night sky because some of the sun-light that strikes it is reflected toward us. The planet is easy to recognize because of its red color. In fact it is sometimes called the Red Planet. Scientists believe that rust-colored substances, called iron oxides, give the surface of Mars its color. The color led the ancient Romans to name the planet Mars, after their god of war.

The Orbit of Mars

Counting outward from the sun, Mars is the fourth planet of the solar system. The path, or **orbit**, that Mars follows around the sun lies between the orbits of the earth and Jupiter. The planets follow orbits that are elliptical, like flattened circles. However, with Mars the flattening is greater than with most of the other planets. As a result, the distance between Mars and the sun can change a great deal. The closest that the planet comes to the sun is 206,700,000 kilometers (128,400,000 miles). This nearest approach is called **perihelion**, meaning "near the sun." When it is at **aphelion** ("away from the sun"), the distance is 249,100,000 kilometers (154,800,000 miles). The average distance is 227,900,000 kilometers (141,600,000 miles). The large distance between perihelion and aphelion means that there is a difference of about 40 percent in the heat and light that Mars gets from the sun at different times of the year. On earth that difference is only about 3 percent.

Planets near the sun revolve around it faster than those farther out. The earth makes one revolution around the sun in about 365 days. This is our year. Mars, farther out from the sun, moves more slowly. It must also go a longer distance to make one revolution. So a year on Mars is 687 earth days, about twice the length of our year.

The earth moves faster than Mars, so that it regularly catches up to that planet and passes it in a little over 2 years. Each time this happens there is a close approach of the two planets, called **opposition**. Before there were planetary probes, astronomers looked forward to oppositions with Mars. It was during those times that they were best able to study the planet in detail. The distance between Mars and the earth is not the same in all their oppositions. (See the diagram on page 104.) The two planets

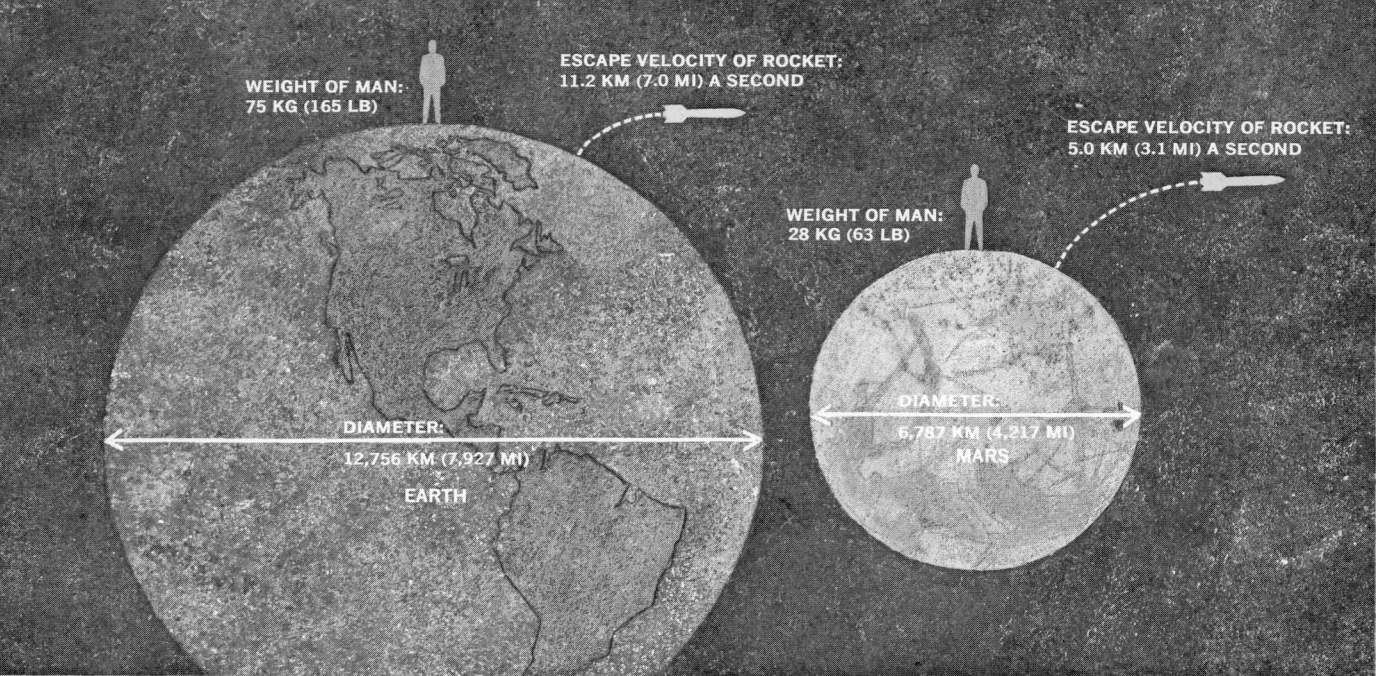

WEIGHT OF MAN:
75 KG (165 LB)

ESCAPE VELOCITY OF ROCKET:
11.2 KM (7.0 MI) A SECOND

ESCAPE VELOCITY OF ROCKET:
5.0 KM (3.1 MI) A SECOND

WEIGHT OF MAN:
28 KG (63 LB)

DIAMETER:
6,787 KM (4,217 MI)
MARS

DIAMETER:
12,756 KM (7,927 MI)
EARTH

Diagram shows earth's size and gravitational pull compared with those of Mars.

come closest in years when Mars is closest to the sun. These especially close oppositions take place once every 15 or 17 years. The planets are then only about 56,000,000 kilometers (35,000,000 miles) apart. The last such close opposition was in 1971.

The Rotation and Size of Mars

Mars and the earth are very different kinds of worlds, but they are very much alike in two ways. The earth turns on its axis, in a motion called **rotation**. It takes 23 hours and 56 minutes to rotate once. Mars rotates in 24 hours and 37 minutes, so a day on Mars is only a little longer than a day on the earth.

Mars and the earth are also very much alike in the way the axis of each planet is tilted. The earth's axis is tilted at an angle of 23½ degrees. Because of the tilt, the northern and southern hemispheres receive unequal amounts of the sun's heat and light as the earth follows its yearly orbit around the sun. As a result, we have seasons. Mars also has seasons for the same reason. Its axis is tilted 25 degrees, about the same amount as the earth's. The Martian seasons are longer than ours, because the planet takes nearly two earth years to make one complete trip around the sun.

If you have seen motion pictures of astro-

nauts on the moon, you know they move with long, bounding steps. They can do this because the moon's gravity is much weaker than the earth's gravity. The strength of gravity depends on the mass, or amount of matter, of a planet or a moon. The moon's mass is much less than the earth's, so the pull of gravity there is weaker. Mars, too, has less mass than the earth, so gravity there is also weak, although not so weak as on the moon.

The diameter of Mars is 6,787 kilometers (4,217 miles), about one half the earth's diameter. And the rock material of Mars is less dense. The smaller size and lower density of Mars mean that a man who weighs 75 kilograms (165 pounds) on earth would weigh 29 kilograms (64 pounds) on Mars. A rocket leaving the earth must travel at 11.2 kilometers (7 miles) per second to overcome the earth's gravitational pull. This speed is known as the **escape velocity**. The escape velocity on Mars is much less: only 5 kilometers (3.1 miles) per second.

The earth has a magnetic field. The field is caused by the liquid metal that makes up the center, or core, of the earth. Scientists reasoned that a magnetic field around Mars could mean that Mars, like the earth, has a core of molten metal. The probes that flew by and landed on Mars did not detect any magnetic field. Some scientists believe this is proof that Mars does not have a liquid metal core, but other scientists do not agree.

▶ THE SATELLITES

Two satellites, or moons, move in orbit around Mars. They are nothing like our moon, whose diameter is one fourth the size of the earth's diameter. The Martian moons are tiny, each being only a few kilometers long. But scientists have been interested in them for a long time. One of these men was Johannes Kepler, the great German astronomer who worked out the laws of motion of the planets. Kepler believed that Mars had satellites. He was proved right more than 200 years later, when the satellites were finally seen in 1877 by Asaph Hall, an American astronomer working at the United States Naval Observatory. Mars was unusually close to the earth that year, and Hall decided to carry on a search for satellites. He found the two tiny moons on two successive nights. Because they moved with Mars, Hall named the moons after the servants of Mars. He called one of them Phobos, which means "fear," and the other Deimos, meaning "terror."

The Mystery of Phobos and Deimos

Phobos and Deimos are a puzzle, because they are so small and so close to their parent planet. Several theories have been suggested to explain how they arose. One theory is that the satellites are actually **planetoids**. Many thousands of these objects travel in orbits between Mars and Jupiter, like miniature planets. Some are a kilometer or two long, while the largest is 770 kilometers (480 miles) in diameter. According to the theory, two planetoids came too close to Mars and were captured by its gravitational pull, becoming the satellites Phobos and Deimos.

Another theory states that Mars, Phobos, Deimos, and our own moon all came into being when the earth was very young. At that time the earth spun much faster than it does today, and its crust was much softer. The fast spinning caused masses of crust to be thrown out into space, to form the moon, Mars, and its satellites.

Still another theory suggests that the satellites are artificial, placed in orbit by inhabitants of Mars, in the same way that artificial satellites now circle the earth, placed there by its inhabitants. But the photographs from the probes, and measurements of the size and density of Phobos and Deimos have convinced most scientists that the artificial satellite theory is wrong.

During its hundreds of orbits of Mars, Mariner 9 gathered information that took some of the mystery away from Phobos and Deimos. Its cameras showed that the two satellites are very much alike. Both are thickly covered with craters. These were made by collisions with tiny meteoroids that streak through space at speeds of hundreds of miles per minute.

The large numbers of craters on the satellites shows that the Martian satellites are probably more than 4,000,000,000 (billion) years old. The color of both is dark enough to suggest that they are made up largely of iron or carbon. Finally, both satellites are elongated and irregular in shape, rather than spherical like the earth. Phobos is about 16 kilometers (10 miles) long, and Deimos stretches about half that length.

For every rotation of Mars, Phobos orbits the planet three times. Therefore Phobos, as seen from Mars, would appear to rise in the west and set in the east.

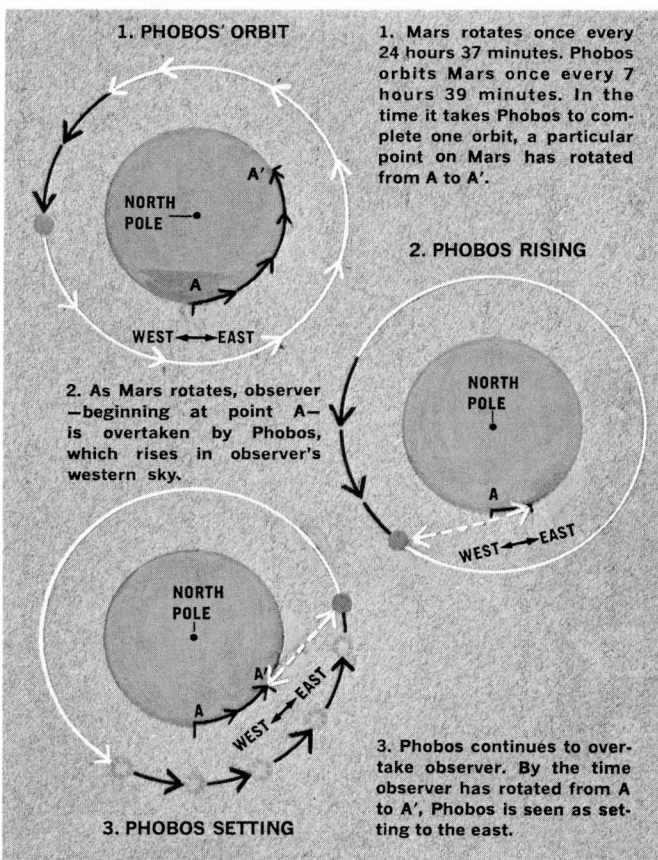

1. PHOBOS' ORBIT

1. Mars rotates once every 24 hours 37 minutes. Phobos orbits Mars once every 7 hours 39 minutes. In the time it takes Phobos to complete one orbit, a particular point on Mars has rotated from A to A'.

2. PHOBOS RISING

2. As Mars rotates, observer —beginning at point A— is overtaken by Phobos, which rises in observer's western sky.

3. Phobos continues to overtake observer. By the time observer has rotated from A to A', Phobos is seen as setting to the east.

3. PHOBOS SETTING

Since Phobos is so small, you might not expect to be able to see it from Mars. But it could be seen easily, because it is only about 6,000 kilometers (3,700 miles) above the surface of the planet. At that distance Phobos would appear to be a disk, rather like our moon. It would even go through phases, or apparent changes of shape, like our moon. But the way Phobos moves would seem strange to us. Because it is so close to Mars, it travels very fast. It circles Mars once in less than 8 hours. The length of one day on Mars is a bit over 24 hours, so a visitor on Mars would see Phobos rise in the west and set in the east three times per day.

Deimos is smaller than Phobos and is more than 20,000 kilometers (12,400 miles) above the surface of Mars. It would appear no bigger than a bright star in the Martian sky. Deimos takes a little more than 30 hours to orbit Mars. Mars takes only a few hours less to make one turn on its axis, so Deimos would appear to move very slowly through the sky, taking more than 60 hours from its rising in the east to its setting in the west.

▶ THE ATMOSPHERE OF MARS

Long before space probes were developed, astronomers knew that Mars has an atmosphere. From time to time the surface of the planet became hazy, as dust storms swept over it. This meant that there must be winds on Mars. Winds are movements of air of some kind, so the dust storms were one proof of the existence of an atmosphere. Scientists know now that it is less than 1/100th as dense as the earth's atmosphere.

The winds of the widespread Martian storms must reach speeds of 320 kilometers (200 miles) per hour or more. One of these great storms was raging when Mariner 9 began sending pictures to earth, so the early pictures were very hazy. The Vikings found less violent wind conditions on the ground, with wind speeds ranging from calm to 32 kilometers (20 miles) per hour.

What kinds of gases make up the atmosphere of Mars? An astronomer can learn a good deal about distant planets and their atmospheres by using an instrument called a **spectroscope**. Attached to a telescope, or carried aboard a space probe, the spectroscope breaks up the light from the sun, a planet, or a star into a rainbow-like pattern called a **spectrum**. Every substance has its own special pattern. By studying the spectrum of a planet an astronomer can get an idea of the kinds of substances present there.

Photographs taken from the earth and from the Mariners show thin clouds above a few places on Mars. Spectroscopic study shows that some of these clouds are composed of water ice and others of carbon dioxide.

But one especially interesting question— Is there nitrogen in the Martian atmosphere? —could not be answered at a distance. All living things on earth contain nitrogen. If there were living things on Mars, but no nitrogen, life on Mars would have to be chemically very different from life on earth. The Viking probes were able to test actual samples of the Martian air. They found nitrogen, but it makes up only 2.5 percent of the atmosphere. Nearly all the rest, 96 percent, is carbon dioxide. This is almost the opposite of what we find on earth. Our atmosphere is almost 80 percent nitrogen, and only a fraction of one percent is carbon dioxide.

The Viking tests also showed that about 1 percent of the Martian atmosphere consists of hydrogen, oxygen, and argon.

Phobos, a satellite of Mars, photographed by Mariner 9 from a distance of about 5,600 km (3,500 mi). Part at upper right is in deep shadow.

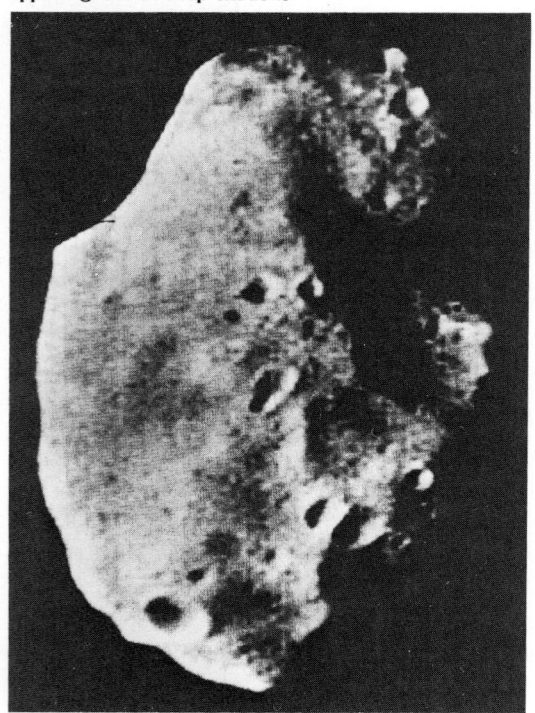

▶ THE SURFACE OF MARS

People are always curious about Mars. One reason for this is that Mars is the only planet whose surface is visible from the earth. Through a telescope, large parts of Mars appear reddish-yellow. It was thought that these areas might be great sandy deserts. But photographs made by the Mariners and Vikings showed a surprisingly varied surface.

About half of the Martian surface is pitted with craters of all sizes. One of the biggest is about 2,000 kilometers (1,200 miles) in diameter, and there are hundreds of thousands of smaller ones. Some were formed by volcanic eruptions. Others were dug by meteorites that crashed onto the surface of Mars. Younger craters have sharp, clear outlines, while the older ones have been smoothed down and partly filled in by the windblown sands.

Great mountains, far higher than any on earth, rise in some places on Mars. One volcanic mountain, Olympus Mons (Mons means mountain), is over 25 kilometers (15 miles) high and over 500 kilometers (300 miles) wide at its base. Its crater is more than 65 kilometers (40 miles) wide. Three other great volcanoes are nearby.

Are these gigantic volcanoes still active? The photographs show some lava flows with sharp, unworn outlines, indicating that the flows are young in a geological sense. The volcanoes do not seem to be active now, but they may be dormant for a time. We know that this has happened with some of the volcanoes on the earth.

Canyons that are longer, deeper, and wider than any on the earth were photographed. One of them is over 4,000 kilometers (2,500 miles) long. The canyons look like enormous riverbeds. This is puzzling, because rivers of flowing water seem impossible in the low temperatures and atmospheric pressure of Mars.

Could the rivers have existed a long time ago, when conditions on Mars were very different? If so, the blowing sands would have smoothed and filled in the canyon walls and floors. But that has not happened. Was there ever enough liquid water on Mars to form rivers? That is one of the mysteries about Mars that is yet to be solved.

A Viking lander. Part of its work was to search for evidence of present or past life on Mars. The long arm was used to collect samples of the planet's soil for analysis within the lander.

Olympus Mons, a huge volcano on Mars. Picture was assembled from several Mariner 9 photographs.

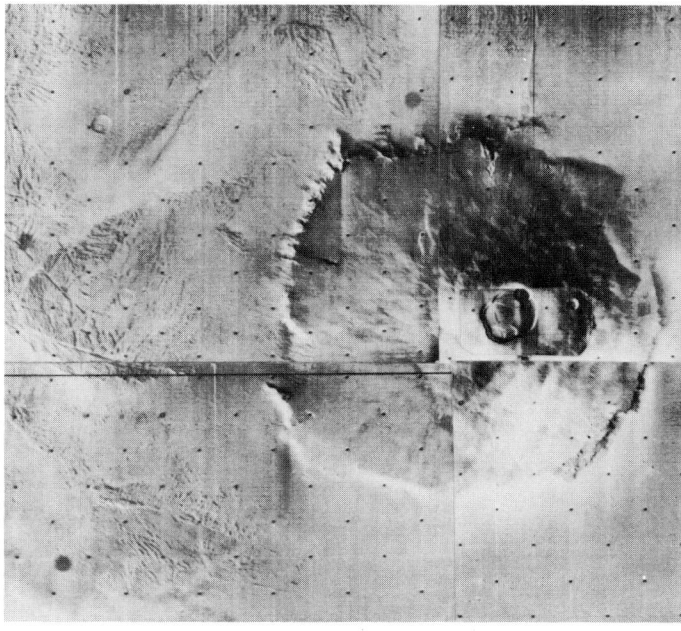

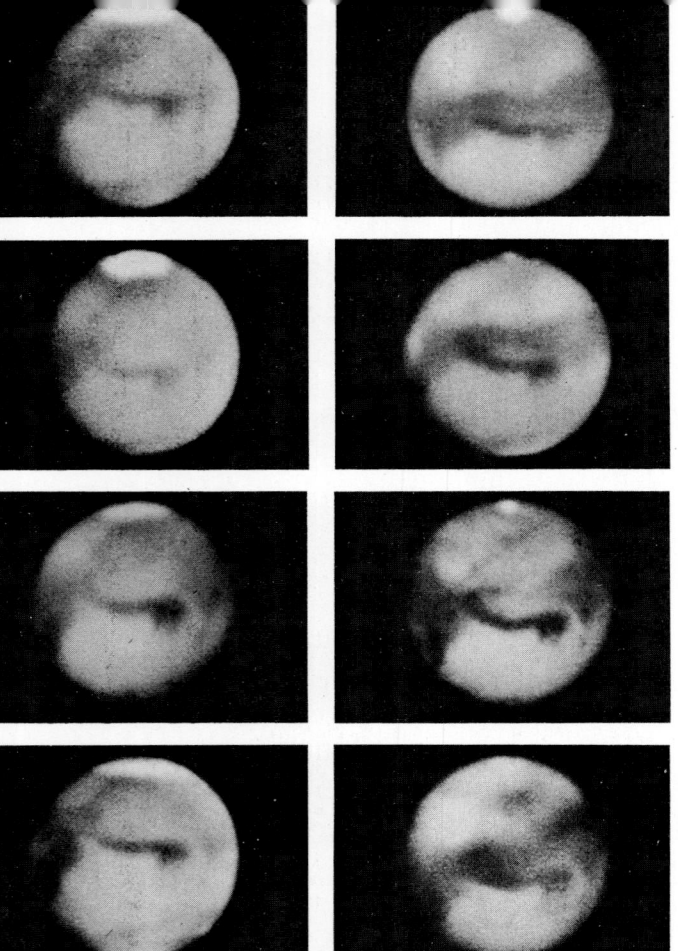

In spring (*left column*) polar caps are fairly large; the dark areas are greenish. During summer (*right column*) size of polar cap shrinks; areas around the tropics darken.

Surface of Mars from Mariner 9, at a distance of about 800 km (500 mi). Threadlike features, called rilles, may be ancient riverbeds or lava channels.

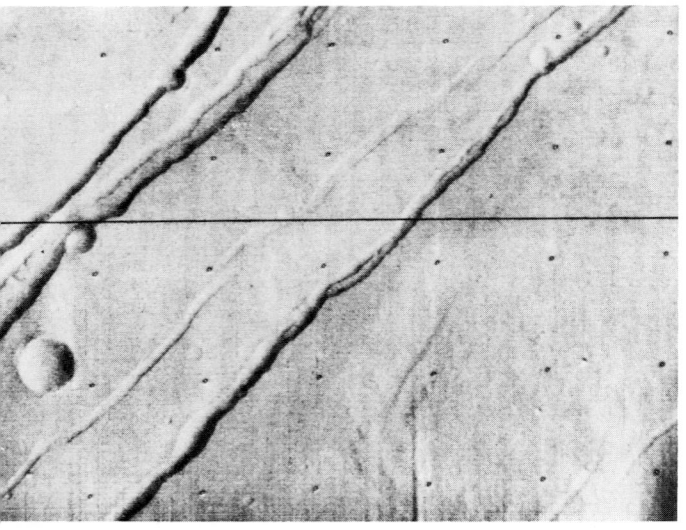

The Polar Caps

Through a powerful telescope white areas can be seen at the north and south polar regions of Mars. The white areas, called polar caps, grow and shrink as the seasons change. For example, the south polar cap is at its largest as winter is drawing to a close in the southern hemisphere.

What are the polar caps made of? The Mariner probes found very little water vapor in the atmosphere of Mars. So it seems unlikely that the caps are thick ice like that at the earth's poles. Some scientists think that the caps may be a very thin coating of ice covering the ground. However, the ice may not be frozen water, but frozen carbon dioxide, the substance we call dry ice. Other scientists believe the caps may be a mixture of frozen carbon dioxide and a small amount of frozen water.

The Mariners and Vikings measured the air temperatures on different parts of Mars. The polar temperature is about $-123°$ C ($-190°$ F), cold enough to freeze carbon dioxide gas. At the equator, temperatures reach $16°$ C ($60°$ F) or more in the daytime, but fall to $-90°$ C ($-130°$ F) at night.

The planets of the solar system are lighted and warmed by the sun. Temperatures on Mars are lower than on the earth because Mars is farther away from the sun. Even when Mars is at its nearest to the sun, it is some 56,000,000 kilometers (35,000,000 miles) farther away than the earth is.

The Dark Areas

The dark areas on the surface of Mars are perhaps the most puzzling of the planet's features. They have been of great interest because they were thought to have a connection with living things on Mars. Some of these huge areas change their shape slowly, taking years to do so. Sometimes, after an area has changed so that it is hard to recognize, it changes back to its original form. One of the areas especially known for changes of shape is Solis Lacus, which means "lake of the sun." Astronomers once thought the dark areas might be lakes and seas. But the probes found very little water vapor on Mars, so it seems unlikely that such bodies of water could have existed in recent times.

Changes in the color and brightness of

A photograph taken by the Viking 2 lander shows a thin layer of ice on the Martian surface. Thus there is some water on Mars. Water is one of the necessities for life as we know it.

Mars could be caused by the seasonal growth and fading of lichens and mosses. You may have seen these plants growing on rocks or in moist shady places. Such plants can endure great extremes of heat and cold. It is exciting to think that living things, even if they are only simple plants, exist on another planet.

But recent observations of Mars have suggested new reasons for the changes. These reasons have nothing to do with living things. Thin clouds drift over Mars. They are composed of crystals of water ice and carbon dioxide ice. The movement of the clouds causes changes in color and brightness. Also, long-range and seasonal changes cause regular shifts in the wind pattern. The winds blow the sands regularly from place to place. The moving light- and dark-colored sands cause the changing pattern of color and brightness.

▶ IS THERE LIFE ON MARS?

The very small amounts of oxygen, nitrogen, and water vapor in the atmosphere of Mars make it unlikely that the planet could support the kind of living things that we know on the earth. However, it may be possible that some kinds of life exist that are not based on these substances.

Viking 1 and Viking 2 landed on two widely separated parts of Mars in 1976. The landers took photographs and recorded temperatures, wind speeds, pressures, magnetism, and other measurements.

The landers also searched for evidence of past and present life on Mars. A clawlike device in the lander reached out to pick up samples of the soil. Each lander contained a small but complex chemical laboratory. The laboratory tested the soil samples for chemicals that could show that life exists, or once existed, on Mars. The laboratories worked well, but the results were not conclusive. Is there, or was there ever, life on Mars? The answer is still unknown.

HAROLD MASURSKY
Center of Astrogeology
U.S. Geological Survey

MARSHALL, GEORGE C. (1880–1959)

The life of George Catlett Marshall was a combination of two brilliant careers. As an officer in the United States Army, he commanded the largest U.S. military force ever assembled. In peacetime, he served his country as a distinguished statesman.

Marshall was born in Uniontown, Pennsylvania, on December 31, 1880. When he was 16, he entered the Virginia Military Institute. He was commissioned a second lieutenant in 1902, and he married Elizabeth Carter Coles that same year. After tours of duty in the Philippines and the United States, Marshall studied and then taught at the Army Staff College. Over the following years he received periodic advances in rank.

Marshall served with distinction in World War I. From 1919 to 1924 he was aide to General John J. Pershing in Washington, D.C. In 1930, three years after the death of his first wife, Marshall married Katherine Boyce Brown, a widow with three children.

In World War II, Marshall directed the operations of all U.S. Army ground and air forces and was a member of the Combined Chiefs of Staff. In 1944 he became the first officer to receive the new rank of five-star general of the Army. He retired in 1945.

Shortly afterward, President Harry Truman named Marshall his special envoy to help solve internal conflicts in China. In 1947, Marshall became secretary of state, the first professional soldier to hold that post. He helped formulate the Truman Doctrine, which aided Greece, and Turkey. He also suggested the Marshall Plan, later called the European Recovery Program, for giving large-scale economic aid to foreign nations.

Marshall resigned in 1949 and served as president of the American Red Cross. In 1950 he became secretary of defense, a post he held until he retired to private life in 1951. In 1953 Marshall received the Nobel peace prize. He once described war as "the most terrible tragedy of the human race." He died in Washington, D.C., on October 16, 1959.

Reviewed by FORREST C. POGUE
Author, *George C. Marshall*

MARSHALL, JOHN (1755–1835)

The story of Chief Justice John Marshall is the story of how the Supreme Court truly became the third great branch of the United States Government. It is also the story of the United States Constitution. For in his 34 years as chief justice, Marshall gave a new, broader meaning to the Constitution, strengthening not only the Supreme Court but also the federal government itself.

John Marshall was born on September 24, 1755, in a log cabin near Germantown, on the Virginia frontier. He had almost no formal schooling, receiving most of his education from his father, Thomas Marshall, a planter. But the vigorous frontier life did much to develop young Marshall's independent, self-reliant character. During the Revolutionary War both father and son joined the patriot army. John Marshall's service in the Revolution had a great influence on his life and career. Years later, he said of this period: "I was confirmed in the habit of considering America as my country and Congress as my government." At that time most Americans felt greater loyalty to their own states than to the country as a whole.

Marshall studied law at the College of William and Mary in Virginia, and in 1780 he was admitted to the bar. Later he opened a law office in Richmond. In 1783 he married Marie Ambler. They had ten children.

As his law practice grew, Marshall rose to political prominence. He became Federalist Party leader in Virginia, and President Washington twice offered him important posts—as attorney general and as minister to France. Marshall refused both for financial reasons. But in 1797, he joined Charles C. Pinckney and Elbridge Gerry on a diplomatic mission to France. In 1799 he was elected to Congress, serving until 1800, when President John Adams appointed him secretary of state. In 1801, Adams appointed him chief justice. Two months later, Marshall administered the oath of office to the new president, Thomas Jefferson. Jefferson, as leader of the Democratic-Republican Party, believed in the strict interpretation of the Constitution. Marshall's view was different. He believed that the Constitution was "intended to endure for ages to come" and must be "adapted to the various *crises* of human affairs."

Of Marshall's hundreds of decisions, only a few can be cited here. His first important case, and one of the most important in the history of the Court, was *Marbury* v. *Madison* (1803). William Marbury was one of the Federalist "midnight" justices of the peace appointed by President Adams during the last days of his administration. Secretary of State James Madison, acting under President Jefferson's orders, refused to deliver Marbury's commission of appointment. Marbury then asked the Supreme Court to issue a writ forcing Madison to deliver it. In his decision Marshall declared that Marbury was entitled to the writ. But he added that the Supreme Court could not issue it because the section of the law authorizing such a writ was unconstitutional. Marbury did not get his appointment. But Marshall had firmly established the principle of judicial review, under which the Court could declare a law of Congress unconstitutional. Later, in *Fletcher* v. *Peck* (1810), Marshall ruled that the Court could also find a state law unconstitutional.

The most important of Marshall's decisions in establishing the supremacy of the federal government was *McCulloch* v. *Maryland* (1819). James McCulloch, cashier of the Baltimore branch of the Bank of the United States, had refused to pay a tax levied by Maryland. Maryland then sued him. Marshall first declared that the law creating the bank was constitutional because it was within "the letter and spirit of the Constitution." He then ruled that no state could tax a federal agency.

The question of control of interstate commerce (commerce between states) was decided by *Gibbons* v. *Ogden* (1824). New York State had claimed the right to grant a monopoly on a steamboat route between New York and New Jersey. Marshall ruled that Congress alone could regulate interstate and foreign commerce.

John Marshall, who has been called the Great Chief Justice, died on July 6, 1835.

Reviewed by RICHARD B. MORRIS
Editor, *Encyclopedia of American History*
See also SUPREME COURT OF THE UNITED STATES.

MARX, KARL (1818–1883)

Karl Marx, a German thinker and revolutionist, has become one of the most influential figures of our time—and perhaps of all time. He first developed his ideas about human beings, society, and nature as a criticism of all religions. Yet he inspired mass movements—Communism and socialism—that include more people and a greater area of the earth than any organized religion. Marx's influence is due to his ideas, which spread most rapidly after his death. To understand the history of our times, one must know what Marx taught.

Karl Marx was born to a Jewish family in Trier, Prussia (now West Germany), on May 5, 1818. While Marx was still a child, his father was converted to Christianity. But as a youth, Marx renounced all religion. He believed that people are a part of nature and that what happens to them depends on the kind of society they live in, not on any god or person.

After completing his studies of law and philosophy, Marx married Jenny von Westphalen in 1843. He turned to writing and threw himself into the struggle for greater political freedom in Germany. Marx observed the miserable conditions under which workers lived during the early days of industrialization. Their lives were marked by poverty, unemployment, child labor, and other evils. He called on them to organize, destroy existing governments, and start a new economic system. These ideas are found in the *Communist Manifesto,* written in 1848 by Marx and his lifelong friend Friedrich Engels.

Marx's call for revolution disturbed government officials in countries where many people were discontented. He was arrested in Germany and was expelled from France and Belgium. In 1849 he found refuge in England, where he and his family lived in acute poverty.

Marx continued to encourage workers everywhere to organize and take revolutionary action. He also devoted long years to studying the existing economic system, called capitalism. This system is based on a continuous quest for profit. Profit is made possible when workers sell their labor power to employers who own the means of production. "Means of production" are factories, farmlands, mills, and the like. As a result of his study, Marx wrote his now famous book *Das Kapital* (*Capital*) and other works. The first volume of *Das Kapital* appeared in 1867. Two other volumes were edited and published by Engels after Marx's death in London on March 14, 1883.

In his writings, Marx predicted that capitalism would be replaced by a socialist society, in which all the people would own the means of production. In countries where democracy did not exist, he called for revolution. In democracies, he expected the change to come peacefully after capitalism had failed and people were in extreme need.

Four main ideas are found in Marx's writings. The first is his belief that the most important feature of a society is the way in which people earn their living—that is, the economic system. It is the basis of the society's art, science, philosophy, and religion.

The second idea is that in all societies (except primitive societies of the past and socialist societies of the future) the economic system divides people into classes— masters and slaves, capitalists and workers. These classes are always in conflict. "All history is the history of class struggles," he wrote.

The third idea is that labor is the source of all value. Under capitalism, profit results when workers produce goods that have more value than the wages they earn. In this way, the labor of workers brings profit for employers. Marx thought that unfair treatment of workers would stop if society as a whole owned the means of production.

Finally, Marx thought of history as a process in which human freedom is always being extended. He thought that people will determine what happens to them on the basis of their needs. They will be free to choose their way of living only when private ownership of the means of production is abolished.

Social scientists who study Marx interpret his ideas in different ways. They disagree about whether his ideas are sound and about the success of his predictions. He was right in predicting that science and technology would have a great influence on how people live. But many of his other ideas have proved to be false. Workers everywhere have not become poorer. Capitalism has not collapsed. Class conflict has not always been more important than racial or national conflict.

Marx expected socialism to come first to highly industrialized countries, but this was not the case. He did not foresee the development of absolute, centralized power in countries such as the Soviet Union that adopted economic systems based on his ideas. Above all, he underestimated the ability of democratic nations to modify the capitalist system in ways that lead to a democratic welfare state, with rising standards of living and increased freedoms for all.

Those who see Marx as an apostle of human freedom believe that the move toward democracy through the welfare state is in keeping with his ideas of socialism. Others insist that the only way to introduce socialism is through revolution and the absolute dictatorship of a minority party. The modern history of many countries reflects these different ways of interpreting Marx. That is why the study of his thought is still important today.

SIDNEY HOOK
Author, *The Ambiguous Legacy: Marx and the Marxists* and *From Hegel to Marx*

See also COMMUNISM; SOCIALISM; CAPITALISM.

MARY, VIRGIN

The Virgin Mary is the mother of Jesus Christ. Tradition has it that she was the daughter of Anne and Joachim and was a member of the house of David, the royal house of Israel. As a young woman, she was promised in marriage to Joseph. He, too, was a descendant of David's.

The Gospels tell us that the Angel Gabriel visited Mary and told her that she would have a son, whose name was to be Jesus. Mary and Joseph married in Nazareth and then went to Bethlehem, where Jesus was born about 6 B.C. The Gospels state that God, through the Holy Spirit, caused the birth of Jesus and that Mary was a virgin when he was born.

Matthew's Gospel tells how the Wise Men, or Magi, came from the east to Bethlehem to worship Jesus and found him "with Mary his mother." It also tells of the anger of King Herod of Judea, who had heard the Magi calling Jesus king of the Jews. Fearing a rival king, Herod ordered that all male infants in Bethlehem under 2 years of age be slain. An angel appeared to Joseph in a dream, telling him to flee with his family to Egypt. Joseph and his family left at once and remained in Egypt until after Herod's death. They then returned to Nazareth.

Once when they made a trip to Jerusalem to celebrate Passover, Jesus became separated from his parents. After three days of searching, they found the boy in the Temple, listening to the teachers and asking them questions.

The next mention of Mary in the Gospels occurs at a wedding feast in Cana. Here Jesus performed his first public miracle. The Scripture says that at Mary's request, Jesus turned water into wine.

Mary was also present at the Crucifixion of Jesus. At that time Jesus entrusted his mother to the care of the Apostle John. The last mention of Mary in Scripture is in the Acts of the Apostles. There we read that after the Resurrection and Ascension of Jesus, Mary was with his followers in Jerusalem, praying and waiting for the coming of the Holy Spirit. There is a tradition that she later went with John to Ephesus, where she died.

The early Christian church had to deal with the problem of what Christians should believe. Meetings—called councils—were held. At the

The Virgin and Child with Angels by Sandro Botticelli, a painter of the Italian Renaissance.

council of Ephesus in A.D. 431, the bishops decided that Jesus was really God and really man and that it was therefore proper to call Mary the Mother of God. For over ten centuries the church honored Our Lady, as Mary is sometimes called.

Many Christians still honor Mary as the greatest of the saints and ask her to pray for them to Jesus. But the leaders of the Protestant Reformation thought too much attention was being paid to Mary. Most of them did not think that Christians should pray to anyone but God and Jesus.

In the 20th century, Christians have been trying to come together again and resolve their differences. One of the questions they have to deal with is the role of Mary. The different churches have tried to find ways of talking about her that will be true to their own traditions and that other churches will be able to understand and accept.

Reviewed by MSGR. GEORGE E. TIFFANY
Editor in Chief, *The Contemporary Church*

MARYLAND

The white oak became the official state tree of Maryland in 1941. One particular white oak, known as the Wye Oak, is owned by the state. This magnificent tree stands on a small plot of land at Wye Mills, on the Eastern Shore. It is shown in the picture on page 117.

Besides a state tree, a state flower (adopted in 1918), and a state bird (adopted in 1947), Maryland has a state sport, a state fish, and a state dog. Jousting was made the state sport in 1962, although it has been popular in eastern Maryland since colonial times. It is a modern version of medieval knights' jousting contests. The contestants, or "knights," ride on galloping horses under a series of arches. They carry lances, on the tips of which they try to collect small rings that are suspended from the arches. Originally only men rode in the tournaments. But women now ride and sometimes become state champions. The rockfish, or striped bass, was made the state fish in 1962. It is the fish most commonly caught in Chesapeake Bay. The Chesapeake Bay retriever was chosen as the state dog in 1964. This large hunting dog was developed in Maryland.

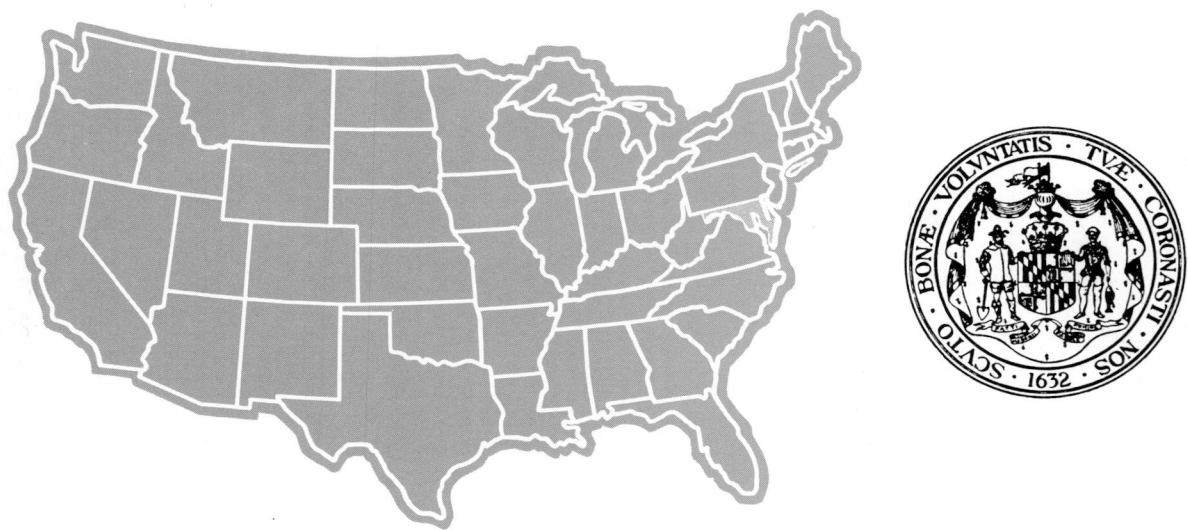

The first European colonists came to Maryland in 1634. Ever since that time Maryland has been a crossroads. Into its sheltered harbors on the Chesapeake Bay sailed some of the first transatlantic ships, bringing people and goods from other lands. The early shipbuilders of Maryland developed sailing ships called Baltimore Clippers. These swift vessels continued to bring cargoes and passengers into the United States through Maryland ports. The first national highway began in Maryland. The nation's first passenger railroad, the Baltimore and Ohio, started on its way west from Maryland.

In wartime, Maryland has been a meeting place or a transfer point for troops and supplies. During the Revolutionary War the Continental Congress fled to Baltimore to avoid capture by the British. In 1783 Congress met at the State House in Annapolis to ratify the Treaty of Paris, which formally ended the Revolutionary War. At that session General George Washington resigned his commission as commander in chief of the Continental Army. During the War of 1812 the British bombarded Fort McHenry in Baltimore harbor. This event inspired Francis Scott Key to write "The Star-Spangled Banner." During the Civil War troops marched north and south to battles, seesawing across the state. In World Wars I and II, Baltimore was an important port of embarkation for troops.

Maryland has been an educational crossroads as well. Each year hundreds of young persons come to Annapolis to study at the United States Naval Academy. Others come to Baltimore to study medicine at Johns Hopkins University or the University of Maryland.

Maryland has a special relationship to the national capital. All the land now in the District of Columbia was donated by Maryland. The part donated by Virginia was later returned. The suburbs of Washington, D.C., are in Maryland and Virginia.

In earlier days Maryland was a land of farming and fishing and of hunting and riding to hounds. These activities are still carried on in Maryland, but few Marylanders take part. Most Marylanders are city dwellers, earning a living in trade, manufacturing, government, or personal service. Most of the state is linked with a chain of great cities on the Atlantic seaboard. This chain forms a super city, or megalopolis, that stretches from Washington, D.C., to Boston, Massachusetts.

▶ **THE LAND**

Maryland is known as an Atlantic coastal state because it has shoreline on the Atlantic

STATE FLAG.

STATE TREE: White oak.

STATE BIRD: Baltimore oriole.

STATE FLOWER: Black-eyed Susan.

MARYLAND

CAPITAL: Annapolis.

STATEHOOD: April 28, 1788; the 7th state.

SIZE: 27,092 km² (10,460 sq mi); rank, 42nd.

POPULATION: 4,216,975 (1980 census); rank, 18th.

ORIGIN OF NAME: Named *Terra Mariae* ("Land of Maria," or "Maryland") by the British king Charles I for his wife, Queen Henrietta Maria. Charles I granted the charter for Maryland to George Calvert, the first Lord Baltimore, who died before it was signed. His son, Cecil Calvert, the second Lord Baltimore, inherited the charter.

ABBREVIATION: Md.; MD.

NICKNAMES: Old Line State; Free State.

STATE SONG: "Maryland, My Maryland," by James R. Randall, to the tune of "O Tannenbaum."

STATE MOTTO: *Scuto bonae voluntatis tuae coronasti nos* (Thou has crowned us with the shield of Thy good will) or *Fatti maschii, parole femine* (usually translated "Manly deeds, womanly words"). The second motto is the Calvert family motto.

STATE SEAL: In the center is the personal shield of the Lords Baltimore. It bears the arms of the Calvert and the Crossland families. (The mother of George Calvert, the first Lord Baltimore, belonged to the Crossland family.) The two men on either side of the shield represent Lord Baltimore's two grants in the New World. The farmer stands for Maryland. The fisherman represents Avalon, an earlier grant in Newfoundland. The earl's coronet above the shield and the ermine background show that Lord Baltimore had royal powers in the colony. On the scroll beneath the shield is the Calvert motto. The other motto, together with the date 1632 (the date of the signing of the charter), is in the border.

STATE FLAG: The flag bears the arms, or design, shown on the shield in the state seal.

117

Ocean. It is irregular in shape, narrowing sharply to the west. At Hancock, in Washington County, the state is scarcely 2 kilometers (1½ miles) wide. It widens again but narrows at Cumberland to about 8 kilometers (5 miles). In the east the Chesapeake Bay extends so far inland that it almost cuts the state in two. Because of these features various parts of Maryland have local names. The part east of the Chesapeake Bay is called the Eastern Shore. The part bordering the bay on the west is called the Western Shore. Beyond the Western Shore is the Piedmont. The rest of the state is known as Western Maryland.

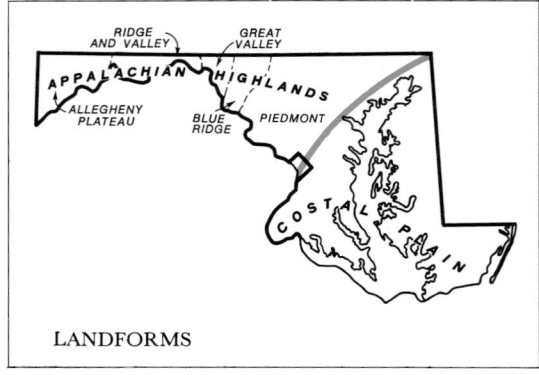

LANDFORMS

Landforms

Maryland extends inland from the Atlantic Ocean across belts of landforms that stretch from New England almost to the Gulf of Mexico.

The Coastal Plain. The lowlands surrounding the Chesapeake Bay belong to the natural region known as the Coastal Plain. This region in Maryland makes up almost half the state. It covers both the Eastern and the Western shores. Large areas on the Eastern Shore are low-lying and marshy.

The Appalachian Highlands. The Piedmont is the easternmost of five sections that make up the Appalachian Highlands in Maryland. It extends from the fall line at the edge of the Coastal Plain to the foot of the Blue Ridge. The Piedmont, or foothills region, is made up of the worn-down remains of ancient moun-

tains. The exposed rocks are among the oldest in the world. The countryside is rolling and not very high.

The Blue Ridge is a long line of mountains. On the top of the mountains is the Appalachian National Scenic Trail, a footpath for hikers that follows the crests of the Appalachians from Maine to Georgia.

The Great Valley is a famous north-south corridor, or passageway. It was used by warring Indians before Columbus discovered America. During the Civil War it was used by Robert E. Lee's invading armies when they penetrated as far north as Antietam Creek, Maryland, and Gettysburg, Pennsylvania. In Maryland the Great Valley is called the Hagerstown Valley.

West of the Great Valley is the Ridge and Valley Region. Its jumbled ridges run roughly north and south. The western edge of this area is a steep-sided ridge called Dans Mountain.

The Allegheny Plateau covers a small area

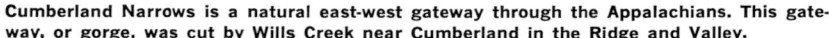

Cumberland Narrows is a natural east-west gateway through the Appalachians. This gateway, or gorge, was cut by Wills Creek near Cumberland in the Ridge and Valley.

in the extreme western part of the state. This is a region of coal-bearing rocks.

Rivers, Lakes, and Coastal Waters

Maryland has two important waterways—the Chesapeake Bay and the Potomac River. The Chesapeake Bay is the drowned valley of the Susquehanna River. The bay once isolated the Eastern Shore from the rest of the state. Now the Chesapeake Bay Bridge connects the two parts. The entire length of the bay is about 315 kilometers (195 miles). It varies in width from 5 to 48 kilometers (3 to 30 miles).

The Potomac River forms most of Maryland's southern border. Maryland owns the entire watercourse to the shores of Virginia. This unusual arrangement has caused some difficulties with Virginia over fishing and seafood rights. The Potomac and the many other rivers in the state are used for recreation.

Dams in the rivers create large artificial lakes, or reservoirs. Their main purpose is to store water for cities or produce hydroelectric power. Some of them are used for recreation as well. The largest reservoir in the state is Deep Creek Lake, on the Youghiogheny River, of the Ohio River drainage system. It was built to produce hydroelectric power. Another large power development is on the Susquehanna River at Conowingo.

Maryland has only 50 kilometers (31 miles) of shoreline on the Atlantic. But the length of its tidal shoreline is 5,133 kilometers (3,190 miles).

Climate

Maryland's climate is midway between the climate of the warmer southern part of the United States and that of the colder north. The storms that move eastward over the United States have an important influence on the weather in winter. These storms bring cold spells and often much snow, especially in Western Maryland. The higher sections of the west catch the precipitation on their western slopes. Often the eastern slopes are drier.

The presence of the Chesapeake Bay and the Atlantic Ocean modifies the climate of the eastern part of the state. The Coastal Plain has milder winters and summers, higher humidity, and less extreme temperatures than Western Maryland.

THE LAND

LOCATION: Latitude—37° 54′ N to 39° 43′ N. **Longitude**—75° 03′ W to 79° 29′ W. Pennsylvania to the north, Delaware and the Atlantic Ocean to the east, Virginia to the south, West Virginia to the south and the west.

ELEVATION: Highest—Backbone Mountain, 1,025 m (3,360 ft). **Lowest**—Sea level, along Atlantic Ocean and Chesapeake Bay.

LANDFORMS: Lowlands (the Coastal Plain) surrounding Chesapeake Bay; highlands (the Appalachian Highlands) in the rest of the state.

SURFACE WATERS: Major rivers—Potomac, Patuxent, Patapsco, Susquehanna, Elk, Chester, Choptank, Nanticoke, Pocomoke—all tributary to the Chesapeake Bay. **Major artificial lakes**—Deep Creek, Patapsco, Triadelphia, Rocky Gorge, Prettyboy, Loch Raven.

CLIMATE: Temperature—January averages from 4°C (39°F) in the southeast to −2°C (29°F) in the west; July averages from 26°C (78°F) in the south to 20°C (68°F) in the west. **Precipitation**—Local averages vary from 910 mm (36 in) a year to 1,240 mm (49 in). Snowfall varies from 23 cm (9 in) near the coast to 198 cm (78 in) in the highlands. **Growing season**—Varies from more than 225 days in the extreme south to fewer than 130 days in the highlands.

The rainfall throughout the state is usually adequate for the growing of crops. But precipitation varies considerably from year to year. Long periods of dry weather are not common, but often there are short dry periods. These short dry spells damage crops if they occur during the growing season. The remnants of hurricanes from the Caribbean sometimes bring unusually heavy rainstorms to the eastern part of the state in August, September, or October.

The variation in climate enables Garrett County, in the west, to have a ski resort. In the milder east, there is a good deal of fishing and sailing on the bay even in the winter.

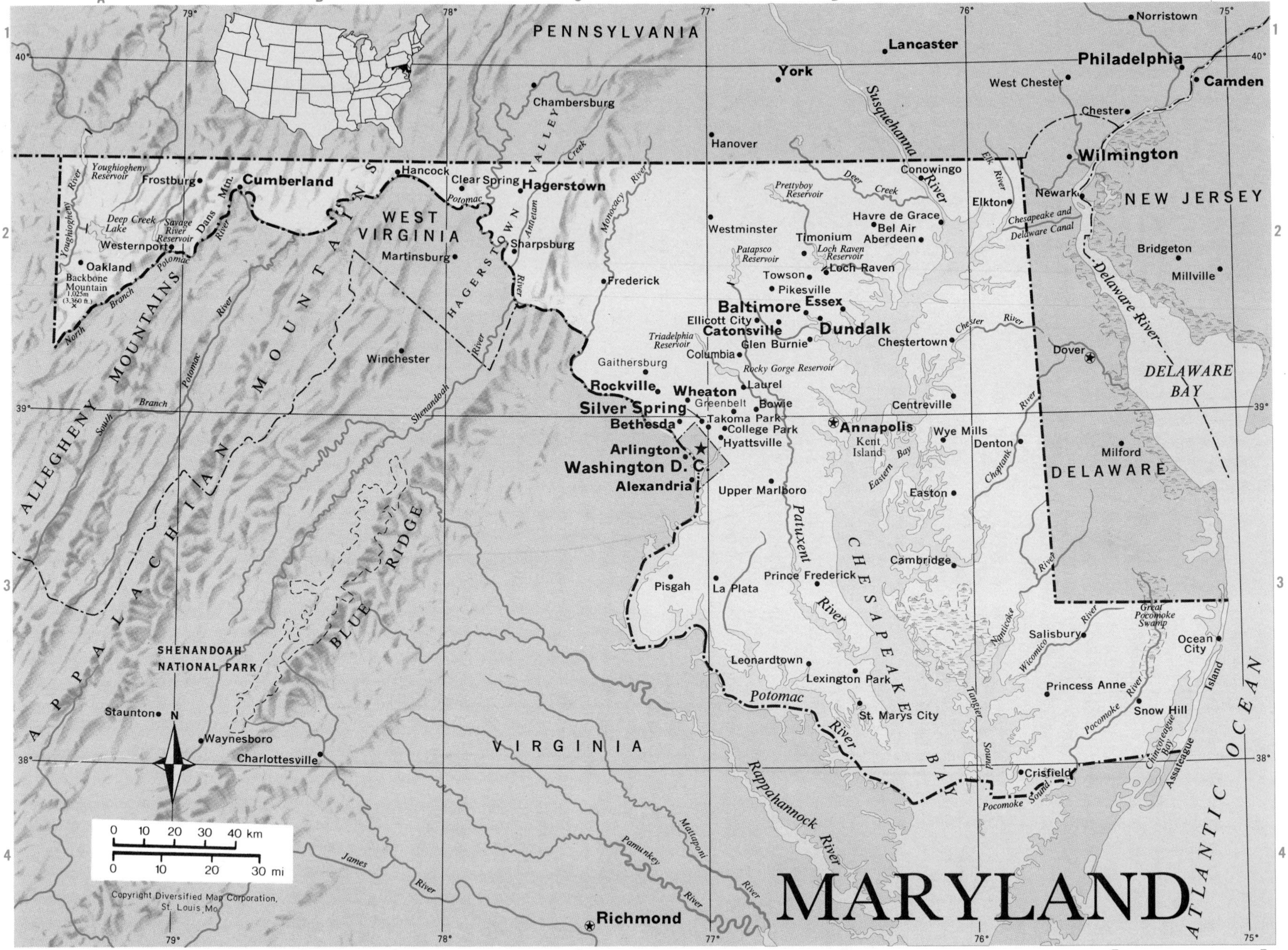

MARYLAND

ATLANTIC OCEAN

PENNSYLVANIA

NEW JERSEY

WEST VIRGINIA

VIRGINIA

DELAWARE

DELAWARE BAY

CHESAPEAKE BAY

APPALACHIAN MOUNTAINS

ALLEGHENY MOUNTAINS

HAGERSTOWN VALLEY

BLUE RIDGE

SHENANDOAH NATIONAL PARK

Norristown
Camden
Philadelphia
Wilmington
Chester
West Chester
Newark
Lancaster
York
Hanover
Chambersburg
Winchester
Martinsburg
Hancock
Clear Spring
Hagerstown
Sharpsburg
Cumberland
Frostburg
Westernport
Oakland
Frederick
Gaithersburg
Westminster
Ellicott City
Columbia
Catonsville
Baltimore
Essex
Dundalk
Towson
Pikesville
Timonium
Aberdeen
Bel Air
Havre de Grace
Conowingo
Elkton
Glen Burnie
Rockville
Wheaton
Silver Spring
Bethesda
Arlington
Washington D.C.
Alexandria
Takoma Park
College Park
Hyattsville
Greenbelt
Bowie
Laurel
Annapolis
Kent Island
Centreville
Chestertown
Wye Mills
Denton
Milford
Dover
Bridgeton
Millville
Ocean City
Snow Hill
Princess Anne
Salisbury
Crisfield
Easton
Cambridge
Prince Frederick
Leonardtown
Lexington Park
St. Marys City
La Plata
Upper Marlboro
Pisgah
Staunton
Waynesboro
Charlottesville
Richmond

Bridgeton
Assateague Island
Great Pocomoke Swamp
Chincoteague Bay

Susquehanna River
Delaware River
Chesapeake and Delaware Canal
Elk River
Deer Creek
Chester River
Choptank River
Nanticoke River
Wicomico River
Pocomoke River
Patuxent River
Potomac River
Rappahannock River
Mattaponi River
Pamunkey River
James River
Shenandoah River
Antietam Creek
Monocacy River
Potomac River
North Branch Potomac River
South Branch Potomac River
Savage River
Deep Creek
Youghiogheny River
Dans Mtn.
Backbone Mountain (3,360 ft.)
Prettyboy Reservoir
Loch Raven Reservoir
Patapsco Reservoir
Rocky Gorge Reservoir
Triadelphia Reservoir
Deep Creek Lake
Savage River Reservoir
Youghiogheny Reservoir

Kent Bay
Eastern Bay
Tangier Sound
Pocomoke Sound

Copyright Diversified Map Corporation, St. Louis, Mo.

0 10 20 30 mi
0 10 20 30 40 km

N

Natural Resources

Maryland's natural resources are as varied as are its landforms and its climate. These resources include forests, farmlands, fishing and hunting grounds, and an abundance of surface and underground water.

Maryland has been a leader among the states in environmental conservation. The legislature has passed strict laws to protect the wetlands of Chesapeake Bay, the quality of the water in rivers and the bay, and the quality of the air.

Soils. There is a great variety of soils derived from the great variety of underlying rocks. Some soils are stony, but most are of medium texture and good drainage. The low-lying soils of the Eastern Shore and some of the stiff clays are exceptions. The sandiest soils are on the south end of the Eastern Shore. Sandy soils warm earliest in the spring. If properly fertilized, they can produce crops of early vegetables.

Minerals. The Piedmont section of Maryland has underlying rocks that contain a great variety of minerals. Unfortunately for Maryland, the minerals exist only in small amounts and so are not profitable to mine. The Piedmont and the Great Valley have deposits of various granites, marbles, and sandstones. Sand and gravel come mostly from the Western Shore counties. Coal and natural gas are found in the western part of the state.

Forests. Forests cover about half the land area of Maryland. Most of them are commercial forests, privately owned. Three fourths of the sawtimber is hardwood, such as oak and hickory. The rest is softwood, chiefly pine.

Fish and Wildlife. The state maintains several wildlife management areas. Those on the Eastern Shore are for wildfowl. The others, in Western Maryland, are for small game and deer. Each contains a public shooting area and an adjoining game refuge. The waters of the Chesapeake Bay provide fish and seafood for the taking. Deep-sea and sport fishing may be enjoyed off Ocean City, Maryland's only ocean resort.

Water. The water resources of the state are adequate to meet the demand, even if demand doubles by the year 2000. The main source of water is rainfall. On the Coastal Plain the rainfall seeps into the ground. In the higher parts of the state, runoff water is collected in reservoirs. One main problem is the control of silt, which may collect in reservoirs. Another is the pollution of water by human and industrial wastes. The water of Chesapeake Bay is unfit for drinking and most industrial uses because it is salty.

▶ **THE PEOPLE AND THEIR WORK**

The first settlers in Maryland came from the British Isles. Among them were wealthy people and farmers and other workers. Black slaves soon arrived to add to the supply of laborers. The native Indians gradually moved away from the area. In the early 1700's farmers of German and Scotch-Irish stock arrived by way of Pennsylvania. They pushed southward into valleys around Frederick and into the Great Valley around Hagerstown.

Baltimore was founded in 1729. Soon the port of Baltimore attracted seafaring people from all over Europe. As manufacturing grew in the Baltimore area, workers from eastern and southern Europe arrived. Today Baltimore's largest foreign-born groups are German, Russian, Polish, and Italian. The languages other than English most frequently heard are German, Italian, Yiddish, and Polish.

Where the People Live

In area, Maryland ranks among the smallest states. But only a few other states have a higher average number of people for each square kilometer. The reason for the density of population is that eight out of every ten Marylanders live in urban areas. Most of them are in a strip of territory extending from Washington, D.C., through Baltimore to the Pennsylvania state line. The eastern and western parts of Maryland either are not growing or are losing population as the number of persons engaged in farming decreases.

Industries, Occupations, and Products

Farming was the first occupation in colonial Maryland. Nowadays fewer than 3 percent of the workers are farmers. Manufacturing flourished in the early days, as it does at the present time. Yet today only about a fifth of all workers earn their living in manufacturing. The rest of Maryland's workers are engaged in wholesale and retail trade, government work, the construction industries, transportation, and many other occupations.

Agriculture. Farms occupy about half of all land in the state. Almost a third of the commercial farms are dairy farms. Dairy products, poultry, and livestock sales bring about two thirds of the farm income. Crop sales make up the rest.

Farming is highly diversified because of the wide variation in soils, elevation, and climate within the state. Most of the farmers in Western Maryland raise livestock, have orchards, or grow potatoes, buckwheat, or oats. They may also sell maple syrup and timber. Farmers in north central Maryland sell dairy products and beef, raise poultry, or grow grains. In southern Maryland farmers cultivate tobacco and raise livestock as well. On the Eastern Shore farmers raise broilers, have cattle for milk or beef, or grow vegetables and grains.

Manufacturing. Manufacturing began in colonial times. Gristmills and textile mills were operated by waterpower. Iron furnaces used iron from the Maryland bogs. Shipbuilders made wooden ships from local timber. Many of these industries still exist, although they are much changed. Now grain is ground by electricity. Maryland's iron furnaces use ores from other states. Shipbuilding includes the construction of huge oceangoing steel freighters.

Once the manufacturing industries made use of local raw materials. Today many of the factories use materials from all over the world. Basic metals, such as iron, aluminum, copper, and tin, are brought by ship and are processed at plants in the Baltimore area. Raw chemical materials also come by ship and leave as sulfuric acid, fertilizer chemicals, and many other products. Raw sugar is processed at a refinery on the harbor. Spices from all over the globe are packed at a plant in Baltimore.

Some industries use the basic metals that are processed in the state. From these metals they fabricate transportation equipment, electrical and other types of machinery, weather and scientific instruments, bottle caps, and telephone and communication cable. Other industries still use local raw materials. For example, the food that is processed in Maryland is largely local seafood, vegetables, and fruits.

Mining. The value of minerals produced in Maryland ranks far below the value of manufactured goods or farm products. The minerals are mainly stone, sand and gravel, coal, and clays. Granite, marble, and limestone are used for trim on buildings. Dimension stone (stone cut to size) was once an important product. Many of the federal government buildings in the District of Columbia were made of Maryland stone. Today the quarries produce mainly crushed stone, which is used in concrete. Sand and gravel come chiefly from the Western Shore counties of the Coastal Plain. The extreme western part of the state produces small amounts of coal and natural gas. Most of the clay is used to make building bricks, tiles, and pottery.

Fisheries. The amount of seafood and fish taken from Maryland waters remains almost the same from year to year, although the weather and other conditions affect the catch. Much also depends on fishing methods and water pollution. Poor farming methods near the bay, for example, can cause soil to wash

Crab fishermen in Chesapeake Bay empty and rebait a trap called a crab pot.

into the streams, covering the oyster beds with silt and smothering the oysters. Oysters rank first in value among the seafoods. Others are crabs and clams.

Striped bass—locally called rockfish or rock—rank first in value among the fish. Others are shad, flounder, and white perch. Most of the people engaged in fishing live on the lower Eastern Shore of the bay, and most of the seafood-processing plants are there.

Transportation and Communication

The first national road in the United States was built west from Cumberland, Maryland, beginning in 1811. This was the Cumberland Road, also known as the National Road. The first section was built earlier. It went from Baltimore over the mountains to Cumberland. Today, a main east-west highway follows the path of this historic road. To speed traffic, the state has built a toll tunnel under Baltimore harbor and a toll bridge across the outer harbor. There are also major north-south highways, as well as many other roads throughout the state. Both Baltimore and Washington, D.C., are ringed by beltways.

The first passenger railroad in the United States was the Baltimore and Ohio. A 21-kilometer (13-mile) section was completed in May, 1830. It extended from Baltimore to Ellicott Mills, now Ellicott City. The first cars

---

WHAT MARYLAND PRODUCES

MANUFACTURED GOODS: Processed foods; electric and electronic equipment, mainly communications equipment; basic steel and other primary metals; nonelectrical machinery; chemicals and related products; transportation equipment; products of printing and publishing; paper and related products.

AGRICULTURAL PRODUCTS: Broilers, milk, corn, soybeans, cattle and calves, tobacco, eggs, greenhouse and nursery products.

MINERALS: Crushed stone, cement, bituminous coal, sand and gravel, natural gas, clays.

were drawn by horses. Today Maryland is served by railroads, which pass through Baltimore and carry freight between Baltimore harbor and the interior of the state. Passenger trains serve the Baltimore and Washington, D.C., areas. But many more Maryland communities are joined by bus lines than by railroads.

Maryland has many commercial airports and heliports. The Baltimore-Washington International Airport, near Baltimore, is a major center of air traffic.

The Chesapeake Bay and its tributaries provide waterways for large oceangoing vessels. Almost any ocean vessel can travel up Chesapeake Bay to the Baltimore harbor and go from there into Delaware Bay by way of the Chesapeake and Delaware Canal. Some ships can go up the Potomac as far as Washington, D.C. Maryland has never had a port on the Atlantic Ocean. The coastline is blocked by the general offshore sandbar that makes up much of the Atlantic coast from Cape Cod to Key West.

The *Maryland Gazette-News,* a weekly newspaper published at Glen Burnie, is the oldest newspaper in the state. It began publication in 1727. Maryland has about a dozen daily newspapers and more than 70 weeklies. The Baltimore *Sun,* established in 1837, is regarded as one of the leading newspapers in the United States.

Maryland has more than 80 radio stations and several television stations. Marylanders can also get a number of television channels from Washington, D.C.

▶ **EDUCATION**

In early colonial days only the sons of the wealthy landowners had a chance for formal education. They were taught by private teachers and sometimes were sent to school in England. Girls were taught household arts in their own homes.

Schools and Colleges

In the early 1700's the government of Maryland authorized schools in each of the counties. They were to be supported by a tobacco tax and other taxes. Few of these early county schools were successful. They lacked both money and teachers. In 1826 an act was passed to establish schools throughout Maryland, but no funds were provided. In the meantime boys and girls were taught separately in the many private schools that were established by churches and by individuals. The present system of public schools, supported by state and local taxes, began in 1864. At that time the state created a board of education and appointed a superintendent of instruction.

Higher education began in 1696 with the founding of King William's School at Annapolis. This school was chartered as St. John's College in 1784. Washington College in

The central building at Johns Hopkins University in Baltimore.

Chestertown was chartered in 1782. It was named for George Washington, with his permission. Both of these are private liberal arts colleges, as are Goucher College in Towson and Hood College in Frederick. There are numerous other private colleges and universities. Johns Hopkins University, which opened in Baltimore in 1876, is one of the country's leading universities. It is known especially for its medical school. The colleges maintained by religious denominations are mainly Roman Catholic.

The majority of Maryland's college and university students are enrolled in state-supported institutions. The University of Maryland System has its largest campus in College Park. Other campuses are located in Baltimore and Princess Anne. The Baltimore area has several other state-supported institutions. They are Towson State University, Morgan State University, Coppin State College, and the University of Baltimore. Other state colleges are located in Bowie (in the Washington, D.C., area); Frostburg, in Western Maryland; Salisbury, on the Eastern Shore; and St. Marys City, in the south.

A recent development in Maryland, as in the rest of the United States, is the growth of two-year colleges. Maryland has nearly 20 such institutions throughout the state. Chiefly they are public institutions administered by local school boards under state supervision.

The United States Naval Academy is at Annapolis. It was opened in 1845.

Music, Libraries, and Museums

Concert series are given at several of the smaller places in Maryland, but the chief musical events take place in Baltimore. The Baltimore Symphony is one of the major orchestras in the nation. The Baltimore Opera Company presents grand opera during the winter. The Peabody Institute of Johns Hopkins University holds a series of candlelight musical events.

Maryland's best-known library is the Enoch Pratt Free Library system in Baltimore. It was established in the 1880's. Today every large community in the state has a public library system. There are many special libraries maintained by colleges, universities, and professional organizations. Some of the museums include libraries.

The Baltimore Museum of Art has important collections of paintings, sculpture, furniture, tapestries, and ceramics covering many periods and cultures. The Cone Collection of French impressionists is especially notable.

The Maryland Academy of Sciences, in Baltimore, maintains a planetarium and a museum of science and industry.

The Maryland Historical Society, in Baltimore, maintains a library of early books and manuscripts and a museum. In the museum visitors may see portraits and letters of the Calvert and the Carroll families of Maryland and the original manuscript of "The Star-Spangled Banner."

The Peale Museum, in Baltimore, was founded in 1813 by the painter Rembrandt Peale. It contains paintings by members of the Peale family and objects of significance to Baltimore.

The United States Naval Academy Museum, at Annapolis, depicts three centuries of American naval history. Exhibited are ship models, marine paintings, naval documents, and battle flags.

The Walters Art Gallery, in Baltimore, includes art of almost every period and country. The library contains more than 1,000 books printed before A.D. 1501.

The Washington County Museum of Fine Arts, at Hagerstown, is an outstanding small museum. It was donated by the wife of the American painter William H. Singer, Jr.

▶ **PLACES OF INTEREST**

Many noted historic places are in the Baltimore and the Washington, D.C., areas or in and around Annapolis. Recreational and scenic areas are found throughout the state.

National Areas

The following list describes places that are part of the National Park System. Most of them are entirely within Maryland, but a few are shared with other states.

Antietam National Battlefield Site, near Sharpsburg, commemorates an important battle of the Civil War fought at Antietam Creek on September 17, 1862. It includes a historical museum and a marked tour of the battlefield. Nearby is **Antietam National Cemetery.**

Assateague Island National Seashore is shared by Maryland and Virginia. It is described in the article VIRGINIA in Volume V.

Catoctin Mountain Park, in Frederick County, contains the presidential retreat Camp David.

The Chesapeake and Ohio Canal National Historical Park follows the route of the 296-kilometer (184-mile) canal that ran from Washington,

D.C., to Cumberland, Maryland. The canal was planned by George Washington and was finished in 1850. In 1924 it was abandoned because of flood damage. The park has facilities for picnicking, boating, and hiking.

Clara Barton National Historic Site, in Glen Echo (near Bethesda), was the home of the founder of the American Red Cross.

Fort McHenry National Monument and Historic Shrine preserves Fort McHenry in Baltimore harbor. The successful defense of this fort on September 13–14, 1814, inspired Francis Scott Key to write the national anthem of the United States.

Fort Washington Park, on the Potomac River south of Washington, D.C., preserves a 19th-century fort that guarded the approaches to Washington.

George Washington Memorial Parkway, shared by Maryland and Virginia, is a landscaped parkway along the Potomac. It connects many landmarks in the life of George Washington.

Hampton National Historic Site, near Towson, is a fine example of a Georgian-style mansion, built in the late 1700's.

Harpers Ferry National Historical Park is shared by West Virginia and Maryland. It is described in the article WEST VIRGINIA in Volume W.

Monocacy National Battlefield, near Frederick, is the site of a Civil War battle. The Union troops lost, but they prevented Washington, D.C., from falling to the Confederates.

Thomas Stone National Historic Site, near La Plata, preserves the home of Thomas Stone, a signer of the Declaration of Independence.

Other Places

Maryland has established some 40 state parks and state forests. The parks preserve scenic or historic places. The main purpose of the forests is conservation. But almost all the parks and forests include places for recreation. The following are among the state parks and other places of special interest:

Calvert Cliffs, in Calvert County, are steep cliffs that extend along Chesapeake Bay. They are world famous among scientists for their fossils.

Deep Creek Lake State Park is a beautiful mountain park in Western Maryland.

Flag House, in Baltimore, is the restored home of Mary Pickersgill, who made the flag that flew over Fort McHenry during the bombardment in 1814.

Fort Frederick State Park, near Clear Spring, includes Fort Frederick, a frontier stone fort that has been restored.

General Smallwood State Park, near Pisgah, contains the restored home of the Revolutionary War general William Smallwood. He was also governor of Maryland (1785–88).

Great Falls of the Potomac, in Montgomery County, mark the edge of the Piedmont and the beginning of the Coastal Plain.

State House, in Annapolis, is the oldest state capitol in the United States still in use. It is also the only state capitol that was once used as the capitol of the United States.

Annual Events

Maryland has many annual celebrations that are based on historic events and the special products or attractions of the state.

March 25—Maryland Day, Baltimore and St. Marys City, celebrating the landing of the first colonists in 1634.

May—Preakness Festival Week, Baltimore.

June—June Week graduation celebrations, Naval Academy, Annapolis.

August—Clam/Seafood Festival, Annapolis.

September—State Fair, Timonium; Old Defenders' Day (September 12), celebration of the defense of Fort McHenry in the War of 1812.

October—Princess Anne Days, Princess Anne; Columbus Day Parade, Baltimore.

▶ CITIES

The two largest clusters of people are in the Baltimore and the Washington, D.C., areas. Incorporated places (cities and towns) elsewhere have fewer than 40,000 people.

Annapolis

Annapolis is the state capital, the county seat of Anne Arundel County, and the site of the United States Naval Academy. About 1648 it was settled by Puritans from Virginia. They called it Providence. Later it was named Anne Arundel for the wife of the second Lord Baltimore. In 1694, when it became the capital, it was given its present name for Princess Anne, who later became Queen Anne of England.

Annapolis is almost a living museum. It has been lived in continuously since colonial times. There are still many houses built before 1800, when it was called the Athens of America. The State House is on a hill dominating the city. Annapolis has no large industries. Its importance is divided between the state government and the Naval Academy.

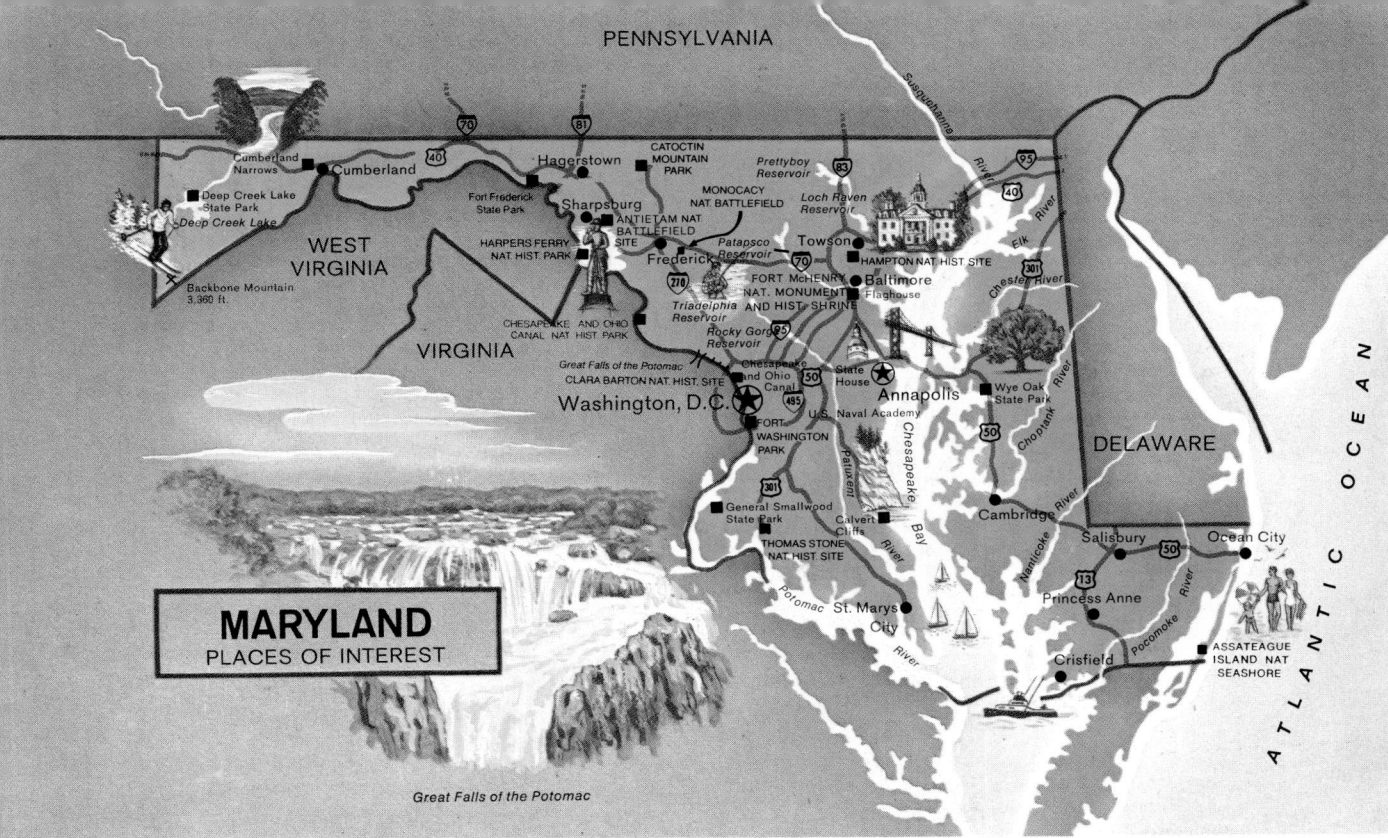

MARYLAND
PLACES OF INTEREST

Great Falls of the Potomac

Baltimore

Baltimore, founded in 1729, is located on the Patapsco River near the Chesapeake Bay. The city and metropolitan area surrounding it contain more than half the population of Maryland. Baltimore itself is a political unit, belonging to no county. An article on Baltimore is included in Volume B.

Hagerstown

Hagerstown is the population and trading center of Maryland's part of the Great Valley. In Maryland this is a fruit and agricultural belt. Hagerstown is the seat of Washington County and a manufacturing center.

Other Cities

Cumberland is the largest population center of Western Maryland. It is an industrial city, located near the Cumberland Narrows. Frederick is a trade center for the valleys east of the Blue Ridge. One of the places of interest in Frederick is the home of Barbara Fritchie. It is said that she hung the United States flag outside her upstairs window when Southern troops marched through town during the Civil War. This event was made famous by John Greenleaf Whittier's poem "Barbara Fritchie." Salisbury is the largest town on the Eastern Shore. It is located in an agricultural and poultry-raising region.

▶ GOVERNMENT

Maryland is governed under its fourth state constitution, which was adopted in 1867.

The governor is at the head of the executive branch of the state government. The other elected executive officials are the lieutenant governor, comptroller, and attorney general. The governor appoints the secretary of state and many other state officials.

The state legislature is called the General Assembly. It has two bodies, the Senate and the House of Delegates. The legislature meets every year.

The Court of Appeals is the highest court in the judicial branch of the state government. The governor appoints the chief judge of this court.

GOVERNMENT

Capital—Annapolis. **Number of counties**—23. **Representation in Congress**—U.S. senators, 2; U.S. representatives, 8. **General Assembly**—Senate, 47 members; House of Delegates, 141 members; all 4-year terms. **Governor**—4-year term; limited to two consecutive terms. **Elections**—General and state, Tuesday after first Monday in November.

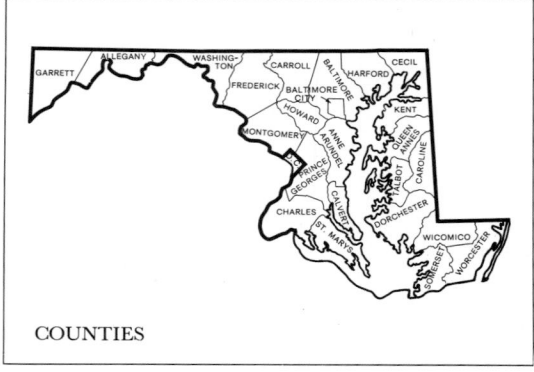

COUNTIES

Who was "the painter of the Revolution"?

He fought valiantly at Trenton and Valley Forge, and in 1777 he was commissioned a captain of volunteers. But this patriot is best remembered as an artist. Even as a soldier he carried his palette and paintbrushes along with his musket. His name was Charles Willson Peale. He can well be called "the painter of the Revolutionary War" because he left records on canvas of many war heroes and founders of the United States of America. The first portrait of George Washington was painted by Peale. And from 1772 to 1795, Peale painted many other portraits of Washington from life. Peale's portraits of Benjamin Franklin, Thomas Jefferson, John Paul Jones, and many other famous people of his time can be seen today in museums.

Peale was born in Queen Annes County, Maryland, in 1741. He lived a long and fruitful life as a patriot, painter, and naturalist. He died in Philadelphia in 1827. Some of his many children were named for famous European painters. And some of those children—including Rembrandt, Raphael, and Titian Peale—became well-known artists themselves.

▶ FAMOUS PEOPLE

The following are among the native-born or adopted citizens of Maryland who became well-known in public affairs, the arts, or industry. They represent different periods in the history of the state and the nation.

Leonard Calvert (1606–47), son of the first Lord Baltimore and younger brother of the second Lord Baltimore, was the first Calvert to come to Maryland. He was the leader of the settlers and the first governor of the colony.

Charles Carroll of Carrollton (1737–1832) was born at Annapolis. He was one of the four Maryland signers of the Declaration of Independence—and the only one who added his address ("of Carrollton"). He was a member of the wealthy and prominent Carroll family, in which Charles was a popular name. He added his address so that everyone would know which Charles Carroll he was. He was one of Maryland's first United States senators (1789–92).

Roger Brooke Taney (1777–1864), born in Calvert County, was the fifth chief justice of the United States. He was appointed by President Andrew Jackson in 1836 and served until 1864. Before that time, Taney had been attorney general of Maryland and of the United States. He was chief justice at the time of the Dred Scott Decision. The home of Justice Taney is one of the important places of interest in Frederick. It also contains mementos of Francis Scott Key, who was a brother-in-law of Taney.

Francis Scott Key (1779–1843) was born in what is now Carroll County. He was a lawyer who won fame as author of "The Star-Spangled Banner."

Robert Sargent Shriver, Jr. (1915–), was born in Westminster. He served as director of the Peace Corps (1961–66) and the Office of Economic Opportunity (1964–68) and as ambassador to France (1968–70). He was the Democratic candidate for vice-president in 1972.

Spiro T. Agnew (1918–) was born in Baltimore. He attended Baltimore public schools, Johns Hopkins University, and Baltimore Law School. Agnew served as county executive of Baltimore County from 1962 to 1966, when he became governor of Maryland. As Richard M. Nixon's running mate, he was elected vice-president in 1968 and in 1972. He resigned the vice-presidency in 1973 just before pleading no contest to a tax-evasion charge.

Edgar Allan Poe, born in Boston, lived in Baltimore from time to time. His house and his burial place are among the places of interest in Baltimore. The poet Sidney Lanier, born in Georgia, came to Maryland as a prisoner of war during the Civil War. He returned later to become famous as a poet, literary critic, and musician. Henry L. Mencken, a famous critic and author of *The American Language,* was a native of Baltimore.

A remarkable group of wealthy citizens enriched the educational and cultural life of Baltimore. Johns Hopkins, a Quaker merchant and banker, gave funds to establish Johns Hopkins University. Enoch Pratt, ironware merchant, donated money to found the Enoch Pratt Free Library system. George Peabody, a banker who lived in Baltimore as a

Fort McHenry in Baltimore harbor. The defense of this fort during the War of 1812 inspired the writing of "The Star-Spangled Banner."

young man, founded the school of music known today as Peabody Institute of Johns Hopkins University. William Thompson Walters and his son Henry assembled one of the outstanding private art collections in the United States. The elder Walters was associated with Johns Hopkins in the building of railroads. The younger Walters left the Walters Art Gallery to the city of Baltimore.

▶ HISTORY

Before Europeans came to North America, Maryland was the home of many Indian tribes. Most of them were around the inlets of the Chesapeake Bay. The Indians lived in bark houses, usually in stockaded villages. They hunted and fished and raised some crops. Usually they were friendly to the settlers. Sometimes they worked for the settlers as hunters, hoping to get guns that they could use against raiding Indian enemies. Indians who raided the settlers were usually warriors from outside the territory.

Discovery and Exploration

The first European to see Maryland was probably John Cabot, an Italian captain working for the English. Cabot sailed down the Atlantic coast in 1498. In 1524 Giovanni da Verrazano, an Italian working for the French, passed the mouth of the Chesapeake Bay.

In 1608 Captain John Smith, with 14 other men from the Virginia colony, started up the Chesapeake in "an open barge of two tunnes burden." He hoped to find a passage to the Indian Sea. He inspected the inlets and islands of the Eastern Shore and was welcomed by the Indians. He returned to Virginia to make a map of the area. The map, published in England, shows the Eastern Shore and the Potomac River rather well. It is less accurate on the north end of the bay and on the Western Shore.

Settlement and Growth

The first Lord Baltimore, George Calvert, was a native of Yorkshire, England. His service to King James I gained for him a grant of land in Newfoundland. This location proved to be too cold. Lord Baltimore persuaded King Charles I, James's successor, to grant him a charter for a new colony, which became the colony of Maryland.

Lord Baltimore died before the charter was signed on June 20, 1632. His son Cecil, the second Lord Baltimore, succeeded him. Cecil organized a colonizing expedition to Maryland in two vessels, the *Ark* and the *Dove*. The *Ark* was a good-sized vessel for those days. The *Dove* was smaller. It was supposed to run into shallow inlets ahead of the *Ark* to see whether it was safe for the larger vessel to follow. The *Ark* was named for the Ark of Noah, which carried people safely through the Flood described in the Bible. The *Dove* was named for the dove that Noah sent out to see whether the Flood was over.

Lord Baltimore did not go with the ships. In charge was his younger brother, Leonard

Calvert, assisted by Father Andrew White, a Jesuit priest. Father White wrote the account of the journey. The members of the Calvert family were Catholic, as were many of the leaders of the colony. Most of the working settlers were Protestant.

The colonists landed at St. Clements Island (now Blakiston Island) in the Potomac River on March 25, 1634. They fixed that date as the landing of the first settlers in Maryland. Later they bought an Indian village from the Indians and moved into what is now St. Marys City.

The colony centered around St. Marys City for more than 60 years. There were difficulties with traders from Virginia who had been dealing with the Indians. William Claiborne, a Virginian, had settled on Kent Island in 1631. There was even a small naval battle before he was put off the island. Religious difficulties arose when King Charles I was deposed and a Puritan parliament took over the rule of England in 1642. For a time Maryland was in the hands of the Puritans.

In 1649 Lord Baltimore felt that it was time to legalize the idea of religious freedom on which the colony was founded. The Maryland assembly passed the famous "act concerning religion." This act made Maryland's government one of the first in the world to recognize freedom of religion. But from 1689 to 1715 Maryland was a crown colony—a colony belonging to the rulers of England—and the Church of England was the established church. In 1715 the colony was restored to the fifth Lord Baltimore.

The capital of Maryland was moved to Annapolis in 1694. Baltimore was founded in 1729. During this time the population expanded rapidly.

Statehood and Later Times

Meanwhile, events were leading up to the Revolutionary War. Troops from Maryland took part from the first skirmish at Boston to the final surrender. The most famous campaign of the Fifth Regiment, known as the Old Line, was at Brooklyn in the Battle of Long Island. There the Maryland troops delayed the British and covered the retreat of George Washington's army. Maryland's nickname, the Old Line State, comes from this battle. The Third Continental Congress met in Baltimore in

---

IMPORTANT DATES

1498	John Cabot, exploring for England, saw the ocean shore of Worcester County.
1608	Captain John Smith of the Virginia colony explored the Chesapeake Bay.
1631	William Claiborne of the Virginia colony established a trading post on Kent Island in the Chesapeake Bay.
1632	Charles I of England granted the Maryland charter to the first Lord Baltimore.
1634	The *Ark* and the *Dove* brought the first colonists to Maryland.
1638	Calvert forces defeated William Claiborne, and Kent Island became part of Maryland.
1649	An act of the Maryland assembly recognized freedom of religion throughout the colony.
1689	Maryland became a crown colony under the rulers of England; returned to private ownership of the fifth Lord Baltimore in 1715.
1694	Capital moved from St. Marys City to Annapolis.
1729	The town of Baltimore founded.
1776	A regiment from Maryland, the Maryland Old Line, helped to save the American army during the Battle of Long Island in the Revolutionary War.
1783	Ninth Continental Congress met in Annapolis; George Washington came before this congress to resign his commission as commander in chief of the Continental Army.
1784	Continental Congress, meeting at Annapolis, ratified the Treaty of Paris ending the Revolutionary War.
1788	April 28, Maryland became the 7th state.
1791	Maryland ceded to the federal government 60 square miles of land for the national capital.
1811	Construction of the first national road began west from Cumberland.
1814	Francis Scott Key, watching the British attack on Fort McHenry, wrote "The Star-Spangled Banner."
1829	Chesapeake and Delaware Canal opened.
1830	Baltimore and Ohio Railroad, the first passenger railroad in the United States, opened a section of track between Baltimore and Ellicott Mills.
1844	First telegraph message sent from Washington, D.C., to Baltimore.
1845	U.S. Naval Academy opened at Annapolis.
1859	First streetcar in Baltimore began operation.
1862	Battle of Antietam near Sharpsburg, September 17, ended the South's first invasion of the North during the Civil War.
1904	February 7–9, fire destroyed much of the city of Baltimore.
1952	Chesapeake Bay Bridge completed.
1957	Baltimore Harbor Tunnel opened.
1974	Baltimore school system began a large-scale desegregation plan.
1977	Francis Scott Key Bridge opened over the outer harbor, completing the beltway around Baltimore.
1978	Voters elected women to four of Maryland's eight seats in the U.S. House of Representatives.
1981	A new aquarium, designated by Congress as the National Aquarium, opened in Baltimore.

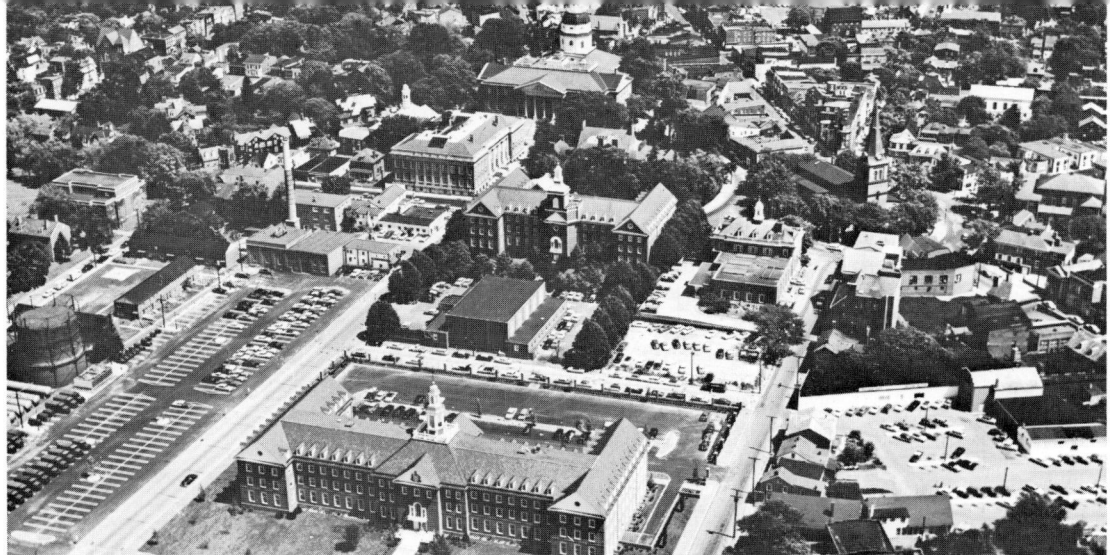

Annapolis, the state capital. Government buildings are in the foreground.

1776 and 1777. The famous Ninth Continental Congress met at the State House in Annapolis in 1783. Two historic events happened at the State House while this congress was in session. George Washington resigned his commission as commander in chief of the Continental Army. The Congress ratified the Treaty of Paris, ending the Revolutionary War. On April 28, 1788, Maryland became the seventh state to ratify the Constitution of the United States.

The War of 1812 brought heavy fighting to Maryland. British troops sailed up the Patuxent River, routed Maryland forces at Bladensburg, and then burned public buildings in Washington, D.C. Later they were fended off from Fort McHenry, a fort in Baltimore harbor. When the British were bombarding the fort, Francis Scott Key was inspired to write the words of the song that became the national anthem of the United States. Maryland privateers, sailing in speedy Baltimore Clippers, captured many of the British ships taken during the war.

The state progressed rapidly after the War of 1812. The first national road was built west from Cumberland. The Chesapeake and Delaware Canal was opened in 1829. The next year the Baltimore and Ohio Railroad opened its first section of track. In 1844, Samuel F. B. Morse sent the first telegraph message over the first telegraph line in the world, from Washington, D.C., to Baltimore. The United States Naval Academy opened in 1845. The first streetcar in Baltimore, a four-horse model, began operation in 1859.

The Civil War

The years just before the Civil War found eastern Maryland with Southern sympathies. Western Maryland shared the feelings of the North. In 1861 mobs of Southern sympathizers in Baltimore attacked some Massachusetts troops as they marched from one railroad station to another on their way to Washington, D.C. Several civilians and soldiers were killed. This was the first blood spilled in the Civil War. Confederate forces invaded Maryland three times. In 1862, at South Mountain and Antietam, two of the bloodiest battles of the war were fought. The next year General Robert E. Lee's army invaded Maryland on its way to Gettysburg, Pennsylvania. In 1864 General Jubal Early's Confederate troops defeated Union forces at the battle of Monocacy.

Modern Times and the Future

After the Civil War more and more federal buildings and installations were built in the Maryland area surrounding Washington, D.C. Recent history has seen great improvements in transportation, particularly in highways. New bridges and tunnels speed traffic through the state.

It is probable that Maryland's main urban centers will continue to grow. Agriculture may become less important. Methods of transportation will change. But the position of Baltimore as a world port seems secure because of its geographical advantages.

GEORGE BEISHLAG
Formerly, Towson State University

MARY QUEEN OF SCOTS (1542–1587)

Mary Stuart, queen of Scotland, was one of the most romantic and tragic figures in British history. She inherited the Scottish throne as a child and later reigned briefly as queen of France. A woman of great beauty, charm, and intelligence, she was also passionate and ambitious. Her romantic involvements cost her the Scottish crown. Her ambition to be queen of England led to years of captivity and, finally, to her execution.

Mary was born at Linlithgow Palace near Edinburgh, Scotland, on December 7 or 8, 1542. She was the daughter of King James V and his French wife, Mary of Guise. Her father died when she was a week old, and the infant princess became queen of Scotland. Her mother governed as regent for her. At the age of 5, Mary was promised in marriage to the French dauphin (the heir to the throne), Francis, and was sent to France to be educated. She was brought up as a Roman Catholic. Her intelligence impressed her teachers, and her grace and charm captivated the elegant French court. In 1558, at the age of 15, she married the young dauphin. The following year he became King Francis II, and Mary became queen of France. She reigned less than two years. The sickly king died in 1560, and Mary returned to Scotland.

She arrived home a Catholic queen in a country that had become largely Protestant. Mary's own religious views were moderate, but her desire to advance the Catholic faith aroused the hostility of many Protestants. Her position as monarch was weak, for much power rested with the Scottish nobility. In 1565, Mary chose as her second husband a cousin, Henry Stewart, Lord Darnley, who was a Catholic. It was a poor choice. Many Scottish lords disapproved of the match, and some took up arms against her.

Mary's great ambition was to gain the throne of England, then occupied by her cousin Elizabeth I. Mary's claims to the English crown were strong. As the great-granddaughter of King Henry VII of England, she was next in line to the throne after Elizabeth. In 1566 Mary gave birth to a son who was to become King James VI of Scotland and, later, King James I of England.

But by then the handsome Darnley had

Mary Queen of Scots, as she appeared in 1560—the year her mother and her first husband died.

proved to be a weak and vicious man, and Mary had grown to hate him. Darnley was jealous of Mary's attentions to her Italian secretary, David Rizzio. Suspecting that Rizzio's influence was turning Mary against him, Darnley and a group of sympathetic lords murdered him in 1566.

Mary never forgave Darnley and turned for affection and support to James Hepburn, Earl of Bothwell. In 1567, Darnley was found murdered. Bothwell was widely believed to have planned the murder, but he was acquitted. Mary's part in the crime has remained unclear. It is thought that she knew of the plan to kill Darnley and probably agreed to it. Soon after, she married Bothwell. The marriage aroused a storm of protest. She was forced to give up the throne in favor of her son, James, and was imprisoned. In 1568 she escaped and raised a small band of loyal followers. But they were defeated in battle and Mary fled to England.

For the next 19 years she was a virtual prisoner. Her presence incited many plots against the English throne and was a constant threat to Elizabeth. Catholics did not recognize Elizabeth's title to the throne and believed Mary to be the rightful queen of England. She was finally put on trial and convicted of having taken part in a plot to assassinate Elizabeth. Fearing the effect that Mary's execution would have, Elizabeth delayed signing the death warrant for three months. At last, on February 8, 1587, Mary—still proclaiming her innocence—was beheaded.

Reviewed by ELLIOT ROSE
University of Toronto

MASARYK, TOMÁŠ (1850–1937)

Tomáš Garrigue Masaryk was a founder and the first president of Czechoslovakia. He was born on March 7, 1850, in Hodonín, Moravia, then part of the Austro-Hungarian Empire. His father was a coachman on an estate belonging to the Austrian imperial family. Masaryk studied at the universities of Vienna and Leipzig. At Leipzig he met an American music student, Charlotte Garrigue. They were married in 1878. In 1882 he was appointed a professor of philosophy at the newly formed Czech University in Prague. There he began his career as a scholar and political leader. His writings quickly made him known as a philosopher.

Prague was the center of Czech nationalism. Masaryk soon became a leader of the Young Czech Party, which sought greater self-government. In 1891 he was elected to the Austrian parliament. But he returned to teaching two years later. In 1900 he formed the Progressive (Realist) Party. He hoped to unite the Slovaks (who were ruled by Hungary) and the Czechs in a self-governing federation within the empire. In 1907 he was again elected to parliament.

When World War I broke out in 1914, Masaryk began to organize a movement for complete independence. He was warned that he might be arrested, and he left Prague for London. There he and other patriots, including Eduard Beneš, formed a Czechoslovak national council. In 1918 Austria was on the brink of defeat, and the council declared itself a provisional government. On October 18 of that year, Masaryk proclaimed the independence of the Czechoslovak nation. He was elected president and returned to Prague. He was re-elected three times and served until his retirement in 1935. His friend Beneš succeeded him as president. Masaryk died near Prague on September 14, 1937. His son, Jan Garrigue Masaryk, held several important posts in the Czechoslovak Government.

Reviewed by R. E. ALLEN
Formerly, Columbia University

MASERS. See LASERS.

MASON-DIXON LINE

The Mason-Dixon line is the southern border of Pennsylvania, just north of 39° 43′ north latitude. The states north of this line abolished slavery during and soon after the Revolutionary War. And the line came to symbolize the entire border between slave and free states, or between the South and the North.

The colonial charters of Maryland and Pennsylvania left their common border in dispute. In 1732, commissioners from both colonies agreed to a border. But minor differences delayed the survey that would mark the actual line. The commissioners finally hired two English astronomers, Charles Mason and Jeremiah Dixon, who made the survey from 1763 to 1767. Their most difficult task was placing their first marker, southwest of Philadelphia. This marker, called the Stargazer's Stone, was set at the point where the borders of Pennsylvania, Maryland, and Delaware meet. It became the point on which all future surveys of federal land west of Pennsylvania rested. From the Stargazer's Stone, Mason and Dixon

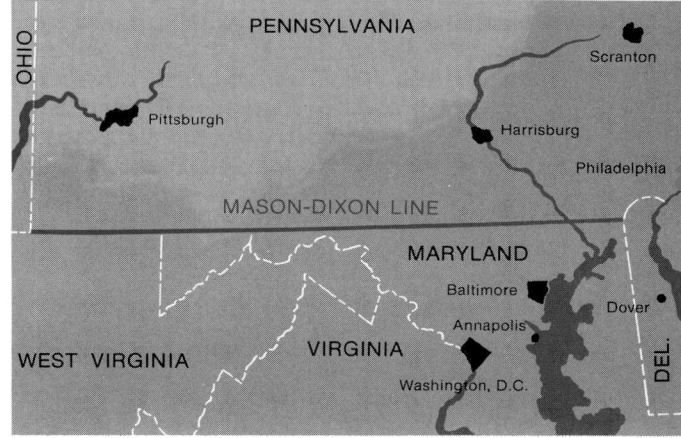

pushed due west to Maryland's western border. Later, Pennsylvania and Virginia extended the line to Pennsylvania's western border.

Mason and Dixon were very accurate. Later surveys resulted in no major changes in their line. Today many people still say the South is located "below the Mason-Dixon line."

ARI HOOGENBOOM
City University of New York, Brooklyn College

MASONRY. See BRICKS AND MASONRY.

MASSACHUSETTS

In 1784 a member of the Massachusetts House of Representatives, John Rowe, rose to make an unusual motion. He proposed that "leave might be given to hang up the representation of a Cod Fish in the room where the House sit, as a memorial of the importance of the Cod Fishery to the welfare of this Commonwealth."

A codfish—1.5 meters (5 feet) long—was carved from a piece of pinewood and hung before the lawmakers. After a new State House was built in 1795, the wooden codfish, or a new likeness, was hung again in the room where the House sits. There it can be seen to this day.

It is no wonder that the wooden figure is called the Sacred Cod. The first explorers wrote of waters filled with codfish. Captain John Smith said that it was a poor fisherman who could not catch 100 or more cod in one day with a hook and line. The Puritans depended on the cod for food. Later the cod fisheries brought much money, which was used to start other industries. Today fishing is only a small part of Massachusetts life, but the cod helped Massachusetts to become a prosperous state.

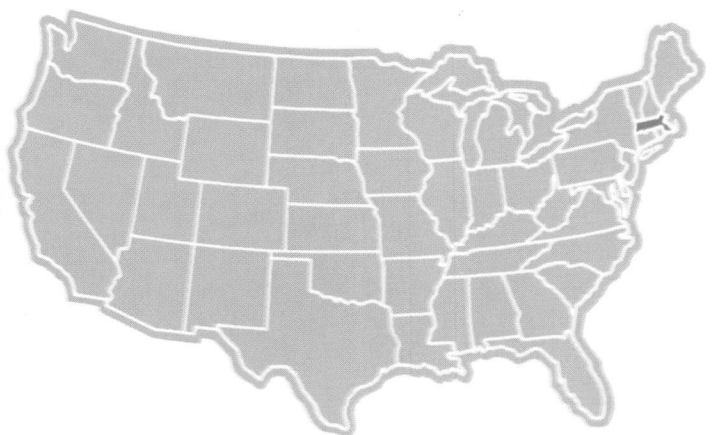

Visitors to Massachusetts often wonder why Boston is nicknamed the Hub of the Universe. Many years ago the writer Oliver Wendell Holmes (1809–94) attributed the nickname to the great pride of his fellow Bostonians. He commented jokingly that many of them thought the dome of the State House on Beacon Hill to be the center, or hub, of the solar system.

Some years later, in the 1930's, Daniel K. Wallingford, an architect and industrial designer, drew a now famous map entitled "A Bostonian's Idea of the United States of America." On this map, Cape Cod is shown as being larger than Florida. Many cities and towns in Massachusetts are on the map, but only a few places in the rest of the country are included. And these are located incorrectly. The point of this humorous map is that Bostonians are so concerned with their own small world—and so proud of it—that they know very little about the rest of the United States.

What truth is there in such a map? Of course, Massachusetts is not large. It could fit into many other states several times. But importance cannot be measured by the amount of land area. Throughout its long history, Massachusetts has contributed people and material goods out of proportion to its size.

Some of the first colonial settlements in North America were in Massachusetts. The fishing, whaling, and shipbuilding industries were launched and developed there. As the frontier pushed westward, Yankees from Massachusetts founded many of the new settlements to the west. When the United States turned from a rural way of life, Massachusetts again led the way. Its busy towns and cities already were producing a large share of the nation's manufactured goods.

Massachusetts also has been concerned with the great ideas that have shaped the nation's history. The Revolutionary War started in Massachusetts. Boston was the first important center of the movement to abolish slavery. Massachusetts' educational institutions and its hospitals have long been known throughout the nation and the world.

Now, in the age of electronics and high technology, Massachusetts is again in the forefront. Much of its modern industry is concerned with research activities and with production of electronic equipment, computer equipment, and other technical machinery.

▶THE LAND

Massachusetts, one of the New England States, is located in the northeastern part of the United States. The Atlantic Ocean forms all of its eastern border. Except for Maine, it is the most easterly of the 50 states.

Landforms

Nothing expresses the varied character of Massachusetts quite so much as its surface

STATE FLAG.

STATE TREE: American elm.

STATE BIRD: Chickadee.

STATE FLOWER: Mayflower (trailing arbutus).

MASSACHUSETTS

CAPITAL: Boston.

STATEHOOD: February 6, 1788; the 6th state.

SIZE: 21,456 km² (8,284 sq mi); rank, 45th.

POPULATION: 5,737,037 (1980 census); rank, 11th.

ORIGIN OF NAME: From the Massachuset Indians, who lived around the Blue Hills near present-day Boston. The name is made up of Indian words meaning "about the big hill."

ABBREVIATIONS: Mass.; MA.

NICKNAME: Bay State; also Old Colony State, Puritan State, Baked Bean State.

STATE SONG: "All Hail to Massachusetts"; words and music by Arthur J. Marsh.

STATE MOTTO: *Ense petit placidam sub libertate quietem* (With the sword she seeks peace under liberty).

STATE SEAL: The seal bears the coat of arms of the Commonwealth of Massachusetts. The arms consist of a blue shield on which are shown a silver star and a golden Indian holding a bow and arrow. The arrow points downward, a sign of friendly welcome. Above the shield is a raised arm with a broadsword, representing defense. The state motto appears on a streamer around the shield. The Latin words in the border mean "Seal of the Republic of Massachusetts."

STATE FLAG: The flag is white, with a different design on each side. The obverse, or front, side shows the coat of arms, as on the seal. On the reverse side a pine tree appears on the shield in place of the Indian.

The rolling farmlands of the Berkshires, in the extreme western part of the state, are among the many scenic areas of Massachusetts.

features. There are some flat areas, but most of the land is broken and hilly. Some parts are quite rugged, even though the elevations are not high. Only a small part of the state is more than 300 meters (1,000 feet) above sea level, and much of it is below 150 meters (500 feet). The topography shows that high elevations are not necessary for a rugged landscape. It shows also that many different kinds of surface features can be found within a small area.

Massachusetts may be divided into several regions—the Coastal Plain, the Seaboard Lowland, the New England Upland, the Connecticut Valley Lowland, and the Taconic Mountains.

Most of the eastern coast of the United States is part of an extensive landform called the Coastal Plain. North of Long Island (a part of New York), the Coastal Plain disappears, except for Cape Cod and the islands of Nantucket and Martha's Vineyard. The northern side of Cape Cod is a long ridge formed by glaciers during the ice ages. The southern side is low and sandy. It is pitted with small lakes and ponds. The hooked end of the Cape was formed after the ice ages by the action of currents and waves. Currents picked up sand from the eastern shore and carried it northward. It was deposited in the form of a curved sandbar, or spit. In this area the wind has whipped up the sand and piled it into huge dunes.

The rest of Massachusetts' coastal land is called the Seaboard, or Coastal, Lowland. This area has a rough terrain, except for a few "pocket-sized" basins. The largest of the basins are the Boston and the Narragansett basins. The Boston Basin contains many oval-shaped hills called **drumlins.** The most famous drumlins are Bunker Hill and Beacon Hill. The coastline is rough and rocky, with many sheltered harbors and small offshore islands. In some places the waves have formed sandbars, or **tombolos,** that tie the islands to the mainland. Good examples of tombolos are found at Duxbury, Nahant, and Marblehead.

Most of the rest of the state belongs to the New England Upland. The Connecticut Valley Lowland cuts into this region, dividing it into the Eastern Upland and the Western Upland. The Eastern Upland rises gradually to elevations as high as 300 meters (1,000 feet). A traveler gets the feeling of ruggedness, emphasized by occasional views of monadnocks—mountains or hills made up of very hard rock that resists erosion. Wachusett Mountain is a monadnock. The drop into the Connecticut Valley Lowland is sharp and distinct. Going toward the center of the lowland,

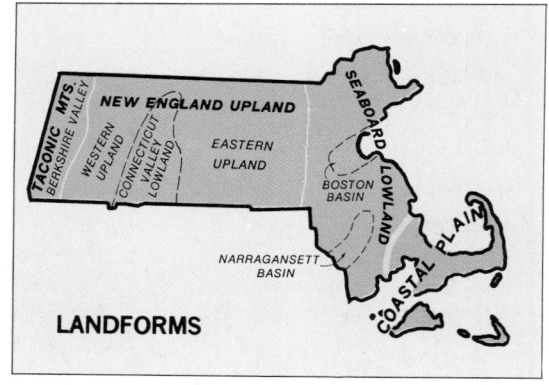

LANDFORMS

one crosses broad terraces that descend like steps. The valley is mostly flat. But it is broken by ridges, which lend a pleasing variety to the landscape. Mount Tom and Mount Holyoke are peaks in these ridges.

The rise from the Connecticut Valley Lowland to the Western Upland is spectacular. This upland is known locally as the Berkshire Hills. It is hilly and wooded. The river valleys are narrow with steep walls. Most of the towns have elevations over 600 meters (2,000 feet).

The Western Upland ends abruptly and drops sharply to the Berkshire Valley—a narrow trough that runs along the base of the Taconic Mountains. The mountains are old and worn down, but they have steep slopes. Mount Greylock, the highest point in the state, is in this range.

Rivers, Lakes, and Coastal Waters

The Connecticut River is the principal river of Massachusetts. Its most important tributaries are the Westfield, Deerfield, Millers, and Chicopee rivers. This river system drains the Connecticut Valley Lowland and the uplands on either side. The Hoosic and Housatonic rivers are to the west in the Berkshire Valley. Northeastern Massachusetts is drained by the Merrimack River and its tributaries, the Concord and the Nashua. In the southeast are the Blackstone and the Taunton rivers.

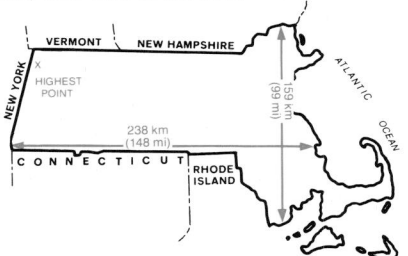

THE LAND

LOCATION: Latitude—41° 14' N to 42° 53' N. **Longitude**—69° 56' W to 73° 30' W.
Vermont and New Hampshire to the north, the Atlantic Ocean to the east, Rhode Island and Connecticut to the south, New York to the west.

ELEVATION: Highest—Mount Greylock, 1,065 m (3,491 ft). **Lowest**—Sea level, along the Atlantic coast.

LANDFORMS: Coastal Plain, Seaboard Lowland, New England Upland, Connecticut Valley Lowland, Taconic Mountains.

SURFACE WATERS: Major rivers—Connecticut, Merrimack, Housatonic, Blackstone, Taunton, **Major artificial lakes**—Quabbin, Wachusett, Cobble Mountain. **Largest natural lakes**—Assawompsett Pond, Watuppa Pond, Long Pond, Lake Chaubunagungamaug (sometimes called Lake Webster).

CLIMATE: Temperature—Boston's January average, −2°C (29°F); July average, 22°C (72°F). **Precipitation**—Rainfall average, 965–1,220 mm (38–48 in), fairly evenly distributed throughout the year. Snowfall in the west varies from 140 to 190 cm (55 to 75 in) a year; in the east, from 50 to 75 cm (20 to 30 in). **Growing season**—In the west, 120–140 days; in the Connecticut Valley Lowland, 140–160 days; along the coast, 160–200 days.

Houses stand like sentinels overlooking the Atlantic Ocean from sand dunes on Cape Cod. The cape is a curving peninsula in southeastern Massachusetts.

Massachusetts has many natural lakes. Most of them are in the eastern part of the state. Often they are called ponds. Among the largest are Assawompsett, Watuppa, and Long ponds. Near the Connecticut border is a lake with a very long name—Lake Chaubunagungamaug. This is the shortened form of an Indian name that is twice as long. Sometimes the lake is called simply Lake Webster. Artificial lakes include Quabbin and Wachusett reservoirs. Both of these supply water to the Boston metropolitan area.

The general coastline of Massachusetts is 309 kilometers (192 miles) long. With all the islands, bays, and inlets, the shoreline measures 2,444 kilometers (1,519 miles). The largest bay is Cape Cod Bay.

Climate

The word for the weather in Massachusetts is variable. A fine day is often followed by two or three stormy or cloudy days. The pattern of climate is about the same throughout the state. Winters are cold and wet. Summers are pleasantly warm. Coastal areas and the higher elevations in the western part of the state have slightly cooler July temperatures than other areas in the state. Average January temperatures increase gradually as one moves from west to east.

Massachusetts does not have a true rainy season. The rainfall is fairly evenly distributed throughout the year. All parts of the state have snow, but snows are heaviest in the west.

Natural Resources

Massachusetts' most valuable natural resource is the marine life found in its offshore waters. The land itself is not richly endowed with minerals, forests, or fertile soils.

The state's conservation programs are run by the Office of Environmental Affairs. It coordinates water-resources development with land management. It is also responsible for, among other things, forest-fire control and forest development and recreation. Massachusetts has passed a "bottle bill," providing for the recycling of some bottles and cans. Hazardous-waste sites are being identified, and many have been cleaned up.

Soils. Scientists classify most of the soils in Massachusetts as podzolic soils. Soils of this kind are somewhat acid. They are best suited to the growing of grass, trees, and root crops. Most of the upland is rough and stony. The largest single expanse of fertile soil is in the Connecticut Valley Lowland.

Forests. In colonial days, Massachusetts was covered with forests. Huge oaks, maples, and white pines supplied the settlers with all their needs for building and fuel. Today nearly 65 percent of the state is forested. But much of this area contains trees of low quality. The high-quality timber was lost 150 years ago by overcutting.

Minerals. Massachusetts has large amounts of sand and gravel and hard building stone, such as granite and traprock. Other mineral deposits include limestone, found in the Berkshire Valley, and clays, found mainly in Plymouth and Bristol counties.

Marine Life. Among the dozens of varieties of fish in the coastal waters are alewife, butterfish, cod, flounder, haddock, halibut, herring, mackerel, pollock, and swordfish. Shellfish are also abundant. They include clams, oysters, lobsters, scallops, and shrimp. Whales once were common in the offshore waters. They are no longer numerous, but occasionally they can be seen.

▶THE PEOPLE AND THEIR WORK

In 1830 most of the citizens of Massachusetts were native-born of Yankee stock—descendants of the original English settlers. Beginning in the 1840's, thousands of immigrants began to arrive in the United States each year. Up to 1890 the largest groups coming to Massachusetts were Irish, English, Scots, Canadians, Germans, Scandinavians, and Finns. After 1890 large numbers arrived from Italy and Portugal and from eastern European countries. The Portuguese were attracted by commercial fishing. But most of the newcomers were attracted to jobs in the growing textile and shoe industries. In the years since 1960, there have been increases in the numbers of Massachusetts citizens from Puerto Rico and from Southeast Asia.

Where the People Live

Most of the people in Massachusetts live in cities and towns. The most heavily populated section is centered on Boston. Other well-settled areas are around Springfield in the Connecticut Valley Lowland, Worcester in the central part of the state, and Lowell and Lawrence in the northeast.

Top: Technicians test desk-top computers manufactured at a plant near Boston. High-technology industries are an important part of the Massachusetts economy. Bottom: A commercial fishing boat docks at a pier in Gloucester.

Industries and Products

Manufacturing and commercial activities—such as banking, insurance, and wholesale and retail trade—provide jobs for large numbers of people in Massachusetts. Many others work in government offices and in various professions and trades.

Manufacturing. In colonial days the main kinds of industries were shipyards, ironworks, mills for grinding grain, and tanneries. The forests provided large quantities of timber for ships. Massachusetts' first shipyard was built at Salem Neck in 1637. Soon, others were built at such ports as Gloucester, Salem, and Boston. The ironworks used deposits of bog iron, mined in swampy areas. One of the first ironworks in the United States was opened at Saugus in 1643. Much of the iron was used for ships' hardware. The gristmills were operated by power from the many small waterfalls. These mills ground corn and other grains from the local farms. Hides for the tanneries came at first from New England. After 1800, hides were brought by ship from California. Plentiful supplies of leather and labor led to shoemaking as a "backyards industry." When the weather was too stormy for fishing, families in small villages from Marblehead to Gloucester worked at making shoes. Gradually the shoe industry began to concentrate in factory towns north and south of Boston.

Major advances in manufacturing took place after 1800. In 1814, Francis Cabot Lowell and his associates established a mill that combined all operations of manufacturing cotton cloth. This mill was at Waltham, on the Charles River. It was not long before Massachusetts and neighboring Rhode Island led the nation in the production of cotton textiles. All the raw cotton had to be shipped from the South. But Massachusetts had advantages that more than balanced this fact. Many people had made fortunes in trade and fishing, and money was available for mills and machinery. The many waterfalls—and later, steam power produced from coal—supplied power to run the mills. The high relative humidity helped to keep threads from breaking in the fast-moving machinery. Finally, labor was in good supply.

Leading producers of cotton textiles were Lowell, Fall River, New Bedford, and Salem.

Woolen textiles and shoes were also of great importance. Lawrence was the largest center of woolen mills. Boston was the financial center for the cotton and woolen textile industries and for the shoe industry. It was also the main importing center for raw wool. The invention of a stitching machine in the 1850's helped to promote factory production of shoes. By 1900 almost half the nation's shoes were made in New England, with Massachusetts the leading state. The production of textiles and shoes led to another industry—the manufacture of machinery for the factories.

Today the chief manufactured products are nonelectrical machinery and electric and electronic equipment, including computers. Other leading manufactures include measuring devices, products made of metal, printed material, and transportation equipment. Textiles and shoes are still produced, but their importance is not so great as in the past.

Agriculture. In colonial days the farmers of Massachusetts grew several kinds of grain and raised a variety of animals on their farms. But most of the land in the state was not suited to general farming. To make a living, farmers eventually turned to special kinds of agriculture. Those who had rich soils grew vegetables to sell in nearby towns and cities. Those living in hilly areas concentrated on dairying. Still others grew specialized crops such as cranberries and cigar tobacco.

Today only a very small number of workers in Massachusetts make a living from agriculture. The main sources of agricultural income are milk and eggs, greenhouse and nursery products, and cranberries and apples. Massachusetts long has been famous for cranberries, which are grown in specially prepared bogs.

Fisheries. Some distance off the shores of New England and Newfoundland, there are extensive shallow areas called banks. Marine life flourishes in these areas. It is said that many people went to the Massachusetts colony not for religious freedom or farming but for the good fishing to be found in that part of the world. Soon their ships were fishing the coastal banks of New England and the Grand Banks of Newfoundland.

The dangers of fishing in the early days were severe. Sometimes whole fleets of boats were lost in storms at sea.

At present the main commercial fish and shellfish include haddock, scallops, flounder, cod, ocean perch, and lobster. But the fishing industry is threatened by overharvesting.

Whaling. Whaling in the coastal waters began as early as 1700. Nantucket and, later, New Bedford were the centers of this industry. The whale furnished oil for lamps, wax for candles, and many other products. By about 1800 there were few whales left in the North Atlantic. Sailors ventured far—even to the Pacific Ocean—in search of new whaling grounds. The industry again prospered until about 1860. At that time, kerosene began to be used as a lighting fuel. There was no longer a great need for other products of the whale, and the whaling industry declined in Massachusetts.

Transportation and Communication

In colonial days the building of roads was not of great importance. Most of the colonists traveled on coastal waterways. Land travel was most common during the winter, when sleighs could be drawn along frozen rivers and streams. By the end of the Revolutionary War, a good system of roads was badly needed because of the growth of industry in different sections of the state. Massachusetts formed private companies to build and maintain roads. Today the state has a network of excellent highways. One of the most notable is the Massachusetts Turnpike, which crosses the state from east to west. Another is the superhighway—Route 128—that circles Boston and its inner suburbs.

Boston has been a leading port since the earliest days. There are numerous other small harbors with port facilities, such as Gloucester and New Bedford. Inland waterways have never been important in Massachusetts. The only canal in operation is the Cape Cod Canal between Cape Cod Bay and Buzzards Bay.

WHAT MASSACHUSETTS PRODUCES

MANUFACTURED GOODS: Nonelectrical machinery; electric and electronic equipment, including computers; measuring devices and other instruments; fabricated metal products; products of printing and publishing; transportation equipment; processed foods; paper and related products; chemicals and related products; rubber and plastic products; clothing and other textile products.

AGRICULTURAL PRODUCTS: Milk, greenhouse and nursery products, cranberries, eggs, apples, cattle and calves, tobacco, potatoes, sweet corn.

MINERALS: Stone, sand and gravel, lime, clays, peat.

Generations of students have passed before the statue of John Harvard at the university in Cambridge that was named for him.

The first railroad track was laid between Quincy and Milton in 1826. By 1836, three important railroads had been completed. They connected Boston and Lowell, Boston and Worcester, and Boston and Providence, Rhode Island. Afterward, railroad building increased rapidly. At one time the most powerful steam engines in the United States were the ones that pulled trains across the rugged Berkshire hills. Today Massachusetts' railroads provide mainly freight service. Commuter lines serve the Boston area.

There are about 50 commercial and municipal airports and several seaplane bases. The major airport is Logan International in Boston.

The Boston *News-Letter*, started in 1704, was the first regularly issued paper in the United States. Some of the largest and best-known newspapers today are *The Boston Globe*, *The Boston Herald*, and *The Christian Science Monitor*, all published in Boston. There are more than 40 other daily newspapers in Massachusetts and more than 200 weeklies and other papers. Massachusetts has about 100 radio stations and about a dozen commercial television stations.

▶ EDUCATION

In 1647 a law was passed requiring an elementary school in every town of 50 families. Towns of 100 families also had to maintain a secondary school to prepare young people for college.

Schools and Colleges

The present-day system of education had its start when the Massachusetts Board of Education was established in 1837. Horace Mann, the first secretary of the board, supervised the founding of an efficient system of public schools. A biography of this famous educator, who was born in Massachusetts, is included in Volume M.

Massachusetts has many private preparatory schools. Among them are Phillips Academy, in Andover; Deerfield Academy, in Deerfield; Groton School, in Groton; and St. Mark's School, in Southboro.

Harvard University, in Cambridge, founded in 1636, is the oldest institution of higher learning in the United States. Other well-known private institutions that were established originally for men are Amherst College, in Amherst; College of the Holy Cross, in Worcester; and Williams College, in Williamstown. Women's colleges include Mount Holyoke College, in South Hadley; Radcliffe College, in Cambridge; Simmons College, in Boston; Smith College, in Northampton; Wellesley College, in Wellesley; and Wheaton College, in Norton. Among the many other private institutions are Boston College, in Chestnut Hill; Boston University, in Boston; Brandeis University, in Waltham; the Massachusetts Institute of Technology, in Cambridge; and Northeastern University, in Boston.

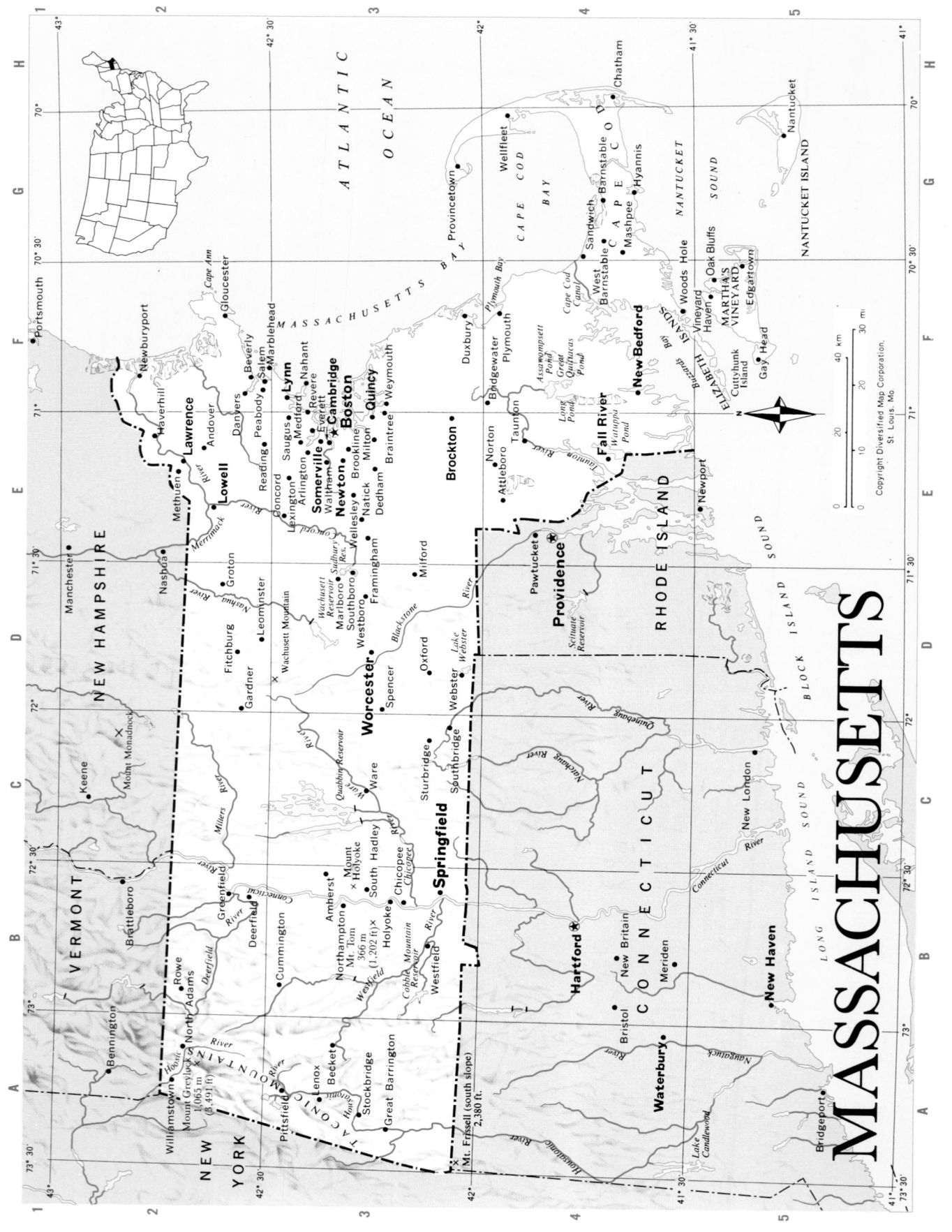

MASSACHUSETTS

INDEX TO MASSACHUSETTS MAP

Massachusetts also has many state-supported institutions of higher education. The University of Massachusetts has campuses in Amherst and Boston. Its medical school is in Worcester. The Massachusetts State College system includes colleges in Bridgewater, Fitchburg, Framingham, North Adams, Salem, Westfield, and Worcester. Other members of the system are the Massachusetts College of Art, in Boston, and the Massachusetts Maritime Academy, in Buzzards Bay. The state also supports the University of Lowell, in Lowell; Southeastern Massachusetts University, in North Dartmouth; and some 15 community colleges.

Libraries, Museums, and the Arts

Massachusetts' first library was established in 1638. In that year, a young minister, John Harvard, died. He left his library and half his fortune to the newly founded college of Massachusetts Bay colony. The college was named Harvard College for him in 1639.

Today there are public libraries in almost every city and town in the state. The Boston Public Library is among the largest in the nation. The Massachusetts Historical Society in Boston, the oldest historical society in the United States, has the private papers of Thomas Jefferson, the Adams Papers, and other historical documents. Important collections pertaining to American history are found also in the Boston Athenaeum, in Boston, and in libraries of the Essex Institute, in Salem, and the American Antiquarian Society, in Worcester. The John Fitzgerald Kennedy Library, in Boston, houses presidential papers and a museum.

POPULATION

TOTAL: 5,737,037 (1980 census). **Density**—283.1 persons to each square kilometer (733.3 persons to each square mile).

GROWTH SINCE 1790

Year	Population	Year	Population
1790	378,787	1900	2,805,346
1820	523,287	1930	4,249,614
1860	1,231,066	1970	5,689,170
1880	1,783,085	1980	5,737,037

Gain Between 1970 and 1980—0.8 percent.

CITIES: Population of Massachusetts' largest incorporated places (cities) according to the 1980 census.

Boston	562,994	Lowell	92,418
Worcester	161,799	Quincy	84,743
Springfield	152,319	Newton	83,622
New Bedford	98,478	Lynn	78,471
Cambridge	95,322	Somerville	77,372
Brockton	95,172	Lawrence	63,175
Fall River	92,574		

Massachusetts is noted for its many museums. The Museum of Fine Arts, in Boston, has an outstanding collection of Asian art. The Isabella Stewart Gardner Museum, in Boston, is a Venetian-style palace with collections of European masterpieces.

The Fogg Art Museum of Harvard University includes a large collection of prints and paintings, objects of ancient and Oriental arts, and wood sculptures. Smith College Museum of Art, in Northampton, has a collection of French paintings that show the development of modern art. The Addison Gallery of American Art of Phillips Academy, in Andover, contains American art—paintings, furniture, glass, silver, and ship models.

The Museum of Science in Boston has exhibits ranging from natural history to nuclear energy. The museum also includes an aquarium and a planetarium. The Peabody Museum of Archaeology and Ethnology of Harvard University has collections acquired by expeditions to many parts of the world. The Peabody Museum of Salem has exhibits on maritime and naval history. Other museums of interest include the Whaling Museum, in New Bedford, and Pilgrim Hall, in Plymouth.

Music, dance, and theater groups are active throughout the state. The Boston Symphony Orchestra, founded in 1881, is one of the world's great orchestras. In the summer the orchestra performs at Tanglewood, near Lenox, where the Berkshire Music Festival is held. Also well known are the Boston Pops Orchestra and the Opera Company of Boston.

▶ PLACES OF INTEREST

Massachusetts has a lovely coastline, many historic places, and pleasant mountain areas.

National Park Areas

The national park areas in Massachusetts include one national seashore. Most of the others commemorate historic sites.

Adams National Historic Site, in Quincy, was the home of the Adams family for more than 100 years.

Boston National Historical Park, in Boston, includes many locations famous in the history of the state and of the nation, such as Bunker Hill

Top: Picnics are part of the fun at the Berkshire Music Festival at Tanglewood. Bottom: Beacon Hill is an elegant and historical residential district in Boston.

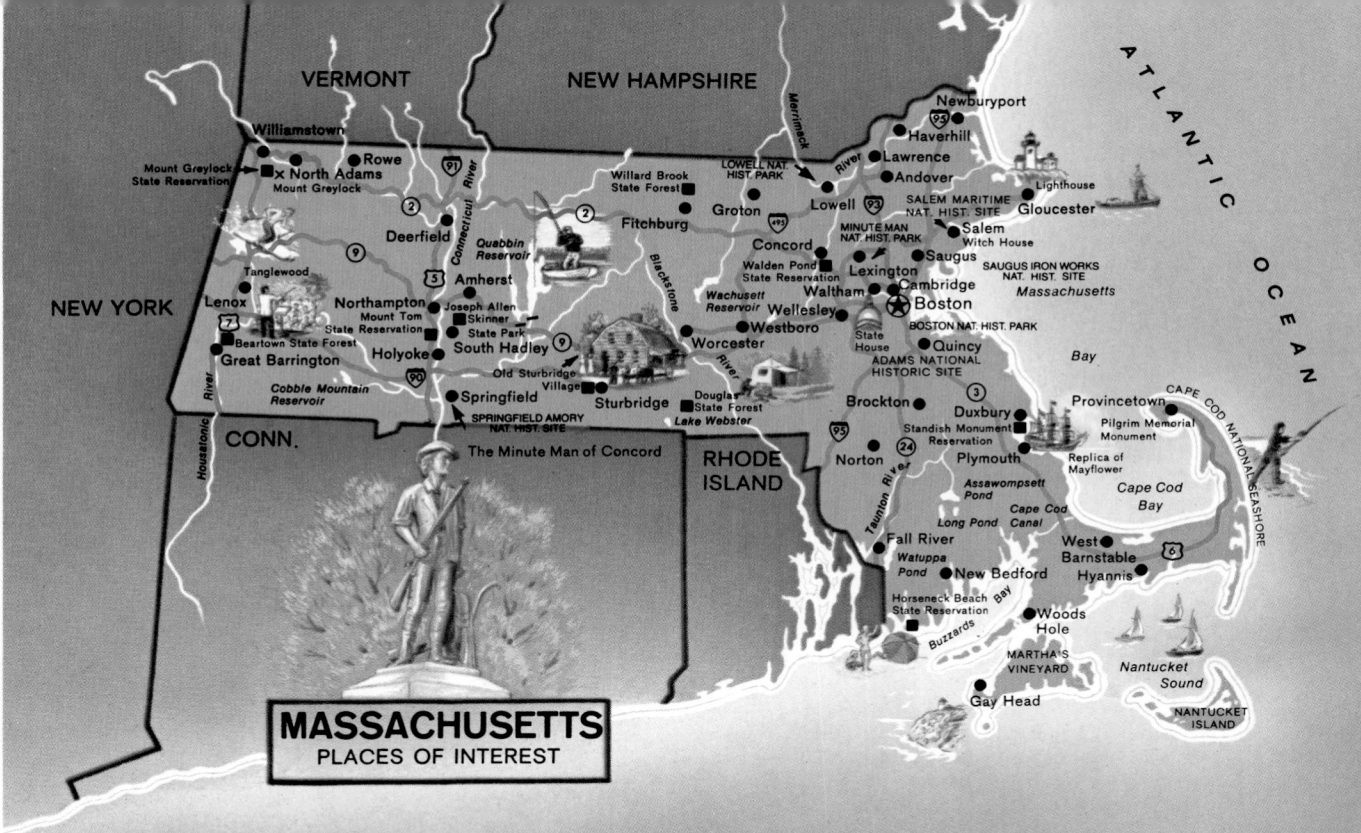

The Minute Man of Concord

MASSACHUSETTS
PLACES OF INTEREST

and the Charlestown Navy Yard, where the U.S.S. *Constitution* is berthed.

Cape Cod National Seashore preserves beaches, dunes, ponds, marshes, and woodlands on outer Cape Cod.

Frederick Law Olmsted National Historic Site, in Brookline, preserves the home of Frederick Law Olmsted (1822–1903), the great landscape architect. A collection of many of his drawings and plans is housed there.

John Fitzgerald Kennedy National Historic Site, in Brookline, was the President's birthplace and early home from 1917 to 1920.

Longfellow National Historic Site, in Cambridge, was the home of the poet Henry Wadsworth Longfellow from 1837 to 1882.

Lowell National Historical Park, in Lowell, commemorates the United States' first planned industrial community.

Minute Man National Historical Park, in Lexington, preserves the site where on April 19, 1775—the first day of the Revolutionary War—minutemen fired on British troops retreating from the battles of Lexington and Concord. Minutemen were armed colonists who were ready to fight at a minute's notice.

Salem Maritime National Historic Site, in Salem, includes a wharf and buildings associated with the seafaring history of New England.

Saugus Iron Works National Historic Site, at Saugus, is a reconstruction of an ironworks that began operating in 1646.

Springfield Armory National Historic Site, in Springfield, preserves an arsenal where U.S. military small arms were manufactured from 1794 to 1968.

State Areas

Areas maintained by the state range from beaches on Cape Cod Bay to ski areas in the Berkshires. Several preserve famous historic sites.

Beartown State Forest, near Great Barrington, is noted for azaleas and laurel. During the winter it is a ski center.

Joseph Allen Skinner State Park, on Mount Holyoke, has interesting volcanic formations. From the top of the mountain, there are beautiful views of the Connecticut Valley Lowland.

Mount Greylock State Reservation, near North Adams, includes Mount Greylock, the highest mountain in the state. On the top of the mountain is the Massachusetts War Memorial Beacon.

Mount Tom State Reservation, near Holyoke, is located on a forested traprock ridge. It includes the Mount Tom Ski Area.

Standish Monument Reservation, in Duxbury, contains a memorial tower dedicated to Myles (or Miles) Standish, who was a Mayflower Pilgrim, colonial leader, and founder of Duxbury.

Walden Pond State Reservation is located near Concord. Walden Pond was a favorite retreat for the writer Henry David Thoreau.

Other Places

Everywhere in Massachusetts, there are other places of special interest.

Cape Cod is a peninsula jutting into the Atlantic Ocean. The cape's lovely beaches, quaint villages, summer theaters, gift shops, and artist colonies are some of the attractions that bring many vacationers.

Concord, near Boston, was settled in 1635. It was the site of the first Provincial Congress in 1774 and of the battle of Concord on April 19, 1775. A famous statue, *The Minute Man of Concord,* by sculptor Daniel Chester French, commemorates the battle. Inscribed on the base of the statue is the first stanza of Ralph Waldo Emerson's ''Concord Hymn.'' By the mid 1800's, Concord had become a literary center. Among the writers who lived and worked there were Ralph Waldo Emerson, Henry David Thoreau, Nathaniel Hawthorne, and Louisa May Alcott.

Martha's Vineyard is an island south of Woods Hole. It is said that the island was named for the many wild grapes that once grew there. It was settled in 1642 and soon became a fishing and whaling center. The many attractions include beaches, small historic towns, and the brightly colored cliffs at Gay Head.

Nantucket Island is located about 40 kilometers (25 miles) south of Cape Cod. Its name comes from an Indian word meaning ''the faraway land.'' Nantucket was settled after 1659. By the time of the Revolutionary War, it had become the most important whaling port in the world. Today the island is a well-known summer resort.

Old Sturbridge Village, near Sturbridge, shows what a New England farming village looked like about 150 years ago. People live and work in the village and dress in period costumes.

Plymouth, located southeast of Boston, is the site of the first permanent white settlement in New England. The best-known monument is Plymouth Rock. It is said that the Pilgrims stepped ashore on this rock when they landed in December, 1620. *Mayflower II,* a reproduction of the ship that brought the Pilgrims to Massachusetts, is moored at State Pier.

Provincetown, on Cape Cod, was the site of the first landing of the Pilgrims in November, 1620. The Pilgrim Memorial Monument commemorates the event. Today Provincetown is a fishing village and a summer resort.

Salem, located near Boston, was established as a farming and fishing village in 1626. In 1692 the village was the scene of famous witchcraft trials. The Witch House, built in 1642, was the home of one of the trial judges. By the end of the 1700's, Salem had become a leading port, trading especially with Asia. Many fine mansions that once belonged tò sea captains are open to the public. The House of the Seven Gables, erected in 1668, was used by Nathaniel Hawthorne as the setting for his novel *The House of the Seven Gables.*

▶CITIES

About 85 percent of the people in Massachusetts live in urban areas. These areas are made up of a group of cities and towns clustered about a central city.

Boston Metropolitan Area

The Boston Metropolitan Area includes Boston, Cambridge, Somerville, Lynn, Newton, Quincy, and many other cities and towns. The total population of the area is about 2,750,000.

Boston, the state capital, is located on an arm of Massachusetts Bay (Boston Bay). It was founded in 1630 by John Winthrop as the main colony of the Massachusetts Bay Company. Boston contains many of the state's most important historical sites. Boston Common is one of the nation's earliest public parks. Faneuil Hall, known as the Cradle of Liberty, is the building where Revolutionary War patriots met. From Old North Church (Christ Church), lanterns gave the signal to Paul Revere to begin his famous ride. The Old State House was the seat of the colonial government and the center of activity for revolutionary patriots. Bunker Hill Monument marks the scene of a famous battle.

Today Boston is the major metropolitan area and the cultural center of New England. An article on Boston appears in Volume B.

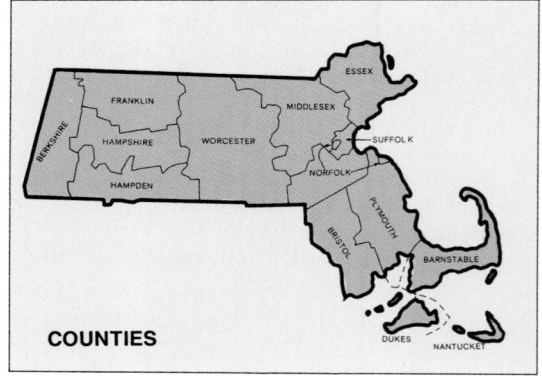

COUNTIES

The city of Boston, with its old neighborhoods and modern skyscrapers, overlooks the lovely Charles River. Boston has been the capital of Massachusetts since 1630.

Other Metropolitan Areas

The Springfield Metropolitan Area includes the cities of Springfield, Chicopee, Holyoke, and other cities and towns. This area is known as a manufacturing center for electrical machinery, chemicals, and paper.

The city of Worcester and about 20 towns make up the Worcester Metropolitan Area. Worcester, the second largest city in the state, is an industrial and educational center.

The Lawrence-Haverhill Metropolitan Area includes Lawrence, Haverhill, and several towns. Lawrence was once the leading woolen textile producer in the United States.

Lowell, Brockton, New Bedford, and Fall River are centers of four other metropolitan areas. Lowell, New Bedford, and Fall River were once the chief centers of cotton textile manufacturing in the United States. Brockton is known for men's shoes.

▶FAMOUS PEOPLE

Massachusetts has produced a host of men and women who have won worldwide fame in politics, literature, art, science, and business. Many of them are members of a family such as the Adams or the Lowell family.

The Adams family of Massachusetts includes a number of distinguished figures. John Adams

(1735–1826) was born in Braintree, now a part of Quincy. He was the first vice president (1789–97) and the second president of the United States (1797–1801). His son, John Quincy Adams (1767–1848), became the sixth president of the United States (1825–29). Samuel Adams (1722–1803), a cousin of John Adams, was a leader of the Boston Tea Party and a signer of the Declaration of Independence. He also served as governor of Massachusetts. Biographies of John Adams, John Quincy Adams, and Samuel Adams are included in Volume A.

The Lowell family includes famous poets, statesmen, educators, industrialists, and scientists. John Lowell (1743–1802) was a jurist and statesman, born in Newburyport. His son, Francis Cabot Lowell (1775–1817), established at Waltham the first complete cotton textile mill in America. His grandson, James Russell Lowell (1819–91), was a poet, editor, and diplomat. Volume L contains a biography of James Russell Lowell. Percival Lowell (1855–1916) was a prominent astronomer. Abbott Lawrence Lowell (1856–1943) was president of Harvard University from 1909 to 1933. Amy Lowell (1874–1925) pioneered in new forms of poetic expression. All of the last three were great-great-grandchildren of John Lowell. Robert Lowell (1917–77) won a Pulitzer prize for poetry in 1947 and in 1974.

Cabot and **Lodge** are other prominent family names in Massachusetts. George Cabot (1752–1823) was a businessman and politician, born in

Salem. Cabot's great-grandson, Henry Cabot Lodge (1850–1924), served as a United States senator from 1893 to 1924. Henry Cabot Lodge (1902–85), grandson of Henry Cabot Lodge, was the Republican nominee for vice president in 1960. He was also a United States senator during the 1930's and 1940's and the United States ambassador to the United Nations and the Security Council during the 1950's.

The Kennedys are another noteworthy political family. Joseph Patrick Kennedy (1888–1969), businessman and diplomat, was born in Boston. His son John F. Kennedy was elected 35th president of the United States in 1960, after serving as United States representative and senator from Massachusetts. Robert F. Kennedy was elected United States senator from New York in 1964, a post he held until his death in 1968. Edward M. Kennedy became a senator from Massachusetts in 1962. Biographies of the Kennedys are in Volume K.

Besides the two Adamses and John Fitzgerald Kennedy, Massachusetts claims another president of the United States—

The State House in Boston, with its gleaming gold dome, is the state capitol. Built in the 1790's, it was designed by the famous architect Charles Bulfinch.

Calvin Coolidge. He was born in Vermont, but he spent most of his life in Massachusetts. He was lieutenant governor of Massachusetts, 1916–18, and governor, 1919–20. A biography of Coolidge is included in Volume C.

A list of all the well-known persons who were born in Massachusetts, going back to colonial days, would cover many pages. Biographies of the following persons are included in this encyclopedia.

Clara Barton (Oxford), founder of the American Red Cross.

William Cullen Bryant (Cummington), poet and editor.

Emily Dickinson (Amherst), poet.

Ralph Waldo Emerson (Boston), poet and essayist.

Cyrus Field (Stockbridge), promoter of the Atlantic telegraph cable.

Benjamin Franklin (Boston), statesman, scientist, and philosopher.

Robert Hutchings Goddard (Worcester), physicist and rocket expert.

John Hancock (Braintree), Revolutionary War statesman.

Nathaniel Hawthorne (Salem), novelist.

Oliver Wendell Holmes (Cambridge), literary figure and physician.

Oliver Wendell Holmes, Jr. (Boston), Justice of the United States Supreme Court.

Winslow Homer (Boston), painter.

Elias Howe (Spencer), inventor.

Samuel Morse (near Boston), inventor and artist.

James Otis (West Barnstable), Revolutionary War statesman.

Paul Revere (Boston), Revolutionary War patriot.

Henry David Thoreau (Concord), writer and naturalist.

James Abbott McNeill Whistler (Lowell), painter.

Eli Whitney (Westboro), inventor.

John Greenleaf Whittier (Haverhill), poet.

▶**GOVERNMENT**

Massachusetts is governed by a constitution adopted in 1780. Amendments may be

---

GOVERNMENT

Capital—Boston. **Number of counties**—14. **Representation in Congress**—U.S. senators, 2; U.S. representatives, 11. **The General Court of Massachusetts** (state legislature)—Senate, 40 members; House of Representatives, 160 members; both 2-year terms. **Governor**—4-year term; no limit on number of terms. **Elections**—General and state, Tuesday after first Monday in November of even-numbered years; town, January through March annually.

proposed by the legislature or by petition of the voters.

The governor, who is elected for a term of four years, is assisted by a governor's council and several other elected executive officers. The state legislature is known as the General Court of Massachusetts. It consists of the Senate and the House of Representatives.

The court system is headed by the Supreme Judicial Court, the oldest court in the United States in continuous existence. Other courts include superior courts, district courts, and the juvenile court of Boston.

IMPORTANT DATES

1602	Bartholomew Gosnold explored Massachusetts Bay and named Cape Cod.
1614	Captain John Smith of the Virginia colony mapped the coast and named the land New England.
1620	Pilgrims established Plymouth, the first permanent colony in Massachusetts.
1621	First Thanksgiving celebrated by the Pilgrims.
1629	Massachusetts Bay Company chartered.
1630	Puritan settlers under John Winthrop arrived in Massachusetts Bay; Boston settled.
1636	Harvard University founded.
1676	Indians defeated in King Philip's War.
1684	England revoked the charter of the Massachusetts Bay Company.
1691	Massachusetts became a royal colony.
1704	The first American newspaper, the Boston *News-Letter*, started.
1770	Boston Massacre—British troops fired into a jeering crowd of colonists.
1773	Boston Tea Party—colonists dumped tea into Boston harbor as a protest against taxes.
1775	First battles of the Revolutionary War fought at Lexington and Concord; the battle of Bunker Hill fought in Boston.
1780	Massachusetts ratified its state constitution.
1788	February 6, Massachusetts ratified the federal Constitution and became the sixth state to enter the Union.
1814	Steam power looms owned by Francis Cabot Lowell began operation in Waltham.
1831	William Lloyd Garrison established the *Liberator,* an antislavery newspaper.
1839	First state teachers college in the United States opened in Lexington under the guidance of Horace Mann.
1852	Boston Public Library established.
1863	Massachusetts Agricultural College, now the University of Massachusetts, chartered at Amherst.
1897	First subway in the United States opened in Boston.
1912	Textile workers in Lawrence struck for higher wages.
1914	Cape Cod Canal opened.
1951	A superhighway around Boston opened, starting a new era of industrial growth.
1957	Massachusetts Turnpike opened.
1966	Edward W. Brooke became the first black elected to the U.S. Senate since Reconstruction days.
1980	Boston celebrated its 350th birthday.
1984	Massachusetts passed a law providing benefits for workers who have lost jobs because of plant closings.

▶HISTORY

Before the Europeans came to North America, several Algonkian Indian tribes inhabited Massachusetts. Most of them lived near the coast or in the Connecticut Valley Lowland. Most of their food came from the forest. If they lived close to the sea, they ate seafood. The Indians also raised a few crops —corn, beans, pumpkins, and squash.

Settlement and Colonial Days

Europeans sailed along the shores of present-day New England long before the first colonists came to Massachusetts. It is thought that the Vikings under Leif Ericson may have explored the coast as early as the year 1000.

In 1602, Bartholomew Gosnold, an English navigator, explored Massachusetts Bay and named Cape Cod, because of the abundance of cod in the area. He also built a fort on Cuttyhunk Island. When Captain John Smith visited the area in 1614, he called it New England. He wrote of the fine timber, the abundance of fish and wildlife, and the gardens cultivated by the Indians. Smith's descriptions and maps of the coast helped to arouse interest in New England.

The first permanent colony in Massachusetts was Plymouth, settled by the Pilgrims in 1620. An article on Plymouth Colony is included in Volume P. Gradually other settlements were established along the coast for fishing and trading. The Massachusetts Bay Company, a company of English Puritans, was formed in 1629 to start a colony on Massachusetts Bay. In 1630 a large group of Puritans under John Winthrop arrived in Massachusetts and founded Boston. The colony prospered. Coastal towns with good harbors became important in cod fishing. Whaling began as early as 1700. Fishing and whaling stimulated shipbuilding, and shipbuilding stimulated trade.

The charter granted to the Massachusetts Bay Company permitted the colonists to govern themselves. But there were laws, passed by the English Parliament, requiring the colony to trade only with England or with other English colonies. When Massachusetts merchants began to ignore the law, the English Government decided to act. In 1684 the king revoked the charter. Massachusetts Bay and Plymouth colonies were combined in 1691 as a royal colony.

At first the Indians and the colonists were friendly. A few Indians, such as Samoset and Squanto, welcomed the English. When the colonists' crops failed, the Indians taught the newcomers how to plant corn, beans, and squash and where to find lobsters and clams. But discontent began to grow among the Indians as the colonists' cows and horses ate up the grass and their hogs spoiled the Indians' clam beds. A few tribes decided to adopt some of the settlers' ways. A mission was established at Natick in 1651. There John Eliot, known as the Apostle to the Indians, led an effort to educate Indians and to convert them to Christianity. This mission was known as the praying town of Natick. Other praying towns were established, and by 1674 more than 1,000 Indians had been converted. Several attended Harvard College.

Other groups of Indians refused to give up their way of life. Some moved far into the interior, and some fought the settlers. The largest group, the Wampanoags under the leadership of Chief Massasoit, aided the English for many years. But Massasoit's son, King Philip (Metacomet), believed that Indian life woud soon be destroyed because of the colonists' increasing need for land. In 1675, war broke out between the Wampanoags and the colonists. After some successes, Philip's forces were defeated, and he was killed in 1676.

The Revolutionary War

From 1691 up to the time of the Revolutionary War, there was constant quarreling between the colonists and the English Government, mostly about taxes. Boston became the center of resistance. Such events as the Boston Massacre in 1770 and the Boston Tea Party in 1773 led finally to the Revolutionary War. The first battles were fought at Lexington and Concord. A description of these and other events of the struggle in Massachusetts are included in the article on the Revolutionary War in Volume R.

Statehood and Later

In 1780 the people of Massachusetts ratified a state constitution. This constitution served as a model for the Constitution of the United States. Eight years later, on February 6, 1788, Massachusetts became the sixth state of the Union.

After the Revolutionary War, a new era of industrial development began. Trade with Asia flourished, especially with China and India. During the years of the clipper ships, sea captains made great fortunes. This period started in the 1840's and lasted for about 20 years. At the same time, Boston was becoming the literary and publishing center of the United States. Writers of this period were concerned with ideas on religion, democracy, the frontier, the common person, and science and industry. Boston also became the center of social movements—such as the abolitionist, or antislavery, movement. During the U.S. Civil War, Massachusetts contributed arms, money, and soldiers to the Union cause.

In the years after the Civil War, Massachusetts continued to develop its industry. By the end of the century, the state was producing a large part of the nation's textiles and shoes and boots. Machinery of all kinds was also being manufactured. Many immigrants came from Europe to work in the factories. By 1900 the mainly rural society of Yankees who farmed and fished had changed to an urban society of many different nationalities.

Industry prospered during this period, but Massachusetts had many labor troubles. Working conditions often were extremely poor, and strikes were frequent. Between 1881 and 1900, there were nearly 2,000 strikes and lockouts. Workers also attempted to get laws passed to protect their interests. In 1911 a labor law reduced the work week for women to 54 hours. The manufacturers struck back by cutting wages. This action led to a strike of textile workers in Lawrence in 1912. This famous strike was a milestone in the struggle of American laborers for better working conditions. Since 1912, Massachusetts has adopted progressive labor laws, and today there are few labor disputes.

During the 20th century, Massachusetts has become one of the great research centers in the United States. The combination of industry, many excellent educational institutions, and "Yankee ingenuity" has stimulated research in the Bay State. Massachusetts will continue to be a great state if it uses its ingenuity to adjust to changing conditions by producing new goods and new ideas.

RICHARD O. RIESS
Salem State College

MASS MEDIA. See ADVERTISING; COMMUNICATION.

MASS PRODUCTION

Two hundred years ago almost everything people used was made either at home or in small workshops. Each pair of shoes, each hat, hammer, shirt, and broom was produced individually, for a particular customer. When a man wanted a new pair of shoes, he did not go to a big store that had hundreds of pairs on the shelves. Instead he went to a small workshop and asked a shoemaker to measure his feet and make him a pair of shoes. The shoemaker marked the leather and cut it, then sewed, trimmed, and colored the shoes. He gave them to his customer and received his payment. This pair of shoes was custom-made, which means that it was specially made for an individual customer or buyer.

Certain things are still sometimes custom-made today, such as men's suits, ladies' hats, and shoes. But most of the shoes, clothing, and other things we use today are made in advance in factories. Hundreds of workers produce not just one item at a time but great quantities of each item. This system is called **mass production**.

With a system of mass production and distribution, such goods as shoes, automobiles, books, and television sets are available for millions of people to buy and use.

Technology, the Factory System, and Markets

Three things are needed for the mass production system used today. The first is **machine technology**—the tools and skills to produce by machinery rather than by hand. The second is the **factory system**—a method of organizing and managing workers and machines. The third is a **mass market**—a large number of people who have the desire and the money to buy mass-produced goods. The mass market needs a system of transportation to move the goods from factory to store. It also needs a system of communication (radio, television, newspapers) to let the people know about the goods through advertising.

The Effects of Mass Production

Mass production is much more efficient than custom manufacturing. This is because of the labor-saving machinery, the skills, and the organization developed in modern mass production. Production costs are lower, and more people can afford to buy the goods.

Mass consumption (many people buying and using a product) is the result of the mass production system. In the United States nine families out of ten have at least one television set in their homes. Three families out of four own an automobile. In such countries as India and China, where mass production is not so common, less than one family in a hundred has a television set or automobile.

Mass production began in western Europe in the late 18th century. It has caused many changes in the way people live. More goods are available today to more people and they do not have to work as hard to get them. But mass production has also helped create another problem—how to fill the increased leisure time wisely.

ROBERT L. DARCY
Executive Director
Ohio Council on Economic Education

See also INDUSTRY; MANUFACTURING.

MATCHES

The human race began using fire many thousands of years ago, but it was only a little over a century ago that matches were invented. It took thousands of years of fire making before mankind managed to leash fire to the end of a little wooden stick.

In the 20th century, matches are one of the cheapest of manufactured items, yet their manufacture is a highly complicated industrial process that is almost completely automated.

▶HISTORY

The ancient Greeks believed that a being named Prometheus stole fire from the gods and gave it to mankind. For this, the Greeks said, Prometheus was punished by the jealous gods.

The Pacific islanders had a story about a young man named Maui who stole the secret of fire making from the fire god.

The Plains Indians of the United States

believed that fire came into the world when a great herd of huge bison stampeded across the plains; their hooves made sparks on the rocks, causing the grass to burst into flames.

The ancient Persians worshiped a fire god. And the ancient Temple in Jerusalem contained an eternal flame as a symbol of the Living God. Even today we light candles in churches.

Fire and fire making have always been vital to human survival.

The various ways to make fire before matches were invented all involved some form of heat produced by friction or by sparks made by striking stones together. In Australia the natives used a fire drill—a pointed wooden rod that was spun between the hands with the point against a flat board. The Plains Indians used a fire drill with a bowstring as the power drive. The Eskimo, too, used a drill with a cord wound around the spindle. The Pacific islanders rubbed a stick on a grooved board.

The early Romans made fire by rubbing two stones against a mixture of sulfur and dry, decayed wood. For hundreds of years Europeans made fire by striking a flint stone against a piece of iron or steel till the sparks ignited some scraps of tinder.

The box that contained the flint, steel, and tinder was called a tinderbox. The tinderbox was used to make fire until early in the 19th century.

Though matches did not become popular until the 19th century, the match was invented in 1669, when Hennig Brand (?–1692?), a German alchemist, discovered phosphorus. At first, this highly flammable element was merely a curiosity. Early methods of obtaining pure phosphorus were very expensive, and the material was so dangerous that it was not used very often. Toward the end of the 18th century, chemists began to experiment with phosphorus. One result of these early experiments was the phosphorus taper. Phosphorus tapers were wax candles coated at the top with white phosphorus and sealed in glass containers. When the glass was broken, the candles flamed.

The experiments to make fire by chemical means culminated in 1827 with the invention of the first friction match by John Walker (1781?–1859), an English druggist. Walker's matches were sticks tipped with a mixture of chemicals that burst into flame when scratched against a rough surface. Walker found that when the mixture dried, he could ignite the stick by drawing the head through a piece of sandpaper. Walker did not patent his idea, and 2 years later other people began making Walker matches. These matches were hard to ignite. They did not always light properly, and the heads often came off.

In 1830 the French inventor Charles Sauria (1812–?) found that Walker matches could be improved by the substitution of white phosphorus for one of the ingredients. Matches of this type were first made in the United States in 1836.

Sulfur was used to help the match-head flame light the wooden splint. The sulfur was later replaced with paraffin, eliminating the bad smell of burning sulfur. Later, fire retardants were added to the wooden match splint.

A big problem in match manufacture resulted from the fact that white phosphorus is poisonous. Many workers in match factories died of phosphorus poisoning before this was discovered. The problem of phosphorus poisoning was not solved in the United States until shortly before World War I. In 1911 an American match company perfected a formula that used a nonpoisonous compound of phosphorus and sulfur. Then in 1913 the United States began taxing white phosphorus matches so heavily that their manufacture became impractical.

▶ TYPES OF MATCH

There are two general types of match. One type is called a strike-anywhere match. It will ignite when struck on any dry, slightly rough surface. The other is called a strike-on-box or strike-on-book match. It ignites only when struck on a phosphorus-coated surface.

All matches are low-priced items. For the manufacturer to make them at a profit, the matches must be made in huge quantities.

To be perfect, a match must flame instantly and silently when struck. It must burn slowly and uniformly down the splint. When it stops burning, it must not leave any afterglow, which might cause it to rekindle.

▶ MANUFACTURE

All matches are made by machines, in much the same way. First the matchstick is

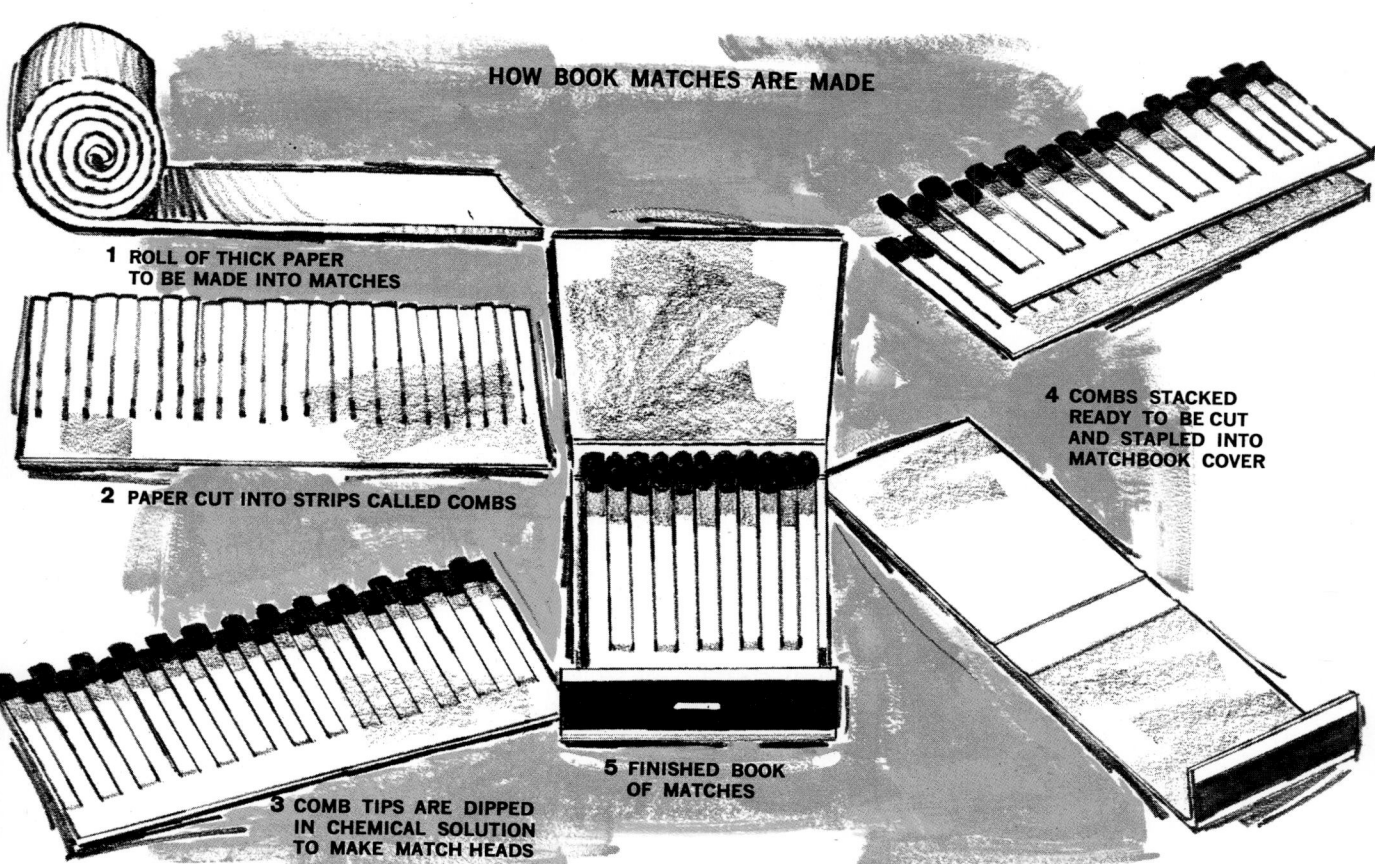

HOW BOOK MATCHES ARE MADE

1 ROLL OF THICK PAPER TO BE MADE INTO MATCHES

2 PAPER CUT INTO STRIPS CALLED COMBS

3 COMB TIPS ARE DIPPED IN CHEMICAL SOLUTION TO MAKE MATCH HEADS

4 COMBS STACKED READY TO BE CUT AND STAPLED INTO MATCHBOOK COVER

5 FINISHED BOOK OF MATCHES

prepared. To make wooden matches, a machine cuts the sticks from a block of wood. Book matches are cut by machine from rolls of cardboard. In order to prevent fires from discarded matches, the matchsticks are chemically treated. This treatment keeps the matchsticks from glowing or smoldering after the flame is blown out.

Next, the matchsticks are dipped in paraffin. The paraffin helps to carry the flame from the match head to the stick. Without the paraffin the match might just flare up and die out when struck.

After the sticks are dipped in paraffin, the match heads are put on the sticks. This is done by dipping the sticks into the match-head mixture. Safety matches get just one dip. Strike-anywhere matches are dipped twice. The second dip gives these matches a small white tip that is very sensitive and can be lit by scraping against any rough surface.

When the match heads have dried, wooden matches are packed, by machine, in boxes. Book matches are stapled into their covers. Strike-anywhere matches have a sand or ground-glass striking surface glued to the side of the box. Safety matches must have a special chemical mixture painted or printed on the box or matchbook.

▶ SAFETY WITH MATCHES

Match manufacturers are very careful to make sure that their matches are safe. But no manufacturer can protect people from their own carelessness. Many people are hurt or killed every year in fires that are started by careless use of matches. Following are a few simple rules that can prevent dangerous fires:

(1) Never keep matches where young children can reach them.

(2) Never put matches in warm places—as in a stove drawer—where the heat might cause them to ignite.

(3) Always make sure a match is out before throwing it away. Never throw away an unused match.

(4) Always close the matchbox or book before striking a match. Many people burn their fingers by accidentally setting fire to the whole box.

Reviewed by FRANK A. HOLLER
Diamond National Corporation

SOME MATHEMATICAL SYMBOLS

+ (plus) means add. $6 + 5 = 11$

Σ means summation. If x is a positive number, then $\sum_{2}^{6}x$ means add all the numbers from 2 to 6. $\sum_{2}^{6}x = 2 + 3 + 4 + 5 + 6 = 20$

— (minus) means subtract. $6 - 5 = 1$

× (times) means multiply. $6 \times 5 = 30$

÷ means divide. $30 \div 6 = 5$

= means equals. One side of an equation has the same value as the other side. $6 + 5 = 11$, or $11 = 11$

≠ means does not equal. The two sides do not have the same value. $6 + 5 \neq 9$, or $11 \neq 9$

! means factorial. Multiply the number beside the factorial sign by each smaller positive whole number. $5! = 5 \times 4 \times 3 \times 2 \times 1 = 120$

∞ means infinity. Anything that increases without bounds is infinite.

π means pi (3.14...). Pi is the ratio of the circumference of a circle to the diameter of the circle.

x^2 means a number squared. A number multiplied by itself is said to be squared. $5^2 = 5 \times 5 = 25$

|| means parallel. Lines that never meet, no matter how far they are extended, are parallel.

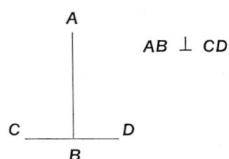

$AB \parallel CD$

⊥ means perpendicular. Two lines meeting one another at an angle of 90 degrees are perpendicular.

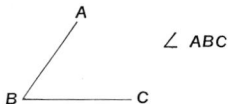

$AB \perp CD$

∠ means angle.

$\angle ABC$

MATHEMATICS

Mathematics is the study of numbers, shapes, and symbols. It also includes the rules for dealing with these things.

Mathematics began with counting. At first, people could not count to large numbers. They often had to use piles of pebbles, notches on a stick, or marks on the ground to help them remember large numbers. Later on, they developed ways of writing down numbers. This made the numbers easier to use when working out mathematical problems. Simple mathematical operations such as adding, subtracting, multiplying, and dividing were also developed long ago.

Measurement

People also used counting for a kind of mathematics called measurement. Measurement concerns the sizes of things. People learned how to measure areas, the sizes of angles, and the weights of objects, for example. As they did so they improved their methods of measurement. These improvements led to new problems in mathematics that had to be solved.

Geometry

About 3,000 years ago people began to notice some interesting facts about measurement. For example, suppose a triangle measured 3 units of length on one side, 4 units on another, and 5 units on the third side. The angle between the 3-unit and the 4-unit sides would always be the same as the angle in the corner of a square. Relationships such as this were not easy to understand at first. People wanted to find out more about them.

In ancient Greece, especially, mathematicians studied relationships they found among measurements of figures. The branch of mathematics they developed came to be called **geometry**. "Geometry" comes from two Greek words meaning "earth" and "to measure," since the idea of geometry started with the measuring of land. Geometry as developed by the Greeks is usually called **Euclidean geometry**, since it is best known through the works of the Greek mathematician Euclid, who lived about 300 B.C.

Men who worked in geometry realized that if some geometric relationships were known, others could be found. Men could use reason to figure out new relationships. The science of reasoning, called **logic**, thus began to be tied in with mathematics.

Geometry was used a great deal by astronomers. There developed an offshoot of geometry and astronomy called **trigonometry**. At first, trigonometry was a kind of mathematical study of parts of circles and of line segments stretching from one point on a circle to another. Later it came to deal mostly with triangles. ("Trigonometry" is from two Greek words meaning "triangle" and "to measure.") Today the ideas of trigonometry are mixed in with other branches of mathematics.

New Numbers

Measuring led to geometry. It also led men to develop new kinds of numbers. At first, men used only the whole numbers that they had used for counting: 1, 2, 3, and so on. But when they used whole numbers for measuring, part of a unit was often left over. This part could not be counted with a whole number. Mathematicians had to find a way of dealing with this problem.

They did so in this way. Suppose the leftover part was half the size of the whole unit. (The whole unit was whatever length seemed most useful.) A half unit compared to a whole unit was like a whole unit compared to 2 whole units. This was written as 1 over 2—that is, ½.

Suppose a leftover part were written as ¾. This would mean that the part was as large compared to a whole unit as 3 whole units are in comparison to 4 whole units. If the whole unit were divided into 4 equal parts, the leftover amount would be equal in size to 3 of the parts together.

These comparisons are called **ratios** or **fractions**. They can be added and multiplied and divided. Therefore they are thought of as numbers. Fractions, together with whole numbers, later came to be called **rational numbers**. This means that these numbers can all be written as ratios. (A whole number such as 2, for example, can be written as ²⁄₁, ⁴⁄₂, ⁸⁄₄, and so on.) As mathematics grew more complex, still other types of numbers were developed.

Number Theory

Mathematicians also found new ways of working with numbers. They studied the ways in which numbers are related to each other. This branch of mathematics is called number theory.

Workers in number theory soon became interested in certain numbers called prime numbers. They noticed that most whole numbers could be written as the product of other whole numbers. For instance, 6 is the product of 3 and 2. But some whole numbers are not the product of any whole numbers but themselves and 1. The number 7, for example, is not the product of any numbers except 7 and 1. The mathematicians called such numbers **prime numbers**. The list of prime numbers begins with 2, 3, 5, 7, 11, 13, and 17.

What is the largest prime number? Early mathematicians proved that there is no largest prime number. Prime numbers can be found among other numbers no matter how high you count. Several other proofs in number theory came from the early mathematicians of Greece and Alexandria, Egypt.

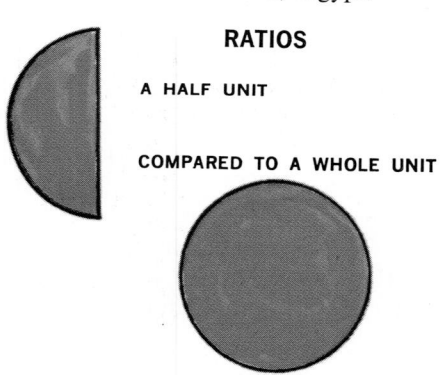

RATIOS

A HALF UNIT

COMPARED TO A WHOLE UNIT

IS AS A WHOLE UNIT

COMPARED TO TWO WHOLE UNITS

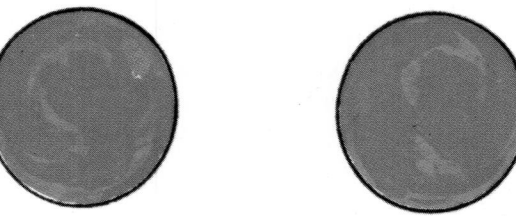

words meaning "earth" and "to measure," since the idea of geometry started with the measuring of land. Geometry as developed by the Greeks is usually called **Euclidean geometry**, since it is best known through the works of the Greek mathematician Euclid, who lived about 300 B.C.

Men who worked in geometry realized that if some geometric relationships were known, others could be found. Men could use reason to figure out new relationships. The science of reasoning, called **logic**, thus began to be tied in with mathematics.

Geometry was used a great deal by astronomers. There developed an offshoot of geometry and astronomy called **trigonometry**. At first, trigonometry was a kind of mathematical study of parts of circles and of line segments stretching from one point on a circle to another. Later it came to deal mostly with triangles. ("Trigonometry" is from two Greek words meaning "triangle" and "to measure.") Today the ideas of trigonometry are mixed in with other branches of mathematics.

New Numbers

Measuring led to geometry. It also led men to develop new kinds of numbers. At first, men used only the whole numbers that they had used for counting: 1, 2, 3, and so on. But when they used whole numbers for measuring, part of a unit was often left over. This part could not be counted with a whole number. Mathematicians had to find a way of dealing with this problem.

They did so in this way. Suppose the leftover part was half the size of the whole unit. (The whole unit was whatever length seemed most useful.) A half unit compared to a whole unit was like a whole unit compared to 2 whole units. This was written as 1 over 2—that is, ½.

Suppose a leftover part were written as ¾. This would mean that the part was as large compared to a whole unit as 3 whole units are in comparison to 4 whole units. If the whole unit were divided into 4 equal parts, the leftover amount would be equal in size to 3 of the parts together.

These comparisons are called **ratios** or **fractions**. They can be added and multiplied and divided. Therefore they are thought of as numbers. Fractions, together with whole numbers, later came to be called **rational numbers**. This means that these numbers can all be written as ratios. (A whole number such as 2, for example, can be written as ²⁄₁, ⁴⁄₂, ⁸⁄₄, and so on.) As mathematics grew more complex, still other types of numbers were developed.

Number Theory

Mathematicians also found new ways of working with numbers. They studied the ways in which numbers are related to each other. This branch of mathematics is called number theory.

Workers in number theory soon became interested in certain numbers called prime numbers. They noticed that most whole numbers could be written as the product of other whole numbers. For instance, 6 is the product of 3 and 2. But some whole numbers are not the product of any whole numbers but themselves and 1. The number 7, for example, is not the product of any numbers except 7 and 1. The mathematicians called such numbers **prime numbers**. The list of prime numbers begins with 2, 3, 5, 7, 11, 13, and 17.

What is the largest prime number? Early mathematicians proved that there is no largest prime number. Prime numbers can be found among other numbers no matter how high you count. Several other proofs in number theory came from the early mathematicians of Greece and Alexandria, Egypt.

RATIOS

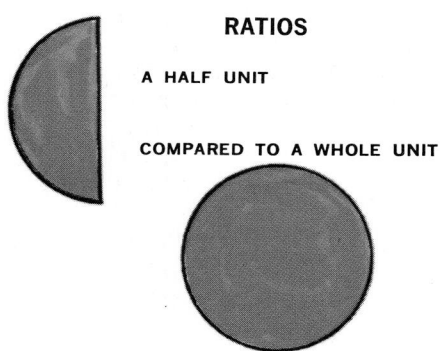

A HALF UNIT

COMPARED TO A WHOLE UNIT

IS AS A WHOLE UNIT

COMPARED TO TWO WHOLE UNITS

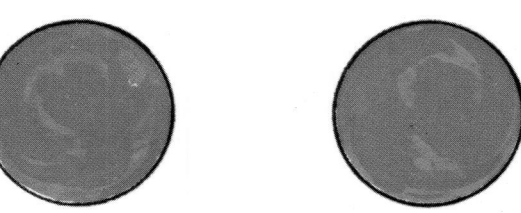

Balls dropped through probability machine pile up at bottom to form bell-shaped pattern illustrating one of the most common curves in probability theory.

Algebra

Another branch of mathematics, called algebra, was developed in early times, along with geometry and number theory. It was developed to help solve the increasingly complicated problems with which mathematicians had to work. Algebra did this through the use of symbols.

Men were already using the number symbols called **numerals**. When they wrote 1, 2, or 3, they were writing down symbols for numbers. Now men began using symbols that could stand for any number at all. For example, the Egyptians used the word *ahau* to represent any unknown number in their mathematical problems.

A symbol used in this way came to be called a **variable**. A variable can stand for any number at all. It can be handled in mathematical operations just as a numeral can. The rules for handling variables make up the branch of mathematics called algebra.

A great advance in algebra took place in the 3rd century A.D. Diophantus, a mathematician of Alexandria, began to use letters of the alphabet as variables. This system is still used. In the term "4x + y," for instance, x and y are variables and can stand for any number.

▶ CLASSICAL MATHEMATICS

Mathematics stayed much the same for several centuries, although mathematicians continued to improve their methods of work. In the 1600's, however, mathematics began to branch in many different directions. The branches developed from the 17th through the 19th centuries are often called classical mathematics. The branches are probability theory, analytic geometry, calculus, projective geometry, topology, non-Euclidean geometry, and Hamilton's algebra.

In the 1600's a French mathematician, Pierre de Fermat (1601–65), made great advances in number theory. He also contributed to another branch of mathematics known as probability theory.

Probability Theory

Fermat and another French mathematician, Blaise Pascal (1623–62), did most of the early important work in probability theory. Some work had been done in this area before by the gambler-mathematician Girolamo Cardano (1501–76), an Italian.

A gambler would have good reason to be interested in probability theory. This branch of mathematics is concerned with chance. It finds out what the chances are of one result happening out of a number of possible results. When a gambler uses dice or cards, he is interested in chance. For example, he may want to know his chances for rolling a 7 instead of a 10 with a pair of dice.

Probability theory is used not only to find betting odds. It is used also in many daily weather reports to give the probability of rain. And it is used in many other areas, such as science and business.

Probability deals with chances. Suppose there are five equally possible results to a situation. The chance of any one result happening is 1 out of 5. In probability the symbol for "1 out of 5" is "⅕." The symbol has the form of a fraction and is treated like any fraction.

Suppose you toss a coin. There are two possible results. The coin can land heads up; or it can land tails up. The probability that the coin will land heads up is 1 out of 2, or ½. The probability that the coin will land tails up is also ½.

Analytic Geometry

Another French mathematician, René Descartes (1596–1650), helped to create analytic geometry, which is a combination of geometry and algebra. Analytic geometry uses methods of logic, and it also uses the operations and symbols of algebra.

Calculus

Two men created calculus independently of each other at about the same time. In Germany it was Wilhelm Leibniz (1646–1716); in England it was Sir Isaac Newton (1642–1727).

Calculus was a very important development for science. In the 1600's the foundations of modern science were being laid. Scientists needed a mathematics that could handle many of the difficult problems about motion and things that change. Motion and rates of growth and change are usually complex, not simple.

Suppose you toss a ball in the air. As the ball moves, its rate of speed changes constantly. Calculus can tell where the ball will be at any time during the ball's motion.

The world is full of complex shapes and motions and changing rates of growth. Chemical reactions often take place at speeds that are changing. Populations of countries have changing rates of growth. The speeds of planets are always changing. Thus calculus is essential to modern science. And it has important applications in almost every kind of study that uses mathematics.

Projective Geometry and Topology

Another branch of mathematics was also developed in the 1600's. This branch was a kind of geometry, but a geometry that was not directly based on measurement. It was called projective geometry.

Imagine that a geometric figure is drawn on a film slide. The slide is inserted into a projector, which is turned on. The figure on the slide appears as an image on a screen. Suppose the slide and the screen are set up parallel to each other. The projected image on the screen will not look very different from the figure on the slide. The only difference between the image and the figure will be a change in size.

Imagine, however, that the screen is not set up parallel to the slide but at an angle to it. Although the projected image will be distorted in some ways, it will not be distorted in others.

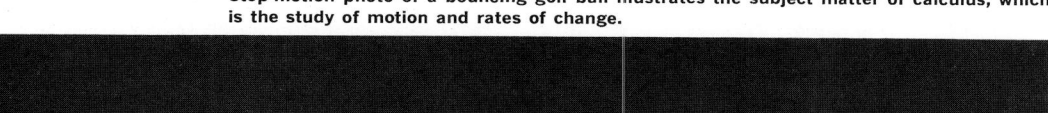
Stop-motion photo of a bouncing golf ball illustrates the subject matter of calculus, which is the study of motion and rates of change.

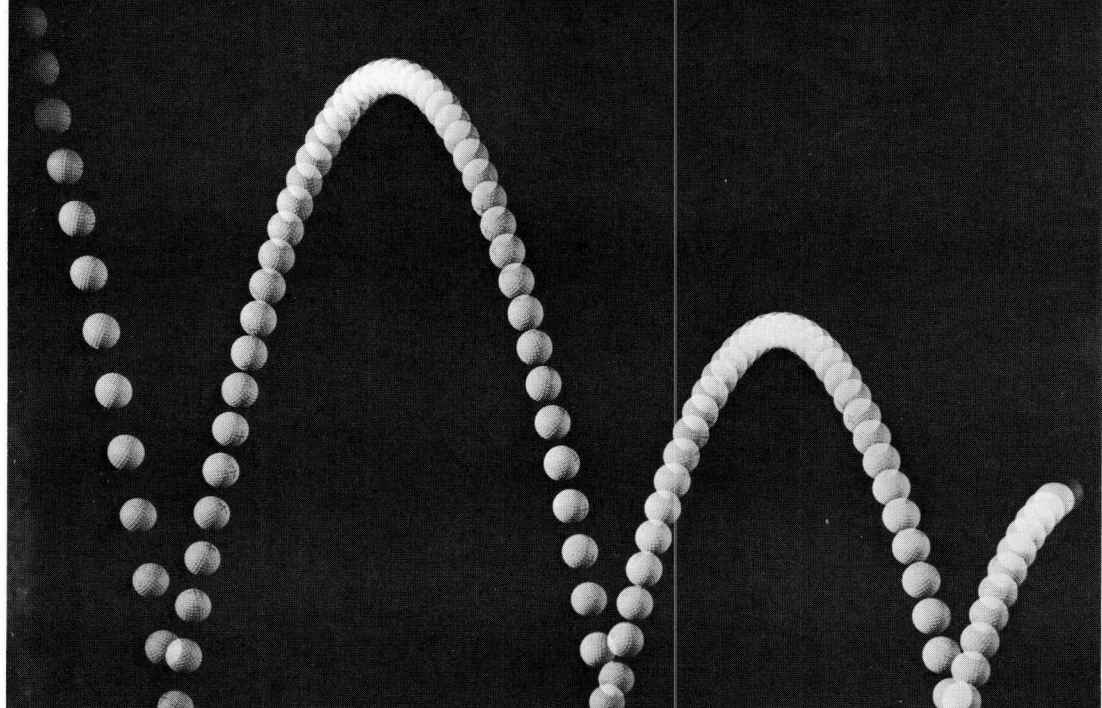

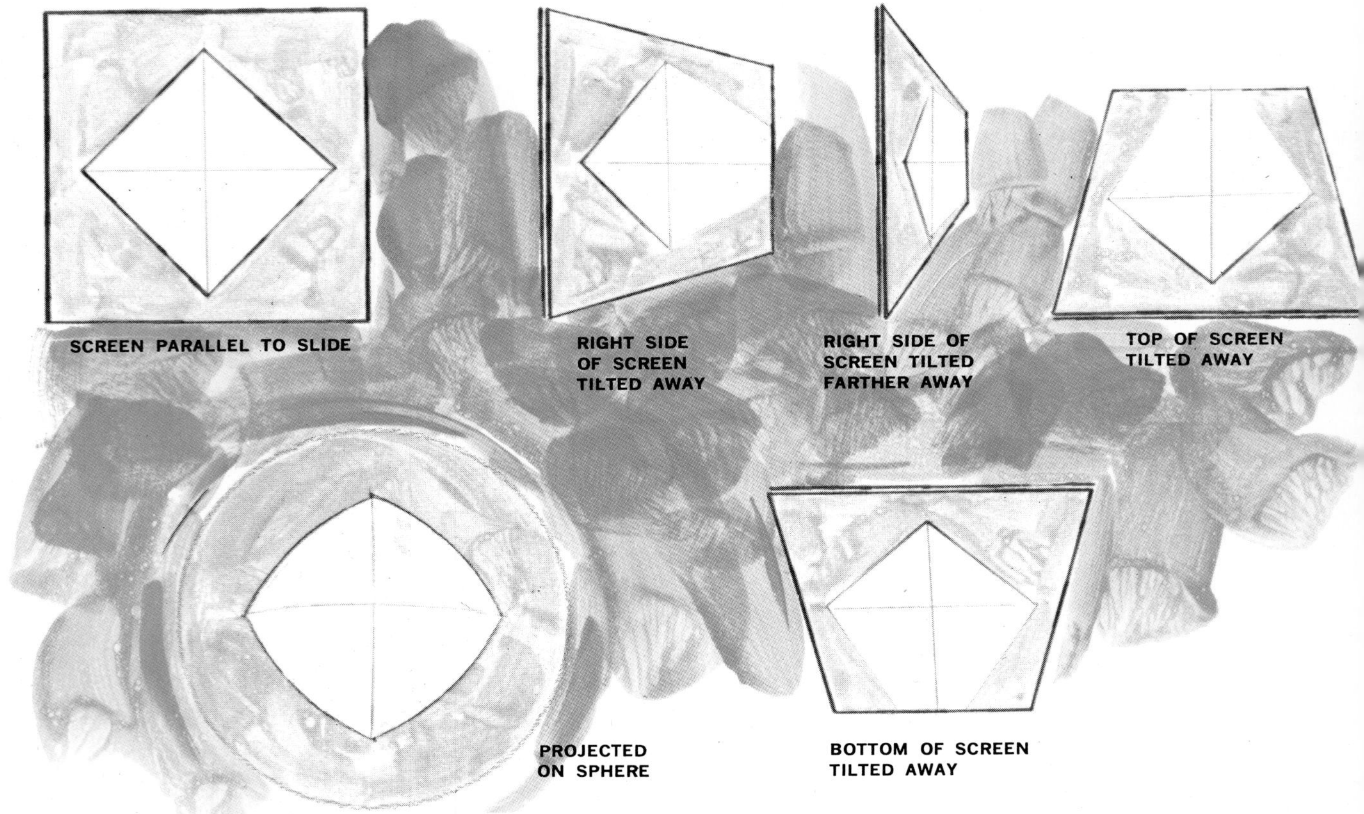

SCREEN PARALLEL TO SLIDE

RIGHT SIDE OF SCREEN TILTED AWAY

RIGHT SIDE OF SCREEN TILTED FARTHER AWAY

TOP OF SCREEN TILTED AWAY

PROJECTED ON SPHERE

BOTTOM OF SCREEN TILTED AWAY

When screen is tilted at an angle, figure is distorted. Projective geometry studies things that do not change when a figure is projected.

Circle drawn on rubber sheet is distorted when sheet is twisted. Topology is the study of properties that do not change when an object is stretched or twisted.

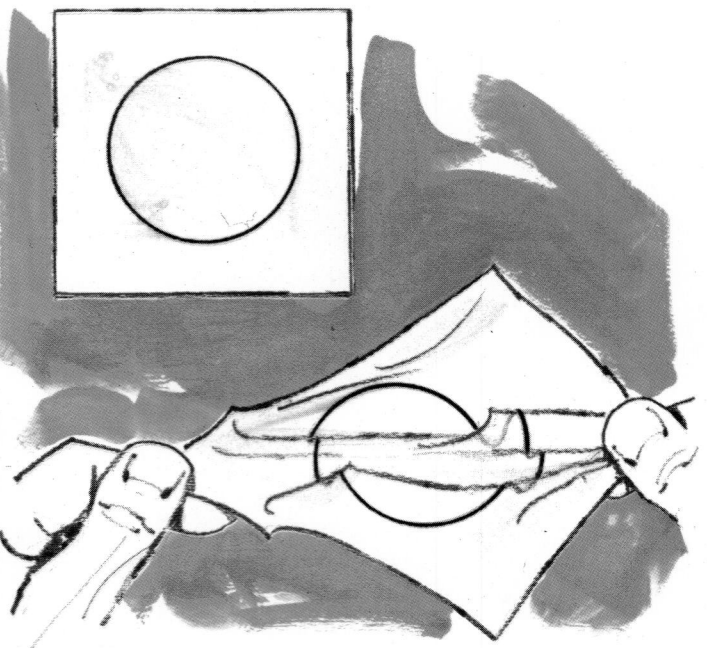

For example, if lines cross in the figure, they will also cross in the projected image. Projective geometry tries to find what things in a figure stay the same when the figure is distorted by being projected.

Mathematicians later developed an even broader kind of geometry called topology. In topology, shapes are changed by stretching, bending, twisting, and so on. Suppose that you have drawn a circle on a rubber sheet. You could stretch and twist the sheet and even tie it up in knots. As long as you did not tear the sheet, you would not change certain properties of the figure. Although the figure is no longer a circle, certain things about it remain the same no matter how you stretch and twist it out of shape. For example, the space inside the figure remains inside it. And the space outside the figure remains outside it. Topology is the study of similar properties that do not change when an object is bent, stretched, or twisted.

Non-Euclidean Geometry

In the 19th century several mathematicians began to question Euclidean geometry. They wondered if it was the only possible geometry or if there could be geometries that disagreed with Euclidean geometry.

The mathematicians who developed non-Euclidean geometries did so at about the same time, but more or less independently of each other. They were Karl Friedrich Gauss (1777–1855), a German; Nikolai Ivanovich Lobachevski (1793–1856), a Russian; and Johann Bolyai (1802–60), a Hungarian.

Euclid's geometry took certain geometric statements for granted. Two examples of such statements are "A straight line segment is the shortest distance between two points" and "Only one straight line can be drawn through two different points." These statements seemed true. So they were not proved mathematically. Unproved statements, or assumptions, are called **axioms** or **postulates**. Euclidean geometry was developed from a few such axioms. This is known as the **axiomatic method**, a method that is important in mathematics. Mathematics always starts with a few axioms—statements that seem true but cannot be proved.

Non-Euclidean geometries also use the axiomatic method. Gauss, Lobachevski, and Bolyai, however, decided to start with some axioms very different from those used in Euclidean geometry.

One axiom of Euclidean geometry, for example, says that through a given point only one straight line can be drawn parallel to another straight line. Suppose you draw a straight line. To one side of that line you mark a point with your pencil. You will find that you can draw through this point only one line that is parallel to the first line.

Lobachevski decided to use a very different axiom. He said that more than one line parallel to the first line could be drawn through the point. If you try to do this it will seem impossible. But there is no mathematical way to prove that this new axiom is not true. Lobachevski developed an entire geometry from his different axiom. This non-Euclidean geometry is just as logical as Euclidean geometry. No statement in this geometry will contradict any other statement in it.

Other non-Euclidean geometries have also been developed. One, for example, uses the axiom that no lines can be drawn parallel to a given line.

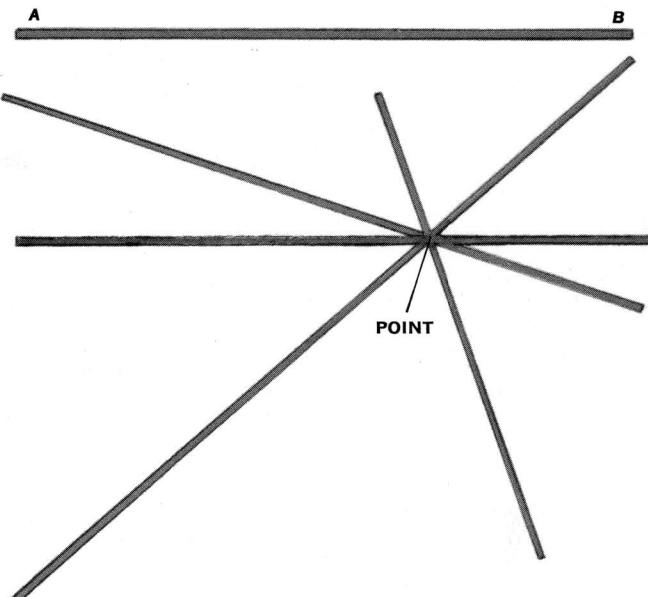

According to Euclidean geometry, only one line that is parallel to line AB can be drawn through any given point.

Hamilton's Algebra

A development in algebra during the 1800's also helped to change men's concept of mathematics. In order to understand this development, let's go back to the whole numbers once again. You probably know that it does not matter in what order you add or multiply whole numbers. The answer will be the same. For example, $2 \times 3 = 6$ and $3 \times 2 = 6$. It does not matter in what order you add or multiply fractions, either. The answer will be the same. This is also true of every other kind of number that was known before the 19th century.

In 1843, however, an Irish mathematician, Sir William Rowan Hamilton (1805–65), made a discovery. He found that certain quantities have different products when their order of multiplication is changed about. For example, vectors have this property. **Vectors** are quantities that are like numbers but have direction. The velocity of a car, for example, is a vector. On paper you can represent velocity as a line, with an arrowhead at one end to show that it has direction.

Hamilton's idea took years to develop. It helped to broaden the field of algebra in the same way that non-Euclidean ideas opened up new fields of geometric study. The algebra of vectors became a separate branch of mathematics.

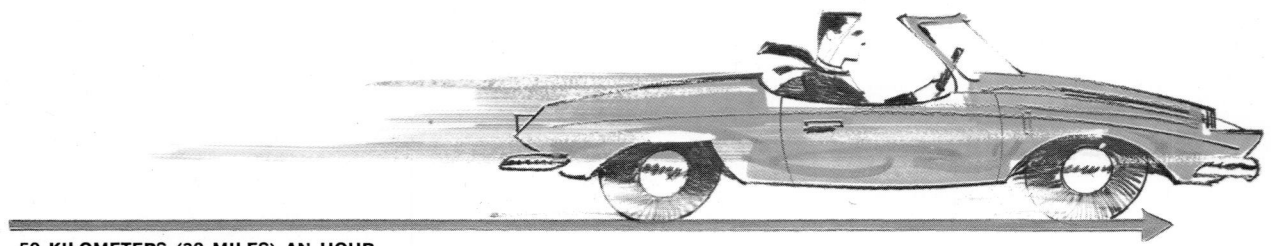

50 KILOMETERS (30 MILES) AN HOUR

VECTOR ARROW

25 KILOMETERS (15 MILES) AN HOUR

VECTOR ARROW

The velocity of a car is a vector—a quantity that has direction.

Non-Euclidean geometries and Hamilton's algebra showed that it is possible to develop whole new branches of mathematics from any axioms a mathematician may choose. But no axiom used in developing such a branch may contradict the other axioms used in that branch. Nothing in the system being developed may contradict anything else in that system. As long as no contradictions appear, mathematicians may develop any kind of mathematical system they choose. Older branches of mathematics, at least in their simple beginnings, seemed to have developed out of common sense. That is, they seemed to have been discovered rather than created. But now mathematicians are really creating new branches of mathematics. The early examples of creating mathematics are the non-Euclidean geometries and Hamilton's algebra.

▶ MODERN MATHEMATICS

Modern mathematics refers to a certain group of topics that includes set theory, mathematical logic, foundations of mathematics, and statistics. These topics were developed about 100 years ago. They continue to be of special interest to mathematicians today.

Set theory, mathematical logic, and foundations are very closely related topics. They all speak the same language—the language of sets. The language and the theory of sets are "modern," but many of the ideas go back to the very beginnings of mathematics—to problems of counting and reasoning.

Set Theory

Set theory, for example, was developed originally to help in counting infinities—numbers so large that we sometimes call them uncountable. But as you will see, some infinities are more countable than others.

A set is a collection. It may be a collection of objects or numbers or points. One set could be the coins in your pocket. If you have no coins in your pocket, that would be the **empty set**. Any set with no members in it is called the empty set. Another set is the whole numbers from 1 to 10. Its members are 1, 2, 3, 4, 5, 6, 7, 8, 9, and 10. The set of points on a line segment has as its members those points that are on the line segment. All other points are not members.

Sets can be compared with one another and can be handled mathematically in many ways. When you deal with infinite sets, the results you get are sometimes surprising.

The set of whole numbers is an infinite set. This is the set that starts with 0, 1, 2, 3 and just keeps going. No matter how many whole numbers you name, there is at least one more number you have not reached. For example, if you name six quintillion, then there is six quintillion and one.

The set of even numbers (0, 2, 4, 6, 8, 10, 12, and so on) is also an infinite set. Are there more whole numbers than even numbers? You might think that there are, since some whole numbers are even and some are not.

But infinity does not work that way.

HERD OF CATTLE

TEAM OF PLAYERS

FLOCK OF BIRDS

BUNCH OF GRAPES

GROUP OF PEOPLE

Notice that you can match every whole number with an even number if you multiply the whole number by two:

WHOLE NUMBERS	0 1 2 3 4 5 6 7 8
	↕ ↕ ↕ ↕ ↕ ↕ ↕ ↕ ↕
EVEN NUMBERS	0 2 4 6 8 10 12 14 16

This process continues through the whole set. For example, 637 from the set of whole numbers would be matched with 1,274 from the set of even numbers. Similarly, for every even number there is a whole number. Because the sets can be matched in this way, they have the same number of members.

Not all infinite sets have the same number of members. The set of points on a line is infinite, but there are more points on a line than there are whole numbers. This is shown by proving that you cannot match the members of the two sets. Sets that can be matched with the set of whole numbers are called "countable." But the set of points on a line truly is an uncountable infinity.

Sets have been used in algebra, geometry, probability, calculus, and other branches of mathematics. Today some of the simpler parts of set theory are often taught in elementary mathematics.

Mathematical Logic

Mathematical logic began with a wider use of symbols in logic. For this reason mathematical logic is sometimes called "symbolic logic." Logic can be thought of as the science of reasoning. Mathematical logic is a fairly recent development.

In mathematical logic, symbols are used to stand for ideas (sentences or parts of sentences) and the relations between the ideas. Take, for example, the sentence, "If the car is not in the garage, then Father drove it to the store, or my sister drove it to work." The ideas in this sentence can be represented by symbols in this way:

$$\sim p \longrightarrow (\, q \; v \; r \,)$$

Here, p means "the car is in the garage"

$\sim$ means "not"

$\longrightarrow$ means "If . . . then . . ."

q means "Father drove it to the store"

v means "or"

r means "my sister drove it to work."

The symbols are a kind of code.

When p, q, and r stand for ideas about mathematics, much of the content of mathematics can be expressed in logical terms. You can then use the rules of logic to find new sentences because, in addition to the code, logic has rules that tell how to find new, true sentences from sentences you have already identified as true.

Once logicians thought that all mathematics could be expressed in terms of logic and that new ideas in mathematics could be found by applying the rules of logic. Neither belief turned out to be true.

SYMBOLS AND TERMS OF SET THEORY

Set: A collection or group.

Examples of sets are: the coins in your pocket, all people who wear glasses, a deck of cards. A set is often shown like this: {dog, cat, rabbit} = set X, or

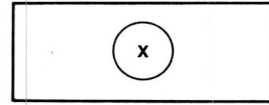

∈ **"Is a member of."**

The symbol ∈ means "is a member of." Suppose set X = {Leonard, Joe, Susan, Florence}. Then "Florence is a member of set X" is written in symbols as:

Florence ∈ X

The symbol ∉ means "is not a member of." "Harry is not a member of set X" is written in symbols as:

Harry ∉ X

∅ **or { }   The empty set.**

The empty set is a set that has no elements (members). Suppose you want to make a set of all the Siamese cats on your block. After searching out all the cats, you find that they are all tabby or Persian. Then your set will have no elements (Siamese cats). Your set is an empty set.

∩ **Intersection of sets.**

The intersection of two sets consists of the elements common to both of them. Suppose set X contains all the people in the room with you: X = {Mother, Father, Anne, John}. Another set, Y, contains all the red-haired people you know: Y = {John, Harry, George, Bruce}. The intersection of sets X and Y is {John}. He is the only person who is a member of both sets. So X ∩ Y = {John}. The intersection of sets is often shown like this:

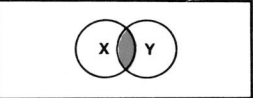

The dark portion where the circles overlap is X ∩ Y.

∪ **Union of sets.**

The union of sets is a set that contains all the objects contained in the two sets. Suppose set X contains all the people in the room with you: X = {Mother, Father, Anne, John}. Suppose another set, Y, contains all the red-haired people you know: Y = {John, Harry, George, Bruce}. The union of X and Y is the set of all the objects in both sets. X ∪ Y = {Mother, Father, Anne, John, Harry, George, Bruce}. Notice that John is listed only once even though he is a member of both sets. Union of sets is often shown like this:

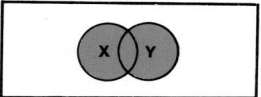

The entire colored area is X ∪ Y.

But the structure of symbolic logic that they built became the basis for electronic computers, which have changed our lives in many ways.

Foundations

When mathematicians use the word "foundations," they are talking about studies of the basic nature of mathematics. Workers in foundations try to find a logical basis for all mathematics. The main tools for these studies are set theory and mathematical logic.

Students of the foundations of mathematics have done as much to indicate what mathematics cannot do as what it can do. During the 1930's several mathematicians proved major theorems concerning the limitations of mathematics.

A mathematical theory, such as set theory or arithmetic, is **complete** if it covers all the results that can be stated in the language of that theory. A theory is **consistent** if it does not contain direct contradictions. For example, "the sun is shining" and "the sun is not shining" are direct contradictions. The mathematicians of the 1930's showed that most theories cannot be complete if they are consistent. Both set theory and arithmetic are among the theories that cannot be complete and consistent at the same time. Often mathematicians can reach such amazing results through simple reasoning.

Statistics

Set theory, logic, and foundations are not very well known to most non-mathematicians. But some recent developments in mathematics are widely known. One subject that has become a part of daily life is statistics. Statistics is that part of mathematics in which knowledge of a part is used to estimate what the whole is like. Statistics is based upon probability.

Today statistics is used in varied ways. For example, it is used to determine how many people watch a particular television show. It is helpful in studying the environment. And it is used to predict the behavior of molecules in a gas. Statistics is important in all these activities because it contains the rules for dealing with large numbers of people, molecules, or any other objects. In most uses of statistics a few objects, called a **sample**, are studied to find out about the behavior of a large number of the same kind of objects. Statistics also tells in what way large numbers of objects will change in time.

For example, we know that atoms of radioactive elements, such as uranium, break down to form atoms of other elements. No one can tell which of the uranium atoms will break down. But statistical theory can tell how much of the uranium will break down in a given period of time.

Mathematics Today

At first, mathematics was entirely practical. It seemed to be a series of natural laws. All these laws seemed to be as firm as the one that states "Two bodies cannot occupy the same place at the same time." But in the 1800's people began to think of mathematics as a game. They realized that they could make up their own rules and that new systems of mathematics could be formed from these rules.

Today mathematicians know that there is no end to the possible systems of mathematics. They know that they cannot make enough rules to include all of these systems.

At the same time, mathematics has become part of our daily lives. Statistics is used to inform and predict in news reports, and the chance of rain is given as a probability. People receive paychecks written by computers, airline tickets are issued by computers, and income tax forms are checked by computers. We may not know the details of the mathematics used in designing bridges and airplanes, in controlling traffic, and

in keeping nuclear reactors working, but our lives are tied up in the results. All of these results require mathematics that was once developed as someone's mathematical game.

What are some of the games mathematicians are playing today? Many of them are working in the branches of modern mathematics that were discussed earlier. Others are working in new directions, such as **catastrophe theory**. For centuries we have had mathematics to deal with changes that take place smoothly. The changes in velocity and altitude throughout the flight of a rocket are examples of such smooth changes. But until very recently no one attempted to find mathematics describing sudden changes that sometimes arise from a series of small changes. This mathematics of "the straw that broke the camel's back" is given the name of catastrophe theory.

One simplified example is the filling of a lake behind a dam. Present-day mathematics can calculate the forces caused by adding water to the lake as long as the dam holds. But new mathematics is needed to describe what happens when the dam breaks. The water no longer flows smoothly. Erosion— the wearing away of the land by the flowing water—is no longer a smooth change taking many years.

In today's mathematics, the computer has become a tool for investigating fundamental problems. For example, a famous problem in topology was solved through the use of the computer. It is the four-color map problem. For over one hundred years, mathematicians had been trying by ordinary means to prove that any map can be colored with just four colors. (The problem is important in map-making because no two countries that share a boundary larger than a point can be of the same color.) Many mathematicians believed that only four colors were needed, but none could find the proof.

Finally, in 1976, two mathematicians programmed a computer to check all possible types of maps. The computer found that all could be colored with just four colors. The proof had seemed beyond the ability of mathematicians because of the enormous number of calculations needed.

Mathematics feeds on itself and on the physical and life sciences. We can be sure that mathematics will continue to grow, although we cannot predict the ways in which it will grow.

MATHEMATICS IN THE WORLD OF WORK

Before the 1940's there was little need for higher mathematics in most careers. Engineers, physical scientists, economists, mathematicians, and mathematics teachers were about the only people who had to know much mathematics beyond arithmetic. These people were a very small part of the total population.

Since the 1940's the situation has changed, largely because of the widespread use of the electronic computer. In time every profession will be affected by the computer. Already biologists and social scientists find higher mathematics essential in their work. Future economists will need to know more and deeper mathematics, and so will every business executive who guides a large corporation or industry.

Biologists and sociologists now use the latest ideas in mathematics, such as catastrophe theory, to carry out research that would otherwise be impossible. Business managers use higher mathematics to learn where to place warehouses and factories, how to route traveling salespeople, and how to control production and quality. Until very recently they had little need for higher mathematics to be successful in their jobs.

Many new branches of science and technology are developing in such fields as space science, traffic and transportation control, and oceanography. These, too, depend heavily on mathematics. Even scholars in the older non-mathematical studies—such as psychology, archeology, and ancient languages—are finding mathematics more and more useful.

Careers in Mathematics

One result of the greater need for mathematics in more careers has been a need for more teachers of mathematics. First mathematicians, and then mathematics teachers, must lead the way for the others who will use mathematics. How do mathematicians and mathematics teachers prepare for such work? What are their lives like? What opportunities are there in mathematics careers?

Some people find it hard to picture what mathematicians do when they are at work. Do they use arithmetic? Sometimes they do, especially those known as **applied mathematicians**. The lines are not sharp, but an applied mathematician usually solves specific problems or develops ways to solve specific problems. A **theoretical mathematician**, on the other hand, works on extending the range of mathematics without worrying about how the mathematics can be used—or, indeed, whether it can be used. The best mathematicians are usually good at both applied and theoretical mathematics. Gauss, who was a great theoretical mathematician, spent years calculating the orbit of an asteroid—which is a problem in applied mathematics.

One thinks of applied mathematicians as persons who work with pencil and paper, calculators, or computers. But they also do a lot of work "in their heads." Theoretical mathematicians use all these tools also, but they do even more of their work in their heads. Thus, a mathematician may be working at any time and in any place at all. Hamilton's great idea came during a walk in the country. He was so excited that he scratched the fundamental statement of the new algebra into the stone pillar of the bridge he was crossing when the idea occurred. Another mathematician, Henri Poincaré, wrote that one of his most original ideas came to him while he was boarding a bus.

Most mathematicians teach part of the time. This is also true of the other scholarly professions, such as economics, physics, and sociology. In a university, mathematicians and other scholars are expected to do research in addition to teaching. In business, mathematicians who have been hired to solve problems or to do research are sometimes encouraged to teach as well.

A very few people seem to be born with a great deal of mathematical ability. Such people can often progress with little formal education. In general, though, a mathematician seeking one of the better careers needs a doctoral degree and one or two years of study beyond that. Applied mathematicians with only a master's degree may find jobs open to them, but their chances for advancement will be quite limited unless they are unusually talented.

Mathematicians today can earn fairly good salaries. A mathematician who teaches at a large university, consults part of the time with industry, and also writes textbooks can earn a great deal. But such a person has little time for research.

Careers in Mathematics Teaching

Most of the people who earn their living from mathematics do so by teaching. These mathematics teachers do not usually do research or solve difficult technical problems. They teach in elementary and secondary schools. Most of them love mathematics, but they may not have the inclination or knack for working mainly with mathematical ideas. The best teachers have, instead, a rare ability and love for teaching.

Less extensive study of mathematics is required to prepare for teaching mathematics in elementary or secondary school than is required for teaching in a college or university.

Members of one small group earn a living from mathematics but do not engage in research, problem solving, or teaching. These people are mathematics editors—people who, for the most part, work on mathematics textbooks. Usually they work on science textbooks or magazines as well. Nearly all mathematics editors were teachers at one time. The education required of editors and the salaries they receive are comparable to those of mathematics teachers.

Mathematics in the Sciences

Everyone uses mathematics at some time. But there are many careers that require extensive use of mathematics. Most of these also require special training in mathematics.

One such group of careers is in the sciences. Physics, especially, has always relied on mathematics. Chemistry and astronomy also require some mathematics. The connection has never been as close as between mathematics and physics. But it would be impossible to become a professional chemist or astronomer without special training in higher mathematics.

Mathematics is being used in many new ways in the other sciences. Geologists use mathematical analysis to determine the interior structure of the earth or the age of a rock. Biologists study the probability of changes in genes or social behavior, the mathematics of energy transfer between living things, and the geometry of proteins. Archeologists make statistical analyses of the shapes of arrow points.

In fact, no physical or biological scientist today can understand what is going on without knowledge of higher mathematics. This is because the other workers in the field use the language of higher mathematics to express their results.

The social sciences are becoming increasingly dependent on mathematics. Economics has always been mathematical. But today even historians may find that they need mathematics to analyze trends in the past or to determine through statistics who is the true author of a document. A person who is interested in both mathematics and one of the social sciences can make a very satisfying career out of being a mathematical social scientist.

Mathematics in Engineering

Engineering is another career that requires considerable higher mathematics. Many engineers do not need to be able to solve new types of problems, as mathematicians do. For that reason engineering courses in college often include special mathematical training that focuses on solving common kinds of problems.

One can become an engineer with somewhat less formal education than many mathematicians and scientists have. Since salaries for engineers are comparable to, or better than, salaries for mathematicians and scientists, engineering is a popular career choice. Many young people who enjoy mathematics become engineers.

Mathematics in Computer Programming

Recently another popular choice has arisen among mathematical careers. This one can require less training than engineering. Yet income in the first few years of employment can be about the same. This career is computer programming. A computer programmer tells a computer what to do. With the great

HOW TO MAKE YOUR OWN SLIDE RULE

The slide rule is a mathematician's tool for multiplying and dividing numbers quickly and easily. You can make your own slide rule from a special type of graph paper called semilog graph paper, available at a stationery store. You will also need a file folder, a pair of scissors, a bobby pin, and some paste.

First cut the file folder about 4 centimeters (1½ inches) above the closed end, as shown in Figure 1. This gives you a double strip with the fold at the bottom. Then, from the top edge of one of the leftover pieces, cut a strip that is 5 centimeters (2 inches) wide. Place this strip into the fold so that the straighter edge can slide in the fold.

Cut two strips of graph paper, as shown in Figure 2. These are your scales. Paste one scale on the outside of the strip with the fold at the bottom. The numbers should increase from left to right. Now paste the other scale on the movable strip. The two scales should line up exactly (Fig. 3). The bobby pin is the scale marker. Clip the bobby pin on the scales as in Figure 3.

▶ HOW TO USE YOUR SLIDE RULE

Your slide rule has two scales. The movable scale is the C scale, and the fixed scale is the D scale. Line up the C and D scales so that each number on the D scale has the same number on the C scale above it. Draw arrowheads on the 1 and 10 lines of the C scale, as shown in Figure 3.

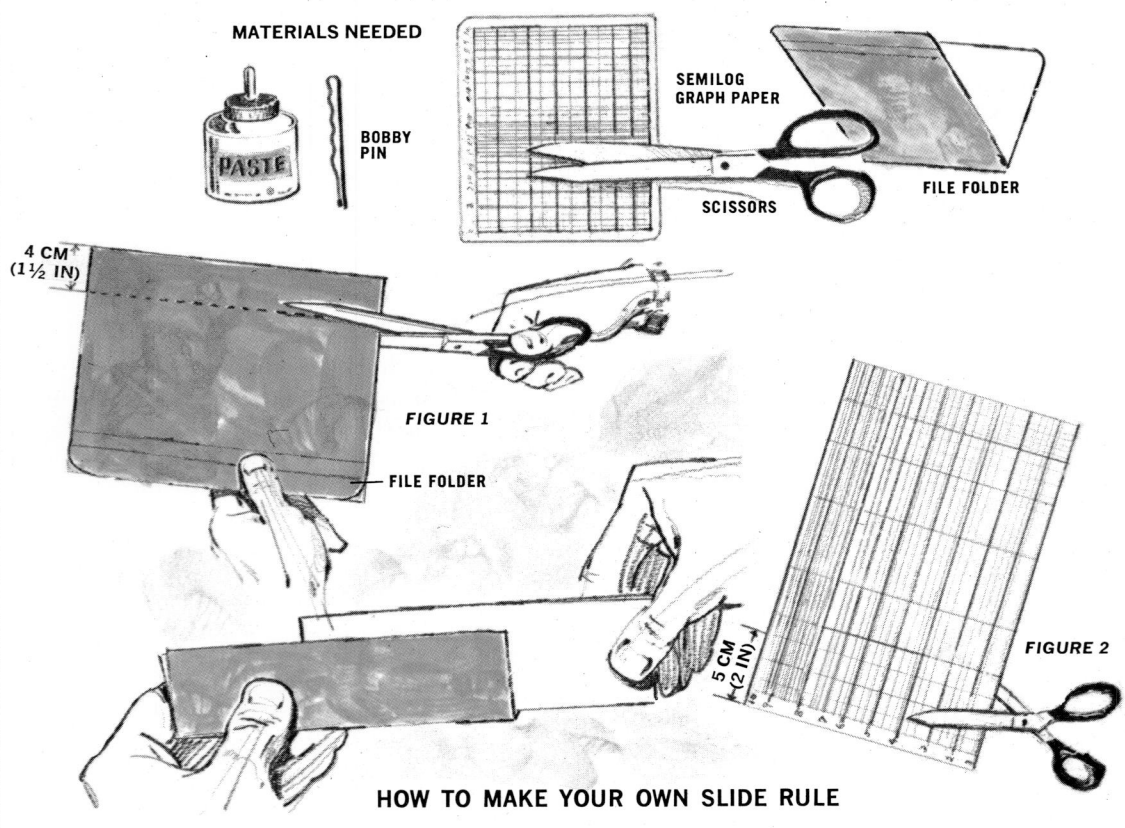

MATERIALS NEEDED

PASTE

BOBBY PIN

SEMILOG GRAPH PAPER

SCISSORS

FILE FOLDER

4 CM (1½ IN)

FIGURE 1

FILE FOLDER

5 CM (2 IN)

FIGURE 2

HOW TO MAKE YOUR OWN SLIDE RULE

increase in computer use, there has been a rising demand for people who know how to do this. Since computers deal only with mathematics, the programmer must understand some mathematical language to be able to communicate with the computer. Programmers do not usually have to apply mathematics, but they do need to have some feeling for mathematical reasoning. It helps if they enjoy mathematics. Several different levels of mathematics are used in programming. A programmer who is working on a scientific program needs more mathematical training than one who is programming a computer in a business situation.

To Multiply with Your Slide Rule

To multiply 3 by 2, slide the C scale along until either arrow on the C scale lines up with the 3 on the D scale. Slide the bobby pin along the rule, being careful not to change the position of the two scales, until you reach the 2 on the C scale. If the bobby pin slides off the end of the D scale, use the other arrow. Your answer now appears on the D scale.

To Divide with Your Slide Rule

To divide 8 by 4, slide the 4 on the C scale along until it lines up with the 8 on the D scale. Without changing the position of the scales, slide the bobby pin to the arrow on the C scale. The answer appears on the D scale.

▶THE NUMBERS ON YOUR SLIDE RULE

Slide the bobby pin along the D-scale until you reach the 3. It is important to realize that the slide rule does not tell you three what. It just tells you 3. You have to decide for each problem what the 3 is to mean. For example, if you decide that the 3 is to mean three tens, then the 3 means thirty. If you decide that the 3 is to stand for ones, then the 3 simply means three.

Let's try an example and see how this works. Multiply 3 by 2. In the example above you saw that the answer on the slide rule was 6. Six what? That depends on what the 3 and 2 are. If 3 is ones and 2 is ones, then three ones times two ones is six ones. If, however, the 3 is tens and the 2 is tens, the 6 is sixty tens, or six hundred.

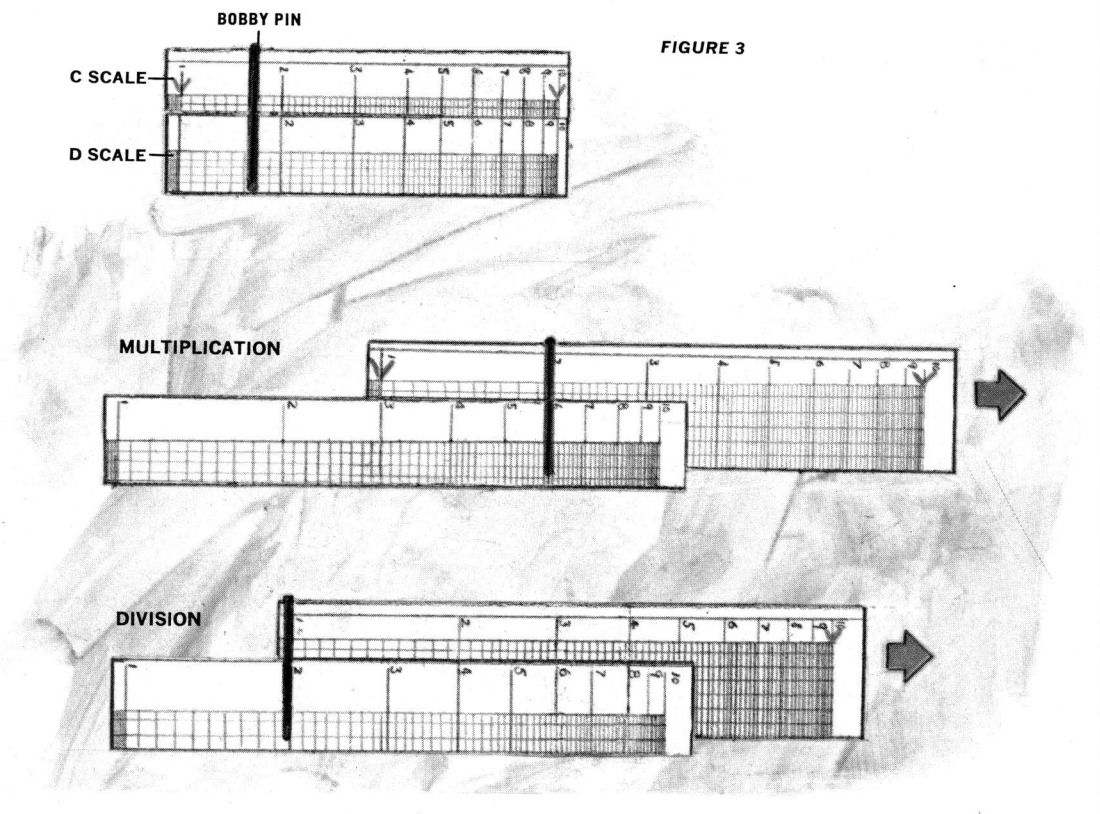

BOBBY PIN

C SCALE

D SCALE

FIGURE 3

MULTIPLICATION

DIVISION

If you have a talent for mathematics but think you would not be interested in any of the careers discussed so far, there are still other opportunities.

Mathematics in Actuarial Work

One career that requires higher mathe-matics is the actuarial profession. Ac-tuaries are the men and women who calculate statistics for the insurance industry. For example, they may determine the life expec-tancy for a woman of 53 or the odds that a male driver under 25, who has had driv-er's training, will have an accident. The mathematics may be difficult, but the kinds of problems that are treated tend to be similar. The challenge is at about the same level as in many engineering jobs, and salaries are comparable. But an actuary's work is more purely mathematical than an engineer's. Actuaries must pass a difficult examination before they can begin this career.

Mathematics in Accounting

Another career that uses mathematics—but is less demanding mathematically than those mentioned so far—is accountancy. Accountants should enjoy working with numbers and should be good at it, but they usually do not need to know higher mathematics. They must combine an excellent understanding of arithmetic with a knowledge of the special problems of business. There are many kinds of accountants, with a great range of salaries. One common but important type is the Certified Public Accountant, or CPA, who must pass an examination to qualify for this title.

▶ WOMEN AND MATHEMATICS

In the past women were not encouraged to follow mathematical careers. Yet there have been women mathematicians in history. Even in this century women mathematicians sometimes had to let men take official credit for their work. Today women are encouraged to enter the careers we have discussed, but there are still unconscious or unofficial restrictions that make this difficult. The basic problem in technical or scientific careers is often that women have not taken the mathematics courses required for advanced work in, for example, biology or engineering.

Most studies of mathematical ability show that up to some point in adolescence girls are better students. Then, on the average, the boys quickly surpass the girls and remain superior. No one is sure why this happens. One popular theory, confirmed by surveys, is that secondary school teachers simply do not expect women to do well in mathematics. Women who do succeed usually have a strong backer who believes in them. For these women, results are as good as for men.

Today, with more teachers aware of the problem—and more women aware of their own abilities—women are increasingly taking the courses they need to enter all of the professions that depend on mathematics.

▶ MATHEMATICS IN EVERYDAY LIFE

Although most careers do not require higher mathematics, it is easy to forget how much mathematics is required in most jobs. Carpenters use geometry. Bookkeepers use arithmetic. And surveyors use trigonometry. Merchants often use algebra in inventory planning. They may also use higher mathematics. Uses of this kind have been common for a long time. Today the use of advanced mathematics is also becoming more important in many careers.

▶ FROM COUNTING TO COMPUTERS

It is believed that the earliest mathematical act performed by people was counting. Today we live in a world where much of the counting and other mathematics are done by electronic computers and where, for a few dollars, you can buy a hand-held calculator that will do your arithmetic for you. It will often do percents, square roots, and other, more complicated functions as well.

When people made their own furniture and houses, forming right angles and computing areas and volumes were important skills. Now furniture and homes can be ordered already assembled. And few people need these skills.

The computer does the mathematical work needed to operate a lathe, direct the cutting and sewing of a garment, put together a budget, or survey a field from a photograph. Do we therefore need to know more mathematics or less? Most people today need to understand more mathematics than used to be required, but they may not need to develop some specific skills as highly as before.

But for those people who hope to follow one of the mathematical careers, there is no question of the need to know more mathematics. Every day there is more to know. People are needed to direct and develop the computers and the mathematics of the future.

BRYAN H. BUNCH
Editor in Chief, American Book Company

See also ALGEBRA; ARITHMETIC; COMPUTERS; DECIMAL SYSTEM; FRACTIONS; GEOMETRY AND GEOMETRIC FORMS; NUMBERS AND NUMBER SYSTEMS; NUMERALS AND NUMERATION SYSTEMS; PROBABILITY; SETS; STATISTICS; TOPOLOGY.

Henri Matisse in his studio, drawing with charcoal attached to a long pole.

MATISSE, HENRI (1869–1954)

The French artist Henri Matisse was born in Le Cateau in northern France on December 31, 1869. He grew up in a nearby town where his father was a grain merchant. When Matisse finished school, his father sent him to Paris to study law. At the end of 2 years he returned home. Matisse worked as a law clerk, but early every morning he took drawing lessons. Then in 1890, while he was recovering from an illness, his mother gave him a box of paints. From that time forward Matisse devoted his life to painting. In 1891, much against his father's wishes, Matisse left for Paris to become an artist.

For 5 years Matisse studied with the painter Gustave Moreau. To earn money, he made copies of famous paintings in the Louvre. In 1899 he married Amélie Parayre. They had two sons and a daughter—Jean, Pierre, and Marguerite. To help support the family, Madame Matisse set up a hat shop.

Matisse became the leader of a group of painters called *Les Fauves* ("wild beasts"). The group was named by an art critic who was shocked by the bright, bold colors these artists used. The public, too, was scandalized by the Fauves' exhibition of 1905. Even so, Matisse's reputation grew. He set up an art school, and collectors were eager to buy his paintings. Soon he became one of the most famous of living painters.

Around 1910 Matisse's style changed. Using calmer colors, he painted simple figures with dark outlines. These paintings have powerful rhythms. During World War I, Matisse's paintings were somber in color and spirit, but after the war they became gay and decorative. About 1925 Matisse again began experimenting. After many lifelike studies he created simple compositions in flat colors.

Matisse was a sculptor as well as a painter. His sculpture follows the same development as his painting. He also illustrated many books and made designs for tapestries and glass.

During World War II, Matisse refused to leave France. In the town of Vence, Matisse designed a chapel. The inside walls are covered with white tiles with simple designs painted in black. Brilliant color floods through stained-glass windows. The chapel was completed in 1951, when Matisse was 82. Because of illness Matisse made many of the designs for the chapel in bed, working with a long stick with charcoal tied to the end. Confined to bed, he began experimenting with arrangements of cutout pieces of paper.

By his constant searching and experimenting, Matisse opened up new paths of art. His works were the result of much planning. Before beginning a painting he made many studies and sketches, but the final work he did quickly. Matisse continued drawing and painting until his death on November 3, 1954.

Reviewed by PIERRE MATISSE

MATTER

Matter is the name given to anything that possesses two qualities, or properties—it must take up space, and it must have mass.

The first property is easy to understand. Everything solid around you—people, books, tables, pens, and so on—takes up space. The amount of space that an object takes up has a special name—it is called **volume**.

The volume of an object is measured in cubic centimeters (or cubic inches). The cubic measurement expresses the volume that the object would have if it were shaped into a cube—that is, a box with sides all of the same length.

You can squeeze a piece of modeling clay into a ball, a cube, or any other shape you wish. But whatever shape you give it, the clay always takes up the same amount of space. Its volume stays the same.

Once you have pushed clay into a particular shape, it will keep that shape if left alone. Anything that keeps its shape when left alone is a **solid**.

What about water? You cannot shape water into a ball, a cube, or any other definite shape—it simply flattens out. But if you place water in an empty container, the water will press against the bottom and sides. No matter what the shape of the container may be, the water will take that shape.

STUDY THE FORMS OF MATTER

Matter may be in the form of a solid, a liquid, or a gas. These easy experiments will help you to see that all matter, whatever its form, takes up space. You will need a toy block, a dishpan or bucket, two or more drinking glasses of different shapes, and a piece of newspaper. Work at a sink or some other place where spilled water will not damage anything.

SOLIDS. Fill the pan with water to the very top. Hold the block with two fingers and push it down into the water so that it is just covered. You will see some of the water running out of the pan. This happens because the solid block takes up space—the space that was taken up by the overflowing water.

LIQUIDS. Pour water into each of the glasses. You can see that the water takes up space inside the glass. Notice also that the water, like any liquid, takes the shape of the container it is in.

GASES. Crumple a piece of newspaper into a ball. Force the ball down into the bottom of the glass. It should fit tightly enough to stay in place when you turn the glass upside down. Push the inverted glass straight down into the water so that it is completely covered. Then lift the glass straight up out of the water, and you will find that the paper ball and the inside wall of the glass are dry. No water can enter because something else is already taking up space in the glass—the mixture of gases that we call air.

Substances that behave in this way are **liquids**. Liquids change their shape easily, but they take up space, as solids do. And no matter what shape a particular amount of liquid may take, its volume remains the same.

Now let us look at the empty container. Was it really empty before the water was poured in? No, the container had air in it. Air is a mixture of several kinds of **gases**, and gases also take up space. When we pour water into the container, we push out the gases.

Solids, liquids, and gases are the three general forms of matter. They are the three **states of matter**. Try the experiments on page 170, and you will see that all matter, whatever state it is in, takes up space.

▶ **MASS**

Here on earth all the space about us is filled with matter. There is rock under our feet and air all around us. Scientists, however, have learned how to take most of the air out of a container. This leaves a volume of space with almost no matter in it. Such space is called a **vacuum**. The space between the planets and between our sun and other stars has practically no matter in it. This means that most of the universe is a vacuum.

Yet can that really be so? What about light, for one thing? Doesn't the blazing sun fill all the space between itself and us with light?

Yes, it does. But scientists think light is both a form of energy and a special form of matter. As matter, it has so little mass that it takes up almost no space.

Now, what is mass?

To understand what it is, let's begin with something that everyone knows. It is harder to throw a large, heavy ball than a small, light one. A very large rock is hard to get moving at all. In the same way, a quickly moving Ping-Pong ball is easy to stop. A quickly moving baseball is harder to stop and calls for a padded glove. A large, heavy rock moving as fast as the baseball is so hard to stop that you had better just get out of the way.

Any piece of matter, if it is at rest (that is, not moving), tends to remain at rest. If it is moving, it tends to keep on moving. That is what people mean when they say that matter possesses **inertia**. It takes an effort to put matter into motion or to bring it to rest. The more effort it takes for a particular piece of matter, the more inertia that matter has. The amount of inertia a particular piece of matter has represents its **mass**.

Mass and Weight

Any piece of matter attracts all other pieces of matter. For ordinary pieces of matter, this attraction is so tiny that no one notices it. For a huge piece of matter, such as the earth, the force of attraction is very strong. We call it the force of **gravity**. The more mass a piece of matter possesses, the more strongly it is attracted by the earth's gravity.

We feel the attraction of the earth as weight. An object with a large mass (a truck, for example) is strongly attracted, so it has a large weight. It is heavy, and you would not expect to be able to lift it. On the other hand, an object of little mass (an insect, let us say) is light and easy to lift.

Since mass and weight go together on the earth's surface, people sometimes talk as though the two were the same thing. They are not. For one thing, weight changes from place to place, but mass does not. An object on a high mountain weighs a little less than it would in the valley below. Up on the mountaintop the object is farther from the center of the earth. It is less strongly attracted toward the center of the earth, so it weighs less.

The moon is a smaller body than the earth. It has less mass. The moon, therefore, produces a weaker force of attraction. An astronaut weighing 70 kilograms (154 pounds) on the earth weighs only about one sixth that much on the moon.

Yet any object would have the same mass, the same amount of inertia—whether it was in a valley, on a mountaintop, or on the moon. An object might feel very light on the moon, but it would be just as hard to set in motion as on the earth. Once in motion, it would be just as hard to stop it as on the earth.

Because mass doesn't change from place to place but weight does, mass is considered the more important property of matter.

Density

It is sometimes useful to speak of mass and volume together. For instance, iron is often said to be "heavier" than aluminum. This means that a certain volume of iron is heavier than the same volume of aluminum.

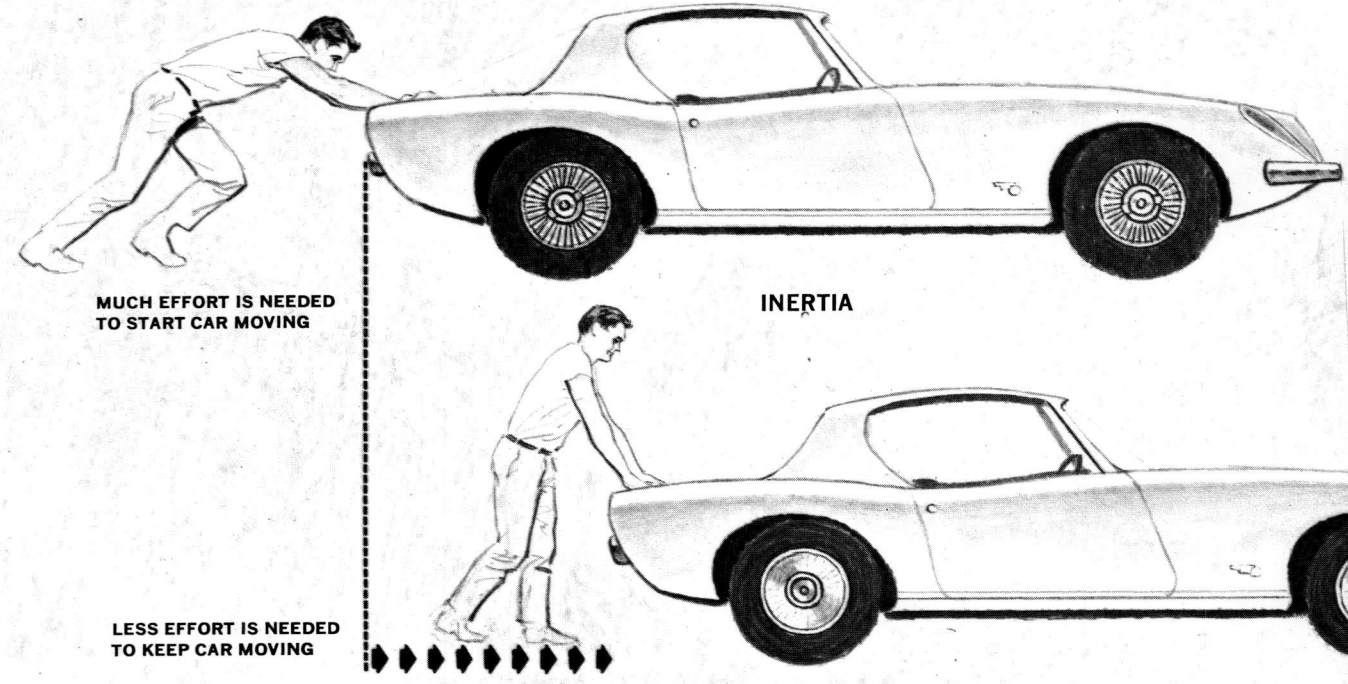

MUCH EFFORT IS NEEDED
TO START CAR MOVING

INERTIA

LESS EFFORT IS NEEDED
TO KEEP CAR MOVING

All matter has inertia. Inertia is the tendency for an object at rest to remain at rest and for a moving object to continue moving. It takes great effort to start a car from resting position, but once started, the car is fairly easy to push.

The quantity of mass in a particular volume is called its density. For example, the density of aluminum is 168.7 pounds per cubic foot, while iron has a density of 491 pounds per cubic foot. This tells us that iron is about three times denser than aluminum.

In the metric system, density is often expressed as grams per cubic centimeter. A cubic centimeter of aluminum weighs 2.7 grams; a cubic centimeter of iron weighs 7.8 grams.

Sometimes it is convenient to compare the density of a substance with the density of water. This comparison is called the **specific gravity**, or **specific weight**, of the substance. For example, the specific gravity of iron is 7.86 because iron weighs 7.86 times as much as an equal volume of water.

▶ TEMPERATURE AND VOLUME

When a solid or a liquid changes shape, it does not change volume. Yet the volume of an object almost always changes with changes in temperature. If a solid or liquid is heated, the volume generally increases. The substance takes up more room. If the solid or liquid is cooled, it takes up less room. You can see this very easily with the colored liquid in a thermometer. Whenever the temperature goes up, the liquid expands (takes up more space). It

rises higher in its tube. When the temperature goes down, the liquid contracts (takes up less space). Its level drops. We tell the temperature by the height of the liquid.

Gases change volume even more easily. In fact, you can make a gas change volume just by compressing it (squeezing it together). As you know, a tire flattens somewhat under the weight of the car. Its air is compressed by the weight. If the little valve in the tire were opened, the air would escape. And if you could trap the air in a container, you would find that it took up much more room outside the tire than inside. As the air escaped, it expanded.

▶ THE CONSERVATION LAWS

Although the volume of a piece of matter can be changed easily, its mass cannot. In the 1800's scientists became certain that it was impossible to change the mass of a particular piece of matter. They felt sure that mass could not be destroyed and could not be created. They stated this as the **law of conservation of mass**. (It could also be called the law of conservation of matter, for matter and mass go hand in hand. You can't have one without the other.)

Scientists also concluded that the same was

true of energy. Energy might change from one form to another, but it could be neither created nor destroyed. This was the **law of conservation of energy**.

In 1905 a scientist named Albert Einstein worked out a theory that matter and energy were not entirely different things. Matter, he said, could be converted (changed) into energy, and energy into matter. Matter is a very rich form of energy, and a little matter could be converted into a great deal of energy. On the other hand, a great deal of energy could be converted into only a small quantity of matter.

However, the sum total of matter and energy could be neither created nor destroyed. For that reason scientists now speak of the **law of conservation of mass-energy**.

The Conversion of Mass and Energy

Scientists have actually been able to measure the changeover. When energy is produced in ordinary fashion, so little mass disappears that it is impossible to measure. However, certain substances are radioactive and give off energy year after year, century after century. Very delicate measurements of these have shown that mass vanishes to supply the energy.

Energy can also be changed into matter. When you make an object move—as when you throw a ball—you are putting energy into it. The more energy you put into it, the faster it moves. Some of the energy is turned into matter. A moving ball, therefore, has more mass than a ball that is not moving.

It takes a great deal of energy to produce even a small quantity of mass. And so the extra mass in an ordinary moving ball is far too tiny to measure. Even a rocket speeding around the earth at 8 kilometers (5 miles) a second gains very little mass.

But the faster an object travels, the more mass it gains. Moving at 257,000 kilometers (160,000 miles) a second, it has twice as much mass as it had when it was standing still. As more energy is put into it to make it go still faster, a larger proportion of the extra energy is changed to mass. By the time it is going 299,000 kilometers (186,000 miles) a second, nearly all the additional energy is changed into mass.

It turns out that the maximum speed at which matter can move is 299,728 kilometers (186,251 miles) a second. By that time, so much energy has been turned into mass that the object is far more massive than it was at the start. It is more massive than anything you can imagine. Additional energy cannot make it go any faster. The additional energy simply turns into more mass, not more motion.

Light travels at the speed of 299,728 kilometers (186,251 miles) a second. (But remember that light is a form of energy.) Thus, you can say that the speed of light is the maximum speed possible in this universe.

The volume of an object changes with changes in temperature. When a thermometer is heated, the volume of liquid in the thermometer tube increases and the liquid rises in the tube.

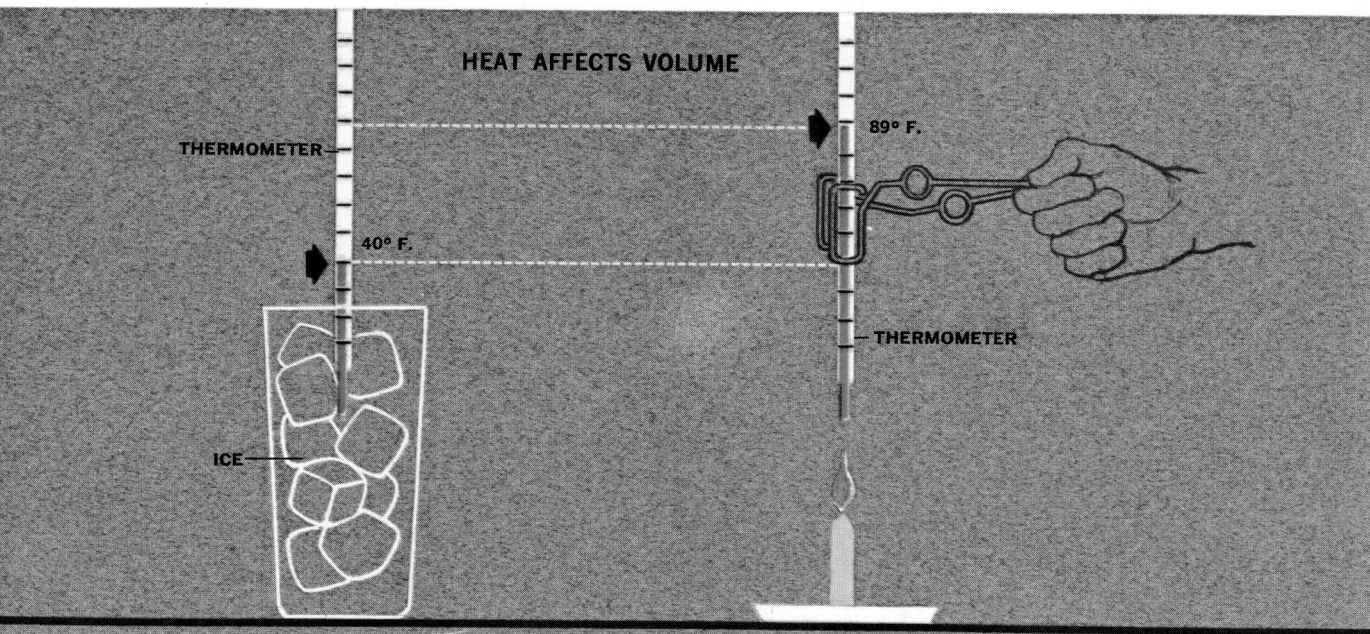

HEAT AFFECTS VOLUME

THERMOMETER

89° F.

40° F.

THERMOMETER

ICE

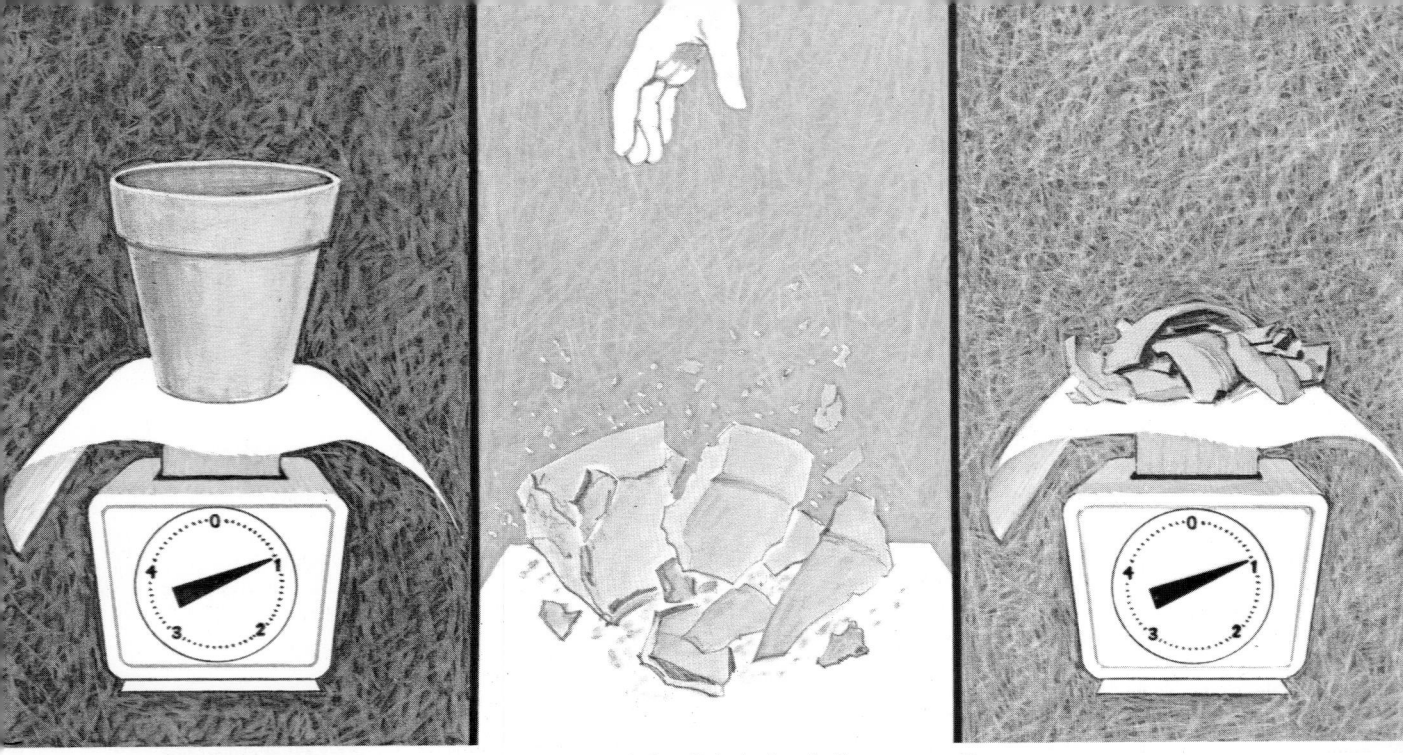

Conservation of mass. The weight of a flowerpot before it is broken is the same as the weight of all the broken pieces.

▶WHAT MATTER IS MADE OF

What is matter made of? There is an important clue in some of the ways that gases differ from liquids and solids.

If water is cooled, it eventually freezes and becomes ice. Ice is the solid form of water. Equal volumes of water and ice differ by less than 10 percent in mass—that is, liquids and solids do not differ very much in density.

If water is heated, it eventually boils and forms steam. Steam is the gaseous form of water, and there is a tremendous difference between the density of steam and the density of water. As steam forms during boiling, it is only about $\frac{1}{1700}$ as dense as water or ice.

That is true of gases generally. Gases are always much less dense than liquids and solids. It is as though matter had been thinned out in forming gases.

Then, too, it is very hard to compress liquids and solids. Even when they are squeezed together under great pressure, they are compressed only very slightly. Gases, on the other hand, are easy to compress. A quantity of a gas that fits into a given amount of space can easily be compressed to fit into $\frac{1}{10}$ of that amount of space.

Gases behave, in this respect, like a sponge or a heap of feathers or a coiled spring, all of which can be easily compressed. Of course, there are air spaces inside a sponge, between the feathers, and between the coils of the spring. The air is squeezed out, and that is what makes compression possible.

It would seem, then, that a gas can be easily compressed because its matter does not really fill up its volume. And that is the case. Gas is made up of tiny particles of matter separated by empty space. That explains why a gas has such a low density. The matter in it is spread out. It would also explain gas compression. The little particles making up gas are just pushed closer together.

In liquids and solids, the little particles are already almost touching. That is why liquids and solids are much denser than gases and hard to compress. The particles cannot be pushed together more closely.

These little particles are called **atoms**. Atoms are usually found in clusters called **molecules**. Molecules differ a great deal in size. Some are small and are made up of only a few atoms—perhaps as few as two. Other molecules are large. Some are clusters of many thousands of atoms.

Atoms come in a number of varieties—at least 105. When a substance is built up of only one variety of atoms, it is called an **ele-**

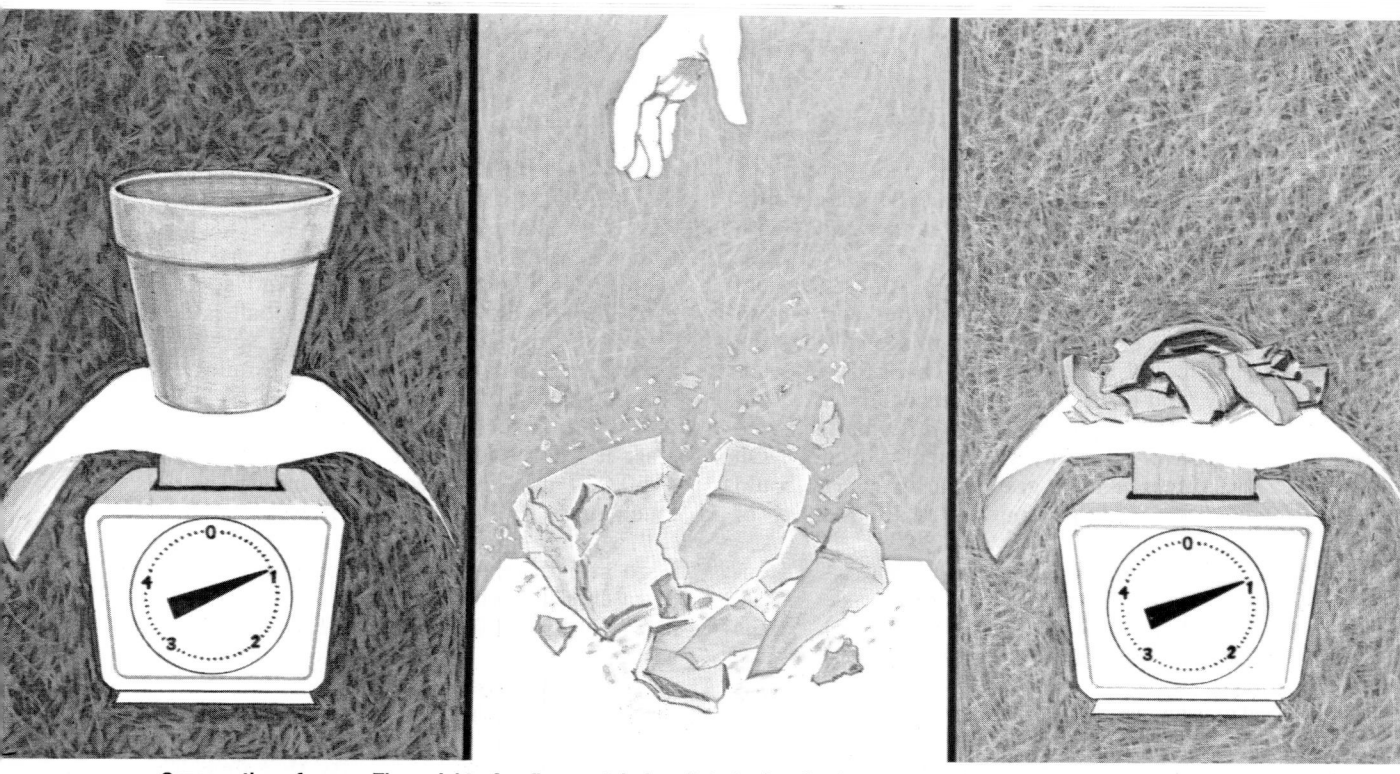

Conservation of mass. The weight of a flowerpot before it is broken is the same as the weight of all the broken pieces.

▶ WHAT MATTER IS MADE OF

What is matter made of? There is an important clue in some of the ways that gases differ from liquids and solids.

If water is cooled, it eventually freezes and becomes ice. Ice is the solid form of water. Equal volumes of water and ice differ by less than 10 percent in mass—that is, liquids and solids do not differ very much in density.

If water is heated, it eventually boils and forms steam. Steam is the gaseous form of water, and there is a tremendous difference between the density of steam and the density of water. As steam forms during boiling, it is only about $\frac{1}{1700}$ as dense as water or ice.

That is true of gases generally. Gases are always much less dense than liquids and solids. It is as though matter had been thinned out in forming gases.

Then, too, it is very hard to compress liquids and solids. Even when they are squeezed together under great pressure, they are compressed only very slightly. Gases, on the other hand, are easy to compress. A quantity of a gas that fits into a given amount of space can easily be compressed to fit into $\frac{1}{10}$ of that amount of space.

Gases behave, in this respect, like a sponge or a heap of feathers or a coiled spring, all of which can be easily compressed. Of course, there are air spaces inside a sponge, between the feathers, and between the coils of the spring. The air is squeezed out, and that is what makes compression possible.

It would seem, then, that a gas can be easily compressed because its matter does not really fill up its volume. And that is the case. Gas is made up of tiny particles of matter separated by empty space. That explains why a gas has such a low density. The matter in it is spread out. It would also explain gas compression. The little particles making up gas are just pushed closer together.

In liquids and solids, the little particles are already almost touching. That is why liquids and solids are much denser than gases and hard to compress. The particles cannot be pushed together more closely.

These little particles are called **atoms**. Atoms are usually found in clusters called **molecules**. Molecules differ a great deal in size. Some are small and are made up of only a few atoms—perhaps as few as two. Other molecules are large. Some are clusters of many thousands of atoms.

Atoms come in a number of varieties—at least 105. When a substance is built up of only one variety of atoms, it is called an **ele-**

| ICE (SOLID) | WATER (LIQUID) | STEAM (GAS) |

Liquids and solids are denser than gases. The matter making up a liquid or solid is much more closely packed together than the matter in a gas. Steam, the gaseous form of water, weighs only about 1/1700 as much as an equal volume of water.

ment. Thus, iron is an element because it is built up only of iron atoms. Aluminum is another element; it is built up only of aluminum atoms. Other metals such as mercury, gold, and copper are elements. So are nonmetals such as sulfur and phosphorus. So are gases such as oxygen, hydrogen, and nitrogen.

There are as many different elements as there are different varieties of atoms. Some elements do not exist on the earth but have been formed in tiny amounts in laboratories. Other elements exist in nature but are very rare. Only about a dozen elements are really common on the earth. Stars like our sun are made up almost entirely of two elements, hydrogen and helium, though many other elements are present in small quantities.

Sometimes two or more different varieties of atoms are found in a single molecule. Substances made up of two or more atom varieties are called **compounds**. Water is an example of a compound. Each molecule of water is made up of three atoms: two hydrogen atoms and one oxygen atom.

Atoms can combine in many thousands of different ways. Every different molecule represents a different substance. That is why matter appears in many different forms and varieties.

In particular, atoms of the element carbon can combine in long chains and complicated rings. Atoms of other varieties can add to these chains and rings, making hundreds of thousands of different molecules. Some of these are very large and complicated. Living organisms contain many such large molecules. And so carbon-containing compounds have come to be called organic substances.

▶ MIXTURES AND SOLUTIONS

Elements and compounds are both examples of pure substances. A **pure substance** is one that has the same atomic makeup in all parts and therefore has the same properties in all parts. For instance, a piece of iron is a pure substance, if it contains nothing but iron. Every part of the iron is just as gray and just as hard as every other part. If the iron is broken into tiny pieces, each piece is attracted by a magnet; each piece will allow an electric current to pass through.

The same is true for limestone (a compound). All pieces of limestone are equally

When you blow up a balloon, you compress air—that is, you push together the particles of the gases that make up air.

SUGAR CINNAMON

WATER SUGAR

GOLD COPPER

MIXTURE

SOLUTION

ALLOY

A mixture is made up of at least two substances—each substance retaining its own atomic makeup and properties. When one of the substances in a mixture is a liquid, the mixture is called a solution. An alloy is a very fine mixture of metals.

white and equally brittle. No pieces will allow an electric current to flow through; no piece is attracted by a magnet.

If iron filings and powdered limestone are mixed, the result is not a pure substance. It is a **mixture**. The mixture seems to be light gray throughout. But if you look at it under a magnifying lens, you will see white pieces and dark pieces. Some pieces will be attracted by a magnet and some won't be. Some pieces will let an electric current flow through and some won't.

Sometimes mixtures are so finely mixed that you can't see the separate parts. For instance, the gold of a wedding ring is a mixture of gold and copper. (Such a mixture of metals is called an **alloy**.) Air is a mixture mostly of oxygen and nitrogen.

When a very fine mixture involves a liquid, it is frequently spoken of as a **solution**. If sugar is added to water, for instance, the sugar breaks up into single molecules. These spread all through the water. The sugar seems to disappear. The water, with the sugar dissolved in it, seems no different from pure water. But if you put the sugar-water on your tongue, you will taste the sweetness. If you allow the water to evaporate, the sugar will

remain behind. It will be the same sugar that it was at the start.

Gases can dissolve in water, too. In fact, the water of the oceans, lakes, and rivers all contains dissolved oxygen and nitrogen from the air. Fish extract the dissolved oxygen from the water. If the oxygen weren't there, the fish would drown as quickly as we would.

Sometimes solutions involve solids, as when a little copper is added to gold to form an alloy in jewelry. The copper breaks up into single atoms that spread evenly through the gold. This is an example of a **solid solution**.

▶ **PHYSICAL AND CHEMICAL CHANGES**

Matter can be made to change its properties in a number of different ways.

For example, a metal like copper can be beaten into different shapes. It can be drawn out into wires. It can be broken up into fragments. It is still copper. An electric current can be passed through it. It can be heated until it glows red-hot. It is still copper. Copper powder can be mixed with iron filings and still be copper. Copper can be heated until it melts. It can then be heated further until it boils and forms gaseous copper. And it is still copper.

Such changes alter the properties of matter but not its atomic makeup. They are called **physical changes**. The science of physics is particularly concerned with energy and with the physical changes of matter.

Often, however, changes in properties also involve changes in atomic makeup. For instance, suppose iron is allowed to stand in damp air. Atoms of oxygen from the air and atoms of hydrogen from the moisture join the iron atoms. The resulting molecules have properties that are entirely different from those of the original iron. In place of a hard, gray metal there is crumbly, reddish-brown rust.

Or suppose copper is dropped into a compound called nitric acid. Nitrogen and oxygen atoms join the copper atoms. In place of the reddish metal, there is a blue, brittle nonmetal, called copper nitrate.

Such changes alter the atomic makeup of the molecules of a substance. They are called **chemical changes**. The science of chemistry is chiefly concerned with such chemical changes.

When wood is heated, a chemical change takes place. The wood does not melt. Instead, its rather complicated molecules break up into smaller ones. The gases, consisting of these simpler molecules, combine very rapidly with the oxygen of the air. As they do so, energy is given off in the form of light and heat. We say the wood is burning.

Many chemical changes produce energy. We use the energy of burning wood, coal, or oil to produce electricity (another form of energy). Chemical changes can produce energy so quickly as to give rise to an explosion. An automobile runs because of the energy of small explosions of gasoline in its cylinders.

The human being—and all other living organisms—makes use of the energy produced by chemical changes within the body.

Chemical changes proceed most rapidly and easily when different substances make a great deal of contact. Molecules can interchange atoms only where such contact takes place. Powdered iron, for instance, will rust much more quickly than a solid piece of iron.

▶ EXTREME COLD AND PRESSURE

In this century scientists have learned how to subject matter to conditions that don't ordinarily exist on the surface of the earth. For instance, they have learned to cool substances to extremely low temperatures. The very lowest possible temperature is $-273.16°C$ ($-459.69°F$). This is called **absolute zero**. Scientists have reached temperatures within a millionth of a degree of it.

At temperatures close to absolute zero, the gas helium becomes a liquid with very unusual properties. It passes through the tiniest holes, and it conducts heat almost perfectly. It is like no other substance in its properties. At temperatures of liquid helium, a number of metals can conduct an electric current perfectly. This is called **superconductivity**. Substances conducting an electric current in this way can be used to build extremely powerful magnets. They can also be used to make tiny switches for complicated computers.

Modern scientists can also subject substances to enormous pressures that force the molecules to take up new, tighter arrangements. For instance, water placed under great pressure produces a series of different ices. These are denser than ordinary ice or water. Some of them remain solid ice at temperatures higher than that of boiling water.

In 1955 scientists discovered how to squeeze carbon together so tightly that carbon atoms took up the arrangement found in diamond. In this way diamonds were made in the laboratory for the first time.

Studying changes under high pressure is important. It provides clues to what goes on deep within the earth, where the pressures are extremely high.

▶ NUCLEAR CHANGES

Atoms are made up of still smaller parts, called subatomic particles. The more massive of these particles are called protons and neutrons. They form a tiny but extremely dense **atomic nucleus** at the very center of the atom. Around this nucleus are the less massive electrons. The protons and electrons carry electric charges, but the neutrons do not.

Ordinary chemical changes affect the electrons at the surface of the atom. However, there are also changes that can take place in the atomic nucleus. These are **nuclear changes**.

Nuclear changes involve much larger quantities of energy than ordinary chemical changes do. The first nuclear change to be

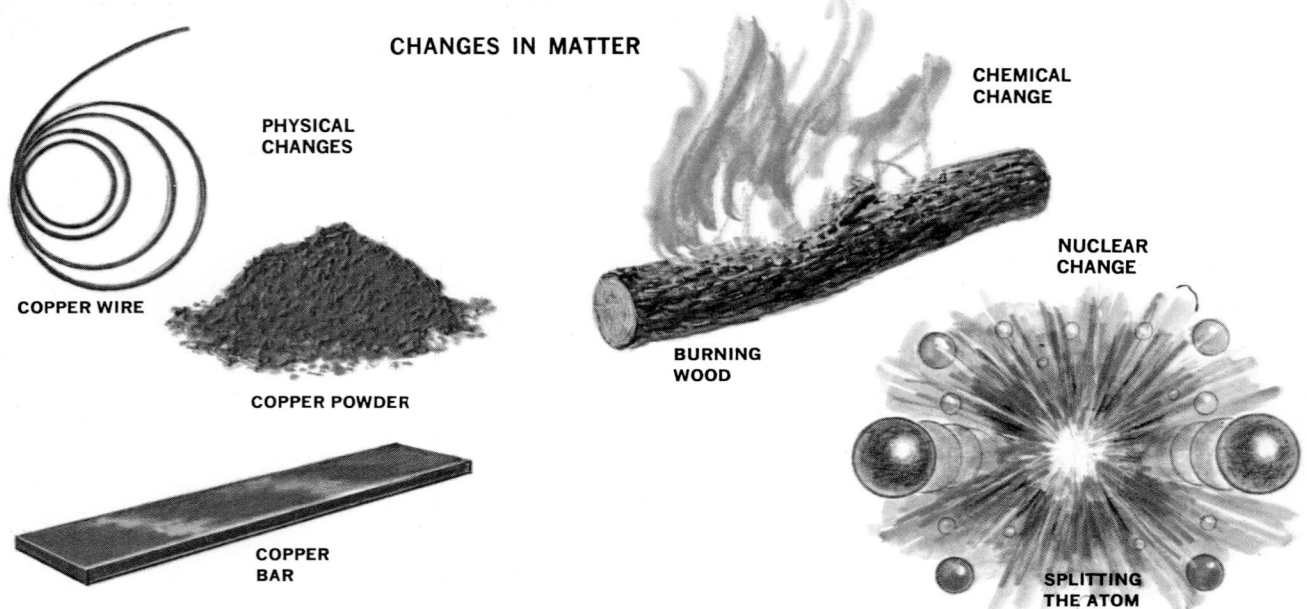

CHANGES IN MATTER

PHYSICAL CHANGES

COPPER WIRE

COPPER POWDER

COPPER BAR

CHEMICAL CHANGE

BURNING WOOD

NUCLEAR CHANGE

SPLITTING THE ATOM

Matter can be made to change its properties in three main ways. In a physical change a substance has the same atomic makeup, but its form is altered. In a chemical change the atomic makeup of a substance is changed, as well as its properties. In a nuclear change the central core, or nucleus, of an atom is altered. In this process great amounts of energy are released.

discovered was radioactivity. The atomic nuclei of radioactive elements give off subatomic particles or little groups of subatomic particles. Energy is released in the process.

Sometimes a nucleus can be made to break apart. More energy is produced in this process of **nuclear fission** than in ordinary radioactivity. Energy can be produced very quickly as a result of fission. This is the kind of energy that powers an atomic bomb.

Still greater energy can be produced with the nuclei of hydrogen atoms. Several of these very tiny nuclei can be made to join together, thus forming the more complicated nucleus of the element helium. This joining together of nuclei is called **nuclear fusion**. Energy released by nuclear fusion is the kind that powers the sun and other stars. A little bit of nuclear fusion on earth powers the hydrogen bomb.

Nuclear scientists have learned to create fission reactions that proceed in a slow and orderly fashion. Taking place within nuclear reactors, these can produce power for ships and submarines. They can produce electricity for peaceful uses. Scientists are trying to tame the more powerful fusion reactions, too.

To bring about controlled fusion reactions, hydrogen must be heated to extremely high temperatures of millions of degrees. At such temperatures the atoms themselves break up into clouds of electrically charged subatomic particles. Matter composed of such broken-up atoms is called **plasma**. Plasma is sometimes called a **fourth state of matter**.

The sun and all other stars are made up of plasma. On earth the gases inside fluorescent bulbs are examples of a low temperature plasma.

The broken atoms in plasma can be packed together much more tightly than ordinary atoms can be. In some stars the plasma is packed together very tightly indeed. The result is that the brightly glowing star shrinks down into a volume no larger, perhaps, than that of our earth. Such a star is a white dwarf. The matter in a white dwarf can be thousands of times as dense as the densest material on earth. Yet it can be packed even more tightly. Eventually, the particles are converted into neutrons, and these are squeezed so tightly that they touch. Such neutron stars may be only a few kilometers across and yet contain as much matter as our sun.

ISAAC ASIMOV
Boston University School of Medicine

See also CHEMISTRY; ELEMENTS; GASES; GRAVITY AND GRAVITATION; HEAT; LIQUIDS; NUCLEAR ENERGY; SOLIDS.

MATTHEW, SAINT. See EVANGELISTS, THE.

MAURITANIA

Mauritania is a large but thinly populated nation located in western Africa, bordering the Atlantic Ocean. Although nearly as large in area as France and Spain combined, Mauritania is mostly a desert or semi-desert land able to support only a relatively small population. Its dominant people are the Moors, or *Maures* in French, from whom the country takes its name. A former French colony, Mauritania gained complete independence in 1960.

▶ THE PEOPLE

The Moors.   The Moors are of mixed Arab and Berber ancestry. Traditionally, they have been nomads of the north, moving from place to place with their herds of camels and flocks of sheep and goats. Their animals provide the Moors with food, transportation, and other necessities of life. Today many Moors live in settled areas, but they still put up tents when entertaining guests.

Black Africans.   About 40 percent of Mauritania's people are black Africans, who live mostly in the southern part of the country. The

Fulani (Fulbe) are herders of cattle who travel with their animals seeking grazing land. The Tukulor and Sarakolé are farmers who live in village communities. Fishing is a traditional occupation of the people living along the Atlantic coast.

Religion and Language.   Almost all Mauritanians are Muslims. Islam (the religion of the Muslims) is the state religion, but freedom of worship is guaranteed by law. French is the

Some of Mauritania's people still follow the traditional nomadic way of life, traveling the vast desert region with their herds of camels and other livestock.

official language of Mauritania, but Arabic is the national language. The people of the south speak a variety of African languages.

Education. Until recently few Mauritanian children went to school. But schools have been built in some towns, and teachers now travel with the nomads, holding classes in tents and other portable classrooms. Classes are taught in Arabic, French, and African languages. This is because black Africans objected to using only Arabic (the language of the Moors) in the schools.

▶ THE LAND

The northern, central, and eastern regions of Mauritania, making up more than half the land, are part of the great Sahara desert. Here, vast stretches of sand are broken only by occasional rocky peaks and plateaus. South of the Sahara is a semi-desert region of scattered grasses and some small, stunted trees called the Sahel. It is grazing land, where cattle, sheep, and goats can be raised. But drought and overuse of the scant vegetation have led to its deterioration and the steady encroachment of the Sahara farther south each year.

Aside from a few desert oases, only about 10 percent of Mauritania's land, in the extreme south along the Senegal River, is fertile enough to grow crops throughout the year.

Natural Resources. Mauritania has several important minerals beneath its barren land, including iron ore, copper, and gypsum. The Atlantic coastal waters are rich in fish. Iron ore and processed fish are Mauritania's two most important exports.

Cities. Mauritania has only a few cities of any size. Nouakchott, the capital, with about 500,000 people, is the largest city. Nouadhibou is the country's chief port.

▶ THE ECONOMY

Mauritania's economy traditionally has been based on its livestock and a few food crops, such as dates, millet, wheat, rice, and corn. Its most important industries are fishing, mining, and the processing of livestock products. A long drought in the 1970's wiped out many of the cattle herds, an economic disaster from which Mauritania has not yet recovered. One of Africa's poorest countries, Mauritania must import most of its food and depends on financial aid from other countries.

▶ HISTORY AND GOVERNMENT

The first Europeans to arrive in what is now Mauritania were the Portuguese in the 15th century. Portuguese, Dutch, French, and British all disputed control of the region. In the late 19th century French explorers penetrated the interior and signed agreements with the Moorish chieftains. The regions became a French protectorate in 1903 and part of French West Africa in 1920.

Mauritania won self-government in 1958 and complete independence in 1960. It acquired part of the former territory of Spanish Sahara (now Western Sahara) in 1976. In 1979, Mauritania relinquished its rights to the territory, which is now claimed by Morocco.

Under a constitution adopted upon independence, Mauritania had a republican form of government with a president, a prime minister, and a legislature, the National Assembly. Mauritania's government was headed by President Moktar Ould Daddah until 1978, when he was overthrown by the armed forces, who suspended the constitution and established a military government. Another coup, in 1984, made Colonel Maouya Ould Sidi Ahmed Taya president and chairman of the ruling Military Committee for National Salvation.

R. J. HARRISON-CHURCH
London School of Economics and Political
Science, University of London
Author, *West Africa*

FACTS AND FIGURES

ISLAMIC REPUBLIC OF MAURITANIA is the official name of the country. It is called République Islamique de Mauritanie in French and Al-Jamhuriya al-Islamiya al-Muritaniya in Arabic.

THE PEOPLE are known as Mauritanians.

LOCATION: Western Africa.

AREA: 397,956 sq mi (1,030,700 km²).

POPULATION: 1,800,000 (estimate).

CAPITAL AND LARGEST CITY: Nouakchott.

MAJOR LANGUAGES: French (official), Arabic (national), various African languages.

MAJOR RELIGION: Muslim.

GOVERNMENT: Republic (under military rule). **Head of state and government**—president and chairman of the Military Committee for National Salvation. **Legislature**—National Assembly (suspended).

CHIEF PRODUCTS: Agricultural—dates, wheat, millet, rice, corn, livestock. **Manufactured**—processed fish, livestock products. **Mineral**—iron ore, copper, gypsum.

MONETARY UNIT: Ouguiya (1 ouguiya = 5 khoums).

NATIONAL ANTHEM: "Mauritania."

MAURITIUS

Mauritius is a small island nation located in the Indian Ocean. It lies about 500 miles (800 kilometers) east of the large island of Madagascar, which is situated off the southeastern coast of Africa. Formerly a French and then a British colony, Mauritius gained its independence in 1968.

The People. The majority of Mauritians are descendants of people from India. Most are Hindus in religion, with smaller numbers of Muslims. The next largest group is formed by the Creoles, who are of mixed African and European descent. Most Creoles are Roman Catholics. Some Chinese and Europeans, mainly of French origin, also live on the islands.

The official language is English. But Creole, a language derived from the French, is widely spoken, as are Hindi and other Indian languages.

Mauritius is a small but densely populated country, and overpopulation has been one of its major problems. Some Mauritians emigrate to other countries to seek a livelihood.

The Land. Mauritius is made up of one main island and several much smaller islands. The main island is volcanic in origin. It is roughly oval in shape, with a high central pla-

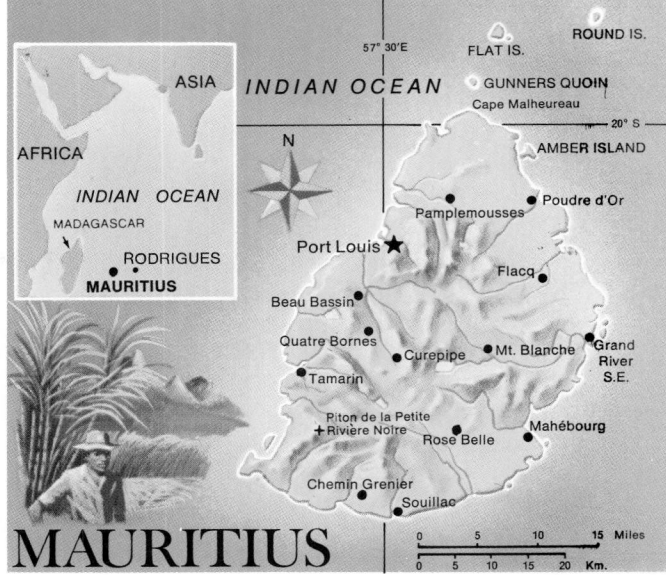

MAURITIUS

teau and mountains with bare black peaks that rise steeply above the lush vegetation. There are several short, fast-flowing rivers. The largest of the other islands is Rodrigues, which lies about 350 miles (560 kilometers) east of the main island. Port Louis, which is located on the main island, is the capital, largest city, and only port of Mauritius.

Economy. Mauritius' economy is largely dependent on sugar, which is its most important export. Tea is the next most important commercial crop. The processing of sugar and sugar by-products, such as molasses, and tea are the islands' most important industries.

History and Government. Mauritius was first settled in the 17th century by the Dutch, who named it after Prince Maurice of Nassau. The islands were ruled by France from 1715 to 1810, when they came under British control. Black Africans were brought as slaves to the islands. After slavery was abolished in the 19th century, Indian laborers were hired to work on the sugarcane plantations.

After gaining its independence in 1968, Mauritius adopted a government based on the British model. The British monarch, represented by a governor-general, is the formal head of state. But the government is led by a prime minister, who heads a Council of Ministers responsible to the elected legislature, the Legislative Assembly. Mauritius's first prime minister, Sir Seewoosagur Ramgoolam, served until 1982. The new prime minister, Anerood Jugnauth, retained his leadership of the government after elections in 1983.

BURTON BENEDICT
Author, *Mauritius: Problems of a Plural Society*

FACTS AND FIGURES

MAURITIUS is the official name of the country.

THE PEOPLE are known as Mauritians.

LOCATION: Indian Ocean, southeast of Africa.

AREA: 790 sq mi (2,045 km^2).

POPULATION: 1,000,000 (estimate).

CAPITAL AND LARGEST CITY: Port Louis.

MAJOR LANGUAGES: English (official), Creole, Hindi.

MAJOR RELIGIONS: Hindu, Roman Catholic, Muslim.

GOVERNMENT: Constitutional monarchy. **Head of state**—British monarch represented by a governor-general. **Head of government**—prime minister. **Legislature**—Legislative Assembly.

CHIEF PRODUCTS: Agricultural—Sugarcane, tea, bananas, tobacco, various vegetables. **Manufactured**—Processed sugar and sugar products, tea.

MONETARY UNIT: Mauritius rupee (1 rupee = 100 cents).

NATIONAL ANTHEM: "Motherland."

May

The month of May was probably named for Maia Majesta, the Roman goddess of spring. In the Southern Hemisphere, May is one of the chilly months of autumn, but in the Northern Hemisphere, May is a warm and merry month. The earth blooms and people rejoice.

Place in year: 5th month.
Number of days: 31.
Flowers: Hawthorne and lily of the valley.
Birthstone: Emerald.
Zodiac signs: Taurus, the Bull (April 20–May 20), and Gemini, the Twins (May 21–June 20).

1
- England, Scotland, and Wales became Great Britain, 1707
- Admiral Dewey won the Battle of Manila Bay, 1898
- Empire State Building dedicated, 1931
- *May Day*

2
- Hudson's Bay Company chartered, 1670
- Prokofiev's *Peter and the Wolf* premiered at a children's concert in Moscow, U.S.S.R., 1936

3
- Constitution Day in Japan; Poland

4
- **Horace Mann** born 1796
- **Thomas Henry Huxley** born 1825
- Rhode Island declared its independence from England, 1776
- Haymarket Riot took place in Chicago, 1886

5
- **Karl Marx** born 1818
- Napoleon died at St. Helena, 1821
- First U.S. suborbital space flight made by Alan B. Shepard, Jr., 1961
- Children's Day in Japan

6
- **Sigmund Freud** born 1856
- **Robert E. Peary** born 1856
- The dirigible *Hindenburg* blew up and burned killing 36 persons, 1937
- Dr. Roger Bannister of England became the first person to run a mile in less than 4 minutes, 1954

7
- **Robert Browning** born 1812
- **Johannes Brahms** born 1833
- **Peter Ilyich Tchaikovsky** born 1840
- The *Lusitania* torpedoed and sunk by a German submarine, 1915

8
- **Harry S Truman** born 1884
- The German High Command surrender to the Allies, ending World War II in Europe, became effective, 1945

9
- **John Brown** born 1800
- **Sir James Matthew Barrie** born 1860
- Anniversary of Liberation in Czechoslovakia

10
- Second Continental Congress met, 1775
- Ethan Allen and his "Green Mountain Boys" captured Fort Ticonderoga in New York during the Revolutionary War, 1775
- First transcontinental railroad in the U.S. completed at Promontory, Utah, 1869
- *Confederate Memorial Day* in North Carolina; South Carolina

11
- **Salvador Dali** born 1904
- Minnesota became the 32nd state, 1858

12
- **Florence Nightingale** born 1820
- **Dante Gabriel Rossetti** born 1828

13
- **Georges Braque** born 1882
- U.S. declared war on Mexico, 1846
- Pope John Paul II wounded in an assassination attempt in Rome, 1981

14
- Lewis and Clark started trip up Missouri River, 1804
- State of Israel established, 1948
- Skylab, first orbiting U.S. space laboratory, launched, 1973
- *National Flag Day in Paraguay*

15
- **Pierre Curie** born 1859

16
- U.S. Senate voted for acquittal in the impeachment trial of Andrew Johnson, 1868

17
- **Edward Jenner** born 1749
- U.S. Supreme Court issued *Brown* v. *Board of Education* decision, ruling segregation of schools unconstitutional, 1954
- *Constitution Day in Nauru; Norway*

18
- **Bertrand Russell** born 1872
- **Pope John Paul II** born 1920

- Mount St. Helens in state of Washington erupted, killing more than 60 people, 1980

19
- Jacques Cartier sailed from France on his second voyage to Canada, 1535

20
- **Honoré de Balzac** born 1799
- Charles Lindbergh took off on first nonstop transatlantic solo flight, 1927
- *National Day in Cameroon*

21
- **Albrecht Dürer** born 1471
- **Alexander Pope** born 1688
- Clara Barton founded American Red Cross, 1881
- Amelia Earhart completed first solo flight by a woman across the Atlantic, 1932

22
- **Richard Wagner** born 1813
- **Mary Cassatt** born 1844
- **Sir Arthur Conan Doyle** born 1859
- The American ship *Savannah* became first steamship to cross the Atlantic, 1819

23
- **Carolus Linnaeus** born 1707
- South Carolina ratified the Constitution, 1788
- New York Public Library incorporated, 1895

24
- **Queen Victoria** born 1819
- First permanent English settlement in the U.S. founded at Jamestown, Virginia, 1607
- First public telegraph message ("What hath God wrought!") sent by Samuel F. B. Morse from Washington, D.C., to Baltimore, Maryland, 1844

25
- **Ralph Waldo Emerson** born 1803
- **Tito (Josip Broz)** born 1892
- Constitutional Convention opened in Philadelphia, 1787

- Organization of African Unity (OAU) charter adopted by heads of most independent African states, 1963
- *Independence Day in Jordan*

27
- San Francisco's Golden Gate Bridge opened, 1937

28
- **William Pitt the Younger** born 1759
- **John Louis Rodolphe Agassiz** born 1807
- **James Francis (Jim) Thorpe** born 1888

29
- **Patrick Henry** born 1736
- **John F. Kennedy** born 1917
- Rhode Island ratified the Constitution, 1790
- Wisconsin became the 30th state, 1848
- Sir Edmund Hillary of New Zealand and Tenzing Norkay of Nepal became first to reach summit of Mount Everest, 1953

30
- **Peter the Great** born 1672
- Joan of Arc burned at the stake, 1431
- Kansas-Nebraska Act passed, 1854
- Memorial Day first celebrated in the U.S., 1868
- First Indianapolis 500 Automobile Race held, 1911

31
- **Walt Whitman** born 1819
- Seventeenth Amendment to U.S. Constitution, providing for direct election of senators, went into effect, 1913
- *Republic Day in South Africa*

Second Sunday in May: *Mother's Day.* **Third Saturday in May:** *Armed Forces Day.* **Last Monday in May:** *Memorial Day.* **Monday before May 25:** Victoria Day in Canada.

The calendar listing identifies people who were born on the indicated day in boldface type, **like this.** You will find a biography of each of these birthday people in *The New Book of Knowledge.* In addition to citing some historical events and historical firsts, the calendar also lists the holidays and some of the festivals celebrated in the United States. These holidays are printed in italic type, *like this.* See the article Holidays for more information.

Many holidays and festivals of nations around the world are included in the calendar as well. When the term "national holiday" is used, it means that the nation celebrates an important patriotic event on that day—in most cases the winning of independence. Consult *The New Book of Knowledge* article on the individual nation for further information on its national holiday.

MAYA. See Indians of North America.

MAYFLOWER

The *Mayflower* was the little three-masted sailing ship that brought the Pilgrims from England to the New World in 1620. It was a tough little ship of 180 tons. About 90 feet long, it was roughly the size of a harbor tugboat. The *Mayflower* was not really a passenger ship at all. It was just a sea "tramp" that usually carried any cargo it could find. On the voyage before the Pilgrims hired it, the ship had been carrying wine from France to England.

On September 20, 1620, the *Mayflower* sailed from Plymouth, England. Aboard were just over 100 men, women, and children, including a crew of about 28 men under Captain Christopher Jones. The *Mayflower* crossed the Atlantic Ocean at its stormiest season.

Sailing a ship westward across the North Atlantic without any engines is difficult. It is a very stormy ocean in the fall and winter. The wind almost always blows strongly right from the direction—west—in which the ship must go.

The Voyage

The winds howled and the storms blew. Sometimes the decks were full of water, and the wind and rain blew through the passengers' quarters. The Atlantic seas almost rolled the little ship over. One young man was washed overboard but managed to hang onto a trailing rope and was rescued. At mealtimes the passengers ate the same food day after day—sea biscuits, salted meat, dried fish, and cheese—and washed it down with beer. Some of them were seasick for weeks on end. The *Mayflower* was so old that once, during a storm, one of the main supporting timbers inside the ship broke. To support the broken beam a printing press was placed underneath it. The press was part of the equipment that the Pilgrims were taking to the New World because they valued knowledge. They did not expect to have to strengthen the ship with it. But they all thanked God and sailed on.

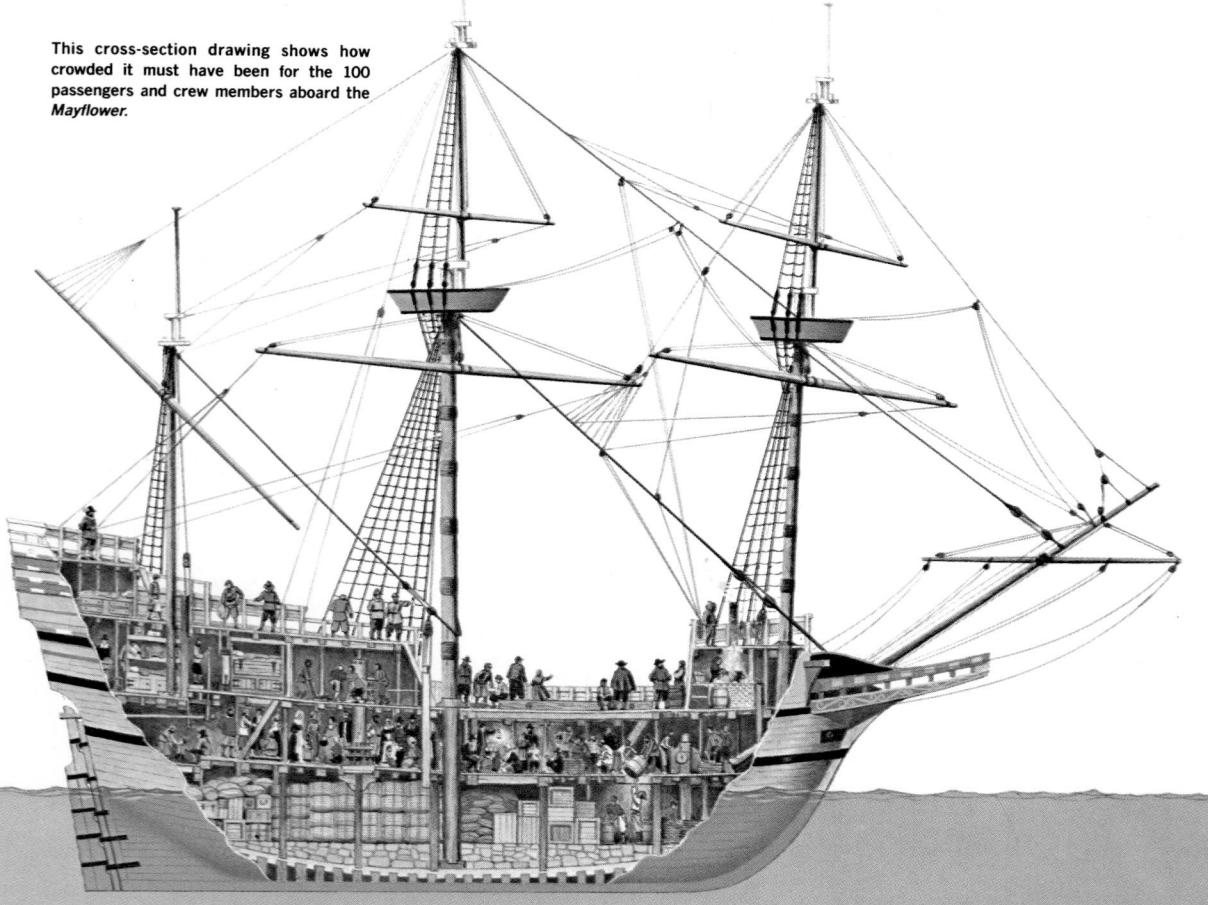

This cross-section drawing shows how crowded it must have been for the 100 passengers and crew members aboard the *Mayflower*.

Shortly before the *Mayflower* reached land, William Butten, the 22-year-old servant of Deacon Samuel Fuller, died and was buried at sea. But the number of passengers remained unchanged. A son, Peregrine, was born on shipboard to William and Susanna White a month after the vessel arrived safely.

After 10 weeks the Pilgrims made the first landfall where Provincetown, Massachusetts, is today, then proceeded to the site of Plymouth, across Cape Cod Bay. The *Mayflower* sailed for England the following April.

The Mayflower Compact

While the *Mayflower* lay at anchor off Provincetown in November, 1620, several discontented members of the Pilgrim band had talked of mutiny. To calm them down, their leaders agreed to prepare a written document. The Mayflower Compact, as this document was called, expressed the idea that everyone would have fair treatment in the government that would be set up to rule the colony. The 41 men who signed the compact in the ship's cabin agreed to obey the laws they themselves would pass. The Mayflower Compact was an important step along the road to self-government in the New World.

Mayflower II

Anchored near a reconstruction of the early colony at Plymouth is a replica of the wonderful old ship that brought the Pilgrims. In 1957 the *Mayflower II* sailed from Plymouth, England to Plymouth, Massachusetts in 55 days. Like the Pilgrim ship, the new *Mayflower* had no engines, only sails to carry it along.

More than 250,000 visitors go aboard the *Mayflower II* each year. They gain a new admiration for the courage and fortitude of the little band of men, women, and children who sailed in such a vessel to America more than 350 years earlier.

ALAN VILLIERS
Master, *Mayflower II*

See also AMERICAN COLONIES; PLYMOUTH COLONY.

MAZZINI, GIUSEPPE (1805–1872)

Giuseppe Mazzini, Italian revolutionist and patriot, was born in Genoa on June 22, 1805. Italy was then divided into separate states. As a young man, Mazzini became fired with a desire to unite them in a republic.

While still a student at the University of Genoa, where his father was a professor, Mazzini joined the Carbonari, a secret revolutionary society. Throughout his life he participated in many plots against Austria, which ruled much of northern Italy, and the Italian states. Though quiet and shy by nature, Mazzini became one of the most feared, loved, and hated men in Europe.

In 1830, Mazzini was imprisoned for conspiracy. After his release he left Italy. In 1831, in France, he founded Young Italy—a society dedicated to the overthrow of the Italian states and to the establishment of a single republic. Mazzini published a newspaper, also called *Young Italy,* and plotted raids against the Italian states. He also formed a group called Young Europe to unite revolutionists from all European countries.

In 1837, Mazzini went to London. There he continued to write and seek help for the Italian cause. He organized a free school for poor Italian children living in London.

In 1848, revolutions broke out in the Italian states. Mazzini returned to Italy. A revolutionary republic was established in Rome, and Mazzini was elected one of its governors. But French troops defeated the republican army, and Mazzini fled once more.

For the next ten years, he continued his revolutionary activities. In 1860, after wars and revolts against Austria and the Italian states, most of Italy was united under King Victor Emmanuel II of Sardinia. In 1861 a united Italian kingdom was officially proclaimed. But Mazzini, still a republican, opposed the monarchy.

In 1870 his attempt to stir up a new republican uprising failed. Sentenced to prison once again, he was pardoned. Though in ill health, he continued to write and work for the Italian people. Mazzini died in Pisa on March 10, 1872. His hopes for a united Italian republic were not realized in his lifetime, but his political ideas strongly influenced Italy's future.

EMILIANA P. NOETHER
University of Connecticut

Cyrus McCormick demonstrated his first reaping machine in a Virginia wheat field in 1831. Later improved models made possible the extensive farming of wheat in the Midwest.

McCORMICK, CYRUS (1809–1884)

Cyrus McCormick is known as the inventor of the reaper, a machine for harvesting grain. The invention of this machine was one of the 19th century's most important developments.

Cyrus McCormick was born on February 15, 1809, on a farm in Rockbridge County, Virginia. He had little schooling. As a boy he spent a lot of time helping his father.

Cyrus' father, Robert McCormick, was also an inventor of farm machines. Like many others, he tried to invent a reaper. And like the others, he was not successful. In 1831, Cyrus McCormick, benefiting from his father's mistakes, built a reaper that worked. He was not entirely satisfied with it, however, and worked to improve his invention. He did not patent the reaper until 1834. Even then he did not try to manufacture or sell it because he had become involved in iron manufacturing.

In 1837, McCormick's iron business failed, and he lost a great deal of money. He decided to return to his work on the reaper, and began manufacturing and marketing his machine.

At first, many farmers chose not to use the reaper. The early models exhausted the horses that pulled them; and the machines often clogged and were generally unreliable.

McCormick realized that the reaper was better suited to the flat fields of the Midwest than to the small, hilly farms of the East. In 1847 he left Virginia to open a factory in Chicago, the center of the wheat country. By 1855 he had completely redesigned his reaper. Even though other people began making reapers, McCormick's business did extremely well. It prospered because he used advanced equipment to make very reliable reapers. McCormick also provided services to his customers that others did not, such as written guarantees and mail-order parts. He advertised heavily and was among the first to offer credit. In addition he established a large network of agencies to sell and service his products. McCormick became a millionaire.

In 1858, McCormick married Nancy Fowler. They had seven children. McCormick died on May 13, 1884. His eldest son, whose name was also Cyrus, continued his father's business.

TERRY S. REYNOLDS
Michigan Technological University
See also FARMS AND FARMING.

WILLIAM MC KINLEY (1843–1901)

25TH PRESIDENT OF THE UNITED STATES

MC KINLEY, WILLIAM. William McKinley was one of the kindliest and most peace-loving of American presidents. Yet he led the United States at a time when most Americans were determined to go to war. And the life of this gentle and sympathetic man was brought tragically to an end by bullets from an assassin's gun.

▶ EARLY YEARS

McKinley was born in Niles, Ohio, on January 29, 1843, the seventh child of William and Nancy Allison McKinley. His father and grandfather were iron founders who had come to Ohio from Pennsylvania. Young McKinley grew up a serious boy, possessed of a quiet determination to succeed. He attended school in Poland, Ohio, and then went to Allegheny College in Meadville, Pennsylvania. He left college before graduating and became a teacher in a rural school. When the Civil War broke out in 1861, the 17-year-old McKinley enlisted as a private in the 23rd Ohio Volunteer Regiment.

Though short and slight, McKinley impressed his superiors with his initiative, and he soon rose through the ranks to become a captain.

One of his commanding officers during these years was Rutherford B. Hayes, who was later to become the 19th president of the United States.

At the war's end, McKinley left the Army and returned to Ohio to study law. In 1867 he opened a law office in Canton, Ohio. There he remained, except when public duty interfered, for the rest of his life. Within 2 years he was elected prosecuting attorney for his county, and a career in politics began to open up for him.

In 1871 McKinley married Ida Saxton, daughter of Canton's most prominent banker. They were devoted to each other. However, after the tragic death of their two young children, both girls, Ida became ill and remained an invalid for the rest of her life.

▶ POLITICAL CAREER

In 1876 McKinley was elected, as a Republican, to the House of Representatives. He was re-elected almost continuously until 1890. In that year the Republican Party lost the election because of a tariff—the McKinley Tariff.

In 1890 the business interests of the country were determined to pass a high tariff, or tax on foreign goods, in order to protect

---

WHEN WILLIAM MC KINLEY WAS PRESIDENT
Dr. Walter Reed proved that yellow fever was caused by a species of mosquito. The Rough Riders, led by Colonel Theodore Roosevelt, served in Cuba during the Spanish-American War. The first practical submarine was launched in 1898.
McKinley's birthplace was Niles, Ohio.

American industry from competition. McKinley firmly believed in such a policy, and overcoming all opposition, he got his tariff bill passed. However, resentment over the tariff, especially in the West and South, cost the Republicans heavily in the election, and McKinley lost his seat in Congress.

Undiscouraged by his defeat, McKinley won the governorship of Ohio in 1891. Earlier he had impressed a wealthy Cleveland businessman, who offered to help McKinley further his political career. This businessman was Marcus Alonzo Hanna (1837–1904), one of the most influential men in the Republican Party. A close relationship developed between the two men and grew into a lifelong friendship. Under Mark Hanna's steady direction McKinley would attain the presidency.

In 1892 McKinley was appointed chairman of the Republican National Convention. Some members of his party were so enthusiastic about McKinley that they wanted him to

During the campaign of 1896 Republicans praised the McKinley tariff bill, as shown in this cartoon.

THE TWO BILLS.
A combination that is hard to beat.

become the Republican presidential candidate. But McKinley felt that he was not yet ready for so important an office. Instead he gave his support to the renomination of President Benjamin Harrison. McKinley's decision not to seek the nomination was a fortunate one. While Harrison was defeated by Grover Cleveland in the election of 1892, McKinley went on to be elected governor of Ohio for a second term.

By 1896 McKinley felt ready to accept his party's nomination for the presidency. At the Republican National Convention in St. Louis, Missouri, he was nominated on the first ballot. The Republicans were confident of victory, for the Democratic administration of President Cleveland had been plagued by an economic depression. Still it was not an easy victory for McKinley.

The Democrats, with William Jennings Bryan as their presidential candidate, campaigned on the issue of "free silver." Many people, especially farmers in the West, felt that their economic hardships would be ended if the government restored unlimited coinage of silver money. Bryan toured the country urging such a policy. He was a forceful orator, and the quiet McKinley was hard pressed to compete with him.

Taking his friend Mark Hanna's advice, McKinley did not try to out-talk Bryan. Instead, he stayed at his home in Canton and conducted a "front-porch" campaign, speaking to groups of people who flocked to his home to listen to him. Businessmen and workers in the East gave him their support, and a good farm crop in the West helped restore prosperity. McKinley received 7,102,246 popular votes to Bryan's 6,492,559 and 271 electoral votes to Bryan's 176.

▶ PRESIDENT

McKinley's first term of office was an eventful one for the United States. The nation was seething with new growth, and many different interests sought dominance. McKinley seemed ideally suited to the task of harmonizing such clashing interests.

Cuba and the Spanish-American War

The most important event in McKinley's administration resulted from a crisis in Cuba. Revolts against Spain by Cuban patriots had broken out, and the Cubans appealed to the United States for help. Stories of Spanish cruelty toward the Cubans began to arouse American public opinion against Spain. Soon an avalanche of sympathy for *Cuba Libre* ("Free Cuba") began to descend on McKinley. The President, above all a man of peace, had already pledged his opposition to any armed interference in another country's affairs. In his annual message to Congress he urged that Spain "be given a reasonable chance" to right the situation. Yet his concern over the plight of the Cuban people was real. He issued a Christmas Eve appeal for public contributions to a Cuban relief fund. And at his initiative over $250,000 of aid was sent to Cuba by the Red Cross.

Early in 1898 two events occurred that left McKinley helpless to avoid war with Spain. The first was a private letter written by the Spanish minister in Washington, D.C. Intercepted by a Cuban, who turned it over to a reporter, the letter was published in American newspapers. In it the minister, De Lôme, called McKinley "a would-be politician . . . weak and a bidder for the admiration of the crowd. . . ." Though the minister promptly resigned and the Spanish Government apologized, the De Lôme letter turned popular opinion even more strongly against Spain.

Then, a few days later, the United States battleship *Maine* was blown up in Havana harbor, with a loss of 260 American lives. Newspapers across the country blazed the headline that Spain was responsible and that war was now certain. Actually, no one knows to this day what caused the disaster. But without waiting further, Congress rushed through a bill appropriating $50,000,000 for national defense.

Though McKinley continued to press for peace, Congress and the vast majority of the American public were convinced that war was the only honorable road left open. A popular newspaper cartoon of the day showed an angry Uncle Sam straining to fight Spain while the President held him back by the coattails. The caption read, "Let go of him, McKinley!"

Soon the President feared that unless he gave way, Congress would declare war over his head. Finally he decided to yield to popular demand, and in April, 1898, war with

IMPORTANT DATES IN THE LIFE OF WILLIAM MC KINLEY	
1843	Born at Niles, Ohio, January 29.
1861–1865	Served in the 23rd Ohio Volunteer Regiment, Union Army.
1867	Opened a law office in Canton, Ohio.
1869	Elected prosecuting attorney of Stark County, Ohio.
1871	Married Ida Saxton.
1877–84; 1885–91	Served in the United States House of Representatives.
1892–1896	Governor of Ohio.
1897–1901	25th president of the United States.
1901	Shot by Leon F. Czolgosz at Buffalo, New York, September 6; died in Buffalo, September 14.

Spain was declared. Yet McKinley always felt that, left to himself, "I could have concluded an arrangement with the Spanish government under which the Spanish troops would have been withdrawn from Cuba without a war."

The Spanish-American War lasted less than 4 months. The United States won control over the former Spanish possessions of Puerto Rico, Guam, and the Philippines, while Cuba gained its independence.

The Issue of Imperialism

After the war some Americans were undecided as to whether the United States should keep the territory won from Spain. They argued that the United States should not hold on to such possessions as the Philippine Islands, which were far from the country's shores. As the islands of Hawaii had also been acquired during this time, there was a growing fear that the United States was becoming an imperialist power.

McKinley was tormented by his conscience as to what course he should take. Though he felt that the United States had had to interfere in Cuba for "humanity's sake," he found it hard to justify holding the Philippines. However, others in his party urged him to keep them as legitimate possessions. Finally, after walking "the floor of the White House night after night until midnight," McKinley decided to accept the islands for the United States.

China and the Open-Door Policy

With major possessions in the Far East, American interest in China and in world

The assassination of President McKinley.

politics in general increased. At the time, Great Britain, France, Germany, and Japan were acquiring large "spheres of influence" in China. In 1899 McKinley's secretary of state, John Hay (1838–1905), called upon the other powers to allow equality of trade in China. After the unsuccessful Boxer Rebellion in 1900, in which the Chinese revolted against foreign domination, Hay declared that it was American policy to respect the independence of China. He called upon the other countries to do the same. This policy of equality of trade with China and respect for its territorial integrity was the basis of the famous Open-Door policy.

The American share of the indemnity exacted from China after the revolt was later turned into a scholarship fund to enable Chinese students to study in the United States.

The Election of 1900

The election of 1900 found McKinley more popular than ever. Bryan, who was again the Democratic candidate, tried to raise the issue of imperialism. But its effect was limited by the fact that the United States was prospering more than ever. The "full dinner pail" became a McKinley slogan. The result was an easy victory for McKinley and his vice-president, Theodore Roosevelt.

▶ASSASSINATION

On the afternoon of September 6, 1901, at a public reception in Buffalo, New York, President McKinley was happily shaking hands with his many admirers. Suddenly a man walked up to the President with a handkerchief-covered revolver in his outstretched hand. Two shots rang out, striking McKinley at point-blank range. While being carried to an ambulance, he pleaded with police not to beat the assassin. Eight days later McKinley died, and Vice-President Theodore Roosevelt was sworn in as 26th president. The assassin, an anarchist named Leon F. Czolgosz, was speedily brought to trial and sentenced to death on September 26. He was executed in the prison at Auburn, New York, on October 29.

Amid great mourning, McKinley was buried in Canton, Ohio. Ida McKinley died in 1907 and was buried beside her husband in a great memorial tomb. Another memorial to McKinley was erected at Niles.

With the passing of McKinley the United States, too, passed from one era to another—from an era of internal growth and expansion to one of growing interest in world affairs.

ANDREW BRYCE
Author, *Narrative History of the United States*

See also BRYAN, WILLIAM JENNINGS; SPANISH-AMERICAN WAR.

MEAD, MARGARET (1901–1978)

By the time Margaret Mead was 10 years old, she was studying her two younger sisters the way her mother, a sociologist, had studied her. She made notes on how they developed and took their places in the family. Those notes about her own family were her first attempt at cultural anthropology—the study of the culture, or ways of life, of the different peoples who make up the family of humankind.

Margaret Mead was born in Philadelphia, Pennsylvania, on December 16, 1901. She thought she might become a writer, a lawyer, or a psychologist. But as a senior at Barnard College, in New York City, she was inspired by the anthropologist Franz Boas to study age-old ways of life that were rapidly dying out. Her first field trip, in 1925, took her to the Samoan Islands in the Pacific Ocean. The book she wrote after this trip, *Coming of Age in Samoa* (1928), helped change people's thinking all over the world. It showed that what people had thought was unchangeable "human nature" was really learned behavior —behavior formed by a particular culture. This helped people understand their own culture and other human beings.

Margaret Mead was associated with the American Museum of Natural History throughout her career. As a curator of ethnology (the study of races and cultures), she studied other Pacific island cultures. She wrote

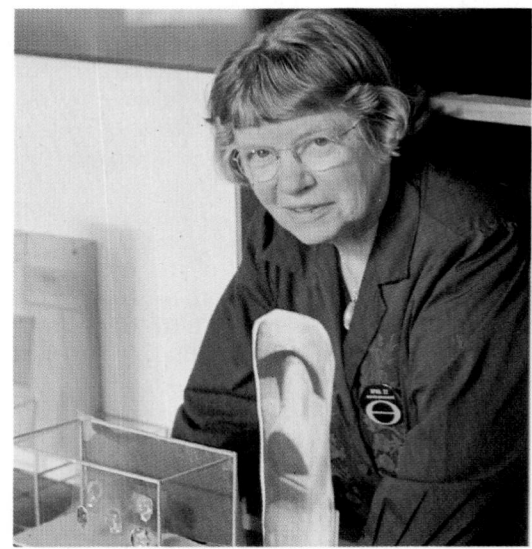

The anthropologist Margaret Mead helped people understand their own culture and that of other human beings.

Growing Up in New Guinea (1930) about one of them. She studied American Indians, too.

When she began to explore relationships between modern men and women, she drew on her work among primitive societies. This is reflected in her book *Male and Female* (1949). She also studied and wrote about relations between generations and between races. As one of the world's best-known and most respected anthropologists, Margaret Mead was a sought-after writer, lecturer, and teacher. She died on November 15, 1978, in New York City.

SAM AND BERYL EPSTEIN

Authors, *She Never Looked Back: Margaret Mead in Samoa*

MEASLES. See DISEASES.

MEASUREMENT. See WEIGHTS AND MEASURES.

MEAT-PACKING

Meat is any part of an animal that people commonly use for food. In ages past, people had fresh meat only when there had been a successful hunt. Later, animals were raised for meat, but usually they were slaughtered only in autumn. To keep the meat from spoiling, people learned to salt it. The modern meat industry supplies fresh meat all year round. The development of railroads and refrigeration made this possible.

▶RAISING ANIMALS FOR MARKET

Methods of raising animals are constantly being changed and improved through scientific research. Farmers depend on this research to be sure that the feed their animals eat keeps the animals healthy and makes them grow as rapidly as possible.

Hogs for Market. The outdoor pigsty, where pigs wallowed in mud and ate raw garbage, is no longer used to raise pigs that go to market. Today many pigs are raised in "pig parlors" that are temperature-controlled, with automatic feeding, watering, and cleaning systems. These systems allow one person to care for several hundred animals. And laws now require that garbage fed to hogs be cooked to destroy harmful bacteria.

Hogs are usually ready for market by the time they are 6 months old. Lean hogs weighing about 100 kilograms (220 pounds) are considered best for market. There are several methods of marketing hogs. Some farmers sell their hogs to livestock dealers, who ship them to livestock centers by rail or truck. At these centers, the animals are sold to packers. Some farmers sell their hogs directly to meat-packers. Others sell through auction or to local dealers in rural areas.

The meat of hogs is called **pork.** Pork may be used fresh, or it may be made into cured ham, bacon, or various kinds of sausages. It is the primary meat in many countries. Austria, Belgium, China, Czechoslovakia, Japan, Poland, Portugal, Spain, Sweden, and the U.S.S.R. all produce more pork than they do any other meat. Great quantities of pork are also produced in the United States.

Cattle for Market. It takes more time and money to raise beef cattle than to raise hogs. The best beef comes from 18- to 24-month-old **steers** (males that were desexed when they were calves) or young **heifers** (females that have not borne calves). **Veal** is meat from very young dairy calves, usually male.

Beef is the primary meat produced in many countries, including Argentina, Australia, Brazil, Britain, Canada, Chile, Italy, Mexico, the United States, and Uruguay.

Sheep for Market. The meat of a mature sheep is called **mutton.** When the sheep is less than a year old, the meat is called **lamb.** In some countries—such as Algeria, New Zealand, and Turkey—mutton and lamb are the most important meats. In the United States and Canada, sheep are far less important than hogs and cattle.

▶**MEAT PROCESSING**

At the packing plant, livestock are changed into meat. Hogs and lambs are moved from pens through narrow chutes to the start of the disassembly line (the line where the animals are taken apart).

The first step is to make the animal unable to feel pain. The animal may be anesthetized by gas or stunned by a hard blow or electric shock. When the animal can no longer feel pain, it is lifted up and attached to a conveyor rail. The main artery above its heart is opened, and the blood drains out.

The next step is not taken until the bleeding has stopped. Some hog carcasses are then placed in hot water to loosen the hair. A dehairing machine scrapes the hair off. The heads and hides are removed from some pork and all beef carcasses. Next, the carcasses are opened and the internal organs removed. A meat inspector examines these and the carcasses. Only the meat of disease-free animals can be sold for people to eat.

The carcass is split by sawing along the backbone. The two sides each go along the overhead rail to be trimmed, washed, and carefully inspected. Then the sides are sent to a cooler to be chilled for 24 to 36 hours. After this, they may be cut into different parts, such as steaks, chops, or roasts. Or the sides may not be cut until they are sent to retail outlets.

▶**MEAT CURING AND SMOKING**

Curing was the best method of preserving meat until about 100 years ago, when meat began to be refrigerated. The basic curing process has not changed in centuries. But modern methods are faster, use less salt and other chemicals, and produce a milder flavor.

In early days, pork was packed in barrels of salt to be cured. The cured meat was dry, tough, and heavily and unevenly salted. Around 1880, hams were rubbed with dry curing salts and then packed in salt water, or brine, for 30 days. Today salt and flavorings in a liquid solution are injected, or pumped, into all parts of the meat. This shortens the curing process to four to six days. With refrigeration, it is not necessary to salt meat heavily to resist spoiling. Nowadays the main purpose of salting meat is to provide flavor.

After curing, many meats are smoked. Smoking has also long been a common method of preservation. Modern smokehouses are air-conditioned rooms, usually made of stainless steel. Controlled amounts of smoke from special hardwood sawdust are sent into the rooms. Sometimes liquid smoke (hardwood smoke distilled and dissolved in water) is used. Smoking is used in preparing ham, bacon, and many kinds of sausage.

▶**SAUSAGES**

There are at least 200 different kinds of sausage made today. Sausages may be fresh, smoked, cooked, smoked and cooked, dry, or

BEEF

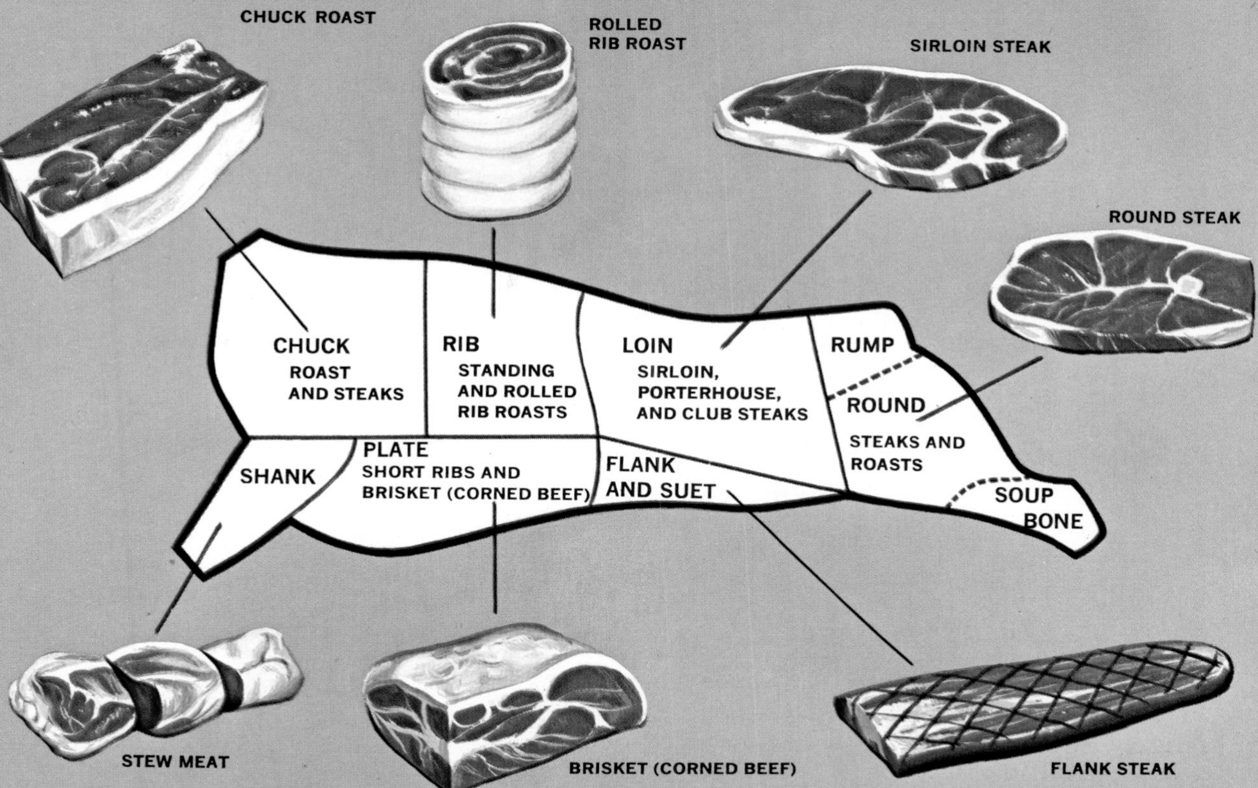

CHUCK ROAST

ROLLED RIB ROAST

SIRLOIN STEAK

ROUND STEAK

CHUCK ROAST AND STEAKS

RIB STANDING AND ROLLED RIB ROASTS

LOIN SIRLOIN, PORTERHOUSE, AND CLUB STEAKS

RUMP

ROUND

SHANK

PLATE SHORT RIBS AND BRISKET (CORNED BEEF)

FLANK AND SUET

STEAKS AND ROASTS

SOUP BONE

STEW MEAT

BRISKET (CORNED BEEF)

FLANK STEAK

PORK

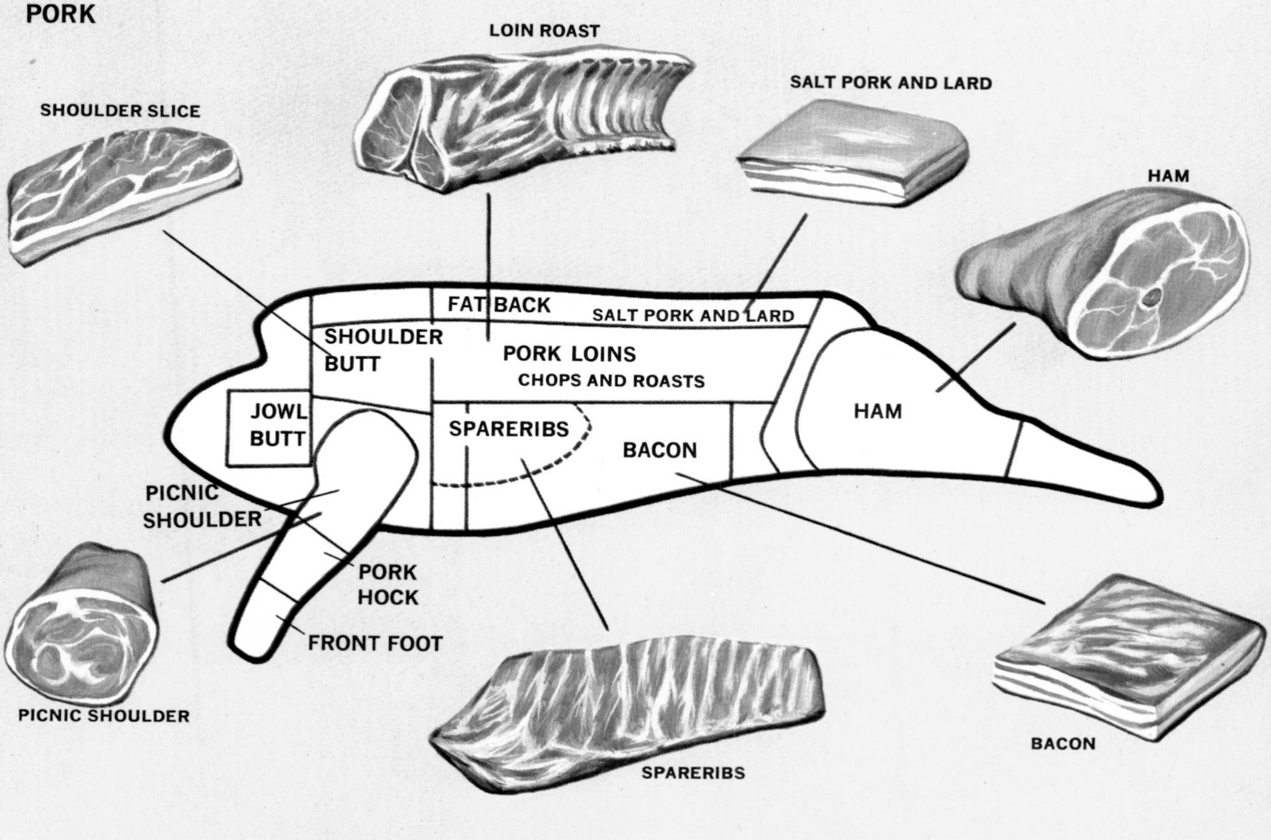

LOIN ROAST

SALT PORK AND LARD

SHOULDER SLICE

HAM

FAT BACK SALT PORK AND LARD

SHOULDER BUTT

PORK LOINS CHOPS AND ROASTS

JOWL BUTT

SPARERIBS

BACON

HAM

PICNIC SHOULDER

PORK HOCK

FRONT FOOT

PICNIC SHOULDER

SPARERIBS

BACON

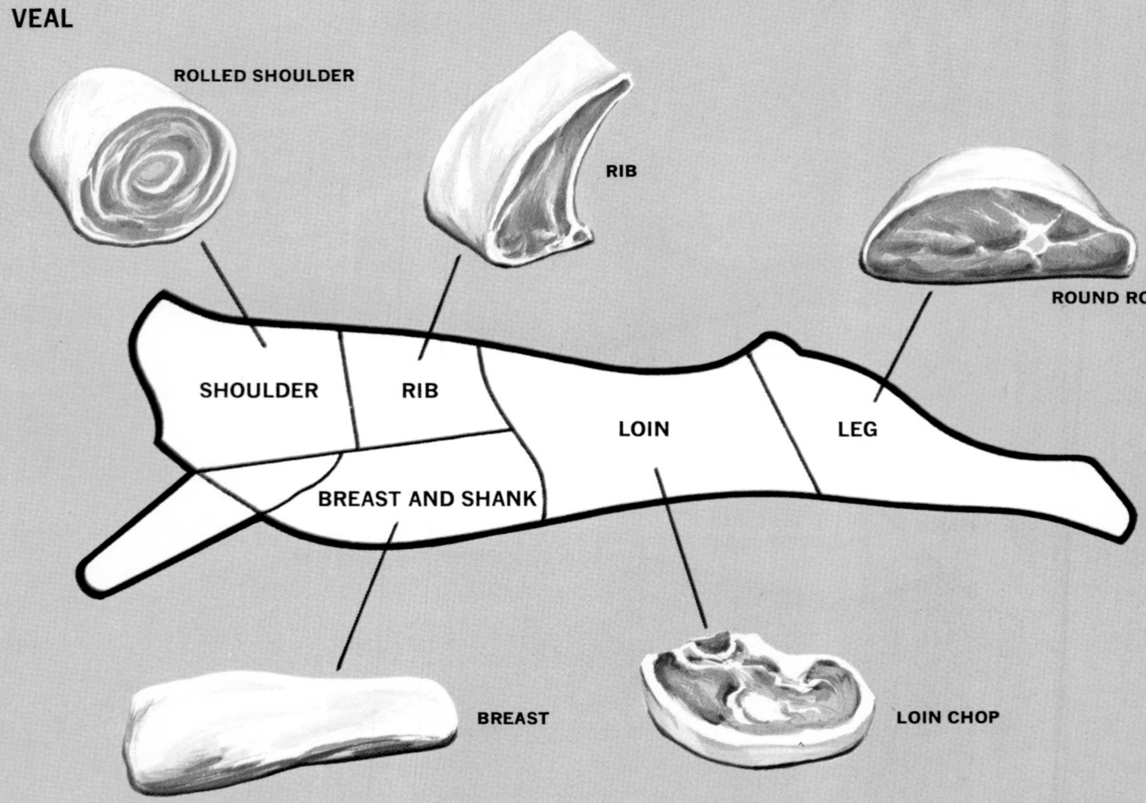

VEAL

ROLLED SHOULDER

RIB

ROUND ROAST

SHOULDER

RIB

LOIN

LEG

BREAST AND SHANK

BREAST

LOIN CHOP

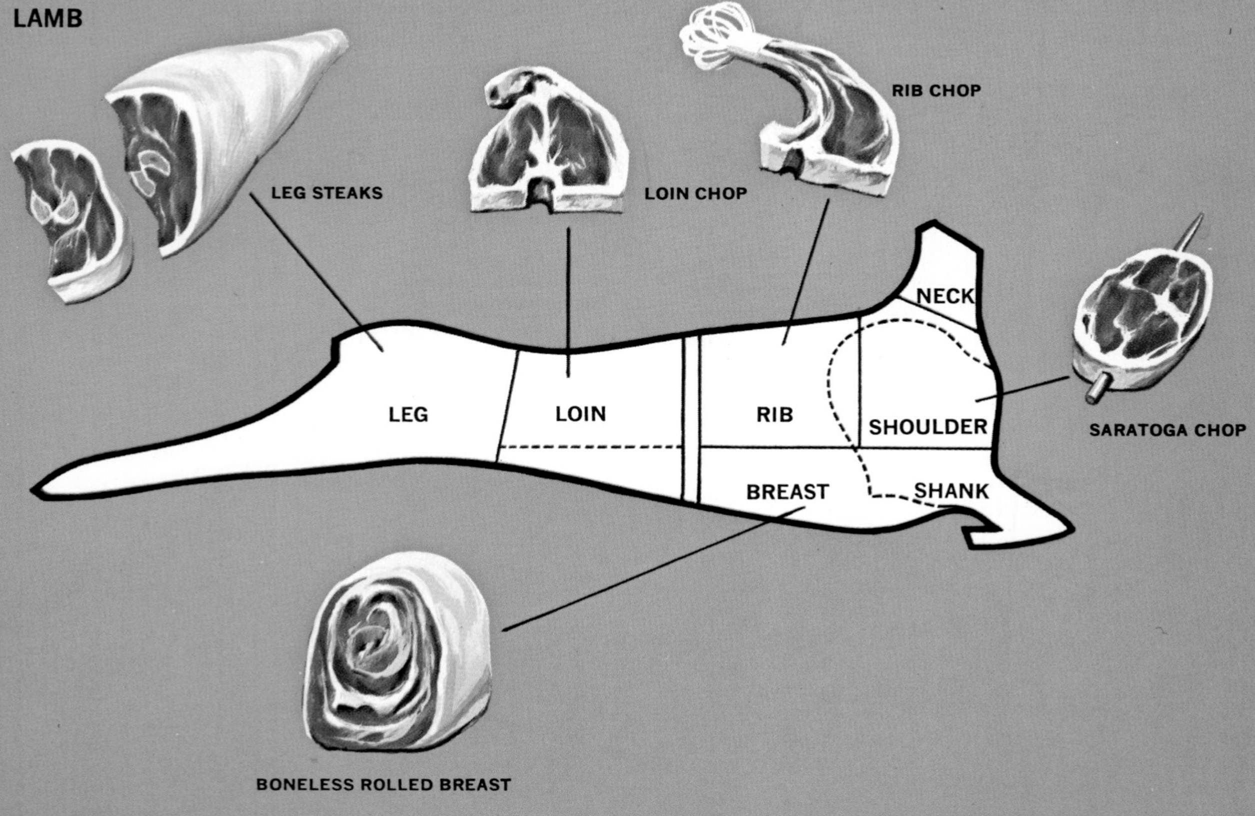

LAMB

LEG STEAKS

LOIN CHOP

RIB CHOP

NECK

LEG

LOIN

RIB

SHOULDER

SARATOGA CHOP

BREAST

SHANK

BONELESS ROLLED BREAST

semi-dry. Frankfurters are the most popular type of sausage in the United States.

Many different kinds of meat are used in sausages. Beef, pork, and veal are often used —separately or in mixtures. Sometimes lamb or chicken is included. The meat must have a certain proportion of fat to lean meat.

The meat is chilled and chopped in a grinder, and blends of spices and flavorings are added to make various kinds of sausages. The sausages may be stuffed into casings made from cellulose, fiber, plastic, or the cleaned, salted intestines of meat animals. Many people prefer sausages to be skinless, or without casings.

Before refrigeration was common, sausages had to be cured and dried to be preserved. Today many kinds of sausage are cured simply because people like the flavor.

▶MEAT IN MANY FORMS

Meat is sold not only fresh, cured, smoked, and in sausages but also canned and frozen. There are many forms of canned meat. They include sandwich spreads, beef stew, chili con carne, and corned-beef hash.

Frozen meats are very popular. The raw meat itself may be directly frozen. There are also many ready-to-serve frozen products, such as precooked dinners and meat pies.

Research to improve the preservation of meat is constantly going on. Freeze-dried meats and poultry have their moisture extracted by a quick-freezing method. The freeze-dried foods are much lighter than the unprocessed product and need little or no refrigeration. When water is added to them in cooking, the foods recover the size, appearance, and taste they had when fresh.

▶MEAT INSPECTION AND GRADING

Meat is inspected and graded in most countries. Inspection and grading systems vary, but most of them accomplish the same goals. Inspection assures that meat is wholesome and safe to eat. **Quality** grades tell how tender, juicy, and flavorful meat is expected to be. **Yield** grades indicate how much of the carcass can be made into cuts that can be sold.

In inspection, animals are checked before they enter the slaughterhouse because diseased or injured animals may not be slaughtered for food. The carcass is inspected during the slaughter process to be sure that there are no diseased tissues. Inspectors also make sure that the plant and equipment are kept clean, that the workers are clean and healthy, and that ingredients added to meat products are clean and wholesome.

All meat that is offered for sale in the United States must pass inspection by either the U.S. Department of Agriculture or an individual state inspection agency that has regulations equal to or better than the federal regulations. Meat that has been inspected is stamped, using a purple dye that is fully edible. A round stamp indicates federal inspection, and a stamp in the shape of the borders of a state indicates state inspection. Both stamps assure the consumer that the product has been inspected and found to be free from disease, clean, unadulterated, and truthfully labeled.

Beef and lamb carcasses may carry a grade stamp in addition to the inspection stamp. There are eight official U.S. grades for beef. The most tender cuts are graded prime and choice. Good and standard grades are leaner. They may be fairly tender but not juicy. Commercial grade will be juicy but tough. It can be made tender by cooking slowly with moist heat. Utility grade is very lean and can be used for ground beef and the like. Canner and cutter grades are extra lean and are used mostly in luncheon meats and frankfurters.

▶ANIMAL BY-PRODUCTS

Much of an animal slaughtered by a meatpacker is not edible. Not more than half the weight of a typical steer, for example, is actually beef. But the rest of the animal does not go to waste. There is a use for almost every part of it. Glands from meat animals are used to produce medicines such as pepsin, cortisone, ACTH, and the insulin used by diabetics.

The packer processes steer hides and pigskins for leather. Hog hair is used to make brushes and upholstery. Fats make soap, cosmetics, and animal feeds. Lambs' wool is turned into yarns and clothing. Other inedible parts become fertilizers and gelatins.

JOHN C. FORREST
Purdue University

See also CATTLE AND OTHER LIVESTOCK; FOOD PRESERVATION AND PROCESSING.

MECCA

Mecca, the birthplace of the prophet Mohammed (570–632), is the holiest city of Islam, the religion of the Muslims. It is also the site of an ancient shrine called the Kaaba. Muslims all over the world face toward Mecca when they pray.

Mecca lies in a hot, sandy valley in west central Saudi Arabia. The valley is unfit for cultivation. But it was on a major ancient caravan route from the southern part of the Arabian Peninsula to Syria, and it has a good water supply. This, together with the presence of the Kaaba, explains why a great and wealthy city grew up on this unfavorable spot.

Mecca was a holy city long before Mohammed was born. Pilgrims from all over Arabia once came to worship the various gods of the Arab tribes at the Kaaba. About 610, a Meccan named Mohammed began to preach the way of life that became known as Islam.

The leaders of Mecca did not accept Mohammed's teachings, and he was forced to move from Mecca to Medina in 622. In 630, Mohammed and his followers conquered Mecca. The city later became part of several great Muslim empires, including those of the Egyptians and the Turks. After World War II, it became part of Saudi Arabia.

All Muslims who are able to do so must make a pilgrimage (*hajj*) to Mecca at least once in their lifetimes. While in Mecca, the pilgrims wear special clothes. They cannot shave, cut their hair or nails, or uproot plants. They pray within the walls of the Great Mosque, a huge temple that encloses the Kaaba. They walk around the windowless Kaaba seven times and kiss the sacred Black Stone embedded in one corner. According to Muslim tradition, this stone was sent down from heaven when the shrine was built by Abraham and his son Ishmael.

Only Muslims can enter the holy city, which has a permanent population of about 370,000. Taking care of pilgrims has been the chief business of the city for centuries. More than 1,000,000 people visit Mecca each year.

JOHN A. WILLIAMS
American University in Cairo

See also ISLAM; MOHAMMED.

Pilgrims from all over the world pray at the Kaaba, Islam's most sacred shrine.

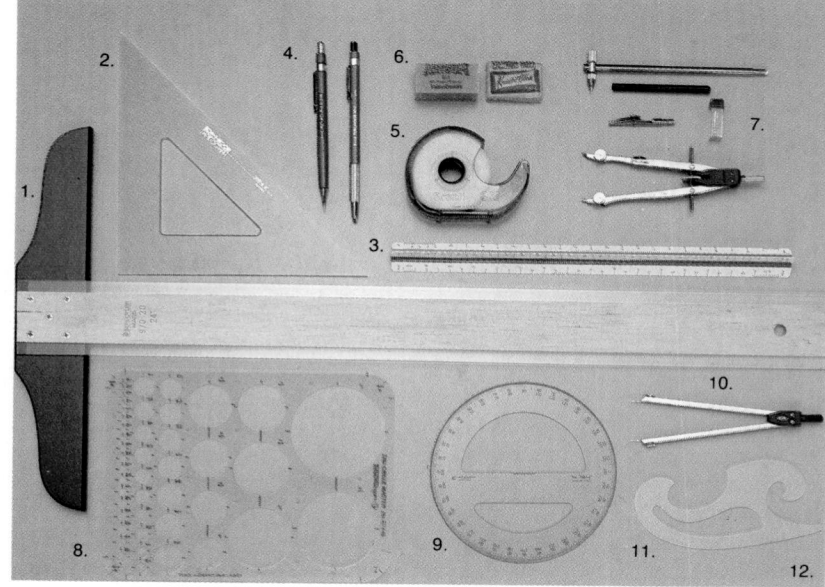

Drafting instruments and tools include:

1. T-square
2. triangle
3. architect's scale
4. pencils
5. drafting tape
6. eraser
7. compass
8. template
9. protractor
10. dividers
11. French curve
12. drafting board

MECHANICAL DRAWING

Before a building is built, a bridge is constructed, or any product manufactured, a plan must be made. Architects, engineers, and designers must sketch pictures of the objects they wish to create. A drawing using special lines and symbols is then made that shows the exact size and shape of the object. These drawings are called mechanical drawings because they are done by hand with drafting instruments and tools. Mechanical drawings require neatness, accuracy, and the skillful use of drafting instruments and techniques. **Drafters** are the people who specialize in making mechanical drawings. Using these drawings as plans, builders and artisans can visualize and make the finished objects.

A multiview mechanical drawing of a portable radio shows three sides separately; a pictorial mechanical drawing shows the radio as it would actually appear.

MULTIVIEW   PICTORIAL

TOP

3

AM

FM

FRONT   RIGHT SIDE

TOP

AM

ON

OFF

FM

FRONT   RIGHT SIDE

Drafters use special drawing sheets made of vellum (a type of paper), cloth, or film. They attach the drawing sheet to a **drafting board,** and draw, or draft, with special pencils and pens. Horizontal lines are drawn along the edge of a **T-square;** vertical and diagonal lines are drawn with **triangles** placed on the top edge of the T-square; and circles and arcs are drawn with a **compass.** Various shapes may also be drawn with **templates.**

Other instruments used by drafters include the **architect's scale,** for measuring distances; **dividers,** for transferring measurements from one place to another on the drawing; **French curves,** for drawing irregular curves; the **protractor,** for measuring angles; the **eraser;** and **drafting tape,** for attaching the paper to the board.

A mechanical drawing may be **multiview,** usually showing two or three sides of an object. Each side (front, top, right side) is shown separately, as if you were looking straight at it. The drafter adds dimensions (size of each part) to the drawing so that a machinist, carpenter, or other builder can make or construct the product. A mechanical drawing may also be **pictorial,** showing the overall appearance of an object.

Today many designs and drawings are created through Computer Aided Drafting (CAD). When done on a computer, a mechanical drawing is made with the same standards and techniques used by an expert drafter.

MARSHALL A. BUTLER
Montclair State College (New Jersey)
MECHANICS. See WORK, POWER, AND MACHINES.

MEDALS AND DECORATIONS

The Jewish historian Josephus (A.D. 37–100?) recorded that in the 3rd century B.C. the high priest Jonathan led the Hebrews in battle to aid Alexander the Great. Alexander "sent to Jonathan . . . honorary awards, as a golden button, which it is the custom to give the king's kinsmen." This is the first mention in history of a medal.

Medals and decorations are given to servicemen for bravery, for outstanding service, for being wounded, and for taking part in a war or a campaign. Medals are awarded in sports, as in the Olympic Games, and for outstanding work in many fields. A medal is part of the Nobel prize.

In ancient Greece and Rome the decoration for merit, military or otherwise, was a laurel wreath. It was placed on the victor's head like a crown. Roman coins bore the head of the current emperor, crowned by such a wreath. On later coins the wreath was placed around the edge of the coin. It still is. You will see it on the back of some American pennies.

Enameled and jeweled decorations became the symbols of orders of knighthood.

During the Crusades medals were used to identify the Knights Templar, the Knights of Saint John of Jerusalem, and others. Through the years most medals were given to nobles or high officers for some special military deed. England's Queen Elizabeth I ordered medals for Sir Francis Drake and the other captains who defeated the Spanish Armada in 1588. Medals were rarely given to common soldiers.

American Medals and Decorations

Medals may be of two kinds: regular (awarded to anyone who earns them) or special (awarded by vote of Congress to particular individuals). The first regular medal for bravery for the common soldier was the **Purple Heart**, established by George Washington in 1782 during the American Revolution (1775–83). It was a heart-shaped patch of purple cloth trimmed with lace, which the wearer could sew on the breast of his uniform. The award gave the one who wore it an unusual privilege. He could pass any sentry whom an officer could pass. Only three Purple Hearts were awarded during the Revolution. Then the award was discontinued. After the Revolution some special medals were awarded by Congress. One went to Washington for driving the British out of Boston, and one to General Horatio Gates (1728?–1806) for winning the battle of Saratoga. Among others, three were awarded to the militia who captured the British spy Major John André (1751–80). But after the Purple Heart was discontinued, there were no regular medals until the Civil War. Americans seemed to feel that medals and democracy did not mix. They associated medals with the European system of knights and nobles and kings.

The Medal of Honor. It was 1862 before Congress voted to give a medal for bravery to both officers and enlisted men. This was the Medal of Honor, often mistakenly called the Congressional Medal of Honor. At first the regulations governing its award were rather vague. Because of this vagueness and because there were no lesser medals, the Medal of Honor was given out freely. Once President Abraham Lincoln promised one to every man in a regiment who would re-enlist. After the war Congress reviewed the awards and canceled 911 of the 2,438 medals that had been given out.

The first men who actually received the Medal of Honor were the Union raiders who went behind Confederate lines, captured a train, and used it to try to wreck a Southern railroad. After doing a good deal of damage, the men were captured by Confederate troops. Later, 20 medals were awarded for this mission. Six were given to survivors. The rest were given posthumously to the next of kin of the men killed trying to escape and of those executed as spies. During the Civil War two Medals of Honor were awarded to 14- and 15-year-old Union drummer boys for rescuing wounded comrades under enemy fire.

Some time after the Civil War a committee of generals and admirals established new, strict rules governing the award of the Medal of Honor. It should be given only to those who performed "a deed of personal bravery or self sacrifice above and beyond the call of duty while a member of the armed forces in actual combat with an enemy of the nation." One exception allows the award to a general commanding troops in the field during war.

Since then Medals of Honor have been

MEDALS AND DECORATIONS OF THE UNITED STATES

PURPLE HEART

DISTINGUISHED SERVICE CROSS

MEDAL OF HONOR (NAVY-MARINE CORPS-COAST GUARD)

NAVY CROSS

BRONZE STAR

SILVER STAR

AIR FORCE CROSS

MEDAL OF HONOR (ARMY)

DISTINGUISHED SERVICE MEDAL (ARMY)

DISTINGUISHED SERVICE MEDAL (NAVY-MARINE CORPS)

AIRMAN'S MEDAL

SOLDIER'S MEDAL

DISTINGUISHED FLYING CROSS

NAVY AND MARINE CORPS MEDAL

LEGION OF MERIT

NATIONAL SECURITY MEDAL

MEDALS AND DECORATIONS OF OTHER COUNTRIES

ORDER OF VICTORY (SOVIET UNION)

LEGION OF HONOR (FRANCE)

DISTINGUISHED SERVICE ORDER (GREAT BRITAIN)

ORDER OF THE RISING SUN (JAPAN)

CROIX DE GUERRE (FRANCE)

ORDER OF LENIN (SOVIET UNION)

VICTORIA CROSS (GREAT BRITAIN)

ORDER OF LEOPOLD (BELGIUM)

ORDER OF MERIT OF THE ITALIAN REPUBLIC (ITALY)

ORDER OF THE AZTEC EAGLE (MEXICO)

IRON CROSS (GERMANY)

awarded very seldom. Perhaps 50,000,000 men have served in the armed forces of the United States during the century of the medal's existence. But throughout the entire period only about 3,400 men have won the medal, mostly soldiers and sailors. By special act of Congress it was awarded to one civilian: Charles A. Lindbergh for his nonstop transatlantic plane flight in 1927.

All other American military medals are pinned to the left breast of the uniform. The Medal of Honor, however, is worn around the neck, suspended by a blue ribbon. The medals for the Army, the Navy, and the Air Force are of different designs. When in civilian clothes, Medal of Honor winners may wear a rosette of blue cloth with 13 white stars on their coat lapels.

FRANK R. DONOVAN
Author, *The Story of the Medal of Honor*

MEDICAL LABORATORY TESTS

To treat a patient, a doctor must know what the sickness is. Medical laboratory tests help the doctor make a diagnosis—that is, identify a disease from its signs or symptoms. Many diseases seem the same but have different causes and need different treatment. For example, certain infections can be correctly identified only through laboratory tests. Other diseases, such as tuberculosis and some kinds of cancer, must be diagnosed very early to be cured easily. Special tests can detect these diseases. Tests also help the doctor make certain the treatment is effective.

Most medical laboratories have several divisions, each dealing with a particular area of testing. Chief among the laboratory divisions are hematology, clinical microscopy, biochemistry, bacteriology, blood banking, and anatomic pathology.

Hematology. This division deals with studies of the elements in the blood. Blood counts performed in a laboratory's hematology section are among the most useful of medical laboratory tests. There are four parts to a blood count—the hemoglobin measurement, the red blood cell count, the white blood cell count, and the differential white blood cell count. Hemoglobin is the oxygen-carrying substance in the red blood cells. The hemoglobin measurement or red blood cell counts are abnormally low in cases of anemia and certain other conditions.

The white blood cell count rises with bacterial infection and with leukemia (cancer of the blood). A differential white blood cell count is especially important when the white blood cell count is abnormally high. There are five different kinds of white blood cells, some of which act against certain kinds of infection. The differential white count reveals which kind of white cell is increasing and thus helps to pinpoint the kind of infection. The differential also gives information about the form and structure of the white cells. This information helps the doctor diagnose and treat the patient with leukemia.

The hematology laboratory also does bone marrow counts. These counts tell the doctor whether the system of the body that makes blood cells is working properly. Tests are also done in hematology to determine whether the blood coagulates, or clots, properly.

At one time, blood counts had to be done one by one, using a microscope. But now all large laboratories have instruments that do the counts automatically.

Clinical Microscopy. Urinalyses (tests of urine) are performed in this division. Color, density, pH (acidity or alkalinity), and tests for sugar, protein, and blood are all part of a urinalysis. In addition, a microscopic examination of a few drops of urine is done to look for bacteria, crystals, cells, and other structures. Such studies may often provide the first clue to kidney or bladder disease, diabetes, or other illnesses.

Stools, or feces, are also examined in this section of the laboratory. Microscopic examinations of stools are done to look for eggs of intestinal worms. Special chemical tests reveal the presence of blood and other substances in the stool.

Biochemistry. The hospital biochemistry laboratory provides a great deal of information about many different parts of the body. Most of the chemistry tests are done on blood. Blood sugar tests help in the detection and treatment of diabetes. Measurements of blood urea (BUN) and blood protein help the doctor to detect and treat kidney disease.

Blood electrolyte tests are of special importance to the doctor treating a seriously ill patient. Blood electrolytes (sodium, potassium, chloride, and bicarbonate) regulate the flow of fluid within the body. Certain sicknesses can change the electrolyte values in the body, upsetting the flow of fluid and causing a drop in blood pressure called shock.

Blood enzyme tests detect heart disease, liver disease, and certain digestive diseases. Hormone tests show how well certain glands are working. In some cases, the doctor needs to know whether a patient is getting the right amount of medicine. A measurement of the amount of medicine in the blood can give this information.

A test may be repeated at regular intervals to reveal how well the body performs a certain function over a period of time. One functional test is the glucose tolerance test. For this test, the patient must not have eaten for eight or ten hours. A sample of blood is taken, and the patient is given a sugar solution to drink. Blood is then taken at different times over a period of several hours. The sugar is measured in all the blood samples. By comparing the blood-sugar measurements, the doctor can see how well the body uses sugar over a period of time. Sugar is an important energy source for the body.

For many years, technicians did the more than 50 different chemistry tests by hand. This could mean many hours of adding different chemicals, timing, filtering, and performing many other chemical procedures. But now the most commonly ordered tests can be done by an automated analyzer. The new instrument can produce as many as 3,000 test results an hour.

Bacteriology. One main task of the bacteriology laboratory is to detect the organism causing an infection. Tests are done on samples of infected tissue, blood, sputum (coughed up mucus), urine, and feces. Sometimes a doctor may send a swab to be tested. This is a bit of cotton on a stick that has been dabbed across an area of the body thought to be infected, such as a sore throat.

In the testing, part of the sample is placed on a glass slide and examined with a microscope. Another part of the sample is added to a special culture medium. This may be a liquid or a gelatinlike material containing substances that will allow the bacteria to grow. Much information comes from studying the form of the organism under the microscope and from observing its growth in the medium. The bacteriology laboratory also determines which antibiotics will kill the bacteria causing the infection. This is called a sensitivity test.

Another major responsibility of the bacteriology laboratory is serology, the testing for antibodies. Antibodies are proteins made by the body in response to infection. The antibodies may kill the disease organisms or neutralize the poisons made by the organisms. Different antibodies form for different diseases. Thus it is possible to diagnose many diseases by determining the antibody present in the blood.

Blood Banking. Often when a patient has lost a great deal of blood for some reason, the doctor may order a blood transfusion. This order goes to the blood bank, where blood drawn from donors is kept stored in huge refrigerators. When the transfusion order is received, the patient's blood type is determined.

Then a unit of blood of the same type as the patient's is selected from the refrigerator. Next a test, called a cross matching, is done to make sure that the patient will not have a serious reaction to certain proteins in the donor's blood. To do a cross matching, a few drops of the patients' blood are mixed in a test tube with a few drops of the donor's blood. If clumps form in the mixture, the donor's blood and the patient's blood are not perfectly matched. The transfusion could make the patient very sick. In this case, cross matching must be done with another unit of donor blood.

Anatomic Pathology. Pathology is the study of the nature of diseases. In the anatomic pathology division of a laboratory, all specimens of abnormal or diseased tissue are carefully studied under the microscope by doctors who are specialists in pathology. They examine all surgical specimens, including tiny tissue samples, called biopsies, and whole organs or limbs removed at major operations. Often the pathologist is consulted during an operation when a diagnosis is in doubt. A small tissue sample is given a rapid microscopic examination to help determine what surgery may have to be performed.

When biopsies are not advisable, diagnoses of cancer or other diseases can be made from samples of cells. This technique is called diagnostic cytology, also known as the Pap test. The method is used to study cells coughed up from the lung, shed into the urine from the urinary tract, or shed from certain organs such as the uterus.

Other special techniques include counting and analyzing the chromosomes in cells. Chromosomes carry the genes that determine heredity. Such an analysis of the chromosomes is called a karyotype. Cell samples may be taken from blood, bone marrow, or other tissues of patients. As more powerful microscopes have been developed, these tests have become even more useful.

A pathologist also performs autopsies, which are anatomic studies of the bodies of dead persons, done to find the cause of death.

MYRON R. MELAMED, M.D.
Attending Pathologist, Memorial Hospital for
Cancer and Allied Diseases (New York City)
Member, Sloan-Kettering Institute
for Cancer Research (New York City)

MEDICAL SUPPLIES. See FIRST AID.

MEDICINE, HISTORY OF

When a caveman got a thorn in his finger, he pulled it out and his finger felt better. He was practicing medicine—that is, doing something to lessen discomfort or pain.

Sometimes the caveman had a pain for which he could not find the reason. But even though he did not understand why he had the pain, he tried to do something about it. His medicine in that case would have been something that we would call magic. This magic might have been a chant or song, a figure carved from stone, a picture on a cave wall, or a stew of herbs and leaves. Since many diseases go away anyway after a period of time, the caveman probably thought that his magic worked. Sometimes, by accident, he may have come upon some kind of treatment that really did help him. The warmth of a fire might ease a sprained shoulder, or an herb drink might help his stomachache.

Among primitive peoples today, medicine and magic are still mixed. The medicine man is the one who knows magic. But he also knows some practical things to do to help the sick and injured. In many primitive tribes the medicine man can set and splint a broken bone. He knows **medicinal plants** that are laxatives and plants that will put people to sleep.

The earliest civilizations that we know about had physicians. The Babylonians left medical writings describing various diseases so clearly that doctors today can recognize them. Among the ancient Egyptians it was widely believed that illness was caused by an evil spirit coming to live in the patient's body. Medical treatments usually included prayers to drive out the evil spirits. But they also included pills and ointments containing drugs such as opium and castor oil. And surgical operations were done on the outer surfaces of the body.

▶**GREEK AND ROMAN MEDICINE**

According to Homer and other sources, the earliest physician in Greek history was Aesculapius. The legend of his healing powers grew until he was thought of as a god. In his honor temples were built to which the sick were brought to sleep overnight. In the morning the patients told their dreams to the priests. The priests interpreted the dreams as messages from Aesculapius and based the treatment on what the god had magically ordered.

Both Greeks and Romans had temples to Aesculapius in which this kind of magical medicine was practiced. But at the same time, nonmagic medicine was beginning in Greece. About 460 B.C. on the small Greek island of Cos, Hippocrates was born. Cos seems to have been a kind of center for men interested in medicine. Hippocrates' father was a physician. Hippocrates himself did so much to rescue medicine from magic and superstition that he is called the Father of Medicine.

Hippocrates did not have the scientific knowledge on which medicine is based today. He did not know about bacteria or chemistry or what the various organs of the body do. Therefore he could not explain the causes of diseases. But he did have the kind of mind and spirit that make a good physician.

In his writings he taught that the physician should observe the patient closely and accurately. Gentle treatment should be used to try to encourage the natural healing process. The physician should never risk harming the patient. The patient's secrets should be kept, and the physician should be in every way worthy of the sick person's trust.

Hippocrates recognized and described many diseases. Some of the medical facts he observed are as true today as they were over 2,000 years ago. For example, he said, "Those naturally very fat are more liable to sudden death than the thin." And he wrote, "Tuberculosis occurs most commonly between the ages of eighteen and thirty-five years."

This nonmagical kind of medicine was advanced further by Aristotle, the great Greek scientist. He studied the bodies of animals closely and described their development. He was not a physician, but he helped establish the science of **biology**, on which nonmagical medicine is based.

After Alexander the Great conquered most of the known world, the city of Alexandria in Egypt became the center of learning. There was a famous library in Alexandria, and there were many schools, including a medical school. Erasistratus (310?–250? B.C.) was one of the greatest teachers in the school. If a patient died, Erasistratus and his students would operate on the body to try to find out the cause of the fatal illness.

The Romans were a very practical people. They did not care as much about study and discovery of new knowledge as the Greeks had. They cared more about putting knowledge to work. They made the world a more healthful place to live in, even though they did little scientific research.

The city of Rome was large and crowded. People could not live so close together without spreading disease from person to person unless they were careful about sanitation. The Romans built huge sewers under the city to carry away the waste. The main sewer of Rome, called the Cloaca Maxima, is still in use today. The Romans also had a supply of pure water for their city. Fourteen great aqueducts brought 300,000,000 gallons of water into Rome every day. There were special Roman officials to inspect the markets and make sure that no spoiled food was sold.

The Romans were also the first to try to organize medical care so that all sick people could have help. They began by sending physicians and medical equipment with the Roman armies so that the wounded soldiers would be cared for. Often in the towns the physician's house had extra rooms, where his patients might stay if they were very ill. This was the beginning of hospitals. The Romans also built public buildings for the care of the sick, especially the slaves and the poor, who might not be able to pay a doctor. The Roman government paid doctors to work in the public hospitals.

The earliest scientific medical book in Latin was written by Celsus (1st century A.D.). He brought together in a kind of encyclopedia most of the Greek learning about medicine.

The greatest physician in Rome was Galen (A.D. 129?–200?). His writings do not show the gentleness and kindliness that Hippocrates' works show. Galen gave some kind of explanation of every organ in the body. Modern scientists know that many of his explanations were completely wrong, but Galen seldom admitted that there was anything he did not know.

Beginning about the year 200, the Western world went through a time of much trouble. Barbarian tribes from the North overran the cities of the Roman Empire. There were wars, earthquakes, and plagues of disease in which thousands of people died. The Christian Church became the main force for law and order. The Church taught that people should be kind to the sick and try to help them. Early Christians risked their lives to nurse the dying during the plagues. But these deeply religious people felt that getting well or dying was in God's hands. They did not try to understand the body and what happened to it in the course of a disease. They were not scientists at all.

Yet even during the Middle Ages interest in scientific medicine continued. From the 9th century to the 14th century one city in southern Italy, Salerno, was a medical center. Monks from western Europe, Jews, Arabs, and Greeks met at Salerno. Many of them brought with them the valuable books of their own languages. The writings of Hippocrates and other earlier doctors were preserved and studied.

▶ MEDICINE AND THE RENAISSANCE (1300–1500)

During the 13th century all of Europe became interested again in Greek learning and in science. By the 1400's the Renaissance, or rebirth of learning, was well under way. Leonardo da Vinci, who was a scientist as well as an artist, was the first to question some of Galen's explanations of the body. Leonardo's notebooks, full of detailed drawings of the heart, the blood vessels, and the muscles, are beautiful examples of his keen observation. One of the great men of Renaissance medicine was Andreas Vesalius (1514–64). He made a great contribution to the study of anatomy, the science of the body's structure. His great book, *The Fabric of the Human Body,* written at the University of Padua, Italy, was printed at Basel, Switzerland. Vesalius was too much a scientist to rely on the work of ancients like Galen and Aristotle. The illustrations in his books were drawn from actual human bodies. He corrected many errors that no one else had found in all the hundreds of years that the work of the ancient masters had been copied and recopied.

Another famous doctor of the same period

was Ambroise Paré (1517?–90), who became surgeon in chief to the kings of France. In Europe surgery was often done by barbers and others with little training. Paré, a student of the new anatomy, helped to make surgery as highly respected as other forms of treatment.

When Paré was a surgeon with the French Army, everyone believed that gunshot wounds contained a poison. Some doctors poured boiling oil on the wounds to drive out the poison. Young Paré ran out of oil and treated some men without it. He was surprised to discover that these patients did better without the treatment. He wrote about his discovery, saying, "Then I resolved within myself never so cruelly to burn poor wounded men."

At about the same time, the Swiss physician Paracelsus (1493?–1541) was bringing back the Greek idea that experience is the key to treating sick people correctly. He angered the other professors at the University of Basel, where he taught, by attacking their belief in the ideas of Galen and by teaching in German instead of Latin. He taught by taking students to the bedsides of the sick instead of lecturing in the classroom. He was one of the first to bring a knowledge of chemistry to medicine and to suggest new kinds of drugs, prepared by rules of science rather than by superstition. For instance, he introduced laudanum, sulfur, and mercury, three substances still used today. However, some of his beliefs would now be called superstitions.

Galileo, the man who first looked at the sky through a telescope, brought a new outlook to the study of nature. He believed that each thing in nature should be examined carefully and, if possible, measured exactly. Galileo stressed mathematics because it is a science that tries to give exact answers. His approach brought changes to all sciences.

At the time of Galileo another Italian, named Fabricius of Acquapendente (1537–1619), was improving surgery and making discoveries about the structure of the human body. He noticed, for example, that the veins have valves, which he described as little doors.

One of Fabricius' most famous students was William Harvey, who became physician to James I and Charles I of England. Harvey holds a unique place in medical history. For about 20 years he did experiments and studied the way the blood moves through the body. When he had found an answer, he published his discovery on the circulation of the blood. Since the time of Aristotle and Galen, doctors had believed that the liver created an unending supply of blood, which ran through the blood vessels and was used up by the body tissues that it reached. But Harvey showed that the same blood actually goes around and around through the body, passing through the lungs on each trip. This constant movement in a circle, he noted, "is brought about by the beat of the heart." Thus, for the first time in history, the heart was seen as what it is: a living pump.

In the Renaissance, barbers practiced medicine.

Marcello Malpighi (1628–95), a professor of anatomy at Bologna, Italy, completed the study of how blood circulates by showing that arteries and veins are connected through a network of tiny channels called capillaries. Malpighi made this discovery with the help of a new invention, the microscope, which enabled him to see details not visible to Harvey's unaided eyes.

The microscope first became a useful tool for medicine in the hands of a skilled Dutch lens maker, Anton van Leeuwenhoek. Although he had no formal training as a scientist, Leeuwenhoek was a scientific observer. He drew the first pictures of the one-celled animals called protozoa, which can be seen only under a microscope.

Meanwhile, Thomas Sydenham (1624–89), a famous London doctor, was bringing a new approach to treating the sick. Or, rather, he was returning to the idea of Hippocrates': study of the patient. This idea had been neglected for hundreds of years by all but a few people, such as Paracelsus. Most doctors preferred to look in books and read complicated theories about disease. Sydenham felt that the surest way to understand a disease was to study people affected with it.

A 17th-century pharmacist supplies medicinal plants.

In Holland, Hermann Boerhaave (1668–1738) carried Sydenham's ideas even further. Skilled in chemistry, anatomy, and botany as well as in practical medicine, Boerhaave tried to bring together the knowledge of these different sciences to help the sick. Like Sydenham, he began at the bedside, by studying the patient.

▶ MEDICINE IN THE 18TH CENTURY

Giovanni Batista Morgagni (1682–1771), an anatomist working at Padua early in the 18th century, made another step forward in relating the effects of disease to its causes. Examining the bodies of people who had died of various diseases, he showed that damage to organs, such as the liver or kidneys, had a direct connection with the signs and symptoms of the disease. Study of organs affected by disease is called pathological anatomy. By introducing it as part of what a practicing physician should consider, Morgagni added greatly to medical progress.

The 18th-century Italian Luigi Galvani (1737–98) was interested in the nervous system. In experiments made with the muscles of a frog, Galvani showed that electric current, then a mystery, affects the nerves and causes muscles to act.

Meanwhile, other men were studying various parts of the body and how they act. In France, Antoine Lavoisier (1743–94) worked on the chemistry of breathing. He made experiments to find out whether the human body uses the same amount of oxygen when it is at rest as when the muscles are working. His experiments proved that more oxygen is needed when the muscles are working.

Another Frenchman, Philippe Pinel (1745–1826), who was a doctor at a Paris hospital, was horrified by the fact that many mentally ill patients were kept in chains. He convinced his government to make reforms in the treatment of the mentally ill. As Pinel had foreseen, the patients improved with kinder treatment. Pinel was the first famous reformer in the field of psychiatry, the branch of medicine that tries to apply science to mental illness.

Not long after Pinel's important reform, René Laennec (1781–1826) brought a different kind of progress to medicine with the invention of the stethoscope. By applying this new tool to the patient's chest and listening

Edward Jenner vaccinates a child against smallpox.

through the earpiece, a doctor could clearly hear breathing sounds and heart sounds. Thus, Laennec made it possible for doctors to find out whether people show signs of heart or lung disease.

While Laennec worked on the problems of chest diseases, a United States Army surgeon, William Beaumont, was learning much about how the stomach digests food. One of Beaumont's patients had been shot in the stomach, and the wound healed leaving an opening like a buttonhole. Through this opening Beaumont could observe the action of the stomach. He found that the stomach gives off certain juices that change food into material that the body can use.

A little later, Claude Bernard (1813–78) of France studied the functions of the liver. Through experiments he found that a dog's liver produces sugar even if the dog has no sugar in its diet. His finding proved the idea that animals, like plants, make sugar inside their bodies. Bernard also studied another organ, the pancreas, and pointed the way to a later explanation of diabetes, a disease in which the body does not use sugar properly.

▶ 19TH-CENTURY MEDICAL CONTRIBUTIONS

Despite all the new medical knowledge, diseases like smallpox that spread rapidly from person to person still caused many deaths. To the English country doctor Edward Jenner goes credit for introducing a way to protect people against smallpox. Jenner learned that people who had had a mild disease called cowpox, which they got from cows, did not catch smallpox. He tried injecting a boy with liquid taken from a cowpox infection on a dairymaid's finger. Later he injected the same boy with liquid from a smallpox infection, and the boy remained well. Working from this discovery, Jenner developed **vaccination**. People who are vaccinated are immune—that is, they will not catch a disease even though they are exposed to it. Jenner's method has saved many thousands of lives. Today vaccinations have been developed to protect people against many other diseases.

Although scientists were discovering more

and more about how the body works, they still did not understand much about the causes of disease. Throughout history, countries and even whole continents had been swept by infectious diseases. In an epidemic, a period when huge numbers of people got a disease, sometimes half the people in a city would die. Yet no one knew how the disease spread from person to person.

There were some dim ideas that the spread of disease had something to do with lack of cleanliness. Finally contagion, or the catching of disease, came to be linked to the little one-celled organisms seen under the microscope. Once people understood that bacteria or germs caused disease, they began to think of ways to stop contagion.

Ignaz Semmelweis (1818–65) and Joseph Lister were two of the first physicians who tried to control the spread of infections. In a Vienna hospital Semmelweis found that many women developed a fatal fever after giving birth. He believed that the fever might be connected with the fact that medical students treated the women after doing work in anatomy. The hands of these students, Semmelweis thought, probably carried infection. So he insisted that the students clean their hands very thoroughly before attending the women giving birth. As a result, the fever practically disappeared from the hospital. Other doctors were insulted when Semmelweis told them they were not clean enough, and they would not believe him.

Like Semmelweis, Lister believed that many patients died because of infection by germs. He insisted on cleanliness when he did operations, and he also used a spray that killed germs in the air. But he realized that it would be even better to avoid the danger of infection by keeping germs out of the operating room. He began using the technique of sterilizing everything that would touch the patient during an operation—that is, he made the instruments completely germfree.

Semmelweis and Lister believed that infections are caused by bacteria, first seen by Leeuwenhoek through his microscope. It was Louis Pasteur who discovered more about the action of bacteria. Pasteur, a chemist, tried to find out what causes fermentation, the process that sours milk and changes wine to vinegar. He decided that bacteria cause these changes.

Then he found that heating wine kills the bacteria and keeps the wine from turning to vinegar. The term "pasteurization," taken from his name, means the process of heating a liquid such as milk until the bacteria are killed.

Pasteur also introduced a vaccination to prevent anthrax, a disease then killing cattle by the thousands. And he discovered a treatment for rabies, often a fatal disease. This remarkable man earned all the honor that he received.

As Pasteur worked in his laboratory to find out more about infection, Edwin Chadwick (1800–90) carried on the same fight in another way. He saw that dirty, crowded living conditions were bad for people's health. When typhoid fever broke out in England, he noticed that the poor died in large numbers, and he began a campaign to improve their way of living. Chadwick wanted better sewers, regular garbage disposal, cleaner streets, and a pure water supply. He led the way to a new attitude by the government toward public health.

In Germany, Robert Koch shared Pasteur's interest in bacteria, and he found new ways to study them through a microscope. His work established bacteriology as a special field of science. Koch proved what doctors since Hippocrates had thought to be true: that tuberculosis is contagious.

▶ MEDICINE IN THE 20TH CENTURY

As medical detectives tried to trace disease to its source, another German supplied medicine with a new tool. Wilhelm Conrad Roentgen (1845–1923) discovered X rays and quickly understood their value to doctors. The newly found rays could go through skin and muscle to make pictures of bones and organs. At first used to see broken bones, X rays soon proved just as useful to find stomach and lung ailments.

A whole concept of mental illness came into being with the work of Sigmund Freud, a Viennese doctor. The branch of medicine in which he worked is called psychoanalysis. Freud was the first to explore the ways in which the unconscious mind works. He found that a patient's dreams and earliest childhood memories often give clues to explain his mental illness.

An 1888 woodcut shows a patient being given ether in Massachusetts General Hospital, Boston. The use of anesthesia was first demonstrated in Boston, in 1846.

In the 19th and 20th centuries, the United States has produced many doctors. Born and trained in Canada, William Osler worked for much of his lifetime in the United States. He was equally famed for helping his patients and for his teaching, much of which he did at the bedside in hospitals. For Osler, as for Sydenham, the direct way to understand a disease was to study the persons affected with it.

William Mayo (1861–1939) and Charles Mayo (1865–1939) made their contribution to 20th-century medicine. Starting as surgeons, the Mayo brothers founded a clinic at Rochester, Minnesota, that offered many types of medical service. Their pattern of a great medical center equipped to deal with every kind of problem has proved useful and has been followed elsewhere.

In the progress of modern surgery a special place belongs to **anesthesia**, which makes the patient unconscious so he does not feel pain during an operation. In 1799 Sir Humphry Davy first suggested having patients breathe nitrous oxide gas, popularly called laughing gas, to put them to sleep before surgery. Horace Wells (1815–48), a Connecticut dentist, had the gas tried on himself when he had a tooth removed and found that he felt no pain. As a result, he began using the gas on his patients.

A Georgia country doctor, Crawford Long (1815–78), is thought to have been the first to use ether as an anesthetic in an operation. Because ether is a liquid, it can be handled more easily than the gas. At about the same time, in 1846, William Thomas Green Morton (1819–68), who had worked with Wells, showed a group of people in Boston how well ether worked. From that point on, its use spread very rapidly and brought new standards to surgery. Sparing patients pain meant that care and neatness could replace speed as the goal of surgery, and a larger range of operations could be done.

In the early 1970's physicians became interested in **acupuncture**, a Chinese medical technique. Western doctors visiting China observed major operations performed on fully conscious patients who felt no pain. Acupuncture has been used in China for treating disease for a long time. Recently Chinese doctors began to use it to produce anesthesia.

In acupuncture fine needles are inserted at certain points under the skin and twirled rapidly. Sometimes a low-voltage electric current is passed through the needles instead of their being twirled. The acupuncturist is trained to know hundreds of specific points on the body's surface that are the places for inserting the needles. The particular points used, and the number of needles, depend on the area in which the feeling of pain is to be deadened.

Acupuncture anesthesia could become an important tool in western medicine. Many doctors would welcome an anesthesia that does not depend on the use of chemicals. These sometimes have unwelcome after-effects in patients. Acupuncture could prove even more useful if it could relieve the pain of headaches, toothaches, and other ailments, as some of its supporters claim it can.

Nobody is sure why acupuncture deadens the feeling of pain. One theory suggests that the acupuncture needles set up a continuous outpouring of painless sensations in the nervous system, blocking the sensations of pain.

Many doctors are impressed with the results of acupuncture anesthesia. But much testing must be done before they can say with certainty that acupuncture belongs among the tools and techniques of modern medicine.

The 20th century has brought a wealth of new scientific knowledge that can be used to help the sick. Perhaps the most important single discovery was that of Sir Alexander Fleming, the British bacteriologist who found the first **antibiotic**, penicillin. Here at last was a substance harmful to many different kinds of bacteria but not harmful to man.

After the discovery of penicillin many other antibiotics were found, of which streptomycin was especially useful. One by one, the diseases caused by bacteria, such as tuberculosis, syphilis, and pneumonia, have been brought almost under control. Surgery is safer also, because infection can be stopped.

Other new drugs have brought relief from many of man's ills. Scientists have learned to make substances that resemble those the body makes itself, such as insulin, cortisone, thyroid extract, and various hormones. These can be used to help people whose bodies do not make these substances properly, and some of them have other uses too.

Drugs that have an effect on the mind have helped many mentally ill persons back to normal life. The most important of these are the tranquilizers, which can keep mentally ill patients from being violent.

As more knowledge about electricity and radioactivity developed, ways to use these forces in medicine soon followed. The electrical impulses in the human brain can be measured with a device called the electroencephalograph. Those in the heart can be mea-

---

THE OATH OF HIPPOCRATES

"I swear by Apollo the physician and Aesculapius and Health and All-Heal and all the gods and goddesses that according to my ability and judgment I will keep this oath and this stipulation—"

This is the beginning of the Oath of Hippocrates, a statement of less than 500 words that has served as a guide for the conduct of doctors for at least 2,000 years.

The Oath is part of the great body of medical works that Hippocrates is commonly thought to have written. No one is sure exactly when the Oath was written. But many historians think it dates from the 5th century B.C., the time in which Hippocrates lived.

In the 10th or 11th century the wording was changed so that there was no mention of the Greek gods. But the ideals of medical conduct expressed in the Oath have remained unchanged through the ages. In many medical schools today the original Oath of Hippocrates still is recited by students as they graduate.

The Oath actually is divided into two main parts. The first part outlines the duties of physicians to their teachers and their teachers' families. Physicians promise to take care of their teachers, if necessary, and to look upon the children of their teachers as brothers and sisters.

The first section had a particular meaning in ancient Greece. The early physicians belonged to family guilds. Each member passed on the art of medicine to his sons. Gradually, people outside the family were admitted to the guilds. The outsiders who were admitted had to promise to assume their share of responsibility for those in the guild. Today physicians carry out this part of the Oath by honoring and respecting their teachers.

In the second part of the Oath, physicians promise to follow certain broad rules in treating the sick. They promise to do whatever they consider best for patients and to avoid doing anything harmful. They promise that they will give no one a "deadly medicine" and will not suggest that anyone take such a medicine.

Physicians pledge, "With purity and with holiness, I will pass my life and practice my art." The physician also makes this promise: "Into whatever houses I enter I will go into them for the benefit of the sick and will abstain from every voluntary act of mischief and corruption."

Physicians finally pledge to keep secret all information about their patients: "Whatever in connection with my professional practice or not in connection with it I see or hear in the life of men which ought not to be spoken of abroad I will not divulge as reckoning that all such should be kept secret."

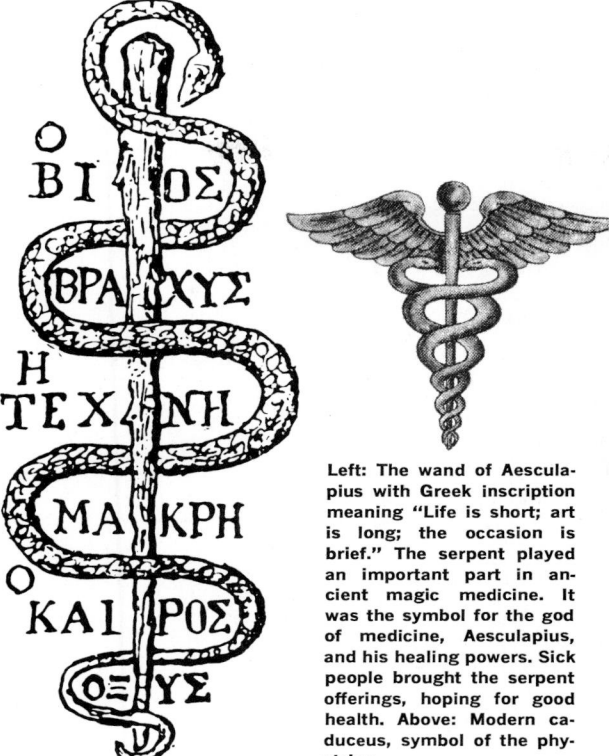

Left: The wand of Aesculapius with Greek inscription meaning "Life is short; art is long; the occasion is brief." The serpent played an important part in ancient magic medicine. It was the symbol for the god of medicine, Aesculapius, and his healing powers. Sick people brought the serpent offerings, hoping for good health. Above: Modern caduceus, symbol of the physician.

Twin babies receiving oral polio vaccine.

sured with the electrocardiograph. These two machines have made it possible for doctors to find injuries or diseased areas in the brain and to observe how a patient's heart is working. There are many new X-ray techniques. Certain radio-opaque substances (chemicals that show up dark on X-ray film) can be given to the patient. X rays of the patient then reveal much information about such areas as the blood vessels or the intestines. An even newer X-ray technique, called CAT (computerized axial tomography), may eventually replace a variety of laboratory and X-ray examinations. In the technique, a computer is used to provide X-ray pictures that show a cross section of the body at any chosen spot.

Measuring blood pressure and giving safe blood transfusions are other medical techniques developed in the 1900's. Scientists have also developed laboratory tests for many diseases. A small sample of blood or a tiny piece of tissue can reveal a wealth of information about the patient's health.

Surgeons have recently made vast progress in replacing parts of the human body. They can put in tubes of synthetic material to replace diseased blood vessels. They can transplant some organs from one person to another. They use tiny electrical devices called pacemakers to keep the heart beating steadily. They can even operate directly on the heart by using a mechanical pump to keep the blood circulating while they work.

Another advance is **microsurgery.** This is surgery performed under a microscope. Tiny scalpels and other tools are used to operate on blood vessels, nerves, and other small structures. Microsurgery makes it possible to reconnect limbs and do difficult brain and eye operations.

Medical progress is often the result of research in many different sciences. Physics, chemistry, biology, and mathematics all contribute to improved human health.

FREDERIC T. JUNG, M.D.
Consultant, American Medical Association

See also ANESTHESIA; ANTIBIOTICS; BIOLOGY; DISEASES (Conquest of Disease); PLANTS, MEDICINAL; VACCINATION AND INOCULATION; articles on outstanding persons in medical history.

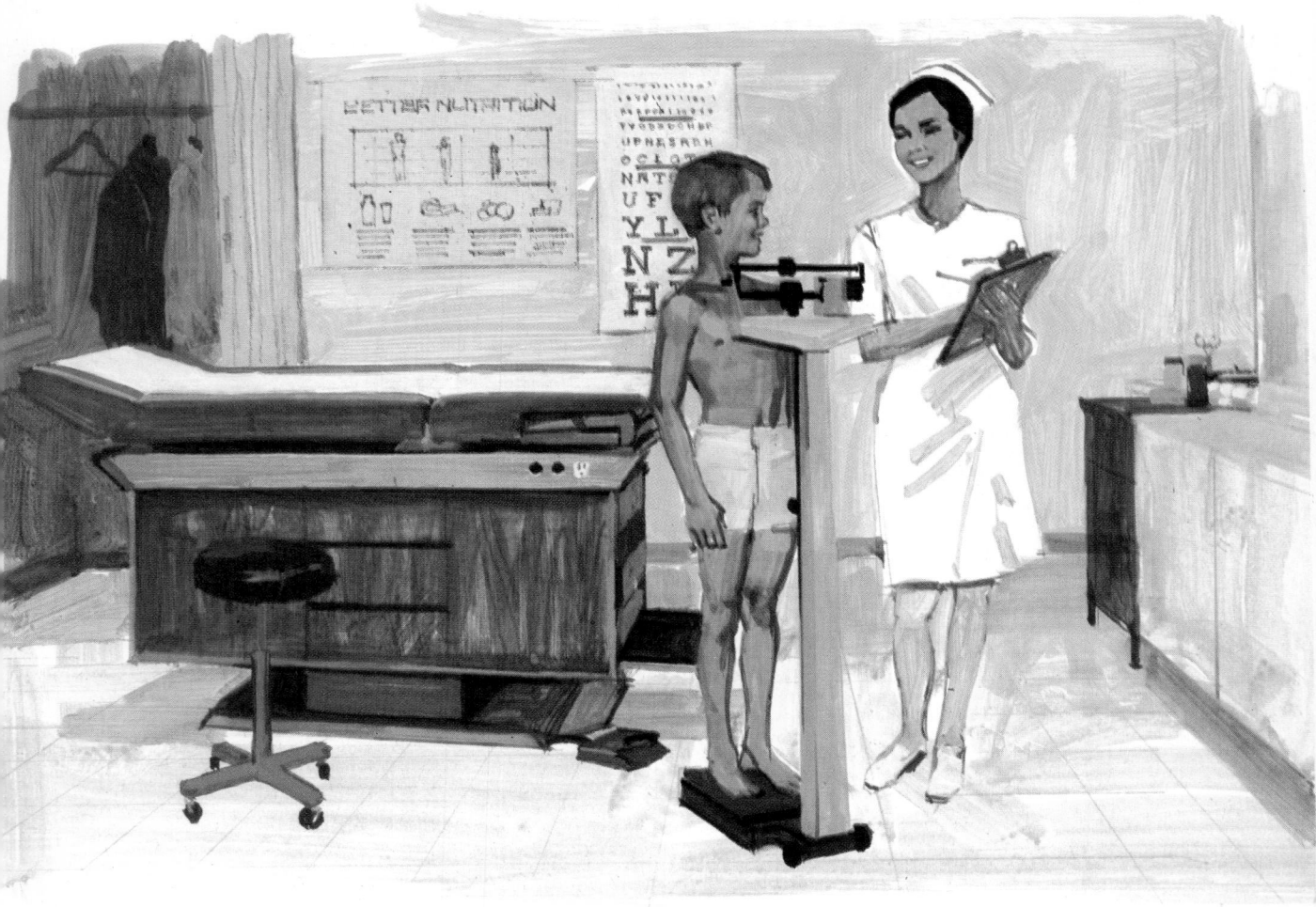

MEDICINE, TOOLS AND TECHNIQUES OF

Doctors are concerned with four broad areas of medical care—prevention of disease, diagnosis, treatment, and rehabilitation. Good health habits, proper nutrition, periodic health examinations, and immunization against contagious diseases, all play a part in **prevention of disease**.

Diagnosis is the identification of the illness, or finding out what is wrong with the patient. **Treatment**, or therapy, is the method used to help cure the disease or injury. **Rehabilitation** begins after the severe part of the patient's illness is over. The aim of rehabilitation is to help the patient recover completely and return to former activities. The doctor knows that the human body has great powers to heal itself. One of the doctor's most important tasks is to help nature in the healing process.

No two illnesses and no two patients are ever exactly alike. Some diseases seem to resemble one another, but symptoms, or signs, can often be misleading. The doctor's experience and observation of patients are guides in deciding the nature of the illness and the treatment that is indicated. Present-day medicine offers many scientific tools that aid the doctor's work.

The doctor who is seeing a patient for the first time needs to know many things about the patient before making a diagnosis. The doctor asks the patient about the chief complaint and past health problems, as well as how the patient feels at the moment. The doctor also needs to know about the health of the patient's family. This information is called a **medical history**. It gives the doctor an understanding of the patient. The doctor learns about the patient's eating, sleeping, exercise, and recreation habits and about whether the patient has pain at any time. Pain can be unpleasant, but it does serve a purpose in the maintenance of health. Pain can be a warning signal to the patient and doctor that something is wrong. Of course, many times a pain is only a passing sensation and does not mean the patient has a disease.

When the doctor is taking a medical history, the patient can be of great help by answering questions as clearly as possible. The patient may wonder at some of the questions the doctor asks, but there is a reason for every question. Every bit of information is important to the doctor in learning everything possible about the patient's health.

PHYSICAL EXAMINATION

After taking the medical history, the doctor performs a careful physical examination of the patient. The trained and experienced eye of the doctor takes in every detail. If necessary, the doctor may order laboratory examinations of body fluids or tissues. Once all the information about the patient has been gathered, the doctor decides what is wrong and what treatment is needed.

The doctor generally begins the examination by noting the patient's height and weight. This information is particularly important with children, for it tells the doctor whether the child is growing properly. A more satisfactory record can be kept when a doctor sees the patient at regular intervals. Every six months the doctor records the height and weight on a special growth chart. It shows the doctor whether the patient is developing normally. If not, there may be some physical condition that should be treated or eating habits that should be changed.

The human body produces a great deal of heat. Muscles are especially good heat producers. Much of this heat is lost through the skin, by breathing out, and by the loss of waste materials. But the body temperature normally changes very little. It is usually 37°C (98.6°F). But it may vary slightly in different people and even in the same person at different times of the day.

A person who has a temperature above normal is said to have a fever. Fever is an important symptom of many diseases. An unusually low temperature may also mean that something is wrong in the temperature-regulating mechanism of the body.

The temperature of a person who is ill is closely watched by the doctor. The amount of change in temperature and the way the changes take place—especially in response to medication—may offer important clues to the diagnosis.

One of the most commonly used doctor's tools, as well as one of the simplest, is the **stethoscope.** It consists of two rubber tubes joined to a small disk- or cone-shaped part, called a chest piece. The two tubes are equipped with earpieces. The earpieces are placed in the doctor's ears, and the chest piece is moved about on the patient's chest. The earpieces keep outside sounds from reaching the doctor's ears. Air moving through the patient's lungs and the thumping sounds of the beating heart can be heard through the earpiece. To the experienced ear, there is a great deal of difference between normal sounds and the sounds that are heard in various kinds of lung or heart diseases.

In examining the chest, the doctor also uses a method called **percussion.** Placing one hand on the patient's chest, the doctor taps one finger with a finger of the other hand. The feel and sound of the tapping tell the doctor whether a lung is healthy or diseased.

The process of breathing in and breathing out is called respiration. The respiratory rate may be as low as 12 breaths per minute or as high as 25. The doctor observes how the patient breathes. Is each breath deep or shallow, quiet or noisy? The answers to these

A stethoscope is used to examine the heart and lungs.

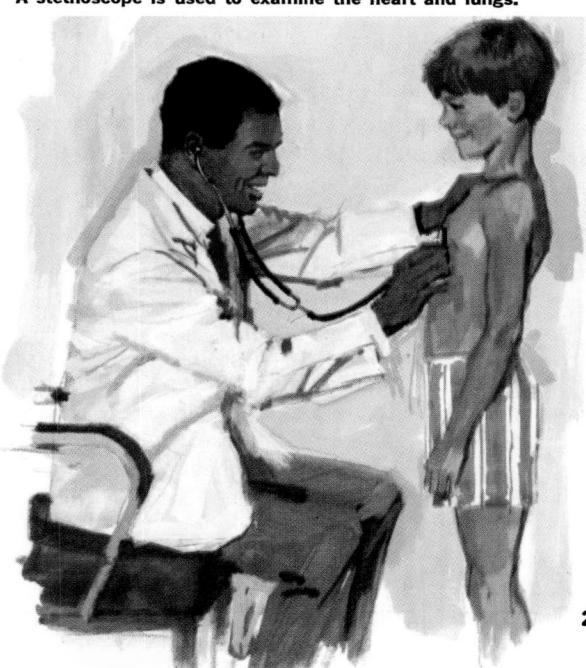

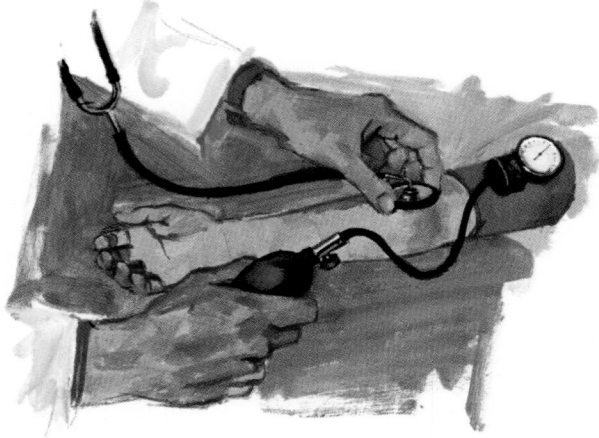
A sphygmomanometer measures the blood pressure.

questions give the doctor information about the condition of the lungs.

Each contraction of the heart is followed by a contraction of the arteries. The contractions can be felt as a pulsation in the places where the arteries are near the surface of the body. The radial artery, which runs along the forearm on the thumb side, is such a place. The doctor counts the pulse by holding two or three fingers gently against the radial artery in the wrist. The number of pulses counted in one minute is exactly the number of times the heart beats in a minute.

The average pulse rate in a healthy person is about 72 beats per minute. Exercise or emotional upsets can cause an increase in the pulse. The pulse rate of very young children is higher than that of older children. Some infections cause an increase in the pulse rate, giving the doctor a clue in making a diagnosis. With a little practice, anybody can take a pulse. But the doctor counts beats and also notes the strength and regularity of the beat. The nature of the beat reveals a great deal about the patient's general health.

Open a faucet and water runs out. Somewhere, perhaps many kilometers away, pumps are putting pressure on the water, forcing it through pipes. Similarly, the heart acts like a pump in the circulatory system. It puts pressure on the blood, forcing it through the blood vessels.

The heart is a hollow, muscular organ about the size of your fist. It is divided into four chambers. When the heart muscle contracts, blood is forced out into blood vessels called arteries. When the heart muscle relaxes, blood enters the heart from blood vessels called veins. The contraction that forces the blood

from the heart is called systole and the relaxation of the heart muscle that follows is called diastole. A blood pressure reading consists of two numbers—for example—125/80. The first number is the systolic pressure, and the second the diastolic. But the numbers for two people cannot be compared as we might compare their weight in kilograms. A doctor must consider many things about the patient before deciding whether the blood pressure is low, normal, or high.

Emotional tension, excitement, or hard exercise can cause a temporary rise in blood pressure. Blood pressure also increases with age in some people. An abnormal blood pressure often alerts a doctor to some disturbance of the kidneys, circulatory system, or nervous system.

To measure blood pressure the doctor uses an instrument called a **sphygmomanometer**. It consists of a long cloth cuff inside of which is a rubber bag. The rubber bag is connected with two tubes. One tube is joined to a rubber bulb that is squeezed to inflate the bag. The other tube is connected with a pressure gauge that measures the pressure in the rubber bag.

Why Must a Fever Thermometer Be Shaken?

A fever, or clinical, thermometer is a glass tube containing mercury, a silvery, liquid metal. The glass tube is marked off in degrees. The thermometer is made so that regardless of the temperature of the surrounding air, the mercury in the tube will remain at the point it registered when last used. To insure an accurate reading when the thermometer is used, the mercury in the glass tube should be below the normal level.

The mercury is contained in the bulging end, or bulb, of the glass tube. The tube has a narrow neck, or constriction, just above the bulb. When the thermometer is placed inside the body, the heat of the body causes the mercury to expand. The column of mercury rises, and the highest point it reaches tells the temperature of the body. The constriction in the tube keeps the mercury at this point until the thermometer is shaken with a quick flip of the wrist. This shaking forces the mercury column down through the constriction, and the thermometer, after being disinfected, is ready for use again.

Clinical thermometers are made in two different forms. One type is for taking the temperature by mouth, and the other for taking the temperature by rectum.

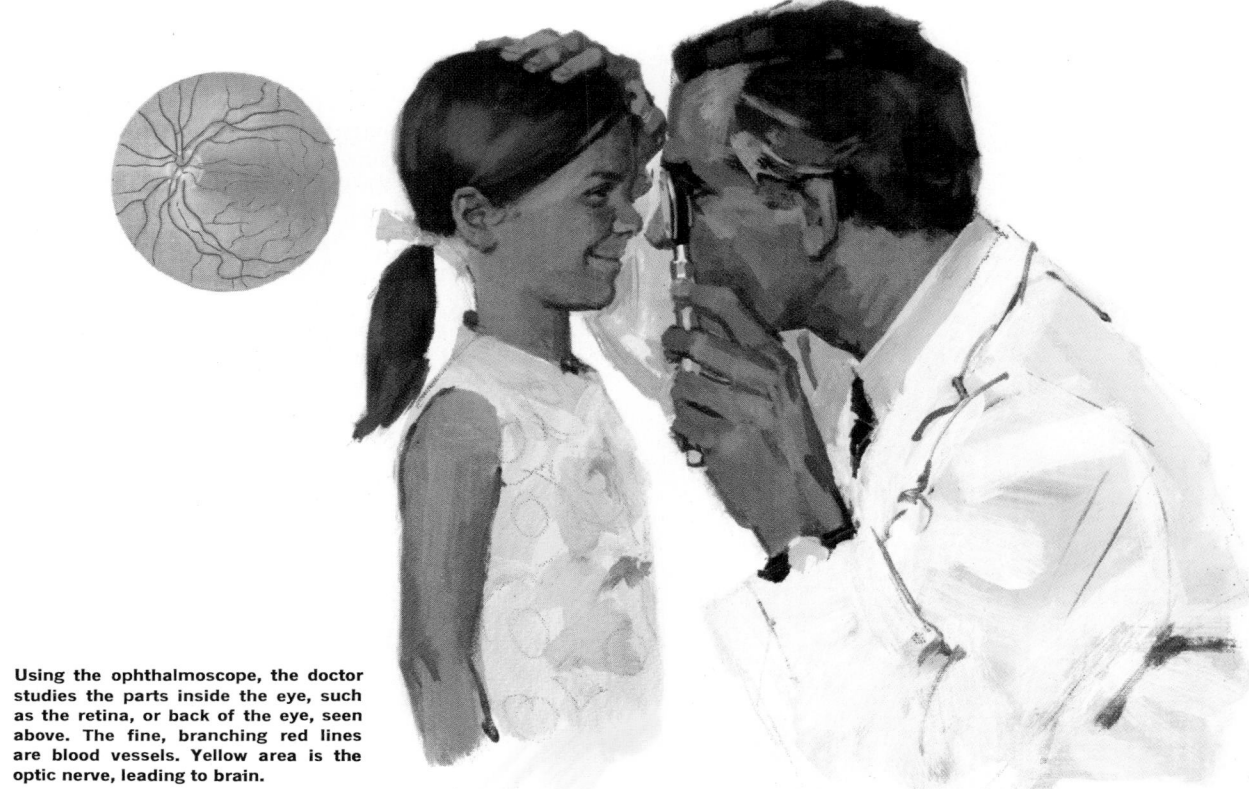

Using the ophthalmoscope, the doctor studies the parts inside the eye, such as the retina, or back of the eye, seen above. The fine, branching red lines are blood vessels. Yellow area is the optic nerve, leading to brain.

The doctor wraps the cuff securely around the patient's arm above the elbow. With the stethoscope, the doctor listens for the sound of the pulse in the main artery of the arm, which can be detected in the bend of the elbow. The doctor inflates the bag. The cuff tightens firmly around the patient's arm. The pressure of the cuff squeezes on the artery as well as on the arm, and soon the artery is squeezed shut. No blood runs through it. At this point no pulse sounds are heard through the stethoscope.

The rubber bag is equipped with a valve that enables the doctor to let the air out of the bag slowly. The pressure decreases and the doctor hears the thumping sound of the blood as it again starts to move in the artery. The pressure shown on the gauge at this point is the same as the pressure the heart puts on the blood each time it contracts. This is the systolic pressure.

The doctor continues to listen to the sound of the pulse as more air is let out of the bag. The sound stops suddenly. The pressure registered on the gauge at this point is the pressure on the blood when the heart muscle relaxes. This is the diastolic pressure.

To examine the front portion of the eyes is a simple matter. Any inflammation or unusual appearance of the eyes or eyelids is seen instantly. It is important to observe the back portion, or fundus, of the eyes. The doctor uses an instrument called the **ophthalmoscope** to see inside the eyes. The wheel-like top of the ophthalmoscope holds a set of tiny lenses that can be focused on various parts inside the eye.

The iris is the colored portion of the eye. The opening in the center of the iris is called the pupil. Just beyond the pupil lies the lens, which focuses light coming through the pupil onto the retina at the back of the eye. The doctor aims the light of the ophthalmoscope through the pupil. The light beam shines through the lens, revealing the liquid that surrounds the lens and the retina. The doctor can also see the optic nerve. The condition of various parts of the eye can be a clue to disease in other parts of the body.

A strong light is needed for an examination of the nose and throat. Doctors may use a flashlight or a head mirror, a device that looks like the round rearview mirror of an automobile. The movable head mirror is at-

An otoscope is used to examine the inside of the ear.

tached to a band that fits around the head, allowing the doctor's hand to be free for using other instruments. The doctor looks through a small hole in the center of the mirror. A bright light placed at the side of the patient shines on the head mirror, which then reflects the light into the patient's nose or mouth.

The doctor inspects the tongue and the smooth lining inside the mouth for the presence of disease. The patient's teeth are examined for normal development. With a flat instrument, or stick, called a **tongue depressor,** the doctor presses the tongue down in order to see the back of the throat and the tonsils.

To make sure that the inside of the nose is normal and that there are no obstructions or inflammation, the doctor looks into the two nasal passages.

A special instrument called an **otoscope** is used to examine the ears. The otoscope has a small funnel-shaped attachment that fits into the patient's ear. A magnifying lens and a light built into the instrument enable the doctor to see clearly a magnified image of the ear canal and the eardrum. The doctor looks for any inflammation or blockage in the ear.

The stethoscope and percussion are used for listening to sounds within the abdomen. But the usual method for examining the abdominal organs is **palpation.** Palpation is a method of feeling with the fingers and the palms of the hand. The doctor can feel the stomach, intestines, liver, and other organs.

A long tubelike instrument, called an **endoscope,** enables the doctor to get a firsthand look at the inside of the stomach and the intestines. The doctor may also order special X rays of these organs, called a **gastro-intestinal** examination, or **GI series.** Soft body parts, such as the intestines and stomach, do not show up sharply on ordinary X-ray pictures, as do bones. To get a clear picture of the stomach and intestines, the doctor has the patient drink a mixture of water and a substance called barium sulfate. Barium has the special property of showing up white on an X-ray picture. It clings to the walls of the stomach and intestines, which then appear as outlines on the X-ray picture. The doctor may use the **fluoroscope.** This is an X-ray machine that permits the doctor to observe the actions of the organs in motion. Another special kind of X ray, called **CAT** (computerized axial tomography), gives the doctor a view of a cross section of the abdomen. CAT can also be used to examine other parts of the body, such as the brain. Similar views can be obtained with **PET** (positron emission tomography). The images reflect the distribution in the body of a positron-emitting substance given to the patient by the doctor. (Positrons are subatomic particles.)

▶ELECTRONIC DEVICES FOR DIAGNOSIS

The **electroencephalograph** (EEG) is a machine used when a doctor wants special information about a patient's brain. The test is a painless procedure. Small electrodes (metal contacts) are applied to different parts of the head. The EEG measures the tiny electric currents that the brain produces. Eight or more automatic styluses, or pens, trace a record of these "brain waves" from as many areas of the brain on graph paper. An unusual wave pattern may indicate some disorder in a particular area of the brain. Highly specialized training and experience are needed to interpret the meaning of the EEG tracings, which are called **electroencephalograms**.

The **electrocardiograph** machine (ECG) is used in examinations of the heart. It detects and records the electric currents produced by a beating heart, just as the electroencephalograph records the brain waves. The electrodes are applied to various parts of the chest, arms, and legs. An automatic stylus records minute electrical currents on graph paper. The ECG tracing is called an **electrocardiogram**, and from it the doctor can tell if the heart is normal.

An electronic device called an **ultrasonoscope** uses ultrasound as an aid in diagnosis. Ultrasound is sound caused by vibrations so fast they cannot be heard by humans. The ultrasonoscope produces ultrasound with 1,000,000 to 10,000,000 vibrations per second. Like ordinary sound, ultrasound can cause an echo when it hits an object and is reflected. The echo cannot be heard, but it can be detected by the ultrasonoscope, and can be seen on a tube like a TV screen.

A doctor using this machine may detect small changes in parts of the brain. Such changes could be caused by a blood clot or some other abnormal condition. The ultrasonoscope has also been used to observe the motion of valves in the heart and to make careful examinations of unborn babies without harming the babies.

▶ **LABORATORY TESTS**

The physical examination provides the doctor with a great deal of information about the patient. As a result of the physical examination, the doctor may want to have laboratory tests made on the patient's blood or other body fluids.

The patient's blood is often a source of information needed to make a diagnosis. **Blood counts** are extremely useful. The doctor takes a few drops of blood, usually by pricking the patient's finger. A drop of blood is examined under a microscope. The number and types of blood cells that are seen are a clue to some infections and to disorders such as anemia and cancer.

When blood chemistry tests are to be done,

a larger sampling of blood is needed. For this, the blood is taken from the arm vein. In the past, a separate test had to be performed for each substance, such as sugar, uric acid, cholesterol, and others. But electronic devices make it possible for modern laboratories to perform 12 to 14 different tests automatically, using just one sample of blood.

Testing a sample of the patient's urine is called **urinalysis**. This test reveals the presence of some disorders, such as diabetes. A urinalysis is an essential part of every medical examination.

In some infections it is important to identify the germ that is responsible for the infection. To determine this, the doctor may order a **bacteriological examination**. Samples of infected tissue, blood, or sputum are examined under a microscope. Part of the sample is usually placed in a culture medium. This is a liquid or gelatin substance in which bacteria or other organisms grow and multiply, so they can be studied further.

Sometimes a small piece of tissue is removed from the body and sent to the pathology laboratory. There it is examined under a microscope. This is called a **biopsy**.

▶ **IMMUNIZATION**

Thanks to immunization, a number of infectious diseases that once took many lives are now almost medical curiosities. Immunization helps the body to defend itself against invading disease germs.

When the body is attacked by disease germs, it makes substances called antibodies. The antibodies fight the germs and the poisons, or toxins, that the germs produce.

Some diseases can be prevented by purposely putting the disease germs or their toxins into the body. This is called a **vaccination**, or **inoculation**, and the material is called a vaccine. In some types of vaccine the germs or toxins have been weakened to make them harmless. In other vaccines, the germs are dead. But even the weak or dead germs or toxins cause the body to make antibodies. Later on, if the body is invaded by the germs causing these diseases, it is protected by the antibodies needed to fight that disease.

There is a quick way to give the patient some short-term protection against infection. This is to give an injection of blood proteins, called globulins. Antibodies are globulins. There are many antibodies within the globulin fraction of the blood. Globulins are obtained from blood plasma.

Most vaccines are given by injection. Immunization procedures can provide protection against a wide variety of diseases, including polio, diphtheria, tetanus, measles, mumps, whooping cough, and one kind of pneumonia.

During the first year of life, a baby is usually given vaccines against a number of diseases. The older child is given booster shots. The boosters strengthen the immunity produced by the original vaccination.

▶ SOME LIFE-SAVING TECHNIQUES

A few hospitals have a special kind of operating room, called a **hyperbaric chamber**. It looks like a huge tank car without wheels. The air pressure inside such a chamber can

HEART—LUNG MACHINE

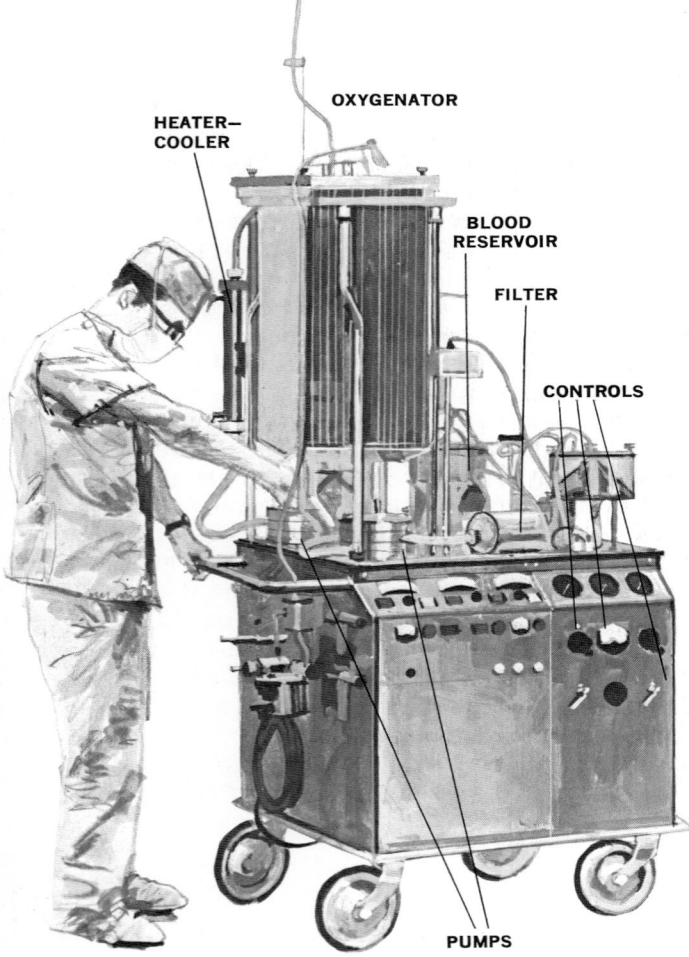

HEATER—COOLER

OXYGENATOR

BLOOD RESERVOIR

FILTER

CONTROLS

PUMPS

be raised to three or four times the normal air pressure. In addition, measured amounts of oxygen or other gases can be pumped into the chamber.

The tanklike chambers are especially valuable for doing certain kinds of operations, such as those on the brain. Brain cells cannot live more than a few minutes without oxygen. The blood supply to the brain must be stopped during the operation so the surgeon can work. The patient is in danger if the operation cannot be done quickly and the blood supply restored.

Hyperbaric chambers are the answer to this problem. The surgeon orders high air pressure with extra oxygen for the chamber. The patient's cells, including the brain cells, build up a reserve of oxygen. Now the brain cells can live a longer time after their blood supply is stopped. In the chambers surgeons can do operations that require extra time.

Hyperbaric chambers are also used in cases of carbon monoxide poisoning. The victim must be supplied with large amounts of oxygen. Another use for the chamber is in treating stubborn infections caused by anaerobic bacteria. These bacteria live without a supply of air. Oxygen kills them, but the concentration of oxygen normally found in the blood is too weak to destroy the bacteria. The high oxygen concentration provided by the hyperbaric chamber has helped to cure many such stubborn infections.

Millions of lives have been saved by **blood transfusions** for people who have lost blood through illness, injury, or during surgical operations. At first, blood was taken from one person, the donor, and injected directly into a vein of the person who needed it, the recipient. Today, nearly all hospitals have a blood bank, or one nearby that they can use.

The blood bank stores blood taken from donors. It is called whole blood. The blood is in glass or plastic containers, which are kept refrigerated. A chemical in the container prevents the blood from clotting.

Whole blood is made up of a liquid portion called plasma and a solid portion made up of red blood cells, white blood cells, and platelets. There are some disadvantages in using whole blood for transfusions. It must be used within two or three weeks. The blood must match the recipient's blood group. There are also many times when only a particular portion of the blood is needed.

Medical scientists developed ways to overcome these disadvantages. They learned how to separate the blood into its parts. These parts are known as blood derivatives.

One of these derivatives is fibrinogen, which hastens blood clotting. Red blood cells, another derivative, are used in treating patients with certain types of anemia.

Plasma is also a derivative. It first came into wide use during World War II. Plasma is needed for patients who have lost a great deal of blood or have been severely burned. It can be stored longer than whole blood. Much plasma is dried and frozen. It can be stored for a year or more in this form. Sterilized water is added when the plasma is to be used. This can be done easily.

Researchers have also developed chemical solutions that can be used as substitutes for plasma. They are not perfect substitutes, but they have some of the effects of plasma. They are easy to obtain and much cheaper than human plasma. They are often used when patients have lost large amounts of blood.

▶ **NEW ORGANS FOR OLD**

A defective automobile battery or starter is easily replaced with a good one. Doctors hoped for a long time to find ways of replacing defective or injured parts of the human body. Today many thousands of people are enjoying life with the help of special machines, artificial body organs, or real organs obtained from other people.

One of the most successful of the lifesaving machines is used for people whose kidneys are defective. Their kidneys, unlike normal ones, are unable to remove certain poisonous wastes from the blood. The kidney machine pumps the patient's blood through special filters for several hours until the wastes have been removed. Because few patients can afford these very costly **renal dialysis** treatments, the U.S. Congress in 1972 passed a law to provide government funds to pay for the treatments.

Many kidney patients live more or less normally with the help of a healthy kidney transplanted from a human donor. Livers, lungs, and hearts from persons who have just died have also been transplanted to recipients whose own organs can no longer keep them alive.

Transplanting organs is a difficult operation, but teams of surgeons can do it. The biggest problem is not the operation but the way in which the recipient's body reacts. The body produces substances called antibodies. These fight off the "foreign" organ by destroying its cells. This rejection process is the same one used by the body to fight off "foreign" disease germs.

The time taken for rejection varies. In kidney transplants, which are the most successful, rejection is slowed if the donor and recipient are close relatives, and slowed still more if identical twins. Doctors can slow down rejection by using X rays and certain drugs to stop production of antibodies. But a lack of antibodies means that the patient cannot fight infections. Scientists are trying to solve the rejection problem.

Some heart defects are cured by placing artificial valves or other artificial parts within the heart. Serious disturbances in the heart's rhythmic beat are corrected by a small battery-operated **pacemaker** worn by the patient. The pacemaker sends electrical impulses to the heart, causing it to beat at a proper and regular rate.

Until recently operations on the heart were especially difficult because the beating action of the heart is needed to pump blood constantly to all parts of the body. Yet an operation to repair a defect within the heart usually cannot be done unless the heart's pumping action is stopped.

Pump-oxygenators, usually called **heart-lung machines**, were developed to meet this problem. The patient's blood is circulated through the machine. Wastes in the blood are removed, and oxygen is added. A pump does the work of circulating the blood through the body. This allows the surgeon to stop the heart safely during the operation.

R. CANNON ELEY, M.D.
Former Chief of Pediatrics
Roger Williams Hospital
Providence, Rhode Island

See also ANTIBODIES AND ANTIGENS; BLOOD; BODY, HUMAN; DOCTORS; IMMUNOLOGY; MEDICAL LABORATORY TESTS; MEDICINE, HISTORY OF; TRANSFUSION, BLOOD; VACCINATION AND INOCULATION.

MEDIEVAL PERIOD. See MIDDLE AGES.

Left: Tripoli, a leading city in Libya and an important North African port on the Mediterranean. Above: Piraeus, the port of Athens, Greece, crowded with fishing boats. Below: Positano, a resort on the Tyrrhenian Sea, an arm of the Mediterranean.

MEDITERRANEAN SEA

The Greeks called it the Great Sea. The Romans, whose empire extended far beyond the shores of the sea, called it *Mare Internum*, "the Inland Sea." Today it is known as the Mediterranean Sea, which means "in the midst of lands."

No sea has played a more important role in the history of Western man. Civilization spread westward from Mesopotamia and the Nile valley to the islands of the Mediterranean and to western Europe. Many centuries later, in the busy Mediterranean port of Genoa, the young Christopher Columbus got his first taste of life as a sailor.

The Mediterranean Sea is nearly land-locked between Europe, Asia, and Africa. In the west the narrow Strait of Gibraltar connects it with the Atlantic Ocean. Its eastern outlet, to the Red Sea, is by way of the Suez Canal.

Several smaller bodies of water that are large enough to be called seas are part of the Mediterranean. They are the Ligurian, Tyrrhenian, Adriatic, Ionian, and Aegean and the Black Sea. The Sea of Azov, an arm of the Black Sea, is usually considered a part of the Mediterranean. The Bosporus, the Sea of Marmara, and the Dardanelles connect the Black Sea and the Aegean Sea.

The Mediterranean has an area of about 1,145,000 square miles. Its greatest length from east to west is 2,400 miles. Its maximum width is about 1,000 miles. At its deepest point the sea is about 14,450 feet deep.

The Mediterranean is a sea of many islands and island groups. The largest islands are Sicily, Sardinia, Corsica, Crete, Cyprus, and Majorca. The island groups include the Balearic, the Ionian, and the Dodecanese and the Cyclades.

The northern coast of the Mediterranean is deeply indented and often mountainous. The Asian and African coasts are more regular and have fewer natural harbors. Earthquakes often shake the entire region, and there are several active volcanoes, including Stromboli, Vesuvius, and Etna.

The salt content of the Mediterranean is higher than that of the Atlantic Ocean and the Black Sea. One reason for this is the sunny climate, which speeds up the rate of evaporation. Another reason is the small number of freshwater rivers that empty into the sea. Important rivers that flow directly into the Mediterranean are the Ebro, the Rhone, the Po, the Tiber, and the Nile. During the dry summer months the recovery of salt along the coasts and bays of the Mediterranean is the basis of a profitable industry.

Climate. The European and part of the African and Asiatic seacoasts have a Mediterranean climate. Summers are usually dry and warm; winters are mild and often rainy. The African and Asian coasts have somewhat higher temperatures.

Some Mediterranean winds are well-known for the sudden effect they have on the region's climate. The **mistral** of the lower Rhone and the **bora** of the Adriatic are cold winter winds that can damage crops. During the spring the **sirocco**, a hot, dry wind from the Sahara, blows across the southern Mediterranean and causes the temperature to rise.

Fisheries. Although many kinds of fish live in the sea, they are too few in number to support a large-scale fishing industry. The only fish of commercial importance is the tuna. Sponges are found in the eastern Mediterranean, and coral near Naples. Anchovies, eels, sardines, lobsters, crabs, prawns, cuttlefish, oysters, and mussels are caught locally.

▶ **INDUSTRIES AND PRODUCTS**

Most of the people who live along the shores of the Mediterranean earn a living by farming. There is an important export trade in citrus fruits, tobacco, olive and other vegetable oils, cotton, wine, and winter wheat. Many people work part- or full-time as fishermen, but the fishing is local and small-scale. Industry has not been highly developed, except in a few places, such as Israel and parts of Italy and Algeria. Mines are worked throughout the Mediterranean region.

The Mediterranean is a key link in the trading route between Europe and Asia via the Suez Canal.

Shipping is not a major industry in Mediterranean countries, except for Greece and Italy. Their merchant fleets are among the largest in the world. Many passenger ships cruise on the Mediterranean, stopping at ports along the way for people to get off and go sight-seeing.

The Mediterranean attracts thousands of

MEDITERRANEAN SEA

tourists every year, especially in winter and early spring. Some come to visit the region's many historic places. Others come to sun themselves on the beaches or to swim and skin dive in the warm, calm, and clear waters of the sea. Leading resort areas are the Balearic Islands; the French and Italian Rivieras; the Costa Brava in Spain; Capri and Taormina; the Dalmatian coast of Yugoslavia; the coasts of Greece, Lebanon, and Israel; and the Black Sea coasts of Bulgaria, Rumania, and the Union of Soviet Socialist Republics.

▶ **HISTORY**

The first histories of the Mediterranean were the myths and legends that told of wars and adventures. The Greek Homer and the Roman Vergil wrote poems about the Trojan War and the subsequent wanderings of Odysseus and Aeneas in the Mediterranean. Perhaps Odysseus and Aeneas were real people. Archeologists have found the ruined sites of some of the places they visited—places that could be reached only by sea. But no one is sure which people first explored the sea and its many basins. It is known that the Phoenicians were among the first to sail beyond the Pillars of Hercules into the Atlantic. During the Greek and especially the Roman eras, colonies were founded on the shores of the Mediterranean, trade routes were developed, and natural resources were tapped. Under the Romans the Mediterranean was virtually a Roman lake.

After the Roman Empire fell in the 5th century A.D., three separate cultures developed in the area. They were the German-Roman, the Slav-Byzantine, and the Arab-Islam empires. During this period city-states, such as Venice, Pisa, and Genoa, grew into important centers of trade.

The Mediterranean lost some of its importance in the late 15th and 16th centuries. As a result of the discovery of lands in the Western Hemisphere, nations facing the Atlantic Ocean grew in importance and power. Meanwhile, the Turks took control of large areas in the Mediterranean region. Piracy became widespread in the western end of the sea, because there was no strong sea power to put an end to it. After the opening of the Suez Canal in 1869, the Mediterranean again became a highway of commerce. The sea became a lifeline to Great Britain's eastern colonies. Gibraltar, Malta, Cyprus, and Port Said were used as bases to protect British commerce. During World Wars I and II control of the sea was very important to the Allied powers. It was vital for Great Britain, which imported most of its oil from the Middle East.

With few exceptions, all the Mediterranean colonies of European countries became independent after World War II. Cyprus, Malta, and the North African colonies have become independent nations. In 1956 Egypt took control of the Universal Company of the Suez Canal from Great Britain and France, and has continued to operate the waterway.

ANTHONY SAS
Madison College (Virginia)

MELBOURNE

Melbourne is Australia's second largest city. It is the capital, largest city, and chief port of the state of Victoria. With a population of nearly 3,000,000, it is an important world metropolis.

Though a large part of Melbourne is a bustling business and industrial area, the city also contains many quiet tree-lined streets with homes fronted by lovely gardens. Broad, attractive avenues are lined with fine, stately buildings. The city's climate is temperate and comfortable, with an average annual temperature of 58°F (14°C).

▶ TRADE, FINANCE, AND INDUSTRY

With its broad, modern harbor Melbourne is one of Australia's major ports. Docks are situated in Melbourne itself and also in Port Melbourne and Williamstown, both of which lie nearby on Hobson's Bay. Because of its location Melbourne is an important agricultural depot.

Melbourne is highly industrialized. Its modern factories produce railway rolling stock (locomotives, passenger and freight cars), power-station equipment, structural steel, and other heavy engineering equipment. Because many leading banks and insurance companies have made Melbourne their headquarters, the city is recognized as the financial center of Australia. The Melbourne Stock Exchange is the largest stock exchange on the continent.

▶ TRANSPORTATION

Melbourne is a vital transportation center. Highways and railway lines connect the city with Sydney, Brisbane, and Adelaide. The new international airport at Tullamarine, on the outskirts of the city, is one of the most modern in the world.

▶ CULTURE AND RECREATION

Melbourne has many excellent theaters and art galleries. The National Gallery of Victoria has one of the finest collections of paintings in the Commonwealth of Nations. The city also maintains an excellent library system and several fine museums, such as the Museum of Applied Science and the National Museum. Centers of learning include the University of Melbourne, the Royal Australian College of Surgeons, the Australian Institute of International Affairs, the Conservatorium of Music, and the Walter and Eliza Hall Institute of Medical Research.

Australians are a sports-minded people. The Melbourne Cup is one of the world's greatest horse races. It is run at Flemington Race Course at Melbourne each year on the first Tuesday in November, a day of national celebration. Melbourne is also the home of the "Australian Rules," an Australian brand of football. In 1956 the city was the site of the Olympic Games.

▶ PLACES OF INTEREST

One attractive sight in Melbourne is the natural beauty of the Botanic Gardens. In Fitzroy Gardens stands a cottage that once belonged to the family of Captain James Cook, the first European to visit eastern Australia. The cottage was brought to Australia from Yorkshire, England, in 1934. Other places of interest are the Victoria Parliament House; the Royal Mint; the Shrine of Remembrance, a World War I memorial; and the recently completed Victorian Arts Center.

▶ HISTORY

Melbourne was first settled in 1835, by two groups of settlers from Tasmania, an island that lies south of Victoria. The city was named in 1837 in honor of Lord Melbourne, prime minister of Great Britain at the time. The discovery of gold at Ballarat and other places in 1851 changed Melbourne into a boom city. From 1901 to 1927, Melbourne was the seat of the federal government pending the development of Canberra. When Parliament House opened in Canberra, the seat of the national government was transferred there. Sydney has surpassed Melbourne as Australia's largest city. But Melbourne is still a major center of commerce, transportation, and culture.

Reviewed by SHARYN KALNINS
Australian Capital Territory Schools Authority

MELONS

The name "melon" refers to the fruit of several closely related plants. Melons belong to the cucurbit family, which also includes cucumbers, pumpkins, squashes, watermelons, and gourds. The plants are either climbing or trailing vines. The leaves may be round, pointed, or folded. Each type of melon has its own leaf shape. The flowers are small and yellow. The fruits are covered with a thick skin, or rind, that may be smooth, wrinkled, warty, netted, or ridged.

Besides watermelons, there are two other main kinds of melons—**summer melons** and **winter melons.** The summer melons, or **muskmelons,** grow quickly during the warm summer months. In the United States, many of the muskmelon varieties are also called **cantaloupe.** The winter melons take most of the summer to grow. Unlike the muskmelons, winter melons may be stored for a few weeks after they are ripe and then sold in the fall. **Casaba, honeydew, Crenshaw,** and **Persian** are the main varieties of winter melons.

History. Melons are generally believed to be native to the Middle East. They were among the fruits grown in early Egypt. The Romans were the first Europeans to grow melons. During the late 1400's, they were introduced to France. Melons were brought to the Americas by Columbus in 1494. They spread rapidly throughout the Americas and were widely grown by the native peoples.

How Melons Are Grown. Melons need a long, warm growing season. They will grow in most soils but do best in sandy and sandy-loam types of soil. Before the melon seeds are planted, the soil must be well fertilized. When the vines are 45 to 60 centimeters (18 to 24 inches) long, more fertilizer is added.

If the soil is a type that drains well, the seeds are planted in hills on level ground. If the soil drains poorly, higher, raised beds are used. Plastic or waxed paper is used to protect the plants from frosts in the early part of the season. In some places, melons are planted in greenhouses, hothouses, or cold frames. After the danger of frost is past, they are transplanted to the field.

For the market, muskmelons are harvested at the "full slip" stage. This is when the stem separates completely from the melon under slight pressure. Muskmelons grown in home gardens are usually picked when the rind develops a yellowish background color. Casaba, Crenshaw, Persian, and honeydew melons do not separate from the vine when ripe and must be cut with a knife. Watermelons are not harvested until they give a muffled sound when thumped. Harvested melons must be handled very carefully to avoid being bruised.

RAYMON E. WEBB
United States Department of Agriculture

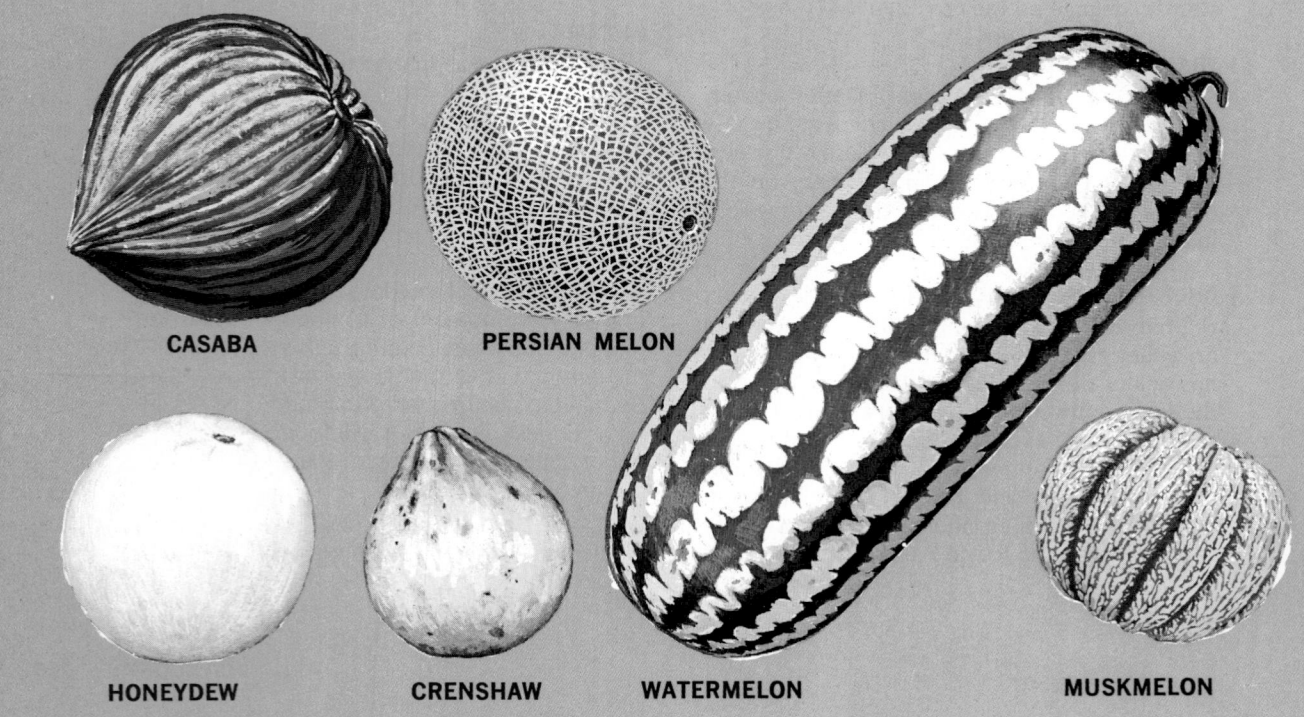

CASABA   PERSIAN MELON

HONEYDEW   CRENSHAW   WATERMELON   MUSKMELON

MELVILLE, HERMAN (1819–1891)

Herman Melville is best known for his novels of the sea. The greatest of these, *Moby Dick,* is not only an exciting adventure story but a complex novel of ideas.

Herman Melville was born in New York City on August 1, 1819. His father was a well-to-do merchant whose business collapsed in 1830. The family then moved to Albany, New York, the home of Mrs. Melville's parents. After his father died in 1832, Herman tried to earn money for his family by working in his uncle's bank and later as a teacher. In 1839 he went to seek his fortune at sea as a member of the crew of a merchant ship.

In 1841, Melville sailed on the whaler *Acushnet* and started on the greatest adventure of his life. When the ship docked at Nuku-Hiva, one of the Marquesas Islands, in 1842, Melville jumped ship and fled into the jungle. He stayed briefly with a native tribe before sailing on an Australian whaler to Tahiti and on another whaler to Hawaii. He reached home in 1844 after spending 14 months on a U.S. Navy frigate.

Melville immediately began to write of his experiences. *Typee* (1846), *Omoo* (1847), *Mardi* (1849), *Redburn* (1849), and *White-Jacket* (1850) followed each other quickly. In 1847, Melville married Elizabeth Shaw, and in 1850 he moved his family to Pittsfield, Massachusetts. There he became a friend of the writer Nathaniel Hawthorne.

When *Moby Dick* was published in 1851, it disappointed readers who preferred Melville's simpler early novels. Its commercial failure was a severe disappointment to Melville. *Pierre,* a novel published in 1852, was even less successful. But Melville continued to write poetry and short stories. *Benito Cereno* and *Bartleby the Scrivener* are among his finest stories.

After attempting unsuccessfully to earn a living by giving public lectures, Melville took a position as a customs inspector in New York City, where he worked until his retirement in 1885. He died on September 28, 1891. The manuscript for *Billy Budd,* a short novel, was discovered among Melville's papers after his death and was published in 1924.

Reviewed by ERWIN HESTER
East Carolina University

Herman Melville drew on his own experiences as a sailor for his novels. *Moby Dick* was a failure when it was first published but is now regarded as a masterpiece.

▶MOBY DICK

Melville's story of Moby Dick, the great white whale, is told by Ishmael, a schoolmaster who signs on a whaling ship, the *Pequod.* Its captain is Ahab, who is obsessed with finding and killing Moby Dick, the great white whale that bit off Ahab's leg on an earlier voyage. When Ishmael arrives at the port of New Bedford, he finds he must share a room in the Spouter Inn with a man who appears to be a savage cannibal. But Queequeg turns out to be the son of a king. In the following passage, Ishmael tells Queequeg's story.

A Sag Harbour ship visited his father's bay, and Queequeg sought a passage to Christian lands. But the ship, having her full complement of seamen, spurned his suit; and not all the King his father's influence could prevail. But Queequeg vowed a vow. Alone in his canoe, he paddled off to a distant strait, which he knew the ship must pass through when she quitted the island. On one side was a coral reef; on the other a low tongue of land, covered with mangrove thickets that grew out into the water. Hiding his canoe, still afloat, among these thick-

Moby Dick is a novel of ideas, but it is also filled with adventure. This illustration by Rockwell Kent shows the crew of the *Pequod* battling a whale.

ets, with its prow seaward, he sat down in the stern, paddle low in hand; and when the ship was gliding by, like a flash he darted out; gained her side; with one backward dash of his foot capsized and sank his canoe; climbed up the chains; and throwing himself at full length upon the deck, grappled a ring-bolt there, and swore not to let it go, though hacked in pieces.

In vain the captain threatened to throw him overboard; suspended a cutlass over his naked wrists; Queequeg was the son of a King, and Queequeg budged not. Struck by his desperate dauntlessness, and his wild desire to visit Christendom, the captain at last relented, and told him he might make himself at home. But this fine young savage—this sea Prince of Wales, never saw the captain's cabin. They put him down among the sailors, and made a whaleman of him. But like the Czar Peter content to toil in the shipyards of foreign cities, Queequeg disdained no seeming ignominy, if thereby he might happily gain the power of enlightening his untutored countrymen. For at bottom—so he told me—he was actuated by a profound desire to learn among the Christians the arts whereby to make his people still happier than they were; and more than that still better than they were. But, alas! the practices of whalemen soon convinced him that even Christians could be both miserable and wicked; infinitely more so than all his father's heathens. Arrived at last in old Sag Harbour; and seeing what the sailors did there; and then going on to Nantucket, and seeing how they spent their wages in *that* place also, poor Queequeg gave it up for lost. Thought he, it's a wicked world in all meridians; I'll die a pagan.

And thus an old idolater at heart, he yet lived among these Christians, wore their clothes, and tried to talk their gibberish. Hence the queer ways about him, though now some time from home.

By hints, I asked him whether he did not propose going back, and having a coronation; since he might now consider his father dead and gone, he being very old and feeble at the last accounts. He answered no, not yet; and added that he was fearful Christianity, or rather Christians, had unfitted him for ascending the pure and undefiled throne of thirty pagan Kings before him. But by and by, he said, he would return,—as soon as he felt himself baptized again. For the nonce, however, he proposed to sail about, and sow his wild oats in all four oceans. They had made a harpooneer of him, and that barbed iron was in lieu of a sceptre now.

I asked him what might be his immediate purpose, touching his future movements. He answered, to go to sea again, in his old vocation. Upon this, I told him that whaling was my own design, and informed him of my intention to sail out of Nantucket, as being the most promising port for an adventurous whaleman to embark from. He at once resolved to accompany me to that island, ship aboard the same vessel, get into the same watch, the same boat, the same mess with me, in short to share my every hap; with both my hands in his, boldly dip into the potluck of both worlds. To all this I joyously assented; for besides the affection I now felt for Queequeg, he was an experienced harpooneer, and as such, could not fail to be of great usefulness to one, who, like me, was wholly ignorant of the mysteries of whaling, though well acquainted with the sea, as known to merchant seamen.

MEMORY. See Learning; Brain.

MEMPHIS

Memphis, Tennessee's largest city, is situated in the southwestern corner of the state. It stands atop a high bluff overlooking the Mississippi River. The "Bluff City" has a rich history and heritage and is today a commercial, medical, and recreational center for much of the Mid-South. Some 650,000 people live in Memphis, and the metropolitan area has a population of about 910,000.

Memphis is one of the largest wholesale and distributing centers in the United States. The city is an important world cotton and lumber market and a distributing center for livestock, grains, and other agricultural products. Memphis processes or manufactures food products, wood and paper products, chemicals, machinery, and a variety of other goods. Each day, thousands of tons of cargo pass through the city's port. A number of large corporations, including Holiday Inns and Federal Express, have their headquarters in Memphis.

The city is a leading medical and educational center. It is the location of the University of Tennessee's Center for the Health Sciences, the state's chief medical school. Memphis State University, with its more than 20,000 students, is one of several institutions of higher education in the city. Others include LeMoyne-Owen College, Christian Brothers College, Memphis Academy of the Arts, Rhodes College, and Southern College of Optometry.

Among the museums of Memphis are the Brooks Memorial Art Gallery and the Memphis Pink Palace Museum, which features natural history exhibits. But the cultural heritage of the city is perhaps best expressed through its music. One of the best-known places in Memphis is Beale Street, where, in the early 1900's, W. C. Handy, the "father of the blues," wrote and played the music for which he was to become famous. In the 1950's, Memphis music—a mixture of blues, rock and roll, and country and western—was popularized by Elvis Presley. Presley, who died in Memphis in 1977, is buried on the grounds of his home, Graceland, where thousands come each year to pay their respects.

For recreation, Memphis has sizable park areas, which include a large zoo. Among the city's annual events are the Cotton Carnival, the Mid-South Fair, and the Liberty Bowl college football game. The city strives to keep its traditions alive in the remodeled Beale Street, Victorian Village, Mud Island River Park, and the historic Peabody Hotel.

The site of the city of Memphis was originally inhabited by Chickasaw Indians. After the Spanish explorer Hernando de Soto visited the area in 1541, a succession of Spanish, French, and English frontiersmen competed for possession of the strategic bluff overlooking the river. A permanent town, however, awaited removal of the Chickasaws by the United States Government in 1818. The next year, the city was founded. By the 1860's, the rough river town had become a busy port.

During the Civil War, Union forces defeated Confederate defenders of the city in a river battle in 1862. Union forces occupied Memphis in spite of efforts to expel them, in 1864, by Nathan Bedford Forrest, the famous Confederate cavalry officer and resident of Memphis.

A series of devastating yellow fever epidemics struck Memphis in the 1870's. By the 1890's, however, the city was growing again. A railroad bridge across the Mississippi was completed in 1892. Memphis entered the 20th century as a leader in the cotton and lumber businesses. It has since grown to become one of the important cities of the modern South.

JAMES R. CHUMNEY
Memphis State University

A 19th-century—style riverboat appears to be out of place against the skyline of modern Memphis. The city is the third largest port on the Mississippi River.

MENDEL, GREGOR JOHANN (1822–1884)

Gregor Johann Mendel, an Austrian priest, first discovered the scientific laws of plant and animal heredity. These laws describe how traits such as eye color in human beings and tallness in plants are passed on from generation to generation.

Mendel, the son of a farmer, was born on July 22, 1822, in a small village in what was then Austria but is now Czechoslovakia. He was named Johann but took the name Gregor when he became a priest. He was an excellent student, and his parents enrolled him in a high school in a nearby city. When his father became ill and had to sell the farm, Mendel turned to tutoring to pay his way through high school. He was helped later by his younger sister who paid his university expenses from her wedding dowry. At the university, Mendel completed a two-year course of philosophy, physics, and higher mathematics. In 1843 he entered the Augustinian monastery in Brünn (now Brno) as a novice. He was ordained into the priesthood at the age of 25 and spent most of the rest of his life at the monastery.

Mendel's first assignment was in the town hospital. But because he could not bear to witness the suffering of the sick, he was transferred to a position as a teacher in an elementary school. Father Gregor, as he was then known, was well liked by his pupils and fellow teachers. In 1851 he was sent to the University of Vienna to study science. It was there that Mendel studied mathematical statistics and experimental botany, the two subjects that were to be of great value to him a few years later.

After two years at the university, Mendel returned to Brünn as a substitute teacher of physics and natural history at the technical school there. He was a good teacher. But his extreme nervousness when taking examinations kept him from completing the university test to become a fully licensed science teacher. For 14 years he remained a substitute teacher, but he did much more than teach. His university courses had given him a sound knowledge of the theory of plant and animal breeding as it was then understood. To satisfy his curiosity about the ways in which such plant traits as color, height, and seed shape were inherited, he used his spare time to carry out a series of

Gregor Mendel, a monk, carried out his experiments in genetics on pea plants in the monastery garden.

experiments with pea plants. Between 1856 and 1863, he grew more than 28,000 plants on which he kept careful records.

From his records, Mendel saw clearly that there was a predictable pattern by which plant traits were passed from generation to generation—a pattern that had never been reported before. He explained this pattern in principles, or rules, that are now known as the Mendelian Laws of Heredity.

In 1868, Mendel became abbot of the monastery. His new duties made it difficult for him to continue with his experiments. He published detailed reports on his findings, but his ideas were ignored, perhaps because he was not a professional scientist. When Mendel died on January 6, 1884, the world of science was still unaware of his genius. But in 1900, three scientists wrote separate articles describing his work and brought it to the attention of biologists everywhere.

Some questions have arisen about Mendel's experimental and statistical methods, questions that cannot be answered because all the facts are not known. Nevertheless, it was Mendel who created a new kind of experiment combining biology and statistics. And it is Mendel and Mendel alone who is still honored as the founder of the modern science of genetics.

LOUIS I. KUSLAN
Southern Connecticut State University

See also GENETICS.

MENDELSSOHN, FELIX (1809–1847)

The composer Jakob Ludwig Felix Mendelssohn-Bartholdy was born on February 3, 1809, in Hamburg, Germany. In 1812 the family moved to Berlin, where Felix began his musical studies. Felix was a true child prodigy. At an early age he developed into an outstanding pianist and organist, as well as composer. His compositions were often played by a group of musicians that gathered at the house of his music-loving parents on Sunday afternoons. Felix received his first training in conducting on these occasions. At 17 he wrote one of his masterpieces, an orchestral overture to Shakespeare's *A Midsummer Night's Dream*. Years later he composed his famous Wedding March for the same play.

In 1829 the young Mendelssohn directed the first performance in almost 100 years of Johann Sebastian Bach's *St. Matthew Passion*. The performance led to a widespread revival of interest in all of the music of this almost forgotten German composer. Today Bach is considered one of the greatest composers in history.

Mendelssohn traveled widely and became famous as both a pianist and a conductor. From 1829 to 1832 he made a tour that included England, Scotland, Germany, Austria, Italy, Switzerland, and France. Both his *Italian Symphony* (1833) and *Scottish Symphony* (1842) were inspired by these travels.

In 1835 he became conductor of the celebrated Gewandhaus Orchestra in Leipzig, Germany. He founded a conservatory of music in this city that became one of the best schools of its kind. Mendelssohn was also a talented painter and poet. He was a friend of the writer Johann Wolfgang von Goethe and set some of Goethe's poems to music. In 1837, Mendelssohn married Cécile Jeanrenaud, whom he had met while serving as director of a choral society in Frankfurt am Main. The marriage was a very happy one.

Despite his full schedule, Mendelssohn continued to compose. In 1836 he completed his oratorio *St. Paul*. He also continued traveling, particularly to England, where the elegance of his music was as much admired as in Mendelssohn's own country. In 1846 he conducted the first performance of his second oratorio, *Elijah*, in Birmingham, England.

The strain of this busy life proved too great for Mendelssohn's health, which had always been delicate. He died of a stroke on November 4, 1847, at his home in Leipzig. Though only 38 at his death, he left rich musical heritage. His best-known works include two piano concertos, the Violin Concerto in E minor, several symphonies, a wealth of chamber music, and many solo piano pieces, including the famous *Songs Without Words*.

KARL GEIRINGER
Professor of Music
University of California—Santa Barbara

MENSTRUATION

Sometime between the ages of 10 and 15, most girls begin to menstruate. Menstruation is a flow of bloody fluid from the uterus, the body organ where babies can develop. Women and girls who are old enough to have children have a menstrual period every month. In fact, the word ''menstruation'' comes from *mensis,* the Latin word for month.

▶ROLE IN REPRODUCTION

Menstruation plays an important role in human reproduction. The uterus, an organ in the pelvis that looks like a small upside-down pear, gets ready for pregnancy every month by thickening its lining, called the endometrium.

Once a month, a tiny egg cell is released from one of two ovaries, small organs on either side of the uterus. The egg cell, or ovum, travels down the Fallopian tube to the uterus. If it is fertilized by a male sperm cell, it settles down on the lining of the uterus. There it will develop into a baby.

If the egg cell is not fertilized, the lining of the uterus breaks down and is washed away. The blood and cells of the lining leave through the vagina, a canal that opens just behind the place where urine leaves the body. The flow normally lasts three to seven days, a time called the menstrual period. The total amount of blood lost is usually less than 30 milliliters

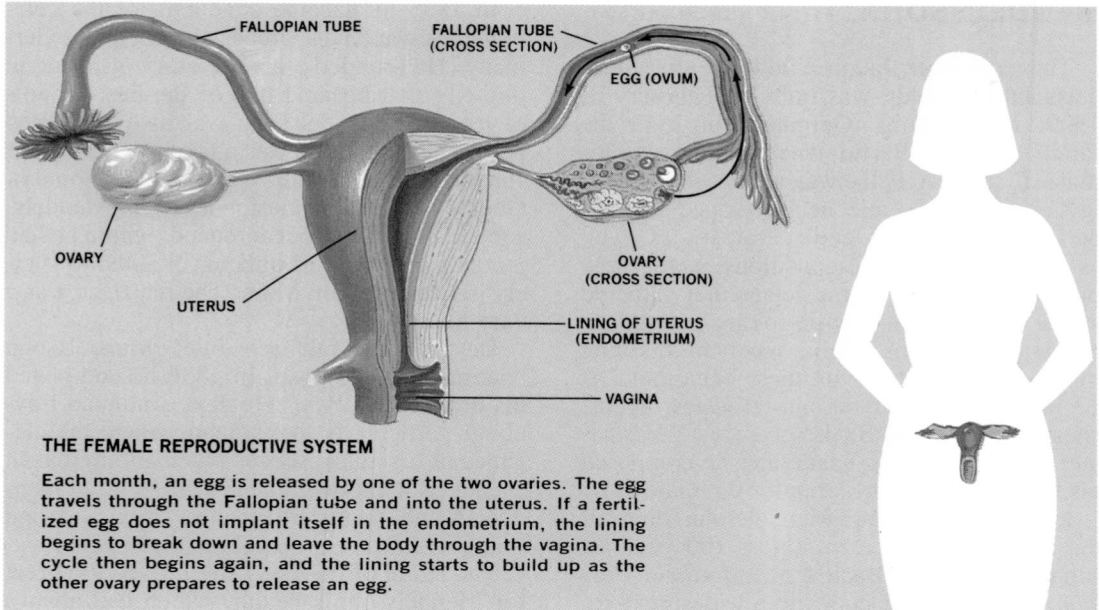

THE FEMALE REPRODUCTIVE SYSTEM

Each month, an egg is released by one of the two ovaries. The egg travels through the Fallopian tube and into the uterus. If a fertilized egg does not implant itself in the endometrium, the lining begins to break down and leave the body through the vagina. The cycle then begins again, and the lining starts to build up as the other ovary prepares to release an egg.

(1 ounce). Then the lining of the uterus begins to thicken again.

This cycle is controlled by hormones, or chemical messengers, that are produced by the ovaries and the pituitary gland. It usually repeats itself about every 28 days, but anywhere from 21 to 40 days is normal. In the first year or so of menstruation, it is common to have irregular periods.

Menstruation starts about two years after the appearance of some other signs that a girl is growing up, such as the first growth of breasts and body hair. Girls who are very thin often begin to menstruate later than others. Menstruation stops when a woman is about 50. This is called menopause. Periods also stop temporarily during pregnancy.

▶MANAGING MENSTRUATION

The flow of blood can be absorbed with a pad (called a sanitary napkin) worn outside the opening of the vagina or with a tampon, a roll of absorbent material that is worn inside. (A tampon cannot get lost inside.) A girl who has her period can continue all her usual activities, including sports and (with tampons) swimming. She need not take unusual care of her health. For example, she will not catch cold if she washes her hair, as was once thought.

Regular periods are a sign of good health, but even healthy women occasionally miss a period. Missed periods can be a sign of pregnancy. They can also result from emotional strain, sudden or extreme weight loss, or a medical problem. A woman who misses several periods or skips periods often should consult a doctor.

Some women have crampy pains in the lower abdomen on the first day or two of their periods. These cramps are caused by contractions of the uterus, which is made of strong muscle. They are not imaginary and are not caused by emotions. The best mild pain relievers for them are ones that contain aspirin. If the pain is severe, a doctor can prescribe other medication and look for less common causes of painful periods.

For a few days before each period, some women have various unpleasant symptoms. These include fatigue, irritability, breast soreness, and bloating of the abdomen. These symptoms together are called premenstrual tension. They are more common in older women than in teenagers. Doctors do not agree on what causes them. Some women find they feel better if they eat less salt for a few days before their periods. If the symptoms are severe, there are a number of treatments that can be tried.

JEAN PASCOE, M.D.
Miriam Hospital/Brown University

See also REPRODUCTION.

MENTAL HEALTH

When your body is well, you have good physical health. When your mind is well, you have good mental health. A great deal has been learned about mental health in this century. Psychiatry and psychology, the sciences that deal with mental health and human behavior, have developed rapidly. Through these sciences it has become possible to understand a great deal about why people feel and behave as they do. More is being learned and understood all the time. As you grow up, your life is sure to be made richer by this increasing understanding.

It is important for you to learn about yourself, to understand your feelings and needs, and to use the information about human behavior that we now have. Through such understanding you can learn to make choices, control your feelings, and express yourself so that you have a full, satisfying life.

▶ MENTALLY HEALTHY PEOPLE

Mentally healthy people are glad to be alive and glad to be themselves. This does not mean that they are always completely happy and confident. They have successes and failures, ups and downs. But they are generally hopeful about the future. And they are reasonably successful in meeting the everyday problems of life.

Having good mental health does not mean being just like everyone else. You may be a quiet person who enjoys spending a lot of time alone, or you may be very sociable and outgoing. You may have different feelings, ideas, and interests from other people.

The important thing is that you are able to live in reality. You can meet the challenges of life in such a way that you use your talents and strengths and enjoy your relationships with other people.

Mentally healthy people have an understanding of themselves. They recognize their limitations, but they like themselves and have a sense of their own worth. They accept the fact that they are human and not perfect. Still, they try to grow and change. They understand that it is normal to have many kinds of feelings—including anger, fear, frustration, and jealousy. But they also learn to control what they do about these feelings.

▶ UNDERSTANDING OUR FEELINGS

All people have many kinds of feelings and impulses that are natural and normal. These are neither good nor bad in themselves. We feel love and the desire to help others. We want to share, to be honest, and to do our work well. It is equally normal to be angry and to hate and to feel frightened, anxious, tense, or defeated.

As young people develop, there are times when they may have impulses to do something that may be dangerous or harmful to themselves or to others. Very young children are not always able to control these impulses. Probably very few children have ever grown up without hitting another child, telling a lie, or taking something that was not theirs. When we are children, parents and other adults have to help us control such behavior. Then as we grow up, we learn to control ourselves.

We do a much better job of controlling ourselves if we recognize and accept our real feelings and understand that it is perfectly normal for us to have them. We do not try to run away from them. At the same time, we are realistic enough to know that we cannot give in to all of our feelings and impulses.

If we do not understand that it is natural to have many kinds of feelings, we may be ashamed of some of our emotions and feel guilty because we have them. Then we punish ourselves in ways that make it harder for us to grow up mentally strong.

Deep down inside, some people may have feelings of anger or jealousy that they just cannot admit they have. They feel ashamed. And they cover these feelings or thoughts up so completely that they do not even know that the feelings are there.

But suddenly they may find that they have trouble studying, or they may have headaches. They may begin to have fears they never had before, or they may break out in a rash. They have no control over any of these things. These are the mind's way of punishing people who feel they deserve to be punished.

Children who feel jealous of a new sister or brother may have the same kind of experience. They think their jealous feelings are wicked, and they try to make up for having them by making a big fuss over the baby.

At the same time, they begin to have nightmares, or they are suddenly afraid of the dark. They may feel sick when it is time to go to school. This is because their feelings of jealousy are still hidden inside them.

It would be better if the older children could admit that the feelings of jealousy are there—and understand that it is normal to have such feelings. This does not mean that they would do anything to hurt the baby. They may not be able to help feeling jealous. But they can control what they do about it.

No one would be hurt if the older children could say, at least to themselves, "That baby is a nuisance!" They might even think, "Sometimes I wish that baby had never been born. I wish someone would pay attention to me once in a while."

Just getting these thoughts out in the open might help them relax. Perhaps they would even begin to enjoy the baby at times, because along with their jealousy the older children have feelings of love for the baby, too.

We punish ourselves in many ways because we feel guilty about what we believe are "bad" feelings. Usually we are the only ones affected. But sometimes others may be hurt. Let us take as an example a boy who has been brought up very strictly. Jim has been told that it is evil to be angry at a parent. This is what his parents were taught, and because of their own unhappy childhood experiences, this is what they believe. Without understanding their own inner anger, they are often harsh and unfair to Jim. After a severe punishment Jim is naturally furious, but he is afraid of that feeling. So it stays buried deep inside himself, and he is hardly aware of it.

When a gang of boys come along and ask Jim to help them steal the bicycle of a new boy who has just moved into the neighborhood, Jim joins them eagerly. All the secret anger bottled up inside him now comes out against a boy he does not even know.

In this case hidden anger is turned against one individual. But sometimes hidden anger can cause a whole group of people to turn against another group. This can have the most serious results.

▶ **FACING PROBLEMS**

Running away from real problems can do a person as much harm as running away from feelings. Of course, there are times when we all want to run away from our problems, and very often we do this. We make excuses for ourselves or treat ourselves to a soda or a movie to forget our troubles. But we know that sooner or later we will be able to gather the strength to solve our problems.

No one has ever grown up without having some troubles and difficulties. One year you may have a teacher you feel is unfair. Another time your family may have to move, and you may have to adjust to a new school and new friends. There may be a bully in your class who picks on you.

These are all normal life experiences. The way you react to them depends on your emotional outlook. Troubled, unhappy people who lack faith in themselves and in others may react in one of several ways. They may try to escape from their problems. They are so afraid of failure or of not being liked that they become shy, withdraw, and give up.

Other unhappy people may react by carrying a chip on their shoulders. They think the only reason things go wrong is that everyone else is against them. They are running away, too—by arguing and blaming others.

Still others may feel they are "no good"—that everyone is against them—but they are going to show the world. They drive themselves hard. Nothing matters but succeeding.

People with healthier emotional outlooks accept their shortcomings but still have faith in themselves. They know that small defeats are part of life, and they take failure as a sign that they must work a little harder and do a little better next time. They strive for achievement, but they do not push too hard.

Sometimes children have to face problems that are much larger than the normal problems of growing up. If a parent is seriously ill for a long time, if a sick child has to be hospitalized, or if there are financial difficulties, the whole family has an emotional problem. Sometimes parents cannot get along and may be separated or divorced. Sometimes someone close may die.

It is hard for most adults—and certainly for children—to adjust to this sort of experience. But when life presents us with serious problems, it is important to remember that other people can help. There are times when even the strongest person needs the comfort and understanding of others.

It is also important to realize that we can deal with feelings of shock, loneliness, and grief. Time and new experiences will help us, and we can help ourselves by being patient with ourselves and riding along with our feelings instead of trying to push them away. We feel better, too, when we try to help others who are hurt and grieving.

▶ KEEPING MENTALLY HEALTHY

All of us who are mentally healthy have some emotional problems, just as people in good physical health may have a cold or some other temporary illness. Today there are many specialists to whom we can go for help with our emotional problems. Psychiatrists, psychologists, social workers, psychiatric nurses, and guidance counselors have all had training in the understanding of these problems.

We know now that much can be done in our growing years to prevent serious emotional problems later. That is why teachers, religious and recreational leaders, parents, and all those who work with young people today are concerned with mental health. That is why mental health ideas are introduced in the schools, and guidance centers are provided where people can go with their problems.

▶ SOME MENTAL HEALTH IDEAS TO REMEMBER

(1) It is normal to have many kinds of feelings. At times we may feel angry, unloving, or violent, but we need not be ashamed about having these feelings. They will not harm other persons. Only our actions can hurt others, and we can control what we do.

(2) By accepting our feelings and facing our problems, we are taking the first step toward gaining a sense of control and mastery over our lives.

(3) Recognizing when we need to go to someone for help with a problem is not a sign of weakness but of maturity and strength.

(4) The mind and body are one. Anything that affects us physically affects us mentally as well. Anything that affects us mentally also affects us physically.

(5) Being oneself is the key to mental health. Discovering what we can do—what our interests, talents, and special qualities are—is the quest for our own identity. We work toward this goal all our lives.

(6) Looking forward to the future with zest and hope is necessary for mental health, as long as we do not expect the impossible of ourselves or demand the impossible of those around us.

EDA J. LeSHAN
Contributing Editor, *Woman's Day*
Author, *What Makes Me Feel This Way?*

MENTAL ILLNESS

People who are so troubled by their thoughts that they cannot control their actions are said to be mentally ill. All of us have moments when we are upset and disturbed and do not think clearly. But most people, given enough time, are able to find a way to solve the problems of everyday living. And there is help for those who cannot. They may seek aid from others who are experienced in helping disturbed people. They may go for advice and help to a trusted friend, to a member of the clergy, to a psychologist or social worker, or to a doctor.

Physicians who have had special training in treating mental and emotional disorders are known as **psychiatrists**. The word **mental** refers to the processes of the mind, or the way a person reasons. **Emotional** refers to a person's feelings, such as fear or joy.

No one knows exactly how many people are mentally ill, because not everyone suffering from mental illness is under treatment. In addition, there is no clear dividing line between those who are mentally ill and those who are not. Some persons with a mild mental disturbance may still be able to carry on the everyday business of life. Others may be able to act properly one day but not the next. Still others may be all right at home but severely troubled when away from home. Or they may feel more upset when they are with their families than when they are with others.

Mental illness may occur at any age. It may come during childhood, middle age, or old age. It is the most widespread illness of our time, affecting people everywhere. How to treat and care for the mentally ill is one of the greatest health problems facing nearly every country in the world. In the

United States alone, it is estimated that services to the mentally ill cost nearly $17,000,000,000 (billion) each year, about ⅛ of all health costs. Experts estimate that at any one time about 15 percent of the population needs some form of mental health services.

Sometimes a severely disturbed person is advised to go to a hospital that specializes in the care of the mentally ill. Mentally ill persons whom doctors consider a danger to themselves or to others may be required by law to enter a hospital. This is known as being **committed** to a hospital. Committed patients are not allowed to leave the hospital until the doctors feel they are ready. Less seriously ill persons may enter and leave mental hospitals as they wish.

In all modern hospitals that use the best methods of treatment, every effort is made to keep the patients active. Hospitals try to keep the patients from becoming so accustomed to **institutional**, or hospital, life that they will not be able to get along in everyday life outside the hospital. Newer types of hospitals are largely "open." Patients must follow certain rules and customs, but may come and go freely unless they are dangerous to themselves or others.

The quality of treatment and care given patients is not the same in all mental hospitals. It ranges from good to very poor. There are still communities with mental hospitals where patients are kept in locked wards and given only **custodial** care. This means they are simply watched over and receive no treatment.

Mental hospitals in the United States are supported by local, state, or federal government or by private organizations. Many general hospitals also care for mental patients.

In the past, people often had to stay in mental hospitals because there was no place near home that could help with their emotional problems. Now there are local community health centers where people can get help while living at home and holding a job. Some patients are also treated by private doctors in office visits. Today 75 percent of those receiving mental care are treated outside of hospitals. Unfortunately, treatment centers are inadequate, or do not exist, in many rural and poor sections. Those that do exist may be overcrowded or hard to reach.

▶ **CAUSES OF MENTAL ILLNESS**

Most mental illnesses, unlike many physical diseases, have no single known cause. Many different things can cause a person to become mentally disturbed. But some types of mental illness have a clearly understood physical cause. Persons who have a high fever caused by an infection can become so confused that they do not know who or where they are. This condition is called **delirium**. It will disappear when the infection goes away. Other persons may become mentally ill when they have not had proper food for a long time. They will recover when their diet is corrected. An elderly person may lose the ability to think clearly. This can be caused by hardening of the arteries of the brain, a disease of old age that harms the brain cells that control behavior.

There is no simple answer to why some other people become mentally ill. Many of them have lived under unhappy conditions, where they could not build up feelings of self-confidence. Some of them may have been kept by themselves, away from the company of others. They may have been made to feel unwanted or unloved. They may not have received approval from their families for their accomplishments. They may have been laughed at for something in their appearance or manner over which they had no control. Any of these persons would be more likely to develop mental illness than those brought up in a home where they were loved and appreciated.

▶ **TYPES OF MENTAL ILLNESS**

The signs and symptoms of mental illness vary as much as the causes. No two persons get sick in exactly the same way. But troubled people show by their behavior that they are in distress. For example, young people may show that something is wrong by behaving in ways that attract undue attention. As a rule, they do not realize that they are behaving in an unusual way. They may suddenly become unable or unwilling to study. They may bully other children. They may steal valueless things for which they have no use. Sometimes children who show some of these forms of disordered behavior can be helped by their parents or teachers.

Children who have lived under conditions that make for poor mental health may not grow up to be good citizens. As they reach adulthood, they may get into automobile accidents often or be unable to hold a job. They may even steal or commit other crimes. They do not seem able to learn from experience. They may also be unable to make friends or may try so hard to make friends that people avoid them. Unlike persons who are brought up in a happy, loving home, they do not feel guilty about their acts. They are unfriendly toward the world, and this is their way of "acting out" their feelings against society.

Persons of this kind are said to have a **character disorder**. They are almost always **emotionally immature** and **unstable**. An emotionally immature person is one who has not grown beyond the emotional development of an infant or small child. It is natural for babies to cry when they want attention. Very young children may fly into a temper when they do not have their way. But as people grow up and become mature, they are expected to control their feelings and make their wants known in other ways. The emotionally immature person does not meet problems thoughtfully or make an effort to find a good way to deal with them. An unstable person is one who changes his or her mind often and cannot be depended upon.

Neuroses are mild forms of mental illness that affect many people. A neurosis can result from a person's early or later life experiences or difficulties. It interferes with a person's ability to be happy and to get along with others. It can show itself in many different ways. People with a neurosis may show signs of a physical disease for which doctors can find no physical cause. Or they may feel driven to follow a course of action that does not make sense. Sometimes they have feelings of great anxiety. Everyone has experienced anxiety at some time. It is a deeper feeling than fear or worry. It is the kind of feeling you might have before an important examination or before going onstage in a school play. The mouth feels dry, and the hands tremble and sweat. Instead of passing quickly, a state of anxiety may last a long time in a disturbed person. It may be set off by harmless things such as a crowd of people in a restaurant, a gentle household pet, or a nameless dread.

Neurotic people often try to meet everyday problems in ways that brought them satisfaction when they were younger but are no longer effective. For example, small children may find that they receive a lot of attention when they are ill. As they grow older, they make up for disappointments by continuing to use illness as a means of attracting attention from those around them. The illness has become a way of solving problems. It is very real to them and gives them pain and discomfort. But it is caused by an emotional state rather than a physical condition. When these people are helped to understand why they behave as they do, they may learn to control their feelings and their actions.

Psychoses are the most severe of all forms of mental illness. "Psychosis" is a term that has come into medical use to replace the word "insanity." The commonest form of psychosis is **schizophrenia**. People with this disease are unable to understand what is going on around them. They may think that people are talking about them or are trying to harm them when this is not true. These ideas are called **delusions**. Or they may see or hear things that are not really happening. These are **hallucinations**.

When patients have a great deal of these unfounded suspicions, they are said to be suffering from **paranoia** or **paranoid schizophrenia**. Persons with paranoia have delusions that they are very important or that people are plotting against them. Often they think that some person or group of persons that they hear about in the news may try to harm them. At times these patients feel that they must take action against such imagined dangers. They may become violent. Schizophrenia may come on gradually. The first symptoms may consist only of sudden forms of very unusual behavior.

Another psychosis is known as **manic-depressive psychosis**. In this condition patients are very low in spirits, or **depressed**. Or their feelings may swing to the other extreme—they may feel joyful, or **elated**. In the slowed-down, or depressed, state these patients feel that they are no good to anyone. They constantly belittle themselves and may even attempt to end their lives. In the elated, or **manic**, state, nothing seems impossible, and they may commit unlawful acts. Depression is more common than elation in patients who have this form of psychosis.

Persons who are judged to be mentally ill are not held responsible for their unlawful acts. They are treated in a mental hospital instead of being sent to prison. It is not always easy for courts of law to decide whether the person accused of a crime is mentally ill or not. When there is doubt, experts on mental illness examine the patient and give their opinions. These opinions are helpful to the judge or jury in reaching a verdict.

▶ TREATMENT OF MENTAL ILLNESS

Mentally ill persons should be treated with kindness. Their needs and feelings should be considered at all times. Their physical condition should receive attention. They should be given a well-balanced diet. Physicians may order medicines that will help them to control any strong, unpleasant feelings, such as depression or anxiety.

The science of **psychopharmacology** deals with the effects of drugs on mental activity. In the 1950's this science developed two new types of drugs that gave physicians powerful tools in the treatment of mental illness.

Physicians prescribe **tranquilizers** to help calm people who are troubled, so that they can live at home instead of in a hospital. Tranquilizers do not produce a lasting cure and are effective only while being taken. **Energizers** stimulate a patient's interest in life. They keep a person from feeling sleepy or tired all the time, but their main use is in the treatment of depression.

Electroshock is another form of treatment sometimes used to help people who are severely depressed. The patient is given a series of electric shocks that cause unconsciousness for a few seconds. These treatments appear to break up the pattern of disturbing thoughts and actions. The sick person is then better able to work with the doctor toward a recovery.

Psychotherapy is the most important of all types of treatment for the mentally ill. In psychotherapy, patients have a series of talks with the doctor, psychologist, or social worker. They discuss what they think about and how they feel about everything around

them. These talks are aimed at helping patients gain an understanding of the events and influences that caused their illness and at finding ways in which they can learn to live with their situation.

Psychotherapy usually consists of interviews once or twice a week for a few weeks. In more severe illnesses the interviews may take place more often and continue for a year or more. **Psychoanalysis** is a more intensive kind of psychotherapy. The physician tries to have patients recall their earliest childhood, in search of the cause of their troubled state. Physicians who treat patients in this way are called psychoanalysts.

Group therapy is a form of treatment in which people get together and discuss their emotional problems with their adviser and with one another. They help one another understand their problems and work them out. Group leaders must have special training in psychiatry, psychology, or social work.

▶ NEED FOR RESEARCH AND TRAINED WORKERS

New clinics and mental health centers and new drugs have enabled many mentally ill people to avoid being hospitalized. The number of patients in mental hospitals has dropped within recent years. But much is still unknown about mental illness. Research has brought about many advances— drugs, electroshock, and other forms of treatment. If the future of the mentally disturbed is to be made brighter, research must continue and more specialists must be trained.

All citizens can help in the fight against mental illness. This can best be accomplished by working with community health centers and mental health associations. There are activities in almost every community that play a part in fighting mental illness. Any group activity that strengthens the family unit, improves relations between persons and groups, keeps people from feeling alone or unfairly treated, or gives people a sense of their own worth is a weapon against mental illness.

DANA L. FARNSWORTH, M.D.
Former Director of University Health Services
Harvard University

MENTAL RETARDATION. See RETARDATION, MENTAL.

MERCHANT MARINE. See UNITED STATES MERCHANT MARINE.

MERCURY. See PLANETS.

METALS AND METALLURGY

Automobiles and airplanes, pens and pencils, roller skates and bicycles, all depend on metals in order to do their jobs. Every day we see, touch, and use hundreds of items in which metals play an important part. But what are metals? How do we get them? How are they shaped into the many things we use?

Pure metals are chemical elements. That is, they cannot be broken down into other substances. Over 100 chemical elements are known to man; of these, about 80 are metals. Although metals differ widely in qualities such as strength and hardness, they all have certain qualities in common. When polished, metals reflect light with a characteristic shine called metallic luster. Metals are good conductors of heat and electricity. Most metals are grayish in color, although copper is reddish and gold is yellow.

Metals can be formed into a number of useful shapes without breaking or cracking—that is, they are workable. Two important working properties of metals are **ductility** and **malleability**. Ductility is that characteristic of a material that allows it to be pulled or stretched into wire. Malleability is that characteristic of a material that allows it to be hammered or squeezed into a sheet. Gold is the most ductile and malleable of all the metals. It can be made into thinner sheets or finer wire than any other material.

The melting points of metals vary greatly. Mercury, which is used in some thermometers, is a liquid at room temperature. Tungsten, the metal used for electric light bulb filaments, has the highest melting point of any metal—over 6000 degrees Fahrenheit.

Metals also differ in density. The lightest metal, lithium, weighs only about half as much as water. Osmium, the heaviest metal, is about three times as heavy as iron and $22\frac{1}{2}$ times as heavy as water. A 1-foot cube of osmium weighs 1,400 pounds.

Metals have many chemical properties in common. They can be **oxidized**—that is, they can combine with oxygen or other nonmetals. Oxidized metals can be **reduced**, or separated, from the nonmetal, and in that way be made pure metals again. Both oxidation and reduction are important in removing metals from their ores and purifying them.

The properties of nonmetals are different from those of metals. Nonmetals are brittle—that is, they are not at all malleable or ductile. They are also poor conductors of heat and electricity.

Some elements, such as carbon and silicon, are called metalloids or semimetals. These are borderline elements. They have some of the properties of metals and some of the properties of nonmetals. They are good conductors of heat and electricity, but they are not so strong or workable as metals.

Metallurgy

The science of metals is called metallurgy. Metallurgy has three principal branches: extractive metallurgy, physical metallurgy, and production metallurgy. Extractive metallurgy deals with the extraction, or removal, of the metal from its ore and the refining of the metal. The physical metallurgist studies the structure and properties of metals and helps decide which metals are best suited for a particular purpose. The physical metallurgist also tries to find new and better mixtures, or alloys, of metals. Finally, methods of fashioning metals into finished products are worked out and studied by production metallurgists.

▶ WHERE DO METALS COME FROM?

A few metals, such as gold, platinum, silver, and sometimes copper, are found in the earth in their pure state. Most metals, however, are not found free in nature. They are found only in chemical combinations with other elements. Chemical compounds that are found in nature are called **minerals**. Minerals that are valuable for the metals they contain are called **ores**.

The value of an ore depends on how much metal is in the ore and how costly it is to remove the metal from the ore. It also depends on the demand for the metal. For example, iron ore containing less than 20 percent iron is considered low-grade, while tin ore containing only 2 percent tin is considered high-grade. A mineral containing only $\frac{1}{28000}$ percent radium is a valuable radium ore.

▶ REMOVING METALS FROM THEIR ORES

Many processes are used to obtain pure metal from ore. Some ores need to go through only a few steps, while other ores must go through many steps.

Concentration

When ore comes from the mine, it usually contains large amounts of unwanted material, such as clay and stone. This worthless material, called **gangue**, is usually removed before the valuable part of the ore is processed further. This is called concentration or mineral dressing. The first step in concentration is to crush the ore, so that the gangue is no longer attached to the valuable part of the ore. Then one of several methods is used to separate them.

Flotation. The most important method of concentration is called froth flotation. This method depends on the fact that certain minerals can be made to attach themselves to

---

SOME IMPORTANT METALS

METAL	IMPORTANT ORES	IMPORTANT MINING COUNTRIES	SPECIAL PROPERTIES	IMPORTANT USES
Aluminum	Bauxite	Jamaica; Soviet Union; Australia; Surinam	Lightweight	Airplanes; buildings; cooking utensils; foil wrapping; cans and containers; power lines
Antimony	Stibnite	China; South Africa; Bolivia; Soviet Union	Hardens lead	Type metal; storage-battery plates; bearing metals; pewter
Chromium	Chromite	South Africa; Turkey; Zimbabwe (Rhodesia); Soviet Union	Resists oxidation and corrosion at high temperature	Chrome plating; stainless steel; electrical resistance wire (toasters, heaters); gas-turbine engines
Cobalt	Nickel and copper ores	Zaïre; Canada; Morocco; Zambia	Resists corrosion at high temperatures; magnetic	Jet aircraft; turbines; magnetic alloy (alnico); cutting-tool steel
Copper	Chalcocite; chalcopyrite	United States; Chile; Soviet Union; Zambia	Second best conductor of heat and electricity; corrosion-resistant	Electrical wire; brass; bronze; water pipes
Gold	Native	Canada; South Africa; United States; Soviet Union	Most malleable and ductile metal; corrosion-resistant	Jewelry and ornaments; dental alloys
Iridium	Nickel and copper ores	Canada; South Africa; Soviet Union	Most corrosion-resistant metal	High-temperature equipment; strengthens platinum
Iron	Hematite; limonite; magnetite	Soviet Union; United States; Canada; Australia	Most useful metal; magnetic	Steel; iron castings
Lead	Galena	Australia; Soviet Union; United States; Canada	Low melting point; high density	Storage batteries; solder; ammunition
Magnesium	Seawater; magnesite	United States; Norway; Canada	Lightest structural metal	Aircraft; tools
Manganese	Pyrolusite; cryptomelane	Soviet Union; Brazil; South Africa; India	Neutralizes sulfur in steel; strengthens steel	Steel; aluminum alloys
Mercury	Cinnabar	Italy; Spain; United States; Soviet Union	Liquid at room temperature	Thermometers; vacuum pumps; dental alloys; electric switches
Molybdenum	Molybdenite; powellite	United States; Chile; Canada	Toughens and strengthens steel; high melting point	Steel; X-ray tubes; radio tubes; solid lubricants
Nickel	Pentlandite; pyrrhotite	Canada; Soviet Union; New Caledonia	Corrosion-resistant; magnetic	Nickel plating; coins; stainless steel; monel metal; noncorrosive equipment; electrical resistance wire
Platinum	Native; nickel and copper ores	Canada; South Africa; Colombia; Soviet Union	Corrosion-resistant; catalyst	Industrial chemical reactions; jewelry
Plutonium	(synthetic)		Radioactive	Nuclear fuel
Silver	Argentite; lead ores	Mexico; Peru; Canada; United States; Soviet Union	Best conductor of heat and electricity; malleable; light-sensitive	Coins; tableware; jewelry; photography
Tin	Cassiterite	Malaysia; China; Bolivia; Thailand	Low melting point; corrosion-resistant	Coating "tin" cans; solder; bronze; type metal; pewter
Titanium	Ilmenite; rutile	United States; Australia; Senegal	Lightweight and strong	Aircraft; gas-turbine engines; paint pigment
Tungsten	Wolframite; scheelite	China; Soviet Union; United States; Korea	Highest melting point of any metal; catalyst	Electric lamp filaments; tungsten carbide tools; industrial chemical reactions
Uranium	Pitchblende; carnotite	United States; Canada; South Africa	Radioactive	Nuclear fuel
Vanadium	Carnotite	United States; South Africa	Makes steel tougher and more elastic	Steel; titanium alloys
Zinc	Sphalerite; smithsonite	United States; Canada; Soviet Union	Corrosion-resistant	Galvanizing; brass; dry-cell batteries

bubbles. The crushed ore is put into a tank of special liquid or solution through which air is bubbled. Each bubble carries a small particle of the valuable part of the ore to the top of the tank, where the particles are collected, while the gangue settles to or remains on the bottom. Zinc, lead, and copper ores are usually concentrated by flotation.

Gravity Concentration. Gravity concentration depends on the fact that in some ores the valuable mineral, which contains the metal being sought, is heavier than the gangue. A current of air or water carries away the gangue, while the rest of the ore sinks.

When prospectors panned for gold, they were using gravity concentration. They would scoop river mud or gravel containing gold dust into a pan. By shaking the pan in the running river water, they washed away the unwanted sand, clay, and pebbles, while the small, heavy particles of gold sank to the bottom of the pan.

Modern gravity concentration is done in large machines rather than in a pan, but the principle is the same. This method is used for a number or ores, including tin, chromium, and tungsten ores, as well as for metallic gold.

Leaching

In leaching, the ore is treated with a liquid that dissolves away the mineral containing the metal being sought, leaving the gangue behind. The metal is then easily removed by treating the solution with other chemicals. This method is particularly useful for low-grade ores. Gold in low-grade ores is recovered by dissolving it in sodium cyanide solution and treating the solution chemically.

Sometimes mercury, which is liquid at ordinary temperatures, is used for leaching. In that case the process is called **amalgamation**.

Pyrometallurgy

Pyrometallurgy is the use of heat in treating ores. Heat is used for a number of different purposes. In **sintering**, for example, heat is used to cause finely divided particles of ore to stick together, forming large chunks that are easy to handle. Other processes use heat to change the ore chemically.

Roasting. In roasting, the ore is heated in air in order to change it to a more useful form.

Roasting is sometimes used before leaching in order to change the valuable parts of an ore into a chemical that will dissolve easily.

The most common use of roasting is in treating sulfide ores—ores in which the metal is combined with sulfur. Roasting gets rid of the sulfur and changes the ore to a form from which the metal can be removed more easily.

Smelting. Smelting is one way of separating a metal from its ore. It is done by heating the ore, a reducing agent, and a flux together in a special furnace. The reducing agent combines with the nonmetal in the ore (usually oxygen), leaving the free metal. In the heat of the furnace the metal is molten and runs to the bottom, where it is collected. The flux combines with gangue and other unwanted material to form slag, which is easily removed from the furnace.

Some metals, including iron, are smelted in a **blast furnace**. In iron smelting the reducing agent is carbon monoxide formed by burning coke (a form of carbon). Limestone is used as the flux. Other metals, including copper, are smelted in a **reverberatory furnace**. Very high temperatures are possible in a reverberatory furnace, because the flame is in the same chamber as the ore. Heat is reflected by the ceiling of the furnace back to the melting material. Very little heat is wasted.

Electrolysis

Some metals, such as magnesium and aluminum, are very active chemically. Because they are so active, powerful methods are needed to separate them from their ores. The only economical way to obtain these metals is electrolysis. Electrolysis is the separation of chemical elements by means of electricity. For electrolysis the ore must first be purified by chemical methods. The pure metal is obtained by running an electric current through the melted purified ore. Aluminum ore is called bauxite. The purified ore is called alumina. Magnesium "ore" is not really an ore at all. Magnesium is usually obtained from seawater. A white chemical called milk of magnesia is extracted from the seawater and must be treated chemically before electrolysis.

▶ REFINING METALS

Once the metal is removed from its ore, it must be refined, or purified. Even very small

Crushed molybdenum ore is separated from waste rock in a spiral classifier. Ore particles cling to froth and rise to top; rock particles sink to bottom.

Purified molybdenum ore is smelted into metal inside huge iron shells resting on a bed of sand. Lifted shell reveals pool of molten molybdenum metal.

amounts of impurities can cause a metal to lose its strength or other valuable properties. The three important methods of refining are electrorefining, distillation, and pyrometallurgy.

Electrorefining

Electrorefining is a process very similar to electroplating. Thin sheets of pure metal and large slabs of impure metal are put into a tank of solution. An electric current is passed through the solution, causing pure metal to be removed from the slabs and to be deposited onto the pure metal strips. The impurities fall to the bottom of the tank or are dissolved in the solution. Copper refined by this method is at least 99.90 percent pure. Zinc and lead are two of the other metals that are often refined by this method.

Distillation

Metals with fairly low boiling points, such as zinc, mercury, and magnesium, may be refined by distillation. In distillation the metal is boiled off, leaving the impurities behind. The vapor is collected and cooled, forming the solid pure metal.

Pyrometallurgy

In refining by pyrometallurgy, the impurities are burned, or oxidized, away. This is done by melting the metal in the presence of air. The impurities, as well as a small amount of metal, combine with the oxygen of the air and either boil off or combine with fluxes to form slag, which is easily removed. This is usually done in a reverberatory furnace. Lead and copper are two of the metals refined by this method.

▶ FASHIONING METALS INTO FINISHED GOODS

A large chunk of metal would not be of much use to anyone if it could not be made into something else. Since people first discovered metals, they have been at work making them into products to meet their needs. Metals have become more and more useful as more and better ways of shaping them have been developed.

Forging

Perhaps the oldest form of metalworking is forging. Forging means beating or squeezing the metal into the desired shape. Blacksmiths used to make horseshoes and other things out of iron bars by forging. The iron was softened by heating it red-hot in a fire. Then the blacksmith, using a pair of tongs, would place the iron on a steel block called an **anvil** and would beat the iron into shape with a hammer. It took a long time and a great deal of work to make even a simple object by this method.

Modern **drop forging** uses the same principles that the blacksmith did. The anvil is much larger, and the hammer is replaced by a steel block called a **ram**, which may weigh as much as several tons. These are parts of a machine called a **drop hammer**. The drop hammer lifts and drops the heavy ram onto the heated piece of metal that is being shaped. By attaching dies—blocks of steel with the desired shape cut into them—to the ram and anvil, very complicated shapes can be made easily. The steam drop hammer can deliver many tons of force by using steam to push the ram down onto the anvil. These great machines can do things in one blow that the blacksmith never dreamed of doing.

Giant steel forgings are reheated to keep them from becoming brittle.

Drop forging is used to make automobile parts, such as crankshafts. It is also used to make tools, such as pliers and wrenches.

Press forging is done in a **hydraulic press**, which is similar in construction to the drop hammer. The ram in the hydraulic press, however, is attached to hydraulic pistons. Instead of pounding the metal into shape, the hydraulic press squeezes it into shape under great force—up to 50,000 tons. Hydraulic presses cost more than drop hammers, but they are faster and quieter.

Casting

Long ago, man learned to melt metals. He learned that molten metal could be poured into holes in stone or clay molds and that when the metal cooled and became solid, it would take the shape of the cavity of the mold. This process is called casting. Today several different casting methods are used.

Sand Casting. In sand casting, the mold is made of sand. A special kind of sand is used that holds together and is not swept away when the liquid metal is poured into the mold.

The first step in sand casting is to make a model, or pattern, of the object that is to be cast. The pattern is put into a special box, and molding sand is packed around it, making the lower half of the mold. The process is repeated in another box to make the top half of the mold. Holes must be made in the mold so that the liquid metal may be poured into it and so that the metal will reach every part of the mold. If the finished piece is to be hollow or is to have holes in it, special pieces called **cores** must be made from molding sand and must be fitted into the mold. The two halves of the mold are then clamped together, and the liquid metal is poured into it. When the metal has solidified, the mold is opened and broken up. The cast piece is then machined to remove rough edges and to give it a smooth surface.

Because the mold is broken when the casting is removed, a new mold must be made for each casting. For this reason sand casting is usually used either when just a few pieces are to be made or when the piece is of such a shape that it cannot be removed from the mold without breaking the mold, since the mold must be broken anyway.

Die Casting. In die casting, metal molds

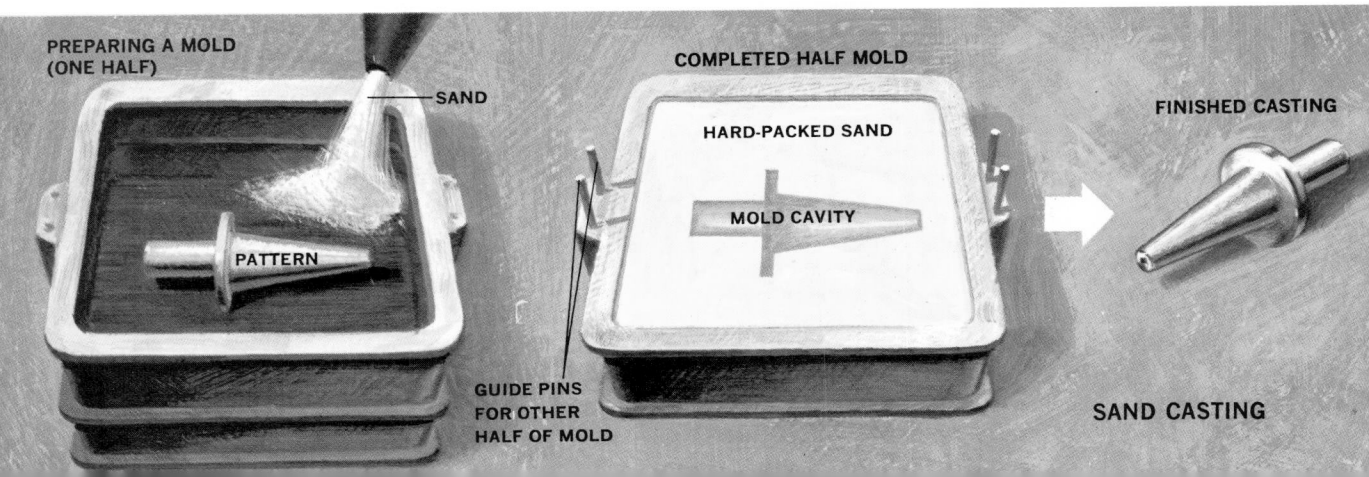

PREPARING A MOLD (ONE HALF)

SAND

PATTERN

GUIDE PINS FOR OTHER HALF OF MOLD

COMPLETED HALF MOLD

HARD-PACKED SAND

MOLD CAVITY

FINISHED CASTING

SAND CASTING

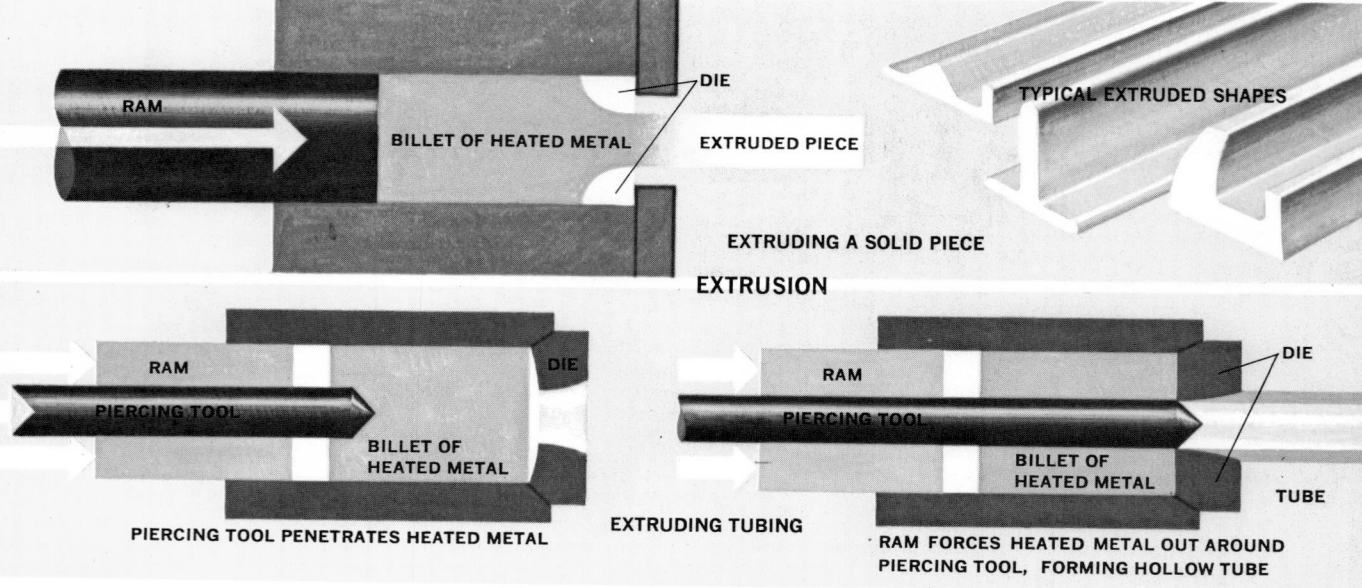

RAM

BILLET OF HEATED METAL

DIE

EXTRUDED PIECE

TYPICAL EXTRUDED SHAPES

EXTRUDING A SOLID PIECE

EXTRUSION

RAM

PIERCING TOOL

BILLET OF HEATED METAL

DIE

PIERCING TOOL PENETRATES HEATED METAL

EXTRUDING TUBING

RAM

PIERCING TOOL

BILLET OF HEATED METAL

DIE

TUBE

RAM FORCES HEATED METAL OUT AROUND PIERCING TOOL, FORMING HOLLOW TUBE

called dies are used. These molds may be used over and over again. In **gravity die casting**, as in sand casting, the molten metal is simply poured into the mold. A much faster method, however, is **pressure die casting**. In this method the molten metal is fed into the mold under great pressure, filling the mold very quickly. Hundreds of parts a minute can be made in this way.

Centrifugal Casting. Still another method is used for casting pipes and other cylindrical (tube-shaped) objects. In this method, centrifugal casting, the mold is spun at high speed as the molten metal is poured into it. Centrifugal force throws the metal against the walls of the mold, leaving the center hollow.

Five-ton aluminum ingot about to enter rolling mill.

Extrusion

Extrusion is a metal-forming method that works on the same principle as squeezing toothpaste from a tube. The metal, in the form of a block, is usually heated to make it softer. Then it is forced by a ram through an opening in a steel plate. The strip of metal that comes out can be made into many different shapes by changing the shape of the opening. Sometimes the extruded strip or bar is sliced to form small parts, such as gears.

Rolling

Metal in sheets or plates has many uses, such as in the manufacture of automobile bodies, refrigerators, and ship hulls. These sheets and plates are made by rolling a metal block between heavy steel or cast-iron rollers. The metal passes back and forth between these rollers, which are gradually brought closer and closer together until the desired thickness is reached. Very thin metal sheets called foil—the aluminum foil used to wrap food, for example—are made by this process.

Shapes other than flat sheets can be made by rolling. Rollers with grooves cut into them are used to form such products as rails for railroad tracks.

Drawing

Wire is made by drawing or pulling a metal rod through dies. This type of die is a block of metal or other hard material having a hole slightly smaller than the rod. A point is made on one end of the rod, and it is put into the die. The pointed end is gripped by a powerful tool, and the rod is pulled through the die.

This is repeated several times using smaller and smaller dies. Each time, the wire comes out longer and thinner.

Powder Metallurgy

In powder metallurgy the metal to be formed is first ground to a fine powder. The powder is poured into a die or mold and compressed under high pressure in a press. The piece is then heated so that the metal powders weld together. The temperature needed for this process is lower than that needed to melt the metal. For this reason powder metallurgy is very useful for forming metals with very high melting points, such as tungsten. Platinum also has a very high melting point and is formed in this way. In the case of platinum, which is very expensive, this process has the added advantage that it wastes very little metal.

Powder metallurgy can also be used to mix certain nonmetals with metals. Graphite—a form of carbon—is an excellent lubricant. It can be mixed with bronze to make self-lubricating bronze bearings. Diamond powder—also a form of carbon—can be mixed with different metals to make grinding wheels.

▶ PROPERTIES AND USES OF METALS

Many metals have special properties that make them very important for certain uses. For example, the high melting point of tungsten makes it a very useful metal for electric lamp filaments as well as for other high-temperature uses. Few chemicals can harm platinum. It is therefore useful for some types of laboratory equipment.

There is almost always more than one reason for choosing a metal for a particular purpose. For example, silver is the best conductor of electricity. But because silver is expensive, copper—the second best conductor—is usually used for electrical wiring. For long-distance power lines, however, aluminum—the fourth best conductor—is used, because it is much stronger and lighter than copper. Gold—the third best conductor—is too expensive.

An engineer who is designing a building, a bridge, or an airplane, for example, must know the properties of all metals in order to choose the ones best suited to the job. Aluminum and magnesium are very light; iron is strong. But very seldom does a single metal have all the properties needed for a particular job. For this reason metallurgists experiment to find alloys—mixtures of metals—that are right for the job.

Some of the properties of metals are changed by special treatment. For example, when a metal is worked without heating it, as is done in some kinds of rolling or forging, the metal becomes hard and brittle. It can be softened and made malleable again by heating it red-hot and allowing it to cool. This is called **annealing**.

If steel—an iron alloy—is heated red-hot

Copper has been prized for cooking utensils since the dawn of history. Left: Copper pots from the ancient city of Ur, about 3200 B.C. Right: An assortment of modern copper kitchenware.

but is cooled quickly by plunging it into water or oil, it behaves differently from other metals. In this case the steel becomes harder and more brittle. This is called **quenching.**

Quenched steel can be made softer and more ductile by **tempering** (heating it again, but not red-hot, and then allowing it to cool at any convenient rate).

▶HISTORY OF METALLURGY

About 8,000 years ago people lived in what is now called the **Stone Age.** At that time they had not yet learned how to use metals—most tools and weapons were made out of stone.

Copper and gold were probably the first metals that ancient people learned how to use. (These metals occur in nature in a free state as well as in ores.) Nuggets of copper and gold can be hammered into shapes without melting them. Scientists do not know precisely when people discovered how to use these metals. But they have determined that copper was used as long ago as 5000 B.C. Gold was first used sometime before 4000 B.C. Within another 1,000 years ancient people had also discovered the metals silver and lead, but copper was the metal most used because it was the strongest and most plentiful metal then known.

By about 3000 B.C. early men and women had discovered some of the most important things about using metals. They had learned to beat metal into useful shapes, such as bowls, tools, and weapons. They soon discovered the processes of annealing, melting, casting, and smelting. And they no longer had to depend on what few nuggets of copper they could find. They learned to get copper from copper ores, which were much more plentiful than the pure metal.

Copper ore is never found pure. It always has ores of other metals—especially tin—mixed with it. Actually the metal that ancient people obtained from copper ore was usually a kind of bronze (a copper-tin alloy). At first they did not know this. But after the discovery of tin, they learned to mix copper and tin to get better alloys than the natural ones. From about 3500 B.C., when the great Egyptian civilization was just beginning, to about 1200 B.C., when many of the stories told in the Bible were taking place, bronze was the most important material for making tools and weapons. This period is called the **Bronze Age.**

The next great development in metallurgy involved iron. Ancient people know about iron from meteorites long before they discovered how to smelt it from its ore. The ancient Egyptian word for iron meant "black copper from heaven." But since meteorites were very rare, iron was not an important metal. Because iron is more difficult to smelt and to shape than copper, early people did not learn to use it until after 1900 B.C. By about 1200 B.C., knowledge of how to work iron had spread all over the civilized world. Iron quickly replaced bronze for most uses. This was the beginning of the **Iron Age.** Even today, iron—in the form of steel—is our most important metal.

By the time of the Romans, seven metals were known—gold, copper, silver, lead, tin, iron, and mercury. Many of the most important processes for extracting and working metals had been discovered. During the Middle Ages two more metals, antimony and bismuth, were discovered. Methods and equipment had improved, but they were still not very different from those of the ancients.

In the middle of the 18th century the Industrial Revolution began. Great advances were made in metallurgy as in other fields. Most important of these were the many improvements in methods of making and working steel. The invention of steam power and later electric power made possible the invention of great machines that could make thousands of identical metal parts in a short time. The invention of the electric battery led to the discovery of electrolysis, which in turn led to the discovery of new metals. Magnesium and aluminum owe their discovery to electrolysis and are produced by electrolysis today.

These are only a few of the important advances in metallurgy that have led to a growing use of metals. As a matter of fact, more metal has been produced since 1900 than in the thousands of years before that date. Metallurgists have accomplished great things, but their work is by no means finished. New and better metals are always needed as our technology changes and calls for special materials and products that may be an important part of our future.

JOHN A. RING
Union Carbide Corporation

See also ALLOYS; DIES AND MOLDS; MINES AND MINING; ROCKS, MINERALS, AND ORES; WIRE; articles on individual metals, such as ALUMINUM.

METAMORPHOSIS

The crawling caterpillar becomes a moth or a butterfly. The tadpole swimming in shallow water changes into a frog or a toad. Many other animals, too, undergo a change in form at some stage in their lives. This change is called metamorphosis. The word comes from a Greek word meaning "change of form." To metamorphose is to undergo metamorphosis.

During metamorphosis more than just the shape of the animal changes. Many parts inside the animal's body change. So does its way of life.

▶ WHY MANY ANIMALS UNDERGO METAMORPHOSIS

There are several reasons why metamorphosis occurs. One is that the eggs of many kinds of marine animals without backbones are smaller than the period after this sentence. Such eggs develop into tiny creatures called **larvae** (singular: **larva**). The larvae must be able to obtain food in order to grow. They are much too small to be at all like the adult in either shape or way of life. They must live and feed in an entirely different way.

The starfish is such a marine animal. The female deposits her eggs in the water. The tiny larva that hatches out of each egg does not look like a starfish. The larva swims near the surface of the sea. It feeds on microscopic plants until it has grown to many times its original size.

The larva then sinks to the sea floor and remains there while it changes into a little crawling starfish. Metamorphosis has taken place.

▶ LIFE HISTORY OF FROGS

A frog undergoes metamorphosis for the same reason as the starfish. Its eggs are much larger than those of a starfish. Still, they are so small that even tiny frogs cannot hatch from them. The frog's eggs must hatch into a different form of the animal.

A frog lives most of its life out of water as a four-legged hopping creature, but it lays its eggs in water. The larva that hatches from each egg must therefore be able to breathe in the water, as a fish does. It must also be able to take its food from the water. The frog larva, called a **tadpole**, has gills like a fish and swims by means of its long, thick tail. It feeds on water plants and grows to many times its original size. Small legs begin to grow. The tadpole's body thickens and begins to look more like that of a little frog.

When the tadpole reaches a certain size, metamorphosis takes place. Quite suddenly, during the course of a day or so, the legs grow larger and the tail starts to shrink. The gills stop working, and lungs, which have been developing inside the tadpole's body, begin to work.

At this time, unless the frog crawls out of the water, it will drown. It has been changed from a fishlike animal that breathes underwater to an air-breathing land animal. It no longer eats plants. It feeds on worms and insects.

Experiments with Metamorphosis in Frogs

Scientists have experimented to learn why metamorphosis takes place at a certain point in the tadpole's life. They have learned that the thyroid gland, a small gland in the throat, controls metamorphosis in frogs. This gland produces a chemical messenger substance containing iodine. The chemical messenger is carried by the bloodstream to all parts of the body. When enough of this chemical messenger is present in the blood, the tadpole changes into a frog.

Starfish egg hatches into (1) microscopic swimming larva. The larva grows (2 and 3); then drops to ocean floor. There, in one day, it metamorphoses into a tiny starfish that takes years to grow to (4) adult size.

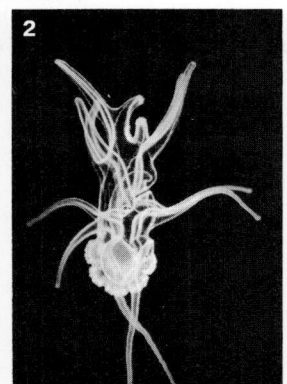

Metamorphosis begins with (1) the larva, or tadpole. For a year it lives in water and breathes through gills. (2) Then in a period of 1 day, the larva's legs grow larger and its lungs begin to work. (3) The tadpole has changed into a frog.

METAMORPHOSIS OF A CECROPIA MOTH

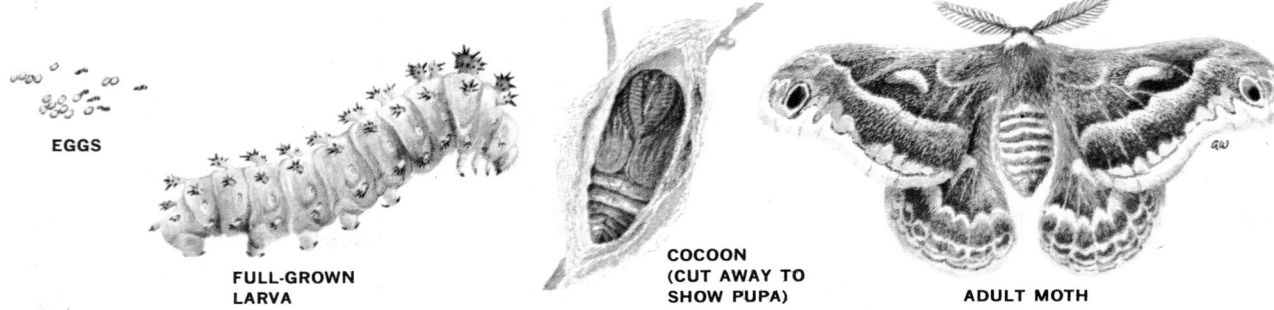

EGGS

FULL-GROWN
LARVA

COCOON
(CUT AWAY TO
SHOW PUPA)

ADULT MOTH

The thyroid gland needs iodine in order to grow. When scientists keep food that contains iodine out of the diet of the tadpole, the thyroid gland can no longer produce its messenger substance. The tadpole keeps on growing—but as a tadpole. It never changes into a frog. The same thing happens if the thyroid gland is removed.

On the other hand, if tadpoles are kept in water rich in iodine, they metamorphose much sooner than they normally would. They also change sooner if they are fed thyroid material. The tadpoles of the leopard frog, for example, metamorphose when they are a little more than 1 inch long. Without their thyroid glands they grow to be tadpoles of 3 or 4 inches. Bullfrog tadpoles normally grow to be about 6 inches long before they change to frogs. On a diet of thyroid material they can be made to change into frogs when they are only 1 or 2 inches long.

▶ METAMORPHOSIS IN INSECTS

Most insects undergo metamorphosis. Insects that fly are able to do so only when they are fully grown. Until then they must live and feed in a way different from that of the adult. In insects, as in frogs, metamorphosis is controlled by a chemical substance in the body.

The greatest change in insects is seen in butterflies and moths. The small moth or butterfly egg usually hatches into a crawling larva, or caterpillar. The caterpillar feeds until it grows to a certain size. Then it spins a covering around itself called a cocoon, or it may burrow into the ground or hide behind loose bark. The caterpillar goes into a resting stage and is now called a pupa. Inside the skin of the pupa, a big change takes place. The larva gradually changes into an adult.

The butterfly or moth that emerges from the pupa is practically a new creature. The metamorphosis of butterflies and moths is more complete than that of any other animal group.

N. J. BERRILL
McGill University

METEOROLOGY. See WEATHER.

METEORS AND METEORITES. See COMETS, METEORS, AND METEORITES.

METRIC SYSTEM. See WEIGHTS AND MEASURES.

METROPOLITAN MUSEUM OF ART

The Metropolitan Museum of Art houses the largest collection of art in the United States. It was incorporated in 1870 by the state of New York. The incentive to establish the museum came from members of the Union League Club, who aroused interest in and support for a public art museum.

In 1880 the City of New York built a permanent home for the Metropolitan Museum on the Fifth Avenue side of Central Park. Though the city still contributes to the maintenance of the building, most of the museum's funds come from private contributions.

▶ **THE COLLECTIONS**

Every year more than 4,000,000 people visit the Metropolitan Museum to see its widely varied collections. The exhibitions include works from every age—from prehistoric pottery to modern paintings—and of every type—from heavy armor to delicate lace. Among the masterpieces are paintings by Raphael, Rembrandt, Vermeer, and El Greco.

One of the outstanding attractions of the museum is its collection of Egyptian art. The exhibit includes the tomb of Perneb and a series of life-size statues of Queen Hapshetsut, dating from about 1500 B.C. The tomb of Perneb, built about 4,400 years ago, has been reconstructed so visitors may enter it. In 1968 the museum added the ancient Temple of Dendur to its collection. This was a gift of the Egyptian Government to the people of the United States for their role in moving ancient monuments away from the danger of flooding when the Aswan High Dam was being built.

Greek and Roman statues have been placed so that you may walk around them and see each one from every possible angle. A bedroom from Boscoreale is decorated with wall paintings that were perfectly preserved under ashes when Vesuvius erupted in A.D. 79. Vases from Greece, China, and Japan, displayed in glass cases, show an endless variety of design and color.

The large and exciting Equestrian Court on the first floor contains life-size figures of armored riders beneath a display of bright heraldic banners. Most of the armor is from the Middle Ages and the Renaissance.

Decorative art objects—including silver, porcelain, and textiles in all styles—are dis-

The Metropolitan Museum of Art's vast collection of Egyptian art is one of the largest in the world outside of Cairo. It is displayed in thirty-two galleries.

played in glass cases. Whole rooms from palaces and great houses have been reconstructed and furnished, to show changes in styles and tastes over a period of 500 years.

In addition to a fine collection of American painting and sculpture, the museum has an entire wing devoted to American decorative arts. Rooms from 17th-, 18th-, and 19th-century houses have been reconstructed with their original woodwork and filled with furniture, silver, glass, and paintings.

Another great attraction of the museum is the Costume Institute, a center for fashion designers. Its collections include clothing from all over the world, representing many styles and periods.

The museum's collection of Islamic art is one of the most comprehensive in the world. In new galleries opened in 1975, the visitor can view a complete survey of Islamic art, from architectural elements to paintings and manuscripts, carpets, ceramics, metalwork, glass, jewelry, and textiles.

The Crosby Brown Collection of Musical Instruments, which came as a gift in 1889, is one of the world's richest and most systematic collections of musical instruments. It forms the nucleus of the museum's musical holdings, which include some 800 instruments from Europe, Asia, the Middle East, Oceania, Africa, and the Americas.

The Michael C. Rockefeller Wing of the Metropolitan is designed to exhibit an unusually extensive collection of primitive art. The museum's holdings include the Michael C. Rockefeller collection, which was transferred to the Metropolitan in 1969, and the museum's collection of pre-Columbian art. These two collections consist of more than 7,500 objects from three separate cultural areas—Africa, Central and South America, and Oceania.

To complement the museum's collection of East Asian art, a reconstruction of a Ming dynasty courtyard was installed in 1981. Twenty-seven engineers and artisans from the People's Republic of China worked for many months to construct the peaceful garden setting.

▶THE CLOISTERS

Overlooking the Hudson River in Fort Tryon Park is the Cloisters—a branch of the Metropolitan Museum devoted to European art of the Middle Ages. The Cloisters looks like a medieval monastery. It is made up of sections from medieval buildings, consisting mainly of five cloisters and a Romanesque chapel. A cloister is a covered walk running around an open court and opening onto it. An entire 12th-century Spanish apse (a large projecting semicircular portion of a building, generally found at the eastern end of a church) was added to the building in 1961. In this authentic medieval setting, many fine examples of sculpture, frescoed walls, painted altarpieces, stained-glass windows, tapestries, and chalices from the 11th to the 15th century are exhibited. The site of the Cloisters, the building, and most of the collections were a gift to the people of New York from John D. Rockefeller, Jr. (1874–1960).

Reviewed by PHILIPPE DE MONTEBELLO
Director, Metropolitan Museum of Art

MEXICAN WAR

In 1846 the United States and Mexico went to war. One of the causes of the war was the annexation by the United States of the former Mexican province of Texas. Americans who had settled in Texas had revolted against Mexico, formed an independent republic, and asked that Texas become part of the United States.

Many Americans wanted to obtain more than just Texas. They sought to acquire, by purchase or conquest, other Mexican territories, including California. These Americans felt that it was necessary for the United States to expand westward. They believed that it was the "manifest destiny" of the United States to span the continent from the Atlantic to the Pacific and from the Canadian border south to the Rio Grande, the river that is now the boundary between the United States and Mexico. This desire for expansion also played a part in bringing about the war.

▶EVENTS LEADING UP TO THE WAR

The years before the war were difficult times for Mexico. Revolutions and changes of government kept the nation in turmoil. Unable to develop the territories of Texas and California, Mexico at first welcomed American settlers there. Later the Mexican Government began to fear the growing power and independence of the settlers, especially in Texas, and passed strict laws to control them. The Texans rebelled and in 1836 declared their independence. Texas then applied to the United States for annexation and statehood.

There was much opposition in the United States to Texas' request. Mexico had threatened war if the United States took over Texas. In addition, Texas would enter the Union as a slave-owning state, and this was unacceptable to the free states, who opposed the expansion of slavery. It was not until 1845 that the United States agreed to annex Texas. Mexico then broke diplomatic relations. Mexico did not declare war, but other disputes arose. The United States claimed the Rio Grande as part of Texas' border. Mexico insisted that the boundary was the Nueces River. There was also a disputed claim by U.S. citizens against Mexico for $3,000,000 for loss of property.

United States President James K. Polk sent a minister, John Slidell, to Mexico. Slidell was to offer to cancel the American money claims and to pay Mexico from $25,000,000 to $40,000,000 if it would accept the Rio Grande boundary and sell California and the New Mexico territory to the United States. The Mexican Government refused to see Slidell.

▶THE WAR BEGINS

President Polk then ordered American forces in Texas to advance to the Rio Grande. On April 25, 1846, Mexican troops crossed the Rio Grande and attacked American soldiers in the disputed area. On May 11, 1846, Polk asked Congress for a declaration of war.

The commander of the American forces in Texas was General Zachary Taylor, who was nicknamed Old Rough and Ready. His victories in the Mexican War later helped him win election as president of the United States. Even before war was formally declared, Taylor had defeated Mexican armies at Palo Alto and Resaca de la Palma. Now, Taylor's men advanced well into Mexico. In September, 1846, they stormed the fortified city of Monterrey, capturing it after a hard-fought battle. It was the first major victory for the United States.

California and New Mexico. Meanwhile the war had spread westward. In June, 1846, American settlers in California rebelled against Mexican rule. An expedition under General Stephen W. Kearny occupied Santa Fe, taking control of New Mexico, and then marched on to California. United States naval forces played an important part in the war in California by lending support to Kearny's troops. The conquest of California was completed in early 1847 with the defeat of Mexican forces near Los Angeles.

In February, 1847, American troops under Colonel Alexander W. Doniphan, marching from Santa Fe, occupied the Mexican city of Chihuahua after heavy fighting.

Buena Vista. At about the same time, General Taylor was advancing on the city of Buena Vista. The Americans and Mexicans clashed in a desperate, hard-fought battle. The advantage swung first to one side, then to the other. As Captain Braxton B. Bragg (a future Confederate general in the U.S. Civil War) brought his artillery into action, Taylor ordered him to "Double-shot your guns and give 'em hell!" When the sounds of battle died away, the Mexicans were in retreat.

Veracruz. Rather than continue the long advance from the north, the United States decided to strike at the heart of Mexico. On March 9, 1847, a seaborne expedition under General Winfield Scott landed near Veracruz on the coast of the Gulf of Mexico. Scott, the highest-ranking general in the U.S. Army, was known as Old Fuss and Feathers because of his strict discipline and handsome uniforms. Artillery commanded by Captain Robert E. Lee (who as a general would command Confederate forces in the Civil War) opened the battle. The shelling forced the surrender of Veracruz. The Americans swept on, winning the battles of Cerro Gordo, Contreras, and Churubusco.

Mexico City. Finally, Mexico City, the capital, loomed before the Americans. Above the city stood the Castle of Chapultepec. The battle for Mexico City was furious, with heavy losses on both sides. Captain Ulysses S. Grant (later the commander of all Union forces in the Civil War) had a light cannon hoisted up into a church tower. From there his gun raked Mexican soldiers in the streets below.

On September 13, 1847, the Americans stormed the Castle of Chapultepec, all that stood between them and victory. It was defended by a small group of soldiers and about 100 young cadets of the Mexican military academy. The cadets, some as young as 14, were known as *los niños* ("the boys"). They fought bravely but were unable to prevent the capture of the castle.

The Peace Treaty. With the fall of Mexico City, the war was practically over. But a treaty of peace remained to be signed. The treaty was signed on February 2, 1848, at the town of Guadalupe Hidalgo. The Treaty of Guadalupe Hidalgo went into effect on July 4, 1848. It established the Rio Grande as the boundary of Texas. Mexico ceded to the United States all of present-day California, Utah, and Nevada, and most of what is now Arizona and New Mexico. In return, the United States paid Mexico $15,000,000, and Mexican debts to American citizens were cancelled.

FAIRFAX DOWNEY
Author, *Texas and the War with Mexico*

See also MEXICO; POLK, JAMES K.; TAYLOR, ZACHARY; TERRITORIAL EXPANSION OF THE UNITED STATES.

MEXICO

Almost every country can be called a land of contrast. But in the nation of Mexico contrasts are sharp and bold. Mexico is a country of parched deserts and lush jungles, of snow-capped mountain peaks and steaming, tropical lowlands. Parts of Mexico are as modern and progressive as any places in the world. And there are isolated areas where people cling to age-old ways. Mexico remains largely a blend of Indian and Spanish cultures. But the rapid growth of industry and population, the shift of people from the countryside to the cities, and the discovery of vast oil reserves are changing Mexico in many ways.

Mexico is the northernmost country of Latin America. It ranks third in population in the Western Hemisphere (after the United States and Brazil) and fifth in area (after Canada, the United States, Brazil, and Argentina).

▶ THE PEOPLE

One of the most important aspects of Mexico's population has been its rapid growth rate. Traditionally the people of Mexico have taken pride in having large families. But during most of Mexico's long history, death rates were high, and the population grew slowly. It was not until after the Revolution of 1910, when the development of modern Mexico began, that health and sanitation services became widely available and the death rate began to drop. But birth rates remained high, causing a "population explosion" by the middle of the 20th century. Until about 1970, most government officials expressed pride in the growing population. They often said that Mexico's wealth was in its people—the more people the more wealth.

Many Mexicans, however, expressed concern about the rapid rate of population increase. It was clear that the government could not keep up in providing such necessities as schools and hospitals. There were not enough jobs for all the people who wanted work. Finally, in 1972, Mexico adopted a government-sponsored program for family planning. By the mid-1980's the population increase seemed to be slowing, and projections for the future indicate a much lower rate of population growth.

The Move to the Cities

During the first half of the 20th century, most people in Mexico lived in rural areas, where their ancestors had lived for generations. Since the 1950's huge numbers of rural people have migrated to the cities. There are many reasons for this. Inexpensive bus service, supported by the government, now connects rural towns and villages with the cities. There is no longer enough productive farmland to support the rural population, and many people had to leave the countryside to find

---

FACTS AND FIGURES

UNITED MEXICAN STATES (Estados Unidos Mexicanos) is the official name of the country.

THE PEOPLE are known as Mexicans.

LOCATION: Southern North America.

AREA: 761,600 sq mi (1,972,547 km²).

POPULATION: 77,000,000 (estimate).

CAPITAL AND LARGEST CITY: Mexico City.

MAJOR LANGUAGES: Spanish (official), various Indian languages.

MAJOR RELIGION: Roman Catholic.

GOVERNMENT: Republic. **Head of state and government**—president. **Legislature**—Congress (made up of a Senate and a Chamber of Deputies).

CHIEF PRODUCTS: Agricultural—corn, beans, wheat, coffee, sugarcane, oilseeds, citrus fruits, bananas, cacao, sorghum, various vegetables, henequen, livestock. **Manufactured**—refined petroleum and petroleum products, chemicals, processed food, textiles, glass, wood products, iron and steel, automobile parts and assembly. **Mineral**—petroleum, natural gas, sulfur, iron ore, copper, zinc, lead, silver, gold.

MONETARY UNIT: Peso (1 peso = 100 centavos).

NATIONAL ANTHEM: *Himno Nacional Mexicana* ("National Anthem of Mexico"). Opening line: *Mexicanos, al grito de guerra* ("Mexicans, to the cry of war").

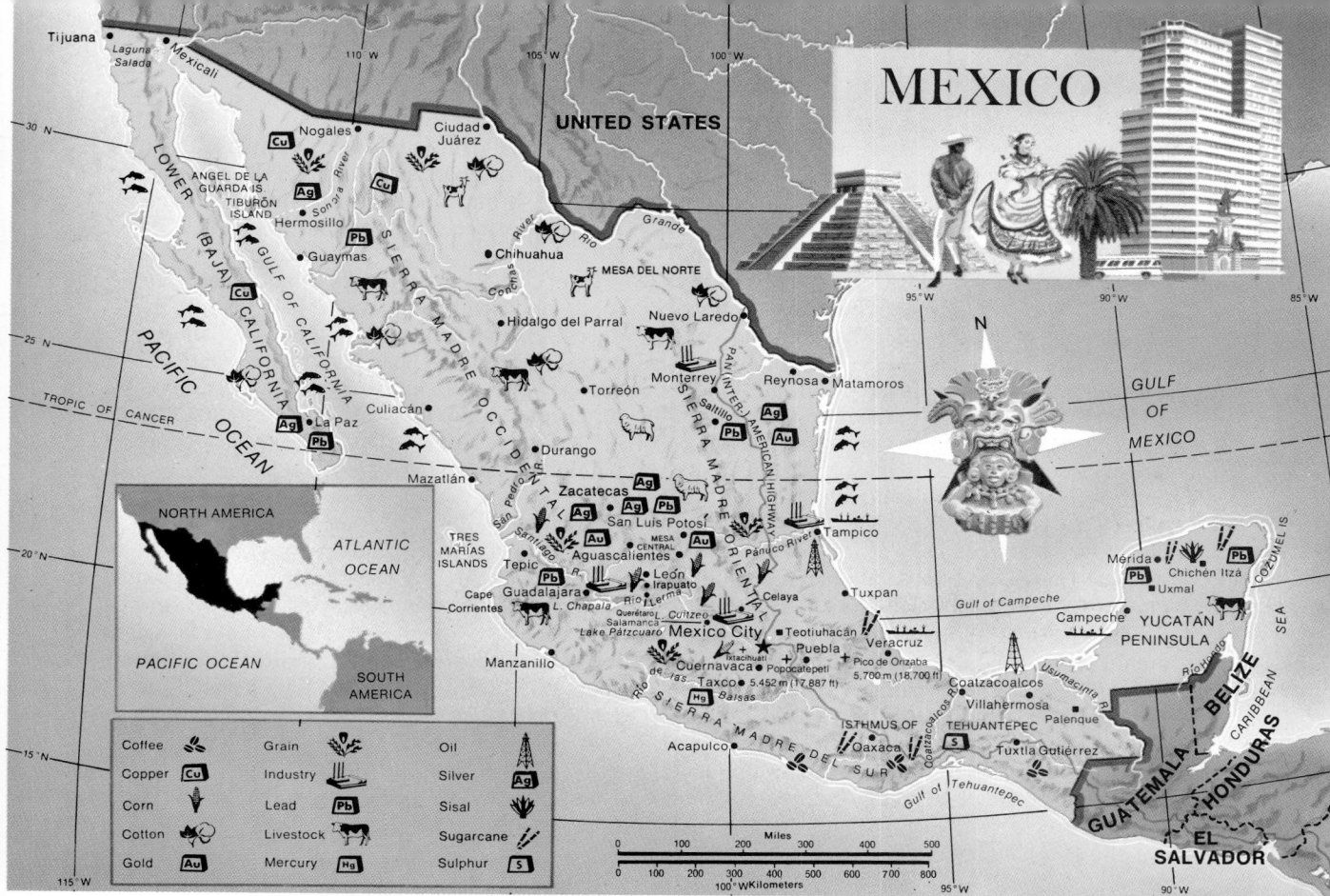

work. Industrial growth and better public services in the cities made many rural people think they could find jobs and a better way of life there.

By the 1980's almost 70 percent of the people lived in urban areas. There were not enough jobs, homes, schools, or other services available in the cities for the many people who moved there. As a result, urban poverty and urban slums became common in the cities.

Mexico City, the capital, has attracted the largest number of people. Already one of the world's largest cities, it has been growing at the rate of 750,000 people a year. In the 1980's about one quarter of Mexico's total population lived in the metropolitan area of Mexico City.

Language and Religion

Most Mexicans are of mixed Spanish and Indian ancestry. As in most other Latin American countries, Spanish is the official language. In fact, Mexico is the world's most populous Spanish-speaking nation. There are regional dialects within the country, just as there are certain regional customs. Numerous Indian groups, generally living in isolated mountain areas, hold to their own languages. But as their contacts with the cities increase, more and more Indians speak Spanish. The overwhelming majority of the people are Roman Catholics.

Education

Mexico has been fighting a battle against illiteracy for nearly a century. At the time of the Revolution of 1910, between 70 and 80 percent of the people could neither read nor write. A system of free public education, from primary schools through the universities, has reduced that figure to about 25 percent. But it is probable that the number of people who cannot read or write is increasing again. Each year the number of children old enough to go to school becomes larger, and the government has not been able to provide enough schools and teachers for them.

There are private and parochial schools as well as state-run schools in the large cities. The law requires that Mexican children attend school up to the age of 15, but the law is not enforced because of the shortage of schools. Secondary and vocational education has expanded rapidly because Mexico's growing industries need skilled workers of all kinds. There are more than 20 universities in Mexico. The National Autonomous University of Mexico, founded in 1551, is the oldest university on the North American continent.

Fine Arts

Mexico has won international recognition during the 20th century for its contribution to the arts. Most of Mexico's famous painters and architects have taken their inspiration from the past. These include painters Diego Rivera (1886–1957), José Clemente Orozco (1883–1949), David Alfaro Siqueiros (1898–1974), and Rufino Tamayo (1899–   ) and architect Juan O'Gorman (1905–82). Composers like Carlos Chávez (1899–1978) and dancers like Amalia Hernández (1917–   ) have expressed the spirit of Mexico's folk music and dance. Many writers have made Mexico and Mexicans the subjects of their works. They include the critic, poet, and scholar Alfonso Reyes (1889–1959), the well-known poet Octavio Paz (1914–   ), and the novelist Carlos Fuentes (1928–   ).

Mexican handicrafts are known around the world. Mountains long have separated one group of Mexicans from another. And each region in the country is known for particular colors and designs for pottery, handicrafts, jewelry, and woven goods. The toys, masks, earthenware, woodwork, ceramics, glass, and jewelry of Mexico combine the best of two cultures—Indian and Spanish.

Foods

The tortilla, a flat, thin corn cake of Indian origin, is eaten everywhere in Mexico with almost every meal. Plain, fried, toasted; rolled or folded and filled with cheese, chicken, or ground meat—it is the basis of such dishes as tacos, enchiladas, and tostadas.

Turkey mole, a famous Mexican dish made of turkey, chocolate, spices, and nuts, was first made in the 16th century by a Spanish nun. Roast kid or goat, sun-dried beef, fish stews, iguana, shrimp and mussels, tropical fruits, and pastries are other regional foods in Mexico.

The cactus and maguey plants also yield foods and drink. One variety of cactus produces tender shoots for salads. Another produces the prickly pear for desserts and preserves. The best-known variety of maguey produces tequila, the country's strongest alcoholic drink. Another maguey produces pulque, a milder drink.

Recreation

Most of the sports that are popular in Mexico have come to the country by way of Spain. Jai alai, a fast handball game of Basque origin, is played by women as well as men. Soccer has as many followers as bullfighting, the sport most closely associated with Mexico. For many people, bullfighting is more than a sport. It is an art in which people pit courage and skill against the bulls. Baseball, from the United States, is becoming more and more popular.

Holidays

The most colorful blending of Mexico's Christian and Indian traditions is evident during the Christmas season. Every night from December 16 through December 24, families re-enact the pilgrimage to Bethlehem with special prayers and songs. The celebration ends each evening when a blindfolded child breaks the *piñata,* an earthen pot covered with brightly colored papier-mâché and filled with fruits, candies, and coins.

All Souls' Day, a day of homage to the dead, is celebrated all over Mexico. Mexicans are taught from childhood not to fear death but to accept it as the beginning of another life. On All Souls' Day families visit the graves of their ancestors to pray, sing, and eat the favorite foods of their dead relatives.

Mexico has several civic holidays, each commemorating a landmark in the country's progress from a Spanish colony to a modern, democratic state. The most important holiday, September 16, celebrates the beginning of the rebellion that brought Mexico freedom from Spain. On the eve of that day, in Mexico City, the president of the country rings a famous

Snow-capped Popocatepetl, an inactive volcano, last erupted in 1702.

bell. This is believed to be the same bell that Father Miguel Hidalgo y Costilla (1753–1811) rang in 1810 to summon his parishioners to rebellion.

On December 12, pilgrims from all over Mexico visit the Basilica of the Virgin of Guadalupe outside Mexico City. They pay homage to the Virgin, the patroness of Mexico and symbol of Hidalgo's rebellion. November 20, the anniversary of the Revolution of 1910, is also an important national holiday. It is marked by parades in every city.

▶ THE LAND

The Mexican landscape is varied and complex. It includes deserts, grasslands, forests, and humid tropical jungles. There are rugged mountain ranges, volcanic peaks, and extensive areas of low-lying plains. But the largest and most important feature of the land is the Central Plateau.

The Central Plateau

In many ways the Central Plateau is the core of Mexico. It contains most of the population and most of the cities, and it accounts for most of the agricultural and industrial production. This region is shaped like an inverted triangle, with its base along the United States border

and its tip extending south to Mexico City. The northern two thirds of the triangle is known as the Mesa del Norte, and the southern third is called the Mesa Central.

The sparsely populated Mesa del Norte is generally flat, with an average height of 1,200 meters (4,000 feet). It is hot and dry in summer and cold and dry in winter. To grow crops, farmers must irrigate the land. Most of the larger cities began as silver-mining towns in colonial days. Small, mineral-rich mountain ranges still yield silver, lead, copper, iron ore, and other minerals.

The plateau rises toward the south and varies from 1,500 to 2,400 meters (5,000 to 8,000 feet) in the Mesa Central. Many rivers and lakes make this rich and fertile region the most productive area in the nation. Farmlands and cities there are crowded. Energy to fuel the region's rapid development comes from a refinery at Salamanca that uses oil piped in from the Gulf Coastal Plain.

Mountains

High, rugged mountain ranges border the Central Plateau to the west and east and come together south of Mexico City. Along the western edge of the Central Plateau is the Sierra Madre Occidental, which has been a severe

Fishing with butterfly nets on Lake Pátzcuaro, in central Mexico.

barrier to east-west travel in Mexico. The only natural pass through this range, at Guadalajara, was the route used in colonial times by numerous Spanish expeditions into California. There are many spectacular volcanoes in the southern part of the Sierra Madre Occidental. The highest and best known are the snow-capped peaks of Popocatepetl ("Smoking Mountain") and Ixtacihuatl ("Sleeping Woman").

Along the eastern edge of the Central Plateau is another range of mountains, the Sierra Madre Oriental. The only natural pass through this range is at Monterrey. To the south of Mexico City, this range joins with the Sierra Madre Occidental. Here is the snow-capped volcanic peak of Pico de Orizaba (Citlaltepetl). It rises to 5,700 meters (18,700 feet) and is one of the highest peaks in North America. The Southern Highlands, or Sierra Madre del Sur, extend south from Mexico City along the Pacific coast.

Mexico's fertile mountain valleys are densely settled. The people cling to their traditional Indian languages, dress, and customs. They have remained rather isolated from the main currents of modern Mexico.

Coastal Plains and Lowlands

Unlike most nations of the world, the development of civilization in Mexico was not centered in the lowlands. Throughout history, the lowlands have been sparsely settled and isolated from the commercial and political centers of the nation. But since 1950, increased attention has been given to the lowlands. With their newly irrigated farmlands, oil wealth, and growing tourist industry, they are Mexico's new frontiers.

One of the two principal lowland regions is the Pacific Coastal Plain in the northwest. It extends from Cape Corrientes to the United States border and includes the peninsula of Baja California. The southern part of the plain is tropical, with humid summers and dry winters. The dry, northern plain is part of the Sonora Desert. An increase in agricultural production due to river-valley irrigation projects and the growth of coastal resorts have contributed to the area's growing prosperity.

The Gulf Coast and the Yucatan Peninsula form the most extensive lowland area in Mexico. The northern part of this lowland is dry. It extends inland almost 160 kilometers (100 miles). Irrigation water from the Rio Grande and its tributaries has helped this region become an important agricultural center. Parts of the southern Gulf Coast are covered by swamps and lagoons. Oil has been an important part of the economy of the Gulf Coast since the turn of the century. And vast new oil discoveries in this region promise to make it even more important. The many temples of the ancient Mayas, such as Chichén-Itzá and Uxmal, make the Yucatan Peninsula a popular tourist attraction.

Natural Resources

Mexico is rich in minerals. But only about 12 percent of the land is suitable for growing crops, and Mexico must import food for its growing population.

Besides the minerals in its mountains and the oil wealth along its Gulf Coast, Mexico has plant and animal life as varied as its climate and terrain. In the arid north, plant life consists of cacti of all kinds, evergreens, and thorny shrubs. On the Central Plateau and in the lower areas of the mountains, there are savannas (grasslands) and forests of oak, pine, poplar, and willow trees. Many kinds of tropical trees grow in the rain forests of the south.

In the cooler north and in the mountains, there are wolves, bears, coyotes, foxes, and deer. Tropical Mexico has jaguars, ocelots, tapirs, monkeys, and anteaters. The burro, "beast of a thousand uses," can be found in every part of the country. In the forests and skies are brilliant birds—parrots, macaws, parakeets, doves, and vultures. Shrimp, tuna, sardines, and other sea creatures live in the waters off the Pacific coast and in the Gulf of Mexico.

▶ THE ECONOMY

Agriculture is of great importance to the economy. But since 1971, the value of manufactured goods sold to other countries has been greater than the export value of agricultural products. This is true even though only about one fourth of all employed Mexicans work in industry.

Agriculture

Mexico's leading crops are maize (corn), beans, cotton, wheat, coffee, sugarcane, and oil seeds. Sugarcane production, mainly along the southern coasts, has doubled since 1959. Sugar now competes with cotton as Mexico's leading agricultural export. Cotton was once the leading crop along the northern Gulf Coast, but animal feeds, especially sorghum and alfalfa, have gained in importance in this region. Cotton is also important in the irrigated farmlands of the northern Pacific Coastal Plain and the Mesa del Norte, where grains and winter vegetables are also grown. An increasing amount of land has been used for growing coffee since 1950, and coffee is Mexico's third most valuable export. Coffee and cacao are the chief crops in the mountains bordering the Gulf Coast.

South of the cotton and grain fields of the northern Gulf Coast is Mexico's citrus belt, with its large orchards of oranges, lemons, and grapefruit. Maize, beans, squash, and other food crops are grown in the mountains and along the southern Gulf Coast for local use. Maize and beans are the chief crops of the Mesa Central during the rainy summer months. Wheat, hay, and vegetables are grown there during the dry winter months. A number of specialty crops are grown on the Mesa Central, such as garlic, strawberries, and

The open-air market in Toluca.

maguey. Henequen has long been the major crop of the Yucatan Peninsula. (Fiber from the henequen plant is used for making inexpensive rope and twine.) But recent competition from henequen grown in Kenya has depressed the economy of rural areas of the peninsula.

Much of the nonirrigated area is used for grazing cattle and goats. Cattle are also raised throughout the Gulf Coast and the Yucatan Peninsula.

Mineral Production and Other Industries

Oil fields along the Gulf Coast made Mexico the world's largest exporter of oil by 1922. Oil exports later declined, but Mexican oil provided a major source of energy for the nation's developing industries. With the discovery in the 1970's of vast new oil reserves along the Gulf Coast and off-shore, Mexico may well become the next major oil-producing nation in the world. Natural gas, found in the same areas, provides another important source of income. Sulfur, iron, copper, zinc, lead, silver, and gold are also mined.

Tourism and fishing are industries of long standing. The traditional light industries of Mexico, such as food processing and the making of glass, textiles, and wood products, have expanded greatly in recent decades. There has also been a rapid growth of such industries as iron and steel production, the manufacture

This oil refinery in central Mexico processes one of the country's most important natural resources.

of automobile parts, automobile assembly, and the manufacture of chemicals and petrochemicals. The value of Mexico's industrial goods is now about three times as great as the value of its agricultural products.

▶ CITIES

Mexico City is the nation's capital and the world's largest city. It is described in an article following this article.

Guadalajara, Mexico's second largest city, is also growing rapidly. But it is much smaller than Mexico City. It is the regional capital for much of the Central Plateau. The city has become a major transportation, industrial, commercial, and distribution center for a large and productive agricultural region.

Monterrey, Mexico's third largest city, was Mexico's first major industrial city. It is the center of the nation's iron and steel industry. Puebla was the traditional cotton textile center of Mexico. More recently it has become known for production of iron and steel, automobiles, and petrochemicals.

Throughout Mexico's history, the Gulf Coast city of Veracruz has been the country's chief seaport. It remains vital to the nation's trade. Most of the major cities of the Mesa del Norte are state capitals, such as Chihuahua, Zacatecas, Durango, San Luis Postosí, and Saltillo or the border towns of Ciudad Juárez and Nuevo Laredo. Cities on the Mesa Central such as León, Celaya, Irapuato, Salamanca, and Querétaro were once small, peaceful towns with long histories and much charm. Today they are rapidly growing commercial and industrial centers.

▶ GOVERNMENT

Mexico is a republic composed of 29 states, two territories, and a federal district. Mexico is governed by the Constitution of 1917. The president is elected by popular vote for a 6-year term. Under the law, a president may not serve two terms in succession. The president appoints a cabinet to assist in governing the country. The Congress consists of two houses, the Senate and the Chamber of Deputies. Senators are elected for 6-year terms and deputies serve for 3 years. All are elected by popular vote. The judicial branch of the government consists of the Supreme Court of Justice, whose members are appointed for

Taxco, southwest of Mexico City, was founded as a silver-mining community in the 16th century.

life. The Supreme Court appoints district and circuit court judges.

▶ HISTORY

Mexico's history is one of the longest in the New World. More than a thousand years before Hernando Cortes landed in what is now called Mexico, great empires had risen and fallen in the area. The Olmec first, then the Maya, followed by the Toltec, Zapotec, Mixtec, and Maya once again, had made many important discoveries in agriculture and science, built great cities, and created great works of art. At the time of the Spanish conquest the Aztecs, ruled by Montezuma, were the most powerful of Mexico's Indians.

The Spanish Conquest

The first Spaniards to reach Mexico came in an expedition led by Francisco Hernández de Córdova. They sailed from Cuba and landed on the coast of Yucatan in 1517, but they were soon driven out of the country by the Maya. In 1518 a second expedition, led by Juan de Grijalva, landed near Veracruz. This time Indians and Spaniards exchanged gifts.

A third expedition, under the leadership of Hernando Cortes, sailed from Cuba in February, 1519. Cortes and his men sailed along the coast of Yucatan. In Tabasco, Cortes received 20 women as a gift. One of these was Malinche, called Doña Marina by the Spaniards.

She spoke the Mayan and Aztec languages, learned Spanish, and became Cortes' wife, guide, and interpreter. She was invaluable in the conquest of Mexico. Cortes and his small army landed on April 21, 1519, on the Gulf Coast, where he founded the first Spanish city in Mexico. He called it Villa Rica de la Vera Cruz, the "Rich City of the True Cross," because it is on remarkably fertile land and because the day was Good Friday.

Three factors were important in helping Cortes conquer Mexico. These were the discipline and ambition of his army, the assistance he received from thousands of Tlaxcalans and other peoples who hated the Aztecs and wished to fight against them, and the belief of many Indians, including the Aztec emperor Montezuma, that the blue-eyed and bearded conqueror was somehow associated with the god Quetzalcoatl. There was a fourth reason for Cortes' victory. When his Indian and Spanish forces besieged Tenochtitlán, the city was caught in an epidemic of smallpox, a disease one of Cortes' men had earlier brought into the city. Tenochtitlán was heroically defended by Cuauhtémoc, who succeeded Montezuma and is one of Mexico's heroes. But in less than three months of fighting and disease, the city fell. By 1522, in less than three years, Cortes had conquered Mexico and had opened for the kings of Spain a vast territory stretching from what is now the southwest of the United States to the Isthmus of Panama.

The sculptured altarpiece of the Church of San Francisco in Huejotzingo dates from the time when Mexico was ruled by Spain.

Colonial Mexico

From 1522 to 1821, Mexico, called New Spain, was a Spanish colony. New Spain was governed first by Cortes and later by viceroys appointed by the king of Spain. Two powerful groups developed in the new colony—the aristocracy of mineowners and landowners and the Roman Catholic Church. The church brought the Christian religion, schools, universities, and learning to the country. But through the Inquisition, the church also suppressed freedom of religion and thought. By the beginning of the 19th century, 50 percent of the land and capital in New Spain was held by the Catholic Church.

Then began the blending of Spanish and Indian civilizations that make up the pattern of Mexican life today. The Indians taught the settlers how to cultivate corn, tomatoes, tobacco, and cacao. The Spanish, in turn, introduced sugarcane, wheat, rice, and onions—crops unknown to the Indians. The Spanish also set up new industries—the making of cotton and woolen goods, mining, and city building. They introduced domestic work animals and a crucial invention, the wheel.

Agriculture and the mining of gold and silver made New Spain a rich colony. But wealth and prosperity were limited to a few. The ruling group was a minority, made up of people born in Spain and known in Mexico as *gachupines* ("those with spurs"). The *gachupines,* proud of their place of birth, controlled all important government jobs and industrial and commercial enterprises and owned the best lands. The *criollos,* or Spaniards born in the colony, were next in importance. They were often wealthy, but they were allowed only minor government posts. Next there were the mestizos, persons of mixed Indian and Spanish descent, who held no government positions at all. They worked as supervisors, storekeepers, soldiers, or parish priests. The largest group was the Indians, who worked for the landowners and mineowners under conditions of virtual slavery.

Independent Mexico

When Napoleon invaded Spain in 1808, he put his brother Joseph on the Spanish throne. This set off a Mexican independence movement.

The leader of the movement was Miguel Hidalgo y Costilla, a *criollo* priest in Dolores, a village in the state of Guanajuato. On the eve of September 16, 1810, Hidalgo summoned his parishioners to revolt. His army soon grew with Indian and mestizo volunteers. The Spaniards defeated Hidalgo's forces, who were poorly armed and inexperienced in war, and Hidalgo was executed within a year. His struggle was kept alive by José María Morelos y Pavón (1765–1815), a mestizo priest and Hidalgo's former student. Morelos, after several victories and two years of fighting, called together a congress in 1813. This congress declared the country independent and drafted a constitution that included many social reforms. But soon after, Morelos was defeated, and in 1815 he was executed by the Spanish. Vicente Guerrero (1783–1831), one of his guerrillas, continued to fight and compelled the leader of the Spanish forces, the *criollo* general Agustín de Iturbide (1783–1824), to agree to independence in 1821.

The First Empire. Mexico was independent, but it had no government. Iturbide seized power and declared himself emperor. Once again Guerrero rose to fight him, as did Antonio López de Santa Anna (1795–1876), a former officer of the Spanish forces. Their successful revolt made the country an independent republic, and for a short time Mexico enjoyed constitutional rule under Guadalupe Victoria (1789–1843), its first president.

The Mexican War. Mexico's progress from independence to nationhood was to take another 30 years. Conflicts between conservatives, upholding strong central government, and liberals, upholding equal responsibility among all states, divided and weakened the country. The conservatives were eager to keep their old privileges, while the liberals were interested in broad social reforms.

The country suffered its greatest loss in the war with the United States, known as the Mexican War (1846–48). In 1835 United States colonists in Texas, then Mexican territory, revolted against Mexico. Santa Anna, the ruler of Mexico, marched into the area. After a victory at the Alamo he was defeated and captured by Sam Houston's troops at San Jacinto. In exchange for his freedom Santa Anna agreed to withdraw all Mexican troops from the territory. Ten years later, Texas, still not recognized as independent by Mexico, was annexed by the United States. And the two countries found themselves at war. Santa Anna, once again in power, led a poorly equipped and poorly supplied army into Texas. Defeated in several battles, he retreated to Mexico City, from which he fled when General Winfield Scott's troops occupied it. Settlement of the war cost Mexico almost half of its territory.

The liberals finally exiled Santa Anna in 1855 and began to lead the country out of chaos. One man began to realize his dream of a nation united and ruled by law. He was Benito Juárez, a Zapotec Indian who saw all Mexicans as one people. He played a leading role in framing the Constitution of 1857, a landmark in the country's history. The constitution abolished the special courts of the army and of the church, forbade the church to own property, recognized civil marriage, and called for freedom of religion, education, assembly, and the press.

Benito Juárez worked to build a united Mexico.

The conservatives violently opposed the constitution, and the country found itself in another three-year war, known as the War of the Reform (1857–61).

Juárez, then provisional president, entered Mexico City triumphantly in 1861. But war had made the country bankrupt. Juárez suspended the country's debts to France, Spain, and Britain. Juárez soon negotiated with Spain and Britain. But France's Napoleon III, urged by Mexican conservatives, seized the opportunity to establish a monarchy in Mexico. Napoleon wanted a Catholic, conservative, French monarchy in the New World. He hoped to rival the Protestant, liberal republic of the United States. He knew the United States, then fighting its own Civil War, could not enforce its policy of opposing European intrusion into the Western Hemisphere. (This policy is known as the Monroe Doctrine.)

French troops invaded Mexico in 1862. With the support of conservative forces the French were victorious at Puebla. Juárez had to flee the capital in 1863. Conservatives declared Mexico a monarchy, and Napoleon III offered the crown to Archduke Maximilian of Austria and his wife Carlota.

The Second Empire. Maximilian, a well-meaning but weak prince, tried to rule Mexico well. But his attempts disappointed his conservative supporters, who betrayed and opposed him. The United States, at peace with

Pancho Villa, one of the leaders of the Revolution of 1910, rides with some of his supporters.

itself after the Civil War and interested in keeping all European powers out of the New World, supported Juárez, who continued to fight Maximilian. Napoleon withdrew his troops from Mexico. Maximilian, now deserted, was made a prisoner and executed in 1867. Juárez, once again free to govern as president, laid the foundations for industry, transportation, and communications—and, most important, for a system of public education that reached out to the illiterate Indians and mestizos. When Juárez died in office in 1872, Mexico had become a nation.

The Age of Don Porfirio. Porfirio Díaz (1830–1915)—one of Juárez' officers and, like him, from Oaxaca—took the presidency by force in 1876 and ruled the country for about 30 years. The church, the traditional aristocracy, and the army regained their old privileges. A newly rich group of business leaders and industrialists also began to attain prominence.

Don Porfirio thought of himself not as a dictator but as a severe but just father of the poor and the oppressed. In 30 years he brought stability to the country. He built railroads, improved harbors, and increased agricultural production. He started the oil industry, promoted good relations with other countries, and encouraged foreign investment in the nation's agriculture and industry. He set a style of life based largely on that of Paris—ornate, elegant, and extravagant but available only to a very few.

The Revolution of 1910

Under Don Porfirio the Indians had less land than ever before. The workers had no right to strike. The country had no real self-government. Members of the legislature were hand-picked, and all opposition was suppressed. In 1910, rebellion broke out. In the north it was led by Pancho Villa (1877–1923), a former cattle bandit and colorful guerrilla fighter. In the south Emiliano Zapata (1877?–1919), a tough peasant leader who wanted land for the Indians, headed the uprising. The rebellion brought about the election of Francisco Madero (1873–1913), a high-minded, wealthy cotton planter. Madero had written a book advocating that no president should have immediate re-election and that land should be given to the Indians.

Many opposed Madero, including Victoriano Huerta (1854–1916), a ruthless general who quickly had Madero assassinated. Villa and Zapata rose against Huerta. So did Venustiano Carranza (1859–1920), a state governor. Carranza called a convention that drafted the Constitution of 1917. The Constitution revived Juárez' ideals of free public education and control of church property and wealth. It also introduced laws to regulate hours and wages for the workers and to uphold the right to unionize and strike. The Constitution affirmed the government's right to reclaim ownership of all land and resources belonging to the nation.

Modern Mexico

Since 1920 no Mexican president has been overthrown by a military uprising, nor has the nation suffered any major civil conflict. In 1929, during the administration of Emilio Portes Gil, the National Revolutionary Party was founded. For the first time there was a civilian party that could compete with, and in time control, the army. The army had always been the chief political power and the only source of presidential candidates. The party, now called the Institutional Revolutionary Party, governs the nation. One-party rule seems undemocratic. But the party's membership includes all important groups in the nation —farmers, urban workers, business and professional people, and students. Although Mexico's presidents all belong to the same political party, their interests and policies have varied greatly. Lázaro Cárdenas nationalized United States and British oil companies, built schools, and distributed land to the poor. General Manuel Ávila Camacho made peace with the church. His government also declared war against Germany in 1941.

Since Camacho, only civilians have been president. Miguel Alemán Valdés improved irrigation, communications, social security, and education. Adolfo Ruiz Cortines made government more efficient. Adolfo López Mateos attracted new foreign investment for developing heavy and light industries. Gustavo Díaz Ordaz continued a policy of domestic development and international co-operation.

In more recent times, Luis Echeverría Alvarez began a national family-planning program to try to reduce the birth rate. José López Portillo used income from petroleum exports and borrowed heavily from abroad to invest in agriculture and industry. His successor, Miguel de la Madrid Hurtado, was elected in 1982. He pledged to end corruption among government officials, curb wasteful programs, and bring Mexico's huge foreign debt under control.

Many people take pride in Mexico's progress. Between 1960 and 1980, the income per person nearly doubled. Industrial production grew at an even more rapid rate. Agricultural output increased during the early 1980's. Acapulco and other tourist centers attracted more visitors than ever before. Mexico has more than enough petroleum to meet its needs for energy. It has many other mineral resources and a large supply of low-cost labor. These are ideal conditions for future industrial growth. This is one view of Mexico, and it is a sound view.

Others are less optimistic. The Revolution of 1910, they say, was supposed to have helped the masses share more equally in the nation's wealth—and perhaps it did. But there is a growing gap between the rich and the poor. At the lower end of the economic scale, there are millions of Mexicans who have not shared in the great economic growth of recent decades. They live in grinding poverty in rural

Aztec temple ruins, a Spanish colonial church, and modern apartment buildings form the Plaza of Three Cultures, Mexico City.

areas and in the slums of cities. These are the poor—without skills, without land, often illiterate, and with little hope for the future. When they find work, they often earn too little to support their families. Most can find only part-time work or no work at all. In spite of the national family-planning program, the population grows so rapidly that the creation of new jobs cannot keep pace with the swelling tide of workers. Thousands of unemployed Mexicans illegally cross the border into the United States every year in search of work to support themselves and their families.

The government supports many industries and pays for a wide range of social programs to provide jobs and help the poor. Because of a worldwide surplus of oil in the early 1980's, Mexico received much less money for its oil exports than had been expected. The government then borrowed large sums of money to pay for its programs. Prices and interest rates rose sharply, and many businesses failed. Mexico's economic difficulties also discouraged individuals and private companies from investing in the country in ways that would provide new jobs.

Mexico's future is unclear. Will it become one of the world's economic giants? It has the resources to do so if the people can find ways to deal with the many serious problems their country faces.

JOHN M. BALL
Georgia State University

EUGENIO C. VILLICAÑA
Author, *Mexico*

See also CORTES, HERNANDO; INDIANS OF NORTH AMERICA; JUÁREZ, BENITO; LATIN AMERICA; MEXICAN WAR; MEXICO CITY.

MEXICO CITY

In the capital of Mexico the old and the new meet in a lovely highland valley near the center of the country. Mexico City rests on a filled-in lake bed more than 2,300 meters (7,800 feet) above sea level. Mountains rise on all sides. These include two snowcapped volcanoes, Ixtacihuatl and Popocatepetl.

Mexico City, with about 17,000,000 people in its metropolitan area, is thought by some to be the world's largest city. It is Mexico's industrial, commercial, and cultural center and a popular attraction for tourists. Large numbers of Mexicans arrive each year from rural areas in search of a better way of life, adding to the size of the great city. Rapid growth has led to a number of problems, including overcrowding and air pollution. Mexico City occasionally has been struck by earthquakes, most recently in 1985, when successive earthquakes caused considerable damage and loss of life.

The Zócalo

Twentieth-century Mexico City rests upon the ruins of ancient Tenochtitlán, the mighty capital of the Aztec Indian Empire, built in 1325. Here the Spanish began construction of a giant cathedral in 1573. The site was the ruins of the temple of the Aztec god of war. The cathedral, the largest in Latin America, was not completed until 1791. Today it proudly stands on the north side of the Zócalo (officially the Plaza de la Constitución). The ruins of the Great Temple of the Aztecs, long buried beneath modern Mexico City, were rediscovered only recently. In 1982, after the site was excavated by archeologists, the ruins were opened to the public.

The Zócalo is the center of old Mexico City. It is surrounded by some of the finest examples of Spanish colonial architecture in the Americas. On its east side is the National Palace. Cortes built his house on this spot. The present building houses the offices of the president. Above the central doorway is the Mexican Liberty Bell. This bell was rung by Miguel Hidalgo y Costilla in 1810 to rally the people to the struggle for freedom from Spain. The bell is rung each year on September 15.

Clustered on the other sides of the Zócalo are government buildings. These include the National Library, National Archives, National Museum, National Pawn Shop, and Municipal Palace. Nearby are many of the city's finest restaurants, hotels, theaters, and shops.

A short distance from the Zócalo, down Avenida Juárez, is the Alameda. This large park contains a beautiful monument to the Mexican president Benito Juárez. Across the street is the massive Palace of Fine Arts. Built by the dictator Porfirio Díaz, it houses the Ministry of Fine Arts. The palace is also the home of the national opera and ballet companies. Here, too, is the national symphony orchestra, organized by the famous Mexican composer Carlos Chávez. The walls of the palace bear murals by Mexico's greatest artists—Rivera, Orozco, Siqueiros, and Tamayo.

Across Avenida Juárez is the Latin-American Tower. This modern skyscraper is 44 stories tall. Rising 181 meters (595 feet) above the ground, it is the tallest building not only in Mexico but in all Latin America.

Where Avenida Juárez ends, the broad, tree-lined Paseo de la Reforma begins. The Paseo, adorned with monuments, is one of the world's loveliest boulevards. Statues of noted Mexicans add a historical luster to the Paseo's calm beauty. The great wrought-iron gates of Chapultepec Park mark the end of the Paseo.

Chapultepec Park

Chapultepec is one of the most popular of the city's many parks. It contains woods of giant bald cypresses, bridle paths, and lakes. Children flock to its zoo. The park also has a castle, where presidents of Mexico used to live. Now the castle has been turned into a historical museum.

The park provides a natural setting for one of the largest and certainly one of the most beautiful museums in the world. In front of the National Museum of Anthropology is a giant stone statue of the Indian rain god Tlaloc. This 168-ton statue is the largest Indian idol ever found. The airy grand patio of the museum is roofed by a huge aluminum umbrella. Soft Indian music can be heard in the galleries surrounding the patio.

Mexico is an archeological treasure land, and the museum has a matchless pre-Columbian collection on display. The excavations for the Mexico City subway unearthed tons of relics from all periods of Mexican history. The museum has many programs to encourage interest in ancient Mexican crafts.

University City

In sharp contrast to Chapultepec's tranquillity is the modern bustle of University City. The famed University of Mexico, one of the oldest universities in the Americas, is located here on the outskirts of the city. The students attend classes in an area that was once nothing but a boulder-strewn lava plain. The area was transformed into a beautiful center of learning by Mexico's best architects, designers, painters, and sculptors. The result is a striking combination of all the varied cultures that have helped form modern Mexico.

Perhaps the most outstanding and representative building is the library. The brainchild of architect-muralist Juan O'Gorman, it blends the clean, straight lines of modern architecture with Aztec symbolism in rich mosaic murals and bas-reliefs.

The rest of the campus shows the same happy blend. Throughout are stunning works by Mexico's best artists. The science building, for example, has a Chávez Morado mural; the administration building, a mural by Siqueiros.

Even in sports, University City combines the old with the new. The thick lava stones of the *frontóns* ("courts") where jai alai is played were designed to suggest the truncated pyramids of the pre-Aztec Indians. Architect Carlos Laza built the giant 110,000-seat Olympic Stadium by pushing volcanic rock into two mounds and placing a concrete shell between them. The outer walls depict, in a "sculpture painting" by Diego Rivera, the history of Mexican sports.

Mexico's Floating Gardens

Mexico's oldest outlying district is the famous pre-Aztec city of Teotihuacán, with its restored pyramids. But equally well-known

Library of the University of Mexico.

is Xochimilco (Aztec for "place where the flowers grow"). It is a favorite excursion point. Before the Spanish Conquest the Aztecs built rafts of twigs and reeds on Lake Xochimilco. These rafts, or chinampas, were covered with rich earth and planted with flowers of all kinds. The roots of the plants gradually grew down to the bottom of the shallow lake. They took root, and the rafts became tiny islands.

Today these floating gardens contain tropical plants, giant eucalyptus trees, and hundreds of different types of flowers. Mexicans love to spend an afternoon floating through the narrow canals in flat-bottom boats. The boats often bear arches of fresh flowers woven to spell out their names. Floating *mariachi* bands lend a musical touch to the scene.

Mexico City has other, poorer sections. The government is making a great effort to improve these areas. So far, it has not been able to provide jobs or housing for all the new arrivals who want them. But the goal is to have whole blocks, or even suburbs, where people with low incomes may live in inexpensive apartments, each with its own garden.

Reviewed by ANDRÉS IDUARTE
Columbia University

See also INDIANS OF NORTH AMERICA; JUÁREZ, BENITO.

MIAMI

Miami is a well-known resort city situated on Biscayne Bay, an arm of the Atlantic Ocean, near the southern tip of Florida. It is noted for winter sunshine, sports, and large hotels along palm-fringed beaches. Miami is also a gateway to the Florida Keys, the Everglades, the West Indies, and South America.

Miami was founded soon after the frost of 1894–95 spoiled central Florida's orange crop. Farmers near the southern trading post of Fort Dallas, where the Miami River empties into Biscayne Bay, escaped the frost. At a settler's suggestion, Henry Flagler (1830–1913), a businessman and promoter, built a railroad line to this settlement and drained the swamps. He installed waterworks, developed the land, and built a resort hotel. The town was incorporated as Miami in 1896 with about 1,500 people. The climate soon drew settlers, vacationers, and real estate dealers. John S. Collins, a New Jersey horticulturist, started the Miami Beach Improvement Company, which drained a mangrove swamp across the bay from Miami and built it into a long,

Miami Beach stands on a narrow Island.

thin island—Miami Beach. It was incorporated in 1915. The company advertised delightful, springlike winter temperatures and balmy summers with gentle trade winds.

A land rush began. During the 1920's thousands of people went to Miami. Almost overnight a cluster of resort towns sprang up around the city. Today Greater Miami, the largest metropolitan area in Florida, includes Miami Beach, Coral Gables, Hialeah, more than 20 other towns, and large urbanized areas.

Miami's main business is tourism. More than 10,000,000 vacationers a year come to the area to enjoy swimming, sunbathing, sailing, golfing, and taking side trips. To preserve its leading position as a resort center, the city is engaged in a massive engineering project to help restore its eroding beaches. This project will also provide for hurricane protection.

Bayfront Park, one of the city's main parks, has an outdoor theater for opera and concerts and a public library. Most of the main parks in the Greater Miami area have beaches, playgrounds, and picnic grounds. Some have rare flowers, such as those found in the Fairchild Tropical Gardens.

Horse racing is enjoyed at Tropical Park, Gulfstream Park, Hialeah Park, or Calder Race Track. Greyhound races, jai alai games, golf tournaments, and boat races attract crowds. On New Year's Day college football teams compete in the Orange Bowl, the home stadium of the University of Miami Hurricanes and the professional Miami Dolphins.

Miami's cultural institutions include the Miami Symphony Orchestra, the Greater Miami Opera Guild, the Museum of Science, and the Villa Vizcaya, a mansion once owned by James R. Deering and now the Vizcaya-Dade County Art Museum. Educational institutions in the area include the University of Miami, in Coral Gables; Florida International University in Miami; and Miami-Dade Community College, in Miami.

Miami's industries turn out furniture, food products, plastics, electrical equipment, clothing, and other products. The subtropical climate that makes Miami a vacationland also makes it a distribution center for vegetables and fruits grown on surrounding farmlands.

Reviewed by ROBERT S. CHAUVIN
Stetson University

The Creation of Adam is one of nine scenes painted by Michelangelo on the ceiling of the Sistine Chapel.

MICHELANGELO (1475–1564)

Michelangelo devoted his whole life to the creation of magnificent works of art. His work was all that interested him, and he had no use for the easy ways of doing things. He lived a long and productive life, creating art that influenced almost all countries in all ages.

Michelangelo Buonarroti was born in Caprese near Florence, Italy, on March 6, 1475. On that day his father, Judge Buonarroti, thought he saw lucky signs in the sky. He was sure the boy would have heavenly powers. For this reason he named his son Michelangelo—*angelo* in Italian means "angel." Michelangelo was a sickly child, but though he remained small and thin throughout his life, he had amazing strength and energy.

Remembering the heavenly signs, Judge Buonarroti sent Michelangelo to school with the hope that the boy would become a great scholar. But Michelangelo was interested in art and sketched or painted day and night. His father and uncles were horrified that he wanted to be an artist. They thought art was a low occupation fit only for peasants. They beat Michelangelo cruelly to make him forget his dream, but the beatings made him more determined. Finally, in 1488, they agreed to let him study with Domenico Ghirlandaio (1449–94), a popular Florentine painter.

In Ghirlandaio's workshop Michelangelo studied the art of the old masters and learned to paint **frescoes**—paintings done on wet plaster. Although he was only 13, Michelangelo was highly skilled. Ghirlandaio paid him a small salary, which the boy gave to his father. The other students did not like Michelangelo because of his hot-tempered, critical ways. And they were jealous of his talent. From the very beginning of his career, he scorned anyone whose goals were less than his—and Michelangelo's goal was perfection in art. He was very outspoken and did not hesitate to attack the ideas of others.

Florence at that time was ruled by the powerful Medici family, who were great lovers of art. When Michelangelo was 16, Ghirlandaio sent him to study sculpture with Bertoldo de Giovanni (1420?–91). Bertoldo supervised the garden of Lorenzo de' Medici, a meeting place for Florentine scholars and artists. Lorenzo, the ruling prince, was so impressed with the ability of the young genius that he gave Michelangelo the privileges of a son. This was a wonderful opportunity for the boy, but his father was sadder than ever. He thought that Michelangelo would be nothing more than a lowly stonecutter and mason.

In the 2 years that Michelangelo lived with Lorenzo he met the most outstanding men of the day. Although he learned a great deal from them, he never copied their courteous ways. These men often talked about the philosophy

The *Last Judgment* (1536–41) was painted on the western wall of the Sistine Chapel.

and art of ancient Greece. Michelangelo came to love the great size and power of Greek sculpture. He admired the Greeks' attempt to capture ideal beauty in their statues. At night he studied anatomy (the structure of the human body). Secretly he cut up dead bodies to see how they were put together. To create overpowering, perfect human forms in marble became his one mission in life.

While living with Lorenzo, Michelangelo once criticized the work of Pietro Torrigiano (1472–1528), a fellow student. Torrigiano became so enraged at Michelangelo's straightforward remarks that he smashed Michelangelo's nose and scarred his face for life. All Florentines came to hate Torrigiano for this black deed.

In 1492 Lorenzo de' Medici died. Within 2

years Michelangelo left Florence and traveled through Italy. He went to Rome in 1496. There he created his first major work. The *Pietà,* completed in 1499, is a sad and graceful statue of Jesus in Mary's lap. Michelangelo's work was well received, and he returned to Florence in 1501 as a famous sculptor.

When Michelangelo was 26, he began a statue that amazed all the critics of his day. The piece of marble that he used was thin and scarred and more than 16 feet long; in fact, other sculptors had refused to use it. But Michelangelo never turned away from a difficult problem. From this poor piece of marble he carved his glorious *David.* The statue of the Bible hero became the most popular work of art in Florence. The citizens felt that the youthful warrior was a symbol of the strength and vigor of their city.

After the *David* was unveiled in 1504, Michelangelo was commissioned to do more work than he could finish. He was asked to design tombs, libraries, and statues. The Medicis ordered a great deal of work. Although the popes also ordered quantities of work from him, they did not give Michelangelo much money or help. When he was 30, the sculptor was chosen by Pope Julius II to design his tomb—the largest in the Christian world. It was so large that a new chapel in St. Peter's Basilica had to be constructed to hold it. For 8 months Michelangelo supervised the quarrying of the marble for the tomb. But when he came to Rome to discuss the project, the Pope refused to see him. Furious, Michelangelo left Rome and went back to Florence. When the Pope threatened war if the sculptor did not return, Michelangelo finally agreed to continue his work.

It took Michelangelo 40 years to finish the tomb. In the meantime he had many more quarrels with Julius and later popes. Julius wanted Michelangelo to paint the ceiling of the Sistine Chapel in St. Peter's. Michelangelo protested at first, saying that he was a sculptor, not a painter. He finally began the project and worked on it feverishly. He locked out his assistants and painted the entire area—over 3,000 square feet—by himself. To paint the ceiling, he had to lie on his back on a scaffold. He slept in his clothes to save time. But Julius was so impatient that he once threatened to throw Michelangelo off the scaffold if he did

The *Pietà* (1498–99) is in St. Peter's Basilica, Rome.

not hurry. Despite the Pope's threats, it took Michelangelo 4 years to finish the fresco.

The overpowering figures on the Sistine ceiling tell the story of man's creation and earliest history according to the Bible. The ceiling is considered by many to be the greatest single work of art ever created by one man. Twenty-four years later, in 1536, Michelangelo began The *Last Judgment,* a fresco on the altar wall of the Sistine Chapel. It is a perfect companion piece to the ceiling painting.

St. Peter's Basilica was constantly being enlarged and changed. Michelangelo was appointed chief architect of St. Peter's in 1547. The dome that he designed for the building has often been called the crowning glory of the Renaissance period. It has been copied in many lands for churches and public buildings.

It is said that when Michelangelo was 60, he could still carve faster than three ordinary sculptors. He lived to be 89, working steadily until his death in Rome on February 18, 1564. Unlike the unhappy Judge Buonarroti, the rest of the world thinks that Michelangelo fulfilled the prophecy of the stars.

Reviewed by AARON H. JACOBSEN
Author, *The Renaissance Sketchbook*

MICHIGAN

"By the shore of Gitche Gumee,/ By the shining Big-Sea-Water,/ At the doorway of his wigwam,/ . . . Hiawatha stood and waited." These lines are from *The Song of Hiawatha,* by Henry Wadsworth Longfellow. Gitche Gumee, the shining Big-Sea-Water, is Lake Superior. "The scene of the poem," as Longfellow himself explained, "is among the Ojibways on the southern shore of Lake Superior, in the region between the Pictured Rocks and the Grand Sable." This area of Michigan is known as the Land of Hiawatha.

Indian legends tell of a great hero who came among the North American Indians to help them and teach them the arts of peace. One of his various names was Hiawatha. In the poem Longfellow used legends and stories that he found in the writings of Henry Rowe Schoolcraft, superintendent of Indian affairs for Michigan, 1836–41. Schoolcraft lived among the Indians for many years and studied their life and culture.

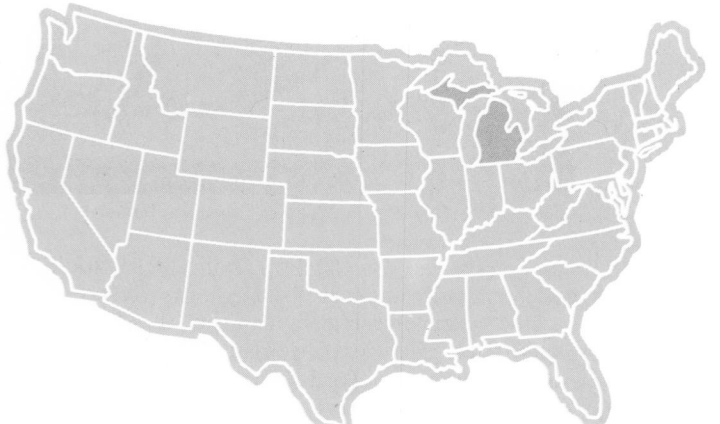

Michigan has a variety of nicknames. Some of them are old, and some are new. Automobile license plates from Michigan boast that it is the "Great Lakes State." Michigan is surrounded by four of the five Great Lakes, which give it a longer freshwater shoreline than any other state of the Union—or any country of the world. Oceangoing ships on the St. Lawrence Seaway call at Michigan's many lake ports. Within its borders Michigan has thousands of smaller lakes, used by vacationers both summer and winter.

At three points—Detroit, Port Huron, and Sault Sainte Marie—great steel bridges span the waters, connecting Michigan with the Canadian province of Ontario. An underwater tunnel below the Detroit River connects Detroit and Windsor, Ontario. Michigan and Canada are also joined along 720 miles (1,160 kilometers) of the international border.

During this century Michigan has been known as the Automobile State. This nickname is well deserved. Michigan's automobile industry is world-famous. But other products and industries have been important, too. In the very early days trappers found wealth in Michigan's furs. The trappers were followed by the first farmers. In the 1840's, miners came to work the rich deposits of iron and copper. For a time Michigan was the leading producer of copper in the United States. In the 1850's loggers found wealth in the forests, and Michigan became a leading lumber state.

Today manufacturing, agriculture, and tourism share importance. Among Michigan's well-known agricultural products are cherries, navy beans, and a kind of cheese known as Pinconning cheese. The iron and copper mines still provide metals. The quarries supply building materials. Grand Rapids is a major furniture center of the United States. Battle Creek is famous for breakfast foods. These and many other industries and products have been developed in keeping with changing times.

▶ THE LAND

The state of Michigan is made up of two peninsulas known as the Lower Peninsula and the Upper Peninsula. The Lower Peninsula, which is shaped like a giant mitten with a "thumb" projecting into Lake Huron, is the larger of the two. It includes about 70 percent of the total area of the state. The two land areas are separated by the Straits of Mackinac, a passageway between Lake Michigan and Lake Huron.

Landforms

There are two major landforms in Michigan. The Lower Peninsula and the eastern half of the Upper Peninsula are part of a large region of the United States known as the Central Lowland. The western section of the Upper Peninsula is part of the Superior Upland, also known as the Laurentian Upland or the Canadian Shield.

The present surface features of Michigan are largely the result of glaciation. During the Ice Age, glaciers covered the land with a thick layer of snow, ice, and rocks. The great weight of the glaciers pressed down on the land, gouging out numerous basins and grinding down entire ranges of hills. Gradually the climate grew warmer, and the great masses of ice began to melt. As they melted, a blanket

STATE FLAG.

STATE TREE: Eastern white pine.

STATE BIRD: Robin.

STATE FLOWER: Apple blossom.

MICHIGAN

CAPITAL: Lansing.

STATEHOOD: January 26, 1837; the 26th state.

SIZE: 58,527 sq mi (151,585 km²); rank, 23rd.

POPULATION: 9,262,078 (1980 census); rank, 8th.

ORIGIN OF NAME: From an Indian word meaning "large lake," or "big water"; applied first to Lake Michigan and then to the state.

ABBREVIATIONS: Mich.; MI.

NICKNAME: Water-Winter Wonderland; also Wolverine State, Automobile State, Great Lakes State.

STATE SONG: "Michigan, My Michigan" (not official).

STATE MOTTO: *Si quaeris peninsulam amoenam, cir-*

cumspice (If you seek a pleasant peninsula, look about you).

STATE SEAL: The state coat of arms is used on the seal. It includes a shield supported by an elk and a moose. Within the shield is a man standing on the shore of a peninsula. Behind him the sun rises over the water. The Latin word *Tuebor* at the top of the shield means "I will defend." The state motto appears on a streamer below the shield. Above the shield are the national emblem—the eagle—and the national motto—*E pluribus unum* ("One out of many," or "One composed of many"). The date 1835 appears in Roman numerals in the border of the seal. The original design was adopted by the Constitutional Convention of that year.

STATE FLAG: The state coat of arms appears in the center of a deep-blue field.

of solid materials called till was deposited on the land. Many low places were filled with water from the melting glaciers. They became some of the thousands of lakes that now dot the landscape.

The Central Lowland. In Michigan, the Central Lowland is known as the Michigan Basin. It is made up of layer upon layer of rocks formed from sediments deposited in an ancient sea long before the Ice Age. A slice deep into the earth would show the many layers of rock —like a stack of saucers with the edges upturned—along the lake shores. The southern half of the Lower Peninsula is level to gently rolling. A moraine—a ridge formed by a glacier—divides the northern half. It separates the rivers flowing west into Lake Michigan from those flowing east into Lake Huron. High bluffs and dunes line the shores of Lake Michigan. The Central Lowland, or eastern, section of the Upper Peninsula is mostly low swampland, although hills rise as high as 1,000 feet (305 meters) along the shores of Lake Superior.

The Superior Upland. The western half of the Upper Peninsula contains crystallized rocks and many metallic minerals. The main surface features are rugged, forested hills. The ranges of hills include the Copper, Gogebic, and Menominee ranges and the Porcupine Mountains. The highest point in the state is found in Baraga County. In 1963 this point was named Mount Curwood in memory of James Oliver Curwood, a Michigan-born writer of adventure stories.

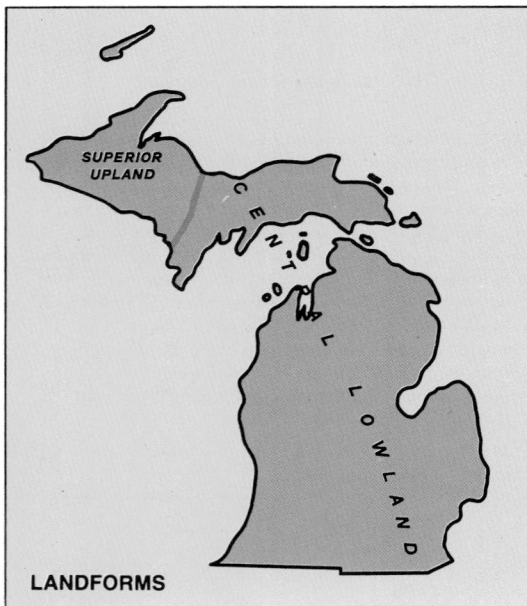

LANDFORMS

THE LAND

LOCATION: Latitude—41° 42′ N to 48° 18′ N. **Longitude**—82° 07′ W to 90° 25′ W. Upper Peninsula—Lake Superior to the north, Lake Huron to the east, Lake Michigan and the state of Wisconsin to the south. Lower Peninsula—Lake Michigan to the west; Lake Huron, the Canadian province of Ontario, and Lake Erie to the east; Ohio and Indiana to the south.

ELEVATION: Highest—Mount Curwood, 1,980 ft (604m). **Lowest**—On the shores of Lake Erie, 572 ft (174 m).

LANDFORMS: Superior Upland in the western half of the Upper Peninsula; Central Lowland in the eastern half of the Upper Peninsula and all the Lower Peninsula.

SURFACE WATERS: Major rivers—Menominee and St. Marys in the Upper Peninsula; Grand, Muskegon, St. Clair, and Detroit in the Lower Peninsula. **Largest natural inland lake**—Houghton.

CLIMATE: Temperature—January average, about 17°F (−8°C) in Upper Peninsula, 25°F (−4°C) in Lower Peninsula. July average, about 66°F (19°C) in Upper Peninsula, 71°F (22°C) in Lower Peninsula. **Precipitation** —Average, 27–38 in (690–970 mm); maximum in summer. Snowfall varies from about 24 in (60 cm) in the southeast to about 170 in (430 cm) in the northwest. **Growing season**—From about 70 days in parts of the north to more than 180 days in the southwest.

Rivers and Lakes

Michigan has two major types of rivers. The first includes rivers that flow into the Great Lakes from the interior of the two peninsulas. Examples are the Escanaba, Menominee, and Tahquamenon rivers in the Upper Peninsula and the Grand, Muskegon, Kalamazoo, Raisin, and Huron rivers in the Lower Peninsula. Second are the rivers that drain one lake into another. The St. Marys, St. Clair, and Detroit rivers are of this type. The three

Tahquamenon Falls, in the Upper Peninsula, is one of Michigan's many scenic recreational areas. The color of the falls is caused by minerals and natural dyes in the water.

rivers serve as international boundaries between the United States and Canada. Rapids and waterfalls are major scenic attractions on the state's nearly 36,000 miles (58,000 kilometers) of rivers. Numerous small dams and reservoirs are located along rivers throughout the state.

Michigan is surrounded by four of the five Great Lakes—Superior, Michigan, Huron, and Erie. Lake St. Clair is a link in the waterway that joins Lake Huron to Lake Erie. Within the borders of the state are more than 11,000 smaller lakes. Houghton Lake in the northern part of the Lower Peninsula is the largest lake in the state.

The Great Lakes shoreline of the two peninsulas is more than 2,000 miles (3,200 kilometers) long. This is about equal to the length of the Atlantic coastline from Maine to Florida. Since the St. Lawrence Seaway was opened in 1959, large ships can reach Michigan ports as easily as they once reached ports on the Atlantic and the Pacific coasts.

Climate

Michigan has a humid continental climate with cold winters and warm summers. The climate close to the shores of the Great Lakes is modified slightly by these lakes and the westerly winds blowing over them.

Spring in Michigan is usually short. Often winter seems to change suddenly to summer. But autumn is somewhat longer. It is a time of great beauty when warm, sunny days and frosty nights change the leaves to brilliant shades of yellow and red. Winters are snowy and cold, especially in the north.

Precipitation is fairly evenly distributed throughout the year, with most occurring in the summer months. Michigan's many winter resorts make good use of the state's often heavy snowfall.

The growing season is shortest in the interior areas of the Upper Peninsula and longest near lakes in the southern part of the Lower Peninsula.

Natural Resources

The natural resources of Michigan have been important since early times, when the fur trade dominated the economy. Water is one of Michigan's most valuable resources today, together with minerals and forests. The state practices timber management, fire control, and water quality control. Industrial pollutants must be treated before they can be dumped

MICHIGAN

Copyright Diversified Map Corporation, St. Louis, Mo.

INDEX TO MICHIGAN MAP

● County Seat   Counties in parentheses   ★ State Capital

POPULATION

TOTAL: 9,262,078 (1980 census). **Density**—162.6 persons to each square mile (62.8 persons to each square kilometer).

GROWTH SINCE 1810

Year	Population	Year	Population
1810	4,762	1940	5,256,106
1840	212,267	1960	7,823,194
1870	1,184,059	1970	8,881,826
1900	2,420,982	1980	9,262,078

Gain Between 1970 and 1980—4.3 percent.

CITIES: Population of Michigan's largest cities according to the 1980 census.

Detroit	1,203,339	Sterling Heights	108,999
Grand Rapids	181,843	Ann Arbor	107,966
Warren	161,134	Livonia	104,814
Flint	159,611	Dearborn	90,660
Lansing	130,414	Westland	84,603

---

into the Detroit River. A number of communities in the western part of the state are recycling their waste water.

Forests. Once the great forests of Michigan were logged without thought of the future. Today more trees are planted than cut. National, state, and privately owned forests are being managed scientifically. Many tree farms have been started or enlarged and woods now cover half the state's area.

Minerals. Michigan is known for its deposits of copper and iron ore. The western part of the Upper Peninsula is part of the iron country —an area that extends into Wisconsin and Minnesota. The copper country is to the north on the Keweenaw Peninsula. Both the Upper and the Lower peninsulas have large deposits of limestone, sandstone, and sand and gravel. The oil and natural-gas fields are in the Lower Peninsula. Other minerals include salt, gypsum,and peat.

Soils. The quality of Michigan's soils varies widely from one part of the state to another. The richest soils are in the southern part of the Lower Peninsula, where vegetables and grain crops are grown. Soils in other areas produce grasses that make good grazing lands. Some soils are suited only to forests.

Wildlife. One of Michigan's nicknames is the Wolverine State. But it is doubtful that wolverines ever inhabited the state in large numbers. The wolverine belongs to the same family as the weasel and the mink. It is a heavy, clumsy animal, blackish in color and noted for its strength and cunning.

Along with its reforestation program, Michigan has made great strides since the 1970's in wildlife conservation. Animals found in the state's forests include moose, elk, black bear, and deer as well as many smaller animals such as beavers, foxes, and rabbits. Game birds include pheasant, partridge, ducks, and wild geese. The lakes and streams are well stocked with such fish as trout, pike, bass, perch, and salmon.

▶THE PEOPLE AND THEIR WORK

Michigan was first settled by French traders and missionaries in the middle 1600's. In 1763 the British took over the area and established several forts. But it was not until the Erie Canal was opened in 1825 that settlers began to pour in from the eastern states and from Europe. Sizable groups from Germany started to arrive in 1830. In 1846 settlers arrived from the Netherlands and established the city of Holland.

The logging boom, which started about 1850, attracted loggers from Finland, Norway, Sweden, and Canada. Many Finns settled in the Upper Peninsula where many evidences of Finnish settlement remain today. Suomi College in Hancock, founded in 1896, is the only Finnish institution of higher learning in the United States. The opening of iron and copper mines brought many miners from Wales and from Cornwall in England. Pasties, a popular food in Michigan, are a reminder of the miners who took these pastry shells filled with meat and potatoes into the mines each day in their lunch pails.

Early in the 1900's, when the automobile industry started to develop, there were new waves of settlement. People came from all over the United States and from many European countries to work in the new automobile plants. One very large group from Poland settled in Hamtramck, a community now entirely surrounded by Detroit.

Many blacks made their way to Michigan from the South during the Civil War era. Racial unrest in urban areas in the 1960's later gave way to greater participation by blacks in the state's political life.

Black, Hispanic, and Asian groups are prominent in the cities. In addition, there are about 20,000 American Indians in Michigan. Many live on the state's four reservations; others live in Detroit and other urban areas.

Where the People Live

About 90 percent of the people of Michigan live in the southern half of the Lower Peninsula. The Upper Peninsula is sparsely settled. The population of rural areas, comprising many retired people, grew during the 1970's.

Industries and Products.

Michigan is an important industrialized state. Its manufactured goods are a main source of income. Tourism, service industries, agriculture, and mining are important.

Manufacturing. The design and manufacture of motor vehicles of all kinds is the leading industry in Michigan. The state leads all others in the production of cars, buses and trucks. The automobile industry had its start in Detroit when, in 1903, Henry Ford founded a motor company. In 1908 the company began to manufacture a car that was to become famous all over the world, the four-cylinder Model T. At about the same time, Ransom Eli Olds produced his "Oldsmobile."

Industrial machinery, metals, and metal products rank next in importance to motor vehicles. Processed foods, especially breakfast cereals, also bring a large income. Other manufactured goods include chemicals, paper, furniture and sports equipment.

Mining. When Michigan became a state in 1837, geologists made a thorough survey of the land. They reported that the state had many minerals that could be mined profitably. The most important were copper and iron.

Iron ore mined in the Marquette, Gogebic, and Menominee ranges of the Upper Peninsula was carried by rail to nearby lake ports. Recently iron mining has been affected by competition from other countries as well as by the fact that most of the high-grade ores have been used up. But Michigan still produces some iron ore.

The first center of copper mining was at Copper Harbor on Lake Superior. Copper in this area existed in an almost pure state. For many years Michigan produced a large part of the nation's copper.

A boom in the early 1980's in the production of oil and natural gas raised the value of these materials. Most of the new production comes from fields in the northern part of the Lower Peninsula. Salt is mined throughout the central section of the state. Most of the salt is produced by the evaporation of brines that have been pumped to the surface of the earth. Iodine, bromine, and magnesium, which have important uses in the chemical and drug industries, are also taken from the brines.

The limestone and sandstone quarried in the state are used mainly in the production of portland cement. Michigan is a leading producer of cement. The state also ranks high in the production of gypsum, which is used in making plaster and other building materials. Large quantities of peat—partly rotted moss and plants—are taken from bogs. Peat is used as a conditioner for soils.

Agriculture. A combination of good pastures and location near large markets has made Michigan a leader in dairying. The major field crops are corn, soybeans, and wheat. Other important farm products are fruits and vegetables. The fruit belt along Lake Michigan produces large quantities of tart cherries, apples, blueberries, peaches, grapes, and other fruits. Vegetables include dry beans, potatoes, cucumbers, and asparagus. Vermontville, in southern Michigan, is noted for maple syrup and maple-sugar candy. Other specialties are peppermint and honey.

Fisheries. Michigan has been noted for its Great Lakes fisheries. The principal kinds of commercial fish are chub, whitefish, lake herring, yellow perch, alewives, and salmon. For many years, the sea lamprey, an eel-like fish, invaded the Great Lakes, killing many other kinds of fish. Scientists first tried to control the lamprey's spread with electric fences.

The manufacture of motor vehicles of all kinds has long been Michigan's leading industry. Today, robots do much of the heavy work on Detroit's assembly lines.

WHAT MICHIGAN PRODUCES

MANUFACTURED GOODS: Transportation equipment, especially motor vehicles and parts and accessories; nonelectrical machinery, especially metalworking machinery; metal forgings, stampings, and other fabricated metal products; basic steel and other primary metals; processed foods; chemicals and related products; electric and electronic equipment; products of printing and publishing; clothing and other textile products, especially for automobile interiors and trim; paper and related products; stone, clay, and glass products; furniture and fixtures.

AGRICULTURAL PRODUCTS: Milk, cattle and calves, corn, soybeans, hogs, dry beans, tart cherries, sugar beets, apples, potatoes, eggs and poultry, wheat, cucumbers.

MINERALS: Petroleum, natural gas, iron ore, cement, sand and gravel, salt, limestone, gypsum, bromine, calcium chloride, magnesium compounds, peat.

Today its spawning grounds are treated with a chemical that kills the lamprey but does not harm other fish. Water pollution and mercury contamination of certain fish have been problems but are being corrected.

Tourism. The tourist industry is one of Michigan's three major sources of income. During the summer and fall, people come to Michigan's lakes and woods to fish and hunt or to camp and explore. The state has many winter sports centers where ski meets and winter carnivals are held.

Transportation and Communication

Some of Michigan's first roads were laid out along Indian trails. The present road system was established in 1913, when the legislature passed a bill providing for the construction of ten highways. Since then Michigan has been a pioneer in highway development as well as a leader in the development of roadside parks.

Huge locks in the Sault Sainte Marie (Soo) Canals join lakes Superior and Huron. The Great Lakes have been important to Michigan's trade since the state's early days.

The first railroads in Michigan were built during the 1830's. Lumbering and mining in the Upper Peninsula soon led to the building of railroads in that area. By 1881 there was railroad ferry service across the Straits of Mackinac, connecting the two peninsulas. Today many of the railroad lines in the lumbering and mining areas have been abandoned. In some areas motor transport has replaced the shorter lines.

The Great Lakes have been important to transportation since pioneer days. Many types of vessels have sailed the lakes, including full-rigged sailing vessels and steamboats. Today the ships on the Great Lakes include ocean-going vessels from the St. Lawrence Seaway. The Seaway links the Great Lakes to the Atlantic Ocean. Another important waterway is the St. Marys River, which joins Lake Superior to the lower Great Lakes.

The famous Sault Sainte Marie Canals are two parallel systems, toll-free and government-operated. They bypass rapids in the St. Marys River at the twin cities of Sault Sainte Marie, Michigan, and Sault Sainte Marie in the Canadian province of Ontario. One canal system is on the Michigan side, and the other is on the Canadian side. They are popularly known as the Soo Canals because the French word *sault* in the name Sault Sainte Marie is pronounced "soo." The two canal systems remain the busiest in the world, although a decline in iron mining has reduced the tonnage shipped through them.

Bridges in Michigan range from huge steel suspension bridges to small covered bridges. Three major steel toll bridges link the United States and Canada. One of the longest bridges in the world is the Mackinac Bridge, or "Big Mac," opened in 1957. It links the Upper and Lower peninsulas.

Michigan has more than 100 public airports, as well as many small airports and emergency landing strips throughout the state. Daily jet flights to all parts of the world are made from the Detroit Metropolitan Airport.

Michigan has more than 50 daily newspapers. The major dailies include the *Free Press* and the *News,* published in Detroit, and the *Press,* published in Grand Rapids.

One of the first commercial radio broadcasting stations in the United States was WWJ in

Detroit. It began operation in 1920. The state now has more than 200 AM and FM radio stations and more than 30 television stations.

▶ EDUCATION

Michigan's first school system was started in the early 1800's by Father Gabriel Richard, a Catholic priest. His idea was to combine the three R's with manual training and domestic arts. Father Richard was also one of the founders of the University of Michigan.

Schools and Colleges

Michigan has been a pioneer in the development of public education. In 1836 the Reverend John Davis Pierce was appointed the first superintendent of public instruction. He drew up a plan for a free school system with three divisions—the elementary school, the high school, and the university.

The University of Michigan was founded at Detroit in 1817. When the school was moved to Ann Arbor in 1841, it had two teachers and six students. Today more than 45,000 students attend the university, which has campuses at Ann Arbor, Dearborn, and Flint. Michigan State University is located at East Lansing. It was chartered in 1855 as the nation's first agricultural college.

Other state-controlled institutions of higher education are Central Michigan University in Mount Pleasant, Eastern Michigan University in Ypsilanti, Ferris State College in Big Rapids, Northern Michigan University in Marquette, Michigan Technological University in Houghton, Wayne State University in Detroit, Western Michigan University in Kalamazoo, Lake Superior State College in Sault Sainte Marie, and Saginaw Valley State College in University Center.

Libraries, Museums, and the Arts

The public library in Detroit is the largest of the state's 300 public library systems. The Hackley Public Library in Muskegon includes an interesting collection on lumbering and local history. The William L. Clements Library at the University of Michigan has a large collection of books on American history.

Michigan has many fine museums. The Detroit Institute of Arts has collections of art ranging from ancient times to the present. The institute also sponsors a theater program for young people. Exhibits at the Detroit Histori-

cal Museum show how life in the United States has changed since pioneer days. The Money Museum in the National Bank of Detroit and the Afro-American Museum of Detroit are special attractions. The Dossin Great Lakes Museum has models and artifacts from Great Lakes vessels. This museum is maintained by the Detroit Historical Museum and is located on Belle Isle in the Detroit River. The Henry Ford Museum in Dearborn includes exhibits of antique automobiles, fire engines, and locomotives.

The Michigan Historical Museum in Lansing has a collection of Indian and pioneer objects. The Netherlands Museum in Holland includes replicas of old Dutch kitchens. The Public Museum in Grand Rapids has a collection of furniture and decorative arts of many different periods and styles.

The Detroit Symphony Orchestra, established in 1914, is one of the nation's leading orchestras. Michigan is also noted for the National Music Camp at Interlochen. Students from all over the United States attend the camp each summer to study and to give performances. Cranbrook is an educational and cultural center in Bloomfield Hills, near Detroit. It includes the Cranbrook Institute of Science and the Cranbrook Academy of Art and Museum. Many of the buildings at the center were designed by the famous Finnish-born architect Eliel Saarinen.

▶ PLACES OF INTEREST

Forests and lakes, sand dunes, and historic forts and villages are among Michigan's many attractions.

National and State Parks

Michigan has one national park, Isle Royale National Park in Lake Superior, and four national forests. The national forests are the Hiawatha and the Ottawa in the Upper Peninsula and the Huron and the Manistee in the Lower Peninsula. Michigan also has two national recreational areas. **Pictured Rocks National Lakeshore** is a scenic area on Lake Superior. The Pictured Rocks are sandstone cliffs that extend almost 20 miles (32 kilometers) along the lakeshore east of Munising. The many-colored cliff walls have been carved into strange formations by wind, rain, and waves. **Sleeping Bear Dunes National Lakeshore,** around Glen Haven, contains two

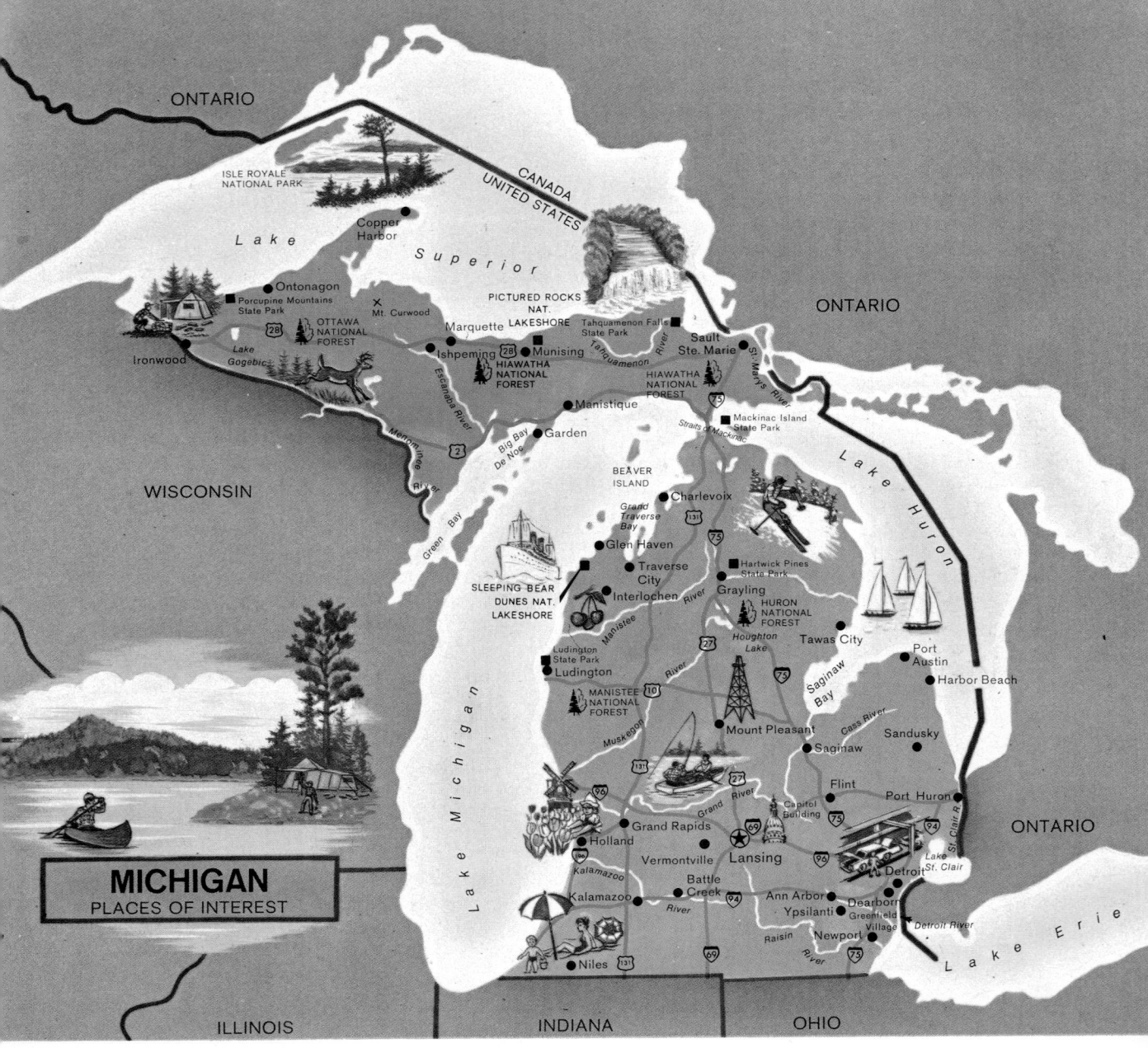

MICHIGAN
PLACES OF INTEREST

islands and 34 miles (55 kilometers) of mainland shore along Lake Michigan. The region is notable for its massive sand dunes.

State park and recreation areas number more than 80. The following list includes several of the best known.

Isle Royale National Park is a wilderness area on Isle Royale and about 200 surrounding islets in the western part of Lake Superior. Much of the area is covered with dense forests, where wolves and moose still roam. Visitors may hike to an ancient pit copper mine or paddle the streams and coves. Isle Royale was named by French trappers, who took possession of the island in 1669 and named it in honor of King Louis XIV.

Hartwick Pines State Park, near Grayling, contains thousands of acres of pine and hemlock, remnants of the great virgin forests that once covered Michigan. The park includes a historical museum and reproductions of parts of a logging camp.

Ludington State Park, near Ludington, has a sand beach on Lake Michigan, sand dunes, and forested areas. The park is adjacent to Big Point Sable Lighthouse. Strong currents sometimes make the lake treacherous in this area.

Mackinac Island State Park includes almost all of Mackinac Island (pronounced *mack-in-aw* by Michiganders). This historic island is located in the Straits of Mackinac between Lake Huron and Lake Michigan. The Indians called it *Michilimackinac*, or Great Turtle. In time the name was shortened to Mackinac. Visitors walk or travel by horse and buggy or by bicycle. No automobiles are allowed on the island. Points of interest include Fort Mackinac, established by the British in 1780, and the John Jacob Astor House, built about 1817. The Astor house served as the headquarters for the American Fur Company.

Porcupine Mountains State Park, near Ontonagon, is a large area of mountains, lakes, and rivers in the copper country. It is said that the Indians named the mountains Kaug (Porcupine) because their outline resembled a crouching porcupine. The park is one of the most popular winter sports centers in the state.

Tahquamenon Falls State Park, near Newberry, includes deep swamps, high hills, and one of the largest falls in the eastern United States. The Tahquamenon River plays an important part in Longfellow's poem *The Song of Hiawatha*.

Other Places

Greenfield Village in Dearborn was built under the auspices of Henry Ford. It includes homes, stores, mills, and other historic structures brought from all over the United States and western Europe. The Thomas Alva Edison buildings portray Edison's career.

Beaver Island is in Lake Michigan, northwest of the town of Charlevoix. It is thought that French loggers had a small settlement on this island in the early 1600's. In the 1800's it was the center of an unusual Mormon community. The Mormons declared a monarchy and for ten years had the only king in the United States.

Annual Events

Michigan has more than 80 winter sports centers. Most of them hold sports carnivals in January and February. Ishpeming has staged a winter carnival since the late 1880's. Springtime festivals include the tulip festival in Holland, the maple syrup festival in Vermontville, the perch festival in Tawas City, and events celebrating local history. The Blossomtime Festival in St. Joseph and Benton Harbor is the oldest in the state. Detroit and Windsor, Ontario, hold an International Freedom Festival on the Fourth of July. Other summer activities are boat races and yacht regattas on the Great Lakes and on the state's many inland lakes. The Michigan State Fair in Detroit is a major autumn event. The Ann Arbor Arts Fair has been held yearly since 1959.

The May Tulip Festival in Holland, Michigan, recalls the state's many early settlers who came from the Netherlands. Holland is known for its tulip-growing industry.

Detroit's Renaissance Center dominates the skyline of Michigan's largest city. Opened in 1977, the center's hotels, shops, and offices overlook the Detroit River.

▶CITIES

All of Michigan's largest cities are in the Lower Peninsula. Approximately half the people of the state live in the Detroit metropolitan area.

COUNTIES

Lansing

The state capital, Lansing, is located in south central Michigan in a shallow valley formed by three rivers—the Grand, the Red Cedar, and the Sycamore. Originally named Michigan, the city was settled in 1837. It has been the seat of government since 1847, when members of the legislature decided to move the capital from Detroit. At that time Lansing consisted of one log house and a sawmill. Today it is an important industrial center, producing automobiles, school buses, trucks, tools, and many other items. It is also a trading center for the surrounding farmlands. Notable buildings are the state capital, completed in 1878, and the Civic Center, dedicated in 1955. East Lansing, a separate community, is the home of Michigan State University.

Detroit

Detroit, the largest city in Michigan, is world famous for its automobile industry. Established in 1701, the city takes its name from a French word meaning ''strait'' or ''channel.'' Large cities in the Detroit metropolitan area include Warren, Sterling Heights, Livonia, Dearborn, and Westland. An article on Detroit appears in Volume D.

Other Cities

Grand Rapids is situated at the rapids of the Grand River. It developed from a lumber town into one of the most important furniture-manufacturing centers in the nation. Flint, northwest of Detroit, is a major automobile-manufacturing city. Saginaw, once a famous lumber city, is now the center of the bean and sugar-beet area of the state. Kalamazoo in southwestern Michigan took its name from an Indian word meaning ''where the water boils in the pot.'' The name was first applied to the river, where there were many bubbling springs, and then to the town. Paper manufacturing is a main industry of Kalamazoo.

Battle Creek is known as the cereal food center of the world. Ann Arbor is the home of the University of Michigan, as well as an agriculture trading center. The hill region surrounding the city is a popular vacation destination. Marquette, the largest city in the Upper Peninsula, is Michigan's major ore-shipping port. Ironwood is a mining, lumbering, and recreation center.

▶GOVERNMENT

Michigan has had four state constitutions. The first one was drawn up in 1835. The most recent one was adopted in 1963.

The state legislature is made up of the Senate and House of Representatives. These two bodies are reapportioned after the census every ten years.

The executive branch of the state government is headed by the governor. The judicial branch is made up of a supreme court, a court of appeals, circuit courts, probate courts, and lower courts.

▶FAMOUS PEOPLE

The following native-born or adopted citizens of Michigan became well known in government, industry, and the arts.

Lewis Cass (1782–1866) is remembered in Michigan's history as the governor of the Michigan territory, 1813–31, and as a United States senator from Michigan, 1845–48 and 1849–57. He was also United States secretary of war (1831–36) under President Andrew Jackson and secretary of state (1857–60) under President James Buchanan. Cass was born in Exeter, New Hampshire.

Stevens Thomson Mason (1811–43), first governor of the state of Michigan, was one of the

youngest persons ever to hold high public office. In 1831, a few months before his 20th birthday, he was appointed secretary of the Michigan territory by President Andrew Jackson. Mason worked so effectively for statehood that he won the confidence of the people. They elected him governor in 1836. Mason was born in Virginia.

Henry Ford (1863–1947) brought the moving assembly line and mass-production methods to the automobile industry. He was born in Greenfield, now a part of Dearborn. A biography of Henry Ford is included in Volume F.

Arthur Hendrick Vandenberg (1884–1951) represented Michigan in the United States Senate from 1928 until the end of his life. He is remembered for his contributions to American foreign policy. Vandenberg was born in Grand Rapids.

Ringgold Wilmer (''Ring'') Lardner (1885–1933) was a journalist and short-story writer known for his realistic humor. Lardner became widely known in 1916, when he published a collection of baseball stories, *You Know Me, Al.* He was born in Niles.

Ralph Johnson Bunche (1904–71), political scientist, educator, and official of the United Nations, was born in Detroit. A biography of Ralph Bunche appears in Volume B.

Walter Reuther (1907–70), labor leader, was born in Wheeling, West Virginia, but moved to Detroit in 1926 and went to work for the Ford Motor Company. Reuther was president of the United Auto Workers Union from 1946 until his death.

Gerald Rudolph Ford (1913–   ), 38th president of the United States, was born in Omaha, Nebraska, but grew up in Grand Rapids. In 1948 he was elected to the House of Representatives, where he served for 35 years. A biography of President Ford appears in Volume F.

Noted writers besides Ring Lardner who were born in Michigan include novelists Edna Ferber (Kalamazoo), James Oliver Curwood (Owosso), and Stewart Edward White (Grand Rapids); science writer Paul de Kruif (Zeeland); and historian Bruce Catton (Petoskey). Others famous in the arts are painter Gari

Melchers (Detroit), actress Julie Harris (Grosse Pointe Park), James Anthony Bailey, circus owner (Detroit), and architect and stage designer Norman Bel Geddes (Adrian). The popular poet Edgar A. Guest was born in England but spent much of his life in Michigan.

Other famous persons born in Michigan are the nuclear scientist Glenn Theodore Seaborg (Ishpeming), who headed the Atomic Energy Commission from 1961 to 1971, and the aviator Charles Lindbergh (Detroit). A biography of Lindbergh is included in Volume L.

▶HISTORY

Before European settlers came, several thousand Indians belonging to three major tribes lived in the forests of Michigan. The Ottawa and the Potawatomi lived along the shores of Lake Michigan. The Ojibwa, or Chippewa, lived in the northern part of the Lower Peninsula and in the Upper Peninsula.

Exploration and Settlement

The French came into the Michigan area in the early 1600's. They came to explore, trade for furs, and establish missions. The French explorer Étienne Brulé may have been the first white man to see Michigan. It is known that he visited Lake Superior, probably in 1622.

French Jesuit missionaries were among the first to settle in Michigan. In 1641 they came to the site of Sault Sainte Marie on the St. Marys River to work among the Indians. Father Jacques Marquette established a mission there in 1668. It became the first permanent settlement in Michigan. The Lower Peninsula was explored and settled later. In 1701, Antoine de la Mothe Cadillac built a fort called Fort Pontchartrain on the site of present-day Detroit.

The area that is now Michigan was held by the French until the end of the French and Indian War in 1763. Then it was transferred to British control. During the Revolutionary War, British posts in Michigan served as bases for attacks against settlements in Ohio and western Pennsylvania. At the end of the war Michigan became a part of the United States.

Territorial Days and the War of 1812

Michigan was included in the Northwest Territory, formed in 1787. In 1794, General Anthony Wayne defeated the Indians at Fallen Timbers near what is now Toledo, Ohio. Indian troubles were ended for a time. In 1796 settlers around Detroit honored General Wayne by naming Wayne County after him. Although Michigan had few settlements, it

Fort Mackinac was once an important military post and center of Indian trade. Today it is part of Mackinac Island State Park, overlooking the Straits of Mackinac.

the strip to Ohio. Michigan gained the Upper Peninsula when it was admitted to the Union in 1837.

Minerals and forests proved to be sources of great wealth. The development of iron and copper mines created a need for a ship canal around the rapids in the St. Marys River. In 1855 the first canal of the present system was completed. During the 1870's and 1880's, Michigan was the leading lumber producer in the United States.

Before and during the Civil War, Michigan was a center of antislavery feelings and a major stop on the "underground railroad" that helped escaped slaves to freedom.

In the early 1900's, Michigan began to turn from an agricultural state into an industrial one. Henry Ford brought moving assembly-line manufacturing to Detroit and started his own automobile empire. Other automobile companies were soon established.

Michigan men and women served valiantly in World Wars I and II, Korea, and Vietnam. Industries in the state furnished large quantities of war materials. After World War II, Michigan's economic activities changed again. Automobile makers suffered losses and looked for ways to produce cars more efficiently. New technological and service industries were developed.

In the 1970's, Michigan lost some population. Severe unemployment in the automotive industry forced many workers to leave the state. In the 1980's, however, the industry regained much of its former strength. New oil and natural gas reserves were discovered. The tourist industry grew rapidly. And although the number of farms in the state declined, the remaining farms increased in size.

The Future

Michigan is a state with many advantages. They include its location on the St. Lawrence Seaway, the Great Lakes, abundant recreational areas, and varied industries. In the future, these industries will continue to adapt to changing times. Cities will grow and become linked by more interstate highways. And Michigan, a pioneer in conservation of natural resources, will continue to protect its environment for the common good.

HERBERT L. ZOBEL
Eastern Michigan University

MICHIGAN, LAKE. See GREAT LAKES.

was organized as a territory in 1805. William Hull, a former Revolutionary War officer, was appointed the first governor.

Within a few years—at the time of the War of 1812—Michigan was again in British hands. After war was declared, Hull surrendered Detroit, and thus Michigan, to the British. During the war the Indians sided with the British and made many attacks on the Americans. In 1813, Oliver Hazard Perry won an important naval victory on Lake Erie. Soon afterward American troops reoccupied Detroit, and Michigan was restored to American control. Lewis Cass was appointed the new territorial governor.

Statehood and Later

With the opening of the Erie Canal in 1825, immigration from states to the east and from Europe increased greatly. In 1834, Michigan applied for statehood. But Congress delayed in granting statehood because Michigan and Ohio were disputing a strip of land along their joint border. Finally, in 1836, Congress gave

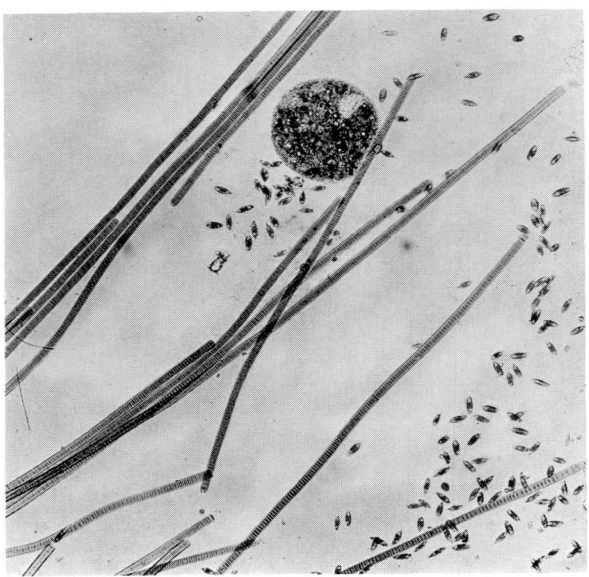

A world of tiny life in a drop of pond water.

MICROBIOLOGY

Three hundred years ago a Dutch store-keeper discovered a new world. He did not cross uncharted oceans or visit far-off lands. He found this new world all around him in his native city of Delft.

The storekeeper's name was Anton van Leeuwenhoek. The world he discovered was the world of living creatures that are present everywhere but are too small to be seen.

▶ LEEUWENHOEK'S NEW WORLD

Leeuwenhoek had often used a magnifying glass to look at things he was selling in his store. Now and then he had glimpsed strange specks moving across a bit of cloth or some other object. He realized that if he had stronger lenses, he could see the specks better.

In his spare time he learned to grind more powerful lenses. He tried out the lenses on all kinds of things—mud, rainwater, vinegar, saliva, and even scrapings from his teeth. One day, to his amazement, he saw hundreds of tiny creatures darting about in a drop of water.

There were, Leeuwenhoek wrote, "unbelievably many small animalcules [little animals] of various sorts; among others, some that were 3 to 4 times as long as broad. . . . These creatures had very short thin legs in front of the head. (Although I can recognize no head, I speak of the head for the reason that this part always went forward during movement.) . . . Close to the hindmost part lay a clear drop; and I judged that the very hindmost part was slightly split. These animalcules are very cute while moving about, sometimes tumbling all over."

Leeuwenhoek carefully drew and described everything he saw. From his records scientists know that he saw bacteria, yeasts, and many other tiny creatures.

Such tiny organisms (living things) are all about us, floating in the air and in water, moving about in the soil and on plants, growing, and multiplying. There are millions inside you and inside all animals. Some cause disease and are sometimes called **germs**. However, most are harmless. And many help make life on earth possible.

Today scientists call these small living things **microbes** or **micro-organisms**, from the Greek word *mikros,* meaning "small." Most micro-organisms are too small to be seen without the aid of a magnifying glass or a microscope.

The scientists who study micro-organisms are called **microbiologists**. Their field of study is **microbiology**.

▶ TOOLS AND METHODS OF MICROBIOLOGY

Leeuwenhoek's new world remained largely unexplored until the 1800's, when improvements in the microscope made it easier to study small life. Then, in the 1930's scientists developed the electron microscope, which enables them to study complicated physical details of extremely small organisms, such as bacteria. It also makes possible the study of viruses and rickettsias—tiny creatures that are invisible under ordinary light microscopes.

The tools of microbiology have greatly improved in the past 100 years. However, many of the basic methods have changed very little since the 1800's. The methods of preparing microbes for study were developed by Robert Koch, a famous German doctor.

Koch believed that each kind of disease is caused by one particular kind of microbe and no other. To prove this, he needed a way to separate different kinds of microbes from one another. In a given blood sample or other liquid there are usually several kinds of mi-

LOCATING A DISEASE-CAUSING ORGANISM: KOCH'S POSTULATES

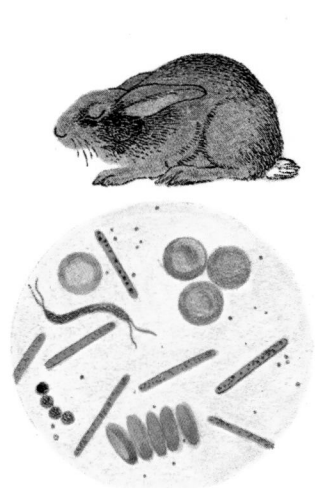

1 ORGANISM MUST ALWAYS BE FOUND IN SICK ANIMAL OR PLANT WHEN DISEASE OCCURS

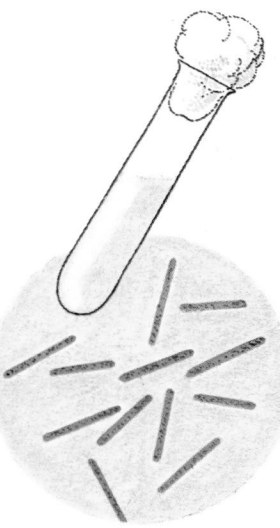

2 SUSPECTED ORGANISM MUST BE ISOLATED AND GROWN IN SUBSTANCE THAT IS FREE OF ANY OTHER ORGANISM

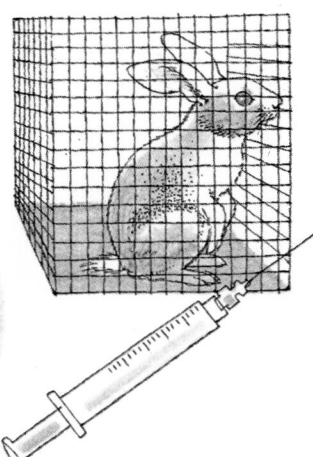

3 ORGANISM TAKEN FROM PURE CULTURE MUST CAUSE DISEASE WHEN INJECTED INTO HEALTHY ANIMAL OR PLANT

4 ORGANISM MUST BE TAKEN FROM DISEASED ANIMAL OR PLANT, ISOLATED, GROWN IN PURE SUBSTANCE, AND COMPARED WITH ORGANISM FIRST INJECTED

crobes. It is impossible to remove just a few individuals of the kind wanted for study. Koch realized that as long as the microbes were mixed, he could not be sure which kind caused the disease he was studying.

Then Koch made an important discovery. When several kinds of microbes were spread on a solid food substance, the individual cells became separated and each kind multiplied into a colony, or group. And each colony of one kind of micro-organism looked somewhat different from the colonies of the other kinds. Since the microbes could not move about freely, as they could in liquid, the colonies tended to stay separate. This meant that by "planting" one colony, Koch could culture, or grow, the kind of micro-organism he wished to study.

These gardens of microbes grew well on gelatin mixtures, which are easy to prepare. Moreover, when gelatin sets, it becomes solid enough to prevent the mixing of colonies. Therefore Koch chose gelatin for his work.

He poured a mixture of liquid gelatin and nutrient (food) into small, clean dishes. He covered these with large glass jars, to prevent microbes in the air from settling on the gelatin. When the gelatin had set, Koch dipped a clean, germ-free needle into the liquid containing the microbes. Then he scratched the surface of the gelatin with the needle.

Later he found he could mix the liquid containing the microbes with the liquid gelatin containing the nutrient. When the gelatin solidified, single microbes would be trapped where they were. They would grow up into colonies, each containing millions of only one kind of microbe, since each started from a single microbe. No matter which method he used, colonies of microbes soon appeared.

A garden of microbes on a gelatin mixture. Each kind of microbe has its own kind of colony.

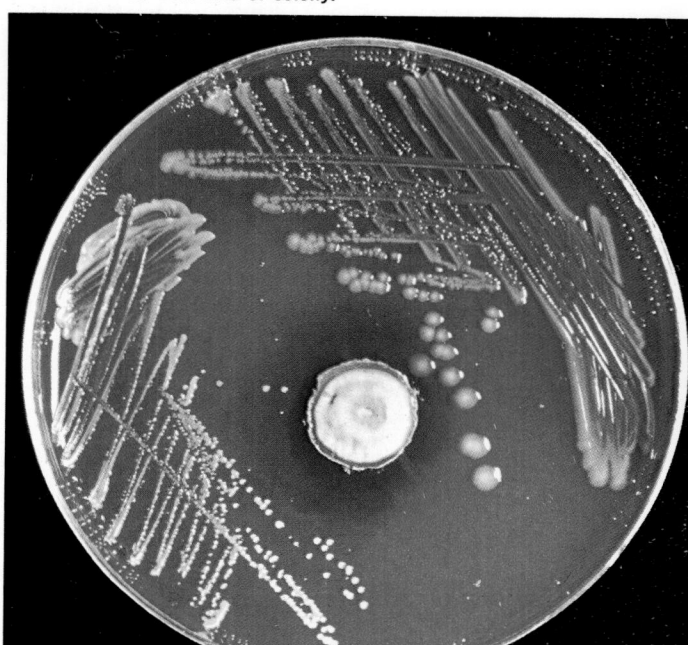

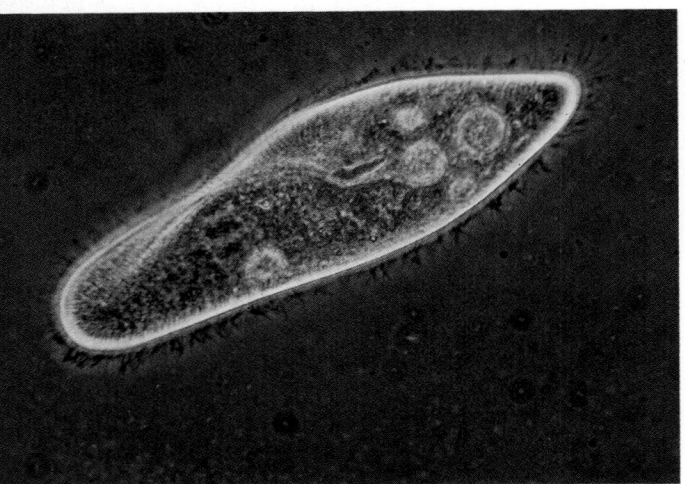

The tiny one-celled **paramecium.** A living animal, it can grow, eat, move, reproduce, and respond to its surroundings.

Scientists today still use these two methods of growing cultures.

THE FIELD OF MICROBIOLOGY

More than 100,000 kinds of micro-organisms have been studied and described since Leeuwenhoek's time. Microbiologists separate micro-organisms into nine general groups, according to body plan and way of life. These groups include protozoans, related to animals; algae, related to plants; fungi, or molds; slime molds; bacteria; rickettsias; and viruses.

Since most microbes do not fit neatly into either the plant or the animal kingdom, many microbiologists classify all simple micro-organisms as **protists,** or "first things." Perhaps when life first appeared on earth several billion years ago, there was no difference between plants and animals. The differences may have come gradually as new forms of life developed.

The basic difference between plants and animals has to do with the way they get food for their life processes. Plants use the energy of sunlight to make their own food. They possess chlorophyll, a green substance that turns carbon dioxide and water into sugar.

Animals, on the other hand, get food by eating plants and other organisms. In general, animals must move about to get food, while plants stay in one place, soaking up light. There are other differences as well.

PROTOZOANS

The first animals may have been something like the tiny animal-like microbes known as **protozoans.** Let us look first at the most highly developed of these creatures, the paramecium (plural: paramecia).

Paramecia

One of the small creatures you may see in a drop of pond water is the paramecium. This micro-organism is just barely visible to the unaided eye. Under a microscope it appears slipper-shaped—rounded at one end and thin at the other. It is longer than it is wide. Its body is almost completely covered with thin, hairlike threads. These are called **cilia,** from a Latin word meaning "eyelid."

The cilia beat rhythmically, somewhat like thousands of tiny oars, driving the body forward or backward or in corkscrew turns. About 5,000 other kinds of protozoans also move this way. Known as ciliates, they are common in fresh and salt water.

The paramecium lives in fresh water, feeding on bacteria, yeasts, and other protozoans. It seems able to control the beating of its cilia, for it can change direction rapidly to get food or to avoid danger.

Along its side the paramecium has a groove lined with cilia. This groove leads like a funnel into the body. As the cilia beat, water and food material are swept in. At the inside end of the funnel a bubble of water gathers about the food. The bubble forms a space, called a **food vacuole,** in the body fluid.

The food vacuole floats slowly along a definite path through the body fluid. As it moves, body chemicals digest the food. At the thin end of the body the vacuole empties out waste materials through a small opening.

There may be several food vacuoles in the body at any one time. There are also two **contractile vacuoles,** one near each end of the body. These vacuoles control the amount of water in the body. The contractile vacuoles fill up with water. When one contains too much water, it moves to the surface of the body and empties its contents. This action prevents the body from swelling up and bursting.

Like all living organisms the paramecium can reproduce, or multiply. When it is fully grown, it may divide in two, forming two new individuals. A paramecium may also reproduce by exchanging body material with another paramecium. The bodies of the two microbes join for several hours, then separate. Each paramecium divides one or more times. As a result, several new microbes are formed that contain living material from two parents.

The Body Plan: One Cell

Though small and barely visible to your eyes, a paramecium carries out many of the same living activities that you and other animals do. It moves about and feeds. It can tell what is food and what is not. It grows. It reproduces.

In your body, however, such activities are carried out by billions of billions of cells (units of living material). These cells are organized in groups, each group performing a specific task.

In a paramecium body these tasks are carried out in a single cell. The entire paramecium body is made of just one cell. With certain exceptions this is true of all other microbes. It is one of the main differences between the protists and the many-celled plants and animals.

The paramecium cell body looks like a grainy glob of jelly surrounded by a thin membrane, or skin. The jellylike material is called **cytoplasm**. The cell membrane walls the cytoplasm off from its surroundings. Chemicals—such as oxygen, carbon dioxide, and water—enter and leave the cell through the cell membrane.

Inside the cell there are two ball-shaped masses, one larger than the other. These are the **nuclei** (singular: **nucleus**). The small nucleus controls reproduction. The large one controls the other activities of the cell. The body cells of most micro-organisms and of most plants and animals contain only one nucleus.

Amoebas

The body of the one-celled amoeba has one nucleus. In other ways, too, the amoeba is simpler than the paramecium. Its body does not even have a definite shape. In fact, the amoeba changes shape almost continually. (Its name comes from a Greek word meaning "to change.") It changes shape as it moves and feeds.

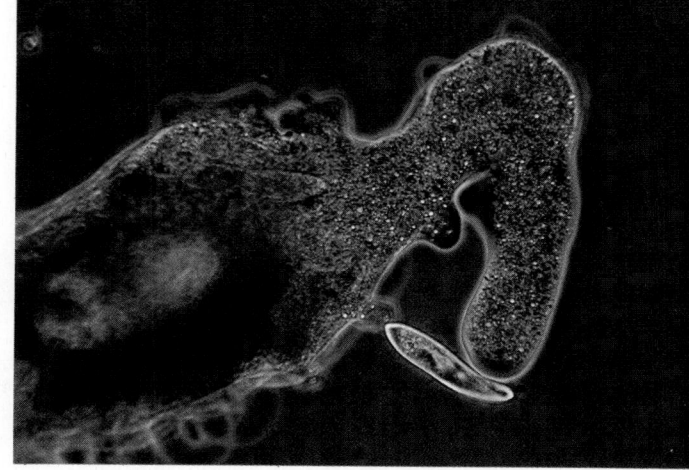

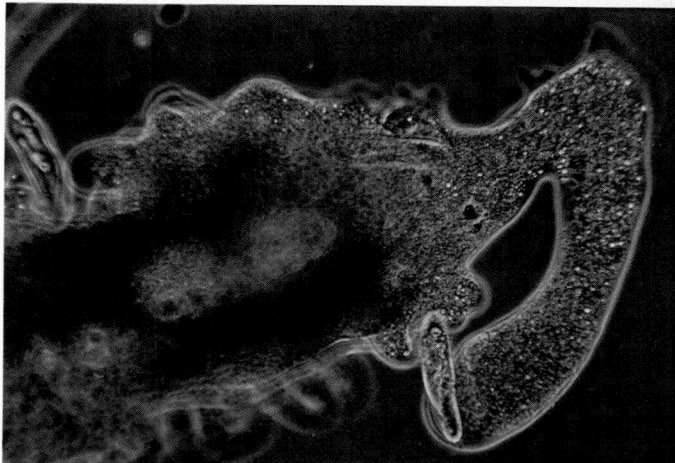

The amoeba feeds on paramecia. A paramecium is much too fast for the amoeba and would never get caught if it were not so curious. The amoeba produces a substance that attracts the paramecium, and the paramecium comes to investigate. (1) The amoeba sends out a pseudopod and surrounds the paramecium. (2) Cytoplasm of the amoeba flows over the paramecium, and (3) the paramecium is caught in a food vacuole. This type of feeding is called phagocytosis.

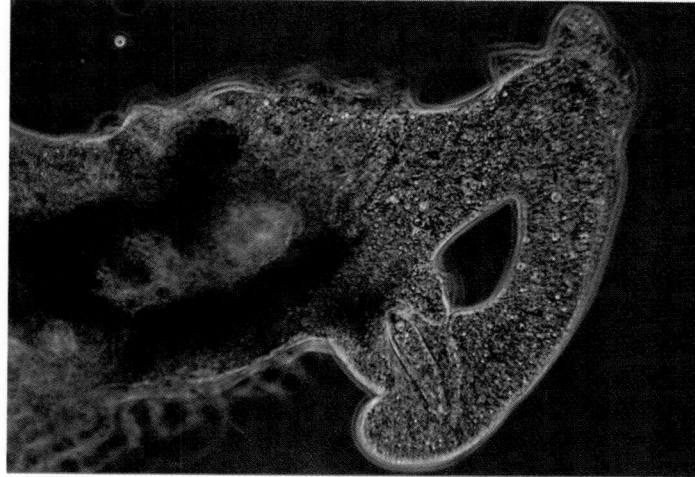

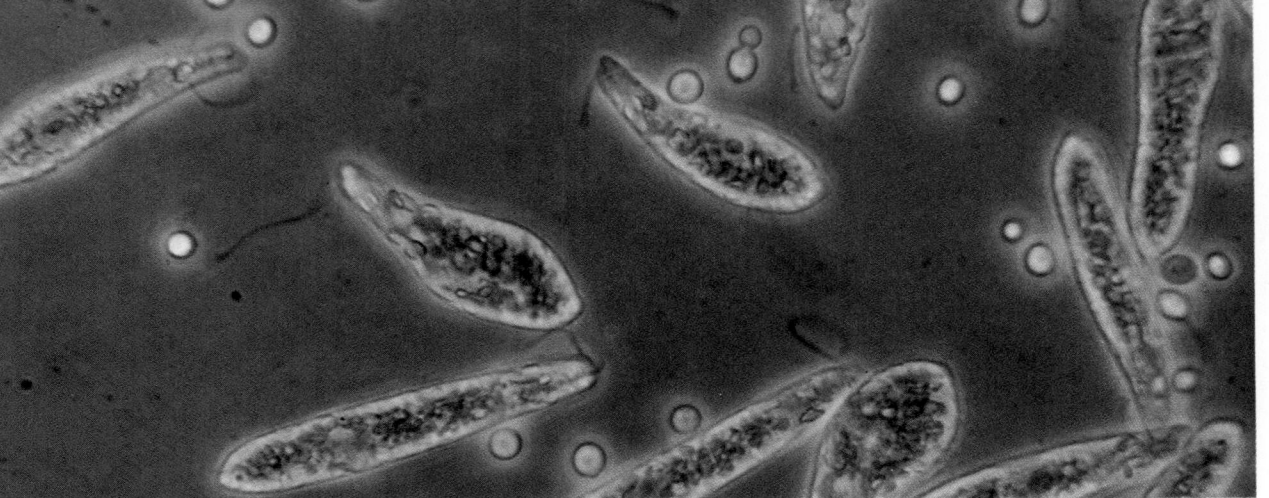

Plant or animal or both? The euglena has many features that are found only in plants. It also has many features common to animals. Many scientists feel that the tiny euglena is a link between the world of plants and the world of animals.

Slime mold forms large colonies that cling to the moist bark of a tree. The colonies shown here contain millions of microscopic organisms.

The amoeba moves in a peculiar way. Its cytoplasm oozes outward, forming a fingerlike tube. This tube is called a pseudopod ("false foot"). As the pseudopod flows outward in one direction, the back end of the cell bunches up. Then a second pseudopod flows outward in a slightly different direction, and then another pseudopod, and another. Slowly the amoeba oozes along. By means of these pseudopods it can move away from harmful objects. It can move toward food.

When an amoeba detects a bacterium or a particle of dead material, its pseudopods flow slowly toward the food. Gradually and without touching the food the pseudopods flow all around it. Soon the food, caught in a drop of the surrounding water, lies inside the cell. A food vacuole has been formed. The food material is digested, and the wastes pass out through the cell membrane.

The amoeba grows and finally reproduces. It does this by splitting in half, forming two new cells.

The common amoeba, found in ponds and in damp soil or oozing along the undersides of leaves, has a soft body. But some of its relatives live in the sea and have shells. They, too, move and feed by means of pseudopods. They reproduce by splitting in half.

In some shelled creatures the pseudopods are long and stiff, spreading out like rays from the cell. The shells are globe-shaped and made of a sandlike substance.

Another shelled group look like tiny snails. The chalk you use is made of the hardened remains of millions of these shells.

In all, there are some 8,000 kinds of amoebas, with and without shells. Certain kinds can live only in other organisms. One such kind is *Entamoeba histolytica,* the microbe that causes amoebic dysentery in man. This microbe is spread in dirty food and water. When not inside another organism, an entamoeba escapes death by forming a tough-walled crust, or **cyst,** about itself. Inside the cyst the microbe can stand extremes of heat, cold, or dryness. However, it usually becomes inactive. That is, it does not feed or grow. Dry cysts may be blown from place to place by the winds. If the cysts land in water or on food, they may enter a human body. Then the entamoebas break out and resume active life. Almost all other kinds of protozoans form cysts. Some kinds have been known to come to life again after 50 years inside a cyst. Most can survive for several months in this state.

Parasites

Microbes, such as entamoebas, that live in and take food from other organisms are called **parasites**. Few can move. They are spread by various outside means, such as wind, water, and insects. Once they enter another organism, parasites feed on materials in the cells or body fluids. Some parasites harm the host organism very little, but others may cause the host's death. One dangerous parasite is *Plasmodium vivax*. When this microbe invades the human bloodstream, it causes malaria.

Flagellates

Still other protozoans are known as flagellates. The flagellates get their name from the way they move. They move about by beating tiny whips called **flagella** (singular: **flagellum**). Flagella are longer than cilia but are otherwise much like them. Thin and hairlike, they can bend in any direction. Some kinds of flagellates have only one such whip. Other kinds have several. When there is more than one flagellum, each one moves separately, unlike cilia, which always move together. The flagella are usually located at one end of the body.

There are about 2,000 kinds of flagellates. Many are parasites, such as the leaf-shaped trypanosome that causes African sleeping sickness. This parasite multiplies in the blood of its human host. Eventually the host's brain is damaged, and death results.

However, certain other flagellate parasites benefit their hosts. An example is the trichonympha that lives inside termites. It digests cellulose, a substance in the wood eaten by these insects. Since the termites cannot by themselves digest this substance, they would starve to death without the flagellates.

Many flagellates are free-living. That is, they do not live inside other organisms. They live in water. In general they possess chlorophyll and produce their own food. Here we find organisms that are related to both plants and animals.

The dinoflagellates ("whirling whips") are among these creatures. Like plants they have thick cell walls of cellulose. Though some dinoflagellates feed on bacteria, most make their own food. For this they need sunshine. (This explains why most dinoflagellates are found in the upper, light-filled regions of the oceans. The dinoflagellates are an important source of food for many water animals.)

You may have noticed green scum on freshwater ponds and swimming pools. The green color often comes from the chlorophyll in masses and masses of tiny, oval-shaped *Euglena* or ball-like *Volvox* colonies. The masses are visible, though the individual cells are not.

A euglena has one flagellum. Near this lies a red spot. Microbiologists believe this spot is sensitive to light and so helps guide the euglena to the light needed for food production. However, when light is lacking, the euglena takes in food particles, dissolved in water, through its cell membrane. Though the euglena has a mouth groove that looks something like a paramecium's, no one has ever seen a euglena get food with it.

A euglena reproduces by dividing in two. Sometimes it does this after forming a cyst. When conditions are right, new euglena cells burst out of the cyst.

A volvox colony looks like a tiny hollow ball of jelly. It is usually made up of thousands of individual cells, which resemble euglenas. The cells are held together by strands of cytoplasm running through a jellylike covering. The beating of all the flagella drives the colony through the water. The cells on the forward side of the colony have light-sensitive spots that guide the movements of the entire colony. The cells of the hind end lack these spots. However, these hind cells are the only ones that can divide.

In a way the members of a volvox colony are like the cells in many-celled organisms. Different groups of cells perform different tasks for the good of the whole.

▶ SLIME MOLDS

In the spring you may be able to find slime molds oozing along, amoebalike, among damp, decaying leaves in a forest. The molds may look like large, spreading masses of yellow, orange, or white jelly.

Like the protozoans, slime molds feed on bacteria, other micro-organisms, and small bits of dead plant and animal material. A slime mold grows and spreads. Eventually it moves to a drier place for reproduction.

At this point it becomes more like a plant than an animal. It slowly produces a number of brightly colored stalks. These are the spore cases, in which tiny spores are formed. In time the wall of the spore case breaks open and the spores are released. When the spores land in a moist spot, they sprout and produce tiny cells. At first the new cells swim about by means of flagella. Then they lose the flagella and pair off. These pairs then develop into new masses of living material.

▶ FUNGI

You have probably seen toadstools sprouting in damp, shady places, mold spreading on stale bread, or mildew growing on old shoes. These organisms are fungi. Fungi are often classified as plants. However, they lack chlorophyll and cannot make their own food. Instead they feed on other organisms, living or dead.

Some fungi feed on dead organisms, such as leaves and fallen logs. Like bacteria they break down dead material and return to the soil chemicals needed for plant growth.

However, some fungi feed on living plants and animals. These parasites cause rusts, smuts, and blights on plants, and various diseases in animals. Athlete's foot and ringworm, for example, are caused by fungi.

As a rule, fungi reproduce by means of spores. The air around us is filled with millions of invisible floating spores. If the spores land on the right sort of substance, they sprout and grow.

▶ ALGAE

The seaweeds you may see growing along rocky beaches or in shallow coastal waters are algae. They possess chlorophyll and make their own food. Many scientists classify these many-celled algae with plants.

Most algae are too small to be seen. These algae are small, one-celled organisms that live in fresh water, in the ocean, and in the soil. Like the seaweeds they produce their own food.

Some of the microscopic algae have shells.

These algae are called diatoms. They live in both fresh and salt water. Like the dinoflagellates, diatoms are an important source of food for many water-dwelling animals.

For millions of years diatom shells have piled up in various parts of the world. Earth formed from these remains is mined and used in industry for filtering and for certain fine polishing.

▶ BACTERIA

Bacteria are distinctly different in their body plan from either plants or animals. Most bacteria, like plants, have thick cell walls outside the cell membrane, but the material in the cell walls of bacteria differs chemically from that in plants. Bacteria have nuclear material, but it is not separated from the rest of the cell by a membrane, as it is in plants and animals. In this way bacteria resemble certain blue-green algae. Bacteria are much smaller than protozoans, fungi, or algae. They can only be seen with a high-powered microscope. Many can move and have flagella, but these are very different from the flagella seen on flagellates.

Most bacteria feed on material produced by other organisms. A few green and purple bacteria, however, can produce their own food out of raw materials such as water and carbon dioxide. Some bacteria get food in both ways.

Some kinds of bacteria are parasites. Among them are the microbes that cause such diseases as scarlet fever, whooping cough, and tuberculosis.

But many more are useful to larger organisms, including man. Without bacteria we would starve to death. Here are two reasons why this is so.

We and all other living things need nitrogen. Even though nitrogen forms a major part of the air, we cannot use this nitrogen. Fortunately certain bacteria can. These microbes make the nitrogen available to us. Colonies of these bacteria live on the roots of clover, bean, and other plants of the pea family. They combine nitrogen from the air with chemicals in the soil. The plants use these substances and so get nitrogen. We and other animals eat the plants and thus obtain the nitrogen we need.

Many other kinds of bacteria break down

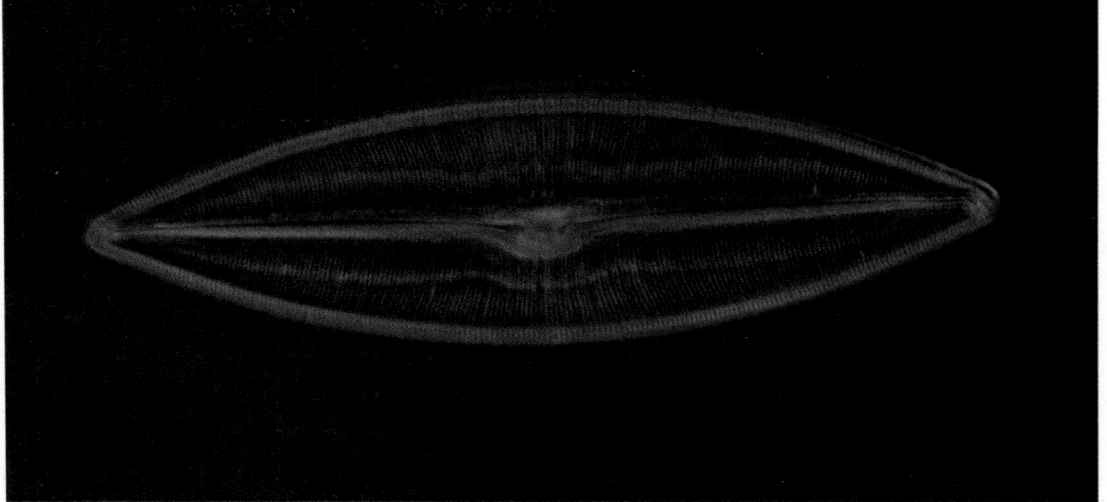

Seen under a special microscope, the tiny plants called diatoms show a symmetrical internal structure. Notice that the diatom has a thin shell around it.

The hills of microscopic plants (*below*) are millions of tiny fungi. Life-saving antibiotics are made by such fungi as these.

GENERALIZED BACTERIUM

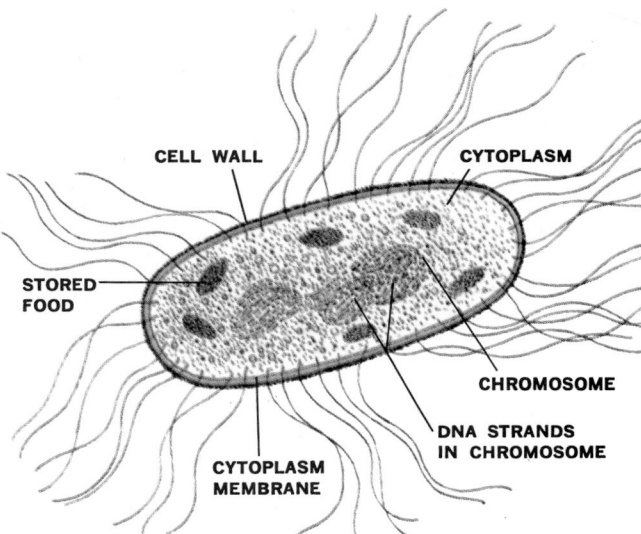

CELL WALL

CYTOPLASM

STORED FOOD

CHROMOSOME

DNA STRANDS IN CHROMOSOME

CYTOPLASM MEMBRANE

dead plant and animal material into its chemical parts. These chemicals may then be used again by growing plants. Without the bacteria the earth's supplies of certain important chemicals would be locked up in dead organisms. Life would soon stop.

▶ VIRUSES AND RICKETTSIAS

Bacteria are the smallest organisms that can feed and grow and reproduce independently of other cells. None can be seen without a high-powered microscope. Still smaller than bacteria are the viruses and rickettsias. None of these can be seen clearly without an electron microscope. Neither viruses nor

GENERALIZED BACTERIOPHAGE

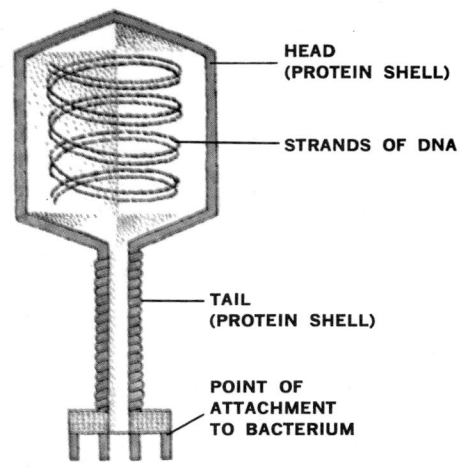

HEAD (PROTEIN SHELL)

STRANDS OF DNA

TAIL (PROTEIN SHELL)

POINT OF ATTACHMENT TO BACTERIUM

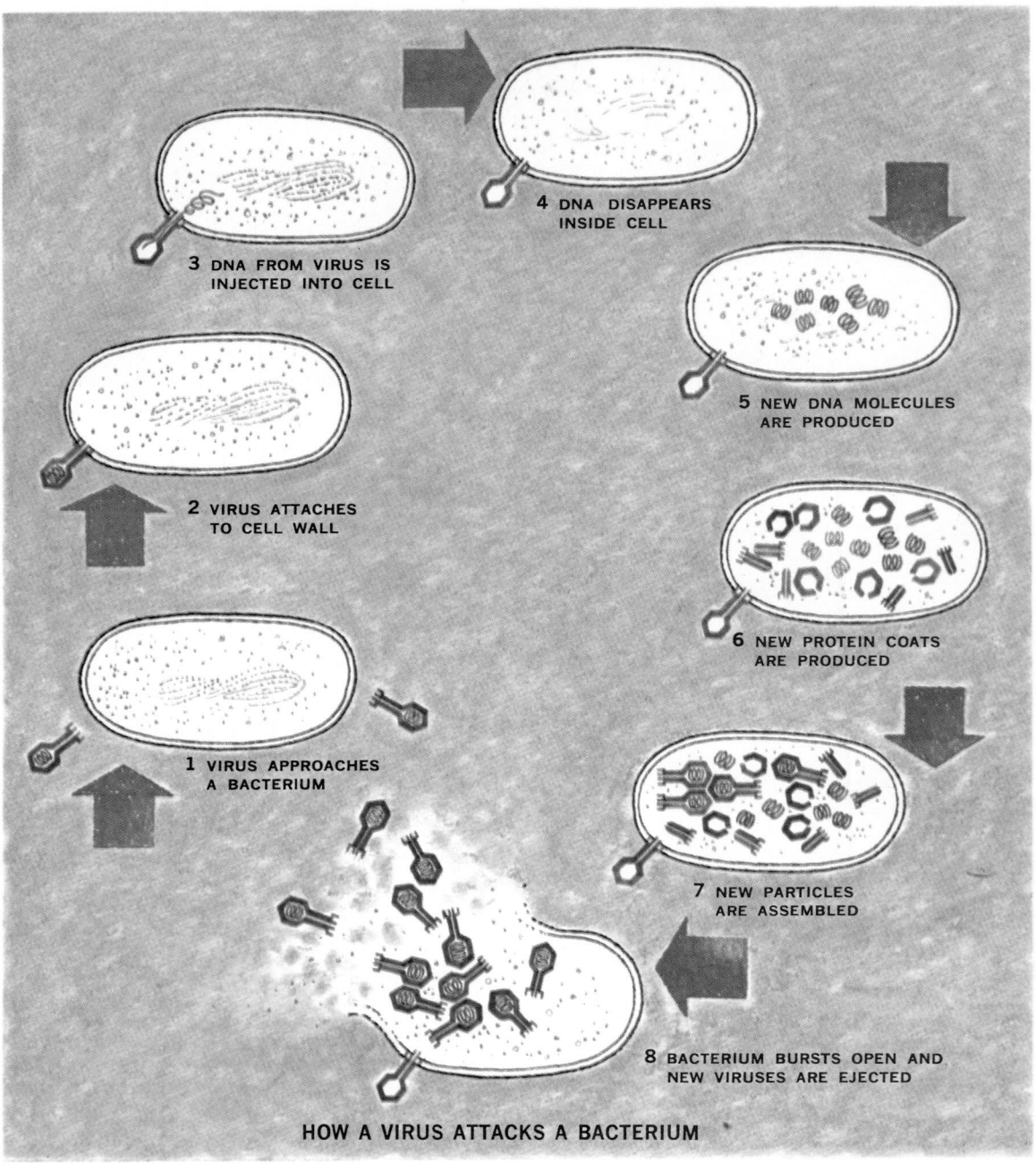

3 DNA FROM VIRUS IS
INJECTED INTO CELL

4 DNA DISAPPEARS
INSIDE CELL

2 VIRUS ATTACHES
TO CELL WALL

5 NEW DNA MOLECULES
ARE PRODUCED

1 VIRUS APPROACHES
A BACTERIUM

6 NEW PROTEIN COATS
ARE PRODUCED

7 NEW PARTICLES
ARE ASSEMBLED

8 BACTERIUM BURSTS OPEN AND
NEW VIRUSES ARE EJECTED

HOW A VIRUS ATTACKS A BACTERIUM

rickettsias, which are somewhat larger than viruses, can use or make food. They can grow and reproduce only when inside a living cell.

All viruses and rickettsias are complete parasites, and most of them are harmful to their hosts. Among the diseases caused in man by viruses are measles, mumps, flu, smallpox, and the common cold. Rickettsias cause typhus, Rocky Mountain spotted fever, and other diseases.

Reviewed by WAYNE W. UMBREIT
Rutgers—The State University

See also ALGAE; ANTIBIOTICS; BACTERIA; CELLS; DISEASES; FERMENTATION; FUNGI; KOCH, ROBERT; LEEUWENHOEK, ANTON VAN; MICROSCOPES; PASTEUR, LOUIS; VIRUSES.

MICROPHONES. See RADIO.

MICROSCOPES

Have you ever looked through a microscope at a drop of pond water? If so, you may have seen tiny animals moving in the water. To the eye alone these animals look no bigger than specks of dust. But the microscope magnifies them and shows the details of their bodies.

The word "microscope" comes from two Greek words meaning "small" and "to see." Microscopes are instruments that enable us to see small things. We can see specks of dust without a microscope, but the specks all look much alike. With a microscope we can see details smaller than the specks themselves. These details tell us that some specks are minerals, some are soot, some are pollen from plants, and so on.

With microscopes we can see objects that are invisible to the eye alone. Scientists can see tiny virus particles and bacteria. They can even distinguish a particular kind of virus from all other kinds of viruses.

There are many kinds of microscopes, each kind best suited to a certain kind of work. It took many years of work by many people to develop and perfect these microscopes. But since the 1930's, improvements and new discoveries have been reported almost every day.

▶ SIMPLE MICROSCOPES

A magnifying glass is a **simple microscope**. It has one glass lens that focuses light. Light rays reflected from a small object pass through the lens, forming an enlarged image of that object.

Lenses were probably first used to magnify objects in the 1200's. In 1268 an English scientist, Roger Bacon, wrote about using a lens in this way.

In the 1600's, Anton van Leeuwenhoek, a Dutch naturalist, made a simple microscope that magnified 200 times. About 1674 he discovered "little animals" in water. These tiny things were bacteria and one-celled animals. This discovery was the beginning of the science of microbiology (the study of small living things).

Today simple microscopes are still used to magnify things up to about 25 times. For higher magnification **compound microscopes** are used.

▶ COMPOUND MICROSCOPES

Compound microscopes have two separate lenses (or sets of lenses). The first one was made in 1590 by two Dutch spectacle makers, Hans and Zacharias Janssen. This microscope was not very powerful. In 1611 the German astronomer Johannes Kepler thought of a better design. Since then, many people have helped to improve compound microscopes. Today they are used in every field of science.

The ordinary compound microscope is used mainly in the fields of biology and medicine. It is called a **medical**, or **biological**, **microscope**. With it doctors can study germs, blood cells, or body tissues to learn why a patient is ill. Biologists can learn how plants and animals grow and multiply and pass on traits, such as eye color, from one generation to the next.

Living material is hard to see with a medical microscope. To make the material more visible, biologists stain it with dyes. But often the dye kills the living material. In 1932 a Dutch physicist, Frits Zernike, invented a microscope that made it easier to see living matter without staining it. Called a **phase-contrast microscope,** this instrument became so useful in biology that in 1953 Zernike received a Nobel prize.

How much magnification can a microscope give?

A microscope shows a magnified image of the specimen (the object being viewed). But magnification alone is not enough. The details of the magnified specimen must be clear, not fuzzy. To show details clearly, a microscope must have good **resolving power**—the ability to separate closely spaced details.

A compound microscope could be designed to have a magnifying power of, let us say, 1,000,000 times. But its resolving power would be no better than that of an ordinary microscope, which has a maximum useful magnifying power of 1,500 times. Resolving power is limited by the comparatively long wavelength of the light coming through the lenses from the specimen. Microscopes that use light are called **optical microscopes.**

Electrons have a much shorter wavelength than light. Scientists developed the **electron microscope,** which uses electrons in place of light. Unlike optical microscopes, electron microscopes can magnify millions of times but show details clearly (see page 288).

Some materials fluoresce (give off visible light) when placed in ultraviolet light. Ultraviolet light, which is invisible to the human eye, has shorter wavelengths than visible light. When bacteria or living tissues are stained with harmless fluorescent dyes they can be studied with **fluorescence microscopes** to detect certain disease conditions.

Scientists use **ultraviolet** and **infrared microscopes** to learn the chemical makeup of small objects such as living cells. This has helped to explain growth and heredity. Not only biologists and doctors but other scientists use microscopes to see small details or work with tiny samples of a substance.

Most solid materials are made of crystals. These crystals can be studied with a **polarizing microscope**. The first polarizing microscopes were developed in the 1800's. At first they were used to identify ores and minerals.

Today they are used to study drugs, chemicals, metals, foods, living tissue, fibers, plastics, poisonous wastes in water and air, radioactivity, and micrometeorites (cosmic dust).

HOW TO CARE FOR YOUR MICROSCOPE

Read the instruction booklet that comes with your microscope. The booklet contains valuable information about the care and use of the microscope.

Keep your microscope in a box when it is not in use. The box protects the microscope from dust.

Keep the lenses clean, and be careful not to scratch them. Clean the lenses with the special tissue called lens-cleaning tissue. Blot the tissue against the lens to pick up bits of dust. Never rub the tissue against the lens. A speck of dust can scratch the lens if pressed against the glass.

Do not touch the lenses with your fingers. The natural oil from your skin is hard to clean off a lens.

SOME THINGS TO LOOK AT THROUGH YOUR MICROSCOPE

Here are a few suggestions of things that you can look at under a microscope that magnifies at least 60 times.

Equipment You Will Need

At least six clean microscope slides. One of them should be a depression slide. (This is a slide with a little hollow in its center. It is used to study liquids, such as a drop of water.)

A cover slip for each of the slides. Cover slips are small, thin pieces of glass or plastic that are used to cover the specimen on a slide.

A pair of sharp-pointed tweezers.

Iodine to use as a stain for some of the specimens.

A medicine dropper.

Two saucers or custard cups.

The Cells of an Onion Skin

(1) Peel the dry skin off an onion. Then peel off a layer of the fleshy part, and from its underside pull off a small piece of the clear skin.

(2) Lay the clear skin flat on a microscope slide. Put a few drops of iodine on the skin. The iodine stains the skin and makes the cells show up clearly. Set the slide aside for a few minutes until the skin absorbs the iodine.

(3) Pick up the cover slip with the tweezers, and cover the onion skin. The cover slip helps prevent the specimen from drying out. Lower the microscope tube carefully until the lens almost touches the cover slip. (Be careful not to lower the tube too far. If you do, you may break the cover slip and damage the microscope lens.) Then slowly raise the tube until the specimen comes into focus.

(4) Examine the slide under the microscope. You should see rows of bricklike cells. Each cell is surrounded by a cell wall and has a spot in the center stained dark brown. The spot is the nucleus of the cell.

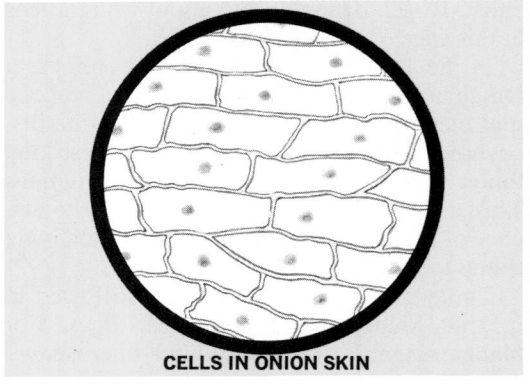

CELLS IN ONION SKIN

Starch Grains in a Potato

(1) Add ¼ teaspoon of iodine to 1 teaspoon of water in a saucer.

(2) Shave a very thin slice of raw potato with a potato peeler. Soak it in the iodine solution for about a minute. The iodine will stain the starch in the potato, turning it dark blue or purple.

(3) Remove the potato slice from the iodine. Put a piece about 1.5 millimeters (1/16 inch) long on a microscope slide and cover it.

(4) Look at the piece of potato under the microscope. If the specimen is too dark to show everything clearly, make another specimen. This time use more water in the iodine solution. The dark-blue circles are starch grains. You can see why a potato is called a starchy vegetable.

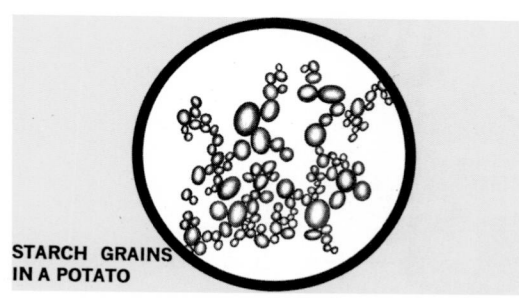

STARCH GRAINS IN A POTATO

The Breathing Pores of a Leaf

(1) Use the tweezers to pull off a piece of colorless skin from the underside of a geranium leaf. You need a piece of skin not much bigger than the head of a pin.

(2) Spread the skin flat on a slide and cover it.

(3) The microscope shows little doughnut-shaped bodies in the cells of the leaf skin. These bodies are the stomata, the breathing pores of green plants. Notice that in some stomata the center is wide open. When the center looks like a dark slit, the pore is closed.

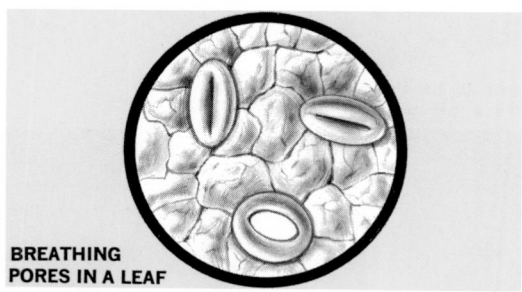

BREATHING PORES IN A LEAF

Flower Pollen

(1) Shake some yellow pollen from a flower onto a microscope slide. Look at the pollen under a microscope.

(2) Examine pollen of various flowers. You can see that the pollen of each kind of flower is different.

Salt Crystals

Examine table salt with your microscope. Cube-shaped crystals show up very clearly.

A Type of Body Cell

(1) Scrape the inside of your cheek lightly with the side of a toothpick.

(2) Put the scrapings on a microscope slide. You can keep the cells from drying out by adding a drop of water to the slide. Be sure to keep the microscope lens dry.

(3) The irregular-shaped cells you see are called squamous epithelial cells. Such cells line the mouth and many other internal parts of the body.

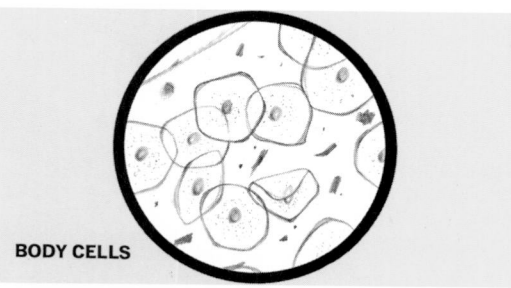

BODY CELLS

Life in Pond Water

Bring home a small jar of water from a pond. If possible, get some water that has scum or bits of water plants in it. Put a drop of the water on a depression slide, and cover it with a cover glass. Examine the drop under the microscope. You will see several different kinds of tiny living things swimming in the drop of water. Some common ones are paramecium, vorticella, stentor, and volvox. You can find the names and pictures of others in almost any biology book.

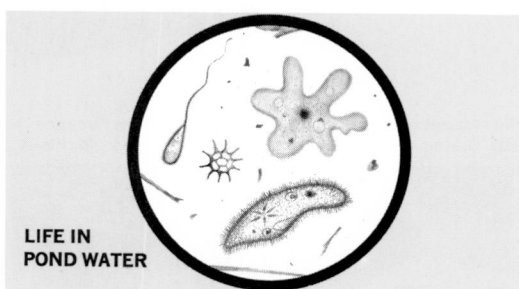

LIFE IN POND WATER

Some Other Ideas

Here are some other things you might look at through your microscope:

A piece of facial tissue.

A crumb from an aspirin tablet while it is dissolving in water.

The wing of a mosquito.

The antenna of a fly.

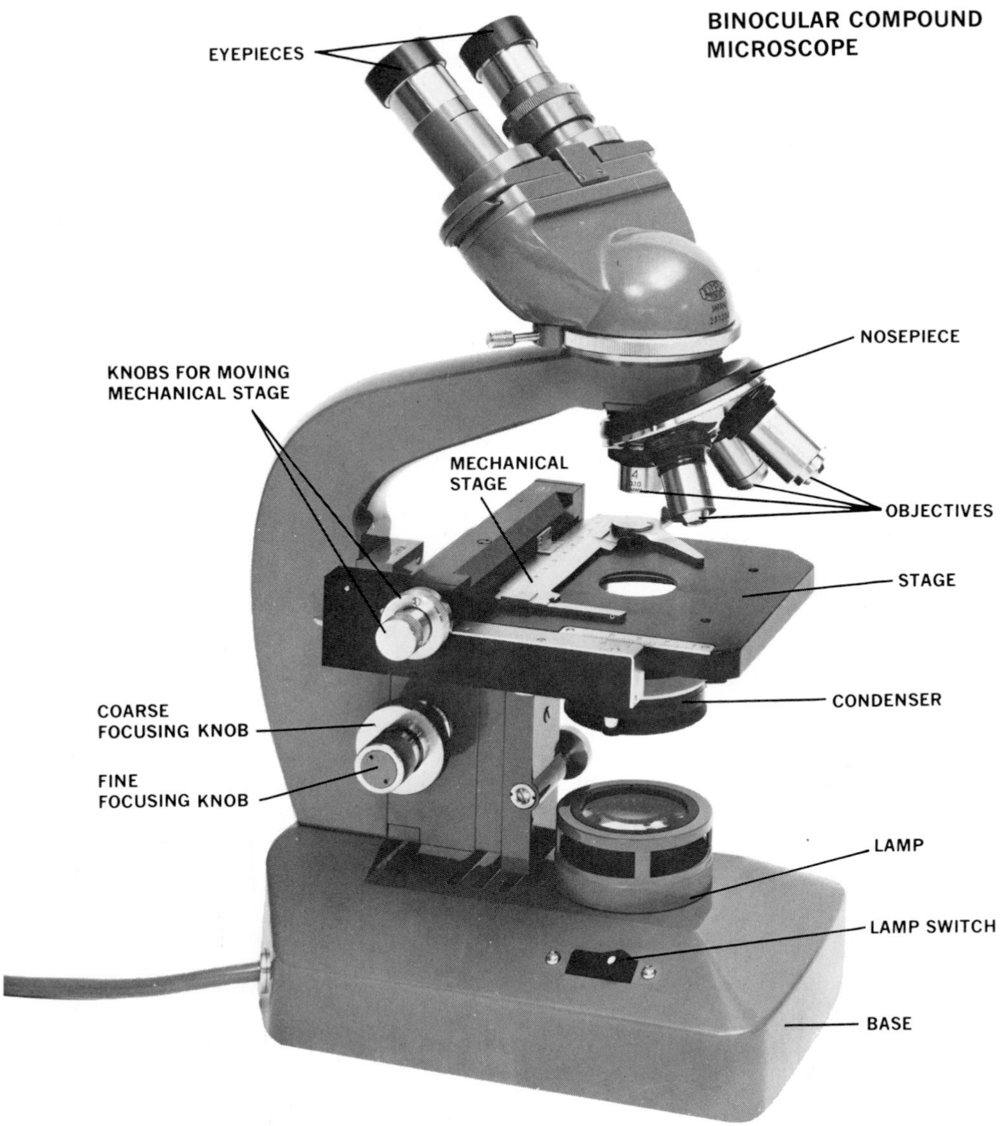

BINOCULAR COMPOUND MICROSCOPE

EYEPIECES

NOSEPIECE

KNOBS FOR MOVING
MECHANICAL STAGE

MECHANICAL
STAGE

OBJECTIVES

STAGE

COARSE
FOCUSING KNOB

CONDENSER

FINE
FOCUSING KNOB

LAMP

LAMP SWITCH

BASE

The scanning electron microscope produces images that appear to be three-dimensional. Below left: Grains of salt are magnified 100 times. Right: A hair from a bat is magnified 1,000 times.

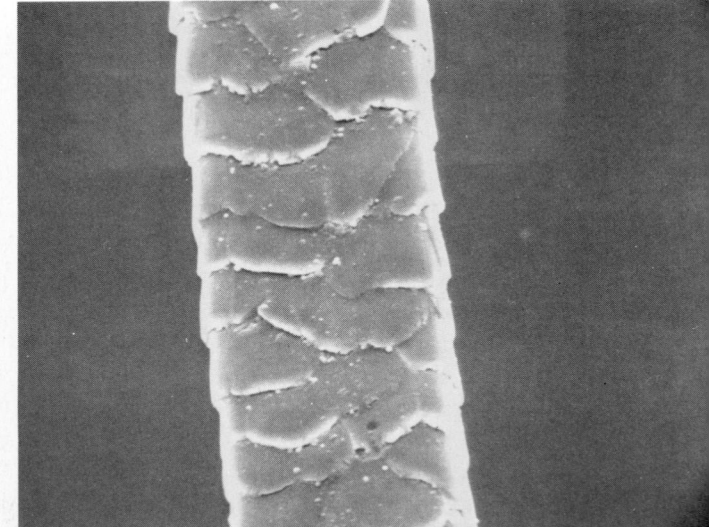

EXPLORING MUSCLE WITH DIFFERENT MICROSCOPES

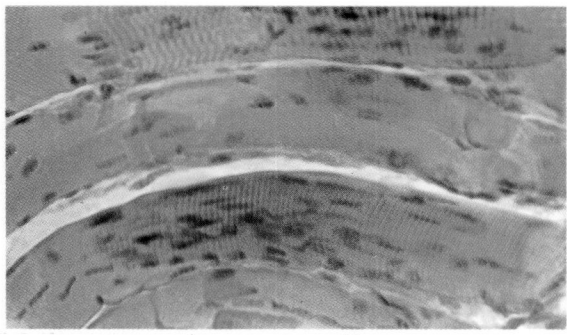

(1) The simple microscope shows large features, such as the muscle surrounded by other kinds of tissue. (2) The compound microscope shows stripes in the muscle fibers. Special stains (dyes) must be used for the stripes to be seen.

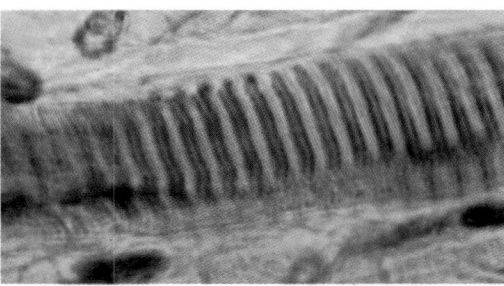

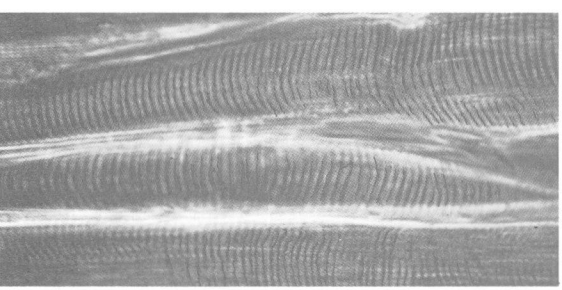

(3) When more detail is desired, the stained muscle can be studied at higher magnification with the compound microscope. (4) With the phase-contrast microscope, the stripes show up without the need for any stain.

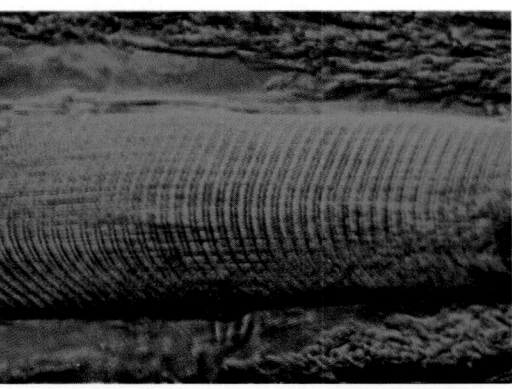

(5) With the interference phase microscope, the detail can be seen without staining. The colors tell scientists much about the structure of the muscles. (6) The polarization differential interference microscope is a newer kind of microscope. With it, even the texture of the muscle can be studied.

(7) The electron microscope shows how much can be seen in the muscle between two stripes. This picture is magnified 70,000 times. (8) With the fluorescence microscope a green glow shows where certain chemicals are located in the muscle fiber. Notice that the stripes do not glow.

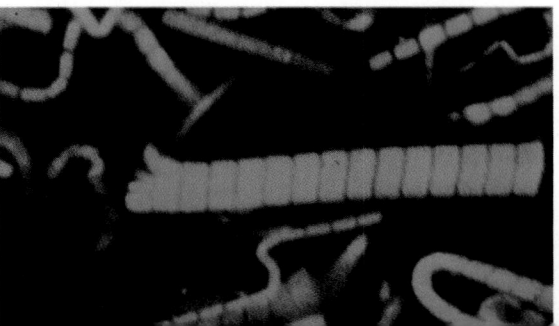

Scientists use **interference microscopes** when they must measure the exact weight of a small object, such as a part of a cell. For example, they have weighed the nucleus of a cell from a human mouth in this way. It weighs only 6/100,000,000,000 (hundred billionths) gram.

Stereomicroscopes, which show objects in three dimensions, are useful for things too small to be studied with the eye alone but too large to be seen with an ordinary microscope. For example, biologists use these microscopes for delicate work like dissecting an insect. Engineers use them when assembling tiny parts for spacecraft.

▶ELECTRON MICROSCOPES

Optical microscopes can magnify objects usefully about 1,400 times. The electron microscope was developed for much higher magnification. In one type, called the **transmission electron microscope**, beams of electrons are sent through the specimen. The beams are focused by magnetic or electric lenses. The image appears on a fluorescent screen somewhat like a television screen. This image can be photographed. The photographs are then enlarged for closer study. Electron microscopes can magnify at least 1,000,000 times.

The first electron microscopes were built in Germany in 1932 by Max Knoll and Ernst

Ruska and by Ernst Brüche and H. Johannson. The electron microscope soon entered almost every field of science. It has been used to see the patterns of molecules in virus crystals and of atoms in metal crystals.

In 1935, Knoll also invented the **scanning electron microscope**. In 1970, Albert V. Crewe, an American physicist, built a special scanning electron microscope with which single atoms of uranium and other heavy elements could be seen and recognized. The scanning electron microscope sweeps a beam of electrons back and forth over the specimen. It forms an image of the surface that is very clear and appears three-dimensional.

The **field ion emission microscope**, invented by Erwin Mueller in the 1950's, is used to study the arrangement of atoms in metals. An extremely sharp needle of the metal being studied is heated electrically in a chamber containing a little helium gas. Helium atoms bounce off the tip of the needle onto a televisionlike screen. They form a pattern that shows the position of the atoms in the tip.

▶X-RAY MICROSCOPES

X rays can pass through objects and thus make it possible to see details impossible to see any other way. Scientists began trying to make X-ray microscopes as soon as X rays were discovered in 1895. But it was not until 1948 that scientists built one that would work. Paul Harmon Kirkpatrick and Albert Vinicio Baez, in the United States, built the first practical one. And in 1951, Vernon Ellis Cosslett and William C. Nixon, in England, built another one of a different type.

With X-ray microscopes, scientists can see through whole living insects or solid pieces of metal. They can also learn what chemical elements make up a small object.

▶ACOUSTIC MICROSCOPES

Sound waves also can pass through solid objects. In the acoustic microscope, sound that has been sent through an object—such as a part of the living human body—is made visible by devices called **transducers**. The acoustic microscope was developed in the 1970's.

LUCY B. McCRONE
Research Microscopist
Walter C. McCrone Associates

See also CRYSTALS; LENSES; LIGHT; RADIATION.

Scientists at work with an electron microscope in France.

Carcassonne is one of the few remaining walled towns in France.

MIDDLE AGES

It is useful to think of a day as being divided into morning, afternoon, evening, and night. It is useful because it makes it possible to be more definite when speaking of time. It is more definite to say that something happened yesterday morning than to say that it happened yesterday. For much the same reason, historians think of the past as being divided into periods. They call the earliest period, which ended about the year A.D. 500, ancient times. They call the last 500 or 600 years modern times, and the period in between, the Middle Ages.

Periods of history are like parts of a day. It is difficult to say just when one ends and another begins. Evening comes between afternoon and night, but just when does evening end and night begin? It is just as hard to pick a certain year as the one when ancient times ended and the Middle Ages began. One historical period fades into another much as evening fades into night. For this reason it is not possible to date the Middle Ages exactly.

Historians usually think of the Middle Ages as a period in the history of Europe that lasted 1,000 years—between the years 500 and 1500. This period covered the years from the fall of the Western Roman Empire to the discovery of the New World by Christopher Columbus in 1492.

A great many things happened in Europe during these years, because this period, like all periods in history, was a time of change.

▶ THE ROMAN EMPIRE AND THE GERMAN TRIBES

Most of western Europe was part of the Roman Empire in later ancient times. But after the death of the Emperor Justinian in 565, Roman rulers had almost no power over the western lands. The capital of the once great empire was in the east, at Constantinople. Roman armies no longer kept tribes of Germans from migrating freely across the Rhine and Danube rivers. The movement of German tribes into the empire had begun long before the time of Justinian. As early as 376 the Visigoths (or West Goths) had moved into the empire. They had secured the Roman emperor's permission, but they soon became dissatisfied and rebelled. They defeated the emperor's army at the battle of Adrianople in 378 and so showed the world that Roman power was no longer what it had once been. Some years later, in 410, the Visigoths invaded Italy and plundered Rome, the old capital. It was hard for people of those times to believe that Roman power had grown so weak. "Who would believe," Saint Jerome, a Christian writer, asked, "that Rome, which had spread over the whole earth by means of its victories, could now fall so low . . . ."

The German tribes settled down in the provinces of the empire, living alongside the old inhabitants. But the Germans lived under their own laws and under the rule of their own chiefs or kings. Several German tribes set up kingdoms in the west: the Visigoths in Spain, the Lombards in Italy, the Anglo-Saxons in

England, and the Franks in France and western Germany.

The Germans did not wish to destroy all signs of Roman civilization. They adopted many of their neighbors' ways, including the Christian religion. Those Germans who settled in places where the Latin-speaking population outnumbered them adopted the Roman tongue in time. This is why modern French, Spanish, Portuguese, and Italian are based on Latin. In places where Latin-speaking people were few, German tongues became the language. Thus, Anglo-Saxon became the language of England and the basis for modern English.

Although the Germans did not intend to destroy the old civilization, their migrations and conquests did in fact greatly change life in the west. There was little trade, with the result that cities and towns became less important. The people in each neighborhood produced almost everything they used, which was little but bare necessities.

Few Germans could read the Latin books, so they learned little about the civilization they had conquered and the Christian religion they had adopted. Some German kings did not understand the Roman system of government, while others had studied it carefully. So the system continued, although in an ever more simplified form.

▶ CHARLEMAGNE'S EMPIRE AND RULE BY FEUDAL LORDS

Historians used to call the early Middle Ages the Dark Ages. These centuries between 500 and 1000 were marked by confusion, disorder, and the breakdown of civilization in western Europe. But elsewhere—in the Muslim world, the Byzantine Empire, and the Far East—great civilizations flourished. Scholars today know more about the so-called Dark Ages. They point out that during this period the great Frankish king Charlemagne (742?–814) established a large empire that included much of western and central Europe.

Charlemagne kept order throughout this realm, and he encouraged interest in the Christian religion and ancient Latin learning. He wanted to rule as the emperors of Rome had done in ancient times. He was even crowned "Emperor of the Romans" by the pope in 800.

Charlemagne kept close check on the great nobles and landlords, who were in the habit of doing as they wished. Into every district he sent special agents who saw that the nobles obeyed his commands. To encourage learning, Charlemagne established a palace school for the sons of nobles. He gave support to scholars, and he set scribes to work copying various ancient books. Because the scribes performed their tasks well, few of the ancient works that had survived until that time were ever lost.

Charlemagne accomplished much, but his empire did not last long after his death. Later Frankish rulers could neither govern nor protect a large empire. Vikings from the Scandinavian lands found that there was no one to keep them from raiding the coast and sailing up the rivers to plunder the countryside. Some of the Vikings settled down in that part of France which is still known as Normandy, land of the Northmen. Muslims threatened in the south, as they had done before Charlemagne became king.

The Muslims were followers of Islam, a religion first preached, in Arabia, by Mohammed. Muslim Arabs conquered North Africa and, in 711, invaded Europe through Spain. They then pressed through the Pyrenees into the land of the Franks. Charlemagne's grandfather, Charles Martel, had defeated the Muslims at the battle of Tours in 732, and Charlemagne fought against them in Spain. But with the collapse of Charlemagne's empire in the 9th century, the Muslims attacked again, particularly in Italy, where they even raided Rome. The Muslims held part of Spain throughout the Middle Ages, and the history of Spain in those years is a story of struggle between Muslims and Christians.

With the breakup of Charlemagne's empire, local lords and their knights offered men the best protection. The system of government in which local lords exchanged land for military service by knights is known as **feudalism**. Feudal lords did give men some protection, but they also disturbed the peace with their private wars. Each lord was a law to himself, and this often led to conflict and disorder.

▶ KINGS AND LORDS

After the year 1000, conditions in Europe again changed—this time for the better. The

Vikings no longer endangered life and property. The Muslims no longer threatened western Europe. Instead, the European Christians carried war to the Muslim lands in the east with a series of "wars for the cross," or **Crusades**.

But the most important change after 1000 resulted from the success that kings in several countries had in bringing the feudal lords under control and checking private wars.

France

Louis VI (1081–1137)—called Louis the Fat—heaved his bulky body into the saddle and personally led campaigns to punish cruel lords who abused their power. His grandson, Philip II (1165–1223), or Philip Augustus, appointed special officials, called bailiffs, who traveled within their districts keeping watch on the lords somewhat as Charlemagne's agents had done. It is interesting to note that a later king, Louis IX (1214–70), found it necessary to appoint other officials to keep check on the bailiffs—watchers to watch the watchmen.

Louis IX was so religious that the Church in 1297 declared him a saint. Louis did his best to see that no man was treated unfairly in his realm. He would seat himself beneath a tree and invite anyone who had been unable to get justice from his lord or the regular courts to come and state his case.

Philip IV (1268–1314), called Philip the Fair because of his fine looks, was not so good a man as Saint Louis. However, he did even more to make the king the real ruler of the kingdom.

England

The kings of England gained greater power over their feudal lords than did the French monarchs. This was partly because William I (1027?–87) was a duke of Normandy who had won the English crown by conquest. He took care that his local lords did not have too much independence or power. William the Conqueror did not want any other duke or lord to do what he had done.

William's son Henry I (1068–1135) and great-grandson Henry II (1133–89) strengthened the crown. Henry II encouraged men to look to the royal courts for justice rather than to their local courts or those of the lords. He

did so partly by having the royal courts offer better and fairer service.

In the local and lords' courts trials often were by ordeal or battle. In a trial by ordeal a man was subjected to some test in order "to offer proof." One form of proof required that a man be bound and cast into a pool of water that had been blessed by a priest. If he sank, he was judged to be in the right and was pulled out. But if he floated, he was judged to be wrong. In a trial by battle, two men having a dispute fought each other with swords or other weapons, and the winner of the duel was judged the winner of the case.

Henry II made it possible for men to have another kind of trial in the royal courts. Twelve men of the neighborhood were required to give information about a case and were then asked questions about it. The judge based his decision on their answers. Although these men were more like witnesses than jurors, this was the beginning of the jury trial in England. It is easy to understand why a man who had a good case but did not want to risk either an ordeal or a trial by battle might be eager to bring his case to a royal court, where he could get a trial by jury.

It was bad for feudal lords to have unchecked powers, but the English discovered that the same was true of kings. A king who could do whatever he wanted could be as cruel and tyrannical as a lord, and he was much more powerful. For this reason the effort by the English lords and others to put checks on royal power was another important event.

King John (1167?–1216) ruled recklessly and unjustly and caused both lords and common people to hate him. It is interesting to note that no later English king was ever given the name of John. It aroused too many unhappy memories.

In 1215 John found himself in so much trouble both at home and abroad that he agreed to issue a great charter, the **Magna Carta**. In it he stated certain limits on his power. Among other things John promised that he would have no freeman arrested or punished except "by the law of the land." This statement has made the Magna Carta one of the world's most famous documents. It meant that the head of the government was not above the law. Constitutional governments today are based on this idea.

The English kings also had their powers limited by Parliament during the latter part of the Middle Ages. Parliament was the king's council, made up of the chief nobles, bishops of the church, and representatives of knights and townsmen. A king called his Parliament before attempting to collect special taxes. Parliament could often obtain privileges and concessions from the king in exchange for the voting of money. This made it possible for Parliament to increase its power over the kings during the Hundred Years War with France. This was the name given to a long series of wars, which lasted more than 100 years, between 1337 and 1453. The Parliament of the Middle Ages was very different from the modern British Parliament, but the modern representative body grew out of the older one.

Germany

The German kings, like those of France and England, tried to reduce the independence of their feudal lords. In general they had less success, even though they re-established Charlemagne's Roman Empire in the west—an empire which included Italy as well as Germany.

▶ PEASANTS AND TOWNSMEN

Kings and feudal lords were important in the Middle Ages, but they made up only a small part of the population. Most people were peasants who spent their lives working in the fields. A great many of the peasants were **serfs**—that is, they were not freemen.

Serfs

A serf could not leave his manor village to try and find a better place. He belonged to the manor on which he was born and was a part of the property. A serf could move or change jobs only if his lord gave permission. The lords did not freely give away their serfs any more than they gave away their land or livestock. When a lord agreed to let one of his serfs marry a serf from another manor, he usually demanded a payment to make up for the loss.

Most serfs led a hard life. A serf had to till the land of the lord, as well as the strips in the manor fields on which he grew his own food. The serf knew little about the world outside

his fields and his village. He could not read. He did not travel himself and rarely met anyone who had. He led a narrow as well as a hard life.

Townsmen

There were few towns, particularly in northwestern Europe, during the early Middle Ages, and so there were few townsmen. The rule of the feudal lords discouraged trade, and towns live by trade. Each lord collected a toll, for "protection," from all merchants who came into his neighborhood. A merchant paid many such tolls in traveling from one land to another. For example, a merchant taking a boatload of goods down the Loire River from Orléans had to pay 74 different tolls. Needless to say, the many tolls made goods expensive and trade difficult even in time of peace. During the frequent private wars trade became still more risky.

As private wars became less frequent, trade became easier. Towns grew in both number and size. The townsman was above the serf, for the townsman was free. But his position was beneath that of the lords. So the townsmen became the **middle class**. Most townsmen were merchants or craftsmen, although there

Merchants had to pay tolls to feudal lords when crossing bridges on their estates.

were a number of lawyers and doctors. Some merchants were little more than peddlers carrying their packs from village to village. Others brought goods by ship, riverboat, or packtrain from distant lands to sell in town markets and fairs.

As towns grew larger, some people kept shops and bought their goods from the traveling merchants. One shopkeeper sold drugs and spices, some brought from distant lands. Another shop had furs or fine cloth and carpets from the East. Towns also had their butchers, bakers, and barbers. Craftsmen manufactured shoes, hats, cloth, ironware, and other goods in their workshops. The craftsmen and merchants probably made the towns more interesting places than the usual manor village. They certainly made them richer.

Guilds

The right to do business in a town was a guarded privilege. The merchants and craftsmen banded together in special organizations for each trade or craft, called guilds. Only members of the guilds could sell goods or practice a trade within the town walls. Guild members all charged the same prices for the

same quality work, and, even more important, they limited the number of men permitted to follow a particular occupation. The shoemakers' guild, for example, wanted to make sure that there were never more shoemakers in a particular town than could make a good living there. They would allow only a limited number of boys each year to begin learning the trade as apprentices. They also often made it difficult for a young man to set up a shop of his own as a master shoemaker after he had learned the trade. There was not much free competition in the Middle Ages.

There were never as many townsmen as peasants, but townsmen were important during the later Middle Ages. The middle class grew richer, and the kings began to choose middle-class lawyers as officials. Many merchants and craftsmen had their sons study law because it opened a way for a young man to get ahead in the world.

▶ PRIESTS, MONKS, AND SCHOLARS

Every town and almost every village in the Middle Ages had its church, where a priest conducted worship services, baptized babies, married young people, and buried the dead in the churchyard. In addition the priests taught

A monastery in the Middle Ages. The monks spent their time in prayer, teaching young scholars who wished to become monks or priests, and working in the fields.

the children at least the most important Christian prayers and beliefs. The church grew great and powerful during the Middle Ages. It had its own courts and laws. Any person who broke church law might be brought before a church court, and the church claimed the priests could be tried in no other court. Heated quarrels broke out between the church and some of the kings, who tried priests in royal courts. The church also collected payments like taxes for its support.

The church was governed by its bishops, archbishops, and, over all, the pope at Rome, who was assisted by cardinals. Some popes were very powerful. Pope Innocent III (1161–1216) forced kings, among them John of England, to accept his decrees by threatening to take away their right to wear a crown. But sometimes kings and emperors opposed the popes in bitter struggles.

The church was also served by monks and nuns. Monks were men who lived together in a house called a monastery. They were under the rule of an abbot, and they devoted their lives mainly to prayer and religious service. The nuns were women who followed a similar life in houses usually called convents. Monks

and nuns gave all of their property to the monastery or convent. They vowed never to marry and agreed to live under strict rules. The most important set of rules had been drawn up in the early Middle Ages by Saint Benedict of Nursia (480?–543?), a Roman Christian.

Monks spent about 8 hours a day in prayer and worship. In Benedict's time they also spent another 6 or 7 hours working in the fields. Later, very few monks did field work, because so many monasteries had been willed or given manors and serfs by great landholders. The monks spent their time in prayer and other work. Some fed the poor who came to the monastery gate or took care of travelers who asked for shelter. Others copied books in the monastery scriptorium, or writing room. Since there were no printing presses, all books had to be copied by hand.

Education

A few monks conducted schools where they taught boys to read and write Latin. It was necessary to learn Latin because both the Bible and the church services were in that language.

Bishops, too, established schools, called cathedral schools. Some cathedral schools, such as those at Paris, became great centers of learning, or universities. A number of the greatest thinkers of the Middle Ages, such men as Peter Abelard (1079–1142), Saint Albertus Magnus (1193?–80), and Saint Thomas Aquinas (1225?–74), studied and taught at Paris.

Students began their studies with the seven liberal arts. These were Latin grammar, rhetoric (how to write and speak), logic (how to reason), arithmetic, geometry, astronomy, and music. A young man who showed in an examination that he had studied the first principles of these arts was known as a Bachelor of Arts (B.A.). One who had mastered the arts well enough to teach them was known as a Master of Arts (M.A.). Students could also go on to studies in law, medicine, arts (philosophy), or theology— the knowledge of God. Those who taught these fields were known as doctors. Modern universities still give the same titles, or degrees, as those used in the Middle Ages. But not all students took degrees in those days. Not all students at the universities even

studied hard, if we are to judge by the letter of a father who said that his lazy son spent his time "strumming a guitar while others are at their studies."

The church not only encouraged learning; it also encouraged artists and builders to produce some of the finest structures ever built anywhere in the world at any time. A number of the famous cathedrals still stand, showing how beautifully and well the men of this age could work in stone and glass.

▶ THE END OF THE MIDDLE AGES

Because one historical period fades into another, it is possible to look at the same times in very different ways. The years between 1300 and 1500 can be seen as the end of an age, for example. France and England fought the costly Hundred Years War between 1337 and 1453. The battles in this war showed clearly that the day of the mounted knight was over. The Black Death, a terrible plague, carried off large numbers of people in the years around 1350, perhaps as many as one third of the population. Business and trade declined, and land that had once been cleared was allowed to stand idle. Discontented peasants rebelled, and landlords grew more fearful of the lower classes.

But this is only part of the story. During these same years the cities of Italy showed a growing spirit of freedom, and there were new fashions in art and thought. The same battles that showed that the age of the knight was over also showed that a new age of warfare had begun. It is possible to see the years between 1300 and 1500 as the beginning of a new age. This age is sometimes called the Renaissance, or rebirth.

It is simply a matter of how we look at these times. But it is important to remember that people living in those days did not think of themselves as living at the end of the Middle Ages. They thought they were living "in the present," just as people always do in any time. The idea of the Middle Ages may be useful for us, but we should not forget that it was invented long after the Middle Ages.

KENNETH S. COOPER
George Peabody College

See also CHARLEMAGNE; CHRISTIANITY, HISTORY OF; CRUSADES; FEUDALISM; GUILDS; HOLY ROMAN EMPIRE; HUNDRED YEARS WAR.

In the 5th century A.D. barbarians from central and northern Europe attacked Rome. This brought an end to the last great empire of the ancient world. For the next 300 years western Europe was dominated by barbarian tribes, such as the Goths, Celts, Franks, Teutons, and Lombards. These conquerors did not try to force their pagan religions on the peoples they defeated. Instead they accepted Christianity and helped to spread it throughout Europe.

▶ BARBARIAN ART OF CHRISTIAN EUROPE

Long before the barbarian tribes overran western Europe, their artists were working in traditional styles. They made ornate jewelry, baskets, pottery, and weapons. Decoration was intricate and geometric—objects were carved with straight lines, curves, circles, triangles, and ovals. Except for a few leaf shapes, the carvings were not made to look like real objects. Very little sculpture and practically no painting was done.

When the barbarians became Christians, they turned to religion as the subject of their art. Monks copied religious books and decorated the pages with brightly colored illustrations. Because few peasants could read, the churches were decorated with sculpture that told stories from the Bible.

The barbarians had abandoned their pagan beliefs, but they did not give up their traditions of art. They decorated jeweled chalices (drinking cups) and great stone crosses with their old geometric designs. Many of these richly carved crosses were placed along the roadside. The barbarians had little interest in architecture. The small churches of the early Middle Ages were made of wood and did not last long.

Gradually the Western Christian Empire grew stronger. Exposed to the ancient architecture and sculpture of Rome, the barbarians began to imitate the techniques of the Romans. But they had had no tradition or training in lifelike art. Saints were carved or painted with gigantic or very tiny heads and stonelike bodies in impossible positions. The figures were often surrounded by the creatures and demons of pagan legends.

The leaders of Christian Rome began to build churches of stone. The designs for these churches were based on ancient Roman temples and law courts. When trade with the Eastern Christian (or Byzantine) Empire increased, Oriental features of Byzantine art began to influence the architecture of the West.

By the 9th century the barbarians had mixed with the more civilized people of southern Europe. Wars were still fought almost constantly, and the life of the peasants remained miserable. But war was no longer the only way of life, and scholarship was increasing. Monasteries, which became centers of learning, were built all over Europe.

▶ ROMANESQUE ART

It is difficult to say exactly when the Romanesque period began in Europe. Late in the 8th and early in the 9th century the Frankish emperor Charlemagne conquered much of Europe and some of the Muslim world. This made the Christian Roman Empire larger and more powerful than it had ever been. Charlemagne told the builders of his new palace to imitate the architecture of ancient Rome. Actually the palace was more Byzantine than Roman in style. In the 10th century the emperor Otto the Great also wanted his churches, monasteries, and schools built in a Roman manner. The new kind of architecture that was developing came to be known as Romanesque, which means "in the Roman manner." But Romanesque was actually a combination of styles and a new kind of art and architecture.

Romanesque buildings are low and heavy-looking, with thick walls, round arches, and small windows. Rows of columns support round, arched ceilings, called **vaults**. The vaults are heavy and tend to create downward force (**thrust**) that could cause the walls to fall. For this reason, great stone supports called **buttresses** were built against the walls of the churches. The Romanesque style had been developing since the 6th century, but all of its features were probably first used together in 1088, when the Church of St. Ambrogio was begun in Milan, Italy. This style was used throughout western Europe, but different countries introduced different elements.

Romanesque carving was almost always done in **relief**—sculpture carved from a background. Early Romanesque buildings have little sculpture. But soon huge figures were created to decorate the doorways and columns of churches. Like the sculpture of the earlier Middle Ages, Romanesque carving was crude and not at all lifelike. But by the 12th century, sculpted figures were beginning to appear with bent legs turned to one side or with the head lowered. They no longer sat unnaturally still, staring straight ahead.

Because the windows of Romanesque churches were so small, there was a great deal of wall space inside. This space was frequently decorated with **frescoes** (paintings done on wet plaster) illustrating Bible stories. Most of these medieval paintings have been destroyed. But we know what they looked like because painting was also done on manuscripts, and these remain. The way the human figure was shown in painting was similar to the style of sculpture. The manuscript pages were skillfully done. The monks were masters of **calligraphy**, the art of beautiful writing. The handsome, intertwining geometric designs of barbarian art still decorated the borders of manuscript pages.

▶ GOTHIC ART

Building skills advanced rapidly. By the 12th century, medieval builders had learned to build higher and more graceful churches. They had developed better ways of constructing vaults, of making larger windows, and of supporting the high, pointed arches that were becoming fashionable. To counteract the thrust from the new, higher vaults, Gothic builders used strong supports called **flying buttresses**. These arched beams extended from the old buttresses to the outsides of the vaults. The first church in which all the features of Gothic architecture were used was probably the Church of St. Denis in France, begun in 1137.

Gothic cathedrals soar high, their windows, arches, and towers reaching heavenward. They are decorated with beautiful stained-glass windows and sculpture more lifelike than any since ancient Rome. Figures are carved in high relief on the columns and doors. Saints appear in active poses with heads turned. Almond-shaped eyes replaced the blank,

The Church of St. Denis, in France, was probably the first church to be constructed entirely in the Gothic style.

round eyes of Romanesque days. Influenced by Byzantine sculpture, Gothic figures are long and graceful.

The Gothic style started in France and quickly spread through all parts of western Europe. More churches were built in this manner than in any other style in history. Even after the Renaissance period, which began in the 15th century, brought the Middle Ages to an end, Gothic churches continued to be built.

Reviewed by Aaron H. Jacobsen
Author, *The Medieval Sketchbook*

See also Architecture; Byzantine Art and Architecture; Cathedrals; Gothic Art and Architecture; Illuminated Manuscripts; Painting; Romanesque Art and Architecture; Sculpture; Stained-Glass Windows.

MIDDLE AGES, MUSIC OF THE

Medieval music, which represents nearly 1,000 years of European musical development, is the ancestor of all later Western music. In the history of music the medieval period extends from about A.D. 500 to about 1450. Since much of the music has been lost, our knowledge of medieval music is incomplete. Though writings of the period tell of many other kinds of music making, church music is almost all that remains of music composed before the year 1000.

▶ GREGORIAN CHANT

The early Christian Church adopted much of the music of the Jewish synagogue. Christian adaptations of Jewish chant were used all over the Mediterranean world of the Roman Empire in the first three centuries A.D. The type of chant used in Rome came to be known as Gregorian chant. This was because the first standard collection of chants was thought to have been ordered by Pope Gregory I (reigned 590–604). It is widely believed now, however, that the standardization took place about 2 centuries later. Gregorian chant is the only music that has been used continuously from the beginning of the Middle Ages to the present day. It consists entirely of vocal melodies without harmony or accompaniments.

The names of the men who shaped the chants are unknown. They were not composers in our modern sense, for they mostly improved, decorated, and added to existing melodies to make new ones. The chant as it exists today is the work of generations of musicians, covering a period of several centuries. It was preserved and developed mainly by monks in monasteries.

▶ SONGS AND DANCES

During the Middle Ages most secular, or nonreligious, music was learned by ear. The composers and performers of this music were the minstrels, most of whom were illiterate vagabonds. The music therefore was usually not written down. Minstrels made their living by chanting long poems about heroic deeds, such as the famous *Song of Roland,* and playing dance music on bagpipes, harps, recorders, and bowed stringed instruments.

Minstrels chanted long poems and played dance music.

They also entertained with acrobatic stunts and magic tricks. From the 11th century onward many minstrels became members of feudal households, and some of them learned to write music. Thus, a few dances of the 13th and 14th centuries have survived.

A new art of song was developed by the **troubadours** of southern France and their northern counterparts, the **trouvères**, who flourished from about 1100 to 1300. Many of them were of noble birth, and all their music was designed for upper-class audiences. Troubadours and trouvères often wrote both the words and music of their songs, which were generally performed with instrumental accompaniment.

▶ THE BEGINNINGS OF PART MUSIC

Simple kinds of part music, or music in which two or more voices sing different notes at the same time, are very ancient. For example, when men and women sing together, the women sing an octave higher than the men. In group singing, if a tune goes too high for some voices, these will sing three or four notes lower than the others. The earliest written part music consisted of short pieces that applied this technique to Gregorian-chant melodies. Separate voices sang the melody on different pitches, three or four notes apart, moving in parallel motion. This music was called **organum**.

Free organum, a more interesting technique, introduced an added part that was

The troubadours often wrote songs about courtly love.

Church music was highly developed in the Middle Ages.

different from the chant melody. This kind of part music, a combination of different melodies, is called **polyphony**, and the individual parts are called **counterpoints**. All part music was performed by a group of soloists, one to each part. The leading composers of organum, Leonin and Perotin, flourished in the late 12th and early 13th century in Paris.

▶ **FURTHER DEVELOPMENT OF PART MUSIC**

The most important form of part music in the 13th and 14th centuries was the **motet**. Usually in three or four parts, motets were based on standard Latin texts, but new words were added in some of the parts. These pieces were called motets because of the added words, since *mot* means "word" in French. Each part had its own text and usually contrasted strongly in rhythm with the others. There were also secular motets written in French.

The leading composer of this period was the Frenchman Guillaume de Machaut (1300?–77). He and his French contemporaries used elaborate rhythmic schemes in which rhythms were repeated exactly but the melodies changed. The Italian composer Francesco Landini (1325–97) was famous not only for his music but also for his organ playing. Landini's favorite instrument was a small *organetto*. It was suspended from the neck and held in the crook of the left arm, the left hand working the bellows and the right hand playing.

Many kinds of musical instruments were used in the late Middle Ages. These included trumpets, shawms (something like very large and noisy oboes), large drums, hunting horns, recorders, flutes, small bagpipes, rebecs and vielles (bowed stringed instruments), psalteries and lutes (plucked stringed instruments), exaquiers (small harpsichords), and organs (both small ones that could be carried about and large ones).

▶ **MUSIC IN MEDIEVAL LIFE**

The music of the people consisted of folk songs and dances. Public concerts did not exist. Paying to hear music would have seemed ridiculous to medieval people. Music making was either an intimate affair of friends or part of courtly or church ceremonial.

Church polyphony was performed only in cathedrals, monasteries, royal chapels, and a few large city churches. Outside of these places polyphony was confined, in most of Europe, to the upper classes. The common man heard polyphonic music if he worshiped in a cathedral or monastic church. Otherwise he would hear it only if there was some unusual public ceremonial, such as a royal wedding procession. For an event like this the king's musicians would perform a piece specially composed for the occasion. They would make, as one medieval writer called it, "hevenly noyse on both sides of the street."

Reviewed by GUSTAVE REESE
Author, *Music in the Middle Ages*

A market in Baghdad, Iraq, with minarets (towers) and domes of a mosque (Muslim place of worship) in the background.

MIDDLE EAST

The Middle East is neither a country nor a continent. It is a geographical region. For centuries it has been important in world affairs because of its location. A look at a map of the area will show why. The Middle East is a great land bridge connecting the continents of Asia, Africa, and Europe.

There has never been agreement on a definition of the Middle East. Sometimes the region is defined as the southwestern part of Asia. Another definition includes the long belt of territory extending along the northern section of Africa. Others consider Afghanistan a part of this region. Still others insist that the southeastern part of Europe, known as the Balkans, is part of the Middle East. These differences of opinion are due to the many changes in the area that have taken place during the course of history.

In this article we shall consider the Middle East to be a region that includes Southwest Asia and the countries of Egypt and Libya in Africa. This region contains many different nations and covers an area about the size of Australia. The northern border lies along the southern frontier of the Soviet Union and Bulgaria and is marked by the Black and Caspian seas. In the south the Middle East is bounded by the Arabian Sea, the Gulf of Aden, and the Sahara. The eastern limit is the borders of Afghanistan and Pakistan. The region extends westward along the Mediterranean Sea to Algeria and Tunisia.

The region known today as the Middle East has been called by different names during the past 2,000 years. Some of these names are still widely used in books and newspapers. Others have been practically forgotten. Although these many names differ, they all have one thing in common. They have been given to the region by Europeans.

Before Vasco da Gama sailed around Africa in 1497 and on to India, Europeans did not know very much about the lands and peoples of Asia. They did not understand how vast the continent really was. As European sailors opened new sea routes to the east, their knowledge was greatly increased. They began to coin new names for the major regions of the Asian continent. The area farthest from Europe was called the Far East. The lands closest to Europe (most of today's Middle East) were often known as the Near East. Sometimes the entire Middle East was called the Levant. Strictly speaking, this term refers to the lands of the eastern Mediterranean, stretching from Greece

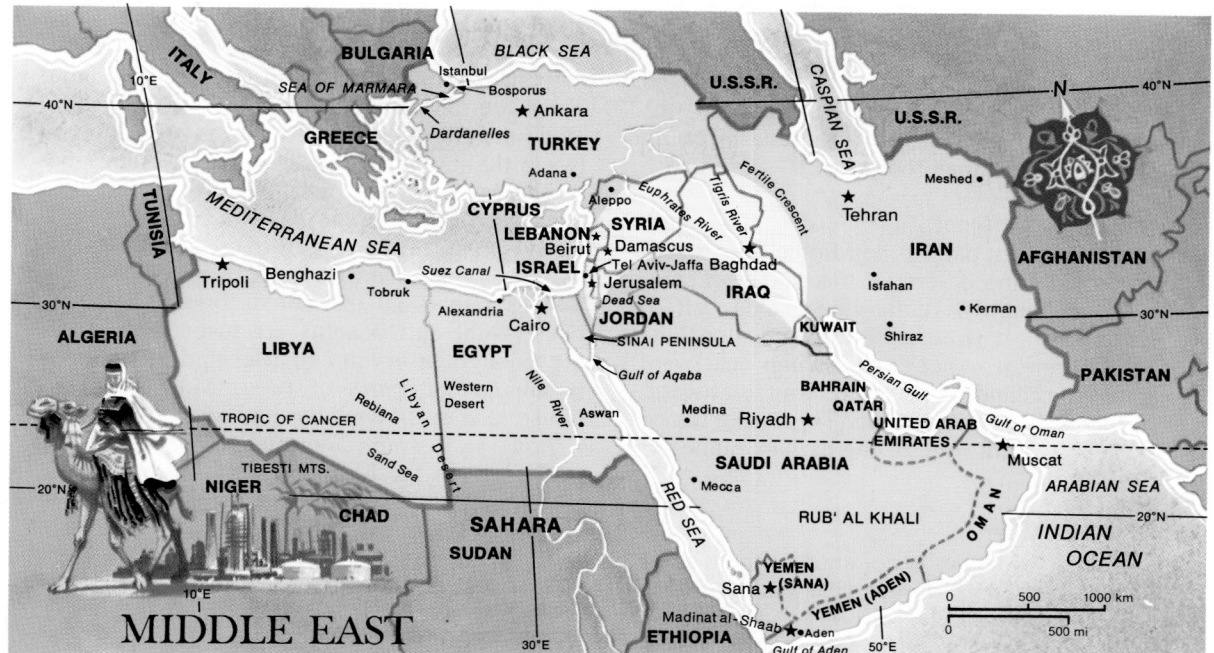

MIDDLE EAST

to Israel. A term often used by geographers is Southwest Asia, since most of the countries of the Middle East lie in that part of the world.

"Middle East" is a fairly new geographical term. Its use was made popular by the British after World War I. They used the name to refer to the many lands situated between Europe and their empire in India. It was quickly adopted by other Europeans and Americans who fought in the region during World War II. Since then it has been picked up by people all over the world.

▶ THE LAND

The Middle East is a vast region, with a total area of about 7,016,000 square kilometers (2,709,000 square miles). It is about three fourths as large as China and more than twice as big as India. Because of its tremendous size, the area was the "world" for most of its inhabitants throughout much of its long history.

To the north the region is almost completely ringed by mountains. Turkey and Iran are hemmed in on all sides by rugged ranges along their frontiers. Other chains of hills and mountains extend along the coastal areas of the eastern Mediterranean, running through Syria, Lebanon, and Israel. The gigantic Arabian Peninsula is nearly enclosed by mountainous

heights in the west and south. Except for the northern section, the interior of the Middle East region is generally flat.

In some places in the Arabian Peninsula there are broad stretches of sandy wastes that resemble the Sahara in northwestern Africa. In other areas of the region, the deserts are great tracts of parched earth and stone. Many

COUNTRIES OF THE MIDDLE EAST

COUNTRY	CAPITAL	AREA	
		(km²)	(sq mi)
Bahrain	Manama	622	240
Cyprus	Nicosia	9,251	3,572
Egypt	Cairo	1,001,499	386,660
Iran	Tehran	1,648,000	636,294
Iraq	Baghdad	434,924	167,925
Israel	Jerusalem	20,770	8,019
Jordan	Amman	97,740	37,738
Kuwait	Kuwait	17,818	6,880
Lebanon	Beirut	10,400	4,015
Libya	Tripoli	1,759,540	679,360
Oman	Muscat	212,457	82,030
Qatar	Doha	11,000	4,247
Saudi Arabia	Riyadh	2,149,690	830,000
Syria	Damascus	185,180	71,498
Turkey	Ankara	780,576	301,381
United Arab Emirates	Abu Dhabi	83,600	32,278
Yemen (Aden)	Madinat al-Shaab	332,968	128,559
Yemen (Sana)	Sana	195,000	75,290

of the hills and mountains are bare of vegetation. Southwest Asia is one of the oldest and most continuously inhabited areas in the world. Yet many places there have probably never known human footprints.

The Fertile Crescent

The northern part of the Middle East is separated from the deserts of the Arabian Peninsula by a narrow, horseshoe-shaped belt of fertile land. It stretches northward along the Mediterranean coast and swings eastward across Syria and Iraq. It then turns southward, ending at the Persian Gulf. This is the famed Fertile Crescent, one of the earliest homes of civilization.

Rain and Water

Hot, dry weather is common to the Middle East during most of the year except in the highest mountains, where snow is frequent. The rainy season in most places lasts from about October to April. In the southern part of the Arabian Peninsula, rain comes mainly between May and September. But there are only light, brief showers in most of the region. In some places it never rains at all. In the desert areas, which are baked each day by the blazing sun, the temperature often rises to over 52°C (125°F). Yet at night the deserts may be cool or even cold.

Life itself in the Middle East has long been dependent upon the amount and location of water. Many rain-bearing winds are not able to penetrate into the interior of the region. They are blocked by the mountain ranges along the edges of the area. Strips of land between the mountains and the sea are some of the best-watered sections. There are actually dense forests along the coasts of Iran facing the Caspian Sea. Still, most of the Middle East suffers from a severe shortage of water. When it does rain—and the rain is brief in many places—the full benefits are lost. There are not enough reservoirs to trap and store the downpour for times of need. Much of the moisture is evaporated by the heat.

Long ago, water determined where people could live in the Middle East and how they would earn their living. The amount of available water limited the farmer's choice of crops. It compelled the nomad to rely on sheep, goats, and camels. Cattle could not easily survive in the harsh environment. The location of water also determined the routes of trade and travel.

From earliest times the power of the empires in the Middle East depended on life-giving water. It is no accident that the basin of the Tigris and Euphrates rivers was a main center of life in the region. Wise rulers were always careful to take steps to conserve and regulate the water supply. Some of the oldest irrigation systems in the world were built in the Middle East. Many are still in use. All kinds of clever methods were invented to control the flow of

THE ARABIAN PENINSULA

The Arabian Peninsula has an area of more than 2,590,000 square kilometers (1,000,000 square miles) and a population of about 21,000,000. The peninsula is bounded on the north by Jordan and Iraq, on the east by the Persian Gulf and the Gulf of Oman, on the south by the Arabian Sea and the Gulf of Aden, and on the west by the Red Sea and the Gulf of Aqaba.

It is largely a flat, arid land. The only fertile regions are found in occasional oases and in some of the coastal areas. A chain of mountains and highlands runs in a north-south direction parallel to the Red Sea coast. Arabia has some of the great deserts of the world, including the vast Rub' al Khali, or Empty Quarter. Summer temperatures are extremely hot, and there is little rainfall except in the highland areas. Cultivation of the land is therefore possible in only a few places. Apart from rich deposits of oil, the land has few natural resources. Oil is the mainstay of the economies of many of the states of the peninsula. Arabia was the birthplace of Mohammed, the prophet of Islam. It was from here, in the 800's, that the Muslim religion spread to many parts of the world.

The Arabian Peninsula is divided politically into the countries listed in the next column.

BAHRAIN is the smallest in area of the countries of the peninsula. It is made up of a group of offshore islands in the Persian Gulf. See BAHRAIN, Volume B.

KUWAIT is a small, oil-rich country in the northeastern corner of the peninsula. See KUWAIT, Volume JK.

OMAN is located along the southeastern coast of the peninsula. See OMAN, Volume O.

QATAR is a small peninsula jutting into the Persian Gulf. See QATAR, Volume QR.

SAUDI ARABIA is the largest country in the region, covering about three fourths of the peninsula. It has vast deposits of oil. See SAUDI ARABIA, Volume S.

UNITED ARAB EMIRATES is a union of seven small states lying along the Persian Gulf. Abu Dhabi, one of the emirates, is especially rich in oil. See UNITED ARAB EMIRATES, Volume UV.

YEMEN (ADEN) is situated along the southern coast of the peninsula on the Gulf of Aden. See YEMEN (ADEN), Volume WXYZ.

YEMEN (SANA) is located in the southwestern corner of the peninsula, fronting the Red Sea. It is one of the few fertile countries of the region. See YEMEN (SANA), Volume WXYZ.

A goatherd and his flock pass by a harbor in Yemen (Aden). The raising of livestock—sheep, goats, cattle, and camels—has long been important on the Arabian Peninsula.

water. Vast underground tunnels, which were the "pipelines" of the ancient Persians, still bring water to croplands.

Today Middle Eastern governments are giving special attention to the building of waterworks. Dams are being constructed, and new irrigation canals are being dug. The Aswan High Dam in Egypt irrigates large areas and provides hydroelectric power. In Israel a long pipeline system has been built to transfer water from the Jordan River to the desert areas of the northern Negev, in the south. Saudi Arabia, Kuwait, and other countries of the Arabian Peninsula are converting seawater into drinking water by various distilling processes. The success of programs to raise the standard of living throughout the Middle East will depend largely on the outcome of the various water projects.

▶ THE PEOPLE

For its size the Middle East is not a very heavily populated region. Its inhabitants number approximately 186,000,000. Besides the descendants of people who have lived in the region since ancient times, there are also immigrants who arrived during the last thousand years. Among them are the Turks and Turkomans, who settled in large parts of the northern Middle East and established the country now known as Turkey. In the 20th century, Jews from all over the world have gone to Israel, joining Jews already in the area. To them, Israel—part of the region called Palestine—has remained the "Promised Land."

Arabs, Iranians, and Turks are the most numerous groups in the Middle East. The Arabs live mainly in the central and southern areas. The Iranians occupy the northeast. The Turks

Many people in the Middle East live in villages like this one in Syria.

are settled in the northwest. The other inhabitants of the Middle East are few in number. Israel is populated largely by Jews (known today in their country as Israelis). There are many Afghans in eastern Iran. A few Armenians, who once lived in what is now eastern Turkey, are now found in Syria, Lebanon, and Iran. Kurds live in parts of Turkey, Iran, Iraq, and Syria.

It is difficult to describe the people of the Middle East. They are of many different physical types. But like Europeans and North Americans, they are chiefly Caucasians. Skin coloring ranges from fair to dark. Both straight and curly hair are common. Brown is the most typical hair color. Most people are brown-eyed, although some have blue eyes. But religious differences have been far more important than ethnic differences.

Languages and Writing

Many different languages are spoken in the Middle East. Arabic is the most important and is the international language of the region. It is spoken in all the lands from the eastern Mediterranean to the Persian Gulf. Hebrew, which is closely related to Arabic, is spoken in Israel. Turkish, another main language, has nothing in common with Arabic. It is similar to languages used in Central Asia, which is where the Turks came from. Persian (Iranian) is spoken in Iran. It is an old and rich language. Educated people throughout the Middle East know either English or French. Nomadic tribes in the deserts of Egypt and Libya often speak Berber dialects.

Many systems of writing originated in the Middle East. The cuneiform symbols invented by the ancient Sumerians have long since disappeared from use. But the influence of the alphabet has lasted to this day. The Arabic alphabet, which has 28 letters, is the system of writing in lands as distant from one another as Morocco and Indonesia. The Koran, the sacred book of Islam, is written in the Arabic alphabet.

Many other writing systems of the Middle East have been based on the Arabic. The Turks used it for many centuries. In 1928 they replaced it with a system of Latin letters. The Persians also borrowed the Arabic alphabet for writing but made a few changes. The Hebrew alphabet of Israel is one of the oldest still used in the world. Like many other ancient systems of writing, it changes slightly from time to time.

Religions

Three of the world's great religions were born in the Middle East. Judaism, the faith of the Jews, emerged in ancient Israel. It was the world's first monotheism (belief in one God). Judaism emphasized morality and social justice. Christianity also began in the Holy Land and has spread all over the globe. The places in Israel that are memorable in the life of Jesus are still visited by pilgrims from many nations. Islam had its origins in Mecca, a city in what is now Saudi Arabia. All Muslims are encouraged to make at least one pilgrimage to Mecca during their lives.

Most inhabitants of the Middle East are followers of Islam. In the Middle East, Judaism is the principal faith only in Israel. Christianity has its only stronghold in tiny Lebanon. Islam dominates religious life in all other countries of the region. In addition to the Arabs, the Turks and the Iranians follow the teaching of Mohammed.

The influences of Islam extend far beyond daily religious worship. Holidays, customs, marriage, and education are in keeping with the message of Mohammed, the Prophet. He also laid down rules for diet. His followers are forbidden to eat pork and must not drink alcoholic beverages. They are also urged to give generously to charity.

Ways of Life

There are many old and great cities in the Middle East. For centuries, Jerusalem has been a familiar name to people everywhere. Other well-known Middle Eastern cities include Baghdad in Iraq, Tehran in Iran, Cairo in Egypt, Beirut in Lebanon, Damascus in Syria, and Ankara and Istanbul in Turkey. Yet only a relatively small number of the people of the Middle East have ever lived in these cities. The village remains the heart of the region's life.

Villages in the Middle East are scattered about the landscape. They are situated along the banks of rivers. They may be found at strategic points along the trade routes. Villages are located along the coasts where trade and fishing are carried on. Many villages have existed for centuries wherever there is fertile soil.

Buildings are of all sizes and shapes. In the large cities, modern government and office buildings tower into the sky. In the villages, most homes are made of packed mud or mud bricks. Forests are scarce, and timber for construction is in short supply. In the deserts of the Arabian Peninsula, wandering nomads live in tents as their ancestors did.

The organization of the family varies from place to place and from people to people in the Middle East. Yet a common feature is the large family. The household is made up of three and sometimes four generations. In the Middle East, poverty is widespread, and people depend for help on their family and relatives. In recent years the old, tightly knit families have begun to break up. Young people have flocked to the cities and towns in search of education and employment.

Birthrates are very high in the Middle East. But for centuries the growth of the population was checked by high death rates. Disease was common, and malnutrition was widespread. As more hospitals, doctors, and medicine have become available, the death rate has declined. Because the birthrate remains high, the population has increased in many parts of the Middle East.

▶THE ECONOMY

Agriculture has been the most important economic activity in the Middle East for

Arabs in a café in Jerusalem exchange news and smoke nargilehs (water pipes).

several thousand years. The main crops throughout the region are cereal grains—wheat, barley, rice, oats, and millet. Olives, grapes, dates, and figs are among the region's staple foods. Citrus fruits from Israel are shipped all over the world. The nomadic way of life is declining, but livestock raising is still an important occupation.

In most Middle Eastern lands the farmers live a bare hand-to-mouth existence. Good lands are often owned by a small number of wealthy families. Many farmers must lease land at high rentals. After paying rent, the farmers usually have little left for themselves. The transfer of the ownership of land from large landlords to the farmers who work it has improved standards of living somewhat in some countries. Israel has many farms called *kibbutzim,* which are owned by groups of farmers. Governments are encouraging changes in inefficient methods of cultivation that have altered little over the centuries.

Until Europeans discovered the sea route to the East, the trade route between Europe and Asia lay across the Middle East. The Suez Canal, connecting the Red Sea and the Mediterranean, was opened in 1869. It led to much development in the region.

Petroleum is the major mineral resource in the Middle East. Saudi Arabia is the world's chief producer and exporter of petroleum. Iran, Iraq, the small nations of the Persian Gulf, Libya, and Egypt also produce large quantities of oil. Natural gas is important in Iran. Chrome, antimony, and magnesite are mined in Turkey, and phosphates are extracted in Jordan. Elsewhere, minerals other than petroleum await large-scale development.

Because the oil-rich nations of the Middle East contain more than half of the world's known petroleum reserves, they have gained worldwide influence. Refineries and petrochemical plants are being built in the oil-producing countries, but other industries in the region are generally small in size. Egypt, Israel, and Turkey are the most highly industrialized nations in the Middle East. Food processing, the making of textiles and handicrafts, construction, and tourism are important in many countries.

▶ **HISTORY**

The Middle East is often called the cradle of civilization. Over 6,000 years ago, people in this part of the world discovered the techniques of agriculture that freed them from the need to wander about in search of food. Towns and methods of government were developed. Between 4000 and 3000 B.C., civilized states began to emerge near the southern part of the Tigris and Euphrates rivers in the region known as the Fertile Crescent.

By the beginning of the Christian era, many kingdoms and empires had risen and fallen in the Middle East. The Egyptians, Hittites, Babylonians, Assyrians, and Persians carved out huge realms. They made great contributions to civilization—law codes, systems of writing, mechanical developments (such as the wheel), and engineering techniques. Alexander the

This airport terminal in Saudi Arabia is one of many projects financed by income from oil.

Great invaded the area in the 4th century B.C. About three centuries later the Romans began their conquests in the region.

When the Roman Empire split up in the 4th century A.D., many contenders for power arose in the Middle East. The Eastern Roman, or Byzantine, Empire, with its capital at Constantinople (now Istanbul), endured for 1,000 years. The Arab countries were the foremost rivals of the Byzantine Empire. After the death of Mohammed in 632 his followers overran most of the Middle East. But their grip on the region was loosened by the impact of many invaders. The Seljuk Turks, the Crusaders from Europe, and the Mongols from Central Asia battled for control of the area. None of these conquerors were so successful as the Ottoman Turks.

Nomads and their camels still roam the oil-rich deserts of Kuwait.

The Ottoman Empire and Arab Nationalism

The Ottoman Empire was founded in the 1300's and lasted until after World War I. It reached the height of its power in the 1500's. All the lands of the Middle East except Persia (now Iran) came under its sway. So did the Balkan region in Europe and the long coast of North Africa. For a while, the Mediterranean Sea was practically a "Turkish lake." But the empire declined after the mid-1500's. In the 1800's, it lost most of its European lands. The weakened empire became known as the "sick man" of Europe and Asia.

During World War I (1914–18), the Ottoman Empire sided with Germany and Austria-Hungary. Many Arabs in the empire revolted against the Turks and fought on the side of the Allied powers, hoping to gain freedom. But after the war, large areas in the Middle East came under British or French control, under charters, or mandates, from the League of Nations. Only Turkey itself and Persia remained independent.

In 1932, the Kingdom of Saudi Arabia was founded, and Mesopotamia became the nation of Iraq. Other Arab nations gained independence during or shortly after World War II. But some had to wait until as late as 1971.

The Middle East Since World War II

Since 1948, the conflict between Israel and the Arab states has been a major source of tension in the Middle East. Israel was created in 1948 as a Jewish homeland in Palestine.

Since that time, there have been four wars between Israel and its Arab neighbors. In 1979, Egypt became the first Arab nation to recognize Israel. But most Arab countries still oppose Israel. The Arabs who had lived in what was once Palestine want a homeland of their own. But the fate of the Palestinians remains undecided.

The Islamic nations have also fought among themselves or have had conflicts within their own borders. Lebanon has suffered a long and destructive civil war that has set Muslim Arabs against Christian Arabs, and Muslims against Muslims. Today Lebanon is a war-torn land with several groups struggling for power. Iran and Iraq have been fighting a long and bitter war since 1980 that neither side seems able to win or end. The war has come to involve neighboring countries.

Income from oil brought change to the Middle East. Because it is such a valuable source of oil and because of its strategic location, the region has become involved in the struggle for influence between Communist and Western powers. These various tensions have kept the Middle East in turmoil and made it a source of worldwide concern.

HYMAN KUBLIN
City University of New York, Brooklyn College
Reviewed by ALEXANDER MELAMID
New York University

See also ANCIENT CIVILIZATIONS; ORGANIZATION OF PETROLEUM EXPORTING COUNTRIES (OPEC); PALESTINE; articles on individual countries.

MIDSUMMER NIGHT'S DREAM, A

Shakespeare invented many things, and one of them was a new kind of fairyland, the one that is found in *A Midsummer Night's Dream.* Before Shakespeare wrote this lovely play, the people of England thought of fairies as dangerous beings that had to be placated. But Shakespeare made them as gay as flowers and small enough to creep into acorn cups. They "hop as light as bird from brier," and the first fairy that appears in the play is given poetry that is as delicate as its wings.

Over hill, over dale,
    Thorough bush, thorough brier,
Over park, over pale,
    Thorough flood, thorough fire,
I do wander everywhere,
Swifter than the moon's sphere;
    And I serve the fairy queen,
    To dew her orbs upon the green.
    The cowslips tall her pensioners be:
    In their gold coats spots you see;
    Those be rubies, fairy favors,
    In those freckles live their savors.
I must go seek some dewdrops here,
    And hang a pearl in every cowslip's ear.

Titania is the queen of the fairies, and when she wishes to go to sleep at night, her bed is made of flowers.

I know a bank where the wild thyme blows,
Where oxlips and the nodding violet grows;
Quite over-canopied with luscious woodbine,
With sweet musk-roses, and the eglantine.
There sleeps Titania sometime of the night,
Lulled in these flowers with dances and delight.

She is also lulled by the charming song that her fairies sing to her.

    Philomel, with melody
    Sing in our sweet lullaby;
Lulla, lulla, lullaby, lulla, lulla, lullaby:
      Never harm,
      Nor spell, nor charm,
    Come our lovely lady nigh;
    So, good night, with lullaby.

Yet a spell does come to the queen of the fairies, for she is put under an enchantment and falls in love with a mortal. Since the play is a comedy, he is a very comic mortal, a workman named Bottom who has been rehearsing a play nearby and who has had an ass's head clapped over his own. Titania thinks he is beautiful, and she gives orders to her little elves to do everything they can to give him pleasure.

Be kind and courteous to this gentleman;
Hop in his walks, and gambol in his eyes;
Feed him with apricocks and dewberries,
With purple grapes, green figs and mulberries;
The honey-bags steal from the humble-bees,
And for night-tapers crop their waxen thighs,
And light them at the fiery glow-worm's eyes,
To have my love to bed and to arise;
And pluck the wings from painted butterflies,
To fan the moonbeams from his sleeping eyes.
Nod to him, elves, and do him courtesies.

The little elves do their best to be helpful to the large, hairy mortal, and they are all very polite to each other. But it turns out that Bottom does not want to be fanned with butterfly wings and fed on berries. He wants to have his ears scratched and be fed on hay.

The whole play is a delicate balance of many things—of fairies, comics, and young lovers all meeting together the same night in a wood near Athens—and the character who holds all the threads of the story together is Puck, the servant of the king of the fairies.

Puck is also an invention of Shakespeare's. In the old days a puck, or pouk, was another name for a goblin or demon. The Puck in this play is also called Hobgoblin, but there is nothing evil or dangerous about Shakespeare's sprite. He is a mischief-maker, but that is because Shakespeare has combined him with another character of English folklore, Robin Goodfellow. Robin Goodfellow used to roam about the countryside and play practical jokes, teasing milkmaids and misleading travelers, and Puck does the same. But he is not like any other spirit in folklore or in books. Puck is just himself, a delightful, energetic messenger who can fly anywhere and do anything. He is fascinated by the behavior of the people from Athens who stray into the enchanted wood, and he loves to get them into and then free them from absurd tangles. It is Puck who speaks, with perfect good cheer, the most famous line in the play:

Lord, what fools these mortals be!

MARCHETTE CHUTE
Author, *An Introduction to Shakespeare*

MIGRATION OF ANIMALS. See HOMING AND MIGRATION.

MIGRATION OF PEOPLE. See IMMIGRATION.

MILK

Early records often mention people's use of milk and milk products. In 1922 a British-American expedition discovered a temple near Babylon. The temple is thought to be 5,000 years old, and on one of the walls is a milking scene. Instead of milking the cows from the side, as people do today, the milker is milking a cow from behind. Other people are straining the milk into a container. Still others are collecting the strained milk in large stone jars. In the Bible, milk stands for riches and plenty. Palestine is described in Exodus 3:8 as a good land because it is "flowing with milk and honey."

What is milk, and why has it been of great importance in human history? Milk is the white liquid produced by the female of the warm-blooded animals for the feeding of her young. Animals that produce milk are called **mammals.** Blood is pumped from the heart to the udder (mammary gland). The mammary gland is able to separate different substances from the blood and combine them to make milk. Milk has been called nature's most perfect food. It provides all the nutrients (nourishing substances) that human babies and other young mammals need for growth until they are able to eat other food. But from ancient times people have continued to drink milk beyond babyhood. They enjoy it, and they know that it provides most of the nutrients needed for good health.

Today the cow and the goat are the major animals that supply milk for human use. But people also use milk from several other animals native to their homelands. In Asia the camel, the horse, and the yak are sources of milk. The Eskimo (Inuit) and the people of Lapland use the milk of caribou and reindeer. Water buffalo and zebu in India and central Asia and the sheep in Europe and Asia also provide milk for human use.

▶ WHAT MILK CONTAINS

Milk contains several hundred different substances. It is best known as a source of calcium, phosphorus, and protein. Since most people can digest milk easily, the calcium, phosphorus, and other materials can be quickly used by the body. Milk contains large amounts of vitamin B_2 (riboflavin) and some

vitamin A. Milk fat, milk sugar (lactose), and the major milk protein, **casein,** are found only in milk and nowhere else in nature.

Milk Fat. The fat in milk is shaped into tiny droplets. They can be seen easily under a microscope. When milk stands for a while, the fat will rise to the surface and form a layer of cream. Farmers used to skim off the cream by repeatedly dipping a dish with tiny holes into the cream layer. In 1877 the Swedish engineer Carl Gustav de Laval invented the centrifugal cream separator, which rapidly removed the cream by spinning the milk in a bowl. The cream was sent out through one spout, and the skim milk flowed out through another. With this machine, there was no need to wait for the cream to rise.

Cream contains five to ten times more fat than the original milk. By adding skim milk, which has almost no fat, the cream can be made less rich. In the United States, whipping cream has at least 30 percent fat. Table, or coffee, cream has at least 18 percent fat, and half-and-half, 10 percent fat or more. The golden color and rich look of cream come from **carotene.** Fresh, green fodder—such as spring pasture grass—provides the carotene pigment in milk fat. In the body, carotene changes into an important nutrient, vitamin A.

Protein. There are two kinds of proteins in milk—the casein and the whey proteins. Milk proteins are noted for their high food value. Casein makes up about 80 percent of the

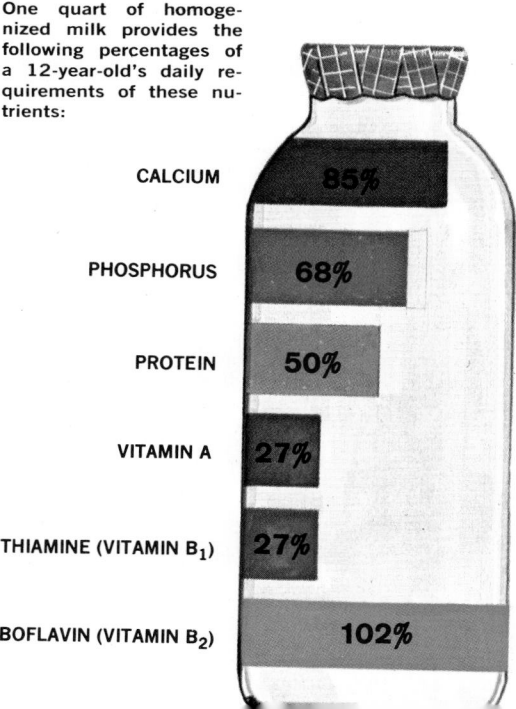

One quart of homogenized milk provides the following percentages of a 12-year-old's daily requirements of these nutrients:

CALCIUM 85%

PHOSPHORUS 68%

PROTEIN 50%

VITAMIN A 27%

THIAMINE (VITAMIN B_1) 27%

RIBOFLAVIN (VITAMIN B_2) 102%

total protein and is the basis of all cheese. When milk sours, the casein forms into a jellylike structure. This lumpy mass is called the curd, or clabber. Cottage cheese, which is made from skim milk, is mostly casein.

Casein has many industrial uses, too. It is used to make some paints; sizing, or paper-coating material; and a strong, water-resistant adhesive. Casein "wool" has been made into clothing. Casein plastic has been used to make ashtrays, buttons, and many other things.

Whey is the pale, greenish-colored liquid that separates from the casein, or curd. Whey has all of the milk sugar, almost all of the minerals, vitamin B_2 (riboflavin), and other water-soluble vitamins. The whey proteins add up to 20 percent of the total milk protein. The whey gets its greenish color from the vitamin B_2. When milk is heated to boiling and allowed to stand for a few minutes, a "skin," or "scum," forms on the surface. This happens because the whey proteins are sensitive to heat. The change in the flavor of milk when it is boiled is caused by changes in the whey proteins as they are heated.

Lactose. Lactose (milk sugar) is a special kind of sugar found in milk. It is not as sweet or as easy to dissolve as table sugar. When milk becomes sour, it does so because the lactose has been fermented by bacteria and has turned into lactic acid. The lactic acid makes the casein firm and gives the milk a sour flavor.

Some people cannot drink milk—or can drink only small amounts—because they have trouble in digesting lactose. This digestive disorder is called **lactose intolerance.**

Lactose may be made in a pure form as a finely ground white powder for use in medicines. Drug companies have used lactose as a base for growing the antibiotic penicillin.

Reviewed by ROBERT L. BRADLEY, JR.
University of Wisconsin

See also CHEESE; DAIRYING AND DAIRY PRODUCTS.

MILKY WAY.   See UNIVERSE.
MILLIPEDES.   See CENTIPEDES AND MILLIPEDES.

MILNE, A. A. (1882–1956)

Winnie-the-Pooh, Piglet, Eeyore, Tigger, and Kanga with little Roo in her pocket—these are some of the best-loved characters in children's literature. They began as stuffed toy animals that belonged to a boy named Christopher Robin. They came to life in the imagination of the boy's father, the writer A. A. Milne.

Alan Alexander Milne was born in London on January 18, 1882. His father, who was headmaster of a small private school, often read aloud to his three sons, Barry, Ken, and Alan.

Milne was very good at mathematics when he was a boy. Later, he attended Trinity College, Cambridge, to study that subject. But he soon became more interested in writing. In 1903, he returned to London to try to make a living as a free-lance writer. He wrote humorous articles and light verse. After two years, publishers were "getting used" to him, as Milne described it. He became an assistant editor for the humor magazine *Punch* in 1906. In 1913 he married Dorothy (Daphne) de Sélincourt.

Milne served in the army in World War I. After the war, he began to write plays, many of which are still performed. The best known is *Mr. Pim Passes By* (1919). He wrote other works for adults—novels, essays, and his autobiography, *It's Too Late Now* (1939). *The Red House Mystery* (1921), a detective

A. A. Milne's stories about young Christopher Robin, his bear Winnie-the-Pooh, and their friends are known to children all over the world.

MISSING

Has anybody seen my mouse?

I opened his box for half a minute,
Just to make sure he was really in it,
And while I was looking, he jumped outside!
I tried to catch him, I tried, I tried. . . .
I think he's somewhere about the house.
Has *anyone* seen my mouse?

Uncle John, have you seen my mouse?

Just a small sort of mouse, a dear little brown one,
He came from the country, he wasn't a town one,
So he'll feel all lonely in a London street;
Why, what could he possibly find to eat?

He must be somewhere. I'll ask Aunt Rose:
Have *you* seen a mouse with a woffelly nose?
Oh, somewhere about—
He's just got out. . . .

Hasn't *anybody* seen my mouse?

novel, is still popular. So is *Toad of Toad Hall* (1929), his dramatization of Kenneth Grahame's *Wind in the Willows.* But it was poems and stories for children that made him famous.

Christopher Robin—or Billy Moon, as he called himself—was born in 1920. One day Milne wrote a poem about him called "Vespers" and gave it to his wife as a present. She sent the poem to a magazine, and it was published. Milne wrote more poems, which were published in two books, *When We Were Very Young* (1924) and *Now We are Six* (1927).

In 1925, the Milnes bought a farmhouse in Sussex. This "enchanted place on the top of the Forest" was the setting for Milne's stories about Christopher Robin and Pooh. Other toy animals, as well as creatures of the forest, joined in the adventures described in *Winnie-the-Pooh* (1926) and *The House at Pooh Corner* (1928).

A. A. Milne had a special talent for presenting small children as they are. He takes us into their private world of make-believe and funny words—of "wheezles and sneezles," "haycorns," "expotitions," and "biffalo-buffalo-bisons." All the pictures in the Christopher Robin books were drawn by the well-known artist Ernest H. Shepard. His tiny pen-and-ink figures exactly capture the mood of the books.

A. A. Milne died on January 31, 1956. Pooh, Piglet, and the others now live in the offices of Milne's New York publisher.

Reviewed by CHRISTOPHER MILNE
Author, *The Enchanted Places*

So they all went off on an Expotition to the North Pole: Rabbit, Christopher Robin, Pooh, Piglet, Owl, Kanga and Roo, and (*opposite page*) Eeyore and all Rabbit's friends-and-relations.

John Milton, from a 1667 miniature by W. Faithorne.

Two of Milton's best-known early poems are *L'Allegro* and *Il Penseroso*. They contrast the outlook of a merry person (L'Allegro) with that of a more thoughtful one (Il Penseroso). In this selection from *L'Allegro,* the poet, in a carefree mood, calls on the spirit of mirth to keep him company.

Haste thee nymph, and bring with thee
Jest and youthful Jollity,
Quips and Cranks, and wanton Wiles,
Nods, and Becks, and Wreathed Smiles,
Such as hang on Hebe's cheek,
And love to live in dimple sleek;
Sport that wrinkled Care derides,
And Laughter holding both his sides.
Come, and trip it as ye go
On the light fantastic toe,
And in thy right hand lead with thee,
The Mountain Nymph, sweet Liberty;
And if I give thee honor due,
Mirth, admit me of thy crew
To live with her, and live with thee,
In unreproved pleasures free.

MILTON, JOHN (1608–1674)

John Milton, one of England's greatest writers, was born into a prosperous London family on December 9, 1608. His father encouraged his early interest in music and languages. John attended St. Paul's School in London before entering Christ's College, Cambridge, at the age of 16. There he began writing poetry in English and Latin.

Milton was graduated in 1632. But he was not satisfied with his formal schooling. In his sonnet "How Soon Hath Time" (1632), he expressed his anxiety about having little to show for his education. While other people of his age were beginning their careers in law or business or the church, Milton lived alone at his father's country house. For nearly six years he read widely in many subjects. Then he rounded out his education with a lengthy stay in Italy. His first important publications were *Comus,* a masque (short play) first performed at Ludlow Castle in 1634, and *Lycidas* (1637), a magnificent elegy on the death of a former classmate.

On the eve of the English Civil War (1642–49), Milton began writing pamphlets supporting the cause of the Puritans, who favored religious liberty and a parliamentary form of government without a king. One of these, *Areopagitica* (1644), is among the earliest and most eloquent pleas for freedom of the press. Milton's writings brought him to the attention of Oliver Cromwell, who became Lord Protector after the execution of Charles I in 1649. He appointed Milton secretary for foreign languages in the new government.

By 1652, Milton had gone blind. He responded to this affliction with renewed creativity. With the help of secretaries, he continued in his government post until the restoration of the monarchy in 1660. He then lived in retirement with his family while he completed his masterpiece, *Paradise Lost* (1667). This work is the greatest epic poem in the English language. It expands the story of the fall of Satan and of Adam and Eve in the Garden of Eden.

In 1671, Milton published *Paradise Regained,* a shorter epic, and *Samson Agonistes,* the story of Samson written in the form of a Greek tragedy. When he died on November 8, 1674, Milton had won a place in English literature next to Shakespeare.

DAYTON HASKIN
Boston College

Located on Lake Michigan, Milwaukee is an important Great Lakes port city and a major industrial center.

MILWAUKEE

Milwaukee, the largest city in Wisconsin, is known as the "machine shop of the world." It produces millions of dollars' worth of heavy machinery each year, and engines and generators made in Milwaukee are used around the world. When Milwaukee was the country's leading center of brewing, it won the nickname "Beer Capital." The city is noted for its excellent government, low crime rate, and beautiful harbor. Milwaukee County is famed for its park system.

Milwaukee is located on the western shore of Lake Michigan where three rivers flow together—the Menomonee, the Kinnickinnic, and the Milwaukee. French fur trappers camped there as early as the mid-1600's. The first permanent settler, Solomon Juneau (1793–1856), built a trading post between the Milwaukee River and Lake Michigan in 1818. Villages grew up around Juneau's post and around the cabins of other nearby pioneers. During the 1830's, many settlers came, including a number of Irish, English, German, and Scandinavian immigrants.

The villages joined in a town, which was incorporated in 1846. Juneau was the first mayor. The Indian name for Milwaukee was Mahn-a-waukee Seepe, meaning "gathering place by the rivers." During the 1840's, the population greatly increased, mainly because of a flood of German immigrants. They were refugees from the Revolution of 1848. Many were important intellectual and political leaders, who set a high cultural tone for the frontier city. The Germans also established the art of making fine beer and set up beer gardens and music societies. Other sizable groups in the population today include blacks and people of Polish and Hispanic descent.

▶THE CITY TODAY

Milwaukee is an important Great Lakes port. The opening of the St. Lawrence Seaway in 1959 provided the city with a route to the Atlantic Ocean. Milwaukee covers 96 square miles (249 square kilometers) and has a population of about 620,000. The city is also the center of a four-county metropolitan area that has a population approaching 1,600,000.

Milwaukee is among the leading industrial cities of the United States. It is known especially for the manufacture of motorcycles, tractors, outboard motors, diesel and gasoline engines, mining machinery, and equipment for electric power plants. Brewing, meatpacking, and the processing of various foods are other important industries.

The Milwaukee County Public Museum is one of the largest science and history museums in the country. The Milwaukee County Zoo, which includes the Children's Zoo, ranks among the country's leading zoos. Milwaukee also has art museums and a performing arts center, where people enjoy symphony concerts, opera, ballet, theater, and other cultural activities. The University of Wisconsin—Milwaukee and Marquette University are the best known of Milwaukee's numerous colleges and universities. Sports fans can watch the Milwaukee Bucks basketball team, the Milwaukee Brewers baseball team, and some of the games of the Green Bay Packers football team.

JAMES JOHN FLANNERY
University of Wisconsin—Milwaukee

MINERALS. See ROCKS, MINERALS, AND ORES.

Open-pit mines, such as this copper mine in Utah, are the chief sources of ore. Ore can be taken more easily from a surface mine than from an underground mine.

MINES AND MINING

Mining is a fascinating—and difficult—task. The earth does not give up its mineral riches easily. People must tear them from the earth with picks and shovels, drills, and explosives. But the work is well worth the trouble. Our modern civilization could not exist without the materials provided by mining.

Most of our food and clothing come from materials on the surface of the earth. But many other important things—including metals, fuels, chemicals, and plastics—are made from materials that are dug out of the earth. Even food and clothing could not be provided in abundance without mineral fertilizers to grow food and without metal machinery to weave cloth.

The materials that miners dig from the earth are minerals. A **mineral** is a chemical element or compound that occurs naturally in the earth. A **rock** is a combination of two or more minerals. An **ore** is a deposit in the earth that is rich enough in some mineral to make mining it worthwhile.

Some of the most important metals that are mined are aluminum, copper, gold, iron, lead, nickel, silver, tin, and zinc. These metals are used every day for hundreds of purposes. Other metals, such as beryllium, are less well known. Beryllium is used to make lightweight alloys (combinations of metals) needed in space vehicles and nuclear equipment.

Not all minerals are metals. Useful nonmetallic minerals include salt and sand and gravel. Precious stones such as diamonds, emeralds, rubies, and sapphires are nonmetallic minerals. Other nonmetals have uses in a variety of industries. Fluorspar is needed for refining aluminum. Gypsum is used for making plaster of paris. Phosphate rock is a main ingredient of fertilizers. Sulfur is used in hundreds of chemical products.

▶WHERE DEPOSITS ARE FOUND

Nonmetallic minerals are found in deposits scattered all over the earth. But the large deposits of metallic ores tend to be grouped in certain areas. The chief centers for gold mining, for instance, are in South Africa, the Soviet Union, northern Canada, Japan, and the southwestern United States. Important copper-producing areas are in the southwestern and northern United States, the Soviet Union, Japan, Chile, and Zambia. Many areas that are rich in deposits of one metallic ore also have other metals. The technical name for such an area is **metallogenetic province.**

Finding and extracting ore is the work of geologists, mining engineers, and metallurgical engineers. Geologists are scientists who study the earth's crust. With their special

Geologists take ore samples for testing. If the samples contain enough high-grade ore, a mine will be opened.

A satellite photograph shows the area around Salt Lake City, Utah. Such pictures help locate ore deposits.

knowledge and instruments, they can find ore deposits that untrained people might never discover. Mining engineers work out ways to get the minerals out of the earth efficiently and safely. Metallurgical engineers figure out how to process the ore to extract valuable metals.

Searching for Ore

The first step in mining is to find a rich mineral deposit, or ore body. Some ore bodies lie exposed on the surface of the earth. This happens when wind, rain, creeks, or rivers have worn away the soil and rock covering them. Because such ore bodies are not hidden from view, most of them have been located by now.

In the past, prospectors—with burros, picks and shovels, and gold pans—searched for rich deposits of gold. Their place has been taken by trained geologists who use scientific instruments and methods to locate deposits of all the important minerals.

One method used to find ore is **geologic analysis.** Geologists carefully study the earth around a known ore deposit. They note such things as the shape of the folded rock layers, the location of faults (breaks in the rock layers), the kinds of rocks and minerals present, and the way the rocks have been changed by forces in the earth's crust. Then the geologists look for another area that has the same char-

acteristics. There is a good chance that there will be ore deposits in that area, too.

To aid in the search for ore, geologists use aerial and satellite photographs and maps that are made from photographs. The formations of land, rocks, and vegetation as seen from the air can reveal much to a trained eye about what lies under the surface of the earth.

Geologists sometimes create small artificial earthquakes to get a better idea of the underlying rock formations. They place sticks of dynamite in shallow holes and set off the blast. This sends vibrations through the earth, which are picked up by devices called **geophones.** Another way of creating vibrations is to "hammer" on the ground with a mechanical device mounted on a truck. Patterns of the vibrations are recorded on graphs by electrically operated pens. A study of the patterns shows what the rock layers and faults, or cracks, are like under the surface.

Measuring differences in the force of gravity with sensitive instruments helps locate mineral-bearing rocks. It is known that rocks containing certain minerals exert more gravity pull than other rocks. When the instruments register very strong gravity forces, samples of the underlying rock may be drilled out for further testing.

Some minerals are magnetic. They can be detected by instruments that measure differences in the strength of the earth's magnetic fields. One magnetic detector, called an **airborne magnetometer,** is trailed behind a low-flying airplane. In this way, a great deal of ground can be checked in a very short time. Magnetic methods led to discoveries of large iron ore deposits in Brazil and Labrador.

Electricity is sometimes used to help locate ore deposits. Ores that contain metals usually conduct more electric current than other minerals and rocks. Metal rods called **electrodes** are stuck into the earth's surface. Electric current is passed through the electrodes, and the amount of current flow is measured. Where the current flow is greatest, metal ore may be present.

Some ores betray their presence by giving off radioactivity—a stream of charged particles. If the ores are not too deep underground, the radioactivity can be detected by a device called a **Geiger counter.** Uranium, thorium, and radium are three important radioactive minerals.

Workers drill holes to attach wire mesh to the ceiling of a nickel mine. The mesh will keep debris from falling.

Geochemical analysis is a newer method for locating ores. Scientists have found that the water in streams, springs, and wells usually contains traces of any metals that are in the area. Many plants also contain traces of the metals. Samples of water and plants are tested with chemicals to find out what metals they contain. When an area shows a concentration of some valuable metal, geologists take a closer look to see whether the deposits are large enough to be mined.

Today, space technology provides valuable new tools to geologists. High-altitude aircraft and earth-orbiting satellites take photographs, radar images, and other measurements that help locate ore deposits.

Drilling and Sampling

When geologists have located a possible ore deposit, they use drilling and sampling to decide whether the deposit is worth mining. Drills with hollow, diamond-tipped cutting bits are used to bore into the rock to get the samples. The drills can cut out a core of rock about 5 centimeters (2 inches) in diameter to a depth of more than 100 meters (330 feet).

The rock samples are tested for the amount of a certain mineral they contain. If the rock has a high percentage of the mineral, the deposit is a **high-grade ore.** Lower percentages of mineral content mean that the deposit is a **low-grade ore** or a **marginal ore.** Low-grade ores usually are considered worth mining if they are not too difficult to dig up. It must also be possible to separate the valuable minerals from the worthless materials cheaply and easily. Marginal ores contain so little of the mineral being sought that they usually are not considered worth mining unless the mineral is extremely valuable. But sometimes marginal ores become worth mining—for example, when a new use is found for a mineral, making it more in demand, or when supplies of higher-grade ores containing the mineral are exhausted.

▶PLANNING A MINE

When it is known how rich and how large the mineral deposit is, a decision must be made about whether to open a mine. A mine, like a highway or a building, is a carefully engineered structure. A team of experts studies the question. The team includes geologists, mining engineers, business managers, and other specialists. They decide what kind of mine should be dug, how much ore could be mined each day, and what the equipment, supplies, labor, and transportation would cost. The mining company will open the mine only if the costs do not seem too high for the amount of ore that could be obtained. The company must make more money from selling the minerals than it spends in mining them.

The method to be used in mining the ore has a great deal to do with how expensive it might be to open a mine. There are two chief methods of mining ore—underground mining and surface mining. Underground mining is usually the more costly method because it requires more labor. In many cases, the large power equipment used in surface mining cannot be put to work underground.

▶ UNDERGROUND MINING

Underground mining is used to extract ores that are deep beneath the earth's surface. To reach the ore, deep shafts and horizontal passageways called **drifts** must be dug. This is very expensive. A large amount of money must be invested before any ore is extracted or any metal produced.

The shaft that is dug down to the ore is usually vertical. An elevator called a **cage** is installed to carry workers and materials up and down. If the ore is not too deeply buried, a sloping shaft may be built, and inclined-rail transportation may be used.

At the bottom of the shaft, a larger opening is dug to make room for workers and equipment. From this spot, working drifts, or roadways, are dug. The ore can now be extracted. How it is removed depends on the kind of ore being mined and how the ore bed, or vein, is placed. Coal, for instance, is usually found in veins that are nearly horizontal. Metallic ores are often found in veins that run almost vertically in the earth. Coal is fairly soft and can be dug out by machines. Most ores must be drilled and blasted out.

Excavating ore from an underground mine is usually called **stoping.** This involves drilling and blasting the ore with explosives so that it is broken into pieces for easy removal.

Open stoping is a system of digging "rooms" out of the ore while leaving pillars of ore to hold up the roof. This is also called

Coils of slow-burning fuse attached to dynamite in the rock are lit to set off the blast.

Timbers are often used to support the mine tunnels.

the room-and-pillar method of mining. Often supports of timber, steel, or concrete are used to help hold the overlying rock in place. Sometimes the pillars of ore are cut away after all the other ore has been extracted. The roof of each room is allowed to collapse as the miners work back toward the main shaft.

If the ore pillars are not strong enough to allow open stoping, **filled stoping** may be used. As ore is cut out, the walls that are left are buttressed with timbers, and the holes are filled with sand. Without support, the weight of rock and earth from above would cause the working areas to cave in. One important type of filled stoping is called the timbered cut-and-fill method.

Many coal deposits and a few ore deposits lie nearly horizontal in the earth. If the overlying ground is not too strong, they can be mined by **longwall stoping.** An excavation (or stope) is dug into the ore vein. The miners drill and blast the ore off the face of one wall of the stope. As the ore is dug out, the rock and ore above will cave in. The stope's walls must be held up by timber or steel supports. When all the ore is taken from one wall of the stope, the supports are removed and that wall caves in. Then the miners start digging ore from the wall on the other side.

Caving is another method that can be used to remove ore. Openings are cut under large blocks of ore. Small pillars are left to hold the ore in place. When everyone is safely out of the openings, the pillars are blasted. The weight of the ore and rock above it causes the ore to cave in. The broken pieces of ore are scooped up, usually by automatic loading machines, and carried away.

Ore is transported to the main shaft by underground railway trains. At the shaft it is loaded onto elevators called **skips** and hoisted to the surface.

Safety in Underground Mines

Huge fans circulate fresh air through the mine tunnels. A fresh air supply is important for several reasons. Drilling and blasting in the passageways and stopes stir up dust. Miners

Ore cars, which run on train tracks, are used to carry mineral-laden rock from an underground mine.

could not work long if they had to breathe this dust-filled air all the time. The dust from quartz, a form of silica, is especially harmful. Inhaling this dust for long periods of time can cause a lung disease called **silicosis.** Gases from explosives are also released into the air when blasting is going on. These gases are harmful to breathe. Besides fouling the air, the dust and gases may cause fires or explosions. Thus, good ventilation of a mine is a necessary safety precaution. Some mines also are very hot from the earth's heat. They must be air-conditioned so that the miners are comfortable while they work.

Another problem is groundwater, which constantly seeps into mines. The water must be pumped out all the time, even when the miners are not working. If pumping stopped even for a few weeks or months, the drifts and stopes might be flooded.

Miners have to be careful of such dangers as falling rock, cave-ins, large digging and loading machinery, and the explosives used for blasting. In spite of all these hazards, the number of mine accidents and deaths has steadily decreased. Mining companies, miners' unions, and the government are continually looking for ways to make mining safer. Miners must take special training courses and safety-education programs.

▶**SURFACE MINING**

Surface mines extract ore that lies near the surface of the earth. The work is faster and easier than underground mining. No shafts, drifts, or stopes have to be dug. All the heavy digging and loading can be done by large power equipment, which cannot be taken into most underground mines.

Surface mines are of two types—open-pit bench mines and strip mines. An open-pit bench mine looks like a bowl lined with a series of benches or terraces. Strip mines are used to mine coal. They follow the coal bed across the countryside.

The ease and speed of surface mining make it less expensive than underground mining. Even very low-grade ores can sometimes be mined with profit in open-pit mines. Huge quantities of ore are taken from open-pit mines. More minerals are obtained from these mines than are obtained from underground mines.

Before the ore can be mined, the soil and rock covering it, called the **overburden,** must be removed. Giant diesel-powered scrapers gouge out tons of the material at a time. The total weight of waste material is usually several times as great as the weight of the ore.

When enough ore is uncovered and blasted loose, large power shovels go into action. They scoop up the ore and dump it into trucks. The largest hauling trucks can carry as much as 350 tons of ore in one load. Because of their great size and weight, these trucks travel on specially built roads from the mines to the processing plants.

▶ PLACER MINING

Valuable minerals are sometimes found in the sand and soil deposited by rivers and streams. Gold, platinum, and zircon, for example, are often found in these **placer deposits.** The minerals are recovered by a specialized type of mining, called **placer mining.**

Large dredges and power shovels dig up the soil and dump it into long troughs. The material is washed over with water. The minerals, which are heavier than the soil, sink to the bottom and are recovered. Placer mining is not used as widely as underground and surface mining. There are not as many placer deposits as there are deposits of minerals buried in the earth.

▶ MILLING AND PROCESSING

Some minerals, such as sulfur and salt, are sometimes found in an almost pure state in the earth. They are not mixed with other materials. They can be sold directly to customers without much processing. But in most cases, minerals must go through several processing treatments before they can be used. Metallic ores, for instance, go through many processing operations before the useful metals are obtained. Sometimes the processing is done in plants at the mine site, and sometimes the ore is shipped to processing plants elsewhere. The ways in which metallic ores are processed are described in the article METALS AND METALLURGY in this volume (Volume M).

▶ HISTORY OF MINING

Mining is such an ancient occupation that no one can say exactly when it began. The

This massive strip-mining machine scoops up 200 tons of earth with each bite. It is used to mine coal.

Greek myth of the Golden Fleece grew out of tales about a primitive kind of mining. The Golden Fleece was a sheepskin used to catch particles of gold washed down a stream.

One of the earliest mining ventures recorded in history was the Egyptian expedition into the Sinai peninsula sometime around 2600 B.C. The Egyptians went to Sinai to mine turquoise. While there, they also found and mined a more useful mineral—copper.

The ancient Greeks mined silver in the mines of Laurion, south of Athens. The mines may have been opened as early as 1400 B.C. by an earlier Greek people, the Mycenaeans. The Greeks worked the mines from about 600 to 350 B.C. Several of the shafts went to a depth of 120 meters (400 feet). Other metals, such as lead, zinc, and iron, were later mined from these old diggings.

By 1940, machines such as this conveyor belt were being used to help miners load coal into cars.

The Romans had mines everywhere, from Africa to Britain. Among their most valuable mines were the Río Tinto mines in Spain, which yielded large quantities of gold, silver, copper, tin, lead, and iron.

Mining became a really large-scale operation in the 1700's and 1800's, when the Industrial Revolution was under way. Large amounts of coal were needed for smelting iron and stoking factory furnaces, and coal mining expanded rapidly. The development of modern mining techniques started at this time.

Most of the exciting stories about mining are connected with the search for precious metals and stones, usually gold and diamonds. Gold fever reached its height in the 1800's. The California gold rush started in 1848, after the discovery of rich gold deposits at John Sutter's sawmill on the American River.

One of the California prospectors was an Australian, Edward H. Hargraves. He noticed that the rocks and terrain of the California goldfields resembled those in his native land. Hargraves went back to Australia and found rich gold deposits there in 1851. This started the Australian gold rush.

Two other large gold deposits were found later in the century. In 1896, a gold strike in the Klondike region of Canada's Yukon Territory started a gold rush in Canada and Alaska. Ten years earlier, in 1886, mining had begun in the richest goldfield ever discovered, the Witwatersrand area in South Africa.

The world's largest diamond deposits were found in South Africa about 1870. These became the famous Kimberley diamond mines.

Some of the money made from these mines led to other mineral discoveries. An Englishman, Cecil Rhodes, used money from his interest in the Kimberley mines to finance exploration into the interior of Africa, where more gold and diamonds were found. Even more valuable were the copper deposits that were discovered.

The widespread prospecting for gold and diamonds often led to the uncovering of other minerals. Prospectors may have been disappointed when they found lead, copper, iron, or other minerals instead of gold, but the discoveries were important. As modern industry grew, these minerals were more in demand.

The radium used in early radioactivity experiments came from ores that eventually also provided the first uranium. Uranium was used to develop the atomic bomb during World War II. Later, atomic, or nuclear, technology developed to include nonmilitary uses.

▶MINING IN THE FUTURE

In the future, mining will probably be more important than ever before. As developing countries build industries to support better living standards for their people, there will be greater demand for minerals. This could result in temporary shortages and higher prices for many minerals.

All over the world geologists are hunting for new mineral deposits. New ways to search for hidden deposits are being developed, as are better mining machines and methods. Gigantic drill bits, able to bore large mine shafts in a single operation, are being tested. Miners are using super-hot torches that can burn through rock too hard for drills.

The demand for minerals is increasing, but it is not likely that the world will run out of minerals. There are still supplies available, especially of low-grade ores and common rocks. As high-grade ores are used up, less rich ores will have to be used. Already modern technology enables us to process ores that were once thought to be too low in grade to be of any value. Scientists and engineers are continually experimenting with ways to extract valuable minerals from these ores.

Reviewed by WILLIAM H. DRESHER
International Copper Research Association, Inc.

See also COAL AND COAL MINING; ENGINEERING; METALS AND METALLURGY.

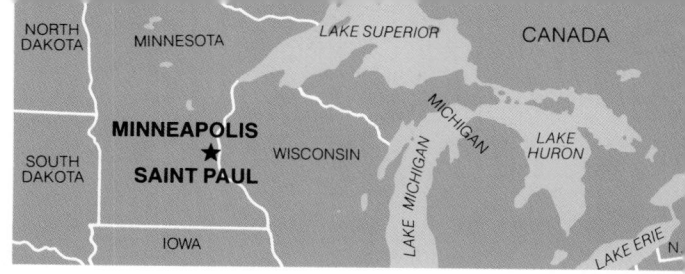

MINNEAPOLIS–SAINT PAUL

Minneapolis and Saint Paul are Minnesota's Twin Cities. Saint Paul is the state capital, Minneapolis the state's biggest city. Both are industrial cities noted for their parks, lakes, and beautiful homes.

The Twin Cities grew up near Fort Snelling, an army post at the junction of the Minnesota and Mississippi rivers. Saint Paul began in 1840 as Pig's Eye—the nickname of its first settler, Pierre "Pig's Eye" Parrant. The next year a priest built a log-cabin church, the Church of Saint Paul, and the settlement became known as Saint Paul. In 1847 a pioneer built a small sawmill upriver on the east side of St. Anthony Falls. Minneapolis (*minne,* Indian for "water," and *polis,* Greek for "city") grew up on the west side and merged with the mill village.

When Minnesota became a territory in 1849 and a state in 1858, Saint Paul, the larger city, was the natural choice for the capital. Yet by 1880, Minneapolis had become the larger of the Twin Cities—a lead it has held ever since. Today the cities co-operate more than they compete. They share big-league baseball and football teams, the Minnesota Twins and Vikings, and serve jointly as a gateway to the Minnesota lake country.

The twin cities are characterized by their diversified economy, with leadership in both trade and industry. Most of the cities' workers are employed in the machinery industry. Some of the biggest flour companies in the world are there, as well as the largest cash grain market in the United States. The South Saint Paul stockyards are among the largest in the country.

Other industries include shipping, graphic arts, food products and processing, apparel, electronics, and instruments. Factories in the Twin Cities produce autos, building materials, computers, guidance systems, electronic equipment, television sets, and plastics. The St. Anthony Falls prevent large-scale shipping north of Minneapolis. Saint Paul is the largest port on the upper Mississippi and is also a busy motor freight terminal. The Twin Cities are a major railroad hub.

Minneapolis is a lake town, a college town, and a trade, industrial, and financial center. Scenic drives link its 22 lakes and more than 150 parks. Enclosed walkways connect many downtown buildings to keep out the winter cold. The University of Minnesota, in Minneapolis, is one of the largest in the country. The city is also the home of the Minnesota Symphony Orchestra and the Tyrone Guthrie Repertory Theatre. Its museums include the Walker Art Center and Minneapolis Institute of Arts. One of the tallest buildings west of the Mississippi River is the 57-story IDS Center, designed by the architect Philip Johnson.

Included among Saint Paul's attractions are the State Historical Society's museum, the Science Museum of Minnesota, and the world-famous Como Park Zoo and Conservatory. The Agricultural College of the University of Minnesota is one of Saint Paul's many colleges, universities, and seminaries.

Saint Paul's modern city hall is famous for its large white onyx statue representing an American Indian peace spirit. It reminds visitors of the Twin Cities' Indian heritage and of the peaceful prosperity they enjoy today.

Reviewed by Lewis Wixon
St. Cloud State University

See also Minnesota.

The 57-story IDS Center dominates the Minneapolis skyline. Minnesota's largest city lies across the Mississippi River from its "twin city," Saint Paul.

MINNESOTA

A long train of two-wheeled carts screeched and rumbled along the dusty trail, traveling along the Red River in western Minnesota. Soon they would turn southeastward and make their way across Minnesota to present-day Saint Paul. They were bringing furs, and maybe buffalo robes and dried meat, from the country to the north.

These were the Red River carts, which helped to make Saint Paul one of the largest fur markets in the country during the middle 1800's. The carts were made entirely of wood, usually oak, held together by wooden pins. At first the wheels were made from sections of tree trunks as much as a meter in diameter. Later the solid disks of wood were cut out to form spokes and rims. Oxen or Indian ponies pulled the carts only about 30 kilometers (20 miles) a day. Red River carts were first used in the 1820's. By the late 1850's as many as 500 were in service. Gradually the use of flatboats and steamboats and the coming of railroads put an end to this cheap but slow and noisy form of transportation.

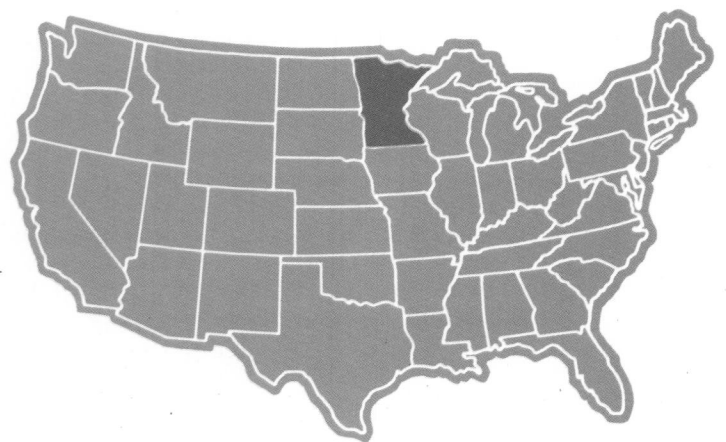

One of Minnesota's nicknames, the Land of 10,000 Lakes, suits the state especially well. Within its borders are more than 10,000 lakes and hundreds of rivers and streams. The Mississippi River has its source near one of these lakes, Lake Itasca. Each year, thousands of people visit Itasca State Park to see the tiny brook that flows from the lake to become the nation's greatest river. Besides its inland waters, Minnesota has more than 240 kilometers (150 miles) of shoreline on Lake Superior, one of the Great Lakes.

An older nickname, the Gopher State, suits Minnesota in a different way. The gopher is a small ground squirrel that once lived in great numbers on the prairies of western and southern Minnesota. The gopher was well known to the prairie settlers. Minnesotans have honored it by calling the athletic teams at the University of Minnesota the Golden Gophers.

Travelers in Minnesota see many different kinds of countryside—woodlands dotted with lakes, level farmlands, and rugged hills. From one part of the state to another, they may see wheat being harvested by modern machines or wild rice being gathered by hand. They may see dairying, logging, quarrying, shipping, fishing, and mining. The largest open-pit iron mine in the United States is near Hibbing in northeastern Minnesota. In the southwest there is an ancient quarry where Indian people obtained the soft stone from which to carve their pipes. Everywhere in the towns and cities of Minnesota, there are modern mills and factories that turn out a variety of products made from Minnesota's own raw materials.

Much of Minnesota's wealth comes directly or indirectly from its agricultural lands and from its forests and mines. But the skills, education, and resourcefulness of its people are equally important to the state. Through the years the people have put their abilities to work to make the Land of 10,000 Lakes a leading agricultural and industrial state as well as a vacationland that is unsurpassed in the nation.

▶ THE LAND

Minnesota is located along the northern border of the United States, about halfway between the Atlantic and the Pacific oceans. It shares an international boundary with the Canadian provinces Ontario and Manitoba.

An unusual part of the state is the Northwest Angle. This piece of land, about 390 square kilometers (150 square miles) in area, is farther north than any other part of the country except Alaska. It became part of the United States through a mistake in geography. The treaty ending the Revolutionary War in 1783 provided that the northern boundary of the United States should extend due west from the northwest point of the Lake of the Woods to the source of the Mississippi River. After

STATE FLAG.

STATE TREE: Red (Norway) pine.

STATE BIRD: Loon.

STATE FLOWER: Showy (pink-and-white) lady's slipper.

MINNESOTA

CAPITAL: Saint Paul.

STATEHOOD: May 11, 1858; the 32nd state.

SIZE: 218,601 km² (84,402 sq mi); rank, 12th.

POPULATION: 4,075,970 (1980 census); rank, 21st.

ORIGIN OF NAME: From the Sioux (Dakota) Indian word *minisota,* meaning "white water" or "sky-tinted water."

ABBREVIATIONS: Minn.; MN.

NICKNAMES: Gopher State, North Star State, Land of 10,000 Lakes, Land of Sky-blue Waters.

STATE SONG: "Hail! Minnesota."

STATE MOTTO: *L'étoile du nord* (The star of the north).

STATE SEAL: A pioneer farmer is shown plowing on the banks of the Mississippi River. His gun and powder horn rest against a tree stump. In the background an Indian flees toward the west. The Falls of St. Anthony are at the right. Above the figures is a streamer bearing the state motto. The date of Minnesota's entry into the Union is shown in the lower part of the border.

STATE FLAG: The state seal appears in the center of a deep-blue field. Around the seal is a wide band of white containing 19 stars. The 19 stars indicate that Minnesota was the 19th state after the original 13. The year of statehood, 1858, is shown above the figures on the seal. Two other dates are woven into the wreath of lady's slippers around the figures—1819, the establishment of Fort St. Anthony (Fort Snelling), and 1893, the year the basic design of the flag was adopted.

Minnesota's iron-rich rock formations tend to divert compass needles. Split Rock Lighthouse is an important guide for navigators on Lake Superior.

some years, explorers proved that the source of the river was south of the Lake of the Woods, not west of it. But the Northwest Angle remained as part of the United States.

Landforms

There are two major landforms in Minnesota—the Central Lowland and the Superior Upland. The Central Lowland covers most of the state. The Superior Upland is in the northeast. All the surface features were created or affected in some way by glaciers that once covered most of the state. In some places the glaciers left tons of drift—sand, gravel, and rocks of all sizes. They also scooped out thousands of lakes and ponds and produced a drainage pattern of more than 400 rivers and streams.

The Superior Upland. The northeastern part of the state belongs to a large upland region that extends southward from Canada. In Minnesota this region is known as the Superior Upland. It is often called the Arrowhead Country because its shape resembles an arrowhead. There are several low ranges of hills, including the Mesabi and the Vermilion

ranges. Both are known for their deposits of iron ore. Eagle Mountain, the highest point in the state, is also in this region. Not far away is the state's lowest point, on the shore of Lake Superior.

The Central Lowland. Most of Minnesota lies within a region of the United States known

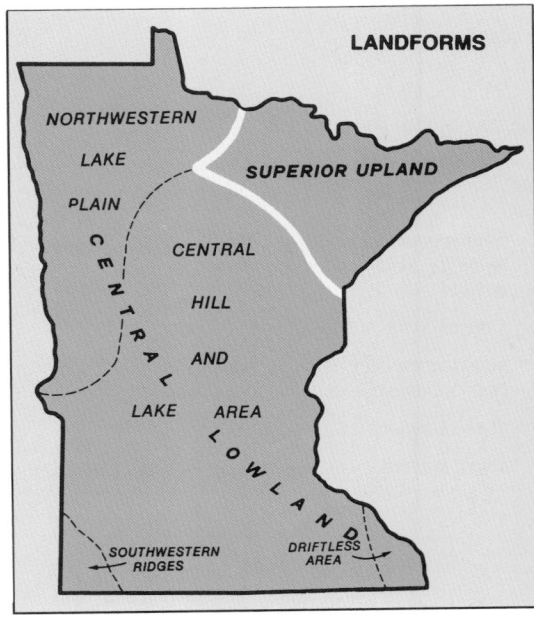

as the Central Lowland. This part of the state may be divided into four areas—the northwestern lake plain, the central hill and lake area, the southwestern ridges, and the southeastern driftless area.

The northwestern lake plain is a very flat area that was once the bottom of an ancient glacial lake called Lake Agassiz. Wide sandy ridges extend through this area in a north-south direction. They were at one time shorelines of this ancient lake. East of the ridges is an area of marshes and peat bogs, known as the Big Bog. Flowing through the plain and into Canada is the Red River of the North.

The central hill and lake area stretches from northern Minnesota to the Iowa border. It is divided by the Minnesota River. North of the river there are many low glacial hills, small valleys, and cold, clear lakes. The land south of the river is gently rolling.

The southwestern ridges contain ridges, or hills, that reach over 540 meters (almost 1,800 feet). These are the second highest elevations in the state. The hills in this area were probably created by the plowlike action of glaciers. Sometimes the hills are called the Coteau des Prairies, French for "hill of the prairies."

The driftless area is a small part of southeastern Minnesota that was not covered by glaciers. It is called driftless because it contains no drift, or glacial deposits. But streams from the glaciers flowed into and across this area, cutting many deep valleys between flat ridges. The Mississippi River flows through this area in a deep, wide valley.

Rivers and Lakes

There are three major river systems in Minnesota. The Red River of the North and the Rainy River flow north toward Hudson Bay. The St. Louis and other rivers in the east drain eastward through the Great Lakes and the St. Lawrence system. The Mississippi and its main tributaries, the Minnesota and the St. Croix, flow south toward the Gulf of Mexico.

The name "Minnesota" comes from a Sioux Indian word that means "sky-tinted water." Among the largest of the state's thousands of freshwater lakes are Red Lake, Leech Lake, Mille Lacs Lake, and Lake Winnibigoshish. Minnesota shares two large lakes with Canada—Lake of the Woods and Rainy Lake. It shares Lake Superior with Canada, Wisconsin, and Michigan.

THE LAND

LOCATION: Latitude—43° 30' N to 49° 24' N.
Longitude—89° 30' W to 97° 14' W.
The Canadian provinces of Manitoba and Ontario to the north, Lake Superior and the state of Wisconsin to the east, Iowa to the south, South Dakota and North Dakota to the west.

ELEVATION: Highest—Eagle Mountain, 702 m (2,301 ft).
Lowest—The shore of Lake Superior, 184 m (602 ft).

LANDFORMS: Superior Upland in the northeast, Central Lowland covering the rest of the state.

SURFACE WATERS: Major rivers—Mississippi, Minnesota, St. Croix, Red River of the North, Rainy, Pigeon.
Largest lakes—Red, Leech, Mille Lacs, Winnibigoshish, and Lake of the Woods and Rainy (both shared with Canada).

CLIMATE: Temperature—July averages, 15 to 24°C (59 to 76°F); January averages, −17 to −8°C (2 to 18°F).
Precipitation—Average, 480 to 790 mm (19 to 31 in). Snowfall varies from 50 cm (20 in) yearly in the southwest to over 180 cm (70 in) in the extreme northeast. **Growing season**—From 90 to 170 days.

Climate

Minnesota is located near the center of North America, about 1,600 kilometers (1,000 miles) from the nearest body of ocean water. For this reason it is subject to great extremes of weather. Summers are often hot, and winters are long and cold.

Generally the southern half of the state is warmer and more humid in summer than the northern half. Occasionally there are hot, cloudless days with temperatures well above average. Such days are often followed by violent thunderstorms.

During the winter the northwest wind often brings very cold air from the Canadian Arctic. Many of the lakes and rivers freeze, and snowfall is heavy in most areas. Often, record-low temperatures are recorded at International Falls during the winter.

Only a moderate amount of precipitation falls in Minnesota. But summer thunderstorms may bring large amounts of rain in one or two hours. A 36-hour winter blizzard may leave as much as 60 centimeters (24 inches) of snow. Severe dry spells are uncommon in eastern Minnesota, but droughts often occur along the western border.

Natural Resources

Minnesota is finding ways to develop its many natural resources while preserving its natural beauty. Air and water pollution, especially of Lake Superior, by mineral-processing plants has been a major concern, but new methods of waste disposal have largely overcome this problem. Also, limits have been placed on mining and logging operations.

Soils and Vegetation. Most of the soils in northeastern Minnesota are acid soils called podzols. They are best suited to growth of coniferous trees. When white settlers first came to this area, they found huge forests of pine, spruce, and fir. After more than a century of lumbering, only small tracts of virgin timber remain.

The southeastern quarter of the state once included forests of both hardwoods and softwoods. The early white settlers prized the brown forest soils in this area, and most of the land was soon cleared for farming.

Before the white settlers came, prairie grasses grew almost everywhere between the rivers in the west and south. Beneath the grasses were rich black soils—the best soils for agriculture. They were so much in demand that very little of the original prairie remains.

Reforestation and scientific forest farming are helping to replace the millions of trees cut during the late 1800's and early 1900's. Most of the forests and woodlands are in the northeastern third of the state. Smaller areas of timber are found in the southeast.

Minerals. Minnesota produces none of the energy-producing minerals—coal, petroleum, or natural gas. But for many years its supplies of iron ore made it the leading producer of this mineral in the United States. Minnesota also has large deposits of granite, limestone, clay, and sand and gravel. Small amounts of other minerals—such as nickel, copper, gold, vanadium, and feldspar—have been discovered.

Wildlife. Most of the original varieties of wildlife are still found in Minnesota, although in much smaller numbers. Moose, elk, bears, and wolves live in the north. Foxes, beavers, deer, and muskrats are found almost everywhere in the state. Muskrats and beavers are trapped for their fur.

In most years there are many pheasant and quail, especially in the west and the south. The rivers and lakes contain northern and walleyed pike, largemouth and smallmouth bass, brook trout, and other fish. Lake Superior has lake herring, lake trout, coho salmon, and small numbers of sturgeon.

▶ THE PEOPLE AND THEIR WORK

The first residents of Minnesota were Sioux (Dakota) and Chippewa (Ojibwa) Indian peoples. Beginning in the 1600's, French Canadian *voyageurs* (travelers) came to barter their goods for the fur pelts of the Sioux. Other traders, soldiers, and missionaries followed the *voyageurs*.

As the whites began to settle the land between 1830 and 1850, workers were needed for farming, lumbering, and the building of towns and railroads. Minnesotans decided to advertise their rich land. Pamphlets describing the state as a land of opportunity were distributed throughout northern Europe. The Germans and the Irish were among the first to arrive. Large numbers of Scandinavians—Swedes, Norwegians, and Danes—also came to Minnesota. At first most of the Norwegians were attracted to lumbering. Later they bought

---

POPULATION

TOTAL: 4,075,970 (1980 census). **Density**—19.8 persons to each square kilometer (51.2 persons to each square mile).

GROWTH SINCE 1850

Year	Population	Year	Population
1850	6,077	1920	2,387,125
1860	172,023	1960	3,413,864
1880	780,773	1970	3,806,103
1900	1,751,394	1980	4,075,970

Gain Between 1970 and 1980—7.1 percent.

CITIES: Population of Minnesota's largest cities according to the 1980 census.

Minneapolis	370,951	St. Louis Park	42,931
Saint Paul	270,230	St. Cloud	42,566
Duluth	92,811	Minnetonka	38,683
Bloomington	81,831	Richfield	37,851
Rochester	57,890	Coon Rapids	35,826
Edina	46,073	Roseville	35,820
Brooklyn Park	43,332		

farms. The Swedes cultivated the land; the Danes developed dairying, the specialty of their homeland. During the 1880's and 1890's, many Finns and Slavic people were attracted to Minnesota by stories of great iron mines and endless tracts of timber.

Descendants of Minnesota's first inhabitants, the Indian peoples, now number about 45,000 (one percent of the total population). More than half of them live in Minneapolis, Saint Paul, and Duluth. Others live on reservations. The largest reservations are Leech Lake, Red Lake, and White Earth.

Where the People Live

Until 1950 more of the people of Minnesota lived in rural areas than in urban areas. Since that time, the reverse has been true. But in recent years many Minnesota cities have lost population to suburbs or nearby rural areas. The southeastern quarter of the state is the most heavily populated area. In the northeast there are areas of dense population along the Mesabi Range and around Duluth.

Industries and Products

Since 1950, manufacturing has replaced farming as the major source of Minnesota's income. In this respect the state has become more like the industrial northeastern part of the United States. But what is called agribusiness —farm employment, food processing and marketing, and farm-supply industries—still adds up to a major industry.

Agriculture. In the late 1800's and early 1900's, grains were the major source of farm income. Huge farms in the Red River valley grew millions of bushels of wheat. In those days, Minnesota produced more flour than any other state, and it was widely known as the nation's breadbasket. Minnesota farmers later became known for both grains and livestock.

Today livestock brings in about half the state's farm income. Farmers in southern Minnesota specialize in raising hogs and Hereford or Aberdeen Angus beef cattle. Meat animals are fattened on corn and oats, which are grown on almost every farm. Dairy farming is concentrated in the east central and southeastern parts of the state and in the north near Duluth. Dairy products include butter and cheese, especially blue cheese that is aged in caves along the Straight River. Turkeys, chickens, and eggs are also important.

Minnesotans stage more than 200 festivals each year. Farm life is the theme of The Harvest Festival at Gibbs Farm Museum in Saint Paul (*above*). King Turkey Day in Worthington (*below*) celebrates the state's ranking as the nation's largest producer of turkeys.

The Red River valley now grows a variety of cash crops. Soybeans and corn are the leading crops in terms of acreage, but soybeans produce more income. Wheat, sugar beets, potatoes, and flax are also grown.

Special products besides blue cheese include wild rice and honey. Wild rice, or Indian rice, grows in some of the lakes and streams. For many years the Chippewa people have been known as harvesters of wild rice, which is sold as a delicacy.

Manufacturing. Minnesota is the home of a large number of major industries that employ about one fifth of the state's labor force. Machinery, principally office and computing machines, heads the list of manufactures in value. Processed foods and paper and allied products are also important.

Most of the manufacturing is done in the larger cities and towns. Minneapolis was once one of the leading flour-milling centers in the United States. South Saint Paul, Austin, St. Cloud, and Albert Lea are major meat-packing centers. Soybeans are processed at Mankato and Minneapolis, and sugar beets at Moorhead, Crookston, Renville, and East Grand Forks. Le Sueur and a number of other towns in southern Minnesota have canneries that process sweet corn and peas. Many small towns and villages throughout the state have creameries, where a variety of dairy products are made.

Minnesota's only steel plant is in Saint Paul. Steel and other metals must be imported for use in many factories that make metal products. Temperature regulators and rocket guidance systems are made in Minneapolis,

---

WHAT MINNESOTA PRODUCES

MANUFACTURED GOODS: Nonelectrical machinery, including office and computing machines; processed foods, notably meat, dairy products, and vegetables; electric and electronic equipment; fabricated metal products; products of printing and publishing; paper and related products; stone, clay, and glass products; instruments of various kinds; chemicals and related products.

AGRICULTURAL PRODUCTS: Milk, soybeans, cattle and calves, hogs, corn, wheat, turkeys, sugar beets, eggs, barley, oats.

MINERALS: Iron ore (accounting for 70 to 80 percent of total value of mineral production), stone, sand and gravel, nickel, copper, gold.

---

business machines in Rochester, and refrigerators in St. Cloud. Printing equipment is made in Saint Paul. Snowmobiles are produced in Roseau.

Cities that make paper and paper products include International Falls, Brainerd, and Saint Paul. The largest plant is at Sartell. Paper from Minnesota wood pulp helps Minneapolis–Saint Paul maintain its place as a large printing and publishing center. Saint Paul also produces a wide variety of tapes, ranging from adhesive tapes to recording tapes. There are oil refineries near Minneapolis–Saint Paul and Duluth.

Mining. Minnesota's leading mineral is iron. Nearly all the ore has come from the Mesabi, Vermilion, and Cuyuna ranges. Of these, the Mesabi is the largest and the only one still producing iron. Most of the best pockets of ore in all of the ranges have been

Duluth's location on the western end of Lake Superior makes it a major shipping center. It also serves as a railroad terminus for nearby mining and agricultural areas.

exhausted. But the iron-bearing taconite rock of the Mesabi Range is still a leading source of iron in the United States. There are many open-pit mines in the range.

Several railroad lines carry the ore to ports on Lake Superior, such as Duluth, Two Harbors, and Silver Bay. From these ports it is shipped to steel mills in the Chicago area and other places outside the state.

Sand and gravel are quarried throughout Minnesota for use in construction of roads and buildings. Central Minnesota has large deposits of granite, which is made into building stone and monuments. Limestone is processed at Mankato, Winona, and other places. Clay, mined in the southern part of the state, is used to make bricks, floor and wall tiles, and other products.

Tourism. Minnesota has long attracted vacationers and tourists. Before the U.S. Civil War, planters from the South traveled up the Mississippi River to spend the summer in Minnesota's cool, forested lake country. Hunting and fishing have always been important activities. Today skiing and other winter sports have become very popular.

Transportation and Communication

Before roads and railroads were built in Minnesota, people traveled on rivers and lakes. Indian canoes made of cedarwood and birch bark were among the first craft. Explorers also found canoes very practical.

Sailing craft were known on Lake Superior in the late 1700's. Vessels of different kinds came to Minnesota after the opening of the Sault Sainte Marie Canals in the 1800's. These canals connect Lake Superior with the other Great Lakes. Duluth became one of the leading freight ports in the world. Today ocean ships reach Duluth through the St. Lawrence Seaway and the Great Lakes.

The first railroad in Minnesota connected Saint Paul and St. Anthony. On July 2, 1862, a train pulled by a wood-burning locomotive, called the "William Crooks," drew into St. Anthony. The engine can still be seen at the Lake Superior Museum at Duluth.

Minnesota's modern highway system had its beginning in 1920, when the legislature authorized a network of roads. Air travel continues to increase in importance. The Minneapolis–Saint Paul International Airport is the largest of more than 140 airports in the state.

Minnesota's first newspaper, the *Minnesota Pioneer*, was printed in Saint Paul in 1849. Today about 30 daily and many weekly newspapers are published in the state. The largest dailies are the *Minneapolis Star and Tribune*, the *St. Paul Pioneer Press*, and the *St. Paul Dispatch*. Another important newspaper is *The Farmer*, published twice a month in Saint Paul. Minnesota has about 12 commercial television stations and more than 100 radio stations.

▶**EDUCATION**

Minnesota is proud of the high quality of education offered in its schools and its public and private colleges and universities. The state's cultural institutions include the Saint Paul-based Minnesota Opera Company and the Minnesota Symphony Orchestra, housed in Orchestra Hall in Minneapolis and known around the world. The equally famed Tyrone Guthrie Theatre in Minneapolis trains actors and presents works by talented playwrights.

Schools and Colleges

The first school in Minnesota was established at Fort Snelling about 1820. Other early schools included mission schools for the Sioux and the Chippewa peoples. Organized education for the children of white settlers began in 1847. In that year, a teacher from the East was brought to Saint Paul to teach in a converted blacksmith shop.

The public school system had its start in 1849, when Minnesota became a territory. Congress granted land in each township for school aid. The land was sold or leased, and the money was used to support schools. In 1858 the new state of Minnesota provided for public schools and teacher-training schools.

Today the leading institution of higher education is the state-supported University of Minnesota, founded in 1851. Besides its main Minneapolis–Saint Paul campus, it includes the Mayo Graduate School of Medicine at Rochester, a university campus and a medical school at Duluth, a university campus at Morris, and technical schools at Crookston and Waseca. Under legislation passed in 1975, the state senior colleges were designated universities. They are at Bemidji, Mankato, Marshall, Moorhead, St. Cloud, Saint Paul, and Winona. A system of community colleges serves all sections of the state.

MINNESOTA

MANITOBA

ONTARIO

Winnepeg

Keewatin • Kenora

NORTHWEST ANGLE

CANADA
UNITED STATES

Hallock • Roseau

Lake of the Woods

Rainy River Fort Frances Rainy Lake

Baudette

International Falls

Thief Lake

Warren
Thief River Falls

Mud Lake

Upper Red Lake

Baptism River

Pigeon River

Grand Forks
East Grand Forks
Red Lake Falls
Crookston

Lower Red Lake

Ely

VERMILION RANGE

Eagle Mtn. × 702 m (2,301 ft)

Grand Portage

Ada

Bagley

Bemidji

Lake Winnibigoshish

Chisholm
Hibbing

MESABI RANGE

Virginia
Eveleth

St. Louis River

Grand Marais

Mahnomen

Cass Lake

Grand Rapids

Baptism River Falls

Silver Bay
Beaver Bay

Lake Itasca

Leech Lake

Walker

Fargo
Moorhead

Park Rapids

Mississippi River

St. Louis R

Two Harbors

LAKE SUPERIOR

Detroit Lakes

Duluth

Cloquet
Carlton

Superior

Breckenridge

Wadena

Aitkin

CUYUNA RANGE

Rice Lake

Otter Tail Lake

Brainerd

Mille Lacs Lake

Kettle River

St. Croix River

WISCONSIN

NORTH DAKOTA

Fergus Falls

Elbow Lake
Alexandria

Little Falls

Mora

Pine City

Wheaton

Kensington

Long Prairie
Sauk Centre

Milaca

Morris

Sartell
Sauk Rapids

Foley

Cambridge

Glenwood

St. Cloud

Elk River

Taylors Falls
Center City

Ortonville

Cold Spring

Anoka

Coon Rapids

Benson

Buffalo

Brooklyn Park
Minneapolis
St. Louis Park
Minnetonka
Edina

Roseville
St. Anthony
Stillwater

Saint Paul

Eau Claire

Madison

Willmar

Litchfield

Lac qui Parle

Montevideo

Bloomington

Richfield

Mendota

Minnesota River

Hutchinson

Granite Falls

Renville
Olivia

Glencoe

Chaska

Shakopee
Apple Valley

Hastings

SOUTH DAKOTA

Gaylord

Morton

Le Sueur

Le Center
Northfield

Red Wing

Marshall

Redwood Falls

St. Peter

Faribault

Lake City
Wabasha

Mississippi

Ivanhoe

New Ulm

Mankato

Owatonna

Mantorville

Pipestone

Slayton

St. James

Waseca

Straight River

Rochester

Winona
La Crescent

La Crosse

Heron Lake

Windom

Des Moines River

Jackson

Fairmont

Austin

Root River

Preston

Caledonia

Sioux Falls

Luverne

Worthington

Albert Lea
Blue Earth

Cedar River

Mason City

Wisconsin River

0 40 80 km
0 20 40 60 mi

Copyright Diversified Map Corporation.
St. Louis, Mo.

The private institutions include Carleton and St. Olaf colleges in Northfield; Gustavus Adolphus College in St. Peter; and Hamline University, Macalester College, and the College of St. Thomas, all in Saint Paul. St. John's University in Collegeville is well known for its Monastic Manuscript Library and Ecumenical Study Center.

Libraries and Museums

Minnesota has approximately 200 public libraries in towns and cities. The largest is the Minneapolis Public Library. The Mayo Clinic and Foundation Library in Rochester has a large collection of works on medicine. The James Jerome Hill Reference Library in Saint Paul specializes in business, economics, technology, and science. The Minnesota Historical Society Library, also in Saint Paul, includes collections on Minnesota, the Old Northwest, and Scandinavians in America.

Most of the well-known museums are in the Minneapolis–Saint Paul area. The Minneapolis Institute of Arts has major works of art. It is situated in the Minneapolis Society of Fine Arts Park, along with the Minneapolis College of Art and Design and the Children's Theatre Company and School. In Saint Paul are the museum of the Minnesota Historical Society and the Saint Paul Arts and Science Center.

Museums in other parts of the state include the Rochester Art Center and the Mayo Medical Museum in Rochester, the Minnesota Museum of Mining in Chisholm, and the United States Hockey Hall of Fame in Eveleth. A beached paddlewheel boat in Winona, the *Julius C. Wilkie*, serves as a museum of the riverboat era.

▶PLACES OF INTEREST

Minnesota is famous for places of historic interest as well as for places of great natural beauty. Most of these places are preserved by the state or by the federal government.

National Areas

Minnesota has two national forests. Superior National Forest includes a large wilderness area, the Boundary Waters Canoe area. Chippewa National Forest contains large lakes and a winter sports arena. The St. Croix National Scenic River and the Lower St. Croix National Scenic River are shared by Minne-

Minnesotans enjoy their long cold winters. The Saint Paul Winter Carnival features parades, ice fishing contests, and ice sculptures such as these in Landmark Center.

sota and Wisconsin. Minnesota also has a national park and two national monuments.

Voyageurs National Park, near International Falls, preserves a vast and beautiful area of woods and lakes. The lakes were once the route of French-Canadian *voyageurs* (men employed by early fur-trading companies to transport goods and guide traders through the wilderness).

Grand Portage National Monument, in northeastern Minnesota, includes a portage from Lake Superior to a navigable point on the Pigeon River. (A portage is an overland path connecting sections of a water route.) Today visitors can see the trail used by the traders and the reconstructed fur depot of the North West Company.

Pipestone National Monument is near Pipestone in southwestern Minnesota. It contains the famous pipestone quarries. Pipestone is a kind of red clay that the Indian peoples used for making their calumets, or ceremonial pipes. Today the stone is called catlinite after George Catlin, a noted artist and traveler who visited the quarries in 1836. Points of interest within the monument include Winnewissa Falls, Lake Hiawatha, numerous Indian shrines, and a museum.

State Park Areas

Minnesota has about 100 state parks and forests. The following list shows the variety.

Interstate State Park, on the St. Croix River near Taylors Falls, is shared by Minnesota and Wisconsin. It is said that this area was known to the Indian peoples as the Valley of Bones because of the fierce battles that took place between the Sioux and the Chippewa. Today the valley is known for lava cliffs that rise to great heights above the river.

Itasca State Park, Minnesota's oldest state park, is near Park Rapids. There the Mississippi River has its source in streams flowing into Lake Itasca. At the point where it leaves the lake, the river is about 3 meters (10 feet) wide and extremely shallow. The importance of the lake was realized in 1832 by Henry Rowe Schoolcraft, an explorer and specialist in the life and culture of the Indian people of the Lake Superior region. It is said that he coined the word "Itasca" from two Latin words meaning "truth" and "head." He believed that Lake Itasca was the "true head" of the Mississippi.

Charles A. Lindbergh State Memorial Park, near Little Falls, maintains the boyhood home of Charles A. Lindbergh, the famous aviator, and tells the story of three generations of the Lindbergh family.

Old Mill State Park is near Warren in Marshall County. Much of the park is typical prairie land. The park takes its name from an old flour mill, build in 1888. The mill still has the original grindstones, which were shipped from France and carried to the site in oxcarts.

Split Rock Lighthouse State Park, near Beaver Bay, overlooks Lake Superior and the Split Rock Lighthouse, which is perched on a high cliff.

Other Attractions

Monuments to Paul Bunyan, the legendary hero of the lumberjacks, may be seen at Bemidji and at Brainerd. Lumbertown, U.S.A., near Brainerd, is a replica of a Minnesota town of the 1870's. Interesting old houses include the Sibley House, built in 1835, and the Faribault House, built a year or so later. Both houses are in Mendota, a village just south of Saint Paul.

Minnehaha Park in Minneapolis contains Minnehaha Falls, made famous by Longfellow's *The Song of Hiawatha*. The Hubert H. Humphrey Metrodome, a sports stadium, is located in Minneapolis, as is the 57-story IDS Tower, the tallest building in the state. Fort Snelling, near Minneapolis, is preserved in a state park area. The fort was one of the first military posts west of the Mississippi River. A museum in Alexandria displays the Kensington Rune Stone. This large stone is said to have been inscribed by a band of Vikings in 1362. The Minnesota Zoo is located in Apple Valley, a suburb south of Minneapolis and Saint Paul.

Annual Events

Each year, Minnesota has many sports events, fairs, and festivals. Some of the events are of local interest. Others attract national attention.

January and February—Winter carnivals, Saint Paul and other places throughout the state.

April—Northwest Sportsmen's Show, Minneapolis.

May—Music Festival, St. Olaf College, Northfield.

June—Paul Bunyan Carnival, Brainerd.

MINNESOTA
PLACES OF INTEREST

The Crystal Court is a popular feature of Minneapolis' 57-story IDS Center. This distinctive skyscraper was designed by architect Philip Cortelyou Johnson.

July—Aquatennial (water sports, parades, and pageants), Minneapolis; Hiawatha Pageant, Pipestone National Monument; Heritagefest, New Ulm.

August—State Fair, Saint Paul; Summer Festival of the Arts, Duluth.

September—Indian Rice Dance, Milaca; Apple Festival, La Crescent.

▶CITIES

Most of Minnesota's large cities, except Duluth, are located in the southeastern part of the state. Minneapolis and Saint Paul with their many suburbs form a metropolitan area that is called Minneapolis–Saint Paul.

Minneapolis–Saint Paul

The Twin Cities of Minneapolis and Saint Paul are located on a bend of the Mississippi River near the mouth of the Minnesota River. Minneapolis is the larger of the two. Saint Paul is the state capital. Cities within the Minneapolis–Saint Paul metropolitan area include Bloomington, St. Louis Park, Richfield, Edina, Minnetonka, Brooklyn Park, Roseville, and Coon Rapids. An article on Minneapolis–Saint Paul appears in this volume.

Duluth

Duluth is situated on Lake Superior at the mouth of the St. Louis River, opposite the city of Superior, Wisconsin. Duluth's location at the western end of the St. Lawrence Seaway and its fine harbor make it one of the world's leading inland ports. It handles large shipments of ore, grain, flour, and dairy products. Duluth is also the gateway to a well-known resort area and the home of the Tweed Museum of Art and a large branch of the University of Minnesota. Duluth was named for a French explorer, Daniel Greysolon, Sieur Duluth (or du Lhut), who visited the area in 1679. The city was settled permanently after 1850.

Other Cities

Rochester, in southeastern Minnesota, is a food-processing center and the home of the Mayo Clinic, a famous medical center. St. Cloud is located in a dairying area northwest of Minneapolis. It is also one of the state's leading industrial cities and its fastest-growing metropolitan area. North of St. Cloud is Brainerd, the center of a well-known resort area. Cities in the Red River valley include Crookston and Moorhead.

▶GOVERNMENT

Minnesota is governed by a constitution adopted in 1857, the year before it was admitted to the Union. The constitution provides for a government of three branches.

The legislative branch consists of two houses, the Senate and the House of Representatives. In 1972 the voters approved a constitutional amendment permitting the legislature to hold regular sessions each year instead of in odd-numbered years.

GOVERNMENT

Capital—Saint Paul. **Number of counties**—87. **Representation in Congress**—U.S. senators, 2; U.S. representatives, 8. **State Legislature**—Senate, 67 members, 4-year terms; House of Representatives, 134 members, 2-year terms. **Governor**—4-year term; no limit on number of terms. **Elections**—General and state, Tuesday after first Monday in November.

The executive branch of the state government is headed by the governor. The judicial branch is headed by the Minnesota Supreme Court. It consists of a chief justice and eight associate justices. The major trial courts in the state are called district courts.

▶FAMOUS PEOPLE

The following people are among Minnesota's native-born or adopted citizens who became well known.

Henry Hastings Sibley (1811–91) was a fur trader who rose to be first governor of the state of Minnesota. He became a territorial delegate to Congress in 1849 and governor of the new state in 1858. Sibley was born in Detroit, Michigan.

James Jerome Hill (1838–1916) was a railroad executive and financier. He built a railroad system with lines stretching from Minnesota to Puget Sound in the state of Washington. Hill played such an important part in the settling and development of the Northwest that he was sometimes called the empire builder. He was born in the Canadian province of Ontario.

Ole Edvart Rölvaag (1876–1931), author and educator, was born in Norway. He came to the United States in 1896. In 1905 he was graduated with honors from St. Olaf College in Northfield. Rölvaag gained fame for his novel *Giants in the Earth,* a story of pioneer life in South Dakota.

Sinclair Lewis (1885–1951), novelist and playwright, was the first American to win the Nobel prize for literature (1930). He was born in Sauk Centre. A biography of Sinclair Lewis is included in Volume L.

Charles Augustus Lindbergh (1902–74), the great aviator, was born in Michigan but was taken to the family home near Little Falls, Minnesota, at an early age. His biography is included in Volume L.

Hubert Horatio Humphrey, Jr. (1902–78), was born in Wallace, South Dakota. In the early 1940's he held government jobs and was also a professor of political science at Macalester College in Saint Paul, He was elected mayor of Minneapolis in 1945 and 1947, United States senator in 1948, and vice president of the United States in 1964. Defeated for the presidency in 1968, he was re-elected senator two years later and served until his death.

The Mayo family consisted of William Worrall Mayo (1819–1911) and his sons, William James Mayo (1861–1939) and Charles Horace Mayo (1865–1939). All three were noted doctors. In 1889 the two sons established the Mayo Clinic in Rochester.

A map laid out in front of the state capitol building in Saint Paul shows all the state's counties. The capitol was constructed of more than 20 kinds of stone.

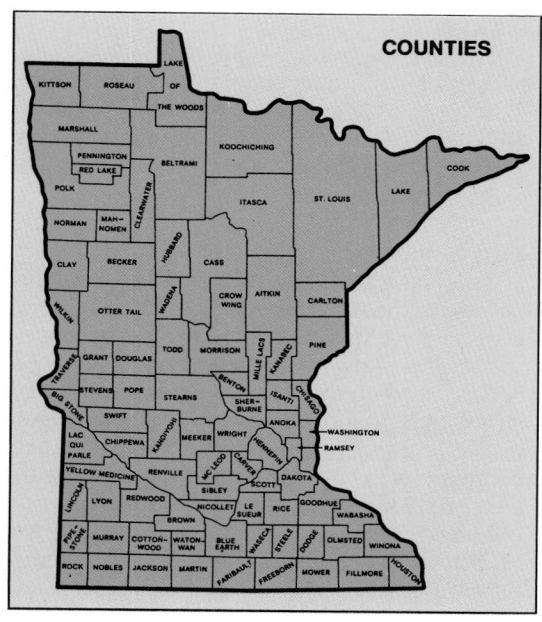

COUNTIES

Minnesota is remarkable for the large number of political figures that have lived there. People who have served the state and the nation include Alexander Ramsey (born in Pennsylvania), first governor of the territory of Minnesota, 1849–53; John Sargent Pillsbury (born in New Hampshire), industrialist and governor of Minnesota, 1876–82; Harold Edward Stassen (born in West Saint Paul), governor of Minnesota, 1938–43, and many times a candidate for the United States presidency; Eugene J. McCarthy (Watkins), U.S. senator from Minnesota, 1959–71; Warren Burger (Saint Paul), chief justice of the United States since 1969; and Walter F. Mondale (Ceylon), U.S. senator from Minnesota, 1964–77, and vice president of the United States, 1977–81.

Other Minnesota writers include novelist F. Scott Fitzgerald (Saint Paul), known for *The Great Gatsby* and other books; Wanda Gág (New Ulm), author and illustrator of children's books; and Charles Alexander Eastman (Redwood Falls), physician and author of books, such as *Indian Boyhood*. Eastman, who was a Sioux Indian, also had an Indian name—Ohiyesa.

Native Minnesotans famous in other activities include singer-actress Judy Garland (Grand Rapids); folk singer Bob Dylan (Duluth); cartoonist Charles Schulz (Minneapolis); and champion golfer Patricia Jane (Patty) Berg (Minneapolis).

▶HISTORY

The early explorers and fur traders found two groups of Indian peoples living in the area that is now Minnesota. The Chippewa, or Ojibwa, lived in northern Minnesota. The Sioux, or Dakota, occupied the western and southern sections.

Early Settlement

The history of the Indian peoples of Minnesota reaches back about 10,000 years. Some historians believe that the first Europeans to see Minnesota were Norse explorers. This belief is based on the Kensington Rune Stone, a large stone found on a farm near Kensington in 1898. Inscriptions on the stone tell of a company of Norse explorers who came to the area on a journey of discovery in 1362.

Later records of exploration show that two French explorers and fur traders—Pierre Esprit Radisson and Médart Chouart, Sieur

de Groseilliers—probably entered Minnesota country about 1660. In 1679, Daniel Greysolon, Sieur Duluth (or du Lhut), reached Mille Lacs Lake and claimed the entire area of Minnesota in the name of King Louis XIV of France. A year later, in 1680, Father Louis Hennepin came up the Mississippi River from Illinois country and reached the Falls of St. Anthony. Soon, others came to claim the land for France, to engage in fur trading with the Indian peoples, and to establish missions.

In 1763 the French lost their lands to the British as a result of the French and Indian War. During the period of British control, fur trading and exploration continued. In 1766–67, Jonathan Carver, a New Englander, visited the area and lived among the Indians for the winter. His book about his journeys was translated into several languages.

At the end of the Revolutionary War in 1783, the United States obtained the part of Minnesota east of the Mississippi. The Louisiana Purchase in 1803 made Minnesota west of the Mississippi part of the United States. In

---

IMPORTANT DATES

1362 According to the Kensington Rune Stone, found in 1898, Norse explorers visited Minnesota.

1660 Radisson and Groseilliers, French explorers and fur traders, probably entered Minnesota about this time.

1679 Daniel Greysolon, Sieur Duluth (or du Lhut), claimed the area for France.

1680 Father Louis Hennepin, exploring the upper Mississippi, reached and named the Falls of St. Anthony.

1763 France ceded its lands east of the Mississippi River to Britain at the end of the French and Indian War.

1783 Britain ceded lands, including the part of Minnesota east of the Mississippi, to the United States at the end of the Revolutionary War.

1803 Minnesota west of the Mississippi became part of the United States through the Louisiana Purchase.

1819 Fort St. Anthony (later named Fort Snelling) established; permanent buildings erected the next year.

1849 Minnesota became a territory with the capital at Saint Paul.

1851 University of Minnesota established by territorial legislature; first collegiate instruction in 1869.

1858 May 11, Minnesota entered the Union as the 32nd state.

1862 Sioux uprising ended in defeat.

1889 Mayo Clinic organized at Rochester.

1892 First iron ore shipped from the Mesabi range.

1950 Value of manufactured goods exceeded total farm income for the first time.

1959 Opening of St. Lawrence Seaway provided Duluth with direct access to the sea.

1975 Regional Native American Center of Minneapolis opened, to serve needs of Indian people in Minnesota and neighboring states.

1984 Minnesotan Walter Mondale ran for the U.S. presidency, losing to the incumbent, Ronald Reagan.

1805, Lieutenant Zebulon Pike was sent to Minnesota to explore and obtain sites for forts. He secured a site at the mouth of the Minnesota River. Josiah Snelling, an army officer, established Fort St. Anthony on this site in 1819. Construction of permanent buildings at the fort began the next year. Later the name was changed to Fort Snelling.

Permanent Settlement

With Fort Snelling to protect them, American traders expanded their operations over most of Minnesota. John Jacob Astor's American Fur Company took over control of trading and trapping in the area. In 1834, Henry Hastings Sibley came to Mendota, a village just south of present-day Saint Paul, as manager of the fur company. This village soon became a terminal for furs brought from the Red River country.

Explorers and mapping parties continued to make Minnesota known in other parts of the nation. In 1832, Henry Rowe Schoolcraft reached the headwaters of the Mississippi River. Joseph Nicholas Nicollet, a French explorer and mathematician, mapped the area northwest of the Mississippi in the 1830's.

During the next ten years, small settlements were made near the Falls of St. Anthony and Fort Snelling. These hamlets later became the city of Minneapolis. Another settlement sprang up on a bluff overlooking the Mississippi. There a priest had built a small church and dedicated it to Saint Paul. By the 1840's, steamboats were bringing increasing numbers of people up the Mississippi to Saint Paul.

The Pioneer Era and Statehood

On March 3, 1849, the territory of Minnesota was established by an act of Congress. Saint Paul became the capital. A month later, President Zachary Taylor appointed Alexander Ramsey of Pennsylvania the first governor of the territory. During the 1850's the population increased enormously. Hundreds of towns were laid out, and farmlands were cleared. The Sioux and Chippewa peoples made treaties, giving up much of their land.

On May 11, 1858, Minnesota was admitted to the Union. Henry Hastings Sibley was governor until the first state election placed Alexander Ramsey in the governor's office in 1860. At the outbreak of the Civil War, thousands of Minnesotans went east and south to fight for the Union. At home, Minnesota was confronted with Indian problems.

After the Civil War the population again expanded greatly. Many railroads were built. Lumbering was a major industry, and wheat-growing continued to be important, as it was during the war. By 1885, Minneapolis was the nation's leading flour-milling center. Farmers began to complain about railroad rates for shipping their wheat and about other farm problems. In 1867, Oliver Hudson Kelley and others founded the National Grange of the Patrons of Husbandry, popularly called the Grange. This organization helped farmers with their problems and supported candidates for the state legislature.

The major event of the 1880's and 1890's was the development of iron mining in the Arrowhead Country. The first carload of iron ore was taken from the Vermilion Range in 1884. In 1892, mining began in the Mesabi Range. The peak of iron ore production was to be reached during World War II.

Modern Times

In 1900, lumber and wheat were still leading products of Minnesota. But dairy products and livestock were soon to become more important. Manufacturing developed, and more and more people left the farms to settle in cities and towns. In 1934, Minnesota was faced with a severe drought that affected most of the western part of the state. After this, farmers began to practice conservation methods to preserve their valuable soil.

Two turning points were reached in 1950. By that time, there were more people living in urban areas than in rural areas, and the value of manufactured goods began to exceed the value of farm products. By the 1980's, two thirds of Minnesota's labor force was employed in transportation, wholesale and retail trade, tourism, and government.

Minnesota faced economic problems in the early 1980's that stemmed largely from the nationwide recession. The number of farms and farmers declined. But the recession did not prevent extensive redevelopment for Minneapolis and Saint Paul. And the high quality of life associated with the state continues to be a source of pride for Minnesotans.

LEWIS WIXON
THOMAS P. DOCKENDORFF
St. Cloud State University

An inspector at the Royal Canadian Mint checks blanks that will be stamped to make pennies.

MINT

A mint is a place where coins are made. Today mints are nearly always under government authority and supervision.

Coins were made in the ancient kingdom of Lydia, in Asia Minor, in the 8th century B.C. From there the art of coining spread throughout the Mediterranean world and into Persia and India. Somewhat later, coining began independently in China. It spread from there to Japan and Korea.

The foundations of modern minting, or coin making, were laid by the Romans. They minted silver coins in the Temple of Juno Moneta as far back as 269 B.C. In Latin, *moneta* came to mean mint or coin. The English words "money" and "mint" developed from this Latin word.

Gold and silver coins existed in Britain before Roman rule. During the Middle Ages, the chief mint in Britain was located in the Tower of London. The British Royal Mint was founded in 1810. It continues to make coins today.

The first coins minted in Britain's North American colonies were made by John Hull in Massachusetts Bay Colony. In 1652, the Boston mint began to make coins that showed a pine tree. Pine-tree shillings and similar six-penny and three-penny coins were widely circulated in New England.

▶ THE UNITED STATES MINT

The states were permitted to coin money immediately after the Revolutionary War, but they do not have that right today. Under the Constitution, only Congress has the right to coin money and to regulate its value.

The first United States mint was established at Philadelphia, Pennsylvania, in 1792. At first the secretary of state supervised the mint. In 1799 it became an independent agency, under the president. Then, in 1873, Congress created the Bureau of the Mint, as part of the Department of the Treasury at Washington, D.C. In 1984 the bureau's name was changed to United States Mint. The director of the mint is appointed by the president.

The bureau mints 1-cent, 5-cent, 10-cent, 25-cent, 50-cent, and 1-dollar coins. It also makes the dies (engraving stamps) and tools used in minting. The bureau mints coins for some foreign governments, and it sells coin sets and commemorative medals to the general public.

The United States Mint is in charge of the mint at Philadelphia and another mint at Denver, Colorado. Coins made at Denver bear a mintmark—the letter D. The bureau also keeps the government's holdings in silver and gold bullion (bars). Gold is kept at Fort Knox, Kentucky, and silver is kept at West Point, New York. The assay office, which judges the value of ores and bullion, is located at San Francisco, California, along with the Mint Museum.

The nation's paper money is designed and printed by the Bureau of Engraving and Printing. This bureau is also a part of the Department of the Treasury.

▶ THE ROYAL CANADIAN MINT

Canada's mint began operation in 1908, as a branch of the British Royal Mint. It was called the Ottawa Mint until 1931, when it became the Royal Canadian Mint. It is headed by a seven-member board of directors, who report to Parliament. Coins for general circulation are produced at a plant in Winnipeg, Manitoba. The mint also buys and sells precious metals and produces medals, plaques, and the like.

STELLA HACKEL SIMS
Former Director, United States Mint
See also COINS AND COIN COLLECTING; MONEY.

MIRACLE PLAYS

Miracle and mystery plays have their source in the Christian church. About the year 900 an antiphonal chant (two choirs responding to each other) was added to the Easter service. Then soloists took parts and sang at the altar.

In England the first church play was called *Quem quaeritis* (*Whom Seek Ye?*). One priest was robed as an angel. Three other priests were robed as women.

"Whom seek ye in the sepulcher?" inquired the angel.

"We seek Jesus of Nazareth who was crucified, O Heavenly One," replied the women.

"He is not here. He has risen. Hallelujah!"

That was about all there was to it. It was sung in Latin. Similar plays were performed in churches throughout western Europe.

Little by little the church dramas became more elaborate. Christmas plays showed the shepherds, the wise men, and the babe in the manger. Before long the churches could not hold all the people who wished to see the plays. So the plays were moved outdoors into the church courtyards. The language of the people took the place of Latin. Comedy, at times coarse and low, entered into the plays. After a time the church prohibited the clergy from taking part.

Guilds and Cycles

In France special companies of amateur, or volunteer, actors, with some paid professionals, presented the plays. In the towns of England trade guilds took over from the church and competed with one another in preparing the productions. The different guilds used their special skills for different scenes. For instance, the shipwrights built Noah's ark while the water carriers created the Flood. The bakers put on the Last Supper. The plays developed into cycles, or groups, presenting the whole story of the Old and New Testaments.

The plays moved through the streets on pageant wagons. The wagons represented paradise, hell, places mentioned in the Old Testament, and various settings from the story of Christ's life.

In general, mystery plays were based on

In cathedral towns, such as Coventry, mystery plays were performed on wagons.

incidents mentioned in the Bible, and they concentrated on the life, death, and resurrection of Christ. Miracle plays dealt with the lives and legends of the saints. However, the terms are often used interchangeably. Gradually miracle plays turned less to the church for their material and developed into a more popular drama.

Chester, York, Coventry, and Wakefield were some of the centers in England for tradesmen's performances of miracle-play cycles. Chester is supposed to have set the example for the others sometime during the 14th century. From York came a great cycle of dramas covering the whole of Biblical history. The Wakefield-Towneley *Second Shepherds' Play* is one of the world's famous plays. Like some of the other Chester and Wakefield plays, it contains much rustic comedy. Four notable collections of English miracle plays have been preserved—the cycles belonging to York, Wakefield, and Chester and one of unknown origin. The plays date from the 14th and 15th centuries.

The English cycles were more extensive than the French, ranging from the Creation to the Day of Judgment. Some of the English plays were adaptations of French originals.

To this day in York, mystery plays are performed as they were in medieval Europe.

The French *Mystère du Viel Testament* corresponds to the English miracle-play cycles. *Adam,* written in the 12th century, is the earliest play in the French language. Few manuscripts have been preserved from other countries of Europe. Yet the tradition of the early mystery plays lives on in the Passion plays performed in Germany, Austria, and Switzerland.

Staging

The plays were sometimes elaborately staged. The settings were rich in color, and the guilds used many mechanical devices to produce thunder and spouting flame and to hide characters in the clouds or send them to hell. Portrayals of the burning and beheading of saints were extremely realistic. Floods covered the earth, and fruit grew on trees in sight of the audience.

In a stationary setting, as at Valenciennes in France, separate enclosures called mansions were grouped in a semicircle around a throne. The mansion for heaven was to the right of the throne. Hell was to the left. Large scenes took place in front of the throne, with the director, holding his book and baton, in the midst of the action. The mouth of hell was an enormous dragon's head, which was sometimes lighted with burning gunpowder. When a soul was carried into hell, the scene was usually accompanied by a great banging of pots and kettles.

When the plays were presented on pageant wagons, each play in the cycle had its own wagon and moved from station to station. At Chester there were three days of plays. At York the plays began at 4:30 in the morning.

For the most part, all the actors came on stage at once. However, when it was time for the Three Kings to enter, they rode up the street on horseback, dismounted, and presented their gifts. Most of the other actors, even Joseph's donkey and the cock that crowed for Peter, had their special places. Each actor was supposed to be invisible until it was his turn to perform. Scene shifting was unknown, so large signs marked hills and groves.

The first costumes were simply priests' robes. Later, the costumes were made fantastic to suit the taste of the people. Christ and the Apostles wore gilt wigs. Evil spirits were painted reptile-green. Souls wore black or white coats, according to their kind.

Miracle plays were taken very seriously by the actors and the spectators. The whole troupe sang a hymn before beginning. The plays represent the birth of modern drama.

ROBERT E. GARD
University of Wisconsin

A mirage of a lake appears on the hot sands of Death Valley in the California desert. The water in the lake is actually an image of the sky.

MIRAGE

Suppose you are riding along a country road on a hot day in summer. If you look ahead about a quarter of a mile, you may suddenly see a silvery lake covering the road. You may even see another car reflected in this lake, as in a mirror. When you come up to the place where you saw the lake, you find that the pavement is perfectly dry. What you saw was not really water. It was only an appearance that is called a **mirage**.

The lake seemed to be there because of something that happens to light rays passing through the air. Usually the light by which you see things travels through the air in straight lines. This is true as long as the air is all at the same temperature. But air, like most other materials, expands and becomes less dense (thinner) when it is warmed. As a result, light is bent aside when it goes from a layer of air at one temperature to a layer at a different temperature.

On a sunny day the road pavement becomes quite hot. This warms the air just above the road, while the air higher up stays cooler. Light coming down from the sky through these layers is bent upward again to your eyes. The bright patch of light looks like water.

Now suppose there is a car on the road ahead of you. You may see both the car and an upside-down mirage of it.

Some of the light rays from the car travel through air that is all at the same temperature, and so these rays are straight. They show you the car where it really is.

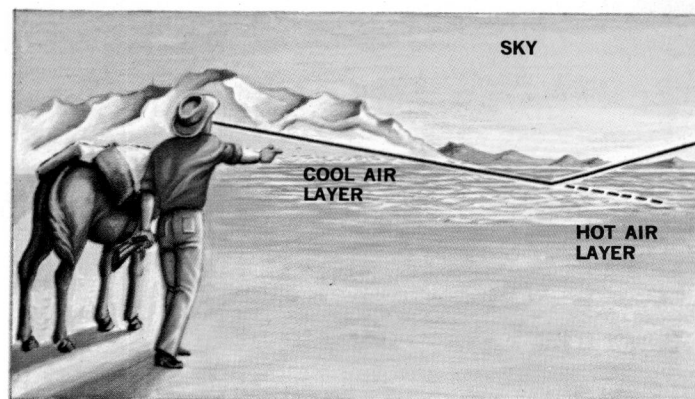

The shallow lower layer of air close to the desert sand is made very hot by the sand. The air above the lower layer is cooler. Light rays passing from the cooler layer to the hot layer of air are refracted (bent) up. They form an image of the sky that looks like a lake.

There are also some rays that reach your eyes by a different path. Rays starting downward from the car will gradually bend upward again when they enter the warmer air near the pavement. These rays come into your eyes from below, and you think you are looking at an upside-down car beneath the real one.

Mirages of this kind are often seen in hot, desert countries. There are stories of thirsty travelers in the desert who imagine they see ahead of them a refreshing pool of water, only to find that it is not really there. What they actually saw was light from the sky, bent upward by hot air just above the sand.

An opposite kind of mirage is sometimes seen over the ocean or in the polar regions. A distant ship or mountain may appear to be

The center iceberg in the distance is a looming mirage. The iceberg is actually out of sight beyond the horizon. Light rays from the iceberg are bent, forming the mirage.

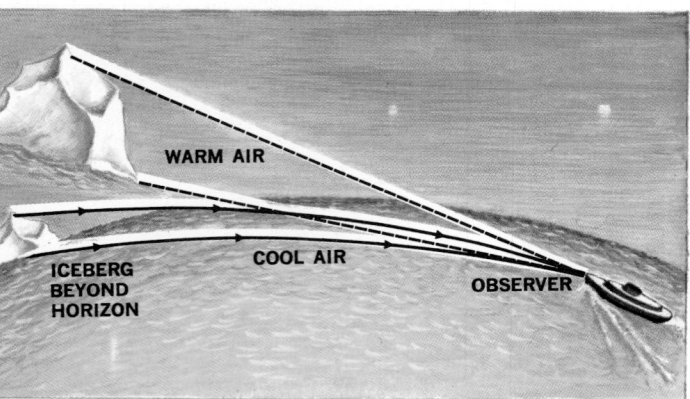

A looming mirage is formed when the layer of air near the cold ocean is cooler than the air above it. Light that usually would pass overhead is bent down, and an observer sees an image of something that may actually be over the horizon.

raised up in the sky. This kind of mirage is called **looming**. The object itself may really be out of the line of sight, below the horizon.

In a looming mirage, air near the ground or near the surface of the ocean is cooler than it is higher up. When this happens, light that would otherwise pass overhead is bent down to the eye. As a result, a person thinks he sees the distant object much nearer and taller than it really is. Travelers have told of seeing whole towns—with their trees, towers, and houses —raised high in the sky as a result of a looming mirage. This is probably where the expression "castles in the air" comes from.

There are other ways in which the air bends light and fools your eyes. These, too, are sometimes called mirages. Look across the top of a car that has been standing in the sun. Things you see in the distance appear to shimmer. The air warmed by the car roof rises and changes the direction of the light that passes through it.

The twinkling of the stars is caused by warm and cool patches of air drifting through the earth's atmosphere. That is why large observatories are usually located on mountaintops or in other places where the temperature of the air is steady, which makes the seeing good.

Astronomers are now using balloons and rockets to send telescopic cameras to great heights. With most of the atmosphere out of the way below them, these instruments are able to get much sharper and clearer pictures of the sun, planets, and stars than ever before.

The bending of light by the air makes the sun look flattened or oval when it is very low in the sky. This bending also makes the sun seem to rise about 2 minutes before it actually comes up over the horizon and keeps it in view about 2 minutes after it really has sunk below the horizon.

IRA M. FREEMAN
Rutgers—The State University

See also LENSES; LIGHT.

MIRRORS. See LIGHT.

MISSILES

Have you ever thrown a ball or shot an arrow? If so, you have launched a missile. A ball or arrow or any other object that is sent toward a target with force may be called a missile.

For modern missiles, that force is provided by the action of a rocket. **Ballistic missiles** are fitted with rockets that give them an initial push into their flight. ("Ballistic" comes from the Greek word *ballein,* meaning "to throw.") Then the rocket turns off, and the missile coasts downward toward its target, pulled by the force of gravity. Another kind of missile is powered all the way to its target by a rocket engine. This is called a **continually powered missile**.

▶ **THE STORY OF MISSILES**

Rocket missiles date back to the 1200's in China. The Chinese invented both gunpowder and the rocket. Their rockets were tubes made of bamboo or heavy paper. The tubes were closed at one end and packed with gunpowder. The Chinese lashed the tubes to arrows. When the gunpowder was set afire, the arrows sped toward the enemy. These "arrows of flying fire," as the Chinese called them, were the first rocket missiles.

The Chinese invention spread to other countries. The rockets were made larger, and explosives were placed in their tips. In the 1790's, troops of the Prince of Mysore, in India, used rocket missiles against British soldiers, killing many of them. These rockets interested an English army officer, William Congreve, who designed rockets of his own. During the War of 1812, between England and the United States, Congreve rocket missiles bombarded Fort McHenry in Baltimore, Maryland. Francis Scott Key mentioned these rockets in his poem "The Star-Spangled Banner," which became the national anthem of the United States.

These early missiles were not very safe or accurate, and big guns were used much more commonly in warfare. But after World War I, work began in many nations to improve the safety, accuracy, range, and payloads (carrying capacity) of missiles. Many people thought it was a waste of time, and in most countries the work went very slowly. There was great

A Tomahawk cruise missile is tested. Cruise missiles are one of the newest kinds of United States missiles.

interest in Germany, though, and the first modern missiles were developed and used by Germany in World War II. Several countries used rocket missiles before the war ended, but the first ballistic missile was the German V-2. Each missile carried more than half a ton of explosives. During the war, more than 1,000 V-2's were fired across the English Channel against Britain.

Since the end of World War II, there has been rapid development of both ballistic and continually powered missiles. They are used for many military purposes. Missiles of both types play a major role today in the military forces of most nations. Another very important use of ballistic missiles is to carry spacecraft into space.

▶ MISSILE DESIGN

Modern missiles contain many thousands of parts—from tiny electronic components to large structures weighing many kilograms. Most missiles have three major systems. They are propulsion, which includes the fuel, fuel

SOME IMPORTANT MISSILES *			
ROCKET	COUNTRY	RANGE	WARHEAD
SSM (surface-to-surface missiles)			
Titan II (B) †	U.S.A.	15,000 km (9,300 mi)	Nuclear
Minuteman III (B)	U.S.A.	13,000 km (8,100 mi)	Nuclear
Pershing (B)	U.S.A.	740 km (460 mi)	Nuclear
Vigilant	England	1,375 m (4,510 ft)	High explosive
Harpoon	U.S.A.	over 90 km (55 mi)	High explosive
Sego/SS-11	U.S.S.R.	10,000 km (6,200 mi)	Nuclear
SS-18	U.S.S.R.	10,500 km (6,500 mi)	Nuclear
SAM (surface-to-air missiles)			
Hawk	U.S.A.	35 km (22 mi)	High explosive
Tartar	U.S.A.	16 km (10 mi)	High explosive
Seacat	England	4.8 km (3 mi)	High explosive
Guideline/SAN-2	U.S.S.R.	43 km (27 mi)	High explosive
Gammon/SA-5	U.S.S.R.	250 km (155 mi)	High explosive
AAM (air-to-air missiles)			
Sparrow III	U.S.A.	25 km (15.5 mi)	High explosive
Red Top	England	12 km (7.4 mi)	High explosive
Matra R 530	France	18 km (11 mi)	High explosive
Sidewinder	U.S.A.	18 km (11 mi)	High explosive
Phoenix	U.S.A.	165 km (102 mi)	High explosive
Atoll/AA-2	U.S.S.R.	6.4 km (4 mi)	High explosive
Acrid/AA-6	U.S.S.R.	50 km (31 mi)	High explosive
ASM (air-to-surface missiles)			
Blue Steel	England	810 km (500 mi)	High explosive
Robot RB-04	Sweden	9.7 km (6 mi)	High explosive
Bullpup/AGM-12C	U.S.A.	17 km (10.5 mi)	High explosive
Kennel/AS-1	U.S.S.R.	90 km (56 mi)	Not known
Kangaroo/AS-3	U.S.S.R.	565 km (350 mi)	Not known
U (Underwater missiles)			
Polaris A-3 (B)	U.S.A.	4,620 km (2,870 mi)	Nuclear
Subroc (B)	U.S.A.	56 km (35 mi)	Nuclear
Asroc (B)	U.S.A.	2–10 km (1.2–6.2 mi)	Nuclear or high explosive
Poseidon C-3 (B)	U.S.A.	4,620 km (2,870 mi)	Nuclear
SS-N-8 (B)	U.S.S.R.	7,800 km (4,840 mi)	Nuclear
Serb/SS-N-5 (B)	U.S.S.R.	1,200 km (745 mi)	Nuclear

* The People's Republic of China has some important missiles, but details about them are not available.

† (B)=Ballistic missile.

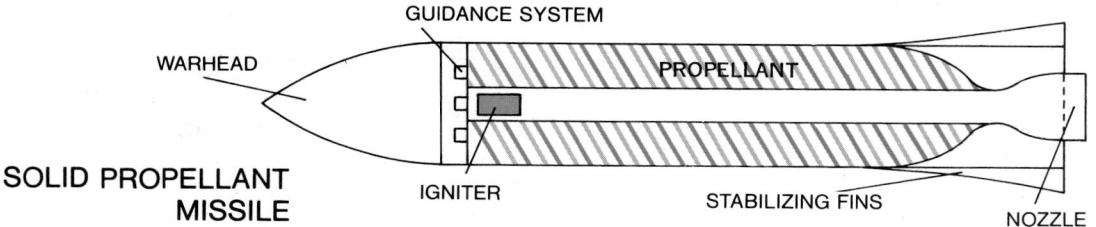

SOLID PROPELLANT MISSILE

WARHEAD · GUIDANCE SYSTEM · PROPELLANT · IGNITER · STABILIZING FINS · NOZZLE

Missiles can be powered by solid or liquid propellants. In solid-fuel missiles, propellants (fuel and oxygen) are pre-mixed. Liquid-fuel missiles are designed so that propellants are mixed during flight.

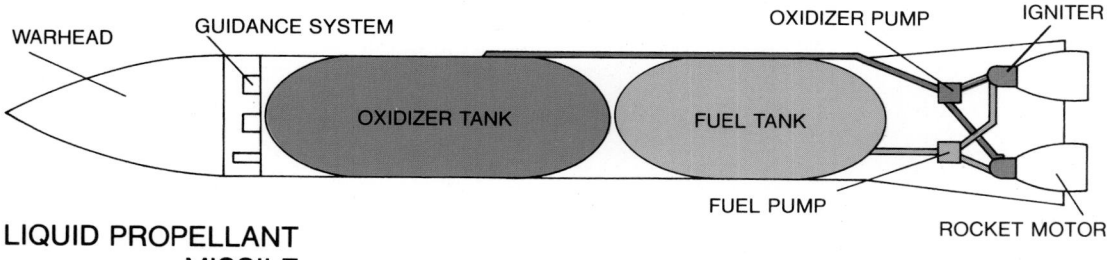

LIQUID PROPELLANT MISSILE

WARHEAD · GUIDANCE SYSTEM · OXIDIZER PUMP · IGNITER · OXIDIZER TANK · FUEL TANK · FUEL PUMP · ROCKET MOTOR

tank, and motor; the guidance and control system, which steers the missile; and the payload, which is usually the explosive warhead that blows up when the missile reaches its target. Other systems, such as the electrical system and the hydraulic system, help the major systems operate correctly.

Propulsion System

The purpose of the propulsion system is to provide the missile with forward motion. The needed energy is stored in the fuel carried by the missile. The energy of the fuel is released during **combustion**, or burning. Combustion is a chemical reaction between the fuel and oxygen. For this reason, both fuel and oxygen are needed to power a rocket. Missiles that fly in the atmosphere at low altitudes can use the oxygen in the air for burning. They are called **air-breathing missiles**. But missiles that fly higher than about 20 kilometers (12 miles) cannot get enough oxygen from the thin air. Such missiles must carry a chemical substance, called an oxidizer, that supplies the necessary oxygen.

Missile Motor. There are two main parts to the missile motor, the combustion chamber and the nozzle. The fuel is burned in the combustion chamber. As the fuel burns, very hot, rapidly moving gases are produced. These gases rush out through the nozzle at the rear of the missile, pushing it forward. Air coming out of an inflated balloon moves the balloon forward in just the same way.

Missile Fuels. Missiles can use **liquid fuels**, like gasoline or kerosene, or **solid fuels**, which can be a mixture of plastic, powdered metal, flammable chemicals, and other dry substances. Fuels and oxidizers are sometimes grouped together and called **propellants**. Solid fuels are easier to store in a missile and are safer. Many liquid fuels contain more energy than a solid fuel of the same volume. Solid fuels were used in all practical missiles until World War II. These early missiles were small and did not need to be very powerful.

Robert Goddard, the pioneer of rocketry in the United States, had flown the first liquid-fuel missile in the 1920's. But liquid-fuel missiles were not used in war until the 1940's. These missiles were the German V-2 rockets. The V-2 used alcohol as the fuel and liquid oxygen as the oxidizer. Some of the early United States missiles, like the Atlas, used kerosene and liquid oxygen as a propellant.

Liquid fuels are very complicated to use. Engines that burn liquids must have many more parts than those that burn solids. Many of these parts are very complicated, expensive to build, and difficult to keep in good working order. It also takes much more time to prepare a liquid-fuel missile for launching

A missile guides itself to a target by sensing the target's heat radiation.

than it does to prepare a solid-fuel missile. To overcome these difficulties, scientists and engineers have developed efficient solid propellants. Today most large missiles, such as the U.S. Minuteman and Poseidon, use solid propellants. Solid propellants are mixed with a compound similar to rubber and poured into a metal or plastic container, where they are allowed to harden. An open space is left in the center, where the burning takes place.

Guidance and Control System

Some missiles are unguided. They have fins, like feathers on an arrow. They are pointed in the direction they are meant to go and then are fired. The pressure of the air on the fins keeps these missiles on a steady course. Once such a missile is on its way, nothing controls or steers it.

But most modern missiles have some kind of guidance system. In ballistic missiles, the guidance operates during the early part of the missile's flight. In continually guided rocket missiles, the guidance system controls the motion of the missile all the way from launch to target.

Guided missiles operate very much as you do when you are going to a certain place. Imagine that you want to go to the supermarket. You start along the street. You know exactly where the supermarket is—it is around the corner from the drugstore. When you see the drugstore, you turn the corner. Then you look for the supermarket's red sign. When you see the sign, you head toward it and enter the supermarket.

Inertial Guidance. As you walked toward the drugstore and then toward the sign, parts of your brain and your eye helped you keep a straight course. Many missiles are kept on a straight course by a guidance system called inertial guidance. This system is made up of devices that can keep track of the distance the missile has traveled and the changes of direction it has made. By comparing the actual path the missile has traveled with the path it must follow to reach the target, the missile "brain," or computer, guides the missile to its target.

Landmark Sensors. Another missile guidance system guides the missile to a target by providing it with a way to "recognize" landmarks in the way the human eye recognizes the corner drugstore and the supermarket signs. In the case of a missile, such landmarks could be mountaintops, rivers, lakes, roads, and railroad tracks. Your brain knows about the familiar landmarks of the neighborhood because it has stored them in a kind of visual map. The missile brain, or computer, knows about the landmarks the missile must recognize because a computer operator has put the coded map information or coded distance information into the computer. The information may say, for example, "Go past three mountains, each a little higher than the last, then turn east," or "The target is 400 kilometers (250 miles) away."

But of course, knowing about these guidance clues is not enough. There must be a way to detect them and recognize them. As you travel toward the supermarket, your eyes see, or sense, the drugstore and the red sign. A signal then moves from your eyes to your brain. And the brain sends out a signal that orders certain muscles in your body to move, or steer, you in a certain direction.

The missile's sensor is like your eyes. It may be radar, a small television camera, or another device that helps it locate landmarks. When the sensor tells the missile's computer that the missile is over a landmark, the computer may decide that it is time to change course. If so, it sends electric signals to the steering devices in the missile that then change its direction.

Steering Systems. There are two basic types of missile steering systems. One system is used in missiles that travel in the atmosphere. It involves moving fins at the end of the missile. Air rushing against the fins changes the direction of the missile. But where the air is very thin or does not exist at all, a rocket steering system is used. The nozzle of the main rocket is moved, so that it points in a direction exactly opposite to the new direction the missile must follow. This makes the gases produced by the burning fuel also move in exactly the opposite direction. Then the force of the rushing gases makes the missile move in the new direction. Another rocket steering system involves firing small rockets built into the sides of the missile.

Missiles may use many combinations of the different guidance devices. Ballistic missiles are guided during the first part of their flight by an inertial guidance system. When the computer on the missile decides that the guidance system has put the missile in the right direction at the right speed, the engines shut off, and the guidance system stops working. From then on, the missile is pulled toward the earth by the force of gravity. If the guidance system has worked properly, the missile is nearing the target area, and it dives directly toward the target.

The biggest missiles are usually ballistic missiles. They may have to travel to targets as far away as 10,500 kilometers (6,500 miles). The Minuteman and the Poseidon are ballistic missiles.

Smaller missiles are usually guided all the way to their target. One such missile, the **cruise missile**, has an inertial guidance system as well as a sensor and a computer with map information. This system allows the missile to follow the contours of the terrain it flies over. For example, the cruise missile can fly just over the tops of mountains and then drop down low over valley floors. Because it can fly so low, the cruise missile is difficult to detect on the radar screens of an enemy. This missile can be launched from a plane, submarine, or ship or from the ground and still find its target thousands of kilometers away.

Homing Devices. Another kind of missile guidance system is the homing device. Homing devices enable a missile to follow a trail in much the same way that a bloodhound follows a smell. For the missile, the trail may be light, heat, or some other kind of energy given off by the target. If, for example, the target is much brighter or warmer than the surrounding area, the missile could home in on it. Homing may be the only guidance system for a short-range missile—one that must travel a short distance. Long-range missiles may be guided by homing devices during the last part of the flight.

Payloads or Warheads

The type of warhead carried by a missile depends on the purpose of the missile. Very early missiles did not carry an explosive. They depended on the weight of the missile to do damage when the missile itself hit the target. During World War II, missiles had warheads consisting of explosives similar to dynamite. Most small missiles today have this type of warhead. They explode either when they hit the target or when they sense that they are close to it.

Large missiles today carry nuclear warheads. Sometimes one missile can carry more than one warhead. These warheads rain down on the target, all falling in an area a few hundred meters in diameter. Such a warhead system is called a MRV (*m*ultiple *r*e-entry *v*ehicle) system. Another missile system involves a cluster of warheads, each of which can hit a separate target. The targets may be many kilometers apart. This warhead system is called a MIRV (*m*ultiple *i*ndependently *t*argeted *r*e-entry *v*ehicle) system. For example, each submarine-launched Poseidon missile can carry as many as 14 MIRV warheads. This means that one Poseidon missile could strike 14 different targets.

Smaller missiles can carry less powerful nuclear warheads, but even these can do a great deal of damage. None of these missiles has ever been used against an enemy. But they are the most powerful weapons that any nation has, and many people consider them an important measure of military strength.

▶ **TYPES OF MISSILES**

Missiles are classified in several different ways. A missile can be either a defensive weapon or an offensive weapon. Missiles are also classified according to their launch and target locations.

A United States Army gunner fires a Redeye surface-to-air missile from a shoulder launcher.

Defensive or Offensive Classification

A missile meant to be fired from a ship at an attacking plane would be a defensive missile. A large missile meant to be fired at a city or a factory could be called an offensive, or attack, weapon. A missile could be defensive or offensive, depending on the mission of the ship or plane from which it is launched.

Launch and Target Classifications

In the United States, it is common to designate this classification by a series of letters. The first letter stands for the launch site of the missile. The second letter stands for the location of the missile's target. The first and second letters are either S, A, or U. An S means the surface of the earth or of the ocean. A stands for air, and U means underwater. The third letter in this system is simply M, for missile. So SSM, for example, is a surface-to-surface missile. It may be launched from the ground toward a target on the ground, or it may be launched from a ship toward a target on the ground.

SSM—Surface-to-Surface Missiles. This group includes the very largest rockets, such as the **intercontinental ballistic missiles** (ICBM's). These are missiles that can travel from continent to continent. They are guided only while gaining speed. An ICBM can carry nuclear warheads. The Soviet SS-18, for example, can carry a nuclear charge with destructive power equal to that of 25,000,000 tons of TNT. It can deliver this incredible destructive force to a target as far as 10,500 kilometers (6,500 miles) away. ICBM's are stored underground in structures called silos to protect them from enemy attack. Many small surface-to-surface missiles are designed for use against tanks, fortifications, and troops. These are mostly continually guided rockets that carry a high-explosive warhead.

SAM—Surface-to-Air Missiles. Surface-to-air, or anti-aircraft, missiles are meant as defensive weapons against enemy planes. Some SAM's, such as the French missile Roland, are placed on mobile launching platforms that can be moved to stay with the tanks they protect.

The United States has a SAM, called Redeye, that can be carried by soldiers very much like a rifle. It is fired from a tube held on the shoulder. The missile homes to the engine heat of low-flying planes.

AAM—Air-to-Air Missiles. Air-to-air missiles are launched by planes toward other planes. Most AAM's have guidance systems that use radar or heat homing sensors to steer the missiles to the other airplane. These missiles usually carry high explosives. The Phoenix of the United States is the most capable air-to-air missile in the world today.

ASM—Air-to-Surface Missiles. ASM's are used by aircraft to attack targets on the ground or on water. Some are used only on targets the pilot can see. The Shrike, which delivers a high-explosive warhead, is such a missile. It was used by the United States in Vietnam and by the Israelis during the 1973 Israeli-Arab War. Other ASM's, such as the nuclear-armed SRAM, a United States Air Force missile, might be called flying bombs. A bomber pilot could launch one or two of them at a point 60 to 160 kilometers (40 to 100 miles) from the target. The missile, using inertial guidance, could then go on to deliver the nuclear warhead by itself while the plane returned to its base. The new cruise missile now being developed by the United States can do the same, traveling to a target as far as 2,500 kilometers (1,550 miles) away from its launch point.

U Missiles. The Polaris, a U missile of the United States, is a long-range ballistic missile that can be fired from a submerged submarine. Each Polaris nuclear submarine carries 16 such missiles and can launch them all within five minutes or so. Polaris missiles, equipped

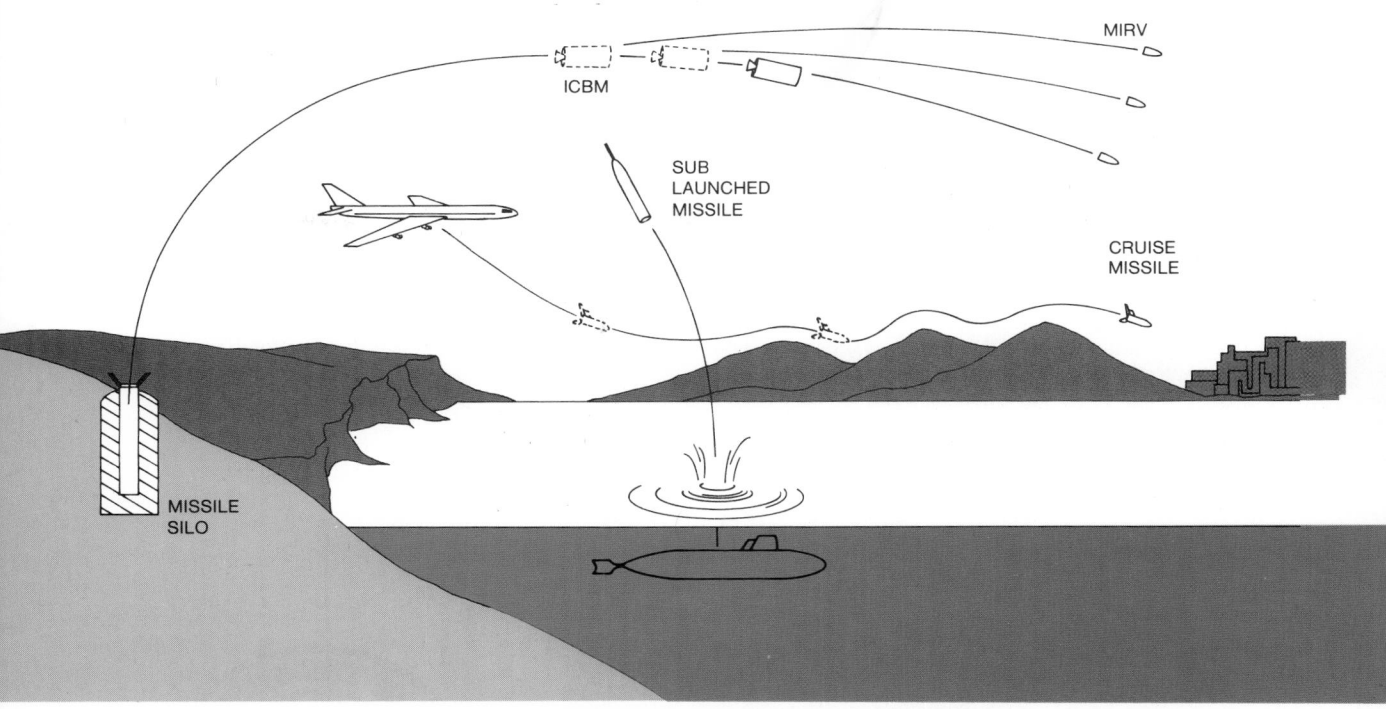

Left to right: An ICBM missile, carrying three warheads (MIRV's) is fired from a silo. A cruise missile is fired from a plane. A submarine-launched missile takes flight.

with MRV warheads, can reach surface targets as far as 4,000 kilometers (2,500 miles) away.

The Poseidon is an improved underwater missile of the United States. Poseidon missiles have a greater accuracy than the Polaris missiles, and they can be fitted with a 14-MIRV warhead.

Cruise Missiles

The United States is developing a new long-range, continually guided cruise missile. The new missile can carry a nuclear warhead almost as far as a ballistic missile. There are three basic types of cruise missiles—ALCM, an air-launched cruise missile; GLCM, a ground-launched cruise missile; and SLCM, a sea-launched cruise missile. All these cruise missiles are different variations of a basic cruise missile developed by the U.S. Navy and originally meant to be a submarine-launched cruise missile.

▶ AN EQUAL THREAT

Any one missile is useful only for a relatively short period of time. Improvements in propulsion, guidance and control, structure, and warheads are made so fast that one type of missile is replaced by a better one in a very few years.

Improvements in missiles have brought us all to the frightening vision of death and destruction. It is now possible to send thousands of powerful nuclear warheads from one continent to another. Many people have begun to realize that most of the life on earth could be killed just by pushing the launching buttons of the U.S. and Soviet ballistic missiles. With this in mind, leaders of the nations possessing the most dangerous weapons have signed agreements that limit the number of nuclear-armed missiles each can have. The goal has been to make certain that no nation has more nuclear weapons than any other. So far, this equalization of nuclear weapons has kept nations from using them.

Without quite realizing what has been happening, people now find themselves and their way of life trapped and threatened by the nuclear weapons they have made. The weapons remain only a threat—so far. But as missiles are improved, it will be necessary to conclude new agreements, keeping the threat so nearly equal for all that the deadly buttons that send forth nuclear destruction will never be pushed.

KOSTA M. TSIPIS
Massachusetts Institute of Technology
See also ROCKETS.

MISSISSIPPI

The Natchez Trace is a famous historic road joining Natchez, Mississippi, and Nashville, Tennessee. The trace began as a series of connected trails made by the Choctaw and Chickasaw Indians. Later, both crews floated goods down the Ohio and Mississippi rivers to ports on the Gulf Coast. The flatboats used could not float upstream so they were sold as lumber, and the crews used the road to walk or ride horses back to their homes in Ohio, Kentucky, and other states to the north. During this time the trace was called the Boatman's Road.

In 1802 the trace was improved by the United States Army, so that the mail could be moved along it more quickly. It was then referred to as the Post Road. By 1811 the first steamboat sailed upstream to Cincinnati, Ohio. With increasing use of steamboats, the Post Road was no longer needed, and by 1830 it was just a memory. Since 1830 the road has been known as the Natchez Trace.

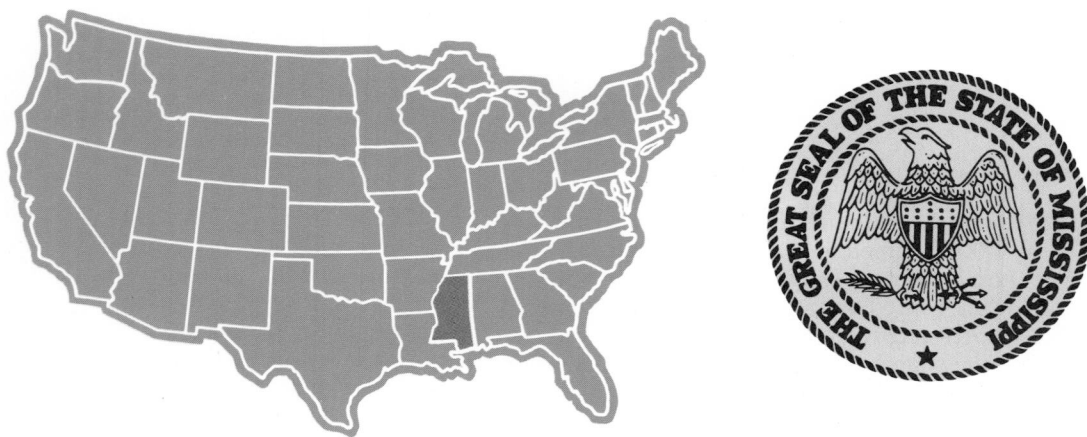

Mississippi takes its unusual name from the Mississippi River, which forms most of its western boundary. It is nicknamed the Magnolia State after the magnolia tree. It is also called the Hospitality State.

The lands along the Mississippi River are the best agricultural lands in the state. But they are low-lying, and people in the area have lived in dread of floods. After an especially disastrous flood in 1927 the federal government took responsibility for flood control. Large dams were built on tributaries of the Mississippi in the northern part of the state. Behind the dams are large reservoirs to store water in times of heavy rainfall. In drier times water is released, and in this way floods are controlled.

Although it has areas of low, flat land, Mississippi is mainly hilly. The highest point is Woodall Mountain, near the place where the Tennessee River makes a nick in the northeast corner of the state. From this area the land slopes southwestward to the Mississippi River and southward to the Gulf of Mexico. In between are strips of prairie and great stretches of hills with woodlands and farms.

Some of the farms are large and are equipped with the most modern machines. Others are small farms. For generations, cotton has been the main crop in Mississippi. Soybeans now rank second and occupy much more land than cotton. Rice, grain sorghum, and wheat are also important crops. Beef cattle and poultry are major sources of income.

Farming is still important in Mississippi, but manufacturing now exceeds agriculture in value. The number of factories has grown steadily since the 1930's, when the state began a campaign to attract new industries. Most of the industries make use of Mississippi's own raw materials—petroleum, agricultural products, and pulpwood and lumber.

▶THE LAND

Mississippi is located in the south central part of the United States. It is roughly rectangular in shape, except for a short, broad panhandle in the southeast. This panhandle gives Mississippi a coastline on Mississippi Sound, an arm of the Gulf of Mexico.

Landforms

Almost all of Mississippi is included in a large region of the United States known as the Coastal Plain. A small part of the northeast corner of the state lies in the Interior Low Plateau. The state can be divided into two land classes based on topography—the Lowlands and the Hill Lands.

The Lowlands form five regions. The largest is the Mississippi Alluvial Plain. These lands along the Mississippi River were deposited as the stream overflowed its banks. Mississippians call the region the Delta. The land is very fertile because of the rich topsoil deposited there by the river. Much of the state's cotton, soybeans, and wheat and all of its rice are grown in the Delta.

Three other Lowland regions form narrow strips of land that angle across the state. They are the Jackson Prairie, the Flatwoods, and the Black Prairie. These lands are called prairies

STATE FLAG.

STATE TREE: Southern magnolia.

STATE FLOWER: Magnolia blossom.

STATE BIRD: Mockingbird.

MISSISSIPPI

CAPITAL: Jackson.

STATEHOOD: December 10, 1817; the 20th state.

SIZE: 47,689 sq mi (123,515 km²); rank, 32nd.

POPULATION: 2,520,638 (1980 census); rank, 31st.

ORIGIN OF NAME: From Indian words meaning "big river"; applied first to the river, then to the state.

ABBREVIATIONS: Miss.; MS.

NICKNAME: Magnolia State.

STATE SONG: "Go, Mississippi," by Houston Davis.

STATE MOTTO: *Virtute et armis* (By valor and arms).

STATE SEAL: An eagle, the emblem of the United States, appears in the center of the seal. In its talons it holds an olive branch and a bundle of arrows—symbols of peace and war. A single star appears in the border at the bottom.

STATE FLAG: A square of red in the upper left-hand corner contains 13 white stars on a cross of blue. The stars stand for the original 13 states. The field of the flag is made up of three horizontal bands—blue, white, and red.

Mississippi's rivers were once the state's major highways, and steamboats its most common means of shipping goods. Today steamboats carry more tourists than cotton.

because much of their area was once covered with grass. The black soil was very fertile, and at one time cotton was important there. Now these lowlands are used mostly for raising beef cattle. The Coastal Pine Meadows occupy a narrow strip of coastal plain along the Gulf of Mexico. The plain is composed mostly of sand and silt. The region is one of the major resort areas of the state.

The Hill Lands also are five in number, but they cover more area than the Lowlands. The Loess-Bluff Hills parallel the Mississippi River and lie east of the Delta. Loess is a fine-grained silt, blown from the edge of the glaciers thousands of years ago. The structure of the material causes it to stand in vertical bluffs. The picturesque bluffs at Vicksburg and Natchez are composed of loess.

The Pine Hills overlie much of the southern part of the state. Once this region was covered with longleaf pine, and many pine trees still grow there. Mississippians call the region the Piney Woods. The North Central Hills are much higher than the Pine Hills. The Pontotoc Ridge lies between two lowlands. Water on the eastern side of the ridge flows into the Tennessee and Tombigbee rivers. Water on the western side drains into Mississippi River. The Tennessee River Hills is the highest upland in Mississippi. Tributary streams of the Tennessee River have cut narrow ravines in the uplands and flow in short, swift courses to the east.

Rivers, Lakes, and Coastal Waters

Abundant year-round rainfall gives Mississippi many rivers and streams. The major river of the state is the Mississippi. It serves as most of the western boundary and then continues southward through the state of Louisiana to the Gulf of Mexico. Its tributaries in the state of Mississippi include the Homochitto, the Big Black, and the Yazoo. The Yazoo is formed by the joining of the Tallahatchie and the Yalobusha rivers.

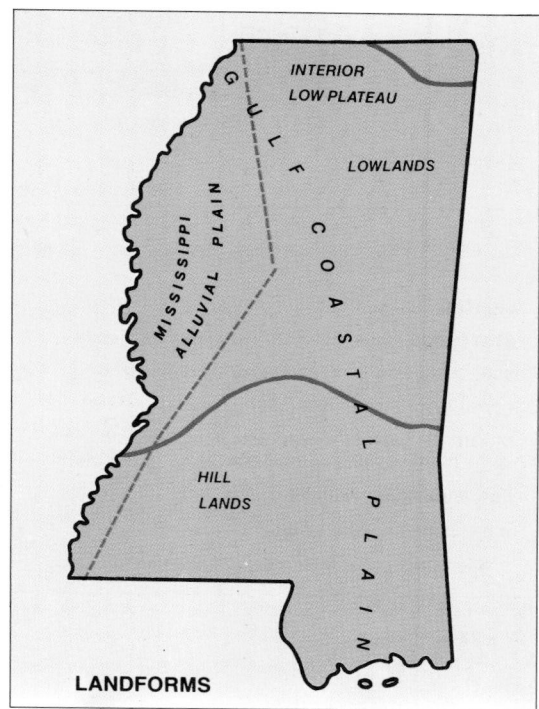

INTERIOR LOW PLATEAU

LOWLANDS

MISSISSIPPI ALLUVIAL PLAIN

GULF COASTAL PLAIN

HILL LANDS

LANDFORMS

Most of the other rivers flow directly into the Gulf of Mexico. These include the Pearl, which forms the western border of the panhandle, and the Pascagoula. The Tombigbee River flows from northeastern Mississippi into Alabama and then continues southward. Small streams called bayous are found along the Mississippi River and the Gulf Coast.

Mississippi has no large natural lakes. But along the Mississippi River, especially north of Vicksburg, there are many oxbow lakes, created when the river changes its course and the original channel is left as a lake.

Levees (artificial banks) have been built along the Mississippi and other rivers. Levees help to keep the rivers from overflowing and causing disastrous floods. Dams have also been built as part of a flood-control system. Their reservoirs are spillways to hold excess water during heavy rains and floods. These reservoirs are used for swimming, fishing, and boating. Northern Mississippi has several large reservoirs on tributaries of the Mississippi River. In the northeast corner of the state is Pickwick Landing Reservoir, also called Pickwick Lake. It is one of a series of lakes on the Tennessee River and is a part of the Tennessee Valley Authority.

Also in the northeast corner of the state is the Tennessee-Tombigbee Waterway, a project completed in 1985 to stimulate the area's economy by increasing shipping. The waterway links the Tennessee River to the Gulf of Mexico through a 234-mile (377-kilometer) system of locks and canals.

Mississippi's coastline is only 44 miles (71 kilometers) long. But numerous bays, rivers and creeks make the tidal shoreline much longer. A number of islands parallel the coast just offshore. They are separated from the mainland by the Mississippi Sound. The largest are Petit Bois, Horn, Ship, and Cat islands.

Climate

Mississippi is located in the humid subtropics and has a warm, moist climate. Rainfall decreases from south to north. Annual totals range between 48 and 66 inches (1,210 and 1,680 millimeters). The greatest rainfall occurs during the winter months, and fall is the state's driest season. Temperatures are mild in winter and hot in summer. The average annual temperature varies from 61°F (16°C) in the north to 68°F (20°C) along the coast. Summer

temperatures reach the mid-eighties (Fahrenheit) and frequently the nineties.

Mississippi is prone to tornadoes in the spring. Hurricanes may occur during the summer and fall, and thunderstorms are present throughout the year. Snow and ice storms occur infrequently in the south and more often in the north.

Natural Resources

Mississippi's natural resources include fertile soils, forests, water, oil and gas, lignite, and sand and gravel.

Soils. The most productive soils are those in the Delta and loess bluff areas of the state. These soils are made up mainly of alluvial and

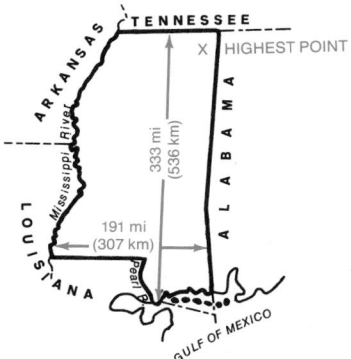

THE LAND

LOCATION: Latitude—30° 10′ N to 35° N. **Longitude**—88° 06′ W to 91° 39′ W.
Tennessee to the north, Alabama to the east, the Gulf of Mexico and part of Louisiana to the south, the Mississippi River on the west forming the boundary with Arkansas and the rest of Louisiana.

ELEVATION: Highest—Woodall Mountain, 806 ft (245 m). **Lowest**—Sea level, along the Gulf of Mexico.

LANDFORMS: Lowland and Hill Lands.

SURFACE WATERS: Major rivers—Yazoo, Big Black, and Homochitto, all draining southwestward into the Mississippi; Pearl, Pascagoula, and Tombigbee, all draining southward into the Gulf of Mexico. **Major lakes**—Sardis, Grenada, Enid, Arkabutla, Ross Barnett.

CLIMATE: Temperature—January average, 44 to 48°F (7 to 9°C) in the north; 50 to 54°F (10 to 13°C) in the south. July average, 81°F (27°C) in the north, 82°F (28°C) in the south. **Precipitation**—Annual average 48–66 in (1,210–1,680 mm). Small amounts of snow or sleet fall on some part of the state almost every year. **Growing season**—Varies from more than 180 days in the north to about 280 days in the southern panhandle.

eolian deposits—material deposited by the rivers and the wind. They produce abundant crops year after year. The soils in the hilly areas and the prairies are less fertile. Constant use of the land for growing cotton has further reduced the fertility of these soils, and erosion has carried much topsoil away. A soil conservation program begun in the 1930's has helped farmers to improve their use of the land. Pasture for livestock is one of Mississippi's major land sources.

Forests. More than half the state is covered by forest lands. Pine, cedar, oak, and hickory are the most important trees in the uplands. Water oak, gum, cypress, tupelo, and cottonwood trees are the most numerous in the lowlands. The major commercial forests are in the southern part of the state and include the famed Piney Woods area. Pine trees there provide resin, turpentine, pulp, and other products, as well as lumber. A tree-planting program started in the 1930's has made Mississippi a leading tree-farm state. Modern forestry practices assure an abundant supply of timber for the future.

Minerals. The most important mineral in the state is petroleum, first produced in 1939. Natural gas was first produced from fields at Amory in 1926. The area along the Gulf Coast contains many salt domes—masses of salt that have pushed through the sedimentary rock. The salt can be used to make table salt and various chemicals. Some of the domes have been chosen as possible sites for underground storage of nuclear wastes. Other minerals found in the state include lignite, sand and gravel, bauxite, limestone, and clays.

Fish and Game. The Mississippi Sound provides excellent breeding and feeding grounds for many kinds of fish and shellfish. Biloxi is the center of the fishing industry. It is especially famous for shrimp. Other major commercial seafoods are menhaden, red snapper, crabs, oysters, and spotted sea trout. People come to the Gulf Coast to enjoy deep-sea fishing for redfish, marlin, and dozens of other varieties of game fish.

Streams and lakes are well stocked with black bass, perch, catfish, and bream. For hunters there are many public hunting areas populated by deer, wild turkey, dove, quail, and numerous small fur-bearing animals.

▶ **THE PEOPLE AND THEIR WORK**

The first Europeans in the Mississippi area were the Spanish. They were followed by the French. During the Revolutionary War many Tories—colonists who favored England—moved from the colonies along the Atlantic coast to southwestern Mississippi. The great migrations came after the Louisiana Purchase in 1803 and after treaties with Mississippi's Indian peoples (1801–32) opened their lands for settlement. Most of the people came from older parts of the South, seeking fresh cotton lands. The Indians, except for 3,000 Choctaw, were moved to lands west of the Mississippi River. Descendants of those Choctaw Indians still live in east central Mississippi.

The first blacks in Mississippi were brought as slaves during colonial days. At present the largest proportion (about 35 percent) of the state's total population is black. However, this percentage has begun to decrease.

Where the People Live

Most Mississippians still live on farms or in small towns rather than in urban areas (places of 2,500 or more), although the percentage of urban residents has been increasing. Hinds County, where the capital city is located, is the state's most densely populated county.

Industries and Products

Before the 1930's most Mississippians earned their living either from farming or from lumbering. There were few industries that produced manufactured goods. In 1936 the state began the BAWI (Balance Agriculture with Industry) program. The number of new industries has grown steadily under the program.

POPULATION

TOTAL: 2,520,638 (1980 census). **Density**—53.4 persons to each square mile (20.6 persons to each square kilometer).

GROWTH SINCE 1800

Year	Population	Year	Population
1800	7,600	1920	1,790,618
1830	136,621	1940	2,183,796
1860	791,305	1970	2,216,994
1890	1,289,600	1980	2,520,638

Gain Between 1970 and 1980—13.7 percent.

CITIES: Population of Mississippi's largest cities according to the 1980 census.

Jackson	202,895	Pascagoula	29,318
Biloxi	49,311	Columbus	27,383
Meridian	46,577	Vicksburg	25,434
Hattiesburg	40,829	Tupelo	23,905
Greenville	40,613	Natchez	22,015
Gulfport	39,676	Laurel	21,897

Agriculture. The early settlers around Natchez grew rice, cotton, tobacco, and flax. The invention of the cotton gin by Eli Whitney in the early 1790's led planters to increase their cotton acreage. In 1806 an improved type of seed was introduced, and cotton was established in Mississippi. Some cotton is grown in almost every part of the state, but the Delta is the chief cotton-growing area.

The boll weevil first attacked Mississippi's cotton in the early 1900's. Year after year the cotton crop was badly damaged by the weevil. As a result many farmers, with the help of agricultural scientists, began to grow a wider variety of crops and to raise livestock. Poultry is now the leading food-producing industry in the state, and beef-cattle production is increasing.

Cotton is still the leading crop in terms of value, but soybeans now rank second. Both rice and grain sorghum are high in value, yet they do not occupy as much land as wheat. Corn, sweet potatoes, and peanuts are among the other crops now grown on land that was once wholly taken up by cotton. Southern Mississippi is a leading producer of cabbages, Irish potatoes, watermelon, and other early vegetables for northern markets. Wiggins is known as the "pickle-packing kingdom" for its production and processing of cucumbers.

WHAT MISSISSIPPI PRODUCES

MANUFACTURED GOODS: Transportation equipment, lumber and wood products, electric and electronic equipment, processed foods, chemicals and related products, clothing, nonelectrical machinery, fabricated metal products, paper and related products.

AGRICULTURAL PRODUCTS: Soybeans, cotton, cattle and calves, broilers, milk, eggs, rice, grain sorghum.

MINERALS: Petroleum (accounting for about two thirds of the total value of mineral production), natural gas, sand and gravel, clays, cement.

Peaches and other fruits are also being grown in this area. Plums, pecans, apples, and pears are grown in different parts of the state.

Manufacturing. In early times the forests of Mississippi were used chiefly for lumber. The pine forests in the Piney Woods section produced large quantities of naval stores—tar, turpentine, rosin, and pitch. The new wood-using industries turn out many different items. Chief among them are paper and paper products, furniture, and processed wood products, such as fiberboard. Laurel, Moss Point, and Hattiesburg are among the leading wood-products centers.

The Marine Division of Litton Industries is the state's largest manufacturing concern. This shipyard, located in Jackson County, special-

Shrimp fishing is a major industry along Mississippi's Gulf Coast. Biloxi's annual Shrimp Festival and blessing of the fleet ceremony is a popular tourist attraction.

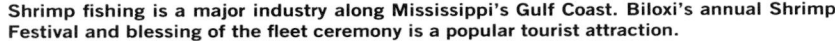

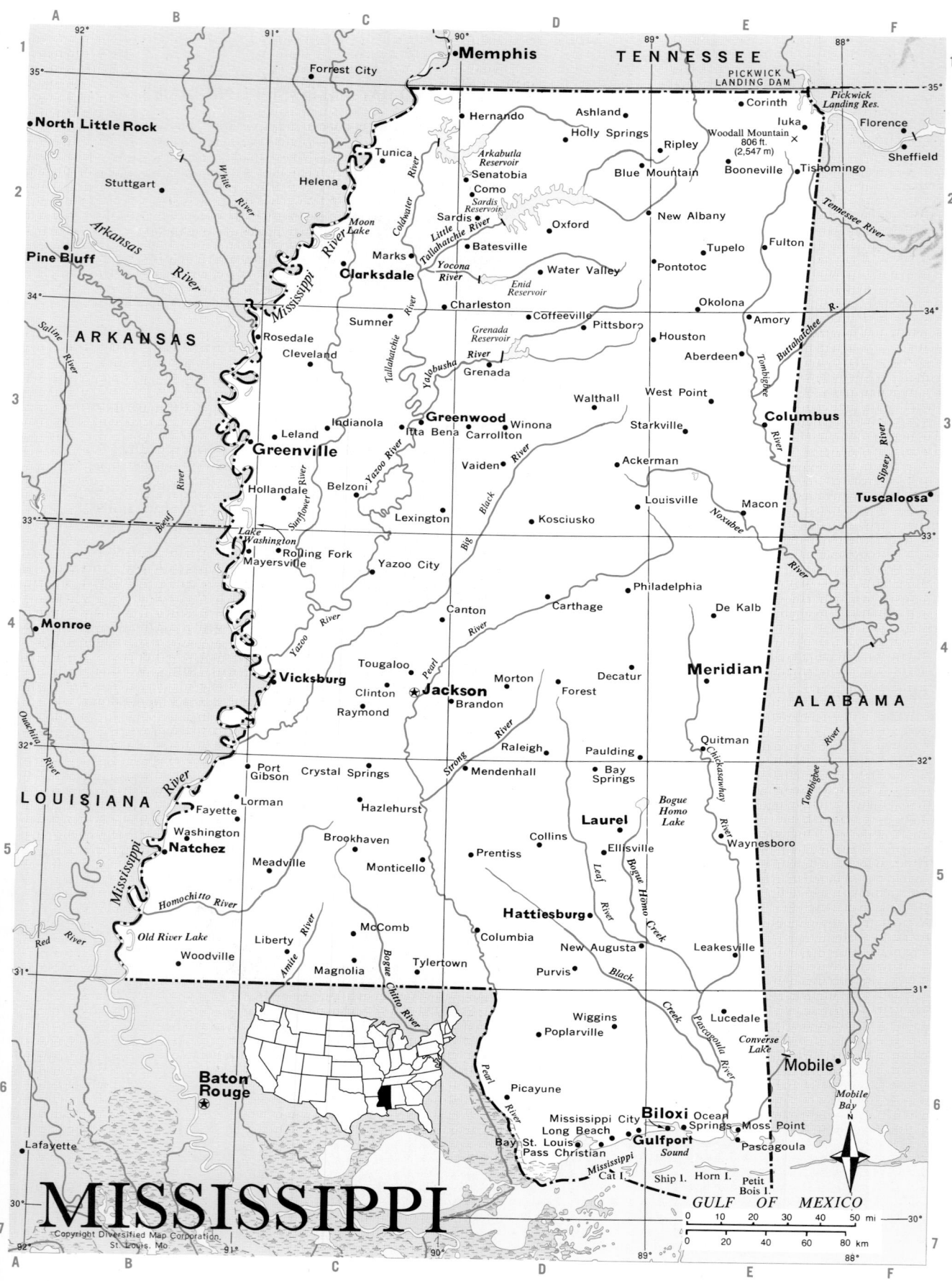

MISSISSIPPI

TENNESSEE

ARKANSAS

LOUISIANA

ALABAMA

GULF OF MEXICO

PICKWICK LANDING DAM

Pickwick Landing Res.

- Memphis
- Forrest City
- North Little Rock
- Hernando
- Ashland
- Holly Springs
- Corinth
- Iuka
- Florence
- Woodall Mountain 806 ft. (2,547 m) ×
- Sheffield
- Tunica
- Senatobia
- Ripley
- Booneville
- Tishomingo
- Helena
- Como
- Blue Mountain
- Stuttgart
- Arkabutla Reservoir
- Sardis Reservoir
- Sardis
- Oxford
- New Albany
- Tupelo
- Fulton
- Marks
- Batesville
- Pontotoc
- Clarksdale
- Water Valley
- Pine Bluff
- Charleston
- Coffeeville
- Okolona
- Amory
- Sumner
- Pittsboro
- Houston
- Aberdeen
- Rosedale
- Enid Reservoir
- Cleveland
- Grenada Reservoir
- Grenada
- West Point
- Columbus
- Indianola
- Greenwood
- Winona
- Walthall
- Starkville
- Tuscaloosa
- Leland
- Itta Bena
- Carrollton
- Greenville
- Vaiden
- Ackerman
- Macon
- Hollandale
- Belzoni
- Louisville
- Lexington
- Kosciusko
- Lake Washington
- Rolling Fork
- Yazoo City
- Philadelphia
- Mayersville
- De Kalb
- Monroe
- Canton
- Carthage
- Tougaloo
- Morton
- Decatur
- Meridian
- Vicksburg
- Clinton
- Jackson
- Brandon
- Forest
- Raymond
- Raleigh
- Paulding
- Quitman
- Port Gibson
- Crystal Springs
- Mendenhall
- Bay Springs
- Lorman
- Bogue Homo Lake
- Fayette
- Hazlehurst
- Washington
- Laurel
- Natchez
- Brookhaven
- Collins
- Ellisville
- Waynesboro
- Meadville
- Monticello
- Prentiss
- Liberty
- McComb
- Columbia
- Hattiesburg
- New Augusta
- Leakesville
- Woodville
- Magnolia
- Tylertown
- Purvis
- Lucedale
- Old River Lake
- Wiggins
- Converse Lake
- Poplarville
- Mobile
- Lafayette
- Baton Rouge
- Picayune
- Mississippi City
- Biloxi
- Ocean Springs
- Moss Point
- Long Beach
- Gulfport
- Pascagoula
- Bay St. Louis
- Pass Christian
- Mobile Bay

Rivers: White River, Arkansas River, Saline River, Mississippi River, Coldwater River, Little Tallahatchie River, Yocona River, Tallahatchie River, Yalobusha River, Tennessee River, Tombigbee River, Buttahatchee R., Sipsey River, Noxubee River, Sunflower River, Yazoo River, Big Black River, Pearl River, Strong River, Ouachita River, Chickasawhay River, Tombigbee River, Homochitto River, Leaf River, Bogue Homo Creek, Amite River, Bogue Chitto River, Black Creek, Pascagoula River, Red River, Moon River Lake, Boeuf River

Moon Lake

Cat I. Ship I. Horn I. Petit Bois I.

Mississippi Sound

N

INDEX TO MISSISSIPPI MAP

izes, plastics, and textiles. Military bases, such as Keesler Air Force Base and Meridian Naval Air Station, employ large numbers of civilian workers.

Mining. During recent years Mississippi has been among the ten leading states in petroleum production. Both petroleum and natural gas are produced in the central and southern parts of the state. Sand and gravel for use in the construction industries come chiefly from the northeast and the south. Clays are used to make tile, brick, and pottery.

Transportation and Communication

In the very early days people in Mississippi walked or traveled by horseback or boat. The Mississippi River and its tributaries became important routes of travel with the introduction of the flatboat and later the steamboat in 1811. Today the major ports on the Mississippi are Greenville, Vicksburg, and Natchez. Three seaports are situated on the Gulf of Mexico— Biloxi, Gulfport, and Pascagoula.

Mississippi has 66,000 miles (106,000 kilometers) of highways. The major traffic arteries focus on Jackson, the Gulf Coast, and the Mississippi River towns.

Most of the railroads in Mississippi are used to move freight. Several railroad companies operate more than 3,600 miles (5,800 kilometers) of mainline track. By far the largest carrier is Illinois Central Gulf. Amtrak operates two major passenger trains that cross the state —the "City of New Orleans," which connects New Orleans and Chicago, and the "Crescent," which runs between New Orleans and New York City via Mississippi. The state has more than 70 commercial and municipal airports.

The first newspaper in the state was the *Mississippi Gazette,* which began publication in Natchez in 1800. The oldest paper still in publication is the weekly Woodville *Republican,* founded in 1824. At present about 22 daily newspapers and more than 140 other papers are published. Mississippi has almost 200 radio stations and 20 television stations.

▶ EDUCATION

In Mississippi's early days the owners of plantations hired private teachers for their children or sent the boys to school in the East or in Europe. After Mississippi became a territory, many private schools were opened.

izes in U.S. Navy and commercial-service ships.

Among other major industries are food processing and the manufacture of electric and electronic equipment, petrochemicals, and nonelectrical machinery, such as farm machines. Petrochemicals are chemicals made from petroleum and natural gas. They are used to make numerous other products, such as fertil-

History survives in Mississippi's recreational areas. Above: Tupeco Swamp is a scenic stop on the Natchez Trace. Right: A now-silent Civil War cannon (*top*) looms over Vicksburg National Military Park, and a Natchez mansion (*below*) retains its antebellum charm.

Schools and Colleges

A system of public education was organized in 1870. But money was scarce, many people were opposed to public education, and the school laws were not enforced. The constitution of 1890 established the state department of education. After that time the state school system began to grow. Consolidation of schools began in 1910, when the first agricultural high schools were opened. The present system of public junior colleges grew out of these agricultural schools.

Like other southern states, Mississippi long maintained separate schools for whites and blacks. In 1954 the Supreme Court of the United States declared this practice to be illegal and ordered all states to integrate their public schools. After some delay, Mississippi began the process of integration in the 1960's.

The state constitution also restricted the state's universities to white students. The first black student at the University of Mississippi was not admitted until 1962.

The largest of the state-supported institutions of higher education are the University of Southern Mississippi in Hattiesburg; Mississippi State University in Mississippi State (near Starkville); and the University of Mississippi, with its main campus in University (near Oxford) and its medical center in Jackson. Mississippi University for Women is in Columbus. Other state universities are located in Cleveland, Itta Bena, Lorman, and Jackson.

Private senior colleges include Belhaven and Millsaps colleges in Jackson, Blue Mountain College in Blue Mountain, Mississippi College in Clinton, Tougaloo College in Tougaloo, and Rust College in Holly Springs.

Libraries and Museums

Most of the cities and larger towns have public libraries. Some of the counties are served by county or regional libraries. The library of the Mississippi Department of Archives and History in Jackson and the University of Mississippi library have important historical collections.

The Old Capitol building in Jackson has been restored as the State Historical Museum. This building housed the state government from 1839 until 1903, when the present capitol was completed. The exhibits in the museum show the various periods in Mississippi's history. The Old Courthouse in Vicksburg is a museum containing thousands of relics of Civil War days and earlier times. The Lauren Rogers Library and Museum of Art in Laurel contains European and American paintings, Indian baskets, and Civil War items. The Mary Buie Museum in Oxford is an art center. It also displays literary prizes awarded to William Faulkner.

▶PLACES OF INTEREST

Interesting places in Mississippi include the many resorts on Mississippi Sound, recreational areas throughout the state, and numerous historic buildings and sites.

National Areas

Mississippi has six national forests. They are the Holly Springs, Tombigbee, Delta, Bienville, Homochitto, and De Soto national forests. De Soto National Forest, in southern Mississippi, is more than twice as large as any of the others. Some other national areas are described in the following list.

Brices Cross Roads National Battlefield Site, north of Tupelo, commemorates a Civil War battle on June 10, 1864. Confederate cavalry under General Nathan B. Forrest defeated Union forces trying to help General William Tecumseh Sherman in his invasion of Georgia.

Gulf Islands National Seashore, shared by Mississippi and Florida, covers a series of offshore islands. Its main features are wildlife sanctuaries, historic forts, and white sand beaches near Pascagoula and Biloxi, Mississippi, and Pensacola, Florida. The islands are reachable only by boat.

Natchez Trace Parkway is shared by Mississippi, Alabama, and Tennessee, but the longest section is in Mississippi. Along the way are picnic sites, nature trails, museums, and historic sites. One of the historic sites is the Ackia Battleground Monument near Tupelo, marking the location of a fortified Chickasaw Indian village. The Chickasaw, aided by the British, defeated the French in the Battle of Ackia in 1736.

Tupelo National Battlefield in Tupelo commemorates the battle of Tupelo, July 13–14, 1864. This battle was part of a plan by General Sherman to protect his communications during his march on Atlanta, Georgia.

Vicksburg National Military Park preserves the scene of the 47-day siege of Vicksburg in 1863. The victory of the Union forces at Vicksburg meant that the Union controlled the Mississippi River. Hundreds of monuments and tablets

MISSISSIPPI
PLACES OF INTEREST

mark the positions of the armies. The park also preserves trenches, rifle pits, and many cannon in their original positions. **Vicksburg National Cemetery,** containing the graves of thousands of soldiers, adjoins the park.

State Parks and Other Places

Mississippi's 14 state parks include a variety of settings—woodlands, lakes and bayous, wildlife refuges, and sand beaches. Other major places of interest are the many stately old homes built before the Civil War. They are located mainly in Natchez, Holly Springs, Columbus, Port Gibson, and Biloxi. The following are among the parks and other places that attract large numbers of visitors.

Beauvoir, near Biloxi, was the last home of Jefferson Davis. The beautiful estate has been completely restored.

Clarkco State Park, south of Meridian, contains a lake and a variety of trees, birds, and small game in a scenic hilly area.

J. P. Coleman State Park is located on Pickwick Landing Reservoir, north of Iuka. It provides fishing, boating, and picnicking.

Connelly's Tavern, in Natchez, was built in 1795 as an inn on the Natchez Trace. It contains original tavern furniture, early newspapers, and other historic items.

Fort Massachusetts, on Ship Island, is a huge fort built in the mid-1800's to protect the entrance of the waterway to New Orleans, Louisiana. During the Civil War the dungeons of the fort held many Confederate prisoners.

Old Spanish Fort, in Pascagoula, is said to be the oldest building still standing in Mississippi. It was built as a fort in 1718. Now it is a museum containing many historic objects.

The Sprague is a retired sternwheel towboat anchored at Vicksburg. It serves as a museum of riverboat days and as an auditorium for showboat musicals.

The U.S. Army Engineer Waterways Experiment Station occupies a government-owned reservation at Vicksburg. The station is a research laboratory for the study of problems that engineers meet in planning ways to control floods, conserve water resources, and build better and safer waterways and harbors. It includes scale models of harbors, spillways, locks, and dams in .various parts of the nation.

Annual Events

Like its neighbors Louisiana and Alabama, Mississippi holds a Mardi Gras festival. Other annual events include agricultural fairs, boating and fishing rodeos, and organized tours of historic homes and gardens.

February or March—Mardi Gras, Biloxi.
March and April—Annual pilgrimages (tours of historic homes and gardens), Natchez, Vicksburg, Columbus, and Holly Springs.
May—Mississippi Arts Festival, Jackson.
June—Shrimp festival and blessing of the fleet, Biloxi.
July—Boating and fishing rodeos on the Gulf Coast; Choctaw Indian Fair, Philadelphia.
September—Central Mississippi fair and livestock and dairy show, Kosciusko.
October—State fair, Jackson.

▶CITIES

Mississippi has no large cities. Jackson is the center of the largest urban area.

Jackson

Jackson was laid out as the state capital in 1821 on the site of a trading post that had been established earlier by Louis Le Fleur, a French-Canadian trader. The plan of the city was suggested by Thomas Jefferson. The name Jackson was chosen to honor Andrew Jackson. Today Jackson is a service and distribution center for the state, a manufacturer of chemicals and furniture, and the home of several educational and welfare institutions. It is one of the most attractive cities of the South, with many green, open spaces.

COUNTIES

Jackson, Mississippi's capital, is one of the South's loveliest cities, with many parks and open spaces. Founded in 1821 on the site of a French trading post, the city was named for U.S. President Andrew Jackson, a Mississippi resident.

Biloxi

Biloxi is located on the Gulf Coast, the oldest settled area of the state. Founded in 1669, the city takes its name from the Biloxi Indians. At various times it has been governed by France, Spain, England, the Confederacy, and the United States. Biloxi is a major resort center, noted for its charming old buidings and oak trees hung with Spanish moss. It is also known for the colorful blessing of the fleet ceremony held annually on Biloxi Bay.

▶GOVERNMENT

Mississippi has been governed under four constitutions. The first was adopted in 1817, the second in 1832, the third in 1869, and the present one in 1890.

The executive branch of the state government is headed by the governor. Governors may not succeed themselves, but a former governor of Mississippi may run for the office again after another governor has served. Other elected executive officers include the lieutenant governor, secretary of state, attorney general, treasurer, and superintendent of public education.

GOVERNMENT

Capital—Jackson. **Number of counties**—82. **Representation in Congress**—U.S. senators, 2; U.S. representatives, 5. **State Legislature**—Senate, 52 members; House of Representatives, 122 members; all 4-year terms. **Governor**—4-year term; may not serve consecutive terms. **Elections**—General and state, Tuesday after first Monday in November.

The legislative branch of the government is made up of the Senate and the House of Representatives. The members of the two bodies meet for regular sessions on Tuesday after the first Monday in January of each year.

The judicial branch of the state government is headed by the Supreme Court. It is made up of nine justices elected for 8-year terms. The major state trial courts in Mississippi are the circuit courts and chancery courts. Circuit and chancery judges are elected for 4-year terms.

▶FAMOUS PEOPLE

Mississippi has been the home of many noted persons. It is known especially for political leaders and writers.

David Holmes (1770–1832), the last territorial governor of Mississippi and the first governor of the state, was born in Pennsylvania. In 1809, President James Madison appointed him governor of the territory. He worked skillfully with both the Indians and the settlers. When Mississippi became a state in 1817, he was elected governor. In 1820 he was appointed to fill a vacancy in the United States Senate, where he served until 1825. He became governor again in 1826 but resigned before the end of the year because of ill health.

Jefferson Davis (1808–89), president of the Confederate States during the Civil War, was born in Kentucky. The family moved to a small plantation near Woodville, Mississippi, when he was a child. A biography of Jefferson Davis is included in Volume D.

Lucius Quintus Cincinnatus Lamar (1825–93), lawyer and statesman, was born in Georgia. He settled in Mississippi during the 1850's. From 1857 to 1860 he represented Mississippi in the United States House of Representatives. In 1885 he became United States secretary of the interior. In 1888 he was appointed to the United States Supreme Court, where he served until his death. Lamar is remembered especially for his attempts to heal differences and to promote good will between the North and the South.

William Faulkner (1897–1962), world-famous novelist and winner of the Nobel prize for literature in 1949, was born in the village of New Albany near Oxford. His home in Oxford attracts many visitors. A biography of William Faulkner is included in Volume F.

Well-known writers besides William Faulkner who were born in Mississippi include novelist and playwright Stark Young (Como), short-story writer and novelist Eudora Welty (Jackson), historian Shelby Foote (Greenville), author Willie Morris (Jackson), novelists Richard Wright (Natchez) and Walker Percy (Greenville), and playwright Tennessee Williams (born Thomas Lanier Williams, Columbus). A biography of Tennessee Williams is included in Volume W.

Elvis Presley was born in Tupelo, opera singer Leontyne Price in Laurel, and country music singer Charlie Pride in Sledge.

▶**HISTORY**

Many Indian tribes once lived in the area that is now Mississippi. The most numerous were the Chickasaw in the north, the Choctaw in the central and southern parts of the area, and the Natchez in the southwest. Some of the minor tribes, such as the Biloxi, the Pascagoula, and the Yazoo, have given their names to present-day cities and rivers.

Exploration and Settlement

A Spaniard, Hernando de Soto, is given credit as the first explorer in Mississippi. He came into eastern Mississippi in December, 1540, searching for gold. By the middle of the next year he had crossed the region and discovered the Mississippi River. The Spanish built no settlements, but Spain claimed the area and ruled it for more than 150 years.

In 1682 the French explorer Robert Cavelier, Sieur de La Salle, came down the Mississippi and claimed all the valley for France. He called the area Louisiana in honor of his king, Louis XIV. Present-day Mississippi was included in that claim. In 1699, Pierre Lemoyne, Sieur d'Iberville, came to Mississippi from New France (now Canada). He established a fort at what is now Ocean Springs. This was Fort Maurepas, the first European settlement in Mississippi. Seventeen years later the French established Fort Rosalie on the site of present-day Natchez.

In 1732 the English extended their claims westward from the Carolinas to the Mississippi River. The Chickasaw Indians sided with the British and kept the French from expanding their control into northern Mississippi. The French defeat at Ackia in 1736 was but a small part of the long struggle between England and France for large territories east of the Mississippi River. By 1762, French defeat was assured. France ceded the Louisiana territory west of the Mississippi to Spain. The next year, at the end of the French and Indian War, England obtained the territory claimed by France east of the Mississippi River. Southern Mississippi became part of West Florida, and most of the rest of the present-day state became part of Georgia.

At the time of the Revolutionary War, Spain saw a chance to re-establish itself in Mississippi. Spanish troops moved into the Gulf area in 1779 while England was at war with its colonies on the Atlantic coast, and a Spanish government was established.

Territorial Days

After the Revolutionary War, England recognized the United States claim to all land north of the 31st degree of latitude. Spain did not do so until 1795, when a treaty ceded the Natchez district to the United States.

The Territory of Mississippi was organized in 1798 with Winthrop Sargent as governor and Natchez as the capital. Four years later the capital was moved to nearby Washington. The southern boundary was the 31st parallel. The western boundary was the Mississippi River, and the eastern boundary was the Chattahoochee River. In 1812 the southern boundary east of the Pearl River was pushed down to the Gulf Coast.

Under the Louisiana Purchase of 1803 the Mississippi River became part of the United States. In 1811 the first steamboat traveled on the river. Both these events had a great influence on the development of Mississippi. Natchez was the most important city during territorial days. After the War of 1812 many people came into the territory.

Statehood and Later Times

In 1817 the United States Congress divided Mississippi into the territory of Alabama and the state of Mississippi. Mississippi joined the Union on December 10, 1817.

By 1840 all the Indian lands in Mississippi had been taken over by the settlers. Most of the Indians were removed to reservations in present-day Oklahoma. With the Indians gone from the northern two thirds of the state, settlers poured in. Many came from southern Mississippi, almost draining this area of people. The cheap, fertile cotton lands also at-

tracted many settlers from the East. A cotton empire was established, based on slave labor, and many Mississippians became rich.

When the Civil War broke out between the North and the South, Mississippi seceded in January, 1861.

Several battles were fought in Mississippi. The most important was at Vicksburg. Union General Ulysses S. Grant conquered this important river port in July, 1863, after almost two months of siege. Capture of this port gave the Union control of the Mississippi River.

After the defeat of the South, Mississippi was placed under military rule. In 1869 a new constitution was adopted, and in 1870, Mississippi was re-admitted to the Union.

Economic recovery started in the mid-1870's. Vast areas in the Delta were drained for farming, and levees were built to protect the drained land from floods. New industries were encouraged to move to the state.

The present state constitution was adopted in 1890. But it contained restrictions that prevented black citizens from gaining political power, or even voting. Segregation of the races continued in many areas until it was abolished by the Civil Rights Act of 1964. Mississippians adjusted slowly to their changing society, but today blacks have full participation in all areas of Mississippi life.

The Future

Mississippi's future looks bright. Many people and industries are moving from other parts of the United States to the Sunbelt region, which includes Mississippi. The state is still considered rural, with 53 percent of the population living in communities of fewer than 2,500 people.

Mississippi's future will depend mainly on attracting new, high-technology industries. Agriculture is expected to increase moderately. Among important resources in the future will be petroleum and natural gas, bauxite, iron ore, and lignite.

An unfavorable national image, based on past racial injustices, is Mississippi's biggest obstacle to growth and development. Today, however, the image is gradually changing. Mississippians are seeking solutions to old problems such as inequality and to new problems such as environmental pollution.

RALPH D. CROSS
University of Southern Mississippi

IMPORTANT DATES

1540 Hernando de Soto, exploring for Spain, entered Mississippi; discovered Mississippi River in 1541.

1699 Pierre Lemoyne, Sieur d'Iberville, established the first settlement, Fort Maurepas, near present-day Biloxi.

1716 Natchez founded as Fort Rosalie.

1763 France ceded its territory east of the Mississippi River to England.

1779 Spain gained control of Fort Rosalie (called Fort Panmure by the British) and set up a Spanish government in the Natchez district.

1783 Mississippi north of the 31st parallel transferred to the United States after the Revolutionary War; Spain refused to recognize the transfer.

1795 Spain signed a treaty giving up its claim.

1798 Territory of Mississippi, including present-day Alabama, created with capital at Natchez.

1802 Capital moved to Washington.

1817 December 10, Mississippi became the 20th state.

1821 Site of new capital selected and named Jackson.

1831 Railroad construction began with a line from Woodville to St. Francisville, Louisiana.

1844 University of Mississippi chartered; opened in 1848.

1861 Mississippi seceded from the Union; Jefferson Davis of Mississippi elected president of the Confederate States.

1863 Union forces captured Vicksburg and gained control of the Mississippi River.

1870 Mississippi re-admitted to the Union.

1890 Present state constitution adopted.

1926 First natural gas field opened at Amory.

1936 BAWI (Balance Agriculture with Industry) program started to encourage growth of industry.

1939 Oil discovered in Yazoo County.

1944 Agricultural and Industrial Board established.

1962 James H. Meredith was the first black student admitted to the University of Mississippi.

1969 Charles Evers elected as first black mayor of a Mississippi city (Fayette) since Reconstruction.

1976 Evelyn Gandy took office as Mississippi's first woman lieutenant governor.

1982 Education Reform Act passed, providing free kindergarten for all children.

1984 Reuben V. Anderson became the first black since Reconstruction to be appointed to the Mississippi Supreme Court.

MISSISSIPPI RIVER

In the language of the Indians of the Great Lakes region, Mississippi means "great river." This is a fitting description for the chief river of the United States and one of the major rivers of the world. The source of the Mississippi is near Lake Itasca in northern Minnesota, an area that was covered by glaciers long ago. The river runs down the length of the United States for about 3,780 kilometers (2,350 miles) and empties into the Gulf of Mexico. The Mississippi River system drains an area of about 3,222,000 square kilometers (1,244,000 square miles), stretching from the western slopes of the Appalachians to the Rocky Mountains. Northward it includes parts of Canada's prairie provinces.

Discovery and Exploration

The first European to discover the river was Hernando de Soto, in 1541. He and his party crossed the river below the present site of Memphis, Tennessee. In 1673, Jacques Marquette, a Jesuit missionary, and Louis Jolliet, a fur trader, explored the Mississippi as far south as the Arkansas River. Father Louis Hennepin explored the upper Mississippi and reached the Falls of St. Anthony (Minnesota) in 1680. In 1682, La Salle descended the Illinois River to its junction with the Mississippi and continued downstream to the Gulf of Mexico.

When the United States gained its independence from England in 1783, the Mississippi became the western boundary of the new nation. In 1803, when the Louisiana Territory was purchased from France, the Mississippi became the center of a vast territory that stretched from the Atlantic to the Rockies.

Course of the River

The Mississippi River flows through the broad central lowland of the United States. It begins as a number of short, rapid rivers connecting a series of lakes. Then the river flows through a broad, shallow valley until it reaches the Falls of St. Anthony, in the city of Minneapolis. From this point to Cairo, Illinois, the Mississippi flows through a valley where the bordering bluffs can rise as high as 150 meters (500 feet) above the river. The valley varies in width from about 1 to 9 kilometers (½ to 6 miles). Before ferries and bridges were built, the wide river and the broad sloughs were effective barriers to east-west trade and travel.

Between Redwing, Minnesota, and the mouth of the Chippewa River, the Mississippi has been broadened into a lake called Lake Pepin. Over the centuries, the Chippewa deposited more sediment than could be removed by the Mississippi, and this barrier of sediment continues to maintain the lake. Below Lake Pepin, between Iowa on the west and Wisconsin and Illinois on the east, the river is a swiftly flowing stream. A series of dams and locks are necessary for boats and other rivercraft to navigate the rapids. At Keokuk, Iowa, a dam provides hydroelectric power. At Cairo the Mississippi is joined by its principal tributary, the Ohio River.

From Cairo to the Gulf of Mexico the Mississippi flows in a meandering (winding) course on a broad plain marked by widely spaced bluffs. The river winds slowly past Memphis and Vicksburg, then on to Baton Rouge and New Orleans. Finally it fans out through a bird-foot delta into the Gulf.

Geologists believe that the Gulf of Mexico once extended northward to the southern tip

MISSISSIPPI RIVER

A powerful tugboat pushes a cargo-laden barge down the Mississippi River.

of Illinois. For millions of years this shallow extension of the sea (called the Mississippi Embayment) received the waters and sediments of the Mississippi, the Arkansas, the Red, and many other rivers. In time, sediments filled the embayment. In this way the Mississippi plain was lengthened from southern Illinois to the delta that juts into the Gulf of Mexico.

The sediments consisted of topsoil from lands drained by the tributaries of the Mississippi. (Soil deposited in this way by rivers is called alluvial soil.) But much of the bottomland is too wet for farming. These wet areas are an immense land resource, which someday can be cleared and drained for agriculture. The broad, natural levees of the Mississippi and its tributaries rise above the wet lowlands and are highly cultivated. Cotton is an important product.

Trade and Transportation

Because the Mississippi River flows north to south, it has always acted as an important waterway to the Gulf of Mexico and the Atlantic Ocean. Before the development of the steamboat most of the commerce was chiefly downstream to New Orleans. It consisted of rafts of logs and barges of lumber and other bulky materials. Steamboat traffic began on the Mississippi and its tributaries in 1811 and lasted for about a century. Today most commerce moves on barges lashed together and pushed by powerful motor tugs. A few steamboats may still be seen on the river, but they carry tourists instead of cargo.

Products consist of corn, wheat, cotton, and soybeans; coal, sand, and gravel; and iron and steel pipe and scrap. Other products are logs, pulpwood, rolled and finished steel products, motor vehicles, sulfuric acid, vegetable oils, animal feed, sugar, cement, fertilizers, and aluminum ore. Special carriers have been designed to handle such cargo as petroleum and petroleum products, industrial chemicals, and molten sulfur.

Improving the River

The Mississippi River is maintained and improved by spending hundreds of millions of dollars of federal funds. ·Improvements include the construction of dams and locks. The river is dredged to remove obstructions and to maintain a uniform channel depth. Water resources are conserved for power, flood control, and irrigation. Recreational facilities are being developed. Thus the Mississippi remains an important part of the national transportation system.

GUY-HAROLD SMITH
Editor, *Conservation of Natural Resources*

See also LA SALLE, ROBERT CAVELIER, SIEUR DE; LOUISIANA PURCHASE; JOLLIET, LOUIS, AND JACQUES MARQUETTE; RIVERS.

MISSOURI

The boat leaped as it hit the rapids. The passengers clung to their seats. It landed with a thump and then shot forward, plunging and bumping over the dark, slick rocks. Suddenly the boat emerged in a quiet pool, and soon it was floating smoothly with the current. Other rapids lay ahead. But now the passengers settled back and got ready to fish. They were enjoying a float trip on the Current River in Missouri's Ozarks.

Float fishing began in the rivers of the Ozarks around the year 1900. Anglers—and many people who do not care to fish—travel in the long, shallow, square-nosed boats called john-boats. They drift along at the current's speed, fishing or simply enjoying themselves. They camp at night and then float on. The Current River, with its clear, spring-fed waters, high bluffs, and gravel bars, is a special favorite for float trips. Sections of this wild, free-flowing stream and of its main tributary, the Jacks Fork, have been designated as the Ozark National Scenic Riverways.

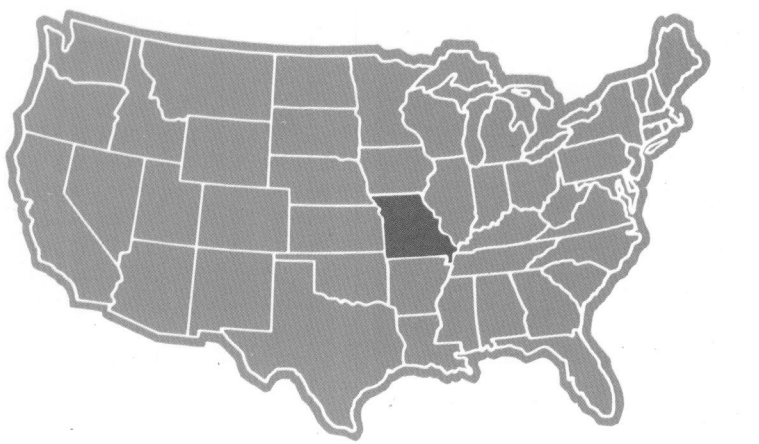

Missouri was the 24th state to be admitted to the Union and the second state (after Louisiana) to be created west of the Mississippi River.

The fur-trading post of St. Louis was founded in 1764. From there the fur traders extended their operations far up the Missouri and the Mississippi rivers. After the Louisiana Purchase in 1803, Missouri was the point of entry and St. Louis was the gateway city for the new western lands. The Lewis and Clark expedition set out from the vicinity of St. Louis in 1804. In the years that followed, pioneers streamed into Missouri. Many stayed. Others joined the growing numbers who were pushing on to Oregon, California, and the Southwest.

The lead mines in the eastern Ozarks were as important as the fur trade in bringing early settlers to Missouri. One of the miners, Moses Austin, was among the many persons who later decided to move on and who helped give Missouri the name Mother of the West. Austin began to operate lead mines at present-day Potosi in the late 1790's. His son, Stephen F. Austin, became known as the founder of Texas.

Missouri's nickname is the "Show Me" State. One story says that a train conductor first used the expression "You'll have to show me" when the passengers insisted that they were entitled to ride on free passes. Another story says that the expression was first used by a politician in a humorous address in 1899.

For many years, Missouri has ranked first among the states in production of lead. It has long been an important agricultural state as well. Today it takes pride in its industrial growth. Missouri also has a wealth of scenic beauty, especially in the rugged hills of the Ozarks.

▶THE LAND

Missouri is located in the heart of the Mississippi Valley. It is near the geographic center of the first 48 states. The 1980 census showed that an area near St. Louis is now the population center of the nation. Missouri is surrounded by more states—eight, in all—than any other state except Tennessee, which also has eight neighbors. Rivers form all of Missouri's eastern boundary and part of its western boundary. In the extreme southeast, a piece of land juts southward into Arkansas. This piece of land, shaped somewhat like the heel of a shoe, is known as the Bootheel.

Landforms

Missouri includes parts of three natural regions of the United States. These are the Ozark Plateaus in the south, the Central Lowland in the north and the west, and the Coastal Plain in the extreme southeast.

STATE FLAG.

STATE TREE: Flowering dogwood.

STATE BIRD: Bluebird.

STATE FLOWER: Hawthorn.

MISSOURI

CAPITAL: Jefferson.City.

STATEHOOD: August 10, 1821; the 24th state.

SIZE: 180,516 km² (69,697 sq mi); rank, 19th.

POPULATION: 4,916,759 (1980 census); rank, 15th.

ORIGIN OF NAME: From Indian syllables meaning "owners of big canoes." First applied to the river, then to the land.

ABBREVIATIONS: Mo.; MO.

NICKNAME: The "Show Me" State.

STATE SONG: "Missouri Waltz," by J. R. Shannon; music arranged by Frederick Logan from a melody by John Valentine Eppel.

STATE MOTTO: *Salus populi suprema lex esto* (Let the welfare of the people be the supreme law).

STATE SEAL: The state coat of arms appears on the seal. The shield in the center is divided into two parts. One half shows a bear and a crescent, representing Missouri. The other half shows the eagle of the United States. The two halves are bound together, or united, by a band ending in a belt buckle. The words in the band, "United we stand; divided we fall," reflect the need for all the states to be united. Two bears support the shield. They stand on a streamer on which the state motto is inscribed. A helmet appears above the shield. The 24 stars above the helmet show that Missouri was the 24th state. The date at the bottom in Roman numerals (1820) is the date of the Missouri Compromise.

STATE FLAG: The field is made up of three horizontal bands—red, white, and blue—of equal width. The state coat of arms appears in the center. It is encircled by a band of blue bearing 24 white stars.

The Mississippi River forms most of the eastern border of Missouri. This wooded spot near the town of Hannibal gives a view of neighboring Illinois.

The Ozark Plateaus. Missouri shares the Ozark Plateaus with Arkansas and Oklahoma. The Ozark region of Missouri has a variety of surface features, resulting from water erosion on the elevated lands.

The greater part of the region is a plateau, or relatively level tableland, cut by steep-sided valleys. Much of it is between 360 and 450 meters (1,200 and 1,500 feet) in elevation. One area of hill country lies well to the north. It is called the Osage-Gasconade Hills. The broken lands there were formed by erosion of the Osage and the Gasconade rivers. Another hill section is in the southwest around the White River. This rugged area is popularly known as the Shepherd of the Hills Country. The name comes from Harold Bell Wright's once popular novel *The Shepherd of the Hills,* published in 1907.

The St. Francois Mountains are in the east. The tallest parts tend to be dome-shaped, with small tops. The name "knob" describes them well. A number of these knobs stand as high as 520 meters (1,700 feet) above sea level. One of them, Taum Sauk Mountain, is the highest point in the state.

The Ozark borderlands encircle the Ozark region on the north and east. The part on the north is a shallow trough, through which the Missouri River flows. But the greater part of the borderlands area is rolling upland.

The Central Lowland. Missouri's second largest landform area belongs to a region of the United States known as the Central Lowland. In Missouri it is divided into two sections. The Dissected Till Plains section lies north of the Missouri River. The Osage Plains section is a triangular-shaped area along the Kansas-Missouri border south of the Missouri River.

The Dissected Till Plains section was once covered by glaciers. The melting ice left behind deposits of earth material, or till. The till was later eroded, or dissected, by streams. This has given much of the area a rolling surface. The Osage Plains section was not covered by glaciers. Here the land rises to the west in a series of steps known as cuestas. Each cuesta has a steep, eastward-facing slope, or scarp, and a gentler western slope that follows the dip or tilt of the rock layer.

The Coastal Plain. The extreme southeastern part of the state belongs to a natural region along the lower Mississippi River known as the Mississippi Alluvial Plain. It, in turn, is part of the larger Gulf Coastal Plain.

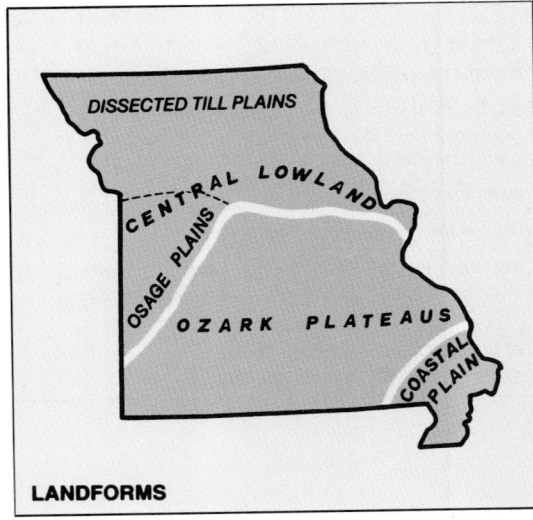

LANDFORMS

In Missouri's early days, part of this lowland was called the Big Swamp. It was covered largely with the stagnant waters of swamps, marshes, and bayous. Everywhere there were mosquitoes, which were deadly enemies of settlers. A series of strong earthquakes around New Madrid in 1811 and 1812 further discouraged settlers for a time. Today the area has been changed through drainage projects into some of the most productive land in the state.

Rivers and Lakes

Missouri has two great rivers—the Missouri and the Mississippi. The Mississippi forms all the eastern boundary of the state except in the extreme northeast. There the Des Moines River separates Missouri from the southeastern tip of Iowa. The Missouri River forms the western boundary as far south as Kansas City.

The chief rivers north of the Missouri are the Grand, the Chariton, and the Salt. Rivers south of the Missouri include the Osage, the Gasconade, and the Meramec—all in the central part of the state—and the White, the Current, and the St. Francis in the south.

The Ozarks region has 11 of the 75 springs in the United States classed as first-magnitude springs. All springs of this kind have a flow of 3 cubic meters (100 cubic feet) or more of water each second. Big Spring in the gorge of the Current River is the largest of Missouri's first-magnitude springs.

Missouri has no large natural lakes, but it has several important artificial lakes. Most of these are in the rugged sections of the Ozarks. The Lake of the Ozarks is formed by Bagnell Dam on the Osage River. This huge lake, with its many arms, stretches about 210 kilometers (130 miles) through west central Missouri. Just west of the Lake of the Ozarks is the Harry S Truman Reservoir, the largest body of water in the state.

Bagnell Dam in central Missouri backs up the Osage River to create the Lake of the Ozarks, one of the state's most popular recreational areas.

THE LAND

LOCATION: Latitude—36° N to 40° 35′ N. **Longitude**—89° 06′ W to 95° 46′ W.

Iowa to the north; Illinois, Kentucky, and Tennessee to the east; Arkansas to the south; Oklahoma, Kansas, and Nebraska to the west.

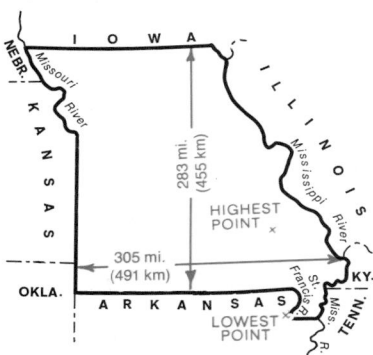

ELEVATION: Highest—Taum Sauk Mountain, 540 m (1,772 ft.). **Lowest**—On the St. Francis River at the Missouri—Arkansas border, 70 m (230 ft).

LANDFORMS: Central Lowland, Ozark Plateaus in south central Missouri, Coastal Plain in the extreme southeast.

SURFACE WATERS: Major rivers—Mississippi, Missouri, Osage, Gasconade, Meramec, Current, St. Francis, Grand, Chariton, Salt. **Major artificial lakes**—Lake of the Ozarks, Table Rock, Harry S Truman Reservoir.

CLIMATE: Temperature—January average from about −3°C (26°F) in the northwest to about 3°C (38°F) in the southeast. July average, about 27°C (80°F). **Precipitation**—From about 810 mm (32 in) a year in the northwest to nearly 1,270 mm (50 in) a year in the southeast. Snowfall averages 46–56 cm (18–22 in) north of the Missouri River; decreases to 20–30 cm (8–12 in) a year in the southernmost counties. **Growing season**—From about 170 days in the extreme north and certain parts of the south to about 210 days in the southeast.

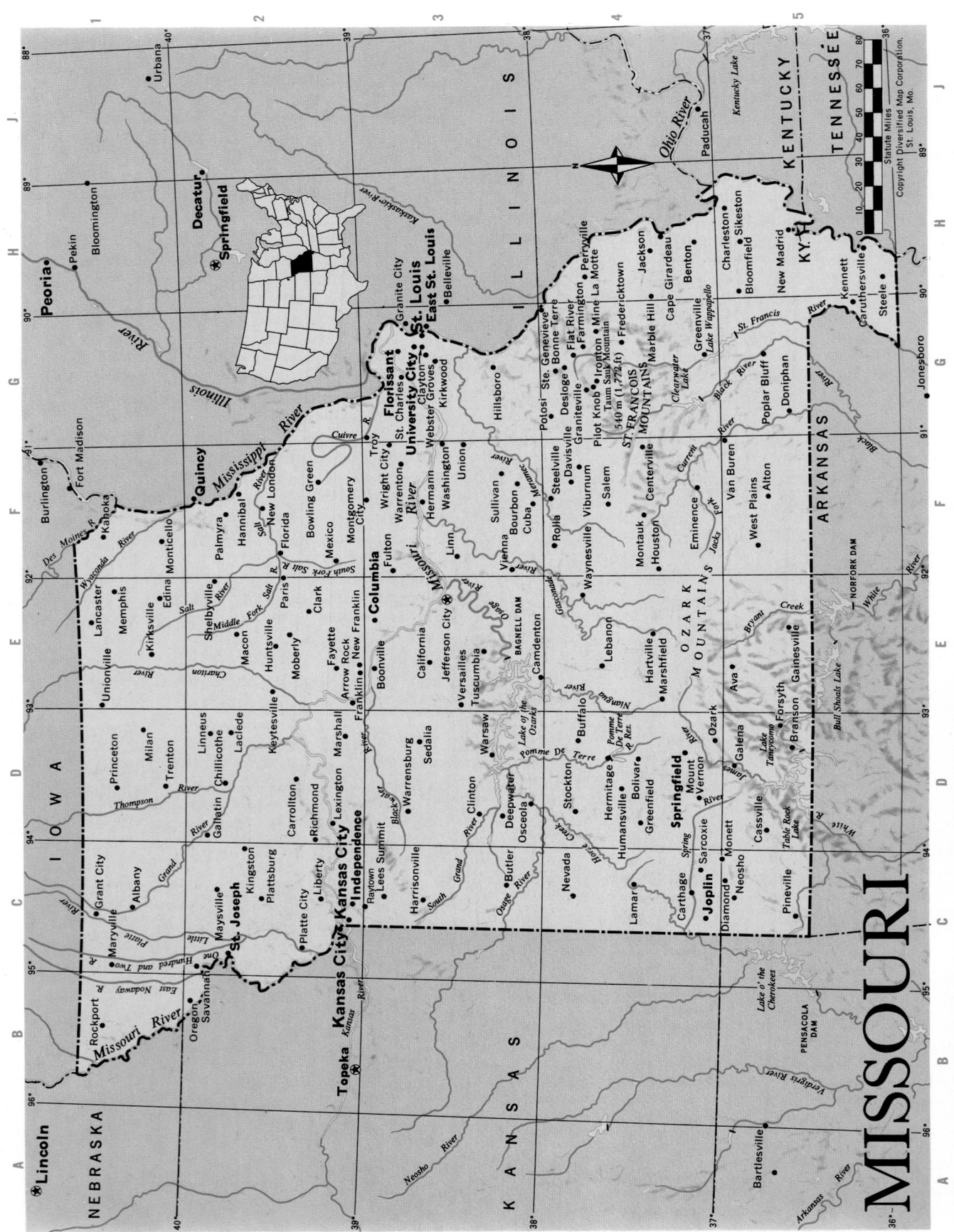

MISSOURI

The White River area of southwestern Missouri includes four large lakes—Table Rock, Taneycomo, Bull Shoals, and Norfolk. All are formed by dams on the White River system in Missouri and neighboring Arkansas. These and other artificial lakes, such as Mark Twain Lake on the Salt River, are good places for recreation. The dams provide hydroelectric power and help to control floods.

Climate

Missouri is located near the center of the North American landmass. This position gives it a continental climate. Summers are long and warm. Winters are long and cold. The most pleasant time of year is early autumn, when cool, dry, and sunny weather prevails.

Missouri's location in a great open plain is a chief factor in temperature changes. There are no significant barriers to air movement. Incoming cold air from the Dakotas or Canada accounts for the most severe cold spells of winter. Temperatures can change more than 10°C (50°F) in less than a day.

The southeastern portion of the state receives more precipitation (rain and melted snow) than the northwest. Snow occurs in all parts of Missouri, but it varies greatly from place to place and from year to year.

Natural Resources

Missouri's greatest natural resource is its soils. Forests, minerals, wildlife, and an abundance of water add to the natural wealth. Missouri's conservation department is active in wildlife management, water control, reforestation and soil conservation programs.

POPULATION

TOTAL: 4,916,759 (1980 census). **Density**—27.5 persons to each square kilometer (71.3 persons to each square mile).

GROWTH SINCE 1810

Year	Population	Year	Population
1810	19,783	1900	3,106,665
1820	66,586	1960	4,319,813
1850	682,044	1970	4,677,623
1880	2,168,380	1980	4,916,759

Gain Between 1970 and 1980—5.1 percent.

CITIES: Population of Missouri's largest cities according to the 1980 census.

St. Louis	453,085	Columbia	62,061
Kansas City	448,159	Florissant	55,372
Springfield	133,116	University City	42,738
Independence	111,806	Joplin	39,023
St. Joseph	76,691	St. Charles	37,379

Soils. There are many different kinds of soil in the state. The soils of the Ozark Plateaus are generally less fertile than the others. They contain much stone and gravel.

The soils of the Dissected Till Plains are largely of fine glacial and wind-deposited materials. Clay loams are extensive in the eastern half of the region. In the level parts and in the larger valleys, the soils are deep and fertile. The soils in the western half of the Dissected Till Plains are among the best in the state. In the Osage Plains, south of the Missouri River, the soils are moderate in depth and fertility.

Most of the soils of the southeast lowlands are made up of alluvial materials—sands, silts, and clays carried in by rivers. In fertility these soils range from some of the richest in Missouri to some of the poorest.

One environmental problem that Missouri has recently faced is contamination of the soil in widely scattered, small areas by dioxin. This highly toxic chemical is a by-product in the manufacture of some chemicals. Waste oil containing dioxin was spread on rural roads to control dust. The town of Times Beach, near St. Louis, was especially badly contaminated when a flood deposited this material over much of the village.

Minerals. Missouri has long been known for its deposits of lead. Other metallic minerals include iron ore, zinc, and copper. By 1715 the French were mining lead at Mine La Motte, a village in the St. Francois Mountains north of Fredericktown. This area in the eastern Ozarks came to be known as the old lead belt. Almost all the zinc in the state came from the Joplin area, but most of the known zinc ores have been used up. Copper has never been found in large quantity. Iron has come from the same general area as lead.

During the 1950's and 1960's, there was much prospecting for new mineral deposits. Important new deposits of lead were found in a belt 80 kilometers (50 miles) wide, west of the old lead belt. This became the leading lead-mining district in the United States. New iron-ore deposits were found at Pilot Knob and Pea Ridge.

Nonmetallic minerals include clays, sand and gravel, and stone, such as limestone, marble, and granite. All these except granite are present in large quantity. The clays include the somewhat rare refractory, or fire, clay found in east central Missouri.

Forests. One third of Missouri is covered with forests. Most of these woodlands are in the Ozarks. The forests supply raw materials for a variety of products—sawlogs, posts, and charcoal. They also help to preserve groundwater, prevent floods, and protect the land from erosion. Finally, they provide a home for wildlife and a source of recreation.

Wildlife. The pioneers reported great numbers of elk, black bear, panthers, antelope, and passenger pigeons. Most of the larger animals and all the passenger pigeons are gone, but smaller animals are perhaps more numerous than ever. Hunting is a popular activity almost everywhere in the state. Deer, quail, ducks, and geese are the chief attractions.

Missouri has many fishing streams and lakes. These waters provide a variety of fish—bass, pike, channel cat, and trout.

▶ **THE PEOPLE AND THEIR WORK**

Indian peoples lived in what was later Missouri as long as 10,000 years ago. The Mound Builders were the state's most notable early inhabitants. Later, European explorers found such groups as the Missouri, Fox, Sauk, and Osage living there.

The first explorers, traders, and settlers in Missouri were the French. They came from settlements in Illinois, from Canada, and from Louisiana. By 1803, settlers from other parts of the United States made up a large share of the population. They followed the Ohio, Tennessee, and Cumberland rivers to the Mississippi. Then they spread out along the Mississippi and Missouri rivers.

After 1830, European immigrants—notably German, Irish, English, and Polish—came in large numbers to St. Louis and surrounding areas. But up to the time of the U.S. Civil War, most of the settlers continued to come from Virginia, North Carolina, Kentucky, and Tennessee. These settlers sympathized with

---

WHAT MISSOURI PRODUCES

MANUFACTURED GOODS: Transportation equipment; processed foods; chemicals and related products; electric and electronic equipment; fabricated metal products; nonelectrical machinery; products of printing and publishing; primary metals; stone, clay, and glass products.

AGRICULTURAL PRODUCTS: Cattle and calves, soybeans, corn, hogs, wheat, milk, grain sorghum, turkeys, eggs, cotton, broilers, rice.

MINERALS: Lead (Missouri ranks first in the nation), cement, stone, coal, lime, zinc, sand and gravel, copper, clays, crude oil, silver, barite.

the South in the Civil War. The counties just north of the Missouri River, where they settled, came to be called Little Dixie.

Slaves were brought to present-day Missouri during early French and Spanish times. But the black population first began to grow when settlers from the South brought slaves to work in the tobacco and hemp fields. By 1840 the state was settled except for the rougher parts of the Ozarks and the southeast lowlands.

Where the People Live

Before 1930 most Missourians lived in rural areas (places with fewer than 2,500 people or in the open countryside). Today more than two thirds of the people live in urban areas. But the rural-to-urban movement changed during the 1970's. The 1980 census showed an increase (from about 30 to 32 percent) in the proportion of the population living in rural areas.

Industries and Products

Once Missouri depended on agriculture for most of its income. Today agriculture ranks third behind manufacturing and tourism in the state's economy. Mining, wholesale and retail trade, and many kinds of service industries are also important.

Agriculture. Corn, wheat, and cotton are all grown in Missouri. The prairie region in the north is known for corn. Wheat is grown mainly in the western and central parts of the state, and cotton in the southeast lowlands. But every county in the state produces some corn, which was the leading crop for many years. Today soybeans bring more cash income than corn.

The largest area of agricultural land is in the north. More than half the Ozarks region is in timber, but agriculture is important. The larger valleys and the uplands produce a variety of crops. The drier southwestern part of the state yields more rye, barley, and sorghum than do other areas. The croplands of southeastern Missouri are especially good for cotton and soybeans, but they also produce large quantities of wheat, corn, and sorghum. An increasing amount of rice is also being planted in this area.

Livestock, especially cattle, bring far more income than crops. Both beef and dairy cattle are raised almost everywhere in the state, as

Hogs and beef and dairy cattle are raised throughout Missouri. Kansas City's stockyards are among the largest in the United States.

are hogs. Dairy farming is of major importance in the Ozarks, especially in the western parts. Poultry has become a large-scale business with the production of eggs, broilers, and turkeys.

Workhorses—and the mules for which Missouri was once famous—have been almost entirely displaced by the use of tractors and other machines on the farms. But riding horses are raised in various parts of the state.

Manufacturing. Gristmills, flour mills, and meat-packing plants were among Missouri's earliest manufacturing industries. Other major industries of the 1840's and 1850's were distilleries and breweries, tobacco factories, tanneries, rope factories, and lumber mills. By the time of the Civil War, iron foundries had also become important.

Most of the major industries of earlier days still exist, although in modern form, and many new types of manufacturing have been added. The two largest industrial centers are St. Louis and Kansas City. The major industries in St. Louis include the manufacture of aircraft, automobiles, chemical products, food products, beer, machinery, and electric equipment. The printing and publishing industry is also important. Kansas City's chief industries include meat-packing, automobile assembling, and the making of flour, chemicals and drugs.

Factories of various kinds are located in every part of the state. Most of them are small. But some are quite large, such as the firebrick plants at Mexico and the milk-processing plant at Springfield. The Ozarks region, with most of the forests, has many lumber mills, furniture factories, and toy and novelty factories.

Mining. The chief lead-mining communities once were located between Bonne Terre and Fredericktown in the eastern Ozarks and at Joplin in the southwest. During the 1950's important new deposits of lead were found to the west of the old deposits.

Although Missouri is famous for lead, it is also noted for stone. Limestone is produced in about two thirds of the counties. It is used in making portland cement, in road construction, and as a fertilizer. Marble is mined in Carthage, and red granite is quarried around Graniteville. St. Louis, St. Charles, and Jefferson counties produce a kind of sand called silica sand. It is used in making glass, enamelware, and cleaning compounds. More than half the counties in the state produce sand and gravel for building and for highway construction. Fireclay is an important clay. It is used to make bricks that can withstand great heat.

Coal is mined in numerous counties, especially Randolph and Macon counties, north of the Missouri River, and Bates, Barton, and Henry counties, south of the river. Almost all of the mining is done by the strip method. The first oil wells were drilled in Jackson County in the 1860's, but only small quantities of oil and gas have been produced in Missouri.

Transportation and Communication

Missouri's first highways were its rivers, especially the Mississippi and the Missouri. Steamboats serving the fur trade began plying the rivers in the early 1800's.

Boone's Lick Trail was the first east-west road across the state. It extended from St. Charles westward to Franklin in the Boone's Lick area, where Daniel Boone's sons and others made salt during the early 1800's. In 1821 a small party of traders led by William Becknell marked out a trail between Franklin and Santa Fe, New Mexico. This was the beginning of the famous Santa Fe Trail. Later the eastern end of the trail was moved to other towns along the Missouri—Independence and then Westport (now Kansas City). Gradually, roads were built throughout the state.

The first railroad construction in Missouri began at St. Louis in 1851. The Hannibal and St. Joseph Railroad was completed in 1859. The railroads were placed where it was easiest to build them and where freight and passenger business was most promising. The Missouri Valley, with its level lands, was a natural route to follow. St. Louis and Kansas City developed rapidly as two of the great railway

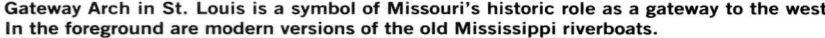

Gateway Arch in St. Louis is a symbol of Missouri's historic role as a gateway to the west. In the foreground are modern versions of the old Mississippi riverboats.

centers of the nation. Today most of the railroads are used for carrying freight. Trucks and buses furnish swift and easy transportation for goods and people.

Missouri has an honored place in the history and development of air transportation. The first international balloon races were held in St. Louis in 1907. Much of St. Louis' early interest in aviation was due to Major Albert Bond Lambert. Major Lambert, who was born in St. Louis in 1875, was an expert balloon pilot and a friend of Orville Wright and other noted air pioneers. In 1920 he opened an airport, known as Lambert Field. Soon after that time, regular airmail service began between St. Louis and Chicago. Soon also a young pilot named Charles A. Lindbergh came to St. Louis and carried mail on the Chicago run. In 1927 he gained fame for making the first nonstop solo flight across the Atlantic Ocean. Lindbergh's flight in the *Spirit of St. Louis* was financed by Major Lambert and other St. Louis businessmen. A biography of Charles A. Lindbergh is included in Volume L.

Lambert Field in St. Louis later became an international airport. The other important air center of Missouri is Kansas City. The state as a whole has about 100 commercial and municipal airports.

The first newspaper in Missouri was the *Missouri Gazette,* established in St. Louis in 1808. Part of the paper was published in French. It continued under various names until 1919, when it was bought by the St. Louis *Globe-Democrat.*

The *Globe-Democrat,* founded in 1852, is one of Missouri's three largest daily newspapers. The *St. Louis Post-Dispatch* was founded by Joseph Pulitzer in 1878. A biography of Joseph Pulitzer is included in Volume P. The *Kansas City Star,* founded in 1880, is also well known outside Missouri. In all, Missouri has approximately 300 newspapers, of which about 50 are dailies.

There are more than 200 radio stations in the state and about 20 television stations.

▶ EDUCATION

Missouri claims several important firsts in education. St. Louis University, which grew out of an academy founded in 1818, is the oldest university west of the Mississippi. The University of Missouri, chartered in 1839, was the first state university to be founded west

of the Mississippi. The School of Journalism at the University of Missouri was the first school in the world to grant a degree in journalism. It was founded in 1908. The first school of osteopathy in the United States was founded at Kirksville in 1892 by Dr. Andrew Taylor Still. Osteopathy is a method of healing. The first public kindergarten in the United States was opened in St. Louis in 1873 by Susan Elizabeth Blow.

Schools and Colleges

The first school in what is now Missouri was a private school for boys, opened in St. Louis in 1774. The teaching was in French. The first schools with instruction in the English language began about 1804. As the population grew, many church-supported schools and academies were opened.

The public school system was founded in 1839, when the legislature voted a fund to support public schools. Public school districts were organized in each county in 1874. After the Civil War the laws of the state required segregation in public education. A decision of the U.S. Supreme Court in 1954 declared this requirement to be unconstitutional.

The University of Missouri was established in Columbia in 1839. Today it includes campuses in Kansas City, Rolla, and St. Louis. Other state-supported universities and senior colleges are in Cape Girardeau, Jefferson City, Joplin, Kirksville, Maryville, St. Joseph, Springfield, and Warrensburg. Most sections of the state have public two-year colleges.

The largest of the private colleges and universities are Washington University and St. Louis University, both in St. Louis. Washington University grew out of Eliot Seminary, founded in 1853 by William Greenleaf Eliot, grandfather of the poet T. S. Eliot. Stephens College in Columbia is well known.

Westminster College in Fulton is the place where in 1946 the British leader Winston Churchill delivered a now-famous speech. In the speech he coined the term "Iron Curtain" to describe an imaginary barrier that had descended across Europe, dividing Communist from non-Communist countries. Today the Winston Churchill Memorial and Library, on the Westminster campus, attracts many visitors. The library is housed in the reconstruction of a historic London church—the Church of St. Mary the Virgin, Aldermanbury.

MISSOURI
PLACES OF INTEREST

JEFFERSON NATIONAL
EXPANSION MEMORIAL

Libraries, Museums, and the Arts

The state constitution of 1945 provided for support of public libraries through state and local taxation. Since that time, the number of libraries has grown until more than 100 cities and towns have public libraries. The largest public library is the St. Louis Public Library. It was started in 1860 in connection with the public schools. In the 1890's it was made free to the public.

The major universities and various private organizations have large libraries with important special collections. The Pope Piux XII Memorial Library at St. Louis University contains microfilm records in many fields of learning from the Vatican Library in Rome. Linda Hall Library in Kansas City contains one of the best collections in science and technology in the Middle West. Other major museums are included in the following list.

The Harry S Truman Library and Museum, in Independence, preserves papers, books, and many historical items pertaining to President Truman's administration and his life. The Truman grave site is in a courtyard.

The City Art Museum of St. Louis is known for its collections of fine art, ranging from ancient to modern times.

The Kansas City Museum of History and Science specializes in history, natural history, and anthropology. Displays of interest to children include Eskimoland and Pioneerland.

The Missouri Historical Society, in the Jefferson Memorial Building, St. Louis, includes both a library and a museum. The Charles A. Lindbergh collection in the museum includes thousands of items commemorating Lindbergh's flight to Paris in the *Spirit of St. Louis.* Other interesting exhibits pertain to the Lewis and Clark expedition, early St. Louis, and the steamboat era.

The St. Joseph Museum, in St. Joseph, emphasizes natural history, wildlife of the area, and American Indian material. **The Pony Express Stables Museum** is housed in the stables used when St. Joseph became the eastern starting point of the Pony Express in 1860.

The State Historical Society of Missouri, in Columbia, has important collections of books and records pertaining to the history of Missouri. The art gallery includes works by two of the state's noted artists, George Caleb Bingham and Thomas Hart Benton.

The William Rockhill Nelson Gallery and Mary Atkins Museum of Fine Arts, in Kansas City, is a single institution usually known as the Nelson. It contains notable exhibits of European, American, and Asian art.

St. Louis and Springfield have symphony orchestras. Both St. Louis and Kansas City have open-air summer theaters. Summer playhouses have been established at Branson, the Lake of the Ozarks, and elsewhere.

▶ PLACES OF INTEREST

Missouri is fortunate to have a variety of places for many kinds of recreation. These include the unspoiled scenery of the Ozarks and many big springs, caverns, lakes, and hunting and fishing areas.

National Areas

The **Mark Twain National Forest** consists of patches of forest scattered throughout the Missouri Ozarks. About 225 kilometers (140 miles) of the Current and Jacks Fork rivers form the Ozark National Scenic Riverways. The other national areas preserve historic sites.

The George Washington Carver National Monument, near Diamond, includes the site where the famous agricultural scientist was born, a statue of him as a boy, and a museum. A biography of George Washington Carver is included in Volume C.

The Jefferson National Expansion Memorial National Historic Site, in St. Louis, commemorates the part that Missouri played in the nation's westward expansion. The memorial includes Gateway Arch, a huge stainless steel arch designed by the architect Eero Saarinen. The underground visitors' center is beneath the arch. Trains in the legs of the arch take visitors to the observation deck at the top.

Wilson's Creek National Battlefield, near Springfield, preserves the place where General Nathaniel Lyon of the Union Army was killed on August 10, 1861, during one of the more than 1,000 Civil War battles that took place in Missouri.

State Parks and Historic Shrines

Missouri has more than 50 state parks and state historic sites. The parks are widely scattered over the state. The following list shows the variety.

Arrow Rock State Historic Site is located between Boonville and Marshall at the old town of Arrow Rock on the Missouri River. At the entrance to the park is the famous old Arrow Rock Tavern, an important stopping place on the Santa Fe Trail.

Big Spring State Park, near Van Buren, is bordered by the swift Current River. The most important feature of the park is Big Spring. Other state parks with large springs are **Bennett Spring State Park** near Lebanon, **Montauk State Park** in Dent County, and **Round Spring State Park** near Eminence.

Battle of Lexington State Historic Site, in Lexington, preserves the site of the battle of Lexington, in September, 1861. The trenches can still

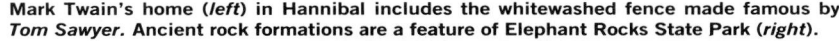

Mark Twain's home (*left*) in Hannibal includes the whitewashed fence made famous by *Tom Sawyer.* Ancient rock formations are a feature of Elephant Rocks State Park (*right*).

be seen. The **Anderson House,** which was used as a field hospital, is preserved as a state historic site.

Johnson's Shut-Ins State Park is in the northeastern corner of Reynolds County. It includes the picturesque shut-ins of the east fork of the Black River. Shut-ins are gorges formed by erosion in an otherwise wide valley.

Lake of the Ozarks State Park is the largest of the state parks, spreading around an arm of the lake. The many recreational facilities include boating, fishing, horseback riding, nature trails, and campgrounds. Other parks with large lakes are **Big Lake State Park** in Holt County, **Lake Wappapello State Park, Table Rock State Park,** and **Thousand Hills State Park** near Kirksville.

Annual Events

Missouri has a variety of yearly events. Some are of local importance, and others are nationally known.

April—Annual Science Fair, St. Louis; Pony Express Commemoration, St. Joseph.

May—May festival and tour of historic homes, Hermann; peony blossom display, Sarcoxie; Journalism Week, University of Missouri.

July—National Tom Sawyer Days, Hannibal; St. Louis Riverfront Festival.

August—State Fair, Sedalia.

September—World Series of Sports Fishing, Branson; Cotton Carnival, Sikeston.

October—The American Royal (livestock show), Kansas City.

▶CITIES

Missouri's major cities—St. Louis and Kansas City—are centers of large metropolitan areas that contain more than 55 percent of the state's total population.

Jefferson City

The state capital is located on the Missouri River near the center of the state. It was named in honor of Thomas Jefferson. The site was chosen in 1821, and the city was laid out the next year. The legislature met there for the first time in 1826. In the meantime, St. Charles had served as the capital.

The state capitol stands in a landscaped park overlooking the steep bluffs of the river. The main floor of the building contains museums. Among works of art in the capitol are Thomas Hart Benton's famous murals dealing with the history of Missouri.

The main business of Jefferson City is state government, but it is also a center for such industries as publishing and the manufacture of electrical equipment and a trading center for nearby farming areas.

St. Louis

St. Louis is the largest city in Missouri. The metropolitan area includes many other cities and towns on both the Missouri side and the Illinois side of the Mississippi River. An article on St. Louis is included in Volume S.

Kansas City

Kansas City, the second largest city in the state, is located on the Missouri River at the mouth of the Kansas River. It adjoins Kansas City, Kansas, to form an important commercial, industrial, and transportation center of the central plains. An article on Kansas City is included in Volume K.

Springfield

Missouri's third largest city, Springfield, is located in the Ozarks resort area of southwestern Missouri. It is surrounded by a highly productive agricultural area. Industries in the city include railroad shops, stockyards, food-processing plants, electrical goods plants, and a large paper-cup factory. Springfield is the home of Drury College and Southwest Missouri State University.

Independence

Settled in 1827, Independence was the starting point for pioneers going west on the California, Oregon, and Santa Fe trails. During the Civil War, Independence was occupied twice by Confederate forces.

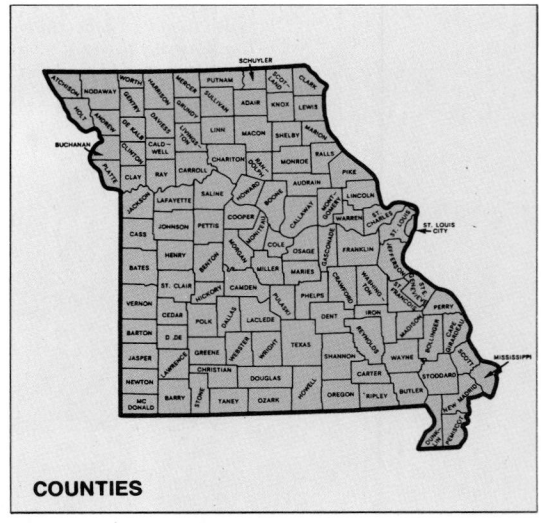

COUNTIES

Today, Independence is a center for oil refining, the manufacture of chemicals and farm and industrial machinery, and other industries. It is the world headquarters of the Reorganized Church of Jesus Christ of Latter Day Saints (Mormons) and the home of the Harry S Truman Library and Museum.

GOVERNMENT

Capital—Jefferson City. **Number of counties**—114.
Representation in Congress—U.S. senators, 2; U.S. representatives, 9. **General Assembly**—Senate, 34 members, 4-year terms; House of Representatives, 163 members, 2-year terms. **Governor**—4-year term; limited to two terms. **Elections**—General and state, Tuesday after first Monday in November.

▶ GOVERNMENT

Missouri is governed by a constitution that was adopted in 1945. Earlier constitutions were adopted in 1820, 1865, and 1875.

The executive branch of the government is headed by the governor. Other elected officials include the lieutenant governor, secretary of state, and attorney general.

The legislative branch is called the General Assembly. It is made up of the Senate and the House of Representatives. The judicial branch is headed by the state Supreme Court. Below it are three courts of appeals—at St. Louis, Kansas City, and Springfield. There are also circuit courts, courts of common pleas, probate courts, and various other courts.

▶ FAMOUS PEOPLE

Missouri has been the birthplace or adopted home of pioneers, political leaders, artists, and writers whose names are widely known.

René Auguste Chouteau (1749–1829), one of the founders of St. Louis, was born in New Orleans. In 1763, he joined the expedition of his stepfather, Pierre Laclède, to establish the fur trade in a large area west of the Mississippi River. Laclède chose the site of the future city and then put the 14-year-old René Auguste in charge of a party that began the work of clearing off trees and erecting buildings. Jean Pierre Chouteau, younger half brother of René Auguste, and two of his sons, Auguste Pierre and Pierre, are remembered for leading expeditions, establishing settlements, and developing the fur trade.

William Clark (1770–1838), born in Virginia, joined Captain Meriwether Lewis in leading the Lewis and Clark expedition. The story of this expedition is told in an article in Volume L. Afterward, Clark was superintendent of Indian affairs at St. Louis and then governor of Missouri territory from 1813 to 1821. His grave is in Bellefontaine Cemetery in St. Louis.

Thomas Hart Benton (1782–1858), born in North Carolina, came to Missouri in 1815. He was elected to the United States Senate and served as senator for 30 years (1821–51). Senator Benton was known for his strong and independent views on many questions. His stand on slavery and his opposition to secession led to his defeat in the 1850 Senate race. His daughter, Jessie, was a writer and the wife of John C. Frémont, explorer and army officer, whose biography is included in Volume F. Senator Benton was the granduncle of **Thomas Hart Benton**

Kansas City is noted for its pleasant downtown shopping areas, fountains, and outdoor attractions. Country Club Plaza was one of the first planned shopping centers in the United States.

(1889–1975), born in Neosho, a noted painter of life in the Middle West.

Mark Twain was the pen name of Samuel Langhorne Clemens (1835–1910). His birthplace is a state memorial site, preserved as a museum, in Mark Twain State Park, near Florida, Missouri. In Hannibal, Mark Twain's boyhood home, visitors may see many of the landmarks mentioned in his novels. A biography of Mark Twain is included in Volume T.

John Joseph Pershing (1860–1948) was commander in chief of the American Expeditionary Force during World War I and chief of staff of the United States Army, 1921–24. His boyhood home in Laclede is a state memorial site. A biography of General Pershing appears in Volume P.

Harry S Truman (1884–1972), 33rd president of the United States, was born in Lamar. He was the first Missourian to become president. Truman's birthplace in Lamar is now a state memorial shrine. A biography of the President is included in Volume T.

St. Louis was the birthplace of several noted writers, including poets Eugene Field, T. S. Eliot, Sara Teasdale, and Marianne Moore. Tennessee Williams, Thomas Wolfe, and Mark Twain lived in St. Louis for some part of their lives. Other Missouri-born writers are poet and playwright Zoë Akins (Humansville), poet Langston Hughes (Joplin), and writer Rupert Hughes (Lancaster). Biographies of T. S. Eliot, Eugene Field, and Langston Hughes are included in Volumes E, F, and H, respectively.

Other well-known Missourians include dancer Ted Shawn (Kansas City), composer Robert Russell Bennett (Kansas City), General Omar N. Bradley (Clark), and clergyman Reinhold Niebuhr (Wright City). Walt Disney's boyhood home was in Marceline.

▶ HISTORY

The first explorers of Missouri found various Indian peoples—Osage, Sauk and Fox, Missouri, Shawnee, and others—living there. During the 30 years after the Louisiana Purchase, the Indians moved on into Kansas and Oklahoma.

Exploration and Settlement

The first explorers to leave a record of their visit to present-day Missouri were Jacques Marquette and Louis Jolliet, in 1673. In 1682, La Salle claimed the entire Mississippi Valley for France. As early as 1700, French missionaries established a mission on the present site of St. Louis. About 1735, French Canadian settlers from Illinois made the first permanent settlement in Missouri. This was Sainte Genevieve.

In 1762, France secretly gave its lands west of the Mississippi to Spain. To encourage settlement the Spanish Government offered generous grants of land. Otherwise the Spanish had little effect on the area. The French, together with American pioneers, developed the fur trade and the lead mines. In 1800,

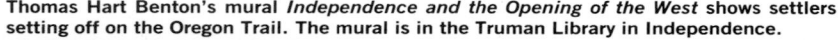
Thomas Hart Benton's mural *Independence and the Opening of the West* shows settlers setting off on the Oregon Trail. The mural is in the Truman Library in Independence.

Spain ceded the territory back to France, and in 1803, France sold it to the United States as part of the Louisiana Purchase.

Territorial Days

From 1804 until 1812, Missouri was part of a territory known as Upper Louisiana, or the District of Louisiana. Meriwether Lewis was governor of this territory from 1807 until his death in 1809. Missouri territory was created in 1812. During territorial days, many settlers came into Missouri.

Statehood and Later Times

Missouri's entry into the Union was delayed because of the struggle in Congress to keep a balance between the free states and the slaveholding states. Finally a compromise was made. Maine entered the Union as a free state in 1820, and Missouri as a slaveholding state in 1821. An article explaining the Missouri Compromise follows this article.

Missouri's first constitution was drawn up by a convention held in St. Louis in 1820. Elections were held the same year. Alexander McNair was elected the first governor. When Missouri was admitted to the Union the next year, the present site of Jefferson City was chosen for the capital. The opening of the Santa Fe Trail and the beginning of steamboat traffic on the Missouri River led to rapid settlement of the western part of the state after 1821. The last of the treaties with the Indians was made in 1832. The Platte Purchase of 1836 added to Missouri a strip of land in the northwest known as the Platte country.

By the 1840's many pioneers were trekking through Missouri to join the wagon trains that were leaving regularly from western Missouri for Oregon and then for Utah and California. Missouri remained in the Union during the Civil War. But the people were divided in their loyalty, and many battles were fought in the state. Much of the warfare was carried out by guerrilla bands. After the war some members of these bands, such as Cole Younger and Frank and Jesse James, became notorious outlaws. An article on Jesse James is included in Volume J.

In the years following the Civil War, steamboat traffic declined, and railroads expanded rapidly. Agriculture and mining continued to be developed, and manufacturing became important. During the present century, Missouri has developed its highway system, diversified its farming, and encouraged the growth of industry.

The Future

In recent years, Missouri's rate of population growth has fallen below the national average, with more and more people and businesses moving to the Sun Belt states. Nevertheless, Missouri's advantages—a central location, abundant water supplies, low energy costs, productive agricultural land, and a low rate of taxation—continue to make it a pleasant place to live.

DALE R. MARTIN
Northeast Missouri State University

IMPORTANT DATES

1673 Marquette and Jolliet came down the Mississippi River and saw the land that is now Missouri.

1682 Robert Cavelier, Sieur de la Salle, reached the mouth of the Mississippi and claimed the entire Mississippi Valley for France.

1700 Jesuit mission established at present-day St. Louis; abandoned in 1703.

1735 Sainte Genevieve established about this time as the first permanent settlement in Missouri.

1762 France ceded lands west of the Mississippi to Spain.

1764 St. Louis founded as a fur-trading post.

1800 Spain ceded lands west of Mississippi back to France.

1803 Louisiana Purchase.

1804 Lewis and Clark expedition set out from the vicinity of St. Louis to explore the Louisiana Purchase.

1805 Upper Louisiana (or District of Louisiana) became a separate territory, with the capital at St. Louis.

1812 Territory of Missouri created.

1820 Missouri Compromise authorized Missouri to enter the Union as a slave state; first state constitution adopted.

1821 August 10, Missouri admitted to the Union as the 24th state.

1836 Platte Purchase ended Indian claims in Missouri.

1859 First railroad completed across the state.

1860 Pony Express began operation between St. Joseph and Sacramento, California.

1861 Missouri remained in the Union during the Civil War.

1873 First public kindergarten in the United States opened at St. Louis.

1908 School of Journalism, the first in the world to grant a degree in journalism, founded at the University of Missouri.

1931 Bagnell Dam, forming Lake of the Ozarks, completed.

1945 Harry S Truman of Missouri became president of the United States.

1964 Ozark National Scenic Riverways authorized.

1979 State court system re-organized into three categories—supreme court, appellate court, and circuit court.

1984 Missouri's first nuclear electric generating plant goes into operation at Fulton.

1985 Harriett Woods, Missouri's first woman lieutenant governor, takes office.

MISSOURI COMPROMISE

Before the issue of slavery finally brought the United States to civil war, there were many attempts at compromise between the North and the South. One of the most important of these attempts was the Missouri Compromise of 1820.

In 1819 Missouri applied for admission to the Union. The question of whether it should be admitted as a slave state stirred up the conflict between those who were for slavery and those who were against it. Many Northerners were against slavery because they thought it morally wrong or economically unfair. Southern planters had already taken their slaves into the Missouri Territory and naturally wanted slavery to be permitted there.

Slave and free states were evenly balanced at the time—11 of each. Therefore each side had the same number of senators. A new slave state would upset the balance and give people who favored slavery control of the United States Senate.

In February of 1819 Representative James Tallmadge (1778–1853) of New York introduced a resolution in Congress proposing that no more slaves be brought into Missouri after it became a state and that children of slaves born after the admission of the state be freed at the age of 25.

Southerners were outraged. Northerners greeted the proposal with enthusiasm, holding mass meetings and signing petitions of support. On February 16 and 17, 1819, the resolution passed in the House of Representatives. But the Senate rejected it. Soon afterward Congress adjourned. The debate raged furiously all over the land.

When Congress met in December, Missouri again asked for statehood. Meanwhile Maine, at that time part of Massachusetts, also asked admission as a separate state. The Senate voted to combine the resolutions, admitting Maine as a free state and Missouri as a slave state. The number of slave and free states would then still be even—12 each.

Then in February, 1820, Senator Jesse Burgess Thomas (1777–1853) of Illinois proposed an amendment to the combined resolutions: Admit Missouri as a slave state, but ban slavery in the future from all territory north of 36° 30' north latitude, Missouri's southern border.

Slave states were already separated from free states by the Mason-Dixon line (the southern boundary of Pennsylvania) and the Ohio River. The new requirement would extend the dividing line westward. If Missouri were admitted as a slave state, it would be the only slave area north of the line.

This proposal angered Southerners. They claimed that all states had equal rights and that Congress had no power to limit the right of a state to decide whether to be slave or free. For months the question of states' rights was debated bitterly in Congress. Thomas Jefferson called the debate "a fire bell in the night" because it appeared to be a warning of great trouble.

The Thomas Amendment passed in the Senate but was rejected in the House. On March 1, 1820, the House voted to admit Missouri as a free state. But in the compromise that both houses of Congress finally accepted, Maine was admitted as a free state (March, 1820), and Missouri was authorized to form a state constitution without restrictions on slavery. The Compromise also banned slavery north of 36° 30'. The South won Missouri, but it lost more than it gained. The area north of the dividing line, where slavery was banned "forever," was larger than the area where slavery would be allowed.

The state constitution Missouri presented to Congress was not approved. According to this constitution freed slaves could not enter Missouri. The "Great Compromiser," Henry Clay, then helped work out a second compromise, which stated that Missouri could not deny free black citizens their constitutional rights. Missouri accepted this and became a state in August, 1821.

In 1854 the Missouri Compromise was repealed by the Kansas-Nebraska Act. By the terms of this law slavery would not be banned in new states north of 36° 30'. Each entering state had the right of popular sovereignty. This meant that these states could decide for themselves whether to be slave or free. The change further divided North and South and led to fighting in Kansas. The repeal of the Missouri Compromise is one of the events that led to the Civil War.

Reviewed by RICHARD B. MORRIS
Columbia University

See also KANSAS-NEBRASKA ACT.

MISSOURI RIVER

The Missouri River is the longest North American river when the Red Rock River is considered as a portion of the Missouri. It rises in the heart of the Rocky Mountains and flows 2,714 miles to join the Mississippi in mid-continent, near St. Louis. The Missouri and Mississippi together stretch 3,892 miles.

History of the Missouri

Historically the Missouri has been both a boundary and a highway. In frontier times it marked the line where the West began. It also provided the main path into the western wilderness. French explorers Louis Jolliet and Father Jacques Marquette discovered the mouth of the Missouri in 1673. Early fur traders traveled the river, and during the late 18th century they began to explore its upper reaches. Meriwether Lewis and William Clark followed the entire course of the Missouri on their journey to the Pacific (1804–06).

For many years settlement stopped at the lower Missouri. On its eastern side were farms; on the west was the prairie, which farmers considered worthless. Then pioneers began going to Oregon, California, and Utah in the 1840's. The Oregon Trail followed the course of one of the Missouri's major branches, the Platte.

The first river carriers were dugout canoes and "bullboats" made of buffalo hide. Then came the keelboats, powered by oars, poles, or sails, or towed by men or animals walking along the banks. Getting keelboats upstream was a backbreaking job, for the Missouri was a tricky, dangerous river. Some said that Missouri mules got their cussedness from drinking its waters. It had a powerful current and was full of sandbars, snags, and rapids.

In 1819 the first steamboat appeared. River traffic, including furs and military and civilian supplies, increased. In the 1870's railroad competition reduced river traffic. Today, the Missouri is again an important waterway.

Course of the River

The Missouri rises in southwestern Montana. Three mountain streams, the Red Rock-Jefferson, the Madison, and the Gallatin, form its headwaters near Three Forks. Here it is over 4,000 feet above sea level. It flows through Montana and in North Dakota is joined by the Yellowstone. Then it runs southeast, forming boundaries between several states. North of St. Louis it pours into the Mississippi at an average rate of 64,000 cubic feet of water per second. There are great seasonal differences in the amount of water.

Some of the Missouri's major branches are the Yellowstone, Big Sioux, James, Cheyenne, Milk, Osage, Kansas, White, and Platte. The whole river system drains an area of 530,000 square miles, which includes a small part of southern Canada. As it cuts through mountains and prairies the Missouri gathers huge quantities of sand and silt, earning its nickname "Big Muddy." It dumps approximately 200,000,000 tons of silt a year into the Mississippi. The water is considered good to drink once the silt is removed.

But the Missouri can be an enemy to man. It can change its channel overnight. At flood stage it is a powerful destroyer. Melting snow in the Rockies and heavy spring rains sometimes swell the volume of water and flood millions of acres. The federal government is building dams and large reservoirs. The program will aid in flood control, increase irrigation, and develop electric power and recreation areas. The river is being deepened to form a 9-foot channel as far upstream as Sioux City, Iowa.

Reviewed by FRANK SEAWALL
Ohio State University

A wagon wheel marks the place where pioneer wagon trains crossed the Missouri River on their journey westward.

MODELING, FASHION

Fashion modeling is big business wherever fashion and advertising exist. Although there are many men and children who are successful models, the vast majority of fashion models are young women who range in age from the teens to the mid-thirties.

A fashion model usually lives and works in a great fashion center, such as Paris, Milan, New York, Tokyo, or Munich. There she may show collections of clothes by famous designers. Or she may be a photographic model whose face smiles at you from the pages of a magazine. She may even lend charm and grace to commercials on national television. Models are usually chosen for their elegance, beauty, and grace. Models are also expressive, animated, and project an image of energy. They set styles of beauty for many women, who copy their makeup, hairdos, and clothes.

Modeling sounds glamorous, but it is really very hard work. To make a picture for a magazine cover, the model may have to stand for hours, holding a difficult pose under strobe lights. The showroom model may be on her feet all day, making hurried changes of clothing in a cramped dressing room. The television model may have to go through many hours of tedious "takes."

A model needs a great deal of patience and stamina. But models who reach the top of their profession make a great deal of money and wear some of the world's most beautiful clothes. They work with great photographers and dress designers. Their assignments can take them all over the world.

Not everyone can be a model. There are stringent physical requirements. Most models are tall and slim and have broad shoulders, long legs, and slender waists. Photographers' models must also have beautiful faces that photograph well. Recently, however, there has been a trend toward using models who look like "real people."

Generally, models must look fresh and young, so their careers are often over by the time they reach their early- to mid-thirties. However, the advertising media have begun to use more mature models in recent years. Many models go on to acting, dress designing, or editorial work on fashion magazines when their active modeling days are over.

Photographic Modeling. Photographers' models pose for department-store catalogs, newspaper advertisements, and the great fashion magazines, such as *Vogue* and *Harper's Bazaar*. A cover on one of these magazines is a prize assignment and means that the model has reached the top of her profession. Many models also appear in the prestige designer fashion shows, which have become showcases for their introduction to editors and advertising directors who ultimately may hire them.

The requirements for photographic modeling are the hardest to meet. Because the camera makes people seem heavier than they are, the models must be trim. Female models must be a minimum of 5 feet 7 inches tall, although heights of 5 feet 8 inches to 5 feet 11 inches are more desirable. Male models are usually over 6 feet tall and may range up to 6 feet 3 inches. In the late 1970's the earnings of male models began to equal that of women, and there are now many more men's fashions and products than ever before.

Photographers' models must also have faces that photograph well. Women often have angular faces with large eyes, hollowed cheeks, and prominent cheek bones.

A photographers' model must learn to stand for hours in a difficult pose. Since magazines plan their issues many months in advance, she may have to pose in a bathing suit in December or wrap up in furs on a sweltering day in July. She must be an expert with makeup and hair styles—and a bit of an actress too. She may be asked to pose as a college girl in one picture and as a society matron in the next. She must know how to change her hair and makeup so that she will feel, act, and look the part.

Top-level models customarily work exclusively through one representative office, or agency, that guides their careers and establishes and negotiates their fees. Such representatives collect from 15 to 20 percent of a model's income as commission.

Showroom Modeling. In fashion houses and some exclusive shops, clothes are shown to customers by showroom models instead of being displayed on racks. In wholesale houses, too, where large quantities of clothing are sold, models wear sample garments from which buyers make their selections.

Some showroom models are hired by a fashion house and work only for that house.

The designers make their clothes on the models, called "fitting models," and often plan clothing with a favorite model in mind. Other models free-lance, through agencies. These models are hired for special showings and are paid by the hour or the day.

The job of the showroom model is to show off the garments at their best. The model must learn to walk gracefully. Graceful movement is more important than classic beauty or a lovely face. Showroom models are usually tall and slender and wear a size 7 to 12 dress.

Television Modeling. Many fashion and photographers' models take classes that will help make them competent for television modeling. There are several different types of television models. Many models appear as background models for TV commercials or, possibly, TV game shows. Some have learned to combine beauty and acting talent for scenes in TV commercials. Others exhibit cosmetics or other products while describing them and urging consumers to use them. Sometimes one model becomes the major spokesperson for a particular product or product line.

Trade Show Modeling. Also referred to as industrial shows, trade shows exhibit merchandise, such as computers, automobiles, or boats, to dealers and the general public. Since the products are exhibited with great fanfare, models are often used to enhance the look of the product and explain its uses. For this type of modeling, height and perfection of features are secondary to personality, general appeal, and a clear speaking voice. A trade show model is usually provided with a brief familiarization of the exhibitor's product or service and is then expected to distribute literature about the product and answer simple questions.

Child Models. Photogenic children are sometimes hired for magazine and television advertisements. Child models range in age from 3 months to 14 years (when they usually become junior models). They are hired through agencies in the same way adult models are hired. Some child models continue their careers into adulthood. Many make the transition from photographic models to TV commercials, TV series, and films.

Model Agencies

Model agencies conduct business transactions for models. They perform such duties as

Posing for photographs may look glamorous, but it is hard work. Models must be able to hold difficult poses for hours under hot studio lights.

arranging test photos, assisting with makeup and grooming, arranging portfolios (groups of pictures of the model), and introducing models to photographers, designers, and other clients. Agencies will also negotiate fees, bill for payment, and advance payment to models before receiving the fees from clients. Agencies collect a percentage of a model's earnings as commission.

Becoming a Model

A person who wishes to become a model must have the required height and photogenic qualities. If such qualities are present, gracefulness of movement, grooming and makeup techniques, and good speaking characteristics can be acquired.

Most reputable agencies will provide a free evaluation of one's potential for modeling, if given a few snapshots, hair and eye color, weight and height measurements, some garment sizes, and age. A model hopeful should not pay for such an evaluation, nor should money be spent on professional photographs, unless a commitment to represent has been made by an agent.

Every field of modeling is highly competitive. Only one person in a hundred can be a successful model. But the lucky few win high pay, independence, and the chance to work in almost every great city in the world.

G. W. FORD
Ford Model Agency

Reviewed and updated by WILLIAM P. WEINBERG
President, Wilhelmina International Ltd.

MODELMAKING. See AIRPLANE MODELS; AUTOMOBILE MODELS; RAILROADS, MODEL; SHIP MODELS.

Impression: Sunrise (1872), by Claude Monet. Musée Marmottan, Paris.

MODERN ART

It is impossible to say exactly when and where modern art began. The history of art is like a chain to which new links are always being added. Every link is attached to the link before it. For example, the many different styles of the 20th century are outgrowths of the styles used during the 19th century. In turn, 19th-century art developed from the styles of the previous century. If we were to trace the origins of modern art as far back as possible, we would find that it really began with the very first link in the chain—the rock scratchings of cavemen.

▶ REALISM

During the first half of the 19th century the artists of France—then the world's center of artistic activity—began to look for new ways to paint. The French Revolution was over, and the Industrial Revolution was under way. Many artists felt that the formal, classical pictures of such artists as Jacques Louis David (1748–1825) no longer expressed the spirit of the times. These young artists preferred the work of Théodore Géricault (1791–1824) and Eugène Delacroix (1798–1863), who were known as **romantics**. The romantics painted dramatic pictures filled with bright, sometimes raw colors. The painters who admired romanticism thought that this informality and passion better expressed an age in which freedom and individuality had become very important.

Gustave Courbet (1819–77), a Frenchman, said that the aim of painting was to set down without change what was seen by the human eye. He called himself a **realist**. Other artists who claimed to be searching for realism were puzzled by Courbet's statement, for the newly invented camera reproduced exactly what was seen by the eye. Was there no difference between a photograph and a painting? For an answer to that question, some French artists looked to the work of an Englishman, J. M. W. Turner (1775–1851). Turner sacrificed details in order to capture atmosphere. He felt that mist, fog, and light were as real in a scene as trees and water. Nature is ever changing, and Turner tried to suggest the changes that occur from hour to hour and season to season.

Around the middle of the century there were several groups and individual artists who were attempting to develop a realistic style. The painters of the French Barbizon school —so called because they worked in the town of Barbizon, south of Paris—went outdoors to paint. They hoped to capture the qualities of nature that were momentary, fleeting, and very real. In this they differed from Courbet, who painted pictures of peasants at work or relaxing. Courbet thought that paintings of day-to-day activities represented a peak of realism. Édouard Manet (1832–83) combined the ideas of Courbet and the Barbizon painters. He liked to depict the quality of a single moment, and his subject matter was often commonplace.

▶ IMPRESSIONISM

On April 15, 1874, a group of Paris artists opened an exhibition of 165 paintings. During the month-long show visitors crowded the gallery, but their opinion of the work was low. The most common reaction was laughter. One critic wrote a humorous article called "Exhibition of the Impressionists." This name, taken from Claude Monet's painting *Impression: Sunrise,* was meant to be sarcastic. Apparently the artists had no objection to it and began calling themselves impressionists.

Most of the impressionists were mature artists. Their exhibition had not been meant to startle or shock. Instead, its purpose was to display the kind of work that had been rejected from official exhibitions for years. The impressionists, after all, had been developing their approach for a long time. Painters like Camille Pissarro (1830–1903) and Claude Monet (1840–1926) had been experimenting with many techniques since before 1860.

Objects themselves were of little importance to the impressionists. The play of light over a surface, the discovery of hidden colors in shadows—these became the subject matter of impressionist paintings. The impressionists studied scientific color theory and tried to apply what they learned to their painting. If an object was supposed to be purple, they did not mix blue and red paint on their palette and then apply the paint to the canvas. Instead they painted the object with many small dabs of blue and red. The eye of the viewer mixed the color, making it appear purple.

Impressionism was not so "scientific" as the impressionists said it was. A painter named Georges Seurat (1859–91) invented a technique called **pointillism**. Seurat's canvases were painted entirely with tiny dots of colors, premixed according to formula. But most of the impressionists did not wish to paint according to formula. Thus, the works of the impressionists bear individual differences.

Rodin

Impressionism is a kind of painting, but the sculptor Auguste Rodin (1840–1917) is sometimes called an impressionist. Like the painters, he wanted to create surfaces that seemed alive. He accomplished this by modeling his surfaces with many distinct little planes. The planes catch and reflect light and make the surface almost appear to breathe.

Monument to Balzac (1897), by Rodin. Museum of Modern Art, New York.

Rodin was also interested in the space that his sculpture occupied. If a figure had its hands placed on its hips, the triangle of space between the arms and the body was, to him, as important a shape as the arms themselves.

Compared to painting, sculpture had been of little importance after the 17th century. It almost always had represented the human form in a classical manner. Soldiers and statesmen were shown in statues to look like Greek gods. Rodin gave new life to the nearly dead art. Trained in the academic tradition, he modeled naturalistic and dramatic figures. His talent was great and his influence strong. Though his work hardly looks revolutionary today, he revived the art of sculpture.

▶ POSTIMPRESSIONISM

Although he was not an impressionist, Edgar Degas (1834–1917) was close to the group and took much from its style. Degas was a collector of Japanese prints. From these prints he learned a great deal about spacious compositions and sharp contrasts of simple shapes. Unlike the impressionists, he used black paint and drew hard edges. But his dancing colors were similar to those used by the impressionists.

Paul Gauguin (1848–1903) was influenced by impressionism and by the work of Degas. But he was not interested in a scientific formula of light. Gauguin liked the flat pattern effects suggested in the work of Degas. He simplified the human figure, treating it as part of an over-all pattern.

Vincent van Gogh (1853–90) loved the effects of shimmering light achieved by the impressionists. He concentrated on this effect, applying paint thickly, in large dabs, making his colors appear to swirl around or explode. The subject matter of his paintings seems to be light alone—its movement and its power.

Gauguin and Van Gogh, along with Seurat and sometimes Degas, are often included in a group called postimpressionists. This term has little meaning because the styles of these painters vary greatly. It does, however, indicate that their styles developed after the impressionists'.

▶ PAUL CÉZANNE

Paul Cézanne (1839–1906) was about the same age as most of the impressionists. But in a discussion of art history Cézanne is always mentioned after the impressionists and after Gauguin, Van Gogh, and Seurat. Although he lived only until 1906, he is regarded as the first 20th-century artist.

Cézanne was impatient with impressionism. He thought that the impressionists had created a veil of pleasing color across the canvas without describing the solid forms of nature. In his paintings he tried to show that natural objects had structure and weight—that they were made of more than atmosphere. A landscape, a human body, and a basket of fruit were solid and real to Cézanne, and he was interested in their every surface, or plane.

In most of Cézanne's pictures there is little suggestion of depth. A tree in the foreground and a mountain in the background appear to be the same distance from the viewer's eye. He divided his objects into planes. A face, for example, would be painted according to its separate surfaces, with a different plane for the forehead, the cheeks, the nose, the chin, and so forth. Cézanne would make the face look solid by varying the amount of light that struck each plane and by varying his shading or brushstroke on each plane.

Cézanne was never fully appreciated when he was alive. He was not an impressionist (though many of his friends were). He desired public recognition, but he died feeling that he had failed. In 1907, a year after his death, a memorial exhibition of his work was held in Paris. Its effect was startling, as we shall see.

▶ FAUVISM

For the Autumn Salon of 1905—the official exhibition of the French Academy of Art—the Academy jury accepted the works of five painters whose styles had certain things in common. Henri Matisse (1869–1954), André Derain (1880–1954), Albert Marquet (1875–1947), Georges Rouault (1871–1958), and Maurice de Vlaminck (1876–1958) painted with bright, rich colors. Their pictures contained only the barest suggestion that they depicted natural scenes. Colors were pure and flat. Very little shading was employed.

The Academy decided to display the pictures of the five artists in one room, apart from the rest of the Salon. One critic, after

Above left: *Rocky Landscape* (1898?), by Cézanne. Right: *Sunflowers* (1888), by Van Gogh. Both pictures are in the National Gallery, London. Below: *The Red Studio* (1911), by Matisse. Museum of Modern Art, New York.

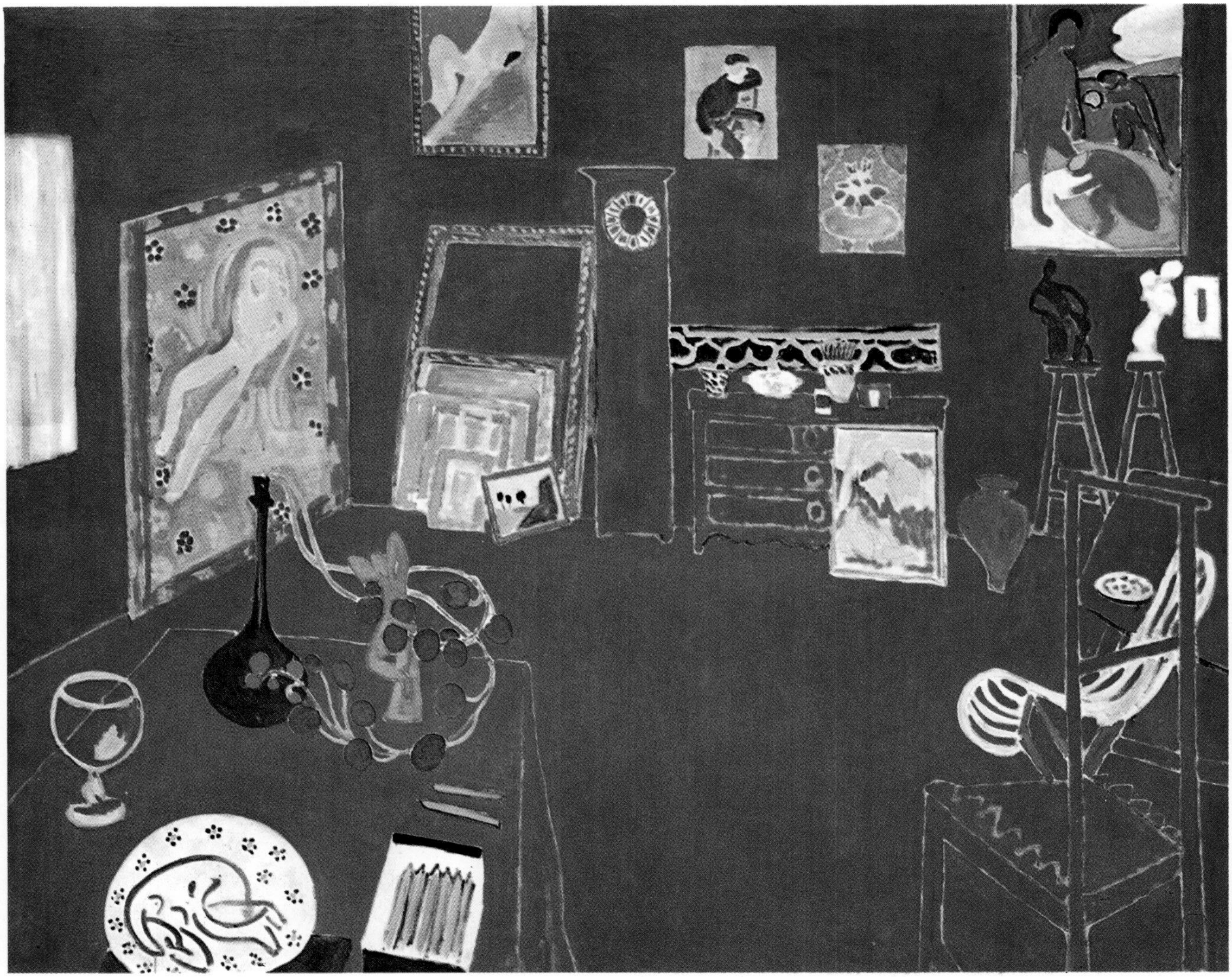

visiting the exhibition, called the five painters *fauves* ("wild beasts").

The fauves learned about color theories from the impressionists. From Van Gogh and Gauguin they learned to use color boldly. From Cézanne they learned how to make separate forms appear solid. They placed complementary colors next to one another, making the canvas seem to vibrate.

Matisse was the greatest painter of the fauve group. Strongly influenced by Cézanne, he continued working with flat, pure colors in patterns. Throughout his long career he produced a tremendous number of pictures and much fine sculpture.

▶CUBISM

The early years of the 20th century were exciting ones. Modern science was exploring everything, replacing superstitions with facts. In all areas of life there were reactions against illusions of any kind. Moreover, the new science of anthropology revealed much about the relationship between art and civilization. By studying so-called primitive societies, the anthropologists realized that art was more than just decoration: it was an important part of life.

Two young painters in Paris were very much aware of the scientific discoveries of their day. The Frenchman Georges Braque (1882–1963) and his Spanish-born friend Pablo Picasso (1881–1973) were interested in African sculpture. They found the simple shapes and sharp contrasts beautiful, and they began to develop a new style influenced by African work. Then, they attended the Cézanne exhibition of 1907. Greatly impressed, they returned to the studio they shared to experiment. Within the year, they developed cubism, a style of painting that dominated art until World War II.

The cubists saw no reason why they should paint a subject from just one view. After all, there are countless ways to look at something. Just as Cézanne had done, they divided their subjects according to planes. But instead of showing only the visible side, they tried to suggest all the sides at once. It was almost as though they had smashed their subjects to bits, put all the pieces on a flat board, and then painted what they saw.

In their early cubist paintings Braque and Picasso used only pale, grayish colors applied in small, even dabs. These neutral colors prevented any part of the picture from appearing to come forward or go backward. Later the cubists began using larger areas of brighter colors. Braque remained within the framework of cubism, experimenting and perfecting, until his death in 1963. Picasso has moved on to other things, working in countless styles.

Cubism, by nature, was very influential in the development of the sculpture of the period. The idea of simplifying a shape into its basic planes and forms was, in fact, a sculptural idea. Picasso did a great deal of three-dimensional work within the cubist framework of ideas.

The cubist idea of **collage** (the gluing of paper, cloth, or other materials to a surface)

Left: *Les Demoiselles d'Avignon* (1907), by Picasso. Museum of Modern Art, New York. Below: *Dog on a Leash* (1912), by Balla. George F. Goodyear and Buffalo Fine Arts Academy, New York.

was soon developed into the school of **constructivism**—the building of sculpture out of ready-made pieces of shaped materials. Picasso did quite a lot of sculpture using construction as his method.

Sculpture that is constructed, rather than modeled or cut from a block, makes wider use of space shapes than the more traditional type of work. This consciousness of space developed into a new form of sculpture. In the work of sculptors like Jacques Lipchitz (1891–1973) the whole piece is actually a network of empty spaces and solid forms.

▶ FUTURISM IN ITALY

Until World War II, Paris remained the art capital of the world. But experiments in art had spread throughout Europe. In Italy, around 1910, a short-lived but important modern movement developed. It was called futurism, and the artists who developed it wanted to express the speed, progress, and even the violence of modern life.

The futurists, led by the poet Filippo Tommaso Marinetti (1876–1944) and the painter Giacomo Balla (1871–1958), were enthusiastic about such modern developments as motion pictures, the airplane, and mechanical weapons. They were actually looking forward to the mechanized war that seemed to be coming. They wanted their art to capture the speed and violence of the new century. They drew objects on their canvases with flowing, overlapping lines, trying to show how things move in ever shifting light.

Futurism lasted until the outbreak of World War I in 1914. Then the war upset the whole scheme of life and the natural development of modern art in Europe.

The futurist artist Umberto Boccioni (1882–1916) was one of the first artists to use space shapes in sculpture. He did this by imitating a natural object in reverse. That is, he would often include a hollowed-out space where one would expect a full, rounded form. A nose, for example, might cut back into the head rather than project from it.

Another method used by futurist sculptors was to exaggerate space in order to give the illusion of movement. For example, the stride of a walking figure would be extended beyond the natural to make it seem as if the figure were really walking.

Composition III (1914), by Kandinsky. Museum of Modern Art, New York.

▶ GERMAN EXPRESSIONISM

The fauves in France had counterparts in Germany. In 1905 several young painters in Dresden rented a studio together and formed a group called *Die Brücke* ("The Bridge"). The most famous of the group are Ernst Ludwig Kirchner (1880–1938) and Emil Nolde (1867–1956). In their paintings they wanted to express their passion for life. They felt that the brightness and darkness of their colors and their generous brushwork could express their innermost feelings.

By 1911 the Bridge group had moved to Berlin. They held exhibitions at the gallery of a magazine, *Der Sturm* ("The Attack"). A year later another group of painters began to exhibit at *Der Sturm* gallery. Calling itself *Der Blaue Reiter* ("The Blue Rider"), this group had begun in Munich in southern Germany. The founders were Wassily Kandinsky

(1866–1944) and Franz Marc (1880–1916).

Kandinsky was a Russian who was strongly influenced by the folk art of his homeland. He came to believe that the strength of all art lay in colors and shapes. He abstracted objects to their simplest forms, and soon no one could identify any natural objects in his paintings. Thus, from 1910 to 1914 he painted the first really abstract works of the 20th century.

Another important Blue Rider artist was Paul Klee (1879–1940). Usually small watercolors, the pictures of this Swiss-born painter are not totally abstract. But his simple figures resemble those that children draw. Although Klee's subject matter is frequently frivolous or fantastic, his pictures are carefully constructed, beautifully painted, and highly sophisticated. Klee is one of the few modern masters whose work is admired universally, and it appeals to artists of all modern schools.

▶ CONSTRUCTIVISM

In 1912 the Russian painter Kazimir Malevich (1878–1935) met Picasso in Paris and discovered cubism. He was enthusiastic and returned to Russia to start a similar movement. The cubists had broken down objects and simplified them to geometric shapes. Malevich's work emphasized only the geometry itself. With the circle, rectangle, triangle, or square he felt that he could suggest any form in the world. One of Malevich's most famous pictures, *White on White*, is

Above: *Twittering Machine* (watercolor and ink; 1922), by Klee. Museum of Modern Art, New York. **Below left:** *White on White* (1918?), by Malevich. Museum of Modern Art. **Below right:** *Opposition of Lines: Red and Yellow* (1937), by Mondrian. Philadelphia Museum of Art.

simply a white square placed on an angle within the square of the canvas.

Malevich called his style **suprematism** because geometric forms were regarded as the simplest and therefore the most pure, or supreme, shapes. His followers, however, changed the name to constructivism.

Sculpture

The brothers Naum Gabo (1890–1977) and Antoine Pevsner (1886–1962) are the best known of the constructivist sculptors. The work of these Russian artists was an outgrowth of the cubist construction, but it relied more on the laws of mathematics and geometry. Whereas cubist work was often expressionistic or emotional in character, the constructivists tried to keep their sculpture as impersonal and scientific as possible.

▶ NEOPLASTICISM

During the war years (1914–18) a movement was developing in the Netherlands. Its ideas were similar to those of Malevich. Piet Mondrian (1872–1944) and Theo van Doesburg (1883–1931) started a magazine called *De Stijl* ("The Style"). For more than 11 years they published their ideas about art. They influenced industrial designers and architects as well as painters.

Mondrian's neoplasticism was an attempt to remove art from the world of natural forms. He said that geometric forms were the only pure ones—the only fully manageable, or plastic, forms in painting. He divided his rectangular white canvas with black lines, drawn up and down or straight across; there were no diagonals. The lines crossed and formed squares and rectangles, which Mondrian sometimes painted with primary colors —red, yellow, and blue. Thus he produced pictures that were perfectly orderly, with the simplest possible shapes and colors. His idea was the opposite of the futurists'. Instead of capturing the speed and violence of life, Mondrian wanted to describe orderliness.

▶ DADAISM

The outbreak of World War I had different effects on the artists of the period. Some artists fought in the war; others continued working in the styles they had developed in the decade before the war. A group of artists from all over

Developable Column (1942), by Pevsner. Museum of Modern Art, New York.

Europe protested against the social ills of the time. Meeting in Switzerland—a neutral country—they created work that was anti-war, anti–modern life, and indeed, anti-art. This group called their art dada because the word had nothing to do with anything—it was pure nonsense.

The dadaists wrote nonsense poetry in which the words were gobbledygook, and they created nonsense objects. For example, Man Ray (1890–1976) attached carpet tacks to the bottom of an iron and exhibited it. Marcel Duchamp (1887–1968) exhibited a printed reproduction of the *Mona Lisa* on which he had painted a moustache. When they held exhibitions, the dadaists sometimes encouraged the public to destroy some of their displays. This was their reaction to the new civilization of the 20th century. They thought that governments had become insane and art too serious.

The dadaists set out to make fun of—or even destroy—art, but they failed. They failed because while trying to destroy art they created it. They used the cubist collage to put all kinds of objects together. They pasted together drawings, photographs, buttons, advertisements, rubbish—anything at all.

Many people found the antics of the dadaists foolish, insane, vulgar, and destruc-

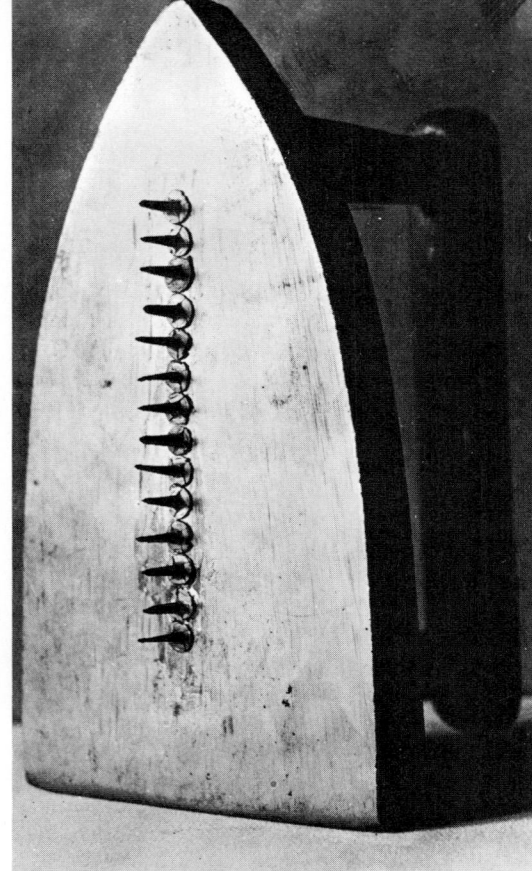

Le Cadeau ("The Gift") (1919), by Man Ray. Collection of Mr. and Mrs. Morton G. Neumann, Chicago.

tive. Nevertheless, new territories of modern art were being opened. Dada forced people to re-examine their opinions of what is ugly and what is beautiful. It forced them to look carefully at everything—even objects that were not supposed to be art. For example, the dada artist Kurt Schwitters (1887–1948) made some of the most admired collages of the period out of ticket stubs, candy wrappers, matchbooks, and similar materials.

One of the most important ideas to develop out of the dada movement was **automatism** —the automatic production of art. This meant that whatever came into the artist's mind was used as part of the work of art. A dada poet would write down any words that his mind formed, regardless of how nonsensical they seemed; a painter would draw the first shapes or objects that appeared to him.

▶ **SURREALISM**

The only style of any importance to develop in the years following World War I was surrealism. This style, an outgrowth of dada,

became the most important art movement in Europe during the late 1920's and 1930's. Many artists who were not members of the movement were strongly influenced by it during this period. Even Pablo Picasso, the cubist painter, was greatly affected by surrealism.

Many of those who were very important in the dada movement—such as the French writer André Breton (1896–1966) and the German-born painter Max Ernst (1891–1976) —were also the founders of surrealism. This new school combined the dada idea of automatism (free and automatic painting) with the psychology of Sigmund Freud. Freud believed that people's real thoughts were hidden in their unconscious minds and in their dreams. He felt that to understand people you must search their dreams. Only dreams are clear. Daytime life is too full of outside events to be understood.

The surrealists believed that the artist should try to understand this world of dreams. They felt that the job of the artist was to show this unconscious world through his work. Obviously they could not paint while asleep. They believed the next best thing was to let the imagination wander and to paint whatever happened to come to mind.

Probably the most important of the surrealist artists was Max Ernst. Not only was he one of the founders of the movement, but he was also a great innovator, developing new ideas in collage. He invented the technique called frottage (texture rubbings). Ernst worked mostly with the idea of automatism, allowing his imagination complete freedom. He often painted or pasted objects next to one another that had no apparent reason for being together. They were placed in this position as an automatic action.

Max Ernst also worked quite often in sculpture, using the same theory of automatism in this medium. Some of the work he did was modeled from clay, using strange and imaginative forms, while other pieces were constructed of ready-made objects in a collagelike technique.

Another very important artist of this period was Joan Miró (1893–1983), who was born in Spain. Although Miró developed no new techniques, his paintings are good examples of surrealism. Completely forgetting the real world, his mind invented humorous abstract paintings made of colorful and unusual forms.

Working a great deal in sculpture, mostly as construction, Jean (Hans) Arp (1887–1966) also was influential as a surrealist artist. Like Miró, Arp created abstract works, using automatism as a means of freeing his imagination and allowing his unconscious mind full reign. Arp's work was based on simple shapes, often symbolic or suggestive of living forms.

A very important surrealist sculptor is Alberto Giacometti (1901–66), who was born in Switzerland. Some of his work seems to use space as its only subject matter. His sculpture often consists of a group of sticklike figures standing on a flat surface. Because the figures are so simple, it becomes obvious to the viewer that the space between them is important. The effect of these strange pieces of sculpture is often eerie and dreamlike.

There were some artists who took an entirely different approach to surrealism; among this group were the Spanish painter Salvador Dali (1904–), French-born Yves Tanguy (1900–55), and an Italian, Giorgio di Chirico (1888–1978). These artists believed in a more literary approach to surrealism. They tried to illustrate dreams the way one would illustrate a story, using symbolic images. Tanguy and di Chirico were very popular during their own period. But they have not influenced more recent artists as much as have Max Ernst and his followers.

Reviewed by RICHARD W. IRELAND
Maryland Institute College of Art

▶ MODERN ART IN THE UNITED STATES

In 1913 an international exhibition of modern art was held in a large armory (military building) in New York City. The Armory Show, as it came to be called, gave the public its first glimpse of some of the important European art movements. And it had a strong influence on American art. During World War I, New York became an active center for modern art. Young artists there came into daily contact with the latest art movements.

In the 1920's, United States artists became convinced that modern art could make a better world. They modeled their art on the highly refined style of the constructivists, and they

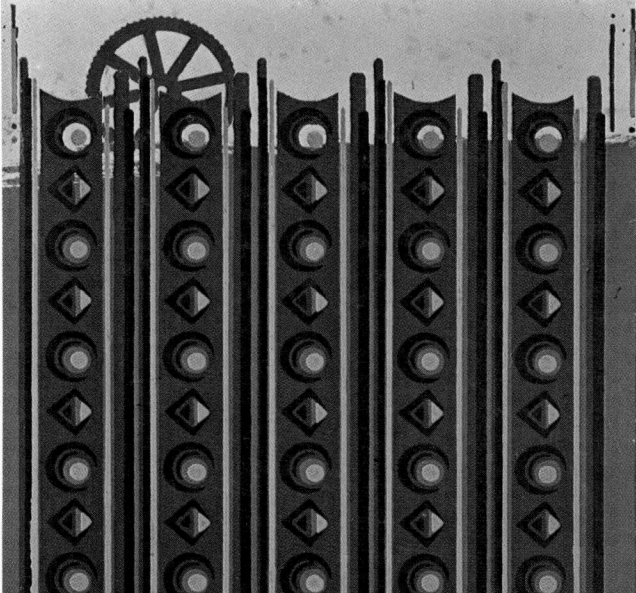

Left: *The Little Tear Gland That Says Tic-Tac* (1920), by Max Ernst. Museum of Modern Art, New York.

Chariot (1950), by Alberto Giacometti. Museum of Modern Art, New York.

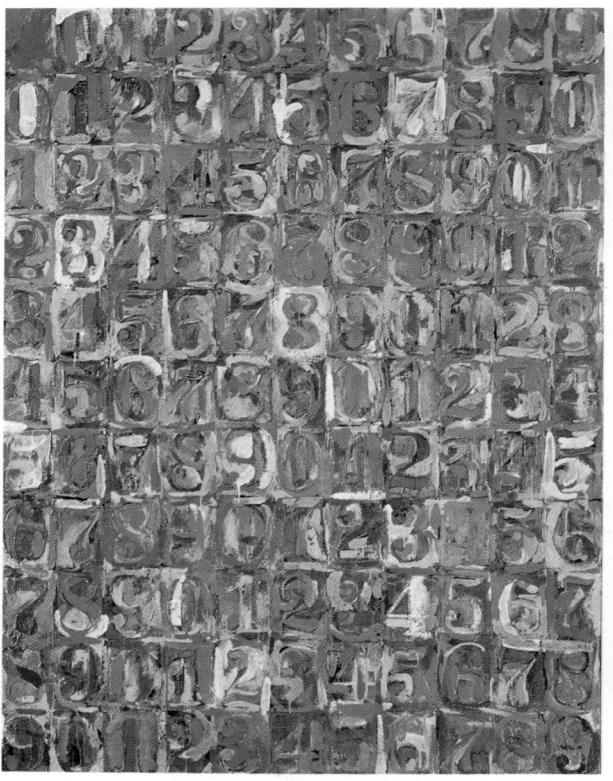

A Tree Grows in Naples (1960), by Willem de Kooning. Janis Gallery, N.Y.

Above: *Numbers in Color* (1958–59), by Jasper Johns. Albright Art Gallery, Buffalo, N.Y.
Below: *Number I* (1948), by Jackson Pollock. Museum of Modern Art, New York.

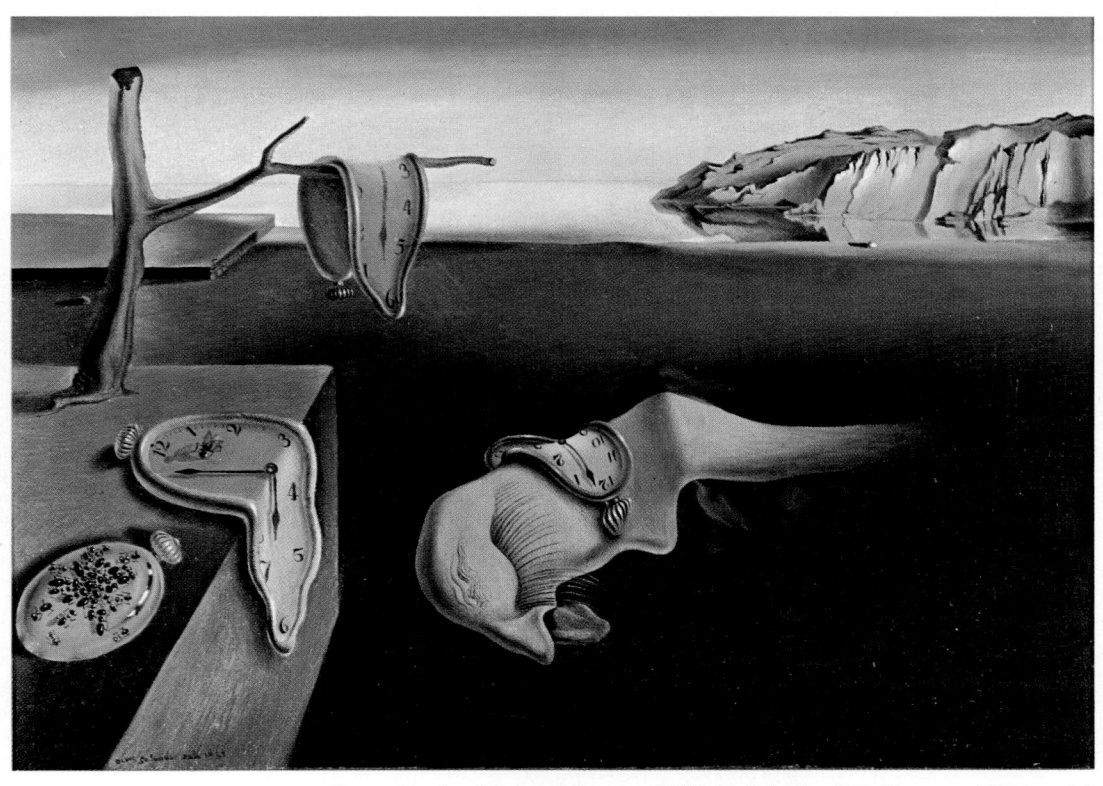

Above: *The Persistence of Memory* (1931), by Salvador Dali. Museum of Modern Art, New York. **Below:** *Landscape* (1922), by Joan Miró. Guggenheim Museum, New York.

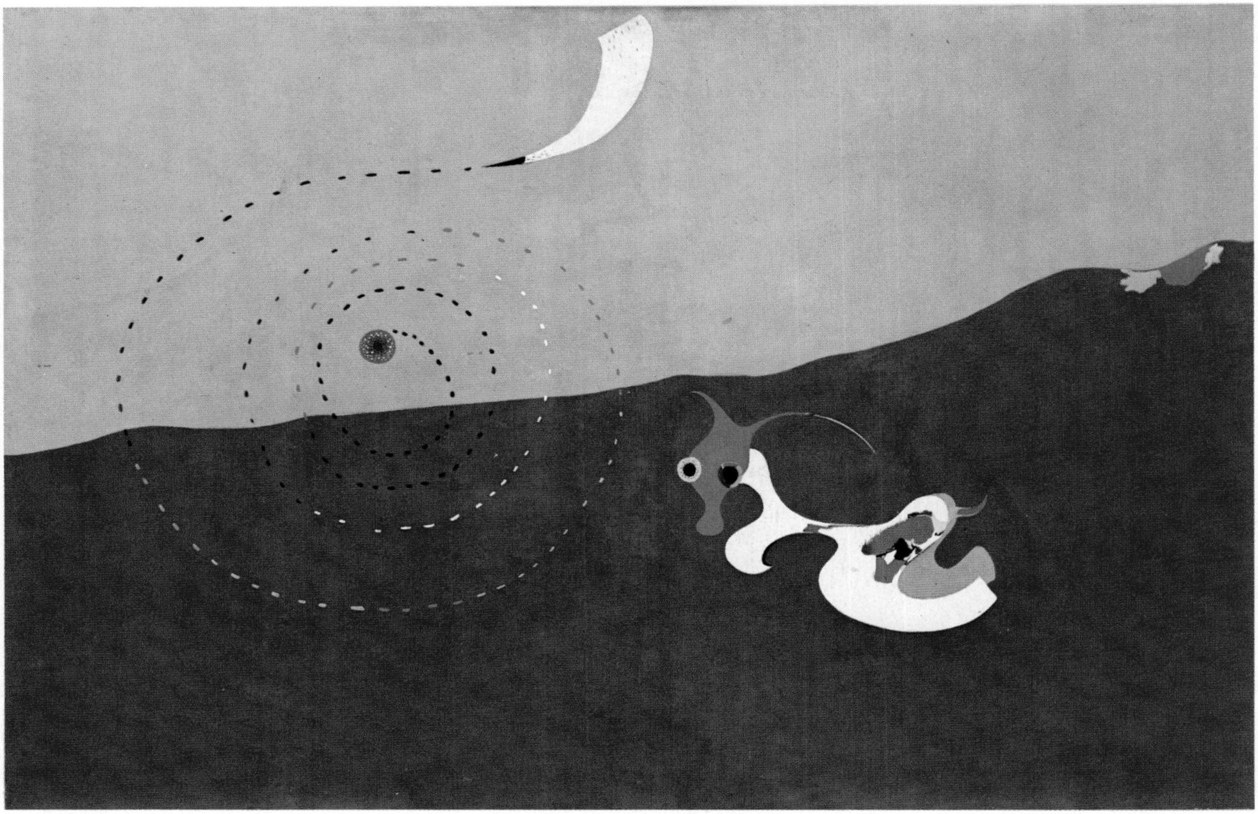

Black Reflections, by Franz Kline. Collection of Ellison Manufacturing Company.

Merzbild mit Regenbogen (Assemblage with Rainbow), by Kurt Schwitters. Collection of Mr. and Mrs. Charles B. Benenson.

Ctesiphon II (1968), by Frank Stella. Collection of Myron Orlovsky.

called for art that associated itself with technology and progress.

During the Depression of the 1930's, when artists found it difficult to support themselves, the U.S. Government stepped in. It provided projects for thousands of artists throughout the country. As a result, the public became much more aware of modern art.

At the start of this period, in 1929, one of the country's major museums—the Museum of Modern Art in New York City—was founded. During the 1930's and 1940's, the Museum of Modern Art expanded its collection and did much to help people understand the importance of modern art and design. Today the museum has the most important collection of modern art in the world.

Many artists escaped the beginnings of war in Europe during this time. They fled to New York City to live and work. As a result of their activities and the activities of the Museum of Modern Art, New York City became the center of modern art.

Abstract Expressionism

During World War II, a significant new style of modern art developed. It became known as the New York school. Arshile Gorky (1904–48), Willem de Kooning (1904–   ), Mark Rothko (1903–70), Jackson Pollock (1912–56), and Franz Kline (1919–62) were among the most important painters of this school. They combined abstraction with emphasis on the expressive quality of paint as it is applied to canvas. Pollock became famous for paintings on which he dripped, swirled, spattered, and pushed the paint in many directions. To do this, he spread the canvas on the floor. His paintings had the look of being unplanned, even though they were carefully planned and controlled. Because Pollock and others valued the action of painting so highly, their work was called **action painting**. The style was known as abstract expressionism because it consisted of expressively created abstract forms.

Significant new forms of sculpture also were being developed in the United States. Alexander Calder (1898–1976) and David Smith (1906–65) were the two most important sculptors during this time.

Calder developed the **mobile**—a construction or sculpture with parts that are delicately balanced and move freely in space. Later came

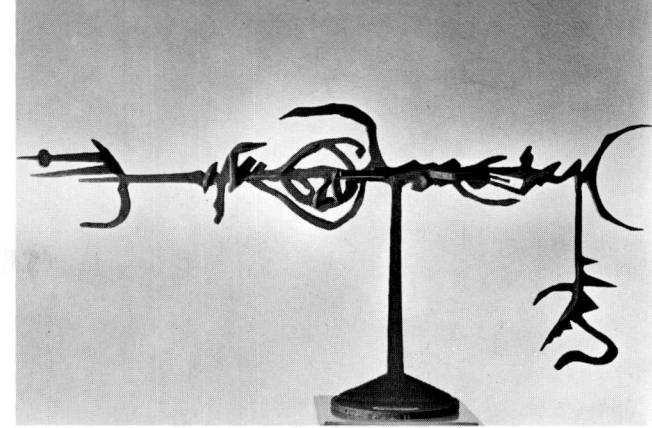

Question and Answer (before 1950), by David Smith. Carnegie Institute, Pittsburgh, Pa.

his **stabiles**. These are abstract sculptures somewhat like mobiles but stationary. They influenced the form of all outdoor sculpture.

David Smith was a highly productive artist who tried to move modern sculpture in the direction of painting. His early works were welded abstractions that were clearly influenced by cubism and surrealism. His later works were simpler and larger pieces, but they were just as complex in their meaning.

Pop Art and Minimal Art

In the 1960's, many artists felt that abstract expressionism was too specialized to appeal to the general public. As a result, pop art ("popular art") came into being. It went back to everyday subject matter and methods. The artists felt that this was a better way for modern art to mirror U.S. society. Jasper Johns (1930–   ) made careful easel paintings of the United States flag, and Robert Rauschenberg (1925–   ) created "combine" paintings. In these, he combined pieces of junk that he found on New York City streets. Andy Warhol (1930?–87) turned out multiple copies of paintings based on subjects featured in newspapers and advertisements, such as motion picture stars and cans of Campbell's tomato soup. Marisol (Marisol Escobar) (1930–   ) and Louise Nevelson (1900–   ) used everyday things or "found objects" to create their sculpture. The observer had to view the subjects, as well as the process of art itself, in a new way.

Some artists objected to the direction that pop art was taking. They felt that the relation between art and the modern world would be better expressed if abstraction was refined and simplified. These feelings were expressed in a kind of art called minimal art ("minimal"

A Two-Faced-Guy, painted steel sculpture by Alexander Calder (1969).

means "the least possible"). It made use mainly of simple geometric forms executed in an impersonal style. The paintings of Frank Stella (1936–) and the sculpture of Donald Judd (1928–) looked simple. Yet they were highly complicated in their meanings. Viewers had to bring their own meanings to these works and wonder what the artist intended. One of minimal art's most important influences on contemporary art was the artists' willingness to join art more closely with an appreciation of beauty. They were concerned with how a simple geometric shape looked in different lights and colors. They wanted to create a more satisfactory means of communication through the use of abstraction.

Conceptual Art and the 1970's

One of the important developments in modern art in the 1970's was the concept that the idea of a work of art is more important than the finished product. Sol Lewitt (1928–) illustrated this development in his many-lined wall drawings and his modular structures.

Artists went on to include the process of thinking out, or acting upon, the idea. They called it conceptual art, or "idea art." The result was a breaking down of boundaries among all the arts. Artists now convey ideas by means of performance, theater, music, dance, video, photography, or the more standard ways of painting, drawing, or sculpture. All of this has revealed a richer field of artistic expression and a new emphasis on variety and complexity. Modern art, as ever, is fully in step with modern life.

PATRICK STEWART
Williams College

See also PAINTING; SCULPTURE; UNITED STATES (Art and Music of the United States).

MODERN MUSIC

Music that has been written from approximately 1900 to the present is usually called modern music. The term "modern music," however, is slightly confusing because not all the music of our time is really modern. In fact, some of it is quite old-fashioned. Many people therefore prefer to use the term "contemporary music" because it is more exact and simply means the music of the present time.

▶ WHAT MAKES MODERN MUSIC DIFFERENT?

Harmony and Melody. Truly modern music is different from older music in several important ways. First, its harmonies and melodies are more complicated and are based on a much greater variety of tones than we find in the music of the old masters. Modern music uses no key (like C major or E-flat minor) acting as a central tone around which the whole piece of music turns. In the older way of writing music one note was always the chief note, and there were usually six other notes, which were used in secondary ways. All these notes had to follow certain strict rules of harmony. The seven tones were called a scale, and they formed the main elements of a key. Five additional tones (called chromatic tones) were used mainly to enrich the seven basic tones of the key.

But in modern music, each of the 12 tones is equal and independent. It is as if the main note (the king), its six related notes (the queen and the king's ministers), and the five remaining notes (the people) had all been put on an equal basis, as in a democracy. In a melody any note is free to move anywhere it wants to. And likewise, in harmony any note can associate with any other notes.

This way of using notes more freely and independently is usually called dissonance. By "dissonance" people often mean sounds that are harsh or ugly. But many people do not find modern music harsh or ugly, just as they do not find the sound of a rocket blast-off uglier than the creaking of old wagon wheels that need oiling.

Rhythm. Second, modern music is different because it uses complicated rhythms. Before the 20th century, music usually had simple, even rhythmic patterns, such as 3/4 (the minuet and the waltz) or 4/4 (the march). In fact, all rhythms were counted either in two, three, or four beats to a measure—sometimes in six or eight. But around 1900, composers began to use rhythms counted in five or seven and even ten or eleven. They used time signatures such as 5/8 (5 eighth notes to a bar) or 7/4 (7 quarter notes to a bar). These new rhythms at first gave people a feeling of lopsidedness—like walking with a limp. Music, like the other arts, had until then been based on symmetry, evenness, and balance. But now composers began to use the opposite of these qualities: asymmetry. Moreover, they learned how to use these odd-numbered rhythms in many strange and contrasting combinations, until music lost its predictable pace and became uneven and unpredictable. Modern rhythms are like the uneven clackety-clack of a train when it goes over some switches in the railroad station.

Form. The third factor that characterizes modern music is probably the most important and the hardest to understand. In modern music much more happens at a much faster rate and there are many more surprises, sudden changes, and contrasts. In older music a melody might last at least eight measures, and it would usually be played by one instrument or by a single group of instruments. It would be in the same rhythm throughout, and it would have an easily recognizable shape. Also, it would usually be repeated several times during the piece.

But in modern music the melodies (or musical ideas) are apt to have very unexpected shapes and may be full of abrupt changes and surprises. They also might be very short and rhythmically complicated. On top of that, they probably will appear only once, never being repeated.

Another way to put it is to say that modern music moves much faster. As a result, the listener's mind, also, has to go faster, to keep up with the music. In older music the musical thoughts change course very rarely and hardly ever abruptly—maybe every 16 or 32 measures or perhaps not at all. But in modern music a sudden change may occur every two measures or—in the most advanced music—almost every beat. That is why modern music takes more concentrated listening.

These changes in harmony, melody, rhythm, and form have made modern music sound like a new musical language. Some people say that this language is ugly. But that is because they don't understand it. Teachers, educators, and parents have made experiments that prove that children like modern music as much as old music, if they haven't been told beforehand that it is supposed to be ugly. Grown-ups listen to modern music when they watch television shows about cowboys or gangsters. Almost always these programs have background music that uses very modern chords and melodies.

To understand and like modern music requires an open mind and a certain amount of practice in listening. We cannot learn a new language without an open mind and some practice. So it is, also, with modern music.

What Are Composers Trying to Say?

In one respect modern music is no different from music of the past. Composers today are still trying to say in music the things they feel about the world. Like the older composers they are trying to talk to us through their music. Their ways of saying these things are more complicated, but so is our life in the 20th century.

▶ THE LEADING COMPOSERS

Schoenberg. Many changes took place in music between 1905 and 1910. In fact, a kind of musical revolution occurred, and when it was all over, music had changed in the ways described above. The most important of the composers who led this revolution were Arnold Schoenberg and Igor Stravinsky.

Schoenberg was born in Vienna. Like all great composers he was at first influenced by some of the modern composers of his day. These were Richard Wagner, Johannes Brahms, and Gustav Mahler. From their styles Schoenberg soon developed a new musical language, which was called atonal. It had no key center, and all the notes of the scale were of equal importance. Between 1907 and 1913 Schoenberg wrote many compositions (operas, songs, orchestra pieces, chamber music), all in the new, atonal style.

But around 1915, Schoenberg began to realize that there was something missing in the new music. It had no rules one could follow, no principles of organization, as music before his time had had. Since all the tones were now equally important, and since all kinds of shapes and surprises were possible, the old rules no longer could be used. And if any note was as good as any other, how could the composer really choose one above the other? If anything and everything was possible, how could the composer decide what was right and what was wrong?

So Schoenberg set out to find some new rules and laws that would govern atonal music. He worked for about 7 years, almost like a research scientist, and developed his new theory, which he called "a method of composing with the 12 tones." It was soon called the 12-tone technique. In this type of music the composer puts the 12 tones of the chromatic scale into a particular order, or sequence, and this sequence of notes becomes the basis for the entire composition. It took the place, in other words, of the old key signature. The 12-tone row, or set, as it is called, is the unifying idea from which everything in the composition grows. In this way law and order were established in atonal music.

From 1923 until he died, Schoenberg composed primarily 12-tone music. Through the years he influenced hundreds of other composers all over the world to follow his lead.

Stravinsky. As a young man in Russia, Stravinsky was influenced by his teacher Nikolay Rimsky-Korsakov (1844–1908) and by the great French composer Claude Debussy. Before Stravinsky was much past 30, he had become world-famous as a composer of modern ballets. One of these, *The Rite of Spring,* composed in 1913, is among the most famous and most important compositions written in the 20th century.

Stravinsky's music was revolutionary mainly in its startling use of rhythm, although his harmonies and melodies were also very advanced. Compared with earlier music, Stravinsky's rhythms seemed wild and completely unpredictable. The form of his music was also radically new: pieces didn't really end—they just stopped. But Stravinsky's sense of form was so great that these sudden endings sounded right. He did not go into atonality, as Schoenberg had. Instead he began to combine two or more keys at one time. (This is called bitonality or polytonality.)

Like Schoenberg, in 1915 Stravinsky, too, began to change his ideas of composition. By the 1920's he had developed a style that was later called neoclassicism ("new classicism"). It was in many ways simpler than his earlier style, taking many familiar ideas from older music and using them in a new manner. Neoclassicism became for many years the most influential school of composition. But around 1950 Stravinsky also began to use the 12-tone technique, or, as it is now called, serial technique.

Debussy. Although much older than his friend Stravinsky, Claude Debussy also wrote several compositions that were very important in the development of modern music. In works like the ballet *Jeux* (1912) (the name means "Games," and the ballet had a story about tennis), Debussy almost did away with themes and motifs. He composed his pieces out of little two- or three-note ideas that one hardly noticed on a first hearing. In his later years Debussy clearly showed that musical sounds could not describe objects or people—at least not without the composer's first telling the listener what he was trying to describe. Debussy realized that a musical sound can only be itself—that is, a chord is only a chord, a certain kind of musical sound. It cannot describe anything specific, such as a chair or an apple. This is one of the most important principles governing modern music, and to understand modern music, one must understand this fundamental idea.

Bartók and Ives. There were two other composers who began writing remarkably daring music in the years around 1910 to 1915. They were Béla Bartók, a Hungarian composer, and Charles Ives, who was born in Danbury, Connecticut. Bartók was not only a composer but also a great collector of Balkan and Arab folk music, and he used these folk elements in his concert music. His works are among the most popular in modern music. But no school of composition developed from his music (as it did in the cases of Schoenberg and Stravinsky).

Ives's music was so advanced that almost everybody thought he was crazy. He made his living as an insurance man. His works were so little performed that he died having heard almost none of his music. But today it is being performed more and more, and Ives is recognized as a remarkable prophet of modern music.

▶THE SECOND WAVE OF MODERN COMPOSERS

World War I ended the whole way of life that had existed in the easygoing, "romantic" 19th century. After the war many countries went through bitter times and depressions. And composers, like painters and poets, began to express these great social changes in their music. They adopted antiromantic attitudes, and in their music many of them made fun of older musical styles or of the troubles of

Igor Stravinsky, one of the most influential composers of the 20th century.

Milton Babbitt with the Mark II synthesizer, an electronic apparatus for producing and controlling sound.

modern life. Among these were Darius Milhaud (1892–1974), Francis Poulenc (1899–1963), Dmitri Shostakovich (1906–75), Paul Hindemith (1895–1963), Ernst Krenek (1900–), and Sergei Prokofiev (1891–1953).

Some composers tried to combine their modern styles with jazz. In the United States, Aaron Copland (1900–) and John Alden Carpenter (1876–1951) experimented with jazz ideas and composed pieces about life in modern America.

Most of these composers belonged in some way to the neoclassic school, and in the 1920's and 1930's there were hundreds of composers writing in this style.

Schoenberg's Pupils.　At the same time, Schoenberg and his two best pupils, Alban Berg (1885–1935) and Anton Webern (1883–1945), were composing music in the 12-tone technique. Webern eventually became one of the most influential composers in modern music. But that was not until the 1950's, after his death. His music at first was ignored by almost everyone. Even musicians could not understand it. But when younger composers began to study Webern's music, they found in it a method of composing that was an extension of Schoenberg's 12-tone technique. This method, called serial technique, made it pos-

sible to apply certain rules and organizational principles not only to notes (pitches) but to other musical elements as well. These include rhythm, dynamics (the music's loudness), and timbre (the music's instrumental colors).

▶**THE NEWEST DEVELOPMENTS**

Webern's influence spread to composers all over the world. In fact, this period was known for a while as the post-Webern era of music. Among the important "serial" composers to follow in Schoenberg's and Webern's footsteps are Roger Sessions (1896–1985), Milton Babbitt (1916–), Pierre Boulez (1925–), and Karlheinz Stockhausen (1928–).

But not all modern composers are serialists. Carl Orff (1895–1982) was influenced by the unusual rhythms of Stravinsky's early music. Composers like Benjamin Britten (1913–76) and Samuel Barber (1910–) retained a simpler tonal style. Others, like Leon Kirchner (1919–) and Oliver Messiaen (1908–), write in a freely atonal style. Still others, like Yannis Xenakis (1922–), use complicated mathematical formulas and equations in writing their compositions. They even use graph paper to plot their music. There is also a whole group of composers who use "improvisational" music, in which the performing musicians may compose part or all of the piece on the spot. The leading members of this group are John Cage (1912–), Earle Brown (1926–), and Morton Feldman (1926–).

The newest area of modern composition is electronic music, which uses computers and electronic instruments, such as synthesizers, to produce sounds. Such compositions are performed on a tape recorder. The leading composers in this field include Milton Babbitt and Mario Davidovsky (1934–).

In recent years, a tendency toward simplification has developed. As composers began to search for ways of simplifying their music, earlier ideas and techniques began to reappear. Repetition, simpler harmonies and forms, and themes and melodies were again heard in many musical compositions.

GUNTHER A. SCHULLER
Artistic Director, Berkshire Music Center

See also BARTÓK, BÉLA; COPLAND, AARON; DEBUSSY, CLAUDE; ELECTRONIC MUSIC; MUSIC; PROKOFIEV, SERGEI; SCHOENBERG, ARNOLD; STRAVINSKY, IGOR.

MODIGLIANI, AMEDEO (1884–1920)

The artist Amedeo Modigliani was born in Leghorn, Italy, on July 12, 1884. At the moment of his birth, moving men were taking away most of the furniture in his house, for the family business had just failed. The Jewish family had been prosperous, but as Dedo—this was Modigliani's childhood nickname—grew up there was little money. In spite of this, his mother encouraged his early interest in art, and he was given painting lessons at 14.

When he was 16, Modigliani was stricken with tuberculosis, and he was sent south to Naples for the winter. He also visited Rome, Florence, and Venice, and was thrilled by the activity of the big cities. For the first time he saw great Italian painting and sculpture. While he was in Venice he decided that his life's ambition was to be a sculptor—to work directly in stone.

Modigliani went to Paris in 1906. He entered an art school, the Colarossi Academy, and rented a studio in Montmartre, a section of Paris where artists lived, worked, and met. While there, he became friendly with the artists Pablo Picasso and Marc Chagall.

Materials for sculpture were expensive, and he begged stone from workers constructing a nearby building. The stone dust irritated his weakened lungs, but he persisted, happy to be pursuing his ambition. When his money ran out, Modigliani moved from place to place, looking for food and lodging. For a few pennies or a drink, he would draw portraits of people sitting in cafés. It is said that he and the painter Maurice Utrillo peeled vegetables together for room and board.

Occasionally he stole ties from subway tracks to make sculptures in wood. His family helped him as much as they could, but he was always in need of money. He started drinking too much and taking drugs. Yet he drew and painted constantly. When he was in moods in which he felt unappreciated, he would destroy some of his paintings. He worked in stone as often as he could, but in 1916 his poor health forced him to stop.

Modi (as he was then called) made friends with many young artists, writers, and poets. He was often seen around the cafés in his corduroy jacket, red scarf, and broad-rimmed hat. In 1914 he sold a few of his paintings for low prices and began to gain recognition. In 1917 he met a young art student named Jeanne Hebuterne; they fell in love. Even her loving care could not restore Modigliani's ruined health, for he died on January 25, 1920. The final tragedy was her suicide the day of the artist's funeral. Their daughter, Jeanne, was adopted by Modigliani's sister.

Portrait painters usually portray their models with noble and serene expressions. But the faces in Modigliani's paintings appear sad. He did not try to portray his subjects realistically. Instead, his human forms are simple and decorative. Modigliani used few colors, and he used them forcefully. He did not soften them with shading.

The figures Modigliani painted have oval faces, long cylindrical necks, and almond-shaped eyes. His painting and sculpture reveal his interest in black African art, which is also created with simplified shapes.

Reviewed by JEANNE MODIGLIANI

In his portraits, such as *Woman with Red Hair*, Modigliani used simple shapes and muted colors.

MOHAMMED (570-632)

Mohammed, the prophet of Islam, was born at Mecca, a city in western Arabia, about 570. His father had died before his birth. His mother died when he was about 6 years old. Mohammed was raised by his grandfather, Abd-al-Muttalib, and later by one of his uncles, abu-Talib.

Although the tribe to which he belonged was very prominent in Mecca, Mohammed's own family was poor. He received no formal education, and it is doubtful that he ever learned to read and write. As a boy he worked as a trader. It is possible that he sometimes went with trading caravans to the north into Syria and Iraq. As a young man he worked for a wealthy widow named Khadijah. When Mohammed was about 25 years old, he and Khadijah were married.

From then on, Mohammed was able to lead a more comfortable life and to give his thoughts to the problems of his people. He saw them warring and feuding almost constantly among themselves and practicing many cruel and selfish acts. Gradually he concluded that their religion was responsible for their evils. It permitted the worship of many different gods and such practices as the abandoning of baby girls to die. Mohammed also objected to all the moneymaking connected with the religion.

Nearly every Arab tribe had special gods of its own, worshiped in the form of stones and trees. Many of them also worshiped the gods they believed to be present in the shrines of other tribes. Mohammed's tribe, the Quraish, was not primarily a nomadic tribe. It was settled in Mecca, at that time a thriving center of trade and commerce. Therefore the tribe's shrine, containing its stone gods, became the object of religious pilgrimages for the many neighboring tribes who did business in Mecca. The shrine was called the Kaaba, and it was located in the center of the city. It brought great profit to the Quraish.

Mohammed had heard that the Jews and Christians believed in only one God. He talked with the Jews and Christians living in Mecca and became convinced that their God was the only true God. Later he belonged to a small group of Meccans called the Hanifs, who, it seems, held ideas similar to his.

The First Revelation

Mohammed used to go to a little cave on a hill outside of Mecca when he wanted to be alone and think. One night, when he was about 40 years old, he was meditating in the cave when suddenly he felt that he himself was called to be a prophet of God. He said that the angel Gabriel visited him and commanded him to recite the word of God to the Arabs in their own language, Arabic. Mohammed asked the angel what words he should recite. The angel's words were the first to become part of the Koran, the book that was to be the foundation of Mohammed's religion. The contents of the Koran were revealed to Mohammed in segments during the remaining years of his life.

At first Mohammed did not feel sure that he was really receiving revelations from God through the angel Gabriel. But his wife Khadijah and her cousin Waraqah, who was a member of the Hanifs, encouraged him to believe in the revelations. Mohammed did not preach his new religion openly until several years after his first revelation. When he began to preach in public, a small group of believers attached themselves to him.

Up to this point the influential Meccans had for the most part shown only indifference toward Mohammed's preaching. Now they began to organize opposition and active resistance to it. In particular, Mohammed's rich relatives and their associates were highly irritated. They did not like Mohammed's preaching against the idols in the name of one God (called Allah), and they did not like his warnings against the last judgment and hell. They refused to trade with Mohammed's followers. Sometimes Mohammed tried to come to terms with them. For instance, three pagan goddesses who were worshiped in and around Mecca were acknowledged in the Koran to be the "daughters of Allah." But such devices were unconvincing to the enemies of Islam, and Mohammed himself soon rejected these "Satanic suggestions."

By 621 Mohammed's prospects for survival seemed dim. Because of differences of opinion within his small community of Muslims and their persecution by the Meccans, Mohammed had already sent about 80 of his followers into Abyssinia. Then his first wife died. So did his uncle, who as a chieftain of the clan had so far prevented the Quraish from taking violent action against his nephew. Suddenly a very fortunate opportunity presented itself. Two of the principal tribes in Medina, a city north of Mecca, had been feuding for years. Some of their members had heard Mohammed preach in Mecca, and they sought him as a mediator in their dispute. Secret arrangements were made for the Muslims to leave Mecca in small groups, and at last Mohammed himself fled to Medina.

The Islamic Era

The year of his flight (called the Hegira, from the Arabic word *hijrah*), 622, was later chosen as the date of the beginning of the Islamic era. It was an appropriate choice of date, because at Medina, Mohammed was able to transform his religion into one that would become a world religion, a powerful state, and, eventually, a world empire. That transformation did not take place immediately, but it did take place rapidly. In a series of skillful moves Mohammed showed himself to be an able political leader in addition to being an inspiring religious leader.

At Medina, Mohammed became a lawgiver and a diplomat as well as a prophet. He established an Islamic community with its own system of government, laws, and institutions. He persuaded many people to accept the teachings of Islam, and he made alliances with neighboring tribes that brought stability to the area. Mohammed's greatest hope was to make Mecca the sacred capital of all Islam. His followers led a successful expedition against a Meccan caravan at Badr in 624, but Meccan resistance continued. In 630, Mohammed and his followers marched to Mecca. The Meccans finally agreed to accept Islam, and the Kaaba has been the center of Muslim worship ever since. Not long after this, in 632, Mohammed died.

JAMES KRITZECK
Princeton University

See also ISLAM; KORAN.

MOLDS.   See DIES AND MOLDS.
MOLDS.   See FUNGI.
MOLECULES.   See ATOMS; MATTER.

MOLIÈRE (1622–1673)

Molière, the great French actor-manager and his country's outstanding comic dramatist, was born in Paris on January 15, 1622. His real name was Jean Baptiste Poquelin. His father was a prosperous upholsterer for King Louis XIII. He made sure that Jean, an intelligent boy, had a good education.

When Jean was 21, his life took a new turn. He joined a troupe of actors who were opening a theater in Paris. At that time he took the name Molière. When this theater failed, the actors decided to try their luck in the provinces. Molière soon became the leader of the troupe. He acted, danced, wrote plays, and directed. After twelve years of touring, the company returned to Paris. This time they were a success, especially in performances of Molière's own comedies. King Louis XIV enjoyed them so much that he commanded the actors to stay and become the King's troupe.

Molière wrote his greatest comedies in this period. Among them are *Tartuffe* (1664), *The Misanthrope* (1666), *The Miser* (1668), *The Learned Ladies* (1672), and *The Imaginary In-valid* (1673). Mostly, the plays portray a character with a typical human failing, which Molière ridicules by exaggerating it. Because misers, hypocrites, and people who worry about their health are always with us, Molière's plays still amuse audiences. They continue to be played at France's national theater, the Comédie-Française in Paris, and in translation all over the world.

The plays offended certain important people who thought they were being laughed at. But Louis XIV always stood by Molière and often summoned him to perform or to compose a play for some royal occasion. Molière worked very hard and suffered from ill health. Even his death, on February 17, 1673, was dramatic. He collapsed during a performance of *The Imaginary Invalid* and died later that evening of a hemorrhage.

Reviewed by WILLIAM D. HOWARTH
Author, *Molière: A Playwright and His Audience*

MOLLUSKS.   See OYSTERS, OCTOPUSES, AND OTHER MOLLUSKS.

MONACO

Monaco is the second smallest independent state in the world, after Vatican City. Situated on the Mediterranean Sea, it occupies a tiny corner of southwestern Europe, surrounded on three sides by France. Monaco has been ruled for centuries by princes, and its official name is Principality of Monaco.

The People. Citizens of Monaco, who are known as Monégasques, make up only about 16 percent of the population. About half of Monaco's residents are French. Most of the remainder include Italians (for Monaco lies near the Italian border) and other Europeans. In addition, several thousand people, mainly French, commute to Monaco each day to work. French is the official language, although Monégasque (a mixture of French and Italian), Italian, English, and other languages also are spoken. Most of the people are Roman Catholics.

The Land. Measuring only a little over half a square mile in area, Monaco is smaller in size than New York City's Central Park.

Monaco is divided into four geographic sections: Monaco-Ville, the capital; La Condamine and Fontvieille, the industrial and business districts; and Monte Carlo, the resort and residential area. Monaco-Ville is the oldest part of the country. It has narrow passageways, shady little squares, and cobblestone streets lined with old houses. The most famous building in Monte Carlo is the Casino, which is always crowded with tourists who have come to gamble, for gambling is legal in Monaco. Its mild climate also has helped to make Monaco a world famous resort.

Economy. Monaco's economy is based mainly on tourism. Manufacturing accounts for about 30 percent of Monaco's income. Additional income is provided by liquor taxes, business registration fees, a small tax on business profits, and tobacco. Monaco also publishes fine art books and issues stamps prized by collectors around the world. Monaco has no unemployment, and legal residents pay no direct taxes on income and property. French citizens, however, pay French taxes.

History and Government. The modern history of Monaco began in the late 13th century when the Grimaldi family (the present ruling house) won control of Monaco. Its independence was recognized by France in 1512. But between 1793 and 1860, Monaco was ruled first by France and then by the Kingdom of Sardinia.

Monaco regained its independence in 1861. Its ruler at that time, Prince Charles III, decided to make an industry of tourism. He built a new town, Monte Carlo (Mount Charles), the Casino, and many fine hotels. Under Charles's son, Albert I, Monaco received its first constitution in 1912. In 1918 a treaty with France guaranteed the independence of

MONACO

FACTS AND FIGURES

PRINCIPALITY OF MONACO (Principauté de Monaco) is the official name of the country.

THE PEOPLE (citizens of Monaco) are known as Monégasques.

LOCATION: Southwestern Europe, on the Mediterranean Sea.

AREA: 0.58 sq mi (1.49 km^2).

POPULATION: 27,000 (estimate).

CAPITAL AND LARGEST CITY: Monaco-Ville.

MAJOR LANGUAGE: French (official).

MAJOR RELIGION: Roman Catholic.

GOVERNMENT: Constitutional monarchy. **Head of state**—prince. **Head of government**—minister of state. **Legislature**—National Council.

CHIEF PRODUCTS: Tourism is the mainstay of the economy. The chief manufactured products include plastics, precision instruments, perfume, jewelry, pottery and glass objects, pharmaceuticals, art books, postage stamps.

MONETARY UNIT: French franc (1 franc = 100 centimes).

NATIONAL ANTHEM: Opening line: *Principauté Monaco, ma patrie* ("Principality of Monaco, my country").

Monaco as long as there is a male heir to the throne. France maintains limited protection over the principality.

Albert's son, Louis II, ruled until 1949. He was succeeded by his grandson, Rainier III. In 1956, Prince Rainier married Grace Kelly, an American motion picture actress. They had three children—Princesses Caroline and Stephanie and Prince Albert, the heir to the throne. Princess Grace died in 1982.

The government of Monaco is based on the Constitution of 1962. The prince, who is the head of state, appoints a minister of state (a French civil servant) as head of government. The members of the legislature are elected directly by the people.

Reviewed by ALBERT LISIMACHIO
Conservateur des Archives et de la
Bibliothèque du Palais de Monaco
GEORGES R. BORGHINI
Consulate General of Monaco (New York)

Monaco-Ville, the capital of Monaco, is the site of the royal palace, the cathedral, government buildings, and the Oceanographic Museum.

MONDRIAN, PIET (1872–1944)

Piet Mondrian, one of the most important artists of the 20th century, is recognized as a founding master of abstract art. His theory of art influenced the clean lines of modern architecture and commercial design.

Mondrian was born in Amersfoort, the Netherlands, on March 7, 1872. He received his first art lessons from his father. Mondrian enrolled in the Amsterdam Academy of Fine Arts in 1892.

In 1911, Mondrian went to Paris. There he saw the work of the cubists, a group of painters who represented objects from all sides, using combinations of flat shapes. Mondrian, too, began to produce paintings using horizontal and vertical lines and no curves. On plain white backgrounds, he painted rectangles of red, yellow, and blue. Mondrian's paintings represent ideas. He believed that there is a logical reason for everything. He expressed his ideas through his use of form and color, which give a sense of order and steadiness.

Mondrian returned to the Netherlands in 1914. There he formed a group of artists that came to be called de Stijl (the Style), after a magazine that he helped to start in 1917. By the 1920's the artists called their work **neoplasticism,** a style in which forms are restricted to simple geometric shapes and primary colors. Reproductions of his paintings from this period appear in the articles DUTCH AND FLEMISH ART and MODERN ART.

Mondrian lived in Paris from 1919 until 1938. At the beginning of World War II, he moved to London and then to New York City. He died in New York on February 1, 1944.

Reviewed by ARIANE RUSKIN BATTERBERRY
Author, *The Pantheon Story of Art
for Young People*

Although it has only a few shapes and colors, *Broadway Boogie-Woogie* (1942–43), by Mondrian, is full of life. Boogie-woogie was popular dance music in the 1930's.

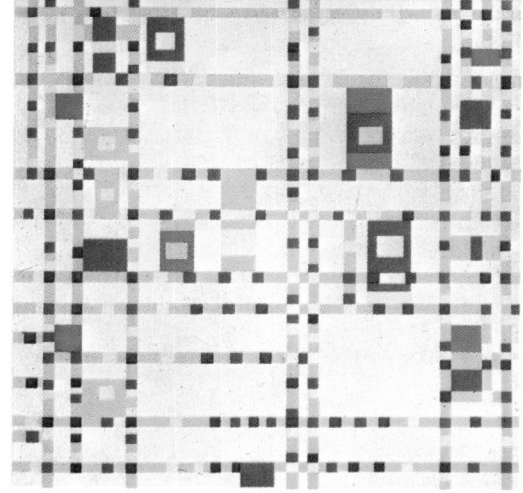

Monet and other impressionists used hundreds of small brushstrokes side by side, often in contrasting colors, to give an impression of solid forms. *Boats at Argenteuil* (1875).

MONET, CLAUDE (1840–1926)

Claude Monet, a French landscape painter, was one of the founders of the style of art known as impressionism. He was born in Paris on November 14, 1840, but spent his childhood in Le Havre. When Monet was 15, he held an exhibit that interested the painter Eugène Boudin. Boudin persuaded him to take his materials outdoors to paint. Monet continued this practice throughout his life.

In 1860, after studying in Paris for a year, Monet joined the army and went to Algeria. He returned to Paris two years later. There he married and had two sons. In the Paris studio of Charles Gleyre, Monet met many other promising young artists, with whom he exhibited in 1874. The critics did not like their works and made fun of these "impressionists." The term was taken from the title of Monet's landscape, *Impression: Sunrise*. This painting is reproduced in the article MODERN ART in Volume M.

Impressionism began at the time (the early 1870's) and in the setting of Monet's painting *Boats at Argenteuil*. Argenteuil is a suburb of Paris, on the Seine River. There the artists Monet, Manet, and Renoir painted together and learned from one another. By watching Monet, Manet became convinced for the first time that it was indeed possible to paint outdoors. Monet and Renoir painted so much alike that it was sometimes difficult for them to tell who had painted certain views.

Monet and the other impressionists placed unmixed colors side by side on their canvases to show how light splits into the colors of the prism—like a rainbow. To show how light could completely change the appearance of an object, Monet painted the same scene at different times of the day and year. For example, he painted the Rouen Cathedral 20 times, in conditions varying from a misty summer dawn to a brilliant winter sunset.

Monet's first wife died in 1879, and he later married a woman with several children of her own. In 1883 the couple moved to Giverny, where the artist created the gardens that inspired his paintings of water lilies.

Monet did not become famous or earn much money until he was over 50 years old. Then his paintings began to sell for higher prices. In 1916 the French Government bought eight of Monet's paintings of water lilies. Although his eyesight began to fail, Monet painted until his death in Giverny on December 5, 1926.

FRANK GETLEIN
Author, *The French Impressionists*

MONEY

More than 2,000 years ago the Romans were using metal coins similar to those we use today. Many of these early coins were made in the temple of the goddess Juno, or Moneta. It is from the name "Moneta" that we get our word "money."

In most places throughout the world people are familiar with some form of what we call money. Yet, in spite of the fact that it is so widely known, money is very difficult to define. A London banker and the chief of an African tribe have widely different ideas of what money is.

Many people think of money as **currency**—metal coins and paper bills. But money is not simply currency—a United States nickel or dollar bill, a Mexican peso, a Canadian dollar, a French franc, an Italian lira, or a Russian ruble. Money is whatever people agree to use in exchange for goods and services.

Money serves people's purposes in several ways. Bakers, for example, cannot live on just the bread they bake. In today's society, they have to sell their bread to other people so that they can get the money they need to buy life's necessities. In this way, money is serving as a **medium of exchange.**

Because the baker knows how much money a loaf of bread will bring, money can do something else. It tells the baker how much work it takes to buy a new oven. Both the bread and the oven have their own price. So, money helps the baker decide whether he or she can afford a new oven by using it to bake and sell more bread. In this way, money is serving as a **standard of value.**

Finally, money can be saved. The baker can hardly set aside a couple of loaves of bread every day until they can be taken down the street to trade for a television set. Even if the television store were willing to take bread as payment, the loaves would be moldy by the time the baker had enough saved up. But the baker can set aside a little money every day. In this way, money serves as a **store of value.**

▶ HISTORY OF MONEY

Down through its long and fascinating history, money has undergone many changes. Long before people thought of making metal coins or paper bills, they needed some way to acquire the things they wanted.

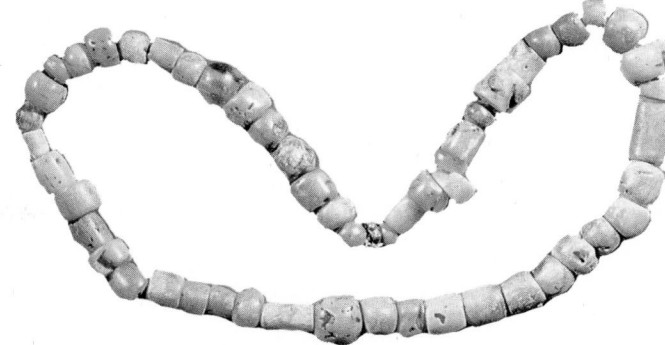

Money is whatever people agree to accept in payment for goods and services. Some American Indians, for example, used beads called wampum during colonial days.

Barter

In early societies, money was unknown, and people relied on a simple system of exchange. Perhaps a good hunter had more animal skins than he could use. His neighbor, a good fisherman, might have too many fish but needed furs to protect his children from the cold. Both soon realized that their problems could be easily solved by exchanging what they did not need, their surplus, for what they did need.

This method of exchanging something not needed for something that is needed is called barter. The word comes from the Italian *barattare* and the French *barater,* which mean "to trade."

On the American frontier, a merchant might let a settler have an ax in return for a sack of wheat. The merchant might then trade the wheat to a miller who would make it into flour. The flour might then be traded to a trapper for animal skins.

Barter is still used today—not only by individuals, but also by corporations. An airline might let people from a fuel company fly on its planes in return for jet fuel. Since the airline probably has a few empty seats on its flights anyway, such a deal could be a significant saving for the airline.

But barter has disadvantages. If the settler on the American frontier had carried his sack of wheat to the merchant just after 40 other settlers had been there, the merchant might have decided that he no longer needed any wheat. That would mean that the settler would not have gotten his ax.

When labor and services became more specialized in growing societies, barter no longer satisfied the demands of payment. A new system of exchange had to be found.

Early Forms of Money

As societies developed, people turned to many different things in the search for a convenient medium of exchange, or money. One of the earliest forms of money was cattle. The richest person was the one who owned the most livestock. Cattle were called *capitale,* and from that Latin word we get our word "capital," meaning "wealth."

But this new method, too, had many drawbacks. A cow or a sheep must be fed and cared for. Some animals are fat and some are lean. A person who wanted to sell something might believe that it was worth much more than one cow. The buyer might not be willing to part with two. A cow and a half was certainly not a practical solution. Difficulties arose over exact values.

The use of cattle as a standard means of exchange decreased when people began to trade with people who lived far away. Again a new medium had to be found. Soon such things as grain and salt came into use. Both of these commodities had certain advantages. They could be weighed exactly. They could be stored in the holds of ships and transported easily. Salt, especially, was fairly scarce, an important quality for something used as a means of exchange. So widespread did the use of salt become that Roman soldiers were sometimes paid in salt. And it is from *salarium,* the Latin word for "salt money," that our own word "salary" comes. We still speak of people as not being worth their salt if they do not do their jobs well.

In early societies around the world, many different objects and products were used as money. The use of colored beads and ornaments was common. After Europeans came to North America, some Indian people began using shell beads, called wampum, as money. (The name "wampum" was taken from the word *wampumpeag,* meaning "string of white beads.") Cowrie shells were used in many areas, including China, India, and Africa.

People on the American frontier used various articles as money. Among these articles were gunpowder, tobacco, and nails, which were in short supply on the frontier. Today, smaller nails are still classified as two-penny nails, for example, and larger nails may be called ten-penny nails. These names are a remnant of the days when nails were used as money.

Coins

The more complex societies became, the less satisfactory livestock and other early media of exchange became. In the search for a better way of trading, people turned to metal. At first they used crude lumps of copper, iron, gold, or silver as money. Decorative metal ornaments became highly valued.

It is difficult to say just when the first metal coins were used. Some historians believe that the Chinese were using miniature metal knives and spades as money as early as 1000 B.C. A few examples of coins made of electrum, a natural alloy of gold and silver, have been found. They were made by the Lydians of Asia Minor about 700 B.C. The Greeks had a silver coin called a drachma; the Roman denarius was a common silver coin during the period of the Empire.

It took many hundreds of years for coins to replace barter and primitive forms of money. As the use of coins increased, their output came to be controlled by the ruler of a country. Governments began to regulate the production of all coins, and it became a crime for individuals to make counterfeits, or imitations, of those issued by authority.

A great step forward in the development of money came with the widespread use of coins in the late Middle Ages. Metals were stamped by the issuing authority and fashioned in uniform weights. People could determine how many coins were required to pay for a particular object or service.

The advantages of coins were many. Coins made it possible for people to trade in a standardized way. They had a set value. They came in various denominations, and prices could be set with some precision. Early coins were made from precious metals, such as gold and silver, which were valuable in their own right and gave people a feeling of wealth.

Paper Money

Paper money came into general use only about three centuries ago. However, some forms of it were known hundreds of years earlier. Many historians believe that the Chinese were printing paper money as early as the 10th century A.D. The Italian explorer Marco Polo saw paper money in China in the 13th century. But it was not commonly used until the 17th century, when international trade was expanding at a rapid rate.

In many nations paper money was strongly distrusted when it was first introduced. It was often difficult to accept the idea that the new form of money stood for something real. Eventually, however, people's confidence increased. Paper currency is now standard in every civilized country in the world.

One advantage of paper money is that it is cheaper to make. Another is that it is easier to carry around in large quantities. But advantages can also create problems. The production of coins was dependent on limited supplies of gold and silver. Paper currency can be produced in virtually unlimited quantities. The danger is that creation of too much money will push prices up because if people have more money to spend, they will be willing to spend more of it on a particular object.

At first, governments tried to limit the creation of paper money by requiring that the paper money be backed by gold or silver. In the United States, for example, a dollar once entitled the holder to exchange the dollar bill for a set amount of gold. This **gold standard** assured that new dollars could be created no faster than the government was able to increase the amount of gold in its vaults. But governments decided that letting the production of gold and silver mines determine the amount of money in circulation was too artificial. At times, the amount of money increased too fast. At other times the amount of money grew too slowly. Most countries stopped using the gold standard in 1933. By 1972 the nations of the world abandoned the final remnants of the gold standard.

CURRENCY AROUND THE WORLD

Every country has its own currency or monetary system. When people travel from one country to another, they must change their money into the currency of the country they are visiting. Here are the currencies of some of the countries of the world:

COUNTRY	CURRENCY
Argentina	100 centavos = **1 peso**
Austria	100 groschen = **1 schilling**
Belgium	100 centimes = **1 franc**
Brazil	100 centavos = **1 cruzado**
Canada	100 cents = **1 dollar**
Chile	100 centavos = **1 peso**
China, People's Republic of	100 fen = **1 yuan**
China, Republic of (Taiwan)	100 cents = **1 new Taiwan dollar**
Denmark	100 øre = **1 krone**
France	100 centimes = **1 franc**
Germany (West)	100 pfennigs = **1 Deutsche mark**
Greece	100 lepta = **1 drachma**
Hong Kong	100 cents = **1 Hong Kong dollar**
India	100 paisa = **1 rupee**
Indonesia	100 sen = **1 rupiah**
Iran	100 dinars = **1 rial**
Ireland	100 pence = **1 Irish pound (punt)**
Israel	100 agorot = **1 shekel**
Italy	100 centesimi = **1 lira**
Japan	100 sen = **1 yen**
Kenya	100 cents = **1 shilling**
Malaysia	100 sen = **1 ringgit**
Mexico	100 centavos = **1 peso**
Netherlands	100 cents = **1 guilder (gulden)**
Philippines	100 centavos = **1 peso**
Portugal	100 centavos = **1 escudo**
Singapore	100 cents = **1 Singapore dollar**
South Africa	100 cents = **1 rand**
Spain	100 céntimos = **1 peseta**
Sweden	100 öre = **1 krona**
Thailand	100 satangs = **1 baht**
U.S.S.R.	100 kopecks = **1 ruble**
United Kingdom	100 pence = **1 pound sterling**
United States	100 cents = **1 dollar**

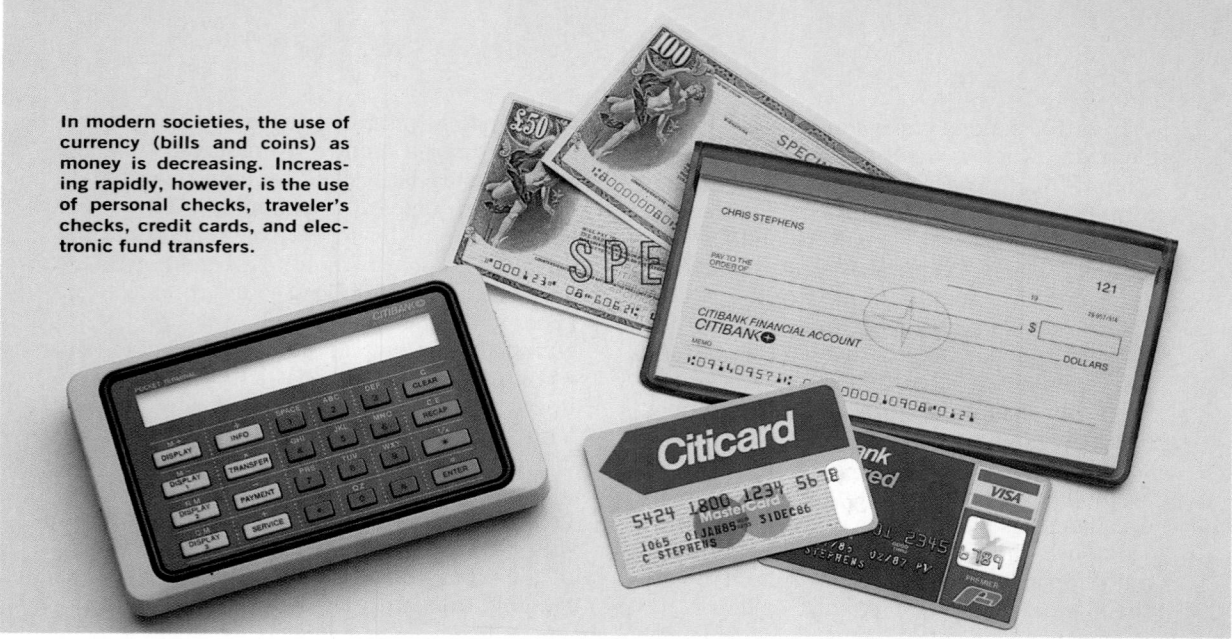

In modern societies, the use of currency (bills and coins) as money is decreasing. Increasing rapidly, however, is the use of personal checks, traveler's checks, credit cards, and electronic fund transfers.

▶MONEY TODAY

In the United States today, the amount of money in circulation is controlled by the **Federal Reserve System.** The Federal Reserve was set up by Congress in 1913. Its purpose is to assure that business gets enough money to expand and to create new jobs. But the Federal Reserve must be careful that new money is not put in circulation so fast that it only pushes prices up. The Federal Reserve controls the amount of money in circulation through its control over banks. In fact, the Federal Reserve is called a **central bank.**

The Federal Reserve controls the amount of money in circulation in two ways. First, it sets the amount of reserves a bank must hold. Lowering the amount required to be held in reserve, for example, increases the amount of money banks can lend. Second, the Federal Reserve buys and sells government securities (bonds). When the Federal Reserve buys government securities, the money goes into the bank accounts of the companies that sold the securities. There, the banks can use the money to make new loans. When the Federal Reserve sells government securities, the money flows out of the banks and into the Federal Reserve, where people cannot use the money for spending.

In a modern society, actual currency—coins and bills—represents a small part of the money in existence. Most money is simply a bookkeeping entry in a bank, representing the value of the goods a merchant has sold or the value of a job a worker has done to earn a paycheck. The money can be moved from one account to another by a **check,** which is a written order from an account holder telling his or her bank to transfer the money to the person or business named in the check. Transfers of money can also be ordered electronically. By passing a plastic card through a special machine that "reads" a coded magnetic tape on the card, a shopper can pay for purchases in a store. The signals picked up from the card are transferred to the banks electronically, where the money is moved from the shopper's account to the merchant's account.

The electronic system is a variation on the **credit card** system. With a credit card, the bank is actually lending its customer money to make purchases. The merchant sends the slip signed by the customer to the bank, the bank pays the merchant, and the customer eventually pays the bank.

Today's system of handling money is far removed from barter, nails, or salt. In the United States, the government decrees that people must accept dollars as payment for debts. In technical terms, the dollar is **legal tender.** It is up to individuals to determine how many dollars—how much money—they will demand as payment for goods or work. Ultimately, the value of money depends on the goods people produce and the work that they do.

Reviewed and revised by G. DAVID WALLACE
Author, *Money Basics*

See also BANKS AND BANKING; COINS AND COIN COLLECTING; CREDIT CARDS; DOLLAR; MINT.

MONGOLIA

In the 13th century, mounted Mongol warriors led by Genghis Khan swept across Asia. They conquered vast territories and created a great empire. The original home of these warriors was the Mongolian plateau of east central Asia. Today when we speak of Mongolia, we usually mean the Mongolian People's Republic, which occupies about half the plateau. The rest of the plateau is now divided between China and the Soviet Union. The Mongolian People's Republic is sometimes referred to as Outer Mongolia. This term was used more commonly in the past to distinguish it from Inner Mongolia, a region of China.

▶ THE PEOPLE

Most of the people of Mongolia are Mongols. The Khalkhas, the largest of the Mongol tribes, make up the great majority of the population. The Kazakhs, one of several Turkic peoples, are the largest non-Mongol group. There are also some Russians and a few Chinese. The various people of Mongolia are known as Mongolians.

Language, Religion, and Education. The official language of the country is Khalkha Mongolian, a Mongolian dialect. It is written in the Cyrillic, or Russian, alphabet.

For centuries, the Mongols have followed Lamaism, a form of Buddhism introduced from Tibet. Before that, their religion was shamanism, a faith with many gods. The Turkic people are Muslims. At one time there were many lamas (or priests), monks, and monasteries in Mongolia. But the Communist government has discouraged religious observance, and few remain.

The number of schools in Mongolia has increased greatly in recent years. Only four years of schooling are required, but many children attend school for seven, eight, or ten years. There is a state university in Ulan Bator, the capital.

Way of Life. At one time most of the people were nomads who lived in the open steppes (level, treeless grasslands) during the entire year. Their homes, called yurts, were made of light wooden frames covered by felt cloth. The yurts, circular in shape, could be set up or taken down quickly. When the nomads traveled, they took their homes with them.

The nomads lived off their herds of sheep, goats, cattle, horses, and camels. The animals provided them with transportation and their staple foods—milk, butter, cheese, and meat. The favorite drinks of the nomads were *airag* (fermented mare's milk) and tea.

Traditional family life usually revolved around the extended family group. This typically consisted of a husband and wife, their unmarried children, and married sons and their wives. The married sons and their wives usually lived in tents nearby to the tent occupied by the father and mother and younger children. Family obligations included providing care for the sick, injured, and elderly.

Because it is discouraged by the government, only a relatively few Mongolians continue to follow the traditional nomadic way of life. Most now live in settled communities. Increasing numbers have moved to the towns

---

FACTS AND FIGURES

MONGOLIAN PEOPLE'S REPUBLIC (Bügd Nairamdakh Mongol Ard Uls) is the official name of the country.

THE PEOPLE are known as Mongolians.

LOCATION: East central Asia.

AREA: 604,248 sq mi (1,565,000 km²).

POPULATION: 2,000,000 (estimate).

CAPITAL AND LARGEST CITY: Ulan Bator.

MAJOR LANGUAGE: Khalkha Mongolian (official).

MAJOR RELIGION: Lamaist Buddhist. (Religious observance is discouraged by the government.)

GOVERNMENT: Communist republic. **Head of state—**chairman of the Presidium of the Great People's Khural. **Head of government—**chairman of the Council of Ministers (premier). (Effective leader of the country is the general secretary of the Mongolian People's Revolutionary Party.) **Legislature—**Great People's Khural.

CHIEF PRODUCTS: Agricultural—wheat, barley, oats, millet, potatoes and other vegetables, hay, livestock (cattle, sheep, goats, horses, camels), livestock products (milk, butter, cheese, animal hides). **Manufactured—**processed food, textiles, leather goods, boots and shoes, cement, wood products, paper. **Mineral—**coal, gold, tungsten, uranium.

MONETARY UNIT: Tögrög (tughrik) (1 tögrög = 100 möngö).

NATIONAL ANTHEM: State Anthem of the Mongolian People's Republic.

MONGOLIA

and cities, where they live in homes resembling those of Europe and the United States. A few of the larger cities have factories, schools, libraries, museums, parks, and theaters. The government buildings in Ulan Bator are very impressive. So are the city's broad streets and avenues.

The appearance of Mongolia has changed greatly. But old customs and habits remain alive. Although the Mongols are becoming city dwellers, they are still enthusiastic about horses. The very survival of their ancestors once depended on the plucky Mongol pony. The Mongols are proud of the fact that they are still among the most skillful riders in the world.

Mongols are fond of sports. The favorites are archery and wrestling. Children start to learn these sports at a very early age. Every Mongol looks forward to the championship contests held in the capital each year. People come from all over the country to watch and compete. At this time horse races also take place. The winners in all of these events are given national honors.

▶ THE LAND

Mongolia is one of the largest countries in Asia. It occupies a large inland plateau that is shaped like a saucer.

Broad, rolling plains cover most of the country. They are somewhat like the prairies of the Midwestern United States. For centuries most Mongols have made their homes on the lush grasslands, where they have been able to find plentiful fodder for their herds.

At some points mountainous regions break through the plains. In the western part of the country are the Altai and Khangai mountains. Long belts of mountains in the north, principally the Tannu-Ola and Kentei ranges, separate Mongolia from eastern Siberia. Much of the northern region is made up of forests and is fairly rich in wildlife. Reindeer are especially common. Northern Mongolia is very lightly populated. People there support themselves largely by hunting and fishing.

The southern part of Mongolia is called the Gobi, which is the Mongol word for "the desert." It is the northernmost desert area of the world. Parched and barren, it has long been uninhabited. Some parts of the Gobi have never been explored or mapped.

The principal river in Mongolia is the Selenga. It begins near the northern slopes of the Khangai Mountains and flows northward, emptying into Lake Baikal in Siberia. Other important rivers are the Kerulen and the Onon in the northeastern part of the country.

The Mongolian climate is marked by sharp extremes. In much of the region, the summers are short and hot. The winters are long and quite cold. Winter temperatures reach as low as –47°C (–52°F). Although summer temperatures may rise to over 32°C (90°F), they average about 18°C (64°F). Mongolia has only light rainfall. The smallest amount, 50 millimeters (2 inches) yearly, falls in the south; the largest amount, about 300 millimeters (12 inches), falls in the north.

THE ECONOMY

The raising of livestock is the basis of the economy. There are many times more domesticated animals than there are people in Mongolia. Sheep and goats are the most numerous. But millions of cattle and horses and large numbers of camels are also raised. The Mongols get most of their food, wool, horsehair, and leather from their herds. Their animals also furnish many other necessities of life, such as clothing, shelter, and transportation. The traditional occupations of hunting and fishing also continue.

In the past, few Mongols engaged in agriculture or trade. These occupations were carried on largely by other people, such as the Chinese who settled in the region. But in recent years the government has been encouraging the growth of agriculture and new industries. Large grassland areas on the steppes have been broken by plows and planted with crops for the first time. Many Mongols are now using modern farm machines, such as tractors and harvesters. But the harsh climate and sparse rainfall still make it difficult to grow crops in many parts of the country. Grains and potatoes are the leading crops, and some farmers raise pigs.

The government has built factories that produce textiles, cement, paper, processed foods, leather goods, boots, shoes, and wood products. Some deposits of coal, gold, tungsten, uranium, petroleum, and salt are now being worked.

Few automobiles and trucks are used in Mongolia. But railroads and airlines now link Ulan Bator directly with Moscow and Peking.

CITIES

Ulan Bator is the capital and largest city of Mongolia. It is the economic as well as the political center of the country. Darkhan and Choibalsan, a railroad terminus on the Kerulen River in the northeast, are other major cities. Also important are Uliassutai, Tsetserlik, Altan Bulak, Kobdo, Undur Khan, and Sukhe Bator.

GOVERNMENT

Political life in Mongolia is dominated by the Communist Party, called the Mongolian People's Revolutionary Party. The party is led by a politburo, whose members are often also government officials. The legislative body is the Great People's Khural, or People's Assembly, whose members are elected for 3-year terms. The Khural meets only briefly each year. It elects a nine-member presidium to conduct its day-to-day affairs. The chairman

Nomads tie their home, a yurt, on a camel when they move from place to place.

Government buildings below rolling hills in Ulan Bator, capital of Mongolia.

of the presidium serves as head of state. The head of government is the premier, who heads the council of ministers.

▶ **HISTORY**

The Mongolian plateau has been inhabited since ancient times. For centuries the people lived a nomadic life. They remained organized in small local tribes that fought among themselves to protect their pasturelands and to win control of richer grazing lands. From time to time tribes made raids against nearby China, but the great Chinese empire was too strong for these tribesmen.

The great era for the Mongols arrived in the 13th century. The many fighting tribes of Mongolia were united and brought under the control of a great military leader, Genghis Khan (1167?–1227). He was one of the most brilliant warriors the world has ever known. Under his leadership the Mongols overran central Asia. Some of his armies invaded the Middle East and even rode as far as southern Russia. By the time of his death he had carved out a tremendous empire.

The victories of Genghis Khan were repeated by his descendants. The greatest of them all was his grandson Kublai Khan (1216–94) who ruled Mongolia and China (the Yüan dynasty) as chief khan of the Mongols. At its height the empire reached from the shores of the Pacific Ocean to eastern Europe. In 1275 Marco Polo visited the court of Kublai Khan in what is now Peking and was astounded by its magnificence.

After the death of Kublai Khan the Mongol Empire fell apart. In the 17th century, the Manchus, a people from Manchuria in northeastern China, conquered all of China. Mongolia soon became part of their empire, and it remained so for over two centuries.

When the Manchus were overthrown in the Chinese revolution of 1911, the Mongols ruled themselves until Chinese troops occupied part of the country in 1919. In 1921 Mongol revolutionaries, led by Sukhe Bator (1893–1923) and aided by the Soviet Union, entered what is now Ulan Bator and seized control of the government. In 1924 they proclaimed the establishment of the Mongolian People's Republic, a Communist state.

But complete independence was some years off. Mongolia was self-governing, but it remained nominally part of China and was dependent on the Soviet Union. In 1945, at the end of World War II, the Allies persuaded China to grant independence to Mongolia. Following a plebiscite (vote) in favor of independence, China formally recognized the Mongolian People's Republic in 1946.

In the years since independence, Mongolia has continued to rely heavily on the Soviet Union for economic assistance. The two nations signed a 20-year treaty of peace and friendship in 1966. Since relations between the Soviet Union and China worsened in the late 1960's, Mongolia has served as an important buffer zone between the two countries.

HYMAN KUBLIN
City University of New York, Brooklyn College

MONGOOSES. See GENETS, CIVETS, MONGOOSES, AND THEIR RELATIVES.

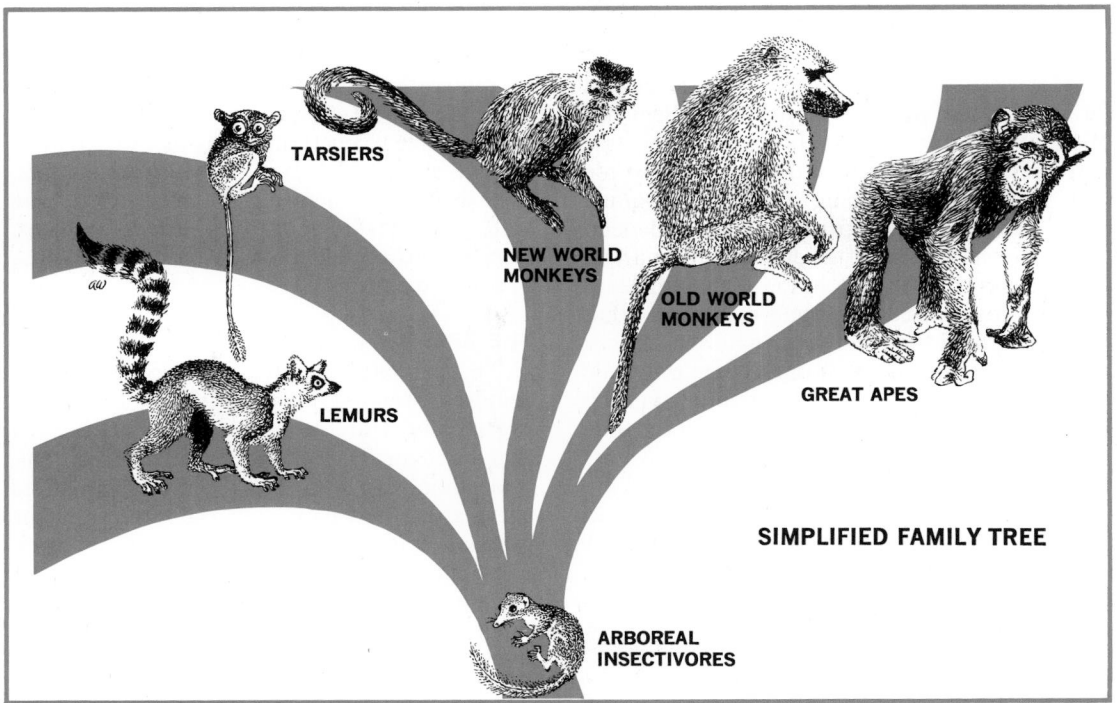

Within the image:
TARSIERS
LEMURS
NEW WORLD MONKEYS
OLD WORLD MONKEYS
GREAT APES
SIMPLIFIED FAMILY TREE
ARBOREAL INSECTIVORES

MONKEYS, APES, AND OTHER PRIMATES

Monkeys and apes belong to the primates, one of the major groups of mammals. Like other mammals, the primates nurse their young with milk. But of all mammals, the primates are of greatest interest to people because people themselves are primates.

The word "primate" comes from the Latin *primus,* meaning "first." The Swedish naturalist Carolus Linnaeus began his classification of all animals with humans. He called humans and their relatives primates because he considered them first in importance.

▶ DEVELOPMENT OF THE PRIMATES

The earliest primates lived approximately 60,000,000 years ago. In the long span of time since then many different primates have evolved. The ones that have developed least, such as the tree shrews, are classified as the lowest of the primates. By studying them, as well as fossils and other living primates, we can trace the development of certain features of the higher primates. Among these are larger brains, better eyes, an upright posture, hands capable of grasping, skillful muscle movement, and a shortening of the face. Such features have reached their greatest development in humans. Although humans long ago

split off from other primates, their bodies still show a basic relationship.

▶ GENERAL CHARACTERISTICS

Most primates (other than humans) live in tropical places. Although a few live on the ground, most spend a good deal of their time in trees. Various parts of their bodies, such as their eyes and feet, are well suited to a life in the trees. An animal that leaps from limb to limb needs good eyes and a firm grip.

Unlike many mammals, most primates have large eyes set in the head so that they look straight forward. The higher primates can focus both eyes on the same object, just as we do. This ability helps them judge how far away an object is. The primates with the best eyesight also see colors.

Primates get a firm grip on a limb with the five toes on each foot. The first toe is usually large. It sticks out from the others like the thumb on a human hand. (A hand is a special type of foot.) While many other mammals have claws, primates tend to have flat nails. The nails help support enlarged pads on the ends of the toes. Like our fingertips, these pads are sensitive to touch and have nonskid bumps, or ridges.

Most primates have large, well-developed brains and are among the most intelligent of mammals. Certain parts of their brains are particularly well developed. Among these are the parts used in seeing and in controlling movement. However, primates do not depend much on their sense of smell, and that part of the brain is smaller than in many mammals.

Primates have fewer young than most other mammals, and the young stay with the mother for a longer period. A mother bears only one or two young at a time. They are nursed at the two milk glands on her chest. The long time that young stay with their mothers allows for learning. In many other mammal groups the young strike out on their own early in life, and so their behavior is based mostly on instinct. Young primates have instincts, too, but they also learn behavior patterns from their mothers and from the group they live in.

▶ THE EXCEPTIONS

There are about 200 living species of primates. The number is approximate because there may be species that have not yet been discovered by scientists. And some now named as separate species may turn out to be races of the same species.

Each of these many species differs from the others. Or as scientists say, each has its own specializations. As a result, for every general characteristic of the primates there is likely to be at least one exception.

For example, many mammals eat only one kind of food (such as meat) and have teeth specially suited to eating this food; that is, their teeth are specialized. Primates eat a variety of foods, including fruits, leaves, and small animals, such as insects and lizards. Their teeth are not specialized except in lemurs. Most lemurs have long lower front teeth, which they use as a comb to clean their hair. The aye-aye, a highly specialized lemur, has big, curved, gnawing teeth that keep growing at the base as they wear off at the tip.

There are a few more exceptions. All primates have five fingers on each foot (counting hands as feet) except the spider monkeys and the guerezas, which have no thumb, and the pottos, which have only a nubbin in place of the first finger. Flat nails occur on the big toe except in tree shrews. Only one pair of mammae (milk glands) occurs on the upper chest except in certain lemurs. These lemurs have two or even three pairs of milk glands; the aye-aye has only one pair, but like a cow's, they are placed between the hind legs. As a rule, primates live only in warm climates. Humans, who make clothes and build houses, are an exception.

▶ THE APES

The primates are divided into several big families. Many of the primates we know best are members of the ape family. This family includes gorillas, chimpanzees, orangutans, and gibbons. The first three are often called great apes. This name sets them off from the gibbons, which are the smallest of the apes. More important, it distinguishes them from certain large primates with names like "black ape" and "Barbary ape," which are not really apes at all, but monkeys.

True apes do not have tails. (Most monkeys do.) True apes have large, projecting jaws. Their front teeth are large and have flat edges. The tusks are big, especially in males.

Apes eat mostly fruits, buds, and other vegetation. Although they have no tails, they are agile in trees, swinging from limb to limb or even from tree to tree with their long, powerful arms. But certain apes also spend a good deal of time on the ground.

Gorillas

Male gorillas are among the ground dwellers. A full-grown male may weigh more than 180 kilograms (400 pounds). This great weight can make tree travel dangerous. But young gorillas and females—much smaller and lighter than males—sometimes do climb trees. When gorillas walk on the ground, they use both feet and hands. The long, curved fingers are doubled up, so that the animals walk on their knuckles.

Gorillas travel in family groups. Like other apes, they feed on fruits, buds, and other vegetation. Gorillas may look fierce, but they are generally peaceful. They are dangerous chiefly when wounded or frightened. Gorillas live in the dense forests of Central Africa. The adult gorillas you often see at zoos were probably caught as babies by hunters.

Chimpanzees

Chimpanzees also live in the tropical forests of Central Africa but not in the same areas as gorillas. For a long time scientists thought that chimpanzees spent most of their time in trees. But a recent study shows that in some places wild chimpanzees spend much of their time on the ground, where they both walk and run on two legs.

Chimpanzees can be told from other apes by the large, hairless ears that stick out from the sides of their heads. These animals weigh slightly less than most humans, but they are very strong. They can lift or move objects that a strong person could not budge.

Chimpanzees are considered the most intelligent of the apes in captivity. They have great curiosity. Chimpanzees trained at research centers have learned to communicate with people by means of sign language. Because they can also learn many tricks, chimpanzees are favorite show animals.

Orangutans and Gibbons

Orangutans are about the same size as chimpanzees. Their bodies are covered with long reddish brown hair. These apes spend a good deal of their time in trees. They travel swiftly through the trees. They rest or sleep on platformlike nests, which they have made out of broken limbs. (The other great apes also make such platforms.) When followed or annoyed, orangutans may break off tree limbs and throw them. These apes are found in Borneo and Sumatra, but they are becoming much rarer as people cut the forests and kill the wildlife.

The gibbons are the smallest of the apes. They eat birds, eggs, insects, and spiders, as well as vegetation. Gibbons can scamper on all fours or walk on their hind legs. Sometimes they are seen walking along a tree limb while holding their long arms up to balance themselves. They are amazing acrobats and can swing across a 9-meter (30-foot) gap between trees. There are five species of gibbons, which vary in color and size. All five live in Southeast Asia and nearby islands, where their loud whoops ring through the forests.

▶ OLD WORLD MONKEYS

Sixty-one species of monkeys found in Asia and Africa are grouped under the name Old World monkeys. (The monkeys in Europe were introduced there by travelers.) But they do not look much alike. Some have short tails, and some have long tails, although none use their tails for hanging from branches. Some have short gray or brown hair. Others have long black and white hair. Some have patches of skin colored a brilliant red, blue, or purple. Some are active at night, and others are active

APE FAMILY

GIBBON

CHIMPANZEE

ORANGUTAN

GORILLA

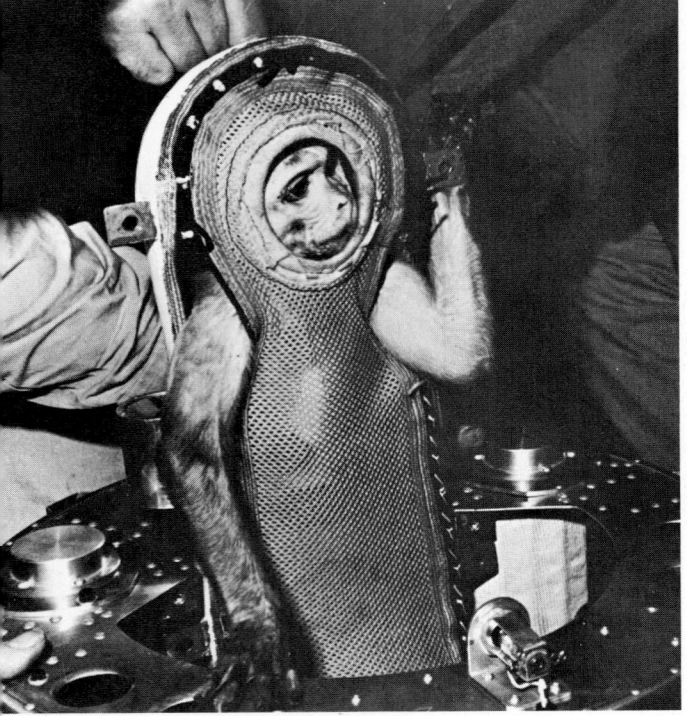

Sam, a rhesus monkey, was one of the first astronauts.

by day. Some live only in trees, and others spend much time hunting for food on the ground.

All of these Old World monkeys have nostrils that are close together, but some have short snouts, and others have long snouts. A monkey in Borneo has a most unusual snout, or proboscis. This monkey has a large bulb of a nose that it blows up with air when excited. The animal is called the proboscis monkey.

Old World monkeys have 32 teeth, as do adult humans. All except the leaf-eating monkeys also have cheek pouches for storing food. The leaf-eaters include the African guerezas, the proboscis monkeys, and the Oriental langurs. Other Old World monkeys eat more varied diets of fruits, eggs, small animals, or whatever else they find at hand.

One of the largest groups of Old World monkeys is the macaques. One kind of macaque is called the long-tailed crab-eating macaque. It lives in the Malay region and the Philippines. These macaques are good swimmers. When frightened, a whole tribe may dive into a river and swim quickly across. On Sumatra there is the pig-tailed macaque. People tame the young and teach them to climb trees and throw down fruit and coconuts. The best-known of the macaques is the rhesus monkey, native to China, India, and

Burma. The rhesus is brown in color and weighs about 4.5 kilograms (10 pounds). Its tail is somewhat shorter than its body. This monkey is often used in medical research.

Baboons and mandrills, the largest of the Old World monkeys, live in large troops on the ground, among rocks, or in forests. They include some of the most brightly colored monkeys. The male mandrill has a brilliant red snout that is framed by blue ridges. Its hind parts are also vividly colored. The hamadryas baboon of the Red Sea area is distinguished by a cape of long hair over its shoulders. This was the sacred baboon of the ancient Egyptians.

Monkeys are greatly respected in some parts of the world. The Hindus of India, for instance, consider certain monkeys sacred and allow them to roam in temples and villages.

▶ NEW WORLD MONKEYS

The New World monkeys of South and Central America are generally smaller than their Old World relatives. Most have more teeth. Their noses are flatter, and the nostrils are widely separated. Most New World monkeys sleep at night and are active only in the daylight.

The 69 species of New World monkeys are divided into two families. One family is made up of the marmosets and the tamarins. Many of these have tufts of hair on their ears or around the face and neck. Unlike most monkeys, they have claws on their toes and fingers, except on the big toe. The members of this family are small. The largest is only about 50 centimeters (20 inches) long. Most of them are under 30 centimeters (12 inches) in length.

All other New World monkeys belong to one family, but they vary greatly in looks and behavior. The owl monkey, for example, has large eyes and is active only at night. The red uakari has a red face and a red, bald head. The squirrel monkeys are well named. They are the size of squirrels, and they scamper about in the trees.

Tails also vary among New World monkeys. Some, such as the capuchins, or sapajous, have medium-length tails covered with hair and use them to grasp tree limbs. Spider monkeys have longer tails with a bare area. This bare area gives them a better grip. These

OLD WORLD MONKEYS

PROBOSCIS MONKEY

STUMP-TAILED MACAQUE

MANDRILL

HAMADRYAS BABOON

NEW WORLD MONKEYS

RED UAKARI

WHITE-EARED MARMOSET

GOLDEN LION-TAMARIN

SPIDER MONKEY

LOWER PRIMATES

TREE SHREW

SLENDER LORIS

RUFFED LEMUR

TARSIER

POTTO

long-legged, skinny creatures with long fingers use their tails as a fifth hand. (Only the woolly spider monkey has a thumb; the other spider monkeys have none.) Sakis have long tails, which they use only for balancing. But howlers use their long tails to grasp limbs or food. The name of these big monkeys refers to the fact that the males have an amazingly loud calling voice.

▶ LOWER PRIMATES

All primates other than humans, apes, and monkeys are called the lower primates because they are less developed. Their braincases are generally smaller. They lack the driving curiosity of the higher primates. Most cannot focus both eyes on the same object. All told, there are six families of lower primates. They are found only in the Old World.

Fossils show that tarsiers are one of the oldest primate families. They once lived in many parts of the world, including North America and Europe. But today only three small species exist; they live in the East Indian region. Tarsiers have huge owl-like eyes and long froglike legs; the ends of their fingers and toes have large pads that improve their grip. At night tarsiers leap from bush to bush in search of insects to eat.

The three families of lemurs are all found on the island of Madagascar, off eastern Africa. They have thrived there because animal life on the island did not offer them much competition. One group of lemurs has the same habit of eating leaves and buds as a group of Old World monkeys. Both lemurs and monkeys have unusually long digestive systems. This is an interesting example of different animals evolving in the same direction.

The true lemurs vary in size from that of a large mouse to that of a medium-sized dog. The mouse lemur is the smallest primate in the world. It fits into the palm of the hand. Lemurs eat many different kinds of food and adapt well to life in captivity.

Another family of lower primates includes the lorises and pottos of Africa and Asia. Like lemurs, lorises and pottos have lower front teeth that form a comb. They have short tails (or no tails) and short ears. In trees they climb slowly and surely. Their close relatives the galagos, or bush babies, have long tails and large movable ears. The galagos are able to jump quickly.

The lowest of the primates are the tree shrews. These are small animals that have long noses. They have claws on all toes. Some look rather like squirrels. "Tree shrews" is not a very good name for these animals. They are not shrews, and many of them do not even live in trees. But they do resemble the earliest primates of all.

SYDNEY ANDERSON
American Museum of Natural History

MONONUCLEOSIS, INFECTIOUS. See DISEASES.
MONOPOLIES. See TRUSTS AND MONOPOLIES.

JAMES MONROE (1758–1831)

5TH PRESIDENT OF THE UNITED STATES

MONROE, JAMES. James Monroe was the last of the Virginia Dynasty presidents. (These also included Thomas Jefferson and James Madison.) He was a professional politician who spent virtually his whole adult life in the public service, steadily rising to ever higher office. A modest man, Monroe was overshadowed by the brilliance of his great contemporaries. Yet his modesty and integrity won him wide esteem and the unwavering loyalty of his friends.

▶ EARLY YEARS

Monroe was born on April 28, 1758, in Westmoreland County, Virginia, the son of Spence and Elizabeth Jones Monroe. At the age of 16 he entered the College of William and Mary, but he left within 2 years, in 1776, to join the Third Virginia Regiment as a lieutenant. He took part in some of the famous battles of the American Revolution. At Valley Forge in the winter of 1777 Monroe served as aide-de-camp to one of George Washington's generals. In the following year, on General Washington's recommendation, the 20-year-old Monroe was commissioned lieutenant colonel of a regiment to be raised in Virginia.

In Virginia the young officer "formed a connection," as he put it, with a man who was to shape his career and affect his whole life. The man was Thomas Jefferson, then governor of Virginia. Jefferson made the young man his protégé and, among other things, taught him law.

The intimacy between the two men lasted for 46 years, until Jefferson's death in 1826. Jefferson, Monroe's senior by 15 years, unfailingly helped the younger man to advance his political career, all the way up to the presidency. His confidence in Monroe never wavered. Jefferson said of him: "He is a man whose soul might be turned wrong side outwards, without discovering a blemish. . . ."

▶ HIS POLITICAL CAREER

Monroe embarked upon his political career with single-minded concentration. No rebuff halted him, and no defeat slowed him for long. From 1782, when he was elected to the Virginia House of Delegates at the age of 24, until 1825, when he left the White House at the age of 66, he was in public office almost without interruption.

Monroe was a member of the Congress of the Confederation, by which the United

WHEN JAMES MONROE WAS PRESIDENT
The *Savannah* became the first steamship to cross the Atlantic; the American ship took 29 days to make the crossing (1819) and used its sails for most of the trip. The Monroe Doctrine was officially proclaimed by President Monroe in his message to Congress on December 2, 1823.
Monroe's birthplace was in Westmoreland County, Virginia.

States was governed before the adoption of the Federal Constitution. He was a delegate to the Virginia Ratification Convention, where he opposed adoption of the Constitution because he felt it centered too much power in the federal government. He was a United States senator, acting in opposition to the Federalist Party. He was four times governor of Virginia. He was minister to France, Spain, and Great Britain. He was secretary of state as well as secretary of war. Finally, he was a two-term president of the United States.

▶ HIS DIPLOMATIC MISSIONS

In 1794 President Washington sent Monroe to Paris. Washington hoped to win a favorable reception among the French revolutionary leaders there and to conciliate their sympathizers in the United States. The French Government gave Monroe an enthusiastic reception. Monroe returned the enthusiasm. But his open pro-French sympathies so antagonized President Washington's anti-French Cabinet that it urged Monroe's recall. The President agreed, even though Monroe's removal deepened the anti-American feelings of the French Government.

The major achievement of Monroe's second mission to Europe involved the Louisiana Purchase. After 1800 there was growing fear in the United States that the Spanish cession of Louisiana to France would bottle up the Mississippi River, a vital artery for western American trade. "The day France takes . . . New Orleans," President Jefferson said, ". . . we must marry ourselves to the British fleet and nation." Jefferson decided, however, upon diplomatic measures first.

For so delicate and grave a mission the President needed a man in whom he and his followers had complete trust. Such a man was James Monroe. Jefferson wrote him in 1803:

"You possessed the unlimited confidence of the administration . . . and generally of the republicans everywhere; and were you to refuse to go, no other man can be found who does this—All eyes, all hopes are now fixed on you."

Monroe carried with him to Paris the President's unlimited confidence and his special instructions. These were, primarily, to buy New Orleans and to acquire the right of free navigation on the Mississippi. He arrived in Paris in April, 1803. There he joined the regular American minister, Robert R. Livingston (1746–1813). The French surprised them with the sudden offer, by Napoleon, to sell the United States the whole Louisiana Territory. After some haggling with the French minister of finance, Monroe and Livingston signed the treaty, which was dated April 30, 1803. By its terms the United States acquired all of the Louisiana Territory for a total cost of 80,000,000 francs (about $15,000,000). The Louisiana Purchase was beyond a doubt the greatest real estate bargain in history. In one stroke it doubled the territory of the United States. The transaction also enhanced Monroe's reputation.

After Paris, Monroe went to London, and then for about a year to Madrid, as American minister. In these wartime capitals (the Napoleonic Wars were then raging) his diplomatic activities were not fruitful, partly because of British hostility. In 1807 he returned home. There his Virginia friends were trying to promote him as successor to Jefferson in the presidency. Monroe was willing, but the nomination and election went to James Madison. Monroe refused the governorship of Louisiana and resumed political life in Virginia, first as member of the state legislature and then as governor.

In 1811 Monroe accepted President Madison's offer of the post of secretary of state. He held this position throughout the War of 1812 and until the end of Madison's second term. In 1814 Monroe also became secretary of war. His energetic policies as war secretary were given some of the credit for the American victories at Plattsburg in 1814 and at New Orleans in 1815. They also helped him toward his nomination for the presidency in 1816.

▶ PRESIDENT

Monroe was elected president in 1816. He received about 84 percent of the electoral votes cast (183 out of 217 votes) and carried 16 of the 19 states of the Union. In 1820, when he ran for a second term, his triumph was even greater. This time he received all but one of the electoral votes (231 out of 232). He would have received all the electoral votes had not one elector felt that nobody should share that historic honor with George Washington.

Monroe's administration came to be known

as the Era of Good Feeling. It was a period of national optimism, expansion, and growth. There were no major domestic problems to trouble the President. The looming slavery issue was settled, at least temporarily, by the Missouri Compromise of 1820. In regard to internal improvements, Monroe in 1822 vetoed the Cumberland Road bill as unconstitutional. However, he recommended a Constitutional amendment to give the federal government power in the field of "great national works."

Foreign Affairs

The Monroe Administration was especially notable in the field of foreign affairs. The able diplomacy of Monroe's secretary of state, John Quincy Adams, resulted in a number of achievements of lasting benefit to the United States. The Convention of 1818, held in London, settled the boundary between the United States and British North America (Canada) and fixed the northern line of the Louisiana Purchase. In the following year the western limit of the Louisiana Territory (from the Sabine River, on the Gulf of Mexico, along the Red and Arkansas rivers to the Pacific Ocean) was defined by the Adams-Onís Treaty with Spain. In the same treaty the United States also acquired East Florida and a claim, which Spain renounced, to West Florida.

The Monroe Doctrine. The most memorable event connected with Monroe's presidency was the proclamation of the Monroe Doctrine. In 1822 the Austrian, French, Russian, and Prussian monarchies considered the possibility of restoring Spanish power in South America. But the British foreign minister, George Canning (1770–1827), was unwilling to see the European nations, especially the French, intrude into the Western Hemisphere. He approached the American minister in London about a joint action on Latin America. This proposal was reported to Monroe. After consulting with his Cabinet and seeking the advice of Jefferson and Madison, Monroe decided to take a step independently of Great Britain. This was a public declaration of American policy, expressed in a message to Congress on December 2, 1823.

The Monroe Doctrine, as embodied in the President's message, comprised four main points: (1) The political system of the Americas was different and separate from that of Europe; (2) the Americas were no longer to be regarded as subjects of European colonization; (3) the United States had no intention of interfering with the European "colonies or dependencies" already existing in the Americas; (4) the United States would be hostile to any extension of European power in the Americas.

For more than a century this doctrine remained the foundation of American foreign policy. It guided United States relations with Europe, particularly in regard to Latin America.

▶ LATER YEARS

Upon his retirement from the presidency, in March, 1825, Monroe returned to Oak Hill, his home in Loudoun County, Virginia. In 1826 he became a regent of the University of Virginia. And in 1829 he presided over the Virginia State Constitutional Convention. After the death of his wife, Eliza, in 1830, Monroe, lonely and ill, went to live with his daughter, Mrs. Samuel L. Gouverneur, in New York City. There he died on July 4, 1831, at the age of 73. In 1858, on the 100th anniversary of his birth, his remains were moved to Richmond, Virginia.

Monroe was about 6 feet tall, with grayish-blue eyes and a lined face that conveyed an expression of kindliness. Somewhat colorless,

---

IMPORTANT DATES IN THE LIFE OF JAMES MONROE

1758	Born in Westmoreland County, Virginia, April 28.
1776	Left the College of William and Mary to join the Continental Army.
1782	Member of the Virginia House of Delegates.
1783–1786	Member of the Congress of the Confederation.
1788	Delegate to the Virginia Ratification Convention.
1790–1794	United States senator.
1794–1796	Minister to France.
1799–1803	Governor of Virginia.
1803	On a diplomatic mission to France; helped negotiate the Louisiana Purchase.
1803	Minister to Great Britain.
1804	Minister to Spain.
1810	Member of the Virginia legislature.
1811	Governor of Virginia.
1811–1817	Secretary of state, also serving as secretary of war (1814–15).
1817–1825	5th president of the United States.
1831	Died in New York City, July 4.

he yet inspired universal respect for his modesty, solid judgment, and quiet administrative ability. The crusty John Quincy Adams, who followed Monroe in the presidency, paid his predecessor this tribute:

"Monroe . . . was . . . of purposes always honest and sincere, of intentions always pure, of labors outlasting the daily circuit of the sun . . . ; of a mind anxious and unwearied in the pursuit of truth and right; patient of inquiry; patient of contradiction; . . . sound in its ultimate judgments; and firm in its final conclusions."

Unavoidably, Monroe has suffered by comparison with his brilliant contemporaries, particularly Jefferson and Madison. But his many years of devoted service to the United States in the country's most formative period entitle him to esteemed remembrance.

SAUL K. PADOVER
Author, *The Genius of America*

See also LOUISIANA PURCHASE; MONROE DOCTRINE.

MONROE DOCTRINE

Hands off the independent states of the New World!

No further European colonization in the Western Hemisphere!

The United States will have nothing more to do with the wars of European powers in matters relating to themselves. But the United States would consider any attempt on the part of European powers to extend their system to any portion of the Western Hemisphere as dangerous to the peace and safety of the New World.

These were the three points of policy that President James Monroe proclaimed to Congress and to the world in his famous annual message of December 2, 1823. At that time the monarchs of Austria, Prussia, and Russia (the Holy Alliance) were debating whether to support France in a plan to restore, by armed intervention, Spain's Latin-American colonies. Early in the 19th century many of Spain's colonies in Latin America had revolted and had become independent nations like the United States. In 1823 Great Britain issued an ultimatum forbidding French interference with the newly independent republics in Latin America. It was this ultimatum rather than the bold words of President Monroe that stopped French intervention in Latin America. But President Monroe and Secretary of State John Quincy Adams did not know of Britain's ultimatum. On his own authority Monroe blazoned his own bold warning to the world. It was not a statement of international law. On the contrary, it was an independent pronouncement of United States policy.

With the passage of years Monroe's message became known as the Monroe Doctrine. For several decades the United States might not have been able alone to enforce this brave warning. Fortunately, wars and rivalries among European powers restrained them from interfering with the independence of the Western Hemisphere; and by the end of the 19th century the United States had grown to be a world power, capable of making the Monroe Doctrine respected.

The Monroe Doctrine Invoked

Several incidents will serve as examples of the Monroe Doctrine's influence.

While the United States was paralyzed by the Civil War, Napoleon III of France planned to take control of Mexico. With the support of French troops he placed the Austrian Archduke Maximilian on the throne of Mexico. By the end of the Civil War in the United States, Napoleon was beset by troubles in Europe. At the insistence of the United States, in the spirit but not the name of the Monroe Doctrine, Napoleon withdrew support from Maximilian's empire in Mexico, and Mexico regained its independence.

In 1895, because of the Monroe Doctrine, Great Britain was persuaded to arbitrate her boundary dispute with Venezuela.

In 1903 Great Britain, Germany, and Italy lifted their naval blockade of Venezuela and agreed to arbitrate their financial claims against that state.

No-Transfer Principle

Associated with the principles of the Monroe Doctrine was an older policy. This was the

No-Transfer Principle—not stated by President Monroe, but equally important. The fathers of American independence were greatly concerned over the possibility that the remaining territory of North America could be united under one great foreign power as a result of wars between the European countries. Such a change in the map of the continent might perhaps place the United States again under control of a European nation. That nation might be the British Empire, the new Napoleonic empire, or the Spanish empire. Actually, the Founding Fathers did not fear Spain. Spain was a weak, declining power. But Spanish Louisiana and Florida transferred to imperial France or to the British Empire would be quite another matter. Therefore, early in the history of the United States it became a policy to oppose the transfer of one colonial possession in North America to another European empire. Such a transfer would upset the balance of power in North America and block United States territorial expansion or even choke off independence itself.

Such a menace loomed large when Napoleon Bonaparte acquired title to Louisiana from Spain in the year 1800. This danger disappeared when Napoleon sold Louisiana to the United States in 1803, before ever occupying it with French troops. The Louisiana Purchase almost doubled United States territory overnight. In 1811, when either Napoleon or Great Britain seemed about to take possession of Spanish Florida, Congress passed (at President James Madison's request) a famous resolution stating the No-Transfer Principle directed at Florida: "That the United States . . . can not without serious inquietude see any part of the said territory pass into the hands of any foreign power." This danger, too, disappeared after the War of 1812. Spain yielded Florida to the United States, together with a large part of her territory between Louisiana and the Pacific Ocean, in the famous Adams-Onís Treaty (Transcontinental Treaty of 1819). After that treaty the No-Transfer Principle extended to the whole of North America. President Grant in 1869 formally made it a part of the Monroe Doctrine.

The wars of the 20th century caused the No-Transfer Principle of the Monroe Doctrine to be extended to cover the entire Western Hemisphere. During World War II, when it seemed likely that Germany might take over some or all of the remaining European colonies in the New World (the Guianas, the islands of the Caribbean, Greenland, or even Iceland), Congress re-affirmed the Principle on June 18, 1940. Congress stated that "the United States would not recognize any transfer and would not acquiesce in any attempt to transfer any geographic region of this hemisphere from one non-American power to another non-American power." In this time of great peril the Latin-American republics supported this expanded concept of the Doctrine. The defeat of Germany in World War II, as in World War I, removed the danger, at least for the time being.

In the period between the two world wars President Franklin D. Roosevelt's Good Neighbor Policy resulted in a series of new inter-American treaties with Latin-American countries. These treaties were based on the Latin-American doctrine of nonintervention: that it is "inadmissable [for any one state to intervene] directly, or indirectly, and for whatever reason, in the internal or external affairs of any of the Parties [states]."

This meant that the United States could not of itself take quick action to defend the Monroe Doctrine in case a dangerous "fact or situation," short of armed attack should present itself. It would first have to secure the agreement of a two-thirds majority of the 21 American republics (article VI of the Inter-American Treaty of Reciprocal Assistance of Rio de Janeiro, 1947). Such at least was the official attitude of the Department of State under presidents Eisenhower and Kennedy. As a result, the Monroe Doctrine was not invoked in 1960 when the Union of Soviet Socialist Republics violated the hands-off principle by intervention in Cuba. The Castro revolution in Cuba had turned that nation into a Soviet satellite.

No president of the United States has actually pronounced the Doctrine lifeless, but it has been left in a state of suspended animation. It remains to be seen whether any president, present or future, will revive the Monroe Doctrine in the defense of independence in the Western Hemisphere.

SAMUEL FLAGG BEMIS
Yale University

MONTANA

One of the nation's largest dams is known by a strange name—Hungry Horse. It is said that this name comes from an event that happened during the fierce winter of 1900–01.

During a blizzard two freight horses named Tex and Jerry wandered away from their sleigh. They were working in the rugged wilderness near the South Fork of the Flathead River, not far from the area now known as Glacier National Park. The wind blew wildly, the snow swirled about them, and soon Tex and Jerry were lost. For a month they wandered, struggling in deep snow. When they were found, they were so weak from hunger that only good care and feeding made them strong enough to be led out of the wilderness.

The name Hungry Horse was given to a mountain, a lake, and a creek in the area where the horses were found. Later the same name was chosen for the dam that was built a short distance downstream. The Hungry Horse Dam, completed in 1953, forms a reservoir about 34 miles (55 kilometers) long. A beautiful highway leads to a parking area high on the canyon wall overlooking the dam. Another highway takes visitors across the crest of the dam.

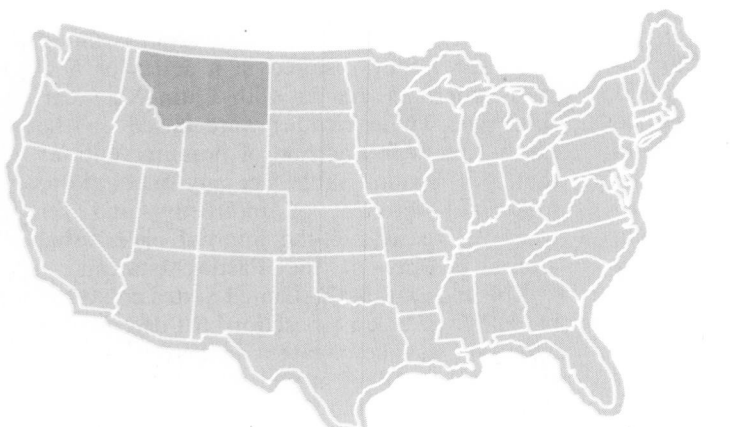

Long ago the Indians called Montana the Land of the Shining Mountains. Today it is often called the Big Sky Country. Such names as these show the call of the out-of-doors in a land of great natural beauty.

In eastern Montana the plains roll endlessly toward the horizon. Cattle and sheep graze on the pasturelands. Wheat and sugar beets spring from the rich soils. Oil flows from deep beneath the surface. In western Montana the peaks of the Rocky Mountains seem to touch the sky. Thick forests cover the foothills and the lower slopes. Only the ore dumps and the smokestacks of metal smelters give a clue to the mineral wealth hidden beneath the surface.

In its earliest days Montana was a place where people came not to settle but to gather riches. The fur traders came for beaver and other furs, and the prospectors for gold. Then ranchers began to bring large herds of cattle to the open ranges. Gradually homesteaders arrived to take up claims. Fences were built, and Montana was settled. Lumbering flourished in the mountains of the west, and mining became an important industry.

Today agriculture, manufacturing, and mining share importance with the tourist industry. Thousands of people visit Montana each year. In summer they come to Glacier National Park and to Yellowstone National Park. They visit the national forests, the wilderness areas, and the many state parks and forests. They camp, hunt, fish, hike, and ride horses along woodland trails bordered by hundreds of different kinds of wildflowers. For variety they visit the early mining camps. Most of the camps are ghost towns now, but a few have been restored to provide a glimpse into Montana's early history. Many people also come to the Big Sky Country to hunt or ski.

▶THE LAND

Montana is located in the northwestern part of the United States, between the Dakotas to the east and Idaho to the west. All of its northern boundary, about 560 miles (900 kilometers) long, is shared with Canada. Except for a ragged western border, the state is shaped somewhat like a rectangle.

Landforms

The western two fifths of Montana lies within the Rocky Mountains. Most of this region is known as the Northern Rocky Mountains. The small section along the Wyoming border is called the Middle Rockies. Eastern Montana is part of the Great Plains.

The Rocky Mountains. Montana's share of the Rocky Mountains includes many mountain ranges. These ranges run generally in a north-south direction. In the northwestern part of the state are the Cabinet Mountains, which Montana shares with Idaho, and the Purcell Mountains, which extend southward from Canada. To the east are a series of ranges—the Whitefish, Mission, Swan, Flathead, Lewis, and Rocky Mountain Front mountains, which face the plains of eastern Montana.

STATE FLAG.

STATE TREE: Ponderosa pine.

STATE FLOWER: Bitterroot.

STATE BIRD:
Western meadowlark.

MONTANA

CAPITAL: Helena.

STATEHOOD: November 8, 1889; the 41st state.

SIZE: 147,046 sq mi (380,848 km²); rank, 4th.

POPULATION: 786,690 (1980 census); rank, 44th.

ORIGIN OF NAME: From the Latin word *montana*, meaning "mountainous regions."

ABBREVIATIONS: Mont.; MT.

NICKNAME: Treasure State; also Land of the Shining Mountains, Big Sky Country.

STATE ANIMAL: Grizzly Bear.

STATE SONGS: "Montana," by Charles C. Cohan; music by Joseph E. Howard; "Montana Melody," by LeGrande Harvey.

STATE MOTTO: *Oro y plata* (Gold and silver).

STATE SEAL: A plow and a miner's pick and shovel in the foreground stand for agriculture and mining. Mountain scenery and the Great Falls of the Missouri River in the background represent Montana's natural beauty. The state motto appears on a streamer at the bottom.

STATE FLAG: The state seal appears in the center of a blue field. Above the seal is the name of the state.

The Continental Divide, a part of the Rocky Mountain chain, towers over St. Mary Lake in Glacier National Park. The park is named for the more than 50 glaciers found there.

The boundary between Idaho and Montana follows the crests of the Bitterroot Range and the Beaverhead and the Centennial mountains. Glaciers have carved out jagged peaks in these wild, almost impassable mountains. Nearby in the southwest are the Spanish Peaks and the Madison and Gallatin ranges. Farther east lies a lofty group of mountains called the Absaroka Range, which extends southward into Wyoming.

Few ranges in the United States are as rugged or as beautiful as the Absaroka. Granite Peak, the highest point in Montana, is located in the Beartooth Mountains just north and east of Yellowstone National Park. The Bighorn Basin separates the Absaroka Range from the Bighorn Mountains, which Montana also shares with Wyoming.

The Continental Divide crosses western Montana from north to south. It follows the crest of the Lewis, Anaconda, Beaverhead, and Centennial mountains.

The many valleys and basins between the mountains are important for agriculture and transportation routes. In the northwest a long valley called the Rocky Mountain Trench extends southward from British Columbia to the vicinity of Kalispell. Valleys south of Kalispell include Mission Valley, which contains Flathead Lake, and Bitterroot Valley.

The Great Plains. The eastern three fifths of Montana lies within the Missouri Plateau, the northern part of a vast landform called the Great Plains. In Montana this region is a broad, rolling plain that slopes gradually eastward.

In the central part of the state are many isolated mountain passes. Some rise as high as 5,000 feet (1,500 meters) above the plain. The Crazy Mountains, the Bearpaw Mountains, and others are groups of old volcanoes.

In the southeast, along the Yellowstone River, is a small badlands area. Badlands are areas of unusual formations carved out by wind and water. Fossils of ancient forms of

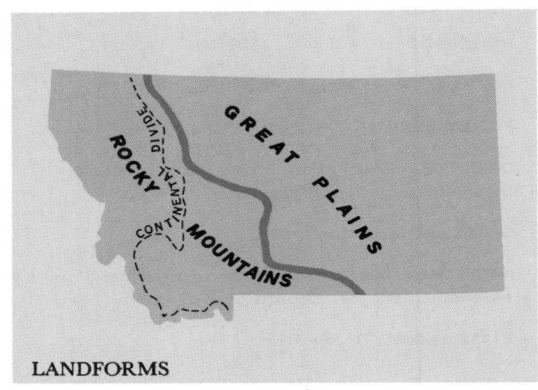

LANDFORMS

life have been found in this area and in other parts of Montana. An almost complete skeleton of *Tyrannosaurus*, a large meat-eating dinosaur, was unearthed in Garfield County. The fossil remains of *Stegosaurus*, an armored dinosaur, were found near Great Falls, and the site of an important find of dinosaur eggs is located near Choteau.

Rivers and Lakes

The major river in northwestern Montana is the Clark Fork of the Columbia River. One of the important tributaries of the Clark Fork is the Flathead River, which drains the Kalispell, Mission, and Flathead valleys. Other tributaries are the Bitterroot River, which drains the valley of the same name, and the Blackfoot River.

East of the Continental Divide the main rivers are the Missouri and the Yellowstone. The Missouri River is formed by the joining of the Jefferson (Beaverhead–Big Hole–Ruby), Madison, and Gallatin rivers near Three Forks. From its source it flows northward through the Townsend and the Helena valleys. At the Gates of the Mountains, a deep gorge, it leaves the Helena Valley and flows northeast past the city of Great Falls.

The Yellowstone River rises in northwestern Wyoming, but most of its course is in Montana. It joins the Missouri in North Dakota near the Montana line. Its major tributaries—the Bighorn, Tongue, and Powder rivers—enter it from the south.

Most of Montana's natural lakes are in the Rocky Mountains. Over a period of time, the ridges formed by mountain glaciers have blocked river valleys, creating many lakes, both large and small. Flathead Lake in Mission Valley is Montana's largest natural lake and one of the largest bodies of fresh water west of the Mississippi River. Quake Lake, near Yellowstone National Park, was formed by an earthquake in 1959.

Numerous dams and reservoirs have been built to provide flood control, water for irrigation, or hydroelectric power. Some of the dams also aid navigation. The Fort Peck Dam on the Missouri River serves all these purposes. It was built by the federal government. Other notable examples of federal projects are Hungry Horse Dam on the South Fork of the Flathead River, Canyon Ferry Dam on the Missouri, Yellowtail Dam on the Bighorn, and

Libby Dam on the Kootenai. Private companies have built many power dams, such as Kerr Dam on the Flathead River and Noxon Rapids Dam on the Clark Fork.

Climate

Montana has great differences in climate. One of the reasons is the great variation in elevation. Others are the barrier effect of the mountains and Montana's location in the inte-

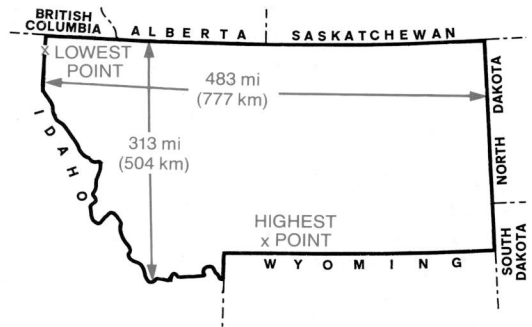

THE LAND

LOCATION: Latitude—44° 22' N to 49° N. **Longitude**—104° 02' W to 116° 03' W.
North Dakota and South Dakota to the east, Wyoming to the south, Idaho to the southwest and west, the Canadian provinces of British Columbia, Alberta, and Saskatchewan to the north.

ELEVATION: Highest—Granite Peak, 12,799 ft (3,901 m). **Lowest**—Kootenai River on the Montana-Idaho border, 1,800 ft (549 m).

LANDFORMS: Rocky Mountains in the west, Great Plains in the east.

SURFACE WATERS: Major rivers—Clark Fork of the Columbia River and its tributaries, the Flathead, Bitterroot, and Blackfoot rivers; Missouri River and its tributaries in Montana, the Marias, Milk, and Musselshell rivers; Yellowstone River and its tributaries, the Bighorn, Tongue, and Powder rivers. **Major artificial lakes**—Fort Peck, Hungry Horse, Canyon Ferry, Tiber, Yellowtail. **Largest natural lake**—Flathead.

CLIMATE: Temperature—January averages vary from 10°F (−12°C) in the northeast to 22°F (−6°C) in the south central and western sections. July averages vary from 64°F (18°C) in the southwest to 72°F (22°C) in the southeast. **Precipitation**—Annual average, 13—19 in. (330—480 mm). Snowfall varies from up to 300 in. (760 cm) in some parts of the mountains to about 24 in. (60 cm) in the north central and northeastern sections. **Growing season**—Four months or more in much of the state.

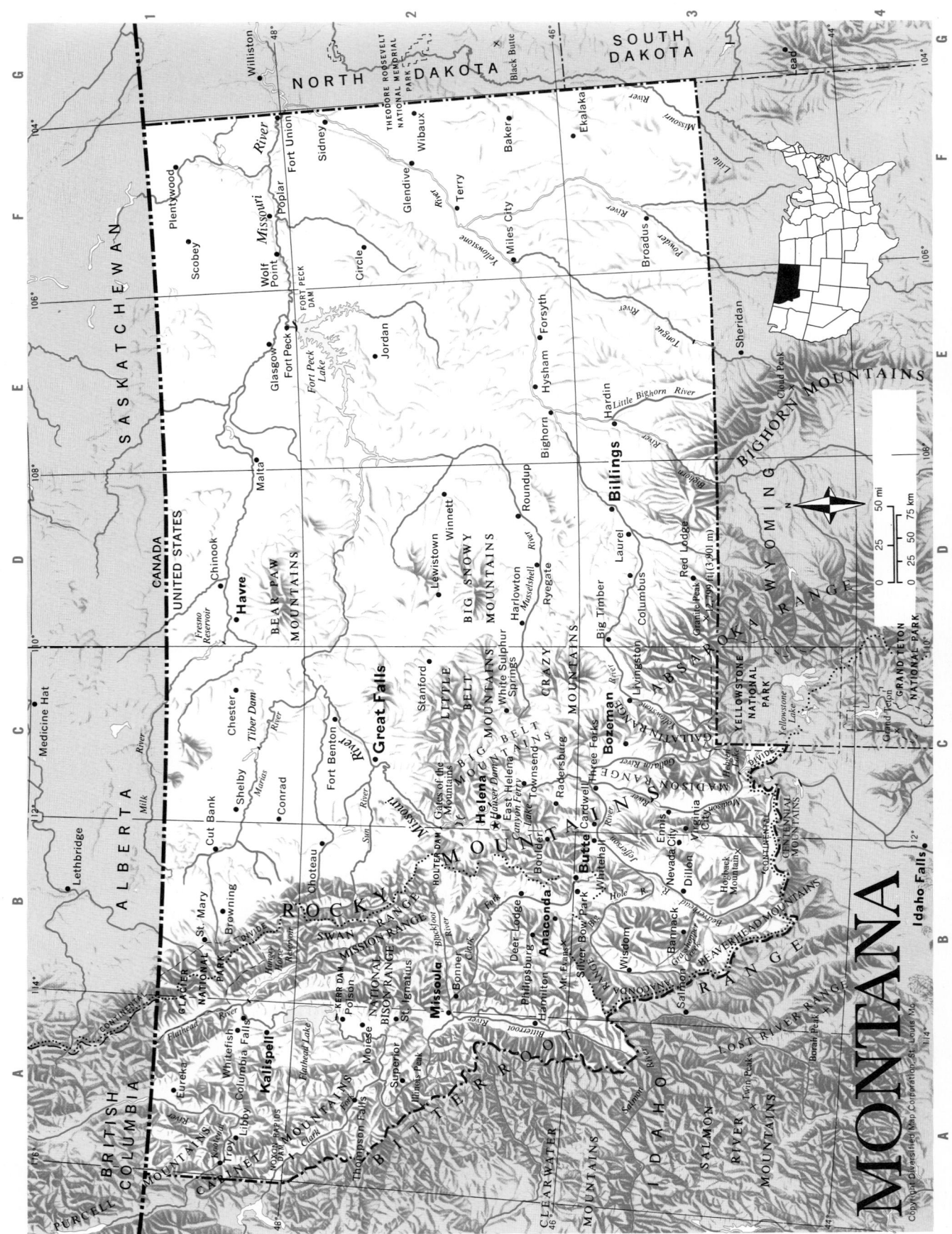

MONTANA

INDEX TO MONTANA MAP

● County Seat   Counties in parentheses   ★ State Capital

rior of the North American continent. West of the Continental Divide the climate of Montana is somewhat like that of the north Pacific Coast. There the winters are generally milder and the summers cooler than in areas east of the Divide.

Western Montana lies in the path of relatively warm Pacific winds. But the mountain barrier keeps these winds from reaching the rest of the state. The mountains also protect western Montana against cold air masses from the Canadian Arctic that sweep down into the Great Plains several times each winter. During one of these cold spells—on January 20, 1954 —the temperature dropped down to −70°F (−57°C) at Rogers Pass, northwest of Helena.

Occasionally most of the cities in Montana have summer daytime temperatures of more than 100°F (38°C).

Because of its location, Montana receives a limited amount of rainfall. Most of the moisture comes from the Pacific Ocean. Fortunately, most of the precipitation falls in late spring and early summer, when it is needed for agriculture. The average number of frost-free days varies from 150 at Miles City to none in many high valleys of the western mountains. Much of the state has a growing season of longer than 130 days, which is ample for a wide variety of crops.

Natural Resources

Montana's chief natural resources are its soils, forests, grazing lands, wildlife, and minerals. Groundwater is probably the most important resource in semi-arid central and eastern Montana. A much greater volume of water exists beneath the surface than on it.

Soils. The poor soils of the forested mountain slopes contrast sharply with the rich, dark soils of the grass-covered plains. In general the mountain soils are thin and not good for cultivation. In the Great Plains and the lowest parts of many western valleys the soils are usually fertile and productive if enough moisture falls or if irrigation is possible. Fertile alluvial soils—soils deposited by rivers—lie along the major rivers and their tributaries, especially along the Missouri and the Yellowstone.

Forests. About one fourth of Montana is covered with forests. Most of the forest land is in mountainous areas. The most important trees in the commercial forests are lodgepole and ponderosa pine, Douglas fir, and larch. All these are trees with needlelike leaves. The broadleaf hardwood forests make up a very small part of the commercial acreage. These forests are found east of the Continental Divide. The most common species include cottonwood and willow.

Grazing Lands. In the eastern part of Montana, where rainfall is relatively light, there is a vast area of grazing land. Most of it is open grassland except for trees along streams. Grazing lands are also found in the broad valleys of the Rocky Mountains, in the foothills of the mountains, and in some forest areas. The grasses are hardy species that can withstand droughts and wide extremes of temperature.

Wildlife. The grasslands that support Montana's livestock industry also supply food for its wild animals. Grizzly bears and the smaller black bears can be seen in Montana's national parks. Big-game animals regularly hunted in the state include moose, mountain goat, elk, deer, bighorn sheep, and antelope. The American bison, or buffalo, is limited to herds in the National Bison Range at Moiese and in a few other areas. Among the game birds are pheasant, duck, and grouse. The many kinds of freshwater fish include trout, whitefish, and grayling.

Minerals. Montana was nicknamed the Treasure State because of its mineral wealth. The Butte district is famous for metallic minerals, especially copper, lead, and zinc. Gold is again being mined in the western mountains.

Montana also has good supplies of mineral fuels. Low-sulfur coal is present under more than one third of the state and is being mined in large strip mines in the Powder River basin. Petroleum and natural gas are found in the eastern counties and in the southern and northern sections.

There are deposits of phosphate rock in southwestern Montana. Clays and limestone are found in several locations. Sand, gravel, and building stone are widely available. Chromium, manganese, tungsten, barite, fluorspar, and vermiculite are among the other minerals in Montana. Numerous deposits of precious and semiprecious stones also have been found. These include sapphire, garnet, and agate.

Montana has been a leader in environmental legislation, particularly concerning its mineral resources. During the 1970's the legislature passed acts to force mining companies to reclaim strip-mined land, to regulate the building of coal-fired electric generation plants and power transmission lines, to maintain air quality, and to protect the quality of Montana's water by banning shipment of the state's coal in the form of slurry (crushed coal mixed with water).

▶ **THE PEOPLE AND THEIR WORK**

Montana was one of the last areas of the United States to be settled. It lay north of the Oregon Trail and other main routes to the Pacific Coast. Although some traders and trappers lived in Montana in the 1840's and 1850's, the state was bypassed by the earliest of the westward-moving pioneers. Rich gold strikes in western Montana during the early 1860's brought the first rush of settlers. Soon afterward, ranchers were attracted to Montana's fertile western valleys.

The railroads were responsible for the greatest gain in population. The first transcontinental railroads were built across the state in the 1880's. The new railroads and others that were built later made it possible for ranch and farm products to be sent easily to eastern markets. The railroad companies advertised in European newspapers, telling of opportunities for settlers in the western part of the United States. Soon people began to arrive from the British Isles, the Scandinavian countries, Germany, Russia, and Canada.

The Indians of Montana now number more than 37,000. Most of them belong to one of eleven major tribes and live on the seven reservations set aside for them.

Where the People Live

Montana is sparsely settled, and the small population is unevenly distributed over the state. People cluster in the valleys of the Rocky Mountains in the west and along the rivers and the railroad lines in the eastern plains. About half the people live in cities with a population of 2,500 or more. Some mountain areas still have no permanent residents.

Industries and Products

Agriculture is Montana's most important economic activity. But manufacturing is expanding, mining continues to be important, and the tourist business adds a large amount to the income each year.

WHAT MONTANA PRODUCES

MANUFACTURED GOODS: Lumber and wood products; processed foods; refined petroleum; products of printing and publishing; concrete, gypsum, and plaster products; chemicals and related products; fabricated metal products.

AGRICULTURAL PRODUCTS: Cattle and calves, milk and other dairy products, sheep and lambs, hogs, poultry and eggs, wheat, barley, hay, sugar beets.

MINERALS: Petroleum, coal, natural gas, clays, talc, sand and gravel, gypsum, phosphate rock, vermiculite, barite, gold.

Top left: Low-sulfur coal lies under more than one third of Montana's land surface. State environmental laws provide for the reclamation of the land after strip-mining. *Top right:* Wheat is Montana's leading grain crop. About two thirds of the state's total area is in agricultural land.

Left: Much of Montana's land is used to pasture livestock. The Flathead River valley is a major cattle-raising area. The irrigated valleys of eastern Montana are mainly grain-growing areas.

Agriculture. About two thirds of Montana's total area is in agricultural land. Many farms and ranches contain at least 3,000 acres (1,214 hectares). Some are much larger, and the trend is toward still larger units.

More than half the agricultural land is classified as pasture for livestock. This land is the base for vast herds of both cattle and sheep. Beef cattle rank first in value among all the agricultural products of the state. The majority of the cattle are slaughtered elsewhere because of the limited local market for meat.

Both winter wheat and spring wheat are grown, chiefly by dry-farming methods. Most of the farms of this type are in the northeastern part of the state and in the area around Great Falls. Barley and oats are grown chiefly in the eastern and central sections.

Some irrigated land is found in every county. The largest areas are in the Bitterroot and the Flathead river valleys west of the Continental Divide, and the Missouri, Yellowstone, Milk, and Jefferson river valleys east of the Divide. Some of the irrigated land is used for pasture, but most of it is used for grains, fruits, vegetables, and sugar beets.

Manufacturing. The production of lumber and wood products is Montana's leading manufacturing activity. It is also one of the oldest industries. The first sawmill was built by Jesuit missionaries in the Bitterroot Valley in the late 1840's. The lumber industry grew as mining expanded and as railroads were built. Most of the early sawmills were small operations. Large mills were built chiefly during the period between 1890 and 1930. Some of these were at Libby, Eureka, Troy, Missoula, and Bonner.

Montana's oil refineries are chiefly in the Billings and Cut Bank areas. Other kinds of manufactured products include processed foods; concrete, gypsum, and plaster products; printed matter; and chemicals and related products.

Mining. Crude petroleum is Montana's most valuable mineral product. Oil production began near Red Lodge in Carbon County in 1915. Later, production began in the Williston Basin. This vast, oil-rich area stretches across several counties of eastern Montana and parts of the Dakotas and Canada. The Cut Bank field in Glacier County is the leading producer of natural gas. Gas is also obtained from some of the oil fields.

Because Montana's coal is near the surface, it can be readily obtained by strip-mining. Much of the coal is also low in sulfur. It causes less pollution when burned than coal with a high sulfur content. A large part of the coal is shipped to other parts of the country. The rest is burned in steam-powered electrical generation plants located near the strip mines. The state has passed strict laws to govern coal mining. The coal producers must restore the strip-mined land. They must also pay a substantial state tax on the value of the high-quality coal that they mine.

Silver Bow County was the center of copper production in Montana for more than a century. Copper mining stopped at Butte in 1983 because the price of copper was not high enough to keep the mines open. Clays, talc, gypsum, phosphate rock, and barite are still mined.

Manganese is mined in Silver Bow and Granite counties. Beaverhead County produces tungsten, and Stillwater County is known for chromium. Fluorspar is mined in Ravalli County.

Montana is the nation's largest supplier of vermiculite, a mineral that is somewhat like mica. It is used as an insulating material in buildings, as a packing material, and in many other ways. Vermiculite comes from Lincoln County. Almost all the counties produce some sand and gravel.

Tourism. Visitors to the state provide one of Montana's main sources of income. An increasing number of people each year visit the two national parks, the forest and wilderness areas, the old mining camps, historical museums, and other places of interest.

In the 1970's and 1980's, Montana also saw a growth in service industries such as health, business and professional services, and transportation.

Transportation and Communication

Good transportation is vital in Montana because distances between places are great. Early travelers came by boat on the Missouri River. In 1862 a wagon road was completed from Fort Benton across the mountains to Walla Walla, Washington. This road was known as the Mullan Trail, or Mullan Wagon Road. Overland trails also connected with the Oregon Trail to the south.

The Northern Pacific Railway, completed in 1883, was the first transcontinental railroad to be built across Montana. It follows a central and southern route through Miles City, Billings, Bozeman, Butte, Helena, and Missoula. The Great Northern Railroad, completed in 1893, follows a northern route. The third transcontinental line—the Chicago, Milwaukee, Saint Paul, and Pacific Railroad—was completed in 1909.

Several interstate highways cross Montana, both from east to west and from north to south. The Going-to-the-Sun Road is a spectacular highway running east and west through Glacier National Park. Another scenic highway leads to the northeast entrance of Yellowstone National Park. This highway dips into Wyoming, where it crosses the Beartooth Pass

---

POPULATION

TOTAL: 786,690 (1980 census). **Density**—5.4 persons to each square mile (2.1 persons to each square kilometer).

GROWTH SINCE 1870

Year	Population	Year	Population
1870	20,595	1920	548,889
1880	39,159	1950	591,024
1890	142,924	1970	694,409
1900	243,329	1980	786,690

Gain Between 1970 and 1980—13.3 percent.

CITIES: Population of Montana's largest incorporated places according to the 1980 census.

Billings	66,842	Bozeman	21,645
Great Falls	56,725	Anaconda—Deer	
Butte—Silver Bow	37,205	Lodge County	12,518
Missoula	33,388	Havre	10,891
Helena	23,938	Kalispell	10,648

at almost 11,000 feet (3,350 meters). All the major cities in Montana have regularly scheduled airline service. Throughout the state there are more than 100 commercial and municipal airports.

Montana's first regular newspaper, the *Montana Post,* was printed in Virginia City in 1864. It moved to Helena in 1866. Today the leading newspapers are the Billings *Gazette* and the Great Falls *Tribune.* About 10 daily newspapers and 70 other papers are published in the state. Montana has 15 television stations and about 95 radio stations.

▶ EDUCATION

The first schools in Montana were started at Bannack, Nevada City, and Virginia City in the 1860's. Until schoolhouses could be built, the teachers held classes in their own homes. In 1864 a boarding school for Indian pupils was opened in the mission at St. Ignatius. This was the first school of its kind in the Northwest. Between 1865 and 1875 numerous private schools were established for both white and Indian pupils.

Schools and Colleges

The first territorial legislature approved the establishment of a school system for the Montana territory in 1865. Virginia City was the first place to organize a school district. A public school opened in a log building there in 1866. A state board of education was created in 1893. By 1897 free county high schools were established.

The public institution of higher education known today as Montana State University, in Bozeman, opened in 1893. The University of Montana, in Missoula, was chartered in the same year, but it did not open until 1895. Today, these universities are part of a system that includes Montana College of Mineral Science and Technology in Butte, Eastern Montana College in Billings, Western Montana College in Dillon, and Northern Montana College in Havre. Private senior colleges include the College of Great Falls in Great Falls, Carroll College in Helena, and Rocky Mountain College in Billings. The state also has several community colleges.

Libraries and Museums

The library in Helena, established in 1886, was the first free public library in the state.

Chief Plenty Coups was a chief of the Crow tribe who worked for better understanding between whites and Indians in Montana. His ranch is now a state park.

Today most counties have some form of library service, and all the major cities have excellent public libraries. The Historical Society of Montana in Helena maintains state archives and a research library noted for its collection of frontier newspapers.

The Historical Society of Montana also maintains a museum. It contains exhibits of frontier photography and displays of historical scenes and artifacts, as well as a collection of paintings, sketches, and bronze sculptures by the noted Western artist Charles M. Russell. Other works by the artist are displayed in the C. M. Russell Museum in Great Falls.

The Museum of the Plains Indian on the Blackfeet Reservation in Browning includes many exhibits showing the history and culture of the Plains Indian. The Museum of the Rockies in Bozeman has historical and paleontological exhibits. The Montana College of Mineral Science and Technology in Butte houses a magnificent collection of minerals. The Butte Historical Society collects and preserves objects relating to the history of southwestern Montana. The Virginia City–Madison County Historical Museum in Virginia City contains reminders of the days when Virginia City was a gold camp and the capital of the territory.

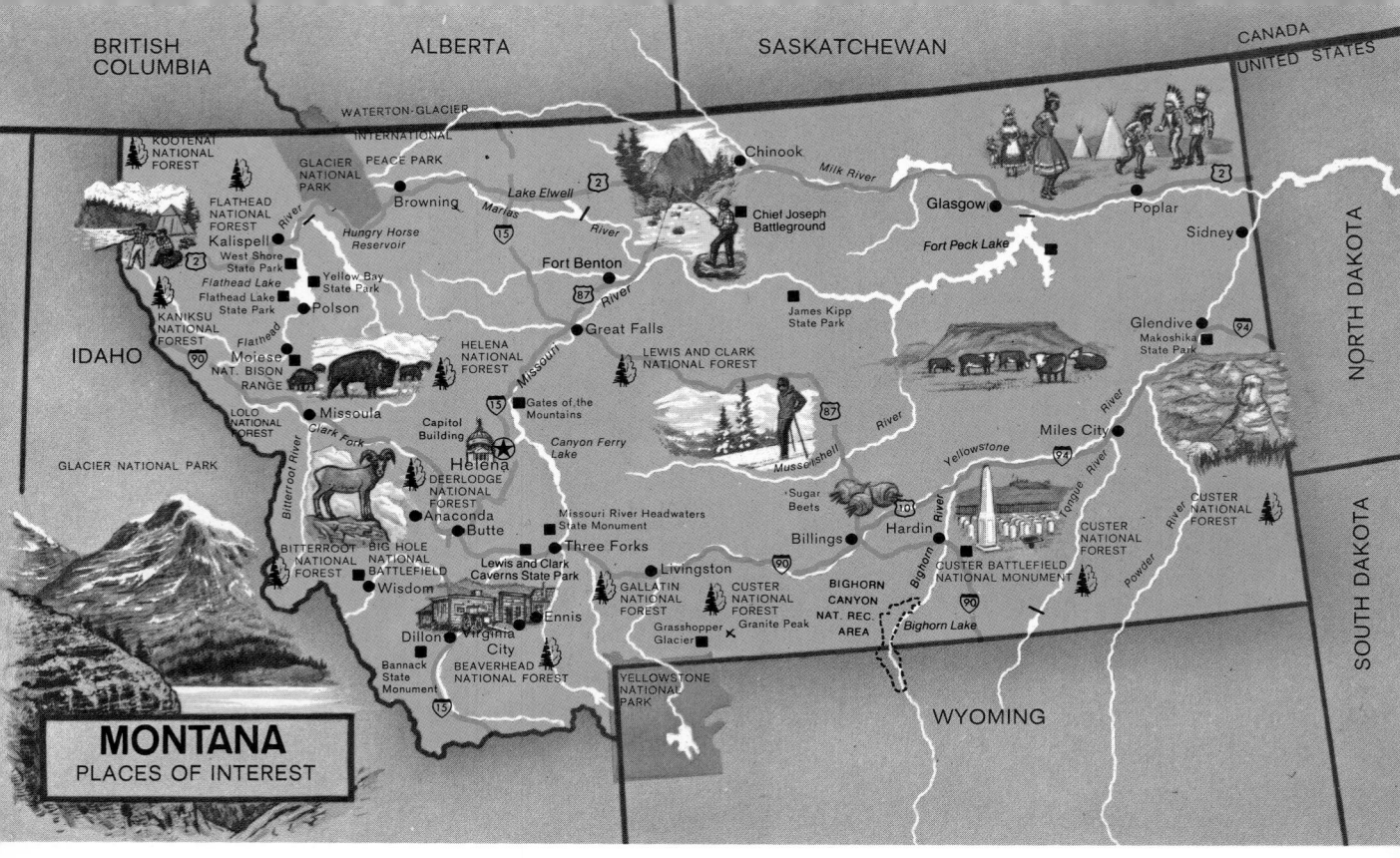

MONTANA
PLACES OF INTEREST

PLACES OF INTEREST

Recreation and tourism are major activities in Montana. The scenic wonders and the opportunities for camping, fishing, hunting, hiking, mountain climbing, and winter sports bring visitors to the Big Sky Country.

National Areas

Montana has eleven national forests, two national parks, two national historic sites, several national historic districts, and one national recreational area, Bighorn Canyon. The Kootenai, Kaniksu, Lolo, Bitterroot, Deerlodge, and Beaverhead national forests—or some sections of these forests—are located along the western border of the state. Paralleling them, from north to south, are the Flathead, Helena, and Gallatin national forests. Sections of the Lewis and Clark National Forest are scattered through western and central Montana. Sections of the Custer National Forest extend from the south central part of the state to the eastern border.

Glacier National Park, in northwestern Montana, contains some of the most spectacular scenery in the Rocky Mountains, including many glaciers, lofty peaks, waterfalls, lakes, and forests. It is part of the Waterton-Glacier International Peace Park, which is shared by the United States and Canada. An article on Glacier National Park is included in Volume G.

Yellowstone National Park lies mainly in the northwestern corner of Wyoming, but it extends into both Montana and Idaho. Three of the park's entrances are in Montana. Volume Y contains an article on Yellowstone National Park.

Big Hole National Battlefield, near Wisdom, marks the site of an important battle in 1877 between United States forces and the Nez Perce Indians from Idaho and Oregon, led by Chief Joseph. After the battle, the Nez Perce pursued a difficult route through Yellowstone Park almost to Canada. A few miles from the border, Chief Joseph surrendered. The place where he surrendered is maintained as a state monument—the Chief Joseph Battleground of the Bear's Paw, south of Chinook. A biography of Chief Joseph is included in the article on Idaho in Volume I.

Custer Battlefield National Monument, southeast of Hardin, commemorates "Custer's Last Stand" at the famous Battle of the Little Bighorn. In June, 1876, Lieutenant Colonel George A. Custer and about 260 soldiers of the Seventh Cavalry were killed by the Sioux and other Indians. A granite memorial marks the battlefield, and headstones show where the soldiers fell.

State Parks and Monuments

Montana has set aside eleven state parks and numerous recreation areas. The following list shows their variety.

Bannack State Monument, west of Dillon, is a reminder of gold-rush days. The first important gold strike in Montana was made on Grasshopper Creek in 1862, and the town of Bannack grew up there almost overnight. The city later became Montana's first territorial capital. Weathered remains of the first capital building, a jail, a hotel, and several log cabins are preserved.

Flathead Lake State Park, northwest of Polson, is one of three state parks located on Flathead Lake, Montana's largest natural lake. **West Shore State Park** is located farther north on the west shore of the lake below Kalispell. **Yellow Bay State Park** is on the eastern shore. All three have facilities for camping and water sports.

Lewis and Clark Caverns State Park, east of Whitehall, affords splendid views of the Madison and Gallatin ranges. It includes limestone caverns that are a wonderland of stalactites, stalagmites, and other formations.

Makoshika State Park preserves a remarkable area of badlands in eastern Montana near Glendive. Centuries of wind and water have eroded the sandstone cliffs into weird formations.

Missouri River Headwaters State Monument near Three Forks is one of the most important geographical sites in the West. The Missouri River begins there at the joining of the Jefferson, Madison, and Gallatin rivers. The Lewis and Clark expedition discovered the site in July, 1805. Lewis and Clark named the rivers in honor of Thomas Jefferson, James Madison, and Albert Gallatin. Gallatin served as United States secretary of the treasury (1801–14) under both President Jefferson and President Madison.

Other Places

Montana has many scenic and historic sites that are not part of the federal or state park system. The following are among those that are especially well known.

Gates of the Mountains, 25 miles (40 kilometers) north of Helena, is a deep gorge cut by the Missouri River. The river has eroded the banks into fantastic shapes. The names of the formations tell what they resemble—Indian Head, Beartooth, Bride and Groom, and the like. During the summer, boats carry tourists on regular trips through the gorge.

Grasshopper Glacier, one of Montana's most remarkable glaciers, is in Custer National Forest southwest of Billings. The glacier gets its name from the millions of grasshoppers embedded in the ice. It is believed that swarms of grasshoppers were trapped in a severe storm and were deposited on the glacier when it was being formed.

Top right: The first territorial legislature of Montana met in 1864 at Bannack, now a state park. *Bottom right:* Custer Battlefield National Monument marks the site of the Battle of the Little Big Horn in 1876. *Below:* Glacier National Park is part of Waterton-Glacier International Peace Park, shared by the United States and Canada.

The **National Bison Range,** near Moiese on the Flathead Indian Reservation, protects one of the few remaining herds of American bison, or buffalo, in the United States. The range is also a home for other big-game animals, such as deer, elk, and bighorn sheep. Tours are conducted throughout the range, but no shooting is allowed—except with cameras.

Virginia City was Montana's second territorial capital. It was near the site of a famous gold strike in Alder Gulch in 1863. Nevada City is about a mile away. These sister cities have been restored in the style of gold-rush days.

Annual Events

The main hunting season in Montana is in October and November. During the winter special fishing areas are open, and skiers may choose from more than 30 ski centers. Other seasons bring a variety of special events.

May—Vigilante Parade, Helena; Bucking Horse Sale and Rodeo, Miles City.

June—Big Sky Logging Championships, Kalispell.

Summer—Summer theater, Virginia City, Fort Peck, Polson.

July or August—State Fair, Great Falls; Northwest Montana Fair, Kalispell; Central Montana Fair, Lewiston; Northeast Montana Fair, Glasgow.

July—Wild Horse Stampede, Wolf Point.

August—Festival of Nations, Red Lodge; Copper Cup Regatta, Polson; Western Montana Fair, Missoula.

September—All Indian Rodeo, Wolf Point.

▶CITIES

Montana's cities are not large. Only Great Falls and Billings have populations of more than 50,000 people.

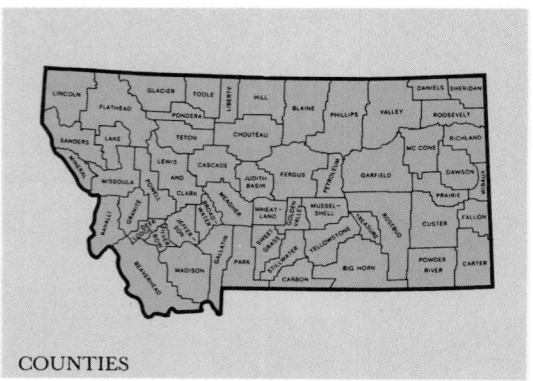

COUNTIES

Helena, Montana's capital, was founded in 1864 by prospectors who discovered gold where the town's main street now runs. The cathedral of St. Helena is a landmark.

Helena

Helena, the capital of Montana, owes its existence to the discovery of gold. In 1864 four prospectors, weary of poor diggings, decided on one ''last chance'' in a gulch they had stumbled upon. They found gold, and the place where they found it was called Last Chance Gulch. A community grew rapidly around the site. In 1875, Helena became Montana's third territorial capital. When Montana became a state in 1889, Helena was the temporary capital. It became the permanent capital in 1894. The original governor's mansion in Helena, in use until 1959, is open to the public.

Helena is situated near the Missouri River in Prickly Pear Valley, a rich agricultural area irrigated by water from Canyon Ferry Reservoir. The city is a center for trade, transportation, and finance as well as government.

Billings

Billings, Montana's largest city, is located on the Yellowstone River in the south central part of the state. It is in the heart of a highly productive area called the Midland Empire. Industries in the city include oil refineries, sugar refineries, and meat-packing plants. Eastern Montana College and Rocky Mountain College are both located in Billings.

Great Falls

Great Falls, Montana's second largest city, is located on the Missouri river at the mouth of the Sun River. It was incorporated as a city in 1888, a year after the arrival of the Great Northern Railroad. Great Falls is the financial, industrial, and supply center of an agricultural and mining area. Waterfalls near the city are used to supply hydroelectric power. Downsteam are the Great Falls of the Missouri River, for which the city is named. Northeast of the city is Giant Springs, one of the world's largest freshwater springs.

Butte

Butte, in southwestern Montana, sits on top of what has been called "the richest hill on earth." A great network of tunnels extends deep beneath the city. The discovery of gold in 1864 brought the first boom to the area. In the 1870's, silver was the leading metal. From the 1880's to the early 1980's, Butte was famous for copper. For government purposes, Butte and the rest of Silver Bow County were consolidated in 1976 into a unit known as Butte–Silver Bow.

▶ GOVERNMENT

Montana adopted a new constitution in 1972. It became effective in 1973. The previous constitution, in effect since statehood in 1889, had been amended many times.

The executive branch of the government includes the governor and other elected officers. There is no limit on the number of terms a governor may serve. The legislative branch, called the Legislative Assembly, is made up of the Senate and the House of Representatives.

The state Supreme Court is the highest court in the state. There are also district, municipal, and other courts.

GOVERNMENT

Capital—Helena. **Number of counties**—56. **Representation in Congress**—U.S. senators, 2; U.S. representatives, 2.
Legislative Assembly—Senate, 50 members, 4-year terms; House of Representatives, 100 members, 2-year terms.
Governor—4-year term; no limit on number of terms.
Elections—General and state, Tuesday after first Monday in November.

▶ FAMOUS PEOPLE

The following adopted and native-born citizens of Montana have made important contributions to the state and to the nation.

Pierre Jean de Smet (1801–73), a Jesuit missionary born in Belgium, is often called the founder of Montana. In 1841 he founded St. Mary's Mission among the Flathead Indians in the Bitterroot Valley. He planted Montana's first crops and helped build the first gristmill. Father de Smet won his greatest fame as a peacemaker between the white settlers and the Indians.

Granville Stuart (1834–1918) came with his brother, James, to Montana from Iowa in 1857. They discovered gold at Gold Creek in 1858. Granville Stuart served in the territorial legislature in 1871 and 1883, was appointed U.S. Minister to Uruguay (1894–99), and was the author of *Forty Years on the Frontier*.

Marcus Daly (1841–1900) was the greatest of Montana's copper kings. He came to the United States from Ireland when he was 15 years old. In 1876 he migrated to Butte, where he acquired an interest in a silver mine. The silver did not last very long, but beneath the mine was a rich deposit of copper. Daly founded Anaconda as a smelting center and organized the Anaconda Mining Company.

Plenty Coups (1848–1932) also had an Indian name, Aleek-chea-akoosh ("many accomplishments"). As the young chief of a band of Crow, Plenty Coups helped organize scouts for Custer in 1876. He worked for understanding between whites and Indians. At his death, Plenty Coups left 40 acres (16 hectares) of his ranch "to be used in perpetuity [forever] for the Crow people." Today it is a state park.

Charles Marion Russell (1865–1926), Western painter and sculptor, was born in St. Louis, Missouri. He went to Montana at the age of 16 to work as a cowboy. He lived among the cowboys and painted scenes of frontier life.

Jeannette Rankin (1880–1973), the first woman to be elected to the U.S. House of Representatives, was born in Missoula. She was a social worker in New York City before returning to Montana, where she helped to get women's suffrage (the right to vote) passed in the state.

Burton Kendall Wheeler (1882–1975) was elected to the U.S. Senate from Montana in 1922. He served as a senator until 1947. In 1924 he was the Progressive Party's candidate for vice president of the United States on a ticket headed by Robert M. La Follette. Senator Wheeler was born in Massachusetts.

Other well-known persons born in Montana include Will (William Roderick) James, writer and illustrator (Great Falls); the actor Gary Cooper

(Helena); actress Myrna Loy (Radersburg); and television comentator Chester (Chet) Huntley (Cardwell). Michael Joseph (Mike) Mansfield of Montana served as majority leader of the U.S. Senate longer than anyone else (1961–77) and later was U.S. ambassador to Japan. He was born in New York.

▶ HISTORY

Tools, weapons, and other clues studied by scientists indicate that people have lived in Montana for perhaps 10,000 years. Little is known about the ancient inhabitants. All the Indians east of the Continental Divide at the time of exploration and settlement had moved there after 1600. Most of them were tribes that had been displaced as Europeans settled eastern North America.

The Kutenai, Flathead, and other tribes occupied the area west of the Continental Divide. The leading Plains tribes were the Blackfoot and the Crow. The Cheyenne roamed the southeast.

Exploration and Settlement

The first white people documented to be in Montana were members of the Lewis and Clark expedition. After the United States bought the area from France in 1803, President Thomas Jefferson sent Meriwether Lewis and William Clark to explore the lands within the Missouri and the Columbia river basins. Members of the expedition crossed Montana on their way to the Pacific in 1805 and again on their return in 1806.

The next 45 years were devoted to the fur trade. Companies in St. Louis, Missouri, excited by reports of an abundance of furs, sent trappers into the eastern part of Montana. The center of American fur activity in Montana was Fort Union, which was built near the junction of the Missouri and the Yellowstone rivers in 1828. The fur trade west of the Rocky Mountains was controlled by British companies. In 1846, Great Britain ceded the Oregon country to the United States, but the British fur trade continued for a while after that time.

Missionaries began to arrive in Montana during fur-trading days. In 1841, Jesuit missionaries, led by Father Pierre de Smet, established St. Mary's Mission in the Bitterroot Valley. Other missions followed.

Development

Traces of gold were found in western Montana during the 1850's. The first important discovery was made on Grasshopper Creek in 1862, and Bannack, Montana's first boom town, soon came into being. Rich finds at Virginia City in 1863 and at Helena in 1864 brought large numbers of miners and prospectors into the area for the first time. On May 26, 1864, Montana became a territory with Bannack as the territorial capital. At the same time a wave of lawlessness swept over the gold towns. Vigilantes (committees of citizens) were organized to combat the numerous robberies and murders and to restore order. Before 1870 the mines had produced more than $100,000,000 in gold. Other metals, especially silver and copper, were also discovered and mined.

While western Montana was being settled by the miners, most of the land east of the

---

IMPORTANT DATES

1805	Lewis and Clark expedition crossed Montana on its way to the Pacific Ocean; returned in 1806.
1841	Father de Smet founded St. Mary's Mission in the Bitterroot Valley.
1846	Western Montana included in territory ceded to the United States by Great Britain.
1862	First important gold strike in Montana made at Bannack.
1864	Territory of Montana created, with first capital at Bannack.
1865	Territorial capital moved to Virginia City.
1866	First cattle from Texas arrived in Montana.
1875	Capital moved to Helena.
1876	Lieutenant Colonel George A. Custer and his company of about 260 men killed in the battle of the Little Bighorn.
1877	Chief Joseph surrendered, ending major Indian resistance in Montana.
1881	Marcus Daly opened Montana's first copper mine.
1883	Northern Pacific Railway completed across Montana.
1889	November 8, Montana became the 41st state.
1893	Montana State College (Bozeman) opened; Montana State University (Missoula) chartered.
1894	Helena became the permanent state capital.
1910	Glacier National Park created by Congress.
1915	Oil discovered near Red Lodge.
1940	Fork Peck Dam on the Missouri River completed.
1951	Oil found in the Williston Basin.
1964	Montana celebrated 75 years as a state and the 100th anniversary of the creation of Montana territory.
1973	New state constitution became effective.
1979	Legislature approved the first general revision of the state legal code since 1947.
1983	Falling copper prices forced the Anaconda Copper Company to close its last mine in Butte.

Rockies was still held by the Indians. After the 1860's, Montana began to be stocked with large herds of cattle. The first herds were driven up from Texas in 1866. Ranching became very profitable, although the severe winter in 1886–87 destroyed many of the herds and temporarily slowed the growth of ranching.

By 1883 the Northern Pacific Railway was completed across the state. Improved transportation, expansion of the cattle range in eastern Montana, and the development of copper mining in Butte brought many more people to Montana. After 25 years as a territory, Montana was ready for statehood. On November 8, 1889, it became the 41st state.

Growth Since Statehood

The copper boom in the Butte district started in the 1880's. The important Anaconda Mining Company, now known as the Anaconda Company, developed copper mines in Butte and the world's largest copper smelter in Anaconda in 1884. Railroads expanded, and timber was in demand. Coal deposits, natural gas, and oil were discovered. The growth of big business was paralleled by the growth of labor unions.

The period before World War I was a period of prosperity for farms. But after the war farm prices dropped, a severe drought crippled agriculture, and Montana lost population during the 1920's. In 1929 a second drought began, and agriculture was further retarded. Beginning in the 1930's the federal government took an important part in helping to conserve and develop Montana's resources. It constructed dams for irrigation, power, flood control, and other purposes. One of these, the Fort Peck Dam, was at the time the largest earth-filled dam in the world.

In the 1960's, Montana's population grew slowly as job shortages forced people to leave the state to find work. The national energy crisis that developed in the 1970's increased the value of the state's oil and coal resources, but falling copper prices in the 1980's led to the close of most of the state's mines. Farmers, too, suffered from falling prices as well as from poor weather.

The Future

Montanans are moving from farms and ranches to the cities. Personal incomes are rising. The major problems are still a sparse population, long distances to markets, and an uncertain economic outlook in mining and agriculture.

VINCENT K. SHAUDYS
Montana State University
Reviewed by WILLIAM L. LONG
Author, *Montana: Our Land and People*

MONTREAL

Montreal, the largest city of Quebec, is also one of the largest cities of Canada and a busy inland port. It stands on an island in the middle of the St. Lawrence River. In the center of the island rises Mount Royal, which is tree-covered and free of buildings on its higher slopes. Montreal is a distinctive and colorful city, with a large French-speaking population and an ''old town'' with 17th-century buildings and houses.

▶HISTORY

Montreal Island was first discovered by the French explorer Jacques Cartier in 1535, but it was not permanently settled until 1642. The settlement was made that year under the leadership of Sieur de Maisonneuve. It was named Ville-Marie de Montreal. To this day a lighted

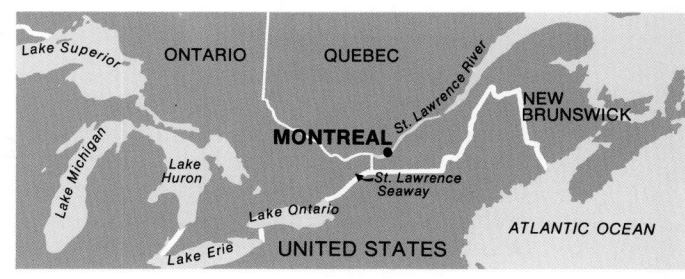

cross stands on Mount Royal in memory of the original cross carried there by Maisonneuve more than three centuries ago.

The settlement's growth was slow at first. In fact, 100 years later Montreal still lay inside confining and protective walls in a small area along the St. Lawrence River. Almost from its beginning the colony lived in great danger of attacks by Indians, who feared to lose their lands. Finally, in 1701, a peace treaty was signed with the Indians.

Montreal served as a base for many famous explorers, traders, and missionaries—Marquette, La Salle, Jolliet, Hennepin, and others. These courageous and daring men fanned out from Montreal to as far north as Hudson Bay and as far south as the Gulf of Mexico.

During the American Revolution an army under the command of General Montgomery occupied Montreal. The Americans hoped that the people of the city would join forces with them in their struggle with the British. But the Montrealers decided to stay loyal to Britain.

Montreal grew rapidly in the first half of the 19th century. Steamboats replaced sailboats. Canals and railways were built. Trade and commerce grew. In 1843 Montreal was important enough to be made the capital of Canada. But this distinction lasted only six years. In 1849 the government buildings were severely damaged during a riot. The capital was moved to Quebec and later to Ottawa.

Today the city of Montreal has spread to the mainland. The old town, recently an area of warehouses and offices, is being restored to its original state. Shops and restaurants now line its narrow streets. Between this area and Mount Royal are large stores, theaters, and modern office blocks. Montreal has grown so much that it has already engulfed about 30 municipalities. Some of these are larger than many Canadian towns.

▶ A COSMOPOLITAN CITY

Montreal was first settled by the French, and two thirds of the population still speak French. Except for Paris, Montreal has more French-speaking people than any other city in the world. At the same time it is very cosmopolitan and has become more so since World War II. Today over 20 percent of the inhabitants are of British origin. There are also many Italians, Chinese, Germans, Greeks, Portuguese, Spanish, and Central Europeans.

The skyline of Montreal formed the backdrop for the Universal and International Exhibition, better known as Expo 67, which opened in April, 1967. For this event, Montreal rushed to complete a new subway, the Métro, modeled after the Paris Métro. Since Expo 67, a large number of new skyscrapers have been added, as well as a complex of structures for the 1976 Olympics, including a massive stadium called the Big O.

The island location of Montreal causes many traffic problems. But the completion of the Métro and the Champlain Bridge to the Southshore in 1967 has improved conditions.

▶ THE INLAND PORT

Because of the Lachine Rapids, west of the island, Montreal was the terminal for large ocean vessels until the construction of the St. Lawrence Seaway. Barges carried wheat, coal, oil, and iron ore from the interior to Montreal, where goods were transferred to oceangoing ships. The opening of the seaway in 1959 has resulted in much more shipping for Montreal harbor.

Montreal has become one of the world's great inland ports because the St. Lawrence River is extremely wide and deep. Ocean liners weighing up to 25,000 tons can sail up the river directly to Montreal and berth at its docks.

The harbor runs for about 20 kilometers (12 miles) along the northern bank of the St. Lawrence River. There is docking space for about 130 ocean vessels. Montreal is the Canadian terminal for over 50 freight transportation companies, including some container lines. The Port of Montreal is open about 360 days a year. It is closed only when ice blocks the St. Lawrence River during severe winter weather.

▶ LAND AND AIR TRANSPORTATION

Since ice is a hazard on the St. Lawrence, land and air transportation are of very great importance. Montreal is the hub of a dense road network. It is the headquarters of Canada's two great railway systems. The Canadian National and the Canadian Pacific railroads, together with the new passenger railroad Via and Amtrak, connect Montreal with all major cities in Canada and the United States.

Montreal has a new international airport, Mirabel, located about 55 kilometers (35 miles) from the center of the city. This airport is used by about 20 major overseas airlines. Flights within the continent are handled by the older airport, Dorval, only 18 kilometers (11 miles) from downtown.

▶ INDUSTRY AND COMMERCE

Montreal is one of the largest and most varied manufacturing centers in Canada. It is a major oil-refining center and is equally important for the manufacture of clothing, textiles, and textile products. Other manufactures are railway rolling stock, boots and shoes, electrical apparatus, chemicals, paints, tobacco, food products, aircraft, and iron and steel products.

Montreal produces half of Quebec's manufactured goods, and the number of factories is still growing. This economic development is due in part to the importance of the port. It is also due to the abundance of hydroelectric power from projects in the Canadian Shield area and the new power plants on the St. Lawrence Seaway.

Montreal is prominent in finance and commerce. Many of the great insurance and banking firms of Canada have their headquarters in the city.

▶ CULTURE AND EDUCATION

Montreal has many fine theaters, libraries, art galleries, and concert halls. The Place des Arts is the home of the Montreal Symphony Orchestra. This is considered one of the most luxurious and modern concert halls in the world.

There are many excellent museums in the city. The Montreal Museum of Fine Arts has a superb collection of paintings of the old masters, French 19th century, and the Canadian school. The Chateau de Ramezay, one of the oldest buildings in Montreal, specializes in history. It has a colorful and impressive display of important historical documents, pictures, furniture, and Indian craft.

The city has several noted universities. McGill and Concordia universities are English-language institutions. The Université de Montréal conducts its classes in French, as does the new Université de Québec. McGill is well known for its medical school.

▶ SPORTS AND RECREATION

The people of Montreal love sports. Hockey in the winter, baseball, soccer, and horse racing in summer, and football in the fall attract many participants and spectators. In the summer many people spend their holidays and weekends in the lake region of the Laurentian

In the streets of Montreal, one can see an interesting blend of the old and the new.

Mountains. It is also to the Laurentians that the skiers swarm in winter. Hockey rinks are crowded all over the city. The Montreal Canadiens have compiled an impressive record and become a famous hockey team throughout North America.

▶ TOURIST CENTER

Montreal holds a great attraction for tourists from all over North America. The charm of the city comes from the blending of its French and English backgrounds and cultures. Many tourists visit the Church of Notre Dame, which was completed in 1829. The twin towers of this beautiful building are called Perserverance and Temperance. Its lovely stained-glass windows tell in glowing colors the history of the city. Among other places much visited are St. Joseph's Oratory and Basilica, the Bonsecours Market, and lovely Dominion Square.

Greater Montreal has a population of over 2,800,000. It is a large metropolis, and yet this Paris of the New World has a character all its own. In the middle of its hustle and bustle there is always the atmosphere—the feeling of its past history, of its part in the building of a new world.

THEODORE L. HILLS
McGill University

MOON

The moon is a great round rock circling the earth. It is the earth's only natural satellite. A satellite is an object that follows a path, or **orbit**, around a larger object. The moon's orbit is an ellipse, a shape like a slightly flattened circle. Because the moon follows this elliptical orbit, its distance from the earth changes. When it is closest, the moon is 356,400 kilometers (221,500 miles) away. It is then said to be at **perigee**. This word comes from Greek words meaning "near" and "earth." At its greatest distance, or **apogee**, the moon is 406,700 kilometers (252,700 miles) away.

The moon moves in its orbit at an average speed of 3,600 kilometers (2,237 miles) per hour. It speeds up when it gets nearer the

earth. The earth's gravitational pull on the moon is stronger then. At greater distances the moon slows down a little.

The diameter of the moon is 3,475 kilometers (2,160 miles), about one fourth the diameter of the earth. No other satellite in the solar system is so large compared to the size of the planet that it circles. The earth and moon are sometimes called a **double planetary system**. They are more like two planets circling each other than a planet with a much smaller satellite.

When you look at the moon, it seems perfectly round, but it is not. It has a slight bulge on the side facing the earth. The bulge can be measured by astronomers only with special instruments. It is believed that the bulge results from the pull of the earth's gravitation.

Spin and Libration

The moon takes 27 days, 7 hours, and 43 minutes to spin, or rotate, once on its axis. It takes just about the same amount of time to orbit the earth. This means that the moon always keeps the same side facing the earth. You would therefore not expect to see the other side of the moon. However, we do see different pieces of it at different times because of motions called **librations**.

The moon's axis, like the earth's, is tilted (Fig. 1). When the moon is at (A) we can see an extra bit of the moon's surface, shown in white. When the moon is at (B) we can see another extra bit of surface.

Another kind of libration occurs because the moon's speed changes a little as it circles the earth. Although the moon's speed changes, its rate of spin on its axis does not change. As a result, we can see a little more around to one side or the other of the moon.

Because of the librations we can see about 59 percent of the moon's surface at one time or another. The back of the moon was a mystery until 1959. Then an unmanned Russian space probe, Lunik III, circled the moon and sent television pictures to the earth. Later, unmanned American and Russian moon probes and the Apollo astronauts took many pictures of the back of the moon.

Phases of the Moon

The moon has no light of its own. Moonlight is really sunlight reflected from the surface of the moon. Sometimes we can see the whole lighted side of the moon, like a big shining disk. At other times we see only a part of the lighted side, so the shape is no longer a disk. The different shapes are called **phases** of the moon.

The phases occur because the moon orbits the earth. When the moon (Fig. 2) is at (A), the side facing us gets no sunlight. We cannot see the moon then. This phase is **new moon**.

After 2 or 3 days the moon has moved on some distance. Now we can see just the thin edge of its lighted side. This is the **crescent moon** (B). The crescent grows, or **waxes**, until, a week after new moon, we see half of the lighted side. This phase is **first quarter** (C). The moon has traveled through one quarter of its orbit.

The moon moves on. We see its **gibbous phase** (D), followed by **full moon** (E). By now, about 2 weeks after new moon, we can see the whole lighted disk, full moon.

After a day or two the full moon begins to shrink, or **wane**. We see a gibbous phase (F), then **last quarter** (G), and then a crescent (H). Finally, we are back to new moon, a little more than 29½ days after the previous new moon.

Sometimes we can see the whole moon

Right: We see varying amounts of the moon's lighted side as it orbits earth. Below: Calendar shows changing shapes of lighted side (phases) seen in a month.

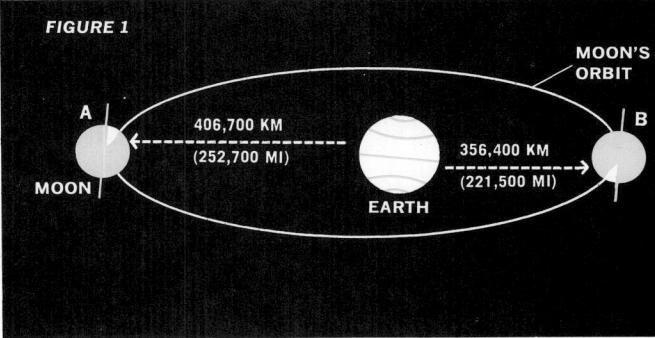

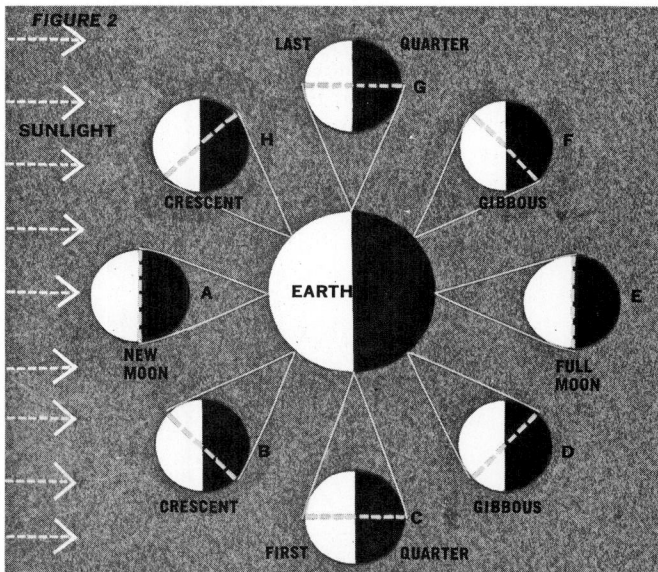

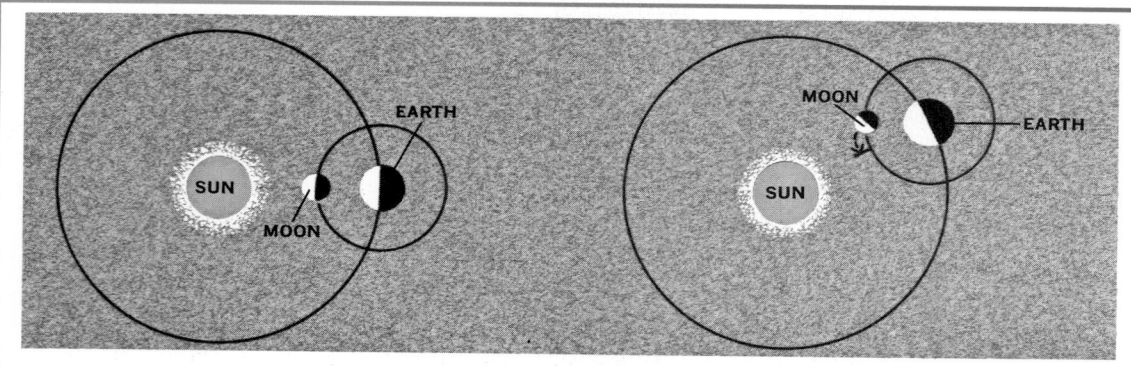

FROM NEW MOON TO NEW MOON

The moon takes a little over 27 days to make one trip around the earth. But the moon takes 29½ days to change from a new moon to the next new moon. There is a difference of more than 2 days between these two periods of time. You may think the times should be the same. But there is a reason for the difference. Can you figure it out before reading the explanation in the next paragraph?

The reason for the difference is that the earth moves around the sun while the moon moves around the earth. By the time the moon completes one orbit, the earth has moved farther in space. The moon has not quite reached its new-moon phase as yet. It must move a little farther around the earth before it is again between the earth and the sun. This extra distance accounts for the 2 extra days the moon takes to change from a new moon to the next new moon.

dimly in the crescent moon. The dim light, called **earthshine**, is sunlight reflected from the earth to the moon and back to the earth.

Eclipses

Since the moon circles the earth, you might think it would pass directly between the earth and the sun on each orbit. The moon's orbit, however, is slightly tilted. This means that the moon does not often pass directly between the earth and the sun. But sometimes it does. When this happens the moon's shadow falls on the earth. The sun's light is blotted out at certain places on earth by the shadow of the moon. This is called an **eclipse of the sun**, or **solar eclipse**. ("Solar" comes from *sol,* the Latin word for "sun.")

During a solar eclipse the diameter of the moon's shadow on the earth varies from about 100 kilometers (60 miles) to about 260 kilometers (160 miles). The shadow crosses the earth at speeds up to about 8,000 kilometers (5,000 miles) an hour. The eclipse may last up to 7½ minutes.

An **eclipse of the moon**, or **lunar eclipse**, occurs when the earth passes directly between the sun and the moon. ("Lunar" comes from *luna,* the Latin word for "moon.") The earth's diameter is nearly four times the size of the moon's diameter. When the moon moves into the earth's wide shadow it may be there, eclipsed, up to 3½ hours.

A lunar eclipse does not happen as often as a solar eclipse. However, a lunar eclipse

SOLAR ECLIPSE: Tape string to Ping-Pong ball ("the moon"). Hold "the moon" so that its shadow falls on the tennis ball ("the earth"), eclipsing a part of it.

LUNAR ECLIPSE: The moon is darkened as it moves into the shadow of the earth. To see the eclipse you must be on the side of the earth where it is nighttime.

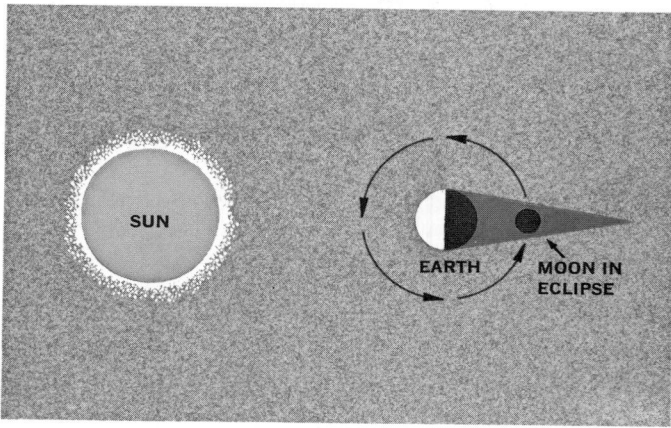

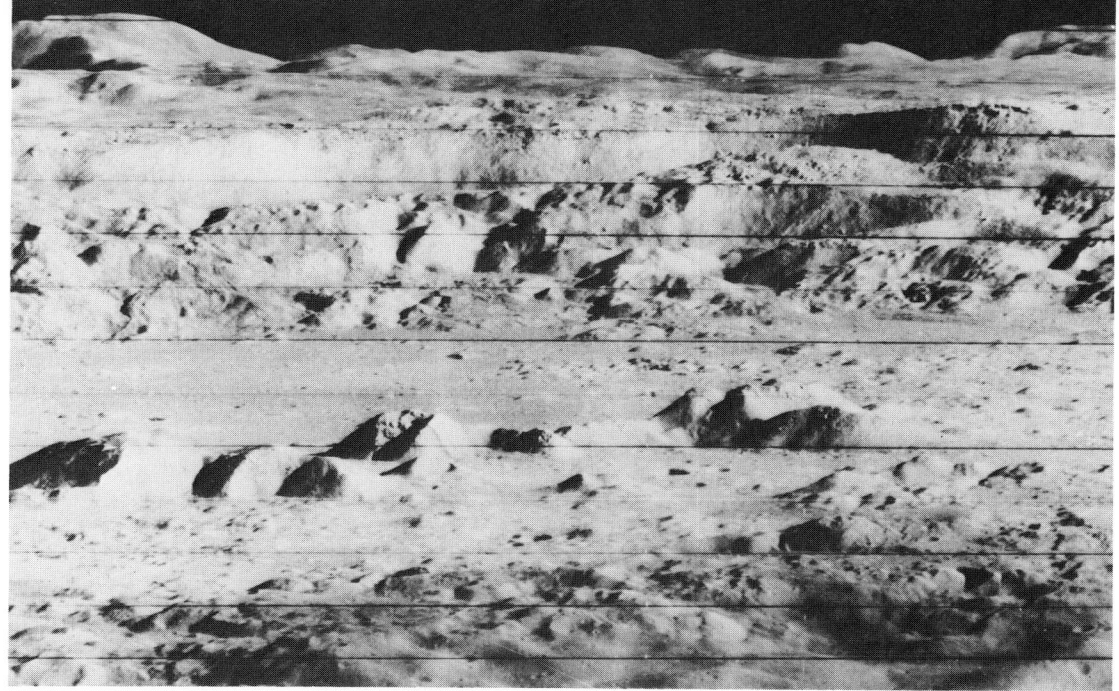

Copernicus crater, photographed by Lunar Orbiter 2. Picture was transmitted in narrow strips. Mountains rising from the crater floor are about 300 m (1,000 ft) high.

can be seen at night from most places on the earth. A total solar eclipse, on the other hand, can be seen only from the very narrow region on earth where the moon's shadow falls. You will probably see several eclipses of the moon in your lifetime, but only rarely will you be able to see a total solar eclipse.

The Moon's Gravitational Pull

If you have seen motion pictures of an astronaut on the moon, you have seen how easily he moves. Each step may be about 2 meters (6½ feet) long. Yet the man, his suit, and the backpack he wears weigh about 160 kilograms (350 pounds) on earth. The moon's gravitation is only one sixth as strong as the earth's. So the weight of the astronaut and his equipment is only about 27 kilograms (60 pounds) on the moon.

The earth and moon pull on each other. The moon's pull is much the weaker, but it is strong enough to cause the **tides,** the daily rising and falling of the ocean's water. Tides occur about 1 hour later each day. This is because the moon takes about 25 hours to reach the place it occupied in the sky the day before. The moon's pull also causes weak tides in the earth's atmosphere and in the earth itself. The earth tides can be measured only with sensitive instruments.

▶ THE SURFACE OF THE MOON

Over 2,000 years ago, Greek astronomers measured the size and distance of the moon. In 1609 Galileo, the famous Italian astronomer, was the first to observe the moon with a telescope. He saw mountains, craters, and dark flat areas that he believed to be seas. As more powerful telescopes were built, smaller lunar features were seen. In the 1960's thousands of photographs of the moon's surface were made by spacecraft in lunar orbit. Between 1969 and 1972, six Apollo landers touched down on the moon. Their crews collected more than 2,000 samples of moon soil and rocks. The samples were brought to the earth for study. Also, a small amount of material was brought to the earth by two unmanned Russian probes.

Scientists found that all the moon rocks, like some rocks on earth, are igneous—that is, they were formed when molten lava cooled and solidified. Moon rocks differ from earth rocks in their chemical makeup. Also, unlike the earth's rocks, moon rocks do not contain any water. Tests of samples showed that the age of the oldest rocks from the moon is 4,600,000,000 years.

Powdery dust and tiny pieces of rock cover much of the moon's surface. This "lunar soil" was formed over billions of years by the constant rain of large and small rocks onto the moon's surface. The process continues.

You may have seen the bright trails left by meteors in the night sky. The trail shows the path of a piece of rock from outer space. Many millions of these pieces reach our atmosphere every day. They fall toward the earth at great speed, burning up from friction with the earth's atmosphere. The moon has no atmosphere, so the rocks, called **meteorites**, crash on the surface. They smash and grind the rocks on the moon into lunar soil.

Mountains on the Moon

Look at the moon. Some parts of it are dark; some are light. With field glasses or a small telescope, you can see many raised areas in the light parts. They are mountains. A few peaks are nearly as high as Mount Everest. Some mountains form ranges but most of them form the rims of craters.

Craters

Craters are flat sunken areas, roughly circular in shape. Millions of craters cover the moon's surface. The largest lunar craters are surrounded by high mountains. Smaller craters are ringed by hills, while the smallest are mere pits in the moon's surface.

There are hundreds of the giant craters. Some, such as Clavius, can be seen without a telescope. Clavius is 235 kilometers (145 miles) across, and it is surrounded by mountains that are up to about 5,200 meters (17,000 feet) in height. On the other hand, there are some craters that are less than 1/100 millimeter (1/2500 inch) in diameter.

The mountains around a large crater form a circular wall. Outside the crater they slope down gently to the surrounding surface. Inside the crater, however, they slope steeply to the flat central plain. In most craters the central plain is lower than the surface outside the crater, sometimes by as much as 3,000 meters (10,000 feet).

Rays and Rilles

When we look at the full moon it is easy to see the light-colored streaks called **rays**. They look like the spokes of a wheel stretching away from some of the craters. The most noticeable rays are those stretching from the crater Tycho. Some of them are more than 2,400 kilometers (1,500 miles) long. Great craters, such as Tycho, were gouged out by gigantic meteorites. The rays are the broken and ground-up rocks thrown up by the explosion of the meteorite.

Powerful telescopes on earth, lunar probes, and the Apollo astronauts have photographed **rilles** in the moon's surface. These are cracks and valleys. They may be straight, or they may twist and turn. Some of them appear to have been formed as a result of cracking in the lunar surface, in the way that parts of the earth's surface may have been cracked by earthquakes.

Seas and Mascons

Galileo thought the flat, dark areas on the moon were seas because they appeared smooth through his telescope. Today we know that the seas are dry, and they are not smooth. Large craters are found in the seas along with millions of small ones.

Space scientists have noted a strange characteristic of those lunar seas that have a roughly circular shape. These seas exert a stronger gravitational pull on orbiting probes and spaceships than do other parts of the moon. The gravitational pull exerted by an object depends on the amount of matter, or **mass**, in the object. Scientists reason that the stronger pull of the circular seas is explained by a greater collection, or **concentration**, of mass in them. The words "mass concentration" have been shortened to **mascons**. The mascons are a problem to astronauts preparing to land on the moon. Mascons pull the spacecraft slightly off its course. These changes in course must be predicted and allowed for if the craft is to land at the selected place on the moon.

▶ THE INTERIOR OF THE MOON

The Apollo astronauts placed a number of seismometers on the moon. These instruments measured the strength of the 3,000 or so weak moonquakes that occur every year. The information, transmitted to earth, enabled scientists to build up a partial picture of the moon's interior.

The moon's outer layer, or **crust**, appears to be about 60 kilometers (37 miles) thick on the side of the moon that always faces the earth. The crust is nearly twice that thick on the far side of the moon. Beneath the crust a thick layer of dense rock, the **mantle**, extends down perhaps 800 kilometers (500 miles). Scientists do not yet know what lies beneath the mantle.

The Lifeless Moon

There is no evidence that life has ever existed on the moon. This is not surprising, for the moon's environment is hostile to the kind of life we know. The moon has no atmosphere of gases that living things must have. On the earth, every living thing contains water and carbon. But on the moon there is no water, and almost no carbon.

Many kinds of rays travel through space. They are called **radiation**. The heat and light of the sun are forms of radiation. Life on earth depends on them. But there are also deadly kinds of radiation. Some of them come from the sun, others come from farther out in space. The earth's atmosphere filters out the most dangerous radiation. But the moon, without a protective blanket of air, is bombarded by deadly radiation.

The earth is warmed by the sun's heat. Heated air moves to cooler areas. It is replaced by cool air that is heated in turn. Moving air currents (winds) even out the temperatures around the earth. But on the airless moon there are no winds. The moon's sunlit, or daytime, side is heated to a temperature of about 120° C (250° F), hotter than boiling water. The 2-week-long lunar day is followed by 2 weeks of night, when the temperature falls to 160° C (255° F) below zero. Such extreme temperatures would kill living things of the kind we know.

Because the moon has no atmosphere, an astronaut on the moon sees a very different sky from the one you see. It is black even in the daytime. On the earth the sun's light is scattered and reflected by the air. The scattering makes the sky look blue. On the moon and in outer space, there is no air to scatter the light. In the black skies over the moon and in outer space, the sun and the stars can be seen at the same time.

▶ PEOPLE ON THE MOON

Many questions had to be answered before astronauts could be sent to the moon. For example, would the moon's surface support

CUTAWAY VIEW OF A MOON CRATER

the weight of a spacecraft? A spacecraft attempting a landing on a soft, spongy surface might sink in and be swallowed up.

Space scientists used unmanned probes to learn more about the moon without risking lives. These craft sent back pictures of the moon's surface, and information about the moon's size and gravitational pull. This information was used in planning manned flights.

Living and Working on the Moon

People can live on the moon only if they can get oxygen for breathing and are protected against radiation and extreme temperatures. Space suits provide oxygen and protection, but for periods of days or weeks, the protection of buildings would be needed. Ways can be developed to produce the large amounts of food, water, oxygen, and energy that would be needed.

Cities on the moon may be far in the future, but scientific uses of the moon may come sooner. Telescopes could operate on the moon without interference from the earth's atmosphere. Radio telescopes, which detect waves of radio energy from the stars, would be free from interference from man-made radio waves on the earth. Once an observatory was set up, the telescopes would operate automatically, sending their findings to earth by radio and television.

Another scientific use of the moon began when the first Apollo crew reached it. Study of the moon rocks that they and later Apollo crews collected is helping to solve the mystery of the moon's beginning and development. And the solution to that mystery will help scientists to understand better how our earth began and developed.

COLIN A. RONAN
Fellow of the Royal Astronomical Society

Apollo 11 astronauts Armstrong and Aldrin were the first men to land on the moon, on July 20, 1969. They took this photograph from a height of 101 km (63 mi). Twisting rilles and many craters are visible. Dark object at left is part of lunar module.

Lunar module, after leaving the moon, is about to rejoin command module piloted by Michael Collins. Cloud-covered earth is visible in moon's black sky.

Lunar module of Apollo 11 landed on Sea of Tranquillity. Aldrin stands on sea's pitted surface. Visor reflects his shadow, figure of Armstrong, and lunar module.

People have wondered for thousands of years how the moon came into being. Many explanations have been offered. One theory is based on the idea that the moon was once a planet, moving in an orbit around the sun, as the earth does. The earth, with its greater force of gravitation, "captured" its nearby neighbor, pulling it into the orbit it now follows around the earth.

A second theory suggests that the earth and moon were once a single mass of material. As the mass grew, it spun so fast that a part of it formed a bulge. After a time the bulge was torn away and thrown out into space, forming the moon. The larger part that remained became the earth.

Still another theory states that the whole solar system was formed at the same time from a great cloud of dust and gas that whirled in space. More than 99 percent of this cloud collected into one mass that became the sun. The rest of the cloud collected into a number of smaller masses. These formed the earth, its moon, and all the other planets and their satellites.

These theories were developed at a time when scientists and their observing instruments were bound to the earth. The moon could be studied only from a distance. What kinds of rocks make up the moon? How old are they? Is there volcanic activity on the moon, as there is on the earth, or is the moon completely "dead"? These questions, and many others, could not be answered. The answers would have to wait until space probes and the Apollo astronauts reached the moon.

Between mid-1969 and late 1972, six Apollo craft landed at six widely separated places on the moon. The astronauts who manned these craft collected samples from the moon's surface. They brought to earth a total of 382 kilograms (840 pounds) of moon rocks and soil. Many scientists in the United States and other countries studied and tested the samples to learn their origins, ages, and chemical compositions.

The astronauts conducted many experiments to collect information about the moon's crust, its gravity, its magnetic field, and the temperatures beneath the crust. They also set up instruments to detect moonquakes.

The mass of information that the astronauts gathered has enabled scientists to begin many new studies of the moon. These studies have suggested new ideas about the way in which the moon and the earth might have begun, and then evolved or changed with time.

Most scientists think that the moon, the earth, and the other planets in the solar system began at about the same time, some 4,600,000,000 years ago. At first, this figure was based on the age of the oldest meteorites that have fallen to earth. It was confirmed when the oldest rocks gathered on the moon were found to be of the same age as the oldest meteorites.

The first stage in the development of the solar system may have been a vast cloud of gases and dust. As parts of the cloud cooled, they condensed into rock. Some of the larger rocks, having more gravitational attraction, pulled other rocks toward them. The larger rock masses attracted still other rocks. In time some of these ever-growing masses collected to form the moon. The moon's growth was unimaginably violent. Rocks ranging from pebble size to boulders many kilometers in diameter crashed onto the moon. The energy of these crashes heated up the surface and melted the rocks. The moon's surface became a sea of glowing liquid rock (lava), hundreds of kilometers deep.

After many millions of years, fewer rocks were left in space, so fewer rocks fell on the moon. The lava cooled slowly. Crystals of solid minerals formed in the cooling liquid. These crystals were not all alike. The lighter or less dense ones floated. In time they formed the moon's outer layer, or **crust**. The denser crystals sank, forming a lower layer of the moon, called the **mantle**. The chemical composition of the crystals was different, so the rocks of the moon's crust and its mantle are different.

After the crust cooled, some rocks continued to fall on the moon, blasting open huge craters in the solid crust. Some of the craters were 50 kilometers (30 miles) in diameter. A few, called basins, were many times that width. During this violent time the upper part of the moon's crust was ground, broken, remelted, and mixed almost completely.

About 4,000,000,000 (billion) years ago, after the moon's outer crust was cool and solid, the mantle was heating up. This hap-

PATH OF AN APOLLO FLIGHT

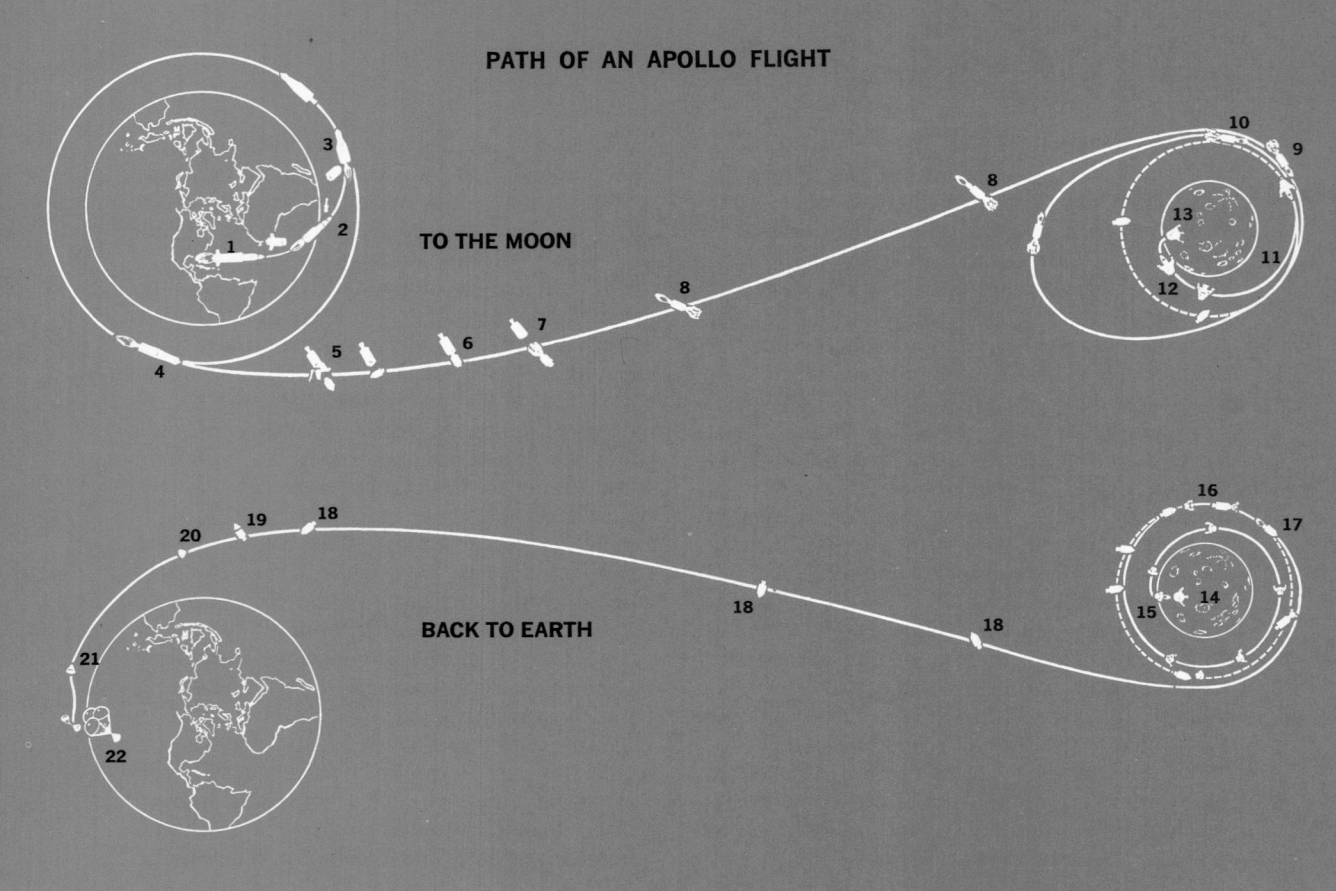

TO THE MOON

BACK TO EARTH

1. First stage of Saturn V rocket fires; lift-off; first stage drops away. 2. Second stage rocket fires and drops away; escape tower drops away. 3. Third stage fires and turns off; craft orbits earth. 4. Third stage refires, pushing craft into course toward moon. 5. Command service module (CSM) separates from third stage, turns around. 6. CSM docks with lunar module (LM). 7. CSM and LM separate from third stage. 8. Course is corrected. 9. Craft turns, fires rockets forward (retrofire) to slow down and go into lunar orbit. 10. Rockets fire to make orbit circular. 11. CSM and LM separate; CSM remains in lunar orbit with one as-tronaut. 12. Two astronauts in LM fire rockets to slow down for descent. 13. LM lands on moon. 14. Ascent stage of LM lifts off from moon. 15. LM goes into lunar orbit, nearly matching orbit of CSM. 16. LM moves closer to CSM; they meet and dock; astronauts climb back into CSM. 17. CSM rockets fire, pushing craft into course toward earth; LM is left behind. 18. Course is corrected. 19. Service module (SM) and command module (CM) separate. 20. Astronauts turn CM to fly with heat shield forward. 21. CM re-enters earth's atmosphere; heat shield burns away. 22. Parachutes lower CM to splashdown in ocean.

pened because the rocks in the deeper part of the moon contained radioactive elements such as uranium. A radioactive substance is unstable. The atoms of which it is composed break down at a constant rate. In one type of uranium, for example, the atoms break down to form atoms of another element, lead. Heat is produced during this process of **radioactive decay**.

The heat of radioactive decay built up within the moon until portions of the interior rocks melted to form lava. The heating up continued for millions of years. As the heat built up, more rocks melted and more and more lava collected in the mantle. In time

some of the lava worked its way up through the moon's crust. In some places the lava spilled across the surface. As it flowed, the fiery lava cooled and solidified, forming great plains of rock. The hot lava also burst into the basins from below, in flow after flow. These gigantic eruptions took place again and again, over a period of nearly 1,000,000,000 (billion) years. Then, about 3,000,000,000 (billion) years ago, the flow of lava came to an end. The lava cooled slowly. The rock that crystallized in the basins was mainly basalt. It was this dark, almost black rock that led Galileo to call the basins "maria," or "seas."

Except for the continuing impact of meteors, asteroids, and comets, the moon has changed little since the last flows of basalt cooled. Great craters like Copernicus were formed during this "quiet" time.

Most scientists now believe that the earth began and developed in the same general way and at the same time as the moon. But a great difference between the two bodies began to appear soon after the time of their formation. Millions of tons of nitrogen, carbon dioxide, water vapor, and other gases formed a shell or blanket around the earth, held in place by the earth's gravity.

Over millions of years, as the earth's crust cooled, the water vapor condensed into drops of water and fell as rain. Torrents of water poured across the earth. The rushing waters, violent winds, and changes in the earth's crust itself, wore away the large craters and other evidence of the world's early history. It was the atmosphere and the oceans of water that made life on earth possible.

No atmosphere collected on the moon. Gases did not remain around it because its gravitational attraction was not strong enough to hold on to them. Without gases to provide an atmosphere or water, no great changes took place on the moon. The changes that have occurred in the last 3,000,000,000 (billion) years were caused mainly by asteroids, comets, and meteors that crashed on the moon's surface. These objects dug out craters of all sizes, and threw up rocks that fell back, digging smaller craters.

For these billions of years the moon has looked much as we see it today. Its surface, cratered and mountainous, is like a partial portrait of our earth when it was young.

▶ **MOON EXPLORATION**

An astronaut climbs down slowly from the *Challenger,* the lunar module of Apollo 17. Some minutes later a second astronaut descends from the module. The two men stand on the moon's surface in their bulky space suits, looking up at the black sky. There they see the faraway shining earth, with its blue oceans and bright white clouds. The colors of the earth contrast strangely with the gray rocks and soil of the moon.

On the moon, away from the lunar module, the space suit is the astronaut's world. It supplies him with oxygen for breathing for up to 8 hours. Then he must return to the lunar module for a fresh supply of oxygen. The suit has a built-in air-conditioning system, needed to protect the astronaut from extremes of heat and cold. The special fabrics of the space suit are the astronaut's shield against the solar heat and the vacuum of space. The communications systems in the suit are the astronaut's link to the earth and to his fellow astronaut. All this equipment makes the suit heavy. But on the moon, whose gravity is only one sixth that of the earth, the suit seems light.

Walking on the moon is fun. Some astronauts prefer a skiing kind of walk, while others make giant kangaroolike hops. On earth the suit and backpack weigh nearly 90 kilograms (200 pounds) but on the moon one can walk a long way in it without tiring. The moon has no atmosphere to carry sound waves, but the astronaut, sealed within his suit, always hears some sounds. Even when his radio is silent, there is the hum of the oxygen blower fan and of the pump that circulates cooling water through the suit.

The sounds are soon forgotten, for there is much work to be done. Equipment for some of the experiments must be checked and set up on the ground. Other equipment is checked and loaded aboard the battery-powered lunar roving vehicle, or "Rover." The Rover itself must be checked before starting out on the first of three moon rides, or "traverses."

The Rover is a very dependable exploration vehicle, but it is not exactly a racing car. On level ground its top speed is about 12 kilometers (7½ miles) per hour. On their three traverses, the Apollo 17 crew drove a total distance of about 32 kilometers (20 miles).

The Rover is usually driven first to the most distant place on the traverse. The astronauts dismount and unload their equipment. Their aim is to gather all the facts they can about the spot. But for safety's sake, many "housekeeping" jobs must be done first. For example, dust thrown up by the wheels must be carefully removed from the surface of the Rover's batteries to prevent overheating. Checks must be made on the space suit batteries, air conditioners, and the supply of oxygen and water within the suit.

The moon explorers use a small hammer to chip off rock samples. They also use a device that drills into the soil. It removes cores of soil for study. Different layers in the core date from different periods in the history of the moon.

In addition to collecting samples of rocks and soil, the astronauts take many photographs at each stopping place. Their cameras are fitted with special controls. These make it possible to operate the camera through the bulky gloves of the space suit. Photography is important in moon exploration. Often the position of rocks and boulders in relation to one another and to the general area can give scientists clues to past events. The astronauts also describe what they see as they move about an area. Their words are recorded for use when the photographs and samples are studied. When the work is done, the Rover is driven to the next work area. Elapsed time must be watched with great care, for the oxygen supply in the space suit is limited, and a breakdown of the Rover could force a long walk back to the lunar module. Fortunately this has never happened.

The astronauts are part of a large group of scientists working together. The scientific team on earth follows the astronauts by television, ready to give suggestions or make changes in the planned programs quickly, if made necessary by new information.

Some members of the scientific team are geologists. There are also astronomers, biologists, engineers, and specialists in various other branches of science. They plan the program of experiments for the trip. The experiments, and the rocks and soil that the astronauts bring back to earth, tell us what the moon is like. They also tell much about the moon's past. And most important of all, they give us a better understanding of the origin and history of our home planet, the earth.

HARRISON H. SCHMITT
Scientist-Astronaut
Apollo 17 Mission

See also ECLIPSES; GRAVITY AND GRAVITATION; SOLAR SYSTEM; SPACE EXPLORATION AND TRAVEL; TIDES.

MOORISH ART AND ARCHITECTURE. See ISLAMIC ART AND ARCHITECTURE.

MORE, SIR THOMAS (1478–1535)

Thomas More was born in London on February 7, 1478, the son of Sir John More, a judge. Thomas attended a grammar school in London. At the age of 13 he was sent to continue his education in the household of John Cardinal Morton, the Archbishop of Canterbury and Lord Chancellor of England. In 1492 More went to Oxford, where he studied Greek and Latin.

At the wish of his father, More returned to London 2 years later to study law. About this time he considered entering the religious life, and for 4 years he lived under the direction of a group of Carthusian monks in London. He decided against becoming a monk and resumed his law career. He entered Parliament in 1504. The next year he married, and his wife bore him four children before she died in 1511. More married again.

Thomas More's deep sense of justice and outstanding legal ability earned for him increasingly important positions. He was knighted in 1521 and made lord chancellor in 1529. As lord chancellor, More became an intimate of King Henry VIII, who occasionally dined at More's house in London. Their friendship was broken when More disapproved of Henry's plan to divorce the Queen, Catherine of Aragon. In 1532 More resigned the chancellorship.

The dispute reached its climax when More refused to take an oath recognizing Henry as head of the Church in England. More was imprisoned in 1534 and the following year brought to trial for treason. He defended himself with great skill, but on the false testimony of a witness he was found guilty and sentenced to death. Just before his execution on July 6, 1535, More stated that he was "the king's good servant, but God's first."

In addition to his brilliance as a lawyer and statesman, More was a scholar. He wrote many works in Latin and in English, notably *Utopia,* which describes an imaginary country with an ideal society.

The Catholic Church declared More a saint in 1935. Catholics honor him as the patron of lawyers and celebrate his feast day on July 9.

KATHLEEN MCGOWAN
Catholic Youth Encyclopedia

MORMONS

When 21-year-old Joseph Smith (1805–44) walked down the pyramid-shaped little hill Cumorah near Palmyra, New York, on a late September night in 1827, he brought with him the beginnings of a new religious idea. This idea was to result in a worldwide religious sect, or group, of over 2,000,000 members—the Church of Jesus Christ of Latter-Day Saints. The people who belong to this church are known to most nonmembers as Mormons. They state that their beliefs are based on a book of golden plates, or tablets—*The Book of Mormon.*

Young Joseph Smith told his family and friends that he had found the book in the earth near the summit of this hill in western New York State. He said that he had been guided there by an angel named Moroni, who reported that he had written the book with Mormon, his father. According to the angel Moroni, its shining pages, written in strange characters, relate the history of two of the "Lost Ten Tribes of Israel." One of these tribes migrated to South America, and its members spread to the other Americas.

Joseph Smith translated *The Book of Mormon* from the "Reformed Egyptian" language with the aid of "magic spectacles" he had also found on Cumorah. He and five of his friends looked upon it as holding truths that should be added to those of the Bible. In April, 1830, they founded a church. Its members believed in both the Bible and *The Book of Mormon.*

At that time, in the mid-19th century, there was much argument among the churches of western New York. Most of the members of older churches thought that the members of the new church were wrong in their beliefs. They treated the Mormons so cruelly that they were forced to move westward. Joseph Smith and his followers, who were steadily growing in number, first stopped in Ohio. They moved on to Missouri, and then to Illinois, where they established the city of Nauvoo. For several years the Mormons found peace in Nauvoo. Then cruel and unjust treatment began again. In 1844 Joseph Smith and his brother Hyrum were murdered by a mob in the nearby town of Carthage. After Smith's death, several groups broke away from the main body of the church and established the Re-organized Church of Jesus Christ of Latter-Day Saints.

In 1844, Brigham Young became the leader of the main body of the church and led the Mormons on a long westward journey from Nauvoo to the valley of Great Salt Lake in Utah. There, gazing out over the valley, Young declared, "This is the place." Young believed in the doctrine of polygamy—that men should marry a number of wives—following the example of prophets described in the Old Testament of the Bible. The church formally did away with this custom in 1890.

When Brigham Young reached the valley of Great Salt Lake, the people who had arrived a short time earlier were already hard at work. They had begun to change the beds of streams that ran down from the mountains. These streams would be made to flow through the dry land on which the Mormons would build "New Jerusalem"—Salt Lake City.

People of other religions who changed to Mormon beliefs went to Salt Lake City from New England and New York State. Some also went from the British Isles, the Scandinavian countries, and other parts of Europe. The migration of many thousands of Mormons helped significantly in opening up the vast American West. These hardworking settlers produced fine crops. Soon they found copper and other minerals in the vicinity of the valley. They became a healthy people. Their religious teachings allow no drinking of alcohol, coffee, or tea and no use of tobacco.

The Mormons also became successful in business and established new towns far out on the sands of Utah. They have built beautiful places of worship in Salt Lake City and other cities in the United States, as well as in Canada, England, Switzerland, and New Zealand. Mormon missionaries are active worldwide.

In 1978 the Mormon church changed a part of its doctrine that banned blacks from becoming priests. Priesthood in the Mormon church is a lay ministry open to faithful males of any race, 12 years of age and older, who are considered deserving. The president of the church announced that the lifting of the ban came as the result of a revelation from God.

CARL CARMER
Author, *Listen for a Lonesome Drum*
See also SALT LAKE CITY; UTAH; YOUNG, BRIGHAM.

MOROCCO

The Kingdom of Morocco is located on the northwestern coast of Africa, bordering both the Atlantic Ocean and the Mediterranean Sea. Part of Morocco lies just a short distance from Spain, across the Strait of Gibraltar. Morocco is sometimes called al-Maghrib al-Aqsa in Arabic, which might be translated as "land farthest west." This name refers to Morocco's location as the farthest west of all the Islamic (Muslim) countries.

▶THE PEOPLE

Most of the people of Morocco are Muslims. Many are distantly related to the Arabs who first came from the Arabian Peninsula

A veiled Moroccan woman, wearing the traditional jellaba, rides by a village in the Atlas Mountains.

during the 7th century. Before the invasion of the Arabs the people living in Morocco were Berbers. The life of the Berbers was greatly changed by the arrival of the Arabs. From the Arabs the Berbers adopted the Muslim religion and learned to speak and write the Arabic language.

Both the Berbers and the Arabs are light-skinned peoples. But there are also many dark-skinned Moroccans. Some have lived on the edges of the Sahara, a vast desert, for thousands of years. Others were brought as slaves from African lands south of the Sahara. Many married light-skinned Moroccans, and all are now Muslims.

At one time there were about 200,000 Jews in Morocco. Most were descendants of Jews who had fled from Spain and other European countries and settled in the coastal cities. Others were Berbers whose ancestors had been converted to Judaism before the Arab invasion. Today most Jews have left Morocco. Morocco also has a number of European residents, many of whom live in Casablanca, a major port on the Atlantic coast.

Moroccans are mainly farmers who grow their own food. They often use camels, donkeys, and mules to pull their plows.

In the south, a few tribes still wander from oasis to oasis in the desert. Their chief foods are dates and camel's milk. Among the tribes are the "Blue Men," whose skin is stained blue from the indigo dye that rubs off their clothes when they perspire.

Some tribes of nomads pitch their tents on the high, dry plateaus, where no crops will grow. There they let their sheep and goats graze. They make their tents from goatskins. Sheep's wool is woven into rugs with bright designs and into fabric for heavy clothing. But the goats and sheep are raised mainly for their meat.

The Muslim religion is important to Moroccans, who are a very religious people. A Muslim boy is first taken to the mosque for prayers when he is 7 years old. From then on, he usually goes to the mosque every Friday and prays every day.

All Muslims fast during the holy month of Ramadan. From sunrise to sunset they do not eat, drink, or smoke. Children learn to fast by first trying it for half a day and then a full day. At night everyone eats a great deal. Before dawn a man goes from house to house beating a drum, so that people will wake up and eat something before daybreak. In the cities a cannon is used to announce the break of dawn.

In the past, city women rarely left their homes. Today the majority of them go out—to the mosque, the public bath, and the movies. But when they go out, some of them still keep their faces covered with a veil and wear long, loose cotton robes called jellabas or white, sheetlike haiks. In the country, women have always had more freedom because they must help in the fields. They do not wear veils, but still they must stay apart from the men. At the weekly open-air markets, or *souks,* the women do not mix with men. Country people come from long distances to buy and sell, to tell and listen to stories, to hear musicians play, and to buy medicine from the herb doctor. In some places the markets are for women only.

In the country Moroccan children help their parents by looking after the sheep. They are often seen carrying buckets of water from the public wells or fountains. Boys, when they are very young, learn to work at their father's trades.

The first thing that many schoolchildren learn is the Koran, the Muslim holy book. They sit cross-legged on the floor and chant in high voices until they memorize it. They learn how to write by copying the Arabic letters.

There are still a large number of people who cannot read or write. But the Moroccan Government is building more schools, and compulsory primary education was begun in 1964. More than 40 percent of Morocco's school-age children are now enrolled in

People come to an open-air market to buy and sell goods and to exchange stories. In the background is a Casbah, an old fortified town.

Animal hides are soaked in vats of tannic acid to make fine leather.

primary schools. They are required to attend school between the ages of 7 and 13. The number of students attending secondary schools, colleges, and universities has increased. The leading institution of higher learning is Mohammed V University in Rabat.

▶THE LAND

The western coastal plain of Morocco has good soil. Winds from the Atlantic Ocean bring rain, and the climate is comfortable. Much of the land is used for farming.

Much of Morocco is cut off from the desert in the south by the Atlas Mountains, the highest mountains in North Africa. Djebel Toubkal, the highest peak, reaches 4,165 meters (13,665 feet). These mountains are covered by snow through much of the year. The Rif mountains are located in the north. Morocco's major rivers begin in the mountains. They are the Moulouya, Sebou, Oum er Rbia, Dra, Sous, Ziz, and Ghéris.

▶THE ECONOMY

About half of Morocco's people work as farmers. The average Moroccan farmer plants cereals, mainly wheat and barley, and often has grapevines and olive, fig, or almond trees. Almost every farmer has a flock of sheep and goats, and some have chickens and cows. But the farms are very small, often just a tiny strip along the mountainside.

In the coastal region there are a few large, modern farms where tomatoes and other vegetables, melons, and oranges are grown. Olive oil and wine are also produced. These products are exported to Europe.

Another important export product is the fiber of the dwarf palm tree, which is used in making stuffing for furniture. More of this fiber is exported from Morocco than from any other country in the world. Cork, which comes from the cork oak tree, is also exported.

The seas off Morocco's coast are filled with fish, especially sardines, tuna, and mackerel. Safi is one of the world's leading sardine ports. Moroccans are making a new kind of flour from sardines that will be less expensive and more nutritious than flour made from grain.

Morocco is also rich in minerals. Mines owned by the government produce 15 percent of the world's phosphates. Manganese, lead, zinc, iron, and coal are also mined.

Morocco's industries are growing rapidly. Factories make cement, trucks, and cars. Leather goods, which used to be made only by hand, are now being made by machine, too. Morocco has good roads, railroads, and electrical and telephone systems that were started by the French and Spanish.

Morocco's largest city and chief port is Casablanca, with a metropolitan population of about 2,500,000. Rabat, the capital, is second in size. Other large cities include Marrakesh, Meknes, and Fez.

▶ GOVERNMENT

Morocco is a constitutional monarchy. The king is both the head of state and the country's spiritual leader, and exercises great authority. A prime minister serves as head of government. Under the 1972 constitution, two thirds of the members of the legislature are elected directly by the people, and the balance by indirect methods.

▶ HISTORY

Morocco was inhabited in the Stone Age by cave dwellers, who left many traces of their presence. About 2000 B.C. it was settled by Berber tribes, who have formed the basis of the population ever since, despite many foreign invasions. Most important were the Arab invasions, beginning in the 7th century A.D. The Arabs converted the Berbers to Islam and joined forces with them to conquer large parts of Spain. Idris, a descendant of Mohammed, established the first Moroccan state, in the 8th century. His son founded the city of Fez, which was a brilliant center of Islamic religion and culture.

The first great Moroccan empire was founded by the Almoravids in the 11th century. Its domain stretched to Algiers and Spain. The empire declined gradually thereafter, but between the 16th and 17th centuries, Morocco ruled much of West Africa.

Morocco remained relatively free of foreign domination until the 19th century, when the European powers began to compete for territory in Africa. In 1912 most of Morocco became a French protectorate. Spain took control of the rest of the country. During World War II, Moroccan troops fought on the side of France. Near the end of the war, a movement for independence began, led by the Istiqlal

Rabat, the capital of Morocco, lies on the Atlantic.

(Independence) Party. Opposition to French rule reached its peak following the exile of the sultan of Morocco, Mohammed V, in 1953. In 1955 he was allowed to return, and independence was granted on March 2, 1956. The sultan took the title of King Mohammed V in 1957. He ruled until his death in 1961, when he was succeeded as king by his son, Hassan II. Spain gave up most of its Moroccan territory at the same time as France but retained control of Ifni until 1969. Spain still maintains two small ports on the Mediterranean coast, Ceuta and Melilla.

Morocco acquired most of Western (formerly Spanish) Sahara in 1976, and the rest of the territory in 1979. A vast, thinly populated desert region, Western Sahara is rich in phosphates, a valuable mineral. The territory also is claimed by the Polisario, which seeks independence as the Saharan Arab Democratic Republic. Fighting between Moroccan troops and Polisario guerrillas has raged in the region.

The dispute over Western Sahara led Morocco to withdraw from the Organization of African Unity in 1984. Morocco and Libya signed a treaty of union in 1984 but canceled it in 1986 due to disagreements.

FRANCES C. L. GASTON
Reviewed by PERMANENT MISSION
OF MOROCCO TO THE UNITED NATIONS

MORSE, SAMUEL F. B. (1791–1872)

Until the middle of the 19th century there was no quick method of sending a message to a person far away. Samuel F. B. Morse was the man who invented a way to send messages quickly by means of electricity. His invention is called the telegraph.

Morse was born in Charlestown, Massachusetts, on April 27, 1791. His father was a minister. At the age of 14 Morse entered Yale University. He attended many lectures on chemistry and electricity. He was fascinated by these subjects, although his main ambition was to become an artist.

Shortly after graduating from Yale University he went to England to study art. He remained there for several years. During those years he became well-known as an artist.

Morse returned to the United States in 1815 and became a portrait painter. Three years later he married Lucretia Pickering Walker. They had four children. In 1823 he settled in New York to lecture and write about art. He was appointed professor of art at the University of the City of New York, now called New York University. The position did not pay him a salary, but it gave him the chance to get private art students. While in New York, Morse also attended a series of lectures on science. Some of these lectures were on the uses of a new device, the electromagnet.

In 1825 Morse's wife died while he was away from the city. He did not learn of her death until days after the funeral, because communication was so slow at that time.

In 1832 Morse was returning from a second trip to Europe. He passed some of the time on shipboard discussing electromagnets with one of the other passengers. Suddenly Morse thought of a way to send messages over great distances with the proper use of an electromagnet, wires, and batteries. When he got back to New York, Morse began to work out his idea. He also invented a message code made up of dots and dashes representing letters of the alphabet.

By this time Morse realized that he would never be a great artist. He was having a hard time making a living as a painter. Fortunately he found friends who were willing to invest money in his invention. Morse then gave up his career as an artist and devoted all his time to perfecting the telegraph. In 1837 he applied for a patent on his invention.

Soon, Morse felt his instrument was good enough for a long-range test—from Washington to Baltimore, 61 kilometers (38 miles) away. He went to the United States Congress for help. But Congress would not grant him any money for the test. Disappointed, he went to Europe to try to interest foreign governments in his invention. But there, too, he was unsuccessful.

Finally, in March, 1843, Congress voted to give $30,000 for the test line. By 1844 the line was finished. The first message, "What hath God wrought!" was sent from the Capitol in Washington on May 24, 1844. The message was received in Baltimore almost as soon as it was sent. "Writing at a distance"—the telegraph—was a fact.

From that moment on, Morse began to receive honors from all over the world. He became a wealthy man. Morse had remained a widower for 23 years. In 1848 he remarried. His second wife, Sarah Elizabeth Griswold, was 31 years younger than he. She, too, bore him four children. On June 10, 1871, the telegraph operators of America unveiled a bronze statue of Samuel F. B. Morse in Central Park in New York. Morse died in New York on April 2, 1872.

DAVID C. KNIGHT
Author, science books for children

MORSE CODE. See RADIO, AMATEUR.
MORTGAGES. See REAL ESTATE.

Samuel F. B. Morse, inventor of the telegraph.

MOSAIC

Mosaic is an art in which small pieces of colored materials are placed in cement or plaster to form a picture or pattern. The pieces, called **tesserae,** can be made of practically anything—marble, glass, tile, minerals, shells, seeds, or pebbles. They can be of any shape—round or square, octagonal (eight-sided), hexagonal (six-sided), or irregular. Mosaic is most often used to decorate floors, walls, ceilings, jewelry, and furniture. Tesserae for floors are usually flat, while those used on walls are often cone-shaped so that they can be pushed into cement.

The Sumerians decorated walls with colored tiles. Egyptians used the beautiful blue stone lapis lazuli as decoration. The Aztecs and Incas covered their masks, shields, and religious statues with turquoise mosaic.

The oldest mosaics are pavements made from colored pebbles. Pavements that were made thousands of years ago have been found in Turkey, northern Greece, and on the island of Crete. The Romans used small cubes of marble and glass for floor mosaics. At first these mosaics had simple abstract patterns in just a few colors. Later, artisans began imitating paintings, using many colors and working in very great detail. Panels of mosaic, like paintings, were used to decorate walls as well as floors.

Mosaic decoration is especially effective in religious buildings because the brilliantly colored and gilded glass reflects light, creating a mysterious, spiritual atmosphere. In the 4th century, mosaic began to be used to cover the entire walls of churches. The use of mosaic in church decoration reached a height during the Byzantine Empire (A.D. 330–1453).

By the 16th century, mosaic had been largely replaced by fresco (painting done on wet plaster). The art of mosaic was revived in the 19th century and is still used today as a form of decoration in religious and public buildings.

Reviewed by CHARLES McCLENDON
Yale University

To make a small mosaic, use a piece of wood as a base. Nail strips of wood around the base to form a bed for the tiles. Trace a design on the base. Carry out the design in tiles of different colors, and glue each tile in place (1). When the tiles are firmly set, fill the spaces between them by pouring grout over the mosaic (2). Clean off the excess grout with a rubber squeegee or scraper (3).

MOSCOW

Moscow is the capital of the Union of Soviet Socialist Republics. It is an ancient city that traces its history to the 12th century. Reminders of the days when the czars ruled Russia can be found all over Moscow. But blocks of modern apartment houses, new hotels, factories, and other buildings are signs of the changes that have been made since the Russian Revolution of 1917.

Moscow, which has a population of about 8,000,000, is the largest city in the Soviet Union. Moscow is in the same latitude as the southern tip of Alaska. Because Moscow is an inland city, it has a continental climate. Winters are long, cold, and snowy. Summers are usually short, but they can be very hot. Moscow is the Soviet Union's center of government, industry, science, trade, and culture. The most important Soviet newspapers are published in Moscow. Besides being the center of the railway system of the Soviet Union, it is also connected by thousands of kilometers of rivers and canals with the Caspian, Baltic, Black, and White seas. Five airports serve the city's air traffic.

Moscow is the center of the country's textile industry. The style of fabrics, footwear, and clothing produced in Moscow influences women's fashions throughout the Soviet Union. Large factories around the city produce machinery, automobiles, electrical equipment, ball bearings, boilers, and many other things.

The Moscow subway, known as the Metro, is world-famous because every station is decorated and the entire line is kept exceptionally clean. Visitors are often taken to see some of the more outstanding stations, such as the one at Revolution Square, which is decorated with sculpture, or the one at Mayakovsky Square, which has paintings on the walls. All the stations are lighted with elaborate electric candles, and most have marble walls.

The Kremlin, center of the Soviet Government, overlooks the Moscow River.

Moscow University is housed in a skyscraper on the Lenin Hills, near the city. There are academies of science, technology, engineering, and agriculture, in addition to excellent libraries and schools for students of all ages. The theaters of Moscow, including the Bolshoi Theater, the Maly Theater, and the Moscow Art Theater, are famous for the quality of their performances of ballet and drama. The many museums are largely devoted to the history of the Russian people and of the Revolution of 1917. The Lenin Museum shows scenes and mementos of the life of Lenin (1870–1924), the Communist leader. The Lenin Library is one of the largest libraries in the world and has over 21,000,000 volumes. Houses of famous people, such as Count Leo Tolstoi (1828–1910), the writer, are kept just as they were during the lifetimes of those people. The Tretyakov Art Gallery contains Russian paintings that date from early times to the present, and the Museum of Eastern Cultures has many exhibits of Asian art. Fine paintings are found also in the Museum of Contemporary Western Art.

Dynamo Stadium, which holds about 70,000 people, is located on the city's outskirts. There are several other stadiums, for the Russians enjoy sports. There are parks in the city, along the river, and in the suburbs. The largest public park is the Gorky Park of Culture and Rest, which lies along the Moscow River. Russian parks have restaurants and amusements, sometimes theaters and concert halls, and always playgrounds and entertainment for children. There are special buildings where children do artistic and scientific handwork. With the help of teachers they learn how to dance and to make up and give their own plays. There are puppet theaters and circuses, and a children's theater that is as fine as those for adults.

▶THE KREMLIN

The Kremlin is an enclosure of about 70 acres that rises on a hill on the left bank of the Moscow River. It is surrounded by solid red brick walls 40 to 50 feet high and 1¼ miles around. The walls form a triangle, one side following the curve of the river. Towers are located at intervals along the walls. Five of these are gates, and over each of them is a tower with a tall spire. On each spire is a red

Most Moscow subway stations are handsomely decorated.

star; the largest of them is 11 feet wide. These stars are lighted at night and can be seen from far off.

The main entrance to the Kremlin is through the Gate of the Savior, whose tower is over 200 feet high. Inside the walls are the palaces formerly used by the czars and the buildings now used by the Soviet Government. There are also three cathedrals, two bell towers, two monasteries, and many churches. The religious buildings have been turned into museums or closed, because the Russians do not encourage religious worship.

Two old palaces and the Great Palace, which was built in the 19th century, are kept just as they were in czarist days and are historical museums. In still another palace are the costumes, jewelry, thrones, crowns, carriages, and personal possessions of former czars and czarinas, as well as the treasures of the churches. The present rulers of the Soviet Union use the reception halls of the Great Palace for state ceremonies and use other buildings for offices and all the business of government. The Soviet Government is often referred to as the Kremlin, just as the United States Government is referred to as Washington, and the British Government as Whitehall.

Muscovites shopping at GUM (State Department Store).

Cathedral Square adjoins the Great Palace and is the home of the Supreme Soviet of the U.S.S.R. Dormition Cathedral, Annunciation Cathedral, and the bell tower of Ivan the Great are grouped together around the square. This slender 300-foot tower is the tallest building in the Kremlin, and its gilded cupola (dome) can be seen above those of the other churches. The cupolas of Russian churches are onion-shaped, and on the points are elaborate crosses. From some of these crosses are hung gilded chains. The cathedrals are white outside. Inside they are dark but full of candlelight and color, gleaming with gold and painted decorations.

The Gate of the Savior opens out from the Kremlin onto Red Square, a vast, open space where the most important public events take place. The anniversary of the Russian Revolution is celebrated here on November 7th, and Labor Day is celebrated on May 1st and 2nd. Colorful parades, such as the one honoring the Soviet cosmonauts, are also held in this square. Red Square was not named by Communists, although red is their color. The name is an old one. In Russian the word for "red" also used to mean "beautiful," and it was known as Beautiful Square. On one side is the Kremlin wall, and in front of it stands the granite tomb of Lenin, where his embalmed body can be seen. Opposite this is a long building that used to be a market and is now the big government department store called GUM. At the third side is the Historical Museum; and at the fourth, St. Basil's Cathedral, with its brilliantly colored domes.

▶ HISTORY

Moscow was founded in 1147 by Yuri Dolgoruki ("George Long-arm") (1120–57). Yuri built a stockade around the hill where the Kremlin now stands. Inside it were built a few log houses and a wooden church.

There was no king or czar at that time. Russia was divided among the many descendants of the first ruler, Rurik. The eldest, called the grand prince, ruled over its principal city at the time—Kiev on the Dnieper River.

When the Mongol Tatars invaded Russia in the early 13th century, they destroyed Kiev and other cities and killed their inhabitants. The Tatars were horsemen who lived in tents and pastured their flocks on the steppes, the vast prairies that stretch across southern Russia into western Asia. The Tatars did not occupy Russia but made their headquarters on the Volga River, near what is now the city of Volgograd. They made the Russians pay tribute—a part of the produce of every province and town—for many years.

One grand prince, Ivan I (?–1341), realized that the forest was safer than the steppes and made the city of Moscow his capital. The head of the church also came to live there, making it a holy city. Ivan realized too that Russia should not be divided among several princes but united under one ruler. He persuaded or forced the other princes to accept him as their leader and collected all their tribute and delivered it to the Tatars. He called himself prince of Moscow and of all the Russias.

Ivan's successors wisely followed his example. Ivan III, called Ivan the Great (1440–1505), was able in 1480 to free Russia from the Tatars. He then called himself Czar of all the Russias and ruled a country that stretched from the steppes to the Arctic Ocean and from the Gulf of Finland to the Ural Mountains. Moscow had expanded by this time and had become the capital. Ivan III sent for Italian architects and built the present wall of the Kremlin, two of the cathedrals, and many other buildings.

Walls were needed not only for protection against enemies but also against fire. Ivan's Russia was heavily forested. Stone was scarce and hard to transport. All the houses and most public buildings were wooden, and when a fire started, nothing could stop it. In every century Moscow has been wholly or partly destroyed by fire and patiently rebuilt.

Under the czars Moscow grew and prospered. It was near the Volga, the Dnieper, and the Dvina rivers or their tributaries, and these were the highways of trade and travel. Under Ivan IV, called Ivan the Terrible (1530–84), the Tatars were driven from the Volga, and Siberia was conquered. Russia was known at this time as Muscovy, and its people as Muscovites. Piles of furs were brought to Moscow on sledges over the snow from Siberia. Tea, silk, spices, and velvets from Asia came on barges up the Volga and were sold in Moscow or sent down the Dvina to other parts of Europe.

There were misfortunes, too, for Ivan tortured and executed thousands of people in Red Square, and fires ravaged Moscow. After he died, there was civil war. He had killed his son, too, and there was no heir. Finally a new family, the Romanovs, the ancestors of the last czars, were chosen to rule the land.

The third Romanov was Peter I, called Peter the Great (1672–1725). He built a new city on the Gulf of Finland and called it St. Petersburg. In 1703 he made it his capital, and for 215 years this city (now called Leningrad) was the capital instead of Moscow. But every czar was crowned in Dormition Cathedral in the Kremlin, for Moscow was still the holy city.

Moscow's last great fire took place in 1812, when Napoleon I (1769–1821), Emperor of France, invaded Russia. He entered Moscow in September but came into an empty city, for its people had abandoned it. The first night he spent there, fires broke out, probably by accident. Winds spread the flames, and the city burned for 4 days. Napoleon stayed for 5 weeks in the Kremlin, whose wall had saved it, and waited for the Czar to surrender. Meanwhile his soldiers looted the ruined city and stabled their horses in its churches. The Czar did not surrender, and in October, Napoleon's army moved out of the city. Most of his soldiers died of cold and hunger during a terrible retreat. The people of Moscow came back and rebuilt their city, adding a fine new church to celebrate the great victory.

The czars remained powerful over the next century as Russia expanded. But revolution broke out in 1917, while Russia was fighting Germany during World War I. The revolution began in St. Petersburg and quickly spread to Moscow. In November, 1917, the revolutionaries captured the Kremlin. Lenin, the head of the Bolsheviks (Communists) and the new leader of the country, made Moscow the capital again in March, 1918. The Communists took over the palaces of the nobles and wealthy people and turned them into clubs, schools, and museums for the workers. The face of Moscow began to change.

The country was again invaded during World War II, when Germany attacked it. People in factories in and around Moscow worked day and night to supply the army. The German armies hoped to capture the city. They were stopped only 40 kilometers (25 miles) from the walls of the Kremlin.

After the war ended in 1945, the Soviet Union began to rebuild. The Communist authorities placed severe restrictions on who could live in Moscow, but many Russians wished to live in the capital. The city grew. Its population has more than tripled since the 1917 Revolution. Massive new apartment complexes now dot the outskirts of the city.

Moscow was the site of the 1980 Summer Olympic Games. The games were boycotted by the United States and many other nations in protest against the Soviet invasion of Afghanistan.

ELIZABETH SEEGER
Author, *The Pageant of Russian History*

MOSES

Moses' story is told in the Bible in the books of Exodus, Leviticus, Numbers, and Deuteronomy. These books, along with Genesis, are sometimes called the Books of Moses. They are known as the Pentateuch.

According to the Bible, Moses was born in Egypt of Hebrew parents in the 13th century B.C., when the Hebrews were slaves of the Egyptians. Pharaoh, the king of Egypt, was afraid that the Hebrews would grow in numbers and become strong. Just before the time of Moses' birth, he ordered that every son born to a Hebrew woman must be cast into the river. Moses' mother put her baby son in a basket among the reeds along the banks of the river. Pharaoh's daughter found him when she came to wash, and she took pity on him. She took him home and raised him as a son.

Moses was treated like a prince at the Egyptian court. He learned to read and write. One day, when he had grown up, he went among his own people, the Hebrews. When he saw a Hebrew slave being beaten by an Egyptian, he killed the Egyptian. Pharaoh heard about Moses' deed and threatened to kill him. Moses fled for his life.

Moses hid in the land of Midian. He lived with Jethro, the priest of Midian, and married Zipporah, one of Jethro's daughters. One day while Moses was tending Jethro's sheep, he

Moses stayed on Mount Sinai for forty days and nights while God instructed him in the law. French painter Marc Chagall shows Moses receiving the Ten Commandments.

saw a flame in the midst of a bush. He stared at it in wonder, for the fire did not burn up the bush. Then God called to Moses from out of the bush. He commanded Moses to return to Egypt and free the Hebrews. God promised to guide Moses and the Hebrews into Canaan, "a land flowing with milk and honey."

Moses obeyed God and returned to Egypt. When Moses asked Pharaoh to free the Hebrews, Pharaoh refused. But each time that he refused, God brought a terrible plague on the land. He turned the waters into blood. He covered the land with frogs and locusts. He made all the cattle of the Egyptians die, but He saved the cattle of the Hebrews. When the tenth plague killed all the firstborn children of the Egyptians, including Pharaoh's own son, Pharaoh finally freed the Hebrews.

Moses took his people out of Egypt and into the wilderness. A pillar of cloud led them by day and a pillar of fire by night. Pharaoh later changed his mind and sent horsemen and chariots after them. His army overtook the Hebrews when they were camped by the Sea of Reeds. The Bible says that God parted the waters, and Moses led his people across on dry land. When the Egyptians tried to follow, the waters closed over them.

The journey through the wilderness was hard, and the people grew tired and hungry. But God provided for them. When they had nothing left to eat, He covered the land with food called manna, and the people ate.

Moses worked to unite his people. At first he settled their quarrels himself. Then he set up courts and judges. In the third month the Hebrews reached Mount Sinai. God called Moses up to the top of the mountain and gave him the Ten Commandments and other laws. This code of laws is called the Law of Moses.

When the people lost faith, they began worshiping other gods. They made a golden calf out of their jewelry and built an altar in front of it. To punish them, God told Moses they would have to wander in the wilderness for 40 years before they enter the promised land.

Moses never lost faith. When he was 120 years old, he led his people to the borders of Canaan. He went to the top of a mountain, and God showed him the promised land. Then Moses died, his work accomplished.

Reviewed by MORTIMER J. COHEN
Author, *Pathways Through the Bible*

See also PASSOVER.

Sugaring Off, painted when Grandma Moses was 83 years old, shows people collecting sap from sugar maple trees and boiling it down to make maple syrup and maple candy.

MOSES, GRANDMA (1860–1961)

The artist Grandma Moses became famous for her simple, bright, cheerful paintings of American farm life. Her full name was Anna Mary Robertson Moses. But she was known to everyone as Grandma Moses because she did not begin to paint seriously until she was in her seventies.

Anna Mary Robertson was born on September 7, 1860, on a farm in Greenwich, New York. She was one of ten children. Life on the farm was hard, and Anna had little schooling. Her days were filled with farm chores—feeding the animals, gathering eggs, making soap, and dipping candles. But she often found time to make pictures. Because she had no proper paints, she used house paint, scraps of colored paper, the juice of wild berries, and even laundry bluing for her colors.

Soon, however, she became too busy to draw or paint. At the age of 12, she went to work as a servant for a family nearby. She worked for other people for many years. Then, when she was 27, she married Thomas Moses, a farmer. And they began raising a family of their own. They moved to a farm near Staunton, Vermont, and later to another at Eagle Bridge, New York. Thomas Moses died there in 1927.

As she grew older, Anna Moses could no longer do heavy farm work. She took up needlework, but her hands became too stiff to continue. Then, in her seventies, she began to paint in oils. Her pictures showed things she remembered from childhood—farm scenes, small villages, picnics, ice-skating, bringing home the Christmas tree. The forms were simple, and the colors bright and cheerful.

Grandma Moses had a remarkable memory for detail, and her pictures made a record of a way of life that was quickly passing away. People everywhere loved these happy scenes of life in days gone by. Soon her paintings were shown in art galleries, and she became the "grand old lady of American art." She continued to paint almost until her death, on December 13, 1961, at the age of 101.

Reviewed by JANE KALLIR
Author, *Grandma Moses: The Artist Behind the Myth*

MOSLEM. See ISLAM.

MOSQUITOES

Mosquitoes are among the most widespread of flying insects. There are more than 2,000 species. They are found on every continent and in every nation, in temperate and tropical climates, and near both freshwater and saltwater. The mosquito is related to the fly.

The Mosquito's Body

Mosquitoes range in length from 0.2 to 6 centimeters (1/12 inch to 2 2/5 inches). The body is very thin and is divided into three main parts, or segments. The **head capsule** is small and round. On it are the large compound eyes (many lenses clustered together), the branching antennae, and the complicated mouthparts.

The **thorax** is a triangular, rigid, boxlike segment just behind the head. The mosquito's six legs are attached to the thorax, and underneath them are the **spiracles,** the vents through which the insect breathes. Two large wings with dumbbell-shaped balancing organs, called **halteres,** are attached to the upper side of the thorax. The wings contain no muscles—they are worked by muscles in the thorax. The wings move in a figure-eight pattern between 250 and 600 times a second, depending on the species. This rapid movement of the wings through the air causes a high-pitched buzzing sound. The mosquito can fly forward or backward and can hover in one spot.

The **abdomen** is the last and longest body segment. It is covered with overlapping plates that allow it to swell. The abdomens of females can become enlarged with blood or eggs.

Life Cycle

Mosquitoes live in places with some of the world's harshest climates, such as Alaska and Greenland. They need only a short season of warmth and moisture to carry out their life cycle. A mosquito goes through four life stages—**egg, larva, pupa,** and **imago** (adult).

In cold climates, where temperatures drop below freezing in winter, fertile females survive in a dormant (resting) state in crevices and holes in barns, houses, and other buildings. When the first warm days of spring arrive, they lay their eggs in a body of still water. This can be a swamp, a puddle, or even water in an old can or paper carton. The entire development from egg to adult takes three to

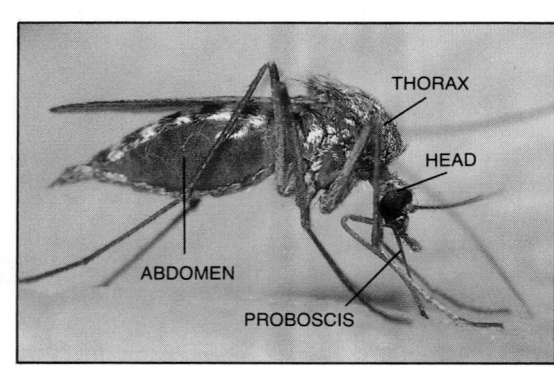

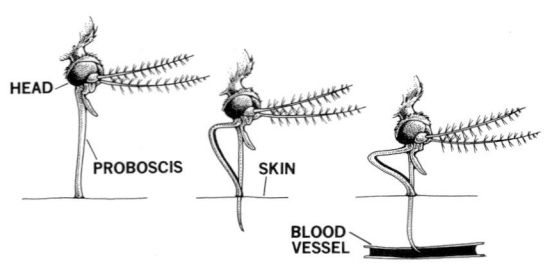

How do mosquitoes bite?

The mosquito feeds primarily on the sugary fluids of plants, flowers, and fruit. Its mouthparts include a long sucking tube, the **proboscis,** with which it drinks these fluids.

Only the female can pierce the skin of animals, including humans, and "bite." Along the sides of the female's proboscis are rodlike blades with spade-shaped ends. The female uses these blades to slice through the skin. Into the wound she secretes an anesthetic chemical, which deadens nerve endings, and an anticoagulant, which keeps the blood from clotting as it is drawn up. The itch of a mosquito bite is the reaction of the body to these chemicals. The female digests the blood, and some of the proteins in it are used to ripen her eggs.

Females are attracted to their victims by means of organs in their heads that are sensitive to heat and chemicals. They can detect the trail of warm, moist carbon dioxide exhaled by all humans and other mammals.

ten days, depending on the species and the climate. If the water in which the eggs are laid is cool, the development will take longer. If the air and water are very warm, then the development will be faster.

Carriers of Disease

Some species of mosquitoes act as vectors, or carriers, of serious diseases. They may transmit disease from animals to humans or from one person to another. Females spread disease by biting, but some parasites are carried on the outside of the mosquito's body and can be spread by touch. The illnesses that are spread by mosquitoes include yellow fever, malaria, and various forms of encephalitis.

For this reason, people have long tried to control populations of mosquitoes and stop their spread. Among the methods tried has been the use of chemical sprays. Since chemical sprays such as DDT have harmful effects on other forms of life, including birds and fish, other methods of control are now favored. These methods include encouraging the spread of natural enemies, such as certain flies, and the spread of diseases that attack mosquitoes. One of the simplest and most effective methods is to drain swamps and puddles and to remove even small quantities of water where the insects develop.

People who live and work in an area of the world where mosquitoes are plentiful should use repellent sprays and should dress to cover most of their bodies. They should avoid wearing dark clothes and should sleep protected by screens or netting.

WILLIAM WHITE, JR.
Author, *The Mosquito: Its Life Cycle*

MOSSES. See FERNS, MOSSES, AND LICHENS.
MOTELS. See HOTELS AND MOTELS.
MOTHS. See BUTTERFLIES AND MOTHS.

MOTION, NEWTON'S LAWS OF

You see things in motion around you everywhere. Cars move along highways. Water flows in rivers. Airplanes cross the skies. The planets move through space around the sun.

All of these motions take place in accord with three simple scientific laws. These laws were thought out about 300 years ago by the English scientist Isaac Newton. Newton's three laws explain how things move and how motions change.

▶NEWTON'S FIRST LAW OF MOTION

When you throw a ball into the air, you say that the ball is in motion. When the ball lands, it rolls along the ground until it comes to a stop. Then it is no longer in motion. Objects that are not in motion are said to be "at rest."

Newton's first law of motion says that **an object in motion tends to stay in motion.** The first law also says that **an object at rest tends to stay at rest.**

You can demonstrate the first law of motion with the following experiments. You will need a toy cart with a smooth, flat top. (Or simply nail a smooth piece of wood over the top of an ordinary toy wagon.) Put a brick or some other heavy object on the cart. If you jerk the cart into motion, you pull it right out from under the brick. The brick does not move along with the cart when you jerk the cart away.

Now put the brick back on the cart and push on the cart. Let it run into a wall while it is moving quickly. The wall stops the cart, but the brick slides along the top of the cart until it also hits the wall.

You have observed two facts about motion. First, when the brick was at rest, it tended to stay at rest. Second, when the brick was in motion, it tended to stay in motion.

You have probably noticed these effects on your own body. If you are in an automobile that starts moving suddenly, your body presses back against the seat of the car. Your body is at rest before the car begins moving, and it tends to stay at rest. If the car comes to a sudden stop, your body pitches forward. Your body is in motion, and it tends to stay in motion. This tendency to continue at rest or continue in motion is called **inertia.**

Forces

A **force**—a push or a pull—is needed to overcome the inertia of an object. That is, a

An object at rest on a cart will tend to stay at rest. It is left behind if the cart is quickly pulled away.

When the object is in motion, it tends to keep moving—even when the cart beneath it suddenly comes to a stop.

force must be used to put a resting object into motion. A force must also be used to stop a moving object or to change its motion while it is moving.

To put the cart in motion, you push on it with your hand. Suppose you want to change the direction in which the cart moves. You must pull or push on the cart from another direction. You can speed the cart up or slow it down, but in each case you have to use force.

If no forces act on a moving object, it will stay in motion forever. It will keep moving along at the same speed and in the same direction.

But you have noticed that things in motion come to a rest even when no force seems to be pushing against them. If you roll a ball on the ground, the ball soon comes to a stop. When your cart is moving along the floor, you do not have to push against it to make it stop. The cart eventually stops moving even if it does not run into anything.

The cart tends to stay in motion at first. Then why does it come to a stop? An unseen force is at work to stop the cart's motion. This force is called **friction.**

Friction is a force between two surfaces that works against movement. One of the surfaces tends to work against, or **resist,** any motion of the other surface. There is friction between the floor and the wheels of the cart. The floor resists the motion of the wheels. That is why the cart soon comes to a stop. Friction exists between any two surfaces that touch, slide, or roll on one another.

▶NEWTON'S SECOND LAW OF MOTION

An object moves because a force is applied to make the object move. The speed of the object depends on how strong the force is.

You can demonstrate the relationship between force and speed by performing a simple experiment with your cart. You also need a spring scale, which you can buy in a hardware store.

Acceleration and Force

Attach a rubber band to the front of the cart, and hook the spring scale to the rubber band. Pull the scale lightly with one hand while holding the cart in place with your other hand. Read the scale to see how hard you are pulling. Then release the cart and notice its speed.

Next, hold the cart in place again and pull twice as hard on the spring scale. When you release the cart this time, it moves forward much more quickly. If you could measure the speed of the cart each time, you would find that the cart moved forward about twice as quickly the second time.

Your cart is accelerating when it starts moving. Any change in the speed of an object is called **acceleration.** An increase in speed is sometimes called positive acceleration. A decrease in speed is negative acceleration, or deceleration.

Pulling twice as hard on the cart made the cart move about twice as fast. If you pulled three times as hard on the cart, you would make it move three times as fast. Newton's second law of motion states this relationship between force and acceleration: **The amount of acceleration depends on the strength of the applied force.**

Acceleration is a change in speed. Acceleration can also mean a change in direction. A force is needed to change the direction of an object. Thus a change in force can mean a change in direction as well as a change in speed. Newton's second law of motion includes change in direction as well as change in speed. According to the law, **the change in direction of a moving object depends on the applied force.**

A football player can kick a football hard and send it into the air quickly. The weaker force of a small child's leg makes the ball move more slowly. This shows that acceleration depends on the strength of the applied force.

Acceleration and Mass

There is another part to Newton's second law of motion. You can observe it in the following experiment. First, weigh your cart. Now attach a rubber band and spring scale to the cart again. Pull on the scale while holding the cart in place. Notice the reading on the scale. Let go of the cart and see how much it accelerates.

Next, add weights to your cart until the cart weighs twice as much as it did before. Hold the cart in place again and pull on the scale. Make sure you are pulling just as hard as you did the first time. When you release the cart, you see that there is less acceleration of the cart and bricks. A certain amount of force will accelerate a light object more than it will a heavy one. The amount of acceleration depends on the weight of the object.

In this experiment the cart and its load weigh twice as much as the cart weighs by itself. A scientist would say that the cart and its load have twice as much mass as the cart by itself. (Mass is the amount of matter in an object.) The cart accelerates twice as much without the load as with the load.

Suppose you try to accelerate a bicycle on which you are carrying a friend. You find that it is much harder than when you ride the bicycle alone. You cannot accelerate the bicycle as easily because you are trying to accelerate a greater mass.

If you could measure the force, mass, and acceleration involved in any motion, you would find that they are always related. Newton's second law of motion states this relationship as follows: **A strong force accelerates a certain mass more than a weak force does.**

▶NEWTON'S THIRD LAW OF MOTION

Another word for force is often used in science. The word is **action.** Newton found that every action is accompanied by a response to an action, or a **reaction.** The reaction is also a force, but it acts in a direction opposite to the action. The strength of the reaction is always equal to the strength of the action. Newton's discovery—that **for every action there is an equal and opposite reaction**—is called the third law of motion.

Action and reaction are involved in every motion. You can observe action and reaction easily with a toy balloon. Blow up the balloon and release it. The balloon flutters around until most of the air has escaped from it.

The air escapes from the balloon with a certain amount of force. This is the action. The movement of the balloon around the room is the reaction to the force of the escaping air.

A giant rocket works on the same principle as the toy balloon. Gases explode from the rocket's engine. The action of the gases is very strong because they escape at high speeds and in large amounts. This means that the reaction is equally strong: The rocket rises from the ground and travels into space.

Anyone who has fired a shotgun or a rifle has felt a reaction to an action. The action is the force that drives the bullet out of the rifle barrel. The reaction is the rifle's "kick"—its push against your shoulder.

The motions of planes in the sky, of planets around the sun, and of people when they walk, all take place in accord with Newton's three laws of motion. All objects at rest tend to remain at rest. Objects in motion tend to remain in motion. The force, mass, and acceleration involved in any motion are always related to each other in the same ways. And whenever there is an action of any sort, there is always an equal and opposite reaction.

Reviewed by SERGE A. KORFF
New York University

See also ENERGY; NEWTON, ISAAC; RELATIVITY.

MOTION PICTURE INDUSTRY

On the downtown streets of most American cities in 1910 a passerby was sure to come across a curious and very gaudy store. Large posters hung outside the store advertising the merchandise inside. One poster in bright colors might picture a sinister man dashing off into the night chased by a policeman. "The Baffled Burglar" would be the words beneath. Another might show a sturdy newsboy helping an old gentleman across the street. "Poor but Honest" would be the title underneath this scene. The store was a **nickelodeon**, where the first movies were shown for the price of a nickel.

Motion picture cameras and projectors were developed at the very end of the 19th century. The first movies were brief scenes without plots and were called **flickers**. Flickers were often no more than travelogues or pictures of sports events.

The man who is usually given the credit for turning movies into a dramatic medium is Georges Méliès (1861–1938). Around the turn of the century he established a studio in Paris and made a series of imaginative fantasies. He used all the known techniques of still photography, such as double exposure (putting one picture on top of another), and dissolving (fading a picture).

▶ **MOVIEMAKING IN THE UNITED STATES**

Edwin S. Porter (1870?–1941) made the first American film to tell a story, *The Great Train Robbery* (1903). The film lasted 8 minutes and was enthusiastically greeted. Other movies with "cops and robbers" plots followed. These movies, of course, were silent.

When movies were young—and women's hats very large—audiences needed reminders like this.

Why do motion pictures seem to have "motion"?

Motion pictures really do not move. They are a series of still shots flashed on the screen so quickly that the eye seems to see a continuous action shot because of "persistence of vision." This enables the human eye to see the picture for a moment even after it has been taken away. Actually the screen goes black for a split second between each picture, as the film is moved into the beam of light inside the projector. The light throws the picture on the screen, and the projector moves on again.

By 1912, printed subtitles were flashed with the action to tell the audience what was happening. A tireless pianist played throughout the picture, switching from fast, dramatic numbers to more sentimental music as the mood of the picture changed.

The great advance in movies came in 1915 when David Wark Griffith (1875–1948) produced a 3-hour film, *The Birth of a Nation*. This was a story about the American Civil War and the Reconstruction (rebuilding of the South). Not only did it deal with a controversial subject—the story was told from the viewpoint of the bitter, defeated South—but it developed and refined camera techniques. Long shots, close-ups, and very imaginative editing (arrangement of shots) brought the audience into the historical setting and held it spellbound. Full orchestras in the theater pits played a specially composed musical and sound-effects score. *The Birth of a Nation* was the first epic of the American screen.

The year before, in April, 1914, the first large theater was built for the showing of films. The theater held 3,000 people. The era of size and grandeur in motion pictures had arrived.

Slowly the little nickelodeons were expanded into large theaters, although the life of the nickelodeons was lengthened by the introduction of the serial. The serials were divided into 20-minute episodes. A new episode was shown each week. Each episode was arranged so that the hero or heroine was left in a perilous predicament at the end. The serials were called cliff-hangers because the hero or heroine was often left hanging dangerously over a cliff. The audience had to wait until the next week to find out what happened.

Silent movies had become a big business in 20 years. No longer were films made by small, independent producers. Big combinations of producers in a few companies, or studios, produced most films. Among these were Paramount, Warner Brothers, Universal, and United Artists. During and after World War I there was a general movement of producers to California. Hollywood, an area within Los Angeles, became the center of production of American films. Soon Hollywood acquired the reputation for glamour that has made it a famous name around the world.

▶ THE STAR SYSTEM AND SILENT PICTURES

Almost from the beginning of movies the public was particularly interested in the leading actors and actresses, called **stars**. The success of a film depended largely on the popularity of these players. Within this **star system** the various actors and actresses had their own distinctive qualities.

Charlie Chaplin was called the Little Tramp, because he always appeared in baggy trousers and a battered derby hat. Buster Keaton always kept a straight face. Harold Lloyd wore horn-rimmed glasses. But these comedians had skill as well as a personal trademark. Their slapstick and pantomime were a real art.

Another kind of trademark was the vampire, or vamp role. A "vamp" meant a sleek, beautiful woman, fatally attractive to men. Theda Bara was the first vamp. She was soon followed by Gloria Swanson and eventually by the "It" girl, Clara Bow. Each created her own brand of vamp.

Rudolph Valentino was the most popular symbol of masculine glamour. His most fa-

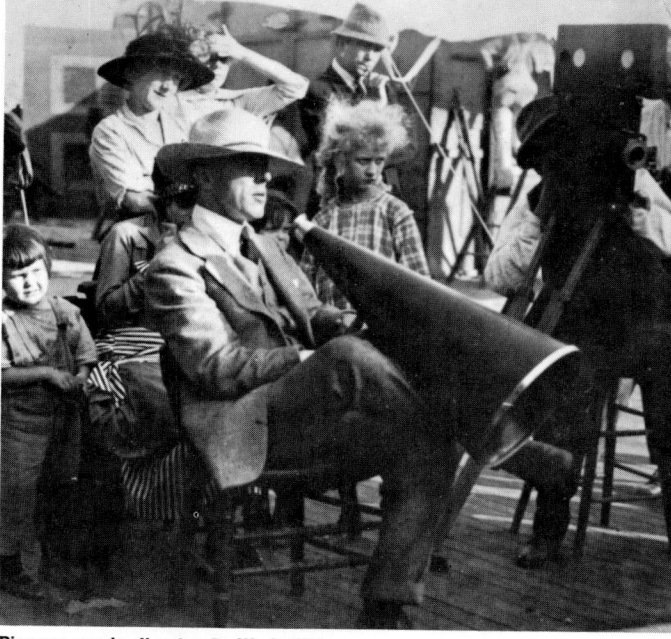

Pioneer movie director D. W. Griffith.

mous picture was a desert picture called *The Sheik* (1921). Lon Chaney was a character actor who played a variety of cripples and monsters in movies such as *The Phantom of the Opera* (1925) and *The Hunchback of Notre Dame* (1923). The Gish sisters, Lillian and Dorothy, were distinguished dramatic stars. William S. Hart and Tom Mix were the leading cowboy actors.

Above all, there were Mary Pickford, "America's Sweetheart," and Douglas Fairbanks, the most dashing, athletic, and romantic of men. Mary Pickford was the ideal of innocence and purity. Douglas Fairbanks played beautifully costumed heroes, as in *The Thief of Bagdad* (1924), *Robin Hood* (1922), and *The Black Pirate* (1926). This

Left: Harold Lloyd in a scene from *Safety Last.* Right: Charlie Chaplin in his famous role of the Little Tramp.

last film was the first outstanding film done in color photography.

Epic films geared for these stars became more frequent and included more startling effects. About this time Cecil B. De Mille directed his first religious spectacle, *The Ten Commandments* (1923). The most expensive production in the era of silent films was Frank Niblo's adaptation of Lew Wallace's novel, *Ben Hur, a Tale of the Christ* (1926). This picture cost over $4,000,000 to make. The chariot race, which climaxed in a spectacular accident, was the high point of the picture. (A second version of *Ben Hur,* made in the 1950's, was equally successful.)

▶ THE ARRIVAL OF SOUND IN MOTION PICTURES

In the mid-1920's movies were threatened by a new rival, radio. Many people stopped going to the movies. The industry was haunted by the fear that movies were doomed.

Then an amazing thing happened. Scientists in the United States and abroad simultaneously discovered a way to add sound to silent pictures. The first sound pictures were short films of concert performers. To the surprise and delight of the audience they could hear the music as the performer played it.

But it wasn't until a film called *The Jazz Singer,* starring Al Jolson, came along in October, 1927, that the possibilities of sound were suddenly revealed. Three song numbers and a few lines of spoken dialogue were introduced in the otherwise silent film. The public response was overwhelming. In a season when other films were doing indifferent

> Sounds consist of vibrations, or waves. Microphones in a movie studio pick up the sound waves and change them into electrical patterns. The electrical patterns are then put along the edge of the film and are known as the sound track. When the film is shown, either a beam of light or an electromagnet changes the patterns of the sound waves back into the original sounds.

business, *The Jazz Singer* packed them in. Customers flocked to see it, fascinated by the picture that "talked." The talking film, or talkies, had met the competition of radio.

After the success of *The Jazz Singer* it took over a year for the full transition from silent to all-talking films. There were many mechanical problems. The equipment had to be perfected. Sound projectors and sound tracks had to be standardized so that films could be shown in all theaters. The sound projectors themselves had to be installed in the theaters. There were also new problems in writing, directing, and acting in pictures with dialogue.

Stage playwrights and top dramatic authors were hastily recruited to write dialogue. Stage directors were rushed out from New York to direct stars who, in most cases, did not know how to talk in their roles. Many romantic leading men turned out to have squeaky voices, and the vamps could not always match their alluring looks with an alluring voice. Many silent-screen stars were finished when sound pictures took over. Sadly enough, sound pictures led to the fall of the great pantomime comics, too.

Pictures with music, in the nature of musical comedies, came into style. *The Coconuts*

Left: Rudolph Valentino as the romantic Arab chieftain in *The Sheik*. Right: Douglas Fairbanks and Mary Pickford in Shakespeare's *Taming of the Shrew*.

Left: Shirley Temple, a child star of the 1930's, with noted tap dancer Bill "Bojangles" Robinson. Right: Clark Gable and Vivien Leigh in a scene from *Gone With the Wind.*

(1929) introduced the four Marx brothers to the movie audience in a new kind of noisy, gag-studded, knockabout farce. Their brand of comedy, like that of W. C. Fields, depended as much on the humor of the dialogue as it did on the art of pantomime. But even these madcap comedians eventually faded.

A type of talking picture known as the sophisticated comedy was developed to fill the vacuum left by the comedians. This kind of film placed people wise in the ways of the world in unexpected situations. Carole Lombard, Irene Dunne, Myrna Loy, and William Powell were memorable performers in these roles.

Soon after the turn to sound came the gangster pictures. The earliest gangster films, such as *Little Caesar* (1930) and *Public Enemy* (1931), were inspired by prohibition racketeering. These violent melodramas introduced a harsh realism. A new crop of masculine stars, including James Cagney, Edward G. Robinson, Clark Gable, and Spencer Tracy, came in with this kind of movie.

The golden age of sound had arrived. The screen was crowded with fine dramas, sleek comedies, and strong adventure films. In the musical field, the top favorites were the Jeanette MacDonald–Nelson Eddy operettas and the dancing team of Fred Astaire and Ginger Rogers.

One of the best-loved movies of this period was *The Wizard of Oz* (1939). This popular children's story was done in color with Judy Garland as its star. Judy Garland was then a 15-year-old girl and one of the top teen-age actors in a period that offered Shirley Temple, Deanna Durbin, Jackie Cooper, and Mickey Rooney.

Walt Disney's feature-length animated cartoon *Snow White and the Seven Dwarfs* delighted grown-ups and children alike. The producer had begun to make cartoon shorts before the transition to sound. These shorts made cartoon characters such as Mickey Mouse as famous as any movie star.

The end of the 1930's and the so-called golden age of sound came to a climax with the production of *Gone With the Wind* (1939). This dramatic story of a southern family during and after the Civil War was made from Margaret Mitchell's best-selling novel. The picture was in color and had an all-star cast headed by Clark Gable and Vivien Leigh. With its elaborate costumes and sets, and spectacular effects, such as the burning of Atlanta, *Gone With the Wind* was the most highly publicized and most commercially successful movie up to that time.

Documentary Films

A documentary film presents factual, historical, political, or social events that sometimes consist of actual news films accompanied by narration. Robert Flaherty (1884–1951) in the United States and John Grierson (1898–1972) in England developed the documentary movie. These men believed that

Filming *Nanook of the North,* one of the first great documentary films.

the film camera offered wonderful possibilities for recording the ways in which people's lives are influenced by their backgrounds.

Working with a silent-movie camera, often under hard conditions, Flaherty journeyed over the globe to make a group of documentaries that today are still recognized as classics. In the frozen Arctic he photographed *Nanook of the North* (1922). *Moana* (1925) was filmed in the South Sea islands. *Man of Aran* (1934) was about Irish fishermen of the barren Aran Islands. Flaherty's documentaries emphasized the raw beauty of these isolated lands and the struggle of people to live in them.

John Grierson's first documentary, *Drifters* (1929), followed a herring fleet at sea and was very much in the spirit of Flaherty's work. But Grierson's real achievement was turning the documentaries into factual studies of problems that all people were facing. His purpose was often to point up an existing evil.

By the mid-1930's moviemakers in many countries were following Grierson's approach. *The March of Time* series began in the United States. These 15-minute surveys covered newsworthy events, with a news commentator to explain the background of the pictures.

With the firing of the guns that began World War II, providing information to the people became very important. John Grierson set up the National Film Board of Canada in 1941. Grierson's film board, along with the

Office of War Information in the United States and the military services themselves, made documentaries throughout the war. These documentaries brought to the screen reports of mobilization (preparation for war) on the home front and actual combat pictures from the battlefields.

Most documentaries were short and dealt strictly with actual happenings. But as the 1940's ended, two feature-length documentaries opened in commercial New York theatres, and they made history. One was *The Quiet One,* a sensitive study of a troubled black child in Harlem. The other was *The Titan. The Titan* was a factual re-creation of the life and career of the Italian artist Michelangelo.

Feature directors started to use an approach to their stories similar to that of the documentary. In Italy the development of the so-called neorealist films was taking place. Neorealist films tried to give the impresssion that a camera had just caught people in their natural actions. The actors were photographed in natural surroundings in ordinary street clothes, but the situation or mood was exaggerated. *Open City* (1945), one of the first neorealist movies, describes Roman resistance to the Nazis. The movie is set in the poor section of Rome, and Nazi brutality is realistically presented. Other Italian movies, such as *Shoe Shine* (1946) and *The Bicycle Thief* (1949), treated their material so realistically that the pictures seem to have been taken from life itself.

In the United States an experienced documentary producer, Louis de Rochemont, used New York City as the setting for *The House on 92nd Street* (1945). This movie was based on an actual case of wartime spying. Other De Rochemont productions showed that movies could be made more lifelike by filming in towns and using nonprofessional supporting actors.

Hollywood was now making more realistic films. But the threat of television was just around the corner, and the industry was soon to need all of its skills.

▶THE EFFECT OF TELEVISION ON THE MOVIE INDUSTRY

The film industry, rich from war profits, at first did not worry about television. But by 1950 the variety of television programs and the number of broadcasting stations had increased tenfold. It was clear to the movie people that the industry was losing attendance in staggering numbers to a competitor even more dangerous than radio.

Hollywood hoped to find a physical improvement in movie projection that would make movies more spectacular than television. They needed something as startling as the addition of sound had been in the twenties.

The technicians first brought back stereoscopic, or **three-dimensional**, films, which had

been developed before the war. When viewers put on special glasses, they seemed to see not flat pictures but three-sided figures. Most 3-D movies specialized in horror and sensation. Pots of boiling wax seemed to be pitched at the audience, and in one sequence a Ping-Pong ball attached to a paddle was batted at the audience. However, the glasses were not comfortable to wear, and 3-D pictures never really caught on.

In 1952 the movie industry brought out a new projection system called **Cinerama**. Cinerama filled a giant wall-to-wall curved screen. The image was thrown by three projectors. Each covered one third of the screen. The three images were joined along

Director Cecil B. De Mille discusses a scene with actors in a 1934 version of *Cleopatra*.

Director Joseph Mankiewicz coaches an actor in the 1964 version of *Cleopatra* while Elizabeth Taylor waits in background.

the match lines to give the appearance of one image.

The pictorial effect was powerful, especially when **stereophonic sound** (several loud-speakers around the theater) made the viewers feel that the action really was taking place all around them. But Cinerama could only be shown in a few theaters specially adapted for it. The mechanism for Cinerama was bulky and difficult to operate. Something more practical was needed for use in all theaters. A wide-angle lens was developed that could be fitted on a single standard projector. This lens threw a reasonably wide, faintly curved image on the screen. The new process was known as **Cinemascope**.

The larger screen, along with stereophonic sound and brilliant color, led to larger and longer films, known as blockbusters in the movie industry. The blockbusters helped the movies regain lost audiences.

The old-time movie studio setup, with emphasis on the attraction of the stars, has become a thing of the past. Rising production costs have brought about fewer films, and the budgets are now watched more carefully. Some large movie companies also house thriving television production plants on their studio lots. United Artists has stopped movie production completely and now only distributes and finances films made by other companies.

More and more pictures are being made outside of Hollywood by independent producers. Independent producers are people who finance and control their own pictures and often get financial backing from private sources.

Furthermore, the studios can no longer afford to keep high-salaried players under permanent contract. Stars used to be under contract to one studio only. They made a certain number of films for set fees. Sometimes they were "loaned" out to another studio if that studio offered an attractive deal. The stars had little choice of the kind of movie made under this kind of contract. But established stars demanded fantastic sums before they would sign a contract. However, many of these famous stars arrived late or not at all for a day's shooting, and the cost of the picture soared as day after day of incomplete work passed.

This system became impossible for both studios and stars. Many established actors have formed their own independent companies. They make their own movies and put themselves in the roles they want to play.

▶ **TELEVISION**

A fair balance appears to have been reached in the realtionship between motion pictures and television. Television offers a great variety of programs, including many of the Hollywood movies turned out during the prosperous movie years in the 1930's and the 1940's. At the same time, attendance at theaters is satisfactory once more.

Today, the television and the movie industries work together. Not only have the Hollywood studios sold their old movies to television, but several of them are now in the business of making movies especially for television. Hollywood stars and directors have long been working in television shows. In turn, television is providing the studios with actors, directors, and story material for films.

Pay television became popular in the 1970's. For a fee, people have been able to watch programs that they would not be able to see on regular commercial television. Pay television brings many fairly new Hollywood movies right into the home. It is not yet known what effect pay television will have on movie theater attendance. Movie attendance remains good. But as rising production costs drive up the prices of movie tickets, many people may prefer to watch movies on pay television.

▶ **HOW A MOVIE IS MADE**

The key people in movie productions are the **producer** and the **director**. The producer usually makes the selection of story or idea behind the movie, borrows the necessary money, and makes the deals with the director and the actors. In general, the producer sets the wheels in motion so that a picture can be made. Occasionally, pictures are produced and directed by one person.

The director controls the filming of the picture and is the mastermind behind the finished movie. In the past, Hollywood directors have been very bitter about the role of studios. They have felt that the studio interfered in the actual making of the movie. Today, many directors have solved this problem by becoming independent.

Skin divers prepare underwater camera for filming Jacques-Yves Cousteau's *World Without Sun*, a documentary of undersea exploration.

Moviemakers often leave the studio lot. Cameramen stand on scaffold to shoot a scene from spy comedy *Blindfold* on location in New York's Central Park.

Before the production of a movie can get under way, the **script** must be prepared. In the early days film stories were usually written specially for the screen. Today, they are drawn mainly from successful stage plays or novels or even from television plays. Such material is often selected with a particular star, or maybe several stars, in mind. The stars themselves sometimes contribute ideas on how the story should be presented.

When the story and actors have been selected, a screenplay is worked out. Writers are assigned to make the adaptation. First, they arrange the story into scenes, called treatments. New scenes are often added. Then the writers either adapt dialogue from the

original or completely rewrite it. The finished script is called the **shooting script**.

Then the technical crew is assembled. The **art director**, the **costume designer**, **makeup people**, the **camera operator**, and many other specialists make up the technical and stage crews.

The art director balances the visual aspect (look) of the locations or sets, the costumes, and the general appearance of the actors and goes over the script to find out what sets will be needed. Movies are photographed either on specially built sets or on location. Movies filmed on location are filmed in natural settings. That is, a movie that is supposed to take place in a well-known city, such as

Between takes of a rain scene in *My Fair Lady* director George Cukor talks to star Audrey Hepburn. Plastic wrappings protect cameras and cameramen from the machine-made rain.

Left: Moviemakers in China prepare to shoot a historical adventure film. Right: Setting up a scene for *The Bible*, filmed in Sicily.

Movies are often shot on location for authenticity. Here a Hollywood company films a pioneer river-crossing scene in Wyoming.

New York, is usually filmed in that city's actual streets and buildings. If part of the movie is set in the mountains or by the sea, the art director will look for a real place that suits the script. The art director must also plan for sets. Perhaps a landslide is part of the plot. Obviously the art director cannot find a real landslide taking place, and it would be too dangerous even if found. Instead, the art director arranges through a department known as **special effects** to have a fake landslide take place on a small copy of a mountain.

The art director also designs houses or sometimes whole towns as sets for the scenes not shot on location. For a costume movie, the art director must reproduce the exact furnishings and architectural style of the period. A walk through a Hollywood studio shows what a wide range of knowledge an art director must have. In just a few steps a visitor might pass an old Western town, a Viking village, and an elegant 18th-century drawing room. These sets cost millions of dollars.

The costume designer works with the art director and matches the style of the costumes with the period of the movie. The designer must also make the actors' clothes suit the characters they are playing.

The job of the makeup crew is to put the right kind and amount of makeup on the actors so that they photograph well. The makeup crew, by drawing lines on an actor's face or even by applying putty to the face, can make an actor look younger, older, or more evil or achieve any effect that may be needed. The makeup people work their magic with a vast supply of jars, tubes, and brushes. But the real magic is the skill with which they handle their materials.

For certain parts of a picture, the director may even call in **assistant directors**. These people have their own crews and camera operators. A spectacular fire, a wild chase, and a sinking ship come under the direction of an assistant director, who is told by the director to film an action sequence. It is often left up to the assistant director to decide how to film it to get the most thrilling effect.

Another specialist is the **montage expert**. "Montage" is a confusing word because it has different meanings in different countries. In Europe, montage is the science of editing the film to arouse feeling in the audience. In Holly-

To simulate a volcanic eruption, a special-effects crew built a volcano of mud about 15 meters (50 feet) high.

wood it has a more limited meaning. Montage is used there mainly to show quick passage of time. For instance, six months of a singer's career can be shown in six minutes by a montage expert. The expert plans a quick sequence of shots of a concert hall, an airplane taking off, a Christmas tree, another concert hall, and finally a spring thunderstorm. If the montage is well done, the audience accepts the time change.

The director and the experts pass on their ideas to the camera operator. Although there is a general camera plan for each scene, the director literally thinks out loud. The chief camera operator is responsible for carrying out the director's orders but rarely touches a camera. The actual filming is done by a crew of assistants working under the chief camera operator's direction.

Hundreds of other people work on a movie, adjusting lighting, arranging for props, and generally helping each head person get the job done.

Filming the Movie

When a film is ready to be photographed, it is not shot from beginning to end. The shooting script is broken down into numbered scenes. All the scenes that will be shot on the same set have the same key. Usually the

For convenience, many scenes are shot by using models, which appear life-size on the screen. Here a special-effects crew films a simulated airplane landing.

A camera operator crouches in a specially built pit to film a charging football team.

Camera crew works waist-deep in water to shoot mine-flooding scene in *How Green Was My Valley.*

outdoor or location scenes are shot first. Then the indoor scenes are shot in a regular film studio.

The director has the controlling hand during shooting, telling the actors what is expected of them in each scene. They work out with the director the gestures and interpretations of dialogue to create the right mood.

Often a scene is rehearsed before it is shot. Even after the scene has been worked out, the director may stop the actual filming if the scene is not going well. Shouts of "Cut!" are part of every picture. "Cut" means that the camera operator is to stop filming. Sometimes the director will be satisfied with the first shot, or "take." But often, dozens of takes are made of one scene. At the end of the day, the director and staff go over the **rushes.** Rushes are prints of the scenes filmed that day. If the rushes do not satisfy the director, the scenes are filmed again.

It may take from 20 days to several months to finish a picture. When all the photography is finished, the prints of the film go to the film editor, or cutter. The editor takes the separate shots and puts them together in a pattern. It is in the editing that the pace and rhythm of the film are created. Most directors, certainly the best ones, also supervise the editing, or cutting, of their pictures. The film is put together in what is called a **rough cut.** The recorded music is placed on the sound track along with the dialogue. The editor then runs the rough cut through and makes the final arrangement of shots.

The completed picture is turned over to the **distributor.** The distributor is usually the company that has contracted for the making of the film and probably also provided the money to make the picture. The distributor sets the release date for the film and starts advertising and publicity in newspapers, magazines, and radio. The distributor also arranges the **bookings,** or showings, of the film, first in theaters in the larger cities and later in smaller communities. The first bookings are usually in New York and Los Angeles.

Most theaters are operated independently of the producing and distributing companies. The theaters pay a percentage of the total amounts of money taken in at their box offices to the distributing company as rental for the film.

A 20-room set was built to speed production of *The Ladies' Man.* Comedy star Jerry Lewis perches on camera crane at left.

An upstate New York town of the early 19th century was re-created on a Hollywood studio lot for a film about life on the Erie Canal.

Alfred Hitchcock, famous director of suspense films, supervises the shooting of *Torn Curtain*.

▶ THE DEVELOPMENT OF FILMS IN EUROPE

Movies began in Europe in much the same way that they did in the United States. In fact, the first spectacle, *Quo Vadis?*, came from Italy in 1912. *Quo Vadis?* inspired movie-makers all over the world to put out huge costume dramas involving gigantic casts and hair-raising dramatic effects.

For a time after World War I, American films were the ones most available to the moviegoing public. The Germans, Russians, Swedes, and Danes were making excellent movies, but they were not being widely distributed. American movies were sold as package lots to English and European distributors. Often the distributor had to buy the rights to a second-rate movie in order to get a big spectacle. Also, if a movie was successful, American film distributors would sell a block of similar movies with the same cast and the same type of situation. This system did not offer much variety of plot or cast to European audiences.

There were many differences between moviemaking in Europe and in America. First of all, there was no European Hollywood. Movie directors did not belong to huge companies. They could choose the kind of picture they wanted to make. Also, they had more control over the actual filming of the picture because they did not have to follow the wishes of a producer.

While American film companies concentrated in general on plots that showed off different stars, European directors tried to combine movie themes with the intellectual movements of the day.

The Cabinet of Doctor Caligari was one of the first movies that tried to draw the audience into another person's mind. The movie was photographed as if seen through the eyes and imagination of an inmate of an insane asylum. It was directed by Robert Weine in Berlin in 1919. Most of the movie's eerie effect came from the strange settings. Wavy lines painted on the floor and walls created a topsy-turvy world. For instance, the absurdity and pomposity of red tape is clearly shown when the protagonist tries to get the attention of an official seated on an exaggeratedly high stool.

Directors in other countries, too, were experimenting with movies. Sergei Eisenstein (1898–1948), a famous Russian director, used a then-new editing technique (montage) in a movie called *Battleship Potemkin* (1925). By cutting his film with great artistry, he achieved powerful effects of rhythm and mood. Like *The Cabinet of Doctor Caligari*, *Potemkin* was silent. *Potemkin* is based on the true story of a revolt by the crew of the battleship *Potemkin*. The crew were starving because they could not eat the rotten food given them. Eisenstein used very realistic close-ups of the meat to shock the viewer into sympathy with the hungry sailors. Later, when soldiers fire into a peaceful crowd, his camera focused on the pain and fear of individuals in the crowd. Eisenstein's use of montage has served as a building block for future movies.

René Clair (1898–1981), the French director, once compared the making of a movie to the building of a house. His movies were so carefully planned that each tiny detail contributed to the over-all mood. He specialized in comedies. His *Italian Straw Hat* (1927), a silent film, followed the chase for a straw hat during a ridiculous wedding. In the next few years Clair used sound very effectively to make several comedies in the same vein. The picture that is considered his best by many critics, *A Nous La Liberté* (1932), was a more serious criticism of life in a world beginning to be mechanized.

Jean Vigo (1905–34), another French director in the 1930's, made two outstanding movies before his death at age 29. His work had great influence on the so-called French New Wave movies of the late 1950's and early 1960's. Vigo's movies had a dreamy, misty quality because of his artistic use of the camera. *Zéro de Conduite* (1932) presents school life through the eyes of a rebellious boy. The head of the school is a dwarf. A pillow fight is shot in slow motion so that the boys seem to be drifting in a snowstorm of flying feathers. Vigo used these unusual approaches to make the audience sympathize with the boys and see the evils of the French school system.

The approach of World War II brought a very moving appeal from the French director Jean Renoir (1894–1979). His movie *La Grande Illusion* (1937) shows the mutual respect and understanding that exist between a French and a German officer during World War I. In the film, Renoir shows that the social structure of prewar European society which was the basis of the officers' relationship was rapidly disappearing.

The British lagged behind other countries in film production because they were in direct competition with the massive output of Hollywood. However, by the mid-1930's, with their characteristic ability to laugh at themselves, the British had become experts at turning out comedies and mysteries.

Alfred Hitchcock (1899–1980) began his career in England in 1920. His movies *The Man Who Knew Too Much* (1934, remade in 1956) and *The 39 Steps* (1935) were among his first exciting spy thrillers. Both films were as full of tricks and surprises as his movies and television shows of 30 years later. *The 39 Steps* had a special Hitchcock ending—the spectacular shooting of the spy Mr. Memory and a chase for the killer through a crowded theater.

▶ FILMS FROM 1940

In 1941, Orson Welles' (1915–) production of *Citizen Kane,* regarded as one of the most important films ever made, was released. It introduced many new and creative cinematic techniques to tell the story of a wealthy man as seen from varying points of view. The film contains montage, deep focus (when everything within the frame is in focus), and unique camera angles to make each scene unusual and effective.

The motion pictures distributed by Hollywood during the war years (1941–45) were generally not of high quality, but the public was eager for entertainment. There were a few distinguished pictures about the dramatic aspects of the war—*Mrs. Miniver* and *The Story of G.I. Joe*—and films strictly for entertainment—*Woman of the Year, Meet Me in St. Louis, Yankee Doodle Dandy,* and *Going My Way.* Preston Sturges (1898–1959) made many satiric comedies during the early 1940's, such as *The Great McGinty, The Miracle of Morgan's Creek,* and *Hail the Conquering Hero.* These films presented a comic view of life in American small towns. The characters and the situations in which they found themselves were often improbable and very funny.

In an improvised outdoor theater near Cairo, Egyptians watch a government film.

Top left: Many airlines show in-flight movies to entertain passengers. Left: Shipboard movies are very popular with sailors of the United States Navy. Above: Crowds line Tokyo's 150-yard-long "Movie House Street," which has 18 movie theaters. Below: Movie theaters are numerous in New York's Times Square district.

The experience of Hollywood talent in making World War II documentary films tended to change the quality of the American film in the late 1940's from romantic stories to more realistic films. *The Set Up* and *Cross Fire* are fine examples of this new style of film making.

During the German occupation of France in World War II, French moviemaking was severely cut back and, of course, under censorship from the Germans. Movies could not be made that commented directly on the times. However, Marcel Carné (1909–) pointed out the basic injustices of the world in his very poetic movie about two separated lovers, *Les Enfants du Paradis*. The hero is a pantomimist. In the last scene, his face made up in the traditional mask of tragedy, he is carried away by a happy carnival crowd just as he catches sight of his first love.

In the 1940's, Michael Powell (1905–) and Emeric Pressburger (1902–) of Britain began to make impressive films that were successful throughout the world. Among these were *One of Our Aircraft is Missing, Stairway to Heaven,* and *The Red Shoes.* British film makers also introduced a string of comedies and suspense movies and sometimes a combination of the two. Alec Guinness did a series of comedies in the late 1940's and early 1950's in which his gentle, whimsical humor endeared him to moviegoers. Even when he played a criminal in *The Lavender Hill Mob* or the several victims of a mass murderer in *Kind Hearts and Coronets,* not one shudder passed through the audience.

In Japan, during the late 1940's, Yasujiro Ozu (1903–63) produced a series of films depicting a family view of Japanese life. The first of these was *Late Spring.* Ozu's personal feeling for life carried through most of his films. Kenji Mizoguchi (1898–1956) is perhaps best known for his films about women

Italian director Federico Fellini adjusts the camera before shooting a scene. Camera's boom is hidden by tree at right.

and the hardships they have faced. One of his most famous films during the late 1940's was *Women of the Night.*

Russian film output during the 1940's was limited, except for documentaries and the memorable films *Ivan the Terrible, Parts I and II,* directed by Sergei Eisenstein. These beautifully filmed historical dramas were a psychological study of the great Russian Czar Ivan IV.

The 1950's. In the 1950's, moviemaking took on a new dimension. Hollywood film makers found themselves threatened with the novelty and challenge of the small home screen, television. Producers turned to new film techniques to bring audiences back into movie houses. *The Robe* is notable for being the first film in Cinemascope, a wide-screen process that was extended in Todd-AO for the movie *Oklahoma.* But this wide screen served only to present films of average quality in a more impressive manner.

During this period of transition, Hollywood also turned out *On the Waterfront, The Man With the Golden Arm, The Moon is Blue, Rebel Without a Cause,* and *Blackboard Jungle,* which were popular and controversial because of the issues they presented.

Hollywood musicals—extremely ambitious

CAMERA TERMS

Close-up—A photograph taken at close range to show a face, hands, a pair of shoes, etc.

Dissolve or **lap dissolve**—Putting one picture on top of another. The top picture slowly fades, and the bottom picture comes on brighter.

Fade in—Gradually putting a picture on a blank screen.

Fade out—Gradually taking a picture away.

Flashback—A break in the sequence of the plot to show a scene, incident, or event that took place earlier.

Moving camera—A camera that moves along with the action, such as for a film taken from a fast-moving car.

Pan shot—Swinging the eye of the camera over a whole scene.

Slow motion—If the camera is speeded up when the picture is taken, and the film is then shown at normal speed, the action on the screen appears to be slowed down.

efforts with opulent color and special effects—were very popular throughout the 1950's. Among the more distinctive films were *The Bandwagon, An American in Paris,* and *Singin' in the Rain.*

In Italy, Federico Fellini (1920–), who worked on the script of Roberto Rossellini's *Open City,* used neorealistic elements in such films as *The Nights of Cabiria* and *La Strada,* the story of the relationship of a simple peasant girl and a brutal carnival player. The movie follows their travels through the poverty-stricken Italian countryside. The contrast of the realistically photographed scenes and the wistful face of the girl tells the story so well that very little dialogue is needed or used.

Michelangelo Antonioni (1915–), another Italian director, filmed his movies realistically, but he used even less plot than Fellini did. Antonioni's most important films during the 1950's were *Le Amiche, Il Grido,* and *L' Avventura.*

French films of the early 1950's hit a peak with Rene Clement's (1915–) *Forbidden Games,* a story of two children on a farm in wartime France. Two other important French films of this decade were by Henri-Georges Clouzot (1907–77)—*The Wages of Fear* and *Diabolique,* an ingenious murder mystery.

The Swedish director Ingmar Bergman (1918–) developed an impressive command of film techniques to explore questions about the inner self, the relationship between men and women, and the meaning of life. In the 1950's he also filmed romantic comedies, such as *Smiles of a Summer Night,* but he became increasingly concerned with people's sense of guilt and failure. In *Wild Strawberries,* a successful doctor questions his life to discover whether he is worthy of the honor he has received. The movie takes place while the doctor is driving with his daughter-in-law on his way to accept an honorary degree. His life is revealed in a series of dreams and flashbacks.

During the 1950's, the Japanese motion picture industry produced many fine films. *Good Morning,* directed by Yasujiro Ozu, is about schoolchildren and their families. In the late 1950's and early 1960's, Ozu did a series of films based on a family and their interrelationships covering the years from World War II to 1962. These were *The Tokyo Story, The End of Summer,* and his last film, one of his most important, *An Autumn Afternoon.* Kenji Mizoguchi, who earlier directed *Women of the Night,* presented *The Life of O-Haru* and *Ugetsu,* a beautiful film about reality and fantasy. Akira Kurosawa's (1910–) best-known films of the 1950's were *Rashomon, The Seven Samurai,* and *Throne of Blood,* a version of Shakespeare's *Macbeth* set in feudal Japan.

India turned out hundreds of motion pictures, many of them showing the beauty as well as the traditions of India, but few were seen by international audiences. Satyajit Ray (1922–) directed the exceptionally beautiful *Apu Trilogy.* These three films describe the struggles of a boy away from his native village.

▶ **THE NEW WAVE AND THE 1960's**

At the beginning of the New Wave era, English directors tended to anchor their pictures in very clear plots—often taken from literature and the stage. The first of these was *Look Back in Anger.* Adapted from a John Osborne (1929–) play, it marked the beginning of a series of the "angry-young-man" films. Pictures following this trend were *Saturday Night and Sunday Morning, Room at the Top,* and *The Loneliness of the Long Distance Runner.* The stark photography and often brutal language marked a new era for socially realistic film making.

The French New Wave, which had its start in 1959, perhaps was not as pungent or powerful as the British in terms of content, but it was extremely vital in changing the form and style of films in many countries. New Wave directors possessed a thorough knowledge of the history of film and a sure sense of style. They elevated the visual aspects of movies and revived devices that had been used by early film makers. Old concepts of plot and character that had lost their force were abandoned. Characterization and mood became more important than conventional plot development.

François Truffaut (1932–84) studied the character of a confused boy in *The 400 Blows.* After a series of notable films, Truffaut made *Stolen Kisses* and later, in 1971, *Bed and Board,* successful sequels to *The 400 Blows.* These three films, somewhat autobiographical in nature, show the character named Antoine Doinel from adolescence to marriage. Another

French director, Alain Resnais (1922–), often deals with the interior of the mind. After the success of his first feature, *Hiroshima, Mon Amour,* he directed *Last Year at Marienbad,* a series of disconnected scenes that attempt to reproduce the fleeting images of two people's minds. A later film by Resnais, *La Guerre est Finie,* shows the motivations of a Communist working to liberate Franco's Spain, and how he comes to realize that the methods of the Communist Party are dated and ineffectual.

Jean-Luc Godard (1930–) began his film career in 1959 with *Breathless,* a film about a Humphrey Bogart-like hero. His later films, such as *La Chinoise* and *Weekend,* are concerned with political ideology and the suffering of people under capitalism.

In the 1960's, Federico Fellini directed *La Dolce Vita,* a portrait of decadence in modern Rome. His later film *8½* examines a director's doubts and fantasies when faced with the ordeal of making a new film that he feels he cannot make. *8½* takes place at an Italian health spa. One scene involves a huge dream-like tower that perhaps symbolizes the fragility of human life and hopes. Pier Paolo Pasolini (1922–75) brought to the screen *The Gospel According to St. Matthew,* a filmed version of the story of Christ, who is seen essentially as a peasant-prophet.

Michelangelo Antonioni, in 1961, directed *La Notte* ("The Night"). Using very little plot, Antonioni's film deals with the strained relationship of a couple during a 24-hour period. By giving the characters vague problems that are never solved, Antonioni is trying to show how people cannot communicate with each other.

Luis Buñuel (1900–83), a Spaniard who began his film career in France in the 1920's, made some of his best films during the 1960's, among them *Viridiana* and *Belle de Jour.*

Interest in films from Czechoslovakia was aroused by the release in the late 1960's of *The Shop on Main Street,* a moving and revealing tale of anti-Semitism in wartime Slovakia, made by Jan Kadar (1918–) and Elmer Klos (1920–). *Loves of a Blonde* and *The Fireman's Ball,* both directed by Milos Forman (1932–), were very popular in many countries.

During the decade of the 1960's, some African countries began to develop motion picture industries. However, most of the early films did not receive worldwide distribution until the 1970's. *Mandabi,* the work of Senegalese novelist-film maker, Sembene Ousmane (1924–), was one of the first, and perhaps the most significant African film, to be released internationally.

In American films, the first half of the 1960's was marked by impressive, spectacular movies. *West Side Story, Lawrence of Arabia, Exodus, The King of Kings,* and *The Guns of Navarone* were extremely successful at the box office. *Cleopatra,* costing in excess of $30,000,000, was one of the most expensive and certainly one of the most talked-about films ever made. Immensely popular, too, in the mid-1960's were *My Fair Lady,* a musical adapted from *Pygmalion,* a play by George Bernard Shaw; *The Sound of Music,* based on the story of the Trapp Family Singers; and *Dr. Zhivago,* a filmed version of the well-known novel about the Russian Revolution.

A popular series of fast-moving, violence-cluttered films, based upon the stories of Ian Fleming (1908–64) and his invincible secret agent James Bond, began with *Dr. No* in 1963 and continued with *From Russia With Love, Goldfinger,* and others. The acceptance of excessive violence in the James Bond films brought about a demand for pictures with similar content. Films like *Bonnie and Clyde, The Dirty Dozen,* and *The Wild Bunch* were only three that emphasized and romanticized the idea of brutality.

It was also during the 1960's that American independent film makers and the film industry produced several successful dramas that explored relationships between blacks and whites. Notable among these films were *One Potato Two Potato, Nothing But a Man, Guess Who's Coming to Dinner,* and *In the Heat of the Night.*

By the late 1960's and early 1970's film producers throughout the world were using words, ideas, and stories that up to that time had never before been shown on the American screen. *Who's Afraid of Virginia Woolf?, Ulysses, Faces, Midnight Cowboy, Chelsea Girls, Trash, Easy Rider,* and *I Am Curious Yellow* are some of the films of this period that caused great controversy and debate over existing censorship laws and boards.

The *Star Wars* series was remarkable for extraordinary special effects and the imaginative re-creation of outer space. In one of the many spectacular scenes in *Return of the Jedi*, an Imperial Star Destroyer approaches the new, unfinished Death Star.

As a result of a series of decisions by the Supreme Court, censorship was almost completely abolished in the United States. In its place, the film industry set up a system of classifying movies according to their suitability for viewing. This system was mainly intended as a guide to parents. It was not intended as a restraint upon filmmakers.

▶ FILMS SINCE 1970

Film directors, rather than motion picture stars, appeared to be the drawing cards at the box office in the 1970's. Mike Nichols (1931–), whose film *The Graduate* was one of the all-time box office hits, followed this success with *Carnal Knowledge, The Day of the Dolphin,* and *The Fortune.* Stanley Kubrick (1928–), the director of the mammoth *2001: A Space Odyssey,* filmed two novels, *A Clockwork Orange* and *Barry Lyndon.* Robert Altman (1925–) made one of 1970's biggest and funniest hits, *M*A*S*H.* Altman's later films were not always consistent moneymakers, but *McCabe and Mrs. Miller, Thieves Like Us,* and *Nashville* all received great acclaim. Francis Ford Coppola (1939–)

made films on organized crime, *The Godfather* Parts I and II, that were successes. So was his *Apocalypse Now,* set in Vietnam.

Italian directors Federico Fellini, Michelangelo Antonioni, and Vittorio De Sica (1901–74) continued to produce impressive movies in the 1970's. Fellini directed *Satyricon* and *Casanova.* Antonioni filmed *Zabriskie Point* and *The Passenger.* And De Sica gave his audiences *The Garden of the Finzi-Continis* and *A Brief Vacation.* Italy's Lina Wertmuller (1930?–) also proved her skill as a director, with *The Seduction of Mimi, Love and Anarchy,* and *Swept Away.*

François Truffaut not only directed but acted in his film *The Wild Child,* about a young boy who lived his early years as a wolf in a forest. In a different mood, Truffaut made the celebrated *Day for Night* and *The Story of Adèle H.*

Ingmar Bergman's stark psychological dramas *Cries and Whispers* and *Scenes from a Marriage* were enhanced by the performances of Liv Ullman. Jan Troell (1931–) made *The Emigrants* and *The New Land,* also starring Liv Ullman. These were films about a group of Swedes who decide to build a new life in America in the 19th century.

Japanese director Akira Kurosawa's film *Dersu Uzala* received worldwide acclaim.

Looking Back. Nostalgia played a major role in American films in the 1970's. *The Last Picture Show, Paper Moon,* and *At Long Last Love,* all dealing with the past, were directed by Peter Bogdanovich (1939–). George Roy Hill (1922–) directed *Slap Shot, The Sting,* and *The Great Waldo Pepper.* John Schlesinger (1926–) brought *The Day of the Locust,* Nathanael West's novel about Hollywood during the 1930's, and *Marathon Man* to the screen. Roman Polanski (1933–) filmed the notable *Chinatown,* a fictional detective melodrama based on actual events in Los Angeles in the 1920's. *Mean Streets,* a film about crime in an ethnic neighborhood in New York City, and *American Graffiti,* about a night in the lives of a group of California teenagers, were set in the early 1960's.

Musicals also dealt with the past. *Let the Good Times Roll* was filmed at concerts in which such famous 1950's musical performers as Fats Domino, Bo Diddley, and Chuck Berry re-created their earlier performances. *That's Entertainment* was a compilation of clips from MGM musicals from 1929 to 1958. *Grease* was about teens in the 1950's.

A number of contemporary musicals were done in the form of documentaries. The 1970's saw the very popular *Woodstock* and *Gimme Shelter.* Other notable musicals were *Tommy, Jesus Christ Superstar, Godspell,* and *The Wiz.* Although not a musical, *Saturday Night Fever* featured excellent music and disco dancing.

Disaster and Laughter. Disaster films made their mark in the 1970's. One of the most successful was *The Towering Inferno,* a film about a fire that envelops the top 50 floors of a new skyscraper. Other popular films of this type included *Airport* and *Airport 1975, The Poseidon Adventure,* and *Earthquake.* On a smaller scale, though more frightening, was *Jaws,* a film about a shark that terrorizes a summer resort community.

Comedy in films was provided by two writer-actors, Mel Brooks (1926?–) and Woody Allen (1935–). Brooks's *Blazing Saddles* and *Young Frankenstein* and Allen's *Bananas, Sleeper,* and *Love and Death* were all popular hits.

Women in Films. Filmmakers showed an increasing awareness of the role of women in films. *Cesar and Rosalie, Happy New Year,* and *Part-time Work of a Domestic Slave* are examples of European films dealing with this theme. In the United States, actresses felt they had finally made some headway in an industry that had seemed to be increasingly dominated by male superstars. Diahann Carroll, the star of *Claudine,* was one of the many American actresses who gave strong performances in substantial roles. Joanne Woodward starred in *The Effect of Gamma Rays on Man-in-the-Moon Marigolds* and *Summer Wishes, Winter Dreams.* Ellen Burstyn gave excellent performances in *The Exorcist* and *Alice Doesn't Live Here Anymore.* Jane Fonda and Vanessa Redgrave won critical acclaim for their roles in *Julia.* Gena Rowlands captured the frustrations of many modern women in *Minnie and Moskowitz* and *A Woman Under the Influence.* Jill Clayburgh was hailed for her performance in *An Unmarried Woman.*

Documentary Films. A number of outstanding documentaries appeared in the 1970's. Marcel Ophuls' *The Sorrow and the Pity* recorded the French reaction to the Nazi occupation of France during World War II. *I. F. Stone's Weekly* was a portrait of I. F. Stone, the well-known American journalist. *Antonia: A Portrait of the Woman* showed the sadness of the conductor Antonia Brico and her long fight to establish herself in the musical world. The film *Hearts and Minds* examined attitudes toward the Vietnam War.

Trends. In the late 1970's and early 1980's, the tendency was toward light entertainment and fanciful, sensational films with many special effects. Especially popular were *Star Wars, Close Encounters of the Third Kind,* the *Star Trek* films, *Jaws,* Sylvester Stallone's *Rocky* series, *Raiders of the Lost Ark,* and *E.T. The Extra-Terrestrial.* Woody Allen turned toward more serious fare, such as his films *Annie Hall, Interiors,* and *Manhattan.* But overall, the prospect was for less serious substance and more spectacle in future films.

BOSLEY CROWTHER
Former Film Critic, *The New York Times*

See also ANIMATED CARTOONS; PHOTOGRAPHY; TELEVISION.

MOTORBOATS. See BOATS AND BOATING.

MOTORCYCLES

Some people say the motorcycle is a modern version of the horse, and in many ways this is true. A rider sits on a motorcycle much as if it were a horse. Like a horse, a motorcycle goes farther and faster than the rider could go on foot. And a motorcycle can be ridden along a trail in the backwoods where a car could not go. But a motorcycle can also be used on streets and highways.

A motorcycle is a two-wheeled vehicle powered by a gasoline engine. On the handlebars are controls for the throttle, the clutch, and the brake. The throttle regulates the speed of the motorcycle by controlling the amount of gasoline flowing into the engine. The clutch puts the motorcycle into gear, and the brake stops the motorcycle.

▶ USES FOR MOTORCYCLES

The first practical motorcycle was built by Gottlieb Daimler, a German inventor, in 1885. Since that time, the motorcycle's special characteristics have made it useful in many ways.

Transportation. Motorcycles generally use much less gasoline than cars. Their engines are simpler and less expensive to tune up and repair than car engines. This makes motorcycles an economical way to drive to school or work.

Recreation. Because motorcycles are fun to ride, many people use them for pleasure.

Some people like to carry light luggage on their motorcycles and take long cross-country tours. Other people enjoy riding their motorcycles along dirt trails in the desert, forest, or mountains. Motorcycle racing is a popular sport. Some races over rough country test the rider's skill as well as the speed of the motorcycle.

Professional Work. Many police departments find that motorcycles are just right for their work. Their motorcycles are fast, and because a motorcycle is narrow, it can get through a traffic jam more easily than a car. Forest rangers use motorcycles to patrol rugged country. Motorcycles are used by the armed forces for transportation in remote areas.

▶ TYPES OF MOTORCYCLES

Motorcycles differ in their design and construction, depending on their intended use. They are all similar in that they have two wheels, an engine, a seat for the rider, and other common features. But because riding on a paved road is very different from riding on soft dirt, the motorcycles designed for these conditions are also different.

Dirt Motorcycles. Motorcycles designed for use on dirt roads and trails tend to be small and light because it is difficult to steer a heavy motorcycle over a rough or rocky surface. To keep their weight low, these motorcycles usually do not have headlights and tail-

Motorcycle competitions are spectacular and exciting. Left: A racer takes his motorcycle into the air to hurdle a barrier. Below: Motorcyclists are bunched together at the start of a cross-country race.

lights, license plates, horns, turn signals, or other equipment required on public roads. Often dirt motorcycles have very large wheels, especially in the front, to help them ride up and over rocks and logs. The tires have deep grooves to give traction in soft dirt and mud.

Dual-Purpose Motorcycles. These motorcycles can be used on public roads and on dirt trails. They are designed and built very much like dirt motorcycles. But they are also fitted with the equipment necessary for legal operation on paved roads—lights, a horn, and turn signals. Often this equipment is designed to be easily removed, to protect it from damage, and to reduce weight on dirt trails.

Street Motorcycles. Motorcycles intended for use on paved roads are available in a wide range of sizes. There are small, light models that provide inexpensive around-town transportation. But street motorcycles can be quite large and heavy. The biggest ones are designed to carry two people and their luggage on long trips.

Mopeds. The word "moped" comes from a combination of "motor" and "pedal." In many ways a moped is just a bicycle with a motor. It is pedaled like a bicycle, but once the moped is under way, the motor can be engaged to keep it going. Mopeds are designed to travel at low speeds. They use very little gasoline and are popular for low-cost transportation in many areas.

▶**MOTORCYCLE SAFETY**

Although motorcycles can be useful and enjoyable, they can also be dangerous. Riders must be completely alert for dangerous traffic situations and road conditions. Because riders are not enclosed as they would be in a car, even a small mishap can cause serious injury. That is why it is important for riders to wear safety helmets. Boots, gloves, and heavy clothing that covers the arms and legs also provide valuable protection.

GEORGE ELLIOTT
Editorial Director, *Popular Cycling*

MOTORS, ELECTRIC. See ELECTRIC MOTORS.

MOUNTAIN CLIMBING

Mountain climbing is actually a part of a wider activity called mountaineering. People who lived for generations in the mountains came to know the ways of the mountains. They learned to live easily in them and to move safely through them and over them. Such people are mountaineers, and the exercise of their skill is called mountaineering. When mountaineers used their knowledge and skill to try to climb a particular summit, they became mountain climbers.

For a long time mountaineering and mountain climbing were practiced only because they were useful. Mountaineers might rescue people or lambs that had strayed. They might go hunting where others would not go. Or they might guide travelers over difficult paths and through high passes. But mountaineers would not climb mountains just for fun. People thought there were demons and monsters up in the highest peaks. They stayed away from them as much as they could.

But then in Europe—starting even in the 1300's—a person here and there began to climb mountains simply for the pleasure of

it, as a sport. For instance, the Italian poet Petrarch climbed Mont Ventoux in France in 1335 and described the experience. Instead of being terrified, he rejoiced in the beauty of the view and the closeness to heaven. By 1786, the number of climbers had increased greatly. Many people were eager to scale the unclimbed peaks of Europe. In that year the successful ascent of Mont Blanc in France—the highest peak in the Alps—gave a tremendous boost to mountain climbing as a sport. By 1850, English climbers were going to the Swiss Alps regularly during their summer vacations. Soon every important peak in Europe had been climbed. The tradition of the trained and dedicated Swiss guide was established. And these guides accompanied expeditions that began to explore and climb the other great mountain areas of the world.

Probably the most famous climb was the first successful ascent of Mount Everest in 1953 by a British expedition under Colonel John Hunt. Two members of the expedition, Edmund Hillary, a New Zealander, and

Tenzing Norkey, a member of the Sherpa ethnic group of Nepal, reached the top on May 29. In the 32 years before this, at least eleven attempts had been made to climb Everest, and many lives had been lost. Among those lost were the famous British climber George Leigh-Mallory and his fellow-climber Andrew Irvine, who were last seen heading for the summit during their 1924 expedition.

MOUNTAIN CLIMBING TODAY

After Everest had been climbed, the sport of mountain climbing became more popular than before. Every year there are more climbers, trying peaks by new routes or even by old ones. The list of countries making serious mountaineering efforts keeps growing. Most European nations, of course, have long been actively represented. But now Latin-American countries, from Argentina to Mexico, compete. India, the Republic of China, Japan, Australia, and New Zealand all have climbing clubs. The sport is worldwide. Most large cities with any kind of cliff or mountain nearby will have a local climbing club. The local clubs are often affiliated with national clubs. The most famous and oldest is the Alpine Club of London. In the United States three of the most important are the Appalachian Mountain Club (with headquarters in Boston), the Sierra Club (San Francisco), and the American Alpine Club (New York). The Alpine Club of Canada has its headquarters in Banff, Alberta.

TYPICAL CLIMB

Starting early, a group of climbers may follow a trail up through pastures and woodland. They can, of course, stay on trails all the way to the top of the mountain. Then they will not need any special equipment— only good lungs and strong, healthy legs. Still, if they are wise, they will take along a pack with first aid supplies, warm clothing, and extra food.

But more probably the climbers will leave the path and head up toward something more difficult, such as some steep rock cliffs and ridges. At first the rock may be easy, Grade I rock, which can be climbed with only an occasional use of the hands. Then steeper (Grade II or III) rock may appear. Now the climbers will rope themselves together so that if one slips, the others can keep him or her from falling. If the rock becomes even steeper and more dangerous (Grade IV or V), all the climbers stop in the safest possible spot. The second climber then pays out the rope to the leader, who goes on climbing. Once at a safe spot, the leader brings the others up one by one. If there are no safe spots, a climber can make one by pounding an iron spike, or piton, into a crack in the rock. A steel snap link called a carabiner is fastened to the piton. The climber then puts the rope through the carabiner and so is less likely to fall. Sometimes there is no crack. The climber may then drill a hole and put in a special bolt, which acts as a piton.

Now the climbers may come to a completely vertical or overhanging section of rock with no way around it (Grade VI and above). There is no way for them to climb it using just their feet and hands, and they may have to turn back. But they may be trained and equipped for the special types of climbing developed in the 20th century, such as artificial and tension climbing. The leader will make a ladder of pitons. The climbers below

FIRST ASCENTS OF MAJOR PEAKS

MOUNTAIN	HEIGHT		DATE CLIMBED	DESCRIPTION	LOCATION
	Meters	Feet			
Matterhorn	4,481	14,701	1865	One of the most famous "impossible" peaks to be climbed (by Edward Whymper and party)	Alps
Mount Elbrus	5,633	18,481	1868	Highest in Europe	Caucasus
Kilimanjaro	5,963	19,565	1889	Highest in Africa	Tanzania
Aconcagua	6,960	22,835	1897	Highest in South America	Andes
Mount McKinley	6,198	20,320	1913	Highest in North America	Alaska
Mount Everest	8,848	29,028	1953	Highest in the world	Himalayas
Mount Godwin Austen, or K2	8,611	28,250	1954	Second highest in the world	Karakoram
Kanchenjunga	8,579	28,146	1955	Third highest in the world	Himalayas

Left: A climber rappels down a Swiss mountain. Center: A roped party climbing with crampons and ice axes. Right: A climber uses stirrups and pitons on an overhang.

hold the leader against the top piton while the leader pounds in the next one above. A climber can stand in a stirrup hooked to the piton and may use a short portable ladder to climb farther up.

After the rock, they may come to some ice and snow. So they cut steps with their ice axes. They take steel frames with sharp spikes, called crampons, and strap the frames to their boots. With these they can walk up even a 40-degree slope without slipping.

At last they get to the top and look out at the wonderful view. They can see the beauty of vast expanses of unspoiled mountains. And they feel elated to be higher than anything else they can see. If the climb was especially difficult, they may feel great pride in having gotten up safely. Because they shared the dangers of the climb together, they are keenly aware of the friendship that binds them. Finally, they are likely to experience a great sense of satisfaction in having done something completely different from anything that goes on in the busy world below. These are some of the values that make all the trouble and difficulty worthwhile.

Carelessness may lead to a slip or a fall. Rock or snow may collapse suddenly underfoot. Equipment may be faulty, as well as judgment and skill in using it. Avalanches may come down on the climber. Weather is notoriously unpredictable. It can blot out all landmarks until the way is lost. It can coat rocks with water or deadly ice in a matter of minutes. It can exhaust and freeze and destroy any climber if it gets bad enough. Finally, any kind of sickness may be fatal. Sometimes a climber cannot be carried out or rescued. But part of the satisfaction of climbing is to meet and overcome all dangers.

On the way down, the climbers rappel over the steep spots. This is a way of letting oneself down a rope. Back at the foot of the mountain, they smile with satisfaction. They have had a fine day of climbing.

WOODROW WILSON SAYRE
Author, *Four Against Everest*

See also EVEREST, MOUNT.

The Jungfrau, in the Swiss Alps, overlooks the village of Wengen.

MOUNTAINS

A mountain is a part of the earth's surface that stands high above its surroundings. Mountains differ greatly in size and ruggedness. Some are huge, steep masses thousands of meters high. Others are low and gentle—hardly more than rolling hills. A mountain rises at least 300 meters (1,000 feet) above the surrounding land.

Some mountains are isolated peaks. But more often they are grouped together in a **mountain range**. Some mountain ranges have hundreds or even thousands of peaks. The peaks are joined by ridges and are separated by canyons through which streams flow. Mountain ranges are generally long in proportion to their width. The Cascade Range is about ten times as long as it is wide. Some ranges, like the Swiss Alps, do not run in a straight line but curve like a great hook.

A group of ranges linked together makes up a **mountain system**. These ranges usually are closely related in age, origin, and general direction. For example, the Cordillera of North America includes all the ranges along the western edge of the continent from Alaska to Central America.

Mountains rise not only from land areas but also from the bottom of the sea. In fact, the deep ocean basins—once thought to be mainly flat-floored—are now known to hold some of the mightiest mountains on earth. The island of Hawaii is the upper part of a hugh volcanic mountain in the Pacific Ocean. It is capped by Mauna Kea, 4,208 meters (13,796 feet) high. Over half of this mountain is submerged. If its full height—9,793 meters (32,128 feet) above the ocean floor—is considered, it ranks as one of the world's tallest mountains. The island lies at the southeast end of a submerged chain of mountains about 2,400 kilometers (1,500 miles) long. Only the tops of a few of the highest peaks stand above the water as islands.

Isolated peaks that rise from the ocean floor are called **seamounts**. A few reach the surface, but many of them are deeply submerged. Some seamounts have curious flat tops. They are called **guyots**.

People have always wondered how mountains form. Early ideas were rooted in mythology and superstition. Today's theories are based on careful study of rocks, the materials of which mountains are made. This study is part of the science of **geology**.

A theory popular for many years held that the earth was once much hotter than it is now. As it cooled, it shrank, forming mountains as wrinkles on its surface. Modern studies have disproved this simple theory and have shown that the true story is much more complicated.

Most mountain systems have developed along narrow belts of heating and movement in the earth's crust. The mountains did not rise immediately. Their rise was preceded by a chain of events that lasted millions of years. This chain of mountain-forming events is called **orogeny**.

Orogeny begins with the sinking of a long, narrow furrow in the earth's surface, usually on the sea floor near the edge of a continent. The furrow deepens, forming an oceanic trench hundreds of kilometers long and thousands of meters deep. The Marianas Trench in the western Pacific, with a depth of 11,033 meters (36,198 feet), is one of the deepest places in the ocean. Sinking of the trench is accompanied by **earthquakes** and often by **volcanism**. Earthquakes are strong shocks that travel through the earth. They are caused by sudden breaking and movement of deeply buried rock—a process called **faulting**. Volcanism is the rise of hot, molten rock from deep in the earth and its eruption onto the surface.

As the trenches sink, they become partly filled with sediment that washes in from their sides. Thousands of meters of sediment accumulate. And the more deeply buried material becomes compacted and hardened into **sedimentary rock**. The sedimentary layers may be interlayered with **igneous (volcanic) rocks** (lava) that were erupted on the sea floor while the sediments were being deposited. A trench might continue to sink and to trap sediment for millions of years. Eventually it stops sinking and fills to the top. Huge sediment-filled troughs like this are called **geosynclines**, and they mark the site of future mountain ranges.

Deep within the geosyncline the layers of sedimentary and volcanic rock become intensely squeezed. Forces press in from the sides, bending the layers into folds. In places the rocks are broken and shoved past one another along slippage (or fault) surfaces, causing earthquakes. In the most deeply buried parts of the geosyncline, the rocks become very hot and are changed into new rocks made of high-temperature minerals. These are called **metamorphic rocks**. In places the rocks get so hot that they melt, forming huge pockets of molten material called **magma**. Under intense pressure this liquid magma is squeezed up along cracks and other weak places in the rocks above, like water being squeezed from a sponge. Some of the magma may work its way up to the earth's surface, where it erupts and builds volcanoes. But much of the magma cools and solidifies (like water turning to ice) while still underground, forming masses of **plutonic rock**. Granite is a familiar example of plutonic rock.

Thus, the geosyncline, which began as a down-sinking trough, has become filled up, heated, and deformed. It now consists of thousands of meters of folded and faulted sedimentary, volcanic, and metamorphic rock, crosscut by masses of plutonic rock. Sinking has stopped, and the geosyncline begins to rise.

Gradually the earth bends upward, forming a belt of rising land dozens of kilometers wide and hundreds of kilometers long. As the land warps up, some rocks bend. Others break and move along faults. As the land becomes higher, **erosion** begins. Water from melting snow trickles down from the high places and collects into creeks. These join to become rivers. The swift-flowing streams wash away the soil and rock and gradually cut channels. Slowly, over tens of thousands of years, these channels are widened and deepened into **canyons** by stream erosion. The canyon walls are eaten back farther by landslides. These landslides carry loose rock and earth to the streams, where they are washed away. Ridges and peaks begin to take form between neighboring canyons. They are the remnants left by erosion.

On high, cold mountains the winter snow does not all melt away. It accumulates into thick masses that compact into ice. When the

NOTABLE MOUNTAIN PEAKS

PEAK	Meters	Feet	LOCATION
AFRICA			
Kilimanjaro	5,963	19,565	Tanzania
Kenya	5,193	17,040	Kenya
Margherita	5,119	16,795	Zaïre-Uganda
Alexandra	5,105	16,750	Zaïre-Uganda
Ras Dashan	4,620	15,158	Ethiopia
Meru	4,566	14,979	Tanzania
Karisimbi	4,505	14,780	Zaïre-Rwanda
Mikeno	4,450	14,600	Zaïre-Rwanda
Elgon	4,321	14,178	Kenya-Uganda
Toubkal	4,165	13,665	Morocco
M'Goun	4,070	13,353	Morocco
Cameroon Mountain	4,069	13,350	Cameroon
ANTARCTICA			
Vinson Massif	5,139	16,859	Sentinel Range
Tyree	4,964	16,285	Sentinel Range
Kirkpatrick	4,449	14,596	Queen Alexandra Range
Markham	4,349	14,268	Queen Elizabeth Range
Kaplan	4,299	14,104	Commonwealth Range
Wade	4,290	14,074	Queen Maud Range
Bell	4,269	14,006	Queen Alexandra Range
Anderson	4,253	13,953	Sentinel Range
ASIA *			
Everest	8,848	29,028	Nepal-China
Godwin Austen, or K²	8,611	28,250	Kashmir
Kanchenjunga	8,579	28,146	Nepal-India
Lhotse I (E¹)	8,501	27,890	Nepal-China
Makalu	8,470	27,790	Nepal-China
Lhotse II	8,400	27,560	Nepal-China
Cho Oyu	8,189	26,867	Nepal-China
Dhaulagiri	8,172	26,810	Nepal
Manaslu	8,125	26,658	Nepal
Nanga Parbat	8,108	26,600	Kashmir
Annapurna	8,078	26,502	Nepal
Gasherbrum I	8,068	26,470	Kashmir
Broad Peak	8,047	26,400	Kashmir
Gosainthan	8,013	26,291	China
Distaghil	7,885	25,868	Kashmir
Masherbrum	7,821	25,660	Kashmir
Nanda Devi	7,817	25,645	India
Rakaposhi	7,788	25,550	Kashmir
Kamet	7,756	25,447	India
Namcha Barwa	7,756	25,445	China
Gurla Mandhata	7,728	25,354	China
Ulugh Muztagh	7,724	25,340	China

* In Asia, there are many more peaks higher than 6,100 meters (20,000 feet).

PEAK	Meters	Feet	LOCATION
ASIA (continued)			
Tirich Mir	7,700	25,263	Pakistan
Minya Konka	7,590	24,900	China
Mount Communism	7,495	24,590	U.S.S.R.
Pobeda Peak	7,439	24,406	U.S.S.R.
AUSTRALIA			
Kosciusko	2,227	7,305	New South Wales
Townsend	2,213	7,260	New South Wales
EUROPE			
Elbrus	5,633	18,481	U.S.S.R.
Dykh-Tau	5,198	17,054	U.S.S.R.
Shkhara	5,193	17,037	U.S.S.R.
Koshtan-Tau	5,145	16,880	U.S.S.R.
Dzhanga	5,050	16,568	U.S.S.R.
Kazbek	5,043	16,545	U.S.S.R.
Mont Blanc	4,810	15,781	France-Italy
Adai-Khokh	4,645	15,239	U.S.S.R.
Monte Rosa	4,634	15,203	Italy-Switzerland
Weisshorn	4,509	14,792	Switzerland
Matterhorn	4,481	14,701	Italy-Switzerland
Finsteraarhorn	4,277	14,032	Switzerland
Jungfrau	4,161	13,653	Switzerland
Barre des Écrins	4,103	13,461	France
Gran Paradiso	4,060	13,323	Italy
Piz Bernina	4,055	13,304	Switzerland
Eiger	3,975	13,040	Switzerland
Grossglockner	3,798	12,460	Switzerland
Wildspitze	3,773	12,379	Austria
Leone	3,561	11,683	Italy-Switzerland
Mulhacén	3,478	11,411	Spain
NORTH AMERICA			
McKinley	6,198	20,320	Alaska
Logan	5,951	19,524	Canada
Orizaba	5,700	18,700	Mexico
St. Elias	5,489	18,008	Alaska-Canada
Popocatepetl	5,452	17,887	Mexico
Ixtacihuatl	5,286	17,342	Mexico
Foraker	5,267	17,280	Alaska
Lucania	5,226	17,147	Canada
King	5,173	16,971	Canada
Steele	5,073	16,644	Canada
Bona	5,005	16,420	Alaska
Sanford	4,940	16,208	Alaska
Blackburn	4,919	16,140	Alaska
Wood	4,842	15,885	Canada
Vancouver	4,785	15,700	Alaska-Canada
Fairweather	4,663	15,300	Alaska-Canada
Toluca	4,577	15,016	Mexico
Hubbard	4,557	15,015	Alaska-Canada
Bear	4,526	14,850	Alaska
Walsh	4,505	14,780	Canada
Malinche	4,461	14,636	Mexico

PEAK	HEIGHT		LOCATION
	Meters	Feet	

NORTH AMERICA (continued)

Hunter	4,442	14,573	Alaska
Alverstone	4,439	14,565	Alaska-Canada
Whitney	4,418	14,495	California
Elbert	4,396	14,423	Colorado
Rainier	4,392	14,410	Washington

SOUTH AMERICA

Aconcagua	6,960	22,835	Argentina-Chile
Ojos del Salado	6,873	22,550	Argentina-Chile
Bonete	6,872	22,546	Argentina
Veladero	6,780	22,244	Argentina
Pissis	6,779	22,240	Argentina
Huascarán	6,768	22,205	Peru
Tocorpuri	6,755	22,162	Bolivia-Chile
Libertador	6,720	22,047	Argentina
Llullaillaco	6,710	22,015	Argentina-Chile
Mercedario	6,671	21,885	Argentina-Chile
Yerupaja	6,632	21,758	Peru
Tres Cruces	6,620	21,720	Argentina-Chile
Incahuasi	6,620	21,720	Argentina-Chile
Coropuna	6,613	21,696	Peru
Carnicero	6,611	21,689	Peru
Ancohuma	6,551	21,490	Bolivia
Tupungato	6,550	21,490	Argentina-Chile
El Muerto	6,538	21,450	Argentina-Chile
Sajama	6,520	21,391	Bolivia
Illampu	6,485	21,275	Bolivia
Illimani	6,457	21,185	Bolivia
Toro	6,380	20,932	Argentina-Chile
Tórtolas	6,323	20,745	Argentina-Chile
Chimborazo	6,272	20,577	Ecuador
Pular	6,210	20,375	Chile

PACIFIC ISLANDS

Puncak Jaya (Carstensz)	5,000	16,400	Indonesia
Daam	4,953	16,250	Indonesia
Idenburg	4,800	15,750	Indonesia
Trikora (Wilhelmina)	4,750	15,585	Indonesia
Mandala (Juliana)	4,700	15,420	Indonesia
Wilhelm	4,694	15,400	Papua New Guinea
J. P. Coen	4,589	15,057	Indonesia
Kubor (Herbert)	4,268	14,000	Papua New Guinea
Leonard Darwin	4,234	13,891	Indonesia
Mauna Kea	4,205	13,796	Hawaii
Mauna Loa	4,168	13,675	Hawaii
Giluwe	4,164	13,660	Papua New Guinea
Bangeta	4,107	13,473	Papua New Guinea
Kinebalu	4,107	13,455	Indonesia
Victoria	4,073	13,240	Papua New Guinea
Albert Edward	3,993	13,100	Papua New Guinea
Kerinchi	3,800	12,467	Indonesia
Cook	3,764	12,349	New Zealand
Mahameru	3,676	12,060	Indonesia

ice becomes more than 60 meters (200 feet) thick, it flows slowly downhill like thick tar, forming rivers of ice called **glaciers**. The glaciers are more effective than streams in eroding (wearing away) their channels and carrying loose rock and earth with them.

Thus, stream and glacial erosion slowly but surely carves the rising geosynclinal rocks into canyons and ridges and transforms them into a rugged mountain range. At first, uplift exceeds erosion, and the range becomes higher. But the time finally comes when uplift slows down and then stops altogether. Erosion continues relentlessly, however. Canyons are widened and ridges cut away between them, until rugged mountains are worn down to low, rounded hills and eventually to flat country. But erosion is very slow, and the destruction of mountains may take many millions of years.

A mountain system that is eroded away may leave its "tracks" behind. The tracks are the folded and faulted metamorphic and plutonic rocks that had formed deep in the roots of the geosyncline. These were exposed when the covering rocks were uplifted and eroded away. The remains of many ancient mountain systems have now been traced. A belt of rocks across the flat central part of Canada and the United States (from northern Quebec to southwestern Montana) marks the site of a mountain system that existed approximately 2,700,000,000 (billion) years ago—the oldest mountain system yet recognized on the North American continent.

People have learned much about the origin of mountains, but unsolved problems remain. What causes the geosyncline to sink? Why does it rise to build mountains? Theories have been formed to explain these things, but much more research must be done before the answers are clear.

▶ **TYPES OF MOUNTAINS**

Mountains are not all the same. They are made of different rocks and were formed in different ways during the long process of orogeny just described.

Volcanoes

When hot molten magma rises from within the earth and flows out onto the surface, it cools and hardens into volcanic rock called

Mount McKinley, in Alaska, is the highest peak in North America.

lava. Repeated eruptions build a cone-shaped hill or mountain where the lava piles up around the vent (opening). Such mountains are called volcanoes. For more information about volcanoes see the article VOLCANOES.

Domed Mountains

Some mountains have a rounded appearance and look nearly circular when viewed from the air. Horizontal sedimentary strata (layers of rock) are abruptly bent upward around their edges. This suggests that they were formed by a force pushing up from beneath. These are called domed mountains.

Some domed mountains, such as Elk Mountain in Wyoming, formed where hot magma pushed it from below, forcing up the rock layers above. These domes were like blisters with liquid inside. But the liquid magma soon solidified into hard igneous rock. Later, erosion wore away the outer layers, exposing the igneous core.

Other domed mountains did not form as blisters but were gradually warped by vertical earth forces acting on already solid rock. The Black Hills (South Dakota) and the Adirondack Mountains (New York) are examples. These domes are many kilometers in diameter, and erosion has cut canyons and ridges across their tops.

Block Mountains

The Sierra Nevada is a high mountain range in California. It slopes gently on the west but drops off abruptly on the east in a steep

mountain wall nearly 3 kilometers (2 miles) high. This range is a great earth block about 640 kilometers (400 miles) long and 110 kilometers (70 miles) wide, pushed up along its eastern side and tilted to the west. Its eastern edge is bordered by steep fractures called **faults,** where the earth's crust has broken and moved. The steep, upraised face of the mountain block is called a **fault scarp**.

Mountain ranges bounded by fault scarps are called block mountains because they are upraised blocks of the earth's crust. Some, like the Sierra Nevada, are tilted blocks with a scarp on one side only. Others were pushed straight up and have scarps on both sides. The mountains in the Basin and Range Region of the western United States are mostly block mountain ranges.

Fold Mountains

Some mountains consist of parallel ridges that stretch for many kilometers. They are carved by erosion from tilted, bent layers of sedimentary rock. These upturned strata (layers) are eroded remnants of great parallel earth folds like the folds in a sheet of corrugated iron. The original horizontal strata were squeezed into folds by the powerful forces that accompany orogeny. Later, streams cut down into the folded strata. The water eroded the weaker layers to form valleys. The harder layers remained as ridges.

The Appalachian Mountains, near the eastern coast of North America, are an example of parallel-fold ridges. The Appalachians are old, deeply eroded mountains. They are not nearly so high and rugged as they were shortly after the folding took place, 200,000,000 to 300,000,000 years ago. Much younger fold mountains are found in the Coast Ranges of California. There is evidence that folding is still going on there today.

Complex Mountains

Many mountain ranges are more complicated than the types just described, although they have many of the same features. They are called complex mountains to indicate their complicated structure. The Rockies, the Appalachians, the Andes, the Alps, and the Himalayas are examples of complex mountains. But they differ greatly from one another in detail.

▶ INFLUENCE AND IMPORTANCE OF MOUNTAINS

Mountains have had a great effect on many things that influence civilization. Mountains affect climate and vegetation, the migration of peoples, the way people make a living, and even the course of history.

From early historical times, mountains have formed barriers that limited travel and trade and have separated peoples of different cultures. Steep slopes, impassable canyons, storms, high-altitude cold, and other natural obstacles made mountain travel difficult. Construction of wagon roads and even horse trails was difficult with crude tools. After completion, these routes were still frequently blocked by slides and avalanches. Thus, big mountain ranges were almost as effective as seas in separating primitive peoples.

The Alps and the Carpathian Mountains shielded the peoples along the Mediterranean Sea from the peoples of northern Europe. In Asia the Himalayas were even more effective in separating India from the rest of Asia. What mountain travel there was went through a few mountain passes where valleys from both sides met at low, easily crossed divides. For centuries the Brenner Pass in the Alps channeled most of the travel and trade, as well as invading armies, back and forth from Italy to Austria and the Germanic kingdoms.

High mountain ranges are equally effective as climatic barriers. Moisture-laden air currents sweep in from the ocean and rise over mountains that block their path. The warm, moist air is cooled as it rises to higher altitudes. Condensation occurs, and rain or snow falls. The world's heaviest rainfalls are recorded on the windward slopes of mountains. Dry areas (called rain shadows) are found on the leeward sides (away from the wind).

Vegetation depends on rainfall. Thus, the location of forests and deserts often shows a clear relation to mountain ranges. The Cascade Range—in California, Oregon, and Washington—cuts off the moist air currents sweeping inland from the Pacific Ocean. These mountains are covered with dense fir forests and underbrush on the rainy western slopes. But a few kilometers east of the mountains there is relatively little vegetation.

The kind of vegetation on high mountains also varies according to temperature and elevation. Forests of broad-leaved trees on the warm lower slopes change to conifers (cone-bearing trees) at higher elevations, where it is cooler. These, in turn, give way to alpine meadows with only sparse, stunted trees. Higher still, where it is always quite cold, there is only bare rock. The upper limit of tree growth is called the **timberline**. This level

The Himalaya mountains in Kashmir.

Mount Kilimanjaro, the highest mountain in Africa.

Mount Fuji, the highest mountain in Japan.

A tributary of the Amazon River in the Peruvian Andes.

Mount Cook, the highest point in New Zealand.

occurs at higher elevations on mountains located closer to the equator.

Some of our most valuable natural resources come from mountains. There are forests that provide trees for lumber. Thick forests of fir and hemlock on the western slope of the Cascade Range supply the great logging and lumber industry of the Pacific Northwest. Much of our mineral wealth also comes from the mountains. The immense copper deposits at Butte, Montana, and Bingham, Utah, are in the heart of the North American Cordillera. The copper deposits (among the world's largest) at Chuquicamata, Chile, and the great tin deposits of Bolivia are both in the Andes mountains. Metallic mineral deposits are often found in the mountains because the igneous activity that goes with mountain building is also responsible for the formation of ore.

Electricity is not often thought of as a product of the mountains. Yet dams, where hydroelectric power is generated, are often located in mountainous areas, where lakes can back up into canyons.

Mountains are becoming increasingly important for recreation. Each year more and more people go to the mountains for camping, hiking, climbing, skiing, fishing, and hunting and just to enjoy the view. These activities have become so popular that tourist resorts and ski centers rival the lumber and mining industries in economic importance.

▶ GREAT MOUNTAIN SYSTEMS OF THE WORLD

The great mountain systems—the Cordilleras of North and South America and the Alpine-Himalayan system of Europe and Asia—include most of the world's highest mountains. That is because they are young, geologically, and are still actively growing. Older mountain systems, such as the Appalachians of eastern North America, have been worn down by erosion.

The Cordilleras border the Pacific Ocean from the tip of South America to Alaska. The high mountains end there. But geologically the system continues around the western rim of the Pacific Ocean as submerged mountain ranges with tops that stick out as islands— the Aleutian and Kurile islands, Japan, Taiwan, the Philippines, New Guinea, and New Zealand. This entire circum-Pacific system, as it is called, is a zone of active mountain building marked by frequent earthquakes and active volcanoes. The volcanoes give the mountains of the Pacific rim the name **Circle of Fire,** or **Ring of Fire**.

In the southern part of the Cordilleras, the Andes form a spine of very high mountains along the west coast of South America. The Andes are a complex range geologically, with folded and faulted mountain forms and a chain of recently active volcanoes. Many peaks exceed 6,100 meters (20,000) feet. Aconcagua—in Argentina, near the border with Chile—is the highest point in the Western Hemisphere. The Andes slope westward into Richards Deep, which is part of the Peru-Chile Trench off the northern coast of Chile. From Richards Deep to the top of nearby Llullaillaco, the difference in elevation is about 14 kilometers (9 miles).

The North American Cordillera widens to include all the ranges from the Rocky Mountains to the Pacific Ocean. The Rocky Mountains extend from New Mexico to northern Alaska. They reach their greatest height in Colorado, where Mount Elbert heads a list of more than 50 peaks that surpass 4,300 meters (14,000 feet).

The North American Cordillera is complex geologically. It has evolved throughout the past 150,000,000 years. Some parts of the system are geologically very young. The Sierra Nevada fault block and the high volcanoes of the Cascade Range have risen in the last 1,000,000 years.

The Alpine-Himalayan system is a great curving chain of ranges that runs east-west for more than 9,700 kilometers (6,000 miles) across Europe and Asia. At one end are the Alps, occupying most of Switzerland and parts of France, Italy, and Austria. These rugged, ice-clad mountains are crowned by Mont Blanc in France. They provide some of the most beautiful scenery in Europe. They are complex mountains that began to be uplifted about 40,000,000 years ago.

At the other end of the system are the Himalayas, located along the border between India and China (including Tibet). The Himalayas are a geologically complex range, and they are still rising. Here the highest mountains on earth are spread out in a huge curving wall about 2,400 kilometers (1,500 miles) long. The highest peak, Mount Everest, is located near the middle of the range.

The longest continuous mountain system on earth, strange to say, went unrecognized until 1958. It is a mid-oceanic ridge that rises from the deep floor of the Atlantic Ocean. Except for a few peaks that project as islands, it is submerged throughout its entire length. The Mid-Atlantic Ridge begins near Iceland and extends down the middle of the North and South Atlantic—a distance of more than 16,000 kilometers (10,000 miles). From there the ridge branches out between South Africa and Antarctica into the Indian Ocean. Then it runs between Australia and Antarctica into the Pacific—a total length of about 65,000 kilometers (40,000 miles). The ridge along the middle of the Atlantic Ocean has been known for years. But only recently has oceanographic mapping with modern echo-sounding equipment revealed the full extent of the system.

CLIFFORD A. HOPSON
University of California—Santa Barbara
See also EVEREST, MOUNT; VOLCANOES; names of principal mountain ranges.

MOZAMBIQUE

The nation of Mozambique is located in southeastern Africa, along the coast of the Indian Ocean. A large territory (nearly twice the size of California), Mozambique was for many centuries a colony of Portugal. It won its independence in 1975 after a long and bitter struggle.

▶ THE PEOPLE

Almost all the people of Mozambique are black Africans who speak various Bantu languages. At one time there was a fairly large Portuguese population. Portuguese is still the official language, but most Portuguese left the country after independence.

About 90 percent of the people are farmers who grow food and raise livestock for their own needs. Most live in villages made up of mud and straw-thatched houses arranged around a central plaza.

The majority of the people practice traditional African religions based on the worship of many gods and spirits. There are some Roman Catholics and a large minority of Muslims, most of whom live in the north.

Maputo, Mozambique's capital and largest city, also serves as a major port for several neighboring countries. The city was formerly called Lourenço Marques.

▶ THE LAND

The Zambezi River divides Mozambique into two distinct regions. South of the river is a wide coastal plain, which rises gradually to a high plateau. North of the Zambezi, the coastal plain is very narrow. It rises abruptly to the central plateau and the mountain ranges far inland. In the extreme north, the coastline is made up of high cliffs broken by many rivers.

The climate is characterized by two main seasons—hot and rainy and cool and dry. During the rainy season, temperatures average between 81 and 84°F (27 and 29°C) but are cooler in the interior highlands. Temperatures are considerably lower during the dry season, which lasts from April to October.

Mozambique has valuable mineral resources, including coal, bauxite (aluminum ore), iron ore, copper, natural gas, and gemstones, but most are still untapped. Forests provide wood for lumber. The country's abundant wildlife includes lions, elephants, crocodiles, zebras, rhinoceroses, hippopotamuses, and many different kinds of birds.

▶ THE ECONOMY

Mozambique's economy is based largely on agriculture. The chief food crops are sorghum (a grain) and corn. Cattle, goats, sheep, and chickens also are raised for food. The most important cash crops, on which Mozambique depends for most of its export income, include

FACTS AND FIGURES

PEOPLE'S REPUBLIC OF MOZAMBIQUE (República Popular de Moçambique) is the official name of the country.

THE PEOPLE are known as Mozambicans.

LOCATION: Southeastern Africa.

AREA: 309,494 sq mi (801,590 km²).

POPULATION: 13,700,000 (estimate).

CAPITAL AND LARGEST CITY: Maputo.

MAJOR LANGUAGES: Portuguese (official), various African languages.

MAJOR RELIGIONS: Traditional African religions, Christian (mainly Roman Catholic), Muslim.

GOVERNMENT: Republic. **Head of state and government**—president. **Legislature**—People's Assembly.

CHIEF PRODUCTS: Agricultural—cassava, sorghum, corn, cashew nuts, sugar, cotton, copra (dried coconut meat), tea, livestock. **Manufactured**—processed agricultural products, textiles, consumer goods, light machinery. **Mineral**—coal.

MONETARY UNIT: Metical (1 metical = 100 centavos).

NATIONAL ANTHEM: Begins: "Viva, viva FRELIMO."

cashew nuts, sugarcane, cotton, cassava (a starchy root used as food throughout much of Africa), coconuts, and tea. Prawns (a shellfish similar to large shrimp), which are caught in coastal waters, also are an important export.

The government, which controls much of the economy, has resettled farmers on communal farms to try to increase agricultural production. But droughts in recent years have reduced harvests.

Aside from the manufacture of textiles, consumer goods, and light machinery, most of Mozambique's industry involves the processing of agricultural products.

Mozambique's economy was badly hurt by the departure of many skilled Portuguese technicians after independence. The government has devoted a large part of its budget to technical training for Mozambicans. The government also hopes to expand manufacturing by using hydroelectric power generated by the huge Cabora Bassa Dam on the Zambezi River. Since the dam was completed in 1979, it has supplied electricity to southern Africa, has irrigated land so that more crops could be grown, and has improved navigation on the Zambezi River.

Although Mozambique has the potential for great mineral wealth, its mining industry is still undeveloped. Coal is the only mineral now being produced in any quantity.

Cities. Many of the chief cities and towns lie along the coast and near the Zambezi River. The capital and largest city is Maputo. It is the chief port and the center of the railroad system. Sofala is the second largest city. Other important cities are Quelimane, Inhambane, Nacala, Tete, and Mutarara.

▶ **HISTORY AND GOVERNMENT**

When the Portuguese explorer Vasco da Gama arrived on the Mozambique coast in 1498, it was the first European contact with the region. In 1505, a settlement was founded at Nova Sofala, where the Portuguese set up a profitable gold trade. Other settlements followed. After gaining control of the coast, the Portuguese gradually began to extend their influence inland along the Zambezi River. From the 1600's to the mid-1800's, the slave trade was the colony's chief source of income.

Under later Portuguese rule, Mozambique was considered to be an overseas province of Portugal. In theory, the people of Mozam-

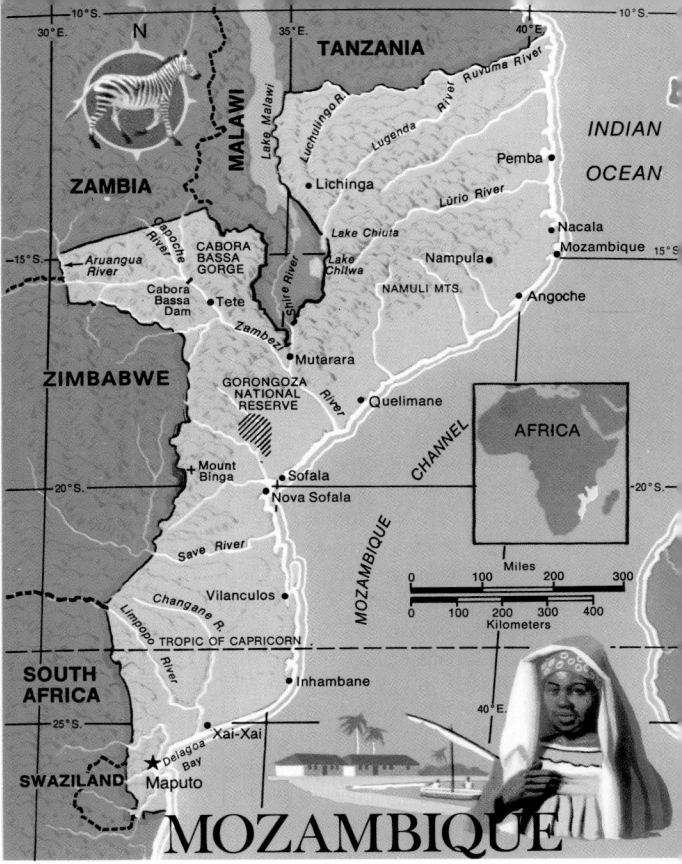

MOZAMBIQUE

bique had equal civil rights and job opportunities with the Portuguese. But they began to demand the right to govern themselves as other colonies in Africa were granted independence. In 1964 the Mozambique Liberation Front (FRELIMO) was formed. It began a guerrilla war that was to last for ten years. When the Portuguese Government was overthrown in 1974, the new government in Portugal acknowledged the right of Mozambique to independence. The country officially became independent in 1975.

The government of Mozambique is dominated by FRELIMO, which is the only political party. The president of the republic, who is head of state and government, is also the leader of FRELIMO. The legislature, the People's Assembly, is made up mostly of party officials.

Samora Machel, a leader in Mozambique's struggle for independence and the nation's first president, was killed in an airplane crash in 1986. He was succeeded as president by Joaquim Alberto Chissano.

ROBERT O. COLLINS
University of California—Santa Barbara
Co-author, *American in Africa*

MOZART, WOLFGANG AMADEUS (1756–1791)

Wolfgang Amadeus Mozart was born on January 27, 1756, in Salzburg, Austria. His father, Leopold, a musician at the Archbishop's court there, was a well-known composer. By the age of 5 Wolfgang was writing little minuets and playing the harpsichord. His father taught him composition, counterpoint, and harmony. His sister, Maria Anna, was an excellent musician too. In 1762 Leopold decided to take his two child prodigies on tour. The children played at the Imperial Court in Vienna. The Emperor was delighted and called Wolfgang "a little magician."

A year later the Mozart family toured Germany, France, and England. Everybody admired Wolfgang. In London, at the age of 8, he wrote his first symphony. Four years later, in Vienna, he composed his first two operas. In 1769 the Archbishop of Salzburg made Wolfgang concertmaster at his court.

In the same year father and son took the first of three trips to Italy, where Wolfgang composed several operas. In Italy the boy studied opera in the country of its origin. He also wrote many symphonies, serenades, sonatas, concertos, and much church music and chamber music.

Wolfgang's salary at the Archbishop's court in Salzburg was rather small. In 1773 his father took him to Vienna to find him a more suitable position but was not successful. In Vienna they heard the latest symphonies and

The Mozarts: Leopold playing the violin, Wolfgang at the keyboard, and Maria singing.

quartets of Joseph Haydn, whose music deeply influenced Wolfgang.

Wolfgang was not happy in Salzburg. In 1777 he took his mother and set off again for Germany and France to seek his fortune. He found no job, and to complete his misery, his mother died in Paris. So once more he returned to his position in Salzburg. In 1781 he quarreled with the Archbishop and was dismissed from his service. Mozart then decided to settle in Vienna.

▶ MOZART'S VIENNA YEARS

In 1782 Mozart married Constanze Weber, whom he loved very much. Although he was plagued by troubles, including the deaths of his four children and his wife's ill health, his greatest works were written during his years in Vienna. There he composed the operas *The Abduction from the Seraglio, The Marriage of Figaro,* and *Così fan tutte.* There, too, he wrote his famous last three symphonies, his finest piano concertos, and many other masterpieces. He became a friend of Haydn's and dedicated six string quartets to him. The Viennese flocked to Mozart's concerts to hear him play his concertos. He made several trips to Prague, where his opera *Don Giovanni* and the *Prague* Symphony were first performed.

About 1788 Mozart began falling seriously into debt. People found his latest music difficult and stayed away from his concerts. He went to Germany in 1790 but returned to Vienna still more in debt.

In the summer of 1791 Mozart began suffering from fever and severe headaches. However, he completed his opera *The Magic Flute,* which was first performed in September, 1791. His last work, the *Requiem* (mass for the dead), he left unfinished. On December 4 Mozart fell into a coma; he died the following day at the age of 35. The cause of his death is believed to have been typhus. Because he was so poor, Mozart's coffin was dumped into an unmarked pauper's grave. To this day no one knows where this great and unique composer lies buried.

H. C. ROBBINS LANDON
Co-editor, *The Mozart Companion*

MUKDEN. See SHENYANG.

MULRONEY, MARTIN BRIAN (1939–   )

As the leader of Canada's Progressive Conservative (or Tory) Party, Brian Mulroney became the nation's 18th prime minister. In a landslide victory on September 4, 1984, the Progressive Conservatives took over a large majority of seats in Parliament. That automatically made their leader the next head of government. On September 17 the 45-year-old Mulroney was sworn in as prime minister. He succeeded John N. Turner of the Liberal Party.

Martin Brian Mulroney was born on March 20, 1939, in the paper-mill town of Baie Comeau, Quebec. He was the third of six children, and his father was an electrician. Brian grew up in a Catholic, middle-class, English-speaking home. At age 13 he was sent to boarding school in New Brunswick, where French was spoken. His ability to speak both French and English would be a great help in his later careers.

Mulroney received a B.A. degree from St. Francis Xavier University in Nova Scotia and a law degree from Laval University in Quebec. He became an active supporter of the Progressive Conservatives while still a student.

Mulroney was a successful businessman as well as a lawyer, becoming president of the Iron Ore Company of Canada in 1977. Although he was unsuccessful in his 1976 bid for the party leadership, he ran again in 1983 and was elected party leader. He won his seat in Parliament in a by-election in Nova Scotia. In 1984 he led his party to victory.

Two of Mulroney's main goals were increased harmony between the federal and provincial governments and a lowering of trade barriers between the United States and Canada. In 1987, Mulroney and the provincial premiers signed a historic accord under which Quebec accepted the Constitution Act. Later in 1987 a free-trade agreement was reached that would eventually eliminate trade barriers between Canada and the United States.

Reviewed by DESMOND MORTON
University of Toronto

MULTIPLICATION.   See ARITHMETIC.
MUMPS.   See DISEASES.

MUNICIPAL GOVERNMENT

Municipal government refers to government in "municipalities," such as cities, towns, villages, and boroughs. Municipal government is also called local government because it is the level of government that is local, or closest to the people it serves.

Cities, counties, towns and townships, boroughs, villages, school districts, and special districts are units of local government in the United States. Citizens of all ages support their local government through the payment of various taxes and fees. In return, local government provides road maintenance, schools, sewers, water, fire and police protection, and other services as required by its citizens.

The various states have different rules under which a unit of local government may be established. Some units are more characteristic of certain parts of the United States—for example, towns in New England, townships in the Midwest, and counties in the South.

Federal and provincial governments in Canada are modeled on those of England, but Canadian local government units, generally called municipalities, are run much like those in the United States. In some parts of Canada, the population is so small that there is no local government at all. These areas are under direct provincial control.

History

American local government received its heritage from English political institutions. Before the Revolutionary War, charters were given to the American colonies by the king of England. The charter is the basic law of a local government, defining its powers, duties, and organization. As small settlements grew into flourishing towns and cities, they were granted their own charters.

A central system of justice, based on the English court system, was established. Each territory was given a county seat where circuit court was held. The court sessions were held in taverns, the central meeting place for the community, until a courthouse could be constructed. In order to pay the costs of the court system, including the courthouses and jails,

City governments in the United States are normally headed by a mayor. A city manager may be hired to help the daily business of the government run more smoothly.

representatives of the towns were elected to set tax rates. They formed a legislative body, the county board of supervisors or commissioners.

After the Revolutionary War, the power to grant charters was placed in the state legislatures. In most states, charters are granted to municipal corporations and, in some cases, to counties and townships. When a city has its own charter (and therefore its own separate government), it is "incorporated." Some states have "home rule" laws, which grant local governments some freedom to draft their own charters and manage their own affairs.

▶TYPES OF LOCAL GOVERNMENT

There are six basic types of local government in the United States. School districts and special districts are formed to provide specific services. Towns, villages, cities, and counties are composed of the executive (or chief officer's) branch, the legislative (law-making) body, and the judicial (court-related) branch.

The County

The county acts as an arm of the state government to carry out programs such as social services for the poor and health and mental health programs. It also provides services and facilities that are too costly for the town government, such as airports, jails, and major road repair.

The county also supervises elections through its board of elections; sees to the accuracy of business scales through the sealer of weights and measures; maintains law enforcement through the sheriff's department; prosecutes crimes through the district attorney; and selects juries and presides over trials in the county court. The county may also provide parks and playgrounds, libraries, and community colleges.

The chief officer of the county may be a county executive, county manager, or the traditional board of supervisors or commissioners. The county treasurer or finance director assists in preparing the budget. County services benefit the people of all the towns and cities within the county.

Towns and Townships

Towns developed as colonial taxing units to meet expenses for items such as roads, public education, relief of the poor, and a share of the county court costs. The town or township may still provide these services, in addition to fire and police protection, street lights, public libraries, recreational facilities, hospitals, water supply, trash disposal, tax assessments (estimates of property value), and building regulations.

The chief officer may be the town supervisor, town manager, town or township board, or, in the case of the New England states, the town meeting. Town meetings are an example of direct democracy in action. In a direct democracy, the people themselves decide on questions by voting. When the town meeting is not in session, the governing body is the board of selectmen, usually consisting of three to nine members. The power to levy taxes rests with the town meeting, not with the board of selectmen. In many New England towns, a town manager is hired for more efficient local government.

The chief officer plans the budget and supervises the various departments. The town justice or justice of the peace presides over the town court for traffic violations and other misdemeanors (lesser crimes).

The Village. Although it may be located within the boundaries of a town, the village has its own government, with an elected mayor and a board of trustees. Villages developed when clusters of people within the sprawling towns began to need specific services of their own. The village may also have its own court and village justice. Villages and towns often contract with each other to share services.

Cities

Cities are municipalities chartered by the state. New Amsterdam (New York City) received its charter in 1653, followed in 1686 by Albany, New York (formerly the Dutch settlement of Fort Orange). Cities provide large-scale services such as police and fire protection, street lighting, health care and hospitals, education, libraries, recreational facilities, traffic control, refuse disposal, water supply, and mass transportation systems.

City governments often face the additional problem of large populations crowded into limited space in deteriorating older buildings. Urban-renewal boards help to halt housing decay and to obtain federal government funds for new housing construction.

This town receives most of its income from property and other taxes. Most of the money is spent on education, which includes buying textbooks and paying teachers. Some money goes for general government expenses, such as the salaries of town officials. Examples of capital expenditures are a new police car or a new typewriter for the town clerk.

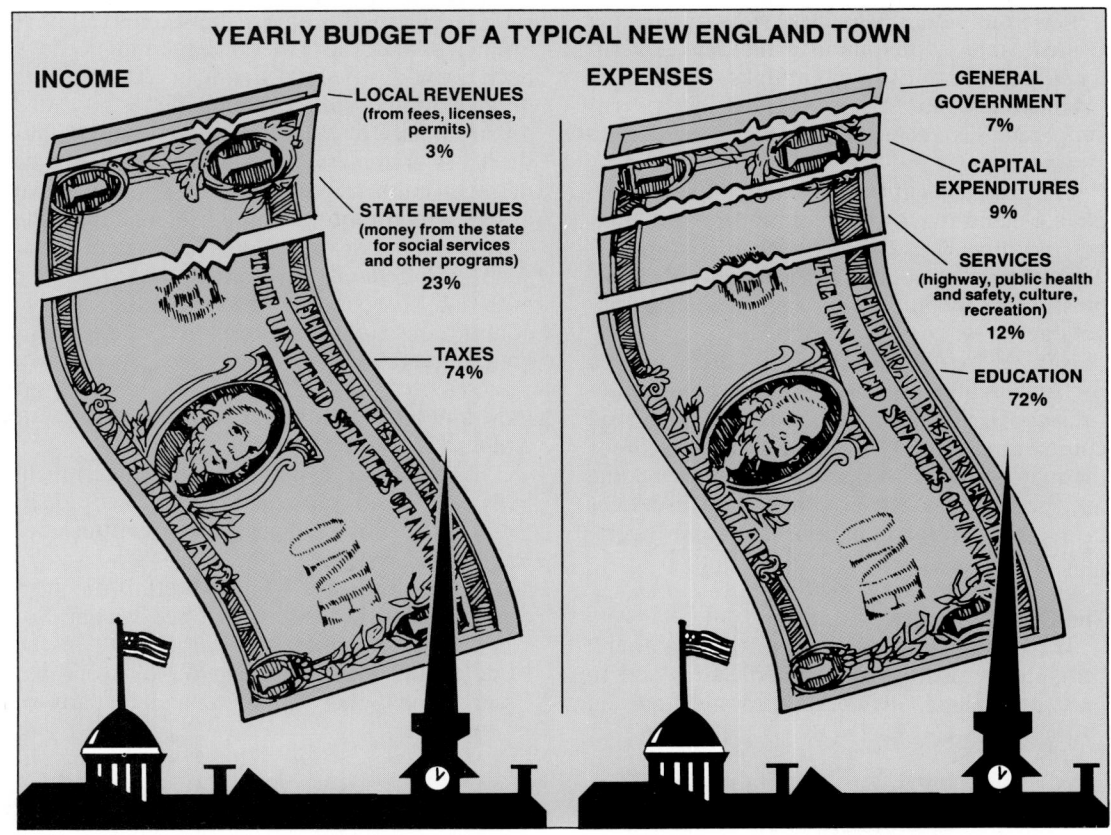

YEARLY BUDGET OF A TYPICAL NEW ENGLAND TOWN

INCOME

LOCAL REVENUES (from fees, licenses, permits) 3%

STATE REVENUES (money from the state for social services and other programs) 23%

TAXES 74%

EXPENSES

GENERAL GOVERNMENT 7%

CAPITAL EXPENDITURES 9%

SERVICES (highway, public health and safety, culture, recreation) 12%

EDUCATION 72%

Forms of City Government. There are four major forms of city government in the United States. One is the **strong mayor-council** form, in which the elected mayor has full power to appoint or remove city officials, administer the departments, prepare the budget, and veto the city council's ordinances or laws.

In the **weak mayor-council** form, the mayor is a ceremonial figure, but the council has strong administrative powers. In the **council-manager** form, the city council hires a professionally trained executive or manager to administer the budget and departments. A **commission** is composed of an elected board whose members administer the various departments and also act as the legislative body or council.

Canadian cities, like those in the United States, are usually headed by an elected mayor and council. Governmental responsibilities are spread among a series of boards and commissions. Canada's largest city, Toronto, has a metropolitan form of government organized like the Canadian federal government, but on a smaller scale.

Cities may have several courts—police court for crimes, city court for civil disputes, and traffic court for traffic violations. They may also have their own jails.

New York City. The largest city in the United States is unique as a regional government, consisting of five boroughs, or counties (Manhattan, the Bronx, Queens, Brooklyn, and Staten Island), with five elected district attorneys.

The chief executive of the city of New York is an elected mayor who administers the budget and supervises the many vast departments. These include social services to the poor, health and mental health facilities, and city colleges.

New York City has a city council headed by the council president, a city comptroller (treasurer), five borough presidents, and 62 community planning districts. The city funds the majority of its services through an income tax, corporation taxes, property taxes, sales taxes, and large amounts of state and federal aid.

The School District

The independent school district is found throughout most of the United States and in parts of Canada. It is organized and financed separately from other units of local government. These districts maintain schools from kindergarten through junior college—depending on the size of the population, the area, and the wealth of the district. A typical school district is governed by an elected board of education, which chooses a superintendent of schools.

Special Districts

Special districts are units that operate separately from the regular governmental machinery. They are established by state law to provide a single service, such as fire protection, water supply, or public housing. These districts may be called authorities, boards, or commissions.

Intergovernmental Relations

Although local units of government are created by the state, they are independent of one another. The county does not control the city, and the school district has no power over the town. State laws have priority over all forms of local government within the state's boundaries, while the laws of the federal government have priority over the state's. But all these units may, and frequently do, co-operate to share services.

In recent years, contacts between local governments and the federal government have been growing. Federal financial aid, which is given mainly to state governments, is now also given directly to local governments. State authority is gradually giving way to the demands of local units for the right to run their own affairs without too much interference from the state. As these developments take place, local, state, and federal governments learn to live with and co-operate with one another. These complex relationships are called intergovernmental relations.

▶MUNICIPAL GOVERNMENTS AROUND THE WORLD

The four basic systems of local government in the world today are the French, the English, the Russian-Soviet, and the non-western, or traditional, systems.

The French System. This pattern is the most common outside the Anglo-American and Soviet world today. It is found mainly in the Middle East and East Asia, Western Europe, Central and South America, and in parts of

Africa. It is structured like a pyramid, with the chief executive at the top and local governments at the bottom.

Metropolitan France has 22 regions, 96 provinces *(departments)*, 322 subprovinces *(arrondissements)*, 3,200 districts *(cantons)*, and about 38,000 municipalities *(communes)*. The municipalities (cities, towns, and villages) are the only units of decentralized local administration.

The chain of governmental authority is from the minister of the interior (national), to the governor *(department)*, to the subgovernor *(arrondissement)*, to the *maire*, or mayor (municipalities). *Cantons*, which are part of the *arrondissements*, are mainly electoral and judicial districts. All public services, such as police and health protection, are under executive jurisdiction. The *maire* of a *commune* is responsible to the local council and the next higher executive official. In this system there is a strong connection between the central, or national, government and the local units.

The English System. English local government can be traced as far back as Anglo-Saxon times. At that time, the English borough, governed by its own officers under crown charters (charters from the king), dominated local government. Modern English local government came into being in the 1800's and was restructured in the 1970's.

England is divided into 6 metropolitan counties that contain 36 metropolitan districts, and 39 non-metropolitan counties that contain 296 county districts and about 10,000 parish councils. The Greater London Council contains 32 London boroughs and the City of London. County councils are responsible for public safety, consumer affairs, housing, highways and roads, traffic control, planning, parks, and waste disposal. District councils are responsible for housing, planning, public health, waste collection, and highways and roads. Other local services are distributed between county and district councils.

The Russian-Soviet System. Before the revolution of 1917, Russia was subdivided into provinces and regions, each headed by a governor with limited power. The provinces were further subdivided into districts, cantons, and villages, or *mirs*. The *mir* was governed by a local council, which elected a leader.

In the Soviet Union today, there are several levels of local government. The first level is made up of large cities and large geographic districts. The second level consists of large towns and medium-sized cities. The lowest level consists of village *soviets* (councils), settlement *soviets*, and small-town *soviets*. All these governments are linked together. Local *soviets* elect a chairperson, a deputy chairperson, a secretary, an executive committee, and standing committees. The Communist Party controls all elections and therefore controls all levels of local government.

Non-Western, or Traditional, Systems. Very few parts of the world have not been influenced by Western forms of local government. But the traditional village community type of government still exists in many places.

Village communities are typically governed by a council, given various names in different lands. In Japan it is the *baraku;* in the Philippines, the *barrio;* and in India, the *panchayat.* Although members of the council and its chief officer are often elected in a modern democratic manner, this type of local government is part of a traditional village way of life that is centuries old.

▶**PROBLEMS OF MUNICIPAL GOVERNMENT**

In the United States and most of the major Western nations, more and more people choose to live in or near cities. Because of the growing populations, municipal and local governments are facing new problems.

They need more money with which to operate and to provide all the services their huge populations require. Even representation in national parliaments and legislatures has become a problem in many Western countries. Populations have shifted, and areas that had many representatives in national government now have small populations. Some areas with large populations have relatively small representation.

It is especially important that these and other problems be solved, for municipal government is the form of government that affects the everyday lives of most people.

EUGENE J. BOCKMAN
Commissioner, Department of Records and
Information Services, City of New York

Reviewed by MARILYN E. ROTHSTEIN
Author, *What Every Citizen Should Know: A Guide to Local Government*

MUSCAT AND OMAN. See OMAN.
MUSCLES. See BODY, HUMAN.

People of all ages enjoy visiting the Louvre art museum in Paris, France. Opened to the public in 1793, the Louvre owns more than 250,000 works of art.

MUSEUMS

Museums are places where collections of objects are preserved and displayed. The objects may be anything found in nature or made by people. There are museums devoted to art, science, history, industry, and technology.

But museums are no longer just storehouses for collections. Today nearly all museums, large or small, carry on educational programs. Museums offer guided tours, lectures, films, music recitals, art lessons, and other attractions. They organize field trips and clubs. They publish pamphlets, guides, and catalogs to help visitors gain a better understanding of the collections. They carry on research programs, the results of which are published so that many people can benefit from them. Many large museums have extensive libraries open to qualified researchers. Often, museums collect more objects than they have room to display. The best are chosen for exhibition, and the rest are kept in a study collection. These study collections can be used by students, researchers, and scholars.

Museums work constantly to improve their collections and ways of displaying them. All museums share a common aim—to attract visitors and help them understand and enjoy the collections. Museums are always on the watch for new additions to their collections. Works of art are bought from art dealers and private collectors or at auction sales. Museums also accept gifts and bequests, but the large museums no longer accept everything that is offered to them. They accept only objects or collections that meet their high standards.

Museums often arrange loan exhibitions of important works from private owners, art dealers, and other museums. In this way, famous works of art may be viewed by people who otherwise might never have had the chance to see them. Several important exhibitions have traveled from their home countries in recent years. Among these are collections of ancient Chinese tomb treasures, art from the buried city of Pompeii, artifacts from the tomb of the Egyptian pharaoh Tutankhamen, and art treasures of the Vatican. Modern shipping methods assure that such priceless treasures can be transported safely.

Almost all the museums in Europe are supported by national or city governments. In the United States the Smithsonian Institution museums are the most important museums that receive support from the federal government. Some of the United States museums are run by the states and some by private groups or colleges. But most museums are supported in part by the cities in which they are located. Additional money is raised through membership dues and private gifts.

What is to be gained from visiting museums? Museum exhibits can teach us about the world in which we live—the materials it is made of, the trees and plants that cover it, and the animals that have lived on it since its beginning. We can learn about the activities of people—their history and development and their accomplishments in arts, crafts, science, and technology. Most people see a great work of art for the first time in a museum. We can see wonderful examples of what people have been able to create out of clay, stone, wood, and metal or with a paintbrush and paints. We cannot all be explorers or collectors in other lands. But in a museum we can see for ourselves the objects that have been gathered from every part of the world.

▶ **HOW MUSEUMS BEGAN**

The word "museum" comes from the Greek word *mouseion,* meaning "temple of the Muses." The Muses were goddesses of the arts, whose lives were removed from the cares of everyday life.

One of the first institutions to be called a *mouseion* was founded in Alexandria, Egypt, in the 3rd century B.C., and adjoined the great Library of Alexandria. The museum collected every sort of information that could be of interest to scholars. Scholars lived and did their research there. The museum displayed a collection of objects of art and curiosities that included statues, instruments used in astronomy and surgery, elephant tusks, and hides of unusual animals. A museum such as the Museum of Alexandria might today be known as an institute for scientific research.

Some of the early Greek temples displayed a jumble of objects with no plan or order. Works of art were shown together with bones of prehistoric animals and other objects of natural history.

In the Middle Ages, cathedral treasuries and monasteries were storehouses for such richly ornamented objects as chalices (cups or goblets, generally used during the celebration of mass), book covers, and reliquaries—containers for relics of saints and martyrs. These treasuries were opened to the public only for special holy days or for the feast day of the patron saint of the church. Museums as we know them did not develop until hundreds of years later. The idea of public service and the wish to spread knowledge did not become an important part of museum work until the 19th century.

During the Renaissance, princes and noble families in Europe took a renewed interest in art and the history of the past. They collected works of art; objects of gold, silver, and other precious metals; and curiosities and rare things found in nature or brought from faraway places. Wealthy families, such as the Medici of Florence, Italy, took pride in surrounding themselves with their beautiful possessions, which their friends could also enjoy. Besides, a well-stocked treasure chamber and art collection impressed visitors with the owner's wealth, power, and taste. These private collections were known by many names —cabinets of rarities, closets of curios, and others. All over Europe, from the south of Italy to Denmark, these private *museos* were visited by scholars, artists, and important persons traveling on the Continent.

The galleries of some of today's great museums include the collections of kings, queens, wealthy merchants, and scholars of the 15th, 16th, and 17th centuries. The large area in the center of Peking, China, known as the Forbidden City, was opened to the public as a museum in 1924. But for centuries it was the court of emperors. Now called the Palace Museum, it includes some 40 buildings filled with every kind of Chinese art and historical object. The Uffizi Gallery in Florence, Italy, contains some of the collection of paintings and sculpture once owned by Lorenzo de' Medici (1449–92), a leading citizen of Florence, who was known as Lorenzo the Magnificent. The Ashmolean Museum at Oxford University, England, opened in 1683, was based on the collection of Elias Ashmole (1617–92), an English collector. The Ashmolean is the oldest science museum in the United Kingdom. Later in the same century, Sir Hans Sloane (1660–1753), a noted British doctor and naturalist, began an important collection of plants and objects related to his scientific work. This collection and others provided the basis of the British Museum, which was founded in the middle of the 18th century.

At that time, the British Museum admitted few people. Even scholars had to wait about two weeks before they could get tickets of admission. Sometimes months passed before the scholars were found to be acceptable. No one was allowed to go through the museum alone. Instead, people were shown through in groups. If there was anything they were especially eager to see, they might have to go through the whole museum to find it because the exhibits were not arranged in any particular order. For example, a Hindu temple ornament might be displayed next to the skeleton of a hippopotamus.

In the mid-19th century, the public was allowed to visit part of the Hermitage collection in St. Petersburg (now Leningrad, Soviet Union). The collection was housed in the Winter Palace and buildings dating from the time of Catherine the Great. Visitors to the museum were obliged to wear the same formal clothes required for court functions. Under this ruling it seems unlikely that the peasants or members of the working classes ever saw the inside of the museum. How different it is today, when visitors to a museum may dress in casual sports clothes if they wish.

It took an event as important as the French Revolution and the overthrow of the monarchy to open the doors of French museums to everyone. In 1793, during the revolution, the Republican Government made the Louvre in Paris a national museum. It contained the collections of the kings of France. Later other royal collections were opened to the public. In 1809, Joseph Bonaparte, then king of Spain, decided that there should be an art museum in Madrid. Later, the Prado, one of Madrid's large civic buildings, was chosen to house the great collections of the kings of Spain.

Museums came to be looked upon as places where knowledge might be gained. They ceased to be showcases to be seen only by a chosen few. Art treasures were moved from old curio cabinets and placed with other precious objects already on exhibit. Objects of scientific interest were collected, and museums of natural history were opened.

In the 19th century, buildings were specially designed as museums. Before that, churches, monasteries, palaces, or state buildings that no longer served their original purposes were used as museums. Among the palaces that later became museums are the Louvre in Paris, France; the Pitti Palace in Florence, Italy; and the Hermitage in Leningrad, Soviet Union. One of the first buildings in Europe planned as a museum was the Altes (Old) Museum in Berlin, Germany. It was constructed in 1830.

Improvements in museum organization followed. Exhibits were arranged according to a plan. Works of art were usually classified and exhibited according to artist, country, and century. Good lighting was installed. Some museums were built with skylights. These replaced the lighting from side windows. The decorative arts—furniture, china, and textiles—were exhibited with paintings and sculpture in period rooms. These rooms showed styles of art and how people lived at a particular time in history.

▶ KINDS OF MUSEUMS

Most museums deal with either science, history, or art. General museums may cover more than one of these subjects, or museums may specialize in one subject, such as natural history, astronomy, modern art, or science in industry. Museums range in size from simple one- or two-room structures to huge buildings that cover many city blocks. Sometimes a museum features a single product, such as glass in the Corning Museum of Glass in Corning, New York, or the work of a single artist, such as that of Auguste Rodin in the Rodin museums in Paris and Philadelphia. Archeological museums, such as the University Museum in Philadelphia, specialize in the art and artifacts made and used by ancient peoples. A great part of their collections has been excavated from tombs, temples, and buried cities.

Science Museums

There are several types of science museums. One is the museum of natural history. It is concerned with all the objects found in nature and all living things, from plants to humans. The anthropology departments of natural history museums deal with the evolution and development of human beings and their environment. There are botanical gardens, which are museums of living plants, and zoos, which are museums of living animals. Aquariums are museums of fish and other marine life.

Museums of industry and technology are museums of applied science. These museums illustrate the ways in which science is put to practical use and made to work for us.

Museums of Natural History. The collections in many of the large museums of natural history have great value for scientists and students. London's Natural History Museum contains a huge collection of mammals, birds, reptiles, and fish. Its collections of insects (entomology) and plants (botany) are so complete that they have been used in much scientific research.

The development of habitat groups has added great interest to the displays in museums of natural history. The word "habitat" comes from the Latin *habitare,* meaning "to inhabit." Habitat displays are prepared on such a large scale that they fill whole exhibition halls. Models of the animals are arranged in settings exactly like the ones the animals lived in while they were alive and free. Each tree, blade of grass, and shrub is carefully copied from the original, and the animals look as if they were alive. Habitat groups were first developed at the Natural History Museum in London, England. The Rijksmuseum in Leyden, the Netherlands, was the first museum to mount animals in a lifelike way.

The American Museum of Natural History in New York City, founded in 1869, has a world-famous display of habitat groups. Many of the mounted specimens were obtained by the museum's own staff members during expeditions.

Not all natural history museums are indoors. Small trailside museums for nature study are to be found outdoors in many places, especially in national, state, or local parks. Various kinds of rock formations, trees, and plants are identified with labels.

Museums of natural hisory all over the world abound in fascinating displays that have something new to teach us on each return visit.

Museums of Industry and Technology. A new museum approach appeared with the opening of the Deutsches Museum in Munich, Germany, in 1903. It exhibited the first diesel engine, the first dynamo (power generator), and early automobiles. For the first time,

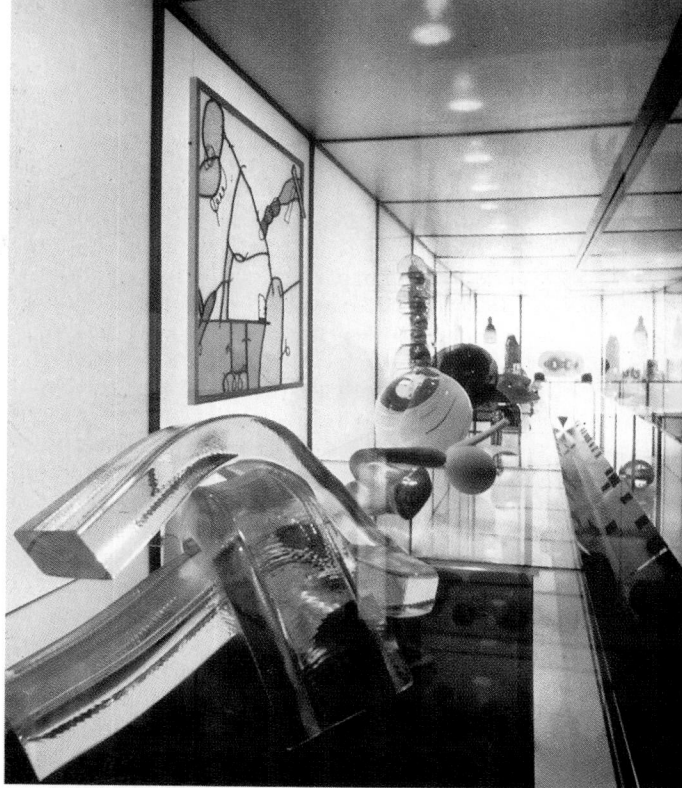

In the Contemporary Glass Gallery (*above*) of the Corning Museum of Glass, in Corning, New York, visitors can see examples of modern sculpture and stained glass. The Field Museum of Natural History (*below*), in Chicago, Illinois, offers exhibits in the fields of anthropology, botany, zoology, and geology.

visitors to a museum were allowed to operate machines or push buttons that set machines in motion. The Museum of Science and Industry in Chicago, Illinois, is modeled after the Deutsches Museum. Visitors are permitted to take part in many of the demonstrations. They may be lowered into a full-size coal mine to see miners at work. They may also see a foundry as it operates, as well as a typical farm with a farmhouse, silo, barn, and brooder with live chicks.

The Museum of History and Technology of the Smithsonian Institution in Washington, D.C., presents some of the most advanced developments of the technological museum. Labels and tape recordings explain exhibits.

Planetariums. A planetarium is actually a museum of astronomy. The motor-driven apparatus for projecting images of the stars and planets on the inner surface of a large dome was a German invention first used in Munich, Germany. The Adler Planetarium and Astronomical Museum in Chicago, built in 1930, was the first of a number of planetariums to appear in the United States.

History Museums

There are probably more history museums than any other type of museum. Many are very small. They may tell the story of a nation, an event, an industry, or a community. They can display the clothing, architecture, coins, and weapons that were part of the early history of the community. The museum may be the home of a national hero, such as George Washington's house at Mount Vernon, Virginia; William Shakespeare's home at Stratford-on-Avon, England; Simón Bolívar's home in Caracas, Venezuela; or the palace of a king at Hampton Court in England.

Peasant life, folk art, and folklore were largely neglected by national museums until Sweden established its first outdoor folk art museum in 1891. Other countries followed Sweden's example and built folk art museums. The Swedish Museum was located at Skansen near Stockholm and was a branch of Sweden's Nordiska Museet. High on a hillside overlooking the city stands a group of peasant cottages, barns, windmills, and other structures. These old buildings were moved to

People can walk through a giant model of the human heart (*left*) at the Museum of Science and Industry in Chicago, Illinois. The Henry Ford Museum (*right*), in Dearborn, Michigan, traces the history of the automobile and other types of transportation.

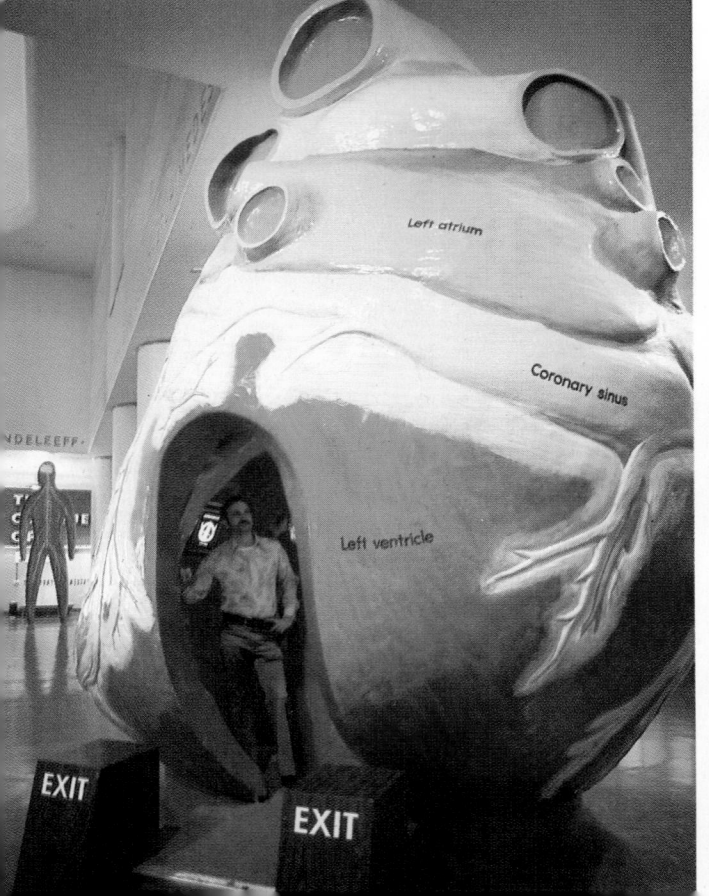

Visitors to the Museum of Fine Arts in Boston, Massachusetts, view a collection of works by French painter Claude Monet, a founder of the impressionist style of art.

Skansen from all parts of Sweden. They illustrate the life of the Swedish people throughout the centuries. Concerts and theatrical performances are presented on the grounds. There is also a zoo.

Skansen led to interest in the reconstruction of whole villages that would show the life and customs of earlier times. Old Sturbridge Village in Massachusetts is a reconstructed New England village with authentic houses and shops. Another noted reconstruction project in the United States is Colonial Williamsburg. This 18th-century capital of Virginia has been rebuilt to look as it did when ladies wore hoopskirts and men wore knee breeches. The Henry Ford Museum and Greenfield Village in Dearborn, Michigan, have many buildings and original houses containing collections from American pioneer days to the present time.

Art Museums

The large 20th-century art museum displays paintings and sculptures from many periods. It may also have collections of furniture, tapestries, medals, and other examples of decorative art.

Some museums of art are called galleries— for example, the National Gallery of Art in Washington, D.C., the National Gallery of Victoria in Australia, and the National Gallery in Norway. Still other art museums may be called institutes, as the Art Institute of Chicago, Illinois.

The greatest collections of Renaissance art in the world are to be found in Florence, Italy. The Uffizi Gallery is noted for its fine collection of paintings, which show the development of Italian art from the 14th to the 18th centuries. The Pitti Gallery is housed in the palace of the Pitti family, a leading 15th-century Florentine family. It contains important works by Raphael, Titian, and Rubens. The Vatican Museum in Rome is a complex of several museums.

The Louvre is the greatest art museum in France. Once a royal palace, the building dates back to the year 1190, when King Philip Augustus ordered that a fortress be built to house "his jewels, his dogs, and his prisoners of war." It later became a royal palace. Anyone determined to see everything on display in the Louvre would have to walk at least 14 kilometers (9 miles).

The British Museum in London is especially rich in its collecton of ancient sculpture. Most famous are the Elgin marbles, which are sculptures from the Parthenon. The British Museum also owns the historic Rosetta stone. The Greek inscription beneath the Egyptian writing on the Rosetta stone provided the clue for deciphering ancient Egyptian hieroglyphics.

The fine objects in museums are often used as sources of design. The Victoria and Albert Museum in London was established in 1852 to help business and industry improve the design of their products by showing the best

examples of old crafts. The museum grouped its collections according to the materials from which objects were made, such as glass, wood, metal, and textile. Similar museums were established in many other cities in Europe and the United States.

Galleries were also established to exhibit the work of modern contemporary artists. There is the Tate Gallery in London, the Museum of Modern Art in Paris, the Museum of Modern Art in Madrid, the Whitney Museum of American Art and the Museum of Modern Art in New York City, and others. Most of these galleries were originally planned for the exhibition of work by native artists, but many now include work by artists from other countries. The Tate, for example, at one time contained only British works, but it now has an international collection.

The art museums in the Soviet Union are known for their excellent work in the conservation of old paintings. In Moscow, parts of the Kremlin, the former palace of the czars, are now public museums. Also in Moscow is the Pushkin State Museum, named after the Russian poet. It is a museum of European art. The Hermitage in Leningrad, the most important art museum of the Soviet Union, is famous for its old masters.

Almost every country in the world has at least one art museum that is a source of national pride. In Cape Town, South Africa, there is the National Art Gallery of South Africa; in Tokyo, Japan, the National Museum; in Karachi, Pakistan, the National Museum of Pakistan; and so on. In the Netherlands the outstanding museum is the Rijksmuseum in Amsterdam. It contains a noted collection of paintings, sculpture, and historical objects. The Gold Museum of the Bank of the Republic in Bogotá, the capital of Colombia, has a collection of over 6,000 objects made of gold. These objects were excavated from ancient tombs in Colombia.

The Dresden Art Gallery in East Germany is known for the *Sistine Madonna* by Raphael. This world-famous painting was taken by the Russians in World War II but returned later in perfect condition.

Most American museums are younger than those in Europe. The first museum in the United States was established by the Charleston Library Society in Charleston, South Carolina, in 1773. The older art museums in

Museum buildings may look very different from one another. The Solomon R. Guggenheim Museum (*above*), in New York City, contains important collections of modern American and European art. The Rijksmuseum (*below*), in Amsterdam, is noted for its fine collection of paintings by Rembrandt and other Dutch artists.

the United States—The Corcoran Gallery of Art in Washington, D.C. (founded in 1859); the Metropolitan Museum of Art in New York City (1870); the Museum of Fine Arts in Boston, Massachusetts (1876); the Art Institute of Chicago (1879); and the M. H. de Young Memorial Museum in San Francisco, California (1895)—used the great museums of Europe, such as the Louvre, the Prado, and the Uffizi, as models for their buildings and collections.

A most unusual museum building is the Solomon R. Guggenheim Museum in New York City. The museum specializes in abstract paintings and sculpture of the 20th and late 19th centuries. The building was designed by the noted American architect Frank Lloyd Wright. Museum visitors take the elevator to the top floor (the sixth) and walk down the gently sloping ramp that circles the inside walls of the building in a continuous spiral. The works of art are displayed in the central lobby and in the exhibition spaces that open off the ramp.

The story of museums will never end, for new museums and collections are constantly being developed. Of international importance was the founding of a Picasso museum in Barcelona, Spain, containing the largest collection of Picassos in the world. Many museums are also becoming increasingly sensitive to the issues of the day. They strive for special exhibitions that reflect the latest trends in art, science, and social issues.

A chart listing some of the best-known museums of the world begins on page 524.

Children's Museums

The first children's museum was organized by the Brooklyn Museum in New York in 1899. The idea of having special museums or departments and exhibition space in museums set aside especially for young people caught on. Today there are hundreds of children's museums, and they are to be found in many countries.

Some museum programs are designed so that children can make their own models and crafts. Others have displays that children can touch, such as Indian artifacts and dinosaur bones. And some museums have exhibits that children can work, such as exhibits on levers, weights and measures, and engines. Some pictures of children's museums follow on the next two pages.

Museum buildings can look quite different inside as well as outside. The inner court of the modern East Building of the National Gallery of Art, in Washington, D.C. (*above*), contrasts greatly with the Uffizi Gallery, in Florence, Italy (*below*), which was once a palace belonging to the Medici family.

CHILDREN'S MUSEUMS

Museums that are especially for children encourage young people to feel, touch, and participate in a wide variety of activities. At the Children's Museum of Denver **(photo 1)**, children plunge into a room filled with 80,000 colored balls. Also featured at the Colorado museum is a water laboratory where youngsters can play with miniature dams, locks, and waterwheels. Bubble blowing is just one activity offered to young visitors at the Please Touch Museum **(2)**, in Philadelphia, Pennsylvania. Children paint on clear plastic easels at the Children's Museum of Rhode Island **(3)**, in Pawtucket. The Capital Children's Museum **(4)**, in Washington, D.C., encourages youngsters to pour water down a slide to make a musical waterfall. Visitors can also experiment with computers or learn to make tortillas and chocolate. The children at right **(5)** play a drum from Ghana at the Brooklyn (New York) Children's Museum. The museum features a variety of authentic tribal musical instruments as well as a greenhouse and one of the largest doll collections in the world. One of the activities at the Los Angeles (California) Children's Museum **(6)** is the recycling of industrial waste material. Visitors are also encouraged to perform plays on a large stage and to build cities with foam blocks that stick together. Young children enjoy Playscape, an exhibit at the Children's Museum **(7)** in Indianapolis, Indiana. Water and sand tables expose children to basic science concepts, letting them experiment with measuring, pouring, and building with sand and water. Older children enjoy an Egyptian room that features hieroglyphics and a Victorian train station. Young people at the Children's Museum **(8)** in San Diego, California, create their own television news programs.

musical
waterfall
MONKEY SLIDE-RAINBOW CHAIR
FUNDS: NATIONAL ENDOWMENT FOR THE AR
DESIGNED BY SKIP LA PLANTE

1 FILL A GALLON JUG
  WITH WATER
2 CARRY IT UPSTAIRS
  AND POUR IT INTO
  CHUTES OR HOSES
  LISTEN. WATCH. ENJOY
3 RETURN ALL WATER
  JUGS TO 1ST LEVEL

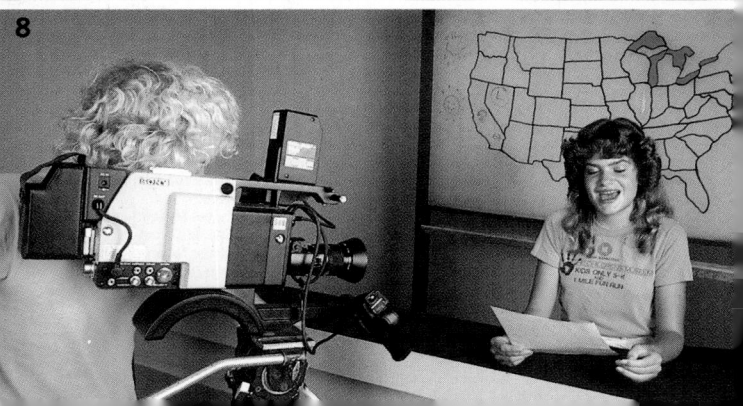

A LISTING OF SOME OF THE WORLD'S MAJOR MUSEUMS

COUNTRY	CITY	MUSEUM	KINDS OF EXHIBITS
Argentina	Buenos Aires	La Plata Museum of Natural Sciences	Science and natural history
		National Museum of Decorative Art	Decorative art
	Rosario	Museum of Fine Arts	European and Argentine art
Australia	Adelaide	Art Gallery of South Australia	World art, Australian history
	Hobart	Tasmanian Museum and Art Gallery	Art, history
	Launceston	Queen Victoria Museum and Art Gallery	Art, natural history
	Melbourne	National Gallery of Victoria	Art
	Perth	Western Australian Art Gallery	Art, aboriginal artifacts
	Sydney	Art Gallery of New South Wales	World art
		Australian Museum	Natural history
		Museum of Applied Arts and Sciences	Decorative arts, technology
Austria	Salzburg	Carolina Augusteum	Archeology, art, history
	Vienna	Albertina Graphics Collection	Graphic art
		Museum of the History of Art	European art, decorative art
		Natural History Museum	Natural history
Belgium	Antwerp	Archives and Museum of Flemish Cultural Life	Modern art
		Plantin-Moretus Museum	Printing, art
		Royal Museum of Fine Arts	Flemish and European art
	Brussels	Royal Museum of Art and History	World art
		Royal Museums of Fine Arts of Belgium	Belgian art
	Ghent	Museum of the History of Art	Belgian, world art
Bolivia	La Paz	National Museum of Art	Archeology, folk art
Brazil	Rio de Janeiro	Museum of Modern Art	Modern art
		National Historical Museum	History, decorative arts
		National Museum	Science, natural history, history
		National Museum of Fine Art	Art
Canada			
Nova Scotia	Halifax	Nova Scotia Museum	Historical objects, science
Ontario	Ottawa	National Gallery of Canada	Canadian art
		National Museums of Man and Natural Sciences	Natural history, Eskimo and Indian art
	Toronto	Art Gallery of Toronto	European, modern art
		Royal Ontario Museum	Archeology, natural history, world art
Quebec	Chambly	Fort Chambly National Historic Park	Restored fort
	Montreal	Montreal Museum of Fine Arts	World art
	Quebec	Museum of Quebec	French-Canadian art, furniture
Chile	Santiago	National Museum of Fine Arts	Spanish, Chilean art
China, People's Republic of	Peking	Imperial Palace	Chinese art, archeology
China, Republic of	Taipei	National Palace Museum	Chinese art, archeology
Colombia	Bogotá	Museum of Gold	Objects made of gold
		Museum of Colonial Art	Spanish Empire art
		National Museum	Art, history
Cyprus	Nicosia	Cyprus Museum	Archeology
Czechoslovakia	Bratislava	National Gallery of Slovakia	European art
	Brno	Moravian Museum	Natural history
	Prague	National Gallery of Modern Art	Czech art
Denmark	Copenhagen	Carlsberg Gallery	Archeology, European art
		Museum of Decorative Art	World decorative art
		National Museum	World art, archeology, history
		State Art Museum	Danish and European art
	Humlebock	Louisiana Museum of Modern Art	Modern art
Egypt	Alexandria	Greco-Roman Museum	Greek and Roman art
	Cairo	Egyptian National Museum	Egyptian art and archeology
England	Brighton	Royal Pavilion Art Gallery	English and European art
	Cambridge	University of Cambridge	Art, decorative arts
	Greenwich	National Maritime Museum	Maritime history
	Liverpool	Merseyside Country Museums	Natural history, archeology
		Walker Art Gallery	English and European art
	London	British Museum	World archeology, art
		Courtauld Galleries	European art
		Geological Museum	Geology, gems
		National Gallery	European art
		Science Museum	Science, technology
		Tate Gallery	European art, 16th–20th century
		Victoria and Albert Museum	Decorative arts
		Wallace Collection	European art
		Wellington Museum	Historic house
	Manchester	City Art Gallery	English, European art
		Manchester Museum	Science, archeology
	Oxford	Ashmolean Museum	World art, archeology
Ethiopia	Addis Ababa	Museum of the Institute of Ethiopian Studies	Ethiopian art
Finland	Helsinki	National Museum of Finland	History, archeology
France	Paris	Guimet Museum	Eastern art
		Jeu de Paume	Impressionist art
		Louvre	World art
		National Museum of Natural History	Natural history
		Palace of Discovery	Science, technology, planetarium
	Versailles	National Museum of the Chateau of Versailles	Palace museum, decorative art
Germany, East	Dresden	Semper Picture Gallery	Art
		Zwinger Gallery	Art, science, natural history
	East Berlin	Pergamon Museum	Ancient art

A LISTING OF SOME OF THE WORLD'S MAJOR MUSEUMS (Continued)

Germany, West	Berlin	Charlottenburg Palace Museums	Art, archeology, science
		Dahlem Museum	World art, antiquities
	Bonn	Rhineland Museum	Archeology, art
	Cologne	Cologne City Museum	European and modern art
	Hamburg	Hamburg Art Hall	European art
	Munich	Bavarian National Museum	European art
		Deutsches Museum	Science, industry
		Old Picture Gallery	European art
	Nuremberg	German National Museum	Decorative arts, art
Ghana	Accra	Ghana National Museum	Archeology, art, history
Greece	Athens	Benaki Museum	Byzantine-Greek art, archeology
		National Archeological Museum	Greek archeology, art
Guatemala	Guatemala City	Museum of History and Fine Arts	History, art
Hong Kong	Hong Kong	City Museum and Art Gallery	Chinese archeology, art
Hungary	Budapest	Hungarian National Gallery	Modern Hungarian art
		Hungarian National Museum	Ancient and modern history, art
Iceland	Reykjavik	National Museum of Antiquities	Archeology and art
India	Bombay	Victoria and Albert Museum	Natural history, art
	Calcutta	Indian Museum	Indian history, art
	New Delhi	National Museum of India	Ancient art, archeology
Iraq	Baghdad	Iraq Museum	Middle Eastern art, archeology
Ireland	Dublin	National Gallery of Ireland	European art
		National Museum	Archeology, art, history, industry
Israel	Haifa	Museum of Ancient and Modern Art	Ancient, modern art
	Jerusalem	Israel Museum	Jewish and world art
		Museum of the Department of Antiquities	Archeology
	Tel Aviv	Alphabet Museum	History of writing
		Tel Aviv Museum	European art
Italy	Florence	National Museum	Italian art
		Uffizi Gallery	Italian art, 14th–18th century
	Milan	Museum of Ancient Art	10th–16th-century art
	Naples	National Archeological Museum	Roman art, archeology
	Rome	Borghese Gallery	Baroque art
		Museum of Rome	Roman history
	Vatican City	Vatican Museums and Libraries	Art
	Venice	Academy Gallery	Venetian art
		Doges' Palace	Palace museum

The Shrine of the Book is part of the Israel Museum in Jerusalem.

The Hermitage in Leningrad is the largest museum in the Union of Soviet Socialist Republics.

Japan	Kyoto	National Museum of Modern Art	Japanese art, handicrafts
	Nara	Nara National Museum	Buddhist, Japanese art
	Tokyo	National Museum	Japanese art, archeology
		National Museum of Modern Art	World modern art
		National Museum of Western Art	European art
Korea, South	Seoul	National Museum of Korea	Ancient art
Lebanon	Beirut	National Museum of Lebanon	Ancient art
Malaysia	Kuala Lumpur	National Museum	Malaysian art, history
Mexico	Mexico City	Museum of Modern Art	Modern art
		National Museum of Anthropology	Mexican art, archeology
		Technological Museum	Science, technology
Monaco	Monte Carlo	Oceanographic Museum	Oceanography
Netherlands	Amsterdam	City Museum	Modern European art
		Rembrandt House	House museum, art
		State Museum (Rijksmuseum)	World art
	Haarlem	Frans Hals Museum	Dutch art, 16th—19th century
	The Hague	Municipal Museum	Decorative art, art, history
New Zealand	Wellington	National Art Gallery	European and New Zealand art
Norway	Oslo	Historical Museum	Norwegian art, antiquities
		National Gallery	Norwegian and European art
		Norwegian Folk Museum	Scandinavian art history
Pakistan	Karachi	National Museum of Pakistan	Ancient art
	Lahore	Lahore Museum	Pakistani and Indian art
Peru	Lima	Museum of Art	Inca and colonial art
Poland	Cracow	National Art Collection	World art
	Warsaw	National Museum	World art
Portugal	Lisbon	National Museum of Ancient Art	World art
Rumania	Cluj	Art Museum	Rumanian, world art
Scotland	Edinburgh	National Galleries of Scotland	Art
		Royal Scottish Museum	Science, archeology, technology
	Glasgow	Art Gallery	Decorative arts, European art
South Africa	Cape Town	South African Museum	History, archeology
		South African National Gallery	African and European art
	Johannesburg	Johannesburg Art Gallery	European and modern art
Spain	Barcelona	Archeological Museum	Ancient art
	Madrid	Prado (National Museum of Painting and Sculpture)	European art
	Toledo	El Greco House and Museum	House museum
Sri Lanka	Colombo	National Museum	Natural history, archeology
Sweden	Stockholm	National Museum of Fine Arts	European and modern art
		Museum of Natural History	Natural history
		Nordic Museum	Swedish culture, history
		Skansen	Swedish folk art
		Swedish Museum	Art and crafts

A LISTING OF SOME OF THE WORLD'S MAJOR MUSEUMS (Continued)

Switzerland	Basel	Public Art Collection	European and American art
	Geneva	Museum of Art and History	Ancient European art
	Zurich	Museum of Art	World art
		Swiss National Museum	Swiss history
Syria	Damascus	National Museum of Damascus	Ancient art, archeology
Tunisia	Tunis	Le Bardo National Museum	Ancient art
Turkey	Istanbul	Archeological Museum of Istanbul	Antiquities
Union of Soviet Socialist Republics	Leningrad	Hermitage Museum	World art
	Moscow	State Museum of Oriental Art	Oriental art
		Tretyakov State Picture Gallery	Russian art
United States			
California	Los Angeles	Los Angeles County Museum of Art	Art
	Oakland	Oakland Museum	Art, natural history
	Pasadena	Pacific Asia Museum	Oriental art
	San Francisco	Fine Arts Museum of San Francisco	World art
		San Francisco Museum of Modern Art	Modern American and European art
Colorado	Denver	Denver Art Museum	Modern art, native American artifacts
Connecticut	Hartford	Wadsworth Atheneum	World art
	Mystic	Mystic Seaport Museum	Maritime village
	New Haven	Yale Center for British Art	British art
Delaware	Winterthur	Winterthur Museum	Decorative arts
Florida	Sarasota	Ringling Museum of Art	European art
Hawaii	Honolulu	Honolulu Academy of Arts	World art
Illinois	Chicago	Art Institute of Chicago	World art
		Chicago Historical Society	American history
		Field Museum of Natural History	Archeology, art, natural history
		Museum of Science and Industry	Science and technology
Maryland	Baltimore	Baltimore Museum of Art	Art, decorative art
Massachusetts	Boston	Museum of Fine Arts	American and Oriental art, decorative art
	Cambridge	Fogg Art Museum	World art
	Plymouth	Plimoth Plantation	Reconstructed Pilgrim village
	Sturbridge	Old Sturbridge Village	Reconstructed colonial village
Michigan	Dearborn	Greenfield Village	Restored town
	Detroit	Detroit Institute of Arts	World art
New Mexico	Santa Fe	Museum of New Mexico	World folk art, history
New York	Albany	Albany Institute of History and Art	History, art
	Buffalo	Albright-Knox Art Gallery	18th–20th-century art
		Buffalo Museum of Science	Natural history
	Corning	Corning Museum of Glass	Glass
	New York	American Museum of Natural History, Hayden Planetarium	Natural history and planetarium
		Brooklyn Botanic Garden	Natural science, botanic garden
		Brooklyn Museum	World art, Egyptian art
		Cooper Hewitt Museum of Design	Decorative arts
		Guggenheim Museum	Modern American and European art
		Metropolitan Museum of Art	World art, archeology
		Museum of Modern Art	Modern art
		Museum of the American Indian	American Indian art and crafts
		Museum of the City of New York	History, decorative arts
		New York Historical Society	American history
		Whitney Museum of American Art	Modern American art
Ohio	Cleveland	Cleveland Museum of Art	World art
Oklahoma	Oklahoma City	National Cowboy Hall of Fame	Western art
Pennsylvania	Philadelphia	Academy of Natural Sciences of Philadelphia	Natural science
		Franklin Institute	Science
		Philadelphia Museum of Art	European and American art
	Pittsburgh	Carnegie Institute Museum of Art	Ancient and modern art
		Carnegie Museum of Natural History	Natural History
Puerto Rico	San Juan	Museum of Fine Arts	Puerto Rican art
		Institute of Puerto Rican Culture	Art, history
Virginia	Newport News	Mariner's Museum	Maritime history, ships
	Williamsburg	Colonial Williamsburg	Restored town
Washington, D.C.		Corcoran Gallery of Art	European and American art
		Dumbarton Oaks Research Library and Collection	Pre-Columbian art
		Freer Gallery of Art (of the Smithsonian Institution)	Oriental and American art
		Hirshhorn Museum and Sculpture Garden	20th-century art, sculpture
		National Air and Space Museum (Smithsonian Institution)	Technology
		National Gallery of Art (Smithsonian Institution)	Art
		National Museum of African Art (Smithsonian Institution)	African art
		National Portrait Gallery	U.S. history
Wisconsin	Baraboo	Circus World Museum	Circus artifacts
Uruguay	Montevideo	National Museum of Fine Art	South American art
Venezuela	Caracas	Museum of Fine Arts	Ancient and modern art
Wales	Cardiff	National Museum of Wales	English and European art
Yugoslavia	Belgrade	Museum of Contemporary Art	Modern art
	Ljubljana	Modern Gallery	Modern art
		National Art Gallery	Slovenian art
Zimbabwe	Salisbury	National Archives of Zimbabwe	History of Zimbabwe

Before becoming part of the permanent collection of the Boston Museum of Fine Arts, these Egyptian artifacts will be carefully studied and classified by museum personnel.

▶WHO WORKS IN A MUSEUM?

The visitor to a large museum is likely to see guards, sales attendants, and perhaps a lecturer. But there may be hundreds more people busy behind the scenes.

The museum director is in charge of all museum activities. The registrar keeps records of all the objects in the museum. The library is staffed by librarians. Large museums are divided into departments. Each department is under the care of a curator. The curator is an expert in a particular field, such as ancient art, modern painting, reptiles, or fossils. A **docent** leads groups through the museum.

Museums often maintain their own workshops, staffed by carpenters, painters, photographers, and other experts. The artists and taxidermists (people who mount animal skins on life-size animal forms) who work on habitat groups for museums of natural history are known as **preparators.** Large art museums employ specialists who take care of the old paintings, sculptures, and other objects that have been damaged by time or accident. They clean the works of art and preserve them. They do as little repainting on old canvases as possible. These people are called **conservators.** Some conservators are responsible for controlling the ''climate'' in the museum to ensure the preservation of the objects. They may also oversee the proper storage and exhibition of the objects.

The building superintendent of the museum takes charge of the maintenance of the building. Museums also employ laborers, gardeners, mechanics, and electricians. Many museums have their own printing plants, where bulletins, announcements, and catalogs are printed.

Secretaries, typists, and, in many cases, volunteer assistants are also needed. Particularly in the smaller museums, the volunteer can be most helpful.

If you wish to work in a leading position in a museum, you must have a college degree, some knowedge of one or more foreign languages, and credits in special courses. The courses should be related to the type of collections in the museum in which you would like to work. You might also attend a course in museology, the general study of museums. In the United States special courses are offered by some museums in co-operation with universities. Grants and scholarships for training in museum work are open to postgraduate students.

Reviewed by ROBERTA PAINE
Senior Lecturer
Metropolitan Museum of Art

See also HERMITAGE MUSEUM; LOUVRE; METROPOLITAN MUSEUM OF ART; NATIONAL GALLERY (LONDON); NATIONAL GALLERY OF ART (WASHINGTON, D.C.); NATIONAL GALLERY OF CANADA; PRADO; SMITHSONIAN INSTITUTION; TAXIDERMY; UFFIZI GALLERY.

MUSHROOMS

Mushrooms are fleshy plants that belong to the fungi group. They grow from decaying materials and have no chlorophyll. They usually grow in the temperate regions of the earth during the time of year when the weather is warm and moist. They are most likely to be found in pastures, meadows, and woodlands.

Mushrooms are of many different colors: white, orange, red, brown, and beautiful glimmering pastels. Mushrooms also have many different shapes and sizes. The most common varieties have short, thick stems and umbrellalike fleshy caps.

Inside each cap are many thin sheets of flesh, which grow between the stem and the cap edge. These are the gills, on which tiny spores grow as the plant ages. The spores are blown away by wind and settle on the ground to grow into new plants, just as the seeds of other plants do.

Some mushrooms are delicious as food. A few kinds of mushrooms, which many people call **toadstools**, are poisonous. Others are too tough or not tasty enough to serve as food, even though they are not poisonous.

Common Edible Mushrooms. The edible mushrooms may be cooked to be eaten by themselves. Often they are eaten with meat, combined with other vegetables, or used in soups and sauces. Mushrooms do not need to be peeled. There is just as much flavor in the stems as in the caps. Mushrooms should be eaten only when they are very fresh. They do not stay fresh long, so many of the mushrooms grown are canned, frozen, or dried before being sold.

There is no completely safe way for anyone but an expert to distinguish wild edible mushrooms from very similar poisonous varieties. So it is much wiser to buy the mushrooms you eat than to collect wild ones.

The **common mushroom**, or field mushroom, is the main kind of mushroom raised. Since the air where mushrooms are grown should always be cool and moist, mushrooms are raised in caves or indoors on shelves filled with partly decayed animal and plant materials. Mushroom **spawn**, or root growth, that is planted in this material grows rapidly and soon fills the bed with tiny threadlike rootlets. The mushrooms do not show above the ground until the rootlets are well grown.

In some European countries wild mushrooms are often sold in the markets. Some of the wild mushrooms popular with Europeans are **morels**, which have unusual pitted, spongelike heads. The **horse mushroom**, which looks very much like the common mushroom with an added collar around its neck, is also popular.

Another delicious wild mushroom is the **puffball**. This is a perfectly round mushroom with no stem at all and no gills. It may be very small, but occasional puffballs have reached 3 feet in diameter. The puffball is good only when the flesh is all white. If you squeeze a dried puffball, its spores will burst out like puffs of smoke.

Poisonous Mushrooms. The **false morels** are among the varieties of poisonous mushrooms. They are easily confused with edible morels. The most deadly poison is contained in the loveliest of all mushrooms—the pure-white, deadly *Amanita verna,* or, as it is sometimes called, the **Destroying Angel**. It has a tall, stately stem and a wide, graceful cap.

Fairy Rings. Sometimes in grassy areas mushrooms are found growing in circles called fairy rings. There was once a superstition that fairies whirled in circles as they danced, thus wearing down the grass so that the mushrooms might grow. Actually, fairy rings are a grass disease that grows steadily and evenly in the soil, spreading out in a larger circle every year.

Reviewed by LEON R. KNEEBONE
Mushroom Research Center
Pennsylvania State University

See also FUNGI.

1500 1600

GUILLAUME DUFAY (1400?-1474)
JEAN D'OCKEGHEM (1425?-1495)
JOSQUIN DES PREZ (1450?-1521)
JACOB OBRECHT (1452-1505)
CRISTOBAL MORALES (1500?-1553)
THOMAS TALLIS (1505-1585) ⟶
PALESTRINA (1525?-1594) ⟶
ROLAND DE LASSUS (1532-1594)
WILLIAM BYRD (1543-1623) ⟶
TOMAS LUIS DE VICTORIA (1549?-1611)
GIOVANNI GABRIELI (1557-1612)
CLAUDIO MONTEVERDI (1567-1643) ⟶
HEINRICH SCHUTZ (1585-1672) ⟶
JEAN-BAPTISTE LULLY (1632-1687) ⟶
ARCANGELO CORELLI (1653-1713) ⟶
HENRY PURCELL (1659?-1695) ⟶
FRANCOIS COUPERIN (1668-1733) ⟶
ANTONIO VIVALDI (1675?-1741) ⟶
JEAN-PHILIPPE RAMEAU (1683-1764) ⟶
JOHANN SEBASTIAN BACH (1685-1750) ⟶
DOMENICO SCARLATTI (1685-1757) ⟶
GEORGE FREDERICK HANDEL (1685-1759) ⟶

CLAUDIO MONTEVERDI

JOSQUIN DES PREZ

WILLIAM BYRD

JOHANN SEBASTIAN BACH

MUSIC

Music may be defined as the art of organizing sounds and silences into meaningful patterns. The word "music" comes from "Muse," the name for the goddesses of ancient Greek mythology who presided over the arts and sciences. Music is one of the oldest of the arts. No civilization in history has been without some form of music.

How did music begin? Scholars differ about the origins of music. Early peoples probably learned to use their voices for singing before they discovered how to make musical instruments. Very likely they sang simple chants to go with their magic rites. (Through magic, primitive people thought they could bring rain, make the sun shine, or help crops grow.) Thus the first melodies were born.

People soon learned how to make musical instruments out of the things they found around them. They made rattles out of nuts or gourds. They blew into bones or reeds to make a whistling sound. Hollow logs made excellent drums. These instruments heightened the effect of people's singing and marked the rhythm of their dances.

When primitive people sang in groups, it is likely that not all the singers sang the melodies on the same pitch. One singer perhaps sang four or five steps higher than the others. If two or three singers did this, several notes were sounded at the same time. Thus groups of people in primitive times experienced the beginnings of **harmony**, the sounding of several tones together.

▶ MUSICAL NOTATION

For a very long time music was not written down. It was sung or played from memory. One singer might teach a song to others, and they in turn would sing it to their friends or teach it to their children. Of course, many changes crept into the tunes in this way. People needed to find a way of writing their music down, so that it would be sung or played exactly as they had composed it. The method that they developed for writing music is called notation.

1700 1800 1900

WOLFGANG AMADEUS MOZART

LUDWIG VAN BEETHOVEN

GIUSEPPE VERDI

FRANZ SCHUBERT

FRÉDÉRIC CHOPIN

JOHANNES BRAHMS

RICHARD WAGNER

IGOR STRAVINSKY

CHRISTOPH WILLIBALD GLUCK (1714-1787)
JOSEPH HAYDN (1732-1809)
WOLFGANG AMADEUS MOZART (1756-1791)
LUDWIG VAN BEETHOVEN (1770-1827)
CARL MARIA VON WEBER (1786-1826)
GIOACCHINO ROSSINI (1792-1868)
FRANZ SCHUBERT (1797-1828)
GAETANO DONIZETTI (1797-1848)
VINCENZO BELLINI (1801-1835)
HECTOR BERLIOZ (1803-1869)
FELIX MENDELSSOHN (1809-1847)
FREDERIC CHOPIN (1810-1849)
ROBERT SCHUMANN (1810-1856)
FRANZ LISZT (1811-1886)
RICHARD WAGNER (1813-1883)
GIUSEPPE VERDI (1813-1901)
CHARLES GOUNOD (1818-1893)
CESAR FRANCK (1822-1890)
ANTON BRUCKNER (1824-1896)
JOHANNES BRAHMS (1833-1897)
GEORGES BIZET (1838-1875)
MODEST MUSSORGSKY (1839-1881)
PETER ILYICH TCHAIKOVSKY (1840-1893)
ANTONIN DVORAK (1841-1904)
EDVARD GRIEG (1843-1907)
NIKOLAY RIMSKY-KORSAKOV (1844-1908)
EDWARD ELGAR (1857-1934)
GIACOMO PUCCINI (1858-1924)
HUGO WOLF (1860-1903)
GUSTAV MAHLER (1860-1911)
CLAUDE DEBUSSY (1862-1918)
FREDERICK DELIUS (1862-1934)
RICHARD STRAUSS (1864-1949)
JEAN SIBELIUS (1865-1957)
RALPH VAUGHAN WILLIAMS (1872-1958)
SERGEI RACHMANINOFF (1873-1943)
ARNOLD SCHOENBERG (1874-1951)
CHARLES IVES (1874-1954)
MAURICE RAVEL (1875-1937)
MANUEL DE FALLA (1876-1946)
BELA BARTOK (1881-1945)
IGOR STRAVINSKY (1882-1971)
ANTON WEBERN (1883-1945)
ALBAN BERG (1885-1935)
SERGEI PROKOFIEV (1891-1953)
DARIUS MILHAUD (1892-1974)
PAUL HINDEMITH (1895-1963)
ROGER SESSIONS (1896-1985)
AARON COPLAND (1900-   )
DMITRI SHOSTAKOVICH (1906-1975)
BENJAMIN BRITTEN (1913-1976)

Musical notation, like written language, is a means of communication. It enables the composers to record their music in written symbols. Musicians can read these symbols and bring a composer's ideas to life in sound, thus communicating them to the listener.

Early Development

The system of musical notation generally used today in the Western world is the result

Why are schools of music often called conservatories?

Have you ever wondered why many schools of music are called conservatories? A conservatory is a place where something is "conserved," that is, kept in good condition. Although it is true that music is kept in good condition in a music conservatory, that is not the reason music schools are called conservatories.

The name "conservatory" actually comes from an Italian word, *conservatorio*, which in turn comes from *conservare*, "to keep." A *conservatorio* was originally a charitable institution where orphans were kept. The children were educated by the state until they were old enough to earn their own living. Since music was a useful profession, they were given excellent musical training for church or court, including court operas. The first orphans' *conservatorio* was established in Naples in 1537.

The oldest surviving music conservatory in Europe was founded in Paris in 1795. Taking its name from the Italian *conservatorio*, the school was called the Conservatoire de Musique. The Conservatoire trained musicians to perform in the concerts, military bands, and theaters of the new French republic. As the Conservatoire broadened its scope to give a more complete musical education, other European cities followed suit and established music conservatories: Milan in 1807; Naples, 1808; Prague, 1811; Brussels, 1813; Vienna, 1817; Geneva, 1835; Leipzig (founded by Mendelssohn), 1843; and Berlin and Cologne, 1850.

In 1774 an English musician, Charles Burney (1726–1814), issued his *Plan for a Music School*. Burney had been in Italy and had made a study of the conservatories for orphans. His proposal for establishing a music school in London in connection with the foundling hospital was not accepted, however. It was not until 1822 that the first professional school of music in England, the Royal Academy of Music, was founded.

During the 1860's a number of conservatories were established in the United States: Oberlin, 1865; New England (Boston) and Cincinnati, 1867; and the Peabody Institute (Baltimore), 1868. The Chicago Conservatory was actually founded in New York in 1857 and later moved to Chicago.

What is the origin of the clef signs?

The clef signs come from the old Gothic letters C, F, and G that were placed on certain lines of the staff to indicate the pitch of that line, and consequently, the pitch of the remaining lines and spaces. In this way singers could locate the pitch of ecclesiastical chants.

The word "clef," which is a French word, comes from the Latin *clavis*, or "key." The signs were called keys because they unlocked the secrets of the staff.

of centuries of development—from about the end of the 9th century to the early 1700's. This development began in the cathedrals and monasteries of the Roman Catholic Church. From early Christian times many of the Church's services were sung. For centuries this music, called Gregorian chant or plainchant, was sung from memory. But toward the end of the 9th century dots and dashes and little squiggles were written over the words in the service books. These signs, called **neumes**, aided the singers' memory by showing the direction in which the melody should go. As a method of notation, however, these signs were very vague. They told the singers only whether the melody went up or down but not exactly how far up or down. Neither did they tell how long each note should be held. They served as little more than reminders to the singers in case they should forget how the melody went. The following example shows neumes written in this manner:

The same example in modern notation looks like this:

About A.D. 900 the music was made a little easier to read. If a note was to be sung high, the neume would be written higher on the page than a note that was to be sung lower. Later a horizontal red line representing the note F was introduced. The neumes were written at certain distances above or below the line, showing how high or low the note should be sung. The following example shows neumes written in this way:

In modern notation it looks like this:

Soon a yellow or green line, which stood for middle C, was drawn above the red line.

The Staff. Guido d'Arezzo (990?–1050), a scholarly monk, is usually given credit for inventing the staff. This early staff was made of four lines. The neumes were written on the lines, as well as in the spaces between lines. It would be hard to overestimate the importance of the staff in the development of notation. Not only was the indication of exact pitch now possible, but also the staff was an aid to composers in writing new melodies. The ancient chants of the Catholic Church are still written on a four-line staff. Neumes written on the four-line staff are shown in the following example:

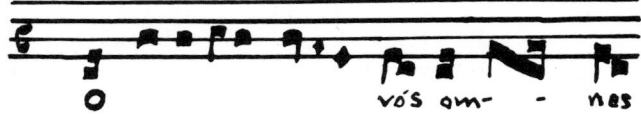

This example in modern notation appears thus:

While chant notation indicated pitch accurately, it did not show the duration, or length, of the notes. A method of notation that made it possible to show the length of each note was developed in the 13th and 14th centuries. This development included the use of the five-line staff, which was introduced about 1200. Notes took on new shapes, and stems were added to some notes according to their length. In the middle 1400's white notes were being used. The following is an example of notation from the 1500's:

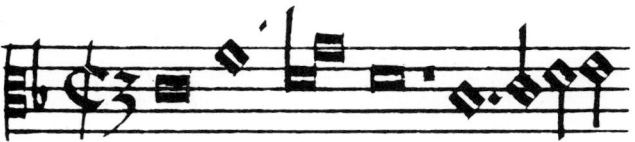

By the 1600's the square- and diamond-shaped notes had become round, and musical notation began to take on the general appearance it has today.

Modern Notation

Clefs. Along with the staff, clefs were introduced. The word *clef* in French means "key." The clefs tell us what each line on the staff stands for. A clef really serves as a key to music. Several clefs were used in early music, but only the clefs commonly used today are shown in the following section.

The **G clef**, or **treble clef**, looks like this:

This clef is used for music written for the soprano voice or high instruments, such as the violin or flute. The curlicue around the second line of the staff shows where the note G above middle C is located. That is why it is called the G clef. In music for the piano, the right-hand part is written in the treble clef.

The **F clef**, or **bass clef**, is used for low voices or instruments. On the staff the line that runs between the two dots of the bass clef marks the place where the note F below middle C is located:

The name "bass clef" is easy to remember, for this clef is usually used for the lowest part, or bass, of a composition. A singer with a deep bass voice would find his part written in this clef. Instruments such as the cello, the trombone, and the bassoon, which play in a low range most of the time, use the bass clef, too. The bass clef is also used for the left-hand part in piano music.

The **C clef** is a movable clef. That is, it can be placed on different lines of the staff, but it always indicates where middle C is located. Here are two ways in which it is used:

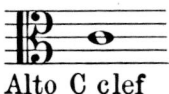
Alto C clef

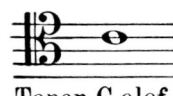
Tenor C clef

Middle C is always located on the line where the two curved arms of the C clef come together. Most of the music for the viola is written in the alto C clef, which is sometimes called the viola clef. (In fact, the French word for "viola" is *alto*.) However, when very high notes are written for the viola, the treble clef is used, for easier reading. The tenor C clef is used for the higher notes of such instruments as the cello and the bassoon. These instruments often play in the range of the tenor singing voice.

It is very important for a serious musician to know these C clefs. Knowing them is necessary for reading much of the music of past composers and the music written for some important instruments. Usually students learn the treble and bass clefs first. But if they want to be good musicians, they will soon learn the C clefs, too.

In writing music, all the lines and spaces on the staff are used. In the treble clef the notes in the spaces are:

This is easy to remember, because if you read the notes from bottom to top, they spell a word: FACE.

The notes on the lines are:

You can remember the notes EGBDF by memorizing this saying: Every Good Boy Deserves Fun.

In the bass clef the notes in the spaces are:

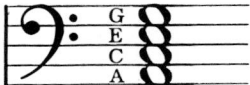

The notes on the lines are:

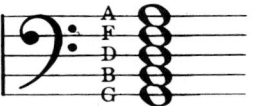

Notes can be written under the bottom line or above the top line of the staff:

Ledger Lines. If you want still higher or lower notes and do not wish to change to another clef, you have to use ledger lines. For example, in the treble clef middle C is written on the first ledger line below the staff:

Middle C

To write notes higher than the usual range of the treble clef, you have to use ledger lines above the staff. For example:

A   C   E

Of course, you can write notes in the spaces between the ledger lines, too.

A B C D E F G A B C D E F G A B C D E F G

In the bass clef, middle C is on the ledger line above the staff:

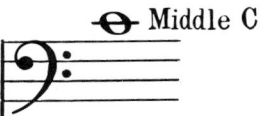

For notes that are lower than the usual range of the bass clef, ledger lines are drawn below the staff:

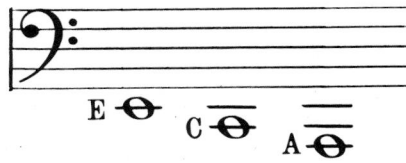

The Octave. The following musical example shows the notes in the treble clef arranged one after the other—line, space, line, space, and so on:

C D E F G A B C

If you play this on the piano or sing it, you will notice that the eighth note sounds like the first note. In fact, these two notes sound so much alike that when you play them at the same time, they blend together perfectly. They are really the same—both are C's—only one is in a higher pitch range than the other. The second C is said to be an **octave** higher than the first. "Octave" comes from a Latin word meaning "eighth." Thus, the octave interval embraces eight tones—for example, from middle C to the next C above it.

The Scale. As you can see, the above musical example is made up of a series of steps—from line to space, from space to line, and so on. You might call it a ladder of tones. And, in fact, the proper name for this structure—**scale**—comes from the ancient Greek word meaning "ladder." (Many of our musical terms—*melody, harmony, rhythm, symphony,* for example—come from Greek words.)

It looks, at first, as if all the steps in this scale are of the same size. However, if you play the scale on the white keys of the piano, you will find this is not so. (Try this on a piano, if you can, as it makes it easier to understand.)

Play middle C, a white key, and then play the next white key, D, on the piano. You will notice that there is a black key between these two white keys. The space between the notes C and D is called a **whole step** or a **whole tone**. This whole step is, in turn, divided into two **half steps** by the black key between the white keys C and D. (These half steps are also known as **half tones**.) The note played by the black key may be called either C sharp (because it is a half step higher than C) or D flat (because it is a half step lower than D).

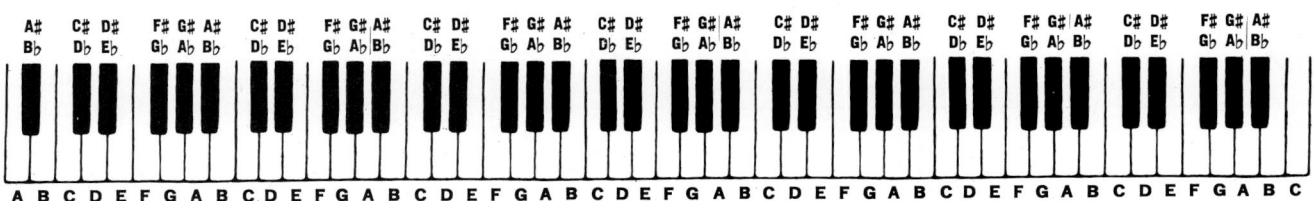

A B C D E F G A B C D E F G A B C D E F G A B C D E F G A B C D E F G A B C D E F G A B C D E F G A B C D E F G A B C

The sharp sign (♯) placed in front of a note always raises the note a half step. The flat sign (♭) placed in front of a note always lowers the note a half step:

C   C sharp
     (half step higher)   B   B flat
                               (half step lower)

If a composer has used a sharp or a flat in front of a note but wants to go back to the note's original pitch, he uses a natural sign (♮). The natural sign placed before a note cancels out the sharp or flat:

G sharp   G natural
               (the ♯ is canceled)

Play the white key E, followed by the white key F. You will notice that there is no black key between the two white keys. In other words, the interval between E and F is a half step. So is the interval between B and C. The following diagram of the scale beginning on C shows where the whole steps and the half steps are:

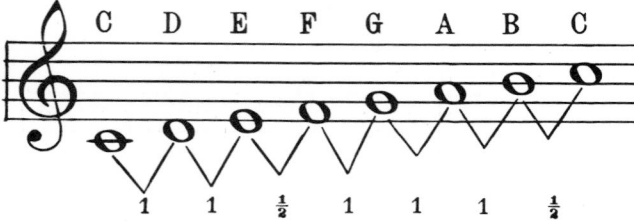

C   D   E   F   G   A   B   C
1   1   ½   1   1   1   ½

Play this scale on the piano, or get someone to play it for you. All major scales are constructed in the same way.

The whole steps and half steps of the minor scale are arranged in the following way:

A   B   C   D   E   F   G   A
1   ½   1   1   ½   1   1

(Composers often use variants of this, the **natural** minor scale. For instance, the second to the last note is usually sharped, forming the **harmonic** minor scale.)

Key Signatures. Now, try to build a major scale on some note besides C. For instance, start on G. Try it on the white keys of the piano first:

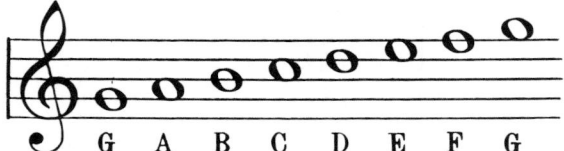

G   A   B   C   D   E   F   G

But this cannot be right, for there is a whole step (F–G) between the seventh and eighth notes. But if you raise the seventh note, F, a half step, to an F♯, you will hear a correct G major scale:

G   A   B   C   D   E   F♯   G

But it would be a bother to have to write a sharp in front of every F that appears in a piece in G major. To avoid this, the F♯ is placed right at the beginning of the piece:

This means that F♯ will be used throughout the piece unless the composer indicates the contrary. The sharps or flats that appear at the beginning of a piece are its **key signature**.

The key signatures of the sharp major and minor keys are:

G major   D major   A major   E major
E minor   B minor   F♯ minor   C♯ minor

B major   F♯ major   C♯ major
G♯ minor   D♯ minor   A♯ minor

The key signatures of the flat major and minor keys are:

F major   B♭ major   E♭ major   A♭ major
D minor   G minor   C minor   F minor

D♭ major   G♭ major   C♭ major
B♭ minor   E♭ minor   A♭ minor

Each major key has the same key signature as its relative minor. You can always find the keynote of the relative minor by counting down a minor third from the keynote of the major. The keys of C major and A minor have no sharps or flats in their key signature.

Chromatic Scale. If you play on the piano all the white and black keys between any note and its upper or lower octave, you have played a **chromatic** scale. Unlike those of the major or minor scale, the intervals (distances, or spaces, between notes) in the chromatic scale are all equal. Each interval is a half step. To write this scale requires several sharp or flat notes, or chromatic tones, as they are often called.

In the following example the top staff shows a chromatic scale beginning on middle C and using only sharps for the chromatic tones. The bottom staff shows exactly the same scale using flats and natural signs instead of sharps. On the piano C♯ and D♭ are the same note, and they are known as **enharmonic tones.** Other enharmonic tones are indicated by the lines drawn between the staffs:

Chords. Often three, four, or more notes are sounded at a time, forming a chord. One of the commonest types of chord is the **triad,** consisting of three tones. Here is a C major triad:

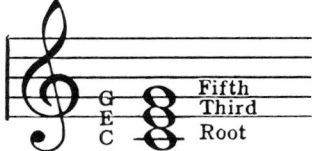

The tone on which the triad is based is called its **root.** The next tone above the root is the triad's **third.** The top tone is the **fifth** of the triad.

You can **invert** a triad in various ways. That is, the root need not always be on the bottom. Here is the same C major triad with its two inversions:

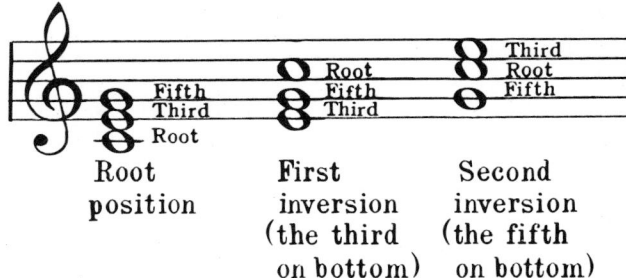

Root position   First inversion (the third on bottom)   Second inversion (the fifth on bottom)

Each tone of the scale can have its own triad. You can build triads on the tones of both the major and minor scales. Each triad is given a Roman numeral to indicate the step of the scale on which it is placed. The triads of the major scale are:

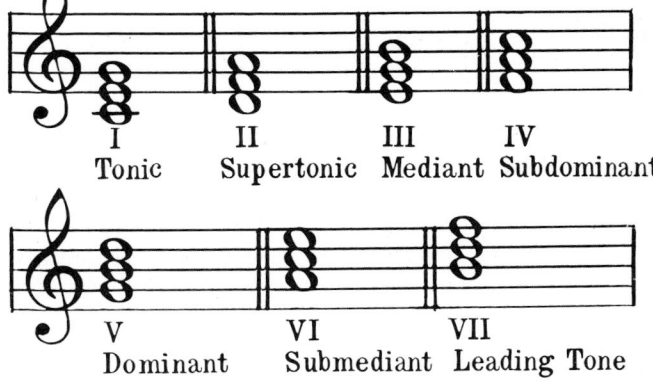

I   II   III   IV
Tonic   Supertonic   Mediant   Subdominant

V   VI   VII
Dominant   Submediant   Leading Tone

Length, or Duration, of Notes. Musical notation tells exactly how long each note should be held. The following diagram shows the

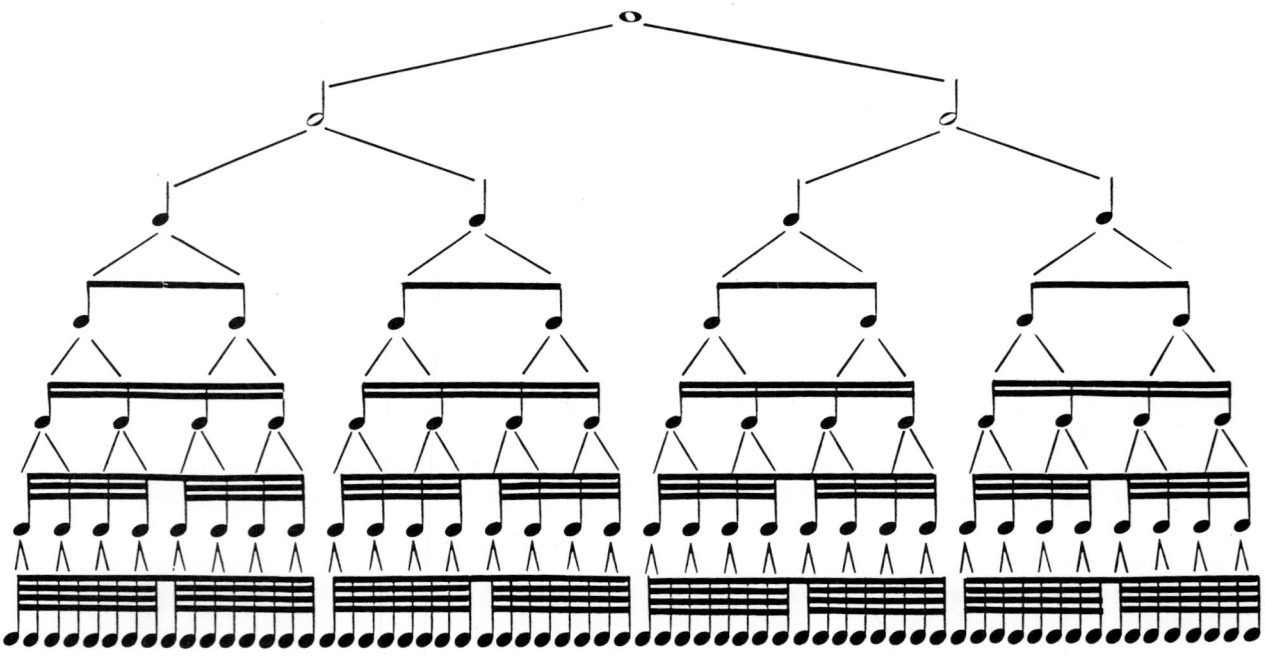

length value of notes in relation to each other. Here is a "pyramid" of note values:

The top note of the pyramid is a **whole note**. If you divide it into halves, you get two **half notes**. As you keep subdividing, you get **quarter notes**, **eighth notes**, **sixteenth notes**, **thirty-second notes**, and (at the base of the pyramid) **sixty-fourth notes**. You could even make one-hundred-and-twenty-eighth notes —but these are very rarely used.

The British terms for notes are:

Semibreve (whole note)
Minim (half note)
Crotchet (quarter note)
Quaver (eighth note)
Semiquaver (sixteenth note)
Demisemiquaver (thirty-second note)
Hemidemisemiquaver (sixty-fourth note)

Rests. Music does not consist only of sound. Rests, or silences, also are necessary, just as you need to take a breath from time to time when reading something aloud.

The **whole rest** hangs down from the fourth line of the staff, while the **half rest** sits on the third line of the staff. You must be careful not to confuse the two:

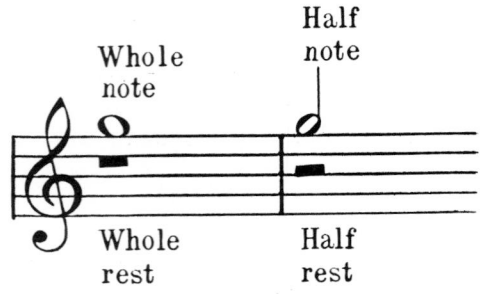

Here are the other rests, corresponding to the various notes shown in the pyramid:

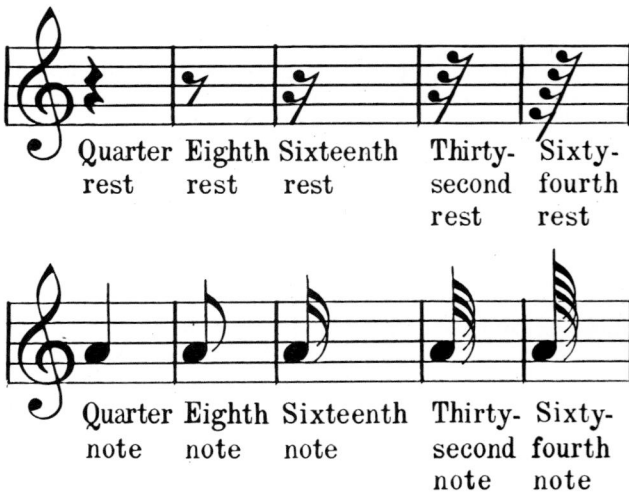

| Quarter rest | Eighth rest | Sixteenth rest | Thirty-second rest | Sixty-fourth rest |

| Quarter note | Eighth note | Sixteenth note | Thirty-second note | Sixty-fourth note |

Dotted Notes. Sometimes you will see a **dot** after a note, as in this example:

The dot adds half again the value of the original note. In other words, a dotted half note equals the length of three quarter notes.

A dotted quarter note equals three eighth notes, and so on, as the following example shows:

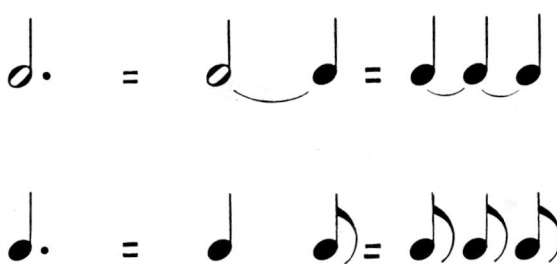

Tied Notes. Sometimes two notes of the same pitch are tied together like this:

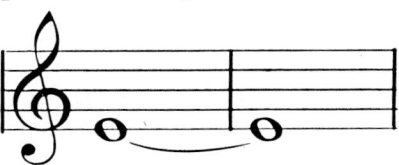

The second note is not sounded anew but simply held, and the sound continues. For example, two quarter notes tied together sound exactly like a half note. Two tied half notes sound exactly like a whole note, and so, also, with the other notes.

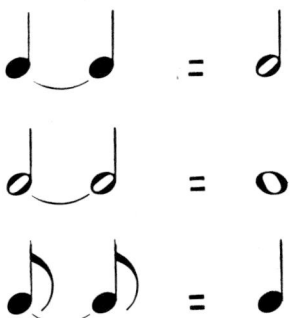

Slurred Notes. A slur is a sign drawn over or under two or more notes of different pitch and means that these notes are to be played or sung smoothly.

The term for such playing or singing is the Italian word *legato.*

Staccato Notes. If, on the other hand, the notes are to be played in a short, detached manner, dots are written under (or over) them like this:

These notes are played *staccato,* which is the Italian word meaning "detached." Do not confuse the dot placed over or under the note with the dot placed after the note. The dot after the note makes it longer—the staccato dot makes it shorter.

Musical Terms. Many Italian words are used as musical terms. A very important group of such terms indicates the **tempo** of the music, or how fast or slow it should be played. Another important group indicates the **dynamics**, or how loud or soft to play. There are many other terms besides these. You will find them listed and explained in the glossary of musical terms in this article. (Some composers prefer to use their own native language instead of Italian words.)

It is very important to know at least the basic musical terms. A good musician knows the exact meaning of every term the composer sets down. And a composer knows how to use terms that will make it clear to the performer exactly how the music should be played.

Meter. Meter is the basic grouping of regular, recurring beats and accents in a piece. Each such group of notes is contained in a **measure**, or **bar**, and each measure is separated from the next by a **bar line**. The meter is indicated at the beginning of each piece of music by a **time signature**. This usually appears in the form of a fraction, such as $\frac{3}{4}$, $\frac{4}{4}$, or $\frac{6}{8}$. The bottom number tells what kind of note will be used in the basic grouping of notes in each measure. The top number of the fraction tells how many of these notes will be used in the basic grouping of notes in each measure. For example, the time signature $\frac{4}{4}$ indicates that four quarter notes (or their equivalent) will appear in every measure.

This is the meter used for marches. Here are some other basic meters with their proper time signatures:

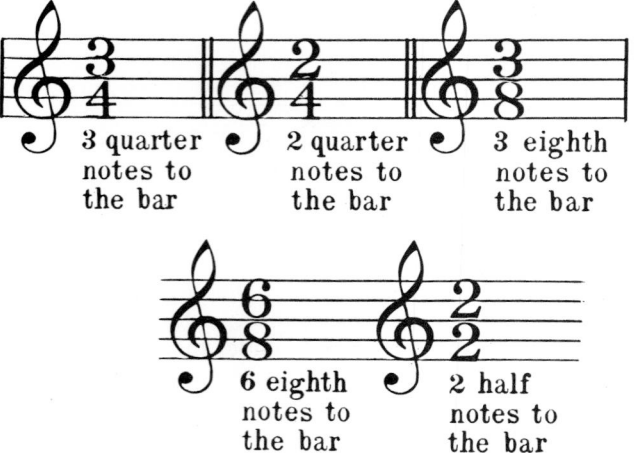

The $\frac{3}{4}$ meter is most often used in the waltz.

Many modern composers are dissatisfied with too much regularity in meter. They like to change the time signature often—sometimes in nearly every measure—or use no time signature at all. Another way composers avoid too much regularity is by using unusual meters, such as $\frac{5}{4}$ or $\frac{7}{16}$.

Sometimes at the beginning of a piece in $\frac{4}{4}$ time the sign C is used as a time signature instead of $\frac{4}{4}$. This sign looks like the letter C, but it is really a half circle. In medieval times, music with a feeling of triple meter (music with three beats to the bar) was given the time signature of a perfect circle. Triple meter was considered perfect. Duple meter (two or four beats to the bar) was considered imperfect. Its time signature was only half a circle. The idea of perfection and imperfection has disappeared from our musical thought. But the half-circle time signature is still often used ($C = \frac{4}{4}$; $\mathcal{C} = \frac{2}{2}$).

Today many composers are creating music that cannot be written down in traditional music notation. They may provide a **verbal score**, telling the performer what to do in words instead of musical symbols. Electronic music is music that does not have to be written down. With electronic equipment, the composer can feed a composition directly into a tape recorder. Computer programs are also used to generate music. Such pieces may or may not use live performers on stage.

But whatever happens to music in the future, the great masterpieces of the past and present cannot be fully appreciated without a knowledge of the basic elements of music.

DIKA NEWLIN
Virginia Commonwealth University
Author, *Bruckner-Mahler-Schoenberg*

MUSICAL TERMS

Absolute music—Music that does not try to suggest non-musical ideas, such as pictures or stories.

A capella—Unaccompanied choral music.

Accelerando—Increasing speed.

Accent—Stress on a beat.

Accidentals—Signs indicating that the normal pitch is to be raised or lowered. Most common are the sharp (♯—raise one halftone), the flat (♭—lower one halftone), and the natural (♮), which cancels a previous accidental at the same pitch.

Accompaniment—Secondary musical material that supports more important material.

Adagio—Slower than *andante*; faster than *lento*.

Ad libitum (ad lib)—At the liberty of the performer.

Affettuoso—With feeling.

Agitato—Agitated.

Al fine—To the end.

Alla breve—Double the speed, so that instead of counting four beats to the measure, count two, each beat represented by a half note.

Allargando—Decreasing speed while increasing loudness.

Allegretto—Moderately fast.

Allegro—Faster than *allegretto*; slower than *vivace*.

Alto—(1) Same as "contralto"; (2) unusually high-pitched male voice.

Andante—Slower than *allegretto*; faster than *adagio*.

Andantino—A little faster than *andante*.

Animato—Lively.

Arco—Indication to play with bow (of a stringed instrument), following a passage in *pizzicato*.

Arpeggio—The tones of a chord played in succession, ascending or descending.

A tempo—Indication to return to the original tempo.

Atonality—The absence of a tonal center, or key.

Augmented—Term used for a type of interval considered as an enlarged version of a certain other interval.

Bar—Same as "measure."

Bar line—A vertical line through a staff, to separate measures.

Baritone—A man's voice of medium pitch (between tenor and bass).

Bass—(1) The lowest male voice; (2) the lowest part in a piece of music.

Basso continuo—See definition of *continuo*, below.

Beat—(1) A regularly recurring brief unit of time that serves as the basis of meter, rhythm, and tempo; (2) the movement of a conductor's hand, which may correspond to the actual beat or may represent groupings of beats.

Bel canto—A style of singing demanding beauty of sound, flexibility, and vocal agility.

Bridge—(1) A wooden or metal arch over which the strings are stretched on stringed instruments; (2) a transitional passage between two themes or sections.

Broken chord—The tones of a chord played in succession in any order.

Cadence—A melodic or harmonic progression having the effect of a temporary or final conclusion.

Cadenza—A passage in which a soloist may display his or her skill.

Cantabile—In a singing style.

Cantillation—Chanted music, especially for a religious service.

Cantus firmus—A preexistent melody used as the basis for a new composition.

Capriccio—A playful or humorous composition.

Chord—The combination of three or more tones.

Chromatic—Refers to melodic or harmonic use of tones other than those of the diatonic scales.

Clef—A sign, such as 𝄢 or 𝄡, that indicates pitches of lines and spaces on a staff.

Coda—A closing section of a movement.

Coloratura—(1) Fast, florid, high passages for a singer; (2) a voice suitable for singing music with high, florid passages.

Common time—Four beats to each measure.

Con—With. (*Con brio*, with spirit; *con moto*, with movement.)

Consonance—A combination of tones considered "pleasing."

Continuo, or basso continuo—(1) The bass part in music of the baroque period; (2) the combination of instruments used to play the bass line and accompanying harmonies.

Contralto—The lower type of female voice.

Counterpoint—(1) The combination of two or more melodic lines; (2) the art, or technique, of writing such music.

Crescendo—Gradually increasing in loudness.

Cyclic—Refers to the use of the same theme in different movements of a large composition.

Da capo (D.C.)—Direction to begin again at the beginning.

Dal segno (D.S.)—Direction to begin again at the point indicated by the sign :S:.

Decrescendo—Gradually decreasing in loudness.

Descant—A countermelody sung above a hymn tune.

Development—The section of a movement in sonata form in which the themes are changed, combined, or otherwise modified.

Diapason—A set of pipes in an organ that provide the foundation of organ tone.

Diatonic—Refers to the seven tones of any major or minor scale.

Diminished—Term used for a type of interval considered as a lessened version of a certain other interval.

Diminuendo—Gradually decreasing in loudness.

Dissonance—An unpleasant combination of tones.

Dolce—Sweet.

Dominant—(1) The fifth tone of a major or minor scale; (2) the chord built on that tone.

Double-stop—Two tones sounded together on a stringed instrument.

Double time—Fast march tempo.

Downbeat—First beat of a bar or downward motion of conductor's baton indicating first beat.

Duet, or duo—A composition featuring two performers.

Duple time—Time that is divided into two or four basic beats to the bar.

Duplet—Two successive notes performed in the time normally filled by three of the same value.

Dynamics—Refers to volume, or loudness and softness.

Enharmonic—A note with alternate names, such as F sharp and G flat.

Ensemble—A group of performers.

Étude—A composition featuring a technical problem in its performance; hence a study or exercise.

Exposition—The first presentation of themes in a composition.

Falsetto—A high, unnatural vocal sound.

Fanfare—A short piece of music, usually for brass instruments, that is used to attract attention.

Fermata—A hold, or pause, indicated by the sign ◠ over a note or rest.

Figured bass—A bass part with numerals to indicate accompanying harmonies.

Finale—A closing scene or movement.

Fine—The end.

Fingerboard—The board against which strings are pressed to change pitch on stringed instruments.

Flat—See definition of "accidentals," above.

Form—The structure, or organization, of a piece of music.

Forte—Loud (*fortissimo*, very loud).

Fret—A small strip of material on the fingerboard of certain stringed instruments to guide the fingers.

Giocoso—Jokingly.

Glissando—A fast scale produced by sliding a finger across a keyboard or the strings of a harp.

Grace note—A very short ornamental note.

Grave—Solemn, in slow tempo.

Ground bass—A bass line repeated many times, with varied upper parts.

Half step—Half tone, such as C to C sharp or B to C.

Harmony—(1) Two or more tones sounded together; (2) the study of chords and how they progress.

Hold—See definition of *fermata*.

Homophonic—Refers to music with one most important melodic line, the other parts being accompaniment.

Imitation—Sounding a melody in one polyphonic part soon after it appears in another part.

Improvisation—Creating new music while performing.

Interval—The difference in pitch between two tones, usually stated in terms of scale steps (such as the interval of a second, a third, and so on).

Invention—Name sometimes given to a short, simple piece "invented" by a composer.

Inversion—(1) Substituting higher tones for lower ones, and vice versa; (2) changing tones of intervals or chords to higher or lower octaves; (3) turning a theme upside-down.

Key—(1) The tonal center of a composition; (2) a lever pressed by a finger on an instrument.

Key signature—Accidentals at the left end of a staff that indicate the key.

Larghetto—Slow; slightly faster than *largo*.

Largo—Very slow; slower than *lento*.

Leading tone—The seventh scale step of a diatonic scale.

Ledger line—A line for a note drawn above or below a staff.

Legato—Smooth, to be played with no interruption of sound between tones.

Leggiero—Light.

Leitmotiv—A musical motif associated with a person, place, thing, or idea, especially in the music dramas of Wagner.

Lento—Slower than *adagio*; faster than *largo*.

Lied—German song.

Maestoso—Majestic.

Major—Refers to (1) a scale having the following succession of intervals (T = tone, H = halftone): T, T, H, T, T, T, H; (2) intervals one halftone larger than minor intervals; (3) chords with a major third above the root, or fundamental tone.

Measure—A group of beats (most commonly two, three, or four) with an accent on the first beat.

Mediant—The third tone of a major or minor scale.

Melody—A succession of tones forming a musical line of individual expressive value.

Meter—The grouping of beats into units of twos, threes, fours, or more by accenting the first beat of each unit.

Metronome—A device used for sounding any desired number of beats per minute.

Mezzo, or mezza—Half or middle (*mezzo forte*, midway between soft and loud; *mezza voce*, with "half" voice).

Minor—Refers to (1) a scale having the following succession of intervals (T = tone, H = halftone): T, H, T, T, H, T, T; (2) intervals one half tone smaller than major intervals; (3) chords with a minor third above the root, or fundamental tone.

Mode—Same as a scale, but usually applied to the scales used in the Middle Ages.

Moderato—Moderate tempo.

Modulation—A change of key, or tonal center.

Molto—Very (*molto maestoso*, very majestic).

Monophonic—Refers to musical texture consisting of a single melodic line.

Motif, or **motive**—A short, distinctive melodic figure.

Mordent—A melodic ornament.

Movement—A self-contained section of a larger work such as a symphony, sonata, or string quartet.

Moto—With motion, or with movement.

Non troppo—Not too much.

Note—A written sign for a tone.

Octave—The interval of an eighth.

Octet—A group of eight performers or a composition for such a group.

Opus (op.)—Work; used in numbering the works of a composer (opus 1, first work).

Ostinato—A melodic phrase repeated again and again.

Parlando—Singing almost as if speaking.

Pause—See definition of *fermata*, above.

Pedal point—A long-held tone (usually in the bass) against which changing harmonies create tension.

Pentatonic—Refers to a five-tone scale, such as C-D-E-G-A.

Period—A segment of musical form, consisting of two or more phrases.

Phrase—A short segment of musical form, consisting of several motifs.

Piano—(1) Soft (*pianissimo*, very soft); (2) short for "pianoforte," a keyboard instrument.

Pitch—The highness or lowness of a tone.

Più—More.

Pizzicato—Plucking the strings of a bowed stringed instrument.

Poco—Little.

Polyphonic—Refers to musical texture consisting of two or more melodic lines sounding at the same time.

Presto—Very fast; faster than *vivace*.

Program music—Music intended to suggest nonmusical ideas, such as pictures or stories.

Quartet—A group of four performers or a composition for such a group.

Quintet—A group of five performers or a composition for such a group.

Rallentando—Decreasing speed.

Recapitulation—The restatement of themes after the development section of a movement in sonata form.

Refrain—A section of a composition that recurs several times.

Resolution—The move to a consonant chord from a dissonant one.

Rest—A sign indicating a silence of specific duration.

Rhythm—The pattern of longer and shorter note values, measured on the basis of the beat; more generally, the organization of music in respect to time.

Ripieno—Indicates full ensemble, as distinguished from small group of soloists.

Ritardando—Gradually decreasing in speed.

Root—The fundamental tone of a chord, from which the other tones of the chord are measured.

Rubato—Slight and short changes (faster or slower) of the basic tempo.

Scale—An ascending or descending series of single tones (usually progressing by means of whole-tone or half-tone steps) that are related to a certain chosen fundamental tone.

Scherzo—Joke; *scherzando*, jokingly.

Score—The notation of a musical composition, showing all its parts.

Segue—Indication to continue without a pause.

Semitone—Same as a half tone.

Sempre—Always (*sempre legato*, always *legato*).

Senza—Without (*senza rallentando*, without slowing down; *senza sordino*, without mute).

Septet—A group of seven performers or a composition for such a group.

Sextet—A group of six performers or a composition for such a group.

Sforzando, or **sforzato**—An accented sound on a single note or chord.

Sharp—See definition of "accidentals," above.

Slur—The sign ⌢, indicating *legato* performance.

Solo—A composition or passage for one performer, alone or with accompaniment.

Soprano—The highest voice.

Sordino—(1) Mute of a stringed or wind instrument; (2) damper of a piano.

Sostenuto—Sustained.

Staccato—A shortened, detached sounding of a tone or chord (the opposite of *legato*).

Staff—Five horizontal lines on and between which notes are written to indicate pitch.

Stretto—(1) In contrapuntal writing, the overlapping of melodic parts, that is, the beginning of a theme in one part before it has been concluded in a previous part; (2) quickening of tempo.

Subdominant—Fourth tone of a major or minor scale.

Subito—Suddenly.

Submediant—The sixth tone of a major or minor scale.

Supertonic—The second tone of a major or minor scale.

Suspension—A note held over from one chord to a new chord, in which it forms a discord.

Syncopation—Stressing of a normally unaccented beat.

Tanto—So much (*non tanto*, not too much).

Tempo—Speed, determined by the length of the beat.

Tenor—The highest natural male voice.

Tenuto—Held, sustained.

Tetrachord—A series of four adjacent tones, usually part of a scale.

Timbre—Quality of tone, or tone color.

Time signature—Figures at the beginning of a composition (such as $\frac{2}{4}$, $\frac{3}{4}$, $\frac{6}{8}$) which indicate how many (upper number) of what kind (lower number) of notes are in each measure.

Tonality—Same as "key" (1), above.

Tone—(1) A single musical sound, represented by a written note; (2) the interval of a major second, such as A to B.

Tonic—(1) The basic tone of a composition, to which all the other tones are related; (2) the lowest and basic tone of a scale.

Transposition—The writing or performing of music in a key different from the original key.

Tremolo—Rapid repetition of a tone or alternation of two tones.

Triad—A three-note chord consisting of a chosen root with intervals of a third and a fifth (such as C-E-G).

Trill—Rapid alternation of a tone with its upper or lower neighbor.

Trio—A group of three performers or a composition for such a group.

Triple time—Time that is made up of three basic beats to the bar.

Triplet—Three successive notes performed in the time normally filled by two notes of the same value.

Turn—A melodic ornament.

Tutti—All, meaning that the whole ensemble is to play.

Unison—The same pitch sounded by two or more performers.

Upbeat—(1) An unaccented beat of a measure; (2) the upward movement of a conductor's baton in preparation for a downbeat.

Vibrato—Rapidly repeated slight changes of pitch.

Vivace—Faster than *allegro*; slower than *presto*.

Whole tone—Same as "tone" (2), above.

Whole-tone scale—A scale made up entirely of whole tones, or major seconds.

RALPH T. DANIEL
Indiana University
Co-author, *The Harvard Brief Dictionary of Music*

MUSICAL FORMS

Form in music is the shape, or structure, of a composition. Usually composers have in mind the general designs of the compositions they are writing, much as architects use ground plans in constructing buildings. These musical "ground plans" serve as foundations on which composers organize their rhythms, melodies, and harmonies. Musical forms are not mere molds into which composers pour music. Rather, musical forms grow out of the way in which composers develop their musical ideas.

Two basic designs that composers use in writing music are **binary form** and **ternary form**. Binary form consists of two nearly equal complementary or contrasting sections (A-B). Ternary form consists of two similar sections that frame a contrasting middle section (A-B-A).

Other basic musical designs are **rondo form** and **variation form**. Rondo form generally follows the pattern A-B-A-C-A-B-A. Variation form consists of a melody followed by sections in which the melody undergoes rhythmic, harmonic, or melodic changes. Each variation is based on the original melody, as in the pattern A1-A2-A3-A4-A5, and so on. Another basic design, commonly used in vocal music, is **strophic form**, in which each stanza of a poem is set to the same music. Any of these basic forms may be altered or extended by the composer.

Sometimes, however, a composer may not want to follow a particular form in a piece. Such a piece is said to have free form. Examples of free forms are the **rhapsody** and the **fantasia**, or **fantasy**. Some important musical forms are described in the following list.

Anthem. A short choral composition written to English words from the Scriptures or some other religious text. It may or may not use vocal soloists and organ accompaniment. Anthems are performed in many Protestant churches. Patriotic songs are often called anthems, hence the term "national anthem."

Aria. A song with instrumental accompaniment, the main lyrical form for solo voice in opera, oratorio, cantata, and passion. Arias in the 18th century were often in A-B-A form.

Bagatelle. A short, light instrumental piece, usually for piano. Ludwig van Beethoven wrote 26 bagatelles.

Ballad. A type of folk song that tells a story. The term is also used for a sentimental popular song.

Ballade. An instrumental piece, usually for piano, that often suggests a story. The most popular examples are the four ballades for piano by Frédéric Chopin. The ballade was an important form of music and poetry in medieval France.

Barcarolle. A piece for voices or instruments that imitates a Venetian gondolier song. The swaying of the boat on the water is suggested by the accompaniment. The barcarolle in *The Tales of Hoffmann* is famous.

Berceuse. A lullaby or instrumental piece in which the rhythm suggests the rocking of a cradle.

Canon. A piece, either sung or played, in which one voice starts a melody and one or more other voices join in with the same melody at successive intervals.

Cantata. A sacred or secular work for voices and instruments. It consists of arias, recitative (speech-song), and parts for chorus. The cantata is sometimes used as part of a religious service, as in the Lutheran Church. The form is similar to the oratorio but on a smaller scale. The most famous examples are those by Johann Sebastian Bach, who wrote over 300 cantatas.

Chaconne. A piece in slow triple (three-beat) time in which a melody is repeated over and over, usually in the bass part. Melodic or rhythmic variations occur in the other parts with each statement of the melody. Bach's chaconne for unaccompanied violin is perhaps the most famous example of this form.

Chorale. A German Lutheran hymn and the central musical portion of the Lutheran service. It was also used as the basis for other forms: chorale prelude, chorale partita, chorale fantasy, chorale motet, and chorale cantata.

Concerto. A work for one or more solo instruments and orchestra. Originally (late 16th century) the term meant a work for voices and instruments. By the end of the 17th century "concerto" generally referred to a work in three or four movements in which two or more solo instruments were contrasted with a larger group of instruments. This form was called the **concerto grosso**. Many important examples of the concerto grosso were written by Arcangelo Corelli (1653–1713), Antonio Vivaldi (1675?–1741), and George Frederick Handel. Bach's six *Brandenburg* concertos are among the most celebrated examples of the form.

The concerto for a single solo instrument and orchestra developed early in the 18th century. At first the solo part was always written for the violin, although the harpsichord and other solo instruments rapidly gained favor. The solo concerto usually consisted of three movements (fast-slow-fast). Late in the 18th century Wolfgang Amadeus Mozart established the standard form of the concerto for solo piano with orchestra. Popular piano concertos were later written by Ludwig van Beethoven, Robert Schumann, Johannes Brahms, Peter Tchaikovsky, and Sergei Rachmaninoff (1873–1943). Mozart, Beethoven, Felix Mendelssohn, Brahms, Tchaikovsky, and Jean Sibelius wrote popular concertos for solo violin and orchestra. In the 20th century important concertos were written by Béla Bartók, Arnold Schoenberg, and Sergei Prokofiev.

Divertimento. A light work in several movements for a small instrumental group. The divertimento, which combines elements of the sonata and the suite, was a very popular form in the 18th century. It often contained two minuets and usually ended with a spirited rondo. Mozart wrote several examples, using various combinations of instruments.

Fantasia, or Fantasy. An instrumental piece in free form that flourished mainly in the 16th and 17th centuries. The fantasia was very important in the early development of instrumental music. In the 18th and 19th centuries a fantasia suggested music of an improvisational character.

Fugue. A composition in which a theme, or subject, is developed throughout in counterpoint. (**Counterpoint** is the art of combining several melodic lines.) A fugue may consist of from two to four or more melodic parts. A fugue begins with a statement of the theme in one part. The theme is then taken up, or imitated, by each part successively, while other parts weave melodic patterns around the theme. In the course of the fugue, the theme reappears at various points in one melodic part or another. Brief sections in which the theme does not appear are called **episodes**.

A double fugue is one in which two themes, or subjects, are developed. There are also triple (three-theme) and quadruple (four-theme) fugues.

A fugue may be written for voices or a group of instruments or a solo instrument. Johann Sebastian Bach, the greatest master of the form, wrote wonderful fugues for single, unaccompanied violin. A fugue may be an independent piece or part of a larger work such as a sonata, suite, or oratorio. Many of the finest examples of the form are found in Bach's organ works and in his *Well-Tempered Clavier* (consisting of 48 preludes and fugues) and *Art of the Fugue*.

Impromptu. A short piece, usually for piano, that sometimes seems to have been improvised, or made up as the performer goes along. But some impromptus are very carefully organized pieces.

Madrigal. A song for several voices and the most important form of vocal chamber music. The madrigal flourished mainly in 16th-century Italy and Elizabethan England. It is a musical setting of a poem for two to six or more voices, using the technique of counterpoint. Leading Italian madrigal composers included Luca Marenzio (1553–99), Carlo Gesualdo (1560?–1613), and Claudio Monteverdi (1567–1643). Among the many important English madrigal composers were William Byrd (1543–1623), Thomas Morley (1557–1603), John Wilbye (1574–1638), and Thomas Weelkes (1575?–1623).

Mass. Musically the term "mass" refers to the sung portions of the main Roman Catholic service. As a musical form, the mass usually consists of those parts of the service known as the **Ordinary**. The Ordinary includes the Kyrie, Gloria, Credo, Sanctus (with the Benedictus), and Agnus Dei. The mass has been an important musical form since medieval times. Among the great mass composers were Guillaume Dufay (1400?–74), Josquin des Prez (1450?–1521), William Byrd, and Giovanni Pierluigi da Palestrina. Important later composers of masses include Johann Sebastian Bach, Wolfgang Amadeus Mozart, Joseph Haydn, Ludwig van Beethoven, Franz Schubert, and Anton Bruckner (1824–96). In the 20th century Igor Stravinsky and Ralph Vaughan Williams (1872–1958) composed outstanding masses.

A **requiem** mass, or mass for the dead, omits the Gloria and Credo but includes several other prayers. Famous requiems were composed by Wolfgang Amadeus Mozart, Hector Berlioz, and Giuseppe Verdi.

Minuet. A dance in triple time (three beats to a bar) of French origin. During the 17th and 18th centuries the minuet was used as a movement in suites, chamber music, and symphonies. It is in A-B-A form.

Motet. A sacred choral composition usually in Latin and sometimes including solo voices and instrumental accompaniment. The motet was one of the most important musical forms of the Renaissance, when it was usually for unaccompanied chorus. The greatest composers of motets in the Renaissance included Josquin, Palestrina, Roland de Lassus (1532–94), Tomás Luis de Victoria (1549?–1611), and William Byrd. Among the important composers of motets since the Renaissance were Heinrich Schütz (1585–1672), Johann Sebastian Bach, and Johannes Brahms. These composers used German instead of Latin for their motets. The medieval motet was characterized by the use of a different text for each melody line. Sometimes each text was even in a different language.

Nocturne. A slow, lyric piano piece with a rich chordal accompaniment. Frédéric Chopin wrote many popular nocturnes. "Nocturne" means "night piece," and these pieces often suggest a dreamy summer evening.

Oratorio. A musical setting of a dramatic or epic text, often on a sacred subject, for voices and instruments. The oratorio uses arias, recitative (speech-song), solo ensembles, and choruses. The form is closely related to the opera, but there is no scenery or stage action. The chorus, rather than the parts for solo voices, is emphasized. Among the important early oratorio composers were Giacomo Carissimi (1605–74) and Heinrich Schütz. But the greatest figure in the history of the form was George Frederick Handel. Handel wrote many oratorios, and his *Messiah* is the most popular example of the form ever composed. Among the famous oratorios by later composers are *The Creation,* by Joseph Haydn, *Elijah,* by Felix Mendelssohn, and the *German Requiem,* by Johannes Brahms. Notable examples of the form in the 20th century include *Belshazzar's Feast,* by William Walton (1902–   ), and *Oedipus Rex,* by Igor Stravinsky.

Overture. An orchestral introduction to an opera, oratorio, or other vocal work. The first movement of an instrumental suite is often given the title overture. Sometimes composers give the name to independent concert pieces for orchestra. Works of this type include Mendelssohn's *Hebrides* Overture and Tchaikovsky's *1812* Overture. Operatic overtures, too, are often performed separately on concert programs.

Partita. An Italian term for "suite." Bach used the term "partita" for several of his suites for harpsichord and for unaccompanied violin.

Passion. The name for the musical setting of the story of Christ's last suffering and crucifixion. The text of the passion, which is in the form of a dramatic oratorio, is taken from the Gospels. The greatest of all passions are those composed by Johann Sebastian Bach to the Gospel according to Saint Matthew and the Gospel according to Saint John.

Plainsong, or Plainchant. The sung prayers of the Roman Catholic Church, also known as Gregorian chant or Roman chant. They consist of a single line of vocal melody without instrumental accompaniment.

Prelude. An instrumental work that is used as an introduction to another piece, as in "Prelude and Fugue." It is sometimes written as an independent composition, as in the piano preludes of Chopin.

Quartet. The title for an instrumental work for four players or a vocal piece for four singers. The string quartet, for two violins, viola, and cello, is the most important instrumental form. The greatest composers of string quartets were Haydn, Mozart, and Beethoven. The literature for the string quartet is one of the richest in music.

Recitative. A type of speech-song. It came into use at the end of the 16th century, when composers tried to capture the inflections of speech through harmonic and melodic accents. Recitative is important in opera, where it serves to advance the action of the story.

Rhapsody. A title for an instrumental work and occasionally for a vocal piece, written in a free, improvisatory style. Among well-known examples are the *Hungarian* rhapsodies for piano by Franz Liszt. Brahms's *Alto* Rhapsody is for solo alto voice, men's chorus, and orchestra. George Gershwin's *Rhapsody in Blue* is for piano and orchestra.

Round. A song in which several voices join in successively with the melody in follow-the-leader fashion. Popular rounds are "Three Blind Mice" and "Frère Jacques."

Scherzo. A title often used for a piece that is humorous or fantastic in character. After about 1750 it was a fast instrumental piece and frequently a movement in a larger work such as a sonata, quartet, or symphony. It is in A-B-A form.

Serenade. A light instrumental form of entertainment music, similar to the divertimento. It combines elements of the suite and the symphony and usually contains minuets, marches, and other dance forms. The serenade was popular in the 18th century, and Mozart wrote several for orchestra and other combinations of instruments. A courting song is also called a serenade. Examples of such songs were written by Schubert and Brahms.

Sonata. See the section on the sonata, which follows.

Song. Literally, song is any music that is sung. Usually, however, a song refers to a piece for one voice with or without instrumental accompaniment. There are three major types of song: art song, folk song, and popular song. Art songs are songs of high artistic merit, written by trained composers. Art songs in German are called **lieder**; in French, **melodies** or **romances**. The more common French word *chanson* usually refers to a popular song. Many of the greatest art songs are set to first-rate poems. Folk songs are songs of the people and are usually of unknown origin. A song cycle is a set of related songs grouped in a particular order and meant to be sung in that order. A song for two voices is called a duet, for three a trio, for four a quartet, and so on. When more than one voice sings each part, the piece is called a part-song or a chorus.

Suite. An important form of instrumental music, particularly in the 17th and 18th centuries. It consisted of a set, or suite, of dance pieces, all in the same key and grouped together to form a larger work. The basic grouping of dances included the *allemande,* courante, saraband, and *gigue.* Optional dances, such as the minuet or gavotte, were often inserted between the saraband and *gigue.* Composers sometimes added a prelude at the beginning. Suites were written for harpsichord, orchestra, and other instrumental ensembles. Those by Bach for keyboard and for unaccompanied violin represent the finest examples of the form. Since the 19th century the suite has usually been a group of instrumental pieces drawn from opera, ballet, or incidental music from a play.

Symphonic Poem, or Tone Poem. An orchestral piece in which nonmusical elements are combined with the principle of development used in sonata form. The form flourished in the 19th century and was an important type of program music. The program may be narrative, as in *Till Eulenspiegel,* by Richard Strauss (1864–1949), or descriptive, as in *The Moldau,* by Bedřich Smetana (1824–84). Literary subjects and paintings have also served as programs for symphonic poems. The form was first developed by Franz Liszt, whose symphonic poem *Les Préludes* is one of his most popular works.

Symphony. See the section on the symphony later in this article.

Toccata. An instrumental piece, usually for keyboard. It is characterized by full chords and rapid runs and is designed to display the resources of the instrument and the skill of the player.

Reviewed by DIKA NEWLIN
Virginia Commonwealth University

Sonata

For the last 3 centuries the sonata has been one of the most important forms of instrumental music. Most sonatas are made up of three or four separate pieces, or movements. Since about 1775, sonatas have usually been written for only one or two instruments, most often for piano alone or for piano with another instrument. A sonatina is a short and simple sonata.

The term "sonata" is used in three different ways: (1) "Sonata" is used in the term "sonata form," which is a special musical design found most often in the first movement of a sonata. (2) "Sonata" can mean the complete work, or cycle of movements. (3) "Sonata" can be the broad term for all instrumental music that falls into the same general class. For example, it can include the symphony, which is basically a sonata for full orchestra. It can include the concerto, as a sonata for soloist (or soloists) and orchestra. And it can include the string quartet, as a sonata for two violins, viola, and cello.

Sonata Form. The sonata form falls into three main sections: exposition, development, and recapitulation. The **exposition** presents at least two main musical ideas, or themes, which usually contrast in style and mood. The **development** freely modifies any or all of these same themes by shifting them about, taking them apart, adding to them, or combining one theme with another. Finally, the **recapitulation** restates the main themes in much the same way that they appeared in the exposition.

Because the recapitulation is so much like the exposition, the three sections of the sonata form make a free A-B-A design (two like sections separated by a contrasting section). But the two outer sections differ in their tonal direction. That is, the exposition modulates, or moves away from the home key to a nearby key, whereas the recapitulation returns to the home key. The departure and the return, along with new modulations to still other keys throughout the development section, create tonal tension and unity. In other words, the modulations help to make the sonata form more exciting and also to hold it together. They are somewhat like stretching a rubber band every which way, with the rubber band finally returning to its original shape.

Sonata Cycle. The sonata form in the first movement is sometimes called the sonata-*allegro* form, because that movement is often marked *allegro,* or "fast." The second movement of the sonata cycle is usually a songful, melodious slow movement. It, too, often has an A-B-A design, but simpler than that of the first movement. Or it may be a series of variations on a clearly phrased melody that makes a little A-B design within itself.

If there are four movements, the third is usually a minuet in a moderate tempo (speed), a *scherzo* in a faster tempo, or some other dancelike piece that has three beats to a measure. Its design is usually A-B-A, too. The B section, or trio, is often the lightest, wittiest section of the whole cycle.

The last movement, or finale, brings the sonata cycle to an effective close, usually be-ing faster, gayer, or more driving and climactic than the previous movements. Sometimes it is a light rondo, in which a tuneful refrain (A) alternates with other sections, as in the design A-B-A-C-A-B-A. Or it may be another movement in sonata form, usually faster in tempo than the first movement.

Occasionally either the first or the last movement has a slow introduction. One or all of the movements may have a **coda,** or final section, that sums up and even throws new light on the whole movement.

Baroque Period. The sonata dates back to the rise of the violin family of instruments in the baroque period (about 1580 to 1750). A favorite baroque type was the trio sonata, with two violins (or flutes or oboes) over a bass part. An organist or harpsichordist played this bass with the left hand, along with a cellist, and filled in the harmony with the right hand.

Baroque sonatas for solo violin and keyboard accompaniment were written by such composers as Arcangelo Corelli (1653–1713), Giuseppe Tartini (1692–1770), Jean-Marie Leclair (1697–1764), Johann Sebastian Bach, and George Frederick Handel. These sonatas were written mainly for use in church or at court. The church sonatas were usually in a slow-fast-slow-fast order. The court type was actually a suite, or set, of contrasting dances.

Classical Period. During the classical period (from about 1750 to 1825) sonatas were written mainly for a keyboard instrument. When the violin or another stringed instrument joined in, it served merely as accompaniment at first, only later becoming a full partner. During this period the piano gradually replaced the harpsichord as the most important keyboard instrument. Joseph Haydn, Wolfgang Amadeus Mozart, Ludwig van Beethoven, and Franz Schubert wrote many sonata masterpieces. Among the most famous examples are Beethoven's *Pathétique, Moonlight,* and *Appassionata* sonatas for solo piano and his *Kreutzer* Sonata for violin and piano. The classical composers perfected both the sonata form and the complete sonata cycle.

Romantic Period. Most composers of the romantic period (from about 1820 to 1910) tended to reduce the sonata to standard formulas. In fact, they tended to think of the sonata as cold and old-fashioned. Yet some of the most important composers—Frédéric Chopin, Robert Schumann, Franz Liszt, and Johannes Brahms—wrote notable large-scale examples of this musical form. These include sonatas for piano alone and for piano with another instrument.

Twentieth Century. In the 20th century the sonata is still a favorite musical form. Many of the leading composers—including Alexander Scriabin (1872–1915), Béla Bartók, Paul Hindemith (1895–1963), and Sergei Prokofiev—have given their best efforts to the sonata. The styles have changed, but the basic forms and sonata idea go on with full force.

WILLIAM S. NEWMAN
Author, A History of the Sonata Idea

Symphony

The word "symphony" dates back to very ancient times. Originally it came from two Greek words meaning "a sounding together."

In the late 16th and early 17th century "symphony" meant an ensemble of voices and instruments. The great Italian composer Giovanni Gabrieli (1557–1612) worked in the magnificent Cathedral of St. Mark in Venice. This building had two choir lofts, so there were wonderful opportunities for echo effects back and forth between different groups of voices and instruments. Double choruses were used, and the brilliant brass instruments played a great part. Gabrieli wrote many compositions for double chorus and brass ensemble. He called these *sacrae symphoniae* ("sacred symphonies"). One of his pupils, the great German composer Heinrich Schütz, also wrote "sacred symphonies."

The 18th Century. In the 18th century composers developed the Italian *sinfonia,* or overture. This was an introduction to an opera. It had three sections: a fast, lively opening section, a quieter middle part, and a brisk close. This form also became well-known in Vienna, Austria, where Italian opera was very popular. There another favorite form was the serenade, or divertimento—basically light music filled with gay dance rhythms. The typical dance was the minuet, in $\frac{3}{4}$ time (that is, with three beats to the bar). Composers brought the minuet into the symphony, inserting it between the slow section and the lively closing section. Thus, the symphony became a four-movement form. (A movement is a self-contained section, with one basic tempo, or speed, throughout.) The symphony became independent of the opera and could stand alone.

The late 18th century was the great age of the "Viennese classical symphony." Each movement of the symphony had its own special characteristics. The first movement sometimes had a slow, dignified introduction to its lively main section. This movement was usually in sonata form. It had three main sections: an exposition (in which the themes were set forth), a development (in which they were elaborated and transformed), and a recapitulation (in which they were restated). The second movement was usually slower and more lyrical. The third movement was the minuet—sometimes very courtly, at other times almost like a peasant dance. The last movement was often a gay rondo, with a lilting refrain theme that was easy to remember.

The great masters of the Viennese classical symphony were Franz Joseph Haydn, Wolfgang Amadeus Mozart, and Ludwig van Beethoven. Haydn, who wrote over 100 symphonies, was famous for his sly humor in music. A typical example of his humor occurs in his *Surprise* Symphony (No. 94). In the second movement, during a quiet passage, the orchestra suddenly plays a loud chord, which was meant to wake the people who sometimes fell asleep at Haydn's concerts. Jokes like this were well known, but Haydn's real importance is shown in the deep seriousness of many of his symphonies. Particularly important are the last 12 that he composed, the "Salomon" symphonies (1791–95).

Mozart brought elegance and refinement, but also passion, to the symphony. During his short life he wrote some 41 works in this form. Mozart's last symphony is perhaps his greatest. It was later nicknamed the *Jupiter* Symphony because, just as Jupiter was ruler of the mythical Roman gods, so this work was considered a leader among symphonies. And it has kept that rank, for it is still much admired and often performed.

Another favorite among Mozart's symphonies, No. 40, is full of passion and feeling. Two others, No. 38 (the *Prague*) and No. 39, also rank among the most glorious works in all symphonic music. Mozart wrote his last three symphonies (Nos. 39–41) in 1788, in the short period of about 2 months.

At first, Beethoven followed in the footsteps of Haydn and Mozart, but he soon went his own way. He enlarged the orchestra. And beginning with his Third Symphony, the *Eroica*, he wrote much longer symphonies than his predecessors had. Beethoven introduced the *scherzo* ("joke") into the symphony, in place of the traditional minuet movement. Probably the most popular of Beethoven's nine symphonies is the Fifth. The Seventh is another favorite, largely because of its fine rhythms. In his last symphony, Beethoven introduced a full chorus and vocal soloists. (The symphonies of Haydn and Mozart were written for orchestra only.)

The 19th Century. During the 19th-century romantic period, composers tried to make their music express their personal feelings more fully than earlier composers had done. Some wanted to make the symphony tell a story. For example, the popular *Fantastic Symphony*, by Hector Berlioz, is subtitled "Episodes in the Life of an Artist." Symphonies became longer, and more instruments were used. Robert Schumann praised the C Major Symphony of Franz Schubert for its "heavenly length." But Schubert's most popular symphony is the *Unfinished*, with only two movements.

Two others who believed in long symphonies were the Austrians Anton Bruckner (1824–96) and Gustav Mahler. Both wrote for massive orchestras, and most of their symphonies play nearly an hour. In general, Bruckner followed the models of Beethoven and Schubert. But he had an individual style of composing, strongly influenced by Richard Wagner. Bruckner's early training as an organist, too, influenced his orchestral style. Bruckner's symphonies are notable for their lovely *adagios* (slow movements).

To Mahler, each symphony was a world with its own laws of construction. He believed that a symphony could use any instruments and have as many movements as the composer wished, instead of following a fixed pattern.

Each of Mahler's ten symphonies is individual. Yet they all bear the mark of his strong personality. Sometimes he used choruses and vocal soloists, after the pattern of Beethoven's Ninth. His Eighth Symphony is called the "symphony of a thousand" because it requires a large orchestra, eight soloists, two mixed choirs, and a children's choir. Like Bruckner, Mahler was influenced by Wagner.

Other important symphony composers of the late 19th century were Johannes Brahms, Antonin Dvořák, and Peter Tchaikovsky. Brahms wrote four great symphonies, which have long been part of the standard orchestral repertory. He wrote for a more traditional-size orchestra than Bruckner or Mahler, and his symphonies are shorter and more classical in structure. As a composer of symphonies, Dvořák was a follower of Brahms. He wrote one of the most popular works in this form— the symphony subtitled "From the New World." The most popular of Tchaikovsky's six symphonies is the *Pathétique* (No. 6).

The 20th Century. Some 20th-century composers reacted against the idea of the big romantic symphony and wrote symphonies for small ensembles. For example, Arnold Schoenberg wrote a chamber symphony for 15 solo instruments. Other composers, called neoclassicists, modeled their works on the Viennese classical symphony. For a time, Igor Stravinsky and Sergei Prokofiev wrote in this way. But composers like Jean Sibelius (1865–1957), Sergei Rachmaninoff (1873–1943), Ralph Vaughan Williams (1872–1958), and Dmitri Shostakovich (1906–75) continued to write very much in the 19th-century manner.

DIKA NEWLIN
Virginia Commonwealth University
Author, *Bruckner-Mahler-Schoenberg*

See also ANCIENT WORLD, MUSIC OF THE; BANDS AND BAND MUSIC; CAROLS; CHAMBER MUSIC; CHORAL MUSIC; COUNTRY MUSIC; DANCE MUSIC; ELECTRONIC MUSIC; FOLK MUSIC; HYMNS; JAZZ; MIDDLE AGES, MUSIC OF THE; MODERN MUSIC; MUSIC FESTIVALS; NATIONAL ANTHEMS AND PATRIOTIC SONGS; OPERA; OPERETTA; ORCHESTRA; ORCHESTRA CONDUCTING; ORIENTAL MUSIC; RENAISSANCE MUSIC; ROCK MUSIC; VOICE TRAINING AND SINGING; names of individual composers, as BACH, MOZART; names of musical instruments, as PIANO, WIND INSTRUMENTS; music of individual countries, as ITALY (Italian Music); and music of periods and styles, as BAROQUE MUSIC.

Comic book characters come to life in *Annie* (1977).

MUSICAL COMEDY

The term "musical comedy" is used to describe almost any form of musical entertainment between grand opera and vaudeville. In opera there is an uninterrupted flow of music and singing. Vaudeville presents a group of unrelated acts. But musical comedy tells its story with speech, songs, and dances. The revue is also considered a form of musical comedy because the production is created as a unit, even though scenes and songs may be unrelated. Other forms of light musical theater are operetta, often costumed and romantic, and the musical play. The musical play is a more serious form of musical comedy.

The musical comedy form has many sources, mostly European. The French *opéra bouffe* (comic opera), the Viennese operetta, and the English comic opera of Gilbert and Sullivan all contributed to its development. Victor Herbert was America's first important composer for the theater. He was greatly in-

fluenced by the European school, particularly the Viennese. George M. Cohan pioneered in establishing a more American form of musical theater. He was followed by Irving Berlin, whose first musical comedy, *Watch Your Step* (1914), introduced American ragtime into the theater. Other important early leaders in advancing the musical comedy form were composer Jerome Kern and lyricists Guy Bolton and P. G. Wodehouse. Their intimate, modern-dress musicals were a refreshing change from the heavy European operettas that had become popular after the success of Franz Lehar's *The Merry Widow* (1907).

The 1920's and 1930's

Many of the great names in the musical theater first appeared in the 1920's. George and Ira Gershwin, Vincent Youmans, Oscar Hammerstein II, Cole Porter, and Lorenz Hart were among those who won fame during this period. Composers were saying something fresh in a typically American way.

Operettas like *Rose Marie,* by Rudolf Friml, and *The Desert Song,* by Sigmund Romberg, continued to attract audiences. But in 1927 the American musical theater came into its own with *Show Boat,* its first modern musical, written by Kern and Hammerstein.

The Depression of the 1930's inspired many topical musicals. The first musical to win a Pulitzer prize, *Of Thee I Sing,* was a satire on politics. With music and lyrics by the Gershwin brothers and story by George S. Kaufman and Morrie Ryskind, it showed that a musical could have a serious side.

Audiences also welcomed entertaining musicals like *The Cat and the Fiddle,* by Kern and Hammerstein. In 1936, Rodgers and Hart collaborated with George Abbott on *On Your Toes.* This was the first musical to use ballet as an important part of the plot. *Porgy and Bess,* with music by George Gershwin and lyrics by Ira Gershwin and DuBose Heyward, was produced in 1935. It is often called the finest American opera. But it had its roots in the Broadway theater.

The 1940's and 1950's

During the 1940's the American musical stage continued to progress. There was *Cabin in the Sky,* a black fantasy by Lynn Root, Vernon Duke, and John LaTouche. There was

Pal Joey, a realistic story about an unpleasant character, by Rodgers and Hart and John O'Hara. There was *Lady in the Dark,* a musical about psychoanalysis by Kurt Weill, Ira Gershwin, and Moss Hart. In 1943 Rodgers and Hammerstein wrote *Oklahoma!* Its blend of songs, dances, and story set a new pattern for the development of musical comedy.

Other musicals of the 1940's took their themes from a variety of sources. From American history came the idea for *Bloomer Girl,* by Harold Arlen, E. Y. Harburg, Sig Herzig, and Fred Saidy; and *Annie Get Your Gun,* by Irving Berlin and Herbert and Dorothy Fields. The themes for *Carousel,* by Rodgers and Hammerstein; *Kiss Me, Kate,* by Cole Porter and Sam and Bella Spewack; and *South Pacific,* by Rodgers and Hammerstein were borrowed from Ferenc Molnár, Shakespeare, and James Michener. From Irish and Scottish folklore came the inspiration for *Finian's Rainbow,* by Burton Lane, E. Y. Harburg, and Fred Saidy; and *Brigadoon,* by Alan Jay Lerner and Frederick Loewe.

Many daring and ambitious musicals were offered during the 1950's. Abe Burrows and Frank Loesser wrote a sparkling show, *Guys and Dolls,* based on Damon Runyon's colorful Broadway stories. In *The King and I,* Rodgers and Hammerstein said some meaningful things about freedom and democracy. Lerner and Loewe's *My Fair Lady,* based on George Bernard Shaw's *Pygmalion,* became one of the most popular musicals of all time. Choreographer Jerome Robbins, composer Leonard Bernstein, lyricist Stephen Sondheim, and librettist Arthur Laurents added new excitement to the musical theater with *West Side Story,* based on *Romeo and Juliet.* Also outstanding were *The Music Man,* by Meredith Willson, and *The Sound of Music* by Rodgers and Hammerstein.

The 1960's and 1970's

The musical theater of the early 1960's presented the Pulitzer-prize-winning Burrows and Loesser musical comedy, *How to Succeed in Business Without Really Trying.* Wit combined with gentle nostalgia won large audiences for *The Fantasticks,* by Tom Jones and Harvey Schmidt. Humor and star performers distinguished hits of the mid-1960's: *I Do! I Do!,* by Jones and Schmidt; *Hello,*

TERMS USED IN MUSICAL COMEDY

Book—Story, or plot.
Choreographer—Person who plans the choreography.
Choreography—Arrangement and composition of the dancing.
Collaboration—Combined effort of the composer, lyricist, and librettist, working together on a production.
Composer—Writer of the music.
Librettist—Writer of the libretto.
Libretto—Text of the words of the musical play or opera.
Lyrics—Words of a song.
Score—Written copy of musical composition.

Dolly!, by Jerry Herman and Michael Stewart; *Funny Girl,* by Jule Styne, Isobel Lennart, and Bob Merrill; and *Mame,* by Jerry Herman, Jerome Lawrence, and Robert E. Lee.

In a more serious vein, *Fiddler on the Roof,* by Jerry Bock, Sheldon Harnick, and Joseph Stein, and *Man of La Mancha,* by Dale Wasserman, Joe Darion, and Mitch Leigh, dealt with courage. *Cabaret,* by John Kander, Fred Ebb, and Joe Masteroff, showed the decay of Berlin society before World War II.

In the late 1960's *Hair,* by Gerome Ragni, James Rado, and Galt MacDermot, was a joyous expression of contemporary life.

In the 1970's *Jesus Christ Superstar,* by Tim Rice and Lloyd Webber, and *Godspell,* by Stephen Schwartz, both based on religious themes, appealed to young people. The long-running *A Chorus Line,* produced by Joseph Papp, won the 1976 Pulitzer prize for drama.

Broadway abounded in nostalgia with revivals of *No, No, Nanette,* by Vincent Youmans, Irving Caesar, and Otto Harbach; and *Irene,* by Joe McCarthy and Harry Tierney. And Shakespeare's classic comedy provided the inspiration for *Two Gentlemen of Verona,* by John Guare and MacDermot.

The Harold Prince productions of *Company,* by George Furth and Sondheim, and *Follies* and *A Little Night Music,* both by Sondheim, represent a trend in the 1970's musical theater to use music to develop plot.

The American musical theater can deal with many subjects in many ways. There is room in it for everything from pure entertainment to more serious work. Oscar Hammerstein once wrote, "There is only one absolutely indispensable element that a musical must have. It must have music. And there is only one thing that it has to be. It has to be good."

RICHARD RODGERS
Composer, *Oklahoma!, South Pacific,*
and *The Sound of Music*

Many different kinds of musical instruments—strings, woodwinds, brass, and percussion—blend their individual sounds to create the music of the orchestra.

MUSICAL INSTRUMENTS

Musical instruments are the devices used in making musical sounds. Most musical instruments fall into three great orders: the **strings,** the **winds,** and the **percussion.**

Stretch a rubber band across the top of an empty, open cigar box. Twang the rubber band in the middle. The vibrations can be seen. Yet they will be rapid enough to produce sound waves in the air. You can hear the twang. That is the working principle of a stringed instrument.

Next, blow across the top of an empty bottle. Try different angles for your breath until you hear a soft, cooing sound. This sound comes from the air in the bottle, which your breath has set quivering with invisible vibrations. But although these vibrations are invisible, they produce sound waves in much the same way as the visible vibrations of the twanged rubber band. You can hear the cooing. That is the working principle of a wind instrument.

Now take a very thin board of wood. Sprinkle some bread crumbs over it. These have nothing to do with the sound, but they will help you to see what is happening. Tap the board sharply with your knuckles. You will not see the wood quivering with vibrations. But you will probably feel the vibrations in the hand that is holding the wood, and you will certainly see the bread crumbs dancing in response to them. These vibrations produce the sound waves that carry the tapping sound

to your ears. That is the working principle of a percussion instrument.

Besides the three traditional orders of instruments, modern science has added a new order: **electronic instruments.** These have loudspeakers, which vibrate much like the wooden board. The vibrations are set up by electrical impulses. Such electrical impulses can be very complicated indeed and can therefore produce all the complex sounds of music. In fact, sounds that no ordinary musical instrument can make can be produced by an electronic apparatus.

▶HOW DO MUSICAL INSTRUMENTS MAKE SOUNDS?

A stone dropped into water makes waves that spread out to the sides of the pond. You can see the force with which the waves break. When a musical instrument is played, it quivers with vibrations. These vibrations spread out through the air till they break against our ears. If the force with which they break is strong enough, we hear the sound.

All musical instruments give off sound waves when they are played. But each instrument gives them off in its own individual pattern. It is through the different patterns in the sound waves that we hear different kinds of sounds.

A choppy sea combines many wave patterns, large and small, which can be seen. Sound waves can also combine into complex patterns, which cannot be seen but can be heard. The more complex the sound waves, the more complicated the sound. Some instruments make more complicated sounds than others. Many instruments playing together sound more complicated than one. The science of sound is called acoustics. The study of the sounds made by musical instruments is therefore called musical acoustics.

Most of the instruments described in this article are those in the modern symphony orchestra, with a few of their ancestors included. Other musical instruments, ancient and modern, are described and pictured in articles throughout the encyclopedia. See the list at the end of this article.

▶ **MAIN TYPES OF STRINGED INSTRUMENTS**

There are three ordinary ways of producing sounds on stringed instruments. These are plucking (twanging), bowing (stroking with horsetail hairs made into a bow), or hammering (hitting with sticks or hammers).

All these ways make the strings vibrate. The vibrations pass into the wooden body of the instrument. This sends them out into the air more loudly than the thin string could by itself.

A normal hunting bow makes a twang when the arrow leaves the string. Prehistoric people attached a gourd or other hollow object to the bow, so that it sounded louder and more musical. This is the musical bow. It first gave the idea for the harp and other stringed instruments.

Harp. The harp, a plucked instrument, dates back to very ancient times and is still used in the modern symphony orchestra. The strings of the modern harp are stretched across a triangular frame.

Viol and Violin Families. The viols are one of these families of older instruments that went out of use. The more brilliant and versatile violin family gradually replaced the viols. Both are families of stringed instruments played with a bow.

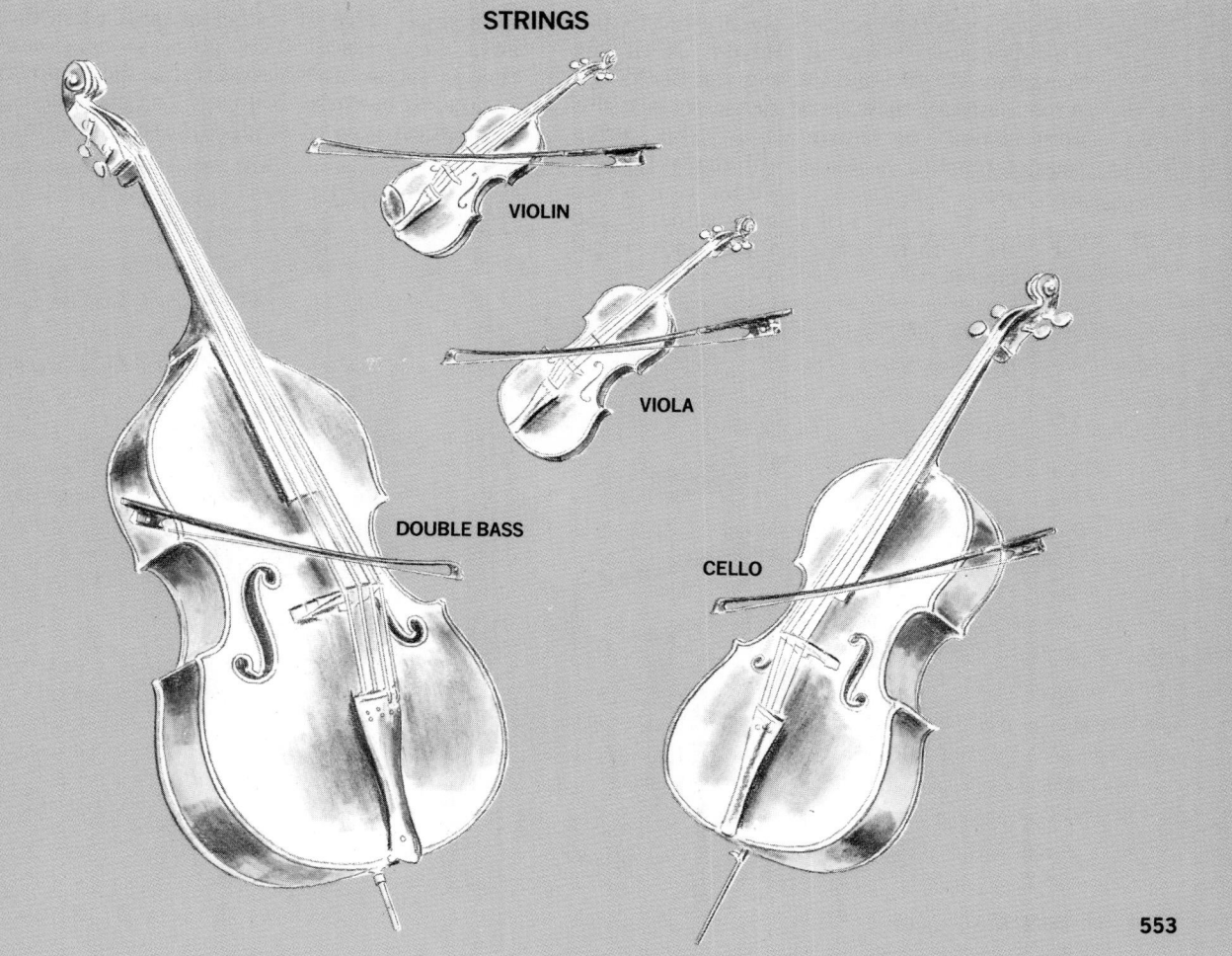

STRINGS

VIOLIN

VIOLA

DOUBLE BASS

CELLO

Bowed instruments are not so ancient as plucked instruments, but there were viols in the late Middle Ages. In the 16th and 17th centuries, they were a complete family—from the highest (treble) to the lowest (double-bass). They were valued especially in chamber music. Some of the best of this music was composed in England during the 17th century. It is now sometimes played again on the family of viols, for which it was originally intended. The sound is sharp yet mellow, and not at all the same as the sound of the violin family.

Violins were first made early in the 16th century, and they, also, came to be a complete family: violin, viola, cello, and double bass. The sound of the violin family is not only unusually beautiful; it is also unusually varied. There are many different colorings of tone and different styles of bowing. These make it a very adaptable family and one of which we do not easily grow tired. The violin family rapidly became the foundation of the orchestra, and it still is.

The string quartet of first and second violins, viola, and cello is equally successful. The composers Joseph Haydn, Wolfgang Amadeus Mozart, and Ludwig van Beethoven wrote some of their finest music for just this combination of instruments. The string quartet remains a favorite of many modern composers. Moreover, the violin itself is one of the most splendid of solo instruments; and the cello, with its deep, mellow tones, is not far behind it.

Stringed Keyboard Instruments. The piano is now the most important stringed instrument played with hammers. These are worked mechanically from the keyboard. When a key is pressed down, a felt-covered hammer is thrown against the string, immediately falling back again when the key is let go. The sound can be made soft and veiled or loud and powerful, exactly as required. This, too, is a most versatile instrument. It is wonderful by itself, in piano solos, and also when it accompanies other instruments or the human voice.

The piano came into the story of music even later than did the violin family. Mozart made it very popular. Beethoven made it essential. Before that, the harpsichord had been the main stringed instrument with a keyboard. Johann Sebastian Bach, for example, composed no music for the piano but much for the harpsichord. Harpsichord music sounds good on the piano, but it sounds even better on its own instrument. For this reason the harpsichord has once more come back into use.

The strings of the harpsichord are plucked by a small piece of leather or quill when the keys are pressed. This gives a clear and ringing sound, not so powerful as the piano at its loudest but more brilliant. The clavichord, the earliest type of stringed keyboard instru-

GRAND PIANO

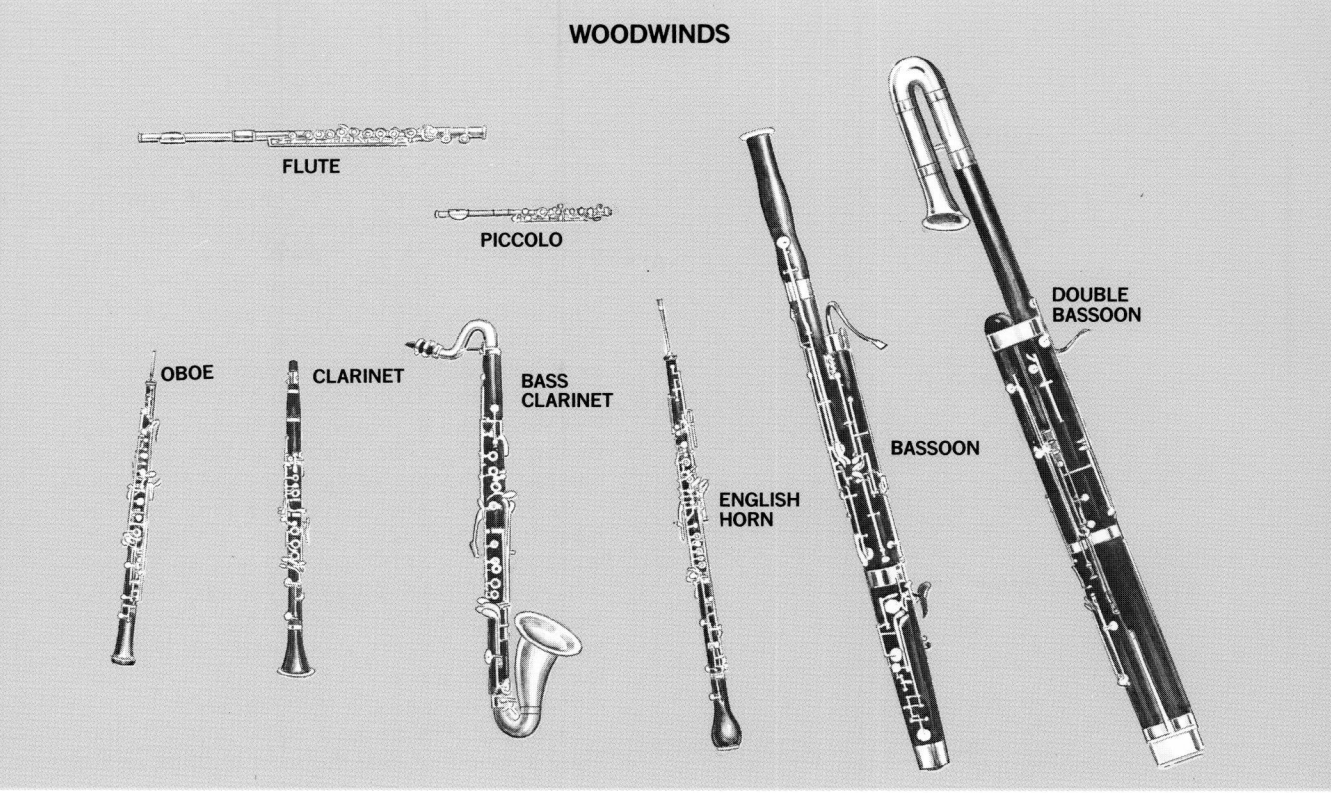

FLUTE

PICCOLO

OBOE CLARINET BASS CLARINET

DOUBLE BASSOON

ENGLISH HORN

BASSOON

ment, is much less powerful. It is so quiet that it can be heard only in a small room. But some consider it more expressive, in its quiet way, than any other keyboard instrument. Unlike those of the harpsichord, the strings of the clavichord are struck by short metal blades called tangents.

There is a story that Handel, as a child, practiced the piano secretly at night in an attic. This cannot be true; the whole house would have been awakened. It was probably a clavichord, which no one would have heard.

▶MAIN TYPES OF WIND INSTRUMENTS

There seem to be many ways of producing sounds on wind instruments. But in fact there are only two.

Sound can be produced by blowing air across a fixed edge. This is what happens, as we have seen, when you blow across the top of a bottle. It is the way in which all flute instruments work.

Or sound can be produced by blowing air across a piece of flexible, springy material (or between two such pieces). Most children can do this with a piece of grass held between their thumbs, making a "squeaker," which can emit a very piercing sound. This is the way in which all reed instruments work.

The piece of grass vibrates, and so do the reeds of reed instruments. In brass instruments the principle is the same, but the player's own lips vibrate instead. In singing, the vocal cords vibrate.

Flute and Piccolo. Flutes have a rather pure and innocent-sounding tone. The flute has a hole in the side, across which the player blows. The piccolo is a small flute, and it makes a higher sound (the highest in the orchestra).

Oboe. The oboe is a reed instrument. Two nearly flat pieces of reed are bound together so that the player's breath flows between them and makes them vibrate. This is called a double reed. The tone is refined and a little sad. But there were ancient oboes whose tone was strong and fiery. The oboe is used as a solo instrument and in chamber music, but it is most often heard in the orchestra.

English Horn. The English horn is closely related to the oboe, but it has a lower and darker sound.

Bassoon. The bassoon is another near relative of the oboe, often playing bass to it in the orchestra. It can sound both tragic and comical. Most often it is eloquent and serious. It produces a tone somewhat like that of the oboe and English horn but deeper and heavier.

BRASS

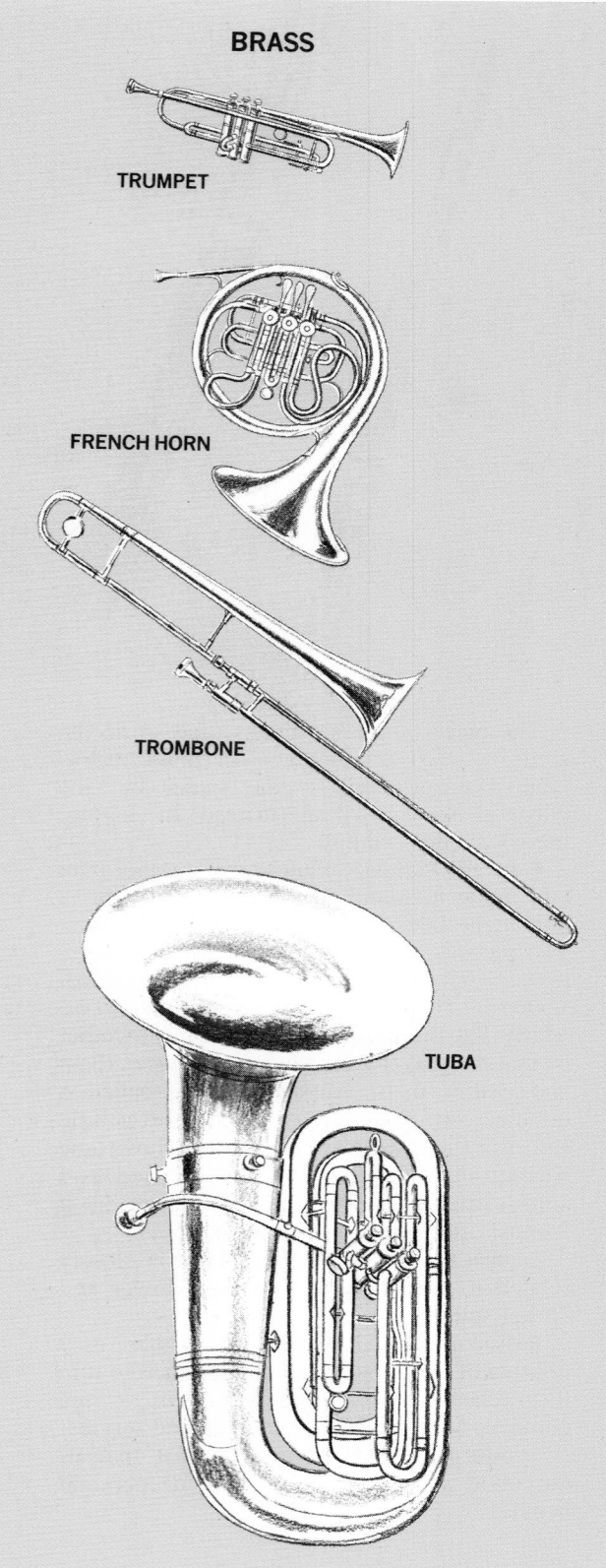

TRUMPET

FRENCH HORN

TROMBONE

TUBA

Clarinet. The clarinet possesses a tone all its own. The reed is single, and the player's breath flows across it to make it vibrate. Oboes and bassoons have tapering tubes, in the shape of a long, narrow cone. But the clarinet has a straight tube, in the shape of a long, narrow cylinder. This in itself gives it a different tone. It is not so innocent-sounding as a flute and not so plaintive as an oboe. On high notes the clarinet sounds clear and silky. It is wonderful in solos and in chamber music. In the orchestra the clarinet creates a telling contrast to the tone of the flutes and oboes.

Saxophone. The saxophone, too, has a single reed. But its tapering tube is very much wider than that of the oboe. This is what gives it its rather fat and oily tone. The saxophone is well adapted to dance music and jazz of all kinds. Its tone flows along easily. It was not invented till about 100 years ago. Very few composers have used it in the orchestra.

Trumpet. The trumpet is the smallest, the highest sounding, and the most brilliant of all the brass instruments. So brilliant is its sound that it was frequently used to stir soldiers to battle. In Britain, trumpets are used at royal weddings and other ceremonial occasions. In the orchestra the trumpets are not only the most brilliant but the loudest of instruments. They could never play all the time, as the violins sometimes do. Even when played softly, the trumpets are sharp and clear. When played loudly, they ring out above all the other instruments.

Trombone. The trombones are like trumpets that have been tamed a little—but not very much. They are larger and their tubes slide in and out to get different notes. Their tone is not quite so dazzling, especially when softly played. They can sound beautifully mellow or extremely powerful.

French Horn. The French horns are prized mainly for their warm, mellow tone. When the French horns are playing, the whole orchestra begins to glow with melting sound. Some of the most tender of all melodies are given to a French horn to play.

Tuba. The tuba is a bass instrument that is not often given the chance to play a tune. It makes a solid and sonorous (full, rich) sound that acts as a firm foundation for the other instruments to stand upon. Military bugles are like very small, high tubas, but they are not used in the orchestra.

PERCUSSION

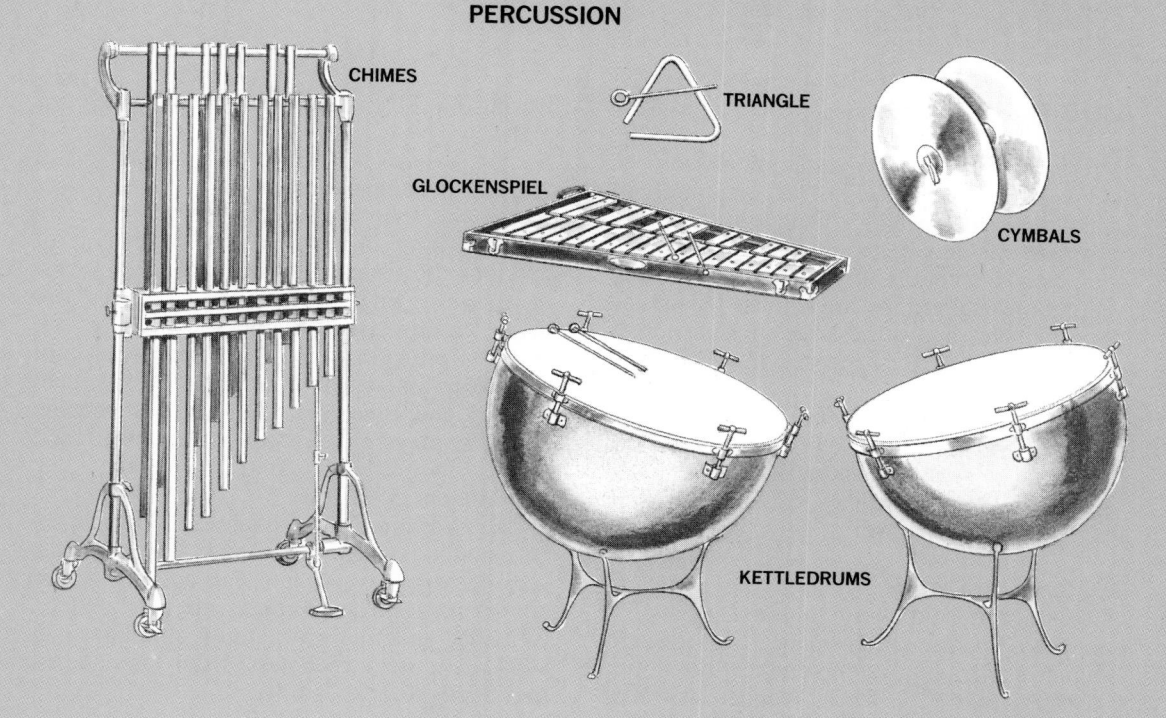

CHIMES

TRIANGLE

GLOCKENSPIEL

CYMBALS

KETTLEDRUMS

Organ. The organ is like a collection of many different wind instruments, linked up by machinery so that one performer can play them all. There may be several keyboards, including one that is played with the feet (the pedal board). The pipes are arranged in groups, which the player controls by stops. The wind is supplied by machinery. The power and variety of a large organ can be almost unlimited. But it needs a good player to prevent it from sounding like what it really is: a huge musical machine.

▶ MAIN TYPES OF PERCUSSION INSTRUMENTS

"Percussion" means "striking." All percussion instruments make a more or less musical sound when struck by the hands, by the fingers, or by some suitable implement.

Bells and gongs, bars of wood or metal, and even bowls and thin stones make fine percussion instruments. The orchestras of Eastern peoples sometimes have a wonderful variety of these and other kinds of percussion instruments, including drums of every size and shape. But in symphony orchestras, percussion instruments are not very numerous. The bowl-shaped kettledrums, or timpani, are almost always present. They give a clear, definite note and a sonorous tone that can be as soft or as loud as the player wishes. Other

types of drums are also used: the snarling side drum, for example, and the deep bass drum.

Cymbals are brass plates that are clashed or jangled together. The triangle is a metal rod left open at one corner. The xylophone is a row of wooden bars, and it has a dry and eerie sound. The glockenspiel has metal bars that sound ringing and enchanting.

But only the kettledrums are regular percussion members of the orchestra in Western music.

▶ GETTING ACQUAINTED WITH THE INSTRUMENTS

All the instruments of the orchestra together make wonderful and varied sounds in many different combinations. Take every opportunity to get to know each instrument. Each has its own personality. Composers take great care in choosing just those instruments that will create the best effect for the music they have in mind. The more familiar you become with the instruments by sight and sound, the greater will be your pleasure in the music.

ROBERT DONINGTON
Author. *The Instruments of Music*

See also FOLK MUSIC INSTRUMENTS; KEYBOARD INSTRUMENTS; PERCUSSION INSTRUMENTS; STRINGED INSTRUMENTS; WIND INSTRUMENTS; articles on individual instruments, such as PIANO; AFRICAN MUSIC; LATIN-AMERICAN MUSIC; ORIENTAL MUSIC; ANCIENT WORLD, MUSIC OF THE.

MUSIC FESTIVALS

A music festival is a series of concerts or opera performances held at regular intervals and often built around a central theme. The central theme may be the music of a particular composer or a certain type of music. Usually, visiting musical groups and soloists are invited to participate, and often large musical forces are used in the performances.

▶MAJOR EUROPEAN FESTIVALS

A great variety of music festivals are held in Europe. Many of them take place during the summer months, and they attract audiences from all parts of the world.

The Bayreuth Festival

This event, held every July and August, is dedicated to the performance of Richard Wagner's operas. It was first held at Bayreuth, Germany, in 1876, when Wagner was still alive. On that occasion, Wagner conducted the first complete performance of his monumental *Ring of the Nibelung*. Since then, Bayreuth has remained the shrine of Wagnerian opera.

The Salzburg Festival

Salzburg, Austria, the birthplace of Wolfgang Amadeus Mozart, is the location of a festival dedicated to Mozart's music. The first Mozart festival was held there in 1877. The Salzburg Festival as we know it today came into being in 1920. The composer Richard Strauss was one of the main organizers. A festival opera house was built in 1926, and a larger, better-equipped theater was added in 1960. Featured in the festival are the Vienna Philharmonic Orchestra, the Vienna State Opera, and many celebrated conductors and soloists. The festival begins in the last week of July and continues through August. The emphasis is still on Mozart's music, but works of other composers, both past and present, are included.

The International Society for Contemporary Music

The festival of the International Society for Contemporary Music was held for the first time in Salzburg in 1923. Only 20th-century music, selected by an international committee, is performed at this festival. The location has shifted from one European city to another.

During World War II, it was held in the United States.

The Glyndebourne Festival

In 1934, John Christie, a wealthy manufacturer of pipe organs, created a festival of opera on the grounds of his estate near Lewes, in Sussex, England. Mozart's operas are given prominence, but other composers are also represented. A small theater was built especially for these operas. The festival, held in May and June of each year, has become one of England's major cultural events.

The Edinburgh Festival

The Edinburgh Festival, in Edinburgh, Scotland, provides one of the richest and most varied programs of musical activity found anywhere. It presents operas, dramas, ballets, concerts, and motion pictures. Organized in 1947, it is held each year from late August into September.

The Casals Festival

In 1950 a Bach festival was organized by the great Spanish cellist Pablo Casals in Prades, France. The Prades Festival was held each June. In April and May of 1957, the festival was moved to Puerto Rico. The works of Bach, Mozart, Schubert, and Brahms are the main features of this annual festival.

▶OTHER EUROPEAN FESTIVALS

The Florence May Festival (the Maggio Musicale Fiorentino), begun in 1933, is an annual event. Opera is the main feature. But there are also symphony concerts by local and visiting orchestras, recitals by famous soloists, and chamber music performances.

One of the major European festivals was founded by the American composer Gian-Carlo Menotti in 1958. This is the Festival of Two Worlds, held every summer in Spoleto, Italy. Its presentations include operas, ballets, chamber music, dramas, and solo recitals.

The famous conductor Arturo Toscanini and several other notable musicians founded the Lucerne Festival in 1939 at Lucerne, Switzerland. Each summer it presents concerts of orchestral, choral, and chamber music and attracts some of the world's most renowned musicians.

The Holland Music Festival, inaugurated in 1949, is held in Amsterdam, The Hague, and

The Boston Symphony Orchestra plays each summer at the Berkshire Festival in Massachusetts. The open "shed" seats 6,000 people, but many more enjoy the music outside.

Scheveningen every summer. The programs consist of orchestral and chamber music concerts, operas, recitals by famous soloists, and performances of choral masterworks.

▶ MAJOR FESTIVALS IN NORTH AMERICA

The United States, too, has many music festivals that attract wide audiences.

The May Music Festival

The first significant American music festival, the May Music Festival in Cincinnati, was founded by the famous conductor Theodore Thomas in 1873. The feature events of this festival are the performances by the Cincinnati Symphony Orchestra.

The Berkshire Festival

The Berkshire Festival of the Boston Symphony is probably the most famous of American music festivals. It is held annually in July and August at Tanglewood, near Lenox, Massachusetts. This festival grew out of a series of concerts held in Stockbridge, Massachusetts, in 1934. In 1937 the Tanglewood estate was acquired by the Boston Symphony as a permanent summer-festival home. Performances by the Boston Symphony Orchestra are still the main attraction of the festival. Operas and chamber music are also performed by the Berkshire Music Center, a summer school created at Tanglewood in 1940.

The Aspen Festival

Another annual music festival takes place in Aspen, Colorado. This festival is an outgrowth of the bicentennial celebration in honor of the German poet Goethe, held at Aspen in 1949. The success of this celebration led to the creation of both a summer music school and a festival. Concerts, recitals, and chamber music performances are given.

Other Festivals

The Wolf Trap Farm Park in Virginia near Washington, D.C., holds an annual festival of music and other fine arts. This festival, established in 1971, is unique because it is sponsored by the U.S. Government under the National Park Service.

The Spoleto Festival, U.S.A., an annual counterpart to the Festival of Two Worlds in Spoleto, Italy, was begun by Gian-Carlo Menotti in Charleston, South Carolina, in May, 1977. It was continued annually thereafter as a late spring event.

The Pacific Northwest Festival in Seattle, Washington, was started in 1975 by the Seattle Opera Company. During the summer of 1978, it presented two weeks of performances of Wagner's *The Ring of the Nibelung*, one series in German, the other in English. The Seattle festival, which takes place during the last two weeks of July, has become one of the main musical-drama festivals in the United States.

An important festival in Chautauqua, New York, grew out of Sunday-school teacher training programs held there, beginning in 1874. Since then the July and August Chautauqua Festival has developed into one of the major cultural events in the United States. It features operas, orchestral concerts, chamber music programs, organ recitals, and many other events.

Ann Arbor, Michigan, has been the location of a significant music festival since 1893. Each May, leading American symphony orchestras, in collaboration with the Michigan Choral Union, perform outstanding symphonic and choral works of the past and present. The Coolidge Festival, held annually at the Library of Congress, Washington, D.C., is devoted to contemporary music.

In 1950 the pianist Rudolf Serkin became a founder and director of a festival of chamber music in Marlboro, Vermont. This festival has been held annually in July and August ever since. May is the month of an annual festival in Bethlehem, Pennsylvania, devoted to the music of Bach. Other important annual festivals include the one held in October in Worcester, Massachusetts; the opera festival in Central City, Colorado, in July and August; and the Ravinia Festival, held every summer in Chicago.

In Canada, summer music festivals are held in Stratford, Ontario, between June and October; in Banff, Alberta, in August; and in Guelph, Ontario, from late April to mid-May.

DAVID EWEN
Author, *Encyclopedia of Concert Music*

MUSLIM. See ISLAM.

MUSSOLINI, BENITO (1883–1945)

From the early 1920's until World War II, Italy was under the complete control of one man—Benito Mussolini. He was called Il Duce (''The Leader''), and he was the founder of Fascism.

Mussolini was born in Dovia, a suburb of Predappio in north central Italy, on July 29, 1883. His father, a blacksmith, taught him socialist ideas. His mother kept a one-room school in their home. As a child, Benito was aggressive, temperamental, and undisciplined. These traits remained with him all his life.

When he was 18, Mussolini qualified to teach school. But his interests and disposition soon led him into politics. His speaking ability quickly made him a leader of the Socialist Party. During this period he met Rachele Guidi, who later became his wife and bore them five children. In 1912, Mussolini became editor of the Socialist newspaper *Avanti!* (''Forward!''). He unexpectedly broke with the Socialists in 1914 and started his own newspaper, *Il Popolo d'Italia* (''The Italian People'').

Italy's role in World War I nearly ruined its economy. Waves of strikes and political demonstrations swept the country. In 1919, Mussolini organized the Fascist Party. His promise to make Italy great gained him the support of Italian nationalists. Conservative business leaders supported him as a defense against a working-class uprising. His small but merciless army of black-shirted Fascists soon became an important political force.

In 1922, Mussolini organized a Fascist march on Rome to gain control of the disunited country. Fearing a revolution, King Victor Emmanuel III asked him to form a new government. In 1923, Mussolini set up what he called the Corporate State, headed by the Grand Council of Fascism. Skillfully using both propaganda and force, he put down individual freedom and turned Italy into a police state.

Mussolini then began to dream of using his army to build an Italian empire. In 1936 he conquered Ethiopia. Unable to find support for his aggressive actions elsewhere, he formed an alliance with the German dictator Adolf Hitler. Soon after World War II began, Italy became Germany's military ally. Losses in the war made Mussolini unpopular at home. In 1943 he was driven from power and imprisoned. Hitler arranged his rescue and made him head of a German-controlled government in northern Italy. On April 28, 1945, he was captured by Italian partisans and executed.

Reviewed by JULES ARCHER
Author, *Twentieth-Century Caesar: Benito Mussolini*

See also FASCISM.

MUSTELIDS. See OTTERS AND OTHER MUSTELIDS.

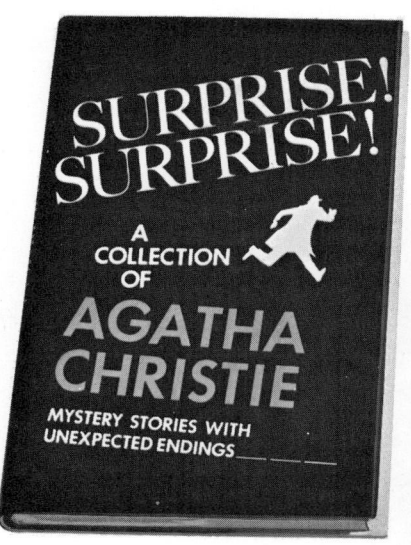

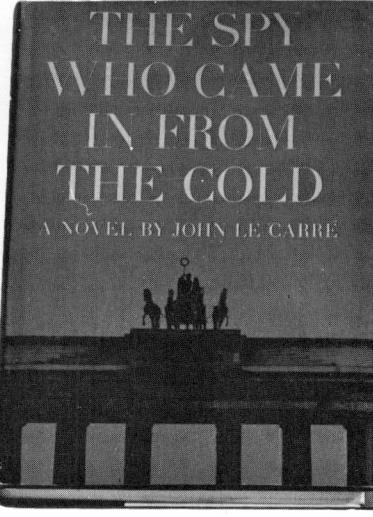

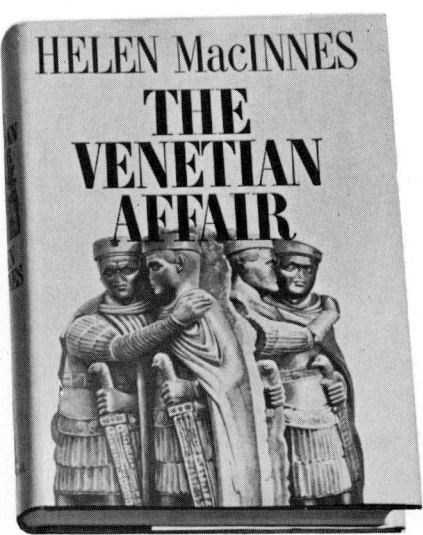

MYSTERY, DETECTIVE, AND SUSPENSE STORIES

The term "mystery story" is loosely used to include many kinds of fiction. There are, however, accepted differences between the mystery story and the detective story. A mystery story has a central character who is not a detective. The reader lives the story, putting himself in the place of the hero or heroine. There may or may not be a policeman or detective who solves the problem or rescues the chief character. The solution is arrived at more through a series of events than by reasoning.

A detective story has a detective as its central character. His object is to solve a given problem and bring a criminal to justice. The reader sees everything through the eyes of the detective or those of a companion who tells the story. The puzzle is solved primarily through reasoning from the evidence.

A suspense story seldom includes a detective but usually does include mystery, pursuit, or adventure. Its conflicts may be chiefly psychological, sometimes leaving out violence al-together, or its conflicts may be expressed in physical danger and action. Some suspense stories probe deeply into character and motivation and thus become more like "straight" novels.

All mysteries employ suspense, but not all suspense stories are mysteries. Fiction classics such as *Treasure Island, A Tale of Two Cities,* and *Jane Eyre* are novels of suspense.

Early Mystery-Detective Fiction

The first mystery-detective fiction appeared in April, 1841, when *Graham's Magazine* published "The Murders in the Rue Morgue," by Edgar Allan Poe. Poe wrote five short tales of mystery. Three of them, about C. Auguste Dupin, are detective stories. Poe, then, is rightly called the father of the detective story. Much of the fiction written since Poe's time has been inspired by his plot patterns or tricks of mystification.

Mystery fiction as an art developed slowly. In the 1860's full-length novels of this type

Arthur Conan Doyle created two memorable characters in detective fiction: Sherlock Holmes and Dr. Watson.

appeared for the first time. In England, Wilkie Collins wrote *The Woman in White,* a mystery-suspense story, published in 1860. In 1868 his *Moonstone,* a detective novel, appeared. Charles Dickens began *The Mystery of Edwin Drood* (1870) but died before it was finished. In France, Émile Gaboriau created the police detective Monsieur Lecoq in 1866. The American detective novelist Anna Katharine Green was the first woman to enter the field, in 1878.

Then, in 1887, Arthur Conan Doyle, in England, wrote *A Study in Scarlet.* This story introduced one of the greatest fictional detectives of all time—Sherlock Holmes. Through a long series of stories Holmes and his companion, Dr. Watson, became such believable characters that many readers thought they actually existed. Sherlock Holmes based much of his detection on principles of scientific observation that have come to be used by modern police. (An excerpt from one of the Holmes stories can be found in the biography of Arthur Conan Doyle in Volume D.)

About the same time, E. W. Hornung was producing a series that reversed the rules of the detective story. His hero was a gentleman thief called Raffles, who stole only from the rich, as Robin Hood had done.

Few American detective or mystery tales appeared for 65 years after Poe's death. In the early 1900's, however, the art was revived. Its popularity grew, although its quality was not uniformly high. Some of the favorite writers of the period, such as Carolyn Wells and Arthur B. Reeve, are now almost forgotten.

Mary Roberts Rinehart, still famous and read by thousands of fans, began her career in 1908 with *The Circular Staircase.* Mrs. Rinehart's novels started the trend toward mystery-romances in which characterization and atmosphere are as important as the plot. In some of her books the heroine keeps secrets from the police or acts foolishly. This delays the investigation and often causes more deaths. This type of story has been called the "Had I But Known" or HIBK.

The English writers of the early 1900's preferred the classic detective story in the manner of Conan Doyle. Although their books seem old-fashioned now, each author had a specialty that was new in his day.

For example, in 1907 R. Austin Freeman presented a scientific sleuth, Dr. John Thorn-

dyke, who appeared in the first **inverted detective stories**. Here the reader knows everything that has happened and wonders only how the criminal will be caught. A. E. W. Mason wrote about Monsieur Hanaud, a professional policeman. Gilbert Keith Chesterton invented Father Brown, who unraveled mysteries more by intuition than by strict reasoning. In 1913 E. C. Bentley wrote *Trent's Last Case,* one of the first detective stories with an easy, humorous style that made its characters sound natural. A few years later, in 1920, Freeman Wills Crofts based his stories on the methods of police routine. His detective was Inspector French of Scotland Yard.

Only one memorable mystery writer appeared at this time in France. This was Gaston Leroux, whose *Mystery of the Yellow Room* (1907) was the first of the full-length locked-room puzzles. In these a criminal seems to have escaped without trace from a murder scene such as a room locked on the inside or a field of unbroken snow. The plot turns on explaining how this trick was brought off.

World War I inspired a crop of spy-adventure books. Names remembered from that time are E. Phillips Oppenheim and John Buchan.

Growth of Mystery-Detective Fiction

Until the 1920's both detective and mystery stories had been rather looked down upon by educated readers. When the stories began to improve, they gained a better reputation. Some authors, especially in England, gave to their detective novels the care and style they would give to a serious novel. Among the first and greatest of these craftsmen were Agatha Christie, Dorothy L. Sayers, Anthony Berkeley, and Philip MacDonald. In America Willard Huntington Wright, whose pen name was S. S. Van Dine, appealed to readers with good literary taste.

It was also in the 1920's that mystery plotting and characterizations began to improve. Readers demanded a fairly presented puzzle, so that they might work out the answer logically for themselves. Later, mystery writers learned the trick of misdirection—giving truthful clues in such a way that readers would misinterpret them.

Mystery-detective story characters came nearer to real life. Villains became more human, with understandable reasons for committing crimes. Detectives grew less eccentric. They now had normal homelives and personal problems.

The next milestone in mystery-detective fiction came in the late 1920's, when Dashiell Hammett published some of the earliest hard-boiled stories. This American writer broke away from the English pattern of refinement and logic. He wrote tough, realistic yarns about private investigators (or "private eyes") and underworld characters. His famous novel *The Maltese Falcon* appeared in 1930. His influence was strong.

The classic detective story, however, was still the more popular form in America as well as England. The year 1929 saw the debut of Ellery Queen, the pen name of Manfred B. Lee and Frederic Dannay. Within the next 5 years some famous American detectives were created. Among them were Rex Stout's "armchair" detective, Nero Wolfe, and Erle Stanley Gardner's Perry Mason. In England, John Dickson Carr invented Sir Henry Merrivale, a locked-room specialist, and in France, Georges Simenon introduced Inspector Maigret.

Mystery and detective fiction came of age in the period about 1935 to 1940. The classic detective story was more like a novel than a puzzle in the hands of such authors as Michael Innes, Ngaio Marsh, and Josephine Tey. Here are some specialized forms of the modern detective story.

Hard-Boiled Detective. This is an American specialty, as begun by Hammett. Raymond Chandler, Ross MacDonald, and Thomas B. Dewey treat sordid or tragic themes without vulgarity. A few others, such as Craig Rice, write hard-boiled novels that are also comedies. Most other writers in this extremely popular field have made great use of crudeness and violence.

Procedural Detective. Scientific methods and realistic teamwork take the place of the single detective hero. Based on actual police procedures, this form was introduced in modern times (1945) by Lawrence Treat. Some of the many authors who use it are Ed McBain in America, Georges Simenon in France, and J. J. Marric (John Creasey) in England.

Adventure-Detective. The threat is personal instead of international, although the action is similar to that of spy-adventure fiction. A detective hero, such as Leslie Charteris' The Saint or Robert L. Fish's Captain Da Silva, performs dangerous escapes and rescues.

Soft-Boiled Detective. The characters do not belong to the criminal world; the detective or policeman is a gentleman, and violence is kept to a minimum. This group includes such writers as Margery Allingham and Frances and Richard Lockridge as well as all the "classic" authors already mentioned.

Locked-Room Detective. This difficult and much admired form is shown at its best in the novels of John Dickson Carr (Carter Dickson), Clayton Rawson, and Anthony Boucher (H. H. Holmes).

Suspense Stories

The mystery-suspense novel has developed in many different ways. Most of these forms tend to overlap, so it is often difficult to place a single label on one piece of fiction. In general, a suspense story can be anything from a study of criminal mentality to the wildest of melodramas.

One of the foremost modern trends is the borderline novel, or **novel with mystery**. The characters and their reactions are the most important factors, although a sound mystery is used as a basis. Daphne du Maurier's *Rebecca* (1938) is one of the best examples of this type. Often the tone of the story is serious, and problems of society may be considered. Julian Symons and Margaret Millar are two of the many notable writers in this field.

Another variety of suspense story is the **crime novel**. The reader of a crime novel often identifies with the criminal, following all his actions and the workings of his mind. The detective or policeman then becomes the antagonist. The "Raffles" type of story, gangster stories, and novels based on true-life cases belong in this group.

What is most commonly defined as a suspense story, however, is the novel of menace and pursuit, the **suspense-thriller**. In many cases the hero, in such danger that rescue seems impossible, works against time to prove himself innocent of a crime. Sometimes, to heighten the sense of menace, the author will reveal the thoughts and actions of the villain. Charlotte Armstrong, Ursula Curtiss, and William Irish (Cornell Woolrich) are well-known for this kind of plotting.

In the **suspense-romance** the action is not so violent as in the thriller, and the love story is more important, as in the books of Mary Stewart. This kind of story is often distinguished by fine description and unusual settings and is generally written from a heroine's point of view.

Spy-adventure stories also are in the suspense group. The chief character is usually a man. Alone or with partners he must outwit spies of some foreign power who try to steal secret weapons or documents. The threat is not only to the hero but to whole countries or the world. These stories often have a wartime background. Most of them are full of violence, disguises, narrow escapes, and wild chases.

The early books of Eric Ambler, who revived the form in the 1930's, are the nearest to realism. The most fantastic are those of Ian Fleming. Helen MacInnes, John Le Carré, and Manning Coles are other excellent writers in this field.

LENORE GLEN OFFORD
Reviewer of mystery books
San Francisco *Chronicle*

MYTHOLOGY

The word "mythology" comes from two Greek words, *mythos* ("story") and *logos* ("word," "talk"). It means, therefore, "storytelling." The word is now used, however, especially for stories that deal with gods. Myths are supposed to explain how things in the world began. Legends also explain things, but legends are usually based on history. Myths go back to a time before history. They often explain happenings in the world for which the people who tell them can find no explanation other than a supernatural one.

Creation Myths

How did everything begin? Where did the world, the stars, and mankind itself come from? Almost every people in the world has some story to explain beginnings. Among the many stories told by ancient peoples is one told by the ancient Babylonians. The Babylonians lived 4,000 years ago in what is now Iraq. Their myth of creation was chanted by their high priest during the new-year ceremonies. The beginning of a new year was the best time to review the beginning of all things.

"When above the sky had not even been mentioned and below the name of firm ground had not even been thought of . . . ." So begins the long myth. Before anything existed, there were only water and clouds, not even any land. Mixed together were the fresh waters, Apsu, and the salt waters, Tiamat. Apsu and Tiamat became parents of Lahmu and Lahamu. In turn Lahmu and Lahamu became parents of Anshar and Kishar. Lahmu and Lahamu were probably thought to be the gods of the land that was formed where the fresh waters ran into the sea. This is the delta on the Persian Gulf where the Tigris and Euphrates rivers meet the salt ocean. Anshar and Kishar were perhaps the horizon, where earth and sky meet. To Anshar and Kishar was born Anu, god of the sky. Anu in turn became the parent of Ea, the earth.

Now there were many beings, each one representing some large part of the natural world. Anu, for example, was in charge of the sky and the things that happened there. Anu was called the sky god, for only a divine being could control the many events occurring there. He could not be limited the way a human being would be. What man could have such power? Yet ancient peoples often described their gods as having the form and habits of men. This helped to make the gods understandable. At the same time the gods were permitted to do things that went far beyond the powers of men. They were also sometimes given a huge size, in keeping with their great powers.

All these gods broke the peaceful, unchanging quiet that had existed in the universe, for they were young gods who danced and moved about. Apsu, the old grandfather, became quite angry at all the noise. He decided to destroy the newly created gods and return to the peace and quiet of the time before the young gods were born. When the gods heard that Apsu was going to destroy them, all except Ea became terror-stricken and helpless. Ea was a master of magic. He set a spell, and soon Apsu sank into a magic sleep. Then Ea killed Apsu and built a house for himself on the huge body of the old god. In this way the Babylonians described how sweet, fresh waters were imprisoned in the earth, for Apsu was the god of fresh water and Ea was the god of the earth.

From among the many gods who now existed Ea chose a wife, Damkina. They became parents of a son, Marduk, who was to become king of the gods. Because he was young and vigorous, Marduk, too, caused commotion in the universe. Some of the older gods went to Apsu's wife, Tiamat, and asked her to do something about Marduk. Tiamat was at first unwilling, but at last she agreed. She set about creating an army to destroy Marduk. She made snakes and serpents and monstrous beasts, the scorpion man, the dragonfly, and the centaur—in all, 11 terrible beings. She placed a god named Kingu in charge of this army. About his neck she hung tablets that gave him the greatest of powers.

Hearing of this army, Anshar asked Ea to destroy the monsters. But Ea could do nothing. Neither could Anu, who ran away when he saw Tiamat and her horrible army.

Only one choice was left. Anshar went to Marduk and asked him to go out and defeat Tiamat. Marduk said he would, if he were made king of the gods. Anshar could not make this decision by himself. A meeting of the gods was called, and at a huge banquet they asked Marduk to prove that he had enough power to fight for them against Tiamat's army. They set a garment before him. With a word Marduk made it disappear. With a word he made it appear again. This was proof that he could control physical things by powers within himself. The gods were willing for Marduk to be king. Marduk then set about gathering weapons to defeat Tiamat's army. He took the rainbow for a bow and the lightning for a whip. He made a net, each corner held by one of the winds. He created hurricanes. At last he got into his chariot and set forth at the head of his forces to face Tiamat.

When Marduk and his terrible weapons approached Tiamat's army, Kingu and all the rest of Tiamat's aides fled. Tiamat stood fast. She opened her huge mouth with a roar, but Marduk was not frightened. He threw the net of winds over her and sent the hurricanes into her mouth. While her mouth was open and her body swollen by the winds, Marduk shot an arrow through her mouth and it pierced her heart. Then Marduk threw his net about Tiamat's monsters. He tied them up and banished them beneath the earth. Kingu was captured and all his powers as a god were taken away from him.

Marduk split Tiamat's body in half. He raised one half to the sky and left the other half below the earth. He filled the space between with the winds. To each of the gods Marduk assigned a duty. Anu was given the sky; Ea, the deep; Enlil, the air. Marduk made the sun, the moon, and the stars, and gave them their paths in the heavens.

The gods complained, saying that gods should not be given such tasks. So Marduk decided to create human beings to serve the gods. From the blood of Kingu, who was no longer immortal, he asked Ea to create humanity. In appreciation for what he had done, the gods built a great temple for Marduk at Babylon. Thereafter man served the gods through religious observance. This gave the gods strength to carry out their tasks.

Astronomical Myths

Less difficult to understand than the Babylonian creation myth is the Korean story of why eclipses occur. We now know that eclipses of the sun are caused by the moon's moving between the earth and the sun, but before people had telescopes and other scientific instruments, they saw only that the light of the sun disappeared. The moon in an eclipse of the sun is visible only as a dark disk. It reflects no light to the earth because it is between the earth and the sun.

According to the Korean myth, there are many countries in heaven. One of the countries is Gamag Nara, land of darkness.

The King of Gamag Nara is not happy with the darkness over his land. Once he told the fiercest of his fire dogs to bring the sun to him. The fire dog tried again and again to seize the sun, but it was too hot. At last he had to give up and return to the land of darkness without it.

The King then sent another dog to try to steal the moon. But the moon was so cold that the dog's mouth froze. So the dog had to let go of the moon and return to Gamag Nara without it.

Gamag Nara is still in darkness, but the King has never given up hope. Again and again he sends out his monster dogs to try to steal the sun or the moon to light his kingdom. That is why pieces of the sun seem to disap-

pear during an eclipse. The sun itself disappears for a time, but it reappears when the dog is forced to release its hold. That is also why the moon, though it darkens during an eclipse, comes back to shine full in the sky.

Origin Myths

On the northwestern coast of the United States live the Quileute Indians. One custom of this tribe is the potlatch. Their potlatch is a feast, accompanied by dancing, singing, and storytelling. The host presents gifts of various kinds to his guests. By giving these gifts, he gains greater standing in the eyes of his neighbors.

According to a Quileute myth, a strange and many-colored bird appeared once in the sea in front of a Quileute village. All the young men of the tribe tried to shoot the bird, but none succeeded.

One day Golden Eagle said to Bluejay, "That bird can be caught by my children."

"Oh, no; they are girls," said Bluejay, laughing.

This conversation was overheard by the two daughters of Golden Eagle. They went off into the woods for a time and secretly made many arrows.

One morning when all the village's hunters were on the ocean in their canoes trying to capture the strange bird, the girls disguised themselves, and collecting all the arrows they had made, set forth in a canoe. By steering an

irregular course, they were able to come near enough to the bird so that the elder daughter could kill it with an arrow. Then they went back to shore and hid the bird in the forest.

In the evening they told their father what they had done. They asked him to invite everyone to a feast the following day and to tell them that they would receive presents. When the guests arrived, the girls gave them feathers—red and brown to Robin, yellow and black to Finch, and so forth. Since that day each bird has had its own colors. This was the first potlatch.

This myth, like the creation myth and the eclipse myth, is an explanatory myth. It tells

The animal gods of ancient Egypt had the heads of animals and the bodies of men.

how the first potlatch took place. It also explains how the bird ancestors of the different Indian clans got their colors. Each clan was closely linked to some bird, which was its totem, or animal counterpart.

Animal gods occur in the mythology of many peoples. Perhaps the best-known are the animal-headed gods of ancient Egypt. Anubis, a god of the dead, had the head of a jackal and the body of a man. Set, the god of evil, had the head of a donkey. Horus, the sun god, had a hawk's head. Sometimes these animal gods can be traced to a place or a group of people that have been identified with the animal, but most often their origin is not clear.

Fragmentary Myths

The myths retold above are all related to ceremony or belief. But during the 19th century, scholars studying the mythology and folktales of the world discovered in folktales what appeared to be parts of myths. Many people who study these stories feel that myths are never told for amusement. They always have a serious meaning, unlike fairy tales or jokes, which are told simply to entertain an audience. However, others have noted that at storytelling time in many places in the world, myths are told along with jokes and other folktales.

Certainly one of the best-known tales is the legend of King Arthur. It is told in Volume A of this encyclopedia. Scholars see in the story of Arthur's drawing the sword from the anvil stuck in the stone the remnant of a myth about the inventor of iron, the one who freed iron from its ore, the rock in which it occurs in nature.

Culture Heroes

The mythical persons who discover or present to the people things that are important to the way people live, but whose origins are lost in time, are called culture heroes. A culture hero may show people how to make fire, the way Prometheus did in Greek mythology, or how to plant grain. Or he may invent an alphabet or change the course of a river. Sometimes he is simply a legendary human being. More often he is a mythical personage, a god or godlike, and belongs to ritual and ceremony.

One of the strangest stories in all history is that of the conquest of Mexico by Hernando Cortes in the 16th century. It is strange because his way was made easy by a myth. The Aztecs, the people whom he conquered, had a myth that described the return of their great culture hero. In many ways their hero resembled Cortes and his small invading force.

Quetzalcoatl, the hero, was adopted by the Aztecs from the Toltecs, who had lived in Mexico in earlier times. According to one version of the myth, the "Master of the Everywhere, who is like the night and the wind," had four children, the Tezcatlipocas, one of whom was Quetzalcoatl. Each had a color, white, black, red, and blue—the colors of fire, water, earth, and air, and also the colors of east, west, north, and south.

At the beginning the children of the master god worked together to build the world—the earth, the heavens, and the underworld. But one of the brothers wanted to be better than the others. He made himself into the sun and created men out of ashes to serve him. The others became angry, and Quetzalcoatl destroyed this first sun and earth in a huge downpour. All was swept away, and the people became fish.

Next, another son created a world of giants. This second son perished when the heavens crumbled and all was destroyed. A third world ended in a rain of fire. Finally, a fourth world was swept away by wind, destroying everything on the earth. At that time there lived beings called ape-men.

Then the gods met to create a new world, the fifth, that of the present. First they had to create the earth once more, for all had been destroyed by the wind. Two of the brothers became serpents and wound themselves around the goddess of the earth, squeezing so hard that she split in two. From one half they made the surface of the earth; from the other, the heavens.

Then they agreed that since she had been so badly treated, the earth goddess should be mother of everything on earth. From her hair came trees and plants. From her eyes they made freshwater springs, and from her many mouths they made rivers and caves. From her nose and her shoulders they created the mountains and the valleys.

But the myth says, "As yet it was night. There was still neither light nor warmth." One of the gods would have to cast himself into the fireplace in their house so that he could become the sun. The time came when the decision had to be made. The lord of the snails gathered his courage and tried four times, but he could not cast himself into the burning fire. Then the gods said the Pimply One should try. With his eyes closed he threw himself in the fire and in a moment was transformed into the sun. The first one then joined his brother in the flames, but he was too late. He could not become the sun, only the moon.

The sun and moon appeared in the sky. But they did not move. The rest of the gods had to sacrifice their lives in turn so that the sun and moon might move, one during the day, the other at night. Had they not done so, creation could not have gone on.

In many ways this myth from ancient Mexico is very much like the creation myth of the Babylonians. Yet the difference between these peoples is obvious in what each myth is meant to teach. The Babylonian myth says that man must serve the gods so that they may continue to do their job in keeping the universe moving. The Toltec myth says that, like the gods before him, man must be prepared to sacrifice his life to prevent everything from coming to an end.

The Toltec myth continues. It was time to create man again to live on earth. The gods met. (Since the gods were immortal, they did not die even though they had sacrificed their lives.) Quetzalcoatl volunteered to go into the place of the dead to bring back the bones of the earlier men who had been destroyed. After fulfilling many tasks set by the lord of this region, he was permitted to bring back to earth the bones of a man and a woman. Over these bones, which the gods ground up in a large basin, Quetzalcoatl dripped some blood drawn from his body. The first man of the present age, the fifth creation of the gods, took form and life.

Before man could take his place on earth, the gods had to supply him with food. Once

The evil sorcerers talk to the priest Quetzalcoatl.

again Quetzalcoatl went off, this time to the "mountain of sustenance," where all food had been stored. Changing himself into an ant, he argued with the ant who guarded the food and received permission to take away some grains of corn. He was aided by the rain gods, the Tlalocs, without whose help the corn could not grow. Quetzalcoatl returned with this precious food, the most important of all the foods in ancient America. The gods chewed on it before putting it into the mouths of the first human couple.

Some students of Aztec mythology say that in the course of time the creation myth of the Toltecs became confused with the story of a priest of the Toltec religion who had taken as his own name that of the god Quetzalcoatl and had attained great power. Thus a human being, a legendary figure, takes his place in the myth alongside the god. In the time of the priest Quetzalcoatl the Toltecs lived in a golden age. The arts of sculpture, painting, and pottery were at their best, and food was so plentiful that few people went hungry. The people were happy. Under the rule of the human Quetzalcoatl it was as if a kind of heaven existed on earth.

Then three evil sorcerers came to the Toltec capital to try to convince Quetzalcoatl that it was necessary to make human sacrifices in order to continue the good time. The priest refused to listen to them, but he was old and could not resist them. The magicians were able to get him to look at himself in a mirror. The mirror bewitched the old priest. While he was under the sorcerers' spell, many Toltecs were sacrificed. Quetzalcoatl finally broke the charm, but his wonderful kingdom was destroyed. He could no longer stay with his people. So he set off toward the east on a raft of serpents, heading for the region where the sun rises. His raft disappeared on the ocean. Yet, though he had left the land, it was foretold that someday he would return to his people.

The Toltec myth was accepted by the people who followed the Toltecs in Mexico and was adapted to their own beliefs. Quetzalcoatl the priest is described as being bearded. (The beard is also part of his identification with the mighty feathered serpent, who is thought to be Quetzalcoatl the god.) Beards were quite rare among Mexicans. Thus, when the bearded Spanish conquistadores under Cortes appeared on the Mexican coast in the early 16th century, the story spread that Quetzalcoatl had returned. It did not cross the minds of the Mexicans that the strangers were invaders who should be resisted. Cortes did his best to foster the idea that he was Quetzalcoatl, since this helped to weaken those who might have driven him off.

Modern Myths

Myths have their place in many religions even today. If a religion has many believers and its secrets are known only to those who follow its observances, its mythology does not become widely known. If it loses its believers, and nonbelievers get to know about the religion, then the mythology becomes more widely known.

In the 19th century there were a number of related religious revivals among the Indians of the United States. First there was the Sun Dance religion of the Plains tribes. A 4-day meeting of the wandering tribes celebrated the Sun Dance. The sun, the gods of the earth and sky, the thunder, the stars, the earth mother, and the four directions were represented in song, dance, and painting.

Later, in the far Northwest, the society of the Dreamers was formed. It was wiped out when the Nez Percé Indians were sent to Indian Territory (now Oklahoma) after the defeat of Chief Joseph. Toward the end of the 19th century the famous Ghost Dance religion, led by a prophet named Wovoka, appeared. The Ghost Dance believers waited for a regenerator, or one who would renew. He would appear to them as a cloud. When he appeared, the earth and all its inhabitants would come to an end. But all would be created again. On this earth the Indians would live close to heaven. The white man would not appear again on this earth, if indeed he would

Plains Indians performed the Sun Dance around the tribe's medicine bundle.

John Frum and his white cargo plane arrive on Tanna.

be reborn into any world at all. The Ghost Dance religion died out after the massacre of Wounded Knee in 1890.

On the islands of the Pacific Ocean, cargo, or trade, cults arose during World War II and gained many followers. In his book *The Golden Haze* Roderick Cameron describes the cult of John Frum, as he found it on the island of Tanna in the New Hebrides. He could not learn much about it, for members of the cult are rather secretive about it. However, from the leading prophet of the Frum cult he learned that the basic belief is that Frum will soon come, bringing many good things for the natives of the island. Frum, who is "Rusfelt's brother," will be dressed in an American Navy uniform with many brass buttons. He will arrive in a white-painted cargo plane, or perhaps in a submarine. The plane will be carrying enough food for all, washing machines, refrigerators, and prefabricated houses. When Frum comes, the island of Tanna will become flat and its volcano will disappear. The area of the island will double.

These American Indian and Pacific Island religions show that mythology is not a collection of ancient stories, but a human activity that has gone on as long as men have existed on this earth and still goes on. The most ancient peoples of whom we have records had mythologies. Their stories explained the universe as well as they could imagine explanations. Who knows which of our own explanations of the world will be looked upon by scholars many centuries from now as a mythological story? The moon is no longer a frozen light that a dog could not hold in his mouth or a fearful god who failed to jump into the fire at the right time. Human beings on the moon's surface will find it as real as the earth. What further advances will change man's outlook on the universe? What beliefs of man will remain unshaken and proved? What new mythologies will arise?

JEROME FRIED
Associate Editor, *Standard Dictionary of Mythology and Legend*

See also GREEK MYTHOLOGY; NORSE MYTHOLOGY.

M, 13th letter of the English alphabet   **M** 1
  See also Alphabet
M-1 rifles, guns   **G** 423

M1, M2, and **M3,** measures of a country's money supply. M1 is the total of currency in public hands plus funds in checking accounts. M2 includes M1 plus savings deposits at commercial banks. M3 includes M1 and M2 plus deposits at savings banks and credit unions. Because M1 represents funds easily available for spending, its growth is considered healthy for a country's economy. But rapid growth is thought to lead to inflation.

MA *see* Mechanical advantage

Ma, Yo Yo (1955–   ), Chinese-American cellist, b. Paris, France. A leading classical cellist, Ma is noted for exceptional technique as well as an engaging stage personality. He gave his first public recital at age 6 in Paris and made his New York City debut at Carnegie Hall in 1964. He studied at The Juilliard School and at Harvard University. In 1978 he received the Avery Fisher Prize, which gave him opportunities to perform with classical music ensembles. He has appeared as a guest artist with major symphony orchestras throughout the world.

Maas, Nicolaes *see* Maes, Nicolaes

Mab, Queen (possibly from Welsh word *mab,* meaning "child"), queen of the fairies in 15th-century English and Welsh folklore, perhaps derived from Queen Maeve (or Mav), a character in old Irish legend. Shakespeare's *Romeo and Juliet* refers to her as "the fairies' midwife," able to bring dreams by driving her chariot over the heads of sleeping people. Queen Mab, mentioned in works by Michael Drayton and Ben Jonson, is the subject of a poem ("Queen Mab") by Shelley, in which she denounces the evils of the world.

Mabus, Ray (1948–   ), governor of Mississippi, Democrat, b. Choctaw County. A former lawyer, he became former governor William Winter's aide (1980–83) and served as legislative liaison for the state's 1982 Education Reform Act. He served as state auditor (1983–87) and was elected governor in 1987.

Mac, Gaelic word for "son of"   **N** 5
  See also names beginning with Mc and Mac in
    alphabetical order as they are spelled

Macadamia nuts, the seeds of the macadamia tree, an evergreen grown in tropical and subtropical climates. Most macadamia nuts have smooth, round shells with flavorful kernels. They are also called Australian nuts and Queensland nuts because macadamia trees were originally grown in Australia. In the late 1800's, the trees were brought to Hawaii, where they are still grown extensively. Macadamia orchards are also found in Florida and California.

Macadam (ma-CAD-am) **roads**   **R** 250; **T** 260

Macao (muh-KOW), a Portuguese overseas province located on the South China Sea at the mouth of the Canton River. It consists of the chief city of Macao and three small adjoining islands—two islands of Taipa, and Coloane

Island. Macao received executive and legislative autonomy in 1976, although its governor is appointed by Portugal. Macao is a resort area and a center of commerce, gambling, and smuggling. Its population is over 300,000. **P** 393
  China   **C** 264

Macapagal (ma-ca-pa-GOL), **Diosdado** (1910–   ), former president of the Philippines, b. Lubao, province of Pampanga. During his presidency (1961–65), Macapagal worked to decentralize government and industry. Earlier, he had served as a member of the Philippine congress (1949–56), vice-president of the country (1957–61), and head of the Liberal Party. In 1979, Macapagal became head of a newly formed political party, the National Union for Liberation, which in 1980 formed an alliance with the Liberal Party.   **P** 188

Macaques (ma-CAKS), Old World monkeys   **M** 420;
    picture **M** 421
Macaroni (mac-a-RO-ni), food made from wheat
    G 281
  jewelry-making   **I** 224
Macaroni penguins   **P** 125
MacArthur, Douglas, American general   **M** 2
  Eisenhower and MacArthur   **E** 108
  Korean War   **K** 303–04
  Truman, Harry S, relations with   **T** 303
  World War II   **W** 293
Macarthur, John, Australian rancher   **A** 516
Macaulay (ma-CAUL-ey), **Thomas Babington,** English
    statesman and writer   **E** 262, 292
Macaws (ma-CAWS), birds, *pictures*   **B** 246
  parrot family   **P** 86–87
Macbeth, play by Shakespeare   **M** 2–3; **S** 132
  background in Scottish history   **S** 88
  outline of the plot   **S** 135
Maccabees, Jewish family   **J** 105
  Hanukkah celebrates victory over Syrians   **H** 28–29
  Jerusalem, history of   **J** 78
  Palestine, history of   **P** 40b
  underground movements   **U** 10
Maccabees I and II, apocryphal books of Bible   **B** 159
Maccabiah Games, for Jewish athletes in Israel   **I** 440
Macchiaioli, group of Florentine painters   **I** 473
Mac Cool *see* Finn Mac Cool
MacDonald, Flora, Canadian political leader, *picture*
    W 213
MacDonald, Golden *see* Brown, Margaret Wise

MacDonald, James Ramsay (1866–1937), English politician, b. Lossiemouth, Scotland. He was a member of Parliament (1906–18, 1922–37). He served as secretary (1900–12) and leader (1911–14, 1922–31) of the national Labour Party. He was the first Labour prime minister (Jan.–Oct., 1924, 1929–31) but left the party and subsequently became leader and prime minister for the coalition government (1931–35). Under Prime Minister Baldwin he was lord president of the council (1935–37).

MacDonald, J. E. H., Canadian artist
  The Solemn Land, painting, *picture*   **C** 83
Macdonald, Sir John A., Canadian statesman   **M** 3–4
  first prime minister of Canada   **C** 75; *picture* **P** 459
  statue in Toronto, *picture*   **T** 230

Macdonough, Thomas, American naval officer **W** 11
MacDowell, Edward, American composer **M** 4
MacDowell Colony, Peterborough, New Hampshire **M** 4
Mace, spice **H** 114; *picture* **H** 115
   See also Nutmeg
Macedonia (ma-ced-O-nia), native kingdom of Alexander
   the Great **A** 151
   Balkan wars **B** 19
   region of Greece and Yugoslavia **G** 333, 334
   Yugoslav state **Y** 358
Maces, clubs used as weapons **K** 273

MacGregor, Ellen (1906–54), American author and librarian, b. Baltimore, Md. She is remembered for her popular science fiction books for children, which include *Miss Pickerell Goes to Mars, Miss Pickerell and the Geiger Counter,* and *Miss Pickerell Goes Undersea.*

Mach (MOCK), **Ernst,** Austrian scientist **A** 40; **S** 469
Machado (ma-CHA-tho), **Antonio,** Spanish writer
   S 372
Machado de Assís (ma-SHA-du day os-SEES), **Joaquim
   Maria,** Brazilian poet and novelist **B** 377; **L** 72
Machado y Morales (ma-CHA-tho e mo-RA-lace),
   Gerardo, president of Cuba (1925–33) **C** 597
Machaut, Guillaume de *see* Guillaume de Machaut
Machel, Samora, president of Mozambique **M** 507
Machiavelli (mac-i-a-VEL-li), **Niccolò,** Italian statesman
   and writer **I** 477–78
   new principle in the writing of history **H** 137–38

Machine age, era in which human and animal labor is largely replaced by mechanical devices to produce goods. The machine age became established through the development of steam and electric power and of extensive transportation networks.

Machine guns G 423; *picture* **G** 424
Machine language, in computer programming **C** 483,
   486
Machine needles N 104
Machines and machinery
   agricultural production, contribution to **A** 99–100
   bulldozers **B** 445–46
   construction equipment **B** 445–48
   dredges **D** 319–20
   earth-moving **B** 446–48
   effect on labor movement **L** 2–3
   elevators and escalators **E** 170–73
   engines **E** 209–11
   environment changed by machines **E** 272c–272d
   farm machinery **F** 53–59
   gears **G** 65–66
   hoisting and loading machinery **H** 146–47
   hydraulic machines **H** 301–03
   industry dependent on **I** 243
   inventions **I** 333–48
   locomotives **L** 327–32
   lubrication **L** 370–71
   manufacturing **M** 87–89
   natural resources, demands on **N** 65
   occupational safety **O** 12, 13
   office machines **O** 53–58
   paper-making machines **P** 52–53; *pictures* **P** 54,
   55
   pneumatic devices **P** 347
   pumps **P** 528–30
   resentment against in folk songs **F** 310
   robots **R** 252–54
   sewing machines **C** 380

simple machines, the lever, the inclined plane, the
   pulley **W** 246–50
wheels, machinery depends on **W** 158
work, power and machines **W** 243–50
See also Automation; Technology
Machine shorthand S 160
Machine tools T 220–23
Machmeters (MOCK-me-ters), instruments to measure
   speed of airplanes **S** 470
Mach (MOCK) **numbers,** measures of supersonic flight
   speed **A** 40; **S** 469–70
Machu Picchu (MA-chu PEEC-chu), ancient Inca city,
   Peru, *pictures* **A** 354, **P** 163, **S** 293
Macias Nguema, Francisco, Equatorial Guinean
   president **E** 274
Macias Nguema Biyogo, island, Equatorial Guinea *see*
   Bioko
Macintosh, Charles, Scottish inventor and chemist
   R 341

Macintosh, William (1775?–1825), American Creek Indian chief, b. Carrol County, Ga. He directed Creek allies of Americans in the War of 1812 and was commissioned brigadier general in the U.S. Army. He signed a treaty (1825) giving Creek lands to white men, and therefore, according to a tribal law prescribing death for cession of land, was executed by a band of Indian warriors.

Mack, Connie, American baseball manager **B** 78, 80
Mackay, John William, American miner and financier
   N 135
Mackenzie, Alexander, Canadian statesman **O** 127
Mackenzie, Sir Alexander, Scottish explorer in North
   America **M** 5
   Arctic region **A** 386d
   British Columbia **B** 407
   Canada's early fur trade **C** 73
   North West Company, fur traders **F** 521–22

Mackenzie, Sir Alexander Campbell (1847–1935), British composer and conductor, b. Edinburgh, Scotland. He taught and served as principal at Royal Academy of Music (1889–1924) and conducted the London Philharmonic Orchestra (1892–99). He was president of the International Music Society (1908–12). His works, often incorporating Scottish themes, include *Pibroch Suite* for violin and orchestra, the oratorio *The Rose of Sharon,* and the choral work *The Cotter's Saturday Night.*

Mackenzie, William Lyon, Canadian leader **M** 5
Mackenzie Highway, Canada **C** 63; **Y** 365
Mackenzie Mountains, Canada **Y** 361
Mackenzie River, Canada **R** 242; **Y** 361, 365
   Arctic Basin of Canada **C** 57
   Mackenzie's explorations **M** 5
Mackerel, fish **F** 188, 214
Mackerel sky, of cirrocumulus clouds **C** 385
Mackinac (MACK-in-aw), **Straits of,** Great Lakes
   G 328; **M** 259, 266
Mackinac Bridge, Michigan **B** 398; **M** 266; *picture*
   G 328
Mackinac Island, Michigan **M** 269; *picture* **M** 272

MacLaine, Shirley (Shirley MacLean Beaty) (1934–   ), American actress, b. Richmond, Va. She won an Academy Award in 1984 for her role in the film *Terms of Endearment.* She was trained from age 3 as a dancer and performed in Broadway musical comedies in the 1950's. Her first film was Alfred Hitchcock's *The Trouble With Harry* (1955). She received four other Oscar nominations—for

Some Came Running (1958), The Apartment (1960), Irma La Douce (1963), and The Turning Point (1977). She has also performed in nightclubs and on television, has been active in social and political causes, and is the author of Out on a Limb (1983), Dancing in the Light (1985), and other books.

MacLeish (mac-LEESH), **Archibald,** American poet and dramatist **A** 210; **I** 85

Macleod, John James Rickard (1876–1935), Scottish physiologist, b. New Clunie. With F. G. Banting he was awarded the 1923 Nobel prize in medicine and physiology for the discovery of insulin and its value in treating diabetes. He taught at a number of British, American, and Canadian institutions.
    Banting and Macleod **B** 52

Maclure, William (1763–1840), American geologist, b. Ayr, Scotland. Noted for his pioneer geological surveys, he made a geological map of the United States (1809, revised 1817) and served as president of the Academy of Natural Sciences, Philadelphia (1817–40). An active supporter of adult education and of Robert Owen's New Harmony community (Indiana), he later founded the New Harmony Working Men's Institute (1838).
    Indiana's New Harmony community **I** 144

MacMillan, Donald Baxter (1874–1970), American Arctic explorer, b. Provincetown, Mass. After accompanying Robert E. Peary on his historic North Pole expedition (1908–09), he engaged in anthropological work among the native peoples of northern Labrador (1910–12). He headed numerous scientific expeditions to Arctic regions (1913–58), including Greenland, Labrador, Baffin Land, and Newfoundland. Among his works are Four Years in the White North, Etah and Beyond, and Kahda.

MacMillan, Harold (Maurice Harold MacMillan, 1st Earl of Stockton), (1894–1986), British statesman, b. London. A member of Parliament (1924–29, 1931–64), he was also director (1920–40), chairman (1963–74), and president (since 1974) of the publishing company Macmillan and Co., Ltd. He served in various governmental posts such as minister of housing and local government (1951–54), secretary of state for foreign affairs (1955), chancellor of the exchequer (1955–57), and prime minister (1957–63). His books include his memoirs and The Middle Way.

MacMillan, H. R., Canadian lumber company executive **B** 406d
Macmillan, Kirkpatrick, Scottish inventor **B** 173
MacNelly, Jeff, American editorial cartoonist **C** 127
Maconochie (mac-ON-ock-ie), **Alexander,** British naval officer **P** 469
Macramé, art of decorative knotting **M** 6–7b
Macromolecules (mac-ro-MOL-e-cules), giant molecules **B** 292
Macronutrients, chemical elements essential to plant growth **F** 96
Macumba (ma-COOM-ba), Brazilian dance music **L** 74

Macy Foundation, Josiah, Jr., association to advance scientific medicine and health care. It grants funds for work in such fields as medical research and medical education. Founded in 1930, it has headquarters in New York, N.Y.

Madagascar **M** 8–9

bricks drying in the sun, picture **B** 390
flag, picture **F** 228
lemurs are an endangered species **E** 195
Madam (or Madame), form of address **A** 20
Madama Butterfly, opera by Giacomo Puccini **O** 146
Madame Bovary (bo-va-RI), novel by Gustave Flaubert **F** 441; **N** 348
Madame Julie Récamier (ray-com-YAY), painting by David **P** 29; picture **P** 26
MADD see Mothers Against Drunk Driving
Madder root, plant used for dyeing **D** 371, 372; picture **D** 369
Maddox, U.S.S., destroyer **V** 336
Madeira (ma-DE-ra), group of islands off northwestern coast of Africa **I** 434; **P** 393
Madeleine (MAD-el-in), **La** (Church of St. Mary Magdalene), Paris **F** 432; **P** 74; picture **P** 74
Madeline's Rescue, picture book by Ludwig Bemelmans, picture **C** 229
Mademoiselle Pogany, sculpture by Constantin Brancusi, picture **B** 370
Madero (ma-DARE-o), **Francisco,** Mexican president **M** 250
Madinat al-Shaab, capital of Yemen (Aden) **Y** 347
Madison, capital of Wisconsin **W** 204, 207
Madison, Dolley (Dorothea Payne Todd Madison), wife of James Madison **F** 166; **M** 13; **N** 320; pictures **F** 167, **M** 12
    first to serve ice cream at White House **I** 30
    White House, history of **W** 162
Madison, James, 4th president of the United States **M** 10–13; picture **P** 448
    Bill of Rights **B** 177
    Federalist, The **F** 78

Madog (or Madoc), in Welsh legend, a prince, son of Owain Gwynedd, king of North Wales. He is said to have gone to America (1170?) and to have founded a settlement on the southern Missouri River. Southey's poem Madoc recounts his exploits and experiences among the Aztecs of the newly founded Mexican empire.

Madonna (Madonna Louise Ciccone) (1958–   ), American rock singer, b. Bay City, Mich. She became well known in 1985 after the release of her hit record album, Like a Virgin. She also appeared in films, including Desperately Seeking Susan and Who's That Girl. Her often outrageous style of dress was much imitated by her fans. In 1985 she married the actor Sean Penn. **R** 262d

Madonna and Angels, sculpture by Luca della Robbia **S** 98
Madonna and Child, altarpiece by Duccio **I** 461
Madonna and Child, ceramic figures by Andrea della Robbia **I** 465
Madonna and Child, sculpture by Michelangelo **R** 168
Madonna and Child Enthroned, painting by Masaccio **I** 466
Madonna and Child with Angels, detail from the painting by Piero della Francesca, picture **F** 448
Madonna del Granduca, The, painting by Raphael **P** 21
Madonna of Pity, statue by Germain Pilon **F** 422
Madonna of the Chair (Madonna della Sedia), painting by Raphael, picture **R** 106
Madonna of the Rocks, painting by da Vinci **P** 21
Madonna of the Trees, painting by Giovanni Bellini, picture **B** 136
Madonna of Vladimir, Byzantine painting **B** 489

Madonna with a Rabbit, detail from the painting by Titian, *picture* **T** 199

Madonna with Saints and Members of the Pesaro Family, painting by Titian **P** 22, 23

Madonna with the Chancellor Rolin, painting by Jan van Eyck, *picture* **D** 352

Madras (ma-DRAS), capital of the state of Tamil Nadu, India **M** 14

Madras, University of, *picture* **I** 122

Madrid (ma-DRID), capital of Spain **M** 15; **S** 355
  at mid-19th century, *picture* **S** 371
  bullfighting, *pictures* **B** 452, **E** 304
  monument to Cervantes, *picture* **S** 354
  Prado **P** 424–25
  Royal Palace, *picture* **S** 364

Madrid, University of, Spain **M** 15

Madrid Hurtado, Miguel de la see De la Madrid Hurtado, Miguel

Madrigal (MAD-rig-al), in music **M** 544
  choral music **C** 283
  English madrigals **E** 269–70
  Italian Renaissance music **I** 483
  Renaissance music **R** 173
  vocal chamber music **C** 183

Madurodam, the Netherlands, *picture* **N** 120a

Maelstrom, Norwegian strait famous for its whirlpool **I** 434

Maeser (MY-ser), **Karl G.,** German-born American educator **U** 253

Maestoso, musical term **M** 541

Maeterlinck (MAE-ter-link), **Count Maurice** (1862–1949), Belgian poet, dramatist, and essayist, b. near Ghent. His writing is marked by a sense of mysticism. Among his well-known works are the collection of poems *Hothouses;* the plays *The Princess Maleine, Pélleas and Mélisande* (transformed by Debussy into an opera), and *The Blue Bird;* and the classic nature study *The Life of the Bee.* He received the Nobel prize for literature (1911).
  drama, history of **D** 302

Mafia see Organized crime

Magars, a people of Nepal **N** 109

Magazines **M** 16–20
  advertising **A** 27–28
  cartoons, history of **C** 127, 129
  comics **C** 453–54
  commercial art **C** 455–56
  illustration and illustrators **I** 91–92, 94–95
  indexes **I** 115
  journalism **J** 137
  libraries, professional publications for **L** 184
  mass communication media **C** 469
  publishing **P** 513
  Reader's Guide to Periodical Literature locates information in magazines **R** 129
  short stories **S** 162

Magdalena (mog-da-LANE-a) **River,** Colombia **R** 242; **C** 405; **S** 277; *picture* **C** 404

Magdalen (MAG-da-len) **Islands,** Canada **I** 434–35

Magdeburg (MAG-de-burg) **hemispheres,** used to illustrate pressure of air **V** 264

Magellan (ma-GELL-an), **Ferdinand,** Portuguese explorer **M** 21
  voyage around the world **E** 382–83

Magellan, Strait of, South America **E** 383; **M** 21

Magellanic (maj-el-LAN-ic) **Clouds,** galaxies **U** 199

Magen David see Star of David

Magenta, color **C** 425

Magi (MAY-ji) (plural of old Persian *magus,* meaning "wizard" or "sorcerer"), priests of ancient Media, northwestern Persia, who were said to have magical skills and knowledge of astrology. Beliefs of the Magi were incorporated into Zoroastrianism. In the Bible reference is made to the Babylonian Rabmag, head of the Magi under Nebuchadnezzar (Jeremiah 39:3, 13). The "wise men of the East" (Matthew 2:1–12) were Magi who, in search of a savior, came to Bethlehem bringing gifts to the child Jesus. English words "magic" and "magician" stem from this term.
  Jesus Christ **J** 84

Magic **M** 22–25
  African tribal religions **A** 56
  dance patterns of the magicians **D** 22
  early religions **R** 145–46
  fetish figures of Pacific Islands **P** 9
  fire to drive away evil spirits **F** 145
  folk art **F** 292–93
  Japanese origami **O** 222
  medicine of cave dwellers **M** 203
  prehistoric art **P** 437
  sculpture in prehistoric times **S** 92
  superstition **S** 473–75
  tricks **T** 288–89
  witchcraft **W** 208–09

Magical Mystery Tour, film **B** 108

Magic Flute, The, opera by Mozart **O** 146; *picture* **O** 147
  work full of lovely melodies sometimes mistaken for folk songs **G** 185

Magic squares, arrangements of numbers **N** 382, 383

Magillycuddy's Reeks, mountains, Ireland, *picture* **L** 30

Maginot (MAJ-in-o) **Line,** line of fortifications constructed by the French just prior to World War II along the eastern frontier of France, from the Swiss to the Luxembourg border. Built to prevent a German invasion, it was considered impregnable. However, in 1940 the Germans skirted the northern end of the line and invaded France across the unprotected Franco-Belgian border.
  World War II **F** 377; **W** 288, 289

Magistrate, judge **J** 155

Magma, liquid underground rock **R** 263–64
  how mountains form **M** 499
  mid-ocean rift being filled **E** 15
  volcanoes, products of **V** 378

Magna Carta, charter to limit the power of the English king **M** 26
  basis for English Bill of Rights **B** 180
  checks on power of kings in Middle Ages **M** 291
  civil rights, historical origins of **C** 330
  English history, barons fight back **E** 218
  taxation principle set forth **T** 26
  what feudal lords owed vassals **F** 101

Magnes, mythical shepherd who was supposed to have discovered lodestone **M** 28

Magnesia (mag-NE-sia), region, Greece **M** 27
  magnetic stone, deposits of **M** 28

Magnesium **M** 27; *chart* **M** 230
  alloys **A** 168
  elements, some facts about **E** 153, 160
  minerals in the ocean **O** 28
  United States is self-sufficient in **N** 293

Magnetic compass see Compass, magnetic

Magnetic disks, storage device for information

computers **C** 480
filmless cameras **P** 203
Magnetic domains, clusters of atoms **M** 32
Magnetic energy E 198, 199
Magnetic equator see Aclinic line
Magnetic field M 29, 30, 32–33
archaeological dating **A** 361–62
earth **A** 474, 475; **E** 8; **G** 113, 115; **M** 30
Jupiter **P** 275
Mars and earth **M** 106, 107
Mercury **P** 270
radiation belts **C** 554
Uranus **U** 231
Venus **P** 271
Magnetic induction
electric generators, Faraday's discovery **E** 132
transformers **E** 134
Magnetic poles see Poles, magnetic

Magnetic resonance imaging (MRI), a medical technique that uses radio waves to create pictures of internal body organs, tissues, and bone. Inside an MRI scanner, huge magnets line up the body's hydrogen atoms. Radio waves momentarily knock the atoms out of alignment. As the atoms re-align, they give off slight radio signals, which a computer interprets to create an image. MRI, though expensive, provides relatively clear pictures of soft body tissues (something that regular X rays cannot do). MRI is especially useful in helping doctors find tumors deep within the body. **D** 208; picture **D** 206
computers in medicine **C** 488, 489

Magnetic tape
automation uses **A** 531
communication, history of **C** 463
computers **C** 481, 484
electronic music **E** 142g
hi-fi and stereo recording **H** 121, 122, 123
videotapes **V** 332c–332d
Magnetite (MAG-net-ite), iron ore **I** 403
Magnetohydrodynamic (mag-NE-to-hy-dro-dy-NAM-ic)
(MHD) **generators P** 423
Magnetometers (mag-net-OM-et-ers), instruments that measure the earth's magnetism
earth's magnetic field, study of **G** 115
exploring for magnetic ores **M** 316
left on moon **S** 340e–340f
petroleum, search for **P** 169
surveying, use in **S** 480
Magnetos (mag-NE-tos), electric generators with permanent magnets **E** 122
Magnetosphere (mag-NE-to-sphere), planet's magnetic field
earth **E** 8; **R** 48
Jupiter **S** 348
Magnetrons (MAG-net-rons), electron tubes **E** 148
Magnets and magnetism M 28–33
earth's magnetism **E** 8; **G** 112–13, 115
electric generators **E** 122
electricity and magnetism **E** 129–31
electric motors **E** 136–41
Faraday's experiments in electromagnetism **F** 47
lines of force due to electric current **E** 130–31
magnetic energy in physics **P** 235
mineral detection **M** 315–16
radiation, effect on **R** 40
radiation belts **R** 47–48
seismographs, use in **E** 32, diagram **E** 33
telegraph, uses in **T** 51
See also Electromagnetism

Magnifiers M 283–88
lenses of magnifiers and microscopes **L** 146–47
optical instruments **O** 168, 169
Magnifying glasses L 144–45; **M** 283; **O** 169
Magnitude, (brightness), of stars **S** 406–07
Magnolia, flowering tree
Louisiana, state flower of, picture **L** 349
Mississippi, state flower of, picture **M** 351
Magnolia State, nickname for Mississippi **M** 350, 351
Magog see Gog and Magog
Magoon, Bob, American boat racer **B** 264

Magpies, group of long-tailed birds found throughout the world. They are usually a glossy black, with blue or green metallic sheen. They are about the size of small crows. The magpie builds an unusually large nest in bushes or tops of trees. It eats almost anything but is especially fond of birds' eggs and young birds. Magpies are noisy birds and have a loud, harsh call. They sometimes are tamed and kept as pets.
crow family **P** 88
nest, picture **A** 273

Magritte (ma-GREET), **René,** Belgian painter **B** 128
Magsat, artificial satellite **S** 54

Magsaysay (MOG-sy-sy), **Ramón** (1907–57), Philippine statesman, b. Iba, Zambales province. After fighting in the Philippine Army during World War II, he was appointed (1945) military governor of Zambales. He represented Zambales in the Philippine Congress (1946–50). He was secretary of the national defense (1950–53) and president of the Philippines (1953–57). **P** 188

Maguey, plant
rope **R** 334
tequila and pulque are made from **M** 242
Magyar, language **H** 283
Magyars, European people **H** 283, 287
Budapest, history of **B** 422b
Mahabharata (ma-HA-ba-ra-ta), epic poem **H** 130;
O 220d; **T** 163
Mahan (ma-HAN), **Alfred T.,** American naval officer and writer **U** 186

Mahathir ibn Mohammed (1925–), prime minister of Malaysia, b. Alor Setar. Mahathir, a physician, became chairman of the United Malay National Organization (a political party) and prime minister in 1981. Before becoming prime minister, he served in the Senate and House of Representatives and held several cabinet posts, including that of deputy prime minister (1976–81).

Mahatma (ma-HAT-ma) ("Great Soul"), name given to Gandhi **G** 24
Mahavira (ma-ha-VI-ra), founder of Jainism **R** 147
Mahayana (ma-ha-YA-na), teachings of Buddha **B** 424
Mahdi, Muslim religious leader **S** 449
Mahé, island, Seychelles **S** 129
Mahendra (ma-HANE-dra), king of Nepal **N** 112
Mahieu (mah-YOH), **Thomas,** French bibliophile and book collector **B** 322
Mahler, Gustav, Austrian composer and conductor
M 34, 549
romantic age in music **G** 189

Mahogany (ma-HOG-any), strong, light to dark reddish-brown wood. Known for its high polish, it was fashionable in 18th century and remains popular in the making of furniture. Mahogany originally came from Central America

Mahogany (continued)
and the West Indies. African and Philippine mahoganies look similar but belong to different species.

uses of the wood and its grain, *picture* **W** 224

Mahony, Roger Michael (1936–), American Roman Catholic clergyman, b. Hollywood, Calif. In 1985 he became the youngest archbishop in the United States as head of the archdiocese of Los Angeles, the country's largest. He was ordained a priest in 1962 and a bishop in 1975. He has served in California throughout his ministry and has been a member of numerous charitable, educational, and civic organizations.

Mahout (ma-HOWT), elephant trainer **E** 169

Mahre (MARE), **Phil** (1957–) and **Steve** (1957–), American skiers, twins, b. White Pass, Wash. During their careers the Mahre brothers were among the best of U.S. men Alpine skiers. At the 1980 Winter Olympics, Phil won the silver medal in the men's slalom. Phil was the first U.S. skier ever to win the World Cup skiing title, a feat he accomplished three times—in 1981, 1982, and 1983. In World Cup competition, Steve finished 4th in 1981 and 3rd in 1982. At the 1984 Winter Olympics, Phil won the gold medal in the men's slalom, and Steve won the silver. Both brothers retired from competition in 1984. **O** 116c; *picture* **O** 116a

Maidan, park, Calcutta **C** 9
Maidenhair ferns, *picture* **F** 93
Maiden of Passamaquoddy, The, nonsense poem, *excerpt* **N** 273
Maid Marian, in the Robin Hood legends **R** 251
queen of the May **M** 182
Maid of Orléans, name for Joan of Arc **J** 112
Maids of Honor, The, painting by Velázquez *see* Meninas, Las
Mail *see* Postal service
Mail, electronic *see* Electronic mail
Mail cars, of railroads **R** 81

Mailer, Norman (1923–), American author, b. Long Branch, N.J. He gained fame for the novel *The Naked and the Dead,* drawn from his World War II experiences. He has also written plays, film scripts, and poetry. His *Armies of the Night* won the National Book Award and the Pulitzer prize for nonfiction (1968). Mailer's works often deal with extremes in politics and social conflicts. His other works include *Miami and the Siege of Chicago, Of A Fire on the Moon, The Executioner's Song,* and *Ancient Evenings.*

American literature, history of **A** 213

Mailgram, combination letter-telegram **P** 400
Mailing lists, for direct-mail advertising **M** 35
Mailing machines O 58
Maillol (ma-YOL), **Aristide,** French sculptor **S** 103
Mail order M 34–35
department store catalogs **D** 120
Maiman, Theodore H., American scientist **L** 46b

Maimonides (my-MON-id-ese), **Moses** (Moses ben Maimon) (1135–1204), Jewish physician, philosopher, and rabbi, b. Cordoba, Spain. Although a respected physician, he was most prominent and influential for his commentaries in the fields of religion and philosophy. An acknowledged authority on Judaism, in 1180 he completed one of his greatest works, the *Mishnah Torah,* a codification of the Jewish law. A second remarkable work was *Moreh Nevukhim (Guide to the Perplexed),* an attempt to reconcile Jewish philosophy with that of the Greeks, particularly Aristotle.

Jews, history of **J** 106

Maine M 36–51
American colonies **A** 186, 190
boundary settlements **T** 108
Portland Head Light, *picture* **L** 276
Maine, University of M 44
Maine, U.S.S., battleship **M** 189; **S** 374, 375
Mainframe computers C 478, 483; **O** 54; *picture* **C** 479
Mainsprings, in watches and clocks **C** 367, 369, 370; **W** 44, 45
Maintenance of membership, in labor contracts **L** 15–16
Maison Carrée, Roman temple, Nîmes, France **A** 381
Maisonneuve (may-zon-nerve), **Paul de Chomedey, Sieur de,** French colonist **M** 443
Maitani, Lorenzo, Italian sculptor **I** 463
Maitreya, wooden statue of Buddha by Kaikei **O** 218
Maize *see* Corn
Majolica (ma-JOL-ic-a), pottery **P** 411; *picture* **P** 409
Major, in music **M** 541
Majorca (ma-YOR-ca), island, Spain **I** 427; *picture* **I** 431
Majority leaders, in Congress **U** 144
Major leagues, in baseball **B** 75, 77
Major medical insurance I 294
Majuro, capital of the Marshall Islands **P** 7

Makarios III (ma-KAR-i-oce), **Archbishop** (1913–77), Greek Orthodox prelate and Cypriot statesman, b. Ano Panayia, Paphos, Cyprus. He was elected archbishop of Cyprus in 1950. A leader in the struggle for freedom from British rule, in 1959 he participated in forming the London agreement granting Cyprus independence. He was president of the new republic from 1960 until he was deposed in July, 1974, by a group of army officers who favored union *(enosis)* with Greece. Forced to flee briefly, he resumed his office from December, 1974, until his death.

Cyprus, history of **C** 603

Makarova, Natalia, Russian dancer, *picture* **B** 29

Makeba (ma-KEE-ba), **Miriam** (1932–), singer, Xhosa tribe, b. Prospect township, Johannesburg, S. Africa. Although she had no musical training, she has spoken for the aspirations of her people through her African melodies and rhythms. She has many best-selling record albums and has made numerous appearances as a television, concert, and nightclub performer.

Makeup
beauty culture **B** 110
clowns **C** 386–87
cosmetics **C** 509–10
motion picture makeup crews **M** 483
plays **P** 341; **T** 156; *pictures* **P** 340
Make Way for Ducklings, book by Robert McCloskey, *picture* **C** 243
Maki, Oili, Finnish artist
Purple Sea, tapestry **T** 24
Mako sharks S 140; *picture* **S** 141
Maksutov, Dmitriy, Russian scientist **T** 63
Maksutov telescope T 63
Malabo, capital of Equatorial Guinea **E** 273
Malacca (ma-LAC-ca) (now Melaka), Malaysia **M** 58, 59

Malachi (MA-la-ky), book of the Old Testament **B** 155
Malagasy, language **M** 8, 9
Malagasy Republic see Madagascar
Malaita, Pacific island **S** 252b

Malamud (MAL-uh-muhd), Bernard (1914–1986), American writer, b. Brooklyn, N.Y. His works portray ordinary people—often American Jews living in New York—whose lives and struggles symbolize the strength of the human spirit. After graduating from the City College of New York and Columbia University, Malamud combined teaching with writing. His novels include The Assistant (1957); The Fixer (1966), which won a Pulitzer Prize and a National Book Award; The Tenants (1971); and God's Grace (1982). Short story collections include The Magic Barrel (1958), a National Book Award winner.
  his place in American literature **A** 214

Malamute see Alaskan malamute
Malapropisms (MAL-a-prop-isms), twisting of words,
    origin of the term **H** 278
Malaria (ma-LAIR-ia), protozoan disease **D** 196
    Anopheles mosquitos **H** 260; **I** 283
    pioneer life **P** 256
    public health **P** 505
Malaspina (ma-la-SPI-na) Glacier, Alaska **A** 131
Malawi (ma-LA-wi) (formerly Nyasaland) **M** 52–53
    flag, picture **F** 228
Malawi, Lake see Nyasa, Lake
Malay (MAY-lay), language **S** 330
    Bahasa Malaysia **M** 54
    Singapore **S** 180
Malaya (ma-LAY-a), Federation of **M** 59
Malaya, University of, Kuala Lumpur, Malaysia **M** 54
Malayan marbled cats **C** 143
Malayan sun bears **B** 107
Malayo-Polynesian languages **A** 460; **L** 40
Malays (MAY-lays), a people of Asia **A** 459
    Indonesian population **I** 216
    Malaysia **M** 54, 55, 58
    Singapore **S** 179
Malaysia (ma-LAY-sia) **M** 54–59
    flag, picture **F** 232
    rubber trees, pictures **A** 464, **R** 343
    Singapore, formerly a part **S** 181
    World War II in Malaya **W** 293
Malcolm III, king of Scotland **S** 88

Malcolm X (1925–65), American civil rights leader, b. Omaha, Neb. When suspended from the Black Muslims, he formed his own protest organization, The Organization for Afro-American Unity (1964). He advocated black pride and believed that black society must become independent before there can be a workable black-white society. His book, The Autobiography of Malcolm X, published shortly after his death (1965), predicted his assassination, which took place on February 21, 1965.
    American literature **A** 214b
    Black Muslims **B** 250o

Maldives (MAL-dives) **M** 60
    flag, picture **F** 232
Male (MA-lay), capital of Maldives **M** 60
Malecite, Indians of North America **I** 170

Malenkov (MA-len-kof), Georgi Maximilianovich (1902–   ), Soviet Communist Party and Government official, b. Orenburg (now Chkalov). He advanced within party ranks to become a deputy premier (1946) under Stalin, and successor to Stalin as premier (1953–55). After taking part in an attempt (1957) to overthrow Khrushchev, he was demoted to a minor post. He was expelled from the Communist Party in 1964.

Maletsunyane Falls, Lesotho **W** 63
Malevich (ma-LAY-vich), Kazimir, Russian painter
    M 392–93
    White on White, painting, picture **M** 392
Malherbe (ma-LAIRB), François de, French poet
    F 435, 437
Mali (MA-li) **M** 61–62
    African epic poetry **A** 76b
    early western African empire **A** 67; **B** 250a—250b
    flag, picture **F** 228
    storytelling **A** 76b
Mali Federation, former union of Senegal and French
    Sudan **M** 62; **S** 120
Malignancy, in cells **V** 367, 369
Malignant tumors, in cancer **C** 90
Maligne (ma-LENE) Lake, Jasper National Park, picture
    J 54

Malik, Adam (1917–84), Indonesian statesman, b. Pematang Siantar, Sumatra. Starting in his teens, he was active in the movement to free Indonesia from Dutch colonial rule and was jailed several times by the Dutch. In 1937 he was one of several journalists who founded the Antara news agency, which later became Indonesia's national press agency. After Indonesian independence (1949), he entered government service and in 1966 was appointed foreign minister. He became vice president of Indonesia in 1978. He was president of the United Nations General Assembly from 1971 to 1972.

Malinche, Aztec adviser to Cortes **M** 247
Malindi, Kenya **K** 232

Malinke (ma-LEEN-kay), African people of the former (13th to 16th century) Mali empire of western Sudan. They now inhabit the republics of Guinea and Mali. **G** 8, 404, 406, 406a; **M** 61
    African epic poetry **A** 76b

Mall, The, Washington, D.C. **W** 29–30
Mallard ducks, birds, pictures **B** 239, **D** 341, **L** 257
Mallarmé, Stéphane, French poet **F** 440
Mallea, Eduardo, Argentine author **L** 72
Malleability (mal-le-a-BIL-ity), property of metals
    M 229
Malle Bobbe, painting by Hals, picture **B** 57
Mallet (mal-LAY), Anatole, Swiss engineer and inventor
    L 332
Mallet brothers, French explorers **N** 92
Mallets, large hammers **T** 215–16
    in croquet **C** 583
Mallorca see Majorca Island
Malls, shopping see Shopping centers
Malmö (MOL-mer), Sweden **S** 484
Malnutrition (poor nutrition) **N** 417–18
    blindness, causes of **B** 251
    food supply **F** 354
    food taboos **F** 335
    nutritional diseases **D** 185
    See also Nutrition
Malocclusion (bad bite), in dentistry **O** 226, 227

Malory, Sir Thomas (lived during 15th century), English writer. While in prison (1451–71), he compiled Morte D'Arthur, a collection of the legendary tales of King Arthur and his knights. It is thought that he served in the Hun-

Malory, Sir Thomas (continued)
dred Years War and in Parliament (1445).
  Arthur, story of **A** 443–45
  English literature, history of **E** 248

Malpeque, Prince Edward Island, Canada **P** 466
Malpighi (mol-PI-ghi), **Marcello,** Italian anatomy
    professor, first to study fingerprints **F** 129
  medicine during the Renaissance **M** 206

Malpractice, improper or negligent practice by a physician, lawyer, or other provider of professional services
(such as a hospital) that results in injury or damage to a
patient or client. A type of insurance called professional
liability insurance, or malpractice insurance, provides protection against losses from lawsuits alleging malpractice.
  doctors **D** 236

Malraux (mal-RO), **André** (1901–76), French writer and
political figure, b. Paris. He participated in and wrote
about revolutionary movements of his day. *Man's Fate,*
winner of the French Goncourt prize (1933), told of China
in 1927. *Man's Hope* had a background of the Spanish
Civil War in which Malraux fought. In World War II he
fought with the French Resistance, was captured by the
Germans, and escaped. An ardent supporter of General de
Gaulle, Malraux served in his governments, the last time
as minister of cultural affairs. **F** 442

Malt, sprouted grain used in brewing and distilling
    G 284–85
  used in brewing beer **B** 116
  whiskey and other distilled beverages **W** 159
Malta, island nation in the Mediterranean **M** 63–64
  flag, *picture* **F** 235
Maltese, language **M** 63

Maltese, a toy spaniel developed on the island of Malta
more than 2,000 years ago. This gentle, affectionate dog
has a compact body, hanging ears, and a plumed tail held
curled over its back. Its pure white coat is long and silky.
The Maltese stands 4 to 7 in (10 to 18 cm) at the shoulder
and weighs 2 to 7 lb (1 to 3.2 kg). **D** 257; *picture*
D 252

Maltese Falcon, The, detective story by Dashiell
    Hammett **M** 563
Malthus, Thomas R., English economist **P** 387–88

Malthusian (mal-THU-sian) **theory,** belief of British economist T. R. Malthus (1766–1834) that if the population
continued to increase at a rapid rate, the world's food supply would become inadequate. The industrial revolution
and advanced methods of agricultural production led to
attack on the theory, but the population explosion since
World War II has revived interest in his ideas.
  overpopulation **P** 387–88

Maltose, malt sugar **S** 453
  how beer is made **B** 116
Maluku *see* Moluccas
Mamaia (ma-MA-ia), Rumania **R** 357; *picture* **R** 359
Mamas and the Papas, The, American rock music group
    R 262c
Mambas, snakes **S** 208; *pictures* **S** 211
Mameli (ma-MAE-li), **Goffredo,** Italian poet **N** 20
Mameluke Sword, Marine officer's sword **U** 182

Mamet, David Alan (1947–   ), American playwright, b.
Chicago, Ill. He won the Pulitzer prize in 1984 for *Glen-
garry Glen Ross,* a satire on dishonest real estate sales-
men. Most of his plays—characterized by vivid dialogue
and short, fast scenes—were first produced in Chicago or
off-off-Broadway in New York City. They include *American
Buffalo* (1976), *A Life in the Theater* (1977), and *The
Water Engine* (1977). He has also been an actor, director,
and screenwriter. **D** 305

Mammals, animals **M** 65–77
  adaptations in the world of life **L** 225–26
  animal communication by scent signals **A** 280
  bats are winged mammals **B** 96
  brain compared with bird's, *diagram* **B** 203
  cetaceans, marine mammals **W** 147–51
  cheetah is the fastest **C** 141
  color vision **C** 428
  dolphins and porpoises **D** 275–80
  earth's history **E** 25
  egg-laying monotremes **P** 333–34
  eggs and embryos **E** 90
  elephants **E** 164–69
  even-toed **F** 81–82
  feet **F** 81–82
  fossils **F** 387–88
  hands **F** 83–84
  hoofed **H** 206–21
  insectivores **I** 259–61
  kangaroos and other pouched mammals **K** 168–73
  kingdoms of living things **K** 249–59
  largest animals **A** 262–63
  life spans **A** 81–83
  milk producers **M** 309
  monkeys, apes, and other primates **M** 417–22
  ocean life **O** 25
  odd-toed **F** 81–82
  organs, compared with birds' **B** 202
  pets **P** 177–78
  prehistoric animals, development of **P** 434
  rodents are gnawing mammals **R** 276–80
  sexual reproduction **R** 179–80
  taxonomy **T** 32
  Viverridae family **G** 92–95
  whales **W** 147–51
  without feet **F** 82–83
  zoos **Z** 374–79
  See also Hoofed mammals; names of mammals
Mammary gland, milk-producing gland **M** 309, 418
  What is a mammal? **M** 65
Mammography, X ray of the breast **C** 92

Mammon (from Aramaic word *māmōnā,* meaning "riches"), material wealth. The term is used in the Talmud and
the New Testament (Matthew 6:24, Luke 16:9, 11, 13) in
the sense of material riches on which too great a value is
put.

Mammoth Cave, Kentucky **C** 156; **K** 212, 215, 221
Mammoth Hot Springs, Yellowstone National Park,
    picture **Y** 346
Mammoths, extinct mammals **E** 338–40; *pictures*
    E 339, 340, **F** 378
  archaeologist working on mammoth skull, *picture*
    A 359
  prehistoric relatives of elephants **E** 168
Mamprusi, a people of Africa **G** 194
Man *see* Human beings
Man, Isle of, in the Irish Sea **I** 435; **U** 79
Manado, Indonesia **I** 221

Management, owners and managers in industry **L** 11
Management and Budget, Office of, of the United States **P** 454
Managua (ma-NA-gua), capital of Nicaragua **N** 247, 248
Managua, Lake, Nicaragua **L** 29
Manama (ma-NA-ma), capital of Bahrain **B** 18
Manassa Mauler, nickname *see* Dempsey, Jack
Manassas (man-AS-sas), Virginia, site of Civil War battles of Bull Run **C** 339, 341; **V** 355
  Jackson, Thomas ("Stonewall") **J** 8
Manasseh (ma-NASS-eh), **Prayer of** **B** 159
Manatees, aquatic mammals **S** 106–07; *picture* **M** 72
Manaus (ma-NOUSE), Brazil **B** 383
Manawyddan (man-a-WUD-dan), legendary Welsh hero **L** 129
Manchester, England **U** 75, 77
Manchester, New Hampshire **N** 159–60
Manchineel (man-chin-EEL), tree **P** 282, 322
Manchu dynasty *see* Ch'ing dynasty
Manchukuo (mon-CHU-ku-o), former puppet state of Japan **W** 284
Manchuria (man-CHU-ria), northeast area of China **C** 264
  Japanese occupation **C** 271
  Shenyang **S** 150
Manchus, Asian people **C** 269
  Korea, history of **K** 303
  See also Ch'ing dynasty
Mandabi, motion picture **M** 491
Mandalay, Burma **B** 462
  Buddha's statue, *picture* **B** 423
Mandan, Indians of North America **N** 336
  painting of a village by George Catlin **U** 119
Mandarin, citrus fruit **O** 179; *picture* **O** 176

Mandarin, a public official in the Chinese Empire. They were required to pass difficult examinations on literature, philosophy, history, and speak the Mandarin dialect. In English, "Mandarin" may refer to any bureaucrat or a person of influence in intellectual circles.

Mandarin Chinese, national language of China **C** 258, 259
Mandarin duck, bird **D** 342

Mandated territory, territory administered by a nation given authority to rule by the League of Nations. The mandate system was established (1919) under the League of Nations Covenant to provide governments for dependent territories of defeated World War I nations (Germany and Turkey) and to aid these territories in attaining independence. Some mandated territories became independent between the world wars; others gained their independence, after first becoming trust territories of the United Nations, in the years after World War II. Namibia (South-West Africa) was made a League of Nations mandate under South African administration. South Africa continues to control it in spite of opposition by the United Nations.
  Namibia **N** 9–10
  Palestine **P** 40c
  Transjordan **J** 132

Mandeans, religious sect of Iraq **I** 378–79

Mandela, Nelson Rolihlahla (1918–   ), South African political leader, b. Umtata. Imprisoned since 1964, he remains a symbol of the hopes of black South Africans. The son of a tribal chieftain, he chose a law career as the best way to serve his people and obtained his degree in

1942. In 1944 he joined the African National Congress and was a co-founder of the ANC's Youth League, which used civil disobedience against the ruling white National Party. But after 69 blacks were killed at a demonstration in Sharpeville in 1961, Mandela became the head of a militant underground protest movement. In 1962 he was arrested and in 1964 was sentenced to life imprisonment for sabotage and treason. Since then he has refused any offers for release that were not unconditional.

Mandela, Nomzamo Winifred (Winnie) (1936–   ), South African political activist, b. Pondoland district. She married black leader Nelson Mandela in 1958, while he was on trial for treason. Since his imprisonment in 1964 she has been his representative at home and abroad. She was born into the Xhosa tribe and received a college education to become her country's first black medical social worker. When she began her clinical training in Johannesburg, she became interested in politics and was among those arrested after riots in Soweto in 1974. In 1977 she was "banned"—forbidden to speak in public and confined to the town of Brandfort. After Brandfort was burned down in 1985, she broke her ban and reappeared in public.

Mandelbaum Gate, in Jerusalem **J** 80
Mandeville, Jamaica **J** 17
Mandingo *see* Malinke
Mandolin **F** 330; *pictures* **F** 329, **S** 439

Mandrake, plant native to the Mediterranean area and eastern Asia. The mandrake has bell-shaped flowers, large leaves, and a thick root. The mandrake was once supposed to have magical properties. Its roots are used in some medicines. A North American plant, the mayapple, also is called a mandrake. The mayapple has a single white flower, poisonous roots, and edible yellow fruit.

Mandrel, ceramic cone for making glass tubing **G** 236
Mandrills, monkeys **M** 420; *picture* **M** 421
Mandyako, African people **G** 406a
Maned wolf, wild dog of South America **D** 247; *picture* **D** 246
Manet (ma-NAY), **Edouard,** French painter **M** 77
  impressionism in painting **P** 29
  Fifer, The, painting **F** 429
  French art **F** 426
  modern art **M** 387
  portrait of Berthe Morisot, *picture* **W** 59
  watercolor painting **W** 60
  Woman with a Parrot, painting, *picture* **M** 77
Manganese, element **E** 153, 160; *chart* **M** 230
  alloys **A** 168
  minerals in the ocean **O** 28
  paints used by prehistoric people **P** 15
  producing regions of North America **N** 293
  steel **I** 395
Mangareva Islands *see* Gambier Islands
Mangles, ironers **L** 84
Mango, tropical fruit **M** 78

Mangroves, group of subtropical and tropical shrubs and trees, usually found in marshes and shore areas. The one American species is common along the shores and in the swamps of Florida. The seeds usually sprout while still on the parent plant. The roots of the young plant dangle in the air. When the seed drops, the roots grow down, settle in the mud, and support the new tree above the water.
  mangrove jungles **J** 152; *picture* **J** 154

Manhattan (man-HATT-an), borough and island, New York City   **N** 228, 234, 235; *picture* **I** 426
  bought by Peter Minuit for $24   **A** 191
Manhattan, icebreaking oil tanker   **N** 338
Manhattan Project, on atomic research   **F** 92
Manic-depressive psychosis (sy-CO-sis), form of mental illness   **M** 227–28

Manichaeism (MAN-ic-e-ism) (or Manicheism), religion founded in Babylonia by Manes (216?–276?). Influenced by Babylonian religion, Christianity, Zoroastrianism, and possibly Buddhism, Manichaeism conceived of humankind as composed of opposing forces of light (good) and darkness (evil). To attain virtue—separation or freeing of the spark of light from darkness or evil—idolatry and animal killing were prohibited and the Elect abstained from meat, wine, and marriage. The movement was influential until the 13th century.

Manifest Destiny, in United States history   **M** 239a
  Polk, James K.   **P** 376
Manila (ma-NIL-a), Philippines   **M** 79; **P** 186–87
Manila Bay, Battle of, 1898   **P** 187; **S** 375
Manila hemp *see* Abaca
Man in White/Woman in Black, Morocco, photograph by Irving Penn, *picture*   **P** 206
Manioc (MAN-i-oc) *see* Cassava
Man is the measure of all things, belief of ancient Greeks   **S** 94
Manito (MAN-it-o), great spirit of American Indians   **I** 171
Manitoba (man-it-O-ba), Canada   **M** 80–86
  Riel rebellions   **C** 75
  Winnipeg   **W** 190

Manitoba, Lake, a lake in in southwestern Manitoba, Canada. It is a remnant of an ancient glacial lake, Lake Agassiz. The third largest lake in the province, Lake Manitoba is more than 130 miles (209 kilometers) long and has many freshwater fisheries.   **M** 80

Manitoba Act, 1870, Canada   **M** 86
Manitoba Escarpment   **M** 80
Manitoulin (man-i-TOO-lin), island in Lake Huron   **G** 327; **O** 119, 120a
Mankiewicz (MAN-kie-witz), **Joseph,** American motion picture director, *picture*   **M** 479
Manley, Michael, prime minister of Jamaica   **J** 17–18
Man-made elements *see* Transuranium elements
Man-made materials *see* Synthetic materials
Man-monkey-crab, game   **G** 19
Mann, Horace, American educator   **M** 87
  battle for the common school   **E** 70
Mann (MONN), **Thomas,** German-born American writer   **G** 180
  Doctor Faustus, a modern Faust story   **F** 73
  themes of his novels   **N** 347
Manna, kind of food   **M** 468
Manned Orbiting Laboratory *see* MOL
Manned Spacecraft Center, Houston, Texas *see* Lyndon B. Johnson Space Center

Mannerheim (MAN-ner-hime) **Line,** World War II line of fortification across the Karelian isthmus, from Lake Ladoga to the Gulf of Finland. The defenses were named for Finnish military leader Baron Carl Gustaf Emil von Mannerheim (1867–1951), who supervised the raising of the line. The line was used by the Finns in Russian invasion of 1939–40.
  Russian Front, 1944   **W** 301

Mannerism, in art and architecture   **I** 470, 472
  Renaissance art   **R** 171
  sculpture   **S** 101
  Tintoretto   **T** 196
Manners *see* Etiquette
Mannheim (MONN-hime), Germany
  classical age of music in   **C** 352
Man of Aran, documentary motion picture   **M** 478
Man of La Mancha, musical   **M** 551
Manolete, Spanish bullfighter   **B** 453
Manon (ma-NON), opera by Jules Massenet   **O** 146
Manors, feudal estates   **F** 102
  agriculture   **A** 98
Man o' War, Kentucky-bred race horse   **K** 212

Manpower Development and Training Act, an act passed by the U.S. Congress in 1962 that provided retraining programs for workers who had lost their jobs to automation. Disadvantaged persons later came under the provisions of the act. Such job training programs were later placed under the sponsorship of the Comprehensive Employment and Training Act (CETA) of 1973.

Manrique (mon-RI-kay), **Gómez,** Spanish poet   **S** 367
Manrique, Jorge, Spanish poet   **S** 367
Mansa Musa, Mali emperor   **B** 250b; **M** 62
Mansard roof, French Renaissance design   **F** 421–22

Mansart (mon-SAR) (or Mansard), **Nicolas François** (1598–1666), French architect, b. Paris. He became architect to King Louis XIII (1636) and designed numerous churches and châteaus in the Paris vicinity. He frequently used a high roof with steep sides that became known as a mansard roof. One of his famous works is the Château de Maisons Lafitte.
  Renaissance design in architecture   **F** 421–22

Mansfield, Katherine, New Zealand-born English writer   **E** 267; **N** 236; **S** 162
Mansfield, Michael Joseph (Mike), American politician   **M** 442
Manta rays, fishes   **S** 140, 142

Mantegna (mon-TAIN-ya), **Andrea** (1431–1506), early Italian Renaissance painter and engraver, b. Vicenza. Commissioned by Pope Innocent VIII, he painted frescoes for the Belvedere Chapel, Rome (1488–90). He is famous for his technique of perspective and the sculpturelike human figures of his paintings and engravings. Among his noted works are *The Triumph of Caesar, Parnassus, The Dead Christ,* and *Saint Sebastian.*
  Adoration of the Shepherds, The, painting   **A** 438a
  art, the meanings of   **A** 438
  Renaissance art in northern Italy   **R** 169

Man That Always Rides, The, painting by Paul Kane, *picture*   **C** 82

Mantis, insect usually called praying mantis because of the way it holds up its forelegs to grasp its insect prey. It is usually 2 to 4 in (5 to 10 cm) long. The mantis has a long, slim, green or brown body, four long walking legs, two forelegs, and strong wings. It is found in Europe, Asia, and the United States. It is useful because it eats harmful insects.
  eating habits   **A** 266; **I** 269
  leg, *diagram*   **I** 273
  newly hatched, *picture*   **I** 265

Mantle, covering of a mollusk   **O** 273, 274, 277

Mantle, of the earth   **E** 6, 8, 19; **G** 113, 114, 116;
   diagram **G** 112
   earthquakes   **E** 29
   earth's plate movement   **E** 9
   seismic waves picture earth's interior   **E** 33;
   diagram **E** 34
Mantle, of the moon   **M** 450, 453

Mantle, Mickey (1931–   ), American baseball player, b. Spavinaw, Okla. An outstanding center fielder and hitter for the New York Yankees from 1951 to 1968, he was voted Most Valuable Player in the American League in 1956, 1957, and 1962, and won the Triple Crown in 1956 for leading the league in batting average, home runs, and runs batted in. Mantle hit 536 home runs in his baseball career. In 1974 he was named to the Baseball Hall of Fame.   **O** 94; *picture* **B** 76

Manu, Hindu Code of
   quoted on women's role   **W** 211
Manual alphabet, of the deaf, *picture*   **D** 49
Manuals (keyboards), of the organ   **K** 236–37
Manuals, type of reference book   **R** 129
Manual training *see* Industrial arts
Manuel, Don Juan *see* Juan Manuel, Don
Manufacturing   **M** 87–89
   advantages of location: Ontario   **O** 121
   Africa   **A** 64
   automation   **A** 530, 533–34
   automobiles   **A** 545, 547–51
   bread   **B** 388–388a
   chemical industry   **C** 197
   clothing industry   **C** 380–81
   explosives industry   **E** 394–95
   hazardous wastes   **H** 72–73
   industrial design   **I** 229–32
   industrial growth   **I** 248–49
   Industrial Revolution   **I** 233–41
   industrial society created in United States   **U** 129–30
   mass production   **M** 151
   New England industry   **N** 139
   North America, producing regions of   **N** 298–302
   patents   **P** 101
   retailing, importance of   **R** 189
   robots, industrial   **R** 253
   technology, development of   **T** 46
   trademarks   **T** 244–45
   See also country, province, and state articles; names of manufactured articles
Manuls (MA-nuls) *see* Pallas cats
Manumission (man-u-MISSION) *see* Emancipation
Manure, organic fertilizer   **F** 97
   agriculture, history of   **A** 98
   methane gas   **B** 12
Manuscript books   **C** 461
   authors' originals prized by collectors   **A** 526
   books in preparation   **B** 330
   Dead Sea Scrolls   **D** 47
   medieval books   **B** 319–21
Manuscripts, illuminated *see* Illuminated manuscripts
Manuscript writing   **H** 22–23
   language arts   **L** 36
Manutius (ma-NU-shi-us), **Aldus,** Italian book publisher   **B** 322
   typeface designs   **T** 345
Man Without a Country *see* Nolan, Philip
Manx cats   **C** 144; *picture* **C** 145
Manx shearwaters, birds   **H** 192

Manych Depression, in the Caucasus Mountains, lowest point in Europe   **E** 309
Manzanares (mon-tha-NAR-ace), river, Spain   **R** 242
Manzini (man-ZI-ni), Swaziland   **S** 481
Manzoni (mon-ZO-ni), **Alessandro,** Italian novelist and poet   **I** 480
   Requiem of Verdi composed in his memory   **C** 285
Manzoni, Piero, Italian painter   **I** 473
Manzu, Giacomo, Italian sculptor   **I** 473
Maoris (MOWR-eez), a people of New Zealand   **N** 236, 241, 242
   art   **P** 10
   top spinning   **T** 228
Mao Tse-tung (MA-o dzu-toong), leader of the People's Republic of China   **M** 90; **C** 267, 271, 272, 273
Mao Tun, Chinese writer   **C** 279
Maple, tree   **M** 91
   acid rain's effects   **A** 9
   leaf, *diagram* **L** 114
   male and female flowers, *pictures* **P** 297
   Rhode Island, state tree of, *picture* **R** 213
   seeds, distribution, *pictures* **F** 281, **L** 233
   sugar maple, *picture* **T** 277
   sugar maple, state tree of New York, West Virginia, Wisconsin, *pictures* **N** 211, **W** 127, 193
   uses of the wood and its grain, *picture* **W** 224
Maple Leaf, The, song by Alexander Muir   **N** 27
Maple syrup and sugar   **M** 91
   American Indians, how prepared by   **I** 178
   Sugaring Off, painting by Grandma Moses, *picture* **M** 469
   tree sap   **T** 280
Mapocho River, Chile   **S** 37
Maps and map making   **M** 92–99
   advances in, at age of exploration   **E** 374
   aerial photography   **P** 217
   be your own map maker   **M** 98
   cartography, as a division of geography   **G** 108
   Champlain, early map maker   **C** 185
   early geographers and map makers   **G** 99
   four-color map problem   **M** 163; **T** 226
   learning about the world from maps   **W** 254
   map and globe terms   **M** 93
   oceanography   **O** 37
   photogrammetry used in making   **O** 173–74
   radio maps   **R** 71
   reference books   **R** 129
   research methods   **R** 183
   satellites, use of   **S** 54
   surveying, use in   **S** 479
   Vespucci, Amerigo   **V** 323
   weather maps   **W** 88–89
   See also continent, country, province, state, and c articles
Mapuche *see* Araucanians
Maputo, capital of Mozambique   **M** 507; *picture* **M** 506
Maquis (ma-KI), French underground   **U** 10–1
   French resistance in World War II   **F** 419
Maquis, Mediterranean scrubby underbrush
   Albania   **A** 145
Marabouts (MARR-a-boots), Muslim holy me
Maracaibo (ma-ra-CA-i-bo), **Lake,** Venezuel
   V 295, 296; *pictures* **L** 29, **P** 167
Marais (ma-RAI), **La,** section of Paris   **P**
Maraschino (mar-a-SKI-no) **cherry**   **P** 1

Marat (ma-RA), **Jean Paul** (1743–93)
cian who became a political figure o

Marat, Jean Paul (continued)
tion, b. Boundry. He took part in the uprising from the onset, founding and editing his revolutionary newspaper, *L'Ami du Peuple* ("The Friend of the People"). Elected (1792) to the National Convention, he was a leading political opponent of the majority Girondist Party. He was a leading advocate of the tactics of the Reign of Terror. Marat was stabbed to death in his bath by Charlotte Corday.

Marathasa Valley, Cyprus, *picture* **C** 601
Marathon, Battle of, 490 B.C. **B** 101
Marathon race, in skiing **S** 185
Marathon race, track event **T** 237
   footrace of Olympic Games **O** 105
   Koreans as long-distance runners **K** 296
Marble, metamorphic rock **R** 269; *picture* **R** 268
   quarries in Vermont **V** 314–15
   sculptors' material **S** 90–91
Marble Faun, The, novel by Nathaniel Hawthorne
   A 202
Marbles **M** 99
Marbury v. Madison, case in constitutional law **M** 113
   Supreme Court decision laying down rule of judicial review **S** 476

Marc, Franz (1880–1916), German painter, b. Munich. He is noted particularly as a pioneer of the German expressionist style, which was one outgrowth of cubism. He often selected animals as subject matter. With Kandinsky he founded (1911) the Blue Rider group. He was killed in action during World War I. His paintings include *The Tower of Blue Horses, Red Horses,* and *Resting Animals.*

   Blue Rider group **G** 170
   German expressionism in modern art **M** 392
   Little Blue Horse, painting, *picture* **G** 170

Marcasite, mineral composed of iron and sulfur. A pyrite, it is a pale brass-yellow color, darkening when exposed to light. It is found throughout the world. The crystals are often used in ornamentation.

Marceau (mar-SO), **Marcel** (1923–), French pantomimist, b. Strasbourg. He first attained fame as Arlequin ~he pantomime *Baptiste* but is most easily recognized as ~" the character he introduced in 1947, a white-faced ~al who wears a middy, culottes, and tall, worn hat. ~peared in the United States in 1955. Known ~lo performer, he has also performed with and ~l of mime in Paris.

   ~be **R** 296
   R 296

   ~r **W** 206
   ~00–01

   ~ntures in

   ~Malaita

   ~Work

founded in 1938 by President Franklin D. Roosevelt as the National Foundation for Infantile Paralysis. Its original purpose was to treat and prevent polio—of which Roosevelt was a victim. When vaccines for polio were developed, the foundation chose birth defects as its concern. The foundation is headquartered in White Plains, N.Y.

March of Time, The, documentary film series **M** 478
March on Washington, 1963 *see* Freedom March
March to the Sea, during the Civil War **C** 345; **S** 150

Marciano, Rocky (Rocco Francis Marchegiano) (1923–69), American boxer, b. Brockton, Mass. Taking up boxing while in the U.S. Army, he turned professional after his discharge. In 1952 he knocked out Jersey Joe Walcott in the 13th round, becoming the world heavyweight champion. When he retired as undefeated heavyweight champion in 1956, Marciano had won 49 straight bouts. **B** 353

Marconi (mar-CO-ni), **Guglielmo,** Italian inventor of wireless telegraphy **M** 102; **C** 467; **R** 55; **T** 54
Marconi Wireless Company **R** 56
Marco Polo *see* Polo, Marco

Marcos, Ferdinand Edralin (1917–), former president of the Philippines, b. Sarrat, Luzon. He was elected president of the Philippines in 1965 and 1969. In 1972, Marcos declared martial law during a period of civil unrest. He assumed broad powers as prime minister the following year. He became both president and prime minister in 1978. In 1981, the constitution was revised, martial law was lifted, and Marcos was elected president for a 6-year term. There were widespread protests against his rule in 1983, following the assassination of opposition leader Benigno Aquino. Defeated in the 1986 presidential elections by Aquino's widow, Corazon, Marcos fled the country. Marcos had entered politics in 1949. He served in the Philippine House of Representatives (1950–60), and Senate (1960–65) and was a delegate to the UN. **P** 188

Marcos, Fray *see* Niza, Marcos de
Marcus, Siegfried, Austrian inventor **A** 542
Marcus Aurelius (MAR-cus au-RE-lius), Roman emperor **G** 355; **R** 305
   equestrian statue, *picture* **S** 95
Mardi Gras (mar-di GRA) (Shrove Tuesday) **H** 158; **R** 153
   carnival **C** 116
   Latin America **L** 50
   Mobile, Alabama, annual event **A** 122
   New Orleans **N** 196
Marduk (MAR-dook), Babylonian god **B** 5; **M** 565, 566
Marek's disease, disease of chickens **A** 100
Marengo, Battle of, 1800 **N** 11
Mares' tails, cirrus clouds **C** 385
Margai (mar-GUY), **Albert,** prime minister of Sierra Leone **S** 171
Margai, Milton, prime minister of Sierra Leone **S** 171
Margaret of Anjou (on-JOO), queen of Henry VI of England **E** 220

Margaret Rose, Princess (1930–), sister of Queen Elizabeth II of England, b. Glamis Castle, Scotland. Her marriage to Anthony Armstrong-Jones, Earl of Snowdon, ended in 1978 with the first divorce in the royal family since Henry VIII. Princess Margaret heads a number of charities and represents the queen at official functions.

Margarine (MARGE-a-rin), butter substitute **B** 470; **O** 76; **P** 111

Margarita, island in the Caribbean, part of Nueva Esparta, a state of Venezuela. Discovered by Columbus on his third voyage (1498), the island became a base for pearl fishing and tourism. Its chief industries are pearl and deep-sea fishing and tourism. The capital is La Asunción. A warm, healthy climate makes it a popular resort area and good agricultural region. **C** 114

Margays, wildcats **C** 143
Marggraf (MARG-grof), **Andreas Sigismond,** German chemist **S** 455
Margherita, Mount, Zaïre **Z** 366b
Margin, buying stocks on **S** 432
Margrethe I, queen of Denmark **D** 113
Margrethe II, queen of Denmark **D** 113; **S** 58e
Marguerite (or Margarete), character in Goethe's *Faust* **F** 73
Maria, lunar seas **M** 449, 450
Maria Laach, Abbey Church of, West Germany, *picture* **G** 166
Marianas (ma-ri-AN-as), **Northern,** islands in the Pacific Ocean **P** 7; **T** 115; **U** 100
Marianas Islands, Pacific Ocean **U** 100
    Guam **P** 6–7
    Magellan was the discoverer of **M** 21
Marianas Trench, Pacific Ocean **M** 499; **O** 46
    Challenger Deep, site of the **O** 21
    ocean deep of the earth **E** 14

Maria Theresa (ma-RI-a te-RE-sa) (1717–80), Austrian empress, b. Vienna. A daughter of Emperor Charles VI, she married Francis of Lorraine (later Francis I of the Holy Roman Empire). When Charles VI died (1740), she inherited his possessions and became archduchess of Austria and queen of Hungary and Bohemia. Her claim to the throne was disputed by France, Prussia, and Spain in the War of Austrian Succession (1740–48). The only land she lost during the war was Silesia, which she tried unsuccessfully to recover in the Seven Years War (1756–63). An enlightened monarch, she introduced economic, administrative, and cultural reforms. Joseph II (who was a joint ruler, 1765–80), Leopold I, and Marie Antoinette were her children.
    Austria, history of **A** 524–25

Mariculture *see* Sea farming
Marie Antoinette, queen of France **M** 103
    bedroom at Fontainebleau, *picture* **F** 508
    fashion design, history of **C** 381
    French Revolution **F** 465, 467
    pupil of Gluck **G** 241
Marie de France, French fabulist **F** 4
Marie de Médicis (d'may-de-CEES), queen of France **P** 73
Marie de Médicis, Queen of France, Landing in Marseilles, painting by Peter Paul Rubens **P** 25
Marie Louise, empress of the French **N** 12
Marietta, Ohio **O** 64
Marignano (marine-YA-no), **Battle of,** 1515 **S** 502
Marigolds, flowers, *picture* **G** 50
Marijuana (mar-i-WAN-a), drug **D** 330–31
Marimba, musical instrument **L** 74; *pictures* **L** 73, **P** 153
Marin, John, American painter **W** 61
    Boats and Sea, Deer Isle, Maine, painting, *picture* **W** 61

Marinas (ma-RI-nas), boat basins or docks **B** 260; *picture* **B** 260
Marinating, of food **O** 247–48
Marine biology **O** 37, 38–39
    Antarctica's marine ecosystem **A** 301
    chemical pollution endangers species **E** 196
    coral polyps **C** 547–48
    life, distribution in oceans and seas **L** 228–33
    ocean life, kinds of **O** 23–27
    ocean life's environment **O** 17, 18, 19–20
    path of food resources, *picture* **O** 22
    plankton **P** 279–81
    underwater exploration of life in the sea **U** 21–22
Marine Corps, United States *see* United States Marine Corps
Marine Corps Development and Education Command **U** 180
Marine Engineers Beneficial Association **U** 183
Marine fire fighters **F** 153
Marine Hospital Service, United States **P** 502
Marine iguanas (ig-WA-nas), lizards **L** 319
Marineland, Florida **D** 277, 279
Marine Mammal Protection Act, 1972 **D** 280
Marine paints **P** 33–34

Mariner II, U.S. planetary probe launched August 27, 1962, and directed toward the planet Venus. During its flight it detected a continuous "solar wind" of charged particles flowing from the sun. It passed Venus on December 14, 1962, at a distance of 34,751 kilometers (21,594 mi), and relayed back a surface temperature reading of 373.32°C (800°F). It detected no magnetic field around Venus. Radio contact with Mariner II was lost on January 3, 1963.

Mariner space probes
    Mars **M** 105, 108; **O** 8; **P** 273; **S** 345
    Mercury **P** 269, 270; **S** 347
    space flight data **S** 346
    Venus **O** 8; **P** 271
Marines, maritime soldiers **U** 176
Marines' Hymn, "From the Halls of Montezuma" **N** 26; **U** 177, 182
Marinetti, Filippo Tommaso, Italian poet **M** 391
Marine west coast climate, of North America **C** 364
Marine worms **O** 26
    aging process **A** 83
Marini, Marino, Italian sculptor **I** 473
Marino (ma-RI-no), **Giambattista,** Italian poet **I** 479
Marinus, Saint, founder of San Marino **S** 35
Marinus I, pope **R** 296
Marinus II, pope **R** 297
Marion, Francis, American Revolutionary War commander **M** 103; **R** 207
Marionettes *see* Puppets and marionettes
Mariposa (ma-ri-PO-za) **Grove,** California **Y** 352

Maris, Roger Eugene (1934–85), American baseball player, b. Hibbing, Minn. He reached the major leagues in 1957 and played for Cleveland, Kansas City, and New York in the American League and St. Louis in the National League before retiring (1968). In 1961, while with the N.Y. Yankees, he hit a record-breaking 61 home runs. He was named Most Valuable Player in the American League in both 1960 and 1961.

Marisol, American artist **M** 397; **S** 105

Maritain (ma-ri-TAN), **Jacques** (1882–1973), French philosopher and educator, b. Paris. A convert to Catholicism,

Maritain, Jacques (continued)
he became one of the most highly honored of contemporary religious philosophers. During World War II he and his wife went to the United States, where he taught at Columbia (1940–44) and Princeton (1948–53). He served as French ambassador to the Vatican (1945–48). His many works include *Creative Intuition in Art and Poetry,* and *Reflections on America.* **F** 442

Maritime Administration, organization established in 1950 as one of the successors to U.S. Maritime Commission to aid development, promotion, and operation of an American merchant marine.

Maritime Alps, in Italy and France **A** 174

Maritime law, system of law concerning navigation and commerce. It represents agreements between nations over customs relating to shipping. Some cases to which it applies are the ownership and operation of vessels, the rights and duties of master and crew, and the transportation of goods and passengers on the high seas.

Maritime Provinces, Canadian provinces of New
  Brunswick, Newfoundland, Nova Scotia, and
  Prince Edward Island **C** 52, 74; **N** 138–138g,
  140–145, 344a–344h; **P** 460–466a
Maritsa (ma-RI-tsa) **River valley,** Bulgaria **B** 440–41
Marivaux, Pierre Carlet de Chamblain, French writer
  F 439
Marjoram, herb **H** 114; *picture* **H** 115
Mark, Saint **E** 335
  Gospel of **B** 160
Mark, Saint, pope **R** 296
Marka, a people of Africa **M** 61

Mark Antony (83?–30 B.C.), Roman general. When Julius Caesar was assassinated in 44 B.C., Antony and two other leaders, Octavian and Lepidus, formed a triumvirate (group of three) and took control of the Roman Government. Antony had a love affair with Cleopatra, queen of Egypt, and he formed a political alliance with her. Octavian felt threatened by their alliance, and he defeated their armies at the Battle of Actium in 31 B.C. Antony and Cleopatra fled to Egypt, where they later committed suicide. Many poets and playwrights, including Shakespeare, have told the story of Antony and Cleopatra. **R** 303
  Cicero's opposition to **C** 303

Market Cart, The, painting by Gainsborough **E** 239
Market economy, in economics **E** 49, 50, 51
Marketing, of products and services **S** 18d–19
  advertising **A** 27–34
  department stores **D** 118–20
  mail order **M** 34–35
  retail stores **R** 188–89
  supermarkets **S** 468
Marketing geography **G** 108
Market research **A** 33; **O** 160; **R** 182; **S** 18d
Market surveys **O** 159–60
  television **T** 70b
Markets, food *see* Food shopping; Supermarkets
Markham, Edwin, American poet **O** 206

Markle Foundation, The John and Mary R., organization supporting projects primarily in the field of medicine. Grants are made to keep young doctors on the teaching and research staffs of medical schools. Established in 1927, it has headquarters in New York, N.Y.

Markova (mar-KO-va), **Alicia,** English ballerina **B** 28,
  28a
Marksmanship, rifle **R** 231–33
Mark Twain *see* Twain, Mark
Markups, of prices **S** 19
Marlboro, Vermont
  chamber music festival **M** 560

Marlborough (MARL-bor-o), **1st Duke of** (John Churchill) (1650–1722), English general and diplomat, b. Devonshire. After helping to crush the Monmouth rebellion (1685), he shifted his loyalty from James II to William of Orange and supported the Glorious Revolution (1688). He was made (1702) duke of Marlborough and captain general of the English troops by Queen Anne. Marlborough's wife, Sarah, was for many years Queen Anne's confidante. Marlborough was the leader of the English and allied armies against Louis XIV of France during most of the War of the Spanish Succession (1701–13). He won brilliant victories against the French at the battles of Blenheim (1704), Ramillies (1706), Oudenaarde (1708), and, to a lesser extent, Malplaquet (1709). Largely for political reasons, he was recalled to England in disgrace in 1711. He is considered one of Britain's greatest generals.
  England, history of **E** 224

Marlborough s'en va-t-en guerre, song **N** 27

Marlin, any of several game fishes found in warm ocean waters around the world. The marlin, which is related to the sailfish, has a rounded, swordlike extension of the upper jaw. The largest species in the Atlantic Ocean is the blue marlin, which weighs up to 1,000 lbs (450 kg). It has a dark blue back, pale blue sides, and about 13 violet stripes on each side.

Marlowe, Christopher (1564–93), English poet and dramatist, b. Canterbury. He is thought to have written parts of Shakespeare's *Titus Andronicus* and *Henry VI.* He is remembered especially for his poem "The Passionate Shepherd to his Love," beginning "Come live with me, and be my love." *The Tragical History of Dr. Faustus, The Jew of Malta,* and *Tamburlaine the Great* are among his noted plays. Marlowe was a playwright connected with the Earl of Nottingham's theatrical company (1587–93).
  Renaissance drama in England **D** 298; **E** 252–53
  Tragical History of Dr. Faustus, The **F** 72

Marmara, Sea of, Turkey **T** 324

Mármol, José (1817–71), Argentine poet, playwright, and novelist, b. Buenos Aires. His romantic, lyric poetry was often directed against despotism and especially against the Argentine dictator Juan Manuel de Rosas, who imprisoned and exiled him (until Rosas' overthrow in 1852). Marmol's works include the poem *Rosas: El 25 de mayo de 1850,* the book of poems *Harmonies,* and the first historical novel in Argentine literature, *Amalia.*

Marmore waterfall, Italy **W** 63
Marmosets, monkeys **M** 420; *picture* **M** 421
Marmots, rodents **R** 277–78

Marne, river in northeastern France that originates in the Plateau of Langres, flows 325 mi (525 km), and joins the Seine near Paris. The Marne was the scene of two crucial battles of World War I.

Marne, First Battle of the, 1914 **B** 103; **W** 274
  Paris **P** 75

Marne, Second Battle of the, 1918 **W** 280
Maroons, a people of Jamaica **J** 17
Marquand (mar-QUAND), **John P.,** American novelist
    A 213
Marque, letters of *see* Letters of marque
Marquesas (mar-KAY-sas) **Islands,** Pacific Ocean **P** 7
Marquet, Albert, French painter **M** 388
Marquetry (MAR-ket-ri), inlaid furniture **D** 77; **F** 506,
    508
Marquette (mar-KETT), **Jacques,** French Jesuit
    missionary and explorer **J** 127
  exploration of area now called Chicago **C** 221
  exploration of the New World **E** 386
Marquette, Michigan **M** 271
Márquez, Felipe González *see* González Márquez, Felipe

Marquis, Don (Donald Robert Perry Marquis) (1878–
1937), American humorist and journalist, b. Walnut, Ill.
After serving as assistant editor to Joel Chandler Harris on
Uncle Remus' Magazine (1907–09), he wrote his famous
column "The Sun Dial" for the New York *Evening Sun*
(1912–22), creating the immortal characters of archy (the
cockroach), mehitabel (the alley cat), the Old Soak, and
Hermione and Her Little Group of Serious Thinkers. His
works include *archy and mehitabel, The Almost Perfect
State,* and the play *The Old Soak.*

Marranos (mar-RA-nos), Christianized Jews **J** 106–07
Marriage
  divorce **D** 230–31
  family group **F** 37, 38, 39, 41–42, 44
  intermarriage of ethnic groups **E** 303
  matrimony is a sacrament of Roman Catholic Church
    R 301
  women, role of **W** 211
Marriage customs *see* Wedding customs
Marriage of Figaro, The, opera by Mozart **O** 146–47
Marriage of the Waters, The, from *The Hudson,* by Carl
    Carmer, excerpt **E** 279; *picture* **E** 277
Marrow, of bones **B** 273; **S** 184b
  blood corpuscles made in **B** 256, 257
  bone marrow counts **M** 201
  leukemia is cancer of **C** 91
  radiotherapy's effects on **C** 93
Mars, planet **M** 104–11; **P** 273
  Ptolemy's theory **A** 471
  robots in space **R** 254
  space probes **O** 8; **S** 345, 347, 349
  tilt of Mars' axis, *diagram* **P** 277
Mars, Roman god **G** 358, 360
Mars, Soviet spacecraft **S** 346

Marsalis, Wynton (1961–   ), American trumpeter, b.
New Orleans, La. He is the son of jazz pianist Ellis Marsalis. Wynton Marsalis was trained in both classical music
and jazz and attended the Juilliard School of Music. In
1980 he joined drummer Art Blakey's band, the Jazz Messengers, winning acclaim for his dazzling trumpet solos.
He formed his own band in 1982, with his brother Bran-
ford on tenor saxophone. In 1983, Marsalis released both
a jazz album and a recording of trumpet concertos. He won
Grammy awards for both, becoming the first artist to win in
both jazz and classical categories in the same year.

Marsden, Samuel, English missionary **N** 242
Marseillaise (mar-say-AISE), **La,** French national anthem
    N 17–18
Marseilles (mar-SAY), France **F** 407, 412; *picture*
    F 409
Marsh, Dame Ngaio (NY-o), New Zealand writer **N** 236

Marsh, Reginald (1898–1954), American artist, b. Paris,
France. He was an illustrator and cartoonist for New York
magazines and newspapers. His paintings, generally depicting New York City life, include *The Bowery, Coney
Island Beach,* and *Memories of the Stork Club.* He also did
murals for the Washington, D.C., Post Office and the New
York City Customs House. He taught at the Art Students
League in New York from the early 1930's until his
death.

Marshall, George C., American statesman **M** 112
  Eisenhower and Marshall **E** 109
Marshall, John, American jurist **M** 112–13; **S** 476
Marshall, Thomas R., vice-president, United States
    V 331; *picture* **V** 328

Marshall, Thurgood (1908–   ), U.S. Supreme Court justice, b. Baltimore, Md. As special counsel for the National
Association for the Advancement of Colored People, he
won numerous civil rights cases before state and federal
courts. He served as federal judge, U.S. 2nd Circuit Court
of Appeals (1962–65), and was the first black to be
appointed U.S. Solicitor General (1965–67), and the first
to be named to the U.S. Supreme Court (1967).

Marshall Field & Co., department store in Chicago,
    Illinois, *picture* **D** 118
Marshall Islands, Pacific Ocean **P** 7; **T** 115; **U** 100
  World War II **W** 298

Marshall Plan (European Recovery Program), a plan for
economic and technical assistance to Europe following
World War II. It was proposed by George C. Marshall, President Harry S Truman's secretary of state. The plan's
objectives were to restore the war-damaged economies of
European nations by providing funds and encouraging
growth and trade. In 1948 the U.S. Congress established
the Economic Cooperation Administration (ECA) to administer the plan. Sixteen Western European countries formed
the Organization for European Economic Cooperation
(OEEC) to co-ordinate and distribute the funds. The Soviet
Union and other European Communist nations were invited to join the program but rejected participation. From
1948 to 1952 the participating countries received more
than $13,000,000,000 (billion) in U.S. aid, including
food, machinery, and other products. Another of the plan's
goals—to curb the spread of Communism in Western
Europe—also was achieved.
  foreign economic aid under Truman **T** 302
  United States aid to Germany **G** 155

Marshals Service, United States *see* United States
    Marshals Service
Marshes, low, swampy land
  a typical community of living things **K** 257–59
  formed from lakes **L** 25
  natural resource **N** 63
Marshmallows, candy **C** 96
Marsh marigolds, flowers, *picture* **W** 169
Marsupials (mar-SU-pials), pouched mammals **M** 66,
    74–75
  Antarctica, fossil remains in **A** 303
  Australia **A** 505–06
  kangaroos and other pouched mammals **K** 168–73
  opossums **O** 161
Martens, mammals **O** 245–46; *pictures* **O** 244

Martha, in the New Testament, the sister of Mary and Lazarus. When she scolded her sister Mary for listening to
Jesus rather than helping with the housework (Luke

Martha (continued)
10:38–42), Jesus reprimanded her. She was present at the resurrection of Lazarus (John 11:1–39) and at a dinner that Jesus attended at Simon the Leper's house two days before His last Passover (Matthew 26:6–13, Mark 14:3–9).

Martha, opera by Friedrich von Flotow **O** 148
Martha's Vineyard, island, Massachusetts **M** 146
Martí (mar-TI), **José,** Cuban statesman and poet
    C 595, 596
    Latin-American literature **L** 71
Martial (MAR-shal), Spanish-born Roman writer **L** 80

Martial law, rule by military forces. Martial law is usually declared by the head of a nation or state when danger, emergency, or panic creates a situation that cannot be handled by the local government. Martial law is usually temporary. But some nations have been ruled by martial law for long periods of time. The term also applies to law used in occupied territory by the military authority of the occupying power.
    Poland **P** 362
    Reconstruction **R** 119

Martin, Abraham (known as L'Écossais, "the Scot") (1589–1664), French settler in Canada, b. Scotland. After arriving in Canada (1614?) he served with the French colonizing Company of One Hundred Associates, receiving from them plateau land west of Quebec. (The land is now known as The Plains of Abraham in his honor.) Martin remained there after its surrender to the British.

Martin, Alexander (1740–1807), American politician, b. Hunterdon Co., N.J. After serving in the Revolutionary forces (1775–77), he was acting governor (1781–82) and governor (1782–84, 1789–92) of North Carolina and a delegate to the Continental Congress (1786–87) and to the Constitutional Convention (1787). As a United States senator (1793–99), he supported the controversial Alien and Sedition Acts, which probably led to his failure to be re-elected (1798).

Martin, James G. (1935–   ), governor of North Carolina, Republican, b. Savannah, Ga. He was elected governor in 1984 after serving in the U.S. House of Representatives since 1973. Martin had been a member of the Mecklenburg County (N.C.) Board of Commissioners (1966–72). Formerly he was an associate professor of chemistry at Davidson College.

Martin, Luther (1748?–1826), American lawyer, b. near New Brunswick, N.J. He was the first attorney general of Maryland (1778–1805, 1818–22). A member of the Continental Congress (1785) and the Constitutional Convention (1787), he bitterly opposed the concept of a strong centralized government. An opponent of Thomas Jefferson, he supported Justice Samuel Chase during his impeachment trial (1804) and Aaron Burr during his trial for treason (1807).

Martin, Mary (1913–   ), American singer and actress, b. Weatherford, Texas. Her most famous roles were Nellie Forbush in the long-running musical *South Pacific* (1949), the title role in the musical version of *Peter Pan* (1954), and Maria von Trapp in the original production of *The Sound of Music* (1959). She made her Broadway debut in 1938 with a memorable performance of the song

"My Heart Belongs to Daddy." Martin has received many awards, including three Tonys. She is the mother of the actor Larry Hagman.

Martin, Saint, patron saint of France **R** 154–55
Martin I, Saint, pope **R** 296
Martin II, pope *see* Marinus I
Martin III, pope *see* Marinus II
Martin IV, pope **R** 297
Martin V, pope **R** 297
Martin Chuzzlewit, novel by Charles Dickens **D** 149, 150
Martin du Gard, Roger, French writer **F** 442

Martinez, Bob (1934–   ), governor of Florida, Republican, b. Tampa. He was elected governor in 1986. He was mayor of Tampa (1979–86). He owned and operated a restaurant in Tampa (1975–83) and previously worked in the field of education (1963–75).

Martínez, Maria, American potter **N** 194
Martínez, Maximiliano Hernández *see* Hernández Martínez, Maximiliano
Martínez de Toledo (mar-TI-naith day to-LAY-tho), **Alfonso,** Spanish writer **S** 367
Martínez Ruiz, José, Spanish writer **S** 371

Martini (mar-TI-ni), **Simone** (Simone di Martino, Simone Memmi) (1283?–1344), Italian painter, b. Siena. A leading artist of the Sienese school, which predated the Renaissance, he worked at Assisi (1333–39) and for the court of Pope Benedict XII at Avignon (1339–44). His paintings reveal French Gothic influence and are noted for their color and flowing lines. Among his works are *St. Louis of Toulouse, The Annunciation,* and *The Holy Family.*

Martinique (mar-tin-EKE), Caribbean island, overseas department of France, one of the Windward Islands, in the Lesser Antilles. Bananas, rum, and pineapples are exported from Fort-de-France, the capital. Tourism is of growing importance. The island, of volcanic origin, was discovered by Columbus and first colonized by the French in 1635. **C** 114
    lava spine, *picture* **V** 381

Martin Luther King, Jr., National Historic Site, Atlanta, Georgia **G** 141
Martinmas (Feast of St. Martin), religious holiday
    R 154–55
Martyrs, Age of the **R** 288
    Christianity, history of **C** 287
Marunouchi district, Tokyo **T** 205

Marvell, Andrew (1621–78), English poet, b. Yorkshire. He composed some outstanding lyrics (such as "To His Coy Mistress" and "The Garden") and, as an active Puritan, produced political satires in both poetry and prose. Marvell is considered one of the outstanding metaphysical poets.

Marver, metal plate for rolling glass **G** 230
Marx, Karl, German economist and political philosopher
    M 113–14
    ideas of Communism **C** 470–71
    Lenin and Marx **L** 138
    on capitalism **C** 103
    socialism **S** 220

Marx Brothers, Chico (Leonard) (1887–1961), **Harpo** (Adolph or Arthur) (1888–1964), and **Groucho** (Julius

Henry) (1890–1977), American comedians, b. New York, N.Y. Given to zany frolicking, they developed their stage characters in a vaudeville team, appearing at various times with their two other brothers **Gummo** (Milton) (1894–1977) and **Zeppo** (Herbert) (1901–79), and on Broadway in *The Coconuts* and *Animal Crackers.* They also played in such films as *Duck Soup, A Night at the Opera,* and *A Day at the Races.* Groucho also hosted a television quiz program, "You Bet Your Life." **M** 477

Marxism-Leninism, program of Soviet Communism **C** 471

Mary, queen of England, wife of George V **D** 265

Mary I (1516–58), queen of England and Ireland (1553–58), b. Greenwich (now in London). Daughter of Henry VIII and Catherine of Aragon, she became England's first ruling queen upon the death of her younger brother, Edward VI. In 1554 she married King Philip II of Spain. In her determination to restore Catholicism in England, she had nearly 300 Protestants burned at the stake, earning the nickname Bloody Mary.
Mary and Elizabeth I **E** 177, 221

Mary II, queen of England **E** 224
Mary, queen of Scotland *see* Mary Queen of Scots
Mary, Virgin, mother of Jesus Christ **M** 115; **J** 83, 84
Day of Our Lady of Guadalupe, Mexican religious holiday **R** 155

Mary had a little lamb, first line of a poem by American writer and editor Sarah Josepha Hale.

Maryland **M** 116–31
American colonies **A** 193
Baltimore **B** 35
colonial life in America **C** 415
founders of the United States **F** 392
places of interest in black history **B** 250d
Maryland, My Maryland, song by James Randall **N** 25
Maryland, University of **M** 125
Maryland Gazette-News, newspaper **M** 124
Maryland yellowthroats, birds **B** 220
Marylebone Cricket Club, England **T** 90

Mary Magdalene, in the New Testament, a woman whom Christ cured of evil spirits. She became a devoted follower and was present at the crucifixion.

Mary Queen of Scots (Mary Stuart) **M** 132
conflicts between Protestants and Catholics **S** 89
golf, history of **G** 259
guest-prisoner in England **E** 222
Elizabeth I and Mary **E** 177
Mary's Lamb, nursery rhyme **N** 405
Marysville, Ohio
motorcycle assembly plant, *picture* **O** 65
Mary Tudor *see* Mary I, queen of England
Marzipan, candy **C** 96

Masaccio (ma-ZA-cho) (Tommaso Guidi) (1401–28), Italian artist, b. San Giovanni Valdarno. His paintings, noted for their strength and depth, completed the shift from medieval art to that of the early Renaissance. His frescoes in the Brancacci Chapel, Florence, such as *The Tribute Money,* were studied as examples by almost all later Florentine painters and had an important influence on Raphael and Michelangelo.
Expulsion from Paradise, The, painting **R** 166
Italian art **I** 468; **P** 20

Madonna and Child Enthroned, painting **I** 466
Renaissance art **R** 164
Tribute Money, The, fresco, detail, *picture* **P** 20

Masada, mountain fortress in Israel **I** 443; *picture* **I** 444
Roman legions captured **J** 105
Masai (ma-SY), tribal group of Kenya and Tanzania
Kenya **A** 62; **K** 229
Tanzania **T** 16

Masaryk (MA-sar-eek), **Jan Garrigue** (1886–1948), Czechoslovak statesman, b. Prague. He was the son of the Czechoslovak patriot Tomáš Masaryk. Under his father's presidency he held several diplomatic posts, including that of minister to Britain (1925–38). During World War II he was foreign minister (1940–48) and vice-premier (1941–45) of the Czechoslovak government-in-exile. Soon after the Communists took over Czechoslovakia (1948), he died, presumably by suicide. **M** 133

Masaryk, Tomáš, co-founder and first president of Czechoslovakia **M** 133
nation of Czechoslovakia is created **C** 608–09
Mascagni (ma-SCON-ye), **Pietro,** Italian composer **I** 486
Cavalleria Rusticana, opera **O** 142
Mascons, on the moon **M** 450
Mascots, lucky emblems of families **H** 109

Masefield, John (1878–1967), English poet, dramatist, and novelist, b. Ledbury. Joining the merchant marine at 13, he became a sailor on a windjammer. His best-known short poems, such as "Cargoes" and "Sea Fever," express his love of the sea. "Sea Fever" was published in his first book, *Salt Water Ballads* (1902). His work includes plays, essays, novels, and narrative poems. He became England's poet laureate in 1930.
English poetry in the 20th century **E** 265

Masers, devices for amplifying microwaves **L** 46c
use of ammonia **G** 61
Maseru (MAS-er-u), capital of Lesotho **L** 156
M*A*S*H, motion picture **M** 492
Mashona (ma-SHO-na), a people of Africa **Z** 368b
Masked Ball, The, opera by Giuseppe Verdi **O** 148–49
Masks
African art form **A** 72; *pictures* **A** 74, 75, **I** 490
death mask of Tutankhamen, *picture* **A** 220
Eskimos (Inuit) **E** 288
Halloween customs **H** 10
Iroquois Indians **I** 157
Nepalese religious rituals, *picture* **N** 111
skin diving **S** 188
Mason, A. E. W., English author **M** 563
Mason, Charles, English surveyor **M** 133

Mason, George (1725–92), American statesman, b. Virginia. His Declaration of Rights (1776) for Virginia was used as a basis for part of the Declaration of Independence and the United States Constitution. He also wrote most of Virginia's constitution (1776) and outlined the Northwest Ordinance (1780). A member of the Constitutional Convention, he refused to sign the Constitution, principally because of its compromise on slave trade. His insistence on a Bill of Rights led to adoption of the first 10 amendments.

Mason, James Murray (1798–1871), American Confederate statesman, b. Georgetown, Va. (now D.C.). As a sena-

Mason, James Murray (continued)

tor from Virginia (1847–61) he drafted the Fugitive Slave Law of 1850 and in 1861 went to England with John Slidell to win British aid for the South. While aboard the British ship *Trent,* Mason and Slidell were captured (November, 1861) by Union forces (nearly causing war with Great Britain). They were freed in January, 1862. Mason went to England but failed to gain British recognition of the Confederacy.

Mason, John (1586–1635), English settler and founder of New Hampshire, b. King's Lynn. Appointed governor of Newfoundland (1615), he received a grant of New England land (1622). He became deputy governor of New Plymouth (1623) but left for England in 1624. Returning from England (1629), he organized, with Sir Ferdinando Gorges and a group of English merchants, the Laconia Company and founded an agricultural colony on Piscataqua River that became New Hampshire. **A** 190; **M** 51; **N** 162

Mason, Stevens Thomson, governor of Michigan **M** 271
Mason bees **B** 123
Mason-Dixon line **M** 133
   Missouri Compromise **M** 382
   Pennsylvania **P** 145
Mason jar, for canning and bottling **B** 346
Masonry **B** 391–94
   cement and concrete **C** 165
   paints for masonry **P** 32
Masonry dams **D** 16
Masons *see* Freemasons
Masque (MASK), poetic pageant **E** 253
   dancing popular during the Renaissance **D** 25
   development of the opera **O** 132
   Renaissance drama **D** 297
Mass, in music **M** 544–45
   choral music **C** 283
   Dutch and Flemish music **D** 365, 366
Mass, in physics **M** 171–72, 173
   acceleration and mass **M** 473
   change of mass in nuclear reactions **N** 358
   defined **C** 204
   earth's **E** 5
   gravity and gravitation **G** 321, 324
   mass numbers **C** 203
   measurement of **W** 114, 117
   stars, nuclear reactions in the **S** 406
Mass, in Roman Catholic Church **R** 302
Massachusetts **M** 134–50
   American colonies **A** 187–88
   Boston **B** 338–41
   colonial home, *picture* **H** 181
   colonial life in America **C** 409, 411, 415, 418
   colonial sites you can visit today **C** 422
   Congregational church, Groton, *picture* **P** 484
   Federal style home, *picture* **H** 181
   first adoption law **A** 26
   first state to establish free public schools **E** 70
   founders of the United States **F** 392
   Horace Mann and education **M** 87
   Intolerable Acts, 1774 **D** 58–59
   Maine, history of **M** 51
   New Hampshire, history of **N** 162
   places of interest in black history **B** 250d
   Plymouth Colony **P** 343–46
   witches, persecution of **W** 209
Massachusetts, University of **M** 143
Massachusetts Bay Colony **A** 188–89

Plymouth Colony becomes part of Massachusetts Bay Colony **P** 346
   Williams, Roger **W** 172
Massachusetts Bay Colony **M** 149–50
Massachusetts Institute of Technology
   Baker Hall designed by Alvar Aalto **A** 385–86
Massachusetts State College System **M** 143
Massamba-Débat, Alphonse, president of the People's Republic of the Congo **C** 498
Massasoit (MASS-a-soit), American Indian chief **P** 345
   Thanksgiving Day **T** 152
Massawa, Ethiopia **E** 300
Mass communication **C** 469
Massenet (mass-en-AY), **Jules,** French composer **O** 146

Massey, Vincent (1887–1967), Canadian diplomat and political leader, b. Toronto, Ontario. He was governor-general of Canada (1952–59), the first Canadian to be appointed to that office. Massey began his career in public service during World War I. In 1919 he joined his family's business—the largest farm-machinery company in Canada—and rose to become its president. He resigned in 1925 to return to government service. He was Canada's first ambassador to the United States (1926–30) and Canada's high commissioner in Britain (1935–46). From 1949 to 1951 he served as chairman of the Royal Commission on National Development in the Arts, Letters, and Sciences. His brother, **Raymond Massey** (1896–1983) was a famous actor.

Massey, William, New Zealand statesman **N** 242
Massine (mass-ENE), **Léonide,** Russian choreographer **B** 28
Mass media, in communication **C** 469
   advertising **A** 27–34
   television **T** 70–71
Mass numbers, of atoms **N** 356
Mass production **M** 151
   automation **A** 528–34
   clothing **C** 378, 380
   decorative arts **D** 79
   glassmaking process **G** 235
   industrial design **I** 231–32
   Industrial Revolution in America **I** 241
   interchangeable parts developed by Whitney in Connecticut **C** 507
   interchangeable parts of automobiles **A** 548–50
   introduced by Henry Ford **F** 367
   machine tools **T** 221
   manufacturing **M** 88–89
   technology **T** 46
   Whitney, Eli, pioneer of mass production **W** 166
Massys (mass-ICE), **Quentin,** Flemish painter
   Moneylender and His Wife, The, painting **P** 19
Mastabas, tombs of Egyptian noblemen **A** 371; **E** 95–96
MasterCard, credit card **C** 592
Master Francis George Hare, painting by Sir Joshua Reynolds, *picture* **R** 210
Master keys **L** 324
Masters, Edgar Lee, American poet **A** 208, 209; **I** 75; **K** 188
Masters, golf tournament **G** 261
Masters, of craft guilds **G** 403

Masterson, Bat (William Barclay Masterson) (1853–1921), American peace officer and sports writer, b. Iroquois County, Ill. During his colorful and varied career he was a buffalo hunter, railroad contractor, army scout, peace officer in tough frontier towns, and a professional gambler. From 1902 until his death he was sports editor on the New York *Morning Telegraph.* A television series was based on his life.

Dodge City, Kansas **K** 184–85

Mastitis, infection of a cow's mammary gland **D** 8

Mastodon, extinct animal, ancestor of the modern elephant. Mastodons had long, shaggy hair, a trunk like the elephant's, and long, curving tusks. Mastodon skeletons, bones, teeth, tusks, and hair have been found in many parts of the world. **E** 168; *picture* **E** 340

Masuria region, Poland **P** 358
Masurian (mas-UR-ian) **Lakes, Battle of the,** 1914 **W** 274
Mat, of type *see* Matrix
Matabele, a people of Africa *see* Ndebele
Matadors, bullfighters **B** 452–53; *picture* **S** 350

Mata Hari (MA-tah HA-ree) (Margaretha Geertruida Zelle) (1876–1917), dancer and spy for Germany during World War I, b. Leeuwarden, the Netherlands. After an unhappy marriage, she went to Paris in 1903 and began a career as an entertainer. Claiming to be a Hindu temple dancer, she took the name Mata Hari ("eye of the dawn"). She charmed military secrets from the French officials she entertained. She was tried and executed after French intelligence agents discovered her identity as a German agent. **S** 389

Matanuska (ma-ta-NU-ska) **River** and **Valley,** Alaska **A** 133, 137
present-day pioneer life **P** 262
Matches **M** 151–53
fire prevention rules **F** 154–55
Matchlocks, early trigger guns **G** 415; *picture* **G** 414
Match play, in golf **G** 259
Matchstick puzzles **T** 289
Maté (MA-tay) (yerba maté), herb tea of Paraguay and Argentina **A** 393; **P** 63, 65
Materiality, in law **C** 567

Materials science, the research, development, and manufacture of new materials to meet specific needs. Once considered a branch of metallurgy (the science of metals), materials science now includes work with nonmetals, such as ceramics, plastics, and glass.

Mathematical logic **M** 161–62
Mathematicians **M** 164–65
Mathematics **M** 154–68
abacus **A** 2–3
algebra **A** 157–59
arithmetic **A** 398–401
careers requiring background in mathematics **M** 164
decimal system **D** 56
Descartes' analytic geometry **D** 123
geometry and geometric forms **G** 122–31
graphs **G** 309–13
Kepler's laws of planetary motion **K** 234
kindergarten children learn through games, *picture* **K** 242
metric system of measurement **W** 109–12
Newton, Isaac **N** 206–07
number lore **N** 378–83
numbers and number systems **N** 384–88
numerals and numeration systems **N** 389–401

percentage **P** 148–50
probability **P** 470–74
Roman numerals **R** 310
sets **S** 126–27
slide rule, how to make your own **M** 166–67
statistics **S** 416–18
teaching **M** 165
topology **T** 224–27
weather prediction **W** 89–90
Mather, Cotton, American writer **A** 196
nine of his children died as infants **C** 411
Mather, Stephen T., National Park Service director **N** 43
Mathewson, Christy, American baseball pitcher **B** 79; *picture* **B** 81

Mathias (ma-THY-as), **Bob** (Robert Bruce Mathias) (1930–   ), American athlete, b. Tulare, Calif. A highly versatile athlete, he set a record by winning the Olympic decathlon twice in succession, at London (1948) and Helsinki (1952). He also won the American National Decathlon title a record four times (1948, 1949, 1950, 1952) and received the James E. Sullivan Memorial Trophy (1949). Mathias served in the U.S. House of Representatives from 1967 to 1975. He later became the director of the U.S. Olympic Training Center at Colorado Springs, Colo. **O** 110

Matilda, folk song **F** 321
Matisse (mah-TEES), **Henri,** French painter **M** 169
collage **C** 400
drawing, history of **D** 316
French art **F** 431
modern art **M** 388, 390
Red Studio, The, painting **M** 389
Mátra Mountains, Hungary **H** 285
Matriarchal family **F** 43
Matrimony, Roman Catholic sacrament **R** 301
Matrix (MAY-trix) (mat), of type **P** 466i, 466j
Matronymic (mat-ro-NIM-ic) **method,** of name giving **N** 7
Matsu, island off China's mainland **T** 12

Matsunaga, Spark Masayuki (1916–   ), United States senator from Hawaii, Democrat, b. Kukuiula. He was elected to the Senate in 1976 and re-elected in 1982. He previously served in the U.S. House of Representatives (1963–77), the Hawaii House of Representatives (1955–59), and as assistant public prosecutor of Honolulu (1952–54). Matsunaga was a member of the Hawaii statehood delegation to Congress (1950 and 1954). He is the author of *The Rulemakers of the House* (1976).

Matsuo Bashō *see* Bashō
Matter **M** 170–78
atoms of three states compared, *diagram* **A** 485
changes in physical properties with speeds near speed of light **R** 142
definition of the term **C** 204
gases **G** 57–59
gravity and gravitation **G** 321–22, 324
heat and changes of state **H** 89–92
instruments for analyzing **O** 174–75
liquids **L** 306–07
nuclear energy **N** 352–71
properties of matter **P** 232–33
radiation and matter **R** 40–45
relativity **R** 139–44
solids **S** 250

Matter (continued)
theories about, in the history of physics **P** 230–33
vacuum **V** 262–65
Matterhorn, mountain, Switzerland **S** 499
first ascent, *chart* **M** 496
Swiss Alps **A** 174; *pictures* **A** 175, **E** 305
Matthew, Saint, one of the 12 Apostles **A** 333
Evangelists, The **E** 335
Gospel of **B** 160
Matthias (ma-THY-as), **Saint,** one of the 12 Apostles
A 333
Matthias Corvinus (cor-VY-nus), king of Hungary
H 287–88
Mattingly, Thomas K., American astronaut **S** 340k
Matzoth (or matzot), unleavened bread **B** 385;
J 146a; **P** 97, 98
Maudslay, Henry, English engineer **T** 221
Maugham (MAUM), **W. Somerset,** English writer
E 266
comedies of manners **E** 268
Maui (MOW-i), one of the Hawaiian Islands **H** 48, 50
Mauldin, Bill (William Henry Mauldin), American
cartoonist **N** 193
Maulid-an-Nabi *see* Mouloud

Mau Mau (MOW MOW), African movement composed
mainly of Kikuyu tribesmen and organized to oust Europeans from Kenya. It arose chiefly from Kikuyu discontent
over European possession of former Kikuyu land, including fertile highlands of Mount Kenya. Members took secret
oaths to kill whites and African opponents. During a state
of emergency (1952–59), the British government gathered Kikuyus into reserves, imprisoned thousands, and
finally, by military force, quelled the rebellion.
Kenya, history of **K** 233

Maumee (mau-MEE), **Lake,** ancient glacial lake, now
Great Lakes plain **O** 62
Mauna Kea (MOW-na KAY-a), volcano, Hawaii **H** 50;
M 498
observatories **O** 7
Mauna Loa, volcano, Hawaii **H** 50, 58; **V** 379–80,
381
Maundy Thursday **E** 35

Maupassant (mo-pa-SAHN), **Guy de** (1850–1893),
French author, b. Normandy. He was one of the greatest
short-story writers in world literature. His stories, published in many volumes, tell of people from different backgrounds. His characters often show the dark side of human
nature. De Maupassant's stories are also characterized by
unexpected, often unpleasant, endings. Among his best-
known short stories are "The Diamond Necklace" and
"The Piece of String." He also wrote several novels,
including *Bel-Ami* (1885). **F** 441; **S** 162

Maupiti, island in the Pacific Ocean, *picture* **P** 8
Mauretania, ocean liner **O** 33
Mauriac, François, French novelist **F** 442
Mauritania (maur-i-TAY-nia) **M** 179–80
flag, *picture* **F** 228
Mauritius (mau-RISH-us) **M** 181
dodo bird's extinction **B** 229, 231
flag, *picture* **F** 228
Mauro (MOW-ro), **Fra,** Venetian cartographer **E** 374

Maurois (more-WAH), **André** (Emile Herzog) (1885–
1967), French writer, b. Elbeuf. A member of the French
Academy from 1938, Maurois was one of France's most
widely read and celebrated writers. He wrote many novels,

short stories, literary reviews, newspaper and magazine
articles, but he is remembered chiefly for his fine biographies. Because he was a Jew, he had to leave France after
it fell to the Nazis in 1940. He and his wife then spent a
few years in the United States. His biographies include
*Ariel: The Life of Shelley, Proust: Portrait of a Genius,
Lelia: The Life of George Sand, Olympio: The Life of Victor
Hugo,* and *Prometheus: The Life of Balzac.*

Maury, Matthew, American oceanographer **O** 35

Maurya (MOW-ur-ya) **Dynasty,** line of kings of India established about 324 B.C. by Chandragupta Maurya, the first
true emperor of India. The third Maurya ruler, Asoka, was
the most renowned. During his reign (274–232 B.C.),
which was marked by peace, prosperity, and the spread of
Buddhism, the noted Asokan pillars—containing his
edicts, moral precepts, laws, and deeds—were erected.
The last Maurya king was assassinated in 185 B.C.
Asia, history of early civilizations **A** 468

Mauser (MOWS-er) **rifle** **G** 419; *picture* **G** 418
Mausoleum at Halicarnassus, Asia Minor **W** 216;
picture **W** 215
Mauve (MOAV), synthetic dye **D** 372
Mavericks, unbranded cattle on open rangeland
R 104–05
Maxentius (max-EN-tius), Roman emperor **C** 522
Maxillofacial surgeon, in dentistry **D** 115

Maxim, Hiram Percy (1869–1936), American mechanical engineer and inventor, b. Brooklyn, N.Y. The son of Sir
Hiram Stevens Maxim, inventor of the Maxim machine
gun, he is well known for inventing the Maxim gun silenc-
er. He also devised numerous improvements in the automobile field, such as the muffler to deaden motor noise.
His books include *Life's Place in the Cosmos* and his autobiography, *Horseless Carriage Days.*

Maximilian (max-i-MIL-ian), emperor of Mexico
M 249–50
defeated by Juárez **J** 138
Maximilian I (Kaiser Max), Holy Roman emperor
created Habsburg empire **A** 524
Maxim machine guns **G** 423–24
Maxwell, James Clerk, Scottish physicist **P** 236–37;
S 75
predicted radio waves **R** 55
Saturn's rings **P** 277
May, 5th month of year **M** 182–83
folk music **F** 326
Maya (MA-ya), Indians of North America **I** 197–99
art **I** 154
calendar **C** 12
Central America **C** 174
communication, history of **C** 461
Copán, *picture* **H** 199
decorative arts **D** 73
El Salvador **E** 183
Guatemala **G** 390, 391, 392
Honduras **H** 198
numeration system **N** 393–94
painting from a vase from Guatemala, *picture*
A 348
pre-Columbian dance **L** 68
pyramid, *picture* **E** 183
Mayagüez (ma-ya-GUACE), Puerto Rico **P** 521
Mayagüez incident, 1975 **F** 366d
Mayakovski (ma-ya-KOF-ski), **Vladimir,** Russian poet
U 61–62

Mayapán (ma-ya-PON), ancient city of Yucatán **I** 199
Mayapple see Mandrake
May beetles **P** 284; *picture* **P** 285
May Day (International Labor Day) **H** 157
　　celebrated in Union of Soviet Socialist Republics
　　　U 29

Mayer (my-AR), **Jean** (1920–　　), French-born American nutritionist and educator, b. Paris. Mayer is noted for studies on weight control, malnutrition, and world hunger. He has been active in campaigns throughout the world to improve nutrition and eliminate hunger. He pioneered in the study of obesity, advocating exercise as an important part of a weight-loss program. His books include *Overweight: Causes, Cost, and Control* (1968), *A Diet for Living* (1975), and *Food and Nutrition in Health and Disease* (1977). Mayer was professor of nutrition at Harvard University from 1950 to 1976. In 1976 he became president of Tufts University.

Mayer, Maria Goeppert (1906–72), American physicist, b. Kattowitz, Germany (now Katowice, Poland). Professor Mayer and J. H. D. Jensen shared half of the 1963 Nobel prize in physics (E. P. Wigner received the other half) for developing the concept of the shell structure of atomic nuclei. She was the second woman to receive the Nobel prize in physics. (Marie Curie was the first, in 1903.)

Mayflower (trailing arbutus), flower
　　Massachusetts, state flower of, *picture* **M** 135
Mayflower, Pilgrims' ship **M** 184–85
　　Pilgrims' voyage to America **A** 186–87
　　Plymouth Colony, founding of **P** 344
Mayflower II, ship **M** 185
Mayflower Compact, 1620 **M** 185; **P** 344
　　American colonies begin self-government and
　　　democracy **A** 187

Mayflower Descendants, General Society of, organization composed of descendants of the colonists who landed at Plymouth, Mass., from the *Mayflower* in 1620. It was founded in 1897, has its headquarters in Plymouth, Mass., and publishes the *Mayflower.*

Mayfly, *picture* **I** 281
May Music Festival, Cincinnati, Ohio **M** 559

Maynor, Dorothy (1910–　　), American soprano, b. Norfolk, Va. She first sang with choirs and choruses and made her formal New York debut in 1939. She was the first black to sing in Coolidge Auditorium in Washington, D.C., and was soloist at the inauguration of President Harry S Truman. Maynor founded the Harlem School of Music in 1963. In 1975 she became the first black to sit on the board of directors of the Metropolitan Opera.

Mayo, Charles and **William,** American doctors **M** 208a
Mayo family, American doctors **M** 335
Mayombé Escarpment, Congo **C** 497
Mayor-council form, of city government **M** 512
Mayotte, island, Indian Ocean **C** 473
Maypole dance, *picture* **F** 298

Mays, Willie Howard (1931–　　), American baseball player, b. Westfield, Ala. He joined New York (now San Francisco) Giants in 1951 and was chosen Rookie of the Year. An outstanding batter, outfielder, and base runner, he was voted the National League's Most Valuable Player in 1954 and 1965. In 1972 he joined New York Mets and retired at end of the '73 season. He hit 660 home runs in his career, ranking third behind Hank Aaron and Babe Ruth. In 1979, Mays was elected to the Baseball Hall of Fame. *picture* **B** 76

Ma Yüan, Chinese artist **C** 275
Mazama (ma-ZA-ma), **Mount,** ancient peak, Oregon
　　L 29; **O** 192

Mazarin (MAZ-ar-in), **Jules, Cardinal** (1602–61), French statesman, b. Pescina, Italy. He executed diplomatic missions for Pope Urban VIII (1629–34), entered French service under Richelieu (1639), and became cardinal (1641). He succeeded Richelieu as prime minister (1642–61), continuing Richelieu's foreign policy in order to strengthen France's position in Europe and weaken the Holy Roman Empire. Domestically, he broke the power of the nobility and gave all authority to the king, Louis XIV.
　　Palais-Mazarin, Paris **P** 74

Maze, network of paths enclosed by hedges **P** 76
　　animal behavior **P** 495
　　animal trial and error tests **A** 283–84
　　Jordan theorem in topology **T** 227
　　learning ability, test for **L** 104
Mazurka (ma-ZUR-ka), dance of Poland **D** 30

Mazzei (mat-TSA-e), **Philip** (1730–1816), American Revolutionary War figure, b. Poggio-Caiano, Italy. Mazzei practiced medicine briefly in Italy and then moved to London, where he became a wine merchant. In 1773 he went to Virginia, where he tried to introduce the growing of grapes. He was a neighbor and friend of Thomas Jefferson and quickly became involved in the revolutionary cause. Under the pen names Furioso, Citizen of Virginia, and Citizen of the World, Mazzei wrote articles urging the colonists to break ties with Britain. From 1779 to 1784, he acted as Virginia's agent in Europe, arranging trade agreements and sending information to Jefferson. He spent his last years in Europe and died in Italy.

Mazzini (ma-TZI-ni), **Giuseppe,** Italian patriot **M** 185
　　Garibaldi and Mazzini **G** 57
　　Italian unification **I** 457
　　Risorgimento in Italian literature **I** 479
mb see Millibar
Mbabane (um-ba-BA-nay), capital of Swaziland **S** 481
Mbandzeni, king of Swaziland **S** 482
M'Bochi, a people of Africa **C** 496

Mboya (m-BOY-a), **Tom** (Thomas Joseph Mboya) (1930–69), Kenyan statesman, b. Central Province. Formerly a health sanitation inspector, he was then involved in political leadership of the Kenya nationalist movement (from 1953). He served as general secretary of the Kenya Federation of Labor (1953–62), minister of labor (1962–63), minister of constitutional affairs (1963–64), and minister of economic development and planning from 1964 until 1969 when he was assassinated. His autobiography is entitled *Freedom and After.*
　　Kenya, history of **K** 233

Mc, contraction of Mac **N** 5
　　See also names beginning with Mac and Mc in
　　　alphabetical order as they are spelled
McAdam, John Loudon, Scottish engineer **T** 260
　　roads and highways, history of **R** 249, 250
McAliskey, Bernadette Devlin *see* Devlin, Bernadette

McBurney, Charles (1845–1913), American surgeon, b. Roxbury, Mass. He pioneered in antiseptic surgery and

McBurney, Charles (continued)
was an authority on appendicitis operation. He discovered McBurney's point, a tender pressure point important in diagnosis of appendicitis, and McBurney's incision, a technique of appendectomy.

McCain, John (1936–   ), United States senator from Arizona, Republican, b. Panama Canal Zone. He was elected to the Senate in 1986. He served in the U.S. House of Representatives (1983–86) and as director of the Navy Senate Liaison Office (1975–80). Previously, McCain served 22 years in the United States Navy, where he achieved the rank of captain. In 1967, while serving in Vietnam, he was shot down over Hanoi and held as a prisoner of war for more than six years.

McCall's, magazine   **M** 19

McCarran, Patrick Anthony (1876–1954), American politician, b. Reno, Nev. He was elected to the Nevada state legislature (1903) and served as associate justice (1913–17) and chief justice (1917–18) of the Nevada Supreme Court. As U.S. senator from Nevada (1933–54), he sponsored the Internal Security Act of 1950 (known as the McCarran Act), requiring registration of members of Communist organizations with the federal government. He coauthored the McCarran-Walter Immigration Act of 1952, revising American immigration policy.   **N** 135

McCarthy, Charlie, ventriloquist's dummy   **V** 302

McCarthy, Eugene Joseph (1916–   ), American political leader, b. Watkins, Minn. McCarthy became nationally known in 1968, when he ran unsuccessfully for the Democratic presidential nomination. He was then a U.S. senator and an opponent of U.S. involvement in Vietnam. He had served in the U.S. House of Representatives (1949–59) before his election to the Senate in 1958. Before entering politics, McCarthy had been a college professor. He retired from the Senate in 1971, resumed teaching, and wrote a newspaper column. As an independent candidate for the presidency in 1976, McCarthy received about 1 percent of the vote. His attempt to regain a Senate seat in 1982 was unsuccessful. McCarthy authored five books, including *The Limits of Power* (1967) and *The Ultimate Tyranny* (1980).   **M** 336

McCarthy, Joseph Raymond (1908–1957), American politician, b. Grand Chute, Wis. McCarthy was a U.S. senator from 1947 to 1957. As chairman of the Senate Permanent Subcommittee on Investigations, he charged that the State Department and the Army had been infiltrated by scores of Communists. In a series of televised hearings, he failed to prove his accusations, and was formally censured by the Senate. McCarthy's supporters credited him with tightening government security, but his critics said that he violated democratic processes and created an atmosphere of fear. The indiscriminate and bitter nature of his charges gave rise to the term "McCarthyism."   **W** 206
McCarthyism and Kennedy   **K** 209

McCarthy, Joseph Vincent (1887–1978), American baseball manager, b. Philadelphia, Pa. He managed the Chicago Cubs (1926–30), winning one pennant; the New York Yankees (1931–46), winning eight pennants and seven World Series Championships; and the Boston Red Sox (1948–50). He was elected to the Baseball Hall of Fame in 1957.

McCarthy, Mary, American writer   **A** 214b

McCarthyism see McCarthy, Joseph Raymond
McCartney, Paul, English musician and singer   **B** 108
McCauley, Mary see Pitcher, Molly
McCay, Clive M., American scientist   **A** 84–85

McClellan, George Brinton (1826–85), American army officer and politician, b. Philadelphia, Pa. He was commissioned army major general (1861) in command of the department of Ohio when the Civil War broke out. His successful campaign of Rich Mountain led to his appointment as commander and later, general-in-chief, of the Division of the Potomac (1861–62). He directed the unsuccessful Peninsula Campaign and was chosen to reorganize the army's defense of Washington. Accused of being overcautious, he was relieved of duty (1862). He was a Democratic presidential candidate (1865) and governor of New Jersey (1878–81).
Civil War campaigns   **C** 339–41, 342, 345
with Lincoln, *picture*   **L** 294

McClintock, Barbara (1902–   ), American scientist, b. Hartford, Conn. In the 1940's and 1950's, she discovered that genes can move from one spot to another on the chromosomes of a plant. These "jumping genes," as they are sometimes called, can change the inherited traits of future generations produced by the plant. McClintock did her research with maize (corn) plants. Her work was at first ignored by other scientists, but the significance of her research was finally realized. McClintock was awarded the Nobel prize in medicine in 1983. She works at the Cold Spring Harbor Laboratory on Long Island, N.Y.

McCloskey, Robert (1914–   ), American illustrator and author of children's books, b. Hamilton, Ohio. He served as a sergeant in the Army during World War II, drawing training pictures. Primarily an illustrator, he creates stories in picture form and later connects them with sentences. He is author of *Make Way for Ducklings* (Caldecott medal winner, 1941), *Homer Price, Blueberries for Sal,* and other works.
illustration from *Make Way for Ducklings*   **C** 243

McClure, James A. (1924–   ), United States senator from Idaho, Republican, b. Payette. He was elected to the Senate in 1972 and re-elected in 1978 and 1984. He previously served in the U.S. House of Representatives (1967–73). McClure formerly served as state senator, as prosecuting attorney for Payette County, and as city attorney of Payette.

McClure, Sir Robert John Le Mesurier (1807–73), British naval officer and Arctic explorer, b. Wexford, Ireland. He accompanied Arctic expeditions under Sir George Back (1836–37) and Sir James Clark Ross (1848). In command of an expedition in search of Sir John Franklin (1850–54), he first proved the existence of the Northwest Passage. He later served in China (1856–61).
Northwest Passage   **N** 338

McConnell, Mitch (Addison Mitchell McConnell, Jr.) (1942–   ), United States senator from Kentucky, Republican, b. Sheffield, Ala. He was elected to the Senate in 1984. He previously served as Jefferson County judge-executive (1977–85) and as deputy assistant U.S. attorney general (1974–75).

McCord, David (1897–   ), American poet, b. New York, N.Y. McCord's poems are often used to teach young children how to write poetry. His collections of poetry for children include *Far and Few* (1952), *Take Sky* (1962), and *For Me to Say* (1970). **C** 240

McCormack, John (1884–1945), Irish-American tenor, b. Athlone, Ireland. He studied in Italy. After winning the gold medal at the National Irish Festival (Dublin, 1902), he went on to a highly successful concert and opera career. He sang with opera companies in New York, Boston, and Chicago, excelling in Mozart and Verdi. He was also popular as a singer of sentimental ballads.

McCormack, John William (1891–1980), American politician, b. South Boston, Mass. A former member of the state House of Representatives (1920–22) and state Senate (1923–26) of Massachusetts, he served in the U.S. House of Representatives (1929–71). Closely associated with Sam Rayburn, he was House majority leader (1940–45, 1948–52, 1955–62) and minority whip (1946–47, 1953–54). He succeeded Rayburn as Speaker of the House (1962–71).

McCormick, Cyrus, American inventor **M** 186; **I** 85

McCormick, Patricia Keller (1930–   ), American diving champion, b. Seal Beach, Calif. She placed first in both springboard and platform diving competitions in two Olympic Games—1952 and 1956. She is a member of the International Swimming Hall of Fame. **D** 229

McCoy, Elijah (1843–1929), American inventor, b. Canada (of parents who had fled as slaves from Kentucky). McCoy patented numerous lubricators and developed a method of oiling moving machinery that made it unnecessary to stop a machine to lubricate it. His lubricator cup (drip cup) was widely used on factory machines and on engines of trains and steamships. He established the Elijah McCoy Manufacturing Company in Detroit about 1920. It is said that customers shopping for a lubricator often asked, "Is this the real McCoy?" This may have been the origin of the expression "the real McCoy," meaning "the real thing" or "the genuine article."

McCracken, Harold (1894–1983), American Arctic explorer and author, b. Colorado Springs, Colo. He led Ohio State University expedition to Alaska (1915–17) and the Stoll-McCracken expedition of the American Museum of Natural History (1928) to the Aleutian Islands, where Stone Age mummies were discovered. He was director of the Buffalo Bill Historical Center and the Whitney Gallery of Western Art, Cody, Wyoming from 1958 to 1974. His many books include *God's Frozen Children* and *Frederic Remington, Artist of the Old West.*

McCullers, Carson, American novelist **A** 214
McCulloch v. Maryland, Supreme Court case **M** 113

McCully, Emily Arnold (1939–   ), American illustrator of children's books, b. Galesburg, Ill. She illustrated *Journey from Peppermint Street* by Meindert De Jong. *Journey* won a National Book Award in 1969. McCully's illustrations are also found in *Michael Is Brave* (1971) by Helen E. Buckley and *Martha's Mad Day* (1977) by Miranda Hapgood.

McDermott, Terry (Richard McDermott), American speed skater **O** 112
McDivitt, James, American astronaut **S** 340j

McDonald, David Lamar (1906–   ), American naval officer, b. Maysville, Ga. He served with the Navy Bureau of Aeronautics (1947–50), directed the air warfare division of the office of Chief of Naval Operations (1955–57), and served as deputy assistant chief of staff, Supreme Headquarters, Allied Powers in Europe (SHAPE) (1957–60). Attaining the rank of full admiral in 1963, he was chief of naval operations from then until 1967.

McDowell, Irvin, American army officer **C** 339
McElroy (MAC-el-roy), **Mary Arthur,** acting first lady in Arthur's administration **F** 174–75

McEnroe, John Patrick, Jr. (1959–   ), American tennis player, b. Wiesbaden, Germany. In 1979 he became the youngest player to win the U.S. men's singles title since 1948. He also won the Masters and the World Championship of Tennis titles in 1979. McEnroe was a member of the victorious U.S. Davis Cup team in 1978, the year he turned professional. He won the U.S. singles title again in 1980, 1981, and 1984. And he won the All-England (Wimbledon) singles title in 1981, 1983, and 1984. In addition, McEnroe and fellow American Peter Fleming have won numerous doubles titles.

McGill, James (1744–1813), Canadian fur trader, b. Glasgow, Scotland. He established his business headquarters in Montreal (1774?), and he served on the Legislative Assembly of Lower Canada (1792–96, 1800–04) and on the Quebec Executive Council (1793). At his death he left land and funds to found McGill University, Montreal.

McGill, Ralph (Emerson) (1898–1969), American journalist, b. Soddy, Tenn. He worked for the Nashville *Banner* (1922–28) before joining the Atlanta *Constitution* (1929–69) where he held several editorial positions before becoming publisher. An early crusader for civil rights, he won a Pulitzer prize for editorial writing (1958) and was awarded the Presidential Medal of Freedom (1964).

McGill University, Montreal, Canada **C** 65; **M** 445; **Q** 11
   ice hockey's code of rules developed **I** 33

McGillvray, Alexander (1759?–93), Creek Indian chief. During the American Revolution he supported the British, and as a Loyalist, lost his Georgia lands at the beginning of the war. To unite southern Indians and halt American settlement in Georgia, Tennessee, and Kentucky, he concluded a treaty with Spain (1784) and directed raids against southern frontier settlements (1785–87). Though he signed a friendship pact with the United States (1790), he nullified it by signing another treaty with Spain (1792).

McGinley, Phyllis, American poet
   Oregon, famous people of **O** 206

McGovern, George S. (1922–   ), American political leader, b. Avon, S. Dak. After receiving his Ph.D. from Northwestern University in 1953, McGovern served as executive secretary of the South Dakota Democratic Party (1954–65). He represented South Dakota in the U.S. House of Representatives from 1957 to 1961, when President Kennedy appointed him director of the Food for Peace Program. In 1962 he was elected to the U.S. Senate, where he served three terms. In 1972 he won the Democratic presidential nomination but lost the election

McGovern, George S. (continued)
to President Nixon. McGovern lost his bid for re-election to the U.S. Senate in 1980. He was briefly a candidate for the 1984 Democratic presidential nomination. **S** 325

McGuffey, William Holmes (1800–73), American educator, b. near Claysville, Pa. President of Cincinnati College (1836–39) and of Ohio University in Athens (1839–43), he later became professor of moral philosophy, University of Virginia (1845–73). McGuffey was a strong supporter of public education. He is remembered mainly for his widely circulated *Eclectic Readers* for elementary schools, which became known as McGuffey's Readers.
　　textbooks in America **T** 139

McGuffey's Readers, textbooks **T** 139
　　early education in the United States **E** 71
　　part of pioneer life **P** 259

McHenry, Donald F. (1936–　　), American diplomat, b. St. Louis, Mo. He was U.S. ambassador to the United Nations from 1979 to 1981. Earlier, he had served as U.S. deputy representative to the U.N. Security Council (1977–79). McHenry originally served in the U.S. State Department from 1963 to 1973. He was also associated with the Brookings Institution (a social sciences research corporation) and the Carnegie Endowment for International Peace in Washington, D.C. After leaving government service, McHenry became a consultant in the field of international relations.

McHenry, James (1753–1816), American army officer, b. Ballymena, Ireland. After serving on medical staff of Revolutionary forces (1775–78), he became secretary to Washington (1778–80) and to Lafayette (1780–81). He was a member of the Maryland senate (1781–86, 1791–96), the Continental Congress (1783–86), and the Constitutional Convention (1787). He served as secretary of war under Washington and Adams (1796–1800). Historic Fort McHenry in Baltimore was named for him.

McIlwain, Carl, American scientist **R** 47

McIntyre, James Francis Aloysius, Cardinal (1886–1979), American Roman Catholic prelate, b. New York, N.Y. Ordained a priest (1921), he served as coadjutor archbishop of New York under Francis Cardinal Spellman (1946–48). He was archbishop of Los Angeles and San Diego (1948–70), and he was made a cardinal in 1953.

McKay, Alexander (?–1811), Canadian fur trader. He joined Sir Alexander Mackenzie on his expedition to the Pacific Ocean (1793). After trading as a partner with North West Company (1799–1808), he became a partner in the Pacific Fur Company of John Jacob Astor (1810).

McKay, Claude (pseudonym Eli Edwards) (1890–1948), American author, b. Sunny Ville, Jamaica. Arriving in the United States (1912), he became associated with Floyd Dell and Max Eastman as an editor of *The Liberator* (1919–22). His poetry, often deploring racial injustices, includes the collections *Songs of Jamaica, Constab Ballads,* and *Harlem Shadows.* Among his other works are the novels *Home to Harlem, Banjo,* and an autobiography, *A Long Way From Home.* **A** 208

McKay, Donald (1810–80), American shipbuilder, b. Shelburne County, Nova Scotia, Canada. Establishing a shipyard in East Boston, Mass. (1844), he became inter-

nationally known for his rapid packet and clipper ships, including the clippers *James Baines* and *Lightning,* which hold the world speed records for sailing ships. He strongly advocated construction of iron ships for the U.S. Navy, and he built several naval vessels (1864–65).

McKay, Douglas, American politician **O** 206
McKay, Frederick, American dentist **F** 283–84
McKay, Gordon, American inventor **S** 158

McKean, Thomas (1734–1817), American statesman, b. Chester County, Pa. He represented Delaware at the Continental Congress (1774–83), serving as president of the Congress (1881). He was chief justice (1777–99) and governor of Pennsylvania (1799–1808).

McKee, Mary Harrison, acting first lady in Harrison's administration **F** 175

McKenzie, Roderick (1761?–1844), Canadian fur trader, b. Scotland. He took charge of Fort Chipewyan during the absence of his cousin, the explorer Sir Alexander Mackenzie (1789, 1792). He was a partner in a fur-trading company (1800–25), and he served in the Legislative Council of Lower Canada (1817–38). His notes on fur-trading history were used in *Bourgeois de la Compagnie du Nord-Ouest,* by Louis François Rodrigue Masson.

McKernan, John R., Jr. (1948–　　), governor of Maine, Republican, b. Bangor. He was elected governor in 1986. He served in the U.S. House of Representatives (1983–86), where he worked on tax reform. In 1982 he was appointed to the Commission on Presidential Scholars. He previously practiced law with a firm in Portland (1976–81) and was a state representative (1971–75).

McKim, Mead and White, firm of architects **U** 123
McKinley, Ida Saxton, wife of William McKinley
　　F 175; *picture* **F** 174

McKinley, John (1780–1852), American politician, b. Culpeper County, Va. A resident of Alabama, he served in the U.S. Senate (1826–31), the state legislature (1831–33, 1836–37), and the House of Representatives (1833–35). In 1837 President Van Buren appointed him to the U.S. Supreme Court, where he served until his death.

McKinley, Mount, Alaska, *pictures* **A** 131, **M** 502,
　　N 44
　　first ascent, *chart* **M** 496
　　highest point in North America **N** 285
McKinley, William, 25th president of the United States
　　M 187–90; *picture* **P** 453
　　Spanish-American War **S** 375
McKinley Tariff, 1890 **H** 39; **M** 187–88

McKissick, Floyd B. (1922–　　), black civil rights leader, b. Asheville, N.C. He attended Morehouse and North Carolina colleges and received his law degree from the University of North Carolina Law School. He succeeded James Farmer as National Director of the Congress of Racial Equality (CORE) (1966–68), and headed Floyd McKissick Enterprises, Inc (1968–74).

McKuen, Rod (1933–　　), American poet, composer, and singer, b. Oakland, Calif. He started as a late-night disk jockey on an Oakland radio station. He appeared in night clubs and had bit parts in Hollywood films, but achieved his first great success as a poet with *And Autumn Came.* This was followed by *Twelve Years of Christmas* and

Listen to the Warm, a collection of song lyrics. He has written more than 1,000 songs and has also composed musical scores for several motion pictures.

McLaughlin, Ann Dore (1941–   ), United States government official, b. Newark, N.J. She served as director of communications for President Richard Nixon's re-election campaign (1971–72) and as director of public affairs for the Environmental Protection Agency (1973–74). She later became a government relations and communications executive for the Union Carbide Corp. (1974–77), then a public affairs consultant with McLaughlin and Co. (1977–81). She returned to public service as assistant secretary for public affairs at the Treasury Department (1981–84) and later served as undersecretary of the Department of the Interior (1984–87). She was appointed secretary of labor in 1987.

McLeod, John (1788–1849), Canadian pioneer, b. Stornoway, Scotland. McLeod went to Canada and became a fur trader, joining Hudson's Bay Company in 1811. In 1815 the company sent him to organize the Red River settlement, near present-day Winnipeg, against attack by the North West Company, which claimed the region's fur resources. He retired from the company in 1848.

McLoughlin (mac-LOC-lin), **John,** Scottish-born
　　Canadian fur trader **F** 523
　　Oregon **O** 205, 207
　　Washington **W** 25, 26

McLuhan, Herbert Marshall (1911–80), Canadian educator and writer, b. Edmonton, Alberta. In his book *Understanding Media* (1964), McLuhan said that people today live in an electronic age of instant communication made possible by telephones, movies, and especially television. For this reason, each person becomes totally involved in the lives of all other people. Phrases like ''the medium is the message'' brought McLuhan international fame. This phrase means that the content of television programs is less important than the way in which television is changing the human environment. His other books include *The Medium Is the Massage* (1967), written with Quentin Fiore, and *The City as Classroom* (1977).

McMahon (mac-MAY-on) **Line,** boundary line between
　　India and Tibet **T** 178
McMath solar telescope, at Kitt Peak National
　　Observatory, *picture* **O** 9
McMillan, Margaret, English educator **K** 244
McNair, Alexander, American governor **M** 381

McNair, Lesley James (1883–1944), American general, b. Verndale, Minn. As chief of staff of the General Headquarters (1940) he was in charge of a gigantic training program, in which he introduced new, realistic training methods. After the reorganization of the War Department General Staff (1942) he was named commanding general of all United States ground forces. He was killed during World War II in Normandy, July, 1944.

McNamara, Robert Strange (1916–   ), American business executive and public official, b. San Francisco, Calif. McNamara was an executive of the Ford Motor Co. from 1946 to 1961. He served as U.S. secretary of defense from 1961 to 1968 and then became president of the International Bank for Reconstruction and Development (World Bank). He held that position until 1981. In 1983 McNamara joined other former public officials in calling for nuclear disarmament.

McNarney, Joseph Taggart (1893–1972), American general, b. Emporium, Pa. He succeeded (1945) Dwight D. Eisenhower as commander of U.S. forces in Europe and was chief of the occupation army in Germany. He served (1947–52) as senior member of the United Nations military staff committee.

McNary, Charles Linza, American politician **O** 206

McNaughton, Andrew George Latta (1887–1966), Canadian army officer and diplomat, b. Moosomin, Sask. He served as chief of the General Staff (1929–35) and as commander of the Canadian Army in Great Britain (1942–43). He later became minister of national defense (1944), chairman of the Canadian section of the Canadian–United States joint board of defense (1945), and Canadian representative to the United Nations Atomic Energy Commission (1946) and the Security Council (1948).

McPherson, Aimee Semple (1890–1944), American evangelist, b. near Ingersoll, Canada. She began preaching at 17 and traveled widely. After settling in Los Angeles (1918), she founded (1921) the Echo Park Evangelistic Association and built the Angelus Temple Church of the Foursquare Gospel.

McTeague, novel by Frank Norris **A** 206

McWherter, Ned (1930–   ), governor of Tennessee, Democrat, b. Palmersville. He was elected governor in 1986. He served in the state House of Representatives (1969–86) and was speaker for seven consecutive terms. He served 21 years in the Tennessee National Guard, retiring with the rank of captain. McWherter owns several small businesses and a farm headquartered in Dresden.

M.D. (medical doctor), degree **D** 234
Mead, Lake, southwestern United States **D** 20; **L** 28;
　　picture **L** 27
　　Arizona **A** 407
　　Nevada **N** 125, 132
Mead, Margaret, American anthropologist **M** 191

Meade, George Gordon (1815–72), American Union general, b. Cádiz, Spain. His successful participation in the Civil War battles of Mechanicsville, Gaines's Mill, Glendale, Bull Run, and Antietam led to his appointment as commander of the Army of the Potomac shortly before the battle of Gettysburg (1863). His victory at Gettysburg brought him further promotion and the thanks of Congress (1864).
　　Civil War campaigns **C** 343

Meadowlarks, common North American birds of the blackbird family. There are two main kinds of meadowlarks, eastern and western. Both kinds live in fields and nest in the grass. Their throats are yellow, with a black V, and their backs are mottled brown-black, hard to see in grassland. The eastern meadowlark has a whistling call. The western meadowlark has a high-pitched, flute-like song.
　　Audubon painting **A** 490
　　birds, *picture* **B** 241
　　See also Western meadowlarks

Meal, corn **C** 551
Meals
　　Basic Four Food Groups in the diet **N** 417
　　camp meals **C** 44–45
　　mealtime around the world **F** 335–40

Meals (continued)
    table manners **E** 303b–303c
    table settings **T** 2–3
Meals on wheels, old-age assistance **O** 100
Mealybugs P 289; *picture* **P** 288
Mealy Mountains, Newfoundland, Canada **N** 140
Mean (arithmetic mean), kind of average of a set of
    numbers **S** 417
Mean solar days T 188
Mean Streets, motion picture **M** 493
Meany, George, American labor leader **L** 4; *picture* **L** 7

Meares, John (1756?–1809), British naval commander
and explorer. After forming a trading company to gather
furs on the northwestern coast of America, he made two
voyages (1786–87, 1788) and established a post at Nootka Sound (1788). He occupied the coastal land before
Spaniards, who claimed the region, seized the post.
Meares's complaint to the king resulted in the Nootka
Sound controversy between Great Britain and Spain, settled in Great Britain's favor (1790).
    Oregon, history of **O** 207

Mearne, Samuel, English bookbinder **B** 322
Mearns (MERNS), **Hughes**
    "Antigonish," nonsense rhyme **N** 274
Mears, Helen Farnsworth, American sculptor **W** 206
Mears, Otto, Russian-American pioneer **C** 444
Measles, virus disease **D** 196–97
    German measles not related **D** 193
    vaccination **V** 261
Measure (bar), in musical notation **M** 539, 541
Measure for Measure, play by Shakespeare **S** 135
Measurement
    ancient scientific inventions for measuring **I** 346
    barometer measures air pressure **B** 54
    chemistry, history of **C** 207
    experiments and other science activities **E** 354
    mathematics **M** 154
    of energy in foot-pounds **E** 198
    tools for measuring **T** 219–20
    weights and measures **W** 108–17
    with optical instruments **O** 172–74
Measures *see* Weights and measures
Meat and meat-packing M 191–95
    beef cattle **C** 147–48, 153–54
    cooking, methods of **C** 536
    cool storage **F** 343
    curing by salting and smoking **F** 345
    cuts of meat **M** 193–94
    food contamination **F** 353
    food regulations and laws **F** 347
    food shopping **F** 349–50
    food taboos and customs **F** 334
    grades of meat **M** 195
    important agricultural products **A** 90
    nutrition **N** 417
    outdoor cooking **O** 247–48
    pemmican **F** 344, 520; **I** 166, 196
    trichinosis, illness from undercooked pork **D** 204
Mecca, holy city of Islam **M** 196; *picture* **S** 58c
    Islam **I** 414, 415, 416; **S** 58a
    Koran **K** 292, 293
    Mohammed's birthplace **M** 404, 405

Mecham, Evan (1924–   ), governor of Arizona, Republican, b. Duchesne, Utah. He was elected governor in
1986. Mecham owns one of the largest Pontiac automobile dealerships in the United States. He served as a state
senator (1961–63) and was a fighter pilot in World War
II.

Mechanical, in printing
    commercial art **C** 458
    magazine production **M** 17
Mechanical advantage (MA), force-saving feature of
    simple machines **W** 246–47
    hydraulic machines **H** 302
Mechanical bonding, adhesive process **G** 242
Mechanical clocks C 366–67, 369–70
Mechanical dolls D 271–72
Mechanical drawing M 197
    computer-aided drafting **C** 491
Mechanical energy E 198
    basic research in physics **P** 233
Mechanical engineering E 205–06
    building construction **B** 431
Mechanics, branch of physics **P** 233
    Archimedes **A** 367
    Galileo's laws of falling bodies **F** 34; **G** 5–7
    motion, Newton's laws of **M** 471–73
    work, power, and machines **W** 243–50
Mechanics' Union of Trade Associations L 3
Mechanism of action, of drugs **D** 333
Meck, Nadezhda von, patron of Tchaikovsky **T** 36
Meckenem, Israel van, Flemish artist
    Lute Player and Woman Playing the Harp, painting,
        picture **D** 366
Mecklenburg, West Virginia **W** 140
Medallions *see* Medals
Medal of Freedom, Presidential *see* Presidential Medal
    of Freedom
Medal of Honor D 65, 67; **M** 198, 200; *pictures*
    D 66, **M** 199
Medal play, in golf **G** 259
Medals D 65–67; **M** 198–200
    children's book awards **C** 228–31
    Olympic medals **O** 107–08; *picture* **O** 106
    portrait medallions on furniture, *picture* **F** 507
    Syrian and Greek medallions, *pictures* **J** 95, 96
    See also Carnegie Hero Fund Commission
Medan, Indonesia **I** 221

Medaris (me-DAIR-is), **John Bruce** (1902–   ), American
army officer and clergyman, b. Milford, Ohio. He organized and operated the Field Army Ordnance Service of
the 1st U.S. Army in World War II. He served as commanding general of the Army Ballistic Missile Agency at Red-
stone Arsenal in Huntsville, Ala. (1955–58), and as commanding general of the U.S. Army Ordnance Missile Command (1958–60). He retired from the army in 1960 and
in 1970 was ordained an Episcopal priest. He is author of
Countdown for Decision, and received Freedom Foundation awards (1959, 1960).

Medawar (MED-a-war), **Sir Peter Brian** (1915–87), English biologist, b. Rio de Janeiro, Brazil. For the theory and
proof that immunity to foreign substances in the body is
not inherited but acquired in the period before birth, he
and F. M. Burnet won the Nobel prize (1960) in medicine
and physiology. His work made possible many types of
organ transplantation, skin grafts, and nerve repair. He
also gained recognition as a scientific philosopher and
writer. His autobiography, *Memoir of a Thinking Radish,*
was published in 1986.

Medea (me-DE-a), in Greek mythology **G** 363–64

Medellín (may-thel-YEEN), Colombia   C 406, 407
   supermarket, *picture*   L 55
Medes, a people of ancient Iran   A 241
Medfly *see* Fruit flies
Media, of communication   A 27–30; L 195, 197
   propaganda   P 480–81
Media centers (school libraries)   L 175–76, 179;
   pictures L 183
Median (ME-dian), average of a set of numbers   S 417
Mediant, in music   M 541
Mediation, in international relations   I 318, 322
Mediation, labor *see* Federal Mediation and Conciliation
   Service
Medicaid, medical care program   W 120
   aged, medical assistance for the   O 99
Medical education   D 237; P 504
Medical ethics, set of rules for doctors   D 236
Medical examiners, in criminal investigations   D 236
Medical history, of a patient   D 206–07, 234;
   M 208d–208e
   examining the heart   H 82

Medical International Cooperation Organization (MEDI-
CO), nonprofit agency associated with CARE. MEDICO
was founded (1958) by Dr. Peter D. Commanduras and
Dr. Tom Dooley.

Medical laboratory tests   M 201–02, 209
Medical records, of patients   H 249
Medical supplies for the home   F 162
Medicare, insurance program   I 294; O 98; S 222
   part of "Great Society" program   J 123
   Saskatchewan was the first Canadian province to
   have   S 45
Medici (MED-i-chi), Lorenzo de' (Lorenzo the
   Magnificent), Italian statesman and art patron
   I 477
   court masques and dances   D 25
   Florence, history of   F 257
   Michelangelo's patron   M 255–56

Medici (MED-i-chi) family, powerful line of Italian Renaissance rulers. Giovanni (1360–1429) took control of Florence in 1421. His descendants created health and welfare
services for the poor, became patrons of the arts, and
broadened the influence of Tuscany province. Lorenzo
(1449–92), known as the Magnificent, made the palace
the center of Renaissance activity. After Lorenzo's death
the Vatican and foreign invaders began to strip the family
of strength. Cosimo I (1519–74) regained power, but in
1737 the family was banished from Tuscany.
   Botticelli supported by   B 345
   early banking enterprises   B 48
   Florence, Italy   F 257
   Uffizi Gallery   U 2

Medicinal plants *see* Plants, medicinal
Medicine
   acupuncture   M 208a, 208b
   anesthesia   A 256–59
   antibiotics   A 310–16
   computers used in   C 488
   deafness, treatment of   D 49
   dentistry   D 114–16
   disabled, rehabilitation of the   D 177
   disease, types of   D 181–86
   disinfectants and antiseptics   D 214
   doctors   D 234–37
   drug abuse   D 329–32
   drugs   D 332–34

Geiger counter, use in medicine, *diagram*   G 68
gene splicing improves health care   G 91
geriatrics   O 98
god of medicine, Aesculapius   M 203, 208c
health insurance   I 294
home nursing   N 413–14
hospitals   H 247–53
hypnosis   H 316–18
infrared photography   P 217
laser beams   L 46d
medical education, aid to   P 504
medical history of the patient   M 208d–208e
medical laboratory tests   M 201–02
medicinal plants   P 310–15
Nobel prizes   N 263–65
nurses and nursing   N 409–13
occupational health and safety   O 12–13
opium, early use of   N 13
poisons and antidotes   P 355–56
preventing diseases   H 76
public health   P 502–06
supposed medicinal powers of foods   F 335
tools and techniques of   M 208d–211
ultrasonography   R 38
veterinarians   V 324
women, role of   W 212
X rays   P 216; X 340–41
See also First aid
Medicine, history of   M 203–208c
   ancient Egyptian   A 220–21
   Beaumont's research on the human stomach
   B 109
   botanical gardens   B 343
   cancer research   C 92–93
   fire to drive away evil spirits of disease   F 145
   herbs effective in medieval medicine   H 113
   humoral theory in Greek medicine   S 62
   medicinal plants   P 310–15
   pioneer life   P 256
   supposed medicinal powers of foods   F 335
   teamwork on discovery of insulin   B 52
   vaccination and inoculation   V 260–61
Medicine, tools and techniques of   M 208d–211
   Why must a fever thermometer be shaken?   M 208f
Medicine Hat, Alberta, Canada   A 146c, 146g
Medicine Lodge, Kansas   K 185
Medicine men   M 203
   Africa   A 56
   American Indians   I 171, 179
   sand art   S 25
Medici (MED-i-chi) Palace, Florence, Italy   I 465;
   picture I 462
Medici porcelain   P 411
Médicis, Catherine de *see* Catherine de Médicis
Médicis, Marie de *see* Marie de Médicis
MEDICO *see* Medical International Cooperation
   Organization
Medieval architecture *see* Middle Ages, architecture of
Medieval art *see* Middle Ages, art of the
Medieval history *see* Middle Ages
Medieval music *see* Middle Ages, music of the
Medina (med-DI-na), Saudi Arabia   S 58a
   Islamic religion established   I 414
   Mohammed's flight to   M 405
   writing of the Koran   K 293
Medinet Habu (ma-DI-net ha-BU), Egyptian temple
   E 100

Meditation, generally, refers to a method of attaining,
through contemplation (deep thought) and concentration,

Meditation (continued)

greater spiritual awareness or mental and physical calm. The practice of meditation has been observed since ancient times by many of the world's religions, including Hinduism, Buddhism, and Christianity. Its use to reduce mental and physical stress became popular in the West relatively recently. Achieving a meditative state is known to produce certain physical changes in the body related to the lessening of stress, such as lowered blood pressure, slower heartbeat, and decreased intake of oxygen.

    listening prayer **P** 431

    See also Transcendental meditation

Mediterranean (med-it-er-RANE-ean) **climate** **E** 310

    Spain **S** 355

    types of climate **C** 364

Mediterranean fruit fly *see* Fruit flies

Mediterranean scrub forest *see* Maquis

Mediterranean Sea **M** 212–14

    continental drift **G** 117

    Europe's southern boundary **E** 307

    Gibraltar, British military fortress **G** 205

    Malta **M** 63–64

    Venice was chief sea power during the Renaissance **V** 301

Medium (vehicle), for artists' paints **P** 30

Medium, of communication **A** 27

Medium of exchange, in economics **E** 49

    money **M** 409–12

Medtner, Nikolai, Russian composer **U** 62a, 62b

Medulla (me-DUL-la), part of the brain **B** 366; **N** 116

    function in body control **B** 282

Medusa (me-DU-sa), one of the Gorgons in Greek mythology **G** 361

Medusae (me-DU-se), forms of jellyfishes and other coelenterates **J** 70, 75

Meeker, Ezra, American pioneer **O** 206

Meerkats, animals related to mongooses **G** 92, 95

Meerschaum (MEER-shum) (from German, meaning "sea foam"), soft mineral composed of hydrated magnesium silicate, usually white, sometimes with grayish, yellowish, or blue-green color. Its name stems from its light weight and porous texture, which enables it to float. Found mainly in Asia Minor and Greece, it is used chiefly for tobacco pipes and cigar and cigarette holders.

Meese, Edwin, III (1931–   ), United States public official, b. Oakland, Calif. He began his law career as a deputy district attorney for Alameda County, Calif. (1958–66), and then became an aide to Governor Ronald Reagan (1967–74). Meese joined Reagan's staff during the 1980 presidential campaign and, after Reagan's victory, was named counselor to the new president. He was nominated as Attorney General of the United States in 1984, but disclosures during confirmation hearings led to an investigation by a court-appointed independent counsel. After being cleared by the special counsel, Meese was renominated and confirmed in 1985.

Meeting, The, painting by Jean Fragonard, *picture* **F** 402

Meeting at the Golden Gate, painting by Giotto di Bondone **R** 163

Megabytes, of computer-stored information **C** 482

Megahertz (MHz), used to measure very-high-frequency radio waves **R** 53

Megaliths, large stones in prehistoric monuments **P** 441

    Stonehenge **E** 214; *pictures* **E** 215

Megalopolis (meg-a-LOP-o-lis), a supercity **C** 324

    Atlantic states, North America **N** 296

    Maryland area **M** 117

Megalosaurs (MEG-a-lo-saurs), dinosaurs **D** 166

Megapodes (MEG-a-podes) (mound builders), birds **B** 225

Megaron, room in an ancient Greek palace **G** 340–41

Megatons (millions of tons) **N** 354

Meharry Medical College, Nashville, Tennessee **N** 17

Mehemet Ali (ma-HEM-et OL-i), governor of Egypt **E** 92

Mehta, Zubin (1936–   ), symphony orchestra conductor, b. Bombay, India. Mehta won international acclaim for his powerful and energetic interpretations of major symphonic works. He was music director of the Montreal Symphony Orchestra (1961) and of the Los Angeles Philharmonic (1962–78). In 1978 he became music director of the New York Philharmonic.

Meighen (MEE-en), **Arthur** (1874–1960), former Canadian prime minister, b. Anderson, Ontario. Meighen became prime minister in 1920 upon the retirement of Sir Robert Borden. His government was defeated in 1921. He also served as prime minister from June to September, 1926. In 1917 he was secretary of state and then minister of the interior. Through his efforts, Canada acquired the Canadian Northern, Grand Trunk, and Grand Trunk Pacific railways. Meighen wrote the Military Service Act of 1917. He served as Conservative leader in the Senate from 1932 to 1935 and briefly in 1941.

Meiji (MAI-ji) **Shrine,** Tokyo **T** 207

Mein Kampf (mine KOMPF), book by Adolf Hitler **H** 159c

Meiosis, formation of reproductive cells **C** 162

Meir (may-EAR), **Golda** (Goldie Mabovitz Meyerson) (1898–1978), Israeli political leader, b. Kiev, Russia. After growing up in the U.S., she emigrated to Palestine in 1921. One of the signers of Israel's Proclamation of Independence (1948), she served as Israeli ambassador to the Soviet Union in 1948–49. She was foreign minister and minister of labor and social security from 1949 to 1952, minister of labor from 1952 to 1956, and secretary-general of the Mapai (Labor) Party from 1966 to 1968. From 1969 to 1974 she served as prime minister of Israel.

Meissen (MY-sen), East Germany **G** 157

    town depicted on glass tumbler, *picture* **G** 228

Meissen chinaware *see* Dresden porcelain

Meistersingers (MY-ster-singers), German singers **G** 174, 181

Meistersinger von Nürnberg, Die, opera by Richard Wagner **O** 149; *picture* **O** 148

Meitner (MITE-ner), **Lise** (1878–1968), Austrian physicist and mathematician, b. Vienna. With O. Hahn she carried out research in particle physics and discovered the principal isotope of the radioactive element protactinium (1917). In 1939 Meitner and O. Frisch published the correct interpretation of the splitting of the uranium nucleus by bombarding it with neutrons. They showed that a fission reaction had indeed taken place. This research led to development of the atomic bomb.

Mejía Victores, Oscar Humberto, Guatemalan political leader **G** 394

Mekong (may-KONG) **River,** Asia **R** 242

    Kampuchea **K** 164

Laos   **L** 41, 42
  Southeast Asia   **S** 328
  Tonle Sap   **L** 33
  Vietnam   **V** 333, 334
Melancholy and Mystery of a Street, painting by Giorgio
    de Chirico   **I** 472
Melanchthon (mel-ANCK-thon), **Philipp,** German scholar
    and religious reformer   **E** 68
Melanesia (mel-a-NE-sia), Pacific islands   **P** 4
  art   **P** 10
  See also names of islands
Melanesians, Pacific islanders   **P** 4
  New Guinea   **N** 146
  Papua New Guinea   **P** 58d
  Solomon Islands   **S** 252
  Vanuatu   **V** 279
Melanin (MEL-an-in), pigment in hair cells   **H** 2–3

Melba, Dame Nellie (Helen Mitchell) (1861–1931), Australian coloratura soprano, b. near Melbourne. After a celebrated debut as Gilda in *Rigoletto* (Brussels, 1887), she
won international acclaim. Possessing a voice of exceptional clarity, she excelled in such roles as Lucia in *Lucia
di Lammermoor,* Violetta in *La Traviata,* and Marguerite in
Faust. The title role in *Helene,* by Saint-Saëns, was composed for her. She wrote an autobiography, *Melodies and
Memories.*

Melbourne, Australia   **M** 215
  capital of Victoria   **A** 511, 513
  Olympic Games, 1956   **O** 110–11
Melbourne Cup, horse race   **H** 232; **M** 215

Melcher, John (1924–   ), United States senator from
Montana, Democrat, b. Sioux City, Iowa. He was elected
to the Senate in 1976 and re-elected in 1982. He previously served in the U.S. House of Representatives (1969–
77), the state Senate (1963–67), and the state House of
Representatives (1961–63 and 1969). He was mayor of
Forsyth, Montana (1955–61).

Melchers, Gari, American painter   **M** 271–72

Melchior (MELK-i-or), **Lauritz Lebrecht Hommel** (1890–
1973), American tenor, b. Copenhagen, Denmark. An
outstanding interpreter of Wagnerian roles, he made his
operatic debut in 1913, sang with the Danish Royal Opera
(1914–21), and frequently appeared at the Bayreuth Festival (1924–31). He was associated with the Metropolitan
Opera, New York (1926–50), and he performed in major
opera houses in Europe. He also appeared in films and on
television and radio.

Melgarejo (mel-ga-RAY-ho), **Mariano,** Bolivian general
    and dictator   **B** 310
Melies (mail-YAYS), **Georges,** French motion picture
    producer   **M** 474
Melilla, Spanish city, enclave in Morocco   **S** 356
Melisande *see* Mélusine
Melle (MEL-la) *see* Mali
Mellette, Arthur C., American statesman   **S** 325
Mellon, Andrew, American banker and industrialist
    P 143
  founded the National Gallery of Art   **N** 36
Mellon, Paul, American banker and philanthropist
    N 38
Mellon Collection, of art   **N** 36

Melloni (mel-LO-ni), **Macedonio** (1798–1854), Italian
physicist, b. Parma. He is noted for his studies of infrared

radiation and its effect on various substances. He showed
that infrared rays are similar to light rays, in that they can
be reflected, refracted, and so on. Melloni originated the
term "diathermancy," which means the ability to transmit
infrared radiation.

Mellorine, frozen dessert   **I** 32
Melodeon (mel-O-de-on), reed organ   **O** 208
Melodrama, form of drama   **D** 294
Melody, in music   **M** 530, 541
  African   **A** 78
  ancient music   **A** 246
  folk music   **F** 328
  jazz improvisation   **J** 62
  modern music   **M** 399
  orchestra conducting   **O** 190
  Oriental music   **O** 220d
  responsorial singing of American Indians   **I** 160
Melons   **M** 216
  food shopping   **F** 350
  fruits we eat   **P** 308; *picture* **P** 309
  grown from seeds   **G** 52
  seeds, *picture*   **P** 298
  vegetable gardening   **V** 291
Melos (ME-los) (Milo), island between Greece and Crete
    I 435

Melpomene (mel-POM-e-ni), goddess in Greek mythology.
She and her eight sisters, the daughters of Zeus and Mnemosyne, were the muses, or patrons of the arts and sciences. Melpomene was the muse of tragedy. Her symbols
were the tragic mask and the buskin, or high boot worn by
actors in the tragedies of ancient times.
  See also Muses

Meltdown, an accident in a nuclear reactor where uranium
fuel melts and burns out of control. During normal operation of a reactor, uranium is burned under controlled conditions to produce energy. Circulating water is used to cool
the burning uranium, but if the cooling system fails, the
water boils away. The uranium fuel becomes extremely hot
(over 5,000°F, or 2,760°C) and melts. The molten fuel
may sink deep into the earth, or explosions may occur due
to a buildup of steam and chemicals produced by the
melting process. If not contained, the explosions release
radioactive particles into the atmosphere. Such an explosion occurred in May, 1986, at the Chernobyl Nuclear
Power Plant in the Soviet Union.

Melting (fusion), changing from a solid to a liquid
    H 90; **I** 3–4
  how icebergs melt   **I** 26
Melting point   **H** 90
  air pressure affects   **H** 92
  ice   **I** 4
  metals   **M** 229
  solids   **S** 250
Melting pot   **I** 99
  mixed population in United States   **U** 132–33
Melting Pot of the Pacific, nickname for Hawaii   **H** 48

Meltzer, Milton (1915–   ), American author of books
for young readers, b. Worcester, Mass. Meltzer writes historical books and biographies. His books include *Langston
Hughes: A Biography* (1968) and *The Terrorists* (1983).

Mélusine (may-lu-SENE) (Melisande), in French medieval
legend, a water fairy who is claimed to be the ancestor of
the houses of Lusignan, Rohan, Luxembourg, and Sassen-
aye. As punishment for imprisoning her father in a moun-

Mélusine (continued)

tain, every Saturday she was turned into a water fairy, half human and half serpent. Her marriage to Raymond, Count of Lusignan, dissolved when he broke his vow never to see her on Saturday. She had to leave him, fated to rove endlessly as a spirit. The legend was written down by Jean d'Arras (1387).

Melville, Herman, American novelist **M** 217–18
   American literature **A** 202
   Moby Dick, excerpt **M** 217
   themes of his novels **N** 349
Membranes
   body cells **B** 267, 269, 295
   cell membranes **C** 160, 161, 162
   osmosis process **O** 234–35

Memling (or Memlinc), **Hans** (1430?–94), German-Flemish painter, b. Seligenstadt, Germany. A student of Rogier van der Weyden, he specialized in portraits and deeply religious paintings. Characteristic works include *Mystic Marriage of St. Catherine* and the portrait of Thomas Portinari and his wife.
   Flemish painting, history of **D** 353–54

Memnon, in Greek mythology, son of Ethiopian king Tithonus and the goddess of dawn, Aurora. A hero in the Trojan war, he led a large army to aid King Priam of Troy, slew Antilochus, son of the Greek leader Nestor, and was finally killed by Achilles. A statue dedicated to him in Egypt was said to emit a musical sound at each daybreak.

Memorial Day H 154
Memorial University of Newfoundland, St. John's **N** 143
Memory L 105
   brain function **B** 369
   Do you remember everything you perceive? **P** 493
   hypnosis **H** 316, 318
   memory bank of sensations **B** 288
   psychology **P** 493–94
   remembering dreams **D** 317, 318
   study, methods of **S** 441
Memory (storage elements), of computers **C** 482, 483, 484
Memphis, capital of ancient Egypt **E** 94
Memphis, Tennessee **M** 219; **T** 74–75, 85, 89; *pictures* **T** 84, 86
Mena al Ahmadi, Kuwait **K** 307
   oil refinery, *picture* **K** 306
Menageries *see* Zoos
Menam River *see* Chao Phraya
Menander (me-NAN-der), Greek author **G** 353
Menard, John W., American political leader, *picture* **R** 119

Mencius (MEN-shus) (Latinized from Chinese Meng-tzu, meaning "Master Meng") (372?–289 B.C.), Chinese Confucian philosopher, b. present-day Shangtung province. He traveled to many Chinese state courts, boldly explaining Confucian principles to rulers. Believing that people were basically good, he urged princes to fulfill their moral duties by providing for the social and economic welfare of their subjects in order to attain peace. His sayings, compiled in the Book of Mencius, are part of the Confucian Four Books.
   Chinese literature **O** 220a

Mencken, Henry L., American writer and critic **A** 214b; **M** 128

Mendaña de Neyra, Alvaro de, Spanish explorer
   Solomon Islands **S** 252b
   Tuvalu **T** 335
Mende, a people of Africa **S** 170
Mendel, Gregor Johann, Austrian priest and botanist **M** 220
   genetics and heredity **G** 79–82
   science, history of **S** 77
   start of modern biology **B** 194

Mendeleev (mend-yel-YAY-ef), **Dmitri Ivanovich** (1834–1907), Russian chemist, b. Tobolsk, Siberia. He recognized a relation between atomic weight and chemical properties and so established the periodic table of elements. With some revisions, it is still used today. Element 101, discovered in 1955, was named mendelevium in his honor. **C** 210; **E** 154; **P** 231

Mendele Mocher Sefarim (or Mendele Moykher Sforim), Hebrew and Yiddish author **H** 101; **Y** 350
Mendelevium (men-del-LE-vi-um), element **E** 153, 160
Mendelian (men-DE-lian) **Laws,** of heredity **M** 220
Mendelssohn (MEN-dels-sohn), **Felix,** German composer **M** 221
   choral music **C** 284
   Midsummer Night's Dream, A, overture **G** 187
   orchestra-conducting tradition **O** 188
   romantic concert overtures **R** 311
Mendelssohn, Moses, Jewish philosopher **H** 100

Mendès-France (mahn-des-FRAHNS), **Pierre** (1907–82), French lawyer, economist, and political leader, b. Paris. During World War II, he was imprisoned by the Vichy Government but escaped to serve with the Free French Air Force. He later served in the National Assembly and held many important government posts. In 1954 and 1955 he was prime minister. In this position he negotiated an end to French involvement in Indochina.

Mendoza (mend-O-sa), Argentina **A** 394
Menelaus (men-e-LAY-us), in Greek mythology **G** 364
   Trojan War **T** 293
Menelik (MEN-e-lik) **I,** legendary ancestor of Ethiopian kings **E** 300, 301
Menelik II, ruler of Ethiopia **E** 301
Menena (men-AE-na), king of ancient Egypt
   tomb painting, *pictures* **E** 94

Menéndez de Avilés (may-NEN-dathe day a-bi-LACE), **Pedro** (1519–74), Spanish naval officer, b. Avilés. Created captain-general of the Indies fleet by Charles V (1554), he led three journeys to America, and established Spanish colonial rule in Florida.
   St. Augustine, founding of **F** 273

Menes (ME-nese) (Narmer), king of ancient Egypt, united Upper and Lower kingdoms **A** 219; **E** 94

Mengistu Haile Mariam (men-GIS-too HY-lee MA-ree-am) (1937–   ), Ethiopian political leader, b. Ethiopia. It is believed he was born to a family of Galla people and developed a hatred of the Amhara people who dominated the country. He attended military college and became an army officer. He was a member of the military committee that led the overthrow of Emperor Haile Selassie in 1974. In 1977, Mengistu assumed power in Ethiopia as chairman of the Provisional Military Administrative Council. In 1984 he became Secretary General of the newly formed Ethiopian Communist party. **E** 301

Meng-tzu see Mencius
Menhaden (men-HAY-den), fish **F** 214, 221
   fish oil **O** 76
Meninas (may-NI-nas), **Las,** painting by Velázquez
   P 424

Meningitis (men-in-JY-tis), (from Greek *meninx,* meaning
"membrane"), acute inflammation of the membranes
(called meninges) of the brain or spinal cord. Meningitis
can be caused by many types of bacteria and viruses.
Some forms of meningitis are very serious and if left
untreated, can result in blindness, loss of hearing, or
death. Symptoms include headache, vomiting, paralysis,
and coma with fever. Treatment varies according to the
infecting agent; bacterial meningitis can be treated successfully with large doses of antibiotics.

Meniscus, caused by adhesion, *picture* **L** 306
Menken, Adah Bertha, American actress **L** 362
Menkure see Mycerinus
Menninger (MEN-nin-ger), **Karl Augustus,** American
   psychiatrist **K** 188
Mennonites, German religious sect **R** 133
   Manitoba, Canada **M** 81
   Paraguay's Chaco region **P** 62, 64
   settlements in Kansas **K** 178–79
Menomini (men-OM-in-i), Indians of North America
   I 178
   "termination" policy of the United States
    government **I** 200
Menopause, in women **M** 222
Menora, traditional Malay drama **M** 55
Menorah (men-OR-ah), candleholder used for Hanukkah
   H 28, 29; **J** 145, 146a
Menorca see Minorca Island
Menotti (men-OT-ti), **Gian-Carlo,** Italian-born American
   composer **M** 558, 559; **O** 139
   Amahl and the Night Visitors, opera **O** 139–40
Menstruation, in human reproduction **M** 221–22;
   R 180
Mensuration see Measurement
Mental cruelty **D** 230
Mental health **M** 223–25; **H** 77
   adolescence and changes affecting feelings and
    emotions **A** 22–24
   astronauts in space exploration and travel **S** 341
   child abuse **C** 222
   divorce, problems involving **D** 231
   See also Mental illness
Mental illness **M** 225–28
   child abuse **C** 222
   disabled people **D** 176, 177
   diseases **D** 186
   Dix, Dorothea, improves conditions for the insane
    D 231
   Freud's theories **F** 469–70
   hypnosis **H** 318
   hysteria of witchcraft **W** 209
   nursing the emotionally disturbed **N** 410
   Pinel, Philippe, first in field of psychiatry **M** 206
   psychology and mental illness **P** 488
   reserpine, drug from medicinal plant **P** 313
Mental retardation see Retardation, mental
Mental suggestion **H** 316–18
Mental tests see Tests and testing

Menthol, colorless crystalline substance that has the refreshing smell and taste of mint. Chemically an alcohol, it
is soluble in alcohol, ether, chloroform, and basic oils.
Obtained from peppermint oil, it can also be prepared syn-

thetically. Menthol is used in making medicine, perfume,
candy, cigarettes, and liqueurs.

Mentuhotep II (men-tu-HO-tep), king of ancient Egypt
   E 98, 99

Menudo, a Puerto Rican pop music group composed of
five boys who sing in Spanish and English. The name
means "small change" in Spanish. The boys, who also
dance but play no instruments, have toured the United
States, Latin America, and several European countries.
Their records are top sellers, and they have a regular U.S.
television program. Menudo started in 1977 in San Juan,
Puerto Rico, with five cousins (two sets of brothers) who
enjoyed singing together. Since then, the composition of
the group has changed each year, for members must leave
before their 16th birthday.

Menuhin, Yehudi (MEN-you-in, yeh-HOO-dee) (1916–
   ), American violinist, b. New York City, N.Y. Menuhin gave his first public performance at the age of 7 and
made his Carnegie Hall debut at the age of 10. He continued to enjoy great success as a soloist, appearing in
concerts throughout the world. During World War II, he
gave hundreds of concerts for the Allied armed forces and
later performed to raise money to aid victims of the war. In
1963 he opened a school in England for musically gifted
children. Menuhin is a popular recording artist and has
appeared on television as host of a series of programs
based on his book *The Music of Man* (1979). His autobiography is entitled *Unfinished Journey* (1977).

Menus
   camp meals **C** 44–45
   dinner for four **R** 114
   outdoor cooking and picnics **O** 247–48
   party refreshments **P** 91, 93
   restaurants **R** 187
   table settings, rules for **T** 2–3

Menzies, Sir Robert Gordon (1894–1978), Australian
statesman, b. Jeparit. He was attorney general of Australia
(1934–39) and then prime minister and leader of the
United Australian Party (1939–41). He again led the
United Australian Party, at that time the opposition
(1943–49), and was prime minister (1949–66).

Meo (Hmong), a people of Asia **L** 41
Mephistopheles (meph-is-TOPH-el-ese), devil in Faust
   legends **F** 72
Merapi (mer-op-i), volcano, Japan **V** 384
Mercantile law **L** 87

Mercator (mer-CAY-tor), **Gerhardus** (Gerhard Kremer)
(1512–94), Flemish geographer, b. Rupelmonde, Belgium. He invented the Mercator system of map projection,
in which the parallels of latitude and the meridians of longitude intersect at right angles. The name "atlas" was giv-
en to map books because a picture on the cover of his book
of maps (published by his son in 1594) showed the Greek
god Atlas holding up the world.
   maps, history of **M** 97, 98

Mercator projection, of maps **M** 97
Mercedes, Uruguay **U** 238
Merced River, California **Y** 352
Mercenaries, hired soldiers **K** 277
   Hessians, Germans who fought for England in
    Revolutionary War **R** 201, 202, 204

Mercersburg Academy, Pennsylvania
birthplace of James Buchanan, *picture* **B** 418
Merchandising *see* Advertising; Marketing; Sales
Merchant Adventurers, joint-stock company **P** 344
Merchant guilds **G** 401
Merchant marine
ships and shipping **S** 151–57
United States Merchant Marine **U** 182–84
Merchant Marine Safety Program **U** 183
Merchant of Venice, The, play by Shakespeare **S** 136;
picture **S** 130
Merchant ships **S** 157
Mercier (mair-ci-AY), **Philippe,** French painter
The Music Party, painting **E** 269
Mercury, element **E** 153, 160; *chart* **M** 230
acid rain **A** 8
amalgamation **M** 231
barometer **B** 54
fish, concentration in **F** 215, 224, 353
fluorescent lamps and mercury lamps **L** 285
gold extracted from ores by **G** 249
mercury poisoning endangers species **E** 196
superconductivity, property of **H** 88
thermometers **H** 92; **M** 208f; **N** 414; **T** 165
unusual properties as a liquid **L** 307
water pollution **W** 66–67
Mercury, planet **P** 269–70, 271–72
orbit, *diagram* **R** 144
seen from earth both morning and evening **S** 244
space probes **S** 347
Mercury, Roman god **G** 358, 359–60
Mercury, series of manned United States space flights
S 340j
Mercury barometer **B** 54
Mercury-vapor turbines **T** 322
Meredith, George, English novelist and poet **E** 264

Meredith, James Howard (1933–   ), American lawyer, b. Kosciusko, Miss. He was the first black to enroll
(1961) in the University of Mississippi after passage of the
school desegregation bill. He graduated from that school
in 1963, and from Columbia Law School in 1969. He has
been a civil rights leader in New York City and chairman of
National Community Improvement Association, Inc.

Meredith, Sir William Ralph (1840–1923), Canadian jurist, b. Westminster Township, Upper Canada. He was a
member of the Legislative Assembly of Ontario (1872–
94), chief justice of the common pleas division of the High
Court of Justice in Ontario (1894–1912), and chancellor
of the University of Toronto (1900–23).

Merengue (mer-EN-gay), Latin-American dance **L** 74

Merezhkovski (mair-esh-KOF-ski), **Dmitri Sergeevich**
(1865–1941), Russian novelist and critic, b. St. Petersburg (now Leningrad). He is best-known for his triology of
philosophical novels, *Christ and Antichrist,* about Julian
the Apostate, Leonardo da Vinci, and Peter the Great.
Strongly religious (he founded a religion called the New
Road), he opposed the Bolsheviks and was sent to prison
in Siberia (1918). He escaped (1920) and fled to Paris,
where he died during the German occupation.

Merganser, duck **D** 342

Mergenthaler (MAIRG-en-ta-ler), **Ottmar** (1854–99),
American inventor, b. Hachtel, Germany. In 1872 he emigrated to the United States, where he invented the linotype printing machine (1884), first used by the New York

Tribune (1886). The modern machine, based on Mergenthaler's, sets one line at a time.
linotype machines in printing **I** 345; **P** 466i

Mergers and consolidations, businesses **T** 306
newspapers **N** 199–200
Merida (MAY-ri-da), **Carlos,** Guatemalan artist **L** 66
Meridians, of longitude **L** 83
great circles on maps and globes **M** 96
Greenwich meridian **G** 372
International Date Line **I** 314
time **T** 189–91
Mérimée (may-ri-MAY), **Prosper,** French novelist **F** 441
Merina (ma-RI-na), a people of Madagascar **M** 8, 9
Merino (mer-RI-no), breed of sheep **C** 152; *picture*
A 92
Australia **A** 508, 516
finest wool **W** 234, 235
Merisi, Michelangelo *see* Caravaggio, Michelangelo
Merisi da
Merit badges, Boy Scouts **B** 359
Merit system, in civil service **C** 332–33
administration of Chester A. Arthur **A** 440, 441
Merlin, magician in tales of King Arthur **A** 443
Merlons, part of a battlement **C** 131
Mermaids, legendary sea creatures **S** 106
Mermaid's purses *see* Witch's purses

Merman, Ethel (Ethel Agnes Zimmermann) (1909–84),
American musical comedy actress, b. Astoria, N.Y. Often
described as "brassy" and best known for the way she
belted out a song, Ethel Merman was first seen and heard
on Broadway singing "I Got Rhythm" in *Girl Crazy* in
1930. The song made her a star and became her signature
over a 50-year career. She had no formal training in music
and was working as a secretary when composer George
Gershwin hired her for *Girl Crazy.* Triumphs in *Anything
Goes, Annie Get Your Gun, Call Me Madam, Gypsy,* and
other musicals followed. Merman also made 14 movies
and appeared on radio and television.

Merrill, Robert (1919–   ), American opera singer, b.
Brooklyn, N.Y. After winning the Metropolitan Opera's
Auditions of the Air (1945), he made his Metropolitan
Opera debut (1945) and has since become one of its foremost baritones. His extensive activities include concert,
nightclub, radio, and TV performances. He has written an
autobiography, *Once More from the Beginning.*

Merrimack, ironclad ship **C** 340
Merrimack River, Massachusetts and New Hampshire
M 137; **N** 151
Merritt Parkway, Connecticut **C** 508
Merry Mount, early settlement in Massachusetts
P 346
Merry Widow, The, operetta by Franz Lehár **O** 158
Merry Wives of Windsor, The, play by Shakespeare
S 136

Merton, Thomas (Father M. Louis) (1915–68), American
Trappist monk, poet, and religious writer, b. Prades,
France. A convert to Roman Catholicism, he entered the
Trappist monastery near Gethsemane, Ky. (1941).
Through his writings he became a revered religious and
literary figure. Among his writings are *The Seven Storey
Mountain* (1949), a best-selling autobiography; *No Man Is
an Island* (1955); and *Mystics and Zen Masters* (1967).

Merz, Mario, Italian painter **I** 473

Merzbild mit Regenbogen, collage by Kurt Schwitters, *picture* **M** 396b
Mesa (MAY-sa), Arizona **A** 412
Mesabi Range, Minnesota **M** 328–29
Mesas, small, high plateaus **C** 433
Mesa Verde (VER-day), Colorado **C** 433, 440; *picture* **C** 443
Mescal (mesc-AL) (century plant) **I** 194
Mescaline, drug obtained from peyote cactus **C** 5
Meseta (me-SAY-ta), tableland section of Spain **S** 352, 354, 357
Meseta Central, Costa Rica **C** 556, 557
Meshed, Iran **I** 375

Mesmer, Friedrich (Anton Franz) (1734–1815), Austrian physician, b. Weil, Germany. After experimenting with the powers of the magnet for curing illness, he developed a theory of animal magnetism, or mesmerism, the basis for modern-day hypnosis. Mesmer believed he possessed supernatural powers. In 1788 he moved to Paris, where he was denounced as an imposter.
    mesmerism **H** 318

Mesolithic period *see* Middle Stone Age
Mesons, subatomic particles **A** 486
    cosmic rays **C** 554
    nuclear energy **N** 368, 369

Mesopotamia (mes-o-po-TAY-me-a), a historic region in southwestern Asia that included the valleys of the Tigris and the Euphrates rivers. The name comes from Greek words meaning "land between rivers." Mesopotamia has been called the cradle of civilization because, beginning around 3000 B.C., several early city-states and kingdoms developed there. Among the earliest known people of the region were the Sumerians. A Semitic people, the Akkadians, arrived several centuries later, and were succeeded by the Babylonians and Assyrians. Mesopotamia was conquered by the Persians in the 6th century B.C., and later by the Arabs. It formed part of the Ottoman Turkish Empire until World War I, when it came under British control. Today the region is part of Iraq. **I** 378, 383
    ancient art **A** 233–37, 240–43
    ancient civilizations **A** 216, 217–19
    architecture **A** 371
    art as a record **A** 438b
    building construction **B** 435
    calendars **C** 12
    ceramics and mosaics **P** 15
    cities, history of **C** 316–17
    early agriculture **A** 97–98
    early cities **U** 231
    "land between rivers," Tigris and Euphrates **R** 246
    pottery **P** 408
    sculpture **S** 93
    wheel, invention of the **W** 157
    See also Assyria; Babylonia; Sumerians

Mesopotamia, region of Argentina **A** 392, 393
Mesoscaphe (MES-o-scaph), underwater ship **P** 244
Mesosphere, layer of the atmosphere **A** 481; **E** 16–17
Mesozoic (mes-o-ZO-ic) **time,** in geology **E** 24–25; **F** 382, 383, 386–87; *chart* **E** 21
    mammals, origin of **M** 67
    prehistoric animals, development of **P** 433–34
Mesquakie, Indians of North America **I** 361

Mesquites (MES-keets), group of thorny shrubs belonging to the pea family. Mesquite plants are found in the deserts of the southwestern United States and of Mexico. Their pods, rich in sugar, are used as livestock feed. The bark is sometimes used for grilling meat, giving the food a distinctive flavor.

Mesquite Area Indians, of North America **I** 177
Messenger RNA, nucleic acid **V** 370
Messiaen, Olivier, French composer **F** 448
Messiah (mes-SY-ah), oratorio by Handel **C** 284; **G** 183; **H** 21
Messiah, to the Jewish people **J** 84, 140
Messiah War, 1890 **S** 327
Messier (mess-YAY), **Charles,** French astronomer **U** 199
Mestizos (mes-TI-zos), Latin Americans of mixed Indian and European ancestry **L** 48–49
    dances **L** 69
    South America **S** 282
    See also people section of Latin-American countries

Meštrović (MESH-tro-vich), **Ivan** (1883–1962), Yugoslav sculptor, b. Vrpolje. He studied in Vienna, then Paris, where he met and was influenced by Rodin. Among his most famous busts is one of the British conductor Sir Thomas Beecham. Meštrović had a one-man show at the Metropolitan Museum of Art in New York in 1947.
    the arts in Yugoslavia **Y** 355

Metabolic (met-a-BOL-ic) **diseases** **D** 184
Metabolism (met-AB-o-lism), in body chemistry **B** 295
    birds **B** 202
    characteristics of kingdoms of living things **K** 253–54
    life process **L** 210
Metacarpals, bones of the hand **S** 184a
Metacomet, Chief *see* Philip, American Indian chief

Metal fatigue, weakening of metal under exposure to repeated stress. It begins at an imperfection in the metal and shows up as a sharp crack or rift.

Metal foil *see* Foil, metal
Metallic soap **L** 371
    oils and fats **O** 79
Metallogenetic provinces, areas rich in metallic ores **M** 314
Metalloids (semimetals), borderline elements **E** 157; **M** 229
Metallurgy *see* Metals and metallurgy
Metals and metallurgy (MET-al-urge-y) **M** 229–36
    acid rain **A** 8, 9
    alchemy **C** 207
    alloys **A** 168–69
    aluminum **A** 176–77
    bronze and brass **B** 409–10
    building materials **A** 373
    conservation of metals **C** 520
    copper **C** 546
    electric conductors **E** 125, 127–28
    electroplating **E** 149–50
    expansion and contraction of railroad rails, *picture* **H** 92
    fire makes metals **F** 143–44
    Geiger counters, uses, *diagram* **G** 68
    gold **G** 247–49
    hazardous chemical wastes **H** 73
    heat conduction, demonstration of **E** 365
    industrial uses of hydrogen gas **G** 61
    iron and steel **I** 396–407
    lead **L** 94–95
    magnesium **M** 27

Metals and metallurgy (continued)
    metallurgical engineers **E** 205
    mines and mining **M** 314–20
    nitrogen gas, inactivity with metals **G** 59–60
    ores **R** 272–73
    phlogiston, theory of **C** 208
    silver **S** 177–78
    soldering and brazing **S** 249
    tin **T** 195
    tools **T** 215
    uranium **U** 228–29
    water pollution **W** 66–67
    welding **W** 118
    zinc **Z** 370
    See also Alloys; Mineralogy; Precious metals;
       Soldering; and names of metals
Metalworking, giving metal a shape **M** 232–35
    bronze and brass **B** 409–10
    coppersmithing **C** 546
    decorative arts **D** 70, 72, 73–74, 75, 76
    dies and molds **D** 156–57
    electroplating **E** 149–50
    goldsmithing **G** 247–49
    iron and steel **I** 396–407
    Islamic art **I** 422
    jewelry **J** 92–101
    Korean art **K** 297
    prehistoric people **P** 441–42
    soldering and brazing **S** 249
    tinsmithing **T** 195
    welding **W** 118
    wire sculpture **W** 190b, 191
    wrought iron **I** 405
Metamorphic (met-a-MORPH-ic) **rock** **R** 263, 268–70
    geology, history of **G** 118
    mountain building **M** 499
Metamorphoses (met-a-MORPH-o-sese), mythological
    narrative poem by Ovid **L** 80; **O** 267
Metamorphosis **M** 237–38
    butterflies and moths **B** 471–72
    eggs that produce larvae **E** 89
    frogs, toads, and other amphibians **F** 470–78
    how insects develop **I** 264–65
    jellyfishes and other coelenterates **J** 73
Metaphors, figures of speech **F** 118
    slang **S** 194
    use in poetry **P** 354
Metaphysical (met-a-PHIS-ic-al) **poets**, in English
    literature **E** 254–55
Metaphysics, branch of philosophy **P** 192
Metastases (met-AST-as-ese), cancer growths **C** 90;
    D 185
Metastasio, Pietro, Italian poet **I** 479
Metatarsals, bones of the foot **S** 184a
Metaurus (me-TAUR-us), **Battle of**, 207 B.C. **B** 101

Metchnikoff (METCH-ni-koff), **Élie** (Ilya Illich Mechnikov)
(1845–1916), Russian bacteriologist, b. Ivanovka. He
discovered the basis for the theory of immunity—the ability of white blood cells to fight disease by destroying bacteria. He shared the Nobel prize for physiology and medicine (1908) with Paul Ehrlich.

Meteor Crater, in Arizona **C** 452; *picture* **C** 451
Meteorites *see* Meteors and meteorites
Meteorological satellites *see* Weather satellites
Meteorologists, scientists who study the weather **W** 77
Meteorology (me-te-or-OL-ogy), study of weather
    W 77–95
    acid rain **A** 7–9

    atmosphere **A** 479–82
    climate **C** 361–66
    clouds **C** 382–85
    earth science **E** 3
    fog and smog **F** 288–89
    geology and other earth sciences **G** 109
    hurricanes and tornadoes **H** 292–99
    jet streams **J** 91
    precipitation **R** 95
    thunder and lightning **T** 170–73
    weather satellites **S** 55; **W** 87
    winds and weather **W** 184–87
Meteors and meteorites **M** 449, 450–52
    moon, effect on its surface **M** 449, 450
    radar astronomy studies **R** 76
    solar system **S** 246
    trails taken for flying saucers, *picture* **F** 286
Meter, in music **M** 539–40, 541
Meter, in poetry **P** 353–54
Meter, measure of length **W** 110–11
Metered postage **P** 399
Meter per second, measure of speed **W** 116
Meter per second per second, measure of acceleration
    W 117
Meters, electric and gas, *diagrams* **P** 511
Methadone, synthetic narcotic drug **N** 13, 15
Methane (METH-ane), gas **G** 59
    greenhouse effect **C** 366
    natural gas **N** 58, 60
    Neptune's atmosphere **N** 113
    produced by bacteria **B** 12
Methaqualone *see* Quaaludes
Methodist Church **C** 294
    Reformation in England **R** 133
    Wesley, John **W** 123
Methodius, Saint *see* Cyril and Methodius, Saints

Methuselah (me-THU-ze-lah) ("man of the dart"), lon-
gest-living person in the Bible. Son of Enoch, father of
Lamech, and grandfather of Noah, he is said to have lived
969 years (Genesis).

Methyl (METH-il) (wood) **alcohol** **A** 147
    distillation **D** 218
    made from synthesis gas **G** 61

Methyl isocyanate, a chemical in the isocyanate group that
is used to make pesticides. Isocyanates are also used to
manufacture paints, varnishes, and adhesives. Methyl isocyanate is a colorless liquid that becomes a gas at 39.1°C
(102.4°F). It is highly flammable and very poisonous,
even in small quantities. It is easily absorbed through the
skin and lungs and produces symptoms that may include
burning eyes and throat, swollen tissue, skin burns, fluid-
filled lungs, or death. Methyl isocyanate was the cause of
more than 2,500 deaths when it leaked from a pesticide-
manufacturing plant in Bhopal, India, in 1984.

Métis (may-TECE) (French for "half-caste"), Canadians of
mixed Indian and European ancestry, often descended
from French fur trappers. Many Métis settled in Red River
in the Canadian Northwest after 1818. When the Northwest Territories were annexed to Canada (1869), the
threat to the Métis' landholdings, their way of life, and
their survival as a group led to the Red River Insurrection
(1869) and the Northwest Rebellion (1885). The Métis'
defeat brought about their disintegration as a separate
group. **C** 75
    Prairie Provinces **M** 83, 86; **S** 45, 51

Metonymy (me-TON-imy), figure of speech **F** 119
Metric system, of measures **W** 109–17
   international trade problems **I** 328
   metric conversion, *tables* **W** 112, 113
Metric ton, unit of weight **W** 114
Metro Manila, Philippines **M** 79; **P** 187
Metronome, device for keeping time **M** 541; **O** 190

Metropolitan (met-ro-POL-it-an) **area,** densely populated area, including a large city (or cities) and the surrounding areas, dependent on the city for livelihood and amusement. According to the U.S. Census Bureau, which specifies that the core city must have a population of at least 50,000, there were more than 300 metropolitan areas in the United States in 1980.
   the Standard Metropolitan Statistical Area **U** 98

Metropolitan Museum of Art, New York City **M** 239–239a
Metropolitan Opera House, Lincoln Center for the Performing Arts, New York City **L** 296; *picture* **O** 130
Metropolitan police **P** 366
Metropolitan Toronto Library, Ontario, Canada, *picture* **L** 193

Metternich (MET-ter-nick), **Prince Klemens Wenzel Nepomulk Lothar von** (1773–1859), Austrian statesman, b. Coblenz, Germany. As minister of foreign affairs (1809–48), he made Austria a first-rank European power. He was a leading figure at the Congress of Vienna (1814–15), and he also did much to bring about the Holy Alliance, formed by Austria, Russia, and Prussia to suppress revolutionary movements. However, Metternich gradually lost power as revolutionary forces grew, and he was forced to flee Austria in 1848.
   Austria, history of **A** 525

Metzenbaum, Howard Morton (1917–   ), United States senator from Ohio, Democrat, b. Cleveland. He was appointed to the Senate in January, 1974—to fill the vacancy created by the resignation of Senator William B. Saxbe—and served until December, 1974. Metzenbaum was elected to the Senate in 1976 and re-elected in 1982. He previously served in the Ohio House of Representatives (1943–46) and the Ohio Senate (1947–50). A business executive, Metzenbaum was chairman of the board of several corporations.

Meuse River, Europe **R** 242
Mev, unit of energy in nuclear physics *see* Electron volt
Mexican Americans, ethnic group **H** 132–33
   immigration **I** 100
Mexican hairless, toy dog **D** 257
Mexican jumping beans *see* Jumping beans
Mexican Liberty Bell **M** 252
Mexican War, 1846–48 **M** 239a–239b, 249
   boundary changes **T** 112
   California **C** 18, 33
   Carson, Kit **C** 121
   dead and veterans buried in Mexico City National Cemetery **N** 26
   Grant, Ulysses S. **G** 294
   Perry, Matthew C. **P** 156
   Pierce, Franklin **P** 246
   Polk's administration **P** 377
   Taylor, Zachary **T** 35
   territory gained and the slavery question **C** 477
   United States Marine Corps campaigns **U** 177
   United States Navy **U** 186

Mexican yam, plant from which cortisone can be extracted **P** 313; *picture* **P** 312
Mexico **M** 240–51
   Aztec civilization **I** 195, 197
   Chichén Itzá, *picture* **I** 153
   Christmas customs **C** 301
   climate **N** 291
   corn meal dishes **C** 551
   Cortes, Hernando **C** 551
   costume, traditional, *picture* **C** 373
   dances **D** 30
   education **E** 80
   emigration to the United States **I** 100
   favorite foods **F** 338–39; *picture* **F** 331
   flag, *picture* **F** 237
   immigration to the United States **H** 132–33
   Indian art **I** 153–54
   Indian folk dances **L** 69; *picture* **L** 51
   Juárez, Benito **J** 138
   Lake Chapala **L** 29
   Latin-American art **L** 67
   life in Latin America **L** 47–61
   limes, leading producer and exporter of **L** 137
   Mesquite Area Indians **I** 177
   Mexican War **M** 239a–239b
   Mexico City **M** 252–53
   national anthem **N** 22
   Pan-American Highway **P** 50
   patriotic songs **N** 27
   Texas, history of **T** 137–38
   Tula, *picture* **I** 154
Mexico, Gulf of **A** 113, 115
   embayment of the Mississippi River **M** 365
   mined for minerals dissolved in the water **T** 129
   Texas shoreline **T** 125
Mexico, National Autonomous University of **M** 242, 253
Mexico City, capital of Mexico **M** 241, 252–53; *pictures* **C** 321, **L** 47
   Mexican War **M** 239b
   oil refinery, *picture* **N** 294
   Olympic Games, 1968 **O** 112–13
   Paseo de la Reforma, *picture* **N** 297
   Plaza of Three Cultures, *picture* **M** 251

Meyerbeer (MY-er-bare), **Giacomo** (Jakob Liebmann Beer) (1791–1864), German opera composer, b. Berlin. He is remembered chiefly for his elaborate grand operas, which include *Robert le Diable, Les Huguenots, Le Prophète,* and *L'Africaine.* He also wrote songs, marches, and other works. His treatment of opera as a stage spectacle influenced Richard Wagner.
   foreign-born composers in France **F** 445
   romanticism in music **R** 310

Meyerson, Goldie Mabovitz *see* Meir, Golda
Mez, Libyan festival **L** 202
Mezuzah (mez-UZ-ah), Jewish religious symbol **J** 146a–146b
Mezzanine, first level above orchestra in theaters **T** 156
Mezzetin (mez-za-TAN), painting by Watteau **F** 424
Mezzo-soprano (met-zo-so-PRAN-o), female voice **C** 283; **V** 375
Mezzotint (MET-zo-tint), printmaking technique **G** 307
MHD generators *see* Magnetohydrodynamic generators
MHz *see* Megahertz
Miacis (MY-a-cis), prehistoric ancestor of carnivores **D** 239

Miami (my-AM-i), Florida   **M** 254; **F** 265, 270
　　Cuban exile population   **H** 134
Miami and Erie Canal, Ohio   **O** 66
Miami Beach, Florida   **M** 254; *picture* **F** 271
Miami University, Oxford, Ohio   **O** 68

Miantonomo (mi-an-to-NO-mo) (?–1643), Narragansett Indian chief. Cleared in Boston of charges of hostility against the English (1636), he aided the colonists in the Pequot War (1637). He concluded a peace pact with the English and Mohegan chief Uncas (1638), and deeded island of Rhode Island to William Coddington (1638). In Narragansett war with Mohegans (1643) he was captured by Uncas and delivered to hostile English officials, who tried him and returned him to Uncas for execution.

Miasmas, gases that were thought to cause diseases
　　S 32
Mica (MY-ca), mineral
　　crystals, *picture* **R** 265
　　mica schist, rock, *picture* **R** 268
Micah (MY-cah), book of Bible, Old Testament   **B** 155
Micah, Hebrew prophet   **J** 104
Mice, rodents   **R** 278–79
　　forelimb, *picture* **F** 80
　　household pests   **H** 263–64
　　"Lion and the Mouse, The," fable by Aesop   **F** 4
　　memory testing, *picture* **A** 283
　　pets   **P** 178
　　tracks, *picture* **A** 271

Michael (from Hebrew, meaning "who is like God"), in the Bible, an archangel who battled Satan and other evil angels. He fought with the devil over Moses' body (Jude 9) and defended the Israelites against the spirit princes of Greece and Persia (Daniel 10:13, 20–21).

Michael (Mihai), king of Rumania   **R** 360
Michaux (mi-SHO), **Ernest,** French inventor of an early bicycle   **B** 173
Michelangelo (my-kel-AN-gel-o), Italian artist   **M** 255–57
　　art of the artist   **A** 438f
　　Creation of Adam, painting   **M** 255
　　David, statue, *pictures* **I** 468, **S** 100
　　dome of St. Peter's   **A** 378
　　drawing, history of   **D** 315
　　Italian art and architecture   **I** 468, 469
　　Last Judgment, The **V** 282; *picture* **M** 256
　　lyric poetry   **I** 478
　　Madonna and Child, sculpture   **R** 168
　　monumental style of painting   **P** 21
　　Moses, statue   **S** 100
　　paintings of prophets   **B** 158
　　Pietà, sculpture   **F** 17; **V** 282; *picture* **M** 257
　　Raphael influenced by Michelangelo   **R** 106
　　red chalk sketches, *picture* **D** 313
　　Renaissance, golden age of the arts   **R** 162
　　Renaissance art and architecture   **R** 167, 169
　　sculpture, place in the history of   **S** 100–01
　　Sistine Chapel ceiling   **V** 282
Michelino, Domenico di, Italian painter
　　Dante and His Book, picture **I** 475

Michelozzo (mi-kel-OTZ-so) **de Bartolommeo** (1396–1472), Italian architect and sculptor, b. Florence. Associated with Ghiberti and Donatello in the development of Renaissance art, Michelozzo is chiefly remembered for his masterpiece, the Medici Palace in Florence.
　　Medici Palace, Florence   **I** 465; *picture* **I** 462

Michelson (MY-kel-son), **Albert Abraham** (1852–1931), American physicist, b. Strelno, Prussia. Michelson made accurate measurements of the speed of light and developed a number of important optical devices, among them the interferometer. With this device he and E. W. Morley conducted a famous experiment (first done in 1881) to determine the earth's speed through the "ether," which was thought to fill an "absolute" space. Their work led to the abandonment of these concepts and influenced the development of the theory of relativity. Michelson received the 1907 Nobel prize in physics.
　　speed of light and relativity   **L** 264–65; **R** 140–41

Michelson-Morley experiment, on the ether concept
　　R 140–41

Michener, James Albert (1907–   ), American novelist, b. New York, N.Y. His books include the short story collection *Tales of the South Pacific,* which received the Pulitzer prize (1948) and was adapted to the stage as *South Pacific.* His many best-selling novels include *The Bridges at Toko-Ri* (1953), *Sayonara* (1954), *Hawaii,* (1959), *The Source* (1965), *Centennial* (1974), *The Covenant* (1980), *Space* (1982), *Poland* (1983), and *Texas* (1985). Several of these have been made into films. Among his works of nonfiction are *Kent State: What Happened and Why* (1971) and *James A. Michener's U.S.A.* (1981).

Michener, Roland (Daniel Roland Michener) (1900–   ), Canadian statesman, b. Lacombe, Alberta. Michener received an Ontario law degree in 1924. He was elected to the Ontario legislature (1945–48) and was a member of the Canadian Parliament (1953–62), where he was Speaker of the House of Commons from 1957 to 1962. He later served as Canada's High Commissioner to India (1964–65) and as ambassador to Nepal (1965–67). In 1967 he was appointed governor-general of Canada, a post he held until his retirement in 1974.

Michigan (MISH-i-gan)   **M** 258–73
　　Detroit   **D** 142–43
　　places of interest in black history   **B** 250d
Michigan, Lake, one of Great Lakes   **G** 328; **I** 73
　　Chicago located on   **C** 218; *picture* **C** 220
　　discovered by Jean Nicolet   **N** 250
　　Indiana   **I** 139, 141
Michigan, University of **M** 267
Michigan City, Indiana   **I** 149
Michigan Road, Indiana   **I** 143
Michigan State University, East Lansing   **M** 267

Mickelson, George S. (1941–   ), governor of South Dakota, Republican, b. Mobridge. He was elected governor in 1986. He served as a state representative (1975–80) and was speaker of the House (1979–80). He was Brookings County states attorney (1970–74) and assistant attorney general (1968–70). He joined the U.S. Army (1965–67) and served in Vietnam.

Mickey Mouse, cartoon character   **A** 297; **D** 215
Mickey Mouse Club, The, television program, *picture* **D** 216
Micmac, Indians of North America   **I** 171–72
　　Nova Scotia   **N** 344g
　　Prince Edward Island   **P** 460, 461
Micombero, Michel, Burundi president   **B** 466
Microbes (MY-crobes) (micro-organisms)   **G** 89–91;
　　M 274–75
　　antibiotics   **A** 310, 312, 315; *pictures* **A** 314

bacteria **B** 10–12
diseases caused by **D** 181–83
fermentation **F** 91
food spoilage **F** 351–52
food storage **F** 341
Pasteur's work with wine and milk **P** 100
smallest forms of plant and animal life **A** 265
soils, countless numbers in **S** 232
viruses **V** 361–370a
Microbiology **M** 274–82
bacteria **B** 10–12
biological research in the 20th century **B** 195–96
dyes, use of **D** 368
food chains **L** 241
Koch, Robert **K** 291
Pasteur's work **P** 99–100
plankton **P** 279–81
viruses **V** 361–370a

Microchemistry, analysis of very tiny amounts of chemical substances by means of special techniques and equipment. Microchemical methods were first developed by Austrian chemist Friedrich Emich.

Microchip, or chip, a tiny silicon wafer that contains thousands of miniaturized circuits. These chips are built into computers, telephones, video sets, and other electronic equipment. Chips replaced vacuum tubes and hand-soldered wires as a way of creating electrical circuits. **C** 481, 482, 490; **E** 142e
credit cards **C** 592
electronic watches **W** 44
video games **V** 332b

Microcomputer **C** 478, 483; **O** 54
libraries' use of **L** 174
Microfiches (MY-cro-fi-shes), information storage technique **L** 173, 199–200; **O** 58
Microfilm, for information storage **O** 58
libraries **L** 173, 199–200
Micrographics, miniaturized storage of information **O** 58
Microliths, flint tools **P** 440
Micrometeoroids (my-cro-ME-te-or-oids), very small particles moving through space **S** 341

Micrometer (my-KROM-uht-er), an instrument designed for making very fine measurements, on the order of 0.025 mm (1/1000 in). A micrometer caliper is used in manufacturing to measure the thickness of objects. Micrometers are also used in microscopes and telescopes to measure the diameters of images.

Micronesia (my-cro-NE-sia), Pacific islands **P** 4, 5
art **P** 10
Micronesia, Federated States of, Pacific Ocean **P** 6, 7; **T** 115; **U** 100
Ponape **P** 8
Truk **P** 8
Yap **P** 9
Micronesians, Pacific Islanders **P** 4
Micronutrients see Trace elements
Micro-organisms (my-cro-OR-gan-isms) see Microbes
Microphones, used in transmitting sound **T** 56
hi-fi recording process **H** 121
phonograph recording **P** 195
radio broadcasting **R** 53, 61
stereo recording **H** 122, 123
Microphotography **O** 58

Microprocessor, computer processor on a single chip **C** 481, 483, 486
Microscopes **M** 283–88
cytology, use in **B** 195–96
development of, as aid to biologists **B** 190
Galileo perfected compound microscope **G** 6
How much magnification can a microscope give? **M** 283
Leeuwenhoek's new world **L** 127; **M** 274
lenses **L** 146–47
medicine, early uses in **M** 206
optical instruments **O** 169–70
photomicrography **P** 216
scanning electron microscopes, *picture* **C** 576
science, advances in **S** 69
Microscopy, clinical see Clinical microscopy
Microsurgery, operations performed under a microscope **M** 208c
disabled, rehabilitation of the **D** 177

Microwave oven, an oven that cooks food by way of radio waves rather than direct heat. The waves are produced by an electronic vacuum tube. They penetrate the food and make its molecules vibrate. Friction between the vibrating molecules produces the heat that cooks the food. Microwave ovens cook food much more quickly than conventional ovens. China, glass, or paper dishes are used in these ovens because the waves pass through these materials without heating them. The waves cannot penetrate metal, so metal pans cannot be used. **C** 534

Microwave radio relay systems, *picture* **T** 59
carrier telephony **T** 60
telegraph **T** 54
Microwaves
electronic communication **E** 142e
masers **L** 46c
radar's use of electric waves **L** 269
television **T** 67

Midas (MY-das), in Greek mythology, king of Phrygia and son of Gordius and Cybele. In return for Midas' kindness to Dionysus' teacher Silenus, Dionysus granted Midas his request that all he touched would turn to gold. When even his food became gold, he implored Dionysus for relief and was directed to bathe in river Pactolus, which has since had golden sands.

Mid-Atlantic Ridge, underwater mountains in the Atlantic Ocean **A** 478; **E** 14; **M** 505; **O** 21
Middens see Kitchen middens
Middle Ages **M** 289–95
agriculture **A** 98
alchemy and the beginnings of the chemical industry **C** 196
architecture see Middle Ages, architecture of the
armor **A** 433–34
art see Middle Ages, art of the
beer and brewing **B** 116
castles **F** 375
Charlemagne **C** 188–89
Christianity, history of **C** 290–91
cities **C** 317–19; **U** 232
citizenship idea replaced by feudal system **C** 327
clocks **C** 369
clothing, history of **C** 375–76
court jesters **J** 125
craft-guild labor system **G** 401–03
Crusades **C** 586–88
dance manias **D** 24

Middle America, geographical term referring to Central America, Mexico, and sometimes the Caribbean islands.

Middle Atlantic States, a group of three states on the eastern coast of the United States. They are situated between New England and the southern coastal states. All three Middle Atlantic states—New York, New Jersey, and Pennsylvania—have outlets to the Atlantic Ocean. Their harbors have made this region one of the major shipping centers of the United States. The three states are also leaders in manufacturing, industry, and commerce. Their major cities—New York and Philadelphia—are world centers of culture and education.

Middleton, Arthur (1742–87), American Revolutionary war leader, b. near Charleston, S.C. He served in the South Carolina House of Assembly (1764–68, 1772). Engaging in revolutionary activity (from 1772), he helped formulate the South Carolina constitution (1776), served in the Continental Congress (1776–78, 1781–83), and signed the Declaration of Independence (1776).

Middleton, Thomas (1570?–1627), English dramatist, b. probably London. He wrote plays with several partners. *The Changeling* (written with William Rowley) is one of the most powerful tragedies of the early 17th century.

Midianites (MID-ian-ites), in the Old Testament, a nomadic people who lived in the northwestern Arabian desert, east of the Gulf of Aqaba. They were the descendants of Midian, a son of Abraham and Keturah. Joseph was taken to Egypt by Midianite traders, and Moses married Zipporah, a daughter of Midianite leader Jethro. During the rule of the Judges, Israel was invaded by Midianites, who were finally expelled by Gideon (Judges 6–8).

Mid-latitudes (temperate zones) **Z** 372–73
    prairies **P** 426–29
Midnight, start of a new day **T** 188
Midnight Special, railroad song **F** 319
Midnight Sun, Land of the see Land of the Midnight
    Sun
Mid-oceanic ridges, of mountains **G** 114–15, 116
Mid-ocean rifts **E** 15
Midrash, body of Jewish literature **H** 99; **J** 139, 143
Midribs, of leaves **L** 114
Midshipmen, at U.S. Naval Academy **U** 191
Midsummer Night's Dream, A, play by Shakespeare
    M 308; **S** 132
    outline of the plot **S** 136
Midway, amusement area of fairs **F** 15
Midway, Battle of, 1942 **W** 294–95
Midway, islands in the Pacific Ocean **H** 50; **P** 7
    occupied by United States **T** 113
    rails are extinct birds **B** 231

Midwest, or **Middle West,** a geographic region of the United States, comprising twelve states: Ohio, Indiana, Illinois, Michigan, Wisconsin, Missouri, Iowa, Minnesota, Kansas, Nebraska, South Dakota, and North Dakota. The Midwest is a largely flat, fertile lowland that constitutes one of the most productive agricultural areas of the world. It is also rich in minerals and contains some of the country's major industrial centers.

Midwives, nurse **N** 409

Mies van der Rohe (ME-es von d'RO-e), **Ludwig** (1886–1969), American architect, b. Aachen, Germany. Last director of the Bauhaus, he closed the German art school in 1933 because of Nazi pressure. He went to the United States in 1937 and became a citizen in 1944. He was tremendously influential in the development of modern skyscraper architecture. His most famous building is New York's Seagram Building (1958), which he designed with his student Philip Johnson.
    architecture in the 20th century **A** 383, 385
    Barcelona chair, *picture* **D** 78
    international style **G** 171
    modern furniture **F** 510
    Seagram Building, *picture* **A** 382
    United States, architecture of the **U** 125

Mieszko I (mi-ESH-ko), Polish ruler **P** 361

Mifflin, Thomas (1744–1800), American Revolutionary leader, b. Philadelphia, Pa. A radical political leader, he sat in the Pennsylvania provincial assembly (1772–76) and in the Continental Congress (1774–76, 1782–84), serving as its president from 1783 to 1784. The quartermaster general of American forces (1775–78), attaining the rank of major general (1777), he was implicated in a plot to supplant Washington with Horatio Gates but denied involvement and resigned from the Army (1779). He was the first governor of Pennsylvania (1790–99).

Mighty Fortress, A, hymn, words and music **H** 311

Mighty Handful, Russian group of musicians **U** 62a

Migraine (MY-graine) (from Greek *hemikrania,* "half cranium"), severe recurrent head pain, usually on one side of the head. An attack of migraine is often preceded by blurring of the vision and an impression of flashing lights, and it may be accompanied by nausea and vomiting. During a migraine attack, the arteries leading to the brain first narrow, then swell, causing a disturbance in blood flow. An attack may last minutes or days. The cause of migraine is unknown, though certain drugs can be used to reduce the pain. Migraine tends to run in families, and attacks may be brought on by certain foods, such as cheese, chocolate, or red wine.

Migrant farm workers
    child labor **C** 227
    fruit harvesting **F** 484
    Mexican Americans **H** 133
    nursery school in a trailer serves workers' children,
        picture **K** 243
Migrant Mother, Nipomo, California, photograph by
    Dorothea Lange, *picture* **P** 206
Migrants, people who continually travel from one place
    to another **I** 98
Migration, of animals see Homing and migration
Migration, of people **P** 385
    Indians of North America **I** 98, 162–63
    overland trails, United States **O** 251–67
    pioneer "movers" to western United States **P** 252
    refugees **R** 137–38
    See also Immigration
Migratory agriculture **J** 153–54
    Burma **B** 461
    milpa practices in Zaïre **Z** 366a
    rain forest **R** 100
    Southeast Asia **S** 332
    world distribution of economic activities, *diagram*
        W 267

Mihajlović (mi-HY-lo-vich), **Draža** (1893?–1946), Yugoslav general, b. Ivanitza, Shumadya, Serbia. During World War II he organized (1941) the Chetniks to fight against German and Italian armies of occupation and was appointed (1942) minister of war and head of the army by the exiled Yugoslav Government. The Chetniks and Tito's Partisans, a more active resistance force, were rivals. Helped by the Allies, Tito's forces gained control and arrested (1946) Mihajlović. Accused of collaborating with the enemy, he was tried, convicted, and executed in Belgrade.
    opposed Tito **T** 199
    Yugoslavia, history of **Y** 358

Mikado (mi-KA-do), **The,** operetta by Gilbert and
    Sullivan **G** 210; *picture* **G** 211

Mikan (MY-kan), **George Lawrence** (1924–   ), American basketball player, b. Joliet, Ill. As a student at De Paul University (1941–46) the 6 ft 9 in (206 cm) tall athlete was considered the best college basketball player in the country. He played professional basketball (1946–54) and was on six championship teams, maintaining a per game average of 22.6 points. An Associated Press poll (1950) voted him the greatest basketball player of the first half of the 20th century, and he was one of the first players elected to the Basketball Hall of Fame (1960).

Mikhalkov (mi-HALL-koff), **Sergey,** Russian poet **N** 19

Mikoyan (mik-o-YAN), **Anastas Ivanovich** (1895–1978), Soviet administrator, b. Sanain, Armenia. He joined the Communist Party in 1915, fought in the Russian civil war (1917–20), and later served on the Central Committee of the Communist Party. He held several important offices, including minister of foreign trade (1946–49) and chairman of the Presidium of the Supreme Soviet (1964–65), before retiring in 1974.

Mikulski, Barbara A. (1936–   ), United States senator from Maryland, Democrat, b. Baltimore. She was elected to the Senate in 1986, the first woman to be elected to this office from Maryland. Previously, she served five consecutive terms in the U.S. House of Representatives (1977–86), where she was the first woman appointed to serve on the Interstate and Foreign Commerce Committee. She was also a founding member of the Congressional Women's Caucus. She served on the Baltimore City Council (1971–76) and was a social worker and community organizer.

Mikvah, Jewish ritual bath **J** 146a
Milan (mi-LON), **Edict of,** A.D. 313 **R** 289, 308
Milan, Italy **I** 450; *picture* **I** 449
   Lambretta factory, *picture* **I** 453
   Renaissance, growth of city states **R** 157
Milbank Papyrus, Egyptian scroll, *picture* **B** 318
Mildew, fungi **F** 498
Mile, measure of length **W** 112, 115
   nautical mile **W** 115
Mile-High City, nickname for Denver, Colorado **D** 116
Miles, Miska, American author **C** 238

Miles, Nelson Appleton (1839–1925), American army officer, b. near Westminster, Mass. After leading successful campaigns against Indian tribes in the West and receiving Medal of Honor (1892) for his services in the Civil War he was appointed (1895) commander in chief of United States Army. He organized an expedition to Cuba during Spanish-American War, dictated terms of the Spanish surrender, and led expedition to Puerto Rico. His several books include *Serving the Republic.*
   Chief Joseph and General Miles **I** 67

Milford Haven, port, Wales **W** 4
Milford Sound, New Zealand, *picture* **N** 237

Milhaud (mi-YO), **Darius** (1892–1974), French composer, b. Aix-en-Provence. After 1940 he taught and conducted in both the United States and France. With French playwright Paul Claudel he wrote the opera *Christophe Colomb* and operas from Claudel's adaptation of the Aeschylus trilogy *Oresteia.* A versatile composer, known as one of Les Six, a group of French composers, his other works include ballets, symphonies, chamber works, piano, and vocal music. **F** 447

Milhous, Katherine (1894–1977), American author and illustrator of children's books, b. Philadelphia, Pa. She served as staff artist on the Philadelphia *Record* (1925–29). Her travels through the Pennsylvania Dutch country and in Europe and South America furnished material for many of her drawings and books, including *Lovina, The First Christmas Crib,* and *Through These Arches, The Story of Independence Hall.* Her book *The Egg Tree* was awarded the Caldecott medal in 1951.

Military Airlift Command **U** 162
Military alliances, in international relations **I** 321; **U** 139

Military engineering **E** 204
Military intelligence, spy networks **S** 389–90
   aerial photography **P** 217
   balloons in war **B** 32
   kites, spy carrying **K** 267
   military satellites **S** 56
Military Order of Foreign Wars of United States *see* Foreign Wars of United States, Military Order of
Military parks, national *see* National military parks
Military service
   draft, or conscription **D** 291–92
   feudalism **F** 100
   military etiquette **E** 303a
   Sparta **A** 228–29
   United States Air Force **U** 159
   United States Army **U** 166–75
   United States Marine Corps **U** 176–82
   United States Navy **U** 184–93
Military Traffic Management Command **U** 174
Militia (mil-ISH-a), local army **D** 291
   forerunner of Canadian Armed Forces **C** 80
   National Guard **N** 41
   War of 1812 **W** 10
Milk **M** 309–10
   baby's food **B** 3
   butter from milk of different animals **B** 470
   care of, on dairy cattle farms **C** 149
   cheese from milk of different animals **C** 195
   condensed milk used in candy making **C** 96
   dairying and dairy products **D** 3–13
   different mammals milked in different parts of the world **F** 332
   food taboos **F** 335
   goat's milk **C** 152
   mammals **M** 65
   nutrition **N** 417
   pasteurization **D** 204, 212
   Pasteur's experiments **P** 100
   primates **M** 418
   processing **D** 9–10
   uses in cooking **C** 534
   vitamin D fortified milk **V** 371
Milk bottle **B** 346
Milk chocolate **C** 281
Milk goats **C** 150
Milking, of dairy cattle **D** 7–8
Milking parlors, for dairy cattle **D** 78
Milking Shorthorn, breed of dual-purpose cattle **C** 149; *picture* **D** 4
Milk of magnesia, laxative **M** 27
Milk River, Montana, Alberta **A** 146c; *picture* **A** 146b
Milk sickness **P** 323
Milk snake, *picture* **S** 205
Milkweed, plant
   controls migration of butterflies **B** 474
Milky Way, galaxy **U** 196–98; *pictures* **U** 196, 197, 198
   astronomy, history of **A** 476–77
   constellations **C** 525
   quasars and pulsars **Q** 7–8
   radio astronomy explores **R** 75–76

Mill, John Stuart (1806–73), English philosopher, b. London. He advocated utilitarianism—a philosophy of "the greatest good for the greatest number"—and wrote on political and economic reform, the rights of women, and scientific methods. Mill was director of the East India Company and was elected to Parliament in 1865. His books include *On Liberty, A System of Logic,* and *Princi-*

ples of Political Economy.   **E** 262
   arguments for civil rights   **C** 328–29

Millais (mil-LAY), **Sir John Everett** (1829–96), English painter, b. Southampton. A child prodigy, he became a fashionable portrait and historical painter and a founder of the Pre-Raphaelite movement, a group of artists who favored medieval and early Italian painting. He later became less concerned with the ideas of the movement. His works include *Christ in the House of His Parents.*
   Pre-Raphaelite Brotherhood   **E** 241

Millay (mil-LAY), **Edna St. Vincent,** American poet
   A 210; **M** 49
Miller, Arthur, American playwright   **A** 215; **D** 304
   Death of a Salesman, scenes from, *pictures*   **D** 304
Miller, Dorie, American sailor   **B** 250L
Miller, Jason, American playwright   **A** 215
Miller, Joaquin, American poet   **A** 205
Miller, John, American governor   **N** 335
Miller, Perry, American historian   **A** 214a
Miller of Dee, occupation song   **F** 319
Millers, moths   **H** 261
Miller's Wife, occupation song   **F** 319

Milles (MIL-les), **Carl** (Vilhelm Carl Emil Anderson) (1875–1955), Swedish sculptor, b. near Uppsala. He was influenced by Rodin. His dramatic figures are often set in fountains that form parts of buildings. He designed the fountain at the Metropolitan Museum of Art and sculptures at Rockefeller Center, New York, N.Y.

Millet, hardy, small-seed cereal grass. The grain is a staple food in parts of Asia and Africa. The whole plant is used to feed cattle. It is used in the United States and Europe for forage and for birdseed.   **G** 284, 285, 286, 318; *picture* **G** 283

Millet (mil-LAY), **Jean François,** French painter   **F** 426

Millett, Kate (Katharine Murray Millett) (1934–   ), American feminist, b. St. Paul, Minn. She is considered a leading theorist of the women's liberation movement and is the author of *Sexual Politics,* a work that is credited with having given stature to the movement. She also wrote a memoir, *Flying,* and *Sita,* a novel.

Millibar, unit of air pressure   **W** 78

Millikan, Robert Andrews (1868–1953), American physicist, b. Morrison, Ill. He was the first to isolate the electron, to show that it carried a constant charge, and to measure this charge. For this work he was awarded the Nobel prize in physics in 1923. He also studied X rays and the high-energy rays from outer space, which he named cosmic rays. Among his books are *The Electron* and *Science and the New Civilization.*

Millimeter (MILL-i-me-ter), measure of length   **W** 111–12

Millin, Sarah Gertrude Liebson (1889–1968), South African writer, b. Russia. As a child she went to South Africa, where she wrote many novels of life in that country, such as *God's Stepchildren* and *The Burning Man.* She also wrote biographies of South African statesmen Cecil Rhodes and Jan Christiaan Smuts, the history *The People of South Africa,* and war diaries.

Milliners, makers of women's hats   **H** 45

Milliner's Model, type of doll   **D** 269
Milling machines   **T** 223
Millions of Cats, book by Wanda Gág   **C** 238;
   illustration **I** 97
Millipedes (MILL-i-pedes), many-legged animals   **C** 168, 169
   compared to insects, *picture*   **I** 263
Mill on the Floss, The, novel by George Eliot   **E** 175
Mills, Billy, American runner   **O** 111
Mills, in industry
   flour milling   **F** 274–75; **W** 156
   Industrial Revolution   **I** 236, 238
   mini-mills in steelmaking   **I** 407
   steel rolling and finishing   **I** 399–402
   water mills   **W** 71–72

Mills, Robert (1781–1855), American architect and engineer, b. Charleston, S.C. After designing the former State House, Harrisburg, Pa. (1810), he designed the country's first important monument to George Washington, in Baltimore. Thereafter his style became simpler, neoclassical, and less influenced by baroque architecture. At the apex of his career (1836–51) he worked in Washington, D.C., where he designed the Washington Monument and the Treasury and Post Office buildings.   **S** 309

Millstones, used in grinding grain   **W** 71
Milluni (mi-YU-ni), **Lake,** South America, *picture*
   S 274
Milne, A. A., English author   **M** 310–11
   Missing, poem   **M** 311
   Shepard drawing for *Winnie-the-Pooh*   **I** 97
Milo (MY-lo), Greek athlete   **O** 103
Milo (MI-lo), island between Greece and Crete *see*
   Melos
Milpa agriculture, of Zaïre   **Z** 366a

Milstein, Nathan (1904–   ), American violinist, b. Odessa, Russia. He left the Soviet Union in 1925, gave concerts in Europe, and made his American debut in 1929. He is noted for his brilliant technique and for his interpretations of the classical violin repertory.

Miltiades, Saint, pope   **R** 296
Milton, John, English poet   **M** 312
   freedom of the press upheld in his *Areopagitica*
      E 255
   L'Allegro, excerpt   **M** 312
   place in English literature   **E** 255
   sonnets   **S** 256
Milwaukee (mil-WAU-kee), Wisconsin   **M** 313; **W** 204
   Performing Arts Center, *picture*   **W** 204
Milwaukee Brewers, baseball team   **B** 80
Milkweed, plant
   controls migration of butterflies   **B** 470
Mime, acting without using words
   ballet   **B** 26, 27
Mime (MI-may) (Regin), dwarf in Norse mythology
   N 280–81
Mimeograph, duplicating machine   **O** 57
   former trademark   **T** 245
Mimicry (MIM-ic-ry)
   humor   **H** 279
   insect protective device   **I** 275
   talking birds   **P** 85
Mimosa, tree
   leaves, responses to light, *picture*   **P** 301

Min, Queen (?–1895), wife of the king of Korea. Member of a powerful family that had helped to rule Korea for gen-

Min, Queen (continued)
erations, she fought Japanese attempts to run the Korean government after the Sino-Japanese War (1894–95). Assassinated by the Japanese, she became a symbol of Korean opposition to Japan.

Minahassa, a people of Indonesia **I** 219
Minamoto no Yoritomo *see* Yoritomo
Minarets (min-a-RETS), towers of mosques **I** 416;
  pictures **B** 485, **M** 300
  Islamic architecture **I** 419
  Taj Mahal **T** 14
Minas Gerais, state, Brazil **B** 378
Mince pie, Christmas dessert **C** 299
Mind **P** 491–92
  dreaming **D** 317–18
  extrasensory perception **E** 396–98
  hypnosis **H** 316–18
  memory **L** 105
  mental health **M** 223–25
  mental illness **M** 225–28
  sleep **S** 200–01
  See also Brain
Mindanao (min-da-NA-o), Philippines **P** 184, 185, 186
Mindanao Trench *see* Philippine Trench
Mindoro, Sea of *see* Sulu Sea
Mind reading, kind of extrasensory perception **E** 396
Mind-reading tricks **T** 288
  digit problem **M** 25

Mindszenty (MINT-sen-ty), **Joseph, Cardinal** (1892–1975), Hungarian Roman Catholic churchman, b. Csehimindszent. Archbishop of Esztergom and Primate of Hungary, he became a cardinal in 1946. Sentenced to life imprisonment by the Hungarian Communist regime in 1949, he was released during the brief anti-Communist revolution of 1956. He was granted asylum in the U.S. Legation in Budapest until 1971, when he left Hungary for Vienna. He lived there until his death.

Mineral collecting **R** 273
Mineral dressing *see* Concentration
Mineralogy (min-er-OL-ogy), study of minerals **G** 118
Mineral oils **O** 76
  cosmetic creams made of **C** 553
Minerals and mineral resources **R** 270–72
  Africa **A** 52–53
  Arctic region **A** 386d
  Asia's resources **A** 450
  Australia **A** 509
  bones contain mineral salts **S** 184b
  collecting minerals **R** 273
  conservation of **C** 520
  deficiency diseases **D** 185
  deserts rich in **D** 127
  Europe **E** 315
  gemstones **G** 68–76
  geologists at work **G** 119
  geology, history of **G** 117
  Law of the Sea Treaty **I** 316
  magnesium, sources of **M** 27
  mineral fibers **N** 425
  mines and mining **M** 314–20
  mountain resources **M** 504
  North America **N** 292–94
  nutrition **N** 416
  ocean, uses of the **O** 28
  soils **S** 230
  South America **S** 279

Where do metals come from? **M** 229
Why is ocean water salty? **E** 16
world distribution **W** 260–61
See also natural resources section of continent, country, province, and state articles

Mineral water, a natural water containing dissolved minerals. Mineral waters contain varying amounts of elements such as iron, sulfur, salt, and hydrogen sulfide. The waters dissolve these elements as they flow under the earth. Most often, mineral waters are clear, with many small bubbles formed by natural gases. Since ancient times some people have believed that mineral waters have medicinal value. They often traveled great distances to bathe in the waters or to drink them. Today mineral waters are popular bottled beverages. Well-known mineral springs are found at Saratoga, New York; Hot Springs, Arkansas; and Vichy, France.

Minerva (min-ER-va), Roman goddess **G** 358, 360
Mines, explosives
  mine warfare ships of U.S. Navy **U** 193
Mines and mining **M** 314–20
  Africa **A** 64
  Asia **A** 462
  Beckley Exhibition Coal Mine, West Virginia **W** 133
  Canada **C** 59, 62
  coal mining **C** 389–90
  diamonds **D** 145
  dredges used in **D** 319, 320
  explosives used in **E** 394, 395
  gold **G** 249
  iron ore **I** 404
  Law of the Sea Treaty **I** 316
  miner's safety fuse **E** 392
  mining engineers **E** 205
  occupational health and safety **O** 12–13
  safety lamp invented by Davy **D** 44
  salt **S** 20–21
  silver **S** 177–78
  South America **S** 292
  underwater mining **U** 21
  See also names of specific types of mines and mining, as Coal and coal mining; country, province, and state articles
Ming Cho Lee, American stage designer
  setting for *King Lear, picture* **T** 158
Ming dynasty, ancient rule of China **C** 269
  Chinese art **C** 275, 277
  jade carving **D** 71
  porcelain **P** 411
Minho (MEEN-yo) **River,** Spain and Portugal **P** 392
Miniature cameras **P** 214
Miniatures, illustrations in illuminated manuscripts
  I 88; *picture* **B** 48
  Kells, Book of **K** 202
  medieval painting **P** 17–18
Miniatures, objects reduced to a very small scale *see* Dollhouses; Models and model making
Minicomputers **C** 478, 483; **O** 54
Minie (MIN-e) **ball,** gun bullet **G** 420
Minimal art **M** 397–98
Minimata disease (mercury poisoning) **W** 67
Minimum till, agricultural practice **A** 95, 100
Minimum wages **L** 5, 18
Mining *see* Mines and mining
Mining Act, 1866 **P** 507
Miniskirt, in fashion, *picture* **C** 380
Mink, animals of mustelid family **O** 245; *picture* **O** 244

furs **F** 518–19
in cages on a fur farm, *picture* **F** 513
mutations for fur colors **F** 514
Minneapolis (min-ne-AP-olis), Minnesota **M** 321, 328, 334, 337
IDS Center, *picture* **M** 334
Minnelli, Liza *see* Garland, Judy
Minnesingers (MIN-ne-singers), medieval German singers **G** 181
Minnesota (min-ne-SO-ta) **M** 322–37
eskers, snakelike ridges left by glaciers, *picture* **I** 14
Minneapolis-Saint Paul **M** 321
Minnesota, University of **M** 321, 329
cheerleading founded at **C** 192
Minnesota River, Minnesota **M** 325
Minoan (mi-NO-an) **civilization,** of ancient Crete **A** 226–27
art **A** 236–38; **P** 15–16
art as a record **A** 438b
clothing, history of **C** 374
palaces **A** 238, 372
sculpture **S** 94
Minor, in music **M** 541
Minorca (min-OR-ca), island, Spain **I** 427
Minority groups *see* Ethnic groups
Minority leaders, in Congress **U** 144
Minor leagues, in baseball **B** 75
Minos (MY-nos), in Greek myth, king of Crete **G** 364
in story from *Tanglewood Tales* **H** 66
palace in Knossos, *picture* **A** 355
wall painting in the palace in Knossos, *picture* **A** 226
Minot (MY-not), North Dakota **N** 335
Minotaur (MIN-o-taur), monster in Greek myth **G** 364
in story from *Tanglewood Tales* **H** 66
Theseus in combat against the Minotaur, painting on a Greek amphora, *picture* **D** 73
Minstrels (jongleurs), medieval entertainers
Africa's bards and minstrels **A** 76b
communication, method of **C** 461
music of the Middle Ages **M** 298
storytellers **C** 232; **S** 434
Mint, herb **H** 114; *picture* **H** 115
Mint, place where coins are made **M** 338
Mint stamps, those not canceled **S** 396
Minuend (MIN-u-end), in subtraction **A** 399
Minuet, musical form **M** 545, 548
Minuet, dance **D** 27; *picture* **D** 26
Minuet-trio, musical form **C** 350

Minuit (MIN-u-it), **Peter** (1580–1638), Dutch official in America, b. Wesel, Duchy of Cleves (now the Netherlands). He landed on Manhattan Island about 1626 and bought it from the Indians for about $24 in his capacity as director general of the Dutch West India Company. In 1637, in Sweden's employ, he landed near Delaware Bay, set up a colony called New Sweden, and built Fort Christina, site of present-day Wilmington.
Dutch colonies in America **A** 191; **N** 234

Minute, measure of time **W** 115
Minute Man, statue by Daniel French **M** 146; *picture* **U** 115
Minuteman, missile **M** 346, 347
Minutemen, American colonial militia **R** 198
alerted by Paul Revere's ride **R** 193
"fired the shot heard round the world" **A** 201
Revolutionary War begins **M** 145

Minyan, group necessary to conduct a Jewish worship service **J** 144
Miocene epoch, in geology **E** 21, 25; **F** 387
Miquelon *see* Saint Pierre and Miquelon, islands
Mira (MY-ra), star **S** 408
Mirabeau (mi-ra-BO), **Comte de,** French revolutionary leader **F** 464
Miracle plays, medieval drama **M** 339–40
drama, history of **D** 297
Middle English drama **E** 249–50
theater in England **T** 159–60
Miracles, of Jesus Christ **J** 85, 87
Miraculous Draught of Fishes, The, tapestry from a drawing by Raphael, *picture* **J** 85
Mirage (mir-AHGE) **M** 341–42
light refraction **L** 263
Miramichi River, New Brunswick, Canada **N** 138a
Miranda (mi-RON-da), **Francisco de,** Venezuelan patriot **V** 298–99
Bolívar and Miranda **B** 305
Miranda, satellite of Uranus **P** 277; **U** 231

Miranda card, a card from which legal rights are read to arrested persons. The term comes from the case *Miranda v. Arizona* (1966), in which the U.S. Supreme Court ruled that statements made by suspects may not be used as evidence unless the suspects have been informed of their rights and warned that their statements may be used in court against them. These rights include the right to remain silent and to consult a lawyer.

Miriam, in the Old Testament, Hebrew prophetess, sister of Moses and Aaron. The Song of Miriam (Exodus 15:20–21) is a hymn celebrating the Israelites' deliverance from Egypt.

Miró (mee-RO), **Joan** (1893–1983), Spanish artist, b. Montroig, near Barcelona. Miró was a well-known abstract artist. In his paintings, people and things appear as imaginative, rounded shapes that seem to float in air. His works are also characterized by the use of brilliant color. His paintings include *Tilled Field* (1923–24) and *Painting* (1953). Miró also created the ceramic murals *Night* and *Day* for the UNESCO building in Paris. His sculpture *Chicago* stands in Daley Plaza in Chicago. **M** 394–95
Landscape, painting **M** 396a
Wall of the Sun, painting **S** 362

Mirrors
first glass mirrors made by Venetians **G** 229
heliograph signaling **C** 465; **T** 50
kaleidoscope **K** 162
laser mirror left on moon **S** 340e
light reflection **L** 260, 262–63
optical instruments **O** 170, 171, 173
superstition about **S** 475
Mirror writing
used by Leonardo da Vinci **L** 154
MIRV (multiple independently targeted re-entry vehicle) **system,** missile system **M** 347
Misbranding, of food **F** 346
Misdemeanor (mis-de-MEAN-or), in law **C** 567, 574, 575
judge usually decides guilt **J** 155
Misdirection, art of, in magic **M** 23–24
Misérables (mi-zay-RA-ble), **Les,** novel by Victor Hugo, *excerpt* **H** 275–77
Mishima, Yukio, Japanese novelist **O** 220d
Mishnah, ancient Hebrew laws **H** 98

Mishnah (continued)
Jewish Oral Law **J** 143
Talmud **T** 15
Mishneh Torah, Jewish law **J** 143
Miskito (or Mosquito) **Indians,** of Nicaragua **N** 245
Miskolc (MISH-kolts), Hungary **H** 286
Miss, form of address **A** 19
Missiles M 343–49
jet propulsion **J** 88–90
liquid gases **L** 305
rocket power **R** 255–62
United States Air Force **U** 161
United States Army **U** 171
United States Navy **U** 193
See also MX
Missing, poem by A. A. Milne **M** 311
Mission of St. Francis of Assisi, Rancho de Taos, New
Mexico, *picture* **U** 122
Missions and missionaries
Africa **A** 56
Christianity, history of **C** 286–87
Indians of North America **I** 176
Indians of South America **I** 210
International Missionary Council **P** 486
Jesuits to North American Indians **I** 171; **O** 128
Livingstone, David **S** 400
overland trails, United States **O** 260; *picture*
O 261
Patrick, Saint **P** 102
Paul, Saint **P** 103
praying towns of Massachusetts **M** 150
Roman Catholic Church **R** 294
Schweitzer, Albert **S** 59
Mississippi M 350–63
Mississippi, University of, University, Mississippi
M 358
Mississippi River M 364–65, 352; *pictures* **I** 358,
M 368, 374, **V** 107
Civil War **C** 343
delta **W** 51
discovered by De Soto **D** 138
explorations of Marquette and Jolliet **J** 127
flood-plain area in Mississippi **M** 350
Kentucky **K** 215
La Salle **L** 46
Louisiana **L** 350, 351, 353
"old" and "young" river features **R** 239
silt from the Missouri **M** 383
source is near Lake Itasca **M** 322, 332
Twain, Mark, river pilot **T** 336
Mississippi River-Gulf Outlet, waterway in Louisiana
L 356
Miss Muffet, nursery rhyme **N** 404
Missouri M 366–81
events leading to Civil War **C** 336
Kansas City **K** 190
Missouri Compromise **M** 382
places of interest in black history **B** 250d
Saint Louis **S** 18
Missouri, University of, Columbia, Missouri **M** 375
Missouri, U.S.S., battleship
Japanese surrender, 1945, *picture* **W** 307
Missouri Botanical Gardens, St. Louis, Missouri **B** 343
Missouri Compromise, 1820 **M** 382
black history **B** 250f
Civil War, events leading to **C** 335–36
Clay, Henry **C** 353
Dred Scott decision **D** 321
Maine and Missouri receive statehood **M** 51

repealed by Kansas-Nebraska Act, 1854 **K** 191
slavery issue **S** 199
Missouri Escarpment, North Dakota **N** 324
Missouri Fur Company F 522
Missouri Plateau, North Dakota **N** 324
Missouri River M 383
lakes, formation of **L** 28
Lewis and Clark expedition **L** 163, 164
source **M** 431, 439
Missouri River basin development program, South
Dakota **S** 327
Mistletoe, plant **P** 318
Christmas customs **C** 297
in Norse mythology **N** 279
state flower of Oklahoma, *picture* **O** 81
Mistletoe cactus C 5
Mistral (mi-STROL), **Gabriela** (Lucila Godoy de
Alcayaga), Chilean poet **C** 250
Latin-American literature **L** 72
Mistral, winter wind of Mediterranean region **M** 213;
W 80
Misty of Chincoteague, book by Marguerite Henry
V 344
M.I.T. *see* Massachusetts Institute of Technology
Mitchell, Alexander, American banker and railroad
builder **W** 206

Mitchell, Arthur (1934–   ), American dancer and
choreographer, b. New York City. One of the world's leading classical dancers, he was the first black performer to
become principal dancer with a major company (the New
York City Ballet). He founded the Dance Theater of Harlem
in 1968 and has choreographed original ballets for the
company.

Mitchell, Billy (William Mitchell) (1879–1936), Ameri-
can soldier and aviator, b. Nice, France. He rose from
private (1898) to the rank of brigadier general (1920) and
was commander of U.S. air forces in France (1917–18).
He was an early advocate of air power and his criticism of
the War and Navy departments' aviation policies led to
Mitchell's court-martial (1925) and resignation from the
Army (1926). Many of his ideas were successfully used in
World War II.
United States Air Force, history of **U** 160

Mitchell, Edgar D., American astronaut **S** 340k

Mitchell, George John (1933–   ), United States senator from Maine, Democrat, b. Portland. He was appointed
to the Senate in 1980 to fill the unexpired term of Senator
Edmund S. Muskie, and was elected to the Senate in
1982. He previously served as a U.S. district judge
(1979–80) and as U.S. attorney for Maine (1977–79).
Mitchell was a practicing attorney (1965–77).

Mitchell, John, American labor leader **L** 5

Mitchell, John Newton (1913–   ), American government
official, b. Detroit, Mich. A former law partner of Richard
Nixon, he was named attorney general in 1969. He resigned to head the President's 1972 re-election campaign. Mitchell was acquitted of charges of malfeasance
(wrongdoing) in campaign funding in 1974. But in 1975
he was convicted of conspiracy to obstruct justice in the
Watergate cover-up and was sentenced to 3 years in prison.

Mitchell, Joni, Canadian singer **C** 67
Mitchell, Margaret, American novelist **A** 213; **G** 146

Mitchell, Maria (1818–89), American astronomer, b. Nantucket, Mass. Under her father's guidance she became a mathematician and astronomer. Among her achievements was discovery of a comet (1847). She was the first woman elected (1848) to Academy of Arts and Sciences. In 1922 she was elected to the Hall of Fame.

Mitchell, Mount, North Carolina **N** 285, 309
Mitchell, Thomas, Scottish explorer **A** 516
Miter gate, of canals **C** 87
Miters, hats **H** 47
Miter saws, tools **T** 216–17
Mites, relatives of spiders **P** 286; **S** 388
Mitochondria (my-to-CON-dria), of cell **C** 160
Mitosis (my-TO-sis), cell division **C** 161–62
 cell division of tumors and cancer **C** 89

Mitre (MI-tray), **Bartolomé** (1821–1906), Argentine military leader, statesman, historian, and journalist, b. Buenos Aires. An exile, he returned to Buenos Aires (1852) to help overthrow Juan Manuel de Rosas, became active in the government, and was first president (1862–68) of the Argentine Republic. He had founded the newspaper *La Nación* in 1852, and later he wrote books, among them *History of San Martín*. **A** 395

Mitropoulos (mi-TROP-oo-los), **Dimitri** (1896–1960), American conductor, composer, and pianist, b. Athens, Greece. He was conductor of Minneapolis Symphony Orchestra (1937–49) and New York Philharmonic (1950–58).

Mittermaier, Rosi, West German skier **O** 115

Mitterrand (MEE-ter-ahn), **François Maurice** (1916–   ), president of France, b. Jarnac. Mitterrand took office in 1981. He entered politics after having fought in the Resistance in World War II, winning election to the National Assembly in 1946. In 1965 he ran unsuccessfully for president. In 1971 he joined the Socialist Party and became its leader. After an unsuccessful campaign for the presidency in 1974, he defeated Valéry Giscard d'Estaing in 1981. As president, Mitterrand granted additional benefits to workers, encouraged scientific research in high technology, and began to transfer more power from the central government to local authorities. **F** 420

Mixed media drawings **D** 311
Mixed metaphor, figure of speech **F** 118
Mixed numbers, combinations of whole numbers and
  fractions **F** 397
Mixtec Indians, of Mexico
  ancient writing, *picture* **H** 22
Mixtures, in chemistry **M** 176
Mizoguchi, Kenji, Japanese motion picture director
  M 489, 490
Mjolnir (m'YERL-nir), hammer of Thor, Norse god
  N 279
Mlanje Mountains, Malawi **M** 52
Mnemonics (ne-MON-ics), memory-improving technique
  L 106
  musical notes **M** 534
  poem to remember how many days in each month
  C 12

Moabites (MO-ab-ites), ancient Semitic people of Moab, a land east of the Dead Sea that is now part of Jordan. Little is known of the Moabites or Moab except for a few Old Testament references, such as those found in the Book of Ruth (Ruth was a Moabite woman).

Moabite stone, inscribed slab of stone erected by Mesha of Moab in 850 B.C. to mark a victory against Israel. The stone was discovered in 1868. Its inscription reveals that the Moabites' language closely resembled Hebrew. The stone is now in the Louvre in Paris.

Moana, documentary motion picture **M** 478
Moas (MO-as), extinct birds **B** 231; *picture* **O** 236b
  giants of nature **G** 200, 204
  New Zealand **N** 239
Moat, of a castle **C** 132; **F** 375; **H** 178
Mobile (mo-BELE), Alabama **A** 124
Mobile Bay, Alabama **A** 113, 115, 126
  naval battle in Civil War **C** 345
Mobile homes, movable houses **H** 177
  camping **C** 41
Mobile (mo-BELE) **River,** Alabama **A** 115

Mobiles (MO-beles), sculpture made of movable parts, usually suspended by wire and rods and balanced to respond to a gentle touch or breeze.
  Calder, Alexander **M** 397; **S** 105; *picture* **N** 38
  modern sculpture of the United States **U** 116;
    picture **U** 117
  three-dimensional design **D** 136
  toys **T** 235a
  wire sculpture **W** 190b

Möbius, August F., German mathematician **T** 226
Möbius (MER-bi-us) **strip,** in topology **T** 226
Mobs, of kangaroos **K** 170

Mobutu (mo-BU-tu) **Sese Seko** (1930–   ), Zaïrian leader, b. Lisala, Upper Congo (now Zaïre). He was secretary of state for national defense after the Congo gained its independence (1960). He led a military coup (1960) to neutralize the conflict between Premier Lumumba and President Kasavubu, directed the government for three months, returned power to President Kasavubu, and was appointed commander in chief (1961). In 1965, Mobutu deposed Kasavubu and named himself president. In elections held in 1970, 1977, and 1984, Mobutu, running unopposed, retained the presidency. **Z** 366d

Moby Dick, novel by Melville **N** 349; *excerpt* **M** 217–
  18; *picture* **A** 203
  American literature, place in **A** 202
  illustrations by Rockwell Kent, *pictures* **I** 92,
    M 218
  whale hunting **W** 152
Moccasin flower *see* Lady's-slipper
Moccasin snakes **S** 209; *picture* **S** 210
Mocha (MO-ca), Yemen (Sana) **Y** 349
  coffee named for **C** 397
Mochica (mo-CHI-ca) (Moche), early Indian culture of
  Peru **P** 163
  art **I** 156; *pictures* **I** 204, 205
Mock-heroic poetry **E** 258

Mockingbirds, American birds of the family commonly called mimic-thrushes. They grow to a length of about 10 in (25 cm). Grayish in color, the bird has white patches on its wings and tail. The mockingbird is found in southern Canada, the United States, Mexico, and the West Indies. It lives in shrubs and thickets and eats fruit, berries, and insects. It is so named because it imitates the calls and songs of other birds. *picture* **B** 239
  Arkansas, state bird of, *picture* **A** 418
  Florida, state bird of, *picture* **F** 259
  Mississippi, state bird of, *picture* **M** 351

Mockingbirds (continued)
Tennessee, state bird of, *picture* **T** 75
Texas, state bird of, *picture* **T** 123

Mock suns *see* Sundogs
Mock-ups, design models **I** 231
Mode, kind of average of a set of numbers **S** 417
Mode, musical scale **M** 541
ancient Greek modes **A** 247
Model Cities Program **C** 324
Modeling, fashion **M** 384–85
Modeling, in drawing **D** 309
Modeling, in sculpture **S** 90
Modeling clay (plasticine) **C** 354
Models and model making
airplane models **A** 104–07
automobile **A** 535–37
railroads, model **R** 91–92
taxidermy **T** 27
Model T, automobile **A** 548
Henry Ford's part in automobile history **F** 367
importance to history of transportation **T** 264
Modem, computer system peripheral **C** 480–81, 483;
E 142b
Moderato, musical term **M** 541
Moderator, of a discussion **D** 53
Modern architecture **A** 381–386a
cathedrals **C** 135
industrial design **I** 232
Sullivan, Louis **S** 457
United States **U** 124–25
Wright, Frank Lloyd **W** 316
Modern art **M** 386–98
art of the artist **A** 438g
Canada **C** 83
Cézanne's influence **C** 179
Chagall, Marc **C** 182
collage **C** 400–01
French art, 20th-century **F** 431–32
furniture design **F** 510
Germany **G** 169–71
Modigliani, Amedeo **M** 403
Mondrian, Piet **M** 407
painting **P** 29–32
Picasso, Pablo **P** 243–44
Pollock, Jackson **P** 378
Pop and Op art **P** 31–32
sculpture of the 20th century **S** 103–05
tapestry **T** 24
United States **U** 116, 122; *pictures* **A** 438d, 438e
Utrillo, Maurice **U** 256
Modern dance **D** 33–34; *pictures* **D** 23, 32
Modern Jazz Quartet, American musicians **J** 61

Modern Language Association of America (MLA), organization of college and university teachers of English and modern foreign languages. Founded in 1883, MLA works to advance all phases of literary and linguistic study. It publishes a quarterly magazine, *PMLA,* and, among other activities, conducts a Foreign Language Program comprised of a research center in New York, N.Y., and a Center for Applied Linguistics in Washington, D.C.

Modern music **M** 399–402
French *musique concrète* **F** 448
sonatas **M** 548
symphonies **M** 549
See also names of composers

Modern Poetry Association (MPA), organization that promotes modern poetry. Founded in 1946, with headquarters in Chicago, Ill., MPA publishes *Poetry Magazine* monthly and sponsors lectures and readings in an effort to bring modern poetry to a larger audience.

Modern roman typefaces **T** 345
Modern Times, film starring Charlie Chaplin **C** 186
Modified American plan, of hotel rates **H** 256
Modigliani (mo-deel-YA-ni), **Amedeo,** Italian painter and sculptor **M** 403
Woman with Red Hair, painting **M** 403

Modjeska (mod-JES-ka), **Helena** (1840–1909), Polish actress, b. Cracow. She married her tutor, Gustav Modrzejewski, when she was about 17 and toured with him in a stock company. After his death she married Count Bozenta Chlapowski (1868) and sailed with him and other political refugees to America (1876). Her first American appearance was in San Francisco (1877). Noted for her portrayal of Shakespearean heroines, she starred with Edwin Booth (1889–90) and toured with Otis Skinner and Maurice Barrymore before retiring in 1905.

Modoc Plateau, California **C** 20
Modred (MO-dred), knight of King Arthur's court **A** 442
Modular furniture **F** 510
Modulation, in music **M** 541
Modulation, in radio broadcasting **R** 54
Moeritherium (mir-i-THE-ri-um), prehistoric ancestor of the elephant **E** 168
Moffat, Robert, Scottish missionary in Africa **B** 340a
Moffat Tunnel, Colorado **D** 117
Mogadishu, capital of Somalia **S** 255; *picture* **S** 254
Mogollon Rim, Arizona **A** 404, 407

Mogul (mo-GUL), dynasty of Mongol rulers of India. Though it dates from Baber, a descendant of Tamerlane (Timur), who ruled (1526–30) over a large part of northern India, it was Baber's grandson, **Akbar** (1542–1605), who established the Mogul empire when he became king (1556). He conquered all of North India, built a sound administrative system, and promoted mutual understanding with the Hindus. When **Aurangzeb** (1658–1707) reversed Akbar's religious policy and drove non-Muslims into revolt, the Mogul rulers lost their power. The last, **Bahadur Shah II** (1768?–1862), was sentenced to prison by the British after the Sepoy Mutiny (1857). The greatness of the Mogul empire has survived in its art and architecture.
India, history of **I** 131, 133

Mogul runs, in skiing **S** 184f
Mohács (MO-hotch), **Battle of,** 1526 **H** 288
Mohair goats **C** 150, 152
animal fibers **F** 107
Mohammad Abdullah Hassan, Somali leader **S** 255
Mohammed (or Muhammad), Arab prophet, founder of Islam **M** 404–05
Arabic education spread by Muslim followers **E** 66
Islam **I** 414–16
Jews and Mohammed disliked each other **J** 106
Koran **K** 292-93
Mecca **M** 196
Mouloud, Muslim holiday **H** 150
Mohammed V, king of Morocco **M** 461
Mohammed Ali *see* Mehemet Ali, governor of Egypt
Mohammedans *see* Islam

Mohammed Reza Pahlavi (PAH-lah-vee) (1919–80), shah of Iran, b. Tehran. He became shah (king) in 1941. In 1953, he was briefly deposed by Premier Mohammed Mossadegh. The Shah returned to power determined to become a strong leader and to make Iran a modern industrial nation. His critics charged him with corruption and the destruction of traditional values, and he used harsh methods to silence them. In 1979, he was overthrown in a revolution led by Ayatollah Ruhollah Khomeini, a Muslim religious leader. When the Shah went to the United States for medical treatment later that year, militant Iranians seized the U.S. embassy in Tehran. The Shah died in exile in Egypt. **I** 376–77

Mohave (mo-HA-vay), **Lake,** Arizona **A** 407
Mohave Desert see Mojave Desert
Mohawk, Indians of North America **I** 184
    Champlain made enemies for France **I** 186
    Joseph Brant, chief **B** 370–71
Mohawk River, New York **N** 213
Mohawk Valley, New York **N** 212, 214
    overland trail through the valley **O** 254

Mohenjo-Daro (mo-HEN-jo DA-ro) ("mound of the dead"), most important ancient city of the Indus valley in Pakistan. Mohenjo-Daro was inhabited continuously from about 3000 to 2000 B.C., when it came to a sudden end, probably at the hands of invaders.
    ancient Indus cities **A** 223–24; **I** 116

Moho, boundary between earth's crust and mantle
    E 6, 33; *diagrams* **E** 34, **G** 114
    How do scientists learn about the earth's interior?
    E 7
Mohole, Project, to drill a hole through the earth's crust into the mantle **G** 113; **U** 21

Moholy-Nagy (MO-ho-ye-NODGE), **László** (1895–1946), Hungarian painter, photographer, industrial designer and writer, b. Bacsbarsod. He taught at the Bauhaus in Germany until 1928. In 1937 he went to the United States and founded the New Bauhaus in Chicago, which became part of the Illinois Institute of Technology. His books, in particular *Vision in Motion,* have had a significant influence on art education and industrial design.

Mohorovičić (mo-ho-ro-VI-chich), **Andrija,** Yugoslav geologist **E** 6, 33; **G** 113
Mohorovičić discontinuity see Moho
Mohr, Joseph, Austrian pastor, author of "Silent Night, Holy Night" **C** 119
Mohs, Freidrich, German mineralogist **G** 69
Mohs' scale, measure for hardness **G** 69
    mineral's hardness **R** 270
Moi, Daniel arap, president of Kenya **K** 233
Moiré (mwa-RAY), fabric **T** 144
Mojave (mo-HA-vay) **Desert,** California and Arizona **C** 20
Molars, teeth **T** 47
Molasses **S** 453
    Sugar Act, 1764, angers American colonists
    R 195
    sugarcane, a source of molasses, *picture* **G** 318
Moldau River see Vltava River
Moldavia (mol-DAVE-ia), former principality, now a region of Rumania **R** 355
Moldavian Soviet Socialist Republic (Moldavia) **U** 44
Moldboard plows **F** 54
Molders, tools
    preparing wood for furniture making **F** 503

Molding, industrial process
    plastics **P** 329
    rubber **R** 347
Molds, for shaping materials **D** 156–57
    candles **C** 94
    candy and candy making **C** 96
    ceramics **C** 177
Molds, fungi **F** 496, 497
    antibiotics **A** 310, 311, 334; *pictures* **A** 314
    bioluminescence **B** 197
    cheese making **D** 12–13
    food spoilage **F** 341, 351
Molecular (mo-LEC-ular) **biology** **B** 196
Molecular weight **C** 204
Molecules (MOL-ec-ules), combinations of atoms
    A 483, 485; **C** 198, 201, 204
    crystals **C** 591–92
    detergents and soaps **D** 139
    gases, diffusion of particles **G** 57–58
    macromolecules in body chemistry **B** 292
    matter and molecules **M** 174, 175; **P** 231
    plastics **P** 324
    polymers and polymerization **P** 324
    separation with heating, *picture* **G** 58
    solids, particles in **S** 250
    water molecule **W** 47, 48
    See also Brownian movement
Molenaer (MO-len-ar), **Jan Miense,** Dutch painter
    Family Group, painting, *picture* **D** 367
Moles, animals of insectivore group **I** 259–60; *picture* **M** 73
    bristles, a variety of mammal hair, *picture* **M** 68
Moles, marsupial **K** 171
Molière (mo-li-AIR), French actor-manager and dramatist **M** 405; *picture* **D** 295
    drama, history of **D** 299; **F** 438
    Tartuffe, scene from, *picture* **D** 299
Molina, Tirso de see Tirso de Molina
Mollusks, group of animals **O** 273–78
    animal plankton **P** 280–81
    benthic ocean life **O** 26
    pearls **P** 113
    shells **S** 147–49
Mollweide (MOL-vy-da) **projection,** of maps **M** 97
Molly Maguires, secret labor union **L** 3
Molly Pitcher see Pitcher, Molly

Molnár (MOL-nar), **Ferenc** (1878–1952), Hungarian playwright and novelist, b. Budapest. His most famous work was *Liliom*, a mixture of realism and fantasy. It was adapted as the musical *Carousel* by Rodgers and Hammerstein. **H** 284

Molokai (mo-lo-KI), one of the Hawaiian Islands
    H 50–51

Molotov (MOL-ot-off), **Vyacheslav Mikhailovich** (Vyacheslav Mikhailovich Skryabin) (1890–1986), Soviet politician, b. Kukarka (now Sovetsk, Kirov oblast). He was a member of the Political Bureau of the Communist Party (1926–57), chairman of the Council of People's Commissars (1930–41), deputy chairman of the Council of Ministers (1941–57), minister for foreign affairs (1939–49, 1953–56), and minister for state control (1956–57). He served as member of the Presidium of the Central Committee of the Communist Party until 1957, when he was charged with leading an anti-party group and was removed from office. He was expelled from the Communist Party in 1962 but reinstated in 1984.

Molotov cocktail, hand grenade made of a bottle filled with a flammable liquid, such as gasoline. A wick or saturated rag is taped to the bottom and ignited when the grenade is thrown. Named for Soviet statesman Vyacheslav M. Molotov, it was used by the Russians against German armored vehicles in World War II.

Molten rock *see* Magma
Molting, of animals
    birds **B** 200, 216, 244
    crustaceans **C** 589
    horseshoe crab **H** 245
    lobsters **L** 322
    shrimps **S** 167
    silkworms **S** 175
    snakes **S** 214
    waterfowl **D** 342

Moltke (MOLT-ka), **Count Helmuth Karl Bernhard von** (1800–91), Prussian general, b. Pachim, Mecklenburg. He became chief of the Prussian general staff in 1858 and developed new ideas on military organization and strategy that helped Prussia (now part of Germany) win wars over Denmark (1864), Austria (1866), and France (1870–71). The victories over Austria and France paved the way for the unification of Germany. His nephew, **Count Helmuth Johannes Ludwig von Moltke** (1848–1916), was chief of the German general staff from 1906 to 1914.
    World War I **W** 273

Molto, musical term **M** 541
Moluccas (mo-LUCC-as) (Maluku, Spice Islands), Indonesia **I** 220
    Magellan's explorations **M** 21
    Netherlands **N** 120d
    spice trade **H** 113

Molucca (mol-UC-ca) **Sea,** part of the Pacific Ocean between Celebes Island and the northern Molucca islands. It is connected to the Pacific on the north through the Molucca Passage, and it contains the Indonesian Sula Islands.

Molybdenum, element **E** 153, 160; *chart* **M** 230
    Colorado leading producer **C** 437
    flotation and smelting, *pictures* **M** 232
    producing regions of North America **N** 293
Mombacho (mome-BA-cho), volcano, Nicaragua, *picture* **N** 246
Mombasa (mom-BA-sa), Kenya **K** 232; *picture* **K** 231
Moment of truth, in bullfighting **B** 453
Momoh, Joseph Saidu, president of Sierra Leone **S** 171
Monaco (MON-a-co), principality on Mediterranean coast of France **M** 406–07
    flag, *picture* **F** 235
    Grand Prix race, *picture* **A** 539
Monaco-Ville (mo-NA-co-vi), capital of Monaco **M** 406; *picture* **M** 407
Monadnocks (mon-AD-nocks), hills or mountains rising above eroded land surface **M** 136
    New Hampshire **N** 150
    Oregon **O** 194
    South Carolina **S** 298
    Stone Mountain, Georgia, *picture* **G** 134
Mona Lisa (MO-na LI-sa), portrait painting by Leonardo da Vinci **L** 153, 154
    hangs in the Louvre **L** 367
Monarch (MON-arc) **butterflies** **B** 474; *picture* **B** 477
    adult life begins, *pictures* **B** 473
    chrysalis, *picture* **I** 265
    migration **H** 188
    Viceroy butterfly resembles, *picture* **I** 275
Monarchy, government by single person **G** 273
    constitutional monarchy of the United Kingdom **U** 77–78
Monasteries, **C** 289; *pictures* **C** 291, **M** 294
    architecture **A** 377
    Burma **B** 458
    centers of learning for Europe **R** 290
    Greece's Mount Athos **G** 332
    libraries **L** 188
    medieval books **B** 319–21
    medieval herb gardens **H** 113
    Thai Buddhist monastery, *picture* **A** 460
    See also Monks and monasticism
Monaural (mon-AUR-al) **recorders** **T** 20, 21

Monck, Sir Charles Stanley (1819–94), Irish statesman, b. Templemore. Appointed (1861) captain general, he became (1866) the first governor-general of the Dominion of Canada after confederation. He was privy councillor of Canada (1867–68).

Moncton, New Brunswick, Canada **N** 138f

Mondale, Walter Frederick (1928–), 42nd vice president of the United States, b. Ceylon, Minn. Mondale practiced law in Minnesota before being named state attorney general in 1960. He was appointed to the U.S. Senate seat held by Hubert Humphrey when Humphrey was elected vice president in 1964. Mondale was elected to a full term in 1966 and was re-elected in 1972. As a senator, he was known for his support of liberal legislation. He served as vice president in the administration (1977–81) of President Jimmy Carter. Mondale was the unsuccessful Democratic candidate for the presidency in 1984. **C** 123; **M** 336; **V** 331; *picture* **C** 124
    Ferraro, Geraldine A. **F** 95

Monday, origin of name **D** 46
Monde Bilingue (bi-LANG), **Le** (Bilingual World, The), French movement for joint use of French and English **U** 195
Mondrian (MON-dri-on), **Piet,** Dutch painter **M** 407
    Broadway Boogie-Woogie, painting, *picture* **M** 407
    Composition, paintings, *pictures* **D** 132, 364
    Dutch art **D** 364
    modern art **M** 393
    Opposition of Lines: Red and Yellow, painting **M** 392
Moneda, Palacio de la, Santiago, Chile **S** 37
Monégasques (mon-e-GASKS), people of Monaco **M** 406
Monet (mo-NAY), **Claude,** French painter **M** 408
    Beach at Sainte-Adresse, painting **A** 438d
    Boats at Argenteuil, painting, *picture* **M** 408
    French art **F** 426
    impressionism in painting **P** 29
    Impression: Sunrise, painting **M** 386
    modern art **M** 387
    Water Lilies, painting **F** 428

Moneta (mo-NAY-ta), ("the adviser" or "admonisher"), name given to the temple erected to Roman goddess Juno after she had advised the Romans during wartime. Because the Romans produced their first silver coins in the temple (269 B.C.), they called them *moneta,* to distinguish them from copper coins. The words "money,"

"mint," and "monetary" come from the Latin *moneta*.
money, history of   **M** 409

Monetary policy, of a government   **I** 253
Monetary units, of countries *see* country articles
Money   **M** 409–12
  banks and banking   **B** 44d–51
  budgets, family   **B** 425–26
  coins and coin collecting   **C** 398–400
  credit cards   **C** 572
  currency table of values for representative countries
    M 411
  dollar   **D** 259–61
  economic institution   **E** 48–49
  free silver coinage was Bryan's political issue
    B 416
  gold standard for official currencies   **G** 247
  inflation and deflation   **I** 252–53
  installment buying   **I** 288
  international trade problems   **I** 327–28
  mint is place where money is coined   **M** 338
  monetary economy of trade and commerce   **T** 243
  monetary units *see* facts and figures section of
    country articles
  silver   **S** 177–78
  silver money under Cleveland   **C** 360
  traveler's checks   **V** 259
  wealth, redistribution of, through income tax   **I** 110
Moneylender and His Wife, The, painting by Massys
    P 18, 19

Money market mutual funds, investment trusts. Money market mutual funds pool the money of many individuals to buy bonds and similar securities. Some funds buy only U.S. Government securities. Others also invest in the securities of foreign governments and blue-chip (highly regarded) corporations. The interest earned on the investment changes with the rate these institutions pay to borrow money. Money market mutual funds became popular with small investors in the late 1970's and early 1980's, chiefly because they paid higher interest than savings accounts.

Money orders, issued at post offices   **P** 399
Mongkut, king of Thailand   **T** 151
Mongo, African people
  African epic poetry   **A** 76b
Mongol Empire   **M** 416
Mongolia (mon-GO-lia)   **M** 413–16; *picture* **C** 261
  Communism   **C** 471
  flag, *picture*   **F** 232
  nomads, *pictures*   **A** 458, **M** 415, **N** 271
Mongolian People's Republic   **M** 413–16
Mongolian wild horse   **H** 243–44
Mongolism (MON-go-lism) *see* Down's syndrome
Mongoloid race   **A** 459
  Eskimos descended from   **E** 284

Mongols, nomadic tribes of central Asia, united during the 13th century by Genghis Khan. They established the greatest land empire in history, including practically all of Asia and Russia. By 1368 they had lost their power and importance in China. However, they remained powerful in Russia until about 1500. The Mongols, no longer a ruling power, now live in the Mongolian People's Republic and neighboring districts of China and the Soviet Union.
  China, conquest of   **C** 269
  Genghis Khan   **G** 96
  Gobi Desert dwellers   **D** 128; *picture* **D** 129
  Mongolia   **C** 257; **M** 413–16; *picture* **C** 261

  Russia invaded by   **U** 48
  yurt homes   **H** 175–76; *pictures* **A** 458, **M** 415,
    N 271
  See also Tatars

Mongooses, mammals   **G** 92, 94–95
Monitor, receiver used in television production   **T** 70a
Monitor, Christian Science *see* Christian Science
  Monitor
Monitor and Merrimack, ironclad warships that fought a
  Civil War battle   **C** 340
  See also Ericsson, John
Monitoring systems, in hospitals   **H** 248
Monitor lizard   **L** 319, 321
Monitors, computer peripherals *see* Video display
  terminals

Monk, Thelonious (1917–82), American jazz pianist and composer, b. Rocky Mount, N.C. He was one of the founders of the jazz style that became known as bop. Monk grew up in New York City. In the early 1940's he began to play piano in clubs in Harlem, working with other jazz greats such as Charlie Parker, Dizzy Gillespie, and Coleman Hawkins. Beginning in the late 1950's, Monk won widespread acclaim for his brilliant, complex piano arrangements. Many of his compositions—notably " 'Round Midnight," "Misterioso," and "Criss Cross"— have become jazz standards.   **J** 61

Monkey fists, knots   **K** 289
Monkeys   **M** 419–22
  animal communication   **A** 280, 281
  animal learning   **A** 285, 286, 287
  have four hands   **F** 83
Monkey wrenches, tools   **T** 219
Mon-Khmer, language   **L** 41
Monks and monasticism (mo-NAST-i-cism)   **M** 294
  art, the meanings of   **A** 438
  Buddhism   **B** 424, 458; *pictures* **A** 447, 460,
    S 331
  Christianity, history of   **C** 289; *picture* **C** 291
  early bridge builders   **B** 395
  early Christianization of Europe   **R** 290
  founding of Dominicans and Franciscans   **R** 292
  Jesuits   **L** 369; **R** 294
  libraries   **L** 188
  Orthodox Eastern Churches   **O** 228–29
  Tibet   **T** 175
  writing preserved by medieval monks   **C** 461
Monk seals, animals   **W** 8
Monkshood (aconite), plant   **P** 322
Monmouth, New Jersey
  Molly Pitcher at the Battle of Monmouth   **R** 206
  Revolutionary War   **R** 204
Monnet (mon-NAY), **Jean,** French statesman   **E** 334
Monocacy National Battlefield, Maryland   **M** 126
Monochord (MON-o-cord), ancient instrument   **K** 237
Monoclinic crystal system, in chemistry, *picture*   **C** 591
Monoclonal antibodies, in cancer treatment   **C** 93
Monocoque (MON-o-coke) **construction,** in airplanes
  A 554; *diagram* **A** 555
Monocotyledons (mon-o-cot-il-E-dons) (monocots), seed
  plants   **P** 292
Monocytes, cells of the body   **I** 104
Monofil, a single filament   **N** 426
Monofilament (mon-o-FIL-a-ment) **fishing lines**   **F** 205,
  206–07, 211
Monogamy, family relationship   **F** 44
Mono Lake, California   **C** 21

Monomers (MON-o-mers) (simple one-part molecules)
P 324
Monongahela National Forest, West Virginia W 135
Monongahela River, *picture* P 130
Mononucleosis, infectious see Infectious mononucleosis
Monophonic (mon-o-PHON-ic) **music** C 282; M 541
Monophonic reproduction, of sound H 121–22
Monoplacophores (mon-o-PLAC-o-phores), mollusks
O 278
Monopolies (mo-NOP-ol-ies) **and trusts** T 303–06;
E 50
capitalism C 103
guilds G 401–03
public utilities P 510–13
Monorail, rapid transit system T 267; *picture* A 467
Monotheism (MON-o-the-ism), belief in one god
R 146
Asia A 460
Judaism J 140
Monotone, expressionless voice S 380
Monotremes, kind of mammal P 333
mammals, orders of M 66
Monotype, machine for typesetting and casting
P 466j; T 345
Monroe, Bill, American musician C 563
Monroe, Louisiana L 361
Monroe, Elizabeth Kortright, wife of James Monroe
F 166; *picture* F 167

Monroe, Harriet (1861?–1936), American editor and
poet, b. Chicago, Ill. The founder of *Poetry: A Magazine of
Verse* (1912), she was more important as a critic and editor than as a poet, introducing to the public many poets
(Carl Sandburg and Ezra Pound, for example).

Monroe, James, 5th president of the United States
M 423–26; *picture* P 448
Liberia's capital named for him L 165
Louisiana Purchase L 365
Monroe Doctrine M 425, 426–27

Monroe, Marilyn (Norma Jean Baker) (1926–1962),
American film actress, b. Los Angeles, Calif. After an
unhappy childhood spent in orphanages and foster homes,
she began to work as a model and actress. Her great beauty caused her to be cast as a sex symbol, and she became
internationally famous in a succession of hit comedies.
These included *Gentlemen Prefer Blondes* (1953), *How to
Marry a Millionaire* (1953), *The Seven-Year Itch* (1955),
and *Some Like It Hot* (1959). She also performed well in
dramatic roles in *Bus Stop* (1956) and *The Misfits*
(1961). But personal problems and the pressures of movie
stardom proved too great, and she died of an overdose of
sleeping pills at age 36. Her tragic story became a Hollywood legend.

Monroe Doctrine, American foreign policy M 426–27
Adams, John Quincy, helped write A 15
foreign affairs of Monroe's administration M 425
isolationism in U.S. history U 137
Polk Doctrine was an extension of P 377
Roosevelt Corollary R 329
Monrovia, capital of Liberia L 165, 166, 167–68
Mons, Battle of, 1914 W 273
Monsieur Verdoux, film starring Charlie Chaplin C 186
Mons Meg, famous cannon G 425; *picture* G 415
Monsoons, seasonal winds W 80, 184–85
Asia A 452
Burma B 460
climate of India I 125–26

prevailing winds are a climatic control C 363
Somalia S 253
Southeast Asia S 329
Sri Lanka S 392c
Mont, geographic term see mountains by name, as
Blanc, Mont
Montage (mon-TODGE) **experts,** for motion pictures
M 483
Montagnais, Indians of North America I 164, 170
Montague, Margaret Prescott, American author W 139
Montaigne (mon-TAIN), **Michel de,** French essayist
E 292; F 437
Montale, Eugenio, Italian poet I 480, 481
Montalvo, Juan, Ecuadorian writer L 71
Montana M 428–43
Montaña, region of Peru P 161
Montana, University of, Missoula M 437
Montanari, Italian family of doll makers D 268–69
Montana State University, Bozeman M 437
Montan wax W 76
Montauk Point, Long Island, New York, *picture* N 222
Mont Blanc Tunnel, between Italy and France, *pictures*
T 313, W 219
Montcalm, Louis Joseph, Marquis de, French general
F 460–61, 462
Mont Cenis (mon ce-NI) **Pass,** through the Alps A 174
Monte Carlo (Mon-tay CAR-lo), Monaco M 406
Monte Cassino (MONE-tay ca-SI-no), abbey, Cassino,
Italy
World War II W 299

Montefiore (mon-te-fi-OR-e), **Sir Moses Haim** (1784–
1885), English philanthropist, b. Leghorn, Italy. He
amassed a fortune on the London Stock Exchange and
retired in 1824. He devoted the rest of his life to serving
the Jewish people, protecting their rights and their liberty.
The spirit of unity he aroused among European Jews led to
the growth of the Zionist movement.

Montego (mon-TE-go) **Bay,** resort, Jamaica J 16–17
Montenegro (mon-te-NE-gro), Yugoslav state Y 358
Balkan wars B 19
Monterrey (mon-ter-RAY), **Battle of,** 1846 M 239b
Monterrey, Mexico M 246
Montesquieu (mon-tes-KU), **Charles de Secondat, Baron
de,** French philosopher F 463
his book, *Spirit of the Laws, The,* influenced
American founding fathers F 439

Montessori (mon-tes-SOR-i), **Maria** (1870–1952), Italian
educator and physician, b. near Ancona. Dr. Montessori
was the first woman in Italy to obtain a medical degree.
She developed methods of teaching children that emphasized the child's initiative and freedom of expression. Her
methods have influenced teaching practices for 3- to 6-
year-olds all over the world. English translations of her
books include *The Montessori Method* and *Advanced Montessori Method.*

kindergartens and nursery schools, growth of
K 243

Monteux (mon-TUH), **Pierre** (1875–1964), French conductor, b. Paris. He was conductor of the Diaghilev Russian Ballet (1911–14, 1916–17). He conducted at the
New York Metropolitan Opera House (1917–18) and led
the Boston Symphony Orchestra (1919–24). He founded
(1929) and was chief conductor (1929–38) of l'Orchestre
Symphonique de Paris. Conductor (1936–52) of the San
Francisco Symphony Orchestra, he was an honored guest
conductor in the United States and Europe.

Monteverdi (mon-tay-VARE-di), **Claudio,** Italian
composer **I** 483–84
baroque music **B** 63
choral music **C** 284
opera **O** 131
pioneer in writing for the orchestra **O** 184
Montevideo (mon-te-vi-DAY-o), capital of Uruguay
U 237, 238; *picture* **U** 235

Montezuma I (mon-te-ZU-ma) (1390?–1464?), Aztec ruler of Mexico. Elected ruler about 1436, he extended Aztec
conquests as far as the Gulf of Mexico, modified and cod-
ified Aztec law, and built many temples and pyramids. The
aqueduct from Chapultepec to Tenochtitlán (Mexico City)
was built during his reign.

Montezuma II (1480?–1520), Aztec ruler of Mexico.
Elected ruler about 1502, he spread the Aztec realm farther than all others before him and organized justice in the
land. He was ruler when the Spaniards landed in Veracruz
(1517) and Cortes marched on Tenochtitlán (1519). Montezuma, believing that Cortes fulfilled the prophecy that
the white god Quetzalcoatl would appear out of the east
that year to rule Mexico, met Cortes with rich gifts but was
taken hostage by the Spaniards in his own palace. He died
from wounds suffered during an Aztec attack on the palace.
Cortes' conquest of the Aztecs **C** 551; **I** 197

Montezuma Castle National Monument, Arizona **A** 414

Montgolfier (mon-golf-YAY), **Jacques Étienne** (1745–99)
and **Joseph Michel** (1740–1810), French inventors, b.
Vidalon. Their hot-air balloon was the first lighter-than-air
craft. After the successful flight of an unmanned balloon
in June, 1783, they sent up a load of animals, and in
November of that year, the first manned balloon. In addition to their pioneer work in flight, the brothers developed
a number of improvements in papermaking processes, and
Joseph patented a hydraulic ram (1797).
balloons in aviation history **A** 568; **B** 30

Montgomery (mont-GUM-ery), **Sir Bernard Law,** 1st Vis-
count Montgomery of Alamein (1887–1976), British general, b. Donegal, Ireland. During World War II he won fame
as commander of the British 8th Army in North Africa for
his decisive victory over the Germans at El Alamein
(1942). He led British forces in the invasions of Sicily and
Italy (1943) and was commander of Allied ground forces
at the invasion of Normandy (1944). From 1945 to 1946
he was commander of the British-occupied zone of
Germany. He served as chief of the imperial general staff
(1946–48), and as deputy supreme commander of NATO
forces (1951–58).
World War II in North Africa **W** 295; *picture* **E** 109

Montgomery, capital of Alabama **A** 122; *picture* **A** 123
bus segregation case **B** 250m–250n; **S** 115
first Confederate capital **C** 338
state capitol, *picture* **A** 124
Montgomery, Lucy Maud, Canadian author **C** 84–85
setting of *Anne of Green Gables* **P** 465
Montgomery, Richard, American military commander
R 201
Montgomery, Wes, American jazz musician **J** 61
Montgomery Ward and Company **M** 35
Month in the Country, A, play by Ivan Turgenev **D** 301
Months, of the year
calendar **C** 11–17
in French **F** 434

in Italian **I** 478
in Spanish **S** 368
rhythms in plant and animal life **L** 244
See also names of months
Monticello (mon-ti-CHEL-lo), Virginia home of Thomas
Jefferson **J** 64; *pictures* **J** 65, **V** 355
American classical architecture **U** 123
Montini, Giovanni Battista *see* Paul VI, pope
Montmartre (mon-MAR-tre), Paris **P** 70
sidewalk café, *picture* **E** 314
Toulouse-Lautrec, Henri de, painter of **T** 231–32
Montmorency cherry **P** 109
Montmorency Falls, Quebec, Canada **W** 63
Montpelier (mont-PEEL-yer), capital of Vermont
V 318; *picture* **V** 319
Montpelier, home of James Madison in Virginia **M** 10;
picture **M** 13
Montreal (mon-tre-ALL), Quebec, Canada **M** 443–45;
C 68; **Q** 11, 12, 13; *picture* **N** 304
Cartier, Jacques **C** 126
Expo 67 **F** 17–18
Habitat, *picture* **H** 183
Olympic Games, 1976 **O** 114–15
Montréal (mon-ray-OL), **Université de,** Quebec, Canada
C 65; **M** 445; **Q** 11
Montreal Canadiens, ice hockey team **I** 39; *picture*
I 33
Montreal Stock Exchange, *picture* **S** 428

Montresor, Beni (1926–), theatrical designer and writer and illustrator of children's books, b. Bussolengo, Italy.
Montresor is a well-known costume and set designer for
films, operas, and stage productions. He is also a noted
illustrator of children's books. His illustrations in *May I
Bring a Friend?* by Beatrice Schenk de Regniers won the
Caldecott medal in 1965. Among the works he has written
and illustrated are *House of Flowers, House of Stars*
(1962), and *Bedtime* (1978).
illustration from *The Witches of Venice* **I** 97

Monts, Pierre du Guast, Sieur de, French colonizer
N 344g
Mont-Saint-Michel (mon-san-mi-SHEL), abbey, France,
pictures **F** 414, **W** 218

Montserrat (mont-ser-RAT), a British crown colony in the
Lesser Antilles in the Caribbean Sea. It was discovered in
1493 by Columbus and colonized by the Irish in 1632.
The island's chief export is cotton. Plymouth is the capital.
C 114

Monument Rocks, Kansas **K** 185
Monuments
art as a record **A** 438b, 438e
Liberty, Statue of **L** 169
monumental sculpture **U** 115–16
Mount Rushmore, South Dakota **S** 312; *picture*
S 322
obelisks **O** 5
sculpture **S** 90–105
Washington Monument **W** 30
See also National monuments; Wonders of the world
Monument to Balzac, statue by Rodin **M** 387
Moodie, Susanna, Canadian writer **C** 84
illustration from *Roughing It in the Bush, picture*
C 85

Moody, Dwight Lyman (1837–99), American evangelist,
b. Northfield, Mass. He retired from business (1860) to
become a missionary, and conducted highly successful

Moody, Dwight Lyman (continued)
evangelistic campaigns in Great Britain and United States. He established Northfield Seminary for girls (1879), Mount Hermon School for boys (1881), and Chicago Bible Institute (1889). **C** 295; **H** 315

Moody, William Vaughn, American poet **A** 208
Moog (MOGE), **Robert,** American composer **E** 142h
Moog synthesizer, for electronic music **E** 142h
Moon, Mountains of the, name given by ancient
    geographers for Ruwenzori Mountains, Uganda
    U 5
Moon, of the earth **M** 446–56; **A** 474
    craters **C** 452
    double planetary system of earth and moon **P** 272
    eclipses of **E** 40–41
    gravity and gravitation **G** 320–21
    lunar, or moon calendar **T** 193
    lunar landing **E** 370; **S** 340–340f
    lunar tides **O** 19
    months of the calendar **C** 11, 12
    observatories in space **O** 8
    planetariums **P** 268
    satellites of planets called moons **P** 272
    solar system, place in the **S** 245
    space exploration and travel **S** 340–340f; *pictures*
    S 342
    space probes **M** 451; **S** 345, 347
    tektites, theory of **C** 452
    tides **T** 180–83

Moon, Sun Myung (1920–), South Korean religious leader and businessman, b. Korea. Moon founded the Unification Church, a Christian sect, in Korea in 1954. Many of his followers believe Moon to be a new Messiah. Members of the church live in communes and work in church-sponsored businesses or engage in raising funds and recruiting others into the church. Critics charge that church members, whom they call "Moonies," are subjected to programs of rigid discipline that rob them of free will and turn them against their families. Church headquarters were relocated to Tarrytown, New York, in 1973. In 1982, Moon was found guilty of income tax evasion, and he spent nearly twelve months in a federal prison (1984–85).

Moonbow, rainbowlike arch, Cumberland Falls,
    Kentucky **K** 221
Moon calendar **T** 193–94
Moonfish *see* Opah

Moonflower, sometimes called night beauty, a tropical vine related to the morning glory, with fragrant white or purple flowers, which bloom at night

Moon jellyfishes **J** 73
Moon landing day, July 20, 1969 **E** 370; **S** 340d–
    340f
Moonlight **L** 286; **M** 447

Moonlight schools, evening classes for adults in isolated regions. The schools were designed to promote literacy and improve community standards. They were opened first in Kentucky in 1911 and spread rapidly through other southern states where illiteracy was high.

Moonrise, Hernandez, New Mexico, 1941, photograph
    by Ansel Adams, *picture* **P** 213
Moons, of planets *see* Moon, of the earth; Satellites
Moonstone, gemstone **G** 76

Moore, Arch Alfred, Jr. (1923–), governor of West Virginia, Republican, b. Moundsville. He was elected governor for the third time in 1984, having previously held the office from 1969 to 1977. He had also served in the U.S. House of Representatives (1957–69) and the West Virginia House of Delegates (1953–57). When not in public office, Moore has been a practicing lawyer.

Moore, Clement Clarke (1779–1863), American scholar, b. New York, N.Y. Best known as the author of "A Visit from Saint Nicholas" ("'Twas the Night before Christmas"), which he wrote as a Christmas gift for his children (1822), he also published a lexicon of the Hebrew language (1809). He gave (1819) the land on which the General Theological Seminary in New York, N.Y., was built, and he was the seminary's professor of Biblical learning and of Oriental and Greek literature (1823–50).
    "A Visit from Saint Nicholas," poem **C** 299

Moore, Colleen, American film actress
    her dollhouse on display in Chicago **D** 266
Moore, Grace, American singer **T** 88

Moore, Henry (1898–1986), English sculptor, b. Castleford, Yorkshire. He is considered to be one of the greatest sculptors of the 20th century. After serving in World War I, Moore studied at the Leeds School of Art and at London's Royal College of Art. His sculpture was influenced by the work of modern artists such as Cezanne and by the sculptures of primitive and ancient peoples. He is best known for his large public sculptures that stand outside museums, offices, and other buildings in many countries. Carved in stone or wood or cast in metal, these works are often massive, simple renditions of human forms. Examples are *North Wind,* for the headquarters of the London underground railway; *Nuclear Energy,* for the University of Chicago; and *Reclining Figure,* for UNESCO headquarters in Paris.
    Reclining Figure, sculpture, *picture* **E** 242
    Rocking Chair II, sculpture, *picture* **D** 137
    20th-century English art **E** 242; **S** 105

Moore, Marianne, American poet **A** 210; **M** 380
    translations of La Fontaine's fables **F** 4
Moore, Merrill, American poet **S** 256

Moore, Thomas (pseudonyms Thomas Little and Thomas Brown) (1779–1852), Irish poet and songwriter, b. Dublin. He gained fame among the London aristocracy as a ballad singer. A strong Irish nationalist, he greatly influenced the growth of Irish literature and music. Among his noted works are poetry collections set to music, including "Irish Melodies," "Sacred Songs," and "National Airs"; the poem *Lalla Rookh; The Twopenny Post* verses of political satire; and biographies of Sheridan and Byron.
    favorite Irish songs **I** 393

Moore's Creek Bridge, Battle of, 1776 **N** 321
Moore's Creek National Military Park, North Carolina
    N 316
Moorhead, Minnesota **M** 334
Moorish art and architecture *see* Islamic art and
    architecture
Moors, Delaware Indian group **D** 94

Moors, usually refers to the descendants of the Berbers and Arabs who invaded Spain from Africa in the 8th century. The Moors rose to great power during the Middle Ages, and many examples of their art and architecture still stand. The last of the Moors were expelled from Spain in

1492. Today the name generally is used to designate the Muslims of northern and northwestern Africa.

    driven from Spain by Ferdinand and Isabella **F** 88
    fountains **F** 394–95
    Mauritania **M** 179
    sour orange introduced to Europe **O** 177
    Spain, history of **S** 351–52, 357, 360–61
    Spanish Inquisition **I** 256

Moose, hoofed mammal **H** 214; *picture* **H** 216
    tracks, *picture* **A** 272
Moosehead Lake, Maine **M** 40
Moose Jaw, Saskatchewan, Canada **S** 49
Moped **M** 495
Moraines, glacial deposits **I** 19; *picture* **I** 18
Morality plays, of the Middle Ages **D** 297; **P** 12
    English literature **E** 250

Moral Majority, Inc., a U.S. political-religious organization. The members are fundamentalists—Christians who believe in a literal interpretation of the Bible—and political conservatives. They work to promote conservative and fundamentalist beliefs. Among its activities, Moral Majority, Inc., publishes the voting records of elected officials on issues of moral concern. It has also campaigned to bring about changes in television programming that it considers morally objectionable. The organization, begun in 1979, is headed by its founder, Jerry Falwell. In a general sense, the term "moral majority" is often used to refer to those who share the values and beliefs of the organization but who are not necessarily members. In 1986, the organization changed its name to Liberty Federation.
    See also Falwell, Jerry

Moral philosophy *see* Ethics
Moral Re-Armament *see* Buchmanism
Morandi, Giorgio, Italian painter **I** 473
Morava (MOR-a-va) **River,** Czechoslovakia **C** 606
Moravia, Alberto, Italian author **I** 481
Moravia (mo-RAY-via), province of Czechoslovakia
    C 606

Moravians (mo-RAY-vians), members of a reformed church that traces its origin to Bohemia and the followers of John Huss (1369–1415) and Jerome of Prague (1360?–1416). Moravian immigrants in the United States founded the towns of Bethlehem and Nazareth, Pa. They are noted for their missionary work.
    Czechoslovakia, history of **C** 608
    Old Salem section of Winston-Salem, North Carolina **N** 317
    Schoenbrunn Village State Memorial, Ohio **O** 70

Moray eels **E** 85; *picture* **E** 87
Morazán, Francisco, Honduran statesman **H** 199
Mordant, substance used to fix dyes **D** 369, 371, 373, 374
Mordant dyes **D** 373
Mordecai (MOR-de-ky), character in the Bible **P** 539
Mordent, in music **M** 541

Mordvinoff, Nicholas (1911–73), American author and illustrator of children's books, b. St. Petersburg (now Leningrad), Russia. After studying at the University of Paris, he lived in the South Pacific for 13 years. In 1947 he settled in New York, where he met writer William Lipkind. Under the names Will and Nicholas the two collaborated on many books, including *Russet and the Two Reds, Four-Leaf Clover,* and *The Christmas Bunny.* Their *Finders Keepers* won the Caldecott medal (1952).

Moré, language **B** 455
More, Sir Thomas, English statesman and author
    M 456
    English literature **E** 250
Morelos y Pavón (mo-RAE-los e pa-BONE), **José María,** Mexican priest and patriot **M** 248
Morels (mo-RELS), mushrooms **F** 498; **M** 529
Moreri (mor-ay-RI), **Louis,** French encyclopedist **E** 194

Morey (MOR-ey), **Samuel** (1762–1843), American inventor, b. Hebron, Conn. He began experimenting with steamboats about 1790 and later claimed that his ideas were stolen by Fulton. He took out patents for a steam-operated spit, rotary steam engine, windmill, waterwheel, steam pump, and an internal-combustion engine.

Morgagni (mor-GON-yi), **Giovanni Batista,** Italian physician **M** 206
Morgan, Daniel, American military commander **R** 207
    Cowpens, Battle of **S** 303

Morgan, Garrett A. (1875?–1963), American inventor, b. Paris, Ky. He invented the gas inhalator, forerunner of the gas mask. His automatic traffic stop sign was sold to the General Electric Company.

Morgan, Gib, American folk hero **F** 312
Morgan, Sir Henry, English buccaneer **P** 264
Morgan, Morgan, American colonist **W** 140

Morgan, Thomas Hunt (1866–1945), American zoologist, b. Lexington, Ky. The 1933 Nobel prize in medicine and physiology was awarded to him for his demonstration of linkage—the tendency for certain genes to be inherited together. He and his students at Columbia University further showed that this occurrence was due to the lineup of genes along each chromosome; genes closer together were inherited together more frequently. His work with the fruit fly, Drosophila, did much to prove the existence of mutations—inheritable changes in living things.

Morgan family, founders of one of the world's leading banking firms. **Junius Spencer** (1813–90) was president (1864–90) of J. S. Morgan and Co., London. His son, **John Pierpont** (1837–1913), founder of J. P. Morgan and Co., New York, was a leader in government financing and international banking and controlled a huge financial and industrial empire. Most of J. P. Morgan's art collection is at the Metropolitan Museum, and his rare books and manuscripts are at the Morgan Library in New York. His son, **John Pierpont** (1867–1943), succeeded him (1913) as head of J. P. Morgan and Co.
    autograph collection of J. P. Morgan **A** 526

Morgan horses **H** 244; **V** 306; *picture* **H** 239
Morganite, beryl gemstone **G** 71
Morgan le Fay, sorceress in legends of King Arthur
    A 442

Morgenthau (MORG-en-tow), **Henry** (1856–1946), American businessman and diplomat, b. Mannheim, Germany. He went to the United States in 1865. He practiced law in New York, N.Y. (1879–99), and was director and president of many large corporations. He became the U.S. ambassador to Turkey (1913–16) and to Mexico (1920) and the technical expert to the Monetary and Economic Conference at London (1933). He was the Chairman of the Greek Refugee Settlement Commission (1923), which was organized by the League of Nations.

Morgenthau (MORG-en-thau), **Henry, Jr.** (1891–1967), American public official and publisher, b. New York, N.Y. Son of diplomat Henry Morgenthau, he published the *American Agriculturist* (1922–33) and served as the New York State conservation commissioner. He was U.S. secretary of the treasury (1934–45) and general chairman of the United Jewish Appeal (1947–50) and other organizations.

Morin (MO-rin), coloring matter from fustic wood **D** 371

Morison, Samuel Eliot, American writer **A** 214b

Morisot (mo-ri-ZO), **Berthe** (1841–95), French painter, b. Paris. She and Mary Cassatt were the only women to join the impressionists. Her early work shows the effect of Corot. She married Eugène Manet (1874) and had a significant influence on his older brother Édouard. After 1885 her work became bolder and brighter, revealing the influence of Renoir. Among her most famous paintings is *The Cradle*.
    portrait by Edouard Manet, *picture* **W** 59

Morley, Christopher Darlington (1890–1957), American novelist, essayist, and poet, b. Haverford, Pa. A versatile writer, he was on the staff of several magazines, including the *Ladies' Home Journal* (1917–18) and the New York *Evening Post* (1920–24). His more than 50 books are very diverse in nature. *Parnassus on Wheels* and its sequel, *The Haunted Bookshop*, were immediate successes. He also wrote *Kitty Foyle*.

Morley, Edward W., American physicist **R** 140
Morley, Thomas, English composer **E** 269
Mormons, religious sect **M** 457
    colonization of Utah **U** 246, 255
    genealogical research **G** 76d
    Mormon Cemetery, near Omaha, Nebraska **N** 89
    Nauvoo State Historic Site, Illinois **I** 82
    Nevada, history of **N** 136
    Protestantism **P** 484
    Salt Lake City **S** 22–23
    Young, Brigham **Y** 353
Mormon Tabernacle Choir **S** 23; **U** 249
Mormon Trail **O** 265
Morne Gimie, volcano, St. Lucia **S** 18a

Morning glory, flowering vines in the same group as the sweet potato. Most species are tropical in origin. The common morning glory is a garden favorite and is easy to raise from seeds. It has a climbing stem, big leaves, and funnel-shaped flowers. The blossoms may be pink, purple, blue, or white. The plant also grows wild.
    solar-day rhythm, *picture* **L** 245

Morning rounds, of doctors **D** 235
Morning Star, name for Mercury or Venus **P** 272

Moro, Aldo (1916–78), Italian political leader, b. Maglie. Moro was twice premier of Italy (1963–68 and 1974–76). After helping to draw up Italy's constitution (1946), Moro was elected to the Chamber of Deputies in 1948 and then was re-elected regularly. He also held several cabinet posts. As a leader of the Christian Democratic Party, Moro spoke against Communism throughout his career. In 1978 he was kidnapped and murdered by the Red Brigades, an Italian terrorist group. **I** 457

Morocco (mo-ROC-co) **M** 458–61
    dyers' markets, *pictures* **A** 63, **D** 370

flag, *picture* **F** 228
Libya, relations with **L** 204
Marrakesh merchant, *picture* **A** 54
Muslims in prayer in Rabat, *picture* **I** 416
Spanish enclaves of Ceuta and Melilla **S** 356
See also Ifni
Moroni, capital of the Comoros **C** 473
Moros (MO-ros), a people of the Philippines **P** 183
    rebellion subdued by Pershing **P** 157
    women weaving mats, *picture* **A** 463

Morpheus (MOR-phe-us) (from Greek *morphe,* meaning "form"), in Greek mythology, the god of dreams and one of the sons of Hypnos (Sleep). He sends visions of human forms to those who sleep and is often called the god of sleep.

Morphine, narcotic drug **D** 333; **N** 13, 14
    plants, medicinal **P** 311
Morphology (morph-OL-ogy), study of structure of living organisms **B** 191
    kingdoms of living things **K** 252
Morphology, study of changes in word form **L** 299
Morrill, Justin Smith, American legislator **V** 316
    agricultural colleges established **A** 96
Morrill Act, 1862 **P** 507
Morris, Esther Hobart, American women's rights advocate **W** 335

Morris, Gouverneur (1752–1816), American statesman, b. Morrisania, N.Y. A signer of the Articles of Confederation (1775), he was co-author of the New York constitution and a member of the Continental Congress (1778–79). He was appointed assistant minister of finance (1781–85) and two years later was a member of the Constitutional Convention. He was also U.S. commissioner to England (1790–91) and minister to France (1792–94). He served as U.S. senator from New York (1800–03).
    Morris's objection to universal suffrage **E** 113

Morris, Lewis (1726–98), American statesman, b. Morrisania, N.Y. He was half-brother of Gouverneur Morris. He served as New York representative to the Continental Congress (1775–77), during which time he was a signer of the Declaration of Independence (1776). Appointed brigadier general of the Westchester county militia (1776), he also served as judge for that county (1777–78). He was frequently active as member of the state legislature (1777–90). He retired as major general at the end of the Revolutionary War.

Morris, Robert, English-born American financier and statesman **P** 142
Morris, William, English poet and artist **E** 263
    decorative arts defended against ugliness of machine crafts **D** 79–80
    founded Kelmscott Press **B** 322, 324
    influence on illustration **I** 91–92
    tapestry **T** 24
    type design **T** 346
    Victorian age in English art **E** 241
Morris, Willie, American author **M** 362

Morris, Wright (1910–   ), American novelist, b. Central City, Nebr. Many of his books, such as the highly regarded *The Home Place* (1948), were influenced by his youth on the plains. *Will's Boy* (1981), *Solo* (1983), and *A Cloak of Light* (1985) are memoirs. He won a National Book Award for *The Field of Vision* (1956) and an American Book Award for *Plains Song* (1980).

Morris dances D 29; F 301

Morrison, Toni (Chloe Anthony Wofford) (1931–), American novelist, b. Lorain, Ohio. Her well-crafted novels eloquently express the black American experience. Morrison received degrees in English from Howard and Cornell universities. In addition to writing, she has also worked as a teacher, lecturer, and editor. Her first two novels were *The Bluest Eye* (1970) and *Sula* (1973). Her third novel, *Song of Solomon* (1977), won the National Book Critics Circle Award and established her as a major American writer. Morrison's next works, *Tar Baby* (1981) and *Beloved* (1987), also were critical and popular successes.

Morristown National Historical Park, New Jersey N 174
Morrisville, Pennsylvania C 422
Morrow, Anne see Lindbergh, Anne Morrow
Morrow, Bobby, American sprinter O 110
Morrow, Dwight W., American diplomat C 540; W 139
Morse, Samuel F. B., American artist and inventor M 462
    communication, history of C 466
    electronic communication, history of E 142
    telegraph T 51–52

Morse, Wayne Lyman (1900–74), United States senator from Oregon, b. Madison, Wisc. He was professor of law and dean of the law school at University of Oregon before winning election to the Senate (1944). Originally a Republican, he resigned from the party in disagreement with the Republican presidential platform (1952) and became an independent. He was re-elected to the Senate as a Democrat (1956, 1962). He was noted for his independence and outspokenness.

Morse Code, International R 63; T 51
    communication, history of C 466
    electronic communication, history of E 142
    invention by Samuel Morse M 462
Mortality, number of deaths in a population P 385, 386, 387
    countries with highest and lowest infant mortality rates, list of P 387
    life insurance rates based on force of mortality A 81
    world population P 395
Mortar, mixture of cement, sand, and water C 165
    brick masonry B 391–94
    early architecture A 370
Mortarboard cap, part of academic dress H 46; U 206
Mortars, guns G 426
Morte D'Arthur, book by Thomas Malory A 443–45
    early English collection of Arthur legends E 248
Mortgages (MOR-gages)
    held by banks B 45
    real estate R 113
    true interest rates I 289
    See also Installment buying
Mortise, slot or notch to form a joint, in furniture F 503
Morton, Jelly Roll, American jazz musician J 58; *picture* J 59

Morton, John (1724?–77), American patriot, b. Ridley, Pa. Morton was a member of the Pennsylvania provincial assembly (1757–67, 1769–76), a delegate to the Stamp Act Congress (1765), and a judge (1770–74). He was a delegate to the Continental Congress (1774–77) and signed the Declaration of Independence.

Morton, Julius Sterling, American originator of Arbor Day N 90
Morton, Levi P., vice-president, United States V 330; *picture* V 327
Morton, Nathaniel, American writer A 195
Morton, Thomas, English adventurer P 346
    satirized Puritan life A 196
Morton, William T. G., American doctor A 257
    early use of anesthesia M 208a; *picture* A 256

M-O-S, U.S. Army term for "military occupation specialty." This refers to a specialized task a soldier is trained to perform.

Mosaic (mo-ZAI-ic), art form M 463
    ancient Greece G 344; *picture* G 342
    Aztec, *picture* I 155
    Byzantine B 484, 485–86, 488–89
    early Christian and Byzantine artistry P 17
    early Eastern European clothing influenced by C 375
    Islamic decoration of mosques I 420; *picture* I 418
    Italian art I 458
    Justinian and His Court, Byzantine mosaic, *pictures* B 491, P 16
    Mérida mosaic, *picture* L 66
    O'Gorman's mosaic for library of University of Mexico L 67
    Pompeian, *picture* A 348
    Roman art, *pictures* A 232; O 51

Mosbacher (MOSS-backer), **Bus** (Emil Mosbacher, Jr.) (1922–), American yachtsman and government official, b. White Plains, N.Y. Introduced to sailing at an early age, he held the intercollegiate sailing championship for two years. The United States retained the America's Cup sailing trophy owing in large part to his skill as captain of the *Weatherley* (1962) and *Intrepid* (1967). Mosbacher was U.S. chief of protocol under President Richard M. Nixon from 1969 to 1972.

Mosby, John Singleton (1833–1916), American lawyer and soldier, b. Edgemont, Va. He practiced law in Virginia until the outbreak of the Civil War (1861), when he joined the Confederate Army. His cavalry unit (formed 1863), known as Mosby's Rangers, became famous for its daring raids, especially behind Union lines. After the war he served as United States consul in Hong Kong (1878–85) and as assistant attorney for the Department of Justice (1904–10).

Moscow, capital of Union of Soviet Socialist Republics M 464–67; U 35; *pictures* U 27, 42
    Allied Conference, 1943 W 297
    Cathedral of Dormition, *picture* U 55
    early state of Russia U 48
    GUM department store, *picture* U 34
    ice cream vendor, *picture* E 314
    Kremlin, *pictures* C 315, U 55, W 220
    Muscovite period in architecture U 53
    Napoleon's retreat from N 12
    Olympic Games, 1980 O 115–16
    parade to mark the anniversary of the Bolshevik Revolution, *picture* U 41
    Saint Basil, Cathedral of, *picture* C 133
Moscow Art Theater T 161

Moseley, (MOSE-ley), **Henry Gwyn-Jeffreys** (1887–1915), English physicist, b. Weymouth. He carried out important

Moseley, Henry Gwyn-Jeffreys (continued)
investigations in the field of radioactivity and in the study of the X-ray spectra of the elements. He calculated the exact number of elements from hydrogen through uranium (92), which showed that there were several elements lighter than uranium yet to be discovered. Moseley was killed in World War I. **C** 211; **E** 154

Moser, Lukas, German artist **G** 166

Moses, Edwin (Edwin Corley Moses) (1955–   ), American hurdler, b. Dayton, Ohio. He is the best 400-meter hurdler in track-and-field history. He won the event in both the 1976 and the 1984 Olympics and has lowered the world record four times, most recently in 1983 (47.02 seconds). Moses has dominated the 400-meter hurdles completely through 1986 he has won more than 115 consecutive races. **O** 116b

Moses, Grandma, American artist **M** 469
   Christmas at Home, painting, *picture* **F** 40
   Sugaring Off, painting, *picture* **M** 469
Moses, Hebrew leader **M** 468
   Bible, Old Testament **B** 154
   leader and lawgiver of the Jews **J** 103
   Michelangelo's *Moses,* statue **S** 100
   Passover **P** 97
   received the Ten Commandments **T** 72; *picture* **J** 102
   spies to Canaan **S** 388
   See also Joshua
Moses, Law of **M** 468

Moses, Robert (1888–1981), American public official, b. New Haven, Conn. As the head of various commissions (1913–63), Moses became known as New York's "master builder." He helped to create buildings, bridges, highways, parks, and power plants that did much to change the appearance of the city and the state. These include such New York City landmarks as Lincoln Center for the Performing Arts, the United Nations headquarters, and Shea Stadium; the Triborough and Verrazano-Narrows bridges, linking boroughs of the city; the Long Island parkway system and Jones Beach State Park on Long Island; and the Niagara and St. Lawrence power projects. Moses' autobiography is entitled *Public Works: A Dangerous Trade* (1969).

Moses ben Maimon *see* Maimonides, Moses
Moses ibn Ezra *see* Ibn Ezra, Moses
Moshavim, Israeli co-operative settlements **I** 442
Moshi, Tanzania **T** 19
Moshoeshoe I, Basotho chief **L** 157
Moshoeshoe II, king of Lesotho **L** 157
Moslems *see* Islam

Mosley, Sir Oswald Ernald (1896–1980), British fascist leader, b. London. Between 1918 and 1931 he served in Parliament, first as a Conservative, then as an Independent, and finally as a member of the Labour Party. He left the Labour Party to found (1931) the British Union of Fascists. He was imprisoned for a time in World War II. Later he lived in self-imposed exile in France, where he died. **F** 64

Mosques (mahsks), Islamic places of worship **I** 416, 419–20
   Badshahi mosque, Lahore, *picture* **P** 37
   Bobo-Dioulasso, Burkina, *picture* **B** 456
   Delhi's Jama Masjid **D** 104
   Gold Mosque, Baghdad, *picture* **B** 15
   Great Mosque, Djibouti, *picture* **D** 232
   Great Mosque, Mecca, *picture* **I** 415
   Islamic architecture **I** 419–20
   Jerusalem's Dome of the Rock **J** 81
   Jordan, *picture* **J** 132
   Kadhimain, Iraq **I** 382; *picture* **I** 383
   Nigeria, *picture* **R** 150
   Pakistani mosque, *picture* **I** 416
   Rabat, Morocco, *picture* **I** 416
   Sabers, Mosque of the, Kairouan, Tunisia, *picture* **I** 419
   Selimiye Mosque, Edirne Turkey, *picture* **T** 327
   Sultan Ahmed Mosque, Istanbul, *picture* **T** 323
   Tehran, *picture* **I** 372
Mosquito Coast, Honduras **H** 196
Mosquito Coast, Nicaragua **N** 246–247
Mosquitoes, insects **M** 470–71; **I** 269, 283; *picture* **I** 276
   eating habits of male mosquito **A** 266
   household pests **H** 260
   How do mosquitoes bite? **M** 470
   malaria spread by **D** 196
   mouthparts, *diagram* **I** 270
   Reed discovers disease carrier **R** 128
   vectors, or carriers of diseases **V** 282–85
Moss, Spanish *see* Spanish Moss
Moss agate, gem quartz **Q** 7
Mosses **F** 94–95
Mossi, a people of Africa **B** 455, 456
Most favored nation principle *see* Reciprocity
Mosul (MO-sul), Iraq **I** 382
Motels **H** 256–59
Motet, in music **M** 545
   choral music **C** 283
   Dutch and Flemish music **D** 365, 366
   Middle Ages **M** 299
Moth and the Star, The, fable by James Thurber **F** 8
Mother Carey's chickens, tag game **G** 17
Mother Goose rhymes **N** 402–08
   children's literature **C** 233, 234
   Little Bo-peep, illustration by Kate Greenaway **I** 93
   Newbery published first collection **N** 137
   nonsense rhymes **N** 276
   Was Mother Goose a real person? **N** 402
Mothering Sunday, in England **H** 159
Mother-of-pearl (nacre) **G** 76
   inner surface of oyster shell **O** 273
   pearls made of layers of nacre **P** 113
Mother of the West, nickname for Missouri **M** 366

Mothers Against Drunk Driving (MADD), a volunteer organization formed to combat drunk driving. Founded in 1980 by Candy Lightner, whose 13-year-old daughter was killed by a drunk driver, MADD works to educate the public (especially teenagers) on the perils of drinking and driving. It has pushed for stiffer penalties for people convicted of drunk driving and has helped to pass the National Minimum Drinking Age Act of 1984. This law pressures states to raise their legal drinking age to 21. MADD has more than 300 local chapters throughout the United States. Headquarters are in Hurst, Texas.

Mother's Day **H** 159
   how to make a Mother's Day greeting card **G** 374
   See also Jarvis, Anna
Mother Teresa *see* Teresa, Mother

Motherwell, Robert (1915–   ), American painter, b. Aberdeen, Wash. Educated in philosophy and archeology,

Motherwell taught himself to paint. In the late 1940's he emerged as a leading American painter working in the abstract style. His work can be seen in various American museums.

The Voyage, painting **A** 438d

Moths **B** 471–72, 474; *pictures* **B** 478–79
  animal communication **A** 278
  clothes moth **H** 261; *picture* **H** 263
  How can you tell a butterfly from a moth? **B** 471
  how insects protect themselves, *picture* **I** 275
  locomotion **A** 296
  metamorphosis **M** 238
  peppered moths, genetic changes in **G** 87
  silk moth, life cycle of the **S** 174–75
  Yucca pollination **P** 320
  See also names of moths, such as Gypsy moth

Mo Ti (MO-di) (or Mo-tzu) (470?–396 B.C.), Chinese philosopher, b. probably Sung province. He was the founder of Mohism (Moism), which introduced logic into Chinese philosophy. His doctrine was universal love. He believed that all institutions should be judged by their ability to promote human welfare, and opposed aggressive war. Mo's philosophy, forgotten for 12 centuries, has been adopted now by many young Chinese.

Motif, in music **M** 541
Motion, in physics
  heat, theory of **H** 84–85
  jet propulsion principle **J** 88
  kinetic energy **E** 198–202
  Newton's laws of **M** 471–73; **N** 207
  optical illusions **O** 166
  principle of the seismograph **E** 31–32
  reaction engine explained by Newton's third law **E** 209
  relativity **R** 140, 141
  speed and direction of, on electric appliances **E** 120
  Why has no one invented a perpetual-motion machine? **I** 333
Motion, Newton's laws of **M** 471–73; **N** 207
  behavior of rockets explained **R** 255–56
Motion picture directors **M** 480, 483, 484
  European films **M** 486
Motion picture industry **M** 474–93
  animated cartoons **A** 297–99
  arts of the United States **U** 103
  audio-visual aids in education **E** 78
  copyright protection **C** 547
  country music, rise of **C** 564
  cowboy folklore **C** 570
  How can movies "talk"? **M** 476
  movies on TV **T** 71
  television programs **T** 70–71
  Why do motion pictures seem to have "motion"? **M** 474
Motion picture photography **P** 212
  communication, history of **C** 462–63
Motion picture producers **M** 480
Motion pictures *see* Motion picture industry
Motions, in parliamentary procedure **P** 82
Motivation, in psychology
  learning **L** 101, 102
  study, methods of **S** 440
Motivational research, in advertising **A** 33
Motive *see* Motif

Motley, Constance Baker (1912–   ), American lawyer and public official, b. New Haven, Conn. As counsel for the Legal Defense and Educational Fund of the NAACP, she won many court decisions involving school segregation and other civil rights cases. She was the first black woman to be elected to the New York state senate (1964) and the first woman to serve (1965–66) as a borough president of New York City. In 1966 she was appointed a federal district judge for New York. *picture* **W** 213

Motley, John Lothrop, American historian **A** 202
  types of historical writing **H** 139

Motley, Willard (1912–65), American novelist, b. Chicago, Ill. Living in the slums of Chicago, wandering across the United States, and working at many odd jobs provided him with some ideas for his best-selling first novel, *Knock on Any Door,* a powerful story of the criminal hardening of a boy growing up in the slums. He was a naturalistic writer, whose other well-known books include *We Fished All Night* and *Let No Man Write My Epitaph.*

Moto, musical term **M** 541
Motokiyo, Zeami, Japanese dramatist **O** 220d
Motor bicycles, *picture* **B** 128
Motorboats **B** 260–64
Motor centers, of nerves **B** 365
Motorcycles **M** 494–95
  assembly plant in Marysville, Ohio, *picture* **O** 65
  riders required to wear helmets **H** 46
Motor development, of children **C** 225
Motor homes, movable houses **H** 177
Motor nerves **N** 116, 117
Motors *see* Engines
Motors, electric *see* Electric motors
Motor scooters
  assembly plant, Milan, *picture* **I** 453
Motor trucks *see* Trucks and trucking

Mott, John Raleigh (1865–1955), American religious worker, b. Livingston Manor, N.Y. Mott was foreign secretary (1898–1915) and general secretary (1915–31) of the Y.M.C.A. International Committee. He made many trips throughout the world in the interest of the World Mission to Christianity. In 1946 he was co-recipient, with Emily G. Balch, of the Nobel peace prize.

Mott, Lucretia Coffin (1793–1880), American preacher and reformer, b. Nantucket, Mass. She spent two years as a teacher for the Society of Friends (Quakers) boarding school near Poughkeepsie, N.Y. Moving to Pennsylvania, she became an "acknowledged minister" of the Society of Friends. Although her greatest interest was abolition of slavery, she also spoke for woman's rights, temperance, and peace. She helped organize the first Woman's Rights Convention in 1848.
  women, role of **W** 212b

Mottoes, provincial *see* province articles
Mottoes, state **U** 91–93
  See also state articles
Mouflon (moo-FLON), hoofed mammal **S** 145; *picture* **H** 220
Mouloud (Maulid-an-Nabi), Muslim holiday **H** 150

Moulton (MOLE-ton), **Forest Ray** (1872–1952), American astronomer, b. Le Roy, Mich. With T. C. Chamberlin he developed the planetesimal theory of how the solar system was formed. The theory states that a passing star caused the sun to throw off matter, which formed many

Moulton, Forest Ray (continued)

tiny planets, or "planetesimals." The tiny planets slowly came together and formed the large planets of the present solar system. This is only one of several possible explanations known today.

planetesimal theory **S** 246–47

Moultrie, William, American soldier **S** 304
Mound Builders, Indians of North America **O** 60, 74
effigy mounds, Serpent Mound State Memorial, Ohio **O** 70; *picture* **O** 71
Indiana **I** 150
Indian art **I** 157
Mound builders (Megapodes), birds **B** 225
Mounds, at archaeological sites **A** 352–54
Mount, geographic term *see* mountains by name, as Everest, Mount
Mountain beaver (Aplodontia) **R** 278
stores hay **M** 70
Mountain bluebird
Idaho, state bird of, *picture* **I** 55
Nevada, state bird of, *picture* **N** 123
Mountain climbing **M** 495–97; *picture* **G** 225
Everest, Mount **E** 336–37
Himalayas **H** 126, 127
spelunking is underground mountain climbing in the dark **S** 382
Tasman Glacier, New Zealand, *picture* **G** 224
Mountaineering *see* Mountain climbing
Mountain gorilla, animal, *picture* **E** 197
endangered species **E** 195–96
Mountain laurel, shrub **P** 282; *picture* **G** 37
Connecticut, state flower of, *picture* **C** 503
Pennsylvania, state flower of, *picture* **P** 129
Mountain lions **C** 136, 138, 141
Mountain men, pioneer explorers, scouts, and fur traders **F** 523
California trail **O** 263
Oregon Trail guides **O** 260, 261
trappers and traders of the westward movement **W** 146
Mountain parks, grassy plateaus **C** 433; **N** 285
Mountains **M** 498–505
Alps **A** 174–75
Andes **A** 252–53
ascents of major peaks, *chart* **M** 496
Asian mountains' effects on temperature and rainfall **A** 451, 452
barriers preventing spread of life **L** 236
birds of **B** 228
climate and mountain barriers **C** 363–64
continents' mountains compared **C** 530
contour lines show elevation on maps **M** 98; *picture* **M** 95
crustal plates, mountains found over cracks in **G** 116, 117
earth's history **E** 23, 24, 25
earth's mountain building **E** 10, 11
erosion **E** 12
Everest, highest **E** 336–37
formation of igneous rocks **G** 111
geological studies of mountain building **G** 116–17
Himalayas **H** 126–27
landforms of Europe **E** 308–09
North American Cordillera **N** 282, 284
oceanic ridges **O** 21
of the moon **M** 449–50
rainfall **R** 95
Rocky Mountains **R** 275
undersea chains **E** 14; **G** 114–15

volcanoes **V** 377–86
See also landform sections of country, province, and state articles
Mountains of the Moon *see* Moon, Mountains of the
Mountain State, nickname for West Virginia **W** 126, 127
Mountain wild flowers *see* Alpine wild flowers
Mountbatten, Lord Louis, British admiral **W** 297
Mount Desert Island, Maine **M** 39, 50; *picture* **M** 45
Mount Hood National Forest, Oregon, *picture* **G** 105
Mounties *see* Royal Canadian Mounted Police
Mount Maxwell Provincial Park, British Columbia, *picture* **B** 406
Mount McKinley National Park *see* Denali National Park and Preserve
Mount Palomar Observatory, California **C** 30; **O** 7; *picture* **O** 9
reflecting telescope **T** 63; *picture* **T** 62
Mount Rainier National Park, Washington, *picture* **N** 45
Mount Revelstoke National Park, British Columbia **B** 406a
Mount Rushmore National Memorial, South Dakota **S** 312; *pictures* **N** 49, **S** 322
Mount Saint-Victoire with Tall Pine, painting by Cézanne, *picture* **C** 179
Mount Vernon, Virginia **V** 355; **W** 36; *pictures* **C** 423, **V** 354, **W** 42
colonial sites you can visit today **C** 422
Mount Wilson Observatory, California **S** 466
Mourne Mountains, Northern Ireland, *picture* **U** 65
Mourners, at funerals **F** 492–95
Mourning doves *see* Doves
Mourning Monk, statue by Claus Sluter, *picture* **D** 353
Mourning rings **J** 98, 99
Mourning (keening) **songs** **F** 326
Mousáká, Greek dish **F** 337
Mouse, animal *see* Mice
Mouse, device used to operate computer programs **C** 483
Mouse deer (chevrotains) **H** 212
Mouse lemur, primate **M** 421; *picture* **E** 197
Mouse River *see* Souris River
Mouth organ *see* Harmonica
Mouth-to-mouth artificial respiration **F** 158
first aid course demonstration, *picture* **R** 127
Mouton (MOO-ton) **lamb,** fur **F** 518
Movement, section of a musical composition **C** 350; **M** 541
Movements of animals *see* Animals: locomotion
Movies *see* Motion picture industry

Mowat, Farley (1921–   ), Canadian writer, b. Belleville, Ontario. His books are mainly descriptions of nature and life in the wilderness; the best known are *People of the Deer* (1952), *Never Cry Wolf* (1963), *The Boat Who Wouldn't Float* (1969), *A Whale for the Killing* (1972), and *Sea of Slaughter* (1984). He has written novels and short stories for children as well as adults.

Mowatt, Anna Cora, American playwright **D** 304
Mowers, farm machinery **F** 58
Mowgli's Song Against People, poem by Kipling **K** 261–62

Moynihan, Daniel Patrick (1927–   ), American government official, educator, and author, b. Tulsa, Okla. As assistant U.S. secretary of labor (1963–65), he helped draft antipoverty legislation and wrote a controversial report on black family life. He is co-author of *Beyond the*

Melting Pot (1963). He has held various academic posts at Harvard University. Moynihan served as presidential assistant and counsellor (1969–70), ambassador to India (1973–75), and permanent representative to the United Nations (1975–76). He was elected to the U.S. Senate from the state of New York in 1976 and re-elected in 1982.

Mozambique (mo-zom-BEEK) **M** 506–07
  flag, *picture* **F** 228
Mozarabic (moth-AR-a-bic), language **S** 366
Mozart (MO-tzart), **Leopold,** German-born Austrian
  violinist and composer **C** 349; **M** 508
Mozart, Maria Anna, Austrian pianist **M** 508
Mozart, Wolfgang Amadeus, Austrian composer **M** 508
  chamber music **C** 184
  choral music **C** 284
  clarinet was one of his favorite instruments **C** 348
  classical age in music **C** 349, 351, 352
  Cosi Fan Tutte, opera **O** 143
  Don Giovanni, opera **O** 143
  first concert at age seven, *picture* **G** 185
  German music **G** 185
  harp, use of **H** 36
  Haydn and Mozart **H** 67
  influenced by Italian music **I** 485
  Magic Flute, The, opera **O** 146
  Marriage of Figaro, The, opera **O** 146–47
  opera **C** 351; **O** 134
  Salzburg Festival **M** 558
  symphonies **M** 548–49
Mozzarella (mot-za-REL-la), Italian cheese **D** 12
Mphahlele, Ezekiel, South African writer **A** 76c, 76d
Mr., form of address **A** 19
Mr. America, bodybuilding competition **B** 289–90
Mr. Gumpy's Outing, book by John Burningham, *picture* **C** 243
MRI *see* Magnetic resonance imaging
Mr. Olympia contest, bodybuilding competition **B** 290
Mr. Sammler's Planet, book by Saul Bellow **B** 136
Mr. Universe, bodybuilding competition **B** 290
Mrs., form of address **A** 19
MRV (multiple re-entry vehicle) **system,** missile system **M** 347
Mr. Yuk, symbol used as a warning label for poison
  containers **F** 161
Ms., form of address **A** 19
Mswati III, king of Swaziland **S** 482

Mubarak, Muhammad Hosni (1928–), Egyptian political and military leader, b. north of Cairo. Mubarak became president of Egypt in 1981, following the assassination of President Anwar el-Sadat. He was appointed air force chief of staff in 1969 and commander in chief three years later. He planned and led the surprise air attack against Israel in the 1973 war. As vice-president (1975–81), Mubarak handled many of the day-to-day duties of running the country and served as Sadat's emissary to political leaders all over the world. As president, he pledged to support the 1979 Egyptian-Israeli peace treaty and focused his attention on Egypt's economic problems. **E** 92

Much Ado About Nothing, play by Shakespeare **S** 136
Mucilage (MUCE-il-age), type of adhesive **G** 242
Muckrakers, crusading reporters **F** 346
Mucus (MU-cus), body substance
  cystic fibrosis **D** 191–92
  eel's body mucus **E** 85
Mud, dredging of **D** 319–20
Mud eels, land-water animals **F** 475

Mudejar (mu-THE-har) **style,** in art and architecture
  S 360
  Latin-American architecture **L** 62
Mudflows, volcanic **V** 382
Mudge, Isadore Gilbert, American librarian **L** 181
Mud houses **A** 370; **H** 173
Mud-mill, dredging machine **D** 320
Mudpuppies, land-water animals **F** 475; picture **F** 474
Mud shrimps, crustaceans **S** 166
Mud turtles **T** 332
Mueller, O. F., Danish zoologist **T** 30
Muezzin (mu-EZZ-in), Muslim crier **I** 416
Mufflers, engine silencers **I** 311

Mugabe, Robert Gabriel (1924–), prime minister of Zimbabwe (Rhodesia), b. Kutama. Mugabe, a former teacher, became involved in the black nationalist movement in 1960. As head of the Zimbabwe African National Union (ZANU), he led guerrilla raids on white-ruled Rhodesia from neighboring Mozambique. Mugabe was influential in working out the cease-fire agreement of 1979 that led to elections in which all groups took part. He won an overwhelming victory in the elections and in 1980 became the first prime minister of the new nation of Zimbabwe. **Z** 369

Mugwumps, reform Republicans **C** 359
Muhammad, Arab prophet *see* Mohammed

Muhammad, Elijah (Elijah Poole) (1897–1975), leader of the Nation of Islam (Black Muslims), b. Sandersville, Ga. The son of a Baptist minister, he joined the Black Muslim movement in Detroit in the early 1930's and was its leader from 1934 until his death. He favored separation of blacks from whites, a policy he made less extreme in his later years. He also believed that blacks should develop their own businesses and schools, independent of any help from whites.
  Black Muslims **B** 250o

Muhammad, Wallace D. (1933–), American religious leader, b. Detroit, Mich. He is the son of Elijah Muhammad, longtime leader of the Nation of Islam (Black Muslims). He became chief minister when his father died in 1975, and he served until 1978. Wallace Muhammad changed the name of the sect to the World Community of Islam in the West. He also changed its separatist policies by opening membership to all races. His writings include *The Book of Muslim Names* (1976).

Muhammad Ali *see* Ali, Muhammad
Muharraq, Bahrain **B** 18

Muhlenberg (MU-len-berg) **family,** distinguished family of Lutheran clergymen, patriots, statesmen, and educators. The founder, **Henry Melchior** (1711–87), was born in Germany and went to America (1742) and settled in Philadelphia, Pa. He created union and order in the Lutheran Church. Three of his sons, **John Peter** (1746–1807), **Frederick Augustus Conrad** (1750–1801), and **Gotthilf Henry** (1753–1815), made their mark in American political, religious, and academic life. Gotthilf's son **Henry Augustus Philip** (1782–1844) was the first minister to Austria, and Henry Augustus' son **Frederick Augustus** (1818–1901) was first president of Muhlenberg College. **William Augustus** (1796–1877), a grandson of Frederick Augustus Conrad, founded St. Luke's Hospital, New York.

Muir, Alexander, Scottish-born Canadian teacher **N** 27

Muir, John (1838–1914), American naturalist and conservationist, b. Dunbar, Scotland. He made botanical studies in the Midwest, hiked from Indianapolis to California, and later wrote studies of the Yosemite Valley, urging that it become a national park. During travels in the United States, Alaska, Asia, and Australia, he pressed for conservation. One of his books is *Our National Parks*.
  Yosemite National Park **Y** 352–53

Muir Woods National Monument, California **C** 30
Mujibar Rahman (Mujib), president of Bangladesh **B** 44c
Mukden *see* Shenyang
Mukden Incident, 1931 **S** 150; **W** 284
Muktibahini, Bengali guerrillas **B** 44c

Mulatto (from Portuguese and Spanish *mulato*), a person with one black and one white parent. The word is also used to describe people whose ancestors were racially mixed.

Mulberries, group of trees bearing purple or black edible berries. The leaves of one variety that grows in China and Japan are used as food for silkworm larvae.
  silkworms, food of **S** 174, 175

Mulberries, term for artificial harbors, World War II **W** 298, 300; *picture* **W** 299
Mulberry Bush, singing game **G** 12
Mulch, materials to retain soil moistures **G** 41–42
  dust mulches for vegetables **V** 288

Muldoon, Robert David (1921–   ), New Zealand statesman, b. Auckland. He became leader of the National Party in 1974 and served as prime minister from 1975 to 1984. He was succeeded as prime minister by David Lange, leader of the Labor Party.

Mule deer **D** 84; **H** 214; *picture* **H** 215
Mules **H** 235; *pictures* **A** 293, **H** 207

Mullan, John (1830–1909), American army officer and road builder, b. Norfolk, Va. He spent two years (1853–55) exploring a planned railroad route from St. Paul to the Pacific and five years (1858–63) working on a military road from Montana to Washington, which helped open the Northwest to immigrants. Many travelers to the West consulted his *Miners' and Travelers' Guide*.

Muller, Hermann Joseph (1890–1967), American geneticist, b. New York, N.Y. He was awarded the 1946 Nobel prize in medicine and physiology for showing that X rays could cause mutations. With this method for producing mutations he gathered evidence that the majority of mutations are harmful.

Mullet, fish
  habitats, feeding habits, uses **F** 213
Mullins, Priscilla, Pilgrim settler **P** 344
Mulroney (mull-ROON-ee), **Martin Brian,** Canadian prime minister **M** 509; **C** 76
Multilateral (mul-ti-LAT-er-al) **treaties,** among many countries **I** 315; **T** 271

Multinational, an adjective used to describe something involving more than two countries. The word is currently most often applied to giant business enterprises, as in multinational corporations. It is also used to refer to meetings involving more than two countries, as in multinational conferences.
  corporations **I** 327

Multiple-choice tests
  animal learning experiments **A** 285
  computer sensors can read answers **C** 481
  points on test taking **E** 349; **T** 121
Multiple independently targeted re-entry vehicle system *see* MIRV system
Multiple re-entry vehicle system *see* MRV system
Multiple sclerosis **D** 197
Multiple stars **S** 409
Multiplex system, in telegraphy **T** 53
Multiplex telegraphy **E** 142
Multiplicand (mul-ti-pli-CAND), in multiplication **A** 400
Multiplication, in mathematics **A** 400
  abacus **A** 2
  algebra **A** 159
  decimal fraction **F** 401
  fractions **F** 399
  slide rule **M** 167
  using base-4 system **N** 400
Multiplier, in multiplication **A** 400
Multipurpose dams **D** 19
Multistage rockets **R** 259–60
  Goddard's plan for reaching moon **G** 245
Multnomah Falls, Oregon **W** 63
Mu mesons, (muons), subatomic particles **N** 368

Mumford, Lewis (1895–   ), American writer, b. Flushing, N.Y. Although he wrote a study of Melville (*Herman Melville*) and books (such as *Men Must Act*) about U.S. policies, he is best known for his works about urban life and about city and regional planning. Books on these subjects include *The Story of Utopias* and *The City in History*, for which he won a 1961 National Book Award. His other works include *The Myth of the Machine, Architecture as the Home of Man,* and his autobiography, *My Works and Days: A Personal Chronicle*.

Mummers, in medieval drama **D** 297
Mummies, dead bodies preserved from decay
  Egyptian **E** 95; **F** 492
  mummy portraits **P** 17
Mumps, virus disease **D** 197

Munch (MOONSH), **Charles** (1891–1968), French conductor, b. Strasbourg (then Germany). He led the Société des Concerts du Conservatoire de Paris (1938–45) and made his American debut with the Boston Symphony in 1946. He succeeded Serge Koussevitzky as conductor and music director of the Boston Symphony (1949–62). He was noted particularly for his interpretations of works by modern French composers.

Munch (MOONCK), **Edvard** (1863–1944), Norwegian painter, b. Loten. He was interested in the subjects of love and death, and an exhibition of his work in Berlin in 1892 had a great effect on later German painting. Many of his paintings and powerful woodcut prints use swirling, curving lines, and they reveal drama and passion. Most of his paintings are in Oslo, but his prints may be seen in museums throughout Europe and the United States.
  The Scream, lithograph **G** 307

Munchausen (MOONCK-how-sen) (or Münchhausen), **Baron Karl Friedrich Hieronymus von** (1720–97), German soldier, b. Hanover. He fought with the Russians against Turkey and supposedly made up tall tales based on his experiences. Rudolph Erich Raspe was the author of an English collection of the tales: *Baron Munchausen's Narrative of His Marvellous Travels and Campaigns in Russia.*

Later editions included more tales and greater lies, and the name Munchausen came to suggest an improbable story.

Muncie, Indiana, Middletown, U.S.A. **I** 149

Muni (MU-ni), **Paul** (Muni Weisenfreund) (1895–1967), American actor, b. Lemberg, Austria. He arrived in the United States in 1902, became a citizen (1923), and appeared in Yiddish- and English-language stage productions before beginning a movie career in 1928 that brought him an Oscar for *The Life of Louis Pasteur* (1936). New York stage appearances included roles in *Counselor-at-Law* and *Inherit the Wind*.

Munich (MU-nick), West Germany **G** 158
    Oktoberfest **H** 158
    Olympic Games, 1972 **O** 113–14
Munich Pact, 1938 **W** 286
    Sudetenland, Czechoslovakia **C** 609
Municipal (mu-NIS-ip-al) **government M** 509–13
    cities, problems of **C** 322, 324; **U** 233–34
    civil service **C** 333
    education **E** 74
    income tax **I** 111
    local health departments **P** 502–03
    police **P** 366
    public utilities **P** 510–13
    re-apportionment of state legislatures **S** 412, 415
    taxation for levels of government **T** 26
    Tokyo **T** 205
Munin, raven of Odin, Norse god **N** 278

Muñoz Marín (MOON-yose ma-REEN), **Luis** (1898–1980), Puerto Rican political leader, b. San Juan. Muñoz founded Puerto Rico's Popular Democratic Party in 1938. He served as president of the Puerto Rican Senate from 1941 to 1949. During the 1940's, he organized a program called Operation Bootstrap to strengthen Puerto Rico's economy. In 1949, he took office as Puerto Rico's first elected governor. Due largely to his efforts, Puerto Rico became a commonwealth of the United States in 1952. After serving four terms as governor, Muñoz decided not to run again for that office in 1964. He was elected to the Puerto Rican Senate in that year and was re-elected in 1968.
    Puerto Rico, history of **P** 522
    See also Operation Bootstrap

Munro, Alice, Canadian writer **C** 85

Munro, Hector Hugh (pen name: Saki) (1870–1916), English writer, b. Burma. Primarily a writer of short stories and satires, his only serious work was *The Rise of the Russian Empire*. He is remembered for collections such as *The Chronicles of Clovis* and *Beasts and Super-Beasts.* Saki's stories are marked by wit and brevity.

Munsel (mun-SEL), **Patrice** (1925–), American soprano, b. Spokane, Wash. She became, at 18, the youngest singer ever to receive a contract from the Metropolitan Opera Company. She specialized in coloratura roles, winning special fame as Adele in *Die Fledermaus*. She has also starred in motion pictures (*Melba*), appeared on television, and toured in musical comedy. She makes frequent appearances with opera companies in the United States and Europe.

Muntjacs, deer **H** 214, 217
Muons *see* Mu mesons

Muppets, puppets designed for television by puppeteer **Jim Henson** (1936–). Characters such as Kermit the Frog, Bert, Ernie, and the Cookie Monster first won popularity on the TV program "Sesame Street" in the 1970's. Others, such as Miss Piggy and Fozzie Bear, were later created for "The Muppet Show." The Muppets also appeared in *The Muppet Movie* (1979) and other films. Muppets are made of foam rubber covered with cloth and are operated by the puppeteer's hand. Their features are removable, so that one puppet can become several characters. *picture* **T** 70d

Murabba'at, ancient community near Dead Sea **D** 47
Mural painting
    ancient Rome **P** 17; **R** 286; *picture* **I** 301
    cave painting of early man **P** 14–15
    Egypt, ancient **P** 15; *picture* **A** 221
    fresco technique popular during Renaissance **P** 20
    Leonardo da Vinci's *Last Supper* damaged because
      of damp wall **P** 21
    Rivera, Diego, Mexican artist **L** 67
    Romanesque art **R** 309
    wall painting in Minoan palace, *picture* **A** 226
Murasaki, Lady, Japanese writer **J** 43; **O** 220b–220c

Murat (mu-RA), **Joachim** (1767?–1815), marshal of France and king of Naples, b. La Bastide, France. He gave up studies for the priesthood to fight in Egypt (1798–99) with Napoleon, whose sister Caroline he married (1800). Murat was named marshal of France (1804) and king of Naples (1808) and took part in Napoleon's Russian campaign (1812) before military and political defeats sent him into exile on Corsica. He was captured and executed upon trying to return to Italy.

Murchison Falls, Uganda **N** 260; **U** 5; **W** 63
Murder, crime
    Holocaust **H** 159c–159d
    juvenile crime **J** 157
Murder in the Cathedral, verse drama by T. S. Eliot
    E 268
Murders in the Rue Morgue, The, by Edgar Allan Poe
    M 561
Murdoch, Iris, English writer **E** 267
Murdock, William, Scottish engineer **A** 541
    natural gas **N** 59
Murex, sea snail
    shell, *picture* **S** 148
    source of purple dye, *picture* **D** 369
Murillo (mu-RILL-o), **Bartolomé Esteban,** Spanish artist
    S 362

Murkowski, Frank Hughes (1933–), United States senator from Alaska, Republican, b. Seattle, Wash. He was elected to the Senate in 1980 and re-elected in 1986. He previously served as the Alaska commissioner of economic development (1966–70). A banker, Murkowski was president of the Alaska Bank of the North (1971–80).

Murmansk, Union of Soviet Socialist Republics **U** 33

Murray, Mary Lindley (1726–82), American patriot, b. Philadelphia, Pa. During the Revolutionary War she detained a detachment of British troops by offering them the hospitality of her home, Murray Hill (1776), and thus allowed a large company of the American Army to relocate.

Murray, Philip, American labor leader **L** 6

Murray, William, American political leader **O** 93

Murray Harbor, Prince Edward Island, Canada **P** 466

Murray Louis Company, modern dance group, *picture*
  D 34

Murray River, Australia **A** 503; **R** 243

Murre (MURR), birds of the auk family **B** 213–14

Murrow, Edward R. (1908–65), American news commentator, b. Greensboro, N. C. Associated with CBS for more than 25 years (1935–61), he became well-known for his World War II news broadcasts from London. Returning from Europe, he was made a CBS vice-president (1946–47) and soon was famous for his television shows *Person to Person* and *See It Now*. A repeated winner of the Peabody award for excellence in broadcasting, he received the Medal of Freedom (1964), the highest United States civilian honor. He also served as United States Information Agency director (1961–63).

Musangs (mu-SONGS), civet cats **G** 94

Muscat, capital of Oman **O** 116d

Muscat and Oman see Oman

Muscles
  animals: locomotion **A** 294
  birds **B** 200–01
  body, human **B** 273; *diagrams* **B** 272
  bodybuilding **B** 289–90
  child development **C** 230
  fishes **F** 188
  microscopic views of muscle fibers, *pictures*
    M 287
  multiple sclerosis **D** 197
  muscle sense **B** 287
  muscular dystrophy **D** 197
  of insects **I** 273–74
  physical fitness **P** 224–29
  reflex actions **N** 118
  tetanus makes muscles stiff **D** 203
  trichinosis **D** 204
  weight lifting **W** 107

Muscle Shoals, Alabama **A** 119

Muscovites, Russians **M** 467

Muscovy, former name of Russia **M** 467

Muscular dystrophy (DIS-trophy), disease **D** 197

Museo del Prado see Prado

Muses, in Greek mythology, the nine daughters of Zeus and Mnemosyne who were the goddesses of the arts and sciences. They sang and danced at the gods' festivities and were said to make people forget their troubles. In classical and English literature there are many appeals to the Muses. The Muses are: Calliope, Clio, Erato, Euterpe, Melpomene, Polyhymnia, Terpsichore, Thalia, and Urania.
  See also names of the Muses

Museumobile, of Illinois State Museum **I** 80

Museum of Fine Arts, Boston, Massachusetts, *pictures*
  M 519, 528

Museum of History and Technology, Washington, D.C.
  M 518

Museum of Modern Art, New York City **M** 397

Museum of Science and Industry, Chicago, Illinois
  I 80; **M** 518; *picture* **C** 221

Museums **M** 514–28
  "Agassiz" museum at Harvard **A** 80
  botanical gardens **B** 341–43
  doll collections **D** 273
  Eisenhower Museum, Abilene, Kansas **K** 181
  Hermitage Museum, Leningrad **H** 116
  list of the world's major museums **M** 524–27

Louvre, Paris **L** 366–68
Metropolitan Museum of Art, New York City
  M 239–239a
National Gallery, London **N** 34–35
National Gallery of Art, Washington, D.C. **N** 36–38
National Gallery of Canada **N** 39–40
Prado, Madrid **P** 424–25
Smithsonian Institution **S** 202
taxidermy prepares animal models **T** 27
Uffizi Gallery **U** 2–3
See also Presidential libraries; education section of
  country, province, and state articles

Museveni, Yoweri (mu-su-VENN-ee, yo-WERR-ee) (1944–   ), president of Uganda, b. Ntungamo. He led the National Resistance Army (the military wing of his National Resistance Movement) in a coup overthrowing the military regime of Tito Okello, and he became president in 1986. Museveni pledged to improve the country's economy, respect human rights, restore parliamentary democracy, and end tribal strife. A socialist, he declared that Uganda would remain neutral with regard to the superpowers. **U** 7

Mushroom ant, *picture* **A** 322

Mushrooms, plants of the fungi group **M** 529; *picture*
  L 210
  club and sac fungi **F** 498–500
  yellow, orange, or red fly agaric, poisonous **P** 322

Musial (MEW-see-uhl), **Stan** (Stanley Frank Musial) (1920–   ), American baseball player, b. Donora, Pa. Known as "Stan the Man," Musial was an outfielder and first baseman for the St. Louis Cardinals (1941–44, 1946–63). He was voted Most Valuable Player in the National League three times and he won seven league batting titles. Musial became a Cardinals executive after his retirement as a player. He was elected to the Baseball Hall of Fame in 1969.

Music **M** 530–49
  acoustics **S** 260–61
  African **A** 77–79
  American Indian **I** 160–61
  ancient **A** 243–47
  ballads **F** 310–11, 318
  bands and band music **B** 38–41
  baroque period in music **B** 62–66
  bell music **B** 137
  Canada **C** 67
  chamber music **C** 182–84
  Christmas **C** 299
  classical age **C** 349–52
  country music **C** 563–65
  dance music **D** 35–36
  Dutch and Flemish **D** 365–67
  early phonograph recordings **P** 195
  electronic **E** 142g–142h
  English music **E** 268–71
  festivals **M** 558–60
  folk music **F** 318–28
  French music **F** 443–48
  German and Austrian music **G** 181–89
  harmonics **S** 264–65
  Hebrew music **A** 246; **C** 282; **H** 309
  hi-fi and stereo recordings **H** 121–23
  hymns **H** 309–15
  instruments see Musical instruments
  Italian language suited to music **I** 474
  Italian music **I** 482–86

jazz **J** 57–62
Latin-American music **L** 73–75
Middle Ages, music of the **M** 298–99
modern music **M** 399–402
musical comedy **M** 550–51
national anthems and patriotic songs **N** 18–23
opera **O** 130–55
operetta **O** 156–58
orchestra **O** 182–87
orchestra conducting **O** 188–91
Oriental music **O** 220d–221
Renaissance music **R** 172–74
rock music **R** 262a–262d
Romantic Age **R** 310–11
Russian music **U** 62a–62b
sounds, musical **S** 264–65
Spanish music **S** 373–74
United States, music of the **U** 125–27
voice training and singing **V** 375–76
What is the origin of clef signs? **M** 532
Why are schools of music called conservatories?
M 532
See also names of famous composers, musicians,
and singers
Music, choral *see* Choral music
Music, modern *see* Modern music
Musical chairs, group game **I** 226
Musical comedy **M** 550–51
motion picture industry **M** 489–90
Musical composition *see* Composition, music
Musical forms **M** 543–49
baroque period **B** 62–66
classical age **C** 350–51
concert overtures **R** 310–11
English music **E** 268–71
operetta **O** 156–58
symphonic poems and program music **R** 311
Musical glasses, for a demonstration of sound **S** 266
Musical instruments **M** 552–57, 530
African music **A** 78–79
ancient music **A** 245–47; *pictures* **A** 244
bands and band music **B** 38–41
bells and carillons **B** 137–38
classical age, new groups of the **C** 350
dance **D** 35
drum **D** 335–38
electronic music **E** 142g–142h
folk music instruments **F** 301, 329–30
forced vibrations to amplify sound **S** 262
glasses to demonstrate musical sounds **S** 266
harmonics **S** 264–65
Italian music **I** 483
jazz bands **J** 59
keyboard instruments **K** 236–40
Latin-American instruments **L** 70, 74; *pictures*
L 73
Metropolitan Museum of Art collection **M** 239
Middle Ages **M** 299
orchestra **O** 182–87
Oriental, *pictures* **O** 220d, 221
percussion instruments **P** 151–53
stringed instruments **S** 438–39
wind instruments **W** 182–83
See also Folk music instruments; Keyboard
instruments; Percussion instruments; Stringed
instruments; Wind instruments; names of
instruments, as Bugle
Musical notation **M** 530–40
ancient music **A** 246
figured bass in baroque music **B** 65

Musical play, more serious form of musical comedy
M 550
Musical terms **M** 540–42
Music City, U.S.A., nickname for Nashville, Tennessee
N 16
Music drama, kind of opera **O** 136
operatic forms in German music **G** 187
Wagner, Richard **W** 2
Music festivals **M** 558–60
rock music festivals **R** 262d
Musicians, The, painting by Caravaggio **A** 438c
Music industry, American **R** 262a–262d

Musicology, scholarly and systematic study of music,
involving research into the history of music and performance practices, music theory and esthetics, acoustics,
and the development of musical instruments. The compar-
ative study of the indigenous and folk music of different
cultures is called ethnomusicology. Musicology as a separate branch of study in the field of music originated in
Germany during the second half of the 19th century and is
today an important part of the musical curriculum in many
universities in Europe and America.

Music Party, The, painting by Philippe Mercier **E** 269

Musil, Robert (1880–1942), Austrian novelist, b. Klagen-
furt. At the age of 26 he published his first novel, which
dealt with the conflicts of adolescence. His most important work was *The Man without Qualities,* about the life
and history of prewar Austria. **G** 180

Musique concrète (mu-ZEEK con-CRET) **E** 142g
Musk, substance from special glands of animals **G** 93
musk deer **H** 217
perfume **P** 154, 155
skunks **S** 191–92
turtles **T** 332
Musk deer **H** 214, 217; *picture* **H** 216
Muskegs, swamps **N** 288; **T** 11
Muskellunge, fish, *picture* **F** 210
Muskets, guns **G** 415

Muskie, Edmund Sixtus (1914–   ), American political
leader, b. Rumford, Me. Muskie entered politics in 1946
and served for six years in the Maine House of Representatives. In 1954, he was elected as Maine's first Democratic governor in 20 years; and in 1958, as Maine's first
Democratic U.S. senator. Muskie was the Democratic
vice-presidential nominee in 1968. In 1972 he ran unsuccessfully for the Democratic presidential nomination. On
completion of a term as U.S. secretary of state (1980–
81), he returned to private law practice.

Muskmelons (summer melons) **M** 216

Musk-ox, large mammal found in Arctic regions of North
America. The long, shaggy hair is deep brown or black in
color. The horns are somewhat curved. Musk-oxen feed on
low-growing vegetation. *picture* **H** 218

Muskrats, rodents **R** 279; *picture* **K** 257
tracks, *picture* **A** 272
Muslims, followers of Islam *see* Arabs; Islam; Moors
Mussels, mollusks **O** 274; *picture* **S** 148
Musset (mu-SAY), **Alfred de,** French writer **F** 440
Mussolini (mu-so-LI-ni), **Benito,** Italian premier **M** 560
fall of **W** 297
Fascism in Italy **F** 63, 64; **I** 457
rise of dictators before World War II **W** 284

Mussorgsky (mu-SORG-ski), **Modest,** Russian composer
U 62a
Boris Godunov, opera O 140–41
opera O 136
Mustangs, wild horses of Spanish stock C 569;
H 242–43; *picture* H 241

Mustard, vegetable belonging to the same group as the turnip, the cabbage, and the cauliflower. The seeds of several species are the chief source of mustard oil and dressing; these species generally are tall plants with hairy leaves, short pods, and yellow blossoms. The cabbagelike leaves of several other mustard species supply greens for food. Mustards were native to Europe, but now are grown in most agricultural regions.
spices and condiments H 113, 114; *picture*
H 115
supposed medicinal powers F 335

Mustelids, family of animals O 240
Mutations, of genes
evolution E 346
furs, colors of F 514
genetic engineering G 89
permanent genetic change G 83–84, 87
viruses V 364
Mutemua (mu-tay-MU-a), wife of Thutmose IV B 250a
Mutesa I (mu-TAY-sa), king of Buganda U 6
Mutesa II (Sir Edward Mutesa), king, then president, of Uganda U 7
Mute swans, birds D 344
Muths, Guts, German writer P 223

Muti, Riccardo (1941–   ), Italian orchestra conductor, b. Naples. He first studied violin and piano in Naples but went to study in Milan after discovering his love for conducting. In 1967, Muti won an international competition for young conductors and three years later became the principal conductor of the Teatro Comunale in Florence. In 1973 he joined the Philharmonia Orchestra in London, also as principal conductor. Muti first appeared with the Philadelphia Orchestra in 1972 and in 1980 succeeded Eugene Ormandy as the orchestra's musical director. Known for his deep musical intuition, Muti has been a guest conductor of orchestras and operas in major cities around the world.

Mutiny on the Bounty *see* Bligh, William
Mutt and Jeff, comic strip C 128
Mutton, meat from older sheep C 150; M 192
Mutton birds H 188
Mutual insurance companies I 296
Mutual savings banks B 47
Muzzle-loaders, early guns G 417–18
Mwanga, king of Buganda U 7
Mwanza, Tanzania T 19

MX, a long-range missile being developed by the United States. The letters MX stand for "missile, experimental." The MX was proposed in the 1970's as a replacement for the Minuteman missile, to counter the improved strength and accuracy of the Soviet Union's missiles. The MX is designed to carry ten independently targeted warheads, compared to three on the Minuteman. There has been much debate on the usefulness and cost of the MX program. In 1985 the U.S. Senate approved funds for the development of 50 MX missiles, but the House of Representatives approved funds for only 40.

Mycelium (my-CE-li-um), of fungi F 496

Mycenae (my-CE-ne), ancient city of Greece
ancient gate A 372
Schliemann, Heinrich, work of S 58h
Mycenaean Age, of ancient Greece G 340–41
art as a record A 438b
sculpture S 94
Mycerinus (mis-er-INE-us), king of ancient Egypt E 96
Mycology (my-COL-ogy), study of fungi F 496
Myelin, outer covering of neurons N 117
My Fair Lady, motion picture M 491; *picture* M 481
My Heart Leaps Up When I Behold, poem by William Wordsworth W 242
Mykonos, one of the Greek Cyclades Islands, *picture*
I 428
Mylar, plastic tape T 20
Myna (or mynah) **birds** B 246–47
pets P 179
talking birds P 86, 88
My Old Kentucky Home, song by Stephen Collins Foster composed at Bardstown, Kentucky K 223

Myrdal (MEER-dahl), **Alva Reimer** (1902–86), Swedish educator, sociologist, and political official, b. Uppsala. Myrdal was the Swedish ambassador to several countries, including India, Burma, and Sri Lanka (Ceylon). She was active in educational reform and the women's movement, and she served as a delegate to international disarmament conferences. For her efforts toward disarmament, she shared the 1982 Nobel prize for peace with Alfonso García Robles. Among her books is *The Crisis in the Population Question* (1934), written with her husband, Gunnar Myrdal.

Myrdal, Gunnar (Carl Gunnar Myrdal) (1898–1987), Swedish social economist and educator, b. Gustafs. Myrdal was the director (1938–43) of the Study of American Negro Problems. His findings were published in *An American Dilemma: The Negro Problem and Modern Democracy* (1944). This book predicted the racial storms that were to develop in the United States more than two decades later. Myrdal served as Sweden's minister of trade and commerce from 1945 to 1947. From 1947 to 1957, he was the executive secretary of the United Nations Economic Commission for Europe. In 1974, he was awarded the Nobel prize in economics. Among his many works are *Beyond the Welfare State* (1960) and *The Challenge of World Poverty* (1970).

Myrmidons, race of people of ancient Greece who lived in Thessaly and followed their leader, Achilles, to fight in the Trojan War. The present meaning of the term refers to personal followers or subordinate civil officers who follow strict orders.

Myron, Greek sculptor active during 5th century B.C., b. Boeotia. None of his work survives, but Roman copies exist. He was interested in depicting the human body, especially athletes in motion. His most famous work, the *Discus–Thrower,* was copied by a Roman sculptor.
Roman copy of the *Discus–Thrower, picture* G 345

Myrrh (MIRR), resin used in incense R 184

Myrtle (MIRTLE), name for a variety of plants in different groups and families. The true myrtle family consists of mostly tropical or subtropical trees and shrubs, including the eucalyptus tree and the allspice. The myrtles proper have simple, often aromatic leaves and white or pink flowers carried singly or in clusters. The plants are used in medicine and perfumery.

PHOTO CREDITS

The following list credits the sources of photos used in THE NEW BOOK OF KNOWLEDGE. Credits are listed, by page, photo by photo—left to right, top to bottom. Wherever appropriate, the name of the photographer has been listed with the source, the two being separated by a dash. When two or more photos by different photographers appear on one page, their credits are separated by semicolons.